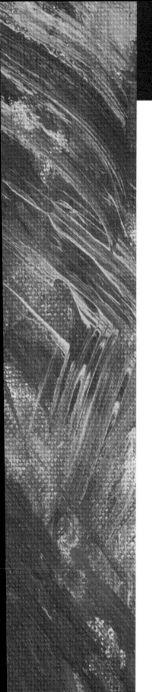

Congratulations!

As a student purchasing *Derivatives Markets*, you are entitled to prepaid access to the downloadable Excel spreadsheets on the book's Companion Web site! Check the Companion Web site to see if there have been any updates to the spreadsheets on the CD-ROM since the book was published.

THE SPREADSHEETS INCLUDE:

- An Excel workbook that implements the option pricing functions described in Appendix E, and contains available Visual Basic code for the pricing routines.
- An Excel workbook that provides analysis of option positions, including Greeks.

TO ACTIVATE YOUR PREPAID SUBSCRIPTION:

1) Go to your book's Companion Web site at http://www.aw.com/mcdonald
2) Click on "Student Software"
3) Select the "New Users Please Register First" link
4) Enter your preassigned Access Code, exactly as it appears below

WSMDM-CROOK-LIPPY-DIVED-TOPAZ-BOARD

5) Select "Submit"
6) Complete the online registration form to establish your personal User ID and Password
7) Once your personal User ID and Password are confirmed, you can begin downloading the *Derivatives Markets* Excel spreadsheets!

This Access Code can only be used once to establish a subscription. This subscription to the software portion of the *Derivatives Markets* Companion Web site is valid for six months upon activation, and the subscription is not transferable.

IMPORTANT:

If you did not purchase this product new and in a shrink-wrapped package, the Access Code above may no longer be valid. Information about purchasing a subscription online can be found on the book's Companion Web site at the above URL.

Derivatives Markets

The Addison-Wesley Series in Finance

Derivatives Markets

ROBERT L. McDONALD
Northwestern University

Addison
Wesley

Boston San Francisco New York
London Toronto Sydney Tokyo Singapore Madrid
Mexico City Munich Paris Cape Town Hong Kong Montreal

Editor-in-Chief: Denise Clinton
Sponsoring Editor: Donna Battista
Senior Project Manager: Mary Clare McEwing
Development Editor: Marjorie Singer Anderson
Managing Editor: James Rigney
Senior Production Supervisor: Nancy Fenton
Marketing Manager: Adrienne D'Ambrosio
Design Manager: Regina Hagen Kolenda
Text Designer: Regina Hagen Kolenda
Cover Designer: Joyce Wells
Senior Manufacturing Buyer: Hugh Crawford
Supplements Editor: Andrea Basso
Project Management: Elm Street Publishing Services, Inc.

Printed in the United States of America.
ISBN: 0-201-72960-1
12345678910–HT–06 05 04 03 02

Library of Congress Cataloging-in-Publication Data

McDonald, Robert L. (Robert Lynch), 1954–
  Derivatives markets / Robert L. McDonald.
    p. cm.
  Includes index.
  ISBN 0-201-72960-1
  1. Derivative securities. I. Title.
HG6024.A3 M3946 2002
332.64'5–dc21   2002026085

For Irene, Claire, David, and Henry

Contents

vii

Foreword

Derivatives have moved to the center of modern corporate finance, investments, and the management of financial institutions. They have also had a profound impact on other management functions such as business strategy, operations management, and marketing. A major drawback, however, to making the power of derivatives accessible to students and practitioners alike has been the relatively high degree of mathematical sophistication required for understanding the underlying concepts and tools.

With the publication of Robert McDonald's *Derivatives Markets,* we finally have a derivatives text that is a wonderful blend of the economics and mathematics of derivatives pricing and easily accessible to MBA students and advanced undergraduates. It is a special pleasure for me to introduce this first edition, since I have long had the highest regard for the author's professional achievements and personal qualities.

The book's orientation is neither overly sophisticated nor watered down, but rather a mix of intuition and rigor that creates an inherent flexibility for the structuring of a derivatives course. The author begins with an introduction to forwards and futures and motivates the presentation with a discussion of their use in insurance and risk management. He looks in detail at forwards and futures on stocks, stock indices, currencies, interest rates, and swaps. His treatment of options then follows logically from concepts developed in the earlier chapters. The heart of the text—an extensive treatment of the binomial option model and the Black-Scholes equation—showcases the author's crystal-clear writing and logical development of concepts. Excellent chapters on financial engineering, security design, corporate applications, and real options follow and shed light on how the concepts can be applied to actual problems.

The last third of the text provides an advanced treatment of the most important concepts on derivatives discussed earlier. This part can be used by itself in an advanced derivatives course, or as a useful reference in introductory courses. A rigorous development of the Black-Scholes equation, exotic options, and interest rate models are presented using Brownian Motion and Itô's Lemma. Monte Carlo simulation methods are also discussed in detail.

Derivatives concepts are now required for every advanced finance topic. Therefore, it is essential to introduce these concepts at an early stage of MBA and undergraduate business or economics programs, and in a fashion that most students can understand. This text is perfectly designed to accomplish this objective. And it is done in such an appealing, inviting way that students will actually enjoy their journey toward an understanding of derivatives.

EDUARDO S. SCHWARTZ, MAY 2002

Preface

Thirty years ago derivatives was an esoteric and specialized subject. Today it is a basic part of modern finance: Corporations routinely hedge and insure using derivatives, finance their activities with structured products, and use derivatives models in capital budgeting. Any financially literate business student must understand the basics of derivatives. This book is intended for anyone who wants to better understand the derivative instruments that exist, how they are used, who sells them, how they are priced, and how the tools and concepts are useful more broadly in finance.

If you flip through the book, you will see a lot of formulas, but I hope that you do *not* come away with the idea that studying derivatives only entails studying an assortment of pricing formulas. Instead, the subject of derivatives provides a unified, systematic, and common-sense way of thinking about an important class of problems. I hope this book conveys both the applicability as well as the logical elegance of the subject. I also hope it conveys that the subject is just plain fun. (It is, admittedly, a structured kind of fun.)

Although much of the material is mathematical, I have tried to emphasize intuition. I assume that a reader of this book already understands basic financial concepts such as present value and elementary statistical concepts such as mean and standard deviation. Thus, the important ideas should be accessible to anyone who has studied elementary finance. For those who want to understand the subject at a deeper level, the last part of the book develops the Black-Scholes *approach* to pricing derivatives and presents some of the standard mathematical tools used in option pricing, such as Itô's Lemma.

I use a "tiered" approach to the mathematics. Chapters 1–9 use only present value calculations, and there is no calculus until Chapter 18. The goal is to make the book accessible to readers with widely varying backgrounds and experiences. There are also chapters dealing with applications: Corporate applications, financial engineering, and real options.

As you read through the book, you will want to experiment with the pricing models and perhaps build your own spreadsheets. Most of the calculations in this book can be replicated using a spreadsheet. This book comes with an Excel spreadsheet containing option pricing functions, written in Visual Basic. These functions are "user-defined functions," which means that you can easily incorporate them into your own spreadsheets. You can also examine and modify the Visual Basic code for the functions. Appendix D explains how to write such functions in Excel, and Appendix E lists the option pricing functions that come with the book. Relevant built-in Excel functions are also mentioned throughout the book.

PLAN OF THE BOOK

This book grew from my teaching notes for two MBA derivatives courses at Northwestern University's Kellogg School of Management. The two courses roughly correspond to the first two-thirds and last third of the book. The first course is a general introduction to derivative products (principally futures, options, swaps, and structured products), the markets in which they trade, and applications. The second course is for those wanting a deeper understanding of the pricing models and the ability to perform their own analysis.

The two courses share the goals that students should understand standard derivatives products and their pricing formulas, comprehend how such products are used and how they are created by market-makers, and appreciate how concepts and tools from derivatives are useful in corporate finance and investment decision making. Additional goals for the advanced course include an understanding of more sophisticated derivatives products; increased computational skills, such as the ability to compute prices and perform Monte Carlo simulations using a spreadsheet; and the facility to read advanced practitioner literature and communicate with financial rocket scientists. This last point is important: No one expects that a 10-week MBA-level course will produce rocket scientists! However, mathematics is the language of derivatives and it would be cheating students to pretend otherwise. Thus, the advanced course assumes that students know basic statistics and have seen calculus, and from that point develops the Black-Scholes option-pricing framework as fully as possible. The aim is to use mathematics to illuminate, without becoming needlessly complex.

You may want to cover the material in a different order than it occurs in the book, so I wrote chapters to allow flexible use of the material. I will indicate several possible paths through the material below. Of course there are dependencies, but it is possible to hop around in the material. For example, I wrote the book expecting that the chapters on lognormality and Monte Carlo simulation might be used in a first derivatives course.

This book has five parts. **Part 1** introduces the basic building blocks of derivatives: Forward contracts and call and put options. Chapters 2 and 3 examine these basic instruments and some common hedging and investment strategies. Chapter 4 illustrates the use of derivatives as risk management tools and discusses why firms might care about risk management. These chapters focus on understanding the contracts and strategies, but not on pricing.

Part 2 considers the pricing of forward, futures, and swaps contracts. In these contracts, you are obligated to buy an asset at a pre-specified price, at a future date. The main question is: What is the pre-specified price, and how is it determined? Chapter 5 examines forwards and futures on financial assets, Chapter 6 discusses commodities, and Chapter 7 looks at bond and interest rate forward contracts. Swaps are just forward contracts with multiple delivery dates and on which multiple payments are made. Chapter 8 shows how swap prices can be deduced from forward prices.

Part 3 studies option pricing. Chapter 9 develops intuition about options prior to delving into the mechanics of option pricing. Chapters 10 and 11 cover binomial option pricing and Chapter 12, the Black-Scholes formula and option Greeks. Chapter 13 explains delta-hedging, which is the technique used by market-makers when managing the risk of an option position. This chapter also introduces the most important pricing result in the book. When you see a complicated option pricing formula, you might wonder how anyone could know that the formula is correct. This chapter begins to explain the answer to that question. Chapter 14 looks at a few important exotic options, including Asian options, barrier options, compound options, and exchange options.

The techniques and formulas in earlier chapters are applied in **Part 4.** Chapter 15 covers financial engineering, which is the creation of new financial products from the derivatives building blocks in earlier chapters. Debt and equity pricing, compensation options, and mergers are covered in Chapter 16. Chapter 17 studies real options—the application of derivatives models to the valuation and management of physical investments.

Finally, **Part 5** explores pricing and hedging in depth. The material in this part explains in more detail the structure and assumptions underlying the standard derivatives models. Chapter 18 covers the lognormal model and shows how the Black-Scholes formula is an expected value. Chapter 19 discusses Monte Carlo valuation, a powerful and commonly used pricing technique. Chapter 20 explains what it means to say that stock prices follow a diffusion process, and also covers Itô's Lemma, which is a key result in the study of derivatives. (At this point you will discover that Itô's Lemma has already been developed intuitively in Chapter 13, using a simple numerical illustration of market-making.)

Chapter 21 derives the Black-Scholes partial differential equation (PDE). Although the Black-Scholes *formula* is famous, the Black-Scholes *equation*, discussed in this chapter, is the more profound result. Chapter 22 covers exotic options in more detail than Chapter 14, including digital barrier options and quantos. Chapter 23 shows how the Black-Scholes and binomial analysis apply to bonds and interest rate derivatives. Finally, Chapter 24 covers risk assessment, including VaR and credit risk.

NAVIGATING THE MATERIAL

There are potentially many ways to cover the material in this book. Although the subject is cumulative, I have tried to make chapters self-contained where feasible. The material is presented in order of increasing mathematical difficulty, which means that related material is sometimes split across distant chapters. For example, fixed income is covered in Chapters 7 and 23, and exotic options in Chapters 14 and 22. Each of these chapters is at the level of the neighboring chapters. As an illustration of one way to use the book, here is the material I cover in the courses I teach (within the chapters I skip some specific topics due to time constraints):

- Introductory course: 1–6, 7.1, 8–10, 11.1–11.2, 12, 13.1–13.3, 14, 15.4–15.5, 16, 17.

• Advanced course: 13, 18–22, 7, 8, 15.1–15.3, 23, 24.

You will note that some material appears in both courses. I do this to emphasize connections within the material. The second time through can be quick, but I find that students appreciate the material at a deeper level the second time.

Table 1 outlines some possible sets of chapters to use in courses that have different emphases. There are a few sections of the book that provide background on topics

TABLE 1

Possible chapters for different courses. Chapters marked with a "y" are strongly recommended, those marked with a "*" are recommended, and those with a "†" fit with the track, but are optional. The advanced course assumes students have already taken a basic course. Sections 1.4, 5.1, 5.2, 7.1, and Appendix B are recommended background for all introductory courses.

	Introductory				Advanced
	General	Futures	Options	Risk Management	
1. Introduction	y	y	y	y	
2. Intro. to Forwards and Options	y	y	y	y	
3. Insurance, Collars, and Other Strategies	y	y	y	y	
4. Intro. to Risk Management	*	*	y	y	
5. Financial Forwards and Futures	y	y	y	y	
6. Commodity Forwards and Futures	*	y	†	*	
7. Interest Rate Forwards and Futures	*	y		*	y
8. Swaps	y	y	†	y	y
9. Parity and Other Option Relationships	*	†	y	†	
10. Binomial Option Pricing: I	y	*	y	y	
11. Binomial Option Pricing: II	*		*		
12. The Black-Scholes Formula	y	*	y	y	
13. Market-Making and Delta-Hedging	†		y	*	y
14. Exotic Options: I	†		y	*	
15. Financial Engineering	*	*	*	y	*
16. Corporate Applications	†		*	*	
17. Real Options	†		*	*	
18. The Lognormal Distribution	†		*	*	y
19. Monte Carlo Valuation	†		*	*	y
20. Brownian Motion and Itô's Lemma					y
21. The Black-Scholes Equation					y
22. Exotic Options: II					y
23. Interest Rate Models					y
24. Risk Assessment				*	y

every reader should understand. These include short-sales (Section 1.4), continuous compounding (Appendix B), prepaid forward contracts (Sections 5.1 and 5.2), and zero-coupon bonds and implied forward rates (Section 7.1).

A NOTE ON EXAMPLES

Many of the numerical examples in this book display intermediate steps to assist you in following the calculations. In most cases it will also be possible for you to create a spreadsheet and compute the same answers starting from the basic assumptions. This creates the following dilemma: Should the answers in the book match the results you would obtain by computing the displayed numbers, which are rounded to a few significant digits, or should they match the results you would obtain by entering the equations directly in a spreadsheet, which are rounded with many more significant digits?

In most cases, the results should match what you would obtain in a spreadsheet. Consequently, you will sometimes encounter displayed calculations that result in a slightly different answer from that in the book. This problem can be more severe the more intermediate steps are displayed, since there is rounding at each step. The problem also arises when there are different ways to compute the same answer. You should not be concerned if an answer you compute from the displayed calculations differs slightly from the answer displayed in the book.

A different issue arises when real companies appear in examples. Some of these companies were subsequently acquired or failed. For example, Times Mirror was acquired by the Tribune Company; Netscape was acquired by AOL Time Warner; Cincinnati Bell is now part of Broadwing, Inc.; and WorldCom was on the verge of failure in June 2002. The moral is that you should bet against the continued independent existence of any company used as an example in this book.

SUPPLEMENTS

A robust package of ancillary materials for both instructors and students accompanies the text.

Instructor's Resources

The derivatives instructor will find a wide variety of materials online at a dedicated **website (www.aw.com/mcdonald)** to facilitate and enhance teaching.

An **Instructor's Solutions Manual** by Mark Cassano, University of Calgary, and Ruediger Fahlenbrach, The Wharton School, University of Pennsylvania, contains complete solutions to all end-of-chapter questions in the text and spreadsheet solutions to selected questions.

The **Test Bank** by Matthew W. Will, University of Indianapolis, features approximately ten to fifteen multiple-choice questions, five short-answer questions, and one longer essay question for each chapter of the book.

PowerPoint slides, developed by Ufuk Ince, University of Washington, and Ekaterina Emm, Georgia State University, provide lecture outlines and selected art from the book. Copies of the slides can be downsized and distributed to students to facilitate note taking during class.

Student Resources

A printed **Student Solutions Manual** by Mark Cassano, University of Calgary, and Ruediger Fahlenbrach, The Wharton School, University of Pennsylvania, provides answers to all the even-numbered questions in the textbook.

Three **spreadsheets** with user-defined option pricing functions in Excel are included on a CD-ROM packaged with the book. These Excel functions are written in VBA, with the code accessible and modifiable via the Visual Basic editor built into Excel. These spreadsheets and any updates are also posted on the book's website.

ACKNOWLEDGMENTS

Numerous students over the course of several years contributed to this book, offering complaints, praise, and corrections. Kellogg student Tejinder Singh catalyzed the book in 1994 by persuading colleague Kathleen Hagerty and me that MBA students at Kellogg were interested in an advanced derivatives course. Kathleen and I initially co-taught that course. My part of the course notes (developed with Kathleen's help and feedback) evolved into the last third of this book.

I benefited enormously from conversations, comments, and complaints from colleagues at Northwestern and elsewhere. I am also grateful to the many others who read and commented upon chapters, answered questions, shared their expertise, and provided a sounding board, including Tom Arnold, Louisiana State University; David Bates, University of Iowa; Luca Benzoni, University of Minnesota; Mark Broadie, Columbia University; Mark A. Cassano, University of Calgary; George M. Constantinides, University of Chicago; Kent Daniel, Northwestern University; Jan Eberly, Northwestern University; Steven Freund, Suffolk University; Rob Gertner, University of Chicago; Kathleen Hagerty, Northwestern University; David Haushalter, University of Oregon; James E. Hodder, University of Wisconsin–Madison; Avraham Kamara, University of Washington; Kenneth Kavajecz, Wharton School, University of Pennsylvania; Arvind Krishnamurthy, Northwestern University; Dennis Lasser, State University of New York at Binghamton; Cornelis A. Los, Kent State University; Deborah Lucas, Northwestern University; Alan Marcus, Boston College; Mitchell Petersen, Northwestern University; Todd Pulvino, Northwestern University; Ernst Schaumburg, Northwestern University; Eduardo Schwartz, University of California–Los Angeles; David Shimko, Risk Capital Management Partners, Inc.; Costis Skiadis, Northwestern University; Donald Smith, Boston University; Alex Triantis, University of Maryland; and Zhenyu Wang, Columbia University. The following served as software reviewers: James Bennett, University of Massachusetts–Boston; Gordon H. Dash, University of Rhode Island; Adam Schwartz, University of Mississippi; and Robert E. Whaley, Duke University.

I want to provide special thanks to Ken Kavajecz, Alan Marcus, and Alex Triantis for their willingness to read and comment upon some of the material multiple times and to George Constantinides, Kathleen Hagerty, Alan Marcus, and Costis Skiadis for class-testing the manuscript. Mark Broadie patiently responded to a number of e-mailed queries and generously provided his pricing software, which I used both to compute the Heston model and to double-check my own calculations.

Ruediger Fahlenbrach, Paskalis Glabadanidis, Jeremy Graveline, Dmitry Novikov, and Krishnamurthy Subramanian served as accuracy checkers for the book and Andy Kaplin provided programming assistance.

Among practitioners who contributed to the book, Andy Moore of El Paso Corporation assisted with the peak-load electricity example in Chapter 17, and Brice Hill of Intel provided the example of Intel using real options. I learned a great deal about practical aspects of options from Alex Jacobson (now of the International Securities Exchange, formerly of the Chicago Board Options Exchange), including the paylater strategy discussed in Chapter 4. I also thank Galen Burghardt of Carr Futures and Blair Wellensiek of Tradelink, L.L.C. for answering specific questions.

With any book, there are many long-term intellectual debts. From the many, I want to single out two. I had the good fortune to take several classes from Robert Merton at MIT while I was a graduate student. Every derivatives book is deeply in his debt, and this one is no exception. His classic papers from the 1970s, as well as his recent writings on the role of derivatives and functional regulation, are essential reading. I also learned an enormous amount working with Dan Siegel, with whom I wrote several papers on real options. Dan's death in 1991 at the age of 35 was a great loss to the profession as well as to me personally.

I am very pleased to have worked with the Addison Wesley team, who made it clear from the outset that their goal was not just to produce a book but to produce a high-quality book. Mary Clare McEwing juggled many balls, offered excellent advice, and answered numerous questions while expertly overseeing the project. Among her thankless tasks was calling me to ask whether I was adhering to the schedule. (The answer, of course, was always "no.") Development editor Marjorie Singer Andersen offered innumerable suggestions, improving the manuscript significantly. Nancy Fenton, the production supervisor, marshalled forces (including the excellent team at Elm Street Publishing Services) to produce a physical book in (what I can only assume will be) an astonishingly short period of time. It has also been a pleasure to work with the exceptional Finance Editor Donna Battista and Editor-in-Chief Denise Clinton.

The Addison Wesley team and I have tried hard to minimize errors, including the use of the accuracy checkers noted above. Nevertheless, of course, I alone bear responsibility for remaining errors. Errata and software updates will be available at **www.aw.com/mcdonald.** Please let us know if you do find errors so we can update the list.

I wrote this book using Gnu Emacs and MikTeX (a Windows implementation of LaTeX), and produced the graphs and figures using Matlab and XFig. Except for Matlab, all of this extraordinary, high-quality software is open source. I am indebted to the Free Software Foundation (**www.fsf.org**) for Emacs and to Christian Schenk for MikTeX (**www.miktex.org**). I also learned from, and received help from, the talented denizens of the newsgroups gnu.emacs.help and comp.text.tex. I wrote a great deal of this book fueled by the caffeine and ambience of Peet's coffee in Evanston, Illinois.

Last, but certainly not least, it is customary for authors to thank their families. If you haven't written a book, you might think that this is a *pro forma* acknowledgment. It is anything but. Particularly in the final stages of manuscript preparation (also known as "crash mode"), I relied heavily on my family's understanding, love, support, and tolerance. I also benefited from my children's occasional plea to roughhouse. This book is dedicated to my wife, Irene Freeman, and children Claire, David, and Henry, with love and heartfelt thanks.

RLM

Robert L. McDonald is Erwin P. Nemmers Distinguished Professor of Finance at Northwestern University's Kellogg School of Management.

Chapter 1

Introduction to Derivatives

Risk is the central element that influences financial behavior.

—*Robert C. Merton (1999)*

The world of finance and capital markets has undergone a stunning transformation in the last 30 years. Simple stocks and bonds now seem almost quaint alongside the dazzling, fast-paced, and seemingly arcane world of futures, options, swaps, and other "new" financial products. (The word "new" is in quotes because it turns out that some of these products have been around for hundreds of years.)

Frequently this world pops up in the popular press: Procter & Gamble lost $150 million in 1994, Barings bank lost $1.3 billion in 1995, Long-Term Capital Management lost $3.5 billion in 1998 and (according to some press accounts) almost brought the world financial system to its knees.[1] What is *not* in the headlines is that, most of the time, for most companies and most users, these financial products are an everyday part of business. Just as companies routinely issue debt and equity, they also routinely use swaps to fix the cost of production inputs, futures contracts to hedge foreign exchange risk, and options to compensate employees, to mention just a few examples.

1.1 WHAT IS A DERIVATIVE?

Options, futures, and swaps are examples of derivatives. A **derivative** is simply a financial instrument (or even more simply, an agreement between two people) which has a value determined by the price of something else. For example, a bushel of corn is not a derivative; it is a commodity with a value determined by the price of corn. However, you could enter into an agreement with a friend that says: If the price of a bushel of corn in one year is greater than $3, you will pay the friend $1. If the price of corn is less than $3, the friend will pay you $1. This is a derivative in the sense that you have an agreement with a value depending on the price of something else (corn, in this case).

You might be tempted to say: "That's not a derivative; that's just a bet on the price of corn." So it is: Derivatives can be thought of as bets on the price of something. But

---

[1] A readable summary of these and other infamous derivatives-related losses is in Jorion (2001).

1

don't automatically think the term "bet" is pejorative. Suppose your family grows corn and your friend's family buys corn to mill into cornmeal. The bet provides insurance: You earn $1 if your family's corn sells for a low price; this supplements your income. Your friend earns $1 if the corn his family buys is expensive; this offsets the high cost of corn. Viewed in this light, the bet hedges you both against unfavorable outcomes. The contract has reduced risk for both of you.

Investors could also use this kind of contract simply to speculate on the price of corn. In this case the contract is not insurance. And that is a key point: *It is not the contract itself, but how it is used, and who uses it, that determines whether or not it is risk-reducing.* Context is everything.

Although we've just defined a derivative, if you are new to the subject the implications of the definition will probably not be obvious right away. You will come to a deeper understanding of derivatives as we progress through the book, studying different products and their underlying economics.

Uses of Derivatives

What are reasons someone might use derivatives? Here are some motives:

Risk management   Derivatives are a tool for companies and other users to reduce risks. The corn example above illustrates this in a simple way: The farmer—a seller of corn—enters into a contract which makes a payment when the price of corn is low. This contract reduces the risk of loss for the farmer, who we therefore say is **hedging.** It is common to think of derivatives as forbiddingly complex but many derivatives are simple and familiar. Every form of insurance is a derivative, for example. Automobile insurance is a bet on whether you will have an accident. If you wrap your car around a tree, your insurance is valuable; if the car remains intact, it is not.

Speculation   Derivatives can serve as investment vehicles. As you will see later in the book, derivatives can provide a way to make bets that are highly leveraged (that is, the potential gain or loss on the bet can be large relative to the initial cost of making the bet) and tailored to a specific view. For example, if you want to bet that the S&P 500 stock index will be between 1300 and 1400 one year from today, derivatives can be constructed to let you do just that.

Reduced transaction costs   Sometimes derivatives provide a lower-cost way to effect a particular financial transaction. For example, the manager of a mutual fund may wish to sell stocks and buy bonds. Doing this entails paying fees to brokers and paying other trading costs, such as the bid-ask spread, which we will discuss later. It is possible to trade derivatives instead and achieve the same economic effect as if stocks had actually been sold and replaced by bonds. Using the derivative might result in lower transaction costs than actually selling stocks and buying bonds.

Regulatory arbitrage   It is sometimes possible to circumvent regulatory restrictions, taxes, and accounting rules by trading derivatives. Derivatives are often used, for example, to achieve the economic sale of stock (receive cash for it and eliminate the risk of holding it) while still maintaining physical possession of the stock. This transaction may allow the owner to defer taxes on the sale of the stock, or retain voting rights, without the risk of holding the stock.

These are common reasons for using derivatives. The general point is that derivatives provide an alternative to a simple sale or purchase, and thus increase the range of possibilities for an investor or manager seeking to accomplish some goal.

Perspectives on Derivatives

How you think about derivatives depends on who you are. In this book we will think about three distinct perspectives on derivatives:

The end-user perspective   End-users are the corporations, investment managers, and investors who enter into derivative contracts for the reasons listed in the previous section: To manage risk, speculate, reduce costs, or avoid a rule or regulation. End-users have a goal (for example, risk reduction) and care about how a derivative helps to meet that goal.

The market-maker perspective   Market-makers are intermediaries, traders who will buy derivatives from customers who wish to sell, and sell derivatives to customers who wish to buy. In order to make money, market-makers charge a spread: They buy at a low price and sell at a high price. In this respect market-makers are like grocers who buy at the low wholesale price and sell at the higher retail price. Market-makers are also like grocers in that their inventory reflects customer demands rather than their own preferences: As long as shoppers buy paper towels, the grocer doesn't care whether they buy the decorative or super-absorbent style. After dealing with customers, market-makers are left with whatever position results from accommodating customer demands. Market-makers typically hedge this risk and thus are deeply concerned about the mathematical details of pricing and hedging.

The economic observer   Finally, we can look at the use of derivatives, the activities of the market-makers, the organization of the markets, the logic of the pricing models, and try to make sense of everything. This is the activity of the economic observer. Regulators must often don their economic observer hats when deciding whether and how to regulate a certain activity or market participant.

These three perspectives are intertwined throughout the book, but as a general point, in the early chapters the book emphasizes the end-user perspective. In the late chapters, the book emphasizes the market-maker perspective. At all times, however, the economic observer is interested in making sense of everything.

Financial Engineering and Security Design

One of the major ideas in derivatives—perhaps *the* major idea—is that it is generally possible to create a given payoff in multiple ways. The construction of a given financial product from other products is sometimes called **financial engineering.** The fact that this is possible has several implications. First, since market-makers need to hedge their positions, this idea is central in understanding how market-making works. The market-maker sells a contract to an end-user, and then creates an offsetting position which pays him if it is necessary to pay the customer. This creates a hedged position.

Second, the idea that a given contract can be replicated often suggests how it can be customized. The market-maker can, in effect, turn dials to change the risk, initial premium, and payment characteristics of a derivative. These changes permit the creation of a product that is more appropriate for a given situation.

Third, it is often possible to improve intuition about a given derivative by realizing that it is equivalent to something we already understand.

Finally, because there are multiple ways to create a payoff, the regulatory arbitrage discussed above can be difficult to stop. Distinctions existing in the tax code, or in regulations, may not be enforceable, since a particular security or derivative that is regulated or taxed may be easily replaced by one which is treated differently but has the same economic profile.

A theme running throughout the book is that derivative products can generally be constructed from other products.

1.2 THE ROLE OF FINANCIAL MARKETS

We take for granted headlines saying that the Dow Jones Industrial Average has gone up 100 points, the dollar has fallen against the Yen, and interest rates have risen. But why do we care about these things? Is the rise and fall of a particular financial index (such as the Dow Jones Industrial Average) simply a way to keep score, to track winners and losers in the economy? Is watching the stock market like watching sports, where we root for certain players and teams—a tale told by journalists, full of sound and fury, but signifying nothing?

Financial markets in fact have an enormous, often underappreciated, impact on everyday life. To help us understand the role of financial markets we will consider the Average family, living in Anytown. Joe and Sarah Average have 2.3 children and both work for the XYZ Co., the dominant employer in Anytown. Their income pays for their mortgage, transportation, food, clothing, and medical care. What is left over goes toward savings earmarked for their children's college tuition and their own retirement.

What role do global financial markets and derivatives play in the lives of the Averages?

Financial Markets and the Averages

The Averages are largely unaware of the ways in which financial markets affect their lives. Here are a few:

- The Average's employer, XYZ Co., has an ongoing need for money to finance operations and investments. It is not dependent on the local bank for funds because it can raise the money it needs by issuing stocks and bonds in global markets.

- XYZ Co. insures itself against certains risks. In addition to having property and casualty insurance for its buildings, it uses global derivatives markets to protect itself against adverse currency, interest rate, and commodity price changes. By being able to manage these risks, XYZ is less likely to go into bankruptcy, and less likely to throw the Averages into unemployment.

- The Averages invest in mutual funds. As a result they pay lower transaction costs than if they tried to achieve comparable diversification by buying individual stocks.

- Since both Averages work at XYZ, they run the risk that if XYZ does fall on hard times they will lose their jobs. The mutual funds in which they invest own stocks in a broad array of companies, ensuring that the failure of any one company will not wipe out their savings.

- The Averages live in an area susceptible to tornadoes and insure their home. If their insurance company were completely local, it could not offer tornado insurance because one disaster would leave it unable to pay claims. By selling tornado risk in global markets, the insurance company can in effect pool Anytown tornado risk with Japan earthquake risk and Florida hurricane risk. This pooling makes insurance available at lower rates.

- The Averages borrowed money from Anytown bank to buy their house. The bank sold the mortgage to other investors, freeing itself from interest rate and default risk associated with the mortgage, leaving that to others. Because the risk of their mortgage is borne by those willing to pay the highest price for it, the Averages get the lowest possible mortgage rate.

In all of these examples, particular financial functions and risks have been split up and parceled out to others. A bank that sells a mortgage does not have to bear the risk of the mortgage. An insurance company does not bear all the risk of a disaster. Risk-sharing is one of the most important functions of financial markets.

Risk-Sharing

Risk is an inevitable part of all lives and all economic activity. As we've seen in the example of the Averages, financial markets enable this risk to be shared. To demonstrate how risk may be shared, let's examine one brief time period. Within the span of a few weeks in 1999 earthquakes devastated Turkey and Taiwan, floods ravaged North Carolina, and war loomed in the former Soviet Union, as well as in India and Pakistan. Drought and pestilence destroy agriculture every year in some part of the world. Some economies surge as others falter. On a more personal scale, people are born, die, retire, find jobs, lose jobs, marry, divorce, and become ill.

In the face of this risk, it seems natural to have arrangements where the lucky share with the unlucky. Risk-sharing occurs informally in families and communities. The insurance market makes formal risk-sharing possible. Buyers pay a premium to obtain various kinds of insurance, such as homeowner's insurance. Total collected premiums are then available to help those whose houses burn down. The lucky, meanwhile, did not need insurance and have lost their premium. The market makes it possible for the lucky to help the unlucky.

In the business world, changes in commodity prices, exchange rates, and interest rates can be the financial equivalent of a house burning down. If the dollar becomes expensive relative to the Yen, some companies are helped and others are hurt. It makes sense for there to be a mechanism enabling companies to exchange this risk, so that the lucky can, in effect, help the unlucky.

You might be wondering what this discussion has to do with the notions of diversifiable and nondiversifiable risk familiar from portfolio theory. Risk is **diversifiable risk** if it is unrelated to other risks. The risk that a lightning strike will cause a factory to burn down, for example, is idiosyncratic and hence diversifiable. If many investors share a small piece of this risk, it has no significant effect on anyone. Risk that does not vanish when spread across many investors is **nondiversifiable risk.** The risk of a stock market crash, for example, is nondiversifiable.

Financial markets in theory serve two purposes. Markets permit diversifiable risk to be widely shared. This is efficient: By definition, diversifiable risk vanishes when it is widely shared. At the same time, financial markets permit nondiversifiable risk, which does not vanish when shared, to be held by those most willing to hold it. Thus, *the fundamental economic idea underlying the concepts and markets discussed in this book is that the existence of risk-sharing mechanisms benefits everyone.*

A risk-management problem faced by Tokyo Disneyland illustrates how it was able to diversify risk using capital markets. Disney decided that it would profit by opening a theme park in Japan. However, Japan is in a high-earthquake region. This location creates unavoidable risk for a theme park, or any business. Disney had several alternatives. First, it could have self-insured. In this case, Disney shareholders would have absorbed the earthquake risk. Second, Disney could have bought earthquake insurance from an insurance company. Because the insurance company's payout would be large if an earthquake did occur, that insurance company would likely have bought insurance for itself from *other* insurance companies, in what is called the reinsurance market. (Reinsurance is insurance for insurance companies, and it is one way for insurance risks to become more widely held.) In the end, the shareholders and bondholders of the reinsurance companies would have held the risk.

Disney took a third alternative, essentially bypassing intermediaries by issuing earthquake bonds, held directly by investors. The box on page 7 discusses these bonds.

All three alternatives—self-insurance, conventional insurance, and earthquake bonds—would have resulted in risk being held by numerous investors. The earthquake bond allowed earthquake risk to be borne by exactly those investors who wished to bear it.

1.3 DERIVATIVES IN PRACTICE

Derivatives use and the variety of derivatives have grown over the last 30 years.

The Tokyo Disneyland Bond

Oriental Land Co. Ltd. is licensed by the Walt Disney Co. to operate theme parks in Japan, including Tokyo Disneyland. In May 1999, the company issued a $100m 5-year earthquake bond, designed both to raise money and to provide earthquake insurance. The bond is structured so that in the event of a severe earthquake, Tokyo Disneyland is not obligated to repay the entire bond. Bondholders thus suffer a loss if an earthquake occurs.

Damage to Tokyo Disneyland would increase with the severity and proximity of the earthquake. The bond was structured to account for this, with the forgiveness of principal linked to the magnitude and location of the earthquake. If an earthquake rated above Richter 7.5 occurs within a 10km radius of the park, the entire bond is forgiven.

There is then a sliding scale down to Richter 6.5, at which point only 25% of the bond's principal is forgiven. The bond also specifies a middle and outer ring, extending to 75km from the park, with increasingly severe earthquakes necessary to trigger nonpayment of principal. The bond coupon was set to equal the London Interbank interest rate (LIBOR) plus 310 basis points.

This deal was the first in which a private company, rather than a reinsurer, issued a catastrophe bond. The bond is not perfect insurance for Oriental Land Co. since the bond payout is related to the severity of the earthquake, not specifically to damage to the park. A second $100m bond called for temporary nonpayment of interest in the event of an earthquake.

Growth in Derivatives Trading

If we examine recent history, the introduction of derivatives has coincided with increases in price risk in various markets. Currencies were officially permitted to float in 1971 when the gold standard was officially abandoned. OPEC's 1973 reduction in the supply of oil was followed by high and variable oil prices. U.S. interest rates became more volatile following inflation and recessions in the 1970s. The market for natural gas has been deregulated gradually since 1978, resulting in a volatile market in recent years. The deregulation of electricity began during the 1990s. Figures 1.1, 1.2, and 1.3 show the changes for oil prices, exchange rates, and interest rates. The link between price variability and the development of derivatives markets is natural—there is no need to manage risk when there is no risk.[2] When risk does exist, we would expect that markets will develop to permit efficient risk-sharing. Investors who have the most tolerance for risk will bear more of it, and risk-bearing will be widely spread among investors.

---

[2]It is sometimes argued that the existence of derivatives markets can increase the price variability of the underlying asset or commodity. Without some price risk in the first place, however, the derivatives market is unlikely to exist.

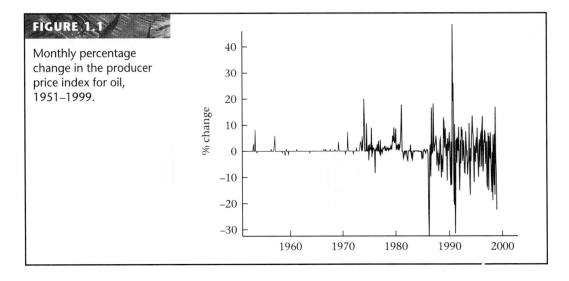

FIGURE 1.1

Monthly percentage change in the producer price index for oil, 1951–1999.

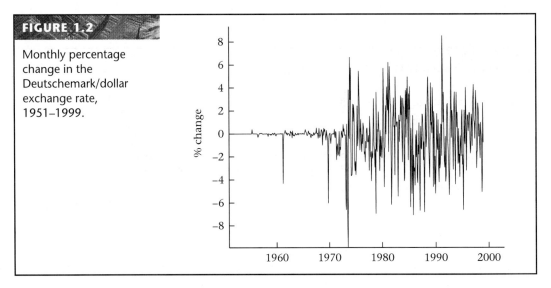

FIGURE 1.2

Monthly percentage change in the Deutschemark/dollar exchange rate, 1951–1999.

Figure 1.4 depicts contract volume for the three largest U.S. futures exchanges over the last 25 years. Table 1.1 illustrates the kinds of futures contracts traded at these exchanges.[3] Futures exchanges are an organized and regulated marketplace for trading

---

[3]The table lists only a fraction of the contracts traded at these exchanges. For example, in January 2002, the Chicago Mercantile Exchange Web page listed futures contracts on over 75 different underlying assets ranging from butter to a bankruptcy index.

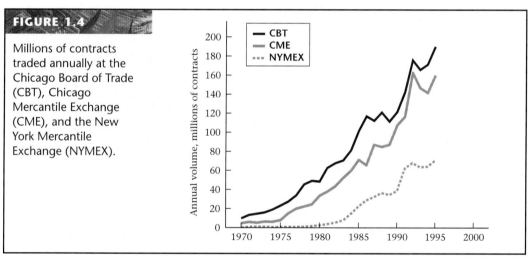

FIGURE 1.3

Monthly change in 3-month Treasury bill rate, 1951–1999.

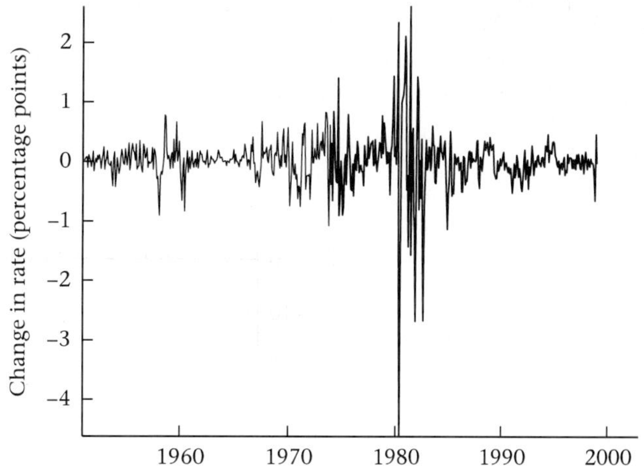

FIGURE 1.4

Millions of contracts traded annually at the Chicago Board of Trade (CBT), Chicago Mercantile Exchange (CME), and the New York Mercantile Exchange (NYMEX).

Source: CRB Commodity Yearbook.

futures contracts, a kind of derivative, but much commercial derivatives trading occurs in the **over-the-counter market,** where buyers and sellers transact with banks and dealers rather than on an exchange. It is difficult to obtain statistics for over-the-counter volume. However, in some markets, such as currencies, it is clear that the over-the-counter market is significantly larger than the exchange-traded market.

| TABLE 1.1 | Examples of futures contracts traded on the Chicago Board of Trade (CBT), Chicago Mercantile Exchange (CME), and the New York Mercantile Exchange (NYMEX). | |

CBT	CME	NYMEX
30-year U.S. Treasury Bonds	S&P 500 Index	Crude Oil
10-year U.S. Treasury Bonds	NASDAQ 100 Index	Natural Gas
Municipal Bond Index	Eurodollars	Heating Oil
Corn	Nikkei 225	Gasoline
Soybeans	Pork Bellies	Gold
Wheat	Heating and Cooling Degree-Days	Copper
Oats	Japanese Yen	Electricity

How Are Derivatives Used?

In recent years the U.S. Securities and Exchange Commission (SEC) and Financial Accounting Standards Board (FASB) have increased the requirements for corporations to report on their use of derivatives. Nevertheless, surprisingly little is known about how companies actually use derivatives to manage risk. The basic strategies companies use are well-understood—and will be described in this book—but it is not known, for example, what fraction of perceived risk is hedged by a given company, or by all companies in the aggregate. We frequently do not know a company's specific rationale for hedging or not hedging.

We would expect the use of derivatives to vary by type of firm. For example, financial firms, such as banks, are highly regulated and have capital requirements. They may have assets and liabilities in different currencies, with different maturities, and with different credit risks. Hence banks could be expected to use interest rate derivatives, currency derivatives, and credit derivatives to manage risks in those areas. Manufacturing firms that buy raw materials and sell in global markets might use commodity and currency derivatives, but their incentives to manage risk are less clear-cut because they are not regulated in the same ways as financial firms.

1.4 BUYING AND SHORT-SELLING FINANCIAL ASSETS

Throughout this book we will talk about buying and selling—and short-selling—assets such as stocks. These basic transactions are so important that it is worth describing the details. First, it is important to understand the costs associated with buying and selling. Second, a very important idea used throughout the book is that of short-sales. The concept of short-selling should be intuitive—a short-sale is just the opposite of a purchase—but for almost everyone it is hard to grasp at first. Even if you are familiar with short sales, spend a few minutes reading this section.

Buying an Asset

Suppose we want to buy 100 shares of XYZ stock. This seems simple: If the stock price is $50, 100 shares will cost $50 \times 100 = 5000. However, this calculation ignores transaction costs.

First, there is a commission, which is a transaction fee you pay your broker. A commission for the above order could be $15, or .3% of the purchase price.

Second, the term "stock price" is, surprisingly, imprecise. There are in fact two prices, a price at which you can buy, and a price at which you can sell. The price at which you can buy is called the **offer price** or **ask price,** and the price at which you can sell is called the **bid price.** Where do these terms come from?

If you want to buy stock, you pick up the phone and call a broker. If the stock is not too obscure and your order is not too large, your purchase will probably be completed in a matter of seconds. Have you ever wondered where the stock comes from that you have just bought? It is possible that at the exact same moment, another customer called the broker and put in an order to sell. More likely, however, a market-maker sold you the stock. Market-makers do what their name implies: They make markets. If you want to buy, they sell, and if you want to sell, they buy. In order to earn a living, market-makers sell for a high price and buy for a low price. If you deal with a market-maker, therefore, you buy for a high price and sell for a low price. This difference between the price at which you can buy and the price at which you can sell is called the **bid-ask spread.**[4] In practice the bid-ask spread on the stock you are buying may be $49.75 to $50. This means that you can buy for $50/share and sell for $49.75/share. If you were to buy immediately and then sell, you would pay the commission twice, and you would pay the bid-ask spread.

Note that when you observe prices in the real world, you will often see them bounce up and down a bit. This can reflect bid-ask bounce. If the bid is $49.75 and the ask is $50, a series of buy and sell orders will cause the price at which the stock was last traded to move between $49.75 and $50. The "true" price has not changed, however, because the bid and ask have not changed.

Example 1.1   Suppose XYZ is bid at $49.75 and offered at $50, and the commission is $15. If you buy 100 shares of the stock you pay ($50 \times 100) + $15 = 5015. If you

---

[4]If you think a bid-ask spread is unreasonable, ask what a world without dealers would be like. Every buyer would have to find a seller, and vice versa. The search would be costly and take time. Dealers, because they maintain inventory, offer an immediate transaction, a service called *immediacy*.

immediately sell them again, you receive ($49.75 × 100) − $15 = $4960. Your round trip transaction cost—the difference between what you pay and what you receive from a sale, not counting changes in the bid and ask prices—is $5015 − $4960 = $55.   ❧

Incidentally, this discussion reveals where the terms "bid" and "ask" come from. Your first thought might have been that the terminology is backward. The bid price sounds like it should be what you pay. It is in fact what the *market-maker* pays; hence it is the price at which you sell. The offer price is what the market-maker will sell for, hence it is what you have to pay. The terminology reflects the perspective of the market-maker.

One last point: What happens to your shares after you buy them? Generally they are held by your broker. If you read the fine print on your brokerage contract carefully, your broker typically has the right to lend your shares to another investor. Why would anyone want to borrow your shares? The answer to that brings us to the next topic, short-sales.

Although we have focused here on shares of stock, there are similar issues associated with buying any asset.

Short-Selling

When we buy something, we are said to have a *long* position in that thing. For example, if we buy the stock of XYZ, we pay cash and receive the stock. Some time later, we sell the stock and receive cash. This transaction is *lending*, in the sense that we pay money today and receive money back in the future. The rate of return we receive may not be known in advance (if the stock price goes up a lot, we get a high return; if the stock price goes down, we get a negative return), but it is a kind of loan nonetheless.

The opposite of a long position is a short position. A **short-sale** of XYZ entails borrowing shares of XYZ and then selling them, receiving the cash. Some time later, we buy back the XYZ stock, paying cash for it, and return it to the lender. The idea is to first sell high and then buy low. (With a long position, the idea is to first buy low and then sell high.) A short-sale can be viewed, then, as just a way of borrowing money. When you borrow money from a bank, you receive money today and repay it later, paying a rate of interest set in advance. This is also what happens with a short-sale, except that you don't necessarily know the rate you pay to borrow.

There are at least three reasons to short-sell:

1. **Speculation** A short-sale, considered by itself, makes money if the price of the stock goes down.

2. **Financing** A short-sale is a way to borrow money, and it is frequently used as a form of financing. This is very common in the bond market, for example.

3. **Hedging** You can undertake a short-sale to offset the risk of owning the stock or a derivative on the stock. This is frequently done by market-makers and traders.

These reasons are not mutually exclusive. For example, a market-maker might use a short-sale to simultaneously hedge and finance a position.

Because short-sales can seem confusing, here is a detailed example that illustrates how short-sales work.

Example: Short-selling pokey babies Consider the (hypothetical) "pokey-baby" phenomenon, in which small dolls representing Japanese cartoon characters become expensive collectors items that are bought and sold worldwide. Suppose, however, that you believe the pokey-baby phenomenon is over and that prices of pokey babies are going to fall. How could you speculate based on this belief?

If you believed prices would rise, you would buy pokey babies today and sell later. However, if you believed prices would fall, you would like to do the opposite: Sell today (at the high price) and buy tomorrow (at the low price). How do you actually accomplish this?

In order to sell today, you must first obtain pokey babies to sell. You can do this by borrowing them from a collector. The collector, of course, will want a promise that the pokey babies will be returned at some point, so suppose you agree to return them in one week. Thus, you borrow them and sell them at the market price. After one week, you acquire replacement pokey babies on the market, then return them to the collector from whom you borrowed them. If the price has fallen, you have made money, while if the price has risen you have lost money. Whatever happens to the price, you have just completed a *short-sale* of pokey babies. The act of buying the pokey baby and returning it to the lender is said to be *closing* or *covering* the short position.

Note that you really have borrowed money. Initially, you received money from selling the pokey babies, and a week later you pay the money back (you had to buy the pokey babies back to return them). The rate of interest you paid was low if the pokey-baby price was low, and high if the pokey-baby price was high.

This example is obviously simplified. We have assumed that

- It is easy to find a pokey-baby lender.

- It is easy to buy, at a fair price, a satisfactory pokey baby to return to the lender. The pokey babies you buy after one week are a perfect substitute for the pokey babies you borrowed.

- The collector from whom you borrowed is not concerned that you will fail to return the borrowed toy.

Example: Short-selling stock Now consider a short-sale of stock. As with the previous example, when you short-sell stock you borrow the stock and sell it, receiving cash today. At some future date you buy the stock in the market and return it to the original owner. You have cash coming in today, equal to the market value of the stock you short-sell. In the future, you repay the borrowing by buying the asset at its then-current market price and returning the asset—this is like the repayment of a loan. Thus, short-selling a stock is equivalent to borrowing money, except that the interest rate you pay is not known in advance. Rather, it is determined by the change in the stock price. The rate of

TABLE 1.2	Cash flows associated with short-selling a share of IBM for 90 days. Note that the short-seller must pay the dividend, D, to the share-lender.		
	Day 0	**Dividend Ex-Day**	**Day 90**
Action	Borrow Shares	—	Return Shares
Security	Sell Shares	—	Purchase Shares
Cash	$+S_0$	$-D$	$-S_{90}$

interest is high if the security rises in price and low if the security falls in price. In effect, the rate of return on the security is the rate at which you borrow. With a short-sale, you are like the *issuer* of a security rather than the buyer of a security.

Suppose you want to short-sell IBM stock for 90 days. Table 1.2 depicts the cash flows. Observe in particular that if the share pays dividends, the short-seller must in turn make dividend payments to the share-lender. This issue did not arise with pokey babies! This dividend payment is taxed to the recipient, just like an ordinary dividend payment, and it is tax-deductible to the short-seller.

Notice that the cash flows in Table 1.2 are exactly the opposite of the cash flows from purchasing the stock. Thus, *short-selling is literally the opposite of buying.*

The Lease Rate of an Asset

We have seen that when you borrow an asset it may be necessary to make payments to the lender. Dividends on short-sold stock are an example of this. We will refer to the payment required by the lender as the **lease rate** of the asset. This concept will arise frequently, and, as we will see, provides a unifying concept for our later discussions of derivatives.

The pokey-baby example did not have a lease payment. But under some circumstances it might be necessary to make a payment to borrow a pokey baby. Pokey babies do not pay an explicit dividend, but they do pay an implicit dividend if the owner enjoys seeing them on the shelf. The owner might thus require a payment in order to lend a pokey baby. This would be a lease rate for pokey babies.

Risk and Scarcity in Short-Selling

The preceding examples were simple illustrations of the mechanics and economics of short-selling, and demonstrate the ideas you will need to understand our discussions of derivatives. It turns out, however, that some of the complexities we skipped over are easy to understand and are important in practice. In this section we return to the pokey-baby example to illustrate some of these practical issues.

Credit risk   As the short-seller, you have an obligation to the pokey-baby lender to return the toys. The pokey-baby lender fears that you will renege on this obligation. This concern can be addressed with collateral: After you sell the pokey babies, the pokey-baby lender can hold the money you received from selling the pokey babies. You have an obligation to return the toy; the lender keeps the money in the event that you don't.

Holding on to the money will help the lender feel more secure, but after thinking the matter over, the lender will likely want more from you than just the value of the pokey babies. Suppose you borrow $5000 worth of pokey babies. What happens, the lender will think, if the price of the pokey babies rises to $6000 one week later? This is a $1000 loss on your short-sale. In order to return the toys, you will have to pay $6000 for toys you just sold for $5000. Perhaps you cannot afford the extra $1000 and you will fail to return the borrowed toys. The lender, thinking ahead, will be worried at the outset about this possibility and will ask you to provide *more* than the $5000 the pokey babies are worth, say an extra $1000. This extra amount is called a **haircut,** and serves to protect the lender against your failure to return the toys when the price rises.[5]   In practice, short-sellers must have funds—called *capital*—to be able to pay haircuts. The amount of capital places a limit on their ability to short-sell.

Scarcity   As the short-seller, do you need to worry about the short-sale proceeds? The lender is going to have $6000 of your money. Most of this, however, simply reflects your obligation, and we could imagine asking a trustworthy third party, such as a bank, to hold the money so the lender cannot abscond with it. However, when you return the toys, you are going to want your money back, *plus interest*. This raises the question: What rate of interest will the lender pay you? Over the course of the short-sale, the lender can invest your money, earning, say, 6%. The lender could offer to pay you 4% on the funds, thinking to keep as a fee the 2% difference between the 6% earned on the money and the 4% paid to you. What happens if the lender and borrower negotiate?

Here is the interesting point: The rate of interest the lender pays on the collateral is going to depend on how many people want to borrow pokey babies and how many are willing to lend them! As a practical matter, it may not be easy to find a lender. If there is high demand for borrowed pokey babies, the lender will offer a low rate of interest, essentially earning a fee for being willing to lend something that is scarce. However, if no one else wants to borrow the toys, the lender might conclude that a small fee is better than nothing and offer you a rate of interest close to the market rate.

The rate paid on collateral is called different things in different markets, the **repo rate** in bond markets and the **short rebate** in the stock market. Whatever it is called, the difference between this rate and the market rate of interest is another cost to your short-sale.

---

[5]Note that the lender is not concerned about your failure to perform when the price goes down because the lender has the money!

CHAPTER SUMMARY

Derivatives are financial instruments with a payoff determined by the price of something else. They can be used as a tool for risk management, for speculation, to reduce transaction costs, or to avoid taxes or regulation.

One important function of financial markets is to facilitate optimal risk-sharing. The growth of derivatives markets over the last 50 years has coincided with an increase in the risks evident in various markets. Events such as the 1973 oil shock, the abandonment of fixed exchange rates, and the deregulation of energy markets have created a new role for derivatives.

A short-sale entails borrowing a security, selling it, making dividend (or other cash) payments to the security lender, and then returning it. A short-sale is conceptually the opposite of a purchase. Short-sales can be used for speculation, as a form of financing, or as a way to hedge. Many of the details of short-selling in practice can be understood as a response to credit risk of the short-seller and scarcity of shares that can be borrowed. Short-sellers typically leave the short-sale proceeds on deposit with lenders, along with additional capital called a haircut. The rate paid on this collateral is called the short rebate, and is less than the interest rate.

FURTHER READING

The rest of this book provides an elaboration of themes discussed in this chapter. However, certain chapters are directly related to the discussion. Chapters 2, 3, and 4 introduce forward and option contracts, which are the basic contracts in derivatives, and show how they are used in risk management. Chapter 13 discusses in detail how derivatives market-makers manage their risk, and Chapter 15 explains how derivatives can be combined with instruments such as bonds to create customized risk-management products.

The various derivatives exchanges have websites which list their contracts. The websites for the exchanges in Figure 1.4 are **www.cbot.com** (Chicago Board of Trade), **www.cme.com** (Chicago Mercantile Exchange), and **www.nymex.com** (New York Mercantile Exchange).

Jorion (1995) examines in detail one famous "derivatives disaster": Orange County in California. Bernstein (1992) is a history of the development of financial markets, and Bernstein (1996) discusses the concept of risk measurement and how it evolved over the last 800 years. Miller (1986) discusses origins of past financial innovation, and Merton (1999) provides a fascinating academic perspective on possible *future* developments in financial markets. Froot and O'Connell (1999) and Froot (2001) examine the market for catastrophe reinsurance. D'Avolio (2001) explains the economics and practices associated with short-sales. Finally, Lewis (1989) is a classic, funny, insider's account of investment banking, offering a different (to say the least) perspective on the mechanics of global risk-sharing.

PROBLEMS

1.1. Heating degree-day and cooling degree-day futures contracts make payments based on whether the temperature is abnormally hot or cold. Explain why the following businesses might be interested in such a contract:

    a. Soft-drink manufacturers.

    b. Ski-resort operators.

    c. Electric utilities.

    d. Amusement park operators.

1.2. Suppose the businesses in the previous problem use futures contracts to hedge their temperature-related risk. Who do you think might accept the opposite risk?

1.3. ABC stock has a bid price of $40.95 and an ask price of $41.05. Assume there is a $20 brokerage commission.

    a. What amount will you pay to buy 100 shares?

    b. What amount will you receive for selling 100 shares?

    c. Suppose you buy 100 shares, then immediately sell 100 shares with the bid and ask prices being the same in both cases. What is your round-trip transaction cost?

1.4. Repeat the previous problem supposing that the brokerage fee is quoted as 0.3% of the bid or ask price.

1.5. Suppose a security has a bid price of $100 and an ask price of $100.12. At what price can the market-maker purchase a security? At what price can a market-maker sell a security? What is the spread in dollar terms when 100 shares are traded?

1.6. Suppose you short-sell 300 shares of XYZ stock at $30.19 with a commission charge of 0.5%. Supposing you pay commission charges for purchasing the security to cover the short-sale, how much profit have you made if you close the short-sale at a price of $29.87?

1.7. Suppose you desire to short-sell 400 shares of JKI stock, which has a bid price of $25.12 and an ask price of $25.31. You cover the short position 180 days later when the bid price is $22.87 and the ask price is $23.06.

    a. Taking into account only the bid and ask prices (ignoring commissions and interest), what profit did you earn?

    b. Suppose that there is a 0.3% commission to engage in the short-sale (this is the commission to sell the stock) and a 0.3% commission to close the short-sale (this is the commission to buy the stock back). How do these commissions change the profit in the previous answer?

c. Suppose the 6-month interest rate is 3% and that you are paid nothing on the short-sale proceeds. How much interest do you lose during the 6 months in which you have the short position?

1.8. When you open a brokerage account, you typically sign an agreement giving the broker the right to lend your shares without notifying or compensating you. Why do brokers want you to sign this agreement?

1.9. Suppose a stock pays a quarterly dividend of $3. You plan to hold a short position in the stock across the dividend ex-date. What is your obligation on that date? If you are a taxable investor, what would you guess is the tax consequence of the payment? (In particular, would you expect the dividend to be tax deductible?) Suppose the company announces instead that the dividend is $5. Should you care that the dividend is different from what you expected?

1.10. Short interest is a measure of the aggregate short positions on a stock. Check an online brokerage or other financial service for the short interest on several stocks of your choice. Can you guess which stocks have high short interest and which have low? Is it theoretically possible for short interest to exceed 100% of shares outstanding?

1.11. Suppose that you go to a bank and borrow $100. You promise to repay the loan in 90 days for $102. Explain this transaction using the terminology of short-sales.

1.12. Suppose your bank's loan officer tells you that if you take out a mortgage (i.e., you borrow money to buy a house) you will be permitted to borrow no more than 80% of the value of the house. Describe this transaction using the terminology of short-sales.

PART 1

INSURANCE, HEDGING, AND SIMPLE STRATEGIES

In this part of the book, Chapters 2–4, we examine the basic derivatives contracts: Forward contracts, futures contracts, call options, and put options. All of these are contracts between two parties, with a payoff at some future date based on the price of an underlying assett (this is why they are called derivatives).

There are a number of things we want to understand about these instruments. What are they? How do they work and what do they cost? If you enter into a forward contract, futures contract, or option, what obligations or rights have you acquired? Payoff and profit diagrams provide an important graphical tool to summarize the risk of these contracts.

Once we understand what the basic derivatives contracts are, what can we do with them? We will see that, among other things, they can be used to provide insurance, to convert a stock investment into a risk-free investment and vice versa, and to speculate in a variety of ways. Derivatives can often be customized for a particular purpose. We will see how corporate risk managers can use derivatives, and some reasons for doing so.

In this part of the book we take the prices of derivatives as given; the underlying pricing models will be covered in much of the rest of the

book. The main mathematical tool is present and future value calcu-
lations. We do, however, develop one key pricing idea: Put-call parity.
Put-call parity is important because it demonstrates a link among the dif-
ferent contracts we examine in these chapters, telling us how the prices of
forward contracts, call options, and put options are related to one another.

Chapter 2

An Introduction to Forwards and Options

This chapter introduces the basic derivatives contracts: forward contracts, call options, and put options. These fundamental contracts are widely used, and serve as building blocks for more complicated derivatives that we discuss in later chapters. We explain here how the contracts work and how to think about their risk. We also introduce an extremely important tool for analyzing derivatives positions, namely payoff and profit diagrams. The terminology and concepts introduced in this chapter are fundamental and will be used throughout this book.

2.1 FORWARD CONTRACTS

To understand how a forward contract works, first consider the simple transaction of buying a share of stock. Buying a share of stock entails at least three separate steps: (1) setting the price to be paid, (2) transferring cash from the buyer to the seller, and (3) transferring the share from the seller to the buyer. With an outright purchase of stock, all three occur simultaneously. However, as a logical matter, we could set a price today and have the transfer of shares and cash occur at a specified date in the future.

This is in fact how a **forward contract** works: The contract sets today the terms at which you buy or sell an asset or commodity at a specific time in the future. The time at which the contract settles is called the **expiration date.** The asset or commodity on which the forward contract is based is called the **underlying asset.** A forward contract:

- Specifies the quantity and exact type of the asset or commodity the seller must deliver.
- Specifies delivery logistics, such as time, date, and place.
- Specifies the price the buyer will pay at the time of delivery.
- Obligates the seller to sell and the buyer to buy, subject to the above specifications.

Apart from commissions and bid-ask spreads (see Section 1.4), a forward contract requires no initial payment or premium. The contractual forward price simply represents the price at which consenting adults agree today to transact in the future, at which time the buyer pays the seller the forward price and the seller delivers the asset.

Futures contracts are similar to forward contracts in that they create an obligation to buy or sell at a predetermined price at a future date. The institutional and pricing differences between forwards and futures will be discussed in Chapter 5. For the time being, think of them as interchangeable.

Figure 2.1 shows futures price listings from the *Wall Street Journal* for futures contracts on several stock indices, including the Dow Jones Industrial Average (DJ 30) and the Standard and Poor's 500 (S&P 500). The indices are the underlying assets for the contracts. (A **stock index** is the average price of a group of stocks. In these examples we work with this group price rather than the price of just one stock.) The first column of the listing gives the expiration month. Following are the price at the beginning of the day (the open), the high and low during the day, and the settlement price, which reflects the last transactions of the day.

The listing also gives the price change from the previous day, the high and low during the life of the futures contract, and open interest, which measures the number of contracts outstanding. (Since each trade of a contract has both a buyer and a seller, a buyer-seller pair counts as one contract.) Finally, the head of the listing tells us where the contracts trade (the Chicago Board of Trade [CBOT] and Chicago Mercantile Exchange [CME]), and the size of the contract, which for the S&P 500 is $250 times the index value. We will discuss such futures contracts in more detail in Chapter 5. There are many more exchange-traded stock index futures contracts than those in Figure 2.1, both in the United States and around the world.

The price quotes in Figure 2.1 are from February. The March and June prices for the two contracts are therefore prices set in February for purchase of the index in later months. For example, the March S&P 500 futures price is $1095.30 and the June price is $1097.30.[1] By contrast, the current S&P index price that day is $1094.44. This is the **spot price** for the index: The market price for immediate delivery of the index.

We will discuss in Chapter 5 how forward and futures prices are determined (why, for example, is the futures price greater than the index value for both contracts in Figure 2.1?) and more details about how futures contracts work. In this chapter we take prices as given and examine profit and loss on a forward contract. We will also see how a position in a forward contract is similar to and different from alternative investments, such as a direct investment in the underlying index.

The Payoff on a Forward Contract

Every forward contract has both a buyer and a seller. The term **long** is used to describe the buyer and **short** is used to describe the seller. Generally, a long position is one that makes money when the price goes up and a short is one that makes money when the price goes down. Because the long has agreed to buy at the fixed forward price, a long position profits if prices rise.

[1]The use and nonuse of dollar signs for futures prices can be confusing. Many futures prices, in particular those for index futures, are in practice quoted without dollar signs, and multiplied by a dollar amount to determine the value of the contract. In this and the next several chapters, we will depart from this convention and use dollar signs for index futures prices. When we discuss the S&P 500 index futures contract in Chapter 5, however, we will follow practice and omit the dollar sign.

FIGURE 2.1

Index futures price listings.

	OPEN	HIGH	LOW	SETTLE	CHANGE	LIFETIME HIGH	LIFETIME LOW	OPEN INT.
INDEX								
DJ Industrial Average (CBOT)-$10 times average								
Mar	9891	9902	9655	9683	– 224	11150	7900	27,474
June	9865	9830	9665	9688	– 228	10951	9080	589

Est vol 21,000; vol Fri 17,070; open int 28,254, +822.
Idx prl: Hi 9905.46; Lo 9677.54; Close 9687.09, –220.17.

S&P 500 Index (CME)-$250 times index								
Mar	112350	112370	109100	109530	– 2810	134960	94100	474,811
June	111950	111950	109350	109730	– 2830	170550	95030	17,224
Dec	111580	111580	110020	110390	– 2930	150070	96130	304

Est vol 79,914; vol Fri 65,250; open int 502,626, –701.
Idx prl: Hi 1122.20; Lo 1092.25; Close 1094.44, –27.76.

Mini S&P 500 (CME)-$50 times index								
Mar	112325	112400	109100	109525	– 2825	117850	99850	100,297

Vol Fri 193,620; open int 100,323, –4,791.

S&P Midcap 400 (CME)-$500 times index								
Mar	502.70	504.00	492.75	493.95	– 10.95	560.00	412.95	13,453

Est vol 1,140; vol Fri 1,101; open int 13,453, –207.
Idx prl: Hi 504.26; Lo 492.74; Close 493.38, –10.88.

Nikkei 225 Stock Average (CME)-$5 times index								
Mar	9690.	9700.	9555.	9580.	– 130	14620.	9245.	15,750

Est vol 667; vol Fri 2,100; open int 15,817, –17.
Idx prl: Hi 9809.82; Lo 9523.99; Close 9631.93, –159.50.

Nasdaq 100 (CME)-$100 times index								
Mar	152900	153550	147300	148700	– 4800	189400	112000	51,803

Est vol 18,215; vol Fri 17,500; open int 51,812, +763.
Idx prl: Hi 1528.30; Lo 1471.52; Close 1479.17, –48.98.

Source: Wall Street Journal, February 5, 2002.

The **payoff** to a contract is the value of the position at expiration. The payoff to a long forward contract is

$$\text{Payoff to long forward} = \text{Spot price at expiration} - \text{forward price} \qquad (2.1)$$

Because the short has agreed to sell at the fixed forward price, the short profits if prices fall. The payoff to a short forward contract is

$$\text{Payoff to short forward} = \text{Forward price} - \text{spot price at expiration} \qquad (2.2)$$

To illustrate these calculations, consider a forward contract on a hypothetical stock index. Suppose the non-dividend-paying S&R ("Special and Rich") 500 index has a current price of $1000 and the 6-month forward price is $1020.[2] The holder of a long position in the S&R forward contract is obligated to pay $1020 in 6 months for one unit of the index. The holder of the short position is obligated to sell one unit of the index for $1020. Table 2.1 lists the payoff on the position for various possible future values of the index.

Example 2.1　Suppose the index price is $1050 in 6 months. A holder who entered a long position at a forward price of $1020 is obligated to pay $1020 to acquire the index, and hence earns $1050 − $1020 = $30 per unit of the index. The short is likewise obligated to sell for $1020, and thus loses $30. ❦

---

[2]We use a hypothetical stock index in order to avoid complications associated with dividends. We discuss dividends—and real stock indices—in Chapter 5.

| TABLE 2.1 | Payoff after 6 months from a long S&R forward contract and a short S&R forward contract at a forward price of $1020. If the index price in 6 months is $1020, both the long and short have a 0 payoff. If the index price is greater than $1020, the long makes money and the short loses money. If the index price is less than $1020, the long loses money and the short makes money. |

S&R Index	S&R Forward	
in 6 Months	Long	Short
900	−$120	$120
950	−70	70
1000	−20	20
1020	0	0
1050	30	−30
1100	80	−80

This example illustrates the mechanics of a forward contract, showing why the long makes money when the price rises and the short makes money when the price falls.

Graphing the Payoff on a Forward Contract

We can graph the information in Table 2.1 to show the payoff in 6 months on the forward contract as a function of the index. Figure 2.2 graphs the long and short positions, with the index price at the expiration of the forward contract on the horizontal axis and payoff on the vertical axis. As you would expect, the two positions have a zero payoff when the index price in 6 months equals the forward price of $1020. The graph for the short forward is a mirror image (about the x-axis) of the graph for the long forward. For a given value of the index, the payoff to the short is exactly the opposite of the payoff to the long. In other words, the gain to one party is the loss to the other.

This kind of graph is widely used because it summarizes the risk of the position at a glance.

Comparing a Forward and Outright Purchase

The S&R forward contract is a way to acquire the index by paying $1020 after 6 months. An alternative way to acquire the index is to purchase it outright at time 0, paying $1000. Is there any advantage to using the forward contract to buy the index, as opposed to purchasing it outright?

If we buy the S&R index today, it costs us $1000. The value of the position in 6 months is the value of the S&R index. The payoff to a long position in the physical S&R

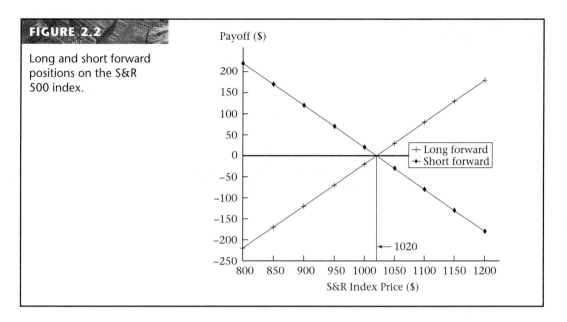

FIGURE 2.2

Long and short forward positions on the S&R 500 index.

index is graphed in Figure 2.3. For comparison the payoff to the long forward position, from Figure 2.2, is graphed as well. Note that the axes have different scales in Figure 2.3 than in Figure 2.2.

To see how the graph is constructed, suppose the S&R index price is $0 after 6 months. (This is just a thought experiment for the purpose of constructing the graph, but if you would like to be concrete, imagine that the S&R index contained Internet firms in the year 2000 which would be bankrupt in 2001.) If the index price is $0, the physical index will be worth $0; hence the physical index graph plots a 0 on the y-axis against 0 on the x-axis. For all other prices of the S&R index, the payoff equals the value of the S&R index. For example, if we own the index and the price in 6 months is $750, the value of the position is $750.

The payoff to the forward contract, using equation (2.1), is

$$\text{Payoff to long forward} = 0 - \$1020 = -\$1020$$

If the index price is $1020, the long index position will be worth $1020 and the forward contract will be worth $0.

With both positions, we own the index after 6 months. What the figure does not reflect, however, is the different *initial* investments required for the two positions. With the cash index, we invest $1000 initially and then we own the index. With the forward contract, we invest $0 initially and $1020 after 6 months; then we own the index. The payoff graph tells us how much money we end up with after 6 months, but does not account for the initial $1000 investment with the outright purchase. Figure 2.3 is accurate, but it does not answer our question, namely whether there is an advantage to either a forward purchase or an outright purchase.

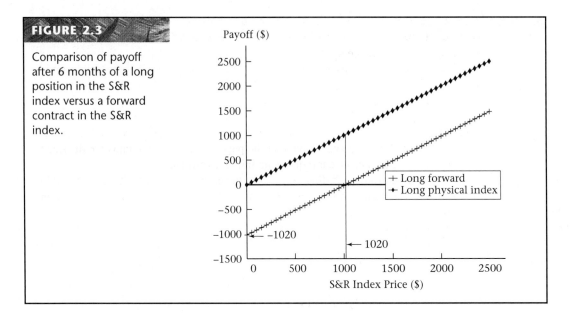

FIGURE 2.3

Comparison of payoff after 6 months of a long position in the S&R index versus a forward contract in the S&R index.

Both positions give us ownership of the S&R index after 6 months. We can compare them fairly if we equate the amounts initially invested and then account for interest earned over the 6 months. We can do this in either of two equivalent ways:

1. Invest $1000 in zero-coupon bonds (for example, Treasury bills) along with the forward contract, in which case each position initally costs $1000 at time 0.

2. Borrow to buy the physical S&R index, in which case each position initially costs $0 at time 0.

Suppose the 6-month interest rate is 2%. With alternative 1, we pay $1000 today. After 6 months the zero-coupon bond is worth $1000 × 1.02 = $1020. At that point, we use the bond proceeds to pay the forward price of $1020. We then own the index. The net effect is that we pay $1000 initially and own the index after 6 months, just as if we bought the index outright. Investing $1000 and at the same time entering a long forward contract mimics the effect of buying the index outright.

With alternative 2, we borrow $1000 to buy the index, which costs $1000. Hence we make no net cash payment at time 0. After 6 months we owe $1000 plus interest. At that time we repay $1000 × 1.02 = $1020 for the borrowed money. The net effect is that we invest nothing initially, and after six months pay $1020. We also own the index. Borrowing to buy the stock therefore mimics the effect of entering into a long forward contract.

We conclude that the only difference between the forward contract and the cash index investment is the timing of a payment that will be made for certain. Therefore, we can compare the two positions by using the interest rate to shift the timing of payments.

In the above example, we conclude that the forward contract and the cash index are equivalent investments, differing only in the timing of the cash flows. Neither form of investing has an advantage over the other.

This analysis suggests a way to systematically compare positions that require different initial investments. We can assume that we borrow any required initial payment. At expiration, we receive the payoff from the contract, and repay any borrowed amounts. We will call this the **net payoff** or **profit.** Because this calculation accounts for differing initial investments in a simple fashion, we will primarily use profit rather than payoff diagrams throughout the book.[3] Note that the payoff and profit diagrams are the same for a forward contract because it requires no initial investment.

To summarize, a **payoff diagram** graphs the cash value of a position at a point in time. A **profit diagram** subtracts from the payoff the future value of the investment in the position.

This discussion begs the question: Should we really expect the forward price to equal $1020, which is the future value of the index? The answer in this case is yes, but we defer a detailed explanation until Chapter 5.

Zero-Coupon Bonds in Payoff and Profit Diagrams

The preceding discussion showed that the long forward contract and outright purchase of the physical S&R index are essentially the same once we take time value of money into account. We saw that buying the physical index is like entering into the forward contract and simultaneously investing $1000 in a zero-coupon bond. We can see this same point graphically by using a payoff diagram where we include a zero-coupon bond.

Suppose we enter into a long S&R index forward position, and at the same time purchase a $1000 zero-coupon bond, which will pay $1020 after 6 months. (This was alternative 1 in the previous section.) Algebraically, the payoff to the forward plus the bond is

$$\text{Forward} + \text{bond} = \underbrace{\text{Spot price at expiration} - \$1020}_{\text{Forward payoff}} + \underbrace{\$1020}_{\text{Bond payoff}}$$

$$= \text{Spot price at expiration}$$

This is the same as the payoff to investing in the physical index.

The payoff diagram for this position is an easy modification of Figure 2.3. We simply add a line representing the value of the bond after 6 months ($1000 × 1.02 = $1020), and then add the bond payoff to the forward payoff. This is graphed in Figure 2.4. The forward plus bond looks exactly like the physical index in Figure 2.3.

What is the profit diagram corresponding to this payoff diagram? For the forward contract, profit is the same as the payoff because there is no initial investment. Profit for

---

[3]The term "profit" is defined variously by accountants and economists. All of our profit calculations are for the purpose of *comparing* one position to another, not computing profit in any absolute sense.

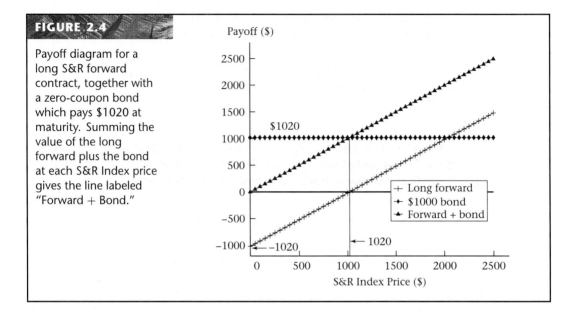

FIGURE 2.4

Payoff diagram for a long S&R forward contract, together with a zero-coupon bond which pays $1020 at maturity. Summing the value of the long forward plus the bond at each S&R Index price gives the line labeled "Forward + Bond."

the forward plus bond is obtained by subtracting the future value of the initial investment. The initial investment was the cost of the bond, $1000. Its future value is, by definition, $1020, the value of the bond after 6 months. Thus, the profit diagram for a forward contract plus a bond is obtained by *ignoring* the bond! Put differently, adding a bond to a position leaves a profit diagram unaffected.

Depending on the context, it can be helpful to draw either payoff or profit diagrams. Bonds can be used to shift payoff diagrams vertically, but do not change the profit calculation.

Cash Settlement versus Delivery

The foregoing discussion assumed that at expiration of the forward contract, the contract called for the seller (the party short the forward contract) to deliver the cash S&R index to the buyer (the party long the forward contract). However, a physical transaction in a broad stock index will likely have significant transaction costs. An alternative settlement procedure which is widely used is **cash settlement.** Instead of requiring delivery of the actual index, the forward contract settles financially. The two parties make cash payment, which is as if delivery had occurred, and both parties had then closed out their positions. We can illustrate this with an example.

Example 2.2   Suppose that the S&R index at expiration is $1040. Because the forward price is $1020, the long position has a payoff of $20. Similarly, the short position loses $20. With cash settlement, the short simply pays $20 to the long, with no transfer of the physical asset, and hence no transaction costs. It is as if the long paid $1020, acquired the index worth $1040, and then immediately sold it with no transaction costs.

If the S&R index price at expiration had instead been $960, the long position would have a payoff of −$60 and the short would have a payoff of $60. Cash settlement in this case entails the long paying $60 to the short.   ⧶

Cash settlement is feasible only when there is an accepted reference price upon which the settlement can be based. Cash settlement is not limited to forward contracts—virtually any financial contract can be settled using cash rather than delivery.

Credit Risk

Any forward or futures contract—indeed, any derivatives contract—has **credit risk,** which means there is a possibility that the counterparty who owes money fails to make a payment. If you agree to sell the index in one year at a fixed price and the spot price turns out to be lower than the forward price, the counterparty is obligated to buy the index for more than it is worth. You face the risk that the counterparty will for some reason fail to pay the forward price for the index. Similarly the counterparty faces the risk that you will not fulfill the contract if the spot price in one year turns out to be higher than the forward price.

With exchange-traded contracts, the exchange goes to great lengths to minimize this risk by requiring collateral of all participants and being the ultimate counterparty in all transactions. We will discuss credit risk and collateral in more detail when we discuss futures contracts in Chapter 5. With over-the-counter contracts, the fact that the contracts are transacted directly between two parties means that each counterparty bears the credit risk of the other.[4]

Credit risk is an important problem with all derivatives, but it is also quite complicated. Credit checks of counterparties and credit protections such as collateral and bank letters of credit are commonly employed to guard against losses from counterparty default.

2.2 CALL OPTIONS

We have seen that a forward contract obligates the buyer (the holder of the long position) to pay the forward price at expiration, even if the value of the underlying asset at expiration is less than the forward price. Because losses are possible with a forward contract, it is natural to wonder: Could there be a contract where the buyer has the right to walk away from the deal?

---

[4]Of course, credit risk also exists in exchange-traded contracts. The specific details of how exchanges are structured to minimize credit risk is a complicated and fascinating subject (see Edwards and Ma, 1992, Chapter 3, for details). In practice, exchanges are regarded by participants as good credit risks.

The answer is yes; a contract where the buyer has the right to buy, but not the obligation to buy, is a **call option.** Here is an example illustrating how a call option works at expiration.

Example 2.3   Suppose that the call buyer agrees to pay $1020 for the S&R index in 6 months, but is not obligated to do so. (The buyer has purchased a call option.) If in 6 months the S&R price is $1100, the buyer will pay $1020 and receive the index. This is a payoff of $80 per unit of the index. If the S&R price is $900, the buyer walks away.

Now think about this transaction from the seller's point of view. The buyer is in control of the option, deciding when to buy the index by paying $1020. Thus, the rights of the option buyer are obligations for the option seller.

Example 2.4   If in 6 months the S&R price is $1100, the seller will receive $1020 and give up an index worth more, for a loss of $80 per unit of the index. If the S&R price is less than $1020, the buyer will not buy, so the seller has no obligation. Thus, at expiration, the seller will have a payoff which is zero (if the S&R price is less than $1020) or negative (if the S&R price is greater than $1020).

Does it seem as if something is wrong here? Because the buyer can decide whether to buy, the seller *cannot* make money at expiration. This situation suggests that the seller must, in effect, be "bribed" to enter into the contract in the first place. At the time the buyer and seller agree to the contract, the buyer must pay the seller an initial price, or **premium.** This initial payment compensates the seller for being at a disadvantage at expiration. Contrast this with a forward contract, for which the initial premium is zero.

Option Terminology

Here are some key terms used to describe options:

Strike price   The **strike price,** or **exercise price,** of a call option is what the buyer pays for the asset. In the example above, the strike price was $1020. The strike price can be set at any value.

Exercise   The **exercise** of a call option is the act of paying the strike price to receive the asset. In Example 2.3, the buyer decided after 6 months whether to exercise the option, that is, whether to pay $1020 (the strike price) to receive the S&R index.

Expiration   The **expiration** of the option is the date by which the option must either be exercised or it becomes worthless. The option in Example 2.3 had an expiration of 6 months.

Exercise style The **exercise style** of the option governs the time at which exercise can occur. In the above example, exercise could occur only at expiration. Such an option is said to be a **European-style option.** If the buyer has the right to exercise at any time during the life of the option, it is an **American-style option.** If the buyer can only exercise during specified periods, but not for the entire life of the option, the option is a **Bermudan-style option.** (The terms "European" and "American," by the way, have nothing to do with geography. European, American, and Bermudan options are bought and sold worldwide.)

To summarize, a European call option gives the owner of the call the right, but not the obligation, to buy the underlying asset on the expiration date by paying the strike price. The option described in Examples 2.3 and 2.4 is a *6-month European-style S&R call with a strike price of $1020.* The buyer of the call can also be described as having a *long position* in the call.

Figure 2.5 presents a small portion of the option price listings for the S&P 500 Index option traded at the Chicago Board Options Exchange. Each row represents a different option, with the expiration month, strike price, a "c" or a "p" to denote call or put, the number of contracts traded that day, the premium at the last trade of the day, the change from the previous day, and open interest. As with futures, every option trade requires a buyer and a seller, so open interest measures the number of buyer-seller pairs. The box below discusses some of the mechanics of buying an option.

How Do You Buy an Option?

How would you actually buy an option? The quick answer is that buying an option is just like buying a stock. Option premiums are quoted just like stock prices. Figure 2.5 provides an example. (For current quotes see, for example, **http://www.cboe.com**; this shows bid and ask prices at the Chicago Board Options Exchange.) Using either an online or flesh-and-blood broker, you can enter an order to buy an option. As with stocks, in addition to the option premium, you pay a commission, and there is a bid-ask spread.

Options on numerous stocks are traded on exchanges, and for any given stock or index, there can be over a hundred options available, differing in strike price and expiration date. (In December 2000, a quick count at the Chicago Board Options Exchange website showed approximately 250 options, with differing strikes and maturities, both puts and calls, with the S&P 500 index as the underlying asset.) Options may be either American or European. If you buy an American option, you have to be aware that exercising the option prior to expiration may be optimal. Thus, you need to have some understanding of why and when exercise might make sense.

You can also sell, or write, options. In this case, you have to post collateral (called margin) to protect others against the possibility you will default. See Appendix 2.A for a discussion of this and other issues.

Closing options prices for S&P 500 index options from the Chicago Board Options Exchange.

STRIKE		VOL.	LAST	NET CHG.	OPEN INT.
			S & P 500(SPX)		
Feb	1080 c	100	26.50	...	...
Feb	1080 p	358	13	+ 8.00	5
Mar	1080 c	10	44	...	...
Mar	1080 p	17	21.40	+ 6.00	412
Feb	1090 c	4	19	...	...
Feb	1090 p	141	15.80	+ 9.00	279
Mar	1090 c	270	32	...	302
Mar	1090 p	343	28	...	302
Feb	1100 c	1,041	15	− 16.20	6,763
Feb	1100 p	3,246	20.10	+ 11.80	26,497
Mar	1100 c	4,439	27	− 15.00	19,083
Mar	1100 p	8,235	33	+ 12.50	30,294
Apr	1100 c	81	37	− 15.00	1,728
Apr	1100 p	2,011	44	+ 14.00	4,126
Feb	1110 c	1,316	9	− 15.00	738
Feb	1110 p	1,032	27	+ 15.50	1,472
Feb	1120 c	805	6.30	− 9.80	1,057
Feb	1120 p	225	33.50	+ 18.50	1,626
Mar	1120 c	838	18	...	5,239
Mar	1120 p	953	43.50	...	5,095
Apr	1120 c	150	33.50	− 6.50	10

Source: Wall Street Journal, February 5, 2002.

For the time being, we will discuss European-style options exclusively. We do this because European options are the simplest to discuss and are also quite common in practice. While most exchange-traded options are American, the options in Figure 2.5 are European. Later in the book we will discuss American options in more detail.

Payoff and Profit for a Purchased Call Option

We can graph call options as we did forward contracts. The buyer is not obligated to buy the index, and hence will only exercise the option if the payoff is greater than zero. The algebraic expression for the *payoff* to a purchased call is therefore

$$\text{Purchased call payoff} = max[0, \text{spot price at expiration} - \text{strike price}] \qquad (2.3)$$

The expression $max[a, b]$ means take the greater of the two values a and b. (Spreadsheets contain a max function, so it is easy to compute option payoffs in a spreadsheet.)

Example 2.5   Consider a call option on the S&R index with 6 months to expiration and a strike price of $1000. Suppose the index in 6 months is $1100. Clearly it is worthwhile to pay the $1000 strike price to acquire the index worth $1100. Using equation (2.3), the call payoff is

$$max[0, \$1100 - \$1000] = \$100$$

If the index is 900 at expiration, it is not worthwhile paying the $1000 strike price to buy the index worth $900. The payoff is then

$$max[0, \$900 - \$1000] = \$0$$

❦

As discussed before, the payoff does not take account of the initial cost of acquiring the position. For a purchased option, the premium is paid at the time the option is acquired. In computing profit at expiration, suppose we defer the premium payment; then by the time of expiration we accrue 6 months' interest on the premium. The option *profit* is computed as

Purchased call profit = max[0, spot price at expiration − strike price]

$$- \text{ future value of option premium} \quad (2.4)$$

The following example illustrates the computation of the profit.

Example 2.6 Use the same option as in Example 2.5, and suppose that the risk-free rate is 2% over 6 months. Assume that the premium for this call is $93.81.[5] Hence, the future value of the call premium is $93.81 × 1.02 = $95.68. If the S&R index price at expiration is $1100, the owner will exercise the option. Using equation (2.4), the call profit is

$$max[0, \$1100 - \$1000] - \$95.68 = \$4.32$$

If the index is 900 at expiration, the owner does not exercise the option. It is not worthwhile paying the $1000 strike price to buy the index worth $900. Profit is then

$$max[0, \$900 - \$1000] - \$95.68 = -\$95.68,$$

reflecting the loss of the premium.   🥢

We graph the call *payoff* by computing, for any index price at expiration, the payoff on the option position as a function of the price. We graph the call *profit* by subtracting from this the future value of the option premium. Table 2.2 computes the payoff and profit at different index values, computed as in Examples 2.5 and 2.6. Note that because the strike price is fixed, a higher market price at expiration of the S&R index benefits the call buyer.

Figure 2.6 graphs the call payoff that is computed in Table 2.2. The graph clearly shows the "optionality" of the option: Below the strike price of $1000, the payoff is zero, while it is positive and increasing above $1000.

The last column in Table 2.2 computes the call profit at different index values. Because a purchased call and a forward contract are both ways to buy the index, it is interesting to contrast the two. Thus, Figure 2.7 plots the profit on both a purchased call

---

[5]It is not important at this point how we compute this price, but if you wish to replicate the option premiums, they are computed using the Black-Scholes formula, which we discuss in Chapter 12. Using the BSCall spreadsheet function (see Appendix E), the call price is computed as $BSCall(1000, 1000, 0.3, 2 \times ln(1.02), 0.5, 0) = 93.81$.

TABLE 2.2	Payoff and profit after 6 months from a purchased S&R call option with a future value of premium of $95.68. The option premium is assumed to be $93.81 and the effective interest rate is 2% over 6 months. The payoff is computed using equation (2.3) and the profit using equation (2.4).

S&R Index in 6 months	Call Payoff	Future Value of Premium	Call Profit
800	$0	−$95.68	−$95.68
850	0	−95.68	−95.68
900	0	−95.68	−95.68
950	0	−95.68	−95.68
1000	0	−95.68	−95.68
1050	50	−95.68	−45.68
1100	100	−95.68	4.32
1150	150	−95.68	54.32
1200	200	−95.68	104.32

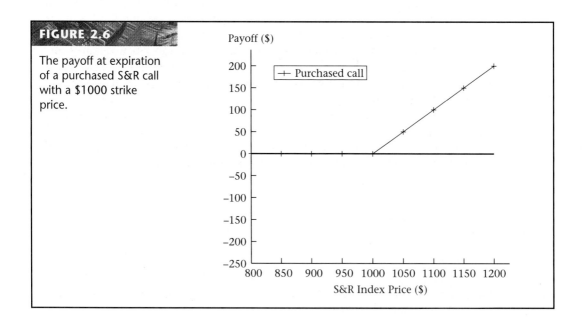

FIGURE 2.6

The payoff at expiration of a purchased S&R call with a $1000 strike price.

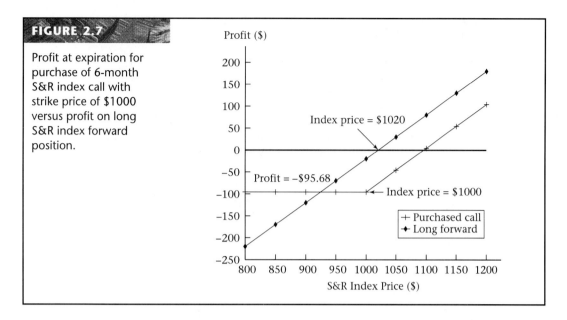

FIGURE 2.7

Profit at expiration for purchase of 6-month S&R index call with strike price of $1000 versus profit on long S&R index forward position.

and a long forward contract. Note that profit and payoff diagrams for an option differ by the future value of the premium, whereas for a forward contract they are the same.

If the index rises, the forward contract is more profitable than the option because it does not entail paying a premium. If the index falls sufficiently, however, the option is more profitable because the most the option buyer loses is the future value of the premium. This difference suggests that we can think of the call option as an *insured* position in the index. Insurance protects against losses, and the call option does the same. Carrying the analogy a bit further, we can think of the option premium as reflecting the cost of that insurance. The forward, which is free, has no such insurance, and potentially has losses larger than those on the call.

This discussion highlights the important point that there are always trade-offs in selecting a position. The forward contract outperforms the call if the index rises and underperforms the call if the index falls sufficiently. When all contracts are fairly priced, you will not find a contract that has higher profits for all index market prices.

Payoff and Profit for a Written Call Option

Now let's look at the option from the point of view of the seller. The seller is said to be the **option writer,** or to have a short position in a call option. The option writer is the counterparty to the option buyer. The writer receives the premium for the option and then has an obligation to sell the underlying security in exchange for the strike price if the option buyer exercises the option.

The payoff and profit to a written call are just the opposite of those for a purchased call:

$$\text{Written call payoff} = -max[0, \text{spot price at expiration} - \text{strike price}] \qquad (2.5)$$

$$\text{Written call profit} = -max[0, \text{spot price at expiration} - \text{strike price}]$$
$$+ \text{future value of option premium} \quad (2.6)$$

This example illustrates the option writer's payoff and profit. Just as a call buyer is long the call, the call seller has a short position in the call.

Example 2.7 Consider a 1000-strike call option on the S&R index with 6 months to expiration. At the time the option is written, the option seller receives the premium of $93.81.

Suppose the index in 6 months is $1100. It is worthwhile for the option buyer to pay the $1000 strike price to acquire the index worth $1100. Thus, the option writer will have to sell the index, worth $1100, for the strike price of $1000. Using equation (2.5), the written call payoff is

$$-max[0, \$1100 - \$1000] = -\$100.$$

The premium has earned 2% interest for 6 months, and is now worth $95.68. Profit for the written call is

$$-\$100 + \$95.68 = -\$4.32.$$

If the index is 900 at expiration, it is not worthwhile for the option buyer to pay the $1000 strike price to buy the index worth $900. The payoff is then

$$-max[0, \$900 - \$1000] = \$0.$$

The option writer keeps the premium, for a profit after 6 months of $95.68. ⚹

Figure 2.8 depicts a graph of the option writer's profit, graphed against a short forward contract. Note that it is the mirror image of the call buyer's profit in Figure 2.7.

2.3 PUT OPTIONS

We introduced a call option by comparing it to a forward contract in which the buyer need not buy the underlying asset if it is worth less than the agreed-to purchase price. Perhaps you wondered if there could also be a contract in which the *seller* could walk away if it is not in his or her interest to sell. The answer is yes. A contract where the seller has the right to sell, but not the obligation, is called a **put option.** Here is an example to illustrate how a put option works.

FIGURE 2.8

Profit for writer of 6-month S&R call with strike of $1000 versus profit for short S&R forward.

Profit ($)

[+ Written call]
[◆ Short forward]

Profit = $95.68

Index price = $1000

Index price = $1020

S&R Index Price ($)

Example 2.8 Suppose that the seller agrees to sell the S&R index for $1020 in 6 months, but is not obligated to do so. (The seller has purchased a put option.) If in 6 months the S&R price is $1100, the seller will not sell for $1020, and will walk away. If the S&R price is $900, the seller *will* sell for $1020, and will earn $120 at that time.

A put must have a premium for the same reason a call has a premium. The buyer of the put controls exercise; hence the seller of the put will never make a profit at expiration. A premium paid by the put buyer at the time the option is purchased compensates the put seller for this no-win position.

It is important to be crystal clear about the use of the terms "buyer" and "seller" in the above example, because there is potential for confusion. The buyer of the put owns a contract giving the right to sell the index at a set price. Thus, *the buyer of the put is a seller of the index!* Similarly, the seller of the put is obligated to *buy* the index, should the put buyer decide to sell. Thus, the buyer of the put is potentially a seller of the index, and the seller of the put is potentially a buyer of the index. (If thinking through these transactions isn't automatic for you now, don't worry. It will become second nature as you continue to think about options.)

Other terminology for a put option is the same as for a call option, with the obvious change that "buy" becomes "sell." In particular, the strike price is the agreed-upon selling price ($1020 in Example 2.8), exercising the option means selling the underlying asset in exchange for the strike price, and the expiration date is that on which you must exercise the option or it is valueless. As with call options, there are European, American, and Bermudan put options.

Payoff and Profit for a Purchased Put Option

We now see how to compute payoff and profit for a purchased put option. The put option gives the put buyer the right to sell the underlying asset for the strike price. The buyer does this only if the asset is less valuable than the strike price. Thus, the payoff on the put option is

$$\text{Put option payoff} = max[0, \text{strike price} - \text{spot price at expiration}] \qquad (2.7)$$

The put buyer has a long position in the put. Here is an example.

Example 2.9   Consider a put option on the S&R index with 6 months to expiration and a strike price of $1000.

Suppose the index in 6 months is $1100. It is not worthwhile to sell the index worth $1100 for the $1000 strike price. Using equation (2.7), the put payoff is

$$max[0, \$1000 - \$1100] = \$0$$

If the index were 900 at expiration, it *is* worthwhile selling the index for $1000. The payoff is then

$$max[0, \$1000 - \$900] = \$100 \qquad \qquad ❧$$

As with the call, the payoff does not take account of the initial cost of acquiring the position. At the time the option is acquired, the put buyer pays the option premium to the put seller; we need to account for this in computing profit. If we borrow the premium amount, we must pay 6 months' interest. The option *profit* is computed as

$$\text{Purchased put profit} = max[0, \text{strike price} - \text{spot price at expiration}]$$
$$- \text{future value of option premium} \quad (2.8)$$

The following example illustrates the computation of profit on the put.

Example 2.10   Use the same option as in Example 2.9, and suppose that the risk-free rate is 2% over 6 months. Assume that the premium for this put is $74.20.[6] The future value of the put premium is $74.20 \times 1.02 = \$75.68$.

---

[6]This price is computed using the Black-Scholes formula for the price of a put: $BSPut(1000, 1000, 0.3, 2 \times ln(1.02), 0.5, 0) = 74.20$. See Appendix E. We will discuss this formula in Chapter 12.

If the S&R index price at expiration is $1100, the put buyer will not exercise the option. Using equation (2.8), profit is

$$max[0, \$1000 - \$1100] - \$75.68 = -\$75.68$$

reflecting the loss of the premium.

If the index is $900 at expiration, the put buyer exercises the put, selling the index for $1000. Profit is then

$$max[0, \$1000 - \$900] - \$75.68 = \$24.32$$

reflecting the payment of premium.

Table 2.3 computes the payoff and profit on a purchased put for a range of index values at expiration. Whereas call profit increases as the value of the underlying asset *increases*, put profit increases as the value of the underlying asset *decreases*.

Because a put is a way to sell an asset, we can compare it to a short forward position, which is a mandatory sale. Figure 2.9 graphs profit from the purchased put described in Table 2.3 against the profit on a short forward.

We can see from the graph that if the S&R index goes down, the short forward, which has no premium, has a higher profit than the purchased put. If the index goes up sufficiently, the put outperforms the short forward. As with the call, the put is like an insured forward contract. With the put, losses are limited should the index go up. With the short forward, losses are potentially unlimited.

TABLE 2.3	Profit after 6 months from a purchased 1000-strike S&R put option with a future value of premium of $75.68.		
S&R Index in 6 Months	**Put Payoff**	**Future Value of Premium**	**Put Profit**
$800	$200	-$75.68	$124.32
850	150	-75.68	74.32
900	100	-75.68	24.32
950	50	-75.68	-25.68
1000	0	-75.68	-75.68
1050	0	-75.68	-75.68
1100	0	-75.68	-75.68
1150	0	-75.68	-75.68
1200	0	-75.68	-75.68

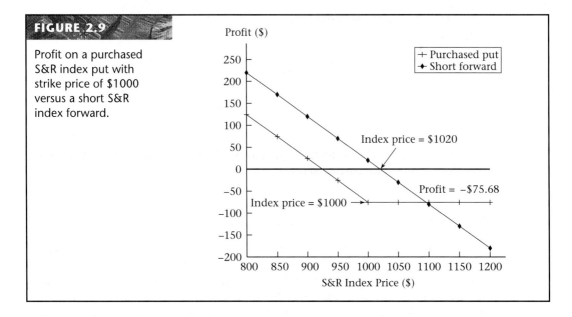

FIGURE 2.9

Profit on a purchased
S&R index put with
strike price of $1000
versus a short S&R
index forward.

Payoff and Profit for a Written Put Option

Now we examine the put from the perspective of the put writer. The put writer is the counterparty to the buyer. Thus, when the contract is written, the put writer receives the premium. At expiration, if the put buyer elects to sell the underlying asset, the put writer must buy it.

The payoff and profit for a written put are the opposite of those for the purchased put:

$$\text{Written put payoff} = -max[0, \text{strike price} - \text{spot price at expiration}] \qquad (2.9)$$

$$\text{Written put profit} = -max[0, \text{strike price} - \text{spot price at expiration}]$$
$$+ \text{future value of option premium} \quad (2.10)$$

The put seller has a short position in the put.

Example 2.11   Consider a 1000-strike put option on the S&R index with 6 months to expiration. At the time the option is written, the put writer receives the premium of $74.20.

Suppose the index in 6 months is $1100. The put buyer will not exercise the put. Thus, the put writer keeps the premium, plus 6 months' interest, for a payoff of 0 and profit of $75.68.

If the index is $900 in 6 months, the put owner will exercise, selling the index for $1000. Thus, the option writer will have to pay $1000 for an index worth $900. Using equation (2.9), the written put payoff is

$$-max[0, \$1000 - \$900] = -\$100$$

The premium has earned 2% interest for 6 months, and is now worth $75.68. Profit for the written put is therefore

$$-\$100 + \$75.68 = -\$24.32$$

Figure 2.10 graphs the profit diagram for a written put. As you would expect, it is the mirror image of the purchased put.

The "Moneyness" of an Option

Options are often described by their degree of *moneyness*. This term describes whether the option payoff would be positive if the option were exercised immediately. (The term is used to describe both American and European options even though European options cannot be exercised until expiration.) An **in-the-money option** is one which would have a positive payoff (but not necessarily profit) if exercised immediately. A call with a strike price less than the asset price and a put with a strike price greater than the asset price are both in-the-money.

An **out-of-the-money option** is one that would have a negative payoff if exercised immediately. A call with a strike price greater than the asset price and a put with a strike price less than the asset price are both out-of-the-money.

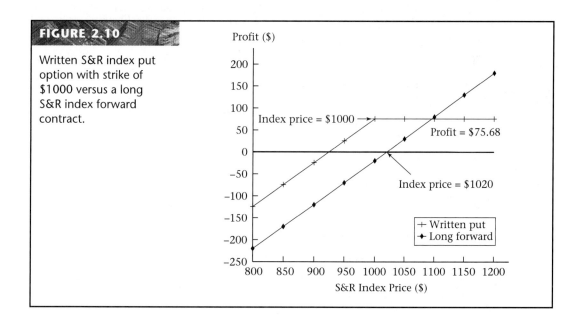

FIGURE 2.10

Written S&R index put option with strike of $1000 versus a long S&R index forward contract.

An **at-the-money option** is one for which the strike price is approximately equal to the asset price.

2.4 Summary of Forward and Option Positions

We have now examined six different positions: Short and long forwards, and purchased and written calls and puts. We can categorize these positions in at least two ways. One way is their potential for gain and loss. Table 2.4 summarizes the maximum possible gain and loss at maturity for forwards and European options.

Another way to categorize the positions is by whether the positions represent buying or selling the underlying asset. Those that represent buying are fundamentally *long* with respect to the underlying asset, while those that represent selling are fundamentally *short* with respect to the underlying asset.

Long Positions

The following positions are long in the sense that there are circumstances in which they represent either a right or an obligation to *buy* the underlying asset:

Long forward A **long forward** represents an *obligation* to buy at a fixed price.

Purchased call A **purchased call** provides the *right* to buy at a fixed price if it is advantageous to do so.

Written put A **written put** *obligates* the put writer to buy the underlying asset at a fixed price if it is advantageous to the option buyer to sell at that price (recall that the option *buyer* decides whether or not to exercise).

TABLE 2.4 Maximum possible profit and loss at maturity for long and short forwards and purchased and written calls and puts. *FV(Premium)* denotes the future value of the option premium.

Position	Maximum Loss	Maximum Gain
Long Forward	−Forward Price	Unlimited
Short Forward	Unlimited	Forward Price
Long Call	−*FV(Premium)*	Unlimited
Short Call	Unlimited	*FV(Premium)*
Long Put	−*FV(Premium)*	Strike Price − *FV(Premium)*
Short Put	*FV(Premium)* − Strike Price	*FV(Premium)*

Figure 2.11 compares these three positions. Note that the purchased call is long when the asset price is greater than the strike price, and the written put is long when the asset price is less than the strike price. *All three of these positions benefit from rising prices.*

Short Positions

The following positions are short in the sense that there are circumstances in which they represent either a right or an obligation to *sell* the underlying asset:

Short forward A **short forward** represents an *obligation* to sell at a fixed price.

Written call A **written call** *obligates* the call writer to sell the underlying asset at a fixed price if it is advantageous to the option holder to buy at that price (recall that the option *buyer* decides whether to exercise).

Purchased put A **purchased put** provides the *right* to sell at a fixed price if it is advantageous to do so.

Figure 2.12 compares these three positions. Note that the written call is short when the asset price is greater than the strike price, and the purchased put is short when the asset price is less than the strike price. *All three of these positions benefit from falling prices.*

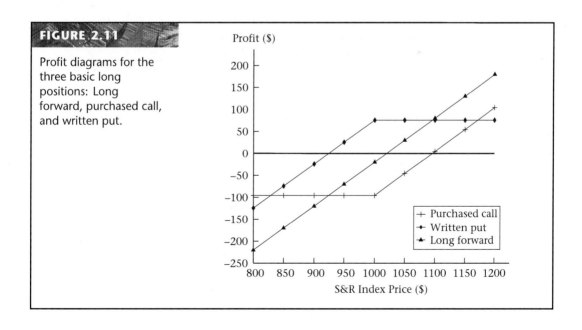

FIGURE 2.11

Profit diagrams for the three basic long positions: Long forward, purchased call, and written put.

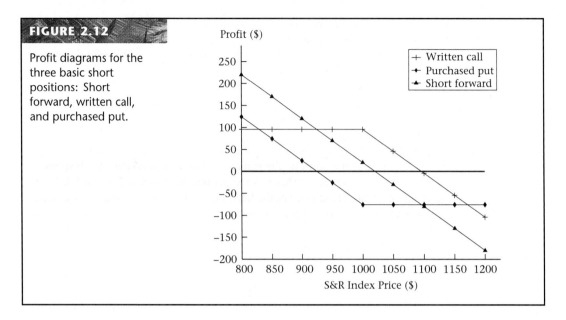

FIGURE 2.12

Profit diagrams for the three basic short positions: Short forward, written call, and purchased put.

2.5 Options Are Insurance

In many investment strategies using options, we will see that options serve as insurance against a loss. In what sense are options the same as insurance? In this section we answer this question by considering homeowner's insurance. You will observe that options are literally insurance, and insurance is an option.

A homeowner's insurance policy promises that in the event of damage to the house, the insurance company will compensate you for at least part of the damage. The greater the damage, the more the insurance company will pay. Your insurance policy thus derives its value from the value of your house: It is a derivative.

Homeowner's Insurance Is a Put Option

To demonstrate how homeowner's insurance acts as a put option, suppose that you own a house that costs $200,000 to build. To make this example as simple as possible, we assume that physical damage is the only thing that can affect the market value of the house.

Let's say you buy a $15,000 insurance policy to compensate you for damage to the house. Like most policies, this has a deductible, meaning that there is an amount of damage for which you are obligated to pay before the insurance company pays anything. Suppose the deductible is $25,000. If the house suffers $4000 damage from a storm, you pay for all repairs yourself. If the house suffers $45,000 in damage from a storm, you pay $25,000 and the insurance company pays the remaining $20,000. Once damage occurs beyond the amount of the deductible, the insurance company pays for all further damage, up to $175,000. (Why $175,000? Because the house can be rebuilt for $200,000, and you pay $25,000 of that—the deductible—yourself.)

Let's graph the profit to you for this insurance policy. Put on the vertical axis the profit on the insurance policy—payoff less the insurance premium—and on the horizontal axis, the value of the house. If the house is undamaged (the house value is $200,000) the payoff is zero, and profit is the loss from the unused insurance premium, $15,000. If the house suffers $50,000 damage, the insurance payoff is $50,000 less the $25,000 deductible, or $25,000. The profit is $25,000 − $15,000 = $10,000. If the house is completely destroyed, the policy pays $175,000, and your profit is $160,000.

Figure 2.13 graphs the profit on the insurance policy. Remarkably, the insurance policy in Figure 2.13 has the same shape as the put option in Figure 2.9. An S&R put is insurance against a fall in the price of the S&R index, just as homeowner's insurance insures against a fall in the price of the house. *Insurance companies are in the business of writing put options!* The $15,000 insurance premium is like the premium of a put, and the $175,000 level at which insurance begins to make payments is like the strike price on a put.

The idea that a put option is insurance also helps us understand what makes a put option cheap or expensive. Two important factors are the riskiness of the underlying asset and the amount of the deductible. Just as with insurance, options will be more expensive when the underlying asset is riskier. Also, the option, like insurance, will be less expensive as the deductible gets larger (for the put option, this means lowering the strike price).

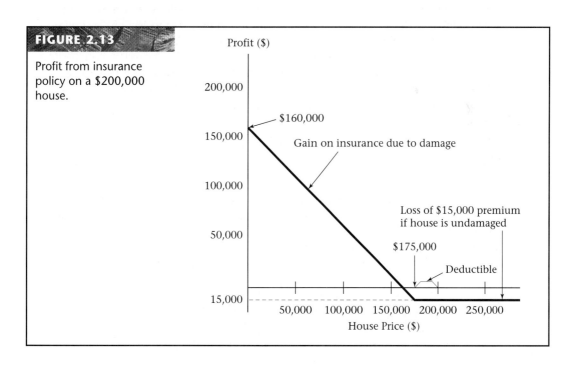

FIGURE 2.13

Profit from insurance policy on a $200,000 house.

You have probably recognized that there are some practical differences between a financial put option and homeowner's insurance. One important difference is that the S&R put pays off no matter why the index price declines. Homeowner's insurance, on the other hand, only pays off if the house declines in value for specified reasons. In particular, a simple decline in real estate prices is not covered by typical homeowner's insurance policies. We avoided this complication by assuming at the outset that only damage could affect the value of the house.

But I Thought Insurance Is Prudent and Put Options Are Risky . . .

If we accept that insurance and put options are the same thing, how do we reconcile this with the common idea that buying insurance is prudent and buying put options is risky?

The risk of a derivative or any other asset or security can only be evaluated in context. Figure 2.13 depicts the risk of an insurance contract *without considering the risk of the insured asset*. This would be like owning insurance on your neighbor's house. It would be "risky" because you would buy the insurance policy, and you would lose your entire investment if there were no insurance claim.[7] We do not normally think of insurance like this, but it illustrates the point that an insurance policy is a put option on the insured asset.

In the same way, Figure 2.9 depicts the risk of a put option without considering the risk of any other positions an investor might be holding. In contrast to homeowner's insurance, many investors *do* own put options without owning the underlying asset. This is why options have a reputation for being risky while homeowner's insurance does not: With stock options it is possible to own the insurance without the asset. Of course, many investors who own put options also own the stock. For these investors, the risk is like that of insurance, which we normally think of as risk-reducing rather than risk-increasing.

Call Options Are Also Insurance

Call options can also be insurance. Whereas a put option is insurance for an asset we already own, a call option is insurance for an asset we plan to own in the future. Put differently, a put option is insurance for a *long* position while a call option is insurance for a *short* position.

Return to the earlier example of the S&R index. Suppose that the current price of the S&R index is $1000 and that we plan to buy the index in the future. If we buy an S&R call option with a strike price of $1000, this gives us the right to buy S&R for a maximum cost of $1000/share. By buying a call, we have bought insurance against an *increase* in the price.

---

[7]Of course, in real life no insurance company will sell you insurance on your neighbor's house. The reason is that you will then be tempted to cause damage in order to make your policy valuable. Insurance companies call this "moral hazard."

2.6 EXAMPLE: EQUITY-LINKED CDs

Although options and forwards are important in and of themselves, they are also commonly used as building blocks in the construction of new financial instruments. For example, banks and insurance companies commonly offer investment products that allow investors to benefit from a rise in a stock index and that provide a guaranteed return if the market declines. We can "reverse-engineer" this kind of product using the tools we have developed thus far.

The box below describes a particular equity-linked CD. At first glance this product *appears* to permit gains but no losses. The appeal of such a product seems obvious. However, by now you are probably skeptical of a phrase like "gains but no losses"; the investor *must* pay something for an investment like this.

We want to understand several things about products like this:

- How to think about the product in terms of options and bonds.
- Where is the cost to the investor?
- How the issuing bank hedges the risk associated with issuing the product.
- How the issuing bank makes a profit.

Graphing the Payoff on the CD

As a first step, we will draw a payoff diagram for the CD described in the box below. Let's begin by describing algebraically the formula used to determine the payoff to a $10,000 investment, assuming that the index is initially 1300.

An Equity-Linked CD

In June 1999, Charles Schwab offered investors an equity-linked Certificate of Deposit, issued by First Union National Bank. This product guaranteed to repay the invested amount after 5.5 years, plus 70% of the simple appreciation in the S&P 500 over that time.

To see how this investment works, suppose the S&P index was 1300 initially and an investor invests $1. If the index is below 1300 after 5.5 years, the CD returns to the investor the original $1 investment. If the index is above 1300 after 5.5 years, the investor receives $1 plus 70% of the percentage gain on the index. If the investor invests $10,000, for example, and the index is 2200, the investor receives

$$\$10,000 \times [1 + (2200/1300 - 1) \times 70\%]$$
$$= \$14,846$$

Schwab also offered a CD paying 105% of the market appreciation, but which defined appreciation based on an *annual average* of index prices over the 5.5-year period. An option with a payoff based on an average of prices over the life of the option is called an **Asian option.** We discuss Asian options in Chapter 14.

We know that we receive at least $10,000. If the index rises to $S_{final} > 1300$, we also receive on our investment 70% of the rate of return

$$\frac{S_{final}}{1300} - 1$$

Thus, the CD pays

$$\$10,000 \times \left(1 + 0.7 \times max\left[0, \frac{S_{final}}{1300} - 1\right]\right) \tag{2.11}$$

Figure 2.14 graphs the payoff at expiration to this investment in the CD.

Recall the discussion in Section 2.1.4 of incorporating a zero-coupon bond into a payoff diagram. Per unit of the index (there are $10,000/1300 = 7.69$ units of the index in a $10,000 investment), the CD buyer receives 0.7 of an index call option, plus a zero-coupon bond paying $1300 at expiration.

Table 2.5 computes the payoff to the equity-linked CD for different values of the index. Figure 2.14 graphs the payoff for a $10,000 investment.

Economics of the CD

Now we are in a position to understand the economics of this product. Think about what happens if the index is below 1300 at expiration. We paid $10,000 and we receive $10,000 back. Thus, we have foregone interest on that amount. Supposing that the effective annual interest rate is 6%, the buyer loses

$$\$10,000 \times (1.06)^{-5.5} - \$10,000 = -\$2,742$$

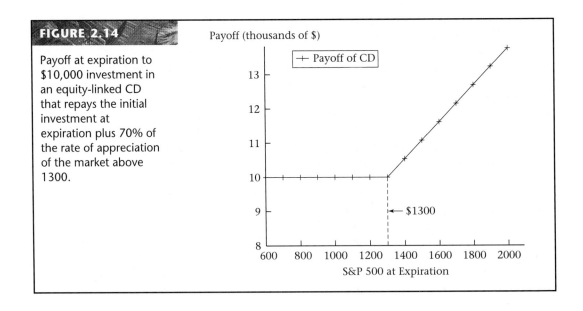

FIGURE 2.14

Payoff at expiration to $10,000 investment in an equity-linked CD that repays the initial investment at expiration plus 70% of the rate of appreciation of the market above 1300.

Payoff (thousands of $)

— Payoff of CD

$1300

S&P 500 at Expiration

TABLE 2.5	Payoff of equity-linked CD at expiration.

S&P Index after 5.5 Years	CD Payoff
500	$10,000.00
1000	10,000.00
1500	11,076.92
2000	13,769.23
2500	16,461.54
3000	19,153.85

in interest on the CD in year −5.5 dollars. Essentially, the buyer foregoes interest in order to pay the option premium.

With this description we have reverse-engineered the CD, decomposing it in terms of an option and a bond. The question of whether the CD is fairly priced turns on whether the $2,742 is a fair price for the index option implicit in the CD. Given information about the interest rate, the volatility of the index, and the dividend yield on the index, it is possible to price the option to determine whether the CD is fairly priced. We perform that analysis for this example in Chapter 15.

Why Equity-Linked CDs?

Our reverse-engineering showed how an investor could "roll his own" equity-linked CD by buying a zero-coupon bond and 0.7 call options. Why, then, do products like this exist?

Consider what must be done to replicate the payoff. If a retail investor were to insure an index investment using options, the investor would have to learn about options, decide what maturity, strike price, and quantity to buy, and pay transaction costs. Exchange-traded options have at most 3 years to maturity, so obtaining longer-term protection requires rolling over the position at some point.

An equity-linked CD provides a prepackaged solution. It may provide a pattern of market exposure that many investors could not otherwise obtain at such low transaction costs.

The idea that a prepackaged deal may be attractive should be familiar to you. Supermarkets sell whole heads of lettuce—salad building blocks, as it were—and they also sell, at a premium price, lettuce already washed, torn into bite-sized pieces, and mixed as a salad. The transaction cost of salad preparation leads some consumers to prefer the prepackaged salads.

What does the financial institution get out of this? Just as the supermarket earns profit on prepackaged salads, the issuing bank wants to earn profit on the CD. When it sells a CD, the issuing bank borrows money (the zero-coupon bond portion of the CD) and receives the premium for writing a call option. The cost of the CD to the bank is the cost of the zero-coupon bond plus the cost of the call option. Obviously the bank would not issue the equity-linked CD in the first place unless it was less expensive than alternative ways to attract deposits, such as standard CDs. The equity-linked CD is risky because the bank has written a call, but the bank can manage this risk in several ways, one of which is to purchase call options from an investment bank to offset the risk of having written calls. Using data from the early 1990s, Baubonis et al. (1993) estimated that issuers of equity-linked CDs earned about 3.5% of the value of the CD as a fee, with about 1% as the transaction cost of hedging the written call.[8]

In this discussion we have viewed the equity-linked CD from several perspectives. The end-user is interested in the product and whether it meets a financial need at a fair cost. The market-maker (the bank in this case) is interested in making a profit without bearing risk from having issued the CD. And the economic observer is interested in knowing why equity-linked CDs exist. The three perspectives overlap, and a full explanation of the product touches on all of them.

Chapter Summary

Forward contracts and put and call options are the basic derivative instruments which can be used directly and which serve as building blocks for other instruments. A long forward contract represents an obligation to buy the underlying asset at a fixed price, a call option gives its owner the right (but not the obligation) to buy the underlying asset at a fixed price, and a put option gives its owner the right (but not the obligation) to sell the underlying asset at a fixed price. Payoff and profit diagrams are commonly used tools for evaluating the risk of these contracts. Payoff diagrams show the gross value of a position at expiration, and profit diagrams subtract from the payoff the future value of the cost of the position.

Table 2.6 summarizes the characteristics of forwards, calls, and puts, showing which are long or short with respect to the underlying asset. The table describes the strategy associated with each: Forward contracts guarantee a price, purchased options are insurance, and written options are selling insurance. Figure 2.15 provides a graphical summary of these positions.

Options can also be viewed as insurance. A put option gives the owner the right to sell if the price declines, just as insurance gives the insured the right to sell (put) a damaged asset to the insurance company.

---

[8]A back-of-the-envelope calculation in Chapter 15 suggests the issuer fees for this product are in the neighborhood of 4%–5%.

TABLE 2.6	Forwards, calls, and puts at a glance: A summary of forward and option positions.

Derivative Position	Position with Respect to Underlying Asset	Asset Price Contingency	Strategy
Long forward	Long (Buy)	Always	Guaranteed Price
Short Forward	Short (Sell)	Always	Guaranteed Price
Long Call	Long (Buy)	> Strike	Insures Against High Price
Short Call	Short (Sell)	> Strike	Sells Insurance Against High Price
Long Put	Short (Sell)	< Strike	Insures Against Low Price
Short Put	Long (Buy)	< Strike	Sells Insurance Against Low Price

FIGURE 2.15

The basic profit diagrams: Long and short forward, long and short call, and long and short put.

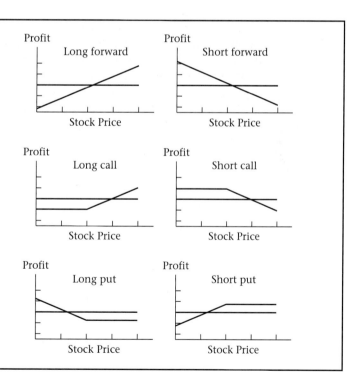

Further Reading

We use the concepts introduced in this chapter throughout the rest of this book. Chapter 3 presents a number of basic option strategies which are widely used in practice, including caps, collars, and floors. Chapter 4 presents the use of options in risk management.

A more general question raised implicitly in this chapter is how the prices of forwards and options are determined. Chapter 5 covers financial forwards and futures in detail, and Chapter 10 introduces the basic ideas underlying option pricing.

Brokerages routinely supply options customers with an introductory pamphlet about options entitled *Characteristics and Risks of Standardized Options*. This is available online from **http://www.cboe.com.** You can also obtain current option prices from websites such as the CBOE's and various brokerage sites.

The notion that options are insurance has been applied in practice. Sharpe (1976), for example, analyzed optimal pension funding policy taking into account pension insurance provided by the Pension Benefit Guaranty Corporation. Merton (1977a) observed that bank deposit insurance and in fact any loan guarantee can be modeled as a put option. Baubonis et al. (1993) discuss equity-linked CDs.

Problems

In the following problems, if the "effective annual interest rate" is r, a $1 investment yields $1 + r$ after one year.

2.1. Suppose XYZ stock has a price of $50 and pays no dividends. The effective annual interest rate is 10%. Draw payoff and profit diagrams for a long position in the stock. Verify that profit is 0 at a price in one year of $55.

2.2. Using the same information as the previous question, draw payoff and profit diagrams for a short position in the stock. Verify that profit is 0 at a price in one year of $55.

2.3. What position is the opposite of a purchased call? The opposite of a purchased put?

2.4.   **a.** Suppose you enter into a long 6-month forward position at a forward price of $50. What is the payoff in 6 months for prices of $40, $45, $50, $55, and $60?

 b. Suppose you buy a 6-month call option with a strike price of $50. What is the payoff in 6 months at the same prices for the underlying asset?

 c. Comparing the payoffs of parts (a) and (b), which contract should be more expensive (i.e., the long call or long forward)? Why?

2.5.   **a.** Suppose you enter into a short 6-month forward position at a forward price of $50. What is the payoff in 6 months for prices of $40, $45, $50, $55, and $60?

 b. Suppose you buy a 6-month put option with a strike price of $50. What is the payoff in 6 months at the same prices for the underlying asset?

c. Comparing the payoffs of parts (a) and (b), which contract should be more expensive (i.e., the long put or short forward)? Why?

2.6. A default-free zero-coupon bond costs $91 and will pay $100 at maturity in 1 year. What is the effective annual interest rate? What is the payoff diagram for the bond? The profit diagram?

2.7. Suppose XYZ stock pays no dividends and has a current price of $50. The forward price for delivery in 1 year is $55. Suppose the 1-year effective annual interest rate is 10%.

a. Graph the payoff and profit diagrams for a forward contract on XYZ stock with a forward price of $100.

b. Is there any advantage to investing in the stock or the forward contract? Why?

c. Suppose XYZ paid a dividend of $2 per year and everything else stayed the same. Now is there any advantage to investing in the stock or the forward contract? Why?

2.8. Suppose XYZ stock pays no dividends and has a current price of $50. The forward price for delivery in one year is $53. *If* there is no advantage to buying either the stock or the forward contract, what is the 1-year effective interest rate?

2.9. An *off-market* forward contract is a forward where either you have to pay a premium or you receive a premium for entering into the contract. (With a standard forward contract, the premium is zero.) Suppose the effective annual interest rate is 10% and the S&R index is 1000. Consider 1-year forward contracts.

a. Verify that if the forward price is $1100, the profit diagrams for the index and the 1-year forward are the same.

b. Suppose you are offered a long forward contract at a forward price of $1200. How much would you need to be paid to enter into this contract?

c. Suppose you are offered a long forward contract at $1000. What would you be willing to pay to enter into this forward contract?

2.10. For Figure 2.7, verify the following:

a. The S&R index price at which the call option diagram intersects the x-axis is $1095.68.

b. The S&R index price at which the call option and forward contract have the same profit is $924.32.

2.11. For Figure 2.9, verify the following:

a. The S&R index price at which the put option diagram intersects the x-axis is $924.32.

b. The S&R index price at which the put option and forward contract have the same profit is $1095.68.

2.12. For each entry in Table 2.4, explain the circumstances in which the maximum gain or loss occurs.

2.13. Suppose the stock price is $40 and the effective annual interest rate is 8%.

   a. Draw on a single graph payoff and profit diagrams for the following options:

   (i) 35-strike call with a premium of $9.12.

   (ii) 40-strike call with a premium of $6.22.

   (iii) 45-strike call with a premium of $4.08.

   b. Consider your payoff diagram with all three options graphed together. Intuitively, why should the option premium decrease with the strike price?

2.14. Suppose the stock price is $40 and the effective annual interest rate is 8%. Draw payoff and profit diagrams for the following options:

   a. 35-strike put with a premium of $1.53.

   b. 40-strike put with a premium of $3.26.

   c. 45-strike put with a premium of $5.75.

Consider your payoff diagram with all three options graphed together. Intuitively, why should the option premium increase with the strike price?

2.15. The profit calculation in the chapter assumes that you borrow at a fixed interest rate to finance investments. An alternative way to borrow is to short-sell stock. What complications would arise in calculating profit if you financed a $1000 S&R index investment by shorting IBM stock, rather than by borrowing $1000?

2.16. Construct a spreadsheet that permits you to compute payoff and profit for a short and long stock, a short and long forward, and purchased and written puts and calls. The spreadsheet should let you specify the stock price, forward price, interest rate, option strikes, and option premiums. Use the spreadsheet's max function to compute option payoffs.

APPENDIX 2.A: MORE ON BUYING A STOCK OPTION

The box on page 31 discusses buying options. There are at least three practical issues that an option buyer should be aware of: Exercise, margins, and taxes. In this section we will focus on retail investors and exchange-traded stock options. Be aware that specific rules regarding margins and taxes change frequently. This section is intended to help you identify issues and is not intended as a substitute for professional brokerage, accounting, or legal advice.

Exercise

Some options, for example those that are cash-settled, are automatically exercised; the option owner need not take any action at expiration. Suppose you own a traded option which is not cash-settled and not automatically exercised. In this case you must provide exercise instructions prior to the broker's deadline. If you fail to do so, the option will expire worthless. When you exercise the option, you generally pay a commission. If you do not wish to own the stock, exercising the option would require that you pay a commission to exercise and then a commission to sell the shares. It would likely involve lower transaction costs to sell the option instead of exercising it. If you do wish to own the underlying asset, you can exercise the option. The option writer who is obligated to fulfill the option exercise (delivering the shares for a call or buying the shares for a put) is said to have been *assigned*. Assignment can involve paying a commission.

American-style options can be exercised prior to expiration. If you own an option and fail to exercise when you should, you will lose money relative to following the optimal exercise strategy. If you write the option, and it is exercised (you are assigned), you will be required to sell the stock (if you sold a call) or buy the stock (if you sold a put). Therefore, if you buy or sell an American option, you need to understand the circumstances under which exercise might be optimal. We discuss early exercise in Chapters 9 and 11.

Margins for Written Options

Purchased options that have been fully paid for require no margin, as there is no counterparty risk. With written option positions, however, you can incur a large loss if the stock moves against you. When you write an option, therefore, you are required to post collateral to insure against the possibility that you will default. This collateral is called margin.

Margin rules are beyond the scope of this book and change over time. Moreover, different option positions have different margin rules. Both brokers and exchanges can provide information about current margin requirements.

Taxes

Tax rules for derivatives in general can be complicated, and they change frequently as the tax law changes. The taxation of simple option transactions is straightforward.

If you purchase a call option or stock and then sell it, gain or loss on the position is treated like gain or loss on a stock, and accorded long-term or short-term capital gains treatment depending on the length of time for which the position has been held. If you purchase a call option and then exercise it, the cost basis of the resulting stock position is the exercise price plus the option premium plus commissions. The holding period for the resulting stock position begins the day after the option is exercised. The time the option is held does not contribute to the holding period.

The rules become more intricate when forwards and options are held in tandem with the underlying asset. The reasons for this complexity are not hard to understand. Tax laws in the United States accord different tax treatment to different kinds of income. The tax code views interest income, dividend income, and capital gains income as distinct and subject to different tax rules. Futures also have special rules. However, using derivatives, one kind of income can be turned into another. We saw in this chapter, for example, that buying zero-coupon bonds and a forward contract mimics a stock investment. Such equivalent positions, however, are often taxed differently.

One category of special rules governs a **constructive sale.** If you own a stock, entering into certain option or forward positions can trigger a constructive sale, meaning that even if you continue to own the stock, for tax purposes you are deemed to have sold it at the time you enter into the forward or option positions. The reason is that by shorting a forward against the stock, for example, the stock position is transformed into a bond position. When you have no risk stemming from stock ownership, tax law deems you to no longer be an owner.

The so-called **straddle rules** are tax rules intended to control the recognition of losses for tax purposes when there are offsetting risks as with constructive sales. Such positions often arise when investors are undertaking tax arbitrage, which is why the positions are accorded special treatment. A stock owned together with a put is a tax straddle.[9] Generally, the straddle rules prevent loss recognition on only a part of the entire position. A straddle for tax purposes is not the same thing as an option straddle, discussed in Chapter 3.

It is probably obvious to you that if you are taxable and transact in options, and especially if you have both stock and offsetting option positions, you should be prepared to seek professional tax advice.

---

[9]For an illustration of the complexity, in this particular case, an exception to the straddle rules occurs if the stock and put are a "married put," meaning that the two are purchased together and the stock is delivered to settle the put.

Chapter 3

Insurance, Collars, and Other Strategies

I n the last chapter we introduced forwards, calls, and puts; showed that options are insurance; and looked at an example of how options can be building blocks. In this chapter we continue these themes, showing how common strategies using options can be interpreted as buying or selling insurance. We also continue the building block approach, examining the link between forward prices and option prices, and looking at some common uses of options, including spreads, straddles, and collars. Among your goals in this chapter should be to understand the reasons for using one strategy instead of another and to become facile with drawing and interpreting profit and loss diagrams.

3.1 BASIC INSURANCE STRATEGIES

There are infinite ways to combine options to create different payoffs. In this section we examine two important kinds of strategies in which the option is combined with a position in the underlying asset. First, options can be used to insure long or short asset positions. Second, options can be written against an asset position, in which case the option writer is selling insurance. In this section we consider four positions: Being long the asset coupled with a purchased put or written call, and being short the asset coupled with a purchased call or written put.

In this section we continue to use the S&R index examples presented in Sections 2.2 and 2.3. We assumed a 2% effective 6-month interest rate, and premiums of $93.809 for the 1000-strike 6-month call and $74.201 for the 1000-strike 6-month put.

Insuring a Long Position: Floors

The analysis in Section 2.5 demonstrated that put options are insurance against a fall in the price of an asset. Thus, if we own the S&R index, we can insure the position by buying an S&R put option. The purchase of a put option in this case is called a **floor**, because we are guaranteeing a minimum for the value of the index.

To examine this strategy, we want to look at the *combined* payoff of the index position and put. In the last chapter we graphed them separately; now we add them together to see the net effect of holding both positions at the same time.

Table 3.1 summarizes the result of buying a 1000-strike put with 6 months to expiration, in conjunction with holding an index position with a current value of $1000. The table computes the payoff for each position and sums them to obtain the total payoff. The final column takes account of financing cost by subtracting cost plus interest from

| TABLE 3.1 | | | Payoff and profit at expiration from purchasing the S&R index and a 1000-strike put option. Payoff is the sum of the first two columns. Cost plus interest for the position is ($1000 + $74.201) × 1.02 = $1095.68. Profit is payoff less $1095.68. | |

Payoff at Expiration				
S&R Index	**S&R Put**	**Payoff**	**−(Cost + Interest)**	**Profit**
$900	$100	$1000	−$1095.68	−$95.68
950	50	1000	−1095.68	−95.68
1000	0	1000	−1095.68	−95.68
1050	0	1050	−1095.68	−45.68
1100	0	1100	−1095.68	4.32
1150	0	1150	−1095.68	54.32
1200	0	1200	−1095.68	104.32

the payoff to obtain profit. "Cost" here means the initial cash required to establish the position. This is positive when payment is required, and negative when cash is received. We could also have computed profit separately for the put and index. For example, if the index is $900 at expiration, we have

$$\underbrace{\$900 - (\$1000 \times 1.02)}_{\text{Profit on S\&R Index}} + \underbrace{\$100 - (\$74.201 \times 1.02)}_{\text{Profit on Put}} = -\$95.68$$

This gives the same result as the calculation performed in Table 3.1. The level of the floor is −$95.68, which is the lowest possible profit.

Figure 3.1 graphs the components of Table 3.1. Panels (c) and (d) show the payoff and profit for the combined index and put positions. The combined payoff graph in panel (c) is created by adding at each index price the value of the index and put positions; this is just like summing columns 1 and 2 in Table 3.1.

Notice in Figure 3.1 that the combined position created by adding the index and the put looks like a call. Intuitively this equivalence makes sense. A call has a limited loss— the premium—and benefits from gains in the index above the strike price. Similarly, when we own the index and buy a put, the put limits losses, but it permits us to benefit from gains in the index. Thus, at a casual level, the call on the one hand and the insured index position on the other seem to have similar characteristics.

Panel (c), however, illustrates that the payoff to the combined position is *not* identical to the payoff from buying a call (compare panel (c) to Figure 2.6). The difference stems from the fact that buying a call entails paying only the option premium, while buying the index and put entails paying for *both* the index and the put option, which together are more expensive than buying a call. The profit diagram in panel (d), however, does look like a call. We discussed in Section 2.1 that adding a bond to a payoff diagram

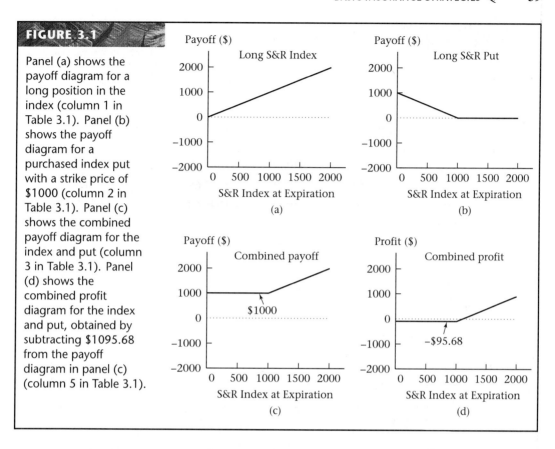

FIGURE 3.1

Panel (a) shows the payoff diagram for a long position in the index (column 1 in Table 3.1). Panel (b) shows the payoff diagram for a purchased index put with a strike price of $1000 (column 2 in Table 3.1). Panel (c) shows the combined payoff diagram for the index and put (column 3 in Table 3.1). Panel (d) shows the combined profit diagram for the index and put, obtained by subtracting $1095.68 from the payoff diagram in panel (c) (column 5 in Table 3.1).

shifts it vertically, but leaves a profit diagram unaffected. The combined position of index plus put in panel (c) is actually equivalent to buying a 1000-strike call and buying a zero-coupon bond which pays $1000 at expiration of the option.

The profit diagram in panel (d) of Figure 3.1 does not merely resemble the profit diagram for buying an S&R index call with a strike price of $1000, graphed in Figure 2.7; it is identical. We can see this by comparing Table 2.2 with Table 3.1. The profit of −$95.68 for prices below $1000 is exactly the future value of the 1000-strike 6-month to expiration call premium above.

The zero-coupon bond thus affects the payoff in panel (c), but leaves profit in panel (d) unaffected. The cash flows in purchasing a call are different from the cash flows in buying an asset and insuring it, but the profit for the two positions is the same. If we had explicitly borrowed the present value of $1000 ($1000/1.02 = $980.39) to offset the cost of the index and put, then the payoff and profit diagrams, panels (c) and (d) in Figure 3.1, would be identical.

The point that buying an asset and a put generates a position that looks like a call can also be seen using the homeowner's insurance example from Section 2.5. There,

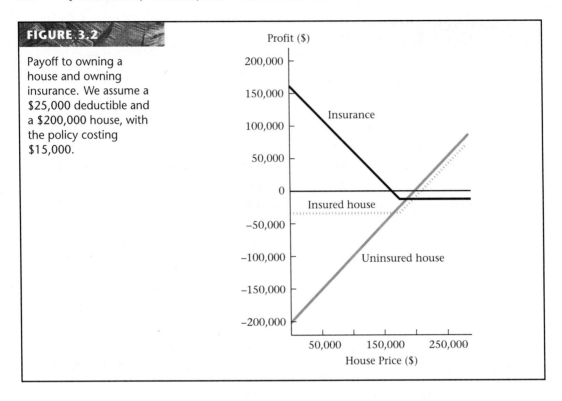

FIGURE 3.2

Payoff to owning a house and owning insurance. We assume a $25,000 deductible and a $200,000 house, with the policy costing $15,000.

we examined the insurance policy in isolation. However, in practice, a buyer of home-owner's insurance also owns the insured asset (the house). Owning a home is analogous to owning the stock index, and insuring the house is like owning a put. Thus, owning a home plus insurance is like owning the index and owning a put. Figure 3.2 depicts the insurance policy from Figure 2.13, together with the uninsured house and the combined position. Interpreting the house as the S&R index and insurance as the put, Figure 3.2 looks exactly like Figure 3.1. *An insured house has a profit diagram that looks like a call option.*

Insuring a Short Position: Caps

If we have a short position in the S&R index, we experience a loss when the index rises. We can insure a short position by purchasing a call option to protect against a higher price of repurchasing the index.[1] This is called a **cap.**

----

[1] Keep in mind that if you have an obligation to buy the index in the future but the price is not fixed, then you have an *implicit* short position (if the price goes up, you will have to pay more). A call is insurance for both explicit and implicit short-sellers.

TABLE 3.2	Payoff and profit at expiration from short-selling the S&R index and buying a 1000 strike call option at a premium of $93.809. The payoff is the sum of the first two columns. Cost plus interest for the position is $(-\$1000 + \$93.809) \times 1.02 = -\$924.32$. Profit is payoff plus $924.32.

Payoff at Expiration				
Short S&R Index	**S&R Call**	**Payoff**	**−(Cost + Interest)**	**Profit**
−$900	$0	−$900	$924.32	$24.32
−950	0	−950	924.32	−25.68
−1000	0	−1000	924.32	−75.68
−1050	50	−1000	924.32	−75.68
−1100	100	−1000	924.32	−75.68
−1150	150	−1000	924.32	−75.68
−1200	200	−1000	924.32	−75.68

Table 3.2 analyzes the payoff and profit for a short position in the index coupled with a purchased call option. Because we short the index, we earn interest on the short proceeds less the cost of the call option, giving −$924.32 as the future value of the cost.

Figure 3.3 graphs the columns of Table 3.2. The payoff and profit diagrams resemble those of a purchased put. As with the insured index position in Figure 3.1, we have to be careful in dealing with cash flows. The *payoff* in panel (c) of Figure 3.3 is like that of a purchased put coupled with borrowing. In this case, the payoff diagram to shorting the index and buying a call is equivalent to that from buying a put and borrowing the present value of $1000 ($980.39). Since profit diagrams are unaffected by borrowing, however, the profit diagram in panel (d) is exactly the same as that for a purchased S&R index put. You can see this by comparing panel (d) with Figure 2.9. Not only does the insured short position look like a put, it has the same loss as a purchased put if the price is above $1000: $75.68, which is the future value of the $74.201 put premium.

Selling Insurance

We can expect that some investors want to purchase insurance. However, for every insurance buyer there must be an insurance seller. In this section we examine strategies in which investors *sell* insurance.

It is possible, of course, for an investor to simply sell calls and puts. More frequently, however, investors also have a position in the asset when they sell insurance. Writing an option when there is a corresponding long position in the underlying asset is called **covered writing, option overwriting,** or selling a covered call. All three terms

FIGURE 3.3

Panel (a) shows the payoff diagram for a short position in the index (column 1 in Table 3.2). Panel (b) shows the payoff diagram for a purchased index call with a strike price of $1000 (column 2 in Table 3.2). Panel (c) shows the combined payoff diagram for the short index and long call (column 3 in Table 3.2). Panel (d) shows the combined profit diagram for the short index and long call, obtained by adding $924.32 to the payoff diagram in panel (c) (column 5 in Table 3.2).

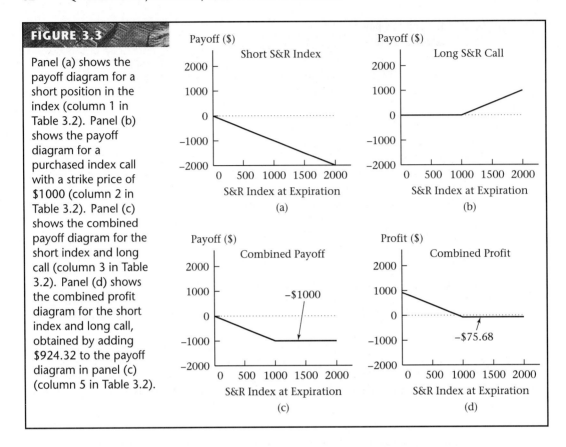

mean essentially the same thing.[2] In contrast, **naked writing** occurs when the writer of an option does not have a position in the asset.

In addition to the covered writing strategies we will discuss here, there are other insurance-selling strategies, such as delta-hedging, which are less risky than naked writing and are used in practice by market-makers. We will discuss these other strategies later in the book, particularly in Chapter 13.

Covered call writing   If we own the S&R index and simultaneously sell a call option, we have written a **covered call**. A covered call will have limited profitability if the index increases, because an option writer is obligated to sell the index for the strike price. Should the index decrease, the loss on the index is offset by the premium earned from

---

[2]Technically, "option overwriting" refers to selling a call on stock you already own, while a "covered write" entails simultaneously buying the stock and selling a call. The distinction is irrelevant for our purposes.

selling the call. A payoff with limited profit for price increases and potentially large losses for price decreases sounds like a written put.

We can compute the maximum profit on this position. Because the covered call looks like a written put, the maximum profit will be the same as with a written put. Suppose the index is $1100 at expiration. The profit is

$$\underbrace{\$1100 - (\$1000 \times 1.02)}_{\text{Profit on S\&R Index}} + \underbrace{(\$93.809 \times 1.02) - \$100}_{\text{Profit on Written Call}} = \$75.68$$

which is the future value of the premium received from writing a 1000-strike put.

The profit from writing the 1000-strike call is computed in Table 3.3 and graphed in Figure 3.4. If the index falls, we lose money on the index but the option premium partially offsets the loss. If the index rises above the strike price, the written option loses money, negating gains on the index.

Comparing Table 3.3 with Table 2.3, we can see that writing the covered call generates *exactly* the same profit as selling a put.

Why would anyone write a covered call? Suppose you have the view that the index is unlikely to move either up or down. (This is sometimes called a "neutral" market view.) If in fact the index does not move and you have written a call, then you keep the premium. If you are wrong and the stock appreciates, you forego gains you would have had if you did not write the call.

Covered puts   A covered put is achieved by writing a put against a short position on the index. The written put obligates you to buy the index—for a loss—if it goes down

TABLE 3.3   Payoff and profit at expiration from purchasing the S&R index and selling a 1000-strike call option. The payoff column is the sum of the first two columns. Cost plus interest for the position is ($1000 − $93.809) × 1.02 = $924.32. Profit is payoff less $924.32.

Payoff at Expiration				
S&R Index	**Short S&R Call**	**Payoff**	**−(Cost + Interest)**	**Profit**
$900	$0	$900	−$924.32	−$24.32
950	0	950	−924.32	25.68
1000	0	1000	−924.32	75.68
1050	−50	1000	−924.32	75.68
1100	−100	1000	−924.32	75.68
1150	−150	1000	−924.32	75.68
1200	−200	1000	−924.32	75.68

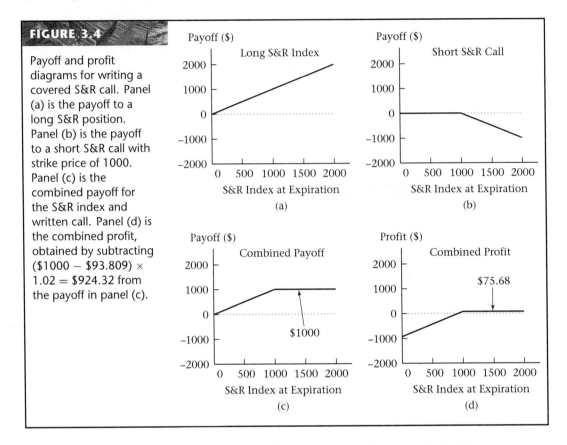

FIGURE 3.4

Payoff and profit diagrams for writing a covered S&R call. Panel (a) is the payoff to a long S&R position. Panel (b) is the payoff to a short S&R call with strike price of 1000. Panel (c) is the combined payoff for the S&R index and written call. Panel (d) is the combined profit, obtained by subtracting ($1000 − $93.809) × 1.02 = $924.32 from the payoff in panel (c).

in price. Thus, for index prices below the strike price, the loss on the written put offsets the short stock. For index prices above the strike price, you lose on the short stock.

A position where you have a constant payoff below the strike and increasing losses above the strike sounds like a written call. In fact, shorting the index and writing a put produces a profit diagram that is exactly the same as for a written call. Figure 3.5 shows this graphically, and Problem 3.2 asks you to verify this by constructing a payoff table.

3.2 SYNTHETIC FORWARDS

It is possible to mimic a long forward position by buying a call and selling a put on the same underlying asset, with each option having the same strike price and time to expiration. For example, we could buy the 1000-strike S&R call and sell the 1000-strike S&R put, each with 6 months to expiration. The result is that in 6 months we will be obliged to pay $1000 to buy the index, just as if we had entered into a forward contract.

To see this, suppose the index in 6 months is at 900. We will not exercise the call, but we have written a put. The put buyer will exercise the right to sell the index for $1000; therefore we are obligated to buy the index at $1000. If the index is at $1100, the

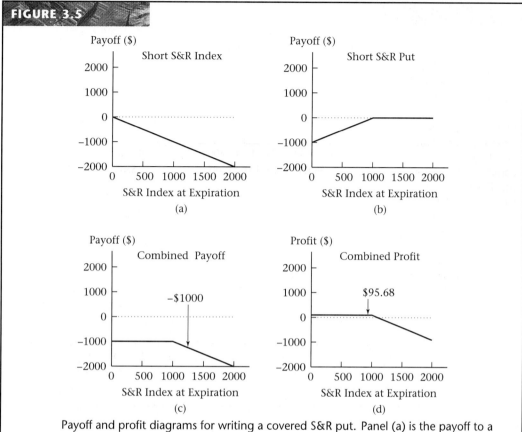

FIGURE 3.5

Payoff and profit diagrams for writing a covered S&R put. Panel (a) is the payoff to a short S&R position. Panel (b) is the payoff to a short S&R put with a strike price of $1000. Panel (c) is the combined payoff for the short S&R index and written put. Panel (d) is the combined profit, obtained by adding ($1000 + $74.201) × 1.02 = $1095.68 to the payoff in panel (c).

put is not exercised, but we exercise the call, buying the index for $1000. Thus, whether the index rises or falls, when the options expire we buy the index for the strike price of the options, $1000.

The purchased call, written put, and combined positions are shown in Figure 3.6. The purchase of a call and sale of a put creates a *synthetic* long forward contract, which has two minor differences from the actual forward:

1. The forward contract has a zero premium, while the synthetic forward requires that we pay the net option premium.

2. With the forward contract we pay the forward price, while with the synthetic forward we pay the strike price.

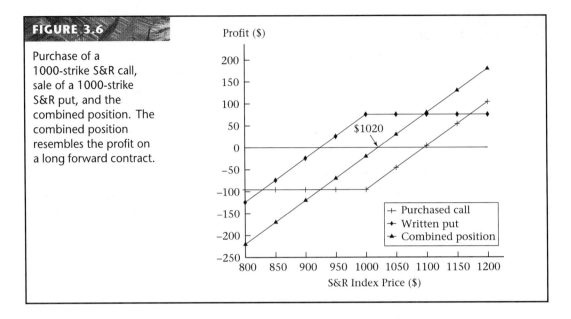

FIGURE 3.6

Purchase of a 1000-strike S&R call, sale of a 1000-strike S&R put, and the combined position. The combined position resembles the profit on a long forward contract.

If you think about it, these two considerations must be related. If we set the strike price low, we are obligated to buy the index at a discount relative to the forward price. Buying at a lower price than the forward price is a benefit. In order to obtain this benefit we have to pay the positive net option premium, which stems from the call being more expensive than the put. In fact, in Figure 3.6, the implicit cost of the synthetic forward—the price at which the profit on the combined call-put position is zero—is $1020, which is the S&R forward price.

Similarly, if we set the strike price high, we are obligated to buy the index at a high price relative to the forward price. To offset the extra cost of acquiring the index using the high strike options, it makes sense that we would receive payment initially. This would occur if the put that we sell is more expensive than the call we buy.

Finally, if we set the strike price equal to the forward price, then to mimic the forward the initial premium must equal zero. In this case, put and call premiums must be equal.

Put-Call Parity

We can summarize this argument by saying that *the net cost of buying the index using options must equal the net cost of buying the index using a forward contract.* If at time 0 we enter into a long forward position expiring at time t, we obligate ourselves to buying the index at the forward price, $F_{0,t}$. The present value of buying the index in the future is just the present value of the forward price, $PV(F_{0,t})$.

If instead we buy a call and sell a put today to guarantee the purchase price for the index in the future, the present value of the cost is the net option premium for buying the call and selling the put, $Call(K, t) - Put(K, t)$, plus the present value of the strike price, $PV(K)$. (The notations "$Call(K, t)$" and "$Put(K, t)$" denote the premiums of options with strike price K and time t until expiration.)

Equating the costs of the alternative ways to buy the index at time t gives us

$$PV(F_{0,t}) = [Call(K, t) - Put(K, t)] + PV(K)$$

We can rewrite this as

$$\boxed{Call(K, t) - Put(K, t) = PV(F_{0,t} - K)} \tag{3.1}$$

In words, the present value of the bargain element from buying the index at the strike price (the right-hand side of equation (3.1)) must be offset by the initial net option premium (the left-hand side of equation (3.1)). Equation (3.1) is one of the most important relations in options.

Example 3.1   As an example of equation (3.1), consider buying the 6-month 1000-strike S&R call for a premium of $93.809 and selling the 6-month 1000-strike put for a premium of $74.201. These transactions create a synthetic forward permitting us to buy the index in 6 months for $1000. Because the actual forward price is $1020, this synthetic forward permits us to buy the index at a bargain of $20, the present value of which is $20/1.02 = $19.61. The difference in option premiums must therefore be $19.61. In fact, $93.809 - $74.201 = $19.61. This result is exactly what we would get with equation (3.1):

$$\$93.809 - \$74.201 = PV(\$1020 - \$1000)$$

A forward contract for which the premium is not zero is sometimes called an **off-market forward.** This terminology arises since a true forward by definition has a zero premium. Therefore, a forward contract with a nonzero premium must have a forward price which is "off the market (forward) price." Unless the strike price equals the forward price, buying a call and selling a put creates an off-market forward.

Equivalence of different positions   We have seen earlier that buying the index and buying a put generates the same profit as buying a call. Similarly, selling a covered call (buying the index and selling a call) generates the same profit as selling a put. Equation (3.1) explains why this happens.

Consider buying the index and buying a put, as in Section 3.1. Recall that, in this example, we have the forward price equal to $1020 and the index price equal to $1000. Thus, the present value of the forward price equals the index price. Rewriting equation (3.1) gives

$$PV(F_{0,t}) + Put(K, t) = Call(K, t) + PV(K)$$
$$\$1000 + \$74.201 = \$93.809 + \$980.39$$

That is, buying the index and buying the put costs the same, and generates the same payoff, as buying the call and buying a zero-coupon bond costing $PV(K)$. (Recall from Section 2.1 that a bond does not affect profit.)

Similarly, in the case of writing a covered call, we have

$$PV(F_{0,t}) - Call(K, t) = PV(K) - Put(K, t)$$

That is, writing a covered call has the same profit as lending $PV(K)$ and selling a put. Equation (3.1) provides a tool for constructing equivalent positions.

3.3 SPREADS AND COLLARS

There are many well-known, commonly used strategies that combine two or more options. In this section we discuss some of these strategies and explain the motivation for using them. Keep in mind that there are infinite variations on the particular strategies we will discuss.

The underlying theme in this section is that there are always trade-offs in designing a position: It is always possible to lower the cost of a position by reducing its payoff. For convenience we will freely refer to the cost of a position as "high" or "low." Be aware that this is a casual use of language. When we are comparing fairly priced positions, a higher cost in some sense reflects a higher payoff. Nevertheless, this use of language is convenient for discussing design trade-offs.

All the examples in this section will use the set of option prices in Table 3.4. We will assume the continuously compounded interest rate is 8%.

Bull and Bear Spreads

An option **spread** is a position consisting of only calls or only puts, in which some options are purchased and some written. Spreads are a common strategy. In this section we define some typical spread strategies and explain why you might use a spread.

TABLE 3.4	Black-Scholes option prices assuming stock price = $40, volatility = 30%, continuously compounded risk-free rate = 8%, dividend yield = $0, and 91 days to expiration.

Strike	Call	Put
35	6.13	0.44
40	2.78	1.99
45	.97	5.08

Suppose you believe the stock will appreciate. One way to speculate on this belief is to enter into a long forward contract, which has zero premium. The drawback to a forward contract is the potential for loss. Buying a call option instead is a way to speculate that the stock will go up while limiting the possible loss. Put-call parity tells us that a call option is essentially a forward contract (which has zero premium) coupled with a put, which provides insurance.

You might ask the question: Is there a way to keep the insurance implicit in the call and still lower the cost of the call? The answer is that you can lower the cost of your strategy if you are willing to reduce your profit should the stock appreciate. You can do this by selling a call at a higher strike price. The owner of this second call buys appreciation above the higher strike price and pays you a premium. Thus, you achieve a lower cost by giving up some portion of profit. A position in which you buy a call and sell an otherwise identical call with a higher strike price is an example of a **bull spread.**

Bull spreads can also be constructed using puts. Perhaps surprisingly, you can achieve the same result either by buying a low-strike call and selling a high-strike call, or by buying a low-strike put and selling a high-strike put.

Spreads constructed with either calls or puts are sometimes called **vertical spreads.** The terminology stems from the way option prices are typically presented, with strikes arrayed vertically (as in Table 3.4).

Example 3.2   To see how a bull spread arises, suppose that as a way to speculate on the stock price increasing, we consider buying a 40-strike call with 3 months to expiration. From Table 3.4, we see that the premium for this call is $2.78. We can reduce the cost of the position—and also the potential profit—by selling the 45-strike call.

An easy way to construct the graph for this position is to emulate a spreadsheet: For each price, compute the profit of each option position and add up the profits for the individual positions. It is worth working through one example in detail to see how this is done.

The initial net cost of the two options is $2.78 − $.97 = $1.81. With 3 months interest, the total cost at expiration is $1.81 \times e^{0.02} = $1.85. Table 3.5 computes the cash flow at expiration for both options and computes profit on the position by subtracting the future value of the net premium.

Figure 3.7 graphs the position in Table 3.5. You should verify that if you buy the 40-strike put and sell the 45-strike put, you obtain exactly the same graph.   🖋

The opposite of a bull spread is a **bear spread.** Using the options from the above example, we could create a bear spread by selling the 40-strike call and buying the 45-strike call. The profit diagram would be exactly the opposite of Figure 3.7.

TABLE 3.5			Profit at expiration from purchase of 40-strike call and sale of 45-strike call.	
Stock Price at Expiration	**Purchased 40-Call**	**Written 45-Call**	**Premium Plus Interest**	**Total**
$35.0	$0.0	$0.0	−$1.85	−$1.85
37.5	0.0	0.0	−1.85	−1.85
40.0	0.0	0.0	−1.85	−1.85
42.5	2.5	0.0	−1.85	0.65
45.0	5.0	0.0	−1.85	3.15
47.5	7.5	−2.5	−1.85	3.15
50.0	10.0	−5.0	−1.85	3.15

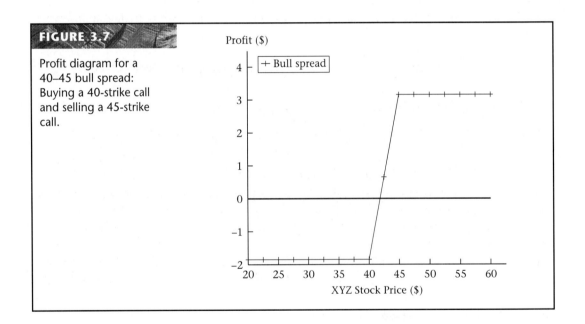

FIGURE 3.7

Profit diagram for a 40–45 bull spread: Buying a 40-strike call and selling a 45-strike call.

Box Spreads

A **box spread** is accomplished by using options to create a synthetic long forward at one price and a synthetic short forward at a different price. This strategy guarantees a cash flow in the future. Hence, it is an option spread that is purely a means of borrowing or lending money: It is costly but has no stock price risk. Reasons for using a box spread are discussed in the box on page 71.

The Use of Box Spreads

A box spread is an alternative to buying a bond. Option market-makers in particular have low transaction costs and can sell box spreads, which is equivalent to borrowing. Box spreads can therefore be a source of funds. In the past, box spreads also provided a tax benefit for some investors. Although a change in the tax law in 1993 ostensibly eliminated this use of box spreads, the issue provides an illustration of why derivatives create problems for the tax authorities.

Consider a taxable investor who has sold stock investments at a loss. This loss is classified for tax purposes as a capital loss. In the United States, capital gains are always taxed, but capital losses are only deductible against capital gains. (The exception to this is that individual investors are allowed to deduct a limited amount of capital losses against ordinary income.) Thus, a taxable investor with large capital losses would like to find a mechanism to generate income which can be labeled as capital gains. This is not as easy as it sounds. A risk-free zero-coupon bond—which is certain to appreciate over its life—generates interest income, which cannot be used to offset capital losses. A stock held to generate gains could instead go down in price, generating additional losses.

A box spread sounds as if it should enable investors to generate capital gains as needed: It is a synthetic bond, guaranteed to appreciate in value just like a bond. Moreover, the gain or loss on an option is a capital gain or loss. *If the change in value of a box spread were taxed as a capital gain, box spreads could be used to create risk-free capital gains income, against which capital losses could be offset.*

Lawmakers in the United States have anticipated strategies like this. Section 1258 of the U.S. Tax Code, enacted in 1993, explicitly states that capital income should be taxed as ordinary income if all expected return is due to time value of money on the investment (in other words, if the investment is equivalent to a bond). This would seem to eliminate the tax motive for entering into box spreads. The problem for the tax authorities, however, is how to identify taxpayers using box spreads for this purpose. There is nothing wrong with entering into a box spread; the law is only violated if the taxpayer reports the resulting income as a capital gain. This is difficult to detect. The fundamental problem is that the tax code calls for different taxation of bonds and options, but options can be used to create bonds. There are many similar illustrations of this problem.

Example 3.3 Suppose we enter into the following two transactions:

1. Buy a 40-strike call and sell a 40-strike put, and simultaneously

2. Sell a 45-strike call and buy a 45-strike put.

The first transaction is a synthetic forward purchase of a stock for $40, while the second transaction is the synthetic forward sale of the stock for $45. Clearly the payoff at expiration will be $5; hence, the transaction has no stock price risk. Using the assumptions in Table 3.4, the cost of the strategy should be

$$5e^{-0.08 \times 0.25} = \$4.90$$

In fact, using the premiums in Table 3.4, the initial cash flow is

$$(\$1.99 - \$2.78) + (\$0.97 - \$5.08) = -\$4.90$$

Another way to view this transaction is that we have bought a 40–45 bull spread using calls (buy 40 call, sell 45 call), and bought a 40–45 bear spread using puts (sell 40 put, buy 45 put). ❧

Ratio Spreads

A **ratio spread** is constructed by buying m calls at one strike and selling n calls at a different strike, with all options having the same time to maturity and same underlying asset. Ratio spreads can also be constructed with puts. You are asked to construct ratio spreads in problem 3.15. Also, a ratio spread constructed by buying a low-strike call and selling two higher-strike calls is one of the positions depicted in the chapter summary in Figure 3.17.

Since ratio spreads involve buying and selling unequal numbers of options, it is possible to construct ratio spreads with zero premium. The significance of this may not be obvious to you now, but we will see in Chapter 4 that by using ratio spreads we can construct insurance strategies that cost nothing if the insurance is not needed. The trade-off to this, as you might guess, is that the insurance is *more* costly if it *is* needed.

Collars

A **collar** is the purchase of a put option and the sale of a call option with a higher strike price, with both options having the same underlying asset and having the same expiration date. If the position is reversed (sale of a put and purchase of a call), the collar is written.[3] The **collar width** is the difference between the call and put strikes.

Example 3.4   Suppose we sell a 45-strike call with a $.97 premium and buy a 40-strike put with a $1.99 premium. This collar is shown in Figure 3.8. Because the purchased put has a higher premium than the written call, the position requires investment of $1.02. ❧

----

[3] Some writers define a collar as the purchase of a put, the sale of a call, *and* the purchase of stock.

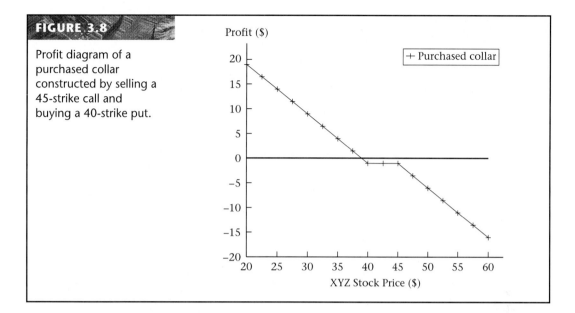

FIGURE 3.8

Profit diagram of a purchased collar constructed by selling a 45-strike call and buying a 40-strike put.

If you hold the book at a distance and squint at Figure 3.8, the collar resembles a short forward contract. Economically, it *is* like a short forward contract in that it is fundamentally a short position: The position benefits from price decreases in the underlying asset and suffers losses from price increases. A collar differs from a forward contract in having a range between the strikes in which the expiration payoff is unaffected by changes in the value of the underlying asset.

In practice collars are frequently used to implement insurance strategies, for example by buying a collar when we own the stock. This position, which we will call a *collared stock*, entails buying the stock, buying a put, and selling a call. It is insurance because we own the asset and buy a put. The sale of a call helps to pay for the purchase of the put. The collared stock looks like a bull spread; however, it arises from a different set of transactions. The bull spread is created by buying one option and selling another. The collared stock begins with a position in the underlying asset that is coupled with a collar.

Example 3.5 Suppose that you own shares of XYZ for which the current price is $40, and you wish to buy insurance. You do this by purchasing put options. A way to reduce the cost of the insurance is to sell an out-of-the-money call. The profit calculations for this set of transactions—buy the stock, buy a 40-strike put, sell a 45-strike call—are shown in Table 3.6. Comparing this table to Table 3.5 demonstrates that profit on the collared stock position is identical to profit on the bull spread. Note that it is essential to account for interest as a cost of holding the stock.

TABLE 3.6			Profit at expiration from purchase of 40-strike put and sale of 45-strike call.			

Stock Price at Expiration	Purchased 40-Put	Written 45-Call	Premium Plus Interest	Profit on Stock	Total
$35.0	$5.0	$0.0	−$1.04	−$5.81	−$1.85
37.5	2.5	0.0	−1.04	−3.31	−1.85
40.0	0.0	0.0	−1.04	−0.81	−1.85
42.5	0.0	0.0	−1.04	1.69	0.65
45.0	0.0	0.0	−1.04	4.19	3.15
47.5	0.0	−2.5	−1.04	6.69	3.15
50.0	0.0	−5.0	−1.04	9.19	3.15

If you have a short position in the stock, you can collar the position by buying a call for insurance and selling an out-of-the-money put to partially fund the call purchase. The result looks like a bear spread.

Zero-cost collars   The collar depicted in Table 3.6 entails paying a net premium of $1.02: $1.99 for the purchased put, against $0.97 for the written call. It is possible to find strike prices for the put and call such that the two premiums exactly offset one another. This position is called a **zero-cost collar.**

To illustrate a zero-cost collar, suppose you buy the stock and buy the 40-strike put that has a premium of $1.99. Trial and error reveals that a call with a strike of $41.72 also has a premium of $1.99. Thus, you can buy a 40-strike put and sell a 41.72-strike call without paying any premium. The result is depicted in Figure 3.9. At expiration, the collar exposes you to stock price movements between $40 and $41.72, coupled with downside protection below $40. You pay for this protection by giving up gains should the stock move above $41.72.

For any given stock there is an infinite number of zero-cost collars. One way to see this is to first pick the desired put strike. It is then possible to find a different strike such that a call has the same premium.

Understanding collars   One aspect of the zero-cost collar that may seem puzzling is that you can finance an at-the-money put by selling an out-of-the-money call. In the above example, with the stock at $40, you were able to costlessly buy a 40-strike put by also selling a 41.72-strike call. This makes it seem as if you have free insurance with some possibility of gain. Even if you are puzzled by this, you probably realize that "free" insurance is not possible, and something must be wrong with this way of thinking about the position.

This puzzle is resolved by taking into account financing cost. Recall that if you pay $40 for stock and sell it for $40 in 91 days, *you have not broken even.* You have lost

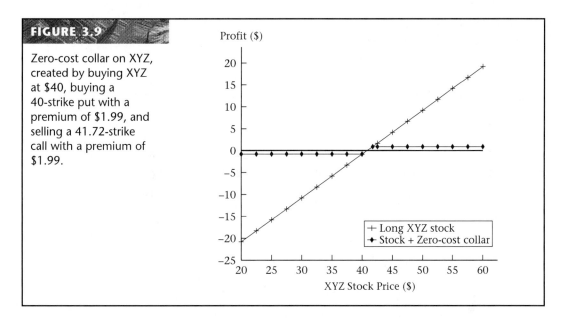

FIGURE 3.9

Zero-cost collar on XYZ, created by buying XYZ at $40, buying a 40-strike put with a premium of $1.99, and selling a 41.72-strike call with a premium of $1.99.

money, because you have foregone $40 \times (e^{0.02} - 1) = \$0.808$ in interest. Thus, the true break-even stock price in this example is $40.808, about halfway between $40 and $41.72.

To make this aspect of the pricing even more obvious, consider a common use of collars: The hedging of a company's stock owned by executives.[4] It is increasingly common for executives with large stock positions to buy zero-cost collars with several years to maturity. Suppose, for example, that Microsoft has a price of $90/share and an executive wishes to hedge 100,000 shares. If the executive buys a 90-strike put, what 3-year call will have the same premium? Using the Black-Scholes formula with a continuously compounded risk-free rate of 6% and a 40% volatility, a 90-strike put has a premium of $15.684. Using trial-and-error (or a numerical solver), a call option with a strike of $144.04 has the same premium. Once again, the collar seems wildly asymmetric because financing cost has not been taken into account. The executive selling stock in three years for $90/share will in fact have lost $90 \times (e^{0.06 \times 3} - 1) = \$17.75$.

The cost of the collar and the forward price   Suppose you try to construct a zero-cost collar in which you set the strike of the put option at the stock price plus financing cost, i.e., the future value of the stock price. In the 91-day example above, this would require that you set the put strike equal to $40.808, which gives a premium of $2.39. The call premium at this strike is also $2.39! *If you try to insure against all losses on the stock, including interest, then a zero-cost collar has zero width.*

---

[4] For an account of this, see "Executive Relief," *The Economist*, April 3, 1999, p. 64.

Note that $40.808 is also the theoretical forward price. Thus we have found that if we set the strike equal to the forward price, the call premium equals the put premium. This is an implication of equation (3.1).

3.4 SPECULATING ON VOLATILITY

The positions we have just considered are all directional: A bull spread or a collar is a bet that the price of the underlying asset will increase. Options can also be used to create positions that are nondirectional with respect to the underlying asset. With a nondirectional position, the holder does not care whether the stock goes up or down, but only how much it moves. We now examine straddles, strangles, and butterfly spreads, which are examples of nondirectional speculations.

Straddles

Consider the strategy of buying a call and a put with the same strike price and time to expiration: This strategy is called a **straddle.** The general idea of a straddle is simple: If the stock price rises, there will be a profit on the purchased call, and if the stock price declines there will be a profit on the purchased put. Thus, the advantage of a straddle is that it can profit from stock price moves in both directions. The disadvantage to a straddle is that it has a high premium because it requires purchasing two options. If the stock price at expiration is near the strike price, the two premiums are lost. The profit diagram for a 40-strike straddle is graphed in Figure 3.10. The initial cost of the straddle at a stock price of $40 is $4.77: $2.78 for the call and $1.99 for the put.

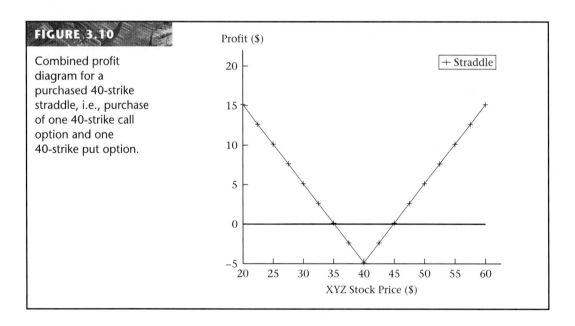

FIGURE 3.10

Combined profit diagram for a purchased 40-strike straddle, i.e., purchase of one 40-strike call option and one 40-strike put option.

Figure 3.10 demonstrates that a straddle is a bet that volatility will be high: The buyer of an at-the-money straddle is hoping that the stock price will move, but does not care about the direction of the move. Because option prices reflect the market's estimate of volatility, the cost of a straddle will be greater when the market's perception is that volatility is greater. If at a given set of option prices all investors found it desirable to buy straddles, then option prices would increase. Thus, purchasing a straddle is really a bet that volatility is greater than the market's assessment of volatility, as reflected in option prices.

Strangle   The disadvantage of a straddle is the high premium cost. To reduce the premium, you can buy out-of-the-money options rather than at-the-money options. Such a position is called a **strangle.** For example, consider buying a 35-strike put and a 45-strike call, for a total premium of $1.41, with a future value of $1.44. These transactions reduce your maximum loss if the options expire with the stock near $40, but they also increase the stock-price move required for a profit.

Figure 3.11 shows the 40-strike straddle graphed against the 35–45 strangle. This comparison illustrates a key point: In comparing any two fairly priced option positions, there will always be a region where each outperforms the other. Indeed, this is necessary to have a fairly priced position.

In Figure 3.11, the strangle outperforms the straddle roughly when the stock price at expiration is between $36.57 and $43.43. Obviously, there is a much broader range in which the straddle outperforms the strangle. How can you decide which is the better investment? The answer is that unless you have a particular view on the stock's performance, you cannot say that one position is preferable to the other. An option pricing

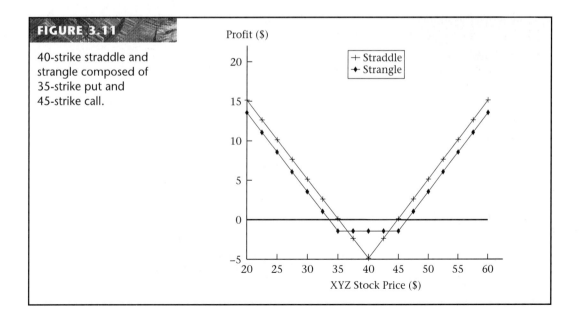

FIGURE 3.11

40-strike straddle and strangle composed of 35-strike put and 45-strike call.

model implicitly evaluates the likelihood that one strategy will outperform the other, and it computes option prices so that the two strategies are equivalently fair deals. One reason for an investor to have a preference for one strategy over the other is having an evaluation of probabilities that differs from the market's.

Written straddle   What if an investor believes that volatility is *lower* than the market's assessment? Because a purchased straddle is a bet that volatility is high (relative to the market's assessment), a **written straddle**—selling a call and put with the same strike price and time to expiration—is a bet that volatility is low (relative to the market's assessment).

Figure 3.12 depicts a written straddle, which is exactly the opposite of Figure 3.10, the purchased straddle. The written straddle is most profitable if the stock price is $40 at expiration, and in this sense it is a bet on low volatility. What is striking about Figure 3.12, however, is the potential for loss. A large change in the stock price in either direction leads to a large, potentially unlimited, loss.

It might occur to you that an investor wishing to bet that volatility will be low could write a straddle and acquire insurance against extreme negative outcomes. That intuition is correct and leads to our next strategy.

Butterfly Spreads

The straddle writer can insure against large losses on the straddle by buying options to protect against losses on both the upside and downside. Buying an out-of-the-money put

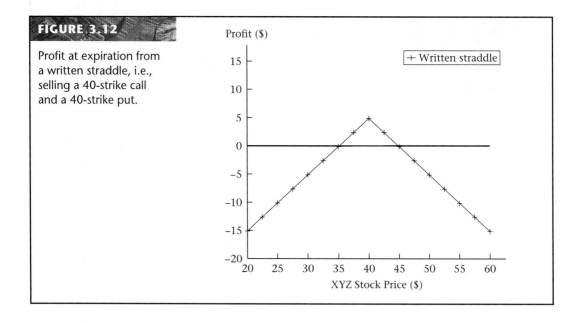

FIGURE 3.12

Profit at expiration from a written straddle, i.e., selling a 40-strike call and a 40-strike put.

provides insurance on the downside, protecting against losses on the at-the-money written put. Buying an out-of-the-money call provides insurance on the upside, protecting against losses on the written at-the-money call.

Figure 3.13 displays the straddle written at a strike price of $40, along with the options to safeguard the position: A 35-strike put and a 45-strike call. The net result of combining these three strategies is an insured written straddle, which is called a **butterfly spread,** graphed in Figure 3.14. It can be thought of as a written straddle for the timid (or for the prudent!).

Comparing the butterfly spread to the written straddle (Figure 3.14), we see that the butterfly spread has a lower maximum profit (due to the cost of insurance) if the stock at expiration is close to $40, and a higher profit if there is a large move in the stock price, in which case the insurance becomes valuable.

We will see in Chapter 9 that by understanding the butterfly spread we gain important insights into option prices. Also, the butterfly spread can be created in a variety of ways: Solely with calls, solely with puts, or by using the stock and a combination of calls and puts. You are asked to verify this in problem 3.18. The spread in Figure 3.14 can also be created by simultaneously buying a 35–40 bull spread and a 40–45 bear spread.

Asymmetric Butterfly Spreads

Examine Figure 3.15. It looks like a butterfly spread except that it is asymmetric: The peak is closer to the high strike than to the low strike. This picture was created by buying two 35-strike calls, selling ten 43-strike calls (with a premium of $1.525, using

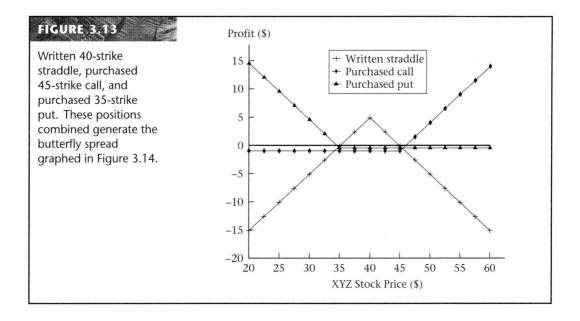

FIGURE 3.13

Written 40-strike straddle, purchased 45-strike call, and purchased 35-strike put. These positions combined generate the butterfly spread graphed in Figure 3.14.

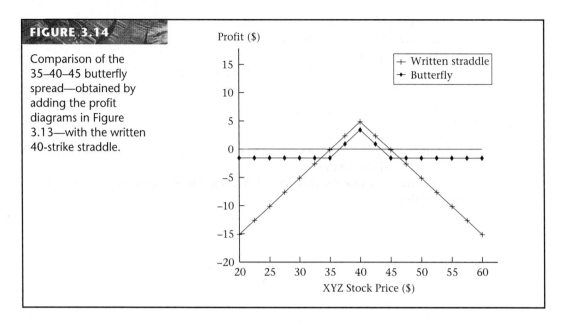

FIGURE 3.14

Comparison of the 35–40–45 butterfly spread—obtained by adding the profit diagrams in Figure 3.13—with the written 40-strike straddle.

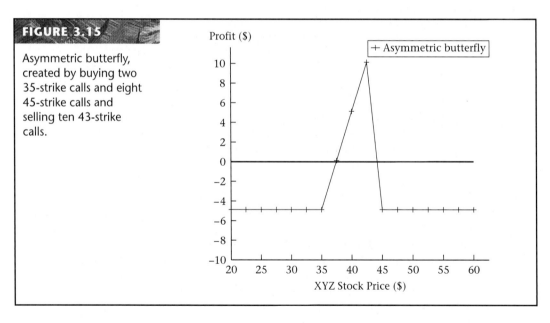

FIGURE 3.15

Asymmetric butterfly, created by buying two 35-strike calls and eight 45-strike calls and selling ten 43-strike calls.

the assumptions in Table 3.4), and buying eight 45-strike calls. The position is like a butterfly in that it earns a profit if the stock stays within a small range, and the loss is the same for high and low stock prices. However, the profit diagram is now tilted to the right, rather than being symmetric.

Suppose you knew that you wanted a position that looks like Figure 3.15. How would you know how many options to buy and sell to construct this position? In order to obtain this position, the strikes clearly have to be at 35, 43, and 45. The total distance between 35 and 45 is 10. The number 43 is 80% ($= \frac{43-35}{10}$) of the way from 35 to 45. In fact, we can write 43 as

$$43 = (0.2 \times 35) + (0.8 \times 45)$$

This way of writing 43 tells us our call position: For every written 43-strike call, we want to buy 0.2 35 calls and 0.8 45 calls. Thus if we sell ten 43-strike calls, we buy two 35 calls and eight 45-strike calls.

In general, consider the strike prices K_1, K_2, and K_3, where $K_1 < K_2 < K_3$. Define λ so that

$$\lambda = \frac{K_3 - K_2}{K_3 - K_1}$$

or

$$K_2 = \lambda K_1 + (1 - \lambda) K_3$$

For example, if $K_1 = 35$, $K_2 = 43$, and $K_3 = 45$, then $\lambda = .2$, as in the above example. In order to construct an asymmetric butterfly, for every K_2 call we write, we buy λ K_1 calls and $1 - \lambda$ K_3 calls.

You should verify that if you buy two 35-strike puts, sell ten 43-strike puts, and buy eight 45-strike puts, you duplicate the profit diagram in Figure 3.15.

3.5 EXAMPLE: ANOTHER EQUITY-LINKED NOTE

In 1996 Times Mirror Co. issued a 5-year note with a 4.25% coupon and an unusual feature: The maturity payment depended upon the price of Netscape stock at maturity of the note. We will discuss in Chapter 16 why Times Mirror issued this note. Our purpose here is to examine its structure, which is similar to that of a collar.

The maturity value of the note was linked to Netscape's stock price in 2001, $S_{Netscape}$.[5] The specific formula is given in Table 3.7.

This structure is called a PEPS (Premium Equity Participating Security). Figure 3.16 depicts this payoff, comparing holding Netscape outright to the PEPS payoff, and also graphing the difference between the two (labeled "Net to Times Mirror" since Times Mirror owned Netscape stock when it issued this security). Investing in the PEPS outperforms investing in Netscape at low prices because Netscape pays no dividend and the PEPS pays a coupon. At high prices, Netscape shares outperform the PEPS because the PEPS only retains 87% of Netscape's appreciation above $45.14. The curve labeled "Net to Times Mirror" shows the result from holding Netscape and issuing the PEPS.

---

[5] When Netscape was acquired by AOL, the structure became defined in terms of AOL shares.

TABLE 3.7	Payment at maturity on Times Mirror PEPS, showing the dependence of the maturity payment on the future price of Netscape stock.

Netscape Share Price	Payment to Times Mirror PEPS-Holders
$S_{Netscape} < 39.25$	$S_{Netscape}$
$39.25 \leq S_{Netscape} \leq 45.14$	39.25
$45.14 < S_{Netscape}$	$39.25 + 0.8696 \times (S_{Netscape} - 45.14)$

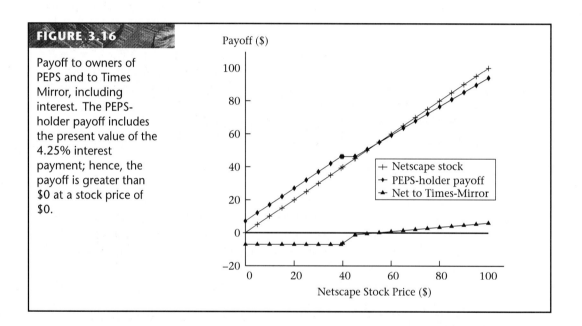

FIGURE 3.16

Payoff to owners of PEPS and to Times Mirror, including interest. The PEPS-holder payoff includes the present value of the 4.25% interest payment; hence, the payoff is greater than $0 at a stock price of $0.

How is a PEPS priced? The "Net" graph should remind you of a bull spread or a collar. We can in fact construct the PEPS using an options spread. Consider the following transactions:

- Buy Netscape.
- Sell one call with a $39.25 strike.
- Buy 0.8696 calls with a $45.14 strike.

The buyer of the PEPS is owed the net option premium because the written call with a strike of $39.25 has a higher premium than the 0.8696 purchased calls with a $45.14 strike. The PEPS coupon is effectively an amortized option premium.

CHAPTER SUMMARY

Puts are insurance against a price decline and calls are insurance against a price increase. Combining a long or short position in the asset with an offsetting position in options (for example, a long position in the asset is coupled either with a purchased put or written call) leads to the various possible positions and their equivalents in Table 3.8.

Buying a call and selling a put with the same strike price and time to expiration creates an obligation to buy the asset at expiration by paying the strike price. This is a synthetic forward. A synthetic forward must have the same cost in present value terms as a true forward. This observation leads to equation (3.1):

$$Call(K, t) - Put(K, t) = PV(F_{0,t} - K) \qquad (3.1)$$

This relationship, called *put-call parity*, explains the difference in call and put premiums for otherwise identical options. It is one of the most important relationships in derivatives.

There are numerous strategies that permit speculating on the direction of the stock or on the size of stock price moves (volatility). Some of these positions are summarized graphically in Figure 3.17. We also categorize in Table 3.9 various strategies according to whether they reflect bullish or bearish views on the stock price direction or volatility.[6]

Netscape PEPS were equivalent to a bond coupled with an option spread, illustrating that the tools in this chapter have applicability beyond speculative investing.

FURTHER READING

In Chapter 4 we will see how firms can use these strategies to manage risk. We will further explore put-call parity in Chapter 9, in which we also will use bull, bear, and butterfly spreads to say more about what it means for an option to be fairly priced.

Put-call parity was first demonstrated in Stoll (1969). Merton (1973a) corrected the original analysis for the case of American options, for which, because of early

TABLE 3.8	Summary of equivalent positions from Section 3.1.	
Position	**Is Equivalent To**	**And Is Called**
Index + Put	Zero-Coupon Bond + Call	Insured Asset (floor)
Index − Call	Zero-Coupon Bond − Put	Covered Written call
−Index + Call	−Zero-Coupon Bond + Put	Insured Short (cap)
−Index − Put	−Zero-Coupon Bond − Call	Covered Written Put

....

[6]Table 3.9 was suggested by David Shimko.

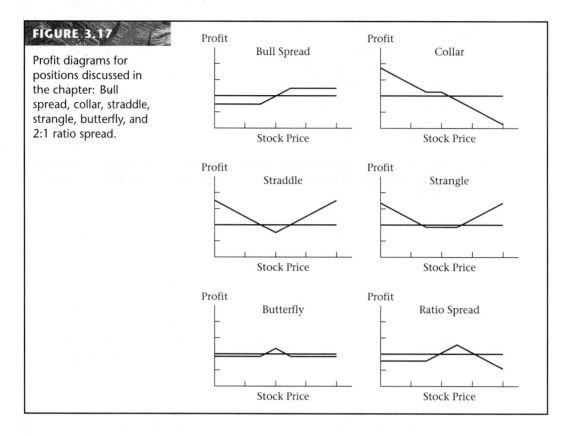

FIGURE 3.17

Profit diagrams for positions discussed in the chapter: Bull spread, collar, straddle, strangle, butterfly, and 2:1 ratio spread.

TABLE 3.9   Positions consistent with different views on the stock price and volatility direction.

	Volatility Will Increase	No Volatility View	Volatility Will Fall
Price Will Fall	Buy Puts	Sell Underlying	Sell Calls
No Price View	Buy Straddle	Do Nothing	Sell Straddle
Price Will Increase	Buy Calls	Buy Underlying	Sell Puts

exercise, parity need not hold. Ronn and Ronn (1989) provide a detailed examination of price bounds and returns on box spreads.

There are numerous practitioner books on option trading strategies. A classic practitioner reference is McMillan (2001).

PROBLEMS

3.1. Suppose that you buy the S&R index for $1000, buy a 1000-strike put, and borrow $980.39. Perform a payoff and profit calculation mimicking Table 3.1. Graph the resulting payoff and profit diagrams for the combined position.

3.2. Suppose that you short the S&R index for $1000 and sell a 1000-strike put. Construct a table mimicking Table 3.1 which summarizes the payoff and profit of this position. Verify that your table matches Figure 3.5.

For the following problems assume the effective 6-month interest rate is 2%, the S&R 6-month forward price is $1020, and use these premiums for S&R options with 6 months to expiration:

Strike	Call	Put
$950	$120.405	$51.777
1000	93.809	74.201
1020	84.470	84.470
1050	71.802	101.214
1107	51.873	137.167

3.3. Suppose you buy the S&R index for $1000 and buy a 950-strike put. Construct payoff and profit diagrams for this position. Verify that you obtain the same payoff and profit diagram by investing $931.37 in zero-coupon bonds and buying a 950-strike call.

3.4. Suppose you short the S&R index for $1000 and buy a 950-strike call. Construct payoff and profit diagrams for this position. Verify that you obtain the same payoff and profit diagram by borrowing $931.37 and buying a 950-strike put.

3.5. Suppose you short the S&R index for $1000 and buy a 1050-strike call. Construct payoff and profit diagrams for this position. Verify that you obtain the same payoff and profit diagram by borrowing $1029.41 and buying a 1050-strike put.

3.6. Verify that you earn the same profit and payoff by (a) buying the S&R index for $1000 and (b) buying a 950-strike S&R call, selling a 950-strike S&R put, and lending $931.37.

3.7. Verify that you earn the same profit and payoff by (a) shorting the S&R index for $1000 and (b) selling a 1050-strike S&R call, buying a 1050-strike put, and borrowing $1029.41.

3.8. Suppose the premium on a 6-month S&R call is $109.20 and the premium on a put with the same strike price is $60.18. What is the strike price?

3.9. Construct payoff and profit diagrams for the purchase of a 950-strike S&R call and sale of a 1000-strike S&R call. Verify that you obtain exactly the same *profit* diagram for the purchase of a 950-strike S&R put and sale of a 1000-strike S&R put. What is the difference in the payoff diagrams for the call and put spreads? Why is there a difference?

3.10. Construct payoff and profit diagrams for the purchase of a 1050-strike S&R call and sale of a 950-strike S&R call. Verify that you obtain exactly the same *profit* diagram for the purchase of a 1050-strike S&R put and sale of a 950-strike S&R put. What is the difference in the initial cost of these positions?

3.11. Suppose you invest in the S&R index for $1000, buy a 950-strike put, and sell a 1050-strike call. Draw a profit diagram for this position. What is the net option premium? If you wanted to construct a zero-cost collar keeping the put strike equal to $950, in what direction would you have to change the call strike?

3.12. Suppose you invest in the S&R index for $1000, buy a 950-strike put, and sell a 1107-strike call. Draw a profit diagram for this position. How close is this to a zero-cost collar?

3.13. Draw profit diagrams for the following positions:

    a. 1050-strike S&R straddle.

    b. Written 950-strike S&R straddle.

    c. Simultaneous purchase of a 1050-strike straddle and sale of a 950-strike S&R straddle.

3.14. Suppose you buy a 950-strike S&R call, sell a 1000-strike S&R call, sell a 950-strike S&R put, and buy a 1000-strike S&R put.

    a. Verify that there is no S&R price risk in this transaction.

    b. What is the initial cost of the position?

    c. What is the value of the position after 6 months?

    d. Verify that the implicit interest rate in these cash flows is 2% over 6 months.

3.15. Compute profit diagrams for the following ratio spreads:

    a. Buy 950-strike call, sell two 1050-strike calls.

    b. Buy two 950-strike calls, sell three 1050-strike calls.

    c. Consider buying n 950-strike calls and selling m 1050-strike calls so that the premium of the position is zero. Considering your analysis in (a) and (b), what can you say about n/m? What exact ratio gives you a zero premium?

3.16. In the previous problem we saw that a ratio spread can have zero initial premium. Can a bull spread or bear spread have zero initial premium? A butterfly spread? Why or why not?

3.17. Construct an asymmetric butterfly using the 950-, 1020-, and 1050-strike options. How many of each option do you hold? Draw a profit diagram for the position.

3.18. Verify that the butterfly spread in Figure 3.14 can be duplicated by the following transactions (use the option prices in Table 3.4):

  a. Buy 35 call, sell two 40 calls, buy 45 call.

  b. Buy 35 put, sell two 40 puts, buy 45 put.

  c. Buy stock, buy 35 put, sell two 40 calls, buy 45 call.

3.19. Here is a quote from an investment website about an investment strategy using options:

> One strategy investors are applying to the XYZ options is using "synthetic stock." A synthetic stock is created when an investor simultaneously purchases a call option and sells a put option on the same stock. The end result is that the synthetic stock has the same value, in terms of capital gain potential, as the underlying stock itself. Provided the premiums on the options are the same, they cancel each other out so the transaction fees are a wash.

Suppose, to be concrete, that the premium on the call you buy is the same as the premium on the put you sell, and both have the same strikes and times to expiration.

  a. What can you say about the strike price?

  b. What term best describes the position you have created?

  c. Suppose the options have a bid-ask spread. If you are creating a synthetic purchased stock and the net premium is zero *inclusive of the bid-ask spread*, where will the strike price be relative to the forward price?

  d. If you create a synthetic short stock with zero premium inclusive of the bid-ask spread, where will the strike price be relative to the forward price?

  e. Do you consider the "transaction fees" to really be "a wash"? Why or why not?

3.20. Construct a spreadsheet for which you can input up to five strike prices and quantities of put and call options bought or sold at those strikes, and which will automatically construct the total expiration payoff diagram for that position. Modify the spreadsheet to permit you to choose whether to graph a payoff or profit function.

Chapter 4
Introduction to Risk Management

Business, like life, is inherently risky. Firms convert inputs such as labor, raw materials, and machines into goods and services. A firm is profitable if the cost of what it produces exceeds the cost of the inputs. Prices can change, however, and what appears to be a profitable activity today may not be profitable tomorrow. Many instruments are available that permit firms to hedge various risks, ranging from commodity prices to weather. A firm that actively uses derivatives and other techniques to alter its risk and protect its profitability is engaging in **risk management.** In this chapter we take a look at how derivatives—such as forwards, calls, and puts—are used in practice to manage risk.

We begin by examining two hypothetical firms—Golddiggers, a gold-mining firm, and Auric Enterprises, a manufacturer using gold as an input—to see what risks they face and to demonstrate the use of derivatives strategies to manage those risks. After looking at these examples we will explore some reasons firms seek to manage risk in the first place.

4.1 BASIC RISK MANAGEMENT: THE PRODUCER'S PERSPECTIVE

Golddiggers is a gold-mining firm planning to mine and sell 100,000 ounces of gold over the next year. For simplicity, we will assume that they sell all of the next year's production precisely 1 year from today, receiving whatever the gold price is that day. The price of gold today is $405/oz. We will ignore production beyond the next year.

Obviously Golddiggers—like any producer—hopes that the gold price will rise over the next year. However, Golddiggers's management computes estimated net income for a range of possible prices of gold in 1 year (Table 4.1). The net income calculation shows that Golddiggers's profit is affected by gold prices.

Should Golddiggers simply shut the mine if gold prices fall enough to make net income negative? The answer depends on the extent to which costs are fixed. The firm incurs the fixed cost whether or not it produces gold. Variable costs are incurred only if the mine operates. Thus, for any gold price above the variable cost of $50/oz., it will make sense to produce gold.[1]

----

[1] Suppose the gold price is $350/oz. If Golddiggers produces no gold, the firm loses its fixed cost, $330/oz. If Golddiggers produces gold, the firm has fixed cost of $330/oz. and variable cost of $50/oz., and so loses $350 − ($330 + $50) = −$30/oz. It is better to lose only $30, so Golddiggers will produce even when they have negative net income. If the gold price were to fall below the variable cost of $50, then it would make sense to stop producing.

TABLE 4.1	Golddiggers's estimated net income one year from today, unhedged.		

Gold Price in One Year	Fixed Cost	Variable Cost	Net Income
$350	−$330	−$50	−$30
$400	−$330	−$50	$20
$450	−$330	−$50	$70
$500	−$330	−$50	$120

Hedging with a Forward Contract

Golddiggers can lock in a price for gold in 1 year by entering into a short forward contract, agreeing today to sell its gold for delivery in 1 year. Suppose that gold to be delivered in 1 year can be sold today for $420/oz. and that Golddiggers agrees to sell forward all of its gold production in 1 year. We will assume in all examples that the forward contract settles financially. As noted earlier, the payoff to a forward is the same with physical or financial settlement.

Profit calculations when Golddiggers is hedged are summarized in Table 4.2. This table adds the profit on the forward contract to net income from Table 4.1. Figure 4.1 contains 3 curves showing:

- **Unhedged profit.** Since cost is $380/oz., the line labeled "unhedged seller" shows zero profit at $380, a loss at lower prices, and profit at higher prices. For example, at $420, profit is $40/oz. Since it has gold in the ground, Golddiggers has a long position in gold.

- **Profit on the short forward position.** The "short gold forward" line represents the profit from going short the gold forward contract at a forward price of $420/oz.

TABLE 4.2	Golddiggers's net income one year from today, hedged with a forward sale of gold.			

Gold Price in One Year	Fixed Cost	Variable Cost	Profit on Short Forward	Net Income on Hedged Position
$350	−$330	−$50	$70	$40
$400	−$330	−$50	$20	$40
$450	−$330	−$50	−$30	$40
$500	−$330	−$50	−$80	$40

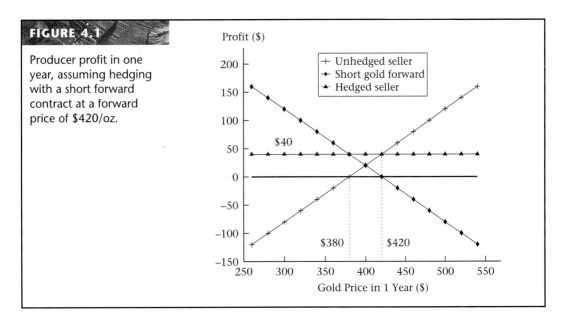

FIGURE 4.1

Producer profit in one year, assuming hedging with a short forward contract at a forward price of $420/oz.

We profit from locking in the price if prices are lower than $420 and we lose if prices are higher.

- **Hedged profit.** The line labeled "hedged seller" is the sum of the other two lines, adding them vertically at every gold price. It is flat at $40/oz., as we would expect from Table 4.2. A quick way to add the lines together is to notice that the "unhedged seller" graph has a positive slope of 1, and the "short gold forward" graph has a slope of −1. Added together vertically, the two graphs will have a slope of 0, so the only question is the height of the line. A profit calculation at a single point tells us that it must be at $40/oz.

Insurance: Guaranteeing a Minimum Price with a Put Option

A possible objection to hedging with a forward contract is that if gold prices do rise, Golddiggers will still receive only $420/oz; there is no prospect for greater profit. Gold insurance, i.e., a put option, provides a way to have higher profits at high gold prices while still being protected against low prices. Suppose that the market price for a 420-strike put is $8.77/oz.[2] This put provides a *floor* on the price.

....

[2]This uses the Black-Scholes formula for the put price with inputs $S = 420$, $K = 420$, $r = 4.879\%$, $\sigma = 5.5\%$, $\delta = 4.879\%$ and $t = 1$ (year).

Since the put premium is paid 1 year prior to the option payoff, we must take into account interest cost when we compute profit in 1 year. The future value of the premium is $8.77 \times 1.05 = \$9.21$. As with the forward contract, we assume financial settlement, although physical settlement would yield the same net income.

Table 4.3 shows the result of buying this put. If the price is less than $420, the put is exercised and Golddiggers sells gold for $420/oz. less the cost of the put. This gives net income of $30.79. If the price is greater than $420, Golddiggers sells gold at the market price.

The insurance strategy—buying the put—performs better than shorting the forward if the price of gold in 1 year is more than $429.21. Otherwise the short forward outperforms insurance. Figure 4.2 shows the unhedged position, profit from the put by itself, and the result of hedging with the put.

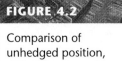

TABLE 4.3   Golddiggers's net income 1 year from today, hedged with a 420-strike put option.

Gold Price in One Year	Fixed Cost	Variable Cost	Profit on Put Option	Net Income
$350	−$330	−$50	$60.79	$30.79
$400	−$330	−$50	$10.79	$30.79
$450	−$330	−$50	−$9.21	$60.79
$500	−$330	−$50	−$9.21	$110.79

FIGURE 4.2

Comparison of unhedged position, 420-strike put option, and unhedged position plus 420-strike put.

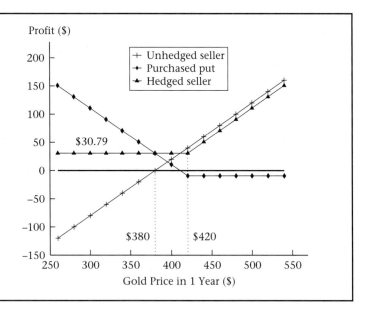

What this analysis does not address is the *probability* that the gold price in 1 year will be in different regions; that is, how likely is it that the gold price will exceed $429.21? The price of the put option implicitly contains information about the likelihood that the gold price will exceed $420, and by how much. The *probability distribution* of the gold price is a key factor determining the pricing of the put. We will see in later chapters how the distribution affects the put price and how to use information about the probability distribution to help us assess risk.

Figure 4.3 compares the profit from the two protective strategies we have examined: Selling a forward contract and buying a put. As you would expect, neither strategy is clearly preferable; rather, there are trade-offs, with each contract outperforming the other for some range of prices.

The fact that no hedging strategy always outperforms the other will be true of all fairly priced strategies. Considerations such as transaction costs and market views are likely to govern the choice of a strategy in practice.

Insuring by Selling a Call

With the sale of a call, Golddiggers receives a premium, which reduces losses, but the written call limits possible profits. One can debate whether this really constitutes insurance, but our interest is in seeing how the sale of a call affects the potential profit and loss for Golddiggers.

Suppose that instead of buying a put, Golddiggers sells a 420-strike call and receives an $8.77 premium. Golddiggers in this case would be said to have sold a *cap*.

Figure 4.4 shows the payoff to this strategy. If we compute the actual profit 1 year from today, we see that if the gold price in 1 year exceeds $420, Golddiggers will show

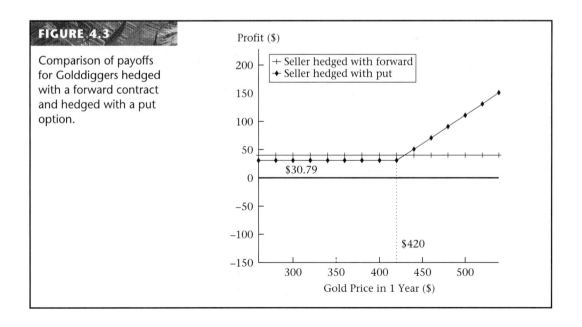

FIGURE 4.3

Comparison of payoffs for Golddiggers hedged with a forward contract and hedged with a put option.

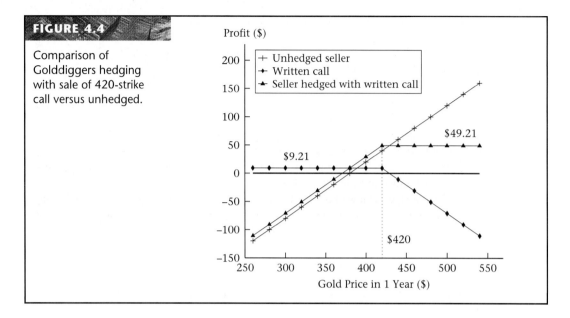

FIGURE 4.4

Comparison of Golddiggers hedging with sale of 420-strike call versus unhedged.

Profit ($)

Legend:
- Unhedged seller
- Written call
- Seller hedged with written call

(Values shown on chart: $9.21, $49.21, $420; x-axis "Gold Price in 1 Year ($)" from 250 to 550; y-axis from −150 to 200)

profits of

$$\$420 + \$9.21 - \$380 = \$49.21$$

That is, Golddiggers sells gold for $420 (since the written call is exercised by the holder), receives the future value of the premium, and has a cost of $380. If the price of gold is less than $420, Golddiggers will make

$$P_{gold} + \$9.21 - \$380$$

On the downside, Golddiggers has exposure to gold, but keeps the option premium.

By writing the call, Golddiggers keeps the $8.77 call premium and 1 year later makes $9.21 more than an unhedged gold seller. On the other hand, if the gold price exceeds $420, the call is exercised and the price Golddiggers receives is thus capped at $420. Thus, for gold prices above $429.21, an unhedged strategy has a higher payoff than that of writing a 420-strike call. Also, for prices below $410.79, being fully hedged is preferable to having sold the call.

Adjusting the Amount of Insurance

Consider again Golddiggers's strategy of obtaining insurance against a price decline by purchasing a put option. A common objection to the purchase of insurance is that it is expensive. Insurance has a premium because it eliminates the risk of a large loss, while allowing a profit if prices increase. The cost of insurance reflects this asymmetry.

There are at least two ways to reduce the cost of insurance:

- Reduce the insured amount by lowering the strike price of the put option.
- Sell some of the gain.

Both of these strategies reduce the asymmetry between gains and losses, and hence lower the cost of insurance. The first strategy, lowering the strike price, permits some additional loss while the second, selling some of the gain, puts a cap on the potential gain.

Reducing the strike price lowers the amount of insurance; therefore the put option will have a lower premium. Figure 4.5 compares profit diagrams for Golddiggers's hedging using put options with strikes of $400 (premium = $2.21), $420 (premium = $8.77), and $440 (premium = $21.54). The 400-strike, low-premium option yields the highest profit if insurance is not needed (the price is high) and the lowest profit if insurance is needed (the price is low). The 440-strike, high-premium option yields the lowest profit if insurance is not needed, and the highest profit if insurance is needed.

The manager's view of the market and willingness to absorb risk will undoubtedly influence the choice among these alternatives. Managers optimistic about the price of gold will opt for low-strike-price puts, whereas pessimistic managers will more likely choose high-strike puts. While corporations *per se* may not be risk-averse, managers may be. Also, some managers may perceive losses to be costly in terms of the public's perception of the firm or the boss's perception of them.

This problem of choosing the appropriate strike price is not unique to corporate risk management. Safe drivers and more careful homeowners often reduce premiums by purchasing auto and homeowner's insurance with larger deductibles. This reflects their proprietary view of the likelihood that the insurance will be used. One important difference between gold insurance and property insurance, however, is that poor drivers would like smaller deductibles for their auto insurance; this differential demand by the quality of the insured is called *adverse selection* and is reflected in the premiums for different deductibles. A driver known to be good would face a lower premium for any

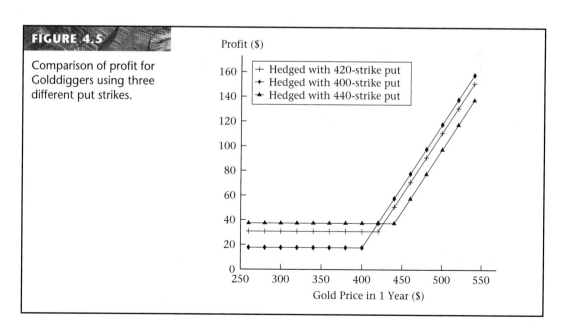

FIGURE 4.5

Comparison of profit for Golddiggers using three different put strikes.

deductible than a driver known to be bad. With gold, however, the price of the put is independent of who is doing the buying.[3]

4.2 BASIC RISK MANAGEMENT: THE BUYER'S PERSPECTIVE

Auric Enterprises is a manufacturer of widgets, a product that uses gold as an input. We will suppose for simplicity that the price of gold is the only uncertainty Auric faces. In particular, we assume that

- Auric sells each widget for a fixed price of $800, a price known in advance.
- The fixed cost per widget is $340.
- The manufacture of each widget requires 1 ounce of gold as an input.
- The non-gold variable cost per widget is zero.
- The quantity of widgets to be sold is known in advance.

Because Auric makes a greater profit if the price of gold falls, Auric's gold position is implicitly short. As with Golddiggers, we will examine various risk-management strategies for Auric. The pro forma net income calculation for Auric is in Table 4.4.

Hedging with a Forward Contract

The forward price is $420 as before. Auric can lock in a profit by entering into a long forward contract. Auric thereby guarantees a profit of

$$\text{Profit} = \$800 - \$340 - \$420 = \$40$$

TABLE 4.4	Auric estimated net income, unhedged, 1 year from today.			
Revenue per Widget	**Gold Price in 1 Year**	**Fixed Cost**	**Variable Cost**	**Net Income**
$800	$350	$340	$0	$110
$800	$400	$340	$0	$60
$800	$450	$340	$0	$10
$800	$500	$340	$0	−$40

....

[3]You might think that a dealer would charge a higher price for a purchased option if the dealer knew that an option buyer had superior information about the market for gold. However, in general the dealer will quickly hedge the risk from the option and then does not care about future movements in the price of gold.

Note that whereas Golddiggers was *selling* in the forward market, Auric is *buying* in the forward market. Thus, Golddiggers and Auric are natural *counterparties* in an economic sense. In practice they need not be direct counterparties since they can enter into forward contracts through dealers or on exchanges. But in an economic sense, one firm's desire to sell forward has a counterpart in the other's desire to buy forward.

Figure 4.6 compares the profit diagrams for the unhedged buyer and a long forward position in gold. It also shows the profit for the hedged buyer, which is generated by summing up the forward position and the unhedged payoff. We see graphically that the buyer can lock in a profit of $40/oz.

Insurance: Guaranteeing a Maximum Price with a Call Option

Rather than lock in a price unconditionally, Auric might like to pay $420/oz. if the gold price is greater than $420/oz., but pay the market price if it is less. Auric can accomplish this by buying a call option. As a future buyer, Auric is naturally short; hence, a call is insurance. Suppose the call has a premium of $8.77/oz. (recall that this is the same as the premium on the put with the same strike price). The future value of the premium is $8.77 \times 1.05 = \$9.21$.

If Auric buys the insurance contract, net income on the hedged position will be as in Table 4.5. If the price is less than $420, the call is worthless at expiration and Auric buys gold at the market price. If the price is greater than $420, the call is exercised and Auric buys gold for $420/oz., less the cost of the call. This gives a profit of $30.79.

If the price of gold in 1 year is less than $410.79, insuring the price by buying the call performs better than locking in a price of $420. At low prices, the option permits

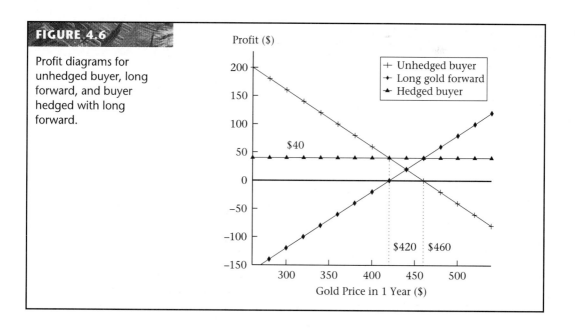

FIGURE 4.6

Profit diagrams for unhedged buyer, long forward, and buyer hedged with long forward.

	Gold Price in 1 Year	Unhedged Net Income from Table 4.4	Profit on Call Option	Net Income
TABLE 4.5 Auric net income 1 year from today, hedged with 420-strike call option.	$350	$110	−$9.21	$100.79
	$400	$60	−$9.21	$50.79
	$450	$10	$20.79	$30.79
	$500	−$40	$70.79	$30.79

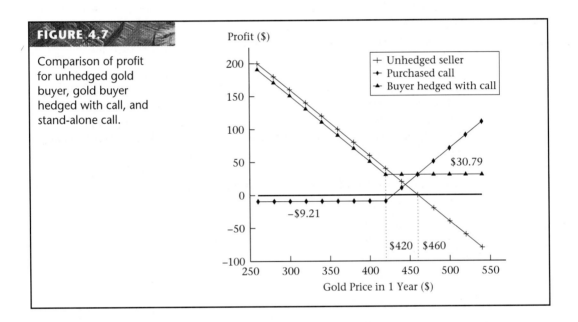

FIGURE 4.7

Comparison of profit for unhedged gold buyer, gold buyer hedged with call, and stand-alone call.

us to take advantage of lower gold prices. If the price of gold in 1 year is greater than $410.79, insuring the price by buying the call performs worse than locking in a price of $420 since we have paid the call premium.

Figure 4.7 shows the profit from the call by itself, along with the results of hedging with the call. As before, the graph does not show the *probability* that the gold price in 1 year will be in different regions; hence, we cannot evaluate the likelihood of different outcomes.

4.3 WHY DO FIRMS MANAGE RISK?

The Golddiggers and Auric examples illustrate how the two companies can use forwards, calls, and puts to reduce losses in case of an adverse gold price move, essentially insuring their future cash flows. Why would a firm use these strategies?

This is a question that seems at first to have an obvious answer—to reduce risk. However, in a world with fairly priced derivatives, no transaction costs, and no other market imperfections such as taxes, derivatives change the *distribution* of cash flows but do not increase the value of cash flows. Moreover, large publicly held firms are owned by diverse shareholders. These shareholders can, in theory, configure their own portfolios to bear risk optimally, suiting their own taste. In order to hedge, the firm must pay commissions and bid-ask spreads, and bear counterparty credit risk. Why incur these costs?

There are in fact several reasons that firms seek to manage risk. Before discussing them, let's think about what derivatives accomplish. To be concrete, suppose that Golddiggers sells gold forward at $420/oz. We saw that this will guarantee a net income of $40/oz.

When hedged with the forward, Golddiggers will have a profit of $40 whatever the price in 1 year. In effect, the value of the reduced profits, should the gold price rise, subsidizes the payment to Golddiggers should the gold price fall. If we use the term "state" to denote a particular gold price in 1 year, we can describe the hedging strategy as shifting dollars from more profitable states (when gold prices are high) to less profitable states (when gold prices are low).

This shifting of dollars from high gold price states to low gold price states will have value for the firm *if the firm values the dollar more in a low gold price state than in a high gold price state*. Why might a firm value a dollar differently in different states?

An Example Where Hedging Adds Value

Consider a firm that produces one unit per year of a good costing $10. Immediately after production, the firm receives a payment of either $11.20 or $9, with 50% probability. Thus, the firm has either a $1.20 profit or a $1 loss. It appears that the firm has an expected profit of

$$[0.5 \times (\$9 - \$10)] + [0.5 \times (\$11.20 - \$10)] = \$.10$$

This calculation ignores taxes.

For example, suppose that when the firm reports a profit, 40% of the profit is taxed, but when the firm reports a loss, it pays no taxes and receives no tax refund. Table 4.6 computes expected after-tax profit under these circumstances. The taxation of profits alone converts an expected $0.10 pre-tax gain into an after-tax $0.14 loss.[4] Because of taxes, the firm values a dollar of profit at $0.60 ($0.40 goes to the government). A dollar of loss pre-tax, however, is a dollar of loss after-tax. In this situation, it is desirable for the firm to trade pre-tax profits for pre-tax losses.

Now suppose that there is a forward market for the firm's output, and that the forward price is $10.10. If the firm sells forward, profit is computed as in Table 4.7. Instead of an expected loss of $0.14, we obtain a certain profit of $0.06. Hedging with

<hr>

[4]Problem 4.15 asks you to compute profit when losses are deductible.

TABLE 4.6	Calculation of after-tax net income in states where the output price is $9.00 and $11.20. Expected after-tax income is $(0.5 \times -\$1) + (0.5 \times \$0.72) = -\$0.14$.

		Price = $9	Price = $11.20
(1)	Pre-Tax Operating Income	−$1	$1.20
(2)	Taxable Income	$0	$1.20
(3)	Tax @ 40% [0.4 × (2)]	0	$0.48
	After-Tax Income [(2) − (3)]	−$1	$0.72

TABLE 4.7	Calculation of hedged after-tax net income in states where the output price is $9.00 and $11.20. Expected after-tax income is $0.06.

		Price = $9	Price = $11.20
(1)	Pre-Tax Operating Income	−$1.00	$1.20
(2)	Income from Short Forward	$1.10	−$1.10
(3)	Taxable Income [(1) + (2)]	$0.10	$0.10
(4)	Tax @ 40% [0.4 × (3)]	$0.04	$0.04
	After-Tax Income [(3) − (4)]	$0.06	$0.06

a forward transfers net income from a less-valued to a more highly valued state, raising the expected value of cash flows.

Figure 4.8 depicts how the nondeductibility of losses affects after-tax cash flows. First, observe that after-tax profit (line ACB) is a concave function of the output price. (A **concave** function is one shaped like the cross section of an upside-down bowl.) When profits are concave, the expected value of profits is increased by reducing uncertainty. We can see this in the graph. If the price is certain to be $10.10, then profit will be given by point C. However, if price can be either $9 or $11.20, expected profit is at point D, on the line ADB at the expected price of $10.10. *Because ACB is concave, point D lies below point C, and hedging increases expected profits.*[5]

Some of the hedging rationales we discuss hinge on concave profits, so that value is increased by reducing uncertainty.

---

[5]This is an illustration of *Jensen's inequality*, which is discussed in Appendix C, and which we will encounter often in this book.

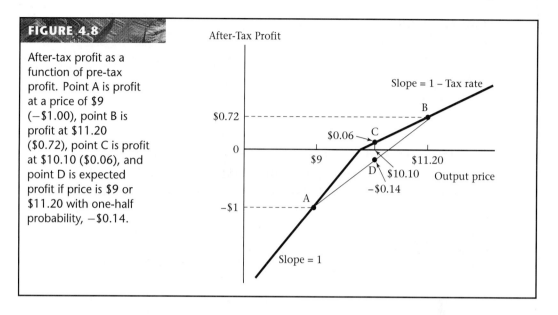

FIGURE 4.8

After-tax profit as a function of pre-tax profit. Point A is profit at a price of $9 (−$1.00), point B is profit at $11.20 ($0.72), point C is profit at $10.10 ($0.06), and point D is expected profit if price is $9 or $11.20 with one-half probability, −$0.14.

Reasons to Hedge

There are in fact a number of reasons why losses might be more harmful than profits are beneficial. We now discuss some of those reasons.[6]

Taxes The previous example illustrating the effect of taxes was oversimplified in assuming that losses are completely untaxed, but it *is* typically the case that governments tax profits but do not give full credits for losses. Tax systems usually permit a loss to be offset against a profit from a different year. However, in present value terms, the loss will have a lower effective tax rate than that applied to profits, which still generates a motive to hedge.

There are other aspects of the tax code that can encourage firms to shift income using derivatives; such uses may or may not appear to be hedging and may or may not be approved of by tax authorities. Tax rules that may entice firms to use derivatives include the separate taxation of capital and ordinary income (derivatives can be used to convert one form of income to another), capital gains taxation (derivatives can be used to defer taxation of capital gains income), and differential taxation across countries (derivatives can be used to shift income from one country to another).

Bankruptcy and distress costs An unusually large loss can threaten the survival of a firm. The most obvious reason is that a firm that is losing money may be unable to meet fixed obligations, such as debt payments and wages. If a firm appears to be in

---

[6]The following are discussed in Smith and Stulz (1985) and Froot et al. (1994).

distress, customers may be less willing to purchase its goods. (Would you buy a car or computer—both of which come with long-term warranties—from a company that appears likely to go out of business and would then be unable to honor its warranties?)

Actual or threatened bankruptcy can be costly; a dollar of loss can cost the company more than a dollar. As with taxes, this is a reason for firms to enter derivatives contracts that transfer income from profit states to loss states, thereby reducing the probability of bankruptcy or distress.

Costly external financing   Even if a loss is not large enough to threaten the survival of a firm, the firm must pay for the loss, either by using cash reserves or by raising funds externally (for example, by borrowing or issuing new securities).

Raising funds externally can be costly. There are explicit costs, such as bank and underwriting fees. There can also be implicit costs. If you borrow money, the lender may worry that you need to borrow because you are in decline, which increases the probability that you will not repay the loan. The lender's thinking this way raises the interest rate on the loan. The same problem arises even more severely with equity issues.

At the same time, cash reserves are valuable because they reduce a firm's need to raise funds externally in the future. So if the firm uses cash to pay for a loss, the reduction in cash increases the probability that the firm will need costly external financing in the future.

The fact that external financing is costly can even lead the firm to forego investment projects it would have taken had cash been available to use for financing.

Thus, however the firm pays for the loss, a dollar of loss may actually cost the firm more than a dollar. Hedging can safeguard cash reserves and reduce the probability of costly external financing.

Increase debt capacity   Because of the deductibility of interest expense for tax purposes, firms may find debt to be a tax-advantaged way to raise funds.[7] However, lenders, fearful of bankruptcy, may be unwilling to lend to firms with risky cash flows. The amount that a firm can borrow is its **debt capacity.**

A firm that credibly reduces the riskiness of its cash flows should be able to borrow more, since for any given level of debt, bankruptcy is less likely. Such a firm is said to have raised its debt capacity. To the extent debt has a tax advantage, such a firm will also be more valuable.

Managerial risk aversion   While large, public firms are owned by well-diversified investors, firm managers are typically *not* well-diversified. Salary, bonus, and compensation options are all tied to the performance of the firm.

An individual who is unwilling to take a fair bet (i.e., one with an expected payoff equal to the money at stake) is said to be **risk-averse.** Risk-averse persons are harmed

---

[7]For a discussion of this issue, see Brealey and Myers (2000, Chapter 17).

by a dollar of loss more than they are helped by a dollar of gain. Thus, they benefit from reducing uncertainty. The effect is analogous to that shown in Figure 4.8.

If managers are risk-averse and have wealth that is tied to the company, we might expect that they will try to reduce uncertainty. However, matters are not this simple: Managers are often compensated in ways that encourage them to take more risk. For example, options given to managers as compensation, which we discuss in Chapter 16, are more valuable, other things equal, when the firm's stock price is riskier. Thus, a manager's risk aversion may be offset by compensation that is more valuable if the firm is riskier.

Nonfinancial risk management   Firms make risk-management decisions when they organize and design a business. For example, suppose you plan to sell widgets in Europe. You can construct a plant in the United States and export to Europe, or you can construct the plant in Europe, in which case costs of construction, labor, interest rates, and other inputs will be denominated in the same currency as the widgets you sell. Exchange rate hedging, to take one example, would be unnecessary.

Of course, if you build in a foreign country, you will encounter the costs of doing business abroad, including dealing with different tax codes and regulatory regimes.

Risk can also be affected by such decisions as leasing versus buying equipment, which determines the extent to which costs are fixed. Firms can choose flexible production technologies that may be more expensive at the outset, but which can be reconfigured at low cost. Risk is also affected by the decision to enter a particular line of business in the first place. Firms making computer mice and keyboards, for example, have to consider the possibility of lawsuits for repetitive stress injuries.

The point is that risk management is not a simple matter of hedging or not hedging using financial derivatives, but rather a series of decisions that start when the business is first conceived.

Reasons *Not* to Hedge

There are also reasons why firms might elect not to hedge:

- Transacting in derivatives entails paying transaction costs, such as commissions and the bid-ask spread.

- The firm must assess costs and benefits of a given strategy; this can require costly expertise.

- The firm must monitor transactions and have managerial controls in place to prevent unauthorized trading.

- The firm must be prepared for tax and accounting consequences of their transactions. In particular, this may complicate reporting.

Thus, while there are reasons to hedge, there are also costs. When thinking about costs and benefits, keep in mind that some of what firms do could be called risk management but may not obviously involve derivatives. For example, suppose Auric enters into a 2-year agreement with a supplier to buy gold at a fixed price. Will management think of this as a derivative? It is similar to a forward contract. (In fact it is a swap, which we will discuss in Chapter 8).

Finally, firms can face collateral requirements if their derivatives position loses money. The box on page 105 illustrates the problems this can cause.

Empirical Evidence on Hedging

What do we know about the risk-management practices of firms in real life? The answer is: Less than you might guess. It is difficult to tell, from publicly available information, the extent to which firms hedge. Beginning in 2000, Statement of Financial Accounting Standards (SFAS) 133 required firms to recognize derivatives as assets or liabilities on the balance sheet, measure them at fair value, and to report changes in their market value.[8] This reporting does not necessarily reveal a firm's hedging position (forward contracts have zero value, for example). Moreover, derivatives that are held to hedge a position need not be marked to market. Existing evidence relies on data from the early and mid-1990s under a different accounting standard.

The research addresses two questions: How much do firms hedge and why do firms hedge? To be clear about the question, *financial* firms—commercial banks, investment banks, broker-dealers, and other financial institutions—transact in derivatives frequently: The risks are identifiable, and regulators encourage risk management. The more open question is the extent to which *nonfinancial* firms use derivatives. We can summarize research findings as follows:

- Half of nonfinancial firms report using derivatives, with usage greater among large firms. Among those that do use derivatives, less than 25% of perceived risk is hedged, with firms likelier to hedge short-term risks (Bodnar et al., 1998).

- Large firms are likelier to use derivatives than small firms (Bodnar et al., 1998).

- Firms with more investment opportunities are likelier to hedge (Géczy et al., 1997).

- Firms that use derivatives have a higher market value (Allayannis and Weston, 2001) and more leverage (Graham and Rogers, 2000 and Haushalter, 2000).[9]

Tufano (1996) and Petersen and Thiagarajan (2000) have examined hedging behavior by gold-mining firms. Tufano finds that most gold firms use some derivatives, with the median firm in his sample (North American firms) selling forward about 25% of 3-year production. Fifteen percent of firms use no derivatives. Firms with large managerial holdings of stock are likelier to hedge.

---

[8] See Gastineau et al. (2001) for a discussion of SFAS 133 and previous accounting rules.

[9] Graham and Smith (1999) find that after-tax profits are concave for a majority of firms, as in Figure 4.8. However, Graham and Rogers (2000) are unable to find a link between hedging and tax-induced concavity.

Ashanti Goldfields

The Golddiggers example considers only 1 year's production. How would you hedge gold reserves that take many years to extract and sell? Selling forward is one obvious strategy. In 1999, Ashanti Goldfields, using forward contracts and collars, had sold forward 11 million ounces of gold, against annual production of 1.4 million ounces and reserves of 23 million ounces (see Cooper, 2000 and *Wall Street Journal*, October 7, 1999, p. C1.).

Ashanti was locking in a selling price for about 8 years' worth of production. From the perspective of financial theory, there is nothing wrong with such a hedging program.

In September 1999, a group of central banks announced that they would be restricting gold sales. The price of gold rose almost 10%, and Ashanti lost an estimated $500 million on its forward gold sales. Under the terms of its contracts, it owed this amount to the group of dealers who were its counterparties. This large debt triggered liquidity problems. Ashanti had assets which had appreciated in value—gold in the ground—offsetting the loss on the forward sales. However, its derivatives contracts called for Ashanti to use cash to pay for losses on the contracts. This was a liquidity problem: Ashanti had assets, but not cash, to cover its losses. Converting the gold in the ground into cash would require that Ashanti extract the gold or sell the land. The gold in the ground was valuable but illiquid. As news of its difficulties spread, Ashanti saw its share price plummet, from $10.125 on September 28, 1999, to $4.125 on October 6, 1999.

If Ashanti's problem was truly just liquidity, not fundamental unprofitability of the business, it would be in everyone's interest to resolve the problems without liquidating Ashanti. In November 1999, Ashanti reached an agreement with the dealers that permitted Ashanti to keep operating, and the dealers received warrants (call options issued by Ashanti) to buy 15% of Ashanti stock.

Petersen and Thiagarajan compared two firms through 1994: American Barrick hedges aggressively and Homestake Mining does no hedging. They argue that Homestake and American Barrick have different business characteristics that account for the difference in their hedging policies. In particular, Homestake adjusts production as the gold price changes, suggesting that changes in production offset the effects of price changes. American Barrick, by contrast, is more like Golddiggers, with a set quantity of production.

The currency hedging operations of a U.S.-based manufacturing firm are examined in detail by Brown (2001), who finds that foreign exchange hedging is an integral part of firm operations, but the company has no clear rationale for hedging. For example, Brown reports one manager saying, "We do not take speculative positions, but the extent we are hedged depends on our views."

The varied evidence suggests that some use of derivatives is common, especially at large firms, and that economic theories may explain why hedging is undertaken.

TABLE 4.8	Call and put premiums for gold options.	

Strike Price	Put Premium	Call Premium
440	21.54	2.49
420	8.77	8.77
400	2.21	21.26

These prices are computed using the Black formula for options on futures, with a futures price of $420, effective annual interest rate of 5%, volatility of 5.5%, and 1 year to expiration.

4.4 GOLDDIGGERS REVISITED

We have looked at simple hedging and insurance strategies for buyers and sellers. We now examine some additional strategies that permit tailoring the amount and cost of insurance. For simplicity we will focus primarily on Golddiggers; however, in every case there are analogous strategies for Auric.

Table 4.8 lists premiums for three calls and puts on gold with 1 year to expiration and three different strikes. The examples use these values.

Selling the Gain: Collars

As discussed earlier, we can reduce the cost of insurance by reducing potential profit, i.e., by selling our right to profit from high gold prices. How do we do this? We can sell someone else the right to buy gold from us at a high fixed price, i.e., we can sell a call. If the gold price is above the strike on the call, we are contractually obligated to sell at the strike. This caps our profits, in exchange for an initial premium payment.

A 420–440 collar Suppose that Golddiggers has bought a 420-strike put option for $8.77 and sold a 440-strike call option for a premium of $2.49. If the price of gold in 1 year is $450/oz., the call owner will exercise and Golddiggers is obligated to sell gold at the strike price of $440, rather than the market price of $450. The $2.49 premium Golddiggers received initially compensates them for the possibility that this will happen.

Figure 4.9 depicts the combination of the purchased put and written call, while Figure 4.10 shows the two profit diagrams for Golddiggers hedged with a 420-strike put, as opposed to hedged with a 420-strike put plus writing a 440-strike call.

Note that the 420–440 collar still entails paying a premium. The 420 put costs $8.77, and the 440 call yields a premium of only $2.49. Thus, there is a net expenditure of $6.28. It is probably apparent, though, that we can tinker with the strike prices and

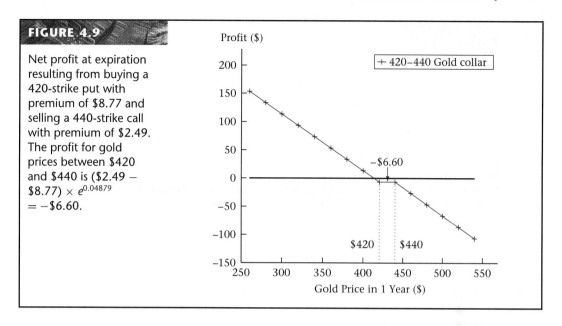

FIGURE 4.9

Net profit at expiration resulting from buying a 420-strike put with premium of $8.77 and selling a 440-strike call with premium of $2.49. The profit for gold prices between $420 and $440 is ($2.49 − $8.77) × $e^{0.04879}$ = −$6.60.

pay a still lower net premium, including zero premium, if we wish. The trade-off is that the payoff on the collar becomes less attractive as we lower the required premium.

A zero-cost collar   To construct a zero-cost collar, we could argue as follows: A 400-strike put and a 440-strike call are equally distant from the forward price of $420. This equivalence suggests that the options should have approximately the same premium. As we can see from the table of premiums for different strike options, the 400-strike put has a premium of $2.21, while the 440-strike call has a premium of $2.49. The net premium we would *receive* from buying this collar is thus $0.28. We can construct a true zero-cost collar by slightly changing the strike prices, making the put more expensive (raising the strike) and the call less expensive (also raising the strike). If we make the strikes $400.78 for the put and $440.78 for the call, we obtain a premium of $2.355 for both options, giving a net premium of zero.

In reality this zero-cost collar of width 40 would be sold at lower strike prices than $400.78 and $440.78. The reason is that there is a bid-ask spread: Dealers are willing to buy a given option at a low price and sell it at a high price.

The put that is purchased will be bought at the dealer's offer price and the call will be sold at the bid. The dealer can earn this spread in either of two ways: Selling the 400.78–440.78 collar and charging an explicit transaction fee, or lowering the strike prices appropriately and charging a zero transaction fee. Either way, the dealer earns the fee. One of the tricky aspects of the more complicated derivatives is that it is relatively easy for dealers to embed fees that are invisible to the buyer. Of course a buyer can mitigate this problem by always seeking quotes from different dealers.

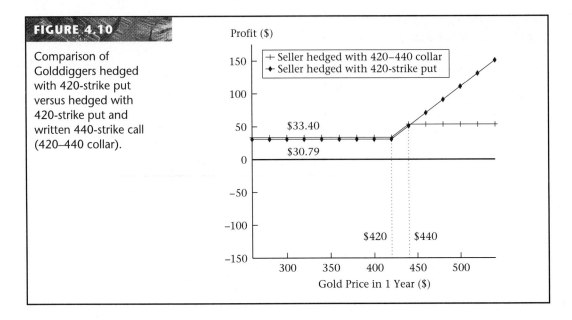

FIGURE 4.10

Comparison of Golddiggers hedged with 420-strike put versus hedged with 420-strike put and written 440-strike call (420–440 collar).

We can examine the payoffs by considering separately the three interesting regions of gold prices:

Price of gold < $400.78. In this region, Golddiggers can sell gold for $400.78 by exercising the put option.

Price of gold between $400.78 and $440.78. In this region, Golddiggers can sell gold at the market price.

Price of gold > $440.78. In this region, Golddiggers sells gold at $440.78. It has sold a call, so the owner of the call will exercise. This forces Golddiggers to sell gold to the call owner for the strike price of $440.78.

Figure 4.11 graphs the zero-cost collar against the unhedged position. Notice that between $400.78 and $440.78, the zero-cost collar graph is coincident with the unhedged profit. Above the 440.78-strike the collar provides profit of $60.78, and below the 400.78-strike, the collar provides profit of $20.78.

The forward contract as a zero-cost collar Because the put and call with strike prices of $420 have the same premiums, we could also construct a zero-cost collar by buying the $420-strike put and selling the $420-strike call. If we do this, here is what happens:

Price of gold < $420. Golddiggers will exercise the put option, selling gold at the price of $420.

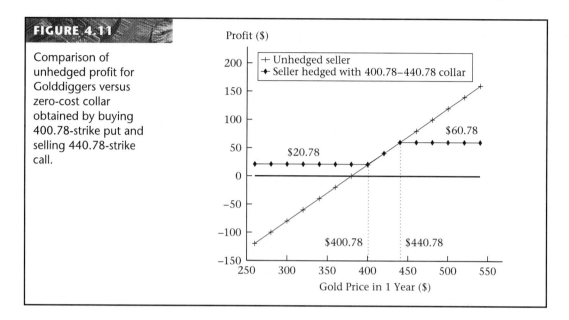

FIGURE 4.11

Comparison of unhedged profit for Golddiggers versus zero-cost collar obtained by buying 400.78-strike put and selling 440.78-strike call.

Price of gold > $420. Golddiggers has sold a 420-strike call. The owner of that call will exercise, obligating Golddiggers to sell gold for $420.

In either case, Golddiggers sells gold at $420. Thus, the "420–420 collar" is exactly like a forward contract, confirming our earlier discussion in Section 3.2. By buying the put and selling the call at the same strike price, Golddiggers has synthetically created a short position in a forward contract. Since a short forward and 420–420 collar have the same payoff, they must cost the same. *This is why the premiums on the 420-strike options are the same.*

Synthetic forwards at prices other than $420   This example is really just an illustration of equation (3.1). We can easily extend this example to understand the relationship between option premiums at other strike prices. In the previous example, Golddiggers created a synthetic forward sale at $420. You might think that you could benefit by creating a synthetic forward contract at a higher price such as $440. Other things equal, you would rather sell at $440 than $420. To accomplish this you buy the 440 put and sell the 440 call. However, there is a catch: The 440-strike put is in-the-money and the 440-strike call is out-of-the-money. Since we would be buying the expensive option and selling the inexpensive option, we have to pay a premium.

How much is it worth to Golddiggers to be able to lock in a selling price of $440 instead of $420? Obviously, it is worth $20 1 year from today, or $20 ÷ (1.05) = $19.05 in present value terms. Since locking in a $420 price is free, it should therefore be the case that we pay $19.05 in net premium in order to lock in a $440 price. In fact, looking at the prices of the 440-strike put and call in Table 4.8, we have premiums of $21.54 for the put and $2.49 for the call. This gives us

$$\text{Net premium} = \$21.54 - \$2.49 = \$19.05$$

Similarly, suppose Golddiggers explored the possibility of locking in a $400 price for gold in 1 year. Obviously, Golddiggers would require compensation to accept a lower price. In fact, they would need to be paid $19.05—the present value of $20—today.

Again we compute the option premiums and we see that the 400-strike call sells for $21.26 while the 400-strike put sells for $2.21. Again we have

$$\text{Net premium} = \$2.21 - \$21.26 = -\$19.05$$

Golddiggers in this case receives the net premium for accepting a lower price.

Other Collar Strategies

Collar-type strategies are quite flexible. We have focused on the case where the firm buys one put and sells one call. However, it is also possible to deal with fractional options. For example, consider the 400.78–440.78 collar above. One variant on this is that we could buy one put to obtain full downside protection, and we could vary the strike price of the call by selling fractional calls at strike prices other than $440.78. For example, we could lower the call strike price below $440.78, in which case we would obtain a higher premium per call. To offset the higher premium, we could buy less than one call. The trade-off is that we cap the gold price on part of production at a lower level, but we maintain some participation at any price above the strike.

Alternatively we could raise the cap level (the strike price on the call) and sell more than one call. This would increase participation in gold price increases up to the cap level, but also have the effect of generating a net short position in gold if prices rose above the cap.

Paylater Strategies

A disadvantage to buying a put option is that Golddiggers pays the premium even when the gold price is high and insurance was, after the fact, unnecessary. One strategy to avoid this problem is a so-called "paylater" strategy, which is a ratio spread. As you might guess from the name, a **paylater** strategy is one where the premium is paid only when the insurance is needed. While it is possible to construct exotic options in which the premium is paid only at expiration and only if the option is in the money, the strategy we discuss here can be constructed using ordinary put options. The goal is to find a strategy where if the gold price is high, there is no net option premium. If the gold price is low, there is insurance, but the effective premium is greater than with an ordinary insurance strategy.

Since we want there to be no premium when the gold price is high, we must have no initial premium. This means that we must sell at least one option. Consider the following strategy for Golddiggers: Sell a 434.6-strike put and buy two 420-strike puts. Using our assumptions, the premium on the 434.6-strike put is $17.55, while the

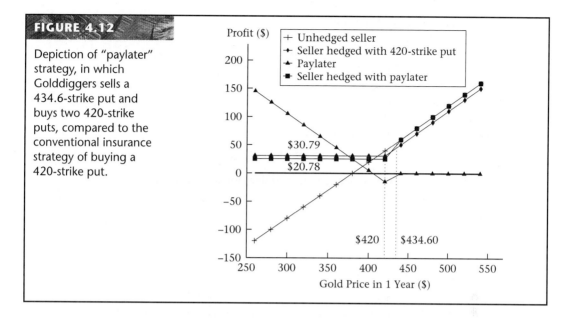

FIGURE 4.12

Depiction of "paylater" strategy, in which Golddiggers sells a 434.6-strike put and buys two 420-strike puts, compared to the conventional insurance strategy of buying a 420-strike put.

premium on the 420-strike put is $8.77. Thus, the net option premium from this strategy is $17.55 − (2 × $8.775) = 0.

Figure 4.12 depicts the result of Golddiggers's hedging with a paylater strategy. When the price of gold is greater than $434.60, neither put is exercised, and Golddiggers's profit is the same as if it were unhedged. When the price of gold is between $420 and $434.60, because of the written $434.6 put the firm loses $2 of profit for every $1 decline in the price of gold. Below $420 the purchased 420-strike puts are exercised, and profit becomes constant. The net result is an insurance policy that is not paid for unless it is needed.

Also depicted in Figure 4.12 is the familiar result from a conventional insurance strategy of hedging by purchasing a single 420-strike put. When the gold price is high, the paylater strategy with a zero premium outperforms the single put. When the gold price is low, the paylater strategy does worse because it offers less insurance. Thus, the premium is paid for later, if insurance is needed.

CHAPTER SUMMARY

A producer selling a risky commodity, such as gold, has an inherent long position in the commodity. Assuming costs are fixed, the firm's profit increases when the price of the commodity increases. Such a firm can hedge profit with a variety of strategies, including selling forward, buying puts, and buying collars. A firm that faces price risk on inputs has an inherent short position in the commodity, with profit that decreases when the price of the input increases. Hedging strategies for such a firm include buying forward, buying calls, and selling collars. All of the strategies involving options can be customized by changing the option strike prices. Strategies such as a paylater can provide insurance with no initial premium, but on which the company has greater losses should the insurance be needed.

Hedging can be optimal for a company when an extra dollar of income received in times of high profits is worth less than an extra dollar of income received in times of low profits. Profits for such a firm are concave, in which case hedging can increase expected cash flow. Concave profits can arise from taxes, bankruptcy costs, costly external finance, preservation of debt capacity, and managerial risk aversion. Such a firm can increase expected cash flow by hedging. Nevertheless, firms may elect not to hedge for reasons including transaction costs of dealing in derivatives, the requirement for expertise, the need to monitor and control the hedging process, and complications from tax and accounting considerations.

FURTHER READING

In this and earlier chapters we have examined uses of forwards and options, taking for granted the pricing of those contracts. Two big unanswered questions are: How are those prices determined? How does the market for them work?

In Chapters 5 through 8, we will explore forward and futures contracts discussing pricing as well as how market-makers function. In Chapters 10 through 13, we will answer the same questions for options. Chapter 14 will discuss how exotic options can be used in risk-management strategies in place of the ordinary puts and calls discussed in this chapter.

Wharton and CIBC regularly survey nonfinancial firms to assess their hedging. One recent survey is summarized by Bodnar et al. (1998). Tufano (1996, 1998) and Petersen and Thiagarajan (2000) have studied hedging practices in the gold-mining industry. Other papers examining hedging include Géczy et al. (1997) and Allayannis and Weston (2001). Brown (2001) provides an interesting and detailed description of the hedging decisions by one (anonymous) firm.

Gastineau et al. (2001) discuss Statement of Financial Accounting Standards 133, which currently governs accounting for derivatives.

Finally, Fleming (1997) relates some of the history of (the fictitous) Auric Enterprises.

PROBLEMS

For the following problems consider the following three firms:

- *XYZ* mines copper, with fixed costs of $0.50/lb and variable cost of $0.40/lb.

- *Wirco* produces wire. It buys copper and manufactures wire. One pound of copper can be used to produce one unit of wire, which sells for the price of copper plus $5. Fixed cost per unit is $3 and non-copper variable cost is $1.50.

- *Telco* installs telecommunications equipment and uses copper wire from Wirco as an input. For planning purposes, Telco assigns a fixed revenue of $6.20 for each unit of wire it uses.

The 1-year forward price of copper is $1/lb. The 1-year continuously compounded interest rate is 6%. One-year option prices for copper are shown in the table below.[10]

Strike	Call	Put
0.9500	$0.0649	$0.0178
0.9750	0.0500	0.0265
1.0000	0.0376	0.0376
1.0250	0.0274	0.0509
1.0340	0.0243	0.0563
1.0500	0.0194	0.0665

In your answers, at a minimum consider copper prices in 1 year of $0.80, $0.90, $1.00, $1.10, and $1.20.

4.1. If XYZ does nothing to manage copper price risk, what is its profit 1 year from now, per pound of copper? If on the other hand XYZ sells forward its expected copper production, what is its estimated profit 1 year from now? Construct graphs illustrating both unhedged and hedged profit.

4.2. Suppose the 1-year copper forward price were $0.80 instead of $1. If XYZ were to sell forward its expected copper production, what is its estimated profit one year from now? Should XYZ produce copper? What if the forward copper price is $0.45?

4.3. Compute estimated profit in 1 year if XYZ buys a put option with a strike of $0.95, $1.00, or $1.05. Draw a graph of profit in each case.

4.4. Compute estimated profit in 1 year if XYZ sells a call option with a strike of $0.95, $1.00, or $1.05. Draw a graph of profit in each case.

4.5. Compute estimated profit in 1 year if XYZ buys collars with the following strikes:

     a. $0.95 for the put and $1.00 for the call.

     b. $0.975 for the put and $1.025 for the call.

     c. $1.05 for the put and $1.05 for the call.

Draw a graph of profit in each case.

4.6. Compute estimated profit in 1 year if XYZ buys paylater *puts* as follows (the net premium may not be exactly zero):

     a. Sell one 1.025-strike put and buy two 0.975-strike puts.

---

[10]These are option prices from the Black formula assuming that the risk-free rate is 0.06, volatility is 0.1, and time to expiration is one year.

b. Sell two 1.034-strike puts and buy three 1.00-strike puts.

Draw a graph of profit in each case.

4.7. If Telco does nothing to manage copper price risk, what is its profit 1 year from now, per pound of copper that it buys? If it hedges the price of wire by buying copper forward, what is its estimated profit 1 year from now? Construct graphs illustrating both unhedged and hedged profit.

4.8. Compute estimated profit in 1 year if Telco buys a call option with a strike of $0.95, $1.00, or $1.05. Draw a graph of profit in each case.

4.9. Compute estimated profit in 1 year if Telco sells a put option with a strike of $0.95, $1.00, or $1.05. Draw a graph of profit in each case.

4.10. Compute estimated profit in 1 year if Telco sells collars with the following strikes:

    a. $0.95 for the put and $1.00 for the call.

    b. $0.975 for the put and $1.025 for the call.

    c. $0.95 for the put and $0.95 for the call.

Draw a graph of profit in each case.

4.11. Compute estimated profit in 1 year if Telco buys paylater *calls* as follows (the net premium may not be exactly zero):

    a. Sell one 0.975-strike call and buy two 1.034-strike calls.

    b. Sell two 1.00-strike calls and buy three 1.034-strike calls.

Draw a graph of profit in each case.

4.12. Suppose that Wirco does nothing to manage the risk of copper price changes. What is its profit 1 year from now, per pound of copper? Suppose that Wirco buys copper forward at $1. What is its profit 1 year from now?

4.13. What happens to the variability of Wirco's profit if Wirco undertakes any strategy (buying calls, selling puts, collars, etc.) to lock in the price of copper next year? You can use your answer to the previous question to illustrate your answer.

4.14. Golddiggers has zero net income if it sells gold for a price of $380. However, by shorting a forward contract it is possible to guarantee a profit of $40/oz. Suppose a manager decides not to hedge and the gold price in 1 year is $390/oz. Did the firm earn $10 in profit (relative to accounting break-even) or lose $30 in profit (relative to the profit that could be obtained by hedging)? Would your answer be different if the manager did hedge and the gold price had been $450?

4.15. Consider the example in Table 4.6. Suppose that losses are fully tax-deductible. What is the expected after-tax profit in this case?

4.16. Suppose that firms face a 40% income tax rate on all profits. In particular, losses receive full credit. Firm A has a 50% probability of a $1000 profit and a 50%

probability of a $600 loss each year. Firm B has a 50% probability of a $300 profit and a 50% probability of a $100 profit each year.

    a. What is the expected pre-tax profit next year for firms A and B?

    b. What is the expected after-tax profit next year for firms A and B?

4.17. Suppose that firms face a 40% income tax rate on positive profits and that net losses receive no credit. (Thus, if profits are positive, after-tax income is $(1 - 0.4) \times$ *profit,* while if there is a loss, after-tax income is the amount lost.) Firms A and B have the same cash flow distribution as in the previous problem. Suppose the appropriate effective annual discount rate for both firms is 10%.

    a. What is the expected pre-tax profit for A and B?

    b. What is the expected after-tax profit for A and B?

    c. What would Firms A and B pay today to receive next year's expected cash flow for sure, instead of the variable cash flows described above?

For the following problems use the *BSCall* option pricing function with a stock price of $420 (the forward price), volatility of 5.5%, continuously compounded interest rate of 4.879%, dividend yield of 4.879%, and time to expiration of 1 year. The problems require you to vary the strike prices.

4.18. Consider the example of Auric.

    a. Suppose that Auric insures against a price increase by purchasing a 440-strike call. Verify by drawing a profit diagram that simultaneously selling a 400-strike put will generate a collar. What is the cost of this collar to Auric?

    b. Find the strike prices for a zero-cost collar (buy high-strike call, sell low-strike put) for which the strikes differ by $30.

4.19. Suppose that LMN Investment Bank wishes to sell Auric a zero-cost collar of width 30 without explicit premium (i.e., there will be no cash payment from Auric to LMN). Also suppose that on every option the bid price is $0.25 below the Black-Scholes price and the offer price is $0.25 above the Black-Scholes price. LMN wishes to earn their spread ($0.25 per option) without any explicit charge to Auric. What should the strike prices on the collar be? (Note: Since the collar involves two options, LMN is looking to make $0.50 on the deal. You need to find strike prices that differ by 30 such that LMN makes $0.50.)

4.20. Use the same assumptions as in the preceding problem, without the bid-ask spread. Suppose that we want to construct a paylater strategy using a ratio spread. Instead of buying a 440-strike call, Auric will sell one 440-strike call, and use the premium to buy two higher-strike calls, such that the net option premium is zero.

    a. What higher strike for the purchased calls will generate a zero net option premium?

    b. Graph the profit for Auric resulting from this strategy.

PART 2

FORWARDS, FUTURES, AND SWAPS

Forward contracts permit the purchase of an asset in the future at terms that are set today. In earlier chapters we have taken forward prices as given. In this part—Chapters 5–8—we explore in detail the pricing of forward and futures contracts on a wide variety of underlying assets: Financial assets (such as stocks, currencies, and bonds) and commodities (such as gold, corn, and natural gas). We also examine swaps, which have multiple future settlement dates, as opposed to forward contracts, which settle on a single date. Swaps are in effect a bundle of forward contracts combined with borrowing and lending. As such, swaps are a natural generalization of forward contracts.

Forward contracts involve deferring receipt of, and payment for, the underlying asset. Thus, computing the forward price requires you to determine the costs and benefits of this deferral. As in Part 1, present and future value calculations are the primary pricing tool.

Chapter 5
Financial Forwards and Futures

Forward contracts—which permit firms and investors to guarantee a price for a future purchase or sale—are a basic financial risk management tool. In this chapter we continue to explore these contracts and study in detail forward and futures contracts on financial instruments, such as stocks, indexes, currencies, and interest rates. Our objectives are to understand more about the use of these contracts, how they are priced, and how market-makers hedge them.

Questions to keep in mind throughout the chapter include: Who might buy or sell specific contracts? What kinds of firms might use the contract for risk management? Why is the contract designed as it is?

5.1 ALTERNATIVE WAYS TO BUY A STOCK

The purchase of a share of XYZ stock has three components: Fixing the price, the buyer making payment to the seller, and the seller transferring ownership to the buyer. If we allow for the possibility that payment and physical receipt can occur at different times, say time 0 and time T, then once the price is fixed there are four logically possible purchasing arrangements: Payment can occur at time 0 or T, and physical receipt can occur at time 0 or T. Table 5.1 depicts these four possibilities, along with their customary names. Let's discuss these different arrangements.[1]

Outright purchase An outright purchase is the typical way to think about buying stock. You simultaneously pay the stock price in cash and receive ownership of the stock.

Fully leveraged purchase A fully leveraged purchase is one in which the investor borrows the entire purchase price of the security. Suppose you borrow the share price, S_0, and agree to repay the borrowed amount at time T. If the continuously compounded interest rate is r, at time T you would owe e^{rT} per dollar borrowed, or $S_0 e^{rT}$.

Prepaid forward contract With a **prepaid forward contract,** you pay for the stock today and receive the stock at an agreed-upon future date. The difference between a prepaid forward contract and an outright purchase is that with the former,

---

[1] All of these arrangements can be reversed in the case of the seller. Problem 5.1 asks you to describe them from that perspective.

	Pay at	**Receive Security**	
Description	**Time:**	**at Time:**	**Payment**
Outright Purchase	0	0	S_0 at time 0
Fully Leveraged Purchase	T	0	$S_0 e^{rT}$ at time T
Prepaid Forward Contract	0	T	?
Forward Contract	T	T	$? \times e^{rT}$

TABLE 5.1 Four different ways to buy a share of stock that has price S_0 at time 0. At time 0 you agree to a price, which is paid either today or at time T. The shares are received either at 0 or T. The interest rate is r.

you receive the stock at time T. We will see that the price you pay is not necessarily the stock price.

Forward contract   With a forward contract you both pay for the stock and receive it at time T, with the time T price specified at time 0.

From Table 5.1 it is clear that you pay interest when you defer payment. The interesting question is how deferring the *physical receipt* of the stock affects the price; this deferral occurs with both the forward and prepaid forward contracts. What should you pay for the stock in those cases?[2]

5.2 PREPAID FORWARD CONTRACTS ON STOCK

A prepaid forward contract entails paying today to receive something—stocks, a foreign currency, bonds—in the future. Prepaid forward contracts permit the sale of an asset while the owner retains physical possession.

We will derive the prepaid forward price using three different methods: Pricing by analogy, pricing by present value, and pricing by arbitrage.

Pricing the Prepaid Forward by Analogy

Suppose you buy a prepaid forward contract on XYZ. By delaying physical possession of the stock, you do not receive dividends and have no voting or control rights. (Here and throughout the book we will assume that we do not care about the value of voting and control.)

---

[2]The arrangements also differ with respect to credit risk, which arises from the possibility that the person on the other side of the transaction will not fulfill his or her end of the deal. (And of course the person on the other side of the deal may be worried about *your* fulfilling your obligation.)

In the absence of dividends, whether you receive physical possession today or in 1 year is irrelevant: In either case you own the stock, and in 1 year it will be exactly as if you had owned the stock the whole time.[3] *Therefore, when there are no dividends, the price of the prepaid forward contract is the stock price today.* Denoting the prepaid forward price for an asset bought at time 0 and delivered at time T as $F_{0,T}^P$, the prepaid forward price for delivery at time T is

$$F_{0,T}^P = S_0 \tag{5.1}$$

Pricing the Prepaid Forward by Discounted Present Value

We can also derive the price of the prepaid forward using present value: We calculate the expected value of the stock at time T and then discount that value at an appropriate rate of return. The stock price at time T, S_T, is uncertain. Thus in computing the present value of the stock price, we need to use an appropriate risk-adjusted rate.

If the expected stock price at time T based on information we have at time 0 is $E_0(S_T)$, then the prepaid forward price is given by

$$F_{0,T}^P = E_0(S_T)e^{-\alpha T} \tag{5.2}$$

where α, the expected return on the stock, is determined using the CAPM or some other model of expected returns.

How do we compute the expected stock price? By definition of the expected return, we expect that in T years the stock will be worth

$$E_0(S_T) = S_0 e^{\alpha T}$$

Thus, equation (5.2) gives

$$F_{0,T}^P = E_0(S_T)e^{-\alpha T} = S_0 e^{\alpha T} e^{-\alpha T} = S_0$$

For a nondividend-paying stock, the prepaid forward price is the stock price.

Pricing the Prepaid Forward by Arbitrage

Classical **arbitrage** describes a situation in which we can generate a positive cash flow either today or in the future by simultaneously buying and selling related assets, with no net investment of funds and with no risk. Arbitrage, in other words, is free money. An extremely important pricing principle, which we will use often, is that the price of a derivative should be such that no arbitrage is possible.

Here is an example of arbitrage. Suppose that the prepaid forward price exceeds the stock price, i.e., $F_{0,T}^P > S_0$. The arbitrageur will buy low and sell high by buying

---

[3] Suppose that someone secretly removed shares of stock from your safe and returned them 1 year later. From a purely financial point of view you would never notice the stock to be missing.

TABLE 5.2	Cash flows and transactions to undertake arbitrage when the prepaid forward price, $F_{0,T}^P$, exceeds the stock price, S_0.

	Cash Flows	
Transaction	**Time 0**	**Time T (expiration)**
Buy Stock @ S_0	$-S_0$	$+S_T$
Sell Prepaid Forward @ $F_{0,T}^P$	$+F_{0,T}^P$	$-S_T$
Total	$F_{0,T}^P - S_0$	0

the stock for S_0 and selling the prepaid forward for $F_{0,T}^P$. This transaction makes money and it is also risk-free: Selling the prepaid forward requires that we deliver the stock in 1 year and buying the stock today ensures that we have the stock to deliver. Thus, we earn $F_{0,T}^P - S_0$ today and at expiration we supply the stock to the buyer of the prepaid forward. We have earned positive profits today and offset all future risk. Table 5.2 summarizes this situation.

Now suppose on the other hand that $F_{0,T}^P < S_0$. Then we can engage in arbitrage by buying the prepaid forward and shorting the stock, earning $S_0 - F_{0,T}^P$. One year from now we acquire the stock via the prepaid forward and we use that stock to close the short position. The cash flows in the above table are simply reversed.

Throughout the book we will assume that prices are at levels that preclude arbitrage. This raises the question: If prices are such that arbitrage is not profitable, who can afford to become an arbitrageur, watching out for arbitrage opportunities? We can resolve this paradox with the insight that in order for arbitrageurs to earn a living, arbitrage opportunities must occur from time to time; there must be "an equilibrium degree of disequilibrium."[4] However, you would not expect arbitrage to be obvious or easy to undertake.

The transactions in Table 5.2 are the same as those of a market-maker who is hedging a position. A market-maker would sell a prepaid forward if a customer wished to buy it. The market-maker then has an obligation to deliver the stock at a fixed price and, in order to offset this risk, can buy the stock. The market-maker thus engages in the same transactions as an arbitrageur, except for the purpose of risk management, not arbitrage. Thus, *the transaction described in Table 5.2—selling the prepaid forward and buying the stock—also describes the actions of a market-maker.*

The no-arbitrage arguments we will make thus serve two functions: They tell us how to take advantage of mispricings, and they describe the behavior of market-makers managing risk.

....

[4]The phrase is from Grossman and Stiglitz (1980), in which this idea was first proposed.

Pricing Prepaid Forwards with Dividends

When a stock pays a dividend, the prepaid forward price is no longer equal to the stock price. The problem is that, although the owner of stock receives dividends, the owner of a prepaid forward contract does not. This difference creates a financial distinction between owning the stock and holding the prepaid forward. It is necessary to adjust the prepaid forward price to reflect dividends that are received by the shareholder, but not by the holder of the prepaid forward contract.

Discrete dividends   To understand the effects of dividends, we will compare prepaid forwards on two stocks: Stock A pays no dividend, and otherwise identical stock B pays a $5 dividend 364 days from today, just before the expiration of the prepaid forwards. We know that the prepaid forward price for stock A is the current stock price. What is the prepaid forward price for stock B?

Since the $5 dividend is paid just before the delivery date for the stock 1 year from today, on the delivery date stock B will be priced $5 less than stock A. Thus, the price we pay today for stock B should be lower than that for stock A by the present value of $5.

In general, the price for a prepaid forward contract will be the stock price less the present value of dividends to be paid over the life of the contract. Suppose there are multiple dividend payments made throughout the life of the forward contract: A stock is expected to make dividend payments of D_{t_i} at times t_i, $i = 1, \ldots, n$. A prepaid forward contract will entitle you to receive the stock at time T but without receiving the interim dividends. Thus, the prepaid forward price is

$$F_{0,T}^P = S_0 - \sum_{i=1}^{n} PV_{0,t_i}(D_{t_i}) \tag{5.3}$$

Example 5.1   Suppose XYZ stock costs $100 today and is expected to pay a $1.25 quarterly dividend, with the first coming 3 months from today and the last just prior to the delivery of the stock. Suppose the annual continuously compounded risk-free rate is 10%. The quarterly continuously compounded rate is therefore 2.5%. A 1-year prepaid forward contract for the stock would cost

$$F_{0,1}^P = \$100 - \sum_{i=1}^{4} \$1.25 e^{-0.025i} = \$95.30 \qquad ❦$$

The calculation in this example implicitly assumes that the dividends are certain. Over a short horizon this might be reasonable. Over a long horizon we would expect dividend risk to be greater, and we would need to account for this in computing the present value of dividends.

Continuous dividends   For stock indexes containing many stocks, it is common to model the dividend as being paid continuously at a rate that is proportional to the level of the index; i.e., the dividend *yield* (the annualized dividend payment divided by the stock price) is constant. This is an approximation, but in a large stock index there can be dividend payments on a large proportion of days.[5] The dividend yield is not likely to be fixed in the short run: When stock prices rise, the dividend yield falls, at least temporarily. Nevertheless, we will assume a constant proportional dividend yield for purposes of this discussion.

To model a continuous dividend, suppose that the index price is S_0 and the annualized daily compounded dividend yield is δ. Then the dollar dividend over one day is

$$\text{Daily dividend} = \frac{\delta}{365} \times S_0$$

Now suppose that we reinvest dividends in the index. Because of reinvestment, after T years we will have more shares than we started with. Using continuous compounding to approximate daily compounding, we get

$$\text{Number of shares} = \left(1 + \frac{\delta}{365}\right)^{365 \times T} \approx e^{\delta T}$$

At the end of T years we have approximately $e^{\delta T}$ more shares than initially.

Now suppose we wish to invest today in order to have one share at time T. We can buy $e^{-\delta T}$ shares today. Because of dividend reinvestment, at time T, we will have $e^{\delta T}$ more shares than we started with, so we end up with exactly one share. Adjusting the initial quantity in this way in order to offset the effect of income from the asset is called **tailing** the position. Tailing enables us to offset the effect of continuous dividends. We will encounter the concept of tailing frequently.

Since an investment of $e^{-\delta T} S_0$ gives us one share at time T, this is the time 0 prepaid forward price for delivery at time T:

$$\boxed{F_{0,T}^{P} = S_0 e^{-\delta T}} \tag{5.4}$$

where δ is the dividend yield and T the time to maturity of the prepaid forward contract.

Example 5.2   Suppose that the index is \$125 and the annualized daily compounded dividend yield is 3%. The daily dollar dividend is

$$\text{Dividend} = (0.03 \div 365) \times \$125 = \$0.01027$$

---

[5]There is significant seasonality in dividend payments, which can be important in practice. A large number of U.S. firms pay quarterly dividends in February, May, August, and November. German firms, by contrast, pay annual dividends concentrated in May, June, and July.

Low Exercise Price Options

In some countries, including Australia and Switzerland, it is possible to buy stock options with very low strike prices—so low that it is virtually certain the option will expire in-the-money. For example, in Australia, the strike price is a penny. Such an option is called a "low exercise price option," or LEPO. These often exist in order to avoid taxes or transaction fees associated with directly trading the stock. LEPOs do not pay dividends and do not carry voting rights. As with any call option, a LEPO is purchased outright, and entitles the option holder to acquire the stock at expiration by paying the (low) strike price. The payoff of a LEPO

expiring at time T is

$$max(0, S_T - K)$$

However, if the strike price, K, is so low that the option is certain to be exercised, this is just

$$S_T - K$$

This option has a value at time 0 of

$$F_{0,T}^P - PV(K)$$

Since the strike price of the option is close to zero, a LEPO is essentially a prepaid forward contract.

or a little more than one penny per unit of the index. If we start by holding one unit of the index, at the end of 1 year we will have

$$e^{0.03} = 1.030455$$

shares. Thus, if we wish to end the year holding one share, we must invest in

$$e^{-0.03} = 0.970446$$

shares. The prepaid forward price is

$$\$125e^{-0.03} = \$121.306$$

5.3 FORWARD CONTRACTS ON STOCK

Now that we have analyzed prepaid forward contracts, it is easy to derive forward prices. The only difference between the prepaid forward and the forward is the timing of the payment for the stock. Thus, *the forward price is just the future value of the prepaid forward.*

Here are forward prices for the cases we have considered:

No dividends Taking the future value of equation (5.1), for the time 0 forward price of a stock that is delivered at time T, we have

$$F_{0,T} = FV(F_{0,T}^P) = S_0 e^{rT} \tag{5.5}$$

This formula shows that the forward contract is a purchase of the stock, with deferred payment. The interest adjustment compensates for that deferral.

Discrete dividends   To obtain the forward price for a stock that pays discrete dividends, we take the future value of equation (5.3). The forward price is the future value of the prepaid forward.

$$F_{0,T} = S_0 e^{rT} - \sum_{i=1}^{n} e^{r(T-t_i)} D_{t_i} \tag{5.6}$$

Whereas for the prepaid forward we subtract the present value of dividends from the current stock price, for the forward we subtract the future value of dividends from the future value of the stock price.

Continuous dividends   When the stock pays continuous dividends, as with an index, we take the future value of equation (5.4):

$$F_{0,T} = e^{rT} S_0 e^{-\delta T}$$

or

$$F_{0,T} = S_0 e^{(r-\delta)T} \tag{5.7}$$

It is important to distinguish between the *forward price* and the *premium* for a forward contract. Because the forward contract has deferred payment, *its initial premium is zero*; it is initially costless. The forward *price*, however, is the future value of the prepaid forward price. This difference between the forward price and premium is in contrast with the prepaid forward, for which price and the premium are the same: The prepaid forward price is the amount you pay today to acquire the asset in the future.

Occasionally it is possible to observe the forward price but not the price of the underlying stock or index. For example, the futures contract for the S&P 500 index trades at times when the NYSE is not open, so it is possible to observe the futures price but not the stock price. The asset price implied by the forward pricing formulas above is said to define **fair value** for the underlying stock or index. Equation (5.7) is used in this case to infer the value of the index.

The **forward premium** is the ratio of the forward price to the spot price, defined as

$$\text{Forward premium} = \frac{F_{0,T}}{S_0} \tag{5.8}$$

We can annualize the forward premium and express it as a percentage, in which case we have

$$\text{Annualized forward premium} = \frac{1}{T} ln \left(\frac{F_{0,T}}{S_0} \right)$$

For the case of continuous dividends, equation (5.7), the forward premium is simply the difference between the risk-free rate and the dividend yield.

Creating a Synthetic Forward Contract

A market-maker or arbitrageur must be able to offset the risk of a forward contract. It is possible to do this by creating a *synthetic* forward contract to offset a position in the actual forward contract.

In this discussion we will assume that dividends are continuous and paid at the rate δ, and hence that equation (5.7) is the appropriate forward price. We can then create a synthetic long forward contract by buying the stock and borrowing to fund the position. To see how the synthetic position works, recall that the payoff at expiration for a long forward position on the index is

$$\text{Payoff at expiration} = S_T - F_{0,T}$$

In order to obtain this same payoff, we buy a tailed position in the stock, investing $S_0 e^{-\delta T}$. This gives us one share at time T. We borrow this amount so that we are not required to pay anything additional at time 0. At time T we must repay $S_0 e^{(r-\delta)T}$ and we sell the stock for S_T. Table 5.3 demonstrates that borrowing to buy the stock replicates the expiration payoff to a forward contract.

Just as we can use the stock and borrowing to synthetically create a forward, we can also use the forward to create synthetic stocks and bonds. Table 5.4 demonstrates that we can go long a forward contract and lend the present value of the forward price to synthetically create the stock. The expiration payoff in this table assumes that equation (5.7) holds. Table 5.5 demonstrates that if we buy the stock and short the forward, we create cash flows like those of a risk-free bond. The rate of return on this synthetic bond—the construction of which is summarized in Table 5.5—is called the **implied repo rate.**

To summarize, we have shown that

$$\text{Forward} = \text{Stock} - \text{zero-coupon bond} \tag{5.9}$$

We can rearrange this equation to derive other synthetic equivalents.

$$\text{Stock} = \text{Forward} + \text{zero-coupon bond}$$

$$\text{Zero-coupon bond} = \text{Stock} - \text{forward}$$

All of these synthetic positions can be reversed to create synthetic short positions.

TABLE 5.3	Demonstration that borrowing $S_0 e^{-\delta T}$ to buy $e^{-\delta T}$ shares of the index replicates the payoff to a forward contract, $S_T - F_{0,T}$.

	Cash Flows	
Transaction	**Time 0**	**Time T (expiration)**
Buy $e^{-\delta T}$ Units of the Index	$-S_0 e^{-\delta T}$	$+S_T$
Borrow $S_0 e^{-\delta T}$	$+S_0 e^{-\delta T}$	$-S_0 e^{(r-\delta)T}$
Total	0	$S_T - S_0 e^{(r-\delta)T}$

TABLE 5.4	Demonstration that going long a forward contract at the price $F_{0,T} = S_0 e^{(r-\delta)T}$, and lending the present value of the forward price creates a synthetic share of the index at time T.

	Cash Flows	
Transaction	Time 0	Time T (expiration)
Long One Forward	0	$S_T - F_{0,T}$
Lend $S_0 e^{-\delta T}$	$-S_0 e^{-\delta T}$	$+S_0 e^{(r-\delta)T}$
Total	$-S_0 e^{-\delta T}$	S_T

TABLE 5.5	Demonstration that buying $e^{-\delta T}$ shares of the index and shorting a forward creates a synthetic bond.

	Cash Flows	
Transaction	Time 0	Time T (expiration)
Buy $e^{-\delta T}$ Units of the Index	$-S_0 e^{-\delta T}$	$+S_T$
Short One Forward	0	$F_{0,T} - S_T$
Total	$-S_0 e^{-\delta T}$	$F_{0,T}$

Synthetic Forwards in Market-Making and Arbitrage

Now we will see how market-makers and arbitrageurs use these strategies. Suppose a customer wishes to enter into a long forward position. The market-maker, as the counterparty, is left holding a short forward position. He can offset this risk by creating a synthetic long forward position.

Specifically, consider the transactions and cash flows in Table 5.6. The market-maker is short a forward contract and long a synthetic forward contract, constructed as in Table 5.3. There is no risk because the total cash flow at time T is $F_{0,T} - S_0 e^{(r-\delta)T}$. All of the components of this cash flow—the forward price, the stock price, the interest rate, and the dividend yield—are known at time 0. The result is a risk-free position.

Similarly, suppose the market-maker wishes to hedge a long forward position. Then it is possible to reverse the positions in Table 5.6. The result is in Table 5.7.

A transaction in which you buy the underlying asset and short the offsetting forward contract is called a **cash-and-carry**. A cash-and-carry has no risk: You have an obligation to deliver the asset but also own the asset. The market-maker offsets the short forward position with a cash-and-carry. An arbitrage that involves buying the underlying asset and selling it forward is called a **cash-and-carry arbitrage.** As you might guess, a

TABLE 5.6 — Transactions and cash flows for a cash-and-carry: A market-maker is short a forward contract and long a synthetic forward contract.

Transaction	Cash Flows	
	Time 0	Time T (expiration)
Buy Tailed Position in Stock, Paying $S_0e^{-\delta T}$	$-S_0e^{-\delta T}$	$+S_T$
Borrow $S_0e^{-\delta T}$	$+S_0e^{-\delta T}$	$-S_0e^{(r-\delta)T}$
Short Forward	0	$F_{0,T} - S_T$
Total	0	$F_{0,T} - S_0e^{(r-\delta)T}$

TABLE 5.7 — Transactions and cash flows for a reverse cash-and-carry: A market-maker is long a forward contract and short a synthetic forward contract.

Transaction	Cash Flows	
	Time 0	Time T (expiration)
Short Tailed Position in Stock, Receiving $S_0e^{-\delta T}$	$+S_0e^{-\delta T}$	$-S_T$
Lend $S_0e^{-\delta T}$	$-S_0e^{-\delta T}$	$+S_0e^{(r-\delta)T}$
Long Forward	0	$S_T - F_{0,T}$
Total	0	$S_0e^{(r-\delta)T} - F_{0,T}$

reverse cash-and-carry entails short-selling the index and entering into a long forward position.

If the forward contract is priced according to equation (5.7), then profits on a cash-and-carry are zero. We motivated the cash-and-carry in Table 5.6 as risk management by a market-maker. However, an arbitrageur might also engage in a cash-and-carry. If the forward price is too high relative to the stock price, i.e., if $F_{0,T} > S_0e^{(r-\delta)T}$, then an arbitrageur or market-maker can use the strategy in Table 5.6 to make a risk-free profit.

An arbitrageur would make the transactions in Table 5.7 if the forward were underpriced relative to the stock, i.e., if $S_0e^{(r-\delta)T} > F_{0,T}$.

As a final point, you may be wondering about the role of borrowing and lending in Tables 5.6 and 5.7. When you explicitly account for borrowing, you account for the opportunity cost of investing funds. For example, if we omitted borrowing from Table 5.6, we would invest $S_0e^{-\delta T}$ today and receive $F_{0,T}$ at time T. In order to know if there is an arbitrage opportunity, we would need to perform a present value calculation to compare the time 0 cash flow with the time T cash flow. By explicitly including borrowing in the calculations, this time-value-of-money comparison is automatic.[6]

Similarly, by comparing the implied repo rate with our borrowing rate, we have a simple measure of whether there is an arbitrage opportunity. For example, if we could borrow at 7%, then there is an arbitrage opportunity if the implied repo rate exceeds 7%. On the other hand, if our borrowing rate exceeds the implied repo rate, there is no arbitrage opportunity.

No-Arbitrage Bounds with Transaction Costs

Tables 5.6 and 5.7 demonstrate that an arbitrageur can make a costless profit if $F_{0,T} \neq S_0 e^{(r-\delta)T}$. This analysis ignores transaction costs. In practice an arbitrageur will face trading fees, bid-ask spreads, different interest rates for borrowing and lending, and the possibility that buying or selling in large quantities will cause prices to change. The effect of such costs will be that, rather than there being a single no-arbitrage price, there will be a no-arbitrage *bound*: A lower price F^- and an upper price F^+ such that arbitrage will not be profitable when the forward price is between these bounds.

Suppose that the stock and forward have bid and ask prices of $S^b < S^a$ and $F^b < F^a$, a trader faces a cost k of transacting in the stock or forward, and the interest rates for borrowing and lending are $r^b > r^l$. In this example we suppose that there are no transaction costs at time T, when the forward is either settled by delivery or cash-settled.

We will first derive F^+. An arbitrageur believing the observed forward price, $F_{0,T}$, is too high, will undertake the transactions in Table 5.6: Sell the forward and borrow to buy the stock. For simplicity we will assume the stock pays no dividends. The arbitrageur will pay the transaction cost k to short the forward and pay $(S_0^a + k)$ to acquire one share of stock. The required borrowing to finance the position is therefore $S_0^a + 2k$. At time T, the payoff is

$$\underbrace{-(S_0^a + 2k)e^{r^b T}}_{\text{Repayment of Borrowing}} + \underbrace{F_{0,T} - S_T}_{\text{Value of Forward}} + \underbrace{S_T}_{\text{Value of Stock}}$$

Arbitrage is profitable if this expression is positive, or

$$F_{0,T} > F^+ = (S_0^a + 2k)e^{r^b T} \qquad (5.10)$$

Thus, the upper bound reflects the fact that we pay a high price for the stock (the ask price), pay transaction costs on both the stock and forward, and borrow at a high rate.

We can derive F^- analogously. Problem 5.14 asks you to verify that the bound below which arbitrage is feasible is

$$F_{0,T} < F^- = (S_0^b - 2k)e^{r^l T} \qquad (5.11)$$

---

[6]In general, arbitrageurs can borrow and lend at different rates. A pro forma arbitrage calculation needs to account for the appropriate cost of capital for any particular transaction.

This expression assumes that short-selling the stock does not entail costs other than bid-ask transaction costs when the short position is initiated.

Notice that in equations (5.10) and (5.11), the costs all enter in such a way as to make the no-arbitrage region as large as possible (for example, the low lending rate enters F^- and the high borrowing rate enters F^+). This makes economic sense: Trading costs cannot help an arbitrageur make a profit.

There are additional costs not reflected in equations (5.10) and (5.11). One is that significant amounts of trading can move prices, so that what appears to be an arbitrage may vanish if prices change when the arbitrageur enters a large order. Another challenge can be execution risk. If trades do not occur instantaneously, the arbitrage can vanish before the trades are completed.

It is likely that the no-arbitrage region will be different for different arbitrageurs at a point in time, and different across time for a given arbitrageur. For example, consider the trading transaction cost, k. A large investment bank sees stock order flow from a variety of sources, and may have inventory of either long or short positions in stocks. The bank may be able to buy or sell shares at low cost by serving as market-maker for a customer order. It may be inexpensive for a bank to short if it already owns the stocks, or it may be inexpensive to buy if the bank already has a short position.

Borrowing and lending rates can also vary. For a transaction that is explicitly financed by borrowing, the relevant interest rates are the arbitrageur's marginal borrowing rate (if that is the source of funds to buy stocks) or lending rate (if stocks are to be shorted). However, at other times, it may be possible to borrow at a lower rate or lend at a higher rate. For example, it may be possible to sell T-bills being held for some other purpose as a source of short-term funds. This may effectively permit borrowing at a low rate. Finally, in order to borrow money or securities arbitrageurs must have available capital. Undertaking one arbitrage may prevent undertaking another.

The overall conclusion is not surprising: Arbitrage may be difficult, risky, and costly. Large deviations from the theoretical price may be arbitraged, but small deviations may or may not represent genuine arbitrage opportunities. The box on page 132 provides a surprising application of the no-arbitrage argument.

Quasi-Arbitrage

The previous section focused on explicit arbitrage. However, it can also be possible to undertake *implicit* arbitrage by substituting a low yield position for one with a higher return. We call this **quasi-arbitrage.**

Consider, for example, a corporation that can borrow at 8.5% and lend at 7.5%. Suppose there is a cash-and-carry transaction with an implied repo rate of 8%. There is no pure arbitrage opportunity for the corporation, but it would make sense to divert lending from the 7.5% assets to the 8% cash-and-carry. If we attempt explicit arbitrage by borrowing at 8.5% in order to earn 8% on the cash-and-carry, the transaction becomes unprofitable. We can arbitrage only to the extent that we are already lending; this is why it is "quasi"-arbitrage.

A No-Arbitrage Proof That Time Travel Is Impossible

You may be surprised to learn that according to finance theory, the ability to travel through time does not exist now, and *it never will exist* (Reinganum, 1986). We can reach this strong conclusion by seeing how time travel would make available new arbitrage opportunities.

Suppose that at some point in the distant future, time travel were to become possible. Investors would immediately form a hedge fund called "Time Travel Capital Management" (TTCM), which would use time travel to undertake arbitrage. TTCM would start with initial capital of $1000. The fund manager would travel back to the year 2000, and invest the $1000 in a Treasury bill maturing in one year. In 2001, the investment would be worth approximately $1005. The traveller would immediately move forward in time to collect the $1005, then travel back to reinvest all proceeds, and so on. *The time traveller does not have to wait a year to earn interest!* In the blink of an eye, the initial investment would be worth trillions of dollars. For TTCM, the only no-arbitrage interest rate would be zero.

Since prices must be at levels that preclude arbitrage, we conclude that because we observe positive interest rates today, there will *never* be time travel! (But see Problem 5.9.)

Does the Forward Price Predict the Future Price?

It is common to think that the forward price reflects some expectation about the asset's future price. However, from the formula for the forward price, equation (5.7), once we know the current asset price, the risk-free rate, and the dividend yield, the forward price conveys no additional information about the expected future stock price. Moreover, the forward price *systematically* errs in predicting the future stock price.

The reason is straightforward. When you buy a stock, you invest money that has an opportunity cost (it could otherwise have been invested in an interest-earning asset), and you are acquiring the risk of the stock. On average you expect to earn interest as compensation for the time value of money. You also expect an additional return as compensation for the risk of the stock—this is the risk premium. Algebraically, the expected return on a stock is

$$\alpha = \underbrace{r}_{\text{Compensation for Time}} + \underbrace{\alpha - r}_{\text{Compensation for Risk}} \tag{5.12}$$

When you enter into a forward contract, there is no investment; hence, you are not compensated for the time value of money. However, the forward contract retains the risk of the stock, so you must be compensated for risk. *This means that the forward contract must earn the risk premium.* If the risk premium is positive, then on average you must expect a positive return from the forward contract. The only way this can happen is if the forward price predicts too low a stock price. In other words *the forward contract is a biased predictor of the future stock price.*

We can see this algebraically. Let α be the expected return on a nondividend-paying stock and let r be the effective annual interest rate. Consider a 1-year forward contract. The forward price is

$$F_0 = S_0(1 + r)$$

The expected future spot price is

$$E_0(S_1) = S_0(1 + \alpha)$$

where E_0 denotes "expectation as of time 0." Thus, the difference between the forward price and the expected future spot price is

$$E_0(S_1) - F_0 = S_0(1 + \alpha) - S_0(1 + r) = S_0(\alpha - r)$$

The expression $\alpha - r$ is the *risk premium* on the asset, i.e., the amount by which the asset is expected to outperform the risk-free asset. This equation verifies that *the forward price is biased by the amount of the risk premium on the underlying asset.*

For example, suppose that a stock index has an expected return of 15%, while the risk-free rate is 5%. If the current index price is 100, then on average we expect that the index will be 115 in 1 year. The forward price for delivery in 1 year will be only 105, however. This means that a holder of the forward contract will on average earn positive profits, albeit at the cost of bearing the risk of the index.[7]

This bias does not imply that a forward contract is a good investment. Rather, it tells us that *the risk premium on an asset can be created at zero cost and hence has a zero value.* Though this seems surprising, it is a result from elementary finance that if we buy any asset and borrow the full amount of its cost—a transaction that requires no investment—then we earn the risk premium on the asset. Since a forward contract has the risk of a fully leveraged investment in the asset, it earns the risk premium. This proposition is true in general, not just for the example of a forward on a nondividend-paying stock.

An Interpretation of the Forward Pricing Formula

The forward pricing formula for a stock index, equation (5.7), depends on $r - \delta$, the difference between the risk-free rate and the dividend yield. This difference is called the **cost of carry.**

Suppose you buy a unit of the index that costs S and fund the position by borrowing at the risk-free rate. You will pay rS on the borrowed amount, but the dividend yield will provide offsetting income of δS. You will have to pay the difference, $(r - \delta)S$, on an ongoing basis. This difference is the net cost of carrying a long position in the asset; hence, it is called the "cost of carry."

....

[7] Accounting for dividends in this example would not change the magnitude of the bias since dividends would lower the expected future price of the index and the forward price by equal amounts.

Now suppose you were to short the index and invest the proceeds at the risk-free rate. You would receive S for shorting the asset, earn rS on the invested proceeds, but you would have to pay δS to the index lender. We will call δ the **lease rate** of the index; it is what you would have to pay to a lender of the asset. The lease rate of an asset is the annualized cash payment that the borrower must make to the lender. For a nondividend-paying stock, the lease rate is zero while for a dividend-paying stock, the lease rate is the dividend.

Here is an interpretation of the forward pricing formula:

$$\text{Forward price} = \text{Spot price} + \underbrace{\text{Interest to carry the asset} - \text{asset lease rate}}_{\text{Cost of Carry}} \qquad (5.13)$$

The forward contract, unlike the stock, requires no investment and makes no payouts and therefore has a zero cost of carry. One way to interpret the forward pricing formula is that, to the extent the forward contract saves our having to pay the cost of carry, we are willing to pay a higher price. This is what equation (5.13) says.

5.4 FUTURES CONTRACTS

Futures contracts are essentially exchange-traded forward contracts. As with forwards, futures contracts represent a commitment to buy or sell an underlying asset at some future date. Because futures are exchange-traded, they are standardized and have specified delivery dates, locations, and procedures. Futures may be traded either electronically or in trading pits, with buyers and sellers shouting orders to one another (this is called **open outcry**). Each exchange has an associated **clearinghouse.** The role of the clearinghouse is to match the buys and sells that take place during the day, and to keep track of the obligations and payments required of the members of the clearinghouse, who are called clearing members. After matching trades, the clearinghouse typically becomes the counterparty for each clearing member.

Although forwards and futures are similar in many respects, there are differences.

- Whereas forward contracts are settled at expiration, futures contracts are settled daily. The determination of who owes what to whom is called **marking-to-market.** Frequent marking-to-market and settlement of a futures contract can lead to pricing differences between the futures and an otherwise identical forward.

- As a result of daily settlement, futures contracts are liquid—it is possible to offset an obligation on a given date by entering into the opposite position. For example, if you are long the S&P 500 in September, you can cancel your obligation to buy by entering into an offsetting obligation to sell the S&P 500 in September. Since the counterparty for the buy and sell orders is the same, your obligation is officially cancelled.[8]

----

[8]Even though forward contracts may not be explicitly marketable, it is generally possible to enter into an offsetting position, although it may not be with the same counterparty.

- Over-the-counter forward contracts can be customized to fit special needs of the buyer or seller. Futures contracts are standardized. For example, available futures contracts may permit delivery of 250 units of a particular index in March or June. A forward contract could specify April delivery of 300 units of the index.

- Because of daily settlement, the nature of credit risk is different with the futures contract. In fact, futures contracts are structured so as to minimize the effects of credit risk.

We will illustrate futures contracts with the S&P 500 index futures contract as a specific example.

The S&P 500 Futures Contract

The S&P 500 futures contract has the S&P 500 stock index as the underlying asset. Figure 5.1 shows a newspaper quotation for the S&P 500 index futures contract, and Figure 5.2 shows its specifications. The notional value, or size, of the contract is the dollar value of the assets underlying one contract. In this case it is by definition $250 \times 1300 = \$325,000$.[9]

The S&P 500 is an example of a cash-settled contract: Instead of settling by actual delivery of the underlying stocks, the contract calls for a cash payment that equals the profit or loss *as if* the contract were settled by delivery of the underlying asset. On the expiration day, the S&P 500 futures contract is marked-to-market against the actual cash index. This final settlement against the cash index guarantees that the futures price equals the index value at contract expiration.

It is easy to see why the S&P 500 is cash-settled. A physical settlement process would call for delivery of 500 shares (or some large subset thereof) in the precise percentage they make up the S&P 500 index. This basket of stocks would be expensive to buy and sell. Cash settlement is an inexpensive alternative.

 **FIGURE 5.1**

Listing for the S&P 500 futures contract from the *Wall Street Journal*, February 5, 2002.

	OPEN	HIGH	LOW	SETTLE	CHANGE	LIFETIME HIGH	LIFETIME LOW	OPEN INT.
S&P 500 Index (CME)-$250 times index								
Mar	112350	112370	109100	109530	−	2810	134960 94100	474,811
June	111950	111950	109350	109730	−	2830	170550 95030	17,224
Dec	111580	111580	110020	110390	−	2930	150070 96130	304

Est vol 79,914; vol Fri 65,250; open int 502,626, −701.
Idx prl: Hi 1122.20; Lo 1092.25; Close 1094.44, −27.76.

---

[9] Because the S&P 500 index is a fabricated number—an average of individual stock prices—the S&P 500 index is treated as a pure number rather than a price and the contract is defined at maturity to have a size of $250× S&P 500 index.

FIGURE 5.2	Underlying	S&P 500 index
	Where traded	Chicago Mercantile Exchange
Specifications for the S&P 500 index futures contract.	Size	$250 × S&P 500 index
	Months	Mar, Jun, Sep, Dec
	Trading ends	Business day prior to determination of settlement price
	Settlement	Cash-settled, based upon opening price of S&P 500 on third Friday of expiration month

Margins and Marking to Market

Let's explore the logistics of holding a futures position. Suppose the futures price is 1100 and you wish to acquire a $2.2 million position in the S&P 500 index. The notional value of one contract is $250 × 1100 = $275,000; this represents the amount you are agreeing to pay at expiration per futures contract. To go long $2.2 million of the index, you would enter into $2.2 million/$.275 million = 8 long futures contracts. The notional value of 8 contracts is 8 × $250 × 1100 = $2, 000 × 1100 = $2.2 million.

A broker executes your buy order. For every buyer there is a seller, which means that one or more investors must be found who simultaneously agree to sell forward the same number of units of the index. The total number of open positions (buy/sell pairs) is called the **open interest** of the contract.

Both buyers and sellers are required to post a performance bond with the broker to ensure that they can cover a specified loss on the position.[10] This deposit, which can earn interest, is called **margin** and is intended to protect the counterparty—in this case the exchange clearinghouse—against default. Because the margin is a performance bond, not a payment, futures contracts are costless (not counting, of course, commissions and the bid-ask spread).

To understand the role of margin, suppose that there is 10% margin and weekly settlement. The margin on futures contracts with a notional value of $2.2 million is $220,000.

If the S&P 500 futures price drops by 1, to 1099, we lose $2000 on our futures position. The reason is that 8 long contracts obligate us to pay $2000 × 1100 to buy 2000 units of the index which we could now sell for only $2000 × 1099. Thus, we lose $(1099 − 1100) × $2000 = −$2000$. Suppose that over the first week, the futures price drops 72.01 points to 1027.99, a decline of about 6.5%. On a mark-to-market basis, we have lost

$$\$2000 × −72.01 = −\$144,020$$

....

[10]The exchange's clearinghouse determines a minimum margin, but individual brokers can and do demand higher margins from individual customers. The reason is that the broker is liable to the clearing corporation for customer failure to pay.

We have a choice of either paying this loss directly, or allowing it to be taken out of the margin balance. It doesn't matter which we do since we can recover the unused margin balance plus interest at any time by selling our position.

If the loss is subtracted from the margin balance, we have earned one week's interest and have lost $144,020. Thus if the continuously compounded interest rate is 6%, our week 1 margin balance is

$$\$220,000e^{0.06 \times 1/52} - \$144,020 = \$76,233.99$$

Because we have a 10% margin, a 6.5% decline in the futures price results in a 65% decline in margin. Were we to close out our position by entering into 8 short index futures contracts, we would receive the remaining margin balance of $76,233.99.

The decline in the margin balance means the broker has signficantly less protection against the possibility that we will default. For this reason, participants are required to maintain the margin at a minimum level, called the **maintenance margin.** This is frequently set at 70–80% of the initial margin level. In this example, where the margin balance declines 65%, we would have to post additional margin. The broker would make a **margin call,** requesting additional margin. If we failed to post additional margin, the broker would close the position by selling 2000 units of the index, and return to us the remaining margin. In practice, marking to market and settling up are performed at least daily.

Since margin is protection against your default, a major determinant of margin levels is the volatility of the underlying asset. The minimum margin on the S&P 500 contract has generally been less than the 10% we assume in this example. In July 1999, for example, the minimum margin on the S&P 500 futures contract was about 7% of the notional value of the contract.

To illustrate the effect of periodic settlement, Table 5.8 reports hypothetical futures price moves and tracks the margin position over a period of 10 weeks, assuming weekly marking to market and a continuously compounded risk-free rate of 6%. As the party agreeing to buy at a fixed price, we make money when the price goes up and lose when the price goes down. The opposite would occur for the seller.

The 10-week profit on the position is obtained by subtracting from the final margin balance the future value of the original margin investment. Week-10 profit on the position in Table 5.8 is therefore

$$\$44,990.57 - \$220,000e^{0.06 \times 10/52} = -\$177,562.60$$

What if the position had been a forward rather than a futures position, but with prices the same? In that case, after 10 weeks our profit would have been

$$(1011.65 - 1100) \times \$2000 = -\$176,700$$

Why do the futures and forward profits differ? The reason is that with the futures contract, interest is earned on the mark-to-market proceeds. Given the prices in Table 5.8, the loss is larger for futures than forwards because prices on average are below the initial price and we have to fund losses as they occur. With a forward, by contrast, losses are not funded until expiration. Earning interest on the daily settlement magnifies the gain or loss compared to that on a forward contract. Had there been consistent gains on

		Futures	Price	Margin
TABLE 5.8	Mark-to-market proceeds and margin balance over 10 weeks from long position in 8 S&P 500 futures contracts. The final row represents expiration of the contract.			

Week	Multiplier ($)	Futures Price	Price Change	Margin Balance($)
0	2000.00	1100.00	—	220,000.00
1	2000.00	1027.99	−72.01	76,233.99
2	2000.00	1037.88	9.89	96,102.01
3	2000.00	1073.23	35.35	166,912.96
4	2000.00	1048.78	−24.45	118,205.66
5	2000.00	1090.32	41.54	201,422.13
6	2000.00	1106.94	16.62	234,894.67
7	2000.00	1110.98	4.04	243,245.86
8	2000.00	1024.74	−86.24	71,046.69
9	2000.00	1007.30	−17.44	36,248.72
10	2000.00	1011.65	4.35	44,990.57

the position in this example, the futures profit would have exceeded the forward profit. Appendix 5.B demonstrates that the ultimate payoff to a forward and futures contract can be equated in this example by adjusting the number of futures contracts so as to undo the magnifying effect of interest.

Comparing Futures and Forward Prices

An implication of Appendix 5.B is that if the interest rate were not random, then forward and futures prices would be the same. However, what if the interest rate varies randomly? Suppose, for example, that on average the interest rate increases unexpectedly when the futures price increases; i.e., the two are positively correlated. Then the margin balance would grow (due to an increased futures price) just as the interest rate was higher. The margin balance would shrink as the interest rate was lower. On average in this case, a long futures position would outperform a long forward contract.

Conversely, suppose that the interest rate declined as the futures price rose. Then as the margin balance on a long position grew, the proceeds would be invested at a lower rate. Similarly, as the balance declined and required additional financing, this financing would occur at a higher rate. Here a long futures contract would on average perform worse than a long forward contract.

This comparison of the forward and futures payoffs suggests that when the interest rate is positively correlated with the futures price, the futures price will exceed the price on an otherwise identical forward contract: The investor who is long futures buys at a higher price to offset the advantage of marking to market. Similarly, when the interest rate is negatively correlated with the forward price, the futures price will be less than an otherwise identical forward price: The investor who is long futures buys at a lower price to offset the disadvantage of marking to market.

As an empirical matter, forward and futures prices are very similar.[11] The theoretical difference arises from uncertainty about the interest on mark-to-market proceeds. For short-lived contracts, the effect is generally small. However, for long-lived contracts, the difference can be significant, especially for long-lived interest rate futures, for which there is sure to be a correlation between the interest rate and the price of the underlying asset.[12] For the rest of this chapter we will ignore the difference between forwards and futures.

Arbitrage in Practice: S&P 500 Index Arbitrage

The S&P 500 futures contract provides a context for illustrating practical issues that arise when we try to apply the theoretical pricing formulas to determine the fair price of a futures contract. In order to compute the theoretical forward price using equation (5.7), we need to determine three things: The value of the cash index (S_0), the value of dividends to be paid on the index over the life of the contract (δ), and the interest rate (r).

Table 5.9 uses newspaper price quotes to see if the theoretical model, equation (5.7), comes close to the actual futures price. On February 1, 2002, the S&P 500 cash index closed at 1130.2, with a current dividend yield of about 1.3%, which we will assume is expected to be constant over time. What interest rate is appropriate? Two obvious possibilities are the yield on U.S. Treasury bills, and LIBOR (the London Interbank Offer Rate), which is a borrowing rate for financial institutions. The LIBOR rates are inferred from Eurodollar futures, which we will discuss in Section 5.7. One interpretation is that the T-bill rate is a lending rate and LIBOR a borrowing rate. Table 5.9 reports the results of computing equation (5.7) using both rates, also taken from the newspaper.[13] For example, for the December contract, the price computed using the T-bill rate is

$$S_0 e^{(r-\delta)T} = 1130.20 e^{(0.0218-0.013)\times 322/365} = 1139.01$$

It is apparent from Table 5.9 that market prices and formula prices are not exactly the same. In fact there are *two* formula prices, depending upon which interest rate we use. To make sense of this, think about the problem facing an arbitrageur. In Section

---

[11] See French (1983) for a comparison of forward and futures prices on a variety of underlying assets.

[12] A practical example of this difference occurs with Eurodollar futures and swaps. Eurodollar futures are marked to market daily, while swaps are settled quarterly and behave more like forward contracts. The difference between actual swap rates and the swap rate implied by the futures curve is sometimes called "convexity bias." See Gupta and Subrahmanyam, 2000, and Chapter 7.

[13] Interest rates are quoted using a variety of conventions for annualizing the rate. This example uses reported rates as if they were continuously compounded, which they are not. In Table 5.9, this simplification makes almost no difference in the computed theoretical prices.

TABLE 5.9	S&P 500 index futures prices and interest rate information from the *Wall Street Journal*, February 1, 2002. The closing S&P 500 spot price was 1130.20. Treasury-bill yields are reported yields on Treasury bills expiring in the same month as the futures contract. LIBOR rates are constructed from Eurodollar prices. The theoretical forward prices are constructed for each maturity from equation (5.7) using the interest rate in the preceding row and assuming a 1.3% dividend yield.

Expiration Month:	March	June	December
Days to Expiration:	42	140	322
S&P 500 Index Futures Price	1130.4	1132.5	1140.3
Treasury-Bill Yield	0.0167	0.017	0.0218
Theoretical Forward Price	1130.68	1131.93	1139.01
LIBOR	0.0187	0.0201	0.0240
Theoretical Forward Price	1130.94	1133.28	1141.22

5.3 we concluded that instead of there being a no-arbitrage price, there is a no-arbitrage *region*, reflecting various costs of arbitrage. An arbitrageur looking at the S&P 500 index futures market faces bid-ask spreads on the futures contract and index, and differential borrowing and lending rates.[14] In Table 5.9, the March futures price is slightly below the theoretical prices. In June and December, however, the observed futures price is bracketed by prices computed using T-bill rates and LIBOR. The actual no-arbitrage bounds are likely wider than in Table 5.9 once costs besides interest rate differentials are taken into account. This example, taking into account only differential borrowing and lending rates, illustrates how there can be a range of prices within which arbitrage is not possible.

One additional complication with S&P 500 index arbitrage is that, because of transaction costs, an arbitrageur will not usually buy the entire 500-stock index, but instead a subset of it.[15] The futures contract and the offsetting position in stocks may

---

[14]A representative bid-ask spread on the index futures contract might be 20–30 basis points (a basis point on the S&P futures contract is 0.01) and 0.25%–0.5% on the stocks in the index when traded in significant quantities.

[15]Another way to trade the cash index is with the use of Standard and Poor's Depository Receipts (SPDRs). These are unit investment trusts that are backed by a portfolio intended to mimic the S&P 500. Investors can convert units of 50,000 SPDR shares into the actual stock and can convert stock into SPDRs. This keeps SPDRs close to the S&P 500 index, but in practice SPDRs may be mispriced relative to the cash S&P 500 just as futures are.

thus not move exactly together. When buying a large number of stocks, there is also execution risk—the possibility that prices move during the time between the order being placed and the stock being actually purchased.

Ultimately, the only way to know if arbitrage is profitable is to be an arbitrageur, facing specific prices, trading costs, borrowing and lending rates, and existing positions. Given this information, you can compute profit and loss and decide whether to trade.

Quanto Index Contracts

At first glance the Chicago Mercantile Exchange's Nikkei 225 futures contract—see a newspaper quotation in Figure 5.3 and the details summarized in Figure 5.4—is a stock index contract like the S&P 500 contract. However there is one very important difference: Settlement of the contract is in a different currency (dollars) than the currency of denomination for the index (yen).[16]

To see why this is important, consider a dollar-based investor wishing to invest in the Nikkei 225 cash index. This investor must undertake two transactions: Changing dollars to yen, and using yen to buy the index. When the position is sold, the investor reverses these transactions, selling the index and converting yen back to dollars. There

FIGURE 5.3

Listing for the Nikkei 225 futures contract from the *Wall Street Journal*, February 5, 2002.

	OPEN	HIGH	LOW	SETTLE	CHANGE	LIFETIME HIGH	LIFETIME LOW	OPEN INT.
Nikkei 225 Stock Average (CME)-$5 times Index								
Mar	9690.	9700.	9555.	9580.	–	130 14620.	9245.	15,750

Est vol 667; vol Fri 2,100; open int 15,817, −17.
Idx prl: Hi 9809.82; Lo 9623.99; Close 9631.93, −159.50.

FIGURE 5.4

Specifications for the Nikkei 225 index futures contract.

Underlying	Nikkei 225 Stock Index
Where traded	Chicago Mercantile Exchange
Size	$5 × Nikkei 225 Index
Months	Mar, Jun, Sep, Dec
Trading ends	Business day prior to determination of settlement price
Settlement	Cash-settled, based upon opening Osaka quotation of the Nikkei 225 index on the second Friday of expiration month

[16]There is also a yen-denominated Nikkei 225 futures contract that trades at the Osaka exchange. Since it is purely yen-denominated, this contract *is* priced according to equation (5.7).

are two sources of risk in this transaction: The risk of the index, denominated in yen, and the risk that the yen/dollar exchange rate will change. From Figure 5.4, the Nikkei 225 futures contract is denominated in dollars rather than yen. Consequently, the contract insulates investors from currency risk, permitting them to speculate solely on whether the index rises or falls. This kind of contract is called a *quanto*. Quanto contracts allow investors in one country to invest in a different country without exchange rate risk.

The dollar-denominated Nikkei contract provides an interesting variation on the construction of a futures contract. Because of the quanto feature, the pricing formulas we have developed do not work for the Nikkei 225 contract. We will discuss quantos and the necessary modification to price a quanto futures contract in Chapter 22.

5.5   Uses of Index Futures

An index futures contract is economically like borrowing to buy the index. Why use an index futures contract if you can easily synthesize one? One answer is that index futures can permit trading the index at a lower transaction cost than actually trading a basket of the stocks that make up the index. If you are taking a temporary position in the index, either for investing or hedging, the transaction cost saving could be significant.

In this section we provide two examples of the use of index futures: Asset allocation and cross-hedging a related portfolio.

Asset Allocation

Asset allocation strategies involve switching investments among asset classes, such as stocks, money market instruments, and bonds. Trading the individual securities, such as the stocks in an index, can be expensive. Our earlier discussion of arbitrage demonstrated that we can use forwards to create synthetic stocks and bonds. The practical implication is that a portfolio manager can invest in a stock index without holding stocks, commodities without holding physical commodities, and so on.

As an example of asset allocation, suppose that we are invested in the S&P 500 index and we wish to temporarily invest in bonds instead of the index. Instead of selling all 500 stocks and investing in bonds, we can simply keep our stock portfolio and take a short forward position in the S&P 500 index. This converts our cash investment in the index into a cash-and-carry, creating a synthetic T-bill. When we wish to revert to investing in stocks, we simply offset the forward position.

To illustrate this, suppose that the current index price, S_0, is \$100, and the effective 1-year risk-free rate is 10%. The forward price is therefore \$110. Suppose that in 1 year, the index price could be either \$80 or \$130. If we sell the index and invest in T-bills, we will have \$110 in 1 year.

Table 5.10 shows that if, instead of selling, we keep the stock and short the forward contract, we earn a 10% return no matter what happens to the value of the stock. In this example 10% is the rate of return implied by the forward premium. If there is no arbitrage, this return will be equal to the risk-free rate.

TABLE 5.10 Effect of owning the stock and selling forward, assuming that $S_0 = \$100$ and $F_{0,1} = \$110$.

		Cash Flows	
Transaction	Today	1 year, $S_1 = \$80$	1 year, $S_1 = \$130$
Own Stock @ $100	−$100	$80	$130
Short Forward @ $110	0	$110 − $80	$110 − $130
Total	−$100	$110	$110

Cross-hedging with perfect correlation Suppose that we have a portfolio that is not the S&P 500, and we wish to shift the portfolio into T-bills. Can we use the S&P 500 futures contract to do this? The answer depends on the correlation of the portfolio with the S&P 500. To the extent the two are not perfectly correlated, there will be residual risk.

Suppose that we own $100 million of stocks with a beta relative to the S&P 500 of 1.4. Assume for the moment that the two indexes are perfectly correlated. Perfect correlation means that there is a perfectly predictable relationship between the two indexes, not necessarily that they move one-for-one. Using the Capital Asset Pricing Model (CAPM), the return on our portfolio, r_p, is related to its beta, β_p, by

$$r_p = r + \beta_p(r_{S\&P} - r)$$

Assume also that the S&P 500 is 1100 with a 0 dividend yield and the effective annual risk-free rate is 6%. Hence the futures price is $1100 \times 1.06 = 1166$.

If we wish to allocate from the index into Treasury bills using futures, we need to short some quantity of the S&P 500. There are two steps to calculating the short futures quantity:

1. *Adjust for the difference in the dollar amounts of our portfolio and the S&P 500 contract.* In this case, one futures contract has a value of $250 \times 1100 = \$275,000$. Thus, the number of contracts needed to cover $100 million of stock is

$$\frac{\$100 \text{ million}}{\$0.275 \text{ million}} = 363.636$$

2. *Adjust for the difference in beta.* Since the beta of our portfolio exceeds 1, it moves more than the S&P 500 in either direction. Thus we need to further increase our S&P 500 position to account for the greater magnitude moves in our portfolio relative to the S&P 500. This gives us

$$\text{Final hedge quantity} = \frac{\$100 \text{ million}}{\$0.275 \text{ million}} \times 1.4 = 509.09$$

Table 5.11 shows the performance of the hedged position. The result, as you would expect, is that the hedged position earns the risk-free rate, 6%.

TABLE 5.11	Results from shorting 509.09 S&P 500 index futures against a $100m portfolio with a beta of 1.4.

S&P 500 Index	Gain on 509 Futures	Portfolio Value	Total
900	33.855	72.145	106.000
950	27.491	78.509	106.000
1000	21.127	84.873	106.000
1050	14.764	91.236	106.000
1100	8.400	97.600	106.000
1150	2.036	103.964	106.000
1200	−4.327	110.327	106.000

Cross-hedging with imperfect correlation   The simplifying assumption in the example above is that the portfolio and the S&P 500 index are perfectly correlated. In practice, correlations between two portfolios can be substantially less than one. Using the S&P 500 to hedge a position in this case would introduce **basis risk,** which is the possibility that the hedging instrument and the hedged asset may not move together as predicted. This hedge is therefore risky.[17]

Assume that we short H futures contracts, each with a notional amount N. Denote the return and invested dollars on our portfolio as r_p and I_p. The futures position earns the risk premium, $r_{S\&P} - r$. Thus, the return on the hedged position is

$$r_{hedged} = r_p I_p + H \times N \times (r_{S\&P} - r)$$

The variance of the return on the hedged position is given by

$$\sigma^2_{hedged} = \sigma^2_p \times I^2_p + (H \times N)^2 \sigma^2_{S\&P} + 2 \times H \times N \times I_p \times Cov(r_p, r_{S\&P}) \quad (5.14)$$

The variance-minimizing hedge position, H^*, is[18]

$$H^* = -\frac{I_p}{N} \frac{Cov(r_p, r_{S\&P})}{\sigma^2_{S\&P}} \quad (5.15)$$

$$= -\frac{I_p}{N} \beta_p$$

The second equality follows because $Cov(r_p, r_{S\&P})/\sigma^2_{S\&P}$ is the slope coefficient when we regress the portfolio return on the S&P 500 return; i.e., it is the portfolio beta with

---

[17]There is additional basis risk in such a hedge because, for reasons discussed in Section 5.4, the S&P 500 futures contract and the cash price of the S&P 500 index may not move perfectly together.

[18]This can be derived by differentiating equation (5.14) with respect to H^*.

respect to the S&P 500 index. Notice that equation (5.15) is the calculation we performed above in concluding that we should short 509.09 contracts.

When we add H^* futures to the portfolio, the variance of the hedged portfolio, σ^2_{hedged}, is obtained by substituting H^* into equation (5.14):

$$\sigma^2_{hedged} = \sigma^2_p I^2_p \left(1 - \rho^2\right) \tag{5.16}$$

where ρ is the correlation coefficient between the portfolio and the S&P 500 index.

In practice, investment banks may be willing to offer forward contracts for indices for which there are no traded futures. In this case the investment bank absorbs the basis risk in exchange for a fee.

General asset allocation   We can use forwards and futures to perform even more sophisticated asset allocation. Suppose we wish to invest our portfolio in Treasury bonds (long-term Treasury obligations) instead of stocks. We can accomplish this reallocation with two forward positions: Shorting the forward S&P 500 index and going long the forward T-bond. The first transaction converts our portfolio from an index investment to a T-bill investment. The second transaction converts the portfolio from a T-bill investment to a T-bond investment. This use of futures to convert a position from one asset category (stocks) to another (bonds) is called a **futures overlay.**

Using forwards to do asset allocation can have benefits beyond just saving transaction costs. Suppose an investment management company has some managers who invest in bonds and some who invest in stocks. The job of these managers is to buy and sell mispriced stocks and bonds, and they are judged on their performance relative to an index. Suppose that on average the company is invested in 60% stocks and 40% bonds. What happens when the company wishes to change the allocation to 75% stocks and 25% bonds because it believes the relative returns to stocks have increased? The investment management company could instruct stock managers to buy more stocks and bond managers to sell some of their holdings. However, this is disruptive to the portfolio managers, and may even be counterproductive. Just because stocks are expected to outperform bonds does not mean that there are increased opportunities to find individual stocks that will outperform a broad stock index.

By using forward contracts, the company can perform asset allocation without disturbing the basic strategies of its stock and bond managers. By shorting treasury bond futures against 15% of the bond portfolio and going long stock index futures in the same amount, the company achieves asset allocation without disturbing the underlying portfolios.

Risk Management for Stock-Pickers

An asset manager who picks stocks is often making a bet about the relative, but not the absolute, performance of a stock. For example, XYZ might be expected to outperform a broad range of stocks on a risk-adjusted basis. If the economy suffers a recession, however, XYZ will decline in value even if it outperforms other stocks. Index futures can be used in this case to help isolate the *relative* performance of XYZ.

Suppose the return of XYZ is given by the capital asset pricing model (CAPM):

$$r_{XYZ} = \alpha_{XYZ} + r + \beta_{XYZ}(r_m - r) \qquad (5.17)$$

The term α_{XYZ} in this context represents the expected abnormal return on XYZ. If we use the S&P 500 as a proxy for the market, then we can select H according to equation (5.15). The result for the hedged position will be that, on average, we earn $\alpha_{XYZ} + r$. The risk of the position will be given by equation (5.16). Since the correlation of an individual stock and the index will not be close to 1, there will be considerable remaining risk. However, the portfolio will not have market risk.

5.6 CURRENCY CONTRACTS

Currency futures and forwards are widely used to hedge against changes in exchange rates. The pricing of currency contracts is a straightforward application of the principles we have already discussed. Newspaper listings for exchange-traded currency contracts are in Figure 5.5.

Many corporations use currency futures and forwards for short-term hedging. An importer of consumer electronics, for example, may have an obligation to pay the manufacturer ¥150 million 90 days in the future. The dollar revenues from selling these products are likely known in the short run, so the importer bears pure exchange risk due to the payable being fixed in yen. By buying ¥150 million forward 90 days, the

FIGURE 5.5

Listings for various currency futures contracts from the *Wall Street Journal*, February 5, 2002.

	OPEN	HIGH	LOW	SETTLE	CHANGE	LIFETIME HIGH	LIFETIME LOW	OPEN INT.
CURRENCY								
Japan Yen (CME)-12.5 million yen; $ per yen (.00)								
Mar	.7528	.7600	.7508	.7576	+ .0050	.8760	.7416	105,563
June	.7570	.7635	.7547	.7611	+ .0050	.8776	.7453	20,834
Est vol 11,091; vol Fri 25,220; open int 126,860, −1,352.								
Canadian Dollar (CME)-100,000 dlrs.; $ per Can $								
Mar	.6282	.6287	.6264	.6266	− .0016	.6725	.6170	60,355
June	.6280	.6287	.6263	.6264	− .0016	.6700	.6180	3,952
Sept	.6265	.6282	.6265	.6266	− .0016	.6590	.6175	1,331
Dec	.6274	.6280	.6265	.6269	− .0016	.6555	.6190	1,075
Est vol 5,343; vol Fri 7,699; open int 66,818, −652.								
British Pound (CME)-62,500 pds.; $ per pound								
Mar	1.4112	1.4206	1.4106	1.4186	+ .0058	1.4700	1.3810	33,978
June	1.4066	1.4140	1.4038	1.4102	+ .0058	1.4550	1.3910	89
Est vol 5,315; vol Fri 4,859; open int 34,067, −174.								
Swiss Franc (CME)-125,000 francs; $ per franc								
Mar	.5836	.5902	.5825	.5892	+ .0061	.6370	.5540	47,600
June	.5866	.5906	.5830	.5895	+ .0061	.6320	.5813	238
Est vol 5,676; vol Fri 6,330; open int 47,871, −587.								
Australian Dollar (CME)-100,000 dlrs.; $ per A.$								
Mar	.5076	.5102	.5074	.5098	+ .0031	.5300	.4810	21,597
June	.5050	.5069	.5046	.5070	+ .0031	.5218	.4885	456
Est vol 944; vol Fri 1,871; open int 22,079, −518.								
Mexican Peso (CME)-500,000 new Mex. peso, $ per MP								
Mar	.10843	.10850	.10810	.10835	+ 00005	.10940	.09770	28,070
June	....	....	....	.10645	+ 00010	.10750	.09730	1,509
Sept	.10450	.10450	.10450	.10453	+ 00010	.10500	.09930	508
Est vol 1,940; vol Fri 2,817; open int 30,163, +626.								
Euro FX (CME)-Euro 125,000; $ per Euro								
Mar	.8601	.8694	.8593	.8686	+ .0085	.9630	.8336	103,910
June	.8663	.8663	.8564	.8657	+ .0085	.9275	.8365	1,492
Dec	.8600	.8600	.8600	.8616	+ .0085	.9175	.8390	236
Est vol 14,904; vol Fri 17,547; open int 105,729, −560.								

importer locks in a dollar price to pay for the yen, which will then be delivered to the manufacturer.

Currency Prepaid Forward

Suppose you want to have ¥1 1 year from today. A prepaid forward allows you to pay dollars today to acquire ¥1 1 year from today. What is the prepaid forward price? Suppose the yen-denominated interest rate is r_y and the exchange rate today (\$/¥) is x_0. We can work backward. If we want ¥1 in 1 year, we must have e^{-r_y} in yen today. To obtain that many yen today, we must exchange $x_0 e^{-r_y}$ dollars into yen.

Thus, the prepaid forward price for a yen is

$$F_{0,T}^P = x_0 e^{-r_y T} \tag{5.18}$$

where T is time to maturity of the forward.

The economic principle governing the pricing of a prepaid forward on currency is the same as that for a prepaid forward on stock. By deferring delivery of the underlying asset, you lose income. In the case of currency, if you received the currency immediately, you could buy a bond denominated in that currency and earn interest. The prepaid forward price reflects the loss of interest from deferring delivery, just as the prepaid forward price for stock reflects the loss of dividend income. This is why equation (5.18) is the same as that for a stock paying a continuous dividend, equation (5.4).

Example 5.3 Suppose that the yen-denominated interest rate is 2% and that the current exchange rate is 0.009 dollars per yen. Then in order to have 1 yen in 1 year, we would invest today

$$0.009\$/¥ \times ¥1 \times e^{-0.02} = \$.008822$$
🖎

Currency Forward

In the prepaid forward discussion above we computed the *dollar* cost of obtaining 1 yen in the future. Thus, to obtain the forward price we take the future value using the dollar-denominated interest rate, r:

$$F_{0,T} = x_0 e^{(r-r_y)t} \tag{5.19}$$

The forward currency rate will exceed the current exchange rate when the domestic risk-free rate is higher than the foreign risk-free rate.[19]

----

[19]Of course if you think about it, every currency transaction can be expressed in terms of either currency, for example as yen/dollar or dollar/yen. If the forward price exceeds the current exchange rate viewed from the perspective of one currency, it must be less from the perspective of the other.

Example 5.4 Suppose that the yen-denominated interest rate is 2% and the dollar-denominated rate is 6%. The current exchange rate is 0.009 dollars per yen. The 1-year forward rate is

$$0.009e^{0.06-0.02} = 0.009367$$ ❧

Notice that equation (5.19) is just like that for stock index futures, equation (5.7), with the foreign interest rate equal to the dividend yield. The interest rate difference $r - r_y$ is the cost of carry for a foreign currency (we borrow at the domestic rate r and invest the proceeds in a foreign money-market instrument, earning the foreign rate r_y as an offset to our cost). If we wish to borrow foreign currency, r_y is the lease rate.

Covered Interest Arbitrage

We can synthetically create a forward contract by borrowing in one currency and lending in the other. If we want to have 1 yen in the future, with the dollar price fixed today, we can pay today for the yen, and borrow in dollars to do so. To have 1 yen in 1 year, we need to invest

$$x_0 e^{-r_y T}$$

in dollars, and we obtain this amount by borrowing. The required dollar repayment is

$$x_0 e^{(r-r_y)T}$$

which is the forward exchange rate.

Example 5.5 Suppose that $x_0 = 0.009$, $r_y = 2\%$, and $r = 6\%$. The dollar cost of buying 1 yen today is $0.009 \times e^{-0.02} = 0.008822$. We defer the dollar payment by borrowing at 6%, for a cost 1 year from today of $0.008822e^{0.06} = 0.009367$. This transaction is summarized in Table 5.12. ❧

The example shows that borrowing in one currency and lending in another creates the same cash flow as a forward contract. If we offset this borrowing and lending position with an actual forward contract, the resulting transaction is called **covered interest arbitrage.**

To summarize, a forward exchange rate reflects the difference in interest rates denominated in different currencies. Imagine that you want to invest $1 for 1 year. You can do so by buying a dollar-denominated bond, or you can exchange the dollar into another currency and buy a bond denominated in that other currency. You can then use currency forwards to guarantee the exchange rate at which you will convert the foreign currency back into dollars. The principle behind the pricing of currency forwards is that *a hedged position in risk-free bonds pays the same return in any currency.*

TABLE 5.12 		Synthetically creating a yen forward contract by borrowing in dollars and lending in yen. The payoff at time 1 is ¥1 − \$0.009367.		

	Cash Flows			
	Year 0		**Year 1**	
Transaction	**\$**	**¥**	**\$**	**¥**
Borrow $x_0 e^{-r_y}$ Dollar at 6% (\$)	+0.008822	—	−0.009367	—
Convert to Yen @ 0.009 \$/¥	−0.008822	+0.9802	—	—
Invest in Yen-Denominated Bill (¥)	—	−0.9802	—	1
Total	0	0	−0.009367	1

5.7 EURODOLLAR FUTURES

Businesses and individuals face uncertainty about future interest rates. A manager may plan to borrow money 3 months from today, but doesn't know today what the interest rate will be at that time. There are forward and futures contracts that permit hedging interest rate risk by allowing the manager to lock in now a borrowing rate for 3 months in the future.

The principles underlying interest rate contracts are exactly those we have been discussing, but interest rates seem more complicated because there are so many of them, depending upon whether you invest for 1 day, 1 month, 1 year, or 30 years. There are also implied forward interest rates between any two points in the future.[20] Because of this complexity, Chapter 7 is devoted to interest rates. However, the Eurodollar contract is so important that we discuss it briefly here. The Eurodollar strip (the set of futures prices with different maturities at one point in time) provides the basic interest rate information that is used to price other futures contracts and to price swaps. Figure 5.6 shows a newspaper listing for the Eurodollar futures contract.

The Eurodollar contract, described in Figure 5.7, is based on a \$1 million 3-month deposit earning LIBOR (the London Interbank Offer Rate), which is the average borrowing rate faced by large international London banks. In addition to the Eurodollar contract, based on 3-month LIBOR, there is also a contract based on 1-month LIBOR. Suppose that current LIBOR is 1.5% over 3 months. By convention, this is annualized by multiplying by 4, so the quoted LIBOR rate is 6%. Assuming a bank borrows \$1 million for 3 months, a change in annualized LIBOR of 0.01% (one basis point) would raise its borrowing cost by 0.0001/4 × \$1 million = \$25.

---

[20]In addition, there are different rates faced by different classes of borrower: Government, private, and municipal. And of course there are different currencies of denomination.

FIGURE 5.6

Listing for the Eurodollar futures contract from the *Wall Street Journal*, February 5, 2002.

	OPEN	HIGH	LOW	SETTLE	CHANGE		YIELD	CHANGE	OPEN INT.
Treasury Bills (CME)-$1 mil.; pts of 100%									
Mar	....	....	....	98.26	+	.01	1.74	−.01	749
Est vol 17; vol Fri 3; open int 749, −10.									
Eurodollar (CME)-$1 Million; pts of 100%									
Feb	98.08	98.09	98.08	98.09	+	.01	1.91	−.01	37,493
Mar	98.02	98.05	98.01	98.04	+	.02	1.96	−.02	758,791
Apr	97.94	97.96	97.94	97.96	+	.04	2.04	−.04	4,565
June	97.67	97.74	97.65	97.73	+	.06	2.27	−.06	684,053
Sept	97.17	97.30	97.17	97.28	+	.09	2.72	−.09	629,125
Dec	96.58	96.74	96.58	96.72	+	.12	3.28	−.12	709,233
Mr03	96.05	96.15	96.05	96.14	+	.12	3.86	−.12	399,549
June	95.57	95.66	95.57	95.64	+	.11	4.36	−.11	260,328
Sept	95.19	95.26	95.19	95.26	+	.11	4.74	−.11	232,148
Dec	94.85	94.92	94.84	94.90	+	.10	5.10	−.10	168,299
Mr04	94.64	94.70	94.63	94.69	+	.09	5.31	−.09	112,715
June	94.42	94.47	94.22	94.46	+	.09	5.54	−.09	116,246
Sept	94.22	94.28	94.22	94.27	+	.09	5.73	−.09	109,477
Dec	94.03	94.08	94.02	94.07	+	.09	5.93	−.09	70,835
Mr05	93.97	94.02	93.97	94.01	+	.08	5.99	−.08	75,902
June	93.86	93.90	93.85	93.90	+	.08	6.10	−.08	67,857
Sept	93.77	93.82	93.76	93.81	+	.08	6.19	−.08	79,848
Dec	93.64	93.69	93.63	93.67	+	.08	6.33	−.08	54,328
Mr06	93.63	93.68	93.62	93.67	+	.07	6.33	−.07	46,271
June	93.59	93.61	93.58	93.61	+	.07	6.39	−.07	35,319
Sept	93.54	93.56	93.54	93.55	+	.06	6.45	−.06	44,724
Dec	93.43	93.45	93.42	93.44	+	.06	6.56	−.06	32,917
Ju07	93.38	93.42	93.38	93.42	+	.05	6.58	−.05	18,263
Sept	93.35	93.39	93.35	93.38	+	.05	6.62	−.05	14,107
Dec	93.24	93.28	93.24	93.27	+	.04	6.73	−.04	13,227
Ju08	93.23	93.26	93.23	93.25	+	.04	6.75	−.04	11,239
Ju09	93.04	93.09	93.04	93.08	+	.02	6.92	−.02	2,406
Est vol 568,992; vol Fri 1,183,059; open int 4,864,582, +85,457.									

FIGURE 5.7

Specifications for the Eurodollar futures contract.

Where traded	Chicaco Mercantile Exchange
Size	3-month Eurodollar time deposit, $1 million principal
Months	Mar, Jun, Sep, Dec, out 10 years, plus 2 serial months and spot month
Trading ends	5 A.M. (11 A.M. London) on the second London bank business day immediately preceding the third Wednesday of the contract month.
Delivery	Cash settlement
Settlement	100 − British Banker's Association Futures Interest Settlement Rate for 3-Month Eurodollar Interbank Time Deposits. (This is a 3-month rate annualized by multiplying by 360/90.)

The Eurodollar futures price at expiration of the contract is

100 − Annualized 3-month LIBOR

Thus, if LIBOR is 6% at maturity of the Eurodollar futures contract, the final futures price will be 100 − 6 = 94. It is important to understand that the Eurodollar contract settles based on current LIBOR, which is the interest rate quoted for the *next* 3 months.

Thus, for example, the price of the contract that expires in June reflects the 3-month interest rate between June and September. With the futures contract, as with a $1 million LIBOR deposit, a change of 0.01% in the rate is worth $25.

Like most money-market interest rates, LIBOR is quoted assuming a 360-day year. Thus, the annualized 91-day rate, r_{91}, can be extracted from the futures price, F, by computing the 90-day rate and multiplying by 91/90. The quarterly effective rate is then computed by dividing the result by 4:

$$ r_{91} = (100 - F) \times \frac{1}{100} \times \frac{1}{4} \times \frac{91}{90} \tag{5.20} $$

Three-month Eurodollar contracts have maturities out to 10 years, which means that it is possible to use the contract to lock in a 3-month rate as far as 10 years in the future. The September 2007 futures price in Figure 5.6, for example, is 93.38. A position in this contract can be used to lock in an annualized rate of 6.62% from September 2007 to December 2007.

The Eurodollar contract can be used to hedge interest rate risk. For a borrower, for example, a short position in the contract pays when the interest rate rises and requires payment when the interest rate falls. To see this, suppose that 7 months from today we plan to borrow $1 million for 90 days, and that our borrowing rate is the same as LIBOR. The Eurodollar futures price for 7 months from today is 94; this implies a 90-day rate of $(100 - 94) \times 90/360 \times 1/100 = 1.5\%$. Now suppose that 7 months hence, 3-month LIBOR is 8%, which implies a Eurodollar futures price of 92. The implied 90-day rate is 2%. Our extra borrowing expense over 90 days on $1 million will therefore be 0.5% $(0.02 - 0.015)$, or $0.005 \times \$1m = \$5,000$.

This extra borrowing expense is offset by gains on the short Eurodollar contract. The Eurodollar futures price has gone down, giving us a gain of $25 per basis point, or $\$25 \times 100 \times (94 - 92) = \$5,000$. The short position in the futures contract compensates us for the increase in our borrowing cost.[21] In the same way, a long position can be used to lock in a lending rate.

The Eurodollar futures price is a construct, not the price of an asset. In this sense Eurodollar futures are different from the futures contracts we have already discussed. Although Eurodollar LIBOR is closely related to a number of other interest rates, there is no one specific identifiable asset that underlies the Eurodollar futures contract.

LIBOR is quoted in currencies other than dollars, and comparable rates are quoted in different locations. In addition to LIBOR, there are PIBOR (Paris), TIBOR (Tokyo), and Euribor (the European Banking Federation).

Finally, you might be wondering why we are discussing LIBOR rather than rates on Treasury bills. Business and bank borrowing rates move more in tandem with LIBOR than with the government's borrowing rate. Thus, these borrowers use the Eurodollar

---

[21] It might occur to you that the Eurodollar contract pays us at the time we borrow, but we do not pay interest until the loan matures, 91 days hence. Since we have time to earn interest on the change in the value of the contract, the hedge ratio should be less than 1 contract per $1 million borrowing. We discuss this complication in Chapter 7.

futures contract to hedge. LIBOR is also a better measure of the cost of funds for a market-maker, so LIBOR is typically used to price forward contracts. We will further discuss Eurodollar futures in Chapter 7.

CHAPTER SUMMARY

The purchase of a stock or other asset entails agreeing to a price, making payment, and taking delivery of the asset. A forward contract fixes the price today, but payment and delivery are deferred. The pricing of forward contracts reflects the costs and benefits of this deferred payment and delivery. The seller receives payment later, so the price is higher to reflect interest owed the seller, and the buyer receives possession later, so the price is lower to reflect dividends not received by the buyer. A prepaid forward contract requires payment today; hence, it separates these two effects. The price of a prepaid forward is

$$\text{Prepaid forward price} = S_0 e^{-\delta T}$$

The prepaid forward price is below the asset spot price, S_0, reflecting dividends foregone by deferring delivery. The forward price also reflects deferral of payment, so it is the future value of the prepaid forward price:

$$\text{Forward price} = S_0 e^{(r-\delta)T}$$

In the case of a currency forward, the dividend yield foregone by holding the forward contract instead of the underlying asset, δ, is the interest rate you could earn by investing in foreign-currency denominated assets. Thus, for currencies, $\delta = r_f$, where r_f is the foreign interest rate.

A forward contract is equivalent to a leveraged position in an asset—borrowing to buy the asset. By combining the forward contract with other assets it is possible to create synthetic stocks and bonds. These equivalences are summarized in Table 5.13. Since a forward contract is risky but requires no investment, it earns the risk premium. The forward price is therefore a biased predictor of the future spot price of the asset, with the bias equal to the risk premium.

The fact that it is possible to create a synthetic forward has two important implications. First, if the forward contract is mispriced, arbitrageurs can take offsetting

TABLE 5.13	Synthetic equivalents assuming the asset pays continuous dividends at the rate δ.

Position	Synthetic Equivalent
Long Forward	$=$ Buy $e^{-\delta T}$ Shares of Stock $+$ Borrow $S_0 e^{-\delta T}$
Bond Paying $F_{0,T}$	$=$ Buy $e^{-\delta T}$ Shares of Stock $+$ Short Forward
Synthetic Stock	$=$ Long Forward $\qquad + $ Lend $e^{-rT} F_{0,T}$

positions in the forward contract and the synthetic forward contract—in effect buying low and selling high—and make a risk-free profit. Second, dealers who make markets in the forward or in the underlying asset can hedge the risk of their position with a synthetic offsetting position. With transaction costs there is a no-arbitrage *region* rather than a single no-arbitrage price.

Futures contracts are similar to forward contracts, except that with futures there are margin requirements and daily settlement of the gain or loss on the position. The contractual differences between forwards and futures can lead to pricing differences, but in most cases forward prices and futures prices are very close.

In addition to hedging, forward and futures contracts can be used to synthetically switch a portfolio invested in stocks into bonds. A portfolio invested in Asset A can remain invested in Asset A but earn the returns associated with Asset B, as long as there are forward or futures contracts on A and B. This is called a futures overlay.

The Eurodollar futures contract, based on LIBOR (the London Interbank Offer Rate) is widely used for hedging interest rate risk. Because the Eurodollar futures contract does not represent the price of an asset (at settlement it is $100 - \text{LIBOR}$), it cannot be priced using the formulas in this chapter.

FURTHER READING

Chapter 6 continues our exploration of forward markets by considering commodity forwards, which are different from financial forwards in important ways. Chapter 7 then examines interest rate forwards. Whereas forward contracts provide a price for delivery at one point in time, swaps, discussed in Chapter 8, provide a price for a series of deliveries over time. Swaps are a natural generalization of forward contracts.

The pricing principles discussed in this chapter also will play important roles when we discuss option pricing in Chapters 10, 11, and 12 and financial engineering in Chapter 15.

To get a sense of the range of traded contracts, look at the futures page of the *Wall Street Journal*, and also explore the websites of futures exchanges: the Chicago Board of Trade (**www.cbot.com**), the Chicago Mercantile Exchange (**www.cme.com**), the New York Mercantile Exchange (**www.nymex.com**), and the London International Financial Futures Exchange (**www.liffe.com**), among others. These sites typically provide current prices, along with information about the contracts: What the underlying asset is, how the contracts are settled, and so forth. At this point you may not understand much of the information you see, but you will get a sense of how these markets operate.

It is well accepted that forward prices are determined by the models and considerations in this chapter. Siegel and Siegel (1990) is a standard reference book on futures. Early papers that examined futures pricing include Modest and Sundaresan (1983), Cornell and French (1983), which emphasized tax effects in futures pricing (see Appendix 5.A), and French (1983), which compares forwards and futures when both exist on the same underlying asset. Brennan and Schwartz (1990) explore optimal arbitrage when there are transaction costs. There is a more technical academic literature focusing on the difference between forward and futures contracts, including Black (1976), Cox et al. (1981), Richard and Sundaresan (1981), and Jarrow and Oldfield (1981).

PROBLEMS

5.1. Construct Table 5.1 from the perspective of a seller, providing a descriptive name for each of the transactions.

5.2. A $50 stock pays a $1 dividend every 3 months, with the first dividend coming 3 months from today. The continuously compounded risk-free rate is 6%.

    a. What is the price of a prepaid forward contract that expires 1 year from today, immediately after the fourth-quarter dividend?

    b. What is the price of a forward contract that expires at the same time?

5.3. A $50 stock pays an 8% continuous dividend. The continuously compounded risk-free rate is 6%.

    a. What is the price of a prepaid forward contract that expires 1 year from today?

    b. What is the price of a forward contract that expires at the same time?

5.4. Suppose the stock price is $35 and the continuously compounded interest rate is 5%.

    a. What is the 6-month forward price, assuming dividends are zero?

    b. If the 6-month forward price is $35.50, what is the annualized forward premium?

    c. If the forward price is $35.50, what is the annualized continuous dividend yield?

5.5. Suppose you are market-maker in S&R index forward contracts. The S&R index spot price is 1100, the risk-free rate is 5%, and the dividend yield on the index is 0.

    a. What is the no-arbitrage forward price for delivery in 9 months?

    b. Suppose a customer wishes to enter a short index futures position. If you take the opposite position, demonstrate how you would hedge your resulting long position using the index and borrowing or lending.

    c. Suppose a customer wishes to enter a long index futures position. If you take the opposite position, demonstrate how you would hedge your resulting long position using the index and borrowing or lending.

5.6. Repeat the previous problem, assuming that the dividend yield is 1.5%.

5.7. The S&R index spot price is 1100, the risk-free rate is 5%, and the dividend yield on the index is 0.

    a. Suppose you observe a 6-month forward price of 1135. What arbitrage would you undertake?

b. Suppose you observe a 6-month forward price of 1115. What arbitrage would you undertake?

5.8. The S&R index spot price is 1100, the risk-free rate is 5%, and the continuous dividend yield on the index is 2%.

   a. Suppose you observe a 6-month forward price of 1120. What arbitrage would you undertake?

   b. Suppose you observe a 6-month forward price of 1110. What arbitrage would you undertake?

5.9. Consider the time travel example on p. 132. Can you think of any omissions in the argument? Under what conditions might time travel be technically possible and yet the interest rate would still be positive?

5.10. The S&R index spot price is 1100 and the continuously compounded risk-free rate is 5%. You observe a 9-month forward price of 1129.257.

   a. What dividend yield is implied by this forward price?

   b. Suppose you believe the dividend yield over the next 9 months will be only 0.5%. What arbitrage would you undertake?

   c. Suppose you believe the dividend yield will be 3% over the next 9 months. What arbitrage would you undertake?

5.11. Suppose the S&P 500 index futures price is currently 1200. You wish to purchase four futures contracts on margin.

   a. What is the notional value of your position?

   b. Assuming a 10% initial margin, what is the value of the initial margin?

5.12. Suppose the S&P 500 index is currently 950 and the initial margin is 10%. You wish to enter into 10 S&P 500 futures contracts.

   a. What is the notional value of your position? What is the margin?

   b. Suppose you earn a continuously compounded rate of 6% on your margin balance, your position is marked to market *weekly*, and the maintenance margin is 80% of the initial margin. What is the greatest S&P 500 index futures price 1 week from today at which will you receive a margin call?

5.13. Verify that going long a forward contract and lending the present value of the forward price creates a payoff of one share of stock when

   a. The stock pays no dividends.

   b. The stock pays discrete dividends.

   c. The stock pays continuous dividends.

5.14. Verify that when there are transaction costs, the lower no-arbitrage bound is given by equation (5.11).

5.15. Suppose the S&R index is 800, and that the dividend yield is 0. You are an arbitrageur with a continuously compounded borrowing rate of 5.5% and a continuously compounded lending rate of 5%.

    a. Supposing that there are no transaction fees, show that a cash-and-carry arbitrage is not profitable if the forward price is less than 845.23, and that a reverse cash-and-carry arbitrage is not profitable if the forward price is greater than 841.02.

    b. Now suppose that there is a $1 transaction fee, paid at time 0, for going either long or short the forward contract. Show that the upper and lower no-arbitrage bounds now become 846.29 and 839.97.

    c. Now suppose that in addition to the fee for the forward contract, there is also a $2.40 fee for buying or selling the index. Suppose the contract is settled by delivery of the index, so that this fee is paid only at time 0.

    d. Make the same assumptions as in the previous part, except assume that the contract is cash-settled. This means that it is necessary to pay the stock index transaction fee (but not the forward fee) at both times 0 and 1. What are the new no-arbitrage bounds?

    e. Now suppose that transactions in the index have a fee of 0.3% of the value of the index (this is for both purchases and sales). Transactions in the forward contract still have a fixed fee of $1 per unit of the index at time 0. Suppose the contract is cash-settled so that when you do a cash-and-carry or reverse cash-and-carry you pay the index transaction fee both at time 1 and time 0. What are the new upper and lower no-arbitrage bounds? Compare your answer to that in the previous part. (Hint: To handle the time 1 transaction fee you may want to consider tailing the stock position.)

5.16. Suppose the S&P 500 currently has a level of 875. The continuously compounded return on a 1-year T-bill is 4.75%. You wish to hedge an $800,000 portfolio that has a beta of 1.1 and a correlation of 1.0 with the S&P 500.

    a. What is the 1-year futures price for the S&P 500 assuming no dividends?

    b. How many S&P 500 futures contracts should you short to hedge your portfolio? What return do you expect on the hedged portfolio?

5.17. Suppose you are selecting a futures contract with which to hedge a portfolio. You have a choice of six contracts, each of which has the same variability, but with correlations of $-0.95, -0.75, -0.50, 0, 0.25$, and 0.85. Rank the futures contracts with respect to basis risk, from highest to lowest basis risk.

5.18. Suppose the current exchange rate between Germany and Japan is $0.02\text{€}/\text{¥}$. The euro-denominated annual continuously compounded risk-free rate is 4% and the yen-denominated annual continuously compounded risk-free rate is 1%. What are the 6-month euro/yen and yen/euro forward prices?

5.19. Suppose the spot $/¥ exchange rate is 0.008, the 1-year continuously compounded dollar-denominated rate is 5% and the 1-year continuously compounded yen-denominated rate is 1%. Suppose the 1-year forward exchange rate is 0.0084. Explain precisely the transactions you could use (being careful about currency of denomination) to make money with zero initial investment and no risk. How much do you make per yen? Repeat for a forward exchange rate of 0.0083.

5.20. Suppose we wish to borrow $10 million for 91 days beginning next June, and that the quoted Eurodollar futures price is 93.23.

   a. What 3-month LIBOR rate is implied by this price?

   b. What will we pay to repay the loan?

APPENDIX 5.A: TAXES AND THE FORWARD PRICE

The formulas in this chapter—and in the book to this point—have ignored taxes. In this appendix we show how taxes enter into the theoretical formula for the forward price, and explain why in practice these tax adjustments are never used.

The impact of taxes on derivative prices was studied by Scholes (1976) and Cornell and French (1983), who showed that prices depend upon taxes when capital gains, dividends, and interest are taxed at different rates.[22] However, a party such as a broker-dealer, who is taxed identically on all forms of income, will have a fair price that is independent of taxes.

Suppose that capital gains on a stock are taxed at the rate τ_g, gains on the forward contract at τ_f, dividends at the rate τ_d, and interest at the rate τ_i. Consider an investor who goes long $(1 - \tau_g)/(1 - \tau_f)$ forward contracts (we will see why in a moment) and hedges by selling one share today. The investor thus receives S_0, which can be invested to earn the risk-free rate.

In 1 year, the investor closes the transaction by buying a share and paying the forward price. After-tax income is

$$S_0[1 + r(1 - \tau_i)] - [S_1 - \tau_g(S_1 - S_0)] - Div(1 - \tau_d) + [S_1 - F_{0,1}]\frac{1 - \tau_g}{1 - \tau_f}(1 - \tau_f)$$

$$(5.21)$$

The first bracketed term is the after-tax value of invested short-sale proceeds, the second is the after-tax cost of buying the share to close the short sale, the third is the after-tax dividend that must be paid to the share-lender, and the fourth is the after-tax gain on $(1 - \tau_g)/(1 - \tau_f)$ futures contracts. If the transaction is to generate no-arbitrage profits,

----

[22]Cornell and French (1983) allowed the timing of the taxation of different forms of income to differ. This could give rise to different "effective" rates across sources of income despite the same statutory tax rate. The issue of taxes and pricing is also discussed in Scholes and Wolfson (1992).

the forward price must be set so that equation (5.21) equals zero. Thus, the after-tax zero-profit forward price is[23]

$$F_{0,1} = S_0 \left(1 + r \frac{1 - \tau_i}{1 - \tau_g} \right) - Div \frac{1 - \tau_d}{1 - \tau_g} \tag{5.22}$$

Note that the tax on the forward contract does not enter the expression at all! The reason is that since the forward contract has a zero value, it is possible to offset the tax by entering into additional forward contracts—this is the reason for going long $(1 - \tau_g)/(1 - \tau_f)$ contracts against one short share. We in effect make the forward contract be taxed at the same rate as the stock.

The important insight is that broker-dealers are marked-to-market for tax purposes and face the same tax rate on all forms of income, i.e., $\tau_i = \tau_g = \tau_d$. Thus, equation (5.22) becomes

$$F_{0,1} = S_0 (1 + r) - Div \tag{5.23}$$

the same as equation (5.5).[24]

Appendix 5.B: Equating Forwards and Futures

Because the futures price exceeds the prepaid forward price, marking to market has the effect of magnifying gains and losses. For example, the futures price on a nondividend-paying stock is $F_{0,T} = S_0 e^{rT}$. If the stock price increases by \$1 at time 0, the gain on the futures contract at time T is e^{rT}. Thus, in order to use futures to precisely hedge a position (with the hedge being settled at time T) it is necessary to hold fewer futures than forward contracts, effectively offsetting the extra volatility induced by the future value factor. In the example in Table 5.8, we can go long fewer than eight contracts, to make up for the effect of marking to market.

Table 5.14 shows the effect of this adjustment to the futures position and how it is adjusted over time. Initially, we go long

$$8 \times e^{-0.06 \times 9/52} = 7.91735$$

contracts. This number of contracts has a multiplier of \$250 × 7.91735 = \$1979.34, the multiplier in the first row of the table. Reducing the number of contracts offsets the effect of earning interest. Each week there is less time until expiration, so we increase the number of index units we are long.

....

[23]With continuously compounded interest and dividends, the zero-profit forward price would be

$$F_{0,T} = S_0 e^{[r(1-\tau_i)/(1-\tau_g) - \delta(1-\tau_d)/(1-\tau_g)]T}$$

[24]In addition to assuming the same tax rate on all forms of income, we are also implicitly assuming that taxes on all forms of income are paid on an accrual basis, and that there is no limit on the ability to deduct losses on one form of income against gains on another form of income.

TABLE 5.14	Mark-to-market proceeds and margin balance from long position in the S&P 500 futures contract, where hedge is adjusted on a weekly basis.

Week	Multiplier ($)	Futures Price	Price Change	Margin Balance ($)
0	1979.34	1100.00	—	217,727.21
1	1981.62	1027.99	−72.01	75,446.43
2	1983.91	1037.88	9.89	95,131.79
3	1986.20	1073.23	35.35	165,372.88
4	1988.49	1048.78	−24.45	117,001.17
5	1990.79	1090.32	41.54	199,738.33
6	1993.09	1106.94	16.62	233,055.86
7	1995.39	1110.98	4.04	241,377.01
8	1997.69	1024.74	−86.24	69,573.25
9	2000.00	1007.30	−17.44	34,813.80
10	2000.00	1011.65	4.35	43,553.99

Profit on this position is

$$\$43,553.99 - \$217,727.21e^{0.06 \times 10/52} = -\$176,700$$

which is exactly the same profit as a forward position. The example in Table 5.14 is unrealistic in the sense that the magnitude is too small for the adjustment to be worth the bother. However, it does demonstrate how to scale the position to offset the magnifying effect of marking to market, and the link between the profit on a forward and futures position.

Chapter 6
Commodity Forwards and Futures

Tolstoy observed that all happy families are all alike; each unhappy family is unhappy in its own way. An analogous idea in financial markets might be: Financial forwards are all alike; each commodity forward, however, has some unique economic characteristic that must be understood in order to appreciate forward pricing in that market. In this chapter we will see how commodity forwards and futures differ from, and are similar to, financial forwards and futures.

In our discussion of forward pricing for financial assets we relied heavily on the fact that for financial assets, the price of the asset today is the present value of the asset at time T, less the value of dividends to be received between now and time T. We will explore the extent to which this relationship also is true for commodities.

6.1 INTRODUCTION TO COMMODITY FORWARDS

Chapter 5 introduced the formula for a forward price on a financial asset:

$$F_{0,T} = S_0 e^{(r-\delta)T} \tag{6.1}$$

where S_0 is the spot price of the asset, r is the continuously compounded interest rate, and δ is the dividend yield on the asset. The difference between the forward price and spot price reflects the cost and benefits of delaying payment for, and receipt of, the asset. In Chapter 5 we treated forward and futures prices as the same; we continue to ignore the pricing differences in this chapter.

On any given day, for many commodities there are futures contracts available that expire in a number of different months. The set of prices for different expiration dates for a given commodity is called the **forward curve** or the **forward strip** for that date. Table 6.1 displays futures prices with up to 6 months to maturity for several commodities. Let's consider these prices and try to interpret them using equation (6.1). To provide a reference interest rate, 3-month LIBOR on May 4, 2001, was 4.01%, or about 1% for 3 months. From May to July, the forward price of corn rose from 202.75 to 210. This is a 2-month increase of $210/202.75 - 1 = 3.58\%$, an annual rate of approximately 22%, far in excess of the 4% annual interest rate. There was a similar increase from July to September. In the context of the formula for pricing financial forwards, equation (6.1), we would need to have a continuous dividend yield, δ, of -17.08% in order to explain

TABLE 6.1	Futures prices for various commodities, May 4, 2001. Corn and soybeans are from the CBOT and unleaded gasoline and crude oil from NYMEX.			
Expiration Month	**Corn (cents/bu)**	**Soybeans (cents/bu)**	**Gasoline (cents/gallon)**	**Crude Oil (dollars/barrel)**
May	202.75	444.50	—	—
June	—	—	108.43	28.36
July	210.00	442.25	102.20	28.96
August	—	438.75	96.52	29.15
September	218.00	433.00	90.17	28.96
October	—	—	83.57	28.56
November	—	436.25	79.87	28.19

Source: Futures data from Futures Industry Institute.

this rise in the forward price over time. In that case, we would have

$$F_{\text{July}} = 202.75e^{[0.04-(-0.1708)]\times(1/6)} = 210$$

How do we interpret a negative dividend yield?

Perhaps even more puzzling, given our discussion of financial futures, is the behavior of forward prices for soybeans and gasoline, in which the forward price went down with time to expiration. In May 2001, gasoline was in relatively short supply. We might guess that high prices would lead producers to increase supply and consumers to reduce demand, resulting in a lower expected gasoline price in subsequent months. It appears this expectation was reflected in forward prices. The lower forward price over time makes sense, but how do we square this logic with our discussion of financial forwards?

Finally, notice that from June to July, crude oil behaved similiarly to corn, rising at a monthly rate of 2%, faster than the interest rate. From July to August, oil rose at 0.6%/month; thereafter it fell. Why? And is there any link with forward prices for gasoline, which is refined from crude oil?

Two terms often used by commodity traders are **contango** and **backwardation.** If on a given date the forward curve is upward-sloping, i.e., forward prices more distant in time are higher, then we say the market is in contango. We observe this pattern with corn in Table 6.1. If the forward curve is downward sloping, as with gasoline, we say the market is in backwardation. Forward curves can have portions in backwardation and portions in contango, as does that for crude oil.

It would take an entire book to cover commodities in depth. Our goal here is to understand the *logic* of forward pricing for commodities and where it differs from the logic of financial forward pricing. What is the forward curve telling us about the market for the commodity?

6.2 SYNTHETIC COMMODITIES

Before we analyze particular commodities, we will discuss some interpretations of forward prices that are true for both commodities and financial assets.

Just as we could create a synthetic stock with a stock forward contract and a zero-coupon bond, we can also create a synthetic commodity by combining a forward contract with a zero-coupon bond. Consider the following investment strategy: Enter into a long commodity forward contract at the price $F_{0,T}$ and buy a zero-coupon bond that pays $F_{0,T}$ at time T. Since the forward contract is costless, the cost of this investment strategy at time 0 is just the cost of the bond, or

$$\text{Time 0 cash flow} = e^{-rT} F_{0,T} \tag{6.2}$$

At time T, the strategy pays

$$\underbrace{S_T - F_{0,T}}_{\text{Forward Contract Payoff}} + \underbrace{F_{0,T}}_{\text{Bond Payoff}} = S_T$$

where S_T is the time T price of the commodity. This investment strategy creates a *synthetic commodity*, in that it has the same value as a unit of the commodity at time T. Note that, from equation (6.2), the cost of the synthetic commodity is the prepaid forward price, $e^{-rT} F_{0,T}$.

Valuing a synthetic commodity is easy if we can see the forward price. Suppose, however, that we do not know the forward price. Computing the time 0 value of a unit of the commodity received at time T is a standard problem: You discount the expected commodity price to determine its value today. Let $E_0(S_T)$ denote the expected time-T price as of time 0, and let α denote the appropriate discount rate for a time-T cash flow of S_T. Then the present value is

$$E_0(S_T)e^{-\alpha T} \tag{6.3}$$

The important point is that *expressions (6.2) and (6.3) represent the same value.* Both reflect what you would pay today to receive one unit of the commodity at time T. Equating the two expressions, we have

$$e^{-rT} F_{0,T} = E_0(S_T)e^{-\alpha T} \tag{6.4}$$

Rearranging this equation, we can write the forward price as

$$F_{0,T} = e^{rT} E_0(S_T)e^{-\alpha T} \tag{6.5}$$
$$= E_0(S_T)e^{(r-\alpha)T}$$

Equation (6.5) demonstrates the link between the expected commodity price, $E_0(S_T)$, and the forward price. As with financial forwards (see Chapter 5), the forward price is a biased estimate of the expected spot price, $E_0(S_T)$, with the bias due to the risk premium on the commodity, $\alpha - r$.

Equation 6.4 deserves emphasis: *The time-T forward price discounted at the risk-free rate back to time 0 is the present value of a unit of commodity received at time T.* If we observe a forward price $F_{0,T}$, the present value of the forward price, $e^{-rT} F_{0,T}$, is the value today of a unit of the commodity at time T. This present value calculation is not dependent upon whether or not you actually have a position in the forward contract. This calculation is useful when performing NPV calculations involving commodities for which forward prices are available. Thus, for example, an industrial producer who buys oil can obtain the present value of future oil costs by discounting oil forward prices at the risk-free rate. We will see an example of this calculation later in the chapter.

Equation (6.5) provides a way of understanding the forward price. However, it would be difficult to implement this formula, which requires forecasting the expected future spot price and estimating α. For our purposes, the more important use of this equation is to interpret observed forward prices. That is, we will take forward prices as given, and use equation (6.5) to try to understand the economics of different commodity markets.

To summarize, forward prices for financial assets and commodities are both the expected future spot price, with a correction for the risk premium on the underlying asset. With financial forwards, our focus was on linking the current spot price to the forward price via equation (6.1). With commodities, the link between the spot price and forward price is less obvious. In the rest of this chapter we will discuss various commodities with different economic characteristics to better understand how the forward price is determined and the link between the spot price and the forward price.

6.3 NONSTORABILITY: ELECTRICITY

The forward market for electricity provides an illustration of the pricing principles we have just discussed. Electricity is produced in different ways: From fuels such as coal and natural gas, or from nuclear power, hydroelectric power, wind power, or solar power. Once it is produced, electricity is transmitted over the power grid to consumers of electricity. Electricity has characteristics that distinguish it not only from financial assets, but from other commodities as well. What is special about electricity?

First, electricity is difficult to store, hence it must be consumed when it is produced or else it is wasted.[1] Second, at any point in time the maximum supply of electricity is fixed. You can produce less but not more. Third, demand for electricity varies substantially by season, by day of week, and by time of day.

To illustrate the effects of nonstorability, Table 6.2 displays 1-day ahead hourly prices for 1 megawatt-hour of electricity in New York City. The 1-day ahead forward price is $31.97 at 4 A.M., and $169.52 at 4 P.M. Since you have learned about arbitrage, you are possibly thinking that you would like to buy electricity at the 4 A.M. price and sell it at the 4 P.M. price. However, there is no way to do so. Because electricity cannot be stored, its price is set by demand and supply at a point in time. There is also no way to buy winter electricity and sell it in the summer, so there are seasonal variations as well as intraday variations. Because of peak-load plants that operate only when prices are

---

[1] There are ways to store electricity. For example, it is possible to use excess electricity to pump water uphill and then, at a later time, release it to generate electricity. Storage is uncommon, expensive, and entails losses, however.

TABLE 6.2			Day-ahead price, by hour, for 1 megawatt-hour of electricity in New York City, June 27, 2001.				
Time	**Price**	**Time**	**Price**	**Time**	**Price**	**Time**	**Price**
0000	$42.41	0600	$40.58	1200	$140.52	1800	$128.81
0100	$38.96	0700	$51.26	1300	$140.64	1900	$123.60
0200	$32.58	0800	$62.86	1400	$149.51	2000	$99.91
0300	$33.79	0900	$86.47	1500	$169.51	2100	$76.79
0400	$31.97	1000	$100.88	1600	$169.52	2200	$73.75
0500	$39.04	1100	$123.29	1700	$149.55	2300	$44.30

Source: Bloomberg.

high, power suppliers are able to temporarily increase the supply of electricity. However, expectations about supply are already reflected in the forward price.

Given these characteristics of electricity, what does the electricity forward price represent? The prices in Table 6.2 are best interpreted using equation (6.5). The large price swings over the day primarily reflect changes in the expected spot price, which in turn reflects changes in demand over the day.

Notice two things. First, the swings in Table 6.2 could not occur with financial assets, which are stored. (It is so obvious that financial assets are stored that we usually don't mention it.) As a consequence, the 4 A.M. and 4 P.M. forward prices for a stock will be almost identical. If they were not, it would be possible to engage in arbitrage, buying low at 4 A.M. and selling high at 4 P.M. Second, whereas the forward price for a stock is largely redundant in the sense that it reflects information about the current stock price, interest, and the dividend yield, the forward prices in Table 6.2 provide information we could not otherwise obtain, revealing information about the future price of the commodity. This illustrates the forward market providing **price discovery,** with forward prices revealing information, not otherwise obtainable, about the future price of the commodity.

6.4 PENCIL FORWARDS

Electricity represents the extreme of nonstorability. However, many commodities are storable. To see the effects of storage, we now consider the very simple, hypothetical example of a forward contract for pencils. We use pencils as an example because they are familiar and you will have no preconceptions about how such a forward should work, because it does not exist.

Suppose that pencils cost $0.20 today and for certain will cost $0.20 in 1 year. The economics of this assumption are simple. Pencil manufacturers produce pencils from wood and other inputs. If the price of a pencil is greater than the cost of production, more pencils are produced, driving down the market price. If the price falls, fewer pencils are produced and the price rises. The market price of pencils thus reflects the cost of production. The economist would say that the supply of pencils is *perfectly elastic*.

There is nothing inherently inconsistent about assuming that the pencil price is expected to stay the same. However, before we proceed, note that a constant price would *not* be a reasonable assumption about the price of a nondividend-paying stock. A nondividend-paying stock must be expected to appreciate, or else no one would own it. At the outset, there is an obvious difference between this commodity and a financial asset.

One way to describe this difference between the pencil and the stock is to say that, in equilibrium, stocks and other financial assets must be held by investors, or *stored*. This is why the stock price appreciates on average; appreciation is necessary for investors to willingly store the stock.

The pencil, by contrast, need not be stored. The equilibrium condition for pencils requires that price equals marginal production cost. This distinction between a storage and production equilibrium is a central concept in our discussion of commmodities.[2]

Now suppose that the continuously compounded interest rate is 10%. What is the forward price for a pencil to be delivered in 1 year? Before reading any further, you should stop and decide what you think the answer is. (Really. Please stop and think about it!)

One obvious possible answer to this question, drawing on our discussion of financial forwards, is that the forward price should be the future value of the pencil price: $e^{0.1} \times \$0.20 = \$0.2210$. However, *common sense suggests that this cannot be the correct answer*. You *know* that the pencil price in one year will be \$0.20. If you entered into a forward agreement to buy a pencil for \$0.221, you would feel foolish in a year when the price was only \$0.20.

Common sense also rules out the forward price being less than \$0.20. Consider the forward seller. No one would agree to sell a pencil for a forward price of less than \$0.20, knowing that the price will be \$0.20.

Thus, it seems as if both the buyer and seller perspective lead us to the conclusion that the forward price must be \$0.20.

An Apparent Arbitrage and Resolution

If the forward price is \$0.20, is there an arbitrage opportunity? Suppose you believe that the \$0.20 forward price is too low. Following the logic in Chapter 5, you would want to buy the pencil forward and short-sell a pencil. Table 6.3 depicts the cash flows in

---

[2]You may be thinking that you have pencils in your desk and therefore you do, in fact, store pencils. However, note that you are storing them to save yourself the inconvenience of going to the store each time you need a new one, not because you expect pencils to be a good financial investment akin to stock. When storing pencils for convenience, you will store only a few at a time. Thus, for the moment, suppose that no one stores pencils. We return to the concept of storing for convenience in Section 6.6.

TABLE 6.3	Apparent reverse cash-and-carry arbitrage for a pencil. These calculations *appear* to demonstrate that there is an arbitrage opportunity if the pencil forward price is below $0.221. However, there is a logical error in the table.

	Cash Flows	
Transaction	**Time 0**	**Time 1**
Long Forward @ $0.20	0	$0.20 - F_{0,1}$
Short-Sell Pencil	+$0.20	-$0.20
Lend Short-Sale Proceeds @ 10%	-$0.20	$0.221
Total	0	$0.221 - F_{0,1}$

this reverse cash-and-carry arbitrage. The result seems to show that there is an arbitrage opportunity.

We seem to have reached an impasse. Common sense suggests a forward price of $0.20, but the application in Table 6.3 of our formulas suggests that any forward price less than $0.221 leads to an arbitrage opportunity, where we would make $0.221 - F_{0,1}$ per pencil.

Once again it is time to stop and think before proceeding. Examine Table 6.3 closely; there is a problem.

The arbitrage assumes that you can short-sell a pencil by borrowing it today and returning it in a year. However, recall that pencils cost $0.20 today and will cost $0.20 in a year. Borrowing one pencil and returning one pencil in a year is an interest-free loan of $0.20. *No one will lend you the pencil without charging you an additional fee.*

If you are to short-sell, there must be someone who is (a) holding the asset and (b) willing to give up physical possession for the period of the short-sale. Unlike stock, nobody holds pencils in a brokerage account. It is straightforward to borrow a financial asset and return it later, in the interim paying dividends to the owner. However, if you borrow an unused pencil and return an unused pencil at some later date, the owner of the pencil loses interest for the duration of the pencil loan since the pencil price does not change.

Thus, *the apparent arbitrage in the above table has nothing at all to do with forward contracts on pencils.* If you find someone willing to lend you pencils for a year, you should borrow as many as you can and invest the proceeds in T-bills. You will earn the interest rate and pay nothing to borrow the money.

You might object that pencils do provide a flow of services, namely making marks on paper. However, this service flow requires having physical possession of the pencil and it also uses up the pencil. A stock loaned to a short-seller continues to earn its return; the pencil loaned to the short-seller earns no return for the lender. Consequently, the pencil borrower must make a payment to the lender to compensate the lender for lost time value of money.

Pencils Have a Positive Lease Rate

How do we correct the arbitrage analysis in Table 6.3? We have to recognize that the lender of the pencil has invested $0.20 in the pencil. In order to be kept financially whole, *the lender of a pencil will require us to pay interest.* The pencil therefore has a *lease rate* of 10%, since that is the interest rate. With this change, the corrected reverse cash-and-carry arbitrage is in Table 6.4.

When we correctly account for the lease payment, this transaction no longer earns profits when the forward price is $0.20 or greater. If we turn the arbitrage around, buying the pencil and shorting the forward, the cash-and-carry arbitrage is in Table 6.5. These calculations show that any forward price greater than $0.221 generates arbitrage profits.

Using no-arbitrage arguments, we have ruled out arbitrage for forward prices less than $0.20 (go long the forward and short-sell the pencil) and greater than $0.221 (go short the forward and long the pencil). However, what if the forward price is between $0.20 and $0.221?

TABLE 6.4   Reverse cash-and-carry arbitrage for a pencil. This table demonstrates that there is an arbitrage opportunity if the pencil forward price is below $0.20. It differs from Table 6.3 in properly accounting for lease payments.

	Cash Flows	
Transaction	Time 0	Time 1
Long Forward @ $.20	0	$0.20 - F_{0,1}$
Short-Sell Pencil @ Lease Rate of 10%	+$0.20	−$0.221
Lend Short-Sale Proceeds @ 10%	−$0.20	$0.221
Total	0	$0.20 - F_{0,1}$

TABLE 6.5   Cash-and-carry arbitrage for a pencil, showing that there is an arbitrage opportunity if the forward pencil price exceeds $0.221.

	Cash Flows	
Transaction	Time 0	Time 1
Short Forward @ $.20	0	$F_{0,1} - \$0.20$
Buy Pencil @ $.20	−$0.20	+$0.20
Borrow @ 10%	+$0.20	−$0.221
Total	0	$F_{0,1} - \$0.221$

TABLE 6.6	Cash and carry arbitrage with pencil lending. When the pencil is loaned, interest is earned and the no-arbitrage price is $0.20.

	Cash Flows	
Transaction	**Time 0**	**Time 1**
Short Forward @ $0.20	0	$F_{0,1}$ − $0.20
Buy Pencil @ $0.20	−$0.20	+$0.20
Lend Pencil @ 10%	0	0.021
Borrow @ 10%	+$0.20	−$0.221
Total	0	$F_{0,1}$ − $0.20

If there is an active lending market for pencils, we can narrow the no-arbitrage price even further: We can demonstrate that the forward price *must* be $0.20. The lease rate of a pencil is 10%. Therefore a pencil *lender* can earn 10% by buying the pencil and lending it. The lease payment for a short seller is a dividend for the lender. Imagine that the forward price is $0.21. We would buy a pencil and sell it forward, *and simultaneously lend the pencil*. To see that this strategy is profitable, examine Table 6.6.

Income from lending the pencil provides the missing piece: Any forward price greater than $0.20 now results in arbitrage profits. Since we also have seen that any forward price less than $0.20 results in arbitrage profits, we have pinned down the forward price as $0.20.

Finally, what about equation (6.5), which we claimed holds for all commodities and assets? To apply this equation to the pencil, recognize that the appropriate discount rate, α, for a risk-free pencil is r, the risk-free rate. Hence, we have

$$F_{0,T} = E_0(S_T)e^{(r-\alpha)T} = 0.20 \times e^{(0.10-0.10)} = 0.20$$

Thus, equation (6.5) gives us the correct answer.

The pencil is obviously a special example, but this discussion establishes the important point that in order to understand arbitrage relationships for commodity forwards, we have to think about the cost of borrowing and income from lending an asset. Borrowing and leasing costs also determine the pricing of financial forwards, but the cash flow associated with borrowing and lending financial assets is the dividend yield, which is readily observable. The commodity analogue to dividend income is *lease income*, which may not be directly observable. We now discuss leasing more generally.

6.5 THE COMMODITY LEASE RATE

The discussion of pencil forwards raises the issue of a lease market. How would such a lease market work in general?

The Lease Market for a Commodity

Consider again the perspective of a commodity lender, who in the previous discussion required that we pay interest to borrow the pencil. More generally, here is how a lender will think about a commodity loan:

"If I lend the commodity, I am giving up possession of a unit worth S_0. At time T, I will receive a unit worth S_T. *I am effectively making an investment of S_0 in order to receive the random amount S_T.*"

How would you analyze this investment? Suppose that α is the expected return on a stock that has the same risk as the commodity; α is therefore the appropriate discount rate for the cash flow S_T. The NPV of the investment is

$$\text{NPV} = E_0(S_T)e^{-\alpha T} - S_0 \tag{6.6}$$

Suppose that we expect the commodity price to increase at the rate g, so that

$$E_0(S_T) = S_0 e^{gT}$$

Then from equation (6.6), the NPV of the commodity loan, without payments, is

$$\text{NPV} = S_0 e^{(g-\alpha)T} - S_0 \tag{6.7}$$

If $g < \alpha$, the commodity loan has a negative NPV. However, suppose the lender demands that the borrower return $e^{(\alpha-g)T}$ units of the commodity for each unit borrowed. If one unit is loaned, $e^{(\alpha-g)T}$ units will be returned. This is like a continuous proportional lease payment of $\alpha - g$ to the lender. Thus, the lease rate is the difference between the commodity discount rate and the expected growth rate of the commodity price, or

$$\delta_l = \alpha - g \tag{6.8}$$

With this payment, the NPV of a commodity loan is

$$\text{NPV} = S_0 e^{(\alpha-g)T} e^{(g-\alpha)T} - S_0 = 0 \tag{6.9}$$

Now the commodity loan is a fair deal for the lender. The commodity lender must be compensated by the borrower for the opportunity cost associated with lending. When the future pencil price was certain to be $0.20, the opportunity cost was the risk-free interest rate, 10%.

Note that if S_T were the price of a nondividend-paying stock, its expected rate of appreciation would equal its expected return, so $g = \alpha$ and no payment would be required for the stock loan to be a fair deal.[3] Commodities, however, are produced; as with the pencil, their expected price appreciation need not equal α.

Forward Prices and the Lease Rate

Suppose we have a commodity where there is an active lease market, with the lease rate given by equation (6.8). What is the forward price?

---

[3] As we saw in Chapter 5, for a nondividend-paying stock, the present value of the future stock price is the current stock price.

The key insight, exactly as in the pencil example, is that *the lease payment is a dividend.* If we borrow the asset, we have to pay the lease rate to the lender, exactly as with a dividend-paying stock. If we buy the asset and lend it out, we receive the lease payment. Thus, the formula for the forward price with a lease market is

$$F_{0,T} = S_0 e^{(r-\delta_l)T} \tag{6.10}$$

Tables 6.7 and 6.8 verify that this formula is the no-arbitrage price by performing the cash-and-carry and reverse cash-and-carry arbitrages. In both tables we tail the position in order to offset the lease income.

The striking thing about Tables 6.7 and 6.8 is that on the surface they are *exactly* like Tables 5.6 and 5.7, which depict arbitrage transactions for a dividend-paying stock. In an important sense, however, the two sets of tables are quite different. With the stock, the dividend yield, δ, is an observable characteristic of the stock, reflecting payment received by the owner of the stock *whether or not the stock is loaned.*

With pencils, by contrast, the lease rate, $\delta_l = \alpha - g$, is income earned only if the pencil is loaned. It is not directly observable except if there is a lease market. However,

TABLE 6.7	Cash-and-carry arbitrage with a commodity for which the lease rate is δ_l. The implied no-arbitrage restriction is $F_{0,T} \leq S_0 e^{(r-\delta_l)T}$.

	Cash Flows	
Transaction	Time 0	Time T
Short Forward @ $F_{0,T}$	0	$F_{0,T} - S_T$
Buy $e^{-\delta_l T}$ Commodity Units and Lend @ δ_l	$-S_0 e^{-\delta_l T}$	$+S_T$
Borrow @ r	$+S_0 e^{-\delta_l T}$	$-S_0 e^{(r-\delta_l)T}$
Total	0	$F_{0,T} - S_0 e^{(r-\delta_l)T}$

TABLE 6.8	Reverse cash-and-carry arbitrage with a commodity for which the lease rate is δ_l. The implied no-arbitrage restriction is $F_{0,T} \geq S_0 e^{(r-\delta_l)T}$.

	Cash Flows	
Transaction	Time 0	Time T
Long Forward @ $F_{0,T}$	0	$S_T - F_{0,T}$
Short $e^{-\delta_l T}$ Commodity Units with Lease Rate δ_l	$+S_0 e^{-\delta_l T}$	$-S_T$
Lend @ r	$-S_0 e^{-\delta_l T}$	$+S_0 e^{(r-\delta_l)T}$
Total	0	$S_0 e^{(r-\delta_l)T} - F_{0,T}$

one of the implications of Tables 6.7 and 6.8 is that the lease rate has to be consistent with the forward price. Thus, when we observe the forward price, we can infer what the lease rate would have to be if a lease market existed. Specifically, if the forward price is $F_{0,T}$, the annualized lease rate is

$$\delta_l = r - \frac{1}{T} ln(F_{0,T}/S) \qquad (6.11)$$

If instead we use an effective annual interest rate, r, the effective annual lease rate is

$$\delta_l = \frac{(1+r)}{(F_{0,T}/S)^{1/T}} - 1 \qquad (6.12)$$

The denominator in this expression annualizes the forward premium.

In some markets, consistent and reliable quotes for the spot price are not available, or are not comparable to forward prices. In such cases, the near-term forward price can be used as a proxy for the spot price, S.

As one final point, contango—an upward-sloping forward curve—occurs when the lease rate is less than the risk-free rate. Backwardation—a downward-sloping forward curve—occurs when the lease rate exceeds the risk-free rate.

6.6 CARRY MARKETS

Sometimes it makes sense for a commodity to be stored, at least temporarily. Storage is also called **carry,** and a commodity that is stored is said to be in a **carry market.**

One reason storage occurs is seasonal variation in either supply or demand, which causes a mismatch between the time at which a commodity is produced and the time at which it is consumed. With some agricultural products, for example, supply is seasonal (there is a harvest season) but demand is constant over the year. In this case, storage permits consumption to occur throughout the year.

Storage also can occur when there is a constant rate of production but there are seasonal fluctuations in demand. We will see that with natural gas, for example, there is high demand in the winter and low demand in the summer, but relatively constant production over the year. This pattern of use and production suggests that there will be times when natural gas is stored.

Storage Costs and Forward Prices

Storage is not always feasible (for example, fresh strawberries are perishable) and when technically feasible, storage is almost always costly. When storage is feasible, how do storage costs affect forward pricing? Put yourself in the position of a commodity merchant who owns one unit of the commodity and ask whether you would be willing to store this unit until time T. You face the choice of selling it today, receiving S_0, or selling it at time T. If you elect to sell at time T, you can sell forward (to guarantee the price you will receive), and you will receive $F_{0,T}$. This is a cash-and-carry.

The cash-and-carry logic with storage costs suggests that *you will only store if the present value of selling at time T is at least as great as that of selling today.* Denote the future value of storage costs for one unit of the commodity from time 0 to T as $\lambda(0, T)$. Indifference between selling today and at time T requires

$$\underbrace{S_0}_{\text{Revenue from Selling Today}} = e^{-rT} \underbrace{\left[F_{0,T} - \lambda(0, T) \right]}_{\text{Net Revenue from Selling at Time } T}$$

This relationship in turn implies that if storage is to occur, the forward price is at least

$$F_{0,T} \geq S_0 e^{rT} + \lambda(0, T) \tag{6.13}$$

In the special case where storage costs are paid continuously and are proportional to the value of the commodity, storage cost is like a continuous negative dividend, and we can write the forward price as

$$F_{0,T} = S_0 e^{(r+\lambda)T} \tag{6.14}$$

When there are no storage costs ($\lambda = 0$), equations (6.13) and (6.14) reduce to our familiar forward pricing formula from Chapter 5.

When there are storage costs, the forward price is higher. Why? The selling price must compensate the commodity merchant for both the financial cost of storage (interest) and the physical cost of storage. With storage costs, the forward curve can rise faster than the interest rate. We can view storage costs as a negative dividend in that, instead of receiving cash flow for holding the asset, you have to pay to hold the asset.

Example 6.1 Suppose that the November price of corn is $2.50/bu, the effective monthly interest rate is 1%, and storage costs per bushel are $0.05/month. Assuming that corn is stored from November to February, the February forward price must compensate owners for interest and storage. The future value of storage costs is

$$\$0.05 + (\$0.05 \times 1.01) + (\$0.05 \times 1.01^2) = (\$0.05/.01) \times \left[(1 + 0.01)^3 - 1 \right]$$
$$= \$0.1515$$

Thus, the February forward price will be

$$2.50 \times (1.01)^3 + 0.1515 = 2.7273$$

Problem 6.9 asks you to verify that this is a no-arbitrage price. ⋛

Keep in mind that just because a commodity *can* be stored does not mean that it *should* (or will) be stored. Pencils were not stored because storage was not economically necessary: A constant new supply of pencils was available to meet pencil demand. Thus, equation (6.13) describes the forward price *when storage occurs.* Whether and when a commodity is stored are peculiar to each commodity.

Storage Costs and the Lease Rate

Suppose that there is a carry market for a commodity, so that its forward price is given by equation (6.13). What is the lease rate in this case?

Again put yourself in the shoes of the commodity lender. If you lend the commodity, you are saved from having to pay storage cost. Thus, the lease rate should equal the *negative* of the storage cost. In other words, the lender will pay the borrower! In effect, the commodity borrower is providing "virtual storage" for the commodity lender, who receives back the commodity at a point in the future. The lender making a payment to the borrower generates a negative dividend.

The Convenience Yield

The discussion of commodities to this point has ignored business reasons for holding commodities. For example, suppose you are a food manufacturer for whom corn is an essential input. You will hold an inventory of corn. If you end up holding too much corn, you can sell the excess. However, if you hold too little and run out of corn, you must stop producing, idling workers and machines. Your physical inventory of corn in this case has value—it provides insurance that you can keep producing in case there is a disruption in the supply of corn.

In this situation, corn holdings provide an extra nonmonetary return that is sometimes referred to as the **convenience yield**.[4] You will be willing to store corn with a lower rate of return than if you did not earn the convenience yield. What are the implications of the convenience yield for the forward price?

Suppose that someone approached you to borrow a commodity from which you derived a convenience yield. You would think as follows: "If I lend the commodity, I am bearing interest cost, saving storage cost, and losing the value I derive from having a physical inventory. I was willing to bear the interest cost already; thus, I will pay a commodity borrower storage cost *less the convenience yield*."

Suppose the continuously compounded convenience yield is c, proportional to the value of the commodity. The commodity lender saves $\lambda - c$ by not physically storing the commodity; hence, the commodity borrower pays $\delta = c - \lambda$, compensating the lender for convenience yield less storage cost. Using an argument identical to that in Table 6.8, we conclude that the forward price must be no less than

$$F_{0,T} \geq S_0 e^{(r-\delta)T} = S_0 e^{(r+\lambda-c)T}$$

This is the restriction imposed by a reverse cash-and-carry, in which the arbitrageur borrows the commodity and goes long the forward.

---

[4]The term "convenience yield" is defined differently by different authors. Convenience yield generally means a return to physical ownership of the commodity. In practice it is sometimes used to mean the lease rate. In this book, the lease rate of a commodity can be inferred from the forward price using equation (6.11).

Now consider what happens if you perform a cash-and-carry, buying the commodity and selling it forward. If you are an average investor, you will not earn the convenience yield (it is earned only by those with a business reason to hold the commodity). You could try to lend the commodity, reasoning that the borrower could be a commercial user to whom you would pay storage cost less the convenience yield. But those who earn the convenience yield likely already hold the optimal amount of the commodity. *There may be no way for you to earn the convenience yield when performing a cash-and-carry.* Those who do not earn the convenience yield will not own the commodity.

Thus, *for an average investor*, the cash-and-carry has the cash flows[5]

$$F_{0,T} - S_T + S_T - S_0 e^{(r+\lambda)T} = F_{0,T} - S_0 e^{(r+\lambda)T}$$

This expression implies that the forward price must be below $S_0 e^{(r+\lambda)T}$ if there is to be no cash-and-carry arbitrage.

In summary, from the perspective of an arbitrageur, the price range within which there is no arbitrage is

$$S_0 e^{(r+\lambda-c)T} \le F_{0,T} \le S_0 e^{(r+\lambda)T} \tag{6.15}$$

The convenience yield produces a no-arbitrage *region* rather than a no-arbitrage *price*. The observed lease rate will depend upon both storage costs and convenience. Also, as in Section 5.3, bid-ask spreads and trading costs will further expand the no-arbitrage region in equation (6.15).

As another illustration of convenience yield, consider again the pencil example of Section 6.4. In reality, everyone stores a few pencils in order to be sure to have one available. You can think of this benefit from storage as the convenience yield of a pencil. However, because the supply of pencils is perfectly elastic, the price of pencils is fixed at \$0.20. Convenience yield in this case does not affect the forward price, but it does explain the decision to store pencils.

The difficulty with the convenience yield in practice is that it can be hard to observe. The concept of the convenience yield serves two purposes. First, it explains patterns in storage, for example, why a commercial user might store a commodity when the average investor will not. Second, it provides an additional parameter to better explain the forward curve. You might object that we can invoke the convenience yield to explain *any* forward curve, and therefore the concept of the convenience yield is vacuous. While convenience yield can be tautological, it is a meaningful economic concept and it would be just as arbitrary to assume that there is never convenience. Moreover, the upper bound in equation (6.15) depends on storage costs but not the convenience yield. Thus, the convenience yield only explains anomalously low forward prices, and only when there is storage.

We will now examine particular commodities to illustrate the concepts from the previous sections.

---

[5]In this expression, we assume we tail the holding of the commodity by buying $e^{\lambda T}$ units at time 0, and selling off units of the commodity over time to pay storage costs.

6.7 GOLD FUTURES

Gold is durable, relatively inexpensive to store (compared to its value), widely held, and actively produced through gold mining. Because of transportation costs and purity concerns, gold often trades in certificate form, as a claim to physical gold at a specific location. There are exchange-traded gold futures, specifications for which are in Figure 6.1.

Figure 6.2 is a newspaper listing for the NYMEX gold futures contract. Figure 6.3 graphs the futures prices for all available gold futures contracts—the forward curve—for the first Wednesday in June, from 1997 to 2000. (Newspaper listings for most futures contracts do not show the full set of available expiration dates, so Figure 6.3 is constructed using more expiration dates than are in Figure 6.2.) What is interesting about the gold forward curve is how relatively uninteresting it is, with the forward price steadily increasing with time to maturity.

From our previous discussion, the forward price implies a lease rate. Short-sales and loans of gold are common in the gold market, and gold borrowers in fact have to pay the lease rate. On the lending side, large gold holders (including some central banks) put

---

FIGURE 6.1

Specifications for the NYMEX gold futures contract. Gold is usually denominated in troy ounces (480 grains), which are approximately 9.7% heavier than the more familiar avoirdupois ounce (437.5 grains). Twelve troy ounces make 1 troy pound, which weighs approximately 0.37 kg.

Underlying	Refined gold bearing approved refiner stamp
Where traded	New York Mercantile Exchange
Size	100 troy ounces
Months	Feb, Apr, Aug, Oct, out two years. Jun, Dec, out 5 years
Trading ends	Third-to-last business day of maturity month
Delivery	Any business day of the delivery month

FIGURE 6.2

Listing for the NYMEX gold futures contract from the *Wall Street Journal*, February 5, 2002.

Gold (Cmx.Div.NYM)-100 troy oz.; $ per troy oz.

	OPEN	HIGH	LOW	SETTLE	CHANGE	LIFETIME HIGH	LIFETIME LOW	OPEN INT.
Feb	286.00	290.00	285.40	289.30	+ 3.30	297.50	248.70	1,612
Apr	287.00	290.50	286.00	290.10	+ 3.30	297.50	267.50	67,838
June	286.90	291.20	286.90	290.80	+ 3.30	385.00	264.50	13,134
Aug	287.40	289.80	287.40	291.30	+ 3.30	297.00	272.60	3,400
Dec	288.50	293.30	288.50	292.60	+ 3.30	358.00	268.10	12,587

Est vol 27,000; vol Fri 34,096; open int 119,504, +1,118.

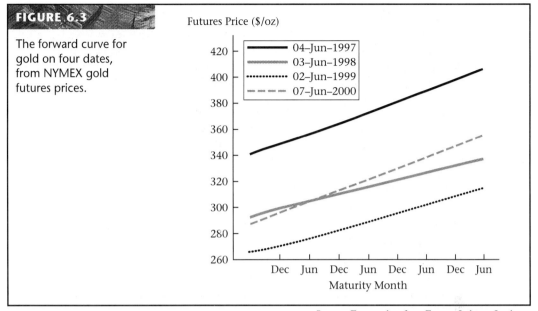

FIGURE 6.3

The forward curve for gold on four dates, from NYMEX gold futures prices.

Futures Price ($/oz)

— 04–Jun–1997
— 03–Jun–1998
········ 02–Jun–1999
– – – – 07–Jun–2000

Maturity Month

Source: Futures data from Futures Industry Institute.

gold on deposit with brokers, in order that it may be loaned to short-sellers. The gold lenders earn the lease rate.

The lease rate for gold, silver, and other commodities is computed in practice using an equation like equation (6.12) and is reported routinely by financial reporting services. Table 6.9 shows the 6-month and 1-year lease rates for the four gold forward curves depicted in Figure 6.3, computed using equation (6.12).

TABLE 6.9   Six-month and 12-month gold lease rates for four dates, computed using equation (6.12). Interest rates are implied by Eurodollar futures prices.

Date	Gold Futures Prices ($)			Lease Rates	
	June	**Dec**	**June**	**6 month**	**1 year**
June 4, 1997	340.9	348.5	356.0	1.45%	1.71%
June 3, 1998	292.7	299.5	304.8	1.07%	1.65%
June 2, 1999	265.9	270.7	276.2	1.68%	1.73%
June 7, 2000	287.2	296.1	304.5	0.78%	1.18%

Source: Futures data from Futures Industry Institute.

Example 6.2 Here are the details of computing the 6-month lease rate for June 2, 1999. Gold futures prices are in Table 6.9. The June and September Eurodollar futures prices on this date were 94.88 and 94.56. Thus, 3-month LIBOR from June to September is $(100 - 94.88)/400 = 1.28\%$, and from September to December is $(100 - 94.56)/400 = 1.36\%$. The June to December interest rate is therefore $(1.0128) \times (1.0136) - 1 = 2.6574\%$. The lease rate is therefore

$$6\text{-month lease rate} = \left(\frac{1.02657}{270.7/265.9}\right)^2 - 1 = 1.6804\%$$

This calculation essentially computes the appreciation of gold from the forward curve, and compares it to the appreciation of a bond. ≋

Gold Investments

Some investors hold gold as part of their investment portofolio. If you wish to hold gold, how should you do it? One possibility is holding physical bars of gold. However, unless you lend the gold, this is an inefficient way to own gold for investment purposes because you do not earn the lease rate. If you do not lend the gold—which is feasible only for large holdings—the positive lease rate implies that it is preferable to hold synthetic gold—created by buying T-bills and going long futures—than to hold physical gold.

We can see why synthetic gold offers a better return than physical gold, held without lending, by comparing two strategies:

1. Buy 1 ounce of gold for S_0 and hold it until time T.

2. Go long one gold forward contract at $F_{0,T}$ and invest $e^{-rT} F_{0,T}$ in zero-coupon bonds.

First, if we simply buy 1 ounce of gold, the cost at time 0 is S_0. At time T, we have one ounce of gold worth S_T.

With the second strategy, we enter into a long gold forward contract and invest the present value of the futures price, $e^{-rT} F_{0,T}$, in zero-coupon bonds. The cost at time 0 is $e^{-rT} F_{0,T} = e^{-\delta T} S_0$. At time T, this strategy pays off

$$e^{rT} (e^{-rT} F_{0,T}) + S_T - F_{0,T} = S_T$$

which is the price of 1 ounce of gold. So we have two strategies that pay S_T at time T, but the first (physical investment) costs S_0, while the second (financial investment) costs $e^{-\delta T} S_0$, which is the price of a prepaid forward on gold. With a positive lease rate, we prefer the financial investment, because *the lease rate is the cost of holding the physical commodity without lending it*. The prepaid forward automatically adjusts for the lease rate.

If we undertake physical investment and lend the gold, then ignoring transaction costs, we should match the return on synthetic gold. Problem 6.5 asks you to verify this.

Some nonfinancial holders of gold will obtain a convenience yield from gold. Consider an electronics manufacturer who uses gold in producing components. Suppose that running out of gold would halt production. It would be natural in this case to hold a buffer stock of gold in order to avoid a stock-out of gold, i.e., running out of gold. For this manufacturer, there *is* a return to holding gold, namely a lower probability of stocking out and halting production. Stocking out would have a real financial cost, and the manufacturer is willing to pay a price—the lease rate—to avoid that cost.

Evaluation of Gold Production

Suppose we have an operating gold mine and we wish to compute the present value of future production. As discussed in Section 6.2, the present value of the commodity received in the future is simply the present value—computed at the risk-free rate—of the forward price. We can use the forward curve for gold to compute the value of an operating gold mine.

Suppose that at times t_i, $i = 1, \ldots, n$, we expect to extract n_{t_i} ounces of gold by paying an extraction cost $x(t_i)$. We have a set of n forward prices, F_{0,t_i}. If the continuously compounded annual risk-free rate from time 0 to t_i is $r(0, t_i)$, the value of the gold mine is

$$\text{PV gold production} = \sum_{i=1}^{n} n_{t_i} \left[F_{0,t_i} - x(t_i) \right] e^{-r(0,t_i)t_i} \qquad (6.16)$$

This equation assumes that the gold mine is certain to operate the entire time and that the quantity of production is known. Only price is uncertain. (We will see in Chapter 17 how the possibility of mine closings due to low prices affects valuation.) Note that in equation (6.16), by computing the present value of the forward price, we compute the prepaid forward price.

Example 6.3 Suppose we have a mining project that will produce 1 ounce of gold every year for 6 years. The cost of this project is $1,100 today, the marginal cost per ounce at the time of extraction is $100, and the continuously compounded interest rate is 6%.

We observe the gold forward prices in the second column of Table 6.10, with implied prepaid forward prices in the third column. Using equation (6.16), we can use these prices to perform the necessary present value calculations.

$$\text{Net present value} = \sum_{i=1}^{6} \left[F_{0,i} - 100 \right] e^{-0.06 \times i} - \$1100 = \$119.56 \qquad (6.17)$$

🦌

6.8 SEASONALITY: THE CORN FORWARD MARKET

Corn in the United States is harvested primarily in the fall, from September through November. The United States is a leading corn producer, generally exporting rather than importing corn. Figure 6.4 shows a newspaper listing for corn futures.

TABLE 6.10	Gold forward and prepaid forward prices on 1 day for gold delivered at 1-year intervals, out to 6 years. The continuously compounded interest rate is 6% and the lease rate is assumed to be a constant 1.5%.

Expiration Year	Forward Price ($)	Prepaid Forward Price ($)
1	313.81	295.53
2	328.25	291.13
3	343.36	286.80
4	359.17	282.53
5	375.70	278.32
6	392.99	274.18

FIGURE 6.4

Listing for the CBOT corn futures contract from the *Wall Street Journal*, February 5, 2002.

	OPEN	HIGH	LOW	SETTLE	CHANGE	LIFETIME HIGH	LIFETIME LOW	OPEN INT.
Corn (CBT) 5,000 bu.; cents per bu.								
Mar	204½	207	204¼	206	+ 1½	270	204¼	231,046
May	211¼	214	211¼	213	+ 1½	266½	211¼	94,496
July	218	220	217¾	219½	+ 1½	279½	210	65,633
Sept	224	226	224	225½	+ 1¼	262	224	21,528
Dec	231½	234½	232½	233¾	+ 1¼	272	232¼	50,689
Mr03	240¼	241¾	240¼	241½	+ 1¼	258½	240	5,531
July	247½	249	247½	248¾	+ 1¼	272	247	2,487
Dec	247¾	248¼	247½	248¼	+ 1	269	246¾	2,360
Est vol 44,500; vol Fri 57,030; open int 473,964, +1,680.								

Given seasonality in production, what should the forward curve for corn look like? Corn is produced at one time of the year, but consumed throughout the year. In order to be consumed when it is not being produced, corn must be stored. Thus, to understand the forward curve for corn we need to recall our discussion of storage and carry markets.

As discussed in Section 6.6, storage is an economic decision in which there is a trade-off between selling today and selling tomorrow. If we can sell corn today for $2/bu and in two months for $2.25/bu, the storage decision entails comparing the price we can get today with the present value of the price we can get in 2 months. In addition to interest, we need to include storage costs in our analysis.

An equilibrium with some current selling and some storage requires that corn prices be expected to rise at the interest rate plus storage costs, which implies that there will be an upward trend in the price between harvests. While corn is being stored, the forward price should behave as in equation (6.14), rising at interest plus storage costs.

Once the harvest begins, storage is no longer necessary; if supply and demand remain constant from year to year, the harvest price will be the same every year. The corn price will fall to that level at harvest, only to begin rising again after the harvest.

The market conditions we have described are graphed in Figure 6.5, which depicts a hypothetical forward curve as seen from time 0. Between harvests, the forward price

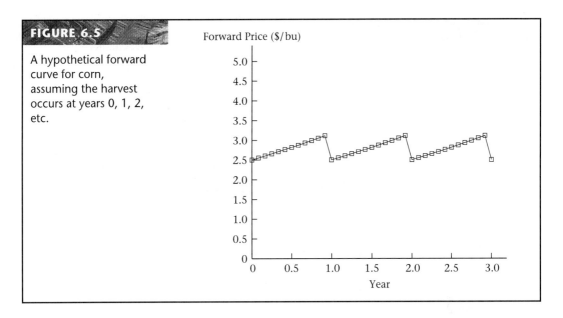

FIGURE 6.5

A hypothetical forward curve for corn, assuming the harvest occurs at years 0, 1, 2, etc.

of corn rises to reward storage, and it falls at each harvest. Let's see how this graph was constructed.

The corn price is \$2.50 initially, the continuously compounded interest rate is 6%, and storage cost is 1.5%/month. The forward price after n months (where $n < 12$) is

$$F_{0,n} = \$2.50 \times e^{(0.005 + 0.015) \times n}$$

Thus, the 12-month forward price is $\$2.50e^{0.06 + 0.18} = \$3.18$. After 1 year, the process starts over.

Farmers will plant in anticipation of receiving the harvest price, which means that it is the harvest price that reflects the cost of producing corn. The price during the rest of the year equals the harvest price plus storage. In general we would expect those storing corn to plan to deplete inventory as harvest approaches and to replenish inventory from the new harvest.

This is a simplified version of reality. Perhaps most important, the supply of corn varies from year to year. When there is a large crop, producers will expect corn to be stored not just over the current year, but into the next year as well. If there is a large harvest, therefore, we might see the forward curve rise continuously until year 2. To better understand the possible behavior of corn, let's look at real corn prices.

Table 6.11 shows the June forward curves for corn over a 10-year period. Some clear patterns are evident. First, notice that from December to March to May (columns 3–5), the futures price rises every year. We would expect there to be storage of corn during this period, with the futures price compensating for storage. A low current price suggests a large supply. Thus, when the near-July price is low, we might also expect storage across the coming harvest. Particularly in the years with the lowest July prices (1993, 1999, and 2000), there is a pronounced rise in price from July to December.

TABLE 6.11				Futures prices for corn (from the Chicago Board of Trade) for the first Wednesday in June, 1991–2000. The last column is the 18-month forward price. Prices are in cents per bushel.				

	Contract Expiration Month							
	Current Year			**Following Year**				
Date	**July**	**Sept**	**Dec**	**Mar**	**May**	**July**	**Sept**	**Dec**
05-Jun-1991	245.75	245.50	246.25	254.25	259.50	264.50	256.00	255.25
03-Jun-1992	262.75	266.00	269.75	276.75	279.25	283.25	267.00	263.50
02-Jun-1993	219.25	223.75	229.75	237.25	242.00	245.75	242.00	240.25
01-Jun-1994	281.00	275.50	268.50	273.75	278.00	278.00	264.50	254.00
07-Jun-1995	265.50	272.25	277.75	282.75	285.25	286.00	269.50	253.50
05-Jun-1996	435.00	373.25	340.75	346.75	350.50	348.00	298.00	286.50
04-Jun-1997	271.25	256.50	254.75	261.00	265.50	269.00	257.00	255.00
03-Jun-1998	238.00	242.25	245.75	253.75	259.00	264.00	261.00	268.00
02-Jun-1999	216.75	222.00	230.75	239.75	244.50	248.25	248.00	251.50
07-Jun-2000	219.75	228.50	234.50	239.25	242.50	248.50	254.50	259.00

Source: Futures data from Futures Industry Institute.

When the price is unusually high (1994 and 1996), there is a drop in price from July to December. Behavior is mixed in the other years.[6] We can also examine the distant–July–December price relationship. In 7 of the 10 years, the distant-December price (column 8) is below the distant July price (column 6). The exceptions occur in years with relatively low current prices (1998, 1999, and 2000). These patterns are generally consistent with storage of corn between harvests, and storage across harvests only occasionally.

Finally, compare prices for the near-July contract (the first column) with those for the distant-December contract (the last column). Near-term prices are quite variable, ranging from 216.75 to 435.00 cents per bushel. In December of the following year, however, prices range only from 240.25 to 286.50. In fact, in 8 of the 10 years, the price is between 251 and 268. The lower variability of distant prices is not surprising: It is difficult to forecast a harvest more than a year into the future. Thus, the forward price is reflecting the market's expectation of a normal harvest 1 year hence.

Although prices in Table 6.11 exhibit variability, if we assume that storage costs are approximately $0.03/month/bushel, the forward price never violates the no-arbitrage

---

[6] It is possible to have low current storage and a large expected harvest, which would cause the December price to be lower than the July price, or high current storage and a poor expected harvest, which would cause the July price to be below the December price.

condition

$$F_{0,T+s} < F_{0,T}e^{rs} + \lambda(T, T + s) \qquad (6.18)$$

which says that the forward price from T to $T + s$ cannot rise faster than interest plus storage costs.

6.9 NATURAL GAS

Natural gas is another market in which seasonality and storage costs are important. The natural gas futures contract, introduced in 1990, has become one of the most heavily traded futures contracts in the United States. The asset underlying one contract is 1 month's worth of gas, delivered at a specific location (different gas contracts call for delivery at different locations). Figure 6.6 shows a newspaper listing for natural gas futures, and Figure 6.7 details the specifications for the Henry Hub contract.

Natural gas has several interesting characteristics. First, gas is costly to transport internationally, so prices and forward curves vary regionally. Second, once a given well has begun production, gas is costly to store. Third, demand for gas in the United States is highly seasonal, with peak demand arising from heating in winter months. Thus, there is a relatively steady stream of production with variable demand, which leads to large and predictable price swings. Whereas corn has seasonal production and relatively constant demand, gas has relatively constant supply and seasonal demand.

Figure 6.8 displays the 3-year strip of gas futures prices for the first Wednesday in June from 1997 to 2000. Seasonality is evident, with high winter prices and low summer prices. The year-2000 strip shows seasonal cycles combined with a downward trend in prices, suggesting that the market considered prices in that year as anomalously high. For the other years, the average price for each coming year is about the same.

FIGURE 6.6

Listing for the NYMEX natural gas futures contract from the *Wall Street Journal*, February 5, 2002.

	OPEN	HIGH	LOW	SETTLE	CHANGE	LIFETIME HIGH	LIFETIME LOW	OPEN INT.
Natural Gas, (NYM) 10,000 MMBtu.; $ per MMBtu's								
Mar	2.110	2.150	2.080	2.117	− .021	5.730	1.960	70,282
Apr	2.175	2.215	2.150	2.184	− .014	4.920	2.060	42,552
May	2.240	2.270	2.220	2.252	− .014	4.775	2.160	32,581
June	2.315	2.330	2.296	2.317	− .014	4.770	2.260	28,497
July	2.370	2.400	2.365	2.377	− .014	4.780	2.320	21,411
Aug	2.425	2.450	2.420	2.432	− .014	4.790	2.380	24,191
Sept	2.420	2.450	2.420	2.432	− .014	4.770	2.375	19,432
Oct	2.450	2.475	2.440	2.459	− .011	4.785	2.410	37,107
Nov	2.675	2.700	2.670	2.679	− .016	4.900	2.630	25,652
Dec	2.890	2.900	2.870	2.879	− .015	5.010	2.720	16,406
Ja03	2.960	2.980	2.960	2.969	− .012	5.049	2.730	21,933
Feb	2.910	2.930	2.910	2.922	− .009	4.874	2.695	14,455
Mar	2.840	2.850	2.830	2.842	− .006	4.710	2.705	12,849
Apr	2.730	2.740	2.730	2.734	+ .005	4.520	2.610	9,032
May	2.750	2.750	2.740	2.744	+ .005	4.490	2.630	6,705
June	2.785	2.800	2.785	2.794	+ .003	4.400	2.610	9,377
July	2.840	2.860	2.829	2.829	+ .003	4.530	2.550	5,696
Aug	2.895	2.895	2.879	2.879	− .002	4.535	2.879	12,031
Sept	2.900	2.900	2.890	2.890	....	4.445	2.890	3,550
Nov	3.100	3.100	3.050	3.069	− .005	4.673	3.050	6,047
Dec	3.250	3.250	3.236	3.236	+ .005	4.820	3.236	7,133
Ja04	3.340	3.340	3.326	3.326	+ .005	4.880	3.300	5,686

Est vol 49,664; vol Fri 53,974; open int 471,875, +3,533.

FIGURE 6.7		
Specifications for the NYMEX Henry Hub natural gas contract.	Underlying	Natural gas delivered at Sabine Pipe Lines Co.'s Henry Hub, Louisiana
	Where traded	New York Mercantile Exchange
	Size	10,000 Million British Thermal Units (MMBtu)
	Months	36 consecutive months
	Trading ends	Third-to-last business day of month prior to maturity month
	Delivery	As uniformly as possible over the delivery month

FIGURE 6.8

Forward curves for natural gas for the first Wednesday in June from 1997 to 2000. Prices are dollars per MMBtu, from NYMEX.

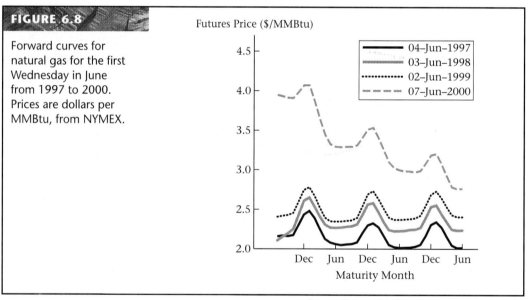

Source: Futures data from Futures Industry Institute.

Gas storage is costly and demand for gas is highest in the winter. The behavior of the forward curve—rising steadily in the fall—suggests that storage occurs just before the heaviest demand. Table 6.12 shows the explicit prices for October through December. The monthly increase in gas prices over these months ranges from $0.08 to $0.18. Assuming the interest rate is about 0.5%/month, using equation (6.13), storage cost in October 1999 would satisfy

$$2.600 = 2.455e^{0.005} + \lambda_{10/99}$$

TABLE 6.12	June natural gas futures prices for October, November, and December in the same year, for 1997 to 2000.		

Date	Oct	Nov	Dec
04-Jun-1997	2.173	2.305	2.435
03-Jun-1998	2.250	2.430	2.610
02-Jun-1999	2.455	2.600	2.745
07-Jun-2000	3.906	3.983	4.070

Source: Futures data from Futures Industry Institute.

and in 2000

$$3.983 = 3.906e^{0.005} + \lambda_{10/00}$$

implying estimated storage costs of $\lambda_{10/99} = \$0.133$ in October 1999 and $\lambda_{10/00} = \$0.057$ in October 2000. Marginal storage costs could vary with the amount of storage used, and it might be that less storage was needed in 2000, with gas evidently in shorter supply.

Because of the expense in transporting gas internationally, the seasonal behavior of the forward curve can vary in different parts of the world. In tropical areas where gas is used for cooking and electricity generation, the forward curve is relatively flat because demand is relatively flat. In the Southern hemisphere, where seasons are reversed from the Northern hemisphere, the forward curve will peak in June and July rather than December and January.

Recent developments in energy markets could alter the behavior of the natural gas forward curve in the United States. Power producers have made greater use of gas-fired peak-load electricity plants. These plants have increased summer demand for natural gas and may permanently alter seasonality.

6.10 OIL

Although both oil and natural gas produce energy and are extracted from wells, the different physical characteristics and uses of oil lead to a very different forward curve. Perhaps most important, oil is easier to transport than gas. Oil takes time to transport, but the price of oil is a worldwide price. Thus, seasonals in the price of crude oil are less pronounced, since demand is high in one hemisphere when it is low in the other. Oil is also easier to store than gas. Specifications for the NYMEX light oil contract are in Figure 6.9. Figure 6.10 shows a newspaper listing for oil futures. The NYMEX forward curve on four dates is plotted in Figure 6.11.

The first thing you are likely to notice about Figure 6.11 is that it is hard to generalize about the shape of the forward curve. On the four dates in the figure, near-term oil prices range from \$15 to \$30, while the 7-year forward price in each case is between \$17 and

FIGURE 6.9

Specifications for the NYMEX light, sweet crude oil contract.

Underlying	Specific domestic crudes delivered at Cushing, Oklahoma
Where traded	New York Mercantile Exchange
Size	1000 U.S. barrels (42,000 gallons)
Months	30 consecutive months plus long-dated futures out 7 years
Trading ends	Third-to-last business day preceding the 25th calendar day of month prior to maturity month
Delivery	As uniformly as possible over the delivery month

FIGURE 6.10

Listing for the NYMEX crude oil futures contract from the *Wall Street Journal*, February 5, 2002.

	OPEN	HIGH	LOW	SETTLE	CHANGE	LIFETIME HIGH	LIFETIME LOW	OPEN INT.
Crude Oil, Light Sweet (NYM) 1,000 bbls.; $ per bbl.								
Mar	20.34	20.36	19.93	20.07	– 0.31	28.00	17.55	121,347
Apr	20.59	20.60	20.24	20.36	– 0.27	27.50	17.95	63,347
May	20.68	20.80	20.40	20.56	– 0.28	27.35	18.20	38,132
June	20.67	20.86	20.60	20.67	– 0.29	27.25	17.35	32,753
July	20.77	20.80	20.60	20.68	– 0.29	26.30	18.75	19,114
Aug	20.90	20.90	20.69	20.69	– 0.29	26.77	18.70	15,316
Sept	20.74	20.80	20.70	20.70	– 0.29	25.50	19.10	16,220
Oct	20.75	20.80	20.60	20.71	– 0.29	26.36	19.50	11,305
Nov	20.76	20.76	20.68	20.72	– 0.29	25.50	19.55	8,906
Dec	20.80	20.92	20.68	20.73	– 0.29	26.95	15.50	31,097
Ja03	20.75	20.75	20.68	20.75	– 0.29	25.75	19.90	14,595
Feb	20.80	20.80	20.75	20.77	– 0.29	24.40	19.70	5,972
Dec	20.90	20.95	20.90	20.95	– 0.31	24.44	15.92	19,705

Est vol 119,158; vol Fri 207,838; open int 459,383, +8,640.

$21. The long-run forward price is considerably less volatile than the short-run forward price, which makes economic sense. In the short run, an increase in demand will cause a price increase since supply is fixed. A supply shock (such as production restrictions by the Organization of Petroleum Exporting Countries [OPEC]) will cause the price to increase. In the long run, however, both supply and demand have time to adjust to price changes with the result that price movements are attenuated. In fact, the high near-term prices in 2000 corresponded to a production decrease by OPEC. The forward curve suggests that market participants in June 2000 did not expect the price to remain at $30/barrel.

6.11 COMMODITY SPREADS

Some commodities are inputs in the creation of other commodities, which gives rise to **commodity spreads.** Soybeans, for example, can be crushed to produce soybean meal and soybean oil (and a small amount of waste). A trader with a position in soybeans and an opposite position in equivalent quantities of soybean meal and soybean oil has a **crush spread** and is said to be "trading the crush."

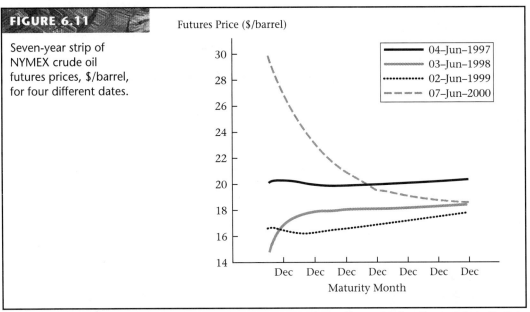

FIGURE 6.11

Seven-year strip of NYMEX crude oil futures prices, $/barrel, for four different dates.

Source: Futures data from Futures Industry Institute.

Similarly, crude oil is refined to make petroleum products, in particular heating oil and gasoline. The refining process entails distillation, which separates crude oil into different components, including gasoline, kerosene, and heating oil. The split of oil into these different components can be complemented by a process known as "cracking"; hence, the difference in price between crude oil and equivalent amounts of heating oil and gasoline is called the **crack spread.**

Oil can be processed in different ways, producing different mixes of outputs. The spread terminology identifies the number of gallons of oil as input, and the number of gallons of gasoline and heating oil as outputs. Traders will speak of "5-3-2," "3-2-1," and "2-1-1" crack spreads. The 5-3-2 spread, for example, reflects the profit from taking 5 gallons of oil as input, and producing 3 gallons of gasoline and 2 gallons of heating oil. A petroleum refiner producing gasoline and heating oil could use a futures crack spread to lock in both the cost of oil and output prices. This strategy would entail going long oil futures and short the appropriate quantities of gasoline and heating oil futures. Of course there are other inputs to production and it is possible to produce other outputs, such as jet fuel, so the crack spread is not a perfect hedge.

Example 6.4 Suppose we consider buying oil in July and selling gasoline and heating oil in August. On June 7, 2000, the July futures price for oil was $29.95/barrel, or $0.71305/gallon (there are 42 gallons/barrel). The August futures prices for unleaded gasoline and heating oil were $0.9713/gallon and $0.7521/gallon. The 3-2-1 crack spread tells us the gross margin we can lock in by buying 3 gallons of oil and producing 2 gallons of gasoline and 1 of heating oil. Using these prices, the spread is

$$(2 \times \$0.9713) + \$0.7521 - (3 \times \$0.71305) = \$0.5555$$

or $\$0.5505/3 = \$0.1852/\text{gallon}$. In this calculation we made no interest adjustment for the different expiration months of the futures contract.   🌿

6.12 COMMODITY HEDGING

Commodity futures and forwards are frequently used to hedge commodity price exposure. There are two issues that arise with commodity hedging (and can also arise when hedging financial assets). First, futures contracts permit you to guarantee a price per unit of the commodity. However, in many cases there is *quantity uncertainty*: The amount to be hedged is uncertain. For example, a farmer growing corn does not know the ultimate yield at the time of planting. How many bushels should a hedging farmer sell forward? The second is *basis risk*: The price of the commodity underlying the futures contract may not be correlated perfectly with the price of the commodity you are hedging. For example, because of transportation cost and time, the price of natural gas in California may differ from that in Louisiana, which is the location underlying the principal natural gas futures contract (see Figure 6.7).

Quantity Uncertainty

In Chapter 4, we saw that Golddiggers could sell forward contracts locking in a price for gold to be produced in the future. We assumed that we knew the amount of gold production, so it was straightforward to sell forward that amount of gold.

Now consider the analogous hedging problem faced by an agricultural producer. Suppose a corn producer wants to take a forward corn position in order to minimize the variability of revenue. Although gold and corn hedging may seem similar, a key difference is that the quantity of corn to be produced is uncertain, depending on factors such as weather and crop disease. It is therefore not obvious how much to sell forward. Moreover, we expect there to be a correlation between quantity and price, because good weather gives rise to bountiful harvests and low prices. This negative correlation between price and quantity is just one possible outcome. We will look at three examples of different relationships between price and quantity: The benchmark case where quantity is certain, an example where quantity and price are negatively correlated, and an example where quantity and price are positively correlated.[7]

---

[7]There are futures contracts intended to mitigate the problem of quantity uncertainty in an agricultural context. Corn yield futures, for example, traded at the Chicago Board of Trade, permit farmers to hedge variations in regional production quantity, and provide an agricultural example of a "quanto" contract. We will discuss quantos further in Chapter 22.

COMMODITY HEDGING ✷ 189

TABLE 6.13   Three scenarios illustrating different correlations between price and quantity for an agricultural producer. Each row is equally likely. In scenario A, there is no quantity uncertainty. In scenario B, quantity is negatively correlated with price, and in scenario C, quantity is positively correlated with price.

	Production Scenario		
Corn Price ($)	A (uncorrelated)	B (negative correlation)	C (positive correlation)
3	1.0m	1.0m	1.5m
3	1.0m	0.6m	0.8m
2	1.0m	1.5m	1.0m
2	1.0m	0.8m	0.6m

In all the examples we will suppose that the corn forward price is $2.50/bu and that there are two equally likely possible prices for corn in one year: $2/bu or $3/bu. In addition, for each corn price there are two equally likely quantities, for a total of four possible price-quantity pairs. Table 6.13 illustrates the three scenarios. Note that in scenario B, average quantity is low when price is high, whereas in scenario C, average quantity is high when price is high.

First, as a benchmark consider scenario A where there is no quantity uncertainty. The analysis of the hedging problem in this case is straightforward because the producer always produces 1m bushels. Let S denote the price in 1 year and Q the quantity. Revenue is SQ. Without hedging, revenue will be either $3m (if the corn price is $3) or $2m (if the corn price is $2).

On the other hand, if the producer sells forward 1m bushels at the forward price $F = 2.50$, revenue is

$$\text{Revenue} = (S \times 1\text{m}) - [1\text{m} \times (S - 2.50)] = 2.5\text{m}$$

We have guaranteed revenue in this case. The calculation is illustrated explicitly in Table 6.14.

TABLE 6.14   When the producer is sure to produce 1m bushels (Scenario A), revenue of $2.5m is assured by selling forward 1m bushels.

		Revenue	
Corn Price	Quantity	Unhedged	Sell Forward 1m bu
3	1.0m	3.0m	2.5m
2	1.0m	2.0m	2.5m

In general, if the producer enters into forward contracts on H units, hedged revenue, $R(H)$, will be

$$\text{Hedged revenue} = R(H) = (S \times Q) + [H \times (S - F)] \tag{6.19}$$

We will want to assess the performance of a given hedging strategy when there is uncertainty. A natural measure is the variability of hedged revenue, $\sigma^2_{R(H)}$. From equation (6.19), this is given by

$$\sigma^2_{R(H)} = \sigma^2_{SQ} + H^2\sigma^2_S + 2H\rho_{SQ,S}\sigma_{SQ}\sigma_S \tag{6.20}$$

Here the standard deviation of total revenue, SQ, is denoted σ_{SQ}, and the correlation of total revenue with price is $\rho_{SQ,S}$. The H that minimizes the variance of hedged revenue will then be

$$H = -\frac{\rho_{SQ,S}\sigma_{SQ}}{\sigma_S} \tag{6.21}$$

This equation should remind you of equation (5.15) in Section 5.5, where we examined hedging a stock with an index futures contract. The formula for the variance-minimizing hedge ratio in equation (6.21) is the negative of the coefficient from a regression of unhedged revenue on price.

We can determine the variance-minimizing hedge ratios for the negative- and positive-correlation scenarios (scenarios B and C) in Table 6.13 either by using equation (6.21) directly, or else we can run a regression of revenue on price.

First, consider what happens if we hedge by shorting the expected quantity of production. As a benchmark, column 3 of Table 6.15 shows that unhedged revenue has variability of $0.654m.

From Table 6.13, expected production in the negative correlation scenario, B, is

$$0.25 \times (1 + 0.6 + 1.5 + 0.8) = 0.975$$

If we short this quantity of corn, column 5 of Table 6.15 shows that there is still variability in hedged revenue. Perhaps more surprising, the variability of total revenue actually *increases*. The reason is that since price decreases when quantity increases, nature already provides a degree of hedging: The increase in quantity partially offsets the decrease in price. Hedging by shorting the full expected quantity actually leaves us overhedged, with a commensurate increase in variability.

The variance-minimizing hedge can be obtained using equation (6.21). By direct calculation, we have $\rho_{SQ,S} = 0.07647$, $\sigma_S = \$0.5$, and $\sigma_{SQ} = \$0.654m$.[8] Thus, we

....

[8]Because Table 6.15 presents the complete population of outcomes, which are equally likely, it is appropriate to use the population estimate of the standard deviation. In Excel, this is *STDEVP* as opposed to *STDEV*. The calculation for σ_{SQ} is obtained as *STDEVP*(3, 1.8, 3, 1.6) = 0.6538.

TABLE 6.15	Results in Scenario B (negative correlation between the price of corn and the quantity of production) from shorting 975,000 corn forwards (columns 4 and 5) and from selling forward 100,000 bushels (columns 6 and 7). Each price-quantity combination is equally likely, with a probability of 0.25. Standard deviations are computed using the population estimate of standard deviation.

Price	Quantity	Unhedged Revenue	Sell Forward 0.975m bu		Sell Forward 0.100m bu	
			Futures Gain	Total	Futures Gain	Total
$3	1.0m	$3.0m	−$0.488m	$2.512m	−$0.050m	$2.95m
$3	0.6m	$1.8m	−$0.488m	$1.312m	−$0.050m	$1.75m
$2	1.5m	$3.0m	$0.488m	$3.488m	$0.050m	$3.05m
$2	0.8m	$1.6m	$0.488m	$2.088m	$0.050m	$1.65m
	σ total revenue	$0.654m		$0.814m		$0.652m

have

$$H = -\frac{0.07647 \times \$0.654m}{\$0.5} = -0.100m$$

Column (7) of Table 6.15 shows that variability is reduced to $0.652m when hedging this amount. The optimal hedge quantity is closer to no hedging than to full hedging. In fact, we gain little by hedging optimally, but we increase the standard deviation of revenue by 25% if we adopt the plausible but incorrect hedging strategy of shorting 975,000 bushels. Problem 6.11 asks you to verify that you obtain the same answer by running a regression of revenue on price.

You might guess by now that when correlation is positive, the optimal hedge quantity exceeds expected quantity. The fact that quantity goes up when price goes up makes revenue that much more variable than when price alone varies, and a correspondingly larger hedge position is required. Problem 6.13 asks you to compute the optimal hedge in scenario C. The answer is to short almost 2 million bushels even though production is never that large.

Basis Risk

Exchange-traded commodity futures contracts call for delivery of the underlying commodity at specific locations and specific dates. The actual commodity to be bought or sold may reside at a different location and the desired delivery date may not match that of the futures contract. Additionally the *grade* of the deliverable under the futures contract may not match the grade that is being delivered.

This general problem of the futures or forward contract not representing exactly what is being hedged is called *basis risk*. Basis risk is a generic problem with commodities because of storage and transportation costs and quality differences. Basis risk can also arise with financial futures, as for example when a company hedges its own borrowing cost with the Eurodollar contract.

Section 5.5 demonstrated how an individual stock could be hedged with an index futures contract. We saw that if we regressed the individual stock return on the index return, the resulting regression coefficient provided a hedge ratio that minimized the variance of the hedged position.

In the same way, suppose we wish to hedge oil delivered on the East Coast with the NYMEX oil contract, which calls for delivery of oil in Cushing, Oklahoma. The variance-minimizing hedge ratio would be the regression coefficient obtained by regressing the East Coast price on the Cushing price. Problems with this regression are that the relationship may not be stable over time or may be estimated imprecisely.

Another example of basis risk occurs when hedgers decide to hedge distant obligations with near-term futures. For example, an oil producer might have an obligation to deliver 10,000 barrels/month at a fixed price for a year. The natural way to hedge this obligation would be to buy 10,000 barrels per month, locking in the price and supply on a month-by-month basis. This is called a **strip hedge.** We engage in a strip hedge when we hedge a stream of obligations by offsetting each individual obligation with a futures contract matching the maturity and quantity of the obligation. For the oil producer obligated to deliver every month at a fixed price, the hedge would entail buying the appropriate quantity each month, in effect taking a long position in the strip.

An alternative to a strip hedge is a **stack hedge.** With a stack hedge, we enter into futures contracts with a *single* maturity, with the number of contracts selected so that changes in the *present value* of the future obligations are offset by changes in the value of this "stack" of futures contracts. In the context of the oil producer with a monthly delivery obligation, a stack hedge would entail going long 1.2m barrels using the near-term contract. (Actually, we would want to tail the position and short less than 1.2m barrels, but we will ignore this.) When the near-term contract matures, we reestablish the stack hedge by going long contracts in the new near month. This process of stacking futures contracts in the near-term contract and rolling over into the new near-term contract is called a **stack and roll.** If the new near-term futures price is below the expiring near-term price (i.e., there is backwardation), rolling is profitable.

Why would anyone use a stack hedge? There are at least two reasons. First, there is often more trading volume and liquidity in near-term contracts. With many commodities, bid-ask spreads widen with maturity. Thus, a stack hedge may have lower transaction costs than a strip hedge. Second, the manager may wish to speculate on the shape of the forward curve. For example, consider the June 3, 1998, forward curve in Figure 6.11. You might decide that the forward curve looks unusually steep in the early months. If you undertake a stack hedge and the forward curve then flattens, you will have locked in all your oil at the relatively cheap near-term price, and implicitly made gains from not having locked in the relatively high strip prices.

TABLE 6.16	One-year forward strip for crude oil on June 3, 1998, and June 22, 1998. The average June 3 strip price is $16.62, while the average June 22 strip price is $15.56.					

Date	Jul	Aug	Sep	Oct	Nov	Dec
Jun 3, 1998	14.81	15.43	15.88	16.26	16.57	16.81
Jun 22, 1998	13.43	13.65	14.38	14.99	15.45	15.80
	Jan	Feb	Mar	Apr	May	Jun
Jun 3, 1998	17.00	17.13	17.24	17.34	17.43	17.51
Jun 22, 1998	16.08	16.30	16.46	16.60	16.74	16.88

Source: Futures data from Futures Industry Institute.

Table 6.16 shows monthly prices in the 1-year forward strips on June 3, 1998, and June 22, 1998, which is the last trading day for the June contract. Suppose an oil marketer had an agreement to deliver oil monthly at a price of $17/barrel. The average monthly price on June 3 is $16.62/barrel. Thus, the marketer has locked in a profit of $0.38/barrel relative to the strip.[9]

Now let's look at a stack hedge. The June futures price is $14.81, which is $2.19 below the contract price of $17/barrel. Why not enter into 12 long June contracts per barrel to be delivered? If the curve gets less steep, we will have locked in the low price plus any additional gain from the reduction in steepness.

Look at the actual prices on June 22 in Table 6.16. The curve is less steep in the early months *but steeper in the later months*. In fact, it is straightforward to calculate that the strip hedge (short one barrel each month) loses $12.65, compared to a loss of $16.56 for the stack hedge (short 12 July barrels). If we were to mark the position to market on June 22, whatever the change in the price of the delivery agreement, we would have lost about $4 more per barrel/year for the stack hedge than the strip hedge. The delivery agreement probably would have dropped in price about $1 per barrel (reflecting the change in the average price). Hence we would have been hedged with the strip, but would have lost all our profits with the stack hedge.

In addition, because the new near-term futures price (August) on June 22 exceeded the old near-term futures price (July), the process of rolling would be costly.

The box on page 194 recounts the story of Metallgesellschaft A. G. (MG), in which MG's large losses on a hedged position might have been caused, at least in part, by the use of a stock hedge.

---

[9]You will note that we are ignoring interest in these calculations. This is for simplicity. Taking account of interest would not change the point of the example.

Metallgesellschaft A. G.

In 1992, a U.S. subsidiary of the German industrial firm Metallgesellschaft A. G. (MG) had a position much like that described in the text on page 193. It had offered customers fixed prices on over 150 million barrels of petroleum products, including gasoline, heating oil, and diesel fuel, over periods as long as 10 years. To hedge the resulting short exposure, MG entered into futures and swaps.

Much of MG's hedging was done using short-dated NYMEX crude oil and heating oil futures. Thus, MG was using stack hedging, rolling over the hedge each month.

During much of 1993, the near-term oil market was in contango (the forward curve was upward sloping). As a result of the market remaining in contango, MG systematically lost money when rolling its hedges and had to meet substantial margin calls. In December 1993, the supervisory board of MG decided to liquidate both its supply contracts and the futures positions used to hedge those contracts. In the end, MG sustained losses estimated at between $200m and $1.3b.

The MG case was extremely complicated and has been the subject of pointed exchanges among academics—see in particular Culp and Miller (1995), Edwards and Canter (1995), and Mello and Parsons (1995). While the case is complicated, several issues stand out. First, was the stack-and-roll a reasonable strategy for MG to have undertaken? Second, should the position have been liquidated when it was and in the manner it was liquidated (as it turned out, oil prices increased—which would have worked in MG's favor—following the liquidation). Third, did MG encounter liquidity problems from having to finance losses on its hedging strategy? While the MG case has receded into history, hedgers still confront the issues raised by this case.

CHAPTER SUMMARY

At a general level, commodity forward prices can be described by the same formula as financial forward prices:

$$F_{0,T} = S_0 e^{(r-\delta)T} \tag{6.22}$$

For financial assets, δ is the dividend yield. For commodities, δ is the commodity *lease rate*. The lease rate is the return that makes an investor willing to buy and then lend a commodity. Thus, for the commodity owner who lends the commodity, it is like a dividend. From the commodity borrower's perspective, it is the cost of borrowing the commodity. As with financial forwards, commodity forward prices are biased predictors of the future spot price when the commodity return contains a risk premium.

While the dividend yield for a financial asset can typically be observed directly, the lease rate for a commodity can typically be estimated *only by observing the forward price*. The forward curve provides important information about the commodity.

Commodities are complex because every commodity market differs in the details. Forward curves for different commodities reflect different properties of storability, storage costs, production, and demand. Electricity, gold, corn, natural gas, and oil all have distinct forward curves, reflecting the different characteristics of their physical markets. These idiosyncracies will be reflected in the commodity lease rate. When there are seasonalities in either the demand or supply of a commodity, the commodity will be stored (assuming this is physically feasible), and the forward curve for the commodity will reflect storage costs. Some holders of a commodity receive benefits from physical ownership. This benefit is called the commodity's *convenience yield*. The convenience yield creates different returns to ownership for different investors, and may or may not be reflected in the forward price. The convenience yield can lead to no-arbitrage regions rather than a no-arbitrage price. It can also be costly to short-sell commodities with a significant convenience yield.

In some contexts there is uncertainty about the quantity of a commodity to be hedged. In this case, the variance-minimizing futures position requires taking into account the correlation between price and quantity. A naive hedge—for example, shorting one futures contract against each unit of expected output—may increase, rather than decrease, the variability of revenue.

FURTHER READING

We will see in later chapters that the concept of a lease rate—which is a generalization of a dividend yield—helps to unify the pricing of swaps (Chapter 8), options (Chapter 10), and commodity-linked notes (Chapter 15). One particularly interesting application of the lease rate arises in the discussion of real options in Chapter 17. We will see there that if an extractable commodity (such as oil or gold) has a zero lease rate, it will never be extracted. Thus, the lease rate is linked in an important way with production decisions.

A useful resource for learning more about commodities is Chicago Board of Trade (1998). The websites of the various exchanges (e.g., NYMEX and the CBOT) are also useful resources, with information about particular commodities and trading and hedging strategies.

Siegel and Siegel (1990) provides a detailed discussion of many commodity futures. There are numerous papers on commodities. Brennan (1991), Pindyck (1993b), and Pindyck (1994) examine the behavior of commodity prices. Schwartz (1997) compares the performance of different models of commodity price behavior. Jarrow and Oldfield (1981) discuss the effect of storage costs on pricing, and Routledge et al. (2000) present a theoretical model of commodity forward curves.

Finally, Metallgesellschaft engendered a spirited debate. Papers written about that episode include Culp and Miller (1995), Edwards and Canter (1996), and Mello and Parsons (1995).

PROBLEMS

6.1. The spot price of a widget is $70.00 per unit. Forward prices for 3, 6, 9, and 12 months are $70.70, $71.41, $72.13, and $72.86. Assuming a 5% continuously compounded annual risk-free rate, what are the annualized lease rates for each maturity? Is this an example of contango or backwardation?

6.2. The current price of oil is $32.00 per barrel. Forward prices for 3, 6, 9, and 12 months are $31.37, $30.75, $30.14, and $29.54. Assuming a 2% continuously compounded annual risk-free rate, what is the annualized lease rate for each maturity? Is this an example of contango or backwardation?

6.3. Given a continuously compounded risk-free rate of 3% annually, at what lease rate will forward prices equal the current commodity price? (Recall the pencil example in Section 6.4.) If the lease rate were 3.5%, would there be contango or backwardation?

6.4. Suppose that pencils cost $0.20 today and the continuously compounded lease rate for pencils is 5%. The continuously compounded interest rate is 10%. The pencil price in 1 year is uncertain and pencils can be stored costlessly.

    a. If you short-sell a pencil for 1 year, what payment do you have to make to the pencil lender? Would it make sense for a financial investor to store pencils in equilibrium?

    b. Show that the equilibrium forward price is $0.2103.

    c. Explain what ranges of forward prices are ruled out by arbitrage in the four cases where pencils can and cannot be short-sold and can and cannot be loaned.

6.5. Suppose the gold spot price is $300/oz., the 1-year forward price is 310.686, and the continuously compounded risk-free rate is 5%.

    a. What is the lease rate?

    b. What is the return on a cash-and-carry in which gold is not loaned?

    c. What is the return on a cash-and-carry in which gold is loaned, earning the lease rate?

For the next three problems, assume that the continuously compounded interest rate is 6% and the storage cost of widgets is $0.03 quarterly (payable at the end of the quarter). Here is the forward price curve for widgets:

2001	2002				2003	
Dec	**Mar**	**Jun**	**Sep**	**Dec**	**Mar**	**Jun**
3.000	3.075	3.152	2.750	2.822	2.894	2.968

6.6.   **a.** What are some possible explanations for the shape of this forward curve?

    b. What annualized rate of return do you earn on a cash-and-carry entered into in December 2001 and closed in March 2002? Is your answer sensible?

c. What annualized rate of return do you earn on a cash-and-carry entered into in December 2001 and closed in September 2002? Is your answer sensible?

6.7. a. Suppose that you want to borrow a widget beginning in December 2001 and ending in March 2002. What payment will be required to make the transaction fair to both parties?

b. Suppose that you want to borrow a widget beginning in December 2001 and ending in September 2002. What payment will be required to make the transaction fair to both parties?

6.8. a. Suppose the March 2002 forward price were $3.10. Describe two different transactions you could use to undertake arbitrage.

b. Suppose the September 2002 forward price fell to $2.70 and subsequent forward prices fell in such a way that there is no arbitrage from September 2002 and going forward. Is there an arbitrage you could undertake using forward contracts from June 2002 and earlier? Why or why not?

6.9. Consider Example 6.1. Suppose the February forward price had been $2.80. What would the arbitrage be? Suppose it had been $2.65. What would the arbitrage be? In each case, specify the transactions and resulting cash flows in both November and February. What are you assuming about the convenience yield?

6.10. Using Table 6.10, what is your best guess about the current price of gold per ounce?

6.11. Using the information in Table 6.15, verify that a regression of revenue on price gives a regression slope coefficient of about 100,000.

6.12. Using the information in Table 6.13 about Scenario C:

a. Compute $\sigma_{\text{total revenue}}$ when correlation between price and quantity is positive.

b. What is the correlation between price and revenue?

6.13. Using the information in Table 6.13 about Scenario C:

a. Using your answer to the previous question, use equation (6.21) to compute the variance-minimizing hedge ratio.

b. Run a regression of revenue on price to compute the variance-minimizing hedge ratio.

c. What is the variability of optimally hedged revenue?

6.14. Using the information in Table 6.13 about Scenario C:

a. What is the expected quantity of production?

b. Suppose you short the expected quantity of corn. What is the standard deviation of hedged revenue?

6.15. Suppose that price and quantity are positively correlated as in this table:

Price	Quantity	Revenue
$2	0.6m bu	$1.2m
$3	0.934m bu	$2.8m

There is a 50% chance of either price. The futures price is $2.50. Demonstrate the effect of hedging if we

a. Short the expected quantity.

b. Short the minimum quantity.

c. Short the maximum quantity.

d. What is the hedge position that eliminates variability in revenue? Why?

6.16. Suppose you know nothing about widgets. You are going to approach a widget merchant to borrow one in order to short-sell it. (That is, you will take physical possession of the widget, sell it, and return a widget at time T.) Before you ring the doorbell, you want to make a judgment about what you think is a reasonable lease rate for the widget. Think about the following possible scenarios.

a. Suppose that widgets do not deteriorate over time, are costless to store, and are always produced, although production quantity can be varied. Demand is constant over time. Knowing nothing else, what lease rate might you face?

b. Suppose everything is the same as in part a except that demand for widgets varies seasonally.

c. Suppose everything is the same as in part a except that demand for widgets varies seasonally and the rate of production cannot be adjusted. Consider how seasonality and the horizon of your short-sale interact with the lease rate.

d. Suppose everything is the same as in part a except that demand is constant over time and production is seasonal. Consider how production seasonality and the horizon of your short-sale interact with the lease rate.

e. Suppose that widgets cannot be stored. How does this affect your answers to the previous questions?

Chapter 7
Interest Rate Forwards and Futures

Suppose you have the opportunity to spend $1 one year from today to receive $2 two years from today. What is the value of this opportunity? To answer this question, you need to know the appropriate interest rates for discounting the two cash flows. This comparison is an example of the most basic concept in finance: using interest rates to compute present values. Once we find a present value for one or more assets, we can compare the cash flows from those assets even if the cash inflows and cash outflows occur at different times. In order to perform these calculations, we need information about the set of interest rates prevailing between different points in time.

We begin the chapter by reviewing basic bond concepts—coupon bonds, yields to maturity, and implied forward rates. Any reader of this book should understand these basic concepts. We then look at interest rate forwards and forward rate agreements, which permit hedging interest rate risk. Finally, we look at bond futures and the repo market.

7.1 BOND BASICS

Table 7.1 presents information about current interest rates for bonds maturing in from 1 to 3 years. *Identical information is presented in five different ways in the table.* Although the information appears differently across columns, it is possible to take the information in any one column of Table 7.1 and reproduce the other four columns.[1]

To see how similar information is presented in practice, Figure 7.1 displays a newspaper listing of U.S. government bond prices. The U.S. government issues Treasury bills, notes, and bonds. At the time of issue, bills have less than 1 year to maturity and make no coupon payments. Consequently, they are issued at a discount—their price is below their maturity value. Notes and bonds both pay coupons and are issued at a price equal to their maturity value (i.e., they are issued at par). Notes have less than 10 years to maturity, and bonds have been issued with maturities out to 30 years, although in 2001 the Treasury announced that it would stop issuing bonds with a maturity exceeding 10 years. The distinctions between bills and notes and bonds are not important for our

---

[1]Depending upon how you do the computation, you may arrive at numbers slightly different from those in Table 7.1. The reason is that all of the entries except those in column 1 are rounded in the last digit, and there are multiple ways to compute the number in any given column. Rounding error will therefore generate small differences among computations performed in different ways.

	(1)	(2)	(3)	(4)	(5)
					Continuously Compounded
	Zero-Coupon	**Zero-Coupon**	**One-Year Implied**	**Par**	
Maturity	**Bond Yield**	**Bond Price**	**Forward Rate**	**Coupon**	**Zero Yield**
1	6.00%	0.943396	6.00000%	6.00000%	5.82689%
2	6.50	0.881659	7.00236	6.48423	6.29748
3	7.00	0.816298	8.00705	6.95485	6.76586

TABLE 7.1 Five ways to present equivalent information about default-free interest rates. All rates but those in the the last column are effective annual rates.

purposes; when it is convenient, we will refer to both bills and notes as bonds. Both a price per $100 of maturity value and a yield to maturity are reported for bonds. We will not cover in detail the conventions for reporting this information. Obviously, there is a great deal of information about interest rates for different maturities.

In addition to government bond information, there is also a listing for STRIPS. A **STRIPS**—Separate Trading of Registered Interest and Principal of Securities—is a claim to a single interest payment or the principal portion of a government bond. These claims trade separately from the bond. STRIPS are zero-coupon bonds since they make only a single payment at maturity. "STRIPS" should not be confused with the forward strip, which is the set of forward prices available at a point in time.

We need a way to represent bond prices and interest rates. Interest rate notation is, unfortunately and inevitably, cumbersome, because for any rate we must keep track of three dates: First, the date on which the rate is quoted, and second, the period of time (this has beginning and ending dates) over which the rate prevails. We will let $r_t(t_1, t_2)$ represent the interest rate from time t_1 to time t_2, prevailing on date t. If the interest rate is current, i.e., if $t = t_1$, and if there is no risk of confusion, we will drop the subscript.

Zero-Coupon Bonds

We begin by showing that the zero-coupon bond yield and zero-coupon bond price, columns (1) and (2) in Table 7.1, provide the same information. A **zero-coupon bond** is a bond that makes only a single payment at its maturity date. Our notation for zero-coupon bond prices will mimic that for interest rates. The price of a bond quoted at time t_0, with the bond to be purchased at t_1 and maturing at t_2, is $P_{t_0}(t_1, t_2)$. As with interest rates, we will drop the subscript when $t_0 = t_1$.

The 1-year zero-coupon bond price of $P(0, 1) = 0.943396$ means that you would pay $0.943396 today to receive $1 in 1 year. You could also pay $P(0, 2) = 0.881659$ today to receive $1 in 2 years and $P(0, 3) = 0.816298$ to receive $1 in 3 years.

FIGURE 7.1

Government bond listing from the *Wall Street Journal*, February 5, 2002.

TREASURY BONDS, NOTES & BILLS

Monday, February 4, 2002

Representative Over-the-Counter quotation based on transactions of $1 million or more.

Treasury bond, note and bill quotes are as of mid-afternoon. Colons in bid-and-asked quotes represent 32nds; 101:01 means 101 1/32. Net changes in 32nds. n-Treasury note. i-Inflation-Indexed issue. Treasury bill quotes in hundredths, quoted on terms of a rate of discount. Days to maturity calculated from settlement date. All yields are to maturity and based on the asked quote. Latest 13-week and 26-week bills are boldfaced. For bonds callable prior to maturity, yields are computed to the earliest call date for issues quoted above par and to the maturity date for issues below par. *-When issued.

Source: eSpeed/Cantor Fitzgerald

U.S. Treasury strips as of 3 p.m. Eastern time, also based on transactions of $1 million or more. Colons in bid-and-asked quotes represent 32nds; 99:01 means 99 1/32. Net changes in 32nds. Yields calculated on the asked quotation. ci-stripped coupon interest. bp-Treasury bond, stripped principal. np-Treasury note, stripped principal. For bonds callable prior to maturity, yields are computed to the earliest call date for issues quoted above par and to the maturity date for issues below par.

Source: Bear, Stearns & Co. via Street Software Technology Inc.

GOVT. BOND & NOTES

RATE	MATURITY MO/YR	BID	ASKED	CHG.	ASKED YLD.
14¼	Feb 02	100:10	100:11	− 2	1.75
6¼	Feb 02n	100:08	100:09	− 1	1.53
6½	Feb 02n	100:09	100:10	....	1.29
6½	Mar 02n	100:22	100:23	....	1.61
6⅝	Mar 02n	100:22	100:23	− 1	1.62
6⅜	Apr 02n	101:01	101:02	− 1	1.68
6⅝	Apr 02n	101:03	101:04	− 1	1.73
7½	May 02n	101:17	101:18	− 1	1.67
6½	May 02n	101:15	101:16	....	1.66
6⅝	May 02n	101:16	101:17	− 1	1.73
6¼	Jun 02n	101:25	101:26	....	1.68
6⅜	Jun 02n	101:26	101:27	....	1.73
3⅝	Jul 02i	101:00	101:01	+ 1	1.28
6	Jul 02n	102:01	102:02	....	1.72
6¼	Jul 02n	102:04	102:05	....	1.78
6⅜	Aug 02n	102:11	102:12	....	1.83
6⅛	Aug 02n	102:11	102:12	+ 1	1.87
6¼	Aug 02n	102:13	102:14	....	1.85
5⅞	Sep 02n	102:17	102:18	....	1.88
6	Sep 02n	102:19	102:20	....	1.88
5¾	Oct 02n	102:23	102:24	+ 1	1.94
11⅝	Nov 02	107:11	107:12	+ 1	1.96
5⅝	Nov 02n	102:27	102:28	....	2.03
5¾	Nov 02n	102:30	102:31	....	2.04
5⅛	Dec 02n	102:21	102:22	+ 1	2.09
5⅝	Dec 02n	103:03	103:04	+ 1	2.10
4¾	Jan 03n	102:16	102:17	+ 1	2.14
5½	Jan 03n	103:07	103:08	+ 1	2.15
6¼	Feb 03n	104:02	104:03	+ 2	2.18
10¾	Feb 03	108:19	108:20	+ 1	2.20
4⅝	Feb 03n	102:16	102:17	+ 2	2.19
5½	Feb 03n	103:13	103:14	+ 1	2.20
4¼	Mar 03n	102:06	102:07	+ 2	2.27
5½	Mar 03n	103:19	103:20	+ 2	2.27
4	Apr 03n	102:00	102:01	+ 3	2.32
5¾	Apr 03n	104:03	104:04	+ 3	2.33
10¾	May 03	110:12	110:13	+ 1	2.39
4¼	May 03n	102:11	102:12	+ 3	2.40
5½	May 03n	104:00	104:00	+ 2	2.39
3⅞	Jun 03n	101:29	101:30	+ 4	2.46
5⅜	Jun 03n	104:00	104:00	+ 3	2.44
3⅞	Jul 03n	101:29	101:30	+ 4	2.54
5¼	Aug 03n	103:30	103:31	+ 3	2.57
5¾	Aug 03n	104:22	104:23	+ 4	2.57
11⅛	Aug 03	112:20	112:21	+ 3	2.61
3⅝	Aug 03n	101:16	101:17	+ 4	2.61
2¾	Sep 03n	100:02	100:03	+ 4	2.68
2¾	Oct 03n	100:00	100:00	+ 5	2.75
4¼	Nov 03n	102:16	102:17	+ 5	2.77
11⅞	Nov 03	115:19	115:20	+ 5	2.77
3	Nov 03n	100:08	100:09	+ 5	2.83
3¼	Dec 03n	100:20	100:21	+ 6	2.89
3	**Jan 04n**	**100:01**	**100:02**	**+ 6**	**2.97**
4¾	Feb 04n	103:14	103:15	+ 6	2.97
5⅞	Feb 04n	105:19	105:20	+ 6	2.99
5¼	May 04n	104:19	104:20	+ 6	3.12
7¼	May 04n	108:27	108:28	+ 6	3.16
12⅜	May 04	120:01	120:02	+ 7	3.16
6	Aug 04n	106:14	106:15	+ 7	3.30
7¼	Aug 04n	109:13	109:14	+ 7	3.32
13¾	Aug 04	125:00	125:00	+ 8	3.35
5⅞	Nov 04n	106:08	106:09	+ 9	3.47
7⅞	Nov 04n	111:13	111:14	+ 7	3.50
11⅝	Nov 04	121:05	121:06	+ 7	3.53
7½	Feb 05n	111:02	111:03	+ 9	3.60
6½	May 05n	108:16	108:17	+ 10	3.71
6¾	May 05n	109:05	109:06	+ 10	3.73
12	May 05	125:05	125:06	+ 9	n.a.
6½	Aug 05n	108:23	108:24	+ 11	3.82
10¾	Aug 05	122:13	122:14	+ 10	3.88
5¾	Nov 05n	106:06	106:07	+ 12	3.96
5⅞	Nov 05n	106:23	106:24	+ 11	3.93
5⅝	Feb 06n	105:29	105:30	+ 12	4.01
9⅜	Feb 06	119:18	119:19	+ 12	4.05
4⅝	May 06n	101:29	101:30	+ 12	4.12
6⅞	May 06n	110:20	110:21	+ 12	4.13
7	Jul 06n	111:07	111:08	+ 12	4.19
6½	Oct 06n	109:13	109:14	+ 14	4.25
3½	**Nov 06n**	**96:30**	**96:31**	**+ 13**	**4.21**
3⅜	Jan 07i	101:26	101:27	+ 7	2.97
6¼	Feb 07n	108:19	108:20	+ 14	4.32
7⅝	Feb 07	100:04	100:05	− 1	n.a.
6⅝	May 07n	110:13	110:14	+ 14	4.38
6⅛	Aug 07n	108:05	108:06	+ 14	4.44
7⅞	Nov 07	104:14	104:15	....	n.a.
3⅝	Jan 08i	102:20	102:21	+ 7	3.13
5½	Feb 08n	105:03	105:04	+ 15	4.52
5⅝	May 08n	105:20	105:21	+ 15	4.58
8⅜	Aug 08	108:12	108:13	+ 5	n.a.
4¾	Nov 08n	100:15	100:16	+ 15	4.66
8¾	Nov 08	110:00	110:01	+ 6	n.a.
3⅞	Jan 09i	103:22	103:23	+ 8	3.27
5½	May 09n	104:21	104:22	+ 16	4.73
9⅛	May 09	112:19	112:20	+ 6	n.a.
6	Aug 09n	107:21	107:22	+ 17	4.77
10⅜	Nov 09	117:16	117:17	+ 8	n.a.
4¼	Jan 10i	106:05	106:06	+ 11	3.36
6½	Feb 10n	111:00	111:00	+ 18	4.83
11¾	Feb 10	122:18	122:19	+ 9	n.a.
10	May 10	118:10	118:11	+ 9	n.a.
5¾	Aug 10n	106:03	106:04	+ 18	4.86
12¾	Nov 10	130:00	130:01	+ 8	n.a.
3½	Jan 11i	101:02	101:03	+ 12	3.36
5	Feb 11n	100:26	100:27	+ 17	4.88
13⅞	May 11	137:13	137:14	+ 9	n.a.
5	**Aug 11n**	**100:23**	**100:24**	**+ 18**	**4.90**
14	Nov 11	141:14	141:15	+ 16	n.a.
3⅜	Jan 12i	100:06	100:07	+ 12	3.35
10⅜	Nov 12	128:23	128:24	+ 16	n.a.
12	Aug 13	140:09	140:10	+ 20	n.a.
13¼	May 14	151:08	151:09	+ 20	n.a.
12½	Aug 14	147:23	147:24	+ 22	n.a.
11¾	Nov 14	143:27	143:28	+ 22	n.a.
11¼	Feb 15	155:19	155:20	+ 28	5.29
10⅝	Aug 15	150:17	150:18	+ 29	5.33
9⅞	Nov 15	143:20	143:21	+ 29	5.35
9¼	Feb 16	137:21	137:22	+ 27	5.39
7¼	May 16	117:28	117:29	+ 26	5.43
7½	Nov 16	120:15	120:16	+ 25	5.46
8¾	May 17	133:26	133:27	+ 28	5.45
8⅞	Aug 17	135:08	135:09	+ 28	5.47
9⅛	May 18	138:25	138:26	+ 32	5.49
9	Nov 18	137:28	137:29	+ 27	5.51
8⅞	Feb 19	136:24	136:25	+ 30	5.51
8⅛	Aug 19	128:25	128:26	+ 29	5.54
8½	Feb 20	133:13	133:14	+ 30	5.54
8¾	May 20	136:17	136:18	+ 31	5.54
8¾	Aug 20	136:25	136:26	+ 29	5.54
7⅞	Feb 21	126:29	126:30	+ 28	5.56
8⅛	May 21	130:02	130:03	+ 29	5.56
8⅛	Aug 21	130:08	130:09	+ 30	5.56
8	Nov 21	129:01	129:02	+ 29	5.56
7¼	Aug 22	120:08	120:09	+ 27	5.58
7⅝	Nov 22	125:01	125:02	+ 29	5.57
7⅛	Feb 23	118:28	118:29	+ 26	5.58
6¼	Aug 23	108:06	108:07	+ 25	5.59
7½	Nov 24	124:17	124:18	+ 30	5.58
7⅝	Feb 25	126:07	126:08	+ 29	5.58
6⅞	Aug 25	116:21	116:22	+ 27	5.59
6	Feb 26	105:10	105:11	+ 24	5.59
6¾	Aug 26	115:10	115:11	+ 26	5.59
6½	Nov 26	112:02	112:03	+ 27	5.59
6⅝	Feb 27	113:26	113:27	+ 28	5.59
6⅜	Aug 27	110:21	110:22	+ 26	5.58
6⅛	Nov 27	107:16	107:17	+ 26	5.57
3⅝	Apr 28i	102:08	102:09	+ 15	3.49
5½	Aug 28	99:05	99:06	+ 25	5.56
5¼	Nov 28	95:26	95:27	+ 24	5.55
5¼	Feb 29	95:29	95:30	+ 26	5.54
3⅞	Apr 29i	106:26	106:27	+ 16	3.48
6⅛	Aug 29	108:11	108:12	+ 27	5.53
6¼	May 30	110:17	110:18	+ 27	5.51
5⅜	**Feb 31**	**100:12**	**100:13**	**+ 24**	**5.35**
3⅜	Apr 32i	99:10	99:11	+ 15	3.41

U.S. TREASURY STRIPS

MATURITY	TYPE	BID	ASKED	CHG.	ASKED YLD.
Feb 02	ci	99:31	99:31	....	1.28
May 02	ci	99:18	99:19	....	1.55
May 02	np	99:17	99:17	....	1.73
Aug 02	ci	99:03	99:03	....	1.72
Aug 02	np	99:01	99:02	....	1.82
Nov 02	ci	98:23	98:24	+ 1	1.65
Feb 03	ci	97:28	97:28	+ 3	2.10
Feb 03	np	97:27	97:28	+ 3	2.11
May 03	ci	97:05	97:06	+ 3	2.26
Jul 03	ci	96:17	96:18	+ 4	2.45
Aug 03	ci	96:09	96:10	+ 4	2.49
Aug 03	np	96:04	96:05	+ 4	2.58
Nov 03	ci	95:20	95:21	+ 5	2.52
Nov 03	np	95:06	95:07	+ 5	2.78
Jan 04	ci	94:15	94:16	+ 5	2.94
Feb 04	ci	94:05	94:06	+ 5	2.98
Feb 04	np	94:03	94:04	+ 5	3.02
May 04	ci	93:01	93:02	+ 6	3.19
May 04	np	92:30	92:31	+ 6	3.24
Jul 04	ci	92:11	92:12	+ 7	3.27
Aug 04	ci	92:00	92:01	+ 7	3.31
Aug 04	np	91:27	91:28	+ 7	3.38
Nov 04	ci	90:20	90:22	+ 8	3.56
Nov 04	bp	90:12	90:14	+ 8	3.66
Nov 04	np	90:18	90:20	+ 8	3.58
Jan 05	ci	89:30	90:00	+ 8	3.62
Feb 05	ci	89:18	89:20	+ 8	3.65
Feb 05	np	89:18	89:20	+ 8	3.66
May 05	ci	88:12	88:14	+ 9	3.79
May 05	bp	88:05	88:07	+ 9	3.87
May 05	np	88:10	88:12	+ 9	3.81
May 05	np	88:13	88:15	+ 9	3.78
Jul 05	ci	87:25	87:27	+ 9	3.80
Aug 05	ci	87:13	87:15	+ 9	3.84
Aug 05	bp	86:28	86:30	+ 9	4.01
Aug 05	np	87:07	87:09	+ 9	3.90
Nov 05	ci	86:22	86:25	+ 10	3.80
Nov 05	np	85:31	86:01	+ 10	4.03
Nov 05	np	86:01	86:03	+ 10	4.01
Jan 06	ci	85:15	85:17	+ 10	4.01
Feb 06	ci	85:01	85:03	+ 10	4.05
Feb 06	bp	84:17	84:19	+ 10	4.20
Feb 06	np	84:28	84:31	+ 10	4.09
May 06	ci	83:28	83:30	+ 11	4.14
May 06	np	83:17	83:20	+ 11	4.23
Jul 06	ci	83:20	83:22	+ 11	4.05
Jul 06	np	82:25	82:27	+ 11	4.28
Aug 06	ci	83:03	83:08	+ 11	4.09
Nov 06	ci	81:29	81:31	+ 12	4.21
Feb 07	ci	80:11	80:13	+ 11	4.39
Feb 07	np	80:06	80:09	+ 11	4.42
May 07	ci	78:29	78:31	+ 11	4.53
May 07	np	79:00	79:02	+ 11	4.50
Aug 07	ci	78:04	78:07	+ 12	4.50
Aug 07	np	77:30	78:01	+ 12	4.54
Nov 07	ci	77:18	77:21	+ 12	4.43
Feb 08	ci	75:18	75:20	+ 12	4.69
Feb 08	np	75:28	75:30	+ 12	4.62
May 08	ci	74:07	74:10	+ 13	4.79
May 08	np	74:20	74:23	+ 13	4.70
Aug 08	ci	73:13	73:16	+ 13	4.77
Nov 08	ci	72:16	72:19	+ 13	4.79
Nov 08	np	72:19	72:22	+ 13	4.76
Feb 09	ci	70:31	71:03	+ 13	4.92
May 09	ci	69:29	70:00	+ 14	4.96
May 09	np	70:15	70:18	+ 14	4.86
Aug 09	ci	69:01	69:04	+ 14	4.97
Aug 09	np	69:10	69:13	+ 14	4.91
Nov 09	ci	68:00	68:03	+ 14	5.00
Nov 09	bp	66:25	66:28	+ 14	5.24
Feb 10	ci	66:22	66:25	+ 14	5.09
Feb 10	np	67:09	67:12	+ 15	4.98
May 10	ci	65:19	65:22	+ 15	5.14
Aug 10	ci	64:25	64:28	+ 15	5.14
Aug 10	np	65:19	65:23	+ 15	4.99
Nov 10	ci	64:02	64:05	+ 15	5.12
Feb 11	ci	62:23	62:26	+ 15	5.22
Feb 11	np	64:01	64:05	+ 16	4.98
May 11	ci	61:22	61:24	+ 15	5.27
Aug 11	ci	60:27	60:29	+ 16	5.27
Nov 11	ci	60:00	60:01	+ 16	5.29

TREASURY BILLS

MATURITY	DAYS TO MAT.	BID	ASKED	CHG.	ASKED YLD.
Feb 07 '02	2	1.68	1.67	+ 0.01	1.69
Feb 14 '02	9	1.67	1.66	+ 0.01	1.68
Feb 21 '02	16	1.66	1.65	....	1.67
Feb 28 '02	23	1.66	1.65	....	1.67
Mar 07 '02	30	1.37	1.66	+ 0.01	1.69
Mar 14 '02	37	1.68	1.67	....	1.70
Mar 21 '02	44	1.68	1.67	....	1.70
Mar 28 '02	51	1.67	1.66	....	1.69
Apr 04 '02	58	1.67	1.66	− 0.01	1.69
Apr 11 '02	65	1.69	1.68	+ 0.01	1.71
Apr 18 '02	72	1.70	1.69	....	1.72
Apr 25 '02	79	1.70	1.69	− 0.01	1.72
May 02 '02	**86**	**1.72**	**1.71**	**− 0.01**	**1.74**
May 09 '02	93	1.73	1.72	....	1.75
May 16 '02	100	1.73	1.72	....	1.75
May 23 '02	107	1.74	1.73	+ 0.01	1.76
May 30 '02	114	1.74	1.73	....	1.76
Jun 13 '02	128	1.74	1.73	− 0.02	1.76
Jun 13 '02	128	1.74	1.73	− 0.02	1.76
Jun 20 '02	135	1.74	1.73	− 0.02	1.77
Jun 27 '02	142	1.74	1.73	− 0.03	1.77
Jul 05 '02	150	1.76	1.75	− 0.02	1.79
Jul 11 '02	156	1.77	1.76	− 0.02	1.80
Jul 18 '02	163	1.80	1.79	− 0.01	1.83
Jul 25 '02	170	1.80	1.79	− 0.02	1.83
Aug 01 '02	**177**	**1.81**	**1.80**	**− 0.02**	**1.84**

OINFLATION-INDEXED TREASURY SECURITIES

RATE	MAT.	BID/ASKED	CHG.	*YLD.	ACCR. PRIN.
3.625	07/02	101-00/01	+ 1	1.290	1107
3.375	01/07	101-26/27	+ 7	2.971	1119
3.625	01/08	102-20/21	+ 7	3.131	1098
3.875	01/09	103-22/23	+ 8	3.272	1081
4.250	01/10	106-05/06	+ 11	3.334	1054
3.500	01/11	101-02/03	+ 12	3.357	1019
3.375	01/12	100-06/07	+ 12	3.345	999
3.625	04/28	102-08/09	+ 15	3.491	1096
3.875	04/29	106-26/27	+ 16	3.483	1079
3.375	04/32	99-10/11	+ 15	3.483	999

*-Yld. to maturity on accrued principal.

The **yield to maturity** (or *internal rate of return*) on a zero-coupon bond is simply the percentage increase in dollars earned from the bond. For the 1-year bond, we end up with $1/0.943396 - 1 = 0.06$ more dollars per \$1 invested. If we are quoting interest rates as effective annual rates, this is a 6% yield.

For the zero-coupon 2-year bond, we end up with $1/0.881659 - 1 = 0.134225$ more dollars per \$1 invested. We could call this a 2-year effective interest rate of 13.4225%, but it is conventional to quote rates on an annual basis. If we want this yield to be comparable to the 6% yield on the 1-year bond, we could assume annual compounding and get $(1 + r(0, 2))^2 = 1.134225$, which implies that $r(0, 2) = 0.065$. In general,

$$P(0, n) = \frac{1}{[1 + r(0, n)]^n} \tag{7.1}$$

Note from equation (7.1) that *a zero-coupon bond price is a discount factor*: A zero-coupon bond price is what you would pay today to receive \$1 in the future. If you have a future cash flow at time t, C_t, you can multiply it by the price of a zero-coupon bond, $P(0, t)$, to obtain the present value of the cash flow. Because of equation (7.1), multiplying by $P(0, t)$ is the same as discounting at the rate $r(0, t)$, i.e.,

$$C_t \times P(0, t) = \frac{C_t}{[1 + r(0, t)]^t}$$

The inverse of the zero-coupon bond price, $1/P(0, t)$, provides a future value factor.

In contrast to zero-coupon bond prices, interest rates such as those in Figure 7.1 are subject to quoting conventions that can make their interpretation difficult (if you doubt this, see Appendix 7.A). Because of their simple interpretation, we can consider zero-coupon bond prices as the building block for all of fixed income.

A graph of annualized zero-coupon yields to maturity against time to maturity is called the zero-coupon **yield curve.** A yield curve shows us how yields to maturity vary with time to maturity. In practice, it is common to present the yield curve based on coupon bonds, not zero-coupon bonds.

Implied Forward Rates

We now see how column (3) in Table 7.1 can be computed from either column (1) or (2). The 1-year and 2-year zero-coupon yields are the rates you can earn from year 0 to year 1 and from year 0 to year 2. There is also an *implicit* rate that can be earned from year 1 to year 2 that must be consistent with the other two rates. This rate is called the **implied forward rate.**

Suppose we could today guarantee a rate we could earn from year 1 to year 2. We know that \$1 invested for 1 year earns $(1 + r_0(0, 1))$ and \$1 invested for 2 years earns $(1 + r_0(0, 2))^2$. Thus, the time 0 forward rate from year 1 to year 2, $r_0(1, 2)$, should satisfy

$$[1 + r_0(0, 1)][1 + r_0(1, 2)] = [1 + r_0(0, 2)]^2$$

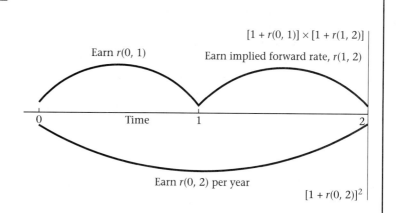

FIGURE 7.2

An investor investing for 2 years has a choice of buying a 2-year zero-coupon bond paying $[1 + r_0(0, 2)]^2$ or buying a 1-year bond paying $1 + r_0(0,1)$ for 1 year, and reinvesting the proceeds at the implied forward rate, $r_0(1,2)$ between years 1 and 2. The implied forward rate makes the investor indifferent between these alternatives.

or

$$1 + r_0(1, 2) = \frac{[1 + r_0(0, 2)]^2}{1 + r_0(0, 1)} \qquad (7.2)$$

Figure 7.2 shows graphically how the implied forward rate is related to 1- and 2-year yields. If $r_0(1, 2)$ did not satisfy equation (7.2), then there would be an arbitrage opportunity. Problem 15 asks you to work through the arbitrage. In general, we have

$$[1 + r_0(t_1, t_2)]^{t_2 - t_1} = \frac{[1 + r_0(0, t_2)]^{t_2}}{[1 + r_0(0, t_1)]^{t_1}} = \frac{P(0, t_1)}{P(0, t_2)} \qquad (7.3)$$

Corresponding to 1-year and 2-year interest rates, $r_0(0, 1)$ and $r_0(0, 2)$, we have prices of 1-year and 2-year zero-coupon bonds, $P_0(0, 1)$ and $P_0(0, 2)$. Just as the interest rates imply a forward 1-year interest rate, the bond prices imply a 1-year forward zero-coupon bond price. The implied forward zero-coupon bond price must be consistent with the implied forward interest rate. Rewriting equation (7.3), we have

$$P_0(t_1, t_2) = \frac{1}{[1 + r_0(t_1, t_2)]^{t_2 - t_1}} = \frac{[1 + r_0(0, t_1)]^{t_1}}{[1 + r_0(0, t_2)]^{t_2}} = \frac{P(0, t_2)}{P(0, t_1)} \qquad (7.4)$$

The implied forward zero-coupon bond price from t_1 to t_2 is simply the ratio of the zero-coupon bond prices maturing at t_2 and t_1.

Example 7.1 Using information in Table 7.1, we want to compute the implied forward interest rate from year 2 to year 3 and the implied forward zero-coupon bond price from year 2 to year 3.

The implied forward interest rate, $r_0(2, 3)$, can be computed as

$$1 + r_0(2, 3) = \frac{[1 + r_0(0, 3)]^3}{[1 + r_0(0, 2)]^2} = \frac{(1 + 0.07)^3}{(1 + 0.065)^2} = 1.0800705$$

or equivalently as

$$1 + r_0(2, 3) = \frac{P_0(0, 2)}{P_0(0, 3)} = \frac{0.881659}{0.816298} = 1.0800705$$

The implied forward 1-year zero-coupon bond price is

$$\frac{P_0(0, 3)}{P_0(0, 2)} = \frac{1}{1 + r_0(2, 3)} = 0.925865$$

≋

Coupon Bonds

Given the prices of zero-coupon bonds—column (1) in Table 7.1—we can price coupon bonds. We can also compute the **par coupon**—column (4) in Table 7.1—the coupon rate at which a bond will be priced at par. To describe a coupon bond, we need to know the date at which the bond is being priced, the start and end date of the bond payments, the number and amount of the payments, and the amount of principal. Some practical complexities associated with coupon bonds, not essential for our purposes, are discussed in Appendix 7.B.

We will let $B_t(t_1, t_2, c, n)$ denote the time t price of a bond that is issued at t_1, matures at t_2, pays a coupon of c per dollar of maturity payment, and makes n evenly spaced payments over the life of the bond, beginning at time $t_1 + (t_2 - t_1)/n$. We will assume the maturity payment is $1. If the maturity payment is different than $1, we can just multiply all payments by that amount.

Since the price of a bond is the present value of its payments, at issuance time t the price of a bond maturing at T must satisfy

$$B_t(t, T, c, n) = \sum_{i=1}^{n} c P_t(t, t_i) + P_t(t, T) \qquad (7.5)$$

where $t_i = t + i(T - t)/n$, with i being the index in the summation. Using equation (7.5), we can solve for the coupon as

$$c = \frac{B_t(t, T, c, n) - P_t(t, T)}{\sum_{i=1}^{n} P_t(t, t_i)}$$

A par bond has $B_t = 1$, so the coupon on a par bond is given by

$$\boxed{c = \frac{1 - P_t(t, T)}{\sum_{i=1}^{n} P_t(t, t_i)}} \qquad (7.6)$$

Example 7.2 Using the information in Table 7.1, the coupon on a 3-year coupon bond which sells at par is

$$c = \frac{1 - 0.816298}{0.943396 + 0.881659 + 0.816298}$$
$$= 6.95485\%$$

Equation (7.5) computes the bond price by discounting each bond payment at the rate appropriate for a cash flow with that particular maturity. For example, in equation (7.5), the coupon occuring at time t_i is discounted using the zero-coupon bond price $P_t(t, t_i)$. An alternative way to write the bond price is using the yield to maturity to discount all payments. Suppose the bond makes m payments per year. Denoting the per-period yield to maturity as y_m, we have

$$B_t(t, T, c, n) = \sum_{i=1}^{n} \frac{c}{(1 + y_m)^i} + \frac{1}{(1 + y_m)^n} \qquad (7.7)$$

It is common to compute the annualized yield to maturity, y, as $y = m \times y_m$. Government bonds, for example, make two coupon payments per year, so the annualized yield to maturity is twice the semiannual yield to maturity.

The difference between equation (7.5) and equation (7.7) is that in equation (7.5), each coupon payment is discounted at the appropriate rate for a cash flow occurring at that time. In equation (7.7), one rate is used to discount all cash flows. By definition, the two expresssions give the same price. However, equation (7.7) can be misleading, since the yield to maturity, y_m, is not the return an investor earns by buying and holding a bond. Moreover, equation (7.7) provides no insight into how the cash flows from a bond can be replicated with zero-coupon bonds.

Zeros from Coupons

We have started with zero-coupon bond prices and deduced the prices of coupon bonds. In practice, the situation is often the reverse: We observe prices of coupon bonds and must infer prices of zero-coupon bonds. This procedure in which zero coupon bond prices are deduced from a set of coupon bond prices is called **bootstrapping.**

Suppose we observe the par coupons in Table 7.1. We can then infer the first zero-coupon bond price from the first coupon bond as follows:

$$1 = (1 + 0.06) P(0, 1)$$

This implies that $P(0, 1) = 1/1.06 = 0.943396$. Using the second par coupon bond with a coupon rate of 6.48423% gives us

$$1 = 0.0648423 P(0, 1) + 1.0648423 P(0, 2)$$

Since we know $P(0, 1) = 0.943396$, we can solve for $P(0, 2)$:

$$P(0, 2) = \frac{1 - 0.0648423 \times 0.943396}{1.0648423}$$

$$= 0.881659$$

Finally, knowing $P(0, 1)$ and $P(0, 2)$, we can solve for $P(0, 3)$ using the 3-year par coupon bond with a coupon of 6.95485%:

$$1 = (0.0695485 \times P(0, 1)) + (0.0695485 \times P(0, 2)) + (1.0695485 \times P(0, 3))$$

which gives us

$$P(0, 3) = \frac{1 - (0.0695485 \times 0.943396) - (0.0695485 \times 0.881659)}{1.0695485}$$

$$= 0.816298$$

There is nothing about the procedure that requires the bonds to trade at par. In fact, we do not even need the bonds to all have different maturities. For example if we had a 1-year bond and two different 3-year bonds, we could still solve for the three zero-coupon bond prices by solving simultaneous equations.

Interpreting the Coupon Rate

A coupon rate—for example the 6.95485% coupon on the 3-year bond—determines the cash flows the bondholder receives. However, except in special cases, it does not correspond to the rate of return that an investor actually earns by holding the bond.

Suppose for a moment that interest rates are certain; i.e., the implied forward rates in Table 7.1 are the rates that will actually occur in years 1 and 2. Imagine that we buy the 3-year bond and hold it to maturity, reinvesting all coupons as they are paid. What rate of return do we earn? Before going through the calculations, let's stop and discuss the intuition. We are going to invest an amount at time 0, reinvest all coupons by buying more bonds, and we will not withdraw any cash until time 3. *In effect, we are constructing a 3-year zero-coupon bond.* Thus, we should earn the same return as on a 3-year zero: 7%. This buy-and-hold return is different than the yield to maturity of 6.95485%. The coupon payment is set to make a par bond fairly priced, but it is not actually the return you earn on the bond except in the special case when the interest rate is constant over time.

Consider first what would happen if we bought the 3-year bond with a $100 principal and a coupon of 6.95485% and we held it for 1 year. The price at the end of the year would be

$$B_1 = \frac{6.95485}{1.0700237} + \frac{106.95485}{(1.0700237)(1 + 0.0800705)}$$

$$= 99.04515$$

The 1-period return is thus

$$
\begin{aligned}
\text{1-period return} \;=\;& \frac{6.95485 + 99.04515}{100} - 1 \\
=\;& 0.06
\end{aligned}
$$

We earn 6%, since that is the 1-year interest rate. Problem 7.13 asks you to compute your 2-year return on this investment.

By time 3, which is maturity, we have received three coupons, two of which have been reinvested at the implied forward rate. The total value of reinvested bond holdings at time 3 is

$$6.95485 \times [(1.0700237)(1.0800705) + (1.0800705) + 1] + 100 = 122.5043$$

The 3-year yield on the bond is thus

$$\left(\frac{122.5043}{100}\right)^{1/3} - 1 = 0.07$$

As we expected, this is equal to the 7% yield on the 3-year zero, different from the coupon rate.

This discussion assumed that interest rates are certain. Suppose that we buy and hold the bond, reinvesting the coupons, and that interest rates are not certain. Can we still expect to earn a return of 7%? The answer in general is no.

The belief that the implied forward interest rate equals the expected future spot interest rate is a version of the **expectations hypothesis.** We saw in Chapters 5 and 6 that forward prices are biased predictors of future spot prices when the underlying asset has a risk premium; the same is true for forward interest rates. When we own a coupon bond, there is risk associated with the rate at which we will be able to reinvest coupons. If this risk carries a risk premium, then the expected return to holding the bond will not equal the 7% return calculated by assuming interest rates are certain. The expectations hypothesis will generally not hold and you should not expect implied forward interest rates to predict future interest rates.

Having said this, if we can enter into hedging agreements to guarantee that we can reinvest coupons at the implied forward rate, then the holding period return on the bond is certain. In this case we will earn 7%. In practice we can guarantee the 7% return by using forward rate agreements to lock in the interest rate we can earn on the reinvested coupons. We discuss forward rate agreements in Section 7.2.

Continuously Compounded Yields

Any interest rate can be quoted as either an effective annual rate or a continuously compounded rate. (Or in a variety of other ways, such as a semiannually compounded rate, which is common with bonds. See Appendix 7.A.) Column (5) in Table 7.1 presents the continuously compounded equivalents of the rates in the "zero yield" column.

In general, if we have a zero-coupon bond paying $1 at maturity, we can write its price in terms of a continuously compounded yield as

$$P(0, t) = e^{-r(0,t)t}$$

Thus, if we observe the price, we can solve for the yield as

$$r(0, t) = \frac{1}{t} ln[1/P(0, t)]$$

We can compute the continuously compounded 3-year zero yield, for example, as

$$\frac{1}{3} ln(1/0.816298) = 0.0676586$$

Alternatively, we can obtain the same answer using the 3-year zero yield of 7%:

$$ln(1 + 0.07) = 0.0676586$$

Any of the zero yields or implied forward yields in Table 7.1 can be computed as effective annual or continuously compounded. The choice hinges on convention and ease of calculation.

7.2 Forward Rate Agreements, Eurodollars, and Hedging

We now consider the problem of a borrower who wishes to hedge against increases in the cost of borrowing. We consider a firm expecting to borrow $100m for 91 days, beginning 120 days from today, in June. This is the borrowing date. The loan will be repaid in September on the loan repayment date. In the examples we will suppose that the effective quarterly interest rate at that time can be either 1.5% or 2%, and that the implied June 91-day forward rate (the rate from June to September) is 1.8%. Here is the risk faced by the borrower, assuming no hedging:

	120 days	**211 days**	
		$r_{quarterly} = 1.5\%$	$r_{quarterly} = 2\%$
Borrow $100m	+100m	−101.5m	−102.0m

Depending upon the interest rate, there is a variation of $0.5m in the borrowing cost. How can we hedge this uncertainty?

Forward Rate Agreements

A **forward rate agreement** (FRA) is an over-the-counter contract that guarantees a borrowing or lending rate on a given notional principal amount. FRAs can be settled either at the initiation or maturity of the borrowing or lending transaction. If settled at maturity, we will say the FRA is settled in arrears. In the example above, the FRA could be settled on day 120, the point at which the borrowing rate becomes known and the borrowing takes place, or settled in arrears on day 211, when the loan is repaid.

FRAs are a forward contract based on the interest rate, and as such do not entail the actual lending of money. Rather, the borrower who enters an FRA is paid if a reference rate is above the FRA rate, and the borrower pays if the reference rate is below the FRA rate. The actual borrowing is conducted by the borrower independently of the FRA. We will suppose that the reference rate used in the FRA is the same as the actual borrowing cost of the borrower.

FRA settlement in arrears First consider what happens if the FRA is settled in September, on day 211, the loan repayment date. In that case, the payment to the borrower should be

$$\left(r_{\text{quarterly}} - r_{\text{FRA}}\right) \times \text{notional principal}$$

Thus, if the borrowing rate is 1.5%, the payment under the FRA should be

$$(0.015 - 0.018) \times \$100\text{m} = -\$300{,}000$$

Since the rate is lower than the FRA rate, the borrower pays the FRA counterparty.

Similarly, if the borrowing rate turns out to be 2.0%, the payment under the FRA should be

$$(0.02 - 0.018) \times \$100\text{m} = \$200{,}000$$

Settling the FRA in arrears is simple and seems like the obvious way for the contract to work. However, settlement can also occur at the time of borrowing.

FRA settlement at the time of borrowing If the FRA is settled in June, at the time the money is borrowed, payments will be less than when settled in arrears because the borrower has time to earn interest on the FRA settlement. In practice, therefore, the FRA settlement is tailed by the reference rate prevailing on the settlement (borrowing) date. (Tailing in this context means that we reduce the payment to reflect the interest earned between June and September.) Thus, the payment for a borrower is

$$\text{Notional principal} \times \frac{\left(r_{\text{quarterly}} - r_{\text{FRA}}\right)}{1 + r_{\text{quarterly}}} \qquad (7.8)$$

If $r_{\text{quarterly}} = 1.5\%$, the payment in June is

$$\frac{-\$300{,}000}{1 + 0.015} = -\$295{,}566.50$$

By definition, the future value of this is $-\$300,000$. In order to make this payment, the borrower can borrow an extra \$295,566.50, which results in an extra \$300,000 loan payment in September. If on the other hand $r_{\text{quarterly}} = 2.0\%$, the payment is

$$\frac{\$200{,}000}{1 + 0.02} = \$196{,}078.43$$

The borrower can invest this amount, which gives $\$200,000$ in September, an amount that offsets the extra borrowing cost.

If the forward rate agreement covers a borrowing period other than 91 days, we simply use the appropriate rate instead of the 91-day rate in the above calculations.

Synthetic FRAs

Suppose that today is day 0 and we plan to lend money 120 days hence. By using a forward rate agreement, we can guarantee the lending rate we will receive on day 120. In particular, we will be able to invest \$1 on day 120 and be guaranteed a 91-day return of 1.8%.

We can synthetically create the same effect as with an FRA by trading zero-coupon bonds. In order to accomplish this we need to guarantee cash flows of 0 on day 0, −\$1 on day 120, and +\$1.018 on day 211.[2]

First, let's get a general sense of the transaction. We want cash going out on day 120 and coming in on day 211. To accomplish this, on day 0 we will need to borrow with a 120-day maturity (to generate a cash outflow on day 120) and lend with a 211 day maturity (to generate a cash inflow on day 211). Moreover, we want the day 0 value of the borrowing and lending to be equal so that there is no initial cash flow. This description tells us what we need to do.

In general, suppose that today is day 0, and that at time t we want to lend \$1 for the period s, earning the implied forward rate $r_0(t, t + s)$ over the interval from t to $t + s$. Recall first that

$$1 + r_0(t, t + s) = \frac{P(0, t)}{P(0, t + s)}$$

The strategy we use is to

1. Buy $1 + r_0(t, t + s)$ zero-coupon bonds maturing at time $t + s$.

2. Borrow 1 zero-coupon bond maturing at time t.

The resulting cash flows are illustrated in Table 7.2, which shows that transactions made on day 0 synthetically create a loan commencing on day t and paying the implied forward rate, $1 + r_0(t, t + s)$, on day $t + s$.

This example can be modified slightly to synthetically create the cash flows from a forward rate agreement that settles on the borrowing date, day t. To make this modification, we sell at time t the bond maturing at time $t + s$. The result is presented in Table 7.3. Note that if we reinvested the FRA proceeds at the market rate prevailing on day t, $r_t(t, t + s)$, we would receive $r_0(t, t + s) - r_t(t, t + s)$ on day t.

Example 7.3 Consider the example above and suppose that $P(0, 211) = 0.95836$ and $P(0, 120) = 0.97561$, which implies a 120-day interest rate of 2.5%. In order to receive \$1.018 on day 211, we buy 1.018 211-day zero-coupon bonds. The cost of this is

$$1.018 \times P(0, 211) = \$0.97561$$

[2]The example in the previous section considered locking in a borrowing rate, but in this section we lock in a lending rate; the transactions can be reversed for borrowing.

TABLE 7.2	Investment strategy undertaken at time 0, resulting in net cash flows of −$1 on day t, and receiving the implied forward rate, $1 + r_0(t, t + s)$ at $t + s$. This synthetically creates the cash flows from entering into a forward rate agreement on day 0 to lend at day t.

	Cash Flows		
Transaction	**0**	t	$t + s$
Buy $1 + r_0(t, t + s)$ Zeros Maturing at $t + s$	$-P(0, t + s) \times (1 + r_0(t, t + s))$	—	$1 + r_0(t, t + s)$
Short 1 Zero Maturing at t	$+P(0, t)$	-1	—
Total	0	-1	$1 + r_0(t, t + s)$

TABLE 7.3	Example of synthetic FRA. The transactions in this table are exactly those in Table 7.2, except that all bonds are sold at time t.

	Cash Flows	
Transaction	**0**	t
Buy $1 + r_0(t, t + s)$ Zeros Maturing at $t + s$	$-P(0, t + s) \times [1 + r_0(t, t + s)]$	$\frac{1 + r_0(t, t+s)}{1 + r_t(t, t+s)}$
Short 1 Zero Maturing at t	$+P(0, t)$	-1
Total	0	$\frac{r_0(t, t+s) - r_t(t, t+s)}{1 + r_t(t, t+s)}$

In order to have zero cash flow initially and a cash outflow on day 120, we borrow 0.97561, with a 120-day maturity. This entails borrowing

$$\frac{0.97561}{P(0, 120)} = 1$$

120-day bond. The result on day 120 is that we pay $1 to close the short position on the 120-day bond, and on day 211 we receive $1.018 since we bought that many 211-day bonds. ❧

To summarize, we have shown that an FRA is just like the stock and currency forwards we have considered, both with respect to pricing and synthesizing. If at time 0 we want to lock in a borrowing rate from time t to time $t + s$, we can create a rate forward synthetically by buying the underlying asset (the bond maturing at $t + s$) and borrowing (shorting) the bond maturing at day t.

In general, if today is t_0 and we want to create a rate forward covering the period t_1 to t_2, we have the following conclusions:

- The forward rate we can obtain is the implied forward rate, i.e., $1 + r_{t_0}(t_1, t_2) = P_{t_0}(t_0, t_1)/P_{t_0}(t_0, t_2)$.

- We can synthetically create the payoff to an FRA, $\frac{r_{t_0}(t_1,t_2)-r_{t_1}(t_1,t_2)}{1+r_{t_1}(t_1,t_2)}$, by borrowing to buy the prepaid forward, i.e., by

  1. Buying $1 + r_{t_0}(t_1, t_2)$ of the zero-coupon bond maturing on day t_2, and

  2. Shorting 1 zero-coupon bond maturing on day t_1.

Eurodollar Futures

Eurodollar futures contracts are similar to FRAs in that they can be used to guarantee a borrowing rate. There are subtle differences between FRAs and Eurodollar contracts, however, that are important to understand.

Let's consider again the example in which we wish to guarantee a borrowing rate for a $100m loan from June to September. Suppose the June Eurodollar futures price is 92.8. Implied 3-month LIBOR is $\frac{100 - 92.8}{4} = 1.8\%$ over 3 months. As we saw in Chapter 5, the payoff on a single short Eurodollar contract at expiration will be[3]

$$[92.8 - (100 - r_{\text{LIBOR}})] \times 100 \times \$25$$

Thus, the payoff on the Eurodollar contract compensates us for differences between the implied rate (1.8%) and actual LIBOR at expiration.

To illustrate hedging with this contract we again consider two possible 3-month borrowing rates in June: 1.5% or 2%. If the interest rate is 1.5%, borrowing cost on $100m will be $1.5m, payable in September. If the interest rate is 2%, borrowing cost will be $2m.

Suppose that we were to short 100 Eurodollar futures contracts. Ignoring marking-to-market prior to June, if the 3-month rate in June is 1.5%, the Eurodollar futures price will be 94. The payment is

$$[(92.8 - 94) \times 100 \times \$25] \times 100 = -\$300,000$$

We multiply by 100 twice: Once to account for 100 contracts, and the second time to convert the change in the futures price to basis points. Similarly, if the borrowing rate is 2%, we have

$$[(92.8 - 92) \times 100 \times \$25] \times 100 = \$200,000$$

---

[3]This calculation treats the Eurodollar contract as if it were a forward contract, ignoring the issues associated with daily settlement, discussed in Appendix 5.B.

This is like the payment on an FRA paid in arrears, except that the futures contract settles in June, but our interest expense is not paid until September. Thus we have 3 months to earn or pay interest on our Eurodollar gain or loss before we actually have to make the interest payment.

Recall that when the FRA settles on the borrowing date, the payment is the *present value* of the change in borrowing cost. The FRA is thus tailed automatically as part of the agreement. With the Eurodollar contract, by contrast, we need to tail the position explicitly. We do this by shorting fewer than 100 contracts, using the implied 3-month Eurodollar rate of 1.8% as our discount factor. Thus, we enter into[4]

$$\text{Number of Eurodollar contracts} = -\frac{100}{1 + 0.018} = -98.2318$$

Now consider the gain on the Eurodollar futures position. If LIBOR = 6% ($r_{\text{quarterly}} = 1.5\%$), our total gain on the short contracts when we initiate borrowing on day 120 will be

$$98.2318 \times (92.8 - 94) \times \$2500 = -\$294,695$$

If LIBOR = 8% ($r_{\text{quarterly}} = 2.0\%$), our total gain on the contracts will be

$$98.2318 \times (92.8 - 92) \times \$2500 = \$196,464$$

Notice that the amounts are different than with the FRA: The reason is that the FRA payment is automatically tailed using the 3-month rate prevailing in June, whereas with the Eurodollar contract we tailed using 7.2%, the LIBOR rate implied by the initial futures price.

We can now invest these proceeds at the prevailing interest rate. Here are the results on day 211, when borrowing must be repaid. If LIBOR = 6% ($r_{\text{quarterly}} = 1.5\%$), we save \$300,000 in borrowing cost, and the proceeds from the Eurodollar contract are

$$-\$294,695 \times (1.015) = -\$299,115$$

If LIBOR = 8% ($r_{\text{quarterly}} = 2.0\%$), we owe an extra \$200,000 in interest and the invested proceeds from the Eurodollar contract are

$$\$196,464 \times (1.02) = \$200,393$$

Table 7.4 summarizes the result from this hedging position. We lock in very close to a 1.8% borrowing cost.

Convexity bias and tailing   In Table 7.4 the net borrowing cost appears to be a little less than 1.8%. You might guess that this is due to rounding error. It is not. Let's examine the numbers more closely.

If LIBOR = 6%, ($r_{\text{quarterly}} = 1.5\%$), we pay \$1.5m in borrowing cost, and we lose \$299,115 on the Eurodollar contract, for a net borrowing expense of \$1.799115m.

---

[4]We assume here that it is possible to short fractional contracts in order to make the example exact.

TABLE 7.4	Results from hedging $100m in borrowing with 98.23 short Eurodollar futures.			
	Cash Flows			
	June		**September**	
Borrowing Rate:	**1.5%**	**2%**	**1.5%**	**2%**
Borrow $100m	+100m	+100m	−101.5m	−102.0m
Gain on 98.23 Short Eurodollar Contracts	−0.294695m	0.196464m		
Gain Plus Interest			−0.299115m	0.200393m
Net			−101.799m	−101.799m

This is a "profit" from the Eurodollar hedge, relative to the use of an FRA, of $1.8m − $1.799115m = $884.

If LIBOR = 8% ($r_{quarterly} = 2.0\%$), we pay $2.0m in borrowing cost, but make $200,393 on the Eurodollar contract, for a net borrowing expense of $1.799607m. We make a profit, relative to an FRA, of $1.8m − $1.799607m = $393.

It appears that we systematically come out ahead by hedging with Eurodollar futures instead of an FRA. You are probably thinking that something is wrong.

As it turns out, what we have just shown is that *the rate implied by the Eurodollar contract cannot equal the prevailing FRA (implied forward) rate for the same loan*. To see this, consider the borrower perspective: When the interest rate turns out to be high, the short Eurodollar contract has a positive payoff and the proceeds can be reinvested until the loan payment date at the high realized rate. When the interest rate turns out to be low, the short Eurodollar contract has a negative payoff and we can fund this loss until the loan payment date by borrowing at a low rate. Thus the settlement structure of the Eurodollar contract works *systematically* in favor of the borrower. By turning the argument around, we can verify that it systematically works against a lender.

The reason this happens with Eurodollars and not FRAs is that we have to make the tailing decision *before* we know the 3-month rate prevailing on day 120. When we tail by a fixed amount (1.8% in the above example), the actual variations in the realized rate work in favor of the borrower and against the lender. The FRA avoids this by automatically tailing—paying the present value of the change in borrowing cost—using the actual interest rate on the borrowing date.

In order for the futures price to be fair to both the borrower and lender, the rate implicit in the Eurodollar futures price must be higher than a comparable FRA rate. This difference between the FRA rate and the Eurodollar rate is called **convexity bias.** For the most part in subsequent discussions we will ignore convexity bias and treat the Eurodollar contract and FRAs as if they are interchangeable. The reason is that in many cases the effect is small. In the above example, convexity bias results in a profit of several hundred dollars out of a borrowing cost of $1.8m. For short-term contracts, the effect can be small, but for longer-term contracts the effect can be important.[5]

In practice, convexity bias also matters before the final contract settlement. We saw in Section 5.4 that marking to market a futures contract can lead to a futures price that is different from the forward price. When a futures contract is marked to market and interest rates are negatively correlated with the futures price, there is a systematic advantage to being short the futures contract. This leads to a futures price that is greater than the forward price. This is exactly what happens with the Eurodollar contract in this example. When interest rates rise, the borrower receives a payment that can be invested at the higher interest rate. When interest rates fall, the borrower makes a payment that can be funded at the lower interest rate. This works to the borrower's benefit. Marking to market prior to settlement is therefore another reason why the rate implied by the Eurodollar contract will exceed that on an otherwise comparable FRA.

LIBOR versus 3-month T-bills   The Eurodollar futures contract is based on LIBOR, but there are other 3-month interest rates. For example, the Treasury-bill futures contract is based on the price of the 3-month Treasury bill. A borrower could use either the Eurodollar contract or the Treasury-bill futures contract to hedge their borrowing rate. Which contract is preferable?

Banks that offer LIBOR time deposits have the potential to default. Thus, LIBOR includes a default premium. (The **default premium** is an increase in the interest rate that compensates the lender for the possibility the borrower will default.) Private companies that borrow also can default, so their borrowing rates will also include a default premium.

The U.S. government, by contrast, is considered unlikely to default, so it can borrow at a lower rate than firms. In addition, in the United States and other

---

[5] If future interest rates were known for certain in advance, then it would be possible to perfectly tail the position. However, with uncertainty about rates, the error is due to interest on the difference between the realized rate, $\tilde{r}$, and the forward rate, r_{forward}. Given that we tail by the forward rate, the error is measured by

$$\frac{\tilde{r}(\tilde{r} - r_{\text{forward}})}{1 + r_{\text{forward}}}$$

The expected error is

$$E\left[\frac{\tilde{r}(\tilde{r} - r_{\text{forward}})}{1 + r_{\text{forward}}}\right] = \frac{1}{(1 + r_{\text{forward}})^2}\left[E\left(\tilde{r}^2\right) - E\left(\tilde{r}r_{\text{forward}}\right)\right]$$

$$= \frac{\sigma^2}{(1 + r_{\text{forward}})^2}$$

where σ^2 is the variance of the interest rate. Given that rates can be 2% or 1.5%, the standard deviation is approximately 25 basis points or 0.0025 and the variance is thus $0.0025^2 = 0.00000625$. Convexity bias is thus

$$100\text{m} \times \frac{0.00000625}{1.018^2} = 603.09$$

The actual average convexity error in the example was $(884 + 393)/2$, or 638.5.

countries, government bonds are more liquid than corporate bonds, and this results in higher prices—a *liquidity premium*—for government bonds.[6]

The borrower will want to use the futures contract that has a price that moves in tandem with its own borrowing rate. It makes sense that a private borrower's interest rate will more closely track LIBOR than the Treasury-bill rate. In fact, the spread between corporate borrowing rates and Treasuries moves around a great deal. The problem with hedging borrowing costs based on movements in the T-bill rate is that a private firm's borrowing costs could increase even as the T-bill rate goes down; this can occur during times of financial distress, when investors bid up the prices of Treasury securities relative to other assets (a so-called "flight to quality"). Thus, LIBOR is commonly used in markets as a benchmark, high-quality, private interest rate.

Figure 7.3 shows historical 3-month LIBOR along with the difference between LIBOR and the 3-month T-bill yield, illustrating this variability.[7] It is obvious that the spread varies considerably over time: Although the spread can be as low as 30 basis points, twice in the 1990s it has exceeded 100 basis points. In September of 1982, when Continental Bank failed, the spread exceeded 400 basis points. A private LIBOR-based borrower who had hedged its borrowing rate by shorting T-bill futures in August of 1982 would by September have lost money on the T-bill contract as Treasury rates declined, while the actual cost of borrowing (LIBOR) would have remained close to unchanged. This example illustrates the value of using a hedging contract that reflects the actual cost of borrowing.

This claim that LIBOR and the Eurodollar contract better reflect private borrowing rates is consistent with trading volume on the Eurodollar and T-bill contracts. Figure 7.4 shows the history of open interest (the number of outstanding contracts) for both Eurodollar and T-bill futures. The dramatic growth of the Eurodollar contract relative to the T-bill contract suggests that market participants find LIBOR much more useful as a reference rate for interest rate hedging. In fact, volume on the T-bill contract has approached zero in recent years.

Interest Rate Strips and Stacks

Suppose a borrower plans to borrow $100m on a short-term basis, rolling over 3-month debt for a period of 2 years, beginning in 6 months. Thus, the borrowing will take place in month 6, month 9, month 12, etc. The borrower in this situation faces eight unknown quarterly borrowing rates. We saw in Section 6.12 that an oil hedger could hedge each commitment individually (a strip) or could hedge the entire commitment using one near-dated contract (a stack). The same alternatives are available with interest rates.

---

[6] In the United States, another reason for government bonds to have higher prices than corporate bonds is that government bond interest is exempt from state taxation.

[7] The TED spread ("T-Bills over Eurodollars") is obtained by going long T-bill futures and short the Eurodollar futures contract. This spread is a measure of preceived default risk.

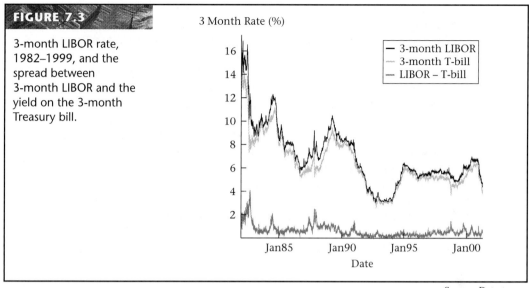

FIGURE 7.3

3-month LIBOR rate, 1982–1999, and the spread between 3-month LIBOR and the yield on the 3-month Treasury bill.

Source: Datastream.

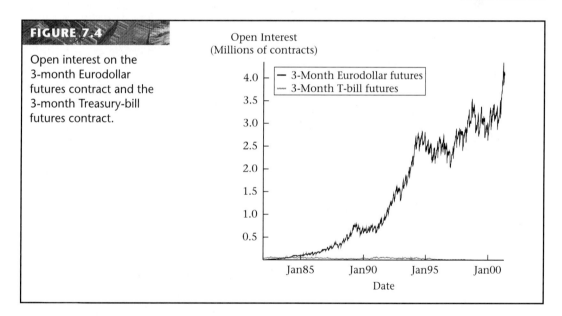

FIGURE 7.4

Open interest on the 3-month Eurodollar futures contract and the 3-month Treasury-bill futures contract.

One way to hedge is to enter into separate $100m FRAs for each future 3-month period. Thus, we would enter into one FRA for months 6–9, another for months 9–12, etc. This strip hedge should provide a perfect hedge for future borrowing costs.

Depending on market conditions, using a strip is not always feasible. For example, forward prices may not be available with distant maturities, or liquidity may be poor and spreads wide at distant maturities. Rather than individually hedging the borrowing cost of each quarter, an alternative in the context of this example is to use a "stack" of short-term FRAs or Eurodollar contracts to hedge the present value of future borrowing costs.

In the above example, we will be borrowing $100 million per quarter for eight quarters. To effect a stack, we would enter into 6-month forward agreements for slightly less than $800 million. (We enter into less than $800 million of forward rate agreements due to tailing for quarters 2 through 8.)

As with the oil example in Section 6.12, the obvious problem with a stacking strategy is basis risk: Quarterly borrowing costs in distant quarters may not move perfectly with borrowing costs in near quarters.

Once we reach the first quarter of borrowing, all of the forward agreements mature. We therefore need to renew our hedge. We now face seven quarters with unknown borrowing costs and therefore we enter into forward agreements for slightly less than $700 million. The constant renewal of the hedging position necessary to effect a stack and roll is exactly like that in the oil example.

7.3 DURATION

An important characteristic of a bond is the sensitivity of its price to interest rate changes, which we measure with a value known as **duration.** We can use the duration of a bond to figure out approximately how much the bond's price will change for a given change in the bond's yield. Duration is thus a summary measure of the risk of a bond, permitting a comparison of bonds with different coupons, times to maturity, and discounts or premiums relative to principal.

Suppose y is the per-period yield to maturity on a bond that will make n payments. Let the ith cash flow on the bond be C_i, $i = 1, \ldots, n$.[8] The price of the bond is then given by

$$B(y) = \sum_{i=1}^{n} \frac{C_i}{(1+y)^i}$$

The change in the bond price for a unit change in the yield is[9]

$$\frac{\text{Change in bond price}}{\text{Unit change in yield}} = -\sum_{i=1}^{n} i \frac{C_i}{(1+y)^{i+1}}$$

$$= -\frac{1}{1+y} \sum_{i=1}^{n} i \frac{C_i}{(1+y)^i} \tag{7.9}$$

....

[8]For a standard coupon bond, the payments prior to maturity are the coupon payments, c, and the payment at maturity is the maturity value plus the coupon, $100 + c$. Thus we have

$$C_i = c \quad i = 1, \ldots, n-1$$
$$C_n = 100 + c$$

[9]This is obtained by computing the derivative of the bond price with respect to the yield, $dB(y)/dy$.

As written, this tells us the *dollar* change in the bond price for a change of 1.0 in y. It is natural to scale this either to reflect a change per percentage point (in which case we divide equation (7.9) by 100) or basis point (divide equation (7.9) by 10,000). Equation (7.9) divided by 10,000 is also known as the **Price Value of a Basis Point** (PVBP). To interpret PVBP for a bond, we need to know the par value of the bond.

Example 7.4 Consider the 3-year bond in Table 7.1 with a yield to maturity of 7%. The bond price per $100 of maturity value is $100/1.07^3 = \$81.62979$. At a yield of 7.01%, one basis point higher, the bond price is $100/1.0701^3 = \$81.60691$, a change of $-\$0.02288$ per $100 of maturity value.

As an alternative way to derive the price change, we can compute equation (7.9) to obtain

$$-\frac{1}{1.07} \times 3 \times \frac{\$100}{1.07^3} = -\$228.87$$

In order for this to reflect a change of 1 basis point, we divide by 10,000 to obtain $-\$228.87/10,000 = -\$0.02289$, almost equal to the actual bond price change. This illustrates the importance of scaling equation (7.9) appropriately. ≷

Equation (7.9) gives the dollar change in the bond price. When comparing bonds with different prices and par values, it is helpful to have a measure of price sensitivity expressed per dollar of bond price. We obtain this by dividing equation (7.9) by the bond price, $B(y)$. This gives us a measure known as *modified duration*. We have

$$\textbf{Modified duration} = -\frac{\text{Change in bond price}}{\text{Unit change in yield}} \times \frac{1}{B(y)}$$

$$= \boxed{\frac{1}{1+y} \sum_{i=1}^{n} i \left[\frac{C_i}{(1+y)^i} \frac{1}{B(y)} \right]} \qquad (7.10)$$

Modified duration is the *percentage* change in the bond price for a unit change in the yield.

We obtain another measure of bond price risk—Macaulay duration—by multiplying equation (7.10) by $1 + y$. This puts both bond price and yield changes in percentage terms and gives us an expression with a clear interpretation:

$$\textbf{Macaulay duration} = -\frac{\text{Change in bond price}}{\text{Unit change in yield}} \times \frac{1+y}{B(y)}$$

$$= \boxed{\sum_{i=1}^{T} i \left[\frac{C_i}{(1+y)^i} \frac{1}{B(y)} \right]} \qquad (7.11)$$

To interpret this expression, examine the term in square brackets. $C_i/(1+y)^i$ is the value of the ith bond payment. $C_i/(1+y)^i B(y)$ is then the fraction of the bond value that is due to the ith payment. Macaulay duration is a *weighted average of the time (number of periods) until the bond payments occur*, with the weights being the percentage of the bond price accounted for by each payment. This interpretation of Macaulay duration as a time-to-payment measure explains why these measures of bond price sensitivity are called "duration." For a zero-coupon bond, equation (7.11) implies that Macaulay duration equals time to maturity.[10]

Macaulay duration illustrates why maturity alone is not a satisfactory risk measure for a coupon bond. A coupon bond makes a series of payments, each with a different maturity. Macaulay duration summarizes bond price risk as a weighted average of these different maturities.

Example 7.5 Returning to Example 7.4, using equation (7.11), Macaulay duration for the 7% bond is

$$-\frac{-\$228.87}{1} \times \frac{1.07}{\$81.62979} = -3.000$$

Many bonds make two or more payments per year. In equations (7.9), (7.10), and (7.11), y is the yield *per period*, where a period is the time between bond payments. It is common to annualize yields and duration. Thus, if a bond makes m payments per year, the annual yield is $y \times m$ and duration is annualized by dividing by m. Under this convention, if a bond makes two payments per year, the annual yield to maturity would be twice the semiannual yield to maturity and duration would be annualized by dividing by two. Typically, spreadsheet functions that compute duration (in Excel they are *Duration* for Macaulay duration and *MDuration* for modified duration) automatically annualize duration in this way.

Example 7.6 Consider the 3-year coupon bond in Table 7.1. For a par bond, the yield to maturity is the coupon, 6.95485% in this case. For each payment we have

$$\%\text{Payment 1} = \frac{0.0695485}{1.0695485} = 0.065026$$

$$\%\text{Payment 2} = \frac{0.0695485}{(1.0695485)^2} = 0.060798$$

$$\%\text{Payment 3} = \frac{1.0695485}{(1.0695485)^3} = 0.874176$$

---

[10]This measure of duration is named after Frederick Macaulay, who wrote a classic history of interest rates (Macaulay, 1938).

Thus, Macaulay duration is

$$(1 \times 0.065026) + (2 \times 0.060798) + (3 \times 0.874176) = 2.80915$$

The interpretation of the duration of 2.81 is that the bond responds to interest rate changes as if it were a pure discount bond with 2.81 years to maturity. Modified duration is $2.80915/1.0695485 = 2.626482$. ≶

Since duration tells us the sensitivity of the bond price to a change in the interest rate, it can be used to compute the approximate bond price change for a given change in interest rates. Suppose the bond price is $B(y)$ and the yield on the bond changes from y to $y + \epsilon$, where ϵ is a small change in the yield. The formula for modified duration, D, can be written

$$D = -\frac{[B(y + \epsilon) - B(y)]}{\epsilon} \frac{1}{B(y)}$$

We can rewrite this equation to obtain the new bond price in terms of the old bond price and duration:

$$B(y + \epsilon) = B(y) - [D \times B(y)\epsilon] = B(y) - [D_{Mac}/(1 + y) \times B(y)\epsilon] \qquad (7.12)$$

Example 7.7 Consider the 3-year zero-coupon bond with a price of $81.63 per $100 maturity value. The yield is 7%. If the yield were to increase to 7.25%, the predicted price (using the fact that $D = D_{Mac}/1 + y$) would be

$$B(7.25\%) = \$81.63 - (3/1.07) \times \$81.63 \times 0.0025 = \$81.058$$

The actual new bond price is $\$100/(1.0725)^3 = \$81.060$. The prediction error is about 0.003% of the bond price. ≶

The formula is close, but only approximate because duration changes as the interest rate changes. It is possible to improve this approximation using the bond's **convexity,** which measures the change in equation (7.9) as the interest rate changes. In Chapter 23 we will explore prediction formulas with more accuracy that use convexity as well as duration.

Although duration is useful, it has a conceptual problem. We emphasized in the previous section that a coupon bond is a collection of zero-coupon bonds, and therefore each cash flow has its own discount rate. Yet both duration formulas are computed assuming a change in "the" yield to maturity. In Chapter 23 we will examine alternative measures of bond price risk that do not have this problem.

Duration Matching

Suppose we own a bond with time to maturity t_1, price B_1, and Macaulay duration D_1. We are considering a short position in a bond with maturity t_2, price B_2, and Macaulay duration D_2. We can ask the question: How much of the second bond should we short-sell in order that the resulting portfolio—long the bond with duration D_1 and short the bond with duration D_2—is insensitive to interest rate changes?

Equation (7.12) gives us a formula for the change in price of each bond. Let N denote the quantity of the second bond. The value of the portfolio is

$$B_1 + NB_2$$

and, using equation (7.12), the change in price due to an interest rate change of ϵ is

$$[B_1(y_1 + \epsilon) - B_1(y_1)] + N[B_2(y + \epsilon) - B_2(y)]$$
$$= -D_1 B_1(y_1)\epsilon/(1 + y_1) - ND_2 B_2(y_2)\epsilon/(1 + y_2)$$

If we want the net change to be zero, we choose N to set the right-hand side equal to zero. This gives

$$N = -\frac{D_1 B_1(y_1)/(1 + y_1)}{D_2 B_2(y_2)/(1 + y_2)} \tag{7.13}$$

When a portfolio is duration-matched in this fashion, the net investment in the portfolio will typically not be zero. That is, either the value of the short bond is less than the value of the long bond, in which case additional financing is required, or vice versa, in which case there is cash to invest. This residual can be financed or invested in very short-term bonds, with duration approximately zero, in order to leave the portfolio duration matched.

Example 7.8   Suppose we own a 7-year 6% coupon bond with a yield of 7%, and want to find the duration-matched short position in a 10-year, 8% coupon bond yielding 7.5%. Assuming annual coupon payments, the duration and price of the two bonds is 5.882 years and $94.611, and 7.297 years and $103.432, respectively. Thus, if we own one of the 7-year bonds, we must hold

$$-\frac{5.882 \times 94.611/(1.07)}{7.297 \times 103.432/(1.075)} = -0.7408$$

units of the 10-year bond. The short position in the 10-year bond is not enough to pay for the 7-year bond; hence, investment in the portfolio is $1 \times 94.611 - 0.7409 \times 103.432 = 17.99$. If the yield on both bonds increases 25 basis points, the price change of the portfolio is

$$-1.289 + (-0.7408) \times -1.735 = -0.004 \qquad ❧$$

The hedge in this example is not perfect. As discussed above, duration changes as the interest rate changes. At the original yields, we computed a hedge ratio of 0.7409. Problem 7.19 asks you to compute the hedge ratio that would have exactly hedged the portfolio had both interest rates increased 25 basis points and decreased 25 basis points.

The two hedge ratios are different, which means that one hedge ratio would not have worked. This idea that the hedge ratio changes as the price changes is not peculiar to bonds; it will appear again in Chapter 13 when we consider the hedging of option positions.

7.4 TREASURY-BOND AND TREASURY-NOTE FUTURES

The Treasury-note and Treasury-bond futures contracts are important instruments for hedging interest rate risk. Figure 7.5 shows newspaper listings for these futures, and the specifications for the T-note contract are listed in Figure 7.6. The bond contract is similar except that the deliverable bond has a maturity of at least 15 years, or if the bond is callable, has 15 years to first call. The two contracts are similar; we will focus here on the T-note contract. In this discussion we will use the terms "bond" and "note" interchangeably.

The basic idea of the T-note contract is that a long position is an obligation to buy a 6% bond with between 6.5 and 10 years to maturity. To a first approximation we can think of the underlying as being like a stock with a dividend yield of 6%. The futures price would then be computed as with a stock index: The future value of the current bond price, less the future value of coupons payable over the life of the futures contract.

This description masks a complication that may already have occurred to you. The delivery procedure permits the short to deliver any note maturing in 6.5 to 10 years. Hence, the delivered note can be one of many outstanding notes, with a range of coupons and maturities. Which bond does the futures price represent?

Of all bonds that *could* be delivered, there will generally be one that is the most advantageous for the short to deliver. This bond is called the **cheapest to deliver.** A description of the delivery procedure will demonstrate the importance of the cheapest-to-deliver bond.

In fulfilling the note futures contract, the short delivers the bond in exchange for payment. The payment to the short—the *invoice price* for the delivered bond—is the

---

FIGURE 7.5

Treasury-bond and Treasury-note futures listings from the *Wall Street Journal*, February 5, 2002.

INTEREST RATE

Treasury Bonds (CBT)-$100,000; pts 32nds of 100%
Mar	103-11	104-08	103-11	104-05	+	26	111-16	97-11	457,263
June	102-17	103-02	102-14	103-00	+	26	110-00	96-30	41,817

Est vol 122,000; vol Fri 193,638; open int 499,310, +10,880.

Treasury Notes (CBT)-$100,000; pts 32nds of 100%
Mar	106-09	106-31	106-08	06-285	+	20.5	11-085	101-23	532,232
June	105-07	05-205	105-04	105-19	+	20.5	107-10	101-10	61,297

Est vol 220,000; vol Fri 272,886; open int 593,529, +1,178.

10 Yr Agency Notes (CBT)-$100,000; pts 32nds of 100%
Mar	102-04	102-14	102-01	102-13	+	18.5	106-04	96-27	36,659

Est vol 1,000; vol Fri 1,519; open int 36,659, +69.

5 Yr Treasury Notes (CBT)-$100,000; pts 32nds of 100%
Mar	06-145	106-27	06-115	106-25	+	12.5	109-08	04-015	531,946
June	105-23	105-29	05-205	105-29	+	14.0	06-105	103-30	30,569

Est vol 107,000; vol Fri 152,108; open int 562,515, +2,338.

2 Yr Treasury Notes (CBT)-$200,000; pts 32nds of 100%
Mar	04-282	105-02	04-282	105-02	+	6.5	105-27	03-255	104,180

Est vol 6,500; vol Fri 11,586; open int 104,180, +858.

FIGURE 7.6

Specifications for the
Treasury-note futures
contract.

Where traded	CBOT
Underlying	6% 10-year Treasury note
Size	$100,000 Treasury note
Months	Mar, Jun, Sep, Dec, out 15 months
Trading ends	Seventh business day preceding last business day of month. Delivery until last business day of month.
Delivery	Physical T-note with at least 6.5 years to maturity and not more than 10 years to maturity. Price paid to the short for notes with other than 6% coupon is determined by multiplying futures price by a conversion factor. The conversion factor is the price of the delivered note ($1 par value) to yield 6%. Settlement until last business day of the month.

futures price times the conversion factor. The conversion factor is the price of the bond if it were priced to yield 6%. Thus, the short delivering a bond is paid

$$\text{Invoice price} = (\text{Futures price} \times \text{conversion factor}) + \text{accrued interest}$$

Example 7.9   Consider two bonds making semiannual coupon payments. Bond A is a 7% coupon bond with exactly 8 years to maturity, a price of 103.71, and a yield of 6.4%. This bond would have a price of 106.28 if its yield were 6%. Thus its conversion factor is 1.0628.

Bond B has 7 years to maturity and a 5% coupon. Its current price and yield are 92.73 and 6.3%. It would have a conversion factor of 0.9435, since that is its price at a 6% yield.   ❧

Now suppose that the futures contract is close to expiration, the observed futures price is 97.583, and the only two deliverable bonds are Bonds A and B. The short can decide which bond to deliver by comparing the market value of the bond to its invoice price if delivered. For Bond A we have

$$\text{Invoice price} - \text{market price} = (97.583 \times 1.0628) - 103.71 = 0.00$$

For Bond B we have

$$\text{Invoice price} - \text{market price} = (97.583 \times 0.9435) - 92.73 = -0.66$$

These calculations are summarized in Table 7.5.

Based on the yields for the two bonds, the short breaks even delivering the 8-year 7% bond and would lose money delivering the 7-year 5% coupon bond (the invoice price

TABLE 7.5	Prices, yields, and the conversion factor for two bonds. The futures price is 97.583. The short would break even delivering the 8-year 7% bond, and lose money delivering the 7-year 5% bond. Both bonds make semiannual coupon payments.

Description	8-Year 7% Coupon, 6.4% Yield	7-Year 5%, 6.3% Yield
Market Price	103.71	92.73
Price at 6% (Conversion Factor)	106.28	94.35
Invoice Price (Futures × Conversion Factor)	103.71	92.09
Invoice − Market	0	−0.66

is less than the market price). In this example, the 8-year 7% bond is thus the cheapest to deliver.

In general there will be a single cheapest-to-deliver bond. You might be wondering why both bonds aren't equally cheap to deliver. The reason is that the conversion factor is set by a mechanical procedure (the price at which the bond yields 6%), taking no account of the current relative market prices of bonds. Except by coincidence, two bonds will not be equally cheap to deliver.

Also, all but one of the bonds must have a negative delivery value. If two bonds had a positive delivery value, then arbitrage would be possible. The only no-arbitrage configuration in general has one bond worth zero to deliver (Bond A in example 7.9) and the rest lose money if delivered. To avoid arbitrage, the futures price is

$$\text{Futures price} = \frac{\text{Price of cheapest to deliver}}{\text{Conversion factor for cheapest to deliver}} \qquad (7.14)$$

This discussion glosses over subtleties involving transaction costs (whether you already own a bond may affect your delivery profit calculation) and uncertainty before the delivery period about which bond will be cheapest to deliver. Also the T-note is deliverable at any time during the expiration month, but trading ceases with 7 business days remaining. Consequently, if there are any remaining open contracts during the last week of the month, the short has the option to deliver any bond at a price that might be a week out of date. This provides a delivery option for the short that is also priced into the contract. There are other complications, but suffice it to say that the T-bond and T-note contracts are complex.

The T-bond and T-note futures contracts have been extremely successful. The contracts illustrate some important design considerations for a futures contract. Consider first how the contract is settled. If the contract designated a particular T-bond as the underlying asset, that T-bond could be in short supply, and in fact it might be possible for someone to corner the available supply. (A **market corner** occurs when someone buys most or all of the deliverable asset or commodity.) A short would then be unable to obtain the bond to deliver. In addition, the deliverable T-bond would change from year to year and the contract would become more complicated, since traders would have to price the futures differently to reflect different underlying bonds for different maturity dates.

An alternative scheme could have had the contract cash-settle against a T-bond index, much like the S&P 500. This arrangement, however, introduces basis risk, as the T-bond futures contract might then track the index but fail to track any particular bond.

In the end, settlement procedures for the T-bond and T-note contracts permitted a range of bonds and notes to be delivered. Since a high-coupon bond is worth more than an otherwise identical low-coupon bond, there had to be a conversion factor, in order that the short is paid more for delivering the high-coupon bond.

The idea that there is a cheapest to deliver is not exclusive to Treasury bonds. The same issue arises with commodities, where a futures contract may permit delivery of commodities at different locations or of different qualities.

7.5 REPURCHASE AGREEMENTS

An extremely important kind of forward contract is a repurchase agreement, or **repo.**[11] A repo entails selling a security with an agreement to buy it back at a fixed price. It is effectively a reverse cash-and-carry—a sale coupled with a long forward contract. Like any reverse cash-and-carry, it is equivalent to borrowing. The particular twist with a repo is that the underlying security is held as collateral by the counterparty, who has bought the security and agreed to sell it at a fixed price. Thus, a repo is collateralized borrowing. Repos are common in bond markets, but in principle a repurchase agreement can be used for any asset.

Example 7.10 Suppose you enter into a 1-week repurchase agreement for a 9-month $1m Treasury bill. The current price of the T-bill is $956,938, and you agree to repurchase it in 1 week for $958,042. You have borrowed money at a 1-week rate of $958,042/956,938 - 1 = 0.115\%$, receiving cash today and promising to repay cash plus interest in a week. The security provides collateral for the loan. ❦

The party who initiates the repo owns the asset when the transaction is completed and is therefore the financial owner of the security. During the repo, however, the counterparty owns the bond. Most repos are overnight. A long-term repurchase agreement is called a **term repo.**

The counterparty is said to have entered into a reverse repurchase agreement, or **reverse repo,** and is short the forward contract. This is a loan of cash for the duration

---

[11] For a detailed treatment of repurchase agreements, see Steiner (1997).

of the agreement with a security held as collateral. It can also be described as a cash-and-carry.

If the borrower does not repay the loan, the lender keeps the security. Thus, the counterparty's view of the risk of the transaction differs according to the quality of the collateral. Collateral with a more variable price and a less liquid market is lower quality from the perspective of the lender. Because collateral quality varies, every security will have its own market-determined repo rate.

In addition to a repo rate that reflects collateral quality, dealers can also charge a **haircut,** which is the amount by which the value of the collateral exceeds the amount of the loan. The haircut reflects the credit risk of the borrower. A 2% haircut would mean that the borrower receives only 98% of the market value of the security, providing an additional margin of protection for the counterparty.

Repurchase agreements are frequently used by dealers to finance inventory. In the ordinary course of business a dealer buys and sells securities. The purchase of a security requires funds. A dealer can buy a bond from a customer and then repo it overnight. The money raised with the repo provides the cash needed to pay the seller. The dealer then has a cost of carrying the bond equal to the repo rate.[12] The counterparty on this transaction is an investor with cash to invest short-term, such as a corporation. The investor buys the bond, promising to sell it back. This is lending.

The same techniques can be used to finance speculative positions. Hedge funds, for example, use repurchase agreements. A hedge fund speculating on the price difference between two Treasury bonds can finance the transaction with repos. An example of this is discussed in the Long-Term Capital Management box on page 228.

How do we engage in a transaction like this—long bond A and short bond B—in practice? The answer is that we undertake the following two transactions simultaneously:

The long position   Buy bond A and repo it. Use the cash raised in the repo to pay for the bond (recall that dealers finance inventory in this fashion). When it is time to reverse the repo, sell the bond and use the cash raised from the sale to buy the bond back and close the repo position (think of the sale and close of the repo as happening simultaneously). Note that a low repo rate for this bond works to the arbitrageur's advantage, since it means that the repurchase price of the bond is low. The arbitrageur also benefits from a price increase on the bond.

The short position   Borrow bond B by entering into a reverse repurchase agreement. We receive the bond (collateral for the loan) via the reverse repo, sell it, and use the proceeds to pay the counterparty. At the termination of the agreement, buy the bond back in the open market and return it, being paid the repo rate. Since we receive interest in this transaction, a high repo rate works to our advantage as does a price decrease on the bond.

....

[12]The repurchase agreement in this example provides financing. The dealer still is the ultimate owner of the bond and thus has price risk that could be hedged with futures contracts.

Long-Term Capital Management

Repurchase agreements are a common financing strategy, but achieved particular notoriety during the Long-Term Capital Management (LTCM) crisis in 1998. LTCM was a hedge fund with a luminous roster of partners, including star bond trader John Meriwether, former Federal Reserve Vice Chairman David Mullins, and academics Robert Merton and Myron Scholes, who won the Nobel prize in Economics while associated with LTCM.

Many of LTCM's strategies involved so-called convergence trades, meaning that they were a bet that the prices of two assets would grow closer together. Typically, the most recently issued bonds at certain maturities—30 years, 10 years, 5 years, and several others—are especially liquid and are said to be "on-the-run." On-the-run bonds have lower yields than adjacent off-the-run bonds.

One well-known convergence trade involves newly issued on-the-run 30-year Treasury bonds, which typically sell at a lower yield than the almost identical off-the-run 29 $\frac{1}{2}$-year Treasury bond. One might bet that the yields of the 30-year and 29 $\frac{1}{2}$-year bonds will converge as the 30-year bond ages and becomes off-the-run. Traders make this bet by short-selling the on-the-run bond and buying the off-the-run bond. When the on-the-run

bond becomes off-the-run, its yield should (in theory) equal that of the other off-the-run bond, and the price of the two bonds should converge. The trader profits from the convergence in price, buying back the former on-the-run bond at its new, cheaper price.

In his book about LTCM, Lowenstein (2000, p. 45) describes the trade like this: "No sooner did Long-Term buy the off-the-run bonds than it loaned them to some other Wall Street firm, which then wired cash to Long-Term as collateral. Then Long-Term turned around and used this cash as collateral on the bonds that *it* borrowed. The collateral it paid equaled the collateral it collected. In other words, Long-Term pulled off the entire $2 billion trade *without using a dime of its own cash*." (Emphasis in original.) Many forward contracts, of course, are entered into without a party "using a dime of its own cash." Long-Term also reportedly paid small or no haircuts.

When Long-Term failed in the fall of 1998, it had many such transactions and thus potentially many creditors. The difficulty of unwinding all of these intertwined positions was one of the reasons the Fed brokered a buyout of Long-Term by other banks, rather than have Long-Term explicitly declare bankruptcy.

Since the investor is betting that there will be a reduction in the price difference between the two bonds, it is necessary to enter into both legs of the transaction. The arbitrageur would like a low repo rate on the purchased bond and a high repo rate on the sold bond, as well as a price increase of the purchased bond relative to the short-sold bond.

In practice, haircuts on both bond positions are a transaction cost. Haircuts are a capital requirement imposed by the counterparty, which means that an arbitrageur must have capital to undertake an otherwise self-financing arbitrage transaction. Differences in repo rates on the assets can be an additional transaction cost. Even if the price gap between the two bonds does not close, the arbitrage can be prohibitively costly if the difference in repo rates on the two bonds is sufficiently great. Cornell and Shapiro (1989) document that in one well-known episode of on-the-run/off-the-run arbitrage (see the box on page 228), the repo rate on an on-the-run (short-sold) bond went to zero, making arbitrage costly even though the price gap remained when the on-the-run bond became off-the-run.

CHAPTER SUMMARY

The price of a zero-coupon bond with T years to maturity tells us the value today of $1 to be received at time T. The set of these bond prices for different maturities is the zero-coupon yield curve and is the basic input for present value calculations. There are equivalent ways to express the same information about interest rates, including the par coupon rate and implied forward rates.

Forward rate agreements (FRAs) permit borrowers and lenders to hedge the interest rate by locking in the implied forward rate. If the interest rate changes, FRAs require a payment reflecting the change in the value of the interest rate as of the loan's maturity day. Eurodollar contracts are an alternative to FRAs as a hedging mechanism. However, Eurodollar contracts make payment on the initiation date for the loan rather than the maturity date, so there is a timing mismatch between the Eurodollar payment and the interest payment date. This gives rise to convexity bias, which causes the rate implied by the Eurodollar contract to be greater than that for an otherwise equivalent FRA. Treasury bill contracts are yet another possible hedging vehicle, but suffer from basis risk since the change in the government's borrowing rate may be different from the change in the borrowing rate for a firm or individual.

Duration is a measure of a bond's risk. Modified duration is the percentage change in the bond price for a unit change in the interest rate. Macaulay duration is the percentage change in the bond price for a percentage change in the discount factor. Duration is not a perfect measure of bond price risk. A portfolio is said to be duration-matched if it consists of short and long bond positions with equal value-weighted durations.

Treasury-note and Treasury-bond futures contracts have Treasury notes and bonds as underlying assets. A complication with these contracts is that a range of bonds are deliverable, and there is a cheapest to deliver. The futures price will reflect expectations about which bond is cheapest to deliver.

Repurchase agreements and reverse repurchase agreements are synthetic short-term borrowing and lending, the equivalent of reverse cash-and-carry and cash-and-carry transactions.

FURTHER READING

Basic interest rate concepts are fundamental in finance and are used throughout this book. Some of the formulas in this chapter will appear again as swap rate calculations in Chapter 8. Chapter 15 shows how to price bonds that make payments denominated in foreign currencies or commodities, and how to price bonds containing options. While the bond price calculations in this chapter are useful in practice, concepts such as duration have conceptual problems. In Chapter 23, we will see how to build a coherent, internally consistent model of interest rates and bond prices.

Useful references for bond and money market calculations are Stigum (1990) and Stigum and Robinson (1996). Sundaresan (2002) and Tuckman (1995) are fixed-income texts that go into topics in this chapter in more depth. Convexity bias is studied by Burghardt and Hoskins (1995) and Gupta and Subrahmanyam (2002). Grinblatt and Longstaff (2000) discuss the market for STRIPS and study the pricing relationships between Treasury bonds and STRIPS.

PROBLEMS

7.1. Suppose you observe the following zero-coupon bond prices per $1 of maturity payment: 0.96154 (1-year), 0.91573 (2-year), 0.87630 (3-year), 0.82270 (4-year), 0.77611 (5-year). For each maturity year compute the zero-coupon bond yields (effective annual and continuously compounded), the par coupon rate, and the 1-year implied forward rate.

7.2. Using the information in Problem 1, find the price of a 5-year coupon bond that has a par payment of $1,000.00 and annual coupon payments of $60.00.

7.3. Suppose you observe the following effective annual zero-coupon bond yields: 0.030 (1-year), 0.035 (2-year), 0.040 (3-year), 0.045 (4-year), 0.050 (5-year). For each maturity year compute the zero-coupon bond prices, continuously compounded zero-coupon bond yields, the par coupon rate, and the 1-year implied forward rate.

7.4. Suppose you observe the following 1-year implied forward rates: 0.050000 (1-year), 0.034061 (2-year), 0.036012 (3-year), 0.024092 (4-year), 0.001470 (5-year). For each maturity year compute the zero-coupon bond prices, effective annual and continuously compounded zero-coupon bond yields, and the par coupon rate.

7.5. Suppose you observe the following continuously compounded zero-coupon bond yields: 0.06766 (1-year), 0.05827 (2-year), 0.04879 (3-year), 0.04402 (4-year), 0.03922 (5-year). For each maturity year compute the zero-coupon bond prices, effective annual zero-coupon bond yields, the par coupon rate, and the 1-year implied forward rate.

7.6. Suppose you observe the following par coupon bond yields: 0.03000 (1-year), 0.03491 (2-year), 0.03974 (3-year), 0.04629 (4-year), 0.05174 (5-year). For each maturity year compute the zero-coupon bond prices, effective annual and continuously compounded zero-coupon bond yields, and the 1-year implied forward rate.

7.7. Using the information in Table 7.1,

  a. Compute the implied forward rate from time 1 to time 3.

    b. Compute the implied forward price of a par 2-year coupon bond that will be issued at time 1.

7.8. Suppose that in order to hedge interest rate risk on your borrowing, you enter into an FRA that will guarantee a 6% effective annual interest rate for one year on $500,000.00. On the date you borrow the $500,000.00, the actual interest rate is 5%. Determine the dollar settlement of the FRA assuming

    a. Settlement occurs on the date the loan is initiated.

    b. Settlement occurs on the date the loan is repaid.

7.9. Using the same information as the previous problem, suppose the interest rate on the borrowing date is 7.5%. Determine the dollar settlement of the FRA assuming

    a. Settlement occurs on the date the loan is initiated.

    b. Settlement occurs on the date the loan is repaid.

Use the following zero-coupon bond prices to answer the next three questions:

Days to Maturity	Zero Coupon Bond Price
90	0.99009
180	0.97943
270	0.96525
360	0.95238

7.10. What is the rate on a synthetic FRA for a 90-day loan commencing on day 90? A 180-day loan commencing on day 90? A 270-day loan commencing on day 90?

7.11. What is the rate on a synthetic FRA for a 180-day loan commencing on day 180? Suppose you are the counterparty for a borrower who uses the FRA to hedge the interest rate on a $10m loan. What positions in zero-coupon bonds would you use to hedge the risk on the FRA?

7.12. Suppose you are the counterparty for a lender who enters into an FRA to hedge the lending rate on $10m for a 90-day loan commencing on day 270. What positions in zero-coupon bonds would you use to hedge the risk on the FRA?

7.13. Using the information in Table 7.1, suppose you buy a 3-year par coupon bond and hold it for 2 years, after which time you sell it. Assume that interest rates are certain not to change and that you reinvest the coupon received in year 1 at the 1-year rate prevailing at the time you receive the coupon. Verify that the 2-year return on this investment is 6.5%.

7.14. As in the previous problem, consider holding a 3-year bond for 2 years. Now suppose that interest rates can change, but that at time 0, the rates in Table 7.1 prevail. What transactions could you undertake using forward rate agreements to guarantee that your 2-year return is 6.5%?

7.15. Consider the implied forward rate between year 1 and year 2, based on Table 7.1.

    a. Suppose that $r_0(1, 2) = 6.8\%$. Show how buying the 2-year zero-coupon bond and borrowing at the 1-year rate and implied forward rate of 6.8% would earn you an arbitrage profit.

    b. Suppose that $r_0(1, 2) = 7.2\%$. Show how borrowing the 2-year zero-coupon bond and lending at the 1-year rate and implied forward rate of 7.2% would earn you an arbitrage profit.

7.16. Suppose the September Eurodollar futures contract has a price of 96.4. You plan to borrow $50m for 3 months in September at LIBOR, and you intend to use the Eurodollar contract to hedge your borrowing rate.

    a. What rate can you secure?

    b. Will you be long or short the Eurodollar contract?

    c. How many contracts will you enter into?

    d. Assuming the true 3-month LIBOR is 1% in September, what is the settlement in dollars at expiration of the futures contract? (For purposes of this question, ignore daily marking to market on the futures contract.)

7.17. A lender plans to invest $100m for 150 days, 60 days from today. (That is, if today is day 0, the loan will be initiated on day 60 and will mature on day 210.) The implied forward rate over 150 days, and hence the rate on a 150-day FRA, is 2.5%. The actual interest rate over that period could be either 2.2% or 2.8%.

    a. If the interest rate on day 60 is 2.8%, how much will the lender have to pay if the FRA is settled on day 60? How much if it is settled on day 210?

    b. If the interest rate on day 60 is 2.2%, how much will the lender have to pay if the FRA is settled on day 60? How much if it is settled on day 210?

7.18. Consider the same facts as the previous problem, only now consider hedging with the 3-month Eurodollar futures. Suppose the Eurodollar futures contract that matures 60 days from today has a price on day 0 of 94.

    a. What issues arise in using the 3-month Eurodollar contract to hedge a 150-day loan?

    b. If you wish to hedge a lending position, should you go long or short the contract?

    c. What 3-month LIBOR is implied by the Eurodollar futures price? Approximately what lending rate should you be able to lock in?

    d. What position in Eurodollar futures would you use to lock in a lending rate? In doing this, what assumptions are you making about the relationship between 90-day LIBOR and the 150-day lending rate?

7.19. Consider the bonds in Example 7.8. What hedge ratio would have exactly hedged the portfolio if interest rates had decreased by 25 basis points? Increased by 25 basis points? Repeat assuming a 50-basis-point change.

7.20. Compute Macaulay and modified durations for the following bonds:

    a. A 5-year bond paying annual coupons of 4.432% and selling at par.

    b. An 8-year bond paying semiannual coupons with a coupon rate of 8% and a yield of 7%.

    c. A 10-year bond paying annual coupons of 6% with a price of $92 and maturity value of $100.

7.21. Consider the following two bonds which make semiannual coupon payments: A 20-year bond with a 6% coupon and 20% yield, and a 30-year bond with a 6% coupon and a 20% yield.

    a. For each bond, compute the price value of a basis point.

    b. For each bond, compute Macaulay duration.

    c. "For otherwise identical bonds, Macaulay duration is increasing in time to maturity." Is this statement always true? Discuss.

7.22. An 8-year bond with 6% annual coupons and a 5.004% yield sells for $106.44 with a Macaulay duration of 6.631864. A 9-year bond has 7% annual coupons with a 5.252% yield and sells for $112.29 with a Macaulay duration of 7.098302. You wish to duration-hedge the 8-year bond using a 9-year bond. How many 9-year bonds must we short for every 8-year bond?

7.23. A 6-year bond with a 4% coupon sells for $102.46 with a 3.5384% yield. The conversion factor for the bond is 0.90046. An 8-year bond with 5.5% coupons sells for $113.564 with a conversion factor of 0.9686. (All coupon payments are semiannual.) Which bond is cheaper to deliver given a T-note futures price of 113.81?

APPENDIX 7.A: QUOTING INTEREST RATES

Typically we want to know the interest rate because we want the answer to a simple question: If we invest $1 today for a specified period of time, how much money will we have at the end? It turns out that in practice there is almost never a simple answer to this question. Conceptually, the question asks for the yield on a zero-coupon bond. In practice, quoting conventions are designed more to make yield quotes comparable across different instruments than to produce a true effective yield.

To illustrate this point, consider standard Treasury-bill yield calculations. On October 28, 1998, the *Wall Street Journal* reported the information in Table 7.6 in its Treasury-bill table. Where do the "ask yields" in this table come from? Stigum and Robinson (1996) provide the formulas for this and other money-market calculations. The goal is to make T-bill yields comparable to Treasury-bond yields, which generally pay semiannual coupons. T-bond yields are quoted as twice the semiannual yield. The

TABLE 7.6		Treasury bill quotations from the *Wall Street Journal* on October 28, 1998.		
Maturity	**Days to Maturity**	**Ask Discount**	**Ask Yield**
Dec 10 1998	43	3.65	3.72
Oct 14 1999	351	3.87	4.04

concept of a "bond-equivalent yield" is designed to make quoted yields for bills, which make no coupon payments, comparable to quoted yields for bonds, which do make semiannual coupon payments, and for which the quoted yield is twice the semiannual yield.

First, T-bill prices are quoted on an annualized discount basis. The discount is the number subtracted from 100 to get the invoice price. The formula, normalizing the face value of the T-bill to be 100, is

$$P = 100 - \frac{discount \times days}{360}$$

The T-bills in Table 7.6 have invoice prices of

$$100 - 3.65 \times 43/360 \ = \ 99.5640$$
$$100 - 3.87 \times 351/360 \ = \ 96.2268$$

Thus, an investor pays 0.995640 per dollar of maturity value for the 43-day bill and 0.962268 for the 351-day bill. Note that these prices give us "true" 43-day and 351-day discount factors. A 43-day bill yields $\frac{100}{99.5640} = 1.004379$ or 0.4379% over 43 days, while the 351-day bill yields 3.9212% over 351 days. Annualizing these yields necessarily involves making somewhat arbitrary assumptions.

For bills less than 182 days from maturity, a bill is directly comparable to a bond since neither makes a coupon payment over that period. In this case the only adjustment needed is to correct for the fact that bonds are quoted on a 365-day basis and bills are quoted on a 360-day basis:

$$r_{be} = \frac{365 \times discount/100}{360 - discount/100 \times days}$$

where r_{be} stands for "bond-equivalent yield." Applying this formula to the Dec 10 T-bill, we see that

$$\frac{365 \times 0.0365}{360 - 0.0365 \times 43} = 0.0372$$

If you use this formula for the 351-day bill, however, it will not work, giving a yield of 4.078 rather than the 4.04 listed in the newspaper. The reason is that a bond with more than 180 days to maturity will make a coupon payment, which is assumed not to be reinvested (since the annual yield is just double the semiannual yield). Thus, to make a bill quote comparable to that for a bond, we need to account for an imaginary coupon. The formula from Stigum and Robinson (1996) is

$$r_{be} = \frac{-\frac{2\times days}{365} + 2\sqrt{\left(\frac{days}{365}\right)^2 - \left(\frac{2\times days}{365} - 1\right)\left(1 - \frac{1}{P}\right)}}{\frac{2\times days}{365} - 1} \tag{7.15}$$

Applying this to the October bond gives

$$\frac{-\frac{2\times 351}{365} + 2\sqrt{\left(\frac{351}{365}\right)^2 - \left(\frac{2\times 351}{365} - 1\right)\left(1 - \frac{1}{0.962268}\right)}}{\frac{2\times 351}{365} - 1} = 0.040384$$

This matches the quoted yield in Table 7.6. In Excel, the function TBILLEQ provides the bond-equivalent yield for a T-bill.

APPENDIX 7.B: PRACTICAL ISSUES WITH COUPON BONDS

There are conventions for handling annualization of coupon rates and yields when there are multiple coupons a year, and for the quotation of bond prices when there is a fractional period until the next coupon payment. This section discusses some of these conventions; a full treatment of bond pricing and quoting conventions is in Stigum and Robinson (1996).

Bond Price Calculations

The standard formula for the price of a bond with periodic coupon C, maturity payment M, per-period yield y, and n remaining coupon payments is

$$B(y) = \sum_{i=1}^{n} \frac{C}{(1+y)^i} + \frac{M}{(1+y)^n} = \frac{C}{y}\left(1 - \frac{1}{(1+y)^n}\right) + \frac{M}{(1+y)^n}$$

This formula assumes there is one full period until the next coupon, with all inputs stated per period, i.e., the coupon is C at each payment, and the yield is y per coupon period. In practice, if a bond makes coupon payments m times a year, the convention is to quote the coupon rate as m times the per-period payment. The yield to maturity is computed per period, and then multiplied by m to obtain the annual quoted yield.

Example 7.11   Consider a 7% $100 maturity coupon bond that makes semiannual coupon payments on February 15 and August 15 and matures on August 15, 2008. Suppose today is August 15, 2000, and the coupon has been paid. There are 16 remaining payments. If the price of this bond is $103.71, the semiannual yield, y, solves

$$\$103.71 = \frac{\$3.5}{y}\left[1 - \frac{1}{(1+y)^{16}}\right] + \frac{\$100}{(1+y)^{16}}$$

The semiannual yield is 3.2%, which would be annualized by multiplying by two. Thus, the yield would be quoted as 6.4%.   ❧

By assuming that the bond has just paid a coupon, this example ignores the problem of fractional periods. In practice, a fractional period until the next coupon is taken into account by discounting for that fractional period. Specifically, suppose there are d days until the next coupon, and m days between the last and next coupon. The price for the bond is

$$B(y) = \sum_{i=1}^{n} \frac{C}{(1+y)^{i-1+d/m}} + \frac{M}{(1+y)^{n-1+d/m}}$$

$$= \left(\frac{1}{1+y}\right)^{d/m} \left(C + \frac{C}{y}\left[1 - \frac{1}{(1+y)^{n-1}}\right] + \frac{M}{(1+y)^{n-1}}\right) \qquad (7.16)$$

Example 7.12   Consider the same bond as in Example 7.11, only suppose that the date is November 11, 2000. There are 96 days until the next coupon payment and 184 days between payments. Thus, the price for the bond at a 6.4% yield (3.2% semiannual) is

$$\left(\frac{1}{1.032}\right)^{96/184} \left(\$3.5 + \frac{\$3.5}{0.032}\left[1 - \frac{1}{(1.032)^{15}}\right] + \frac{\$100}{(1.032)^{15}}\right) = \$105.286 \qquad ❧$$

Clean and Dirty Prices

Equation (7.16) gives a bond price that fully reflects the coming coupon payment. Using this formula, the bond price would rise over time as each coupon payment approached, then fall on the coupon payment date, and so forth. The bond price quoted in this fashion is called the **dirty price.**

In practice, bond prices are quoted net of **accrued interest.** Accrued interest is the pro-rated portion of the coupon since the last coupon date. With $m - d$ days since the last coupon, accrued interest is $C \times (m - d)/m$. Intuitively, if you buy a bond three-fourths of the way from one coupon payment to the next, the price you pay should reflect three-fourths of the coming coupon payment. This pro-rated amount is the accrued interest.

Bond prices are quoted as a **clean price,** which is the dirty price less accrued interest. The clean price does not exhibit the predictable rise and fall in price due to the coming coupon payment.[13]

....

[13]Because accrued interest is amortized linearly rather than geometrically, this statement is not exactly true. See Smith (2002).

Example 7.13 Consider the bond in Example 7.12. Accrued interest as of November 11 would be $3.5 \times (184 - 96)/184 = 1.674$. Thus, the clean price for the bond would be

$$\text{Clean price} = \text{Dirty price} - \text{accrued interest}$$
$$= \$105.286 - \$1.674 = \$103.612$$

Chapter 8

Swaps

Thus far we have talked about derivatives contracts that settle on a single date. A forward contract, for example, fixes a price for a transaction that will occur on a specific date in the future. However, many transactions occur repeatedly. Firms that issue bonds make periodic coupon payments. Multinational firms frequently exchange currencies. Firms that buy commodities as production inputs or that sell them make payments or receive income linked to commodity prices on an ongoing basis.

These situations raise the question: If a manager seeking to reduce risk confronts a risky payment *stream*—as opposed to a single risky payment—what is the easiest way to hedge this risk? One obvious answer to this question is that we can enter into a separate forward contract for each payment we wish to hedge. However, it might be more convenient, and entail lower transaction costs, if there were a single transaction that we could use to hedge a stream of payments.

A **swap** is a contract calling for an exchange of payments over time. One party makes a payment to the other depending upon whether a price turns out to be greater or less than a reference price that is specified in the swap contract. A swap thus provides a means to hedge a stream of risky payments. By entering into an oil swap, for example, an oil buyer confronting a stream of uncertain oil payments can lock in a fixed price for oil over a period of time. The swap payments would be based on the difference between a fixed price for oil and a market price that varies over time.

From this description, you can see that there is a relationship between swaps and forward contracts. In fact, a forward contract is a single-payment swap. It is possible to price a multi-date swap—determine the fixed price for oil in the above example—by using information from the set of forward prices with different maturities (i.e., the strip). We will see that swaps are nothing more than forward contracts coupled with borrowing and lending money.

8.1 AN EXAMPLE OF A COMMODITY SWAP

We begin our study of swaps by presenting an example of a simple commodity swap. Our purpose here is to understand the economics of swaps. In particular we wish to understand how a swap is related to forwards, why someone might use a swap, and how market-makers hedge the risk of swaps. In later sections we present swap-price formulas and examine interest rate swaps, total return swaps, and more complicated commodity swap examples.

An industrial producer, IP Inc., is going to buy 100,000 barrels of oil 1 year from today and 2 years from today. Suppose that the forward price for delivery in 1 year is $20/barrel and in 2 years is $21/barrel. We need interest rates in this discussion, so suppose that annual interest rates are as in Table 7.1 (see page 200): The 1- and 2-year zero-coupon bond yields are 6% and 6.5%.

IP can use forward contracts to guarantee the cost of buying oil for the next 2 years. Specifically, IP could enter into long forward contracts for 100,000 barrels in each of the next 2 years, committing to pay $20/barrel in 1 year and $21/barrel in 2 years. The present value of this cost per barrel is

$$\frac{\$20}{1.06} + \frac{\$21}{1.065^2} = \$37.383$$

IP could invest this amount today and ensure that it had the funds to buy oil in 1 and 2 years. Alternatively, IP could pay an oil supplier $37.383, and the supplier would commit to delivering one barrel in each of the next two years. A single payment today for a single delivery of oil in the future is a prepaid forward. A single payment today to obtain *multiple* deliveries in the future is a **prepaid swap.**

Although it is possible to enter into a prepaid swap, buyers might worry about the resulting credit risk: They have fully paid for oil that will not be delivered for up to 2 years. (The prepaid forward has the same problem.) For the same reason, the swap counterparty would worry about a postpaid swap, where the oil is delivered and full payment is made after 2 years. A more attractive solution for both parties is to defer payment until the oil is delivered, while still fixing the total price.

Note that there are many feasible ways to have the buyer pay; any payment stream with a present value of $37.383 is acceptable. Typically, however, a swap will call for equal payments in each year. The payment per year per barrel, x, will then have to be such that

$$\frac{x}{1.06} + \frac{x}{1.065^2} = \$37.383$$

To satisfy this equation, the payments must be $20.483 in each year. We then say that the 2-year swap price is $20.483. *However, any payments that have a present value of $37.383 are acceptable.*

Physical versus Financial Settlement

Thus far we have described the swap as if the swap counterparty supplied physical oil to the buyer. Figure 8.1 shows a swap that calls for physical settlement. In this case $20.483 is the per-barrel cost of oil.

However, we could also arrange for *financial settlement* of the swap. With financial settlement, the oil buyer, IP, pays the swap counterparty the difference between $20.483 and the spot price (if the difference is negative, the counterparty pays the buyer), and the oil buyer then buys oil at the spot price. For example, if the market price is $25, the swap counterparty pays the buyer

$$\text{Spot price} - \text{swap price} = \$25 - \$20.483 = \$4.517$$

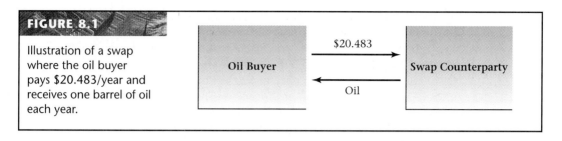

FIGURE 8.1

Illustration of a swap where the oil buyer pays $20.483/year and receives one barrel of oil each year.

If the market price is $18, the spot price less the swap price is

$$\text{Spot price} - \text{swap price} = \$18 - \$20.483 = -\$2.483$$

In this case, the oil buyer makes a payment to the swap counterparty. Whatever the market price of oil, the net cost to the buyer is the swap price, $20.483:

$$\underbrace{\text{Spot price} - \text{swap price}}_{\text{Swap Payment}} - \underbrace{\text{spot price}}_{\text{Spot Purchase of Oil}} = -\text{Swap price}$$

Figure 8.2 depicts cash flows and transactions when the swap is settled financially. *The results for the buyer are the same whether the swap is settled physically or financially.* In both cases, the net cost to the oil buyer is $20.483.

We have discussed the swap on a per-barrel basis. For a swap on 100,000 barrels, we simply multiply all cash flows by 100,000. In this example, 100,000 is the **notional amount** of the swap, meaning that 100,000 barrels is used to determine the magnitude of the payments when the swap is settled financially.

Why Is the Swap Price Not $20.50?

The swap price, $20.483, is close to the average of the two oil forward prices, $20.50. However, it is not exactly the same. Why?

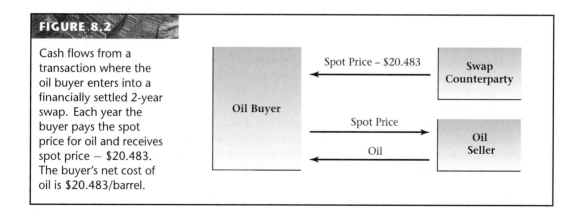

FIGURE 8.2

Cash flows from a transaction where the oil buyer enters into a financially settled 2-year swap. Each year the buyer pays the spot price for oil and receives spot price − $20.483. The buyer's net cost of oil is $20.483/barrel.

Suppose that the swap price were $20.50. The oil buyer would then be committing to pay $0.50 more than the forward price the first year and would pay $0.50 less than the forward price the second year. Thus, *relative to the forward curve, the buyer would have made an interest-free loan to the counterparty.* There is implicit lending in the swap.

Now consider the actual swap price of $20.483/barrel. Relative to the forward curve prices of $20 in 1 year and $21 in 2 years, we are overpaying by $0.483 in the first year and we are underpaying by $0.517 in the second year. Therefore, the swap is equivalent to being long the two forward contracts, coupled with an agreement to lend $0.483 to the swap counterparty in 1 year, and receive $0.517 in 2 years. This loan has the effect of equalizing the net cash flow on the two dates.

The interest rate on this loan is $0.517/0.483 - 1 = 7\%$. Where does 7% come from? We assumed that 6% is the 1-year zero yield and 6.5% is the 2-year yield. Given these interest rates, 7% is the 1-year implied forward yield from year 1 to year 2. (See Table 7.1.) By entering into the swap, we are lending the counterparty money for 1 year beginning in 1 year. If the deal is priced fairly, the interest rate on this loan should be the implied forward interest rate.

The Swap Counterparty

The swap counterparty is a dealer, who is, in effect, a broker between buyer and seller. It's easy to imagine that an oil seller would like to lock in a fixed selling price of oil. In this case, the dealer locates the oil buyer and seller and serves as a go-between for the swap, receiving payments from one party and passing them on to the other. In practice the fixed price paid by the buyer exceeds the fixed price received by the seller. This price difference is a bid-ask spread and is the dealer's fee.

Figure 8.3 illustrates how this transaction would work with financial settlement. The oil seller receives the spot price for oil and receives the swap price less the spot price, on net receiving the swap price. The oil buyer pays the spot price and receives the spot price less the swap price. The situation where the dealer matches the buyer and seller is called a **back-to-back transaction** or "matched book" transaction. The dealer bears the credit risk of both parties, but is not exposed to price risk.

A more interesting situation occurs when the dealer serves as counterparty and hedges the transaction using forward markets. Let's see how this would work.

After entering the swap with the oil buyer, the dealer has the obligation to pay the spot price and receive the swap price. If the spot price rises, the dealer can lose money. The dealer has a short position in 1- and 2-year oil.

The natural hedge for the dealer is to enter into long forward or futures contracts to offset this short exposure. Table 8.1 illustrates how this strategy works. As we discussed earlier, there is an implicit loan in the swap and this is apparent in Table 8.1. The net cash flow for the hedged dealer is a loan, where the dealer receives cash in year 1 and repays it in year 2.

This example shows that *hedging the oil price risk in the swap does not fully hedge the position.* The dealer also has interest rate exposure. If interest rates fall, the dealer will not be able to earn a sufficient return from investing $0.483 in year 1 to repay $0.517

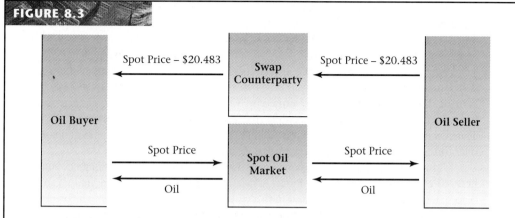

FIGURE 8.3

Cash flows from a transaction where an oil buyer and seller each enters into a financially settled 2-year swap. The buyer pays the spot price for oil and receives spot price − $20.483 each year as a swap payment. The oil seller receives the spot price for oil and receives $20.483 − spot price as a swap payment.

TABLE 8.1

Positions and cash flows for a dealer who has an obligation to receive the fixed price in an oil swap and who hedges the exposure by going long year 1 and year 2 oil forwards.

Year	Payment from Oil Buyer	Long Forward	Net
1	$20.483 − Year 1 Spot Price	Year 1 Spot Price − $20	$0.483
2	$20.483 − Year 2 Spot Price	Year 2 Spot Price − $21	−$0.517

in year 2. Thus, in addition to entering oil forwards, it would make sense for the dealer to use Eurodollar contracts or forward rate agreements to hedge the resulting interest rate exposure.

The Market Value of a Swap

When the buyer first enters the swap, its market value is zero, meaning that either party could enter or exit the swap without having to pay anything to the other party (apart from commissions and bid-ask spreads). From the oil buyer's perspective, the swap consists of two forward contracts plus an agreement to lend money at the implied forward rate of 7%. The forward contracts and forward rate agreement have zero value, so the swap does as well.

Once the swap is struck, however, its market value will generally no longer be zero, for two reasons. First, the forward prices for oil and interest rates will change over time. New swaps would no longer have a fixed price of $20.483; hence, one party will owe money to the other should one party wish to exit or *unwind* the swap.

Second, if oil and interest rate forward prices do not change, the value of the swap will remain zero *until the first swap payment is made.* Once the first swap payment is made, however, the buyer has overpaid by $0.483 relative to the forward curve, and hence, in order to exit the swap, the counterparty would have to pay the oil buyer $0.483. Thus, in general, even if prices do not change, the market value of swaps will change over time due to the implicit borrowing and lending.

A buyer wishing to exit the swap could negotiate terms with the original counterparty to eliminate the swap obligation. An alternative is to leave the original swap in place and enter into an offsetting swap with whoever offers the best price. The original swap called for the oil buyer to pay the fixed price and receive the floating price; the offsetting swap has the buyer receive the fixed price and pay floating. The original obligation would be cancelled except to the extent that the fixed prices are different. However, the difference is known, so oil price risk is eliminated. (There is still credit risk when the original swap counterparty and the counterparty to the offsetting swap are different. This could be a reason for the buyer to prefer offsetting the swap with the original counterparty.)

To see how a swap can change in value, suppose that immediately after the buyer enters the swap, the forward curve for oil rises by $2 in years 1 and 2. Thus, the year-1 forward price becomes $22 and the year-2 forward price becomes $23. The original swap will no longer have a zero market value.

Assuming interest rates are unchanged, the new swap price is $22.483. (Problem 8.1 asks you to verify this.) The buyer could unwind the swap at this point by agreeing to sell oil at $22.483, while the original swap still calls for buying oil at $20.483. Thus, the net swap payments in each year are

$$\underbrace{(\text{Spot price} - \$20.483)}_{\text{Original Swap}} + \underbrace{(\$22.483 - \text{spot price})}_{\text{New Swap}} = \$2$$

The present value of this difference is

$$\frac{\$2}{1.06} + \frac{\$2}{(1.065)^2} = \$3.650$$

The buyer can receive a stream of payments worth $3.65 by offsetting the original swap with a new swap. Thus, $3.65 is the market value of the swap.

If interest rates had changed, we would have used the new interest rates in computing the new swap price.

The examples we have analyzed in this section illustrate the fundamental characteristics of swaps and their cash flows. In the rest of the chapter, we will compute more realistic swap prices for interest rates, currencies, and commodities and see some of the ways in which we can modify the terms of a swap.

8.2 INTEREST RATE SWAPS

Companies use interest rate swaps to modify their interest rate exposure. In this section we will begin with a simple example of an interest rate swap, similar to the preceding oil swap example. We will then present general pricing formulas and discuss ways in which the basic swap structure can be altered.

A Simple Interest Rate Swap

Suppose that XYZ Corp. has $200m of floating-rate debt at LIBOR—meaning that every year XYZ pays that year's current LIBOR—but would prefer to have fixed-rate debt with 3 years to maturity. There are several ways XYZ could effect this change.

First, XYZ could change their interest rate exposure by retiring the floating-rate debt and issuing fixed-rate debt in its place. However, an actual purchase and sale of debt has transaction costs.

Second, they could enter into a strip of forward rate agreements (FRAs) in order to guarantee the borrowing rate for the remaining life of the debt. Since the FRA for each year will typically carry a different interest rate, the company will lock in a different rate each year and, hence, the company's borrowing cost will vary over time, even though it will be fixed in advance.

A third alternative is to obtain interest rate exposure equivalent to that of fixed rate debt by entering into a swap. XYZ is already paying a floating interest rate. They therefore want to enter a swap in which they receive a floating rate and pay the fixed rate, which we will suppose is 6.9548%. This swap is illustrated in Figure 8.4. Notice the similarity to the oil swap.

In a year when the fixed 6.9548% swap rate exceeds 1-year LIBOR, XYZ pays 6.9548% − LIBOR to the swap counterparty. Conversely, when the 6.9548% swap rate is less than LIBOR, the swap counterparty pays LIBOR − 6.9548% to XYZ. On net, XYZ pays 6.9548%. Algebraically, the net interest payment made by XYZ is

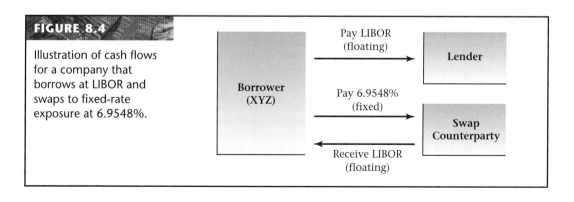

FIGURE 8.4

Illustration of cash flows for a company that borrows at LIBOR and swaps to fixed-rate exposure at 6.9548%.

$$\text{XYZ net payment} = -\underbrace{\text{LIBOR}}_{\text{Floating Payment}} + \underbrace{\text{LIBOR} - 6.9548\%}_{\text{Swap Payment}} = -6.9548\%$$

The notional principal of the swap is \$200m: It is the amount on which the interest payments—and, hence, the net swap payment—is based. The life of the swap is the **swap term** or **swap tenor.**

There are timing conventions with a swap similar to those for a forward rate agreement. At the beginning of a year, the borrowing rate for that year is known. However, the interest payment on the loan is due at the end of the year. The interest rate determination date for the floating interest payment would therefore occur at the beginning of the period. As with an FRA we can think of the swap payment being made at the end of the period (when interest is due).

With the financially settled oil swap, only net swap payments—in this case the difference between LIBOR and 6.9548%—are actually made between XYZ and the counterparty. If one party defaults, they owe to the other party at most the present value of net swap payments they are obligated to make at current market prices. This means that a swap generally has less credit risk than a bond: Whereas principal is at risk with a bond, only net swap payments are at risk in a swap.

The swap in this example is a construct, making payments *as if* there were an exchange of payments between a fixed-rate and floating-rate bond. In practice, a fund manager might own fixed-rate bonds and wish to have floating-rate exposure while continuing to own the bonds. A swap in which a fund manager receives a floating rate in exchange for the payments on bonds the fund continues to hold is called an **asset swap.**

Pricing and the Swap Counterparty

To understand the pricing of the swap, we will examine it from the perspective of both the counterparty and the firm. We first consider the perspective of the counterparty, who we assume is a market-maker.

The market-maker is a counterparty to the swap in order to earn fees, not to take on interest rate risk. Therefore, the market-maker will hedge the transaction. The market-maker receives the fixed rate from the company and pays the floating rate; the danger for the market-maker is that the floating rate will rise. The risk in this transaction can be hedged by entering into forward rate agreements. We express the time 0 implied forward rate between time t_i and t_j as $r_0(t_i, t_j)$ and the realized 1-year rate as $\tilde{r}_{t_i}$. The current 1-year rate, 6%, is known. With the swap rate denoted R, Table 8.2 depicts the risk-free (but time-varying) cash flows faced by the hedged market-maker.

How is R determined? Obviously a market-maker receiving the fixed rate would like to set a high swap rate, but the swap market is competitive. We expect R to be bid down by competing market-makers until the present value of the hedged cash flows is zero. In computing this present value, we need to use the appropriate rate for each cash flow: The one-year rate for $R - 6\%$, the two-year rate for $R - 7.0024\%$, and so forth. Using the rate information from Table 7.1, we compute

Year	Payment on Forward	Net Swap Payment	Net

TABLE 8.2 Cash flows faced by a market-maker who receives fixed and pays floating and hedges the resulting exposure using forward rate agreements.

Year	Payment on Forward	Net Swap Payment	Net
1	—	$R - 6\%$	$R - 6\%$
2	$\tilde{r}_2 - 7.0024\%$	$R - \tilde{r}_2$	$R - 7.0024\%$
3	$\tilde{r}_3 - 8.0071\%$	$R - \tilde{r}_3$	$R - 8.0071\%$

$$\frac{R - 6\%}{1.06} + \frac{R - 7.0024\%}{1.065^2} + \frac{R - 8.0071\%}{1.07^3} = 0$$

This formula gives us an R of 6.9548%, which from Table 7.1 is the same as the par coupon rate on a 3-year bond! In fact, our swap-rate calculation is a round-about way to compute a par bond yield. On reflection, this result should be no surprise. Once the borrower has entered into the swap, the net effect is exactly like borrowing at a fixed rate. Thus the fixed swap rate should be the rate on a coupon bond.

Notice that the unhedged net cash flows in Table 8.2 (the "net swap payment" column) can be replicated by borrowing at a floating rate and lending at a fixed rate. In other words, *an interest rate swap is equivalent to borrowing at a floating rate to buy a fixed-rate bond.*

The borrower's calculations are just the opposite of the market-maker's. The borrower continues to pay the floating rate on its floating rate debt, and receives floating and pays fixed in the swap. Table 8.3 details the cash flows.

Since the swap rate is the same as the par 3-year coupon rate, the borrower is indifferent between the swap and a coupon bond, ignoring transaction costs. Keep in mind that the borrower could also have used forward rate agreements, locking in an escalating interest rate over time: 6% the first year, 7.0024% the second, and 8.0071% the third. By using interest rate forwards the borrower would have eliminated uncertainty about future borrowing rates and created an uneven but certain stream of interest payments

TABLE 8.3 Cash flows faced by a floating-rate borrower who enters into a 3-year swap with a fixed rate of 6.9548%.

Year	Floating Rate Debt Payment	Net Swap Payment	Net
1	-6%	$6\% - 6.9548\%$	-6.9548%
2	$-\tilde{r}_2$	$\tilde{r}_2 - 6.9548\%$	-6.9548%
3	$-\tilde{r}_3$	$\tilde{r}_3 - 6.9548\%$	-6.9548%

over time. The swap provides a way to both guarantee the borrowing rate and lock in a constant rate in a single transaction.

Computing the Swap Rate in General

We now examine more carefully the general calculations for determining the swap rate. We will use the interest rate and bond price notation introduced in Chapter 7. Suppose there are n swap settlements, occurring on dates t_i, $i = 1, \ldots, n$. The implied forward interest rate from date t_{i-1} to date t_i, known at date 0, is $r_0(t_{i-1}, t_i)$. (We will treat $r_0(t_{i-1}, t_i)$ as *not* having been annualized; i.e., it is the return earned from t_{i-1} to t_i.) The price of a zero-coupon bond maturing on date t_i is $P(0, t_i)$.

The market-maker can hedge the floating-rate payments using forward rate agreements. The requirement that the hedged swap have zero net present value is

$$\sum_{i=1}^{n} P(0, t_i)[R - r_0(t_{i-1}, t_i)] = 0 \tag{8.1}$$

where there are n payments on dates $t_1, t_2, \ldots, t_n$. The cash flows $R - r_0(t_{i-1}, t_i)$ can also be obtained by buying a fixed rate bond paying R and borrowing at the floating rate.

Equation (8.1) can be rewritten as

$$\boxed{R = \frac{\sum_{i=1}^{n} P(0, t_i) r(t_{i-1}, t_i)}{\sum_{i=1}^{n} P(0, t_i)}} \tag{8.2}$$

The expression $\sum_{i=1}^{n} P(0, t_i) r(t_{i-1}, t_i)$ is the present value of interest payments implied by the strip of forward rates. The expression $\sum_{i=1}^{n} P(0, t_i)$ is just the present value of a \$1 annuity when interest rates vary over time. Thus, the swap rate annuitizes the interest payments on the floating-rate bond.

We can rewrite equation (8.2) to make it easier to interpret:

$$R = \sum_{i=1}^{n} \left[\frac{P(0, t_i)}{\sum_{j=1}^{n} P(0, t_j)} \right] r(t_{i-1}, t_i)$$

Since the terms in square brackets sum to one, this form of equation (8.2) emphasizes that the fixed swap rate is a weighted average of the implied forward rates, where zero-coupon bond prices are used to determine the weights.

There is another, equivalent way to express the swap rate. Recall from Chapter 7, equation (7.4), that the implied forward rate between times t_1 and t_2, $r_0(t_1, t_2)$, is given by the ratio of zero-coupon bond prices, i.e.,

$$r_0(t_1, t_2) = P(0, t_1)/P(0, t_2) - 1$$

Therefore equation (8.1) can be rewritten

$$\sum_{i=1}^{n} P(0, t_i)[R - r(t_{i-1}, t_i)] = \sum_{i=1}^{n} P(0, t_i) \left[R - \frac{P(0, t_{i-1})}{P(0, t_i)} + 1 \right]$$

Setting this equation equal to zero and solving for R gives us

$$R = \frac{1 - P_0(0, t_n)}{\sum_{i=1}^{n} P_0(0, t_i)} \tag{8.3}$$

You may recognize this as the formula for the coupon on a par coupon bond, equation (7.6), from Chapter 7. This in turn can be rewritten as

$$R \sum_{i=1}^{n} P(0, t_i) + P(0, t_n) = 1$$

This is the valuation equation for a bond priced at par with a coupon rate of R.

The conclusion is that *the swap rate is the coupon rate on a par coupon bond*. This result is intuitive since a firm that swaps from floating-rate to fixed-rate exposure ends up with the economic equivalent of a fixed-rate bond.

The Swap Curve

As discussed in Chapter 5, the Eurodollar futures contract provides a set of 3-month forward LIBOR rates extending out 10 years. It is possible to use this set of forward interest rates to compute equation (8.2) or (8.3). As discussed in Chapter 7, zero-coupon bond prices can be constructed from implied forward rates.

The set of swap rates at different maturities implied by LIBOR is called the *swap curve*. There is an over-the-counter market in interest rate swaps, which is widely quoted. The swap curve should be consistent with the interest rate curve implied by the Eurodollar futures contract, which is used to hedge swaps.[1]

Here is how we construct the swap curve using the set of Eurodollar prices. Column 2 of Table 8.4 lists 2 years of Eurodollar futures prices from June 2000. The next column shows the implied 91-day interest rate, beginning in the month in column 1. For example, using equation (5.20), the June price of 93.18 implies a June to September quarterly interest rate of

$$(100 - 93.18)\frac{91}{90}\frac{1}{400} = 1.724\%$$

Column 4 reports the corresponding implied zero-coupon bond price. In the second row, the price reflects the cost in June of $1 paid in September. The third row is the June cost of $1 paid in December, and so forth. The fourth row is

$$\frac{1}{1.01724} \times \frac{1}{1.01782} \times \frac{1}{1.01827} = 0.9485$$

....

[1] The Eurodollar contract is a futures contract, while a swap is a set of forward rate agreements. Because of convexity bias, discussed in Chapter 7, the swap curve constructed from Eurodollar futures contracts following the procedure described in this section will be somewhat greater than the observed swap curve. This is discussed by Burghardt and Hoskins (1995) and Gupta and Subrahmanyam (2000).

TABLE 8.4		3-month LIBOR forward rates implied by Eurodollar futures prices with maturity dates given in the first column. Prices are from June 7, 2000.		
Maturity Date, t_i	Eurodollar Futures Price	Implied Quarterly Rate, $r(t_i, t_{i+1})$	Implied June 2000 Price of $1 Paid on Maturity Date, t_i, $P(0, t_i)$	Swap Rate
Jun-00	93.18	0.01724	—	6.895%
Sep-00	92.95	0.01782	0.9830	7.011%
Dec-00	92.77	0.01827	0.9658	7.109%
Mar-01	92.75	0.01832	0.9485	7.162%
Jun-01	92.72	0.01840	0.9314	7.201%
Sep-01	92.70	0.01842	0.9146	7.228%
Dec-01	92.67	0.01852	0.8980	7.252%
Mar-02	92.74	0.01835	0.8817	7.263%

Source for Eurodollars futures prices: FII.

which is the June cost of $1 paid in March. The December swap rate, expressed as a quarterly rate, is the fixed quarterly interest rate from June through March, with swap payments in June, September, and December (the months in which the quarterly rate prevailing over the *next* 3 months is known). This is computed using equation (8.3):

$$\frac{1 - 0.9485}{0.9830 + 0.9658 + 0.9485} = 1.778\%$$

Multiplying this by 4 to annualize the rate gives the 7.109% in the swap rate column of Table 8.4.

In Figure 8.5 we graph the entire swap curve against quarterly forward rates implied by the Eurodollar curve. The **swap spread** is the difference between swap rates and Treasury-bond yields for comparable maturities. Thus, Figure 8.5 also displays yields on government bonds.

The Swap's Implicit Loan Balance

An interest rate swap behaves much like the oil swap in Section 8.1. At inception, the swap has zero value to both parties. If interest rates change, the present value of the fixed payments and, hence, the swap rate will change. The market value of the swap is the difference in the present value of payments between the old swap rate and the new swap rate. For example, consider the 3-year swap in Table 8.3 (see page 247). If interest rates rise after the swap is entered into, the value of the existing 6.9548% swap will fall for the party receiving the fixed payment.

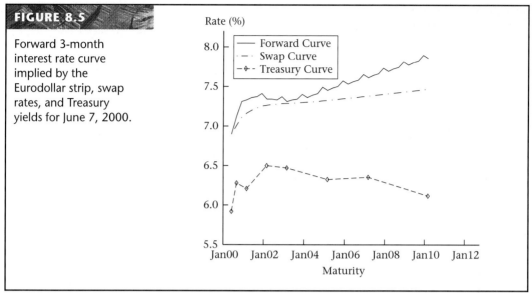

FIGURE 8.5

Forward 3-month interest rate curve implied by the Eurodollar strip, swap rates, and Treasury yields for June 7, 2000.

Source: FII and Datastream.

Even in the absence of interest rate changes, however, the swap in Table 8.3 changes value over time. Once the first swap payment is made, the swap acquires negative value for the market-maker (relative to the use of forwards) because in the second year the market-maker will make a net cash payment. Similarly, the swap will have positive value for the borrower (again relative to the use of forwards) after the first payment is made. In order to smooth payments, the borrower pays "too much" (relative to the forward curve) in the first year and receives a refund in the second year. *The swap is equivalent to entering into forward contracts and undertaking some additional borrowing and lending.*

The 10-year swap rate in Figure 8.5 is 7.4667%. We can use this value to illustrate the implicit borrowing and lending in the swap. Consider an investor who pays fixed and receives floating. This investor is paying a high rate in the early years of the swap, and, hence, is lending money. About halfway through the life of the swap, the Eurodollar forward rate exceeds the swap rate and the loan balance declines, falling to zero by the end of the swap. The fixed rate recipient has a positive loan balance over the life of the swap because the Eurodollar futures rate is below the swap initially—so the fixed-rate recipient is receiving payments—and crosses the swap price once. The credit risk in this swap is therefore borne, at least initially, by the fixed-rate payer, who is lending to the fixed-rate recipient. The implicit loan balance in the swap is illustrated in Figure 8.6.

Deferred Swaps

We can construct a swap that begins at some date in the future, but for which the swap rate is agreed upon today. This type of swap is called a **deferred swap.** To demonstrate this type of swap, we can use the information in Table 7.1 to compute the value of a

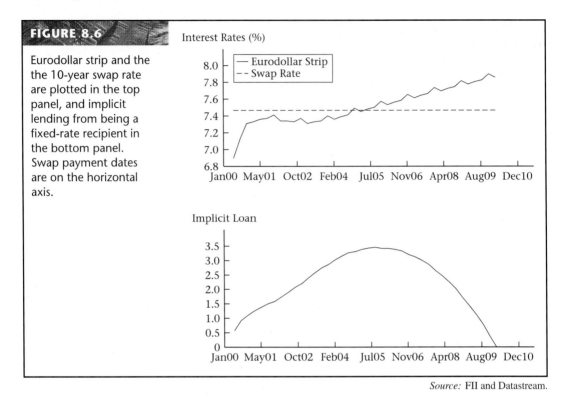

FIGURE 8.6

Eurodollar strip and the the 10-year swap rate are plotted in the top panel, and implicit lending from being a fixed-rate recipient in the bottom panel. Swap payment dates are on the horizontal axis.

Interest Rates (%)

Implicit Loan

Source: FII and Datastream.

2-period swap that begins 1 year from today. The reasoning is exactly as before: The swap rate will be set by the market-maker so that the present value of the fixed and floating payments is the same. This gives us

$$\frac{R - 0.070024}{1.065^2} + \frac{R - 0.080071}{1.07^3} = 0$$

Solving for R, the deferred swap rate is 7.4854%. In general, the fixed rate on a deferred swap beginning in k periods is computed as

$$R = \frac{\sum_{i=k}^{T} P_0(0, t_i) r_0(t_{i-1}, t_i)}{\sum_{i=k}^{T} P(0, t_i)} \tag{8.4}$$

This can also be written as

$$R = \frac{P(0, t_{k-1}) - P(0, t_n)}{\sum_{i=k}^{n} P(0, t_i)} \tag{8.5}$$

Equation (8.4) is equal to equation (8.2) when $k = 1$.

Why Swap Interest Rates?

Managers sometimes say that they would like to borrow short-term because short-term interest rates are on average lower than long-term interest rates. Leaving aside the question of whether this view makes sense theoretically, let's take for granted that a firm wishes to borrow at short-term interest rates. The problem facing the manager is that the firm may be unable to borrow significant amounts by issuing short-term debt.

When a firm borrows by issuing long-term debt, bondholders bear both interest rate risk and the credit risk of the firm. If the firm borrows short-term (for example, by issuing commercial paper), lenders primarily bear credit risk.

In practice, short-term lenders appear unwilling to absorb large issues from a single borrower because of credit risk. For example, money-market mutual funds that hold commercial paper will not hold large amounts of any one firm's commercial paper, preferring instead to diversify across firms. This diversification minimizes the chance that a single bankruptcy will significantly reduce the fund's rate of return.

Because short-term lenders are sensitive in this way to credit risk, a firm cannot borrow a large amount of money short-term without facing a higher interest rate. By contrast, long-term lenders to corporations, for example pension funds and insurance companies, willingly assume both interest rate and credit risk. Thus there are borrowers who wish to issue short-term debt and lenders who are unwilling to buy it. Swaps provide a way around this problem, permitting the firm to separate credit risk and interest rate risk.

Suppose, for example, that a firm borrows long-term and then swaps into short-rate exposure. The firm would receive the fixed rate and pay the floating rate on the swap. The firm therefore pays the short-term rate, which is what it desired in the first place.

The swap does not cause credit risk to vanish; it is still being held by the long-term bondholders who are willing to accept this exposure. By swapping its interest rate exposure, the firm pays the short-term interest rate it desires, *but the long-term bondholders continue to bear the credit risk.* The swap counterparty acquires some credit risk, but much less than if it had loaned short-term to the firm. The swap counterparty has credit risk only if the firm goes bankrupt at the same time that the value of the swap is positive to the counterparty (this would occur if interest rates had risen). The notional principal of the loan is not at risk for the swap counterparty.

If it seems odd to you that the firm can use a swap to convert a high fixed rate into a low floating rate, recognize that any time there is an upward-sloping yield curve, the short-term interest rate is below the long-term interest rate. If you reduce the period for which your borrowing rate is fixed (which happens when you swap fixed for floating), you borrow at the lower short-term interest rate instead of the higher long-term interest rate.

Swaps thus permit separation of two aspects of borrowing: Credit risk and interest rate risk. To the extent these risks are acquired by those most willing to hold them, swaps increase efficiency.

Amortizing and Accreting Swaps

We have assumed that the notional value of the swap remains fixed over the life of the swap. However, it is also possible to engage in a swap where the notional value is changing over time. For example, consider a floating-rate mortgage, for which every payment contains an interest and principal component. Since the outstanding principal is declining over time, a swap involving a mortgage would need to account for this. Such a swap is called an **amortizing swap** because the notional value is declining over time. It is also possible for the principal in a swap to grow over time. This is called an **accreting swap.**

Let Q_t be the relative notional amount at time t. Then the basic idea in pricing a swap with a time-varying notional amount is the same as with a fixed notional amount: The present value of the fixed payments should equal the present value of the floating payments:

$$\sum_{i=1}^{n} Q_{t_i} P(0, t_i)[R - r(t_{i-1}, t_i)] = 0 \tag{8.6}$$

where, as before, there are n payments on dates $t_1, t_2, \ldots, t_n$. Equation (8.6) can be rewritten as

$$R = \frac{\sum_{i=1}^{n} Q_{t_i} P(0, t_i) r(t_{i-1}, t_i)}{\sum_{i=1}^{n} Q_{t_i} P(0, t_i)} \tag{8.7}$$

The fixed swap rate is still a weighted average of implied forward rates, only now the weights also involve changing notional principal.

Many other structures are possible for swaps based on interest rates or other prices. One infamous swap structure is described in the box on page 255, which recounts the 1993 swap between Procter & Gamble and Bankers Trust.

8.3 CURRENCY SWAPS

Firms sometimes issue debt denominated in a foreign currency. A firm may do this as a hedge against revenues received in that currency, or they may perceive borrowing costs in that currency to be lower. Whatever the reason, if the firm later wants to change the currency to which they have exposure, there are a variety of ways to do so.

To be concrete, let's consider the example of a dollar-based firm that has euro-denominated 3-year fixed-rate debt. The annual coupon rate is ρ. The firm is obligated to make a series of payments that are fixed in euro terms, but variable in dollar terms.

Since the payments are known, eliminating euro exposure is a straightforward hedging problem using currency forwards. We have cash flows of $-\rho$ each year, and $-(1 + \rho)$ in the maturity year. If currency forward prices are $F_{0,t}$, we can enter into long euro forward contracts to acquire at a known exchange rate the euros we need to pay to the lenders. Hedged cash flows in year t are $-\rho F_{0,t}$.

As we have seen in other examples, the forward transactions eliminate risk but leave the firm with a variable (but riskless) stream of cash flows. The variability of hedged cash flows is illustrated in the following example.

The Procter & Gamble Swap

In November 1993, consumer products company Procter & Gamble (P&G) entered into a 5-year $200m notional value swap with Bankers Trust. The contract called for P&G to receive a 5.3% fixed rate from Bankers Trust and pay the 30-day commercial paper rate less 75 basis points, plus a spread. Settlements were to be semiannual. The spread would be zero for the first settlement, and thereafter be fixed at the spread as of May 4, 1994.

The spread was determined by the difference between the 5-year constant maturity treasury (CMT) rate (the yield on a 5-year Treasury bond, but a constructed rate since there is not always a Treasury bond with exactly 5 years to expiration) and the price per $100 of maturity value of the 6.25% 30-year Treasury bond. The formula for the spread was

$$\text{Spread} = max \left(\frac{\frac{5-\text{yearCMT}\%}{0.0578} \times 98.5 - \text{price of 30-year bond}}{100}, 0 \right)$$

At inception in November 1993, the 5-year CMT rate was 5.02% and the 30-year Treasury price was 102.57811. The expression in the max function evaluated to $-.17$ (-17 basis points), so the spread was zero.

If the spread were 0 on May 4, 1994, P&G would save 75 basis points per year on $200m for 4.5 years, an interest rate reduction worth approximately $7m. However, notice something important: If interest rates rise before the spread determination date, then the 5-year CMT goes up *and the price of the 30-year bond goes down*. Thus, the swap is really a bet on the *direction* of interest rates, not the difference in rates!

The swap is recounted in Smith (1997) and Srivastava (1998). Interest rates rose after P&G entered the swap. P&G and Bankers Trust renegotiated the swap in January 1994, and P&G liquidated the swap in March, with a loss of about $100m. P&G sued Bankers Trust, complaining in part that the risks of the swap had not been adequately disclosed by Bankers Trust.

In the end P&G and Bankers Trust settled, with P&G paying Bankers Trust about $35m. (Forster [1996] and Horwitz [1996]) debate the implications of the trial and settlement.) The notion that Procter & Gamble might have been uninformed about the risk of the swap, and if so, whether this should have mattered, was controversial. U.S. securities laws are often said to protect "widows and orphans." Nobel-prize–winning economist Merton Miller wryly said of the case, "Procter is the widow and Gamble is the orphan."

Example 8.1 Suppose the euro-denominated interest rate is 3.5% and the dollar-denominated rate is 6%. The spot exchange rate is $0.90/€. A dollar-based firm has a 3-year 3.5% euro-denominated bond with a €100 par value and price of €100. The firm wishes to guarantee the dollar value of the payments. Since the firm will make debt payments in euros, it buys the euro forward to eliminate currency exposure. Table 8.5 summarizes the transaction and reports the currency forward curve and the unhedged

TABLE 8.5		Unhedged and hedged cash flows for a dollar-based firm with euro-denominated debt.	
Year	Unhedged Euro Cash Flow	Forward Exchange Rate	Hedged Dollar Cash Flow
1	−€3.5	0.922	−$3.226
2	−€3.5	0.944	−$3.304
3	−€103.5	0.967	−$100.064

and hedged cash flows. The value of the hedged cash flows is

$$\frac{\$3.226}{1.06} + \frac{\$3.304}{1.06^2} + \frac{\$100.064}{1.06^3} = \$90$$

Example 8.1 verifies what we knew had to be true: Hedging does not change the value of the debt. The initial value of the debt in euros is €100. Since the exchange rate is $0.90/€, the debt should have a dollar value of $90, which it has.

As an alternative to hedging each euro-denominated payment with a forward contract, a firm wishing to change its currency exposure can enter into a **currency swap,** which entails an exchange of payments in different currencies. Compared with hedging the cash flows individually, the currency swap generates a different cash flow stream, but with equivalent value. We can examine a currency swap by supposing that the firm in Example 8.1 uses a swap rather than forward contracts to hedge its euro exposure.

Example 8.2   Make the same assumptions as in Example 8.1. The dollar-based firm enters into a swap where it pays dollars (6% on a $90 bond) and receives euros (3.5% on a €100 bond). The firm's euro exposure is eliminated. The market-maker receives dollars and pays euros. The position of the market-maker is summarized in Table 8.6. The present value of the market-maker's net cash flow is

$$\frac{\$2.174}{1.06} + \frac{\$2.096}{1.06^2} - \frac{\$4.664}{1.06^3} = 0$$

The market-maker's net exposure in this transaction is long a dollar-denominated bond and short a euro-denominated bond. Table 8.6 shows that after hedging there is a series of net cash flows with zero present value. As in all the previous examples, the effect of the swap is equivalent to entering into forward contracts, coupled with borrowing or lending. In this case, the firm is lending to the market-maker in the first 2 years, with the implicit loan repaid at maturity.

TABLE 8.6 Unhedged and hedged cash flows for a dollar-based firm with euro-denominated debt. The effective annual dollar-denominated interest rate is 6% and the effective annual euro-denominated interest rate is 3.5%.

Year	Forward Exchange Rate ($/€)	Receive Dollar Interest	Pay Hedged Euro Interest	Net Cash Flow
1	0.9217	$5.40	$-€3.5 \times 0.9217$	$2.174
2	0.9440	$5.40	$-€3.5 \times 0.9440$	$2.096
3	0.9668	$95.40	$-€103.5 \times 0.9668$	$-$4.664

The fact that a currency swap is equivalent to borrowing in one currency and lending in the other is familiar from our discussion of currency forwards in Chapter 5. There we saw the same is true of currency forwards.

Currency Swap Formulas

Currency swap calculations are the same as those for the other swaps we have discussed. To see this, consider a swap in which a dollar annuity, R, is exchanged for an annuity in another currency, R^*. Given the foreign annuity, R^*, what is R?

We start with the observation that the present value of the two annuities must be the same. There are n payments and the time-0 forward price for a unit of foreign currency delivered at time t_i is F_{0,t_i}. This gives

$$\sum_{i=1}^{n} \left[R P_{0,t_i} - R^* F_{0,t_i} P_{0,t_i} \right] = 0$$

In calculating the present value of the payment R^*, we first convert to dollars by multiplying by F_{0,t_i}. We can then compute the present value using the dollar-denominated zero-coupon bond price, P_{0,t_i}. Solving for R gives

$$R = \frac{\sum_{i=1}^{n} P_{0,t_i} R^* F_{0,t_i}}{\sum_{i=1}^{n} P_{0,t_i}} \tag{8.8}$$

This expression is exactly like equation (8.2), with the implied forward rate, $r_0(t_{i-1}, t_i)$, replaced by the foreign-currency-denominated annuity payment translated into dollars, $R^* F_{0,t_i}$.

When coupon bonds are swapped, we have to account for the difference in maturity value as well as the coupon payment, which is an annuity. If the dollar bond has a par value of $1, the foreign bond will have a par value of $1/x_0$, where x_0 is the current exchange rate expressed as dollars per unit of the foreign currency. If R^* is the coupon rate on the foreign bond and R is the coupon rate on the dollar bond, the present value of the difference in payments on the two bonds is

$$\sum_{i=1}^{n} \left[R P_{0,t_i} - R^* F_{0,t_i} P_{0,t_i} / x_0 \right] + P_{0,t_n} (1 - F_{0,t_n} / x_0) = 0$$

The division by x_0 accounts for the fact that a \$1 bond is equivalent to $1/x_0$ bonds with a par value of 1 unit of the foreign currency. The dollar coupon in this case is

$$R = \frac{\sum_{i=1}^{n} P_{0,t_i} R^* F_{0,t_i} / x_0 + P_{0,t_n} (F_{0,t_n} / x_0 - 1)}{\sum_{i=1}^{n} P_{0,t_i}} \tag{8.9}$$

The fixed payment, R, is the dollar equivalent of the foreign coupon plus the amortized value of the difference in the maturity payments of the two bonds. Problem 16 asks you to verify that equation (8.9) gives 6% using the assumptions in Tables 8.5 and 8.6.

Other Currency Swaps

There are other kinds of currency swaps. The preceding examples assumed that all borrowing was fixed rate. Suppose the dollar-based borrower issues a euro-denominated loan with a *floating* interest rate. In this case there are two future unknowns: The exchange rate at which interest payments are converted, and—because the bond is floating rate—the amount of the interest payment. Swapping this loan to a dollar loan is still straightforward, however; we just require one extra hedging transaction.

We first convert the floating interest rate into a fixed interest rate with a *euro* interest rate swap. The resulting fixed-rate euro-denominated exposure can then be hedged with currency forwards and converted into dollar interest rate exposure. Given the assumptions in Table 8.6, the euro-denominated loan would swap to a 3.5% floating-rate loan. From that point on, we are in the same position as in the previous example.

In general, we can swap fixed-to-fixed, fixed-to-floating, floating-to-fixed, and floating-to-floating. The analysis is similar in all cases.

One kind of swap that might on its face seem similar is a **diff swap,** short for differential swap. In this kind of swap, payments are made based on the difference in floating interest rates in two different currencies, with the notional amount in a single currency. For example, we might have a swap with a \$10m notional amount, but the swap would pay in dollars, based on the difference in a euro-denominated interest rate and a dollar-denominated interest rate. If the short-term euro interest rate rises from 3.5% to 3.8% with the dollar rate unchanged, the annual swap payment would be 30 basis points on \$10m, or \$30,000. This is like a standard interest rate swap, only for a diff swap, the reference interest rates are denominated in different currencies.

Standard currency forward contracts cannot be used to hedge a diff swap. The problem is that we can hedge the change in the foreign interest rate, but doing so requires a transaction denominated in the foreign currency. We can't easily hedge the exchange rate at which the value of the interest rate change is converted *because we don't know in advance how much currency will need to be converted.* In effect there is quantity uncertainty regarding the foreign currency to be converted. We have seen this kind of problem before, in our discussion of dollar-denominated Nikkei index futures in Chapter 5 and in our discussion of crop yields in Chapter 6. The diff swap is an example of a quanto swap. We will discuss quantos in Chapter 22.

8.4 COMMODITY SWAPS

At the beginning of this chapter we looked at a simple two-date commodity swap. Now we will look at commodity swaps more generally, present the general formula for a commodity swap—showing that the formula is exactly the same as for an interest rate swap—and look at some ways the swap structure can be modified.

The Commodity Swap Price

The idea of a commodity swap, as discussed in Section 8.1, is that we use information in the commodity forward curve to fix a commodity price over a period of time. We can derive the swap price following the same logic as before.

Think about the position of the market-maker, who we suppose receives the fixed payment, $\overline{F}$, makes the floating payment, and hedges the risk of the floating payment. If there are n swap payments, the resulting hedged cash flow is

$$\text{Hedged cash flow for payment } i = \overline{F} - F_{0,t_i}$$

With competitive market-makers, the present value of the net *hedged* swap payments will be zero (ignoring bid-ask spreads):

$$\sum_{i=1}^{n} P(0, t_i) \left(\overline{F} - F_{0,t_i} \right) \tag{8.10}$$

As before, $P(0, t_i)$ is the price of a zero-coupon bond paying \$1 at time t_i. Equation (8.10) implies that the present value of the swap payments equals the present value of the forward curve:

$$\overline{F} \sum_{i=1}^{n} P(0, t_i) = \sum_{i=1}^{n} P(0, t_i) F_{0,t_i}$$

Solving for the swap price, we obtain

$$\overline{F} = \frac{\sum_{i=1}^{n} P(0, t_i) F_{0,t_i}}{\sum_{i=1}^{n} P(0, t_i)} \tag{8.11}$$

Compare equation (8.11) with equation (8.2) for an interest rate swap. *They are the same formula, except that the interest swap rate is a weighted average of implied forward interest rates and the commodity swap price is a weighted average of commodity forward prices.*

Natural Gas Swaps

Because of seasonality in both price and quantity, natural gas provides an interesting context for examining commodity swaps. The swap curves for June 1999 and June 2000, computed using equation (8.11), are plotted in Figure 8.7.

You might guess that the implicit loan in the swap switches between borrowing and lending because the forward curve is alternately above and below the swap price. Figure 8.8 shows that this guess is correct. Compare this to Figure 8.6, in which the implicit loan is always positive. The different shapes of the forward curve in Figures 8.6 and 8.8 account for the different behavior of the implicit loan.

Swaps with Variable Quantity and Price

It might make sense for a gas buyer with seasonally varying demand (for example, someone buying gas for heating) to enter into a swap in which quantities vary over time. For example, a buyer might want three times the quantity in the winter months as in the summer months. A buyer also might be willing to fix different prices in different seasons: For example, if there is seasonal variation in the price of the output produced using gas as an input. How do we determine the swap price with seasonally varying quantities?

Let Q_{t_i} denote the quantity of gas purchased at time t_i. Once again, we can think about this from the perspective of the competitive market-maker. The market-maker

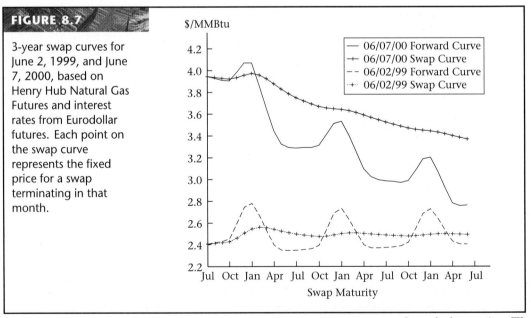

FIGURE 8.7

3-year swap curves for June 2, 1999, and June 7, 2000, based on Henry Hub Natural Gas Futures and interest rates from Eurodollar futures. Each point on the swap curve represents the fixed price for a swap terminating in that month.

$/MMBtu

— 06/07/00 Forward Curve
—⊢ 06/07/00 Swap Curve
– – 06/02/99 Forward Curve
⋯⊹⋯ 06/02/99 Swap Curve

Swap Maturity

Source for futures prices: FII.

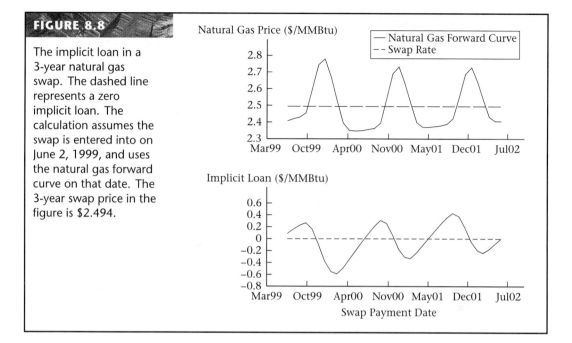

FIGURE 8.8

The implicit loan in a 3-year natural gas swap. The dashed line represents a zero implicit loan. The calculation assumes the swap is entered into on June 2, 1999, and uses the natural gas forward curve on that date. The 3-year swap price in the figure is $2.494.

who hedges the swap will enter into varying quantities of forward contracts in different months to match the variable quantity called for in the swap. The zero-profit condition is still that the fixed and floating payments have zero present value, only in this case they must be weighted by the appropriate quantities. Thus, we have

$$\sum_{i=1}^{n} P(0, t_i) Q_{t_i} \left(\overline{F} - F_{0,t_i} \right)$$

The swap price is thus

$$\overline{F} = \frac{\sum_{i=1}^{n} Q_{t_i} P(0, t_i) F_{0,t_i}}{\sum_{i=1}^{n} Q_{t_i} P(0, t_i)} \tag{8.12}$$

This equation makes perfect sense: If we are going to buy more gas when the forward price is high, we have to weight more heavily the forward price in those months. When $Q_t = 1$, the formula is the same as equation (8.11), when the quantity is not varying.

Example 8.3 The June 1999 3-year swap price is $2.494. If the swap calls for tripling the quantities of gas to be delivered in November through February, the 3-year swap price increases to $2.563. 🦡

We can also permit prices to be time-varying. Suppose, for example, that the buyer is uncomfortable with the varying quantity swap described in Example 8.3 because the high winter quantity raises the price paid in the summer. A solution would be to fix the summer price at a lower value, and then let the winter price be determined by the zero present value condition.

If we let the summer swap price be denoted by $\overline{F}_s$ and the winter price by $\overline{F}_w$, then the summer and winter swap prices can be any prices that satisfy the market-maker's zero present value condition:

$$\overline{F}_s \sum_{i \in summer} P(0, t_i) Q_{t_i} + \overline{F}_w \sum_{i \in winter} P(0, t_i) Q_{t_i}$$
$$= \sum_{i \in summer} P(0, t_i) Q_{t_i} F_{0,t_i} + \sum_{i \in winter} P(0, t_i) Q_{t_i} F_{0,t_i}$$

The notations $i \in summer$ and $i \in winter$ mean to sum over only the months in those seasons. This gives us one equation and two unknowns, $\overline{F}_w$ and $\overline{F}_s$. Once we fix one of the two prices, the equation will give us the other.

8.5 Swaptions

An option to enter into a swap is called a **swaption.** We can see how a swaption works by returning to the two-date oil swap example in Section 8.1. The 2-year oil swap price was $20.483. Suppose we are willing to buy oil at $20.483/barrel, but we would like to speculate on the swap price being even lower over the next 3 months.

Consider the following contract: If in 3 months the fixed price for a swap commencing in 9 months (1 year from today) is $20.483 or above, we enter into the swap, agreeing to pay $20.483 and receive the floating price for 2 years. If, on the other hand, the market swap price is below $20.483, we have no obligation. If the swap price in 3 months is $19.50, for example, we could enter into a swap at that time at the $19.50 price, or we could elect not to enter any swap.

With this contract we are entering into the swap with $20.483 as the swap price only when the market swap price is greater; hence, this contract will have a premium. In this example, we would have purchased a **payer swaption,** since we have the right, but not the obligation, to pay a fixed price of $20.483 for 2 years of oil. The counterparty has sold this swaption.

When exercised, the swaption commits us to transact at multiple times in the future. It is possible to exercise the option and then offset the swap with another swap, converting the stream of swap payments into a certain stream with a fixed present value. Thus, the swaption is analogous to an ordinary option, with the present value of the swap obligations (the price of the prepaid swap) as the underlying asset.

The strike price in this example is $20.483, so we have an at-the-money swaption. We could make the strike price different from $20.483. For example, we could reduce the swaption premium by setting the strike above $20.483.

Swaptions can be American or European, and the terms of the underlying swap—fixed price, floating index, settlement frequency, and tenor—will be precisely specified.

Example 8.4 Suppose we enter into a European payer oil swaption with a strike price of $21. The underlying swap commences in 1 year and has two annual settlements. After 3 months, the fixed price on the underlying swap is $21.50. We exercise the option, obligating us to pay $21/barrel for 2 years. If we wish to offset the swap, we can enter into a swap to receive the $21.50 fixed price. In year 1 and year 2 we will then receive $21.50 and pay $21, for a certain net cash flow each year of $0.50. The floating payments cancel. ❧

A **receiver swaption** gives you the right to pay the floating price and receive the fixed strike price. Thus, the holder of a receiver swaption would exercise when the fixed swap price is below the strike.

Although we have used a commodity swaption in this example, an interest rate or currency swaption would be analogous, with payer and receiver swaptions giving the right to pay or receive the fixed interest rate.

8.6 TOTAL RETURN SWAPS

A **total return swap** is a swap in which one party pays the realized total return (dividends plus capital gains) on a reference asset, and the other party pays a floating return such as LIBOR. The two parties exchange only the difference between these rates. The party paying the return on the reference asset is the *total return payer*.

As with other swaps, there are multiple settlement dates over the life of the swap. The cumulative effect for the total return payer is of being short the reference asset and long an asset paying the floating rate. The cash flows on a total return swap are illustrated in Figure 8.9.

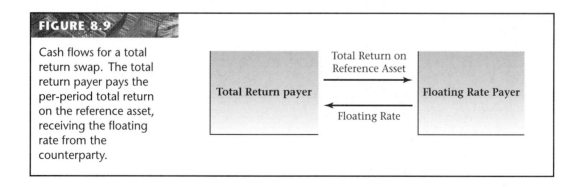

FIGURE 8.9

Cash flows for a total return swap. The total return payer pays the per-period total return on the reference asset, receiving the floating rate from the counterparty.

Example 8.5   ABC Asset Management has a $2 billion investment in the S&P stock index. However, fund managers have become pessimistic about the market and would like to reduce their exposure to stocks from $2 billion to $1 billion. One way to do this is to sell $1 billion of stocks. However, the fund can retain the stock position but financially transfer the return of the stocks by engaging in a total return swap, obligating the fund to pay the total return (dividends plus capital gains) on the swapped stocks, while receiving a floating-rate return such as LIBOR on the swapped $1 billion notional amount. This avoids the transaction costs of a sale of physical stock.

Table 8.7 illustrates the payments on such a swap. In year 1, ABC earns 6.5% on the S&P index. However, on the portion it has swapped, it must pay the 6.5% in exchange for the 7.2% floating rate. The net payment of 0.7% leaves ABC as well off as if it had sold the index and invested in an asset paying the floating rate. In year 2, ABC receives 18%, compensating it for the difference between the 7.5% floating return and the 10.5% loss on the S&P index. Finally, in year 3 the S&P index does well, and ABC pays 16.5% to the counterparty.   ⚡

You might wonder about the economics of a swap like this. The stock index on average earns a higher return than LIBOR. So if the fund swaps the stock index in exchange for LIBOR, it will on average make payments to the counterparty.

This observation is correct, but notice that the fund is paying the difference between the index return and a short-term interest rate—this difference is the risk premium on the index. In Section 5.3, we had a similar result for a forward contract: On average a short position in a forward contract on a stock index loses money because the risk premium has zero value.

The average loss associated with swapping a stock index for LIBOR is the same as the average loss associated with selling the stock and buying a floating-rate note paying LIBOR. It is just that the swap makes the loss obvious since it requires a payment.

Some investors have used total return swaps to avoid taxes on foreign stocks. In many cases, countries impose withholding taxes on foreign investors, meaning that if a

TABLE 8.7	Illustration of cash flows on a total return swap with annual settlement for 3 years.			
Year	S&P Capital Gain	S&P Dividend	Floating Rate	Net Payment to Total Return Payer
1	5%	1.5%	7.2%	0.7%
2	−12%	1.5%	7.5%	18.0%
3	22%	1.5%	7.0%	−16.5%

firm in country A pays a dividend, for example, country A withholds a fraction of that dividend from investors based in country B. A total return swap enables a country-B investor to own country-A stocks without physically holding them, and thus in many cases without having to pay withholding taxes. For example, a U.S. investor could first swap out of a U.S. stock index and then swap into a European stock index, effectively becoming the counterparty for a European investor wanting to swap out of European stock exposure. Because net swap payments are not always recognized by withholding rules, this transaction can be more tax-efficient than holding the foreign stocks directly.

Another use of total return swaps is the management of credit risk. A fund manager holding corporate debt can swap the return on a particular bond for a floating-rate return. If the company that issued the bond goes bankrupt, the debt holder receives a payment on the swap compensating for the fact that the bond is worth a fraction of its face value.

If you think about this use of total return swaps, it is a crude tool for managing credit risk specifically. The problem is that bond prices also change due to interest rate changes. A corporate bond holder might wish to retain interest rate risk but not bankruptcy risk. Thus, there are products called **default swaps.** These are essentially default options, in which the buyer pays a premium, usually amortized over a series of payments. If the reference asset experiences a "credit event" (for example, a failure to make a scheduled payment on a particular bond or class of bonds), then the seller makes a payment to the buyer. Frequently these contracts split the return on the bond into the portion due to interest rate changes (with Treasury securities used as a reference) and the portion due to credit quality changes, with the swap making payments based only on the latter. Tavakoli (1998) discusses such swaps.

CHAPTER SUMMARY

A swap is a contract calling for an exchange of payments, on one or more dates, determined by the difference in two prices. A single-payment swap is the same thing as a cash-settled forward contract. In the simplest swaps, a fixed payment is periodically exchanged for a floating payment. A firm can use a swap to lock in a long-term commodity price, a fixed interest rate, or a fixed exchange rate. Considering only the present value of cash flows, the same result is obtained using a strip of forward contracts and swaps. The difference is that hedging with a strip of forward contracts results in net payments that are time-varying. In contrast, hedging with a swap results in net payments that are constant over time. The value of a swap is zero at inception, though as swap payments are made over time, the value of the swap can change in a predictable way.

The fixed price in a swap is a weighted average of the corresponding forward prices. The swap formulas in different cases all take the same general form. Let $f_0(t_i)$ denote the forward price for the floating payment in the swap. Then the fixed swap

To Obtain Formula for	Substitute in Equation (8.13)	Equation in Chapter
TABLE 8.8 — Equivalent forms of the swap-rate calculation. For the currency swap, F_{0,t_i} is the forward price for the foreign currency. For the commodity swap, F_{0,t_i} is the forward price for the commodity.		
Interest Rate Swap	$f_0(t_i) = r_0(t_{i-1}, t_i)$	Equation (8.2)
Currency Swap (annuity)	$f_0(t_i) = R^* F_{0,t_i}$	Equation (8.8)
Commodity Swap	$f_0(t_i) = F_{0,t_i}$	Equation (8.11)

payment is

$$R = \frac{\sum_{i=1}^{n} P(0, t_i) f_0(t_i)}{\sum_{i=1}^{n} P(0, t_i)} \tag{8.13}$$

Table 8.8 summarizes the substitutions to make in equation (8.13) to get the various swap formulas shown in the chapter. This formula can be generalized to permit time variation in the notional amount and the swap price, and the swap can start on a deferred basis.

An important characteristic of swaps is that they require only the exchange of net payments, and not the payment of principal. So if a firm enters an interest rate swap, for example, it is required only to make payments based on the difference in interest rates, not on the underlying principal. As a result, swaps have less credit risk than bonds.

Total return swaps involve exchanging the return on an asset for a floating rate such as LIBOR. The term *swap* is also used to describe agreements like the Procter & Gamble swap (page 255), which required payments based on the difference in interest rates and bond prices, as well as default swaps.

FURTHER READING

The same formulas used to price swaps will appear again in the context of structured notes, which we will encounter in Chapter 15. We will discuss default swaps in Chapter 24.

Litzenberger (1992) provides an overview of the swap market. Turnbull (1989) discusses arguments purporting to show that the use of swaps can have a positive net present value. Default swaps are discussed by Tavakoli (1998). Because of convexity bias (Chapter 7), the market interest rate swap curve is not exactly the same as the swap curve constructed from Eurodollar futures. This is discussed in Burghardt and Hoskins (1995) and Gupta and Subrahmanyam (2000).

PROBLEMS

Some of the following problems use this table:

TABLE 8.9

Quarter	1	2	3	4	5	6	7	8
Oil forward price	21	21.1	20.8	20.5	20.2	20	19.9	19.8
Gas swap price	2.2500	2.4236	2.3503	2.2404	2.2326	2.2753	2.2583	2.2044
Zero-coupon bond price	0.9852	0.9701	0.9546	0.9388	0.9231	0.9075	0.8919	0.8763
Euro-denominated zero-coupon bond price	0.9913	0.9825	0.9735	0.9643	0.9551	0.9459	0.9367	0.9274
Euro forward price ($/€)	0.9056	0.9115	0.9178	0.9244	0.9312	0.9381	0.9452	0.9524

Assume that the current exchange rate is $0.90/€.

8.1. Consider the oil swap example in Section 8.1 with the 1- and 2-year forward prices of $22/barrel and $23/barrel. The 1- and 2-year interest rates are 6% and 6.5%. Verify that the new 2-year swap price is $22.483.

8.2. Suppose that oil forward prices for 1 year, 2 years, and 3 years are $20, $21, and $22. The 1-year effective annual interest rate is 6.0%, the 2-year interest rate is 6.5%, and the 3-year interest rate is 7.0%.

   a. What is the 3-year swap price?

   b. What is the price of a 2-year swap beginning in one year? (That is, the first swap settlement will be in 2 years and the second in 3 years.)

8.3. Consider the same 3-year oil swap. Suppose a dealer is paying the fixed price and receiving floating. What position in oil forward contracts will hedge oil price risk in this position? Verify that the present value of the locked-in net cash flows is zero.

8.4. Consider the 3-year swap in the previous example. Suppose you are the fixed-rate payer in the swap. How much have you overpaid relative to the forward price after the first swap settlement? What is the cumulative overpayment after the second swap settlement? Verify that the cumulative overpayment is zero after the third payment (be sure to account for interest).

8.5. Consider the same 3-year swap. Suppose you are a dealer who is paying the fixed oil price and receiving the floating price. Suppose that you enter into the swap and immediately thereafter all interest rates rise 50 basis points (oil forward prices are unchanged). What happens to the value of your swap position? What if interest rates fall 50 basis points? What hedging instrument would have protected you against interest rate risk in this position?

8.6. Supposing the interest rate is 1.5% per quarter, what are the per-barrel swap prices for 4-quarter and 8-quarter oil swaps? (Use oil forward prices in Table 8.9.) What is the total cost of prepaid 4- and 8-quarter swaps?

8.7. Using the information about zero-coupon bond prices and oil forward prices in Table 8.9, construct the set of swap prices for oil for 1 through 8 quarters.

8.8. Using the information in Table 8.9, what is the swap price of a 4-quarter oil swap with the first settlement occurring in the third quarter?

8.9. Given an 8-quarter oil swap price of $20.43, construct the implicit loan balance for each quarter over the life of the swap.

8.10. Using the zero-coupon bond prices and oil forward prices in Table 8.9, what is the price of an 8-period swap for which two barrels of oil are delivered in even-numbered quarters and one barrel of oil in odd-numbered quarters?

8.11. Using the zero-coupon bond prices and natural gas swap prices in Table 8.9, what are gas forward prices for each of the 8 quarters?

8.12. Using the zero-coupon bond prices and natural gas swap prices in Table 8.9, what is the implicit loan amount in each quarter in an 8-quarter natural gas swap?

8.13. What is the fixed rate in a 5-quarter interest rate swap with the first settlement in quarter 2?

8.14. Using the zero-coupon bond yields in Table 8.9, what is the fixed rate in a 4-quarter interest rate swap? What is the fixed rate in an 8-quarter interest rate swap?

8.15. What 8-quarter dollar annuity is equivalent to an 8-quarter annuity of €1?

8.16. Using the assumptions in Tables 8.5 and 8.6, verify that equation (8.9) equals 6%.

8.17. Using the information in Table 8.9, what are the *euro-denominated* fixed rates for 4- and 8-quarter swaps?

8.18. Using the information in Table 8.9, verify that it is possible to derive the 8-quarter dollar interest swap rate from the 8-quarter euro interest swap rate by using equation (8.9).

PART 3

OPTIONS

$\mathcal{I}$n earlier chapters we have seen the basics of how options work, and introduced some of the terminology related to options. In this part of the book we return to options, with the goal of understanding how they are priced.

Forward contracts (and futures and swaps) represent a binding commitment to buy or sell the underlying asset in the future. Because the commitment is binding, but deferred, time value of money is the main economic idea used in determining forward prices.

Options, on the other hand, need not be exercised. Intuitively, you would expect the probability distribution of the stock to affect the option price. In this part of the book we will in fact use some concepts from basic probability. However, it turns out that there is much to say about options without needing to think about the probability distribution of the stock. In Chapter 9 we explore concepts such as parity in more depth, and discuss some basic intuition about option prices that can be gleaned using only time value of money arguments.

Chapters 10 and 11 introduce the binomial option pricing model. This model assumes that the stock can move only in a very simple way, but provides the intuition underlying more complicated option pricing calculations. Chapter 12 presents the Black-Scholes option pricing formula, which is one of the most important formulas in finance.

As with forwards, futures, and swaps, option contracts are bought and sold by market-makers who hedge the risk associated with market-making. Chapter 13 looks at how market-makers hedge their option risk, and shows the precise sense in which the price of an option reflects the cost of synthetically creating it. Finally, Chapter 14 discusses exotic options, which are variants of the standard options we have been discussing. ≋

Chapter 9

Parity and Other Option Relationships

W ith this chapter we begin to study option pricing. Up to this point we have primarily studied contracts entailing *firm commitments*, such as forwards, futures, and swaps. These contracts do not permit either party to back away from the agreement. Optionality occurs when it is possible to avoid engaging in unprofitable transactions. The principal question in option pricing is: *How do you value the right to back away from a commitment*?

Before we delve into pricing models, we devote this chapter to refining our common sense about options. For example, Table 9.1 contains call and put prices for IBM for four different strikes and two different expiration dates. These are American-style options. Here are some observations and questions about these prices:

- What determines the difference between put and call prices at a given strike?

- How would the premiums change if these options were European rather than American?

- It appears that, for a given strike, the July options are more expensive than the April options. Is this necessarily true?

- Do call premiums always decrease as the strike price increases? Do put premiums always increase as the strike price increases?

- Both call and put premiums change by less than the change in the strike price. Does this always happen?

Although we will answer these questions, and others, in this chapter, take a minute and think about the answers now, drawing on what you have learned in previous chapters. While doing so, pay attention to *how* you are trying to come up with the answers. What constitutes a persuasive argument? Along with finding the answers, we want to understand how to think about questions like these.

9.1 PUT-CALL PARITY

Put-call parity is perhaps the single most important relationship among option prices. In Chapter 2 we argued that synthetic forwards (created by buying the call and selling the put) must be priced consistently with actual forwards. Therefore, the difference between call and put premiums equals the present value of the difference between the forward price and the strike price. The basic parity relationship for European options with the

271

| TABLE 9.1 | | IBM option prices, dollars per share, March 15, 2002. The closing price of IBM on that day was $106.79. | | | |

		Calls		Puts	
Strike	**Expiration**	**Bid ($)**	**Ask ($)**	**Bid ($)**	**Ask ($)**
95	April	12.90	13.20	0.95	1.10
100	April	8.70	9.00	1.75	1.95
105	April	5.20	5.40	3.20	3.40
110	April	2.60	2.75	5.60	5.90
95	July	15.20	15.90	3.20	3.50
100	July	11.90	12.20	4.70	4.90
105	July	8.90	9.10	6.40	6.70
110	July	6.10	6.50	8.80	9.10

Source: Chicago Board Options Exchange (**www.cboe.com**).

same strike price and time to expiration is

$$\text{Call} - \text{put} = PV(\text{forward price} - \text{strike price})$$

Equation (3.1) from Chapter 3 expresses this more precisely:

$$C(K, T) - P(K, T) = PV_{0,T}(F_{0,T} - K) \tag{9.1}$$
$$= e^{-rT}(F_{0,T} - K)$$

where $C(K, T)$ is the price of a European call with strike price K and time to expiration T, $P(K, T)$ is the price of a European put, $F_{0,T}$ is the forward price for the underlying asset, K is the strike price, T is the time to expiration of the options, and $PV_{0,T}$ denotes the present value over the life of the options. Note that $e^{-rT}F_{0,T}$ is the prepaid forward price for the asset and $e^{-rT}K$ is the prepaid forward price for the strike, so we can also think of parity in terms of prepaid forward prices.

The intuition for equation (9.1) is that buying a call and selling a put with the strike equal to the forward price ($F_{0,T} = K$) creates a synthetic forward contract and hence must have a zero price. If we create a synthetic long forward position at a price lower than the forward price, we have to pay $PV_{0,T}(F_{0,T} - K)$ since this is the benefit of buying the asset at the strike price rather than the forward price.

Parity generally fails for American-style options, which may be exercised prior to maturity. Appendix 9.A discusses a version of parity for American options.

We now consider the parity relationship in more detail for different underlying assets.

Options on Stocks

If the underlying asset is a stock and Div is the stream of dividends paid on the stock, then from Chapter 5, $e^{-rT}F_{0,T} = S_0 - PV_{0,T}(Div)$. Thus, from equation (9.1), the parity relationship for European options on stocks is

$$C(K, T) = P(K, T) + [S_0 - PV_{0,T}(Div)] - e^{-rT}(K) \qquad (9.2)$$

where S_0 is the current stock price and $PV_{0,T}(Div)$ is the present value of dividends payable over the life of the stock. For index options, we know that $S_0 - PV_{0,T}(Div) = S_0 e^{-\delta T}$. Hence, we can write

$$C(K, T) = P(K, T) + S_0 e^{-\delta T} - PV_{0,T}(K)$$

Example 9.1 Suppose that the price of a nondividend-paying stock is $40, the continuously compounded interest rate is 8%, and options have 3 months to expiration. A 40-strike European call sells for $2.78 and a 40-strike European put sells for $1.99. This is consistent with equation (9.2) since

$$\$2.78 = \$1.99 + \$40 - \$40 e^{-0.08 \times 0.25} \qquad ❦$$

Why does the price of an at-the-money call exceed the price of an at-the-money put by $0.79? We can answer this question by recognizing that buying a call and selling a put is a synthetic alternative to buying the stock, with different cash flows than an outright purchase.

Figure 9.1 represents the cash flows for a synthetic and outright purchase. Note that the synthetic purchase of the stock entails a cash outflow of $0.79 today and $40 at expiration, compared with an outright purchase that entails spending $40 today.

Also, both positions result in the ownership of the stock 3 months from today. With the outright purchase of stock, we still own the stock in 3 months. With the synthetic purchase, we will own the stock if the price is above $40 because we will exercise the

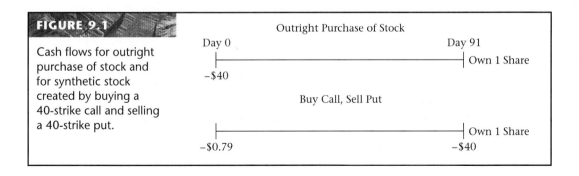

FIGURE 9.1

Cash flows for outright purchase of stock and for synthetic stock created by buying a 40-strike call and selling a 40-strike put.

call. We will also own the stock if the price is below $40, because we sold a put that will be exercised; as the put-writer we have to buy the stock. In either case, in 3 months we pay $40 and acquire the stock.

Finally, the dollar risk of the positions is the same. In both cases, a $1 change in the stock price at 3 months will lead to a $1 change in the value of the position. In other words, both positions entail economic ownership of the stock. You can verify that the risk is the same by drawing a profit and loss diagram for the two positions.

Thus, by buying the call and selling the put we own the stock, but we have deferred the payment of $40 until expiration. To obtain this deferral we must pay 3 months of interest on the $40, the present value of which is $0.79. *The option premiums differ by interest on the deferral of payment for the stock.* Interest is the reason that at-the-money European calls on nondividend-paying stock always sell for more than at-the-money European puts with the same expiration.

Note that if we reverse the position by selling the call and buying the put, then we are synthetically short-selling the stock. In 3 months, the options will be exercised and we will receive $40. In this case, the $0.79 compensates us for deferring receipt of the stock price.

There are differences between the outright and synthetic positions. First, the stock pays dividends and the synthetic does not. This example assumed that the stock paid no dividends. If it did, the cost of the actual stock would exceed that of the synthetic by the present value of dividends paid over the life of the options. Second, the actual stock has voting rights, unlike the synthetic position.

Example 9.2   Make the same assumptions as in Example 9.1, except suppose that the stock pays a $5 dividend just before expiration. The price of the European call is $0.74 and the price of the European put is $4.85. These prices satisfy parity with dividends, equation (9.2):

$$\$0.74 - \$4.85 = (\$40 - \$5e^{-0.08 \times 0.25}) - \$40e^{-0.08 \times 0.25}$$

The call price is higher than the put price by interest on the strike ($0.79) and lower by the present value of the dividend ($4.90), for a net difference of $4.11.   ✽

In this example, the at-the-money call sells for less than an at-the-money put since dividends on the stock exceed the value of interest on the strike price.

It is worth mentioning a common but erroneous explanation for the higher premium of an at-the-money call compared to an at-the-money put. The profit on a call is potentially unlimited since the stock price can go to infinity, while the profit on a put can be no greater than the strike price. This explanation seems to suggest that the call should be more expensive than the put.[1] However, the true reason for the call being

---

[1] In fact, the argument also seems to suggest that every stock is worth more than its price!

more expensive (as in Example 9.1) is time value of money, as expressed by put-call parity.

Synthetic stock Parity provides a cookbook for the synthetic creation of options, stocks, and T-bills.

The example above shows that buying a call and selling a put is like buying the stock except that the timing of the payment for the stock differs in the two cases. Rewriting equation 9.2 gives us

$$S_0 = C(K, T) - P(K, T) + PV_{0,T}(Div) + e^{-rT} K \qquad (9.3)$$

To match the cash flows for an outright purchase of the stock, in addition to buying the call and selling the put, we have to lend the present value of the strike and dividends to be paid over the life of the option. We then receive the stock in 91 days.

Example 9.3 In Example 9.1, $PV_{0,0.25}(K) = \$40e^{-0.08 \times 0.25} = \$39.21$. Hence, by buying the call for \$2.78, selling the put for \$1.99, and lending \$39.21, we invest a total of \$40 today. In 91 days, we have the two options and a T-bill worth \$40. We acquire the stock via one of the exercised options, using the \$40 T-bill to pay the strike price. 🎐

Synthetic T-bills If we buy the stock, sell the call, and buy the put, we have purchased the stock and short-sold the synthetic stock. This transaction gives us a hedged position that has no risk but requires investment. Parity shows us that

$$S_0 + P(K, T) - C(K, T) = PV_{0,T}(K) + PV_{0,T}(Div)$$

We have thus created a position that costs $PV(K) + PV_{0,T}(Div)$ and that pays $K + FV_{0,T}(Div)$ at expiration. This is a synthetic Treasury bill.

Example 9.4 In Example 9.1, $PV_{0,0.25}(K) = \$39.21$. Hence, by buying the stock, buying a put, and selling the call, we can create a T-bill that costs \$39.21 and pays \$40 in 91 days. 🎐

Since T-bills are taxed differently than stocks, the ability to create a synthetic Treasury bill with the stock and options creates problems for tax and accounting authorities. How should the return on this transaction be taxed—as a stock transaction or as interest income? Tax rules call for this position to be taxed as interest, but you can imagine taxpayers trying to skirt these rules.

The creation of a synthetic T-bill in this fashion is called a **conversion.** If we short the stock, buy a call, and sell a put, we have created a synthetic short T-bill position and this is called a **reverse conversion.**

Synthetic options   Parity tells us that

$$C(K, T) = S_0 - PV_{0,T}(Div) - PV_{0,T}(K) + P(K, T)$$

and that

$$P(K, T) = C(K, T) - S_0 + PV_{0,T}(K) + PV_{0,T}(Div)$$

The first relation says that a call is equivalent to a leveraged position on the underlying asset $[S_0 - PV_{0,T}(Div) - PV(K)]$, which is insured by the purchase of a put. The second relation says that a put is equivalent to a short position on the stock, insured by the purchase of a call.

Options on Currencies

Suppose we have options to buy euros by paying dollars. From our discussion of currency forward contracts, we know that the dollar forward price for a euro is $F_{0,T} = x_0 e^{(r-r_\in)T}$, where x_0 is the current exchange rate denominated as \$/€, $r_\in$ is the euro-denominated interest rate, and r is the dollar-denominated interest rate. The parity relationship for options to buy one euro by paying x_0 is then

$$C(K, T) - P(K, T) = x_0 e^{-r_\in T} - K e^{-rT} \tag{9.4}$$

Buying a euro call and selling a euro put is equivalent to lending euros and borrowing dollars. Equation (9.4) tells us that the difference in the call and put premiums simply reflects the difference in the amount borrowed and loaned, in the currency of the country in which the options are denominated.

Example 9.5   Suppose the current \$/€ exchange rate is 0.9, the dollar-denominated interest rate is 6%, and the euro-denominated interest rate is 4%. By buying a dollar-denominated euro call with a strike of \$0.92 and selling a dollar-denominated euro put with the same strike, we construct a position where in 1 year we will buy €1 by paying \$0.92. We can accomplish the same thing by lending the present value of €1 today (with a dollar cost of $\$0.9e^{-0.04} = \$0.8647$) and paying for this by borrowing the present value of \$0.92 ($\$0.92e^{-0.06} = \$0.8664$). The proceeds from borrowing exceed the amount we need to lend by \$0.0017. Equation (9.4) performs exactly this calculation, giving us a difference between the call premium and put premium of

$$x_0 e^{-r_\in T} - K e^{-rT} = 0.9\$/€ \times €e^{-0.04 \times 1} - \$0.92 \times e^{-0.06 \times 1}$$
$$= \$0.8647 - \$0.8664$$
$$= -\$0.0017$$

Options on Bonds

Finally, we can construct the parity relationship for options on bonds. The prepaid forward for a bond differs from the bond price due to coupon payments (which are like dividends). Thus if the bond price is B_0 we have

$$C(K, T) = P(K, T) + [B_0 - PV_{0,T}(Coupons)] - PV_{0,T}(K) \qquad (9.5)$$

Note that for a pure-discount bond, the parity relationship is exactly like that for a nondividend-paying stock.

9.2 GENERALIZED PARITY AND EXCHANGE OPTIONS

The preceding section showed that there is one parity relationship for all assets, not a different one for each underlying asset. Now we will generalize parity to apply to the case where the strike asset is not necessarily cash but could be any other asset. This version of parity includes all previous versions as special cases.

Suppose we have an option to exchange one asset for another. Let the underlying asset, asset A, have price S_t, and the strike asset (the asset which, at our discretion, we surrender in exchange for the underlying asset), asset B, have the price Q_t. Let $F_{t,T}^P(S)$ denote the time t price of a prepaid forward on the underlying asset, paying S_T at time T, and let $F_{t,T}^P(Q)$ denote the time t price of a prepaid forward on asset B, paying Q_T at time T. We use the notation $C(S_T, Q_T, T - t)$ to denote the time T price of an option with $T - t$ periods to expiration, which gives us the right to give up asset B in exchange for asset A. $P(S_T, Q_T, T - t)$ is defined similarly as the right to give up asset A in exchange for asset B. Now suppose that the call payoff at time T is

$$C(S_T, Q_T, 0) = max(0, S_T - Q_T)$$

and the put payoff is

$$P(S_T, Q_T, 0) = max(0, Q_T - S_T)$$

Then for European options we have this form of the parity equation:

$$\boxed{C(S_T, Q_T, T - t) - P(S_T, Q_T, T - t) = F_{t,T}^P(S) - F_{t,T}^P(Q)} \qquad (9.6)$$

The use of prepaid forward prices in the parity relationship completely takes into account the dividend and time value of money considerations. This version of parity tells us that there is nothing special about an option having the strike amount designated as cash. In general, options can be designed to exchange any asset for any other asset, and the relative put and call premiums are determined by prices of prepaid forwards on the underlying and strike assets.

To prove equation (9.6) we can use a payoff table in which we buy a call, sell a put, sell a prepaid forward on A, and buy a prepaid forward on B. This transaction is illustrated in Table 9.2.

If the strategy in Table 9.2 does not pay zero at expiration, there is an arbitrage opportunity. Thus, we expect equation (9.6) to hold. All European options satisfy this formula, whatever the underlying asset.

TABLE 9.2		Payoff table demonstrating that there is an arbitrage opportunity unless $-C(S_T, Q_T, T-t) + P(S_T, Q_T, T-t) + F_{t,T}^P(S) - F_{t,T}^P(Q) = 0$.	

		Expiration	
Transaction	**Time 0**	$S_T \leq Q_T$	$S_T > Q_T$
Buy Call	$-C(S_T, Q_T, T-t)$	0	$S_T - Q_T$
Sell Put	$P(S_T, Q_T, T-t)$	$S_T - Q_T$	0
Sell Prepaid Forward on A	$F_{t,T}^P(S)$	$-S_T$	$-S_T$
Buy Prepaid Forward on B	$-F_{t,T}^P(Q)$	Q_T	Q_T
Total	$\begin{aligned}&-C(S_T, Q_T, T-t)\\&+P(S_T, Q_T, T-t)\\&+F_{t,T}^P(S) - F_{t,T}^P(Q)\end{aligned}$	0	0

Example 9.6 Suppose that nondividend-paying stock A has a price of $20, and nondividend-paying stock B has a price of $25. Because neither stock pays dividends, their prepaid forward prices equal their prices. If A is the underlying asset and B is the strike asset, then put-call parity implies that

$$Call - put = \$20 - \$25 = -\$5$$

The put is $5 more expensive than the call for any time to expiration of the options.

Options to Exchange Stock

Executive stock options are sometimes constructed so that the strike price of the option is the price of an index, rather than a fixed cash amount. The idea is to have an option that pays off only when the company outperforms competitors, rather than one that pays off simply because all stock prices have gone up. As a hypothetical example of this, suppose Bill Gates, chairman of Microsoft, is given compensation options that pay off only if Microsoft outperforms AOL Time Warner. He will exercise these options if and only if the share price of Microsoft, $S_{\text{Microsoft}}$, exceeds the share price of AOL, S_{AOL}, i.e., $S_{\text{Microsoft}} > S_{\text{AOL}}$. From Gates's perspective, this is a call option, with the payoff

$$max(0, S_{\text{Microsoft}} - S_{\text{AOL}})$$

Now consider the compensation option for Steve Case, chairman of AOL. He will receive a compensation option that pays off only if AOL outperforms Microsoft, i.e.,

$$max(0, S_{AOL} - S_{Microsoft})$$

This is a call from Case's perspective.

Here is the interesting twist: Case's AOL call looks to Gates like a Microsoft put! And Gates's Microsoft call looks to Case like an AOL put. Either option can be viewed as a put or call; it is simply a matter of perspective. *The distinction between a put and a call in this example depends upon what we label the underlying asset and what we label as the strike asset.*

What Are Calls and Puts?

The preceding discussion suggests that labeling an option as a call or put is always a matter of convention. It is an important convention because we use it all the time in talking about options. Nevertheless, in general we can interpret calls as being puts, and vice versa. We can see why by using an analogy.

When you go to the grocery store to obtain bananas, you typically say that you are *buying* bananas. The actual transaction involves handing cash to the grocer and receiving a banana. This is an exchange of one asset (cash) for another (a banana). We could also describe the transaction by saying that we are *selling cash* (in exchange for bananas). The point is that an exchange occurs, and we can describe it either as buying the thing we receive, or selling the thing we surrender.

Any transaction is an exchange of one thing for another. Whether we say we are buying or selling is a matter of convention. This insight may not impress your grocer, but it is important for options since it suggests that the labeling we commonly use to distinguish calls and puts is a matter of convention.

To see how a call could be considered a put, consider a call option on a stock. This is the right to exchange a given number of dollars, the strike price K, for stock worth S, if the stock is worth more than the dollars. For example, suppose that if $S > K$, we earn $S - K$. We can view this as either of two transactions:

- Buying one share of stock by paying K. In this case we exercise when $S > K$. This is a call option on stock.

- Selling K dollars in exchange for one share of stock. Again we exercise when $S > K$, i.e., when the dollars we sell are worth less than the stock. This is a put option on dollars, with a share of stock as the strike asset.

Under either interpretation, if $S < K$ we do not exercise the option. If the dollars are worth more than the stock, we would not sell them for the stock.

Now consider a put option on a stock. The put option confers the right to exchange one share of stock for a given number of dollars. Suppose $S < K$; we earn $K - S$. We can view this in either of two ways:

- Selling one share of stock at the price K.

- Buying K dollars by paying one share of stock. This is a call where we have the right to give up stock to obtain dollars.

If $S > K$ we do not exercise under either interpretation. If the dollars are worth less than the stock, we would not pay the stock to obtain the dollars.

Currency Options

The idea that calls can be relabeled as puts is not just academic; it is used frequently by currency traders. A currency transaction involves the exchange of one kind of currency for another. In this context, it is obvious to market participants that referring to a particular currency as having been bought or sold is a matter of convention. Labelling a particular option a call or a put depends upon which currency you regard as your home currency.

In the following example we will show that a dollar-denominated call option on euros, which gives you the right to pay dollars to receive euros, is equivalent to a euro-denominated put option on dollars, which gives the right to sell a dollar for euros. Obviously, the strike prices and option quantities must be chosen appropriately for there to be an equivalence.

We will say that an option is "dollar-denominated" if the strike price and premium are denominated in dollars. An option is "euro-denominated" if the strike price and premium are in euros.

Suppose the current exchange rate is $x_0 = 0.90\$/€$, and consider the following two options:[2]

1. A 1-year *dollar-denominated call option* on euros with a strike price of $0.92 and premium of $0.0337. In 1 year, the owner of the option has the right to buy €1 for $0.92. The payoff on this option, in dollars, is therefore

$$max(0, x_1 - 0.92)$$

2. A 1-year *euro-denominated put option* on dollars with a strike of $\frac{1}{0.92} = €1.0870$. The premium of this option is €0.0407. In 1 year the owner of this put has the right to give up $1 and receive €1.0870; the owner will exercise the put when $1 is worth less than €1.0870. The euro value of $1 in 1 year will be $1/x_1$. Hence, the payoff of this option is

$$max\left(0, \frac{1}{0.92} - \frac{1}{x_1}\right)$$

Since $x_1 > 0.92$ exactly when $\frac{1}{0.92} > \frac{1}{x_1}$, the euro-denominated dollar put will be exercised when, and only when, the dollar-denominated euro call is exercised.

---

[2]These are Black-Scholes prices with a current exchange rate of 0.90 $/€, a dollar-denominated interest rate of 6%, a euro-denominated interest rate of 4%, and exchange rate volatility of 10%.

Though they will be exercised under the same circumstances, the dollar-denominated euro call and the euro-denominated dollar put differ in two respects:

- The scale of the two options is different. The dollar-denominated euro call is based on one euro (which has a current dollar value of $0.90) and the euro-denominated dollar put is based on one dollar.

- The currency of denomination is different.

We can equate the scale of the two options by holding more of the smaller option or less of the larger option. In particular, we can either scale up the dollar-denominated euro calls, holding $\frac{1}{0.92}$ of them, or we can scale down the euro-denominated dollar puts, holding 0.92 of them. To see the equivalence of the euro call and the dollar put, consider the following two transactions:

1. Buy $\frac{1}{0.92}$ 1-year dollar-denominated euro call options. At expiration, if we exercise, we will give up $1 for €$\frac{1}{0.92}$. The cost is $\frac{1}{0.92} \times \$0.0337 = \$0.0366$.

2. Buy one 1-year euro-denominated put option on dollars with a strike of €1.0870. The cost of this in dollars is 0.90$/€ × €0.0407 = \$0.0366$. When the option expires, convert the proceeds back from euros to dollars.

Tables 9.3 compares the payoffs of these two option positions. At exercise, each position results in surrendering $1 for €$\frac{1}{0.92}$ if $x_1 > 0.92$. Thus, the two positions must cost the same, or else there is an arbitrage opportunity.

We can summarize this result algebraically. The price of a dollar-denominated foreign currency call with strike K, when the current exchange rate is x_0, is $C_\$(x_0, K, T)$. The price of a foreign-currency–denominated dollar put with strike $\frac{1}{K}$, when the

TABLE 9.3	This table depicts the equivalence of buying a dollar-denominated euro call and a euro-denominated dollar put. In transaction I, we buy $\frac{1}{0.92}$ dollar-denominated call options permitting us to buy €1 for a strike price of $0.92. In transaction II, we buy one euro-denominated put permitting us to sell $1 for a strike price of €$\frac{1}{0.92}$ = € 1.0870. The option premium is €0.0407.

| | | Year 0 | | Year 1 | | | |
| | | | | $x_1 < 0.92$ | | $x_1 \geq 0.92$ | |
Transaction		$	€	$	€	$	€
I:	Buy $\frac{1}{0.92}$ Euro Calls	−0.0366	—	0	0	−1	$\frac{1}{0.92}$
II:	Convert Dollars to Euros	−0.0366	0.0407				
	Buy Dollar Put		−0.0407	0	0	−1	$\frac{1}{0.92}$

exchange rate is $\frac{1}{x_0}$, is $P_f(\frac{1}{x_0}, \frac{1}{K}, T)$. Adjusting for currency and scale differences, the prices are related by

$$C_\$(x_0, K, T) = x_0 \, K \, P_f \left(\frac{1}{x_0}, \frac{1}{K}, T \right) \tag{9.7}$$

This insight—that calls in one currency are the same as puts in the other—is commonplace among currency traders. While this observation is interesting in and of itself, its generalization to *all* options provides a fresh perspective for thinking about what calls and puts actually are.

9.3 COMPARING OPTIONS WITH RESPECT TO STYLE, MATURITY, AND STRIKE

We now examine how option prices change when there are changes in option characteristics, such as exercise style (American or European), the strike price, and time to expiration. Remarkably, we can say a great deal without a pricing model and without making any assumptions about the distribution of the underlying asset.[3] Thus, *whatever* the particular option model or stock price distribution used for valuing a given option, we can still expect option prices to behave in certain ways.

Here is an example of the kind of questions we will address in this section. Suppose you have three call options, with strikes of $40, $45, and $50. How do the premiums on these options differ? Common sense suggests that, with a call option on any underlying asset, the premium will go down as you raise the strike price; it is less valuable to be able to buy at a higher price.[4] Moreover, the decline in the premium can't be greater than $5. (The right to buy for a $5 cheaper price can't be worth more than $5.)

Following this logic, the premium will drop as we increase the strike from $40 to $45, and drop again when we increase the strike further from $45 to $50. Here is a more subtle question: In which case will the premium drop more? It turns out that the decline in the premium from $40 to $45 *must* be greater than the decline from $45 to $50, or else there is an arbitrage opportunity.

In this section we will explore the following issues for stock options (some of the properties may be different for options on other underlying assets):

- How prices of otherwise identical American and European options compare.

---

[3]The so-called "theory of rational option pricing," on which this section is based, was first presented in 1973 by Robert Merton in an astonishing paper (Merton, 1973b). This material is also superbly exposited in Cox and Rubinstein (1985).

[4]If you're being fastidious, you will say the option premium *cannot increase* as the strike goes up. Saying that the option premium will *decrease* as the strike increases does not account for the possibility that all the premiums are zero, and hence the premium will not go down, but will remain unchanged, as the strike price increases.

- How option prices change as the time to expiration changes.
- How option prices change as the strike price changes.

A word of warning before we begin this discussion: If you examine option price listings in the newspaper, you can often find option prices that seemingly give rise to arbitrage opportunities. There are several reasons for this. One is that some reported option price quotes are stale, meaning that the comparison is among option prices recorded at different times of the day. Moreover, an apparent arbitrage opportunity only becomes genuine when bid-ask spreads (see Table 9.1), commissions, costs of short-selling, and market impact are taken into account. Caveat arbitrageur!

European versus American Options

Since an American option can be exercised at any time, it must always be at least as valuable as an otherwise identical European option. (By "otherwise identical" we mean that the two options have the same underlying asset, strike price, and time to expiration.) Any exercise strategy appropriate to a European option can always be duplicated with an American option: The American option cannot be less valuable. Thus we have

$$C_{\text{Amer}}(S, K, T) \geq C_{\text{Eur}}(S, K, T) \tag{9.8a}$$

$$P_{\text{Amer}}(S, K, T) \geq P_{\text{Eur}}(S, K, T) \tag{9.8b}$$

As we will see, there are times when the right to early-exercise is worthless, and, hence, American and European options have the same value.

Maximum and Minimum Option Prices

It is often useful to understand just how expensive or inexpensive it is possible for an option to be. Here are some basic limits.

Calls   The price of a European call option

- Cannot be negative, because the call need not be exercised.
- Cannot exceed the stock price, because the best that can happen with a call is that you end up owning the stock.
- Must be at least as great as the price implied by parity with a zero put value.

Combining these statements, together with the result about American options never being worth less than European options, gives us

$$\boxed{S \geq C_{\text{Amer}}(S, K, T) \geq C_{\text{Eur}}(S, K, T) \geq max[0, PV_{0,T}(F_{0,T}) - PV_{0,T}(K)]} \tag{9.9}$$

where present values are taken over the life of the option.

Puts Similarly, a put

- Cannot be worth more than the undiscounted strike price, since that is the most it can ever be worth (if the stock price drops to zero, the put pays K at some point).

- Must be at least as great as the price implied by parity with a zero call value.

  Also, an American put is worth at least as much as a European put. This gives us

$$K \geq P_{\text{Amer}}(S, K, T) \geq P_{\text{Eur}}(S, K, T) \geq max[0, PV(K) - PV(F_{0,T})] \qquad (9.10)$$

Early Exercise for American Options

When might we want to exercise an option prior to expiration? An important result is that an American call option on a nondividend-paying stock should never be exercised prior to expiration. You may, however, rationally exercise an American-style put option prior to expiration.

Calls on a nondividend-paying stock We can demonstrate in two ways that an American-style call option on a nondividend-paying stock should never be exercised prior to expiration. This assertion about early exercise is equivalent to saying that the price of an American call prior to expiration satisfies

$$C_{\text{Amer}}(S_t, K, T - t) > S_t - K$$

If this inequality holds, you would lose money by early-exercising (receiving $S_t - K$) as opposed to selling the option (receiving $C_{\text{Amer}}(S_t, K, T - t) > S_t - K$).

We will use put-call parity to demonstrate that early exercise is not rational. If the option expires at T, parity implies that

$$C_{\text{Eur}}(S_t, K, T) = \underbrace{S_t - K}_{\text{Exercise Value}} + \underbrace{P_{\text{Eur}}(S_t, K, T - t)}_{\text{Insurance against } S_T < K}$$

$$+ \underbrace{K(1 - e^{-r(T-t)})}_{\text{Time Value of Money on } K} > S_t - K \qquad (9.11)$$

Since the put price, $P_{\text{Eur}}(S_t, K, T - t)$, and the time value of money on the strike, $K(1 - e^{-r(T-t)})$ are both positive, this equation establishes that the European call option premium on a nondividend paying stock always is at least as great as $S_t - K$. From equation (9.8), we also know that $C_{\text{Amer}} \geq C_{\text{Eur}}$. Thus we have

$$C_{\text{Amer}} \geq C_{\text{Eur}} > S_t - K$$

Since C_{Amer}, the American option premium, always exceeds $S - K$, we would lose money exercising an American call prior to expiration, as opposed to selling the option.

Equation (9.11) is useful because it shows us precisely *why* we would never early-exercise. Early-exercising has two effects. First, we throw away the implicit put protection should the stock later move below the strike price. Second, we accelerate the payment of the strike price.

A third effect is the possible loss from deferring receipt of the stock. However, when there are no dividends, we lose nothing by waiting to take physical possession of the stock.

We have demonstrated that if a stock pays no dividends, you should never see an option selling for less than $S_t - K$. In fact, equation (9.11) like equation (9.9) actually implies the stronger result that you should never see a call on a nondividend-paying stock sell for less than $S_t - Ke^{-r(T-t)}$. What happens if you do observe an option selling for too low a price? If $C < S_t - K$ and the option is American, you can buy the option, exercise it, and earn $S_t - K - C_{Amer}(S_t, K, T - t) > 0$. However, what if the option is European and therefore cannot be exercised early? In this case the arbitrage is: Buy the option, short the stock, and lend the present value of the strike price. Table 9.4 demonstrates the arbitrage in this case. The sources of profit from the arbitrage are the same as those identified in equation (9.11).

It is important to realize that this proposition does *not* say that you must hold the option until expiration. It says that if you no longer wish to hold the call, you should sell it rather than early-exercising it.[5]

Calls may be exercised just prior to a dividend   If the stock pays dividends, the parity relationship is

$$C(S_t, K, T - t) = P(S_t, K, T - t) + S_t - PV_{t,T}(Div) - PV_{t,T}(K)$$

Using this expression, we cannot always rule out early exercise as we did above. Early exercise is not optimal at any time where

$$K - PV_{t,T}(K) > PV_{t,T}(Div) \tag{9.12}$$

TABLE 9.4		Demonstration of arbitrage if a call option with price C sells for less than $S_t - Ke^{-r(T-t)}$. Every entry in the row labeled "total" is nonnegative.	

		Expiration or Exercise, Time T	
Transaction	**Time t**	$S_T < K$	$S_T > K$
Buy Call	$-C$	0	$S_T - K$
Short stock	S_t	$-S_T$	$-S_T$
Lend $Ke^{-r(T-t)}$	$-Ke^{-r(T-t)}$	K	K
Total	$S_t - Ke^{-r(T-t)} - C$	$K - S_T$	0

[5] Some options, such as compensation options, cannot be sold. In practice it is common to see executives exercise options prior to expiration and then sell the stock. The discussion in this section demonstrates that such exercise would be irrational if the option could be sold, or if the stock could be sold short.

That is, if interest on the strike price (which induces us to delay exercise) exceeds the present value of dividends (which induces us to exercise), then we will for certain never early-exercise at that time. If inequality (9.12) is violated, this does not tell us that we *will* exercise, only that we cannot rule it out.

If dividends are sufficiently great, however, early exercise might be optimal. For example, consider a 90-strike American call on a stock selling for $100, which is about to pay a dividend of $99.99. If we exercise—paying $90 to acquire the $100 stock— we have a net position worth $10. If we delay past the ex-dividend date, the option is worthless.

If dividends do make early exercise rational, it will be optimal to exercise at the last moment before the ex-dividend date. By exercising earlier than that, we pay the strike price prematurely and thus at a minimum lose interest on the strike price.

Early exercise for puts   When the underlying stock pays no dividend, a call will not be early-exercised, but a put might be. To see that early exercise for a put can make economic sense, suppose a company is bankrupt and the stock price falls to zero. Then a put that would not be exercised until expiration will be worth $PV_{t,T}(K)$. If we could early-exercise, we would receive K. Since as long as the interest rate is positive, $K > PV(K)$, early exercise would be optimal in order to receive the strike price earlier.

We can also use a parity argument to understand this. The put will never be exercised as long as $P > K - S$. Supposing that the stock pays no dividends, parity for the put is

$$P(S_t, K, T - t) = C(S_t, K, T - t) - S_t + PV_{t,T}(K)$$

$P > K - S$ then implies

$$C(S_t, K, T - t) - S_t + PV_{t,T}(K) > K - S_t$$

or

$$C(S_t, K, T - t) > K - PV_{t,T}(K)$$

If the call is sufficiently valueless (as in the above example of a bankrupt company), parity can not rule out early exercise. This does not mean that we *will* early-exercise; it simply means that we can not rule it out.

We can summarize this discussion of early exercise. When we exercise an option, we receive something (the stock with a call, the strike price with a put). A necessary condition for early exercise is that we prefer to receive this something sooner rather than later. For calls, dividends on the stock are a reason to want to receive the stock earlier. For puts, interest on the strike is a reason to want to receive the strike price earlier. Thus, dividends and interest play similar roles in the two analyses of early exercise. In fact, if we view interest as the dividend on cash, then dividends (broadly defined) become the sole reason to early-exercise an option.

Similarly, dividends on the strike asset become a reason not to early-exercise. In the case of calls, interest is the dividend on the strike asset, and in the case of puts, dividends on the stock are the dividend on the strike asset.

The point of this section has been to make some general statements about when early exercise will not occur, or under what conditions it *might* occur. Early exercise is a trade-off involving time value of money on the strike price, dividends on the underlying asset, and the value of insurance on the position. In general, figuring out when to exercise requires an option pricing model. We will discuss early exercise further in Chapters 10 and 11.

Time to Expiration

How does an option price change as we increase time to expiration? If the options are American, the option price can never decline with an increase in time to expiration. If the options are European, the price can go either up or down as we increase time to expiration.

American options   An American call with more time to expiration is at least as valuable as an otherwise identical call with less time to expiration. An American call with 2 years to expiration, for example, can always be turned into an American option with 1 year to expiration by voluntarily exercising it after 1 year. Therefore, the 2-year call is at least as valuable as the 1-year call.

The same is true for puts: A longer-lived American put is always worth at least as much as an otherwise equivalent European put.

European options   A European call on a nondividend-paying stock will be at least as valuable as an otherwise identical call with a shorter time to expiration. This occurs because, with no dividends, a European call has the same price as an otherwise identical American call. With dividends, however, longer-lived European options may be less valuable than shorter-lived European options. Economic forces that make it optimal to exercise an option early can make a short-lived European option worth more than a long-lived European option.

To see this for calls, imagine a stock that will pay a liquidating dividend 2 weeks from today.[6] A European call with 1 week to expiration will have value since it is exercisable prior to the dividend. A European call with 3 weeks to expiration will have no value since the stock will have no value at expiration. This is an example of a longer-lived option being less valuable than a shorter-lived option. Note that if the options were American, we would simply exercise the 3-week option prior to the dividend.

Longer-lived European puts can also be less valuable than shorter-lived European puts. A good example of this is a bankrupt company. The put will be worth the present value of the strike price, with present value calculated until time to expiration. Longer-lived puts will be worth less than shorter-lived puts. If the options were American, they would all be exercised immediately and hence would be worth the strike price.

----

[6]A liquidating dividend occurs when a firm pays its entire value to shareholders. A firm is worthless after paying a liquidating dividend.

European options when the strike price grows over time   In discussing the effect of changing time to maturity, we have been keeping the option strike price fixed. The present value of the strike price therefore decreases with time to maturity. Suppose, however, that we keep the present value of the strike constant by setting $K_t = Ke^{rt}$. When the strike grows at the interest rate, the premiums on European calls and puts on a nondividend-paying stock increase with time to maturity.[7] We will demonstrate this for puts; the demonstration is identical for calls.

To keep the notation simple, let $P(t)$ denote the time 0 price of a European put maturing at time t, with strike price $K_t = Ke^{rt}$. We want to show that $P(T) > P(t)$ if $T > t$. To show this, we will demonstrate an arbitrage if $P(T) \leq P(t)$.

If the longer-lived put is not more expensive, i.e., if $P(T) \leq P(t)$, buy the put with T years to expiration and sell the put with t years to expiration. At time t the written put will expire. If $S_t > K_t$ its value is zero and we can ignore the shorter-lived option from this point on. If $S_t < K_t$, the put holder will exercise the short-lived option and our payoff is $S_t - K_t$. Suppose that we keep the stock we receive and borrow to finance the strike price, holding this position until the second option expires at time T. Here is the important step: Notice that the time-T value of this time-t payoff is $S_T - K_t e^{r(T-t)} = S_T - K_T$.

Table 9.5 summarizes the resulting payoffs. By buying the short-lived put and selling the long-lived put, we are guaranteed not to lose money at time T. Therefore, if $P(t) > P(T)$ there is an arbitrage opportunity. A practical application of this result is discussed in the box on page 289.

| TABLE 9.5 | Demonstration that there is an arbitrage if $P(T) \leq P(t)$ with $t < T$. The strike on the put with maturity t is $K_t = Ke^{rt}$, and the strike on the put with maturity T is $K_T = Ke^{rt}$. If the option expiring at time t is in-the-money, the payoff, $S_t - K_t$, is reinvested until time T. If $P(t) \geq P(T)$, all cash flows in the "total" line are non-negative. |

		Payoff at Time T			
		$S_T < K_T$		$S_T > K_T$	
		Payoff at Time t			
Transaction	Time 0	$S_t < K_t$	$S_t > K_t$	$S_t < K_t$	$S_t > K_t$
Sell $P(t)$	$P(t)$	$S_T - K_T$	0	$S_T - K_T$	0
Buy $P(T)$	$-P(T)$	$K_T - S_T$	$K_T - S_T$	0	0
Total	$P(t) - P(T)$	0	$K_T - S_T$	$S_T - K_T$	0

....

[7]Dividends can easily be accommodated in the following way. Suppose that all dividends are reinvested in the stock. Call the resulting position a *total return portfolio* and let S_t be the price of this portfolio. Define the options so that the total return portfolio is the underlying asset. The result in this section then obtains for the total return portfolio. The reason is that the total return portfolio is a synthetic nondividend-paying stock.

Portfolio Insurance for the Long Run

Historically, the rate of return from investing in stocks over a long horizon has outperformed that from investing in government bonds in the United States (see, for example, Siegel, 1998). This observation has led some to suggest that if held for a sufficiently long period of time, stocks are a safe investment relative to risk-free bonds.

Bodie (1995) suggests using put option premiums to think about the claim that stocks are safe in the long run. Specifically, what would it cost to buy a put option insuring that after T years your stock portfolio would be worth at least as much as if you had instead invested in a zero-coupon bond? If your initial investment was S_0, you could provide this insurance by setting the strike price on the put option equal to $K_T = S_0 e^{rT}$.

Bodie uses the Black-Scholes model to show that the premium on this insurance increases with T. As Bodie notes, however, this proposition must be true for any valid option pricing model. The payoffs in Table 9.5 demonstrate that the cost of this insurance *must* increase with T or else there is an arbitrage opportunity. Whatever the historical return statistics appear to say, the cost of portfolio insurance is increasing with the length of time for which you insure the portfolio return. Using the cost of insurance as a measure, stocks are riskier in the long run.

Different Strike Prices

We discussed at the beginning of this section some statements we can make about how option prices vary with the strike price. Here is a more formal statement of these propositions. Suppose we have three strike prices, $K_1 < K_2 < K_3$, with corresponding call option prices $C(K_1)$, $C(K_2)$, and $C(K_3)$ and put option prices $P(K_1)$, $P(K_2)$, and $P(K_3)$. Here are the propositions we discuss in this section:

1. A call with a low strike price is at least as valuable as an otherwise identical call with a higher strike price:

$$\boxed{C(K_1) \geq C(K_2)} \tag{9.13}$$

A put with a high strike price is at least as valuable as an otherwise identical put with a low strike price:

$$\boxed{P(K_2) \geq P(K_1)} \tag{9.14}$$

2. The premium difference between otherwise identical calls with different strike prices cannot be greater than the difference in strike prices:

$$\boxed{C(K_1) - C(K_2) \leq K_2 - K_1} \tag{9.15}$$

The premium difference for otherwise identical puts also cannot be greater than the difference in strike prices:

$$P(K_2) - P(K_1) \leq K_2 - K_1 \tag{9.16}$$

3. Premiums decline at a decreasing rate as we consider calls with progressively higher strike prices. This is called **convexity** of the option price with respect to the strike price:

$$\frac{C(K_1) - C(K_2)}{K_2 - K_1} \geq \frac{C(K_2) - C(K_3)}{K_3 - K_2} \tag{9.17}$$

$$\frac{P(K_2) - P(K_1)}{K_2 - K_1} \leq \frac{P(K_3) - P(K_2)}{K_3 - K_2} \tag{9.18}$$

These statements are all true for both European and American options.[8] Algebraic demonstrations are in Appendix 9.B. It turns out, however, that these three propositions are equivalent to saying that there are no free lunches: If you enter into an option spread, there must be stock prices at which you would lose money on the spread. Otherwise the spread represents an arbitrage opportunity. These three propositions say that you cannot have a bull spread, a bear spread, or a butterfly spread for which you can never lose money. If any of these propositions were not true, such a spread would exist. Specifically:

1. If equation (9.13) were not true, buy the low-strike call and sell the high-strike call (this is a call bull spread). If equation (9.14) were not true, buy the high-strike put and sell the low-strike put (a put bear spread).

2. If equation (9.15) were not true, sell the low-strike call and buy the high-strike call (a call bear spread). If equation (9.16) were not true, buy the low-strike put and sell the high-strike put (a put bull spread).

3. If either of equations (9.17) or (9.18) were not true, there is an asymmetric butterfly spread with positive profits at all prices.

We will illustrate these propositions with numerical examples.

Example 9.7 Suppose we observe the call premiums in Panel A of Table 9.6. These values violate the second property for calls, since the difference in strikes is 5 and the difference in the premiums is 6. If we observed these values, we could engage in arbitrage

---

[8]In fact, if the options are European, the second statement can be strengthened: The difference in option premiums must be less than the *present value* of the difference in strikes.

TABLE 9.6	Panel A shows call option premiums for which the change in the option premium ($6) exceeds the change in the strike price ($5). Panel B shows how a bear spread can be used to arbitrage these prices. By lending the bear spread proceeds, we have a zero cash flow at time 0; the cash outflow at time T is always greater than $1.

Panel A

Strike	50	55
Premium	18	12

Panel B

		Expiration or Exercise		
Transaction	Time 0	$S_T < 50$	$50 \leq S_T \leq 55$	$S_T \geq 55$
Buy 55-Strike Call	-12	0	0	$S_T - 55$
Sell 50-Strike Call	18	0	$50 - S_T$	$50 - S_T$
Total	6	0	$50 - S_T$	-5

by buying the 55-strike call and selling the 50-strike call, which is a bear spread. Note that we receive $6 initially and never have to pay more than $5 in the future. This is an arbitrage, whatever the interest rate. ≹

Now consider the third proposition, *strike price convexity*. There is a different way to write the convexity inequality, equation (9.17). Since K_2 is between K_1 and K_3, we can write it as a weighted average of the other two strikes, that is

$$K_2 = \lambda K_1 + (1 - \lambda)K_3$$

where

$$\lambda = \frac{K_3 - K_2}{K_3 - K_1} \qquad (9.19)$$

With this expression for λ, it is possible to rewrite equation (9.17) as

$$C(K_2) \leq \lambda C(K_1) + (1 - \lambda)C(K_3) \qquad (9.20)$$

Here is an example illustrating convexity.

Example 9.8   If $K_1 = 50$, $K_2 = 59$, and $K_3 = 65$, $\lambda = \frac{65-59}{65-50} = 0.4$; hence,

$$59 = 0.4 \times 50 + 0.6 \times 65$$

Call prices must then satisfy

$$C(59) \leq 0.4 \times C(50) + 0.6 \times C(65)$$

Suppose we observe the call premiums in Table 9.7. The change in the option premium per dollar of strike price change from 50 to 59 is $5.1/9 = 0.567$, and the change from 59 to 65 is $3.9/6 = 0.65$. Thus, prices violate the proposition that the premium decreases at a decreasing rate as the strike price increases.

To arbitrage this mispricing, we engage in an asymmetric butterfly spread: Buy four 50-strike calls, buy six 65-strike calls, and sell ten 59-strike calls.[9] By engaging in a butterfly spread, Panel B shows that a profit of at least \$3 is earned.   ❧

TABLE 9.7   The example in Panel A violates the proposition that the rate of change of the option premium must decrease as the strike price rises. The rate of change from 50 to 59 is 5.1/9, while the rate of change from 59 to 65 is 3.9/6. We can arbitrage this convexity violation with an asymmetric butterfly spread. Panel B shows that we earn at least \$3 plus interest at time T.

Panel A

Strike	50	59	65
Call Premium	14	8.9	5

Panel B

Transaction	Time 0	$S_T < 50$	$50 \leq S_T \leq 59$	$59 \leq S_T \leq 65$	$S_T > 65$
Buy Four 50-Strike Calls	−56	0	$4(S_T - 50)$	$4(S_T - 50)$	$4(S_T - 50)$
Sell Ten 59-Strike Calls	89	0	0	$10(59 - S_T)$	$10(59 - S_T)$
Buy Six 65-Strike Calls	−30	0	0	0	$6(S_T - 65)$
Lend \$3	−3	$3e^{rT}$	$3e^{rT}$	$3e^{rT}$	$3e^{rT}$
Total	0	$3e^{rT}$	$3e^{rT} + 4(S_T - 50)$	$3e^{rT} + 6(65 - S_T)$	$3e^{rT}$

[9]Note that we get exactly the same arbitrage with any number of calls as long as the ratio at the various strikes remains the same. We could also have bought 0.4 50 calls, sold one 59 call, and bought 0.6 65 calls.

The formula for λ may look imposing, but there is an easy way to figure out what λ is in any situation. In this example, we had the prices 50, 59, and 65. It is possible to express 59 as a weighted average of 50 and 65. The total distance between 50 and 65 is 15, and the distance from 50 to 59 is 9, which is $9/15 = 0.6$ of the total distance. Thus, we can write 59 as

$$59 = (1 - 0.6) \times 50 + 0.6 \times 65$$

This is the interpretation of λ in expression (9.20).

Here is an example of convexity with puts.

Example 9.9   See the prices in Panel A of Table 9.8. We have $K_1 = 50$, $K_2 = 55$, and $K_3 = 70$. $\lambda = 0.75$ and $55 = 0.75 \times 50 + (1 - 0.75) \times 70$. Convexity is violated since

$$P(55) = 8 > 0.75 \times 4 + (1 - 0.75) \times 16 = 7$$

To arbitrage this mispricing, we engage in an asymmetric butterfly spread: Buy three 50-strike puts, buy one 70-strike put, and sell four 55-strike puts. The result is in Panel B of Table 9.8.   ❧

TABLE 9.8   Arbitrage of mispriced puts using asymmetric butterfly spread.

Panel A			
Strike	50	55	70
Put Premium	4	8	16

		Panel B			
			Expiration or Exercise		
Transaction	**Time 0**	$S_T < 50$	$50 \leq S_T \leq 55$	$55 \leq S_T \leq 70$	$S_T > 70$
Buy Three 50-Strike Puts	-12	$3(50 - S_T)$	0	0	0
Sell Four 55-Strike Puts	32	$4(S_T - 55)$	$4(S_T - 55)$	0	0
Buy One 70-Strike Put	-16	$70 - S_T$	$70 - S_T$	$(70 - S_T)$	0
Lend $4	-4	$4e^{rT}$	$4e^{rT}$	$4e^{rT}$	$4e^{rT}$
Total	0	$4e^{rT}$	$4e^{rT} + 3(S_T - 50)$	$4e^{rT} + 70 - S_T$	$4e^{rT}$

Again, we always make at least 0. Figure 9.2 illustrates the necessary shape of curves for both calls and puts relating the option premium to the strike price.

Exercise and Moneyness

If it is optimal to exercise an option, it is also optimal to exercise an otherwise identical option that is more in-the-money. Consider what would have to happen in order for this *not* to be true.

Suppose a call option on a dividend-paying stock has a strike price of $50, and the stock price is $70. Also suppose that it is optimal to exercise the option. This means that the option must sell for $70 − $50 = $20.

Now what can we say about the premium of a 40-strike option? We know from the discussion above that the change in the premium is no more than the change in the strike price, or else there is an arbitrage opportunity. This means that

$$C\,(40) \leq \$20 + (\$50 - \$40) = \$30$$

Since the 40-strike call is worth $30 if exercised, it must be optimal to exercise it.

Following the same logic, this is also true for puts.

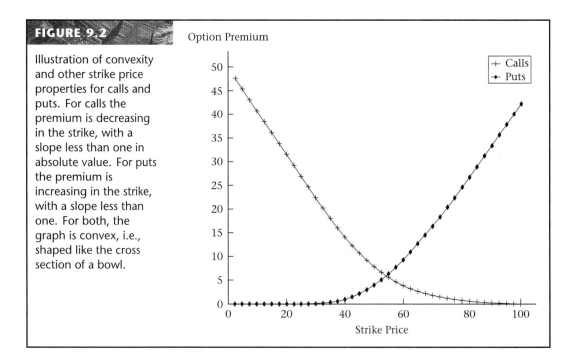

FIGURE 9.2

Illustration of convexity and other strike price properties for calls and puts. For calls the premium is decreasing in the strike, with a slope less than one in absolute value. For puts the premium is increasing in the strike, with a slope less than one. For both, the graph is convex, i.e., shaped like the cross section of a bowl.

CHAPTER SUMMARY

Put-call parity is one of the most important relations in option pricing. Parity is the observation that buying a European call and selling a European put with the same strike price and time to expiration is equivalent to making a leveraged investment in the underlying asset, less the value of cash payments to the underlying asset over the life of the option. Different versions of parity for different underlying assets appear in Table 9.9. In every case the value on the left-hand side of the parity equation is the price of the underlying asset less its cash flows over the life of the option. The parity relationship can be algebraically rearranged so that options and the underlying asset create a synthetic bond, options and a bond create a synthetic stock, and one kind of option together with the stock and bond synthetically create the other kind of option.

The idea of an option can be generalized to permit an asset other than cash to be the strike asset. This insight blurs the distinction between a put and a call. The idea that puts and calls are different ways of looking at the same contract is commonplace in currency markets.

Option prices must obey certain restrictions when we vary the strike price, time to maturity, or option exercise style. American options are at least as valuable as European options. American calls and puts become more expensive as time to expiration increases, but European options need not. European options on a nondividend-paying stock do become more expensive with increasing time to maturity if the strike price grows at the interest rate. Dividends are the reason to exercise an American call early, while interest is the reason to exercise an American put early. A call option on a nondividend-paying stock will always have a price greater than its value if exercised; hence, it should never be exercised early.

There are a number of pricing relationships related to changing strike prices. In particular, as the strike price increases, calls become less expensive with their price

---

TABLE 9.9 Versions of put-call parity. Notation in the table includes the spot currency exchange rate, x_0; the risk-free interest rate in the foreign currency, r_f; and the current bond price, B_0.

Underlying Asset	Parity Relationship
Futures Contract	$e^{-rT} F_{0,T} = C(K, T) - P(K, T) + e^{-rT} K$
Stock, No-Dividend	$S_0 = C(K, T) - P(K, T) + e^{-rT} K$
Stock, Discrete Dividend	$S_0 - PV_{0,T}(Div) = C(K, T) - P(K, T) + e^{-rT} K$
Stock, Continuous Dividend	$e^{-\delta T} S_0 = C(K, T) - P(K, T) + e^{-rT} K$
Currency	$e^{-r_f T} x_0 = C(K, T) - P(K, T) + e^{-rT} K$
Bond	$B_0 - PV_{0,T}(Coupons) = C(K, T) - P(K, T) + e^{-rT} K$

decreasing at a decreasing rate. The absolute value of the change in the call price is less than the change in the strike price. As the strike price decreases, puts become less expensive with their price decreasing at a decreasing rate. The change in the put price is less than the change in the strike price.

Further Reading

Two of the ideas in this chapter will prove particularly important in later chapters.

The first key idea is put-call parity, which tells us that if we understand calls we also understand puts. This equivalence makes it easier to understand option pricing since the pricing techniques and intuition about one kind of option are directly applicable to the other. The idea of exchange options—options to exchange one asset for another—also will show up again in later chapters. We will see how to price such options in Chapter 14.

A second key idea that will prove important is the determination of factors influencing early exercise. As a practical matter, it is more work to price an American than a European option, so it is useful to know when this extra work is not necessary. Less obviously, the determinants of early exercise will play a key role in Chapter 17, where we discuss real options. We will see that certain kinds of investment projects are analogous to options, and the investment decision is like exercising an option. Thus, the early-exercise decision can have important consequences beyond the realm of financial options.

Much of the material in this chapter can be traced to Merton (1973b), which contains an exhaustive treatment of option properties that must hold if there is to be no arbitrage. Cox and Rubinstein (1985) also provides an excellent treatment of this material.

Problems

9.1. A stock currently sells for $32.00. A 6-month call option with a strike of $35.00 has a premium of $2.27. Assuming a 4% continuously compounded risk-free rate and a 6% continuous dividend yield, what is the price of the associated put option?

9.2. A stock currently sells for $32.00. A 6-month call option with a strike of $30.00 has a premium of $4.29, and a 6-month put with the same strike has a premium of $2.64. Assume a 4% continuously compounded risk-free rate. What is the present value of dividends payable over the next 6 months?

9.3. Suppose the S&R index is 800, the continuously compounded risk-free rate is 5%, and the dividend yield is 0%. A 1-year 815-strike European call costs $75 and a 1-year 815-strike European put costs $45. Consider the strategy of buying the stock, selling the 815-strike call, and buying the 815-strike put.

    a. What is the rate of return on this position held until the expiration of the options?

    b. What is the arbitrage implied by your answer to (a)?

c. What difference between the call and put prices would eliminate arbitrage?

d. What difference between the call and put prices eliminates arbitrage for strike prices of $780, $800, $820, and $840?

9.4. Suppose the exchange rate is 0.95 $/€, the euro-denominated continuously compounded interest rate is 4%, the dollar-denominated continuously compounded interest rate is 6%, and the price of a 1-year 0.93-strike European call on the euro is $0.0571. What is the price of a 0.93-strike European put?

9.5. The premium of a 100-strike yen-denominated put on the euro is ¥8.763. The current exchange rate is 95 ¥/€. What is the strike of the corresponding euro-denominated yen call, and what is its premium?

9.6. The price of a 6-month dollar-denominated call option on the euro with a $0.90 strike is $0.0404. The price of an otherwise equivalent put option is $0.0141. The annual continuously compounded dollar interest rate is 5%.

a. What is the 6-month dollar-euro forward price?

b. If the euro-denominated annual continuously compounded interest rate is 3.5%, what is the spot exchange rate?

9.7. Suppose the dollar-denominated interest rate is 5%, the yen-denominated interest rate is 1% (both rates are continuously compounded), the spot exchange rate is 0.009 $/¥, and the price of a dollar-denominated European call to buy one yen with 1 year to expiration and a strike price of $0.009 is $0.0006.

a. What is the dollar-denominated European yen put price such that there is no arbitrage opportunity?

b. Suppose that a dollar-denominated European yen put with a strike of $0.009 has a premium of $0.0004. Demonstrate the arbitrage.

c. Now suppose that you are in Tokyo, trading options that are denominated in yen rather than dollars. If the price of a dollar-denominated at-the-money yen call in the United States is $0.0006, what is the price of a yen-denominated at-the-money dollar call—an option giving the right to buy one dollar, denominated in yen—in Tokyo? What is the relationship of this answer to your answer to (a)? What is the price of the at-the-money dollar put?

9.8. Suppose call and put prices are given by

Strike	50	55
Call Premium	9	10
Put Premium	7	6

What no-arbitrage property is violated? What spread position would you use to effect arbitrage? Demonstrate that the spread position is an arbitrage.

9.9. Suppose call and put prices are given by

Strike	50	55
Call Premium	16	10
Put Premium	7	14

What no-arbitrage property is violated? What spread position would you use to effect arbitrage? Demonstrate that the spread position is an arbitrage.

9.10. Suppose call and put prices are given by

Strike	50	55	60
Call Premium	18	14	9.50
Put Premium	7	10.75	14.45

Find the convexity violations. What spread would you use to effect arbitrage? Demonstrate that the spread position is an arbitrage.

9.11. Suppose call and put prices are given by

Strike	80	100	105
Call Premium	22	9	5
Put Premium	4	21	24.80

Find the convexity violations. What spread would you use to effect arbitrage? Demonstrate that the spread position is an arbitrage.

9.12. In each case identify the arbitrage and demonstrate how you would make money by creating a table showing your payoff.

    a. Consider two European options on the same stock with the same time to expiration. The 90-strike call costs $10 and the 95-strike call costs $4.

    b. Now suppose these options have 2 years to expiration and the continuously compounded interest rate is 10%. The 90-strike call costs $10 and the 95-strike call costs $5.25. Show again that there is an arbitrage opportunity. (Hint: It is important in this case that the options are European.)

    c. Suppose that a 90-strike European call sells for $15, a 100-strike call sells for $10, and a 105-strike call sells for $6. Show how you could use an asymmetric butterfly to profit from this arbitrage opportunity.

9.13. Suppose the interest rate is 0 and the stock of XYZ has a positive dividend yield. Is there any circumstance in which you would early-exercise an American XYZ call? Is there any circumstance in which you would early-exercise an American XYZ put? Explain.

9.14. In the following, suppose that neither stock pays a dividend.

    a. Suppose you have a call option that permits you to receive one share of Apple by giving up one share of AOL. In what circumstance might you early-exercise this call?

b. Suppose you have a put option that permits you to give up one share of Apple, receiving one share of AOL. In what circumstance might you early-exercise this put? Would there be a loss from not early-exercising if Apple had a zero stock price?

c. Now suppose that Apple is expected to pay a dividend. Which of the above answers will change? Why?

9.15. The price of a nondividend-paying stock is $100 and the continuously compounded risk-free rate is 5%. A 1-year European call option with a strike price of $100 × $e^{0.05 \times 1}$ = $105.127 has a premium of $11.924. A $1\frac{1}{2}$ year European call option with a strike price of $100 × $e^{0.05 \times 1.5}$ = $107.788 has a premium of $11.50. Demonstrate an arbitrage.

9.16. Suppose that to buy either a call or a put option you pay the quoted ask price, denoted $C_a(K, T)$ and $P_a(K, T)$, and to sell an option you receive the bid, $C_b(K, T)$ and $P_b(K, T)$. Similarly, the ask and bid prices for the stock are S_a and S_b. Finally, suppose you can borrow at the rate r_H and lend at the rate r_L. The stock pays no dividend. Find the bounds between which you cannot profitably perform a parity arbitrage.

9.17. In this problem we consider whether parity is violated by any of the option prices in Table 9.1. Suppose that you buy at the ask and sell at the bid, and that your continuously compounded lending rate is 2% and your borrowing rate is 4%. Ignore transaction costs on the stock, for which the price is $106.79. Assume that IBM is expected to pay a $0.14 dividend in early May. For each strike and expiration, what is the cost if you

a. Buy the call, sell the put, short the stock, and lend the present value of the strike price?

b. Sell the call, buy the put, buy the stock, and borrow the present value of the strike price?

9.18. Consider the April 95, 100, and 105 call option prices in Table 9.1.

a. Does convexity hold if you buy a butterfly spread, buying at the ask price and selling at the bid?

b. Does convexity hold if you *sell* a butterfly spread, buying at the ask price and selling at the bid?

c. Does convexity hold if you are a market-maker either buying or selling a butterfly, paying the bid and receiving the ask?

d. Suppose the ask price for the 100-strike call had been $9.20 instead of $9.00. Is there a convexity violation? For whom?

Appendix 9.A: Parity Bounds for American Options

The exact parity relationship discussed in Chapter 9 only holds for European options. However, American options often come close to obeying put-call parity, especially when options have short times to expiration.

With a nondividend-paying stock, the call will not be exercised early, but the put might be. The effect of early exercise for the put is to accelerate the receipt of the strike price. Since interest on the strike price is small for short times to maturity, parity will come close to holding for short-lived American options on nondividend-paying stocks.

We now let P and C refer to prices of American options. The American put can be more valuable than the European put, and we have

$$P \geq C + PV(K) - S$$

However, suppose that the put were exercised early. Then it would be worth $K - S$. For example, if we think of synthetically creating the stock by buying the call and selling the put, there is a chance that we will pay K before expiration, in the event the stock price plummets and the put is early-exercised. Consequently, if we replace the present value of the strike with the undiscounted strike, we have a valid upper bound for the value of the put. It will be true (and you can verify with a no-arbitrage argument) that

$$P \leq C + K - S$$

When there are no dividends, we have $C + K - S$ as an upper bound on the put, and European parity as a lower bound (since an American put is always worth at least as much as a European put). The parity relationship can be written as a restriction on the put price or on the call price:

$$C + K - S \geq P \geq C + PV(K) - S$$
$$P + S - PV(K) \geq C \geq P + S - K$$

Thus, when there are no dividends, European parity can be violated to the extent of interest on the strike price. Since this will be small for options that are not long-lived, European parity can remain a good approximation for American options.

Dividends add the complication that the call as well as the put may be exercised early. There exists the possibility of a large parity violation because of the following "whipsaw" scenario: The call is exercised early to capture a large dividend payment, the stock price drops, and the put is then exercised early to capture interest on the strike price. The possibility that this can happen leads to a wider no-arbitrage band. With dividends, the parity relationship becomes (Cox and Rubinstein [1985], p. 152)

$$C + K + PV(D) - S \geq P \geq C + PV(K) - S$$
$$P + S - PV(K) \geq C \geq P + S - PV(D) - K$$

The upper bound for the call is the same as in European parity, except without dividends. The intuition for the upper bound on the call option (the left-hand side) is that we can avoid the loss of dividends by early-exercising the call; hence, it is the same bound as in the European case with no dividends. The lower bound exists because it may not be optimal to exercise the call to avoid dividends, and it may be optimal to early-exercise the put.

Consider the worst case for the call. Suppose $K = \$100$ and $S = \$100$, and the stock is about to pay a liquidating dividend (i.e., $D = \$100$). We will not exercise the call, since doing so gives us nothing. The put will be exercised after the dividend is paid, once the stock is worthless. So $P = \$100$. The relationship then states

$$C \geq P + S - D - K = 100 + 100 - 100 - 100 = 0$$

And indeed, the call will be worthless in this case.

APPENDIX 9.B: ALGEBRAIC PROOFS OF STRIKE-PRICE RELATIONS

In Chapter 9 we demonstrated several propositions about how option prices change when the strike price changes. To prove these propositions we will consider strike prices K_1, K_2, and K_3, where $K_1 < K_2 < K_3$. Define λ so that

$$\lambda = \frac{K_3 - K_2}{K_3 - K_1}$$

or

$$K_2 = \lambda K_1 + (1 - \lambda) K_3$$

Since we are considering options that differ only with respect to the strike price, we can write $C(K)$ and $P(K)$ to denote the option premium for a particular strike K.

The call premium decreases as the strike price increases   Suppose that $C(K_1) < C(K_2)$; i.e., a lower strike call had a lower premium. To effect arbitrage, we would buy the low-strike call and sell the high-strike call (this is a bull spread). Table 9.10 shows the result. We will consider each entry in the "Total" row separately.

TABLE 9.10		Proof that the call premium is a decreasing function of the strike price.		
			Expiration or Exercise	
Transaction	**Time 0**	$S_T < K_1$	$K_1 \leq S_T \leq K_2$	$S_T > K_2$
Buy K_1-Strike Call	$-C(K_1)$	0	$S_T - K_1$	$S_T - K_1$
Sell K_2-Strike Call	$C(K_2)$	0	0	$K_2 - S_T$
Total	$C(K_2) - C(K_1)$	0	$S_T - K_1$	$K_2 - K_1$

Time 0. We earn net premium from selling the more expensive option. The cash flow is positive.

Expiration or Exercise, $S_T < K_1$. Neither option is exercised, so the cash flow is zero.

Expiration or Exercise, $K_1 \leq S_T \leq K_2$. We exercise the option we bought, earning $S_T - K_1$.

Expiration or Exercise, $S_T > K_2$. We exercise the option we bought, earning $S_T - K_1$, and the option we sold is exercised, costing us $K_2 - S_T$. The net is $K_2 - K_1$, which is positive.

What about the fact that the options are American? We then have to account for the possibility that the written option is exercised. If that happens, we can simply exercise the purchased option, earning the payoffs in the table. If it is not optimal to exercise the purchased option, we can sell it, earning even higher payoffs.

The call premium changes by less than the change in the strike price   Suppose that $C(K_1) - C(K_2) \geq K_2 - K_1$. We can make money initially by selling the K_1-strike call, buying the K_2-strike call, and lending $K_2 - K_1$. Table 9.11 summarizes the results.

Time 0. We earn net premium since the initial assumption is that $C(K_1) - C(K_2) \geq K_2 - K_1$.

Expiration or Exercise, $S_T < K_1$. Neither option is exercised, so we keep the future value of the difference between the strikes.

Expiration or Exercise, $K_1 \leq S_T \leq K_2$. The written option is exercised, so we have to sell the stock for K_1. However, the net loss is less than the difference between the strike prices.

		Expiration or Exercise		
Transaction	**Time 0**	$S_T < K_1$	$K_1 \leq S_T \leq K_2$	$S_T > K_2$
Sell K_1-Strike Call	$C(K_1)$	0	$K_1 - S_T$	$K_1 - S_T$
Buy K_2-Strike Call	$-C(K_2)$	0	0	$S_T - K_2$
Lend $K_2 - K_1$	$-(K_2 - K_1)$	$e^{rT}(K_2 - K_1)$	$e^{rT}(K_2 - K_1)$	$e^{rT}(K_2 - K_1)$
Total	$C(K_1) - C(K_2) -$ $(K_2 - K_1)$	$e^{rT}(K_2 - K_1)$	$e^{rT}(K_2 - K_1) -$ $(S_T - K_1)$	$e^{rT}(K_2 - K_1) -$ $(K_2 - K_1)$

TABLE 9.11   Proof that the call premium changes by less than the change in the strike price of the option.

Expiration or Exercise, $S_T > K_2$. We keep the interest on the difference between the strike prices.

What adjustments do we have to make if the options are American? If the written K_1 option is exercised, we can duplicate the payoffs in the table by throwing our option away (if $K_1 \leq S_T \leq K_2$) or exercising it (if $S_T \geq K_2$). Since it never makes sense to discard an unexpired option, and since exercise may not be optimal, we can do at least as well as the payoff in the table if the options are American.

You may have noticed that if the options are European, we can put a tighter restriction on the difference in call premiums, namely $C(K_1) - C(K_2) < PV(K_2 - K_1)$. We would show this by lending $PV(K_2 - K_1)$ instead of $K_2 - K_1$. This strategy does not work if the options are American, since we don't know how long it will be before the options are exercised, and, hence, we don't know what time to use in computing the present value.

The call premium is a convex function of the strike price This proposition says that as the option moves more into the money, its premium increases at a faster rate. To prove it, suppose that $C(K_2) \geq \lambda C(K_1) + (1 - \lambda)C(K_3)$. We can make money initially by selling the K_2-strike call, buying λ K_1-strike calls, and buying $1 - \lambda$ K_3-strike calls. Table 9.12 summarizes the results.

Time 0. We earn net premium since the initial assumption is that $C(K_2) \geq \lambda C(K_1) + (1 - \lambda)C(K_3)$.

Expiration or Exercise, $S_T < K_1$. No options are exercised.

Expiration or Exercise, $K_1 \leq S_T \leq K_2$. The purchased K_1 calls are exercised.

TABLE 9.12 Proof that the call price is a convex function of the strike price.

Transaction	Time 0	Expiration or Exercise			
		$S_T < K_1$	$K_1 \leq S_T \leq K_2$	$K_2 < S_T \leq K_3$	$S_T > K_3$
Buy λ K_1-Strike Calls	$-\lambda C(K_1)$	0	$\lambda(S_T - K_1)$	$\lambda(S_T - K_1)$	$\lambda(S_T - K_1)$
Sell 1 K_2-Strike Call	$C(K_2)$	0	0	$K_2 - S_T$	$K_2 - S_T$
Buy $1 - \lambda$ K_3-Strike Calls	$-(1 - \lambda)C(K_3)$	0	0	0	$(1 - \lambda)$ $(S_T - K_3)$
Total	$C(K_2) -$ $\lambda C(K_1) -$ $(1 - \lambda)C(K_3)$	0	$\lambda(S_T - K_1)$	$(1 - \lambda)$ $(K_3 - S_T)$	0

Expiration or Exercise, $K_2 < S_T \leq K_3$. We exercise our $\lambda \, K_1$ calls, and the written K_2 call is exercised against us. Recall that $K_2 = \lambda K_1 + (1 - \lambda)K_3$; substituting this expression for K_2 explains how we obtain the total in this column.

Expiration or Exercise, $S_T > K_3$. All options are exercised and the payoffs cancel.

Puts   Here are the counterpart propositions for puts, stated more formally.

1. The put premium is increasing in the strike price: $P(K_1) \leq P(K_2)$.

2. The put premium changes by less than the change in the strike price: $P(K_2) - P(K_1) < K_2 - K_1$.

3. The put premium is a convex function of the strike price: $P(K_2) < \lambda P(K_1) + (1 - \lambda)P(K_3)$.

The proofs are identical to the propositions for calls.

Chapter 10

Binomial Option Pricing: I

U p to now we have discussed how the price of one option is related to the price of another, but we have not pinned down the price of an option relative to the underlying asset. In this chapter we discuss binomial option pricing, which will enable us to say what the price of an option should be, given the characteristics of the stock or other underlying asset.

The binomial option pricing model assumes that the price of the underlying asset in each period can move only up or down by a specified amount—that is, the asset price follows a binomial distribution. Surprisingly, this approach to pricing options, which appears at first glance to be overly simplistic, conveys much of the depth and intuition in more complex and seemingly more realistic models that we will encounter in later chapters. It is hard to overstate the value of thoroughly understanding this approach to pricing options.

Because of its usefulness, we devote this and the next chapter to binomial option pricing. In this chapter, we will see how the binomial model works and use it to price both European and American call and put options on stocks, currencies, and futures contracts. As part of the pricing analysis, we will also see how market-makers can create options synthetically using the underlying asset and risk-free bonds. In the next chapter, we will explore the assumptions underlying the model.

10.1 A ONE-PERIOD BINOMIAL TREE

Option pricing can be mathematically complex, but it is possible to understand many important results and properties of option prices using the binomial pricing model. This approach to pricing was first used by Sharpe (1978) as an intuitive way to explain option pricing. Binomial pricing was developed more formally by Cox et al. (1979) and Rendlemann and Bartter (1979), who showed how to implement the model, demonstrated the link between the binomial model and the Black-Scholes model, and showed that the method provides a tractable way to price options for which early exercise may be optimal. The binomial model is often referred to as the "Cox-Ross-Rubinstein pricing model."

Binomial pricing achieves its simplicity by making a very strong assumption about the stock price: At any point in time, the stock price can change to one of only two values: An up value or a down value. In-between, greater, or lesser values are not permitted. The restriction to two possible prices is why the method is called "binomial." The appeal of binomial pricing is that it displays the logic of option pricing in a simple setting, using only algebra to price options.

We begin with a simple example. Consider a European call option on the stock of XYZ, with a $40 strike and 1 year to expiration. XYZ does not pay dividends and its current price is $41. The continuously compounded risk-free interest rate is 8%. We wish to determine the option price.

Since the stock's return over the next year is uncertain, the option could expire either in-the-money or out-of-the-money, depending upon whether the stock price is more or less than $40. Intuitively, the valuation for the option should take account of both possibilities and assign values in each case. If the option expires out-of-the money, its value is zero. If the option expires in-the-money, its value will depend upon how far in-the-money it is. To price the option, then, we need to characterize the uncertainty about the stock price at expiration.

Figure 10.1 represents the evolution of the stock price: Today the price is $41, and in 1 year the price can be either $59.954 or $32.903. This depiction of possible stock prices is called a **binomial tree.** For the moment we take the tree as given and price the option. Later we will learn how to construct such a tree.

Computing the Option Price

Now we compute the price of our 40-strike 1-year call. Consider two portfolios:

Portfolio A Buy one call option. The cost of this is the call premium, which is unknown.

Portfolio B Buy 0.7376 shares of XYZ and borrow $22.405 at the risk-free rate.[1] This position costs

$$0.7376 \times \$41 - \$22.405 = \$7.839$$

Now we compare the payoffs to the two portfolios 1 year from now. Since the stock can take on only two values, we can easily compute the value of each position at each possible stock price.

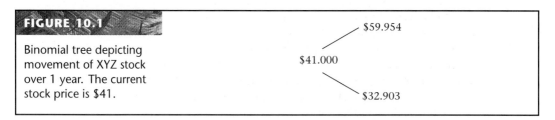

FIGURE 10.1

Binomial tree depicting movement of XYZ stock over 1 year. The current stock price is $41.

$41.000 → $59.954

$41.000 → $32.903

---

[1] If you are worried that you cannot buy fractional shares of stock, you are of course correct. Feel free to multiply all the numbers in the example by 100,000 for greater realism.

For Portfolio A, the value is

	Stock Price in 1 Year (S_1)	
	$32.903	$59.954
Payoff	0	$19.954

In computing the payoff for Portfolio B, we assume that we sell the shares at the market price and that we repay the borrowed amount, plus interest ($22.405 × $e^{.08}$ = $24.271). Thus we have

	Stock Price in 1 Year (S_1)	
	$32.903	$59.954
0.7376 Purchased Shares	$24.271	$44.225
Repay Loan of $22.405	−$24.271	−$24.271
Total Payoff	0	$19.954

Note that Portfolio A and Portfolio B have the same payoff: Zero if the stock price goes down, in which case the option is out-of-the-money, and $19.954 if the stock price goes up. Therefore, Portfolio A and Portfolio B should have the same cost. Since Portfolio B costs $7.839, *the price of one option must be $7.839.*

Moreover, Portfolio B demonstrates that there is a way to create the payoff to a call by buying shares and borrowing. In effect, Portfolio B is a *synthetic* call.

Finally, the example demonstrates that a call option is replicated by holding 0.7376 shares, which implies that one option has the risk of 0.7376 shares. The value 0.7376 is the *delta* (Δ) of the option: The number of shares that replicates the option payoff. Delta is a key concept and we will say much more about it later.

The Binomial Solution

The preceding example appears arbitrary. In particular, how did we know that buying 0.7376 shares of stock and borrowing $22.405 would replicate a call option?

We have two instruments to use in replicating a call option: Shares of stock and a position in bonds (i.e., borrowing or lending). To find the replicating portfolio, we need to find a combination of stock and bonds such that the portfolio mimics the option.

To be specific, we wish to find a portfolio consisting of Δ shares of stock and a dollar amount B in lending, such that the portfolio imitates the option whether the stock rises or falls. We will suppose that the stock has a continuous dividend yield of δ, which we reinvest in the stock. Thus, as in Section 5.2, if you buy one share at time t, at time $t + h$ you will have $e^{\delta h}$ shares. The up and down movements of the stock price reflect the *ex-dividend* price.

We can write the stock price as uS_0 when the stock goes up, and as dS_0 when the price goes down. We can represent the stock price tree as follows:

In this tree u is interpreted as one plus the rate of capital gain on the stock if it goes up, and d is one plus the rate of capital loss if it goes down. (If there are dividends, the total return is the capital gain or loss plus the dividend.)

The tree for the stock implies a corresponding tree for the value of the option:

If the length of a period is h, the interest factor per period is e^{rh}. The problem is to solve for Δ and B such that our portfolio of Δ shares and B in lending duplicates the option payoff. Let C_u and C_d represent the value of the option when the stock goes up or down, respectively. The value of the replicating portfolio at time h, with stock price S_h, is

$$\Delta S_h + e^{rh} B$$

At the prices $S_h = dS$ and $S_h = uS$, a successful replicating portfolio will satisfy

$$(\Delta \times dS \times e^{\delta h}) + (B \times e^{rh}) = C_d$$
$$(\Delta \times uS \times e^{\delta h}) + (B \times e^{rh}) = C_u$$

This is two equations in the two unknowns Δ and B. Solving for Δ and B gives

$$\Delta = e^{-\delta h} \frac{C_u - C_d}{S(u - d)} \tag{10.1}$$

$$B = e^{-rh} \frac{uC_d - dC_u}{u - d} \tag{10.2}$$

Note that when there are dividends, we adjust the number of shares in the replicating portfolio, Δ, to offset the dividend income.

Given the expressions for Δ and B, we can derive a simple formula for the value of the option. The cost of creating the option is the cash flow required to buy the shares and bonds. Thus, the cost of the option is $\Delta S + B$. Using equations (10.1) and (10.2), we have

$$\Delta S + B = e^{-rh} \left(C_u \frac{e^{(r-\delta)h} - d}{u - d} + C_d \frac{u - e^{(r-\delta)h}}{u - d} \right) \tag{10.3}$$

The assumed stock price movements, u and d, should not give rise to arbitrage opportunities. In particular, we require that

$$u > e^{(r-\delta)h} > d \qquad (10.4)$$

To see why this condition must hold, suppose $\delta = 0$. If the condition were violated, we would short the stock to hold bonds (if $e^{rh} \geq u$), or we would borrow to buy the stock (if $d \geq e^{rh}$). Either way, we would earn an arbitrage profit, so the assumed process could not be consistent with any possible equilibrium. Problem 10.21 asks you to verify that the condition must also hold when $\delta > 0$.

Note that because Δ is the number of shares in the replicating portfolio, it can also be interpreted as the sensitivity of the option to a change in the stock price. If the stock price changes by $1, then the option price, $\Delta S + B$, changes by Δ. This interpretation will be quite important later.

Example 10.1 Here is the solution to the numerical example above. Recall the stock price tree depicted in Figure 10.1. There we have $u = \$59.954/\$41 = 1.4623$, $d = \$32.903/\$41 = 0.8025$, and $\delta = 0$. In addition, the call option had 1 year to expiration, hence, $h = 1$, and a strike price of $40. Thus $C_u = \$59.954 - \$40 = \$19.954$, and $C_d = 0$. Using equations (10.1) and (10.2), we have

$$\Delta = \frac{\$19.954 - 0}{\$41 \times (1.4623 - 0.8025)} = 0.7376$$

$$B = e^{-0.08} \frac{1.4623 \times \$0 - 0.8025 \times \$19.954}{1.4623 - 0.8025} = -\$22.405$$

Hence, the option price is given by

$$\Delta S + B = 0.7376 \times \$41 - \$22.405 = \$7.839$$

Note that *if we are only interested in the option price, it is not necessary to solve for Δ and B;* that is just an intermediate step. If we only want to know the option price, we can use equation (10.3) directly:

$$\Delta S + B = e^{-0.08}\left(\$19.954 \times \frac{e^{0.08} - 0.8025}{1.4623 - 0.8025} + \$0 \times \frac{1.4623 - e^{0.08}}{1.4623 - 0.8025}\right)$$

$$= \$7.839$$

Throughout this chapter we will continue to report Δ and B, since we are interested not only in the price, but also in the replicating portfolio. Figure 10.2 summarizes the solution for Example 10.1.

Arbitraging a Mispriced Option

What if the observed option price differs from the theoretical price? Because we have a way to replicate the option using the stock, it is possible to take advantage of the mispricing and fulfill the dream of every trader, namely to buy low and sell high.

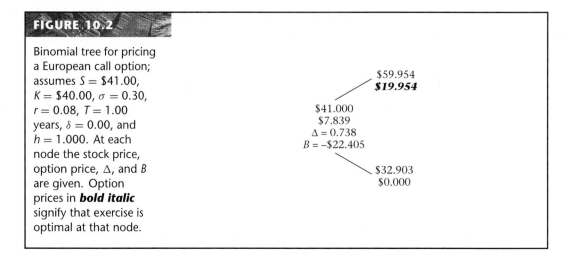

FIGURE 10.2

Binomial tree for pricing a European call option; assumes $S = \$41.00$, $K = \$40.00$, $\sigma = 0.30$, $r = 0.08$, $T = 1.00$ years, $\delta = 0.00$, and $h = 1.000$. At each node the stock price, option price, Δ, and B are given. Option prices in **bold italic** signify that exercise is optimal at that node.

$59.954
$**19.954**

$41.000
$7.839
$\Delta = 0.738$
$B = -\$22.405$

$32.903
$0.000

The following examples illustrate that if the option price is anything other than the theoretical price, arbitrage is possible.

The option is overpriced   Suppose that the market price for the option is $8.50, instead of the theoretical price of $7.839. We can sell the option, but this leaves us with the risk that the stock price at expiration will be $59.954 and we will be required to deliver the stock.

We can address this risk by buying a synthetic option at the same time we sell the actual option. We have already seen how to create the synthetic option by buying 0.7376 shares and borrowing $22.405. If we simultaneously sell the actual option and buy the synthetic, the initial cash flow is

$$\underbrace{\$8.50}_{\text{Option Premium}} - \underbrace{0.7376 \times \$41}_{\text{Cost of Shares}} + \underbrace{\$22.405}_{\text{Borrowing}} = \$0.661$$

We earn $0.661, the amount by which the option is mispriced.

Now we verify that there is no risk at expiration. We have

	Stock Price in 1 Year (S_1)	
	$32.903	**$59.954**
Written Call	0	−$19.954
0.7376 Purchased Shares	$24.271	$44.225
Repay Loan of $22.405	−$24.271	−$24.271
Total Payoff	0	0

By hedging the written option, we eliminate risk.

The option is underpriced   Now suppose that the market price of the option is $7.75. We wish to buy the underpriced option. Of course if the stock price falls at expiration, we lose our investment. Thus, to hedge we will sell a synthetic option. We accomplish this by reversing the position for a synthetic call: We short 0.7376 shares and invest $22.405 of the proceeds in Treasury bills. The cost of this is

$$\underbrace{-\$7.75}_{\text{Option Premium}} + \underbrace{0.7376 \times \$41}_{\text{Short-Sale Proceeds}} - \underbrace{\$22.405}_{\text{Invest in T-Bills}} = \$0.089$$

At expiration we have

	Stock Price in 1 Year (S_1)	
	$32.903	**$59.954**
Purchased Call	$0	$19.954
0.7376 Short-Sold Shares	−$24.271	−$44.225
Sell T-Bill	$24.271	$24.271
Total Payoff	$0	$0

We have earned the amount by which the option was mispriced and hedged the risk associated with buying the option.

A Graphical Interpretation of the Binomial Formula

The binomial solution for Δ and B, equations (10.1) and (10.2), is obtained by solving two equations in two unknowns. Letting C_h and S_h be the option and stock value after one binomial period, and supposing $\delta = 0$, the portfolio describes a line with the formula

$$C_h = \Delta S_h + e^{rh} B$$

This is graphed as line ABD in Figure 10.3, which shows the option payoff as a function of the stock price.

We choose Δ and B to yield a portfolio which pays C_d when $S_h = dS$ and C_u when $S_h = uS$. Hence, by construction this line runs through points B and D. We can control the slope of a payoff diagram by varying the number of shares, Δ, and its height by varying the number of bonds, B. It is apparent that a line that runs through both B and D must have slope $\Delta = C_u - C_d/S_u - S_d$. Also, the point A is the value of the portfolio when $S_h = 0$, which is the time-h value of the bond position, $e^{rh}B$. Hence, $e^{rh}B$ is the y-axis intercept of the line.

You can see by looking at Figure 10.3 that *any* line replicating a call will have positive slope ($\Delta > 0$) and negative intercept ($B < 0$). As an exercise, you can verify graphically that a portfolio replicating a put would have negative slope ($\Delta < 0$) and positive intercept ($B > 0$).

Risk-Neutral Pricing

So far we have not specified the probabilities of the stock going up or down. In fact probabilities were not used anywhere in the option price calculations. Since the strategy of holding Δ shares and B bonds replicates the option whichever way the stock moves, the probability of an up or down movement in the stock is irrelevant for pricing the option.

FIGURE 10.3

The payoff to an expiring call option is the dark heavy line. The payoff to the option at the points dS and uS are C_d and C_u (at point D). The portfolio consisting of Δ shares and B bonds has intercept $e^{rh}B$ and slope Δ, and by construction goes through both points B and D. The slope of the line is calculated as $\frac{\text{Rise}}{\text{Run}}$ between points B and D, which gives the formula for Δ.

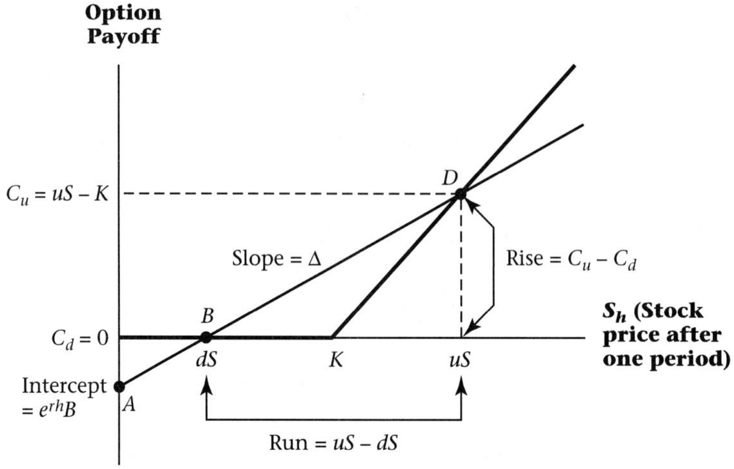

Although probabilities are not needed for pricing the option, there is a probabilistic interpretation of equation (10.3). Notice that in equation (10.3) the terms $(e^{(r-\delta)h} - d)/(u - d)$ and $(u - e^{(r-\delta)h})/(u - d)$ sum to 1 and are both positive (this follows from inequality (10.4)). Thus, we can interpret these terms as probabilities. Let

$$p^* = \frac{e^{(r-\delta)h} - d}{u - d} \tag{10.5}$$

Equation (10.3) can then be written as

$$C = e^{-rh}[p^*C_u + (1 - p^*)C_d] \tag{10.6}$$

This expression has the appearance of a discounted expected value. It is peculiar, though, because we are discounting at the risk-free rate, even though the risk of the option is at least as great as the risk of the stock (a call option is a leveraged position in the stock since $B < 0$). In addition, there is no reason to think that p^* is the true probability that the stock will go up; in fact it is not.

We can also use p^* to compute the expected *undiscounted* stock price. Doing this, we obtain

$$p^*uS + (1 - p^*)dS = e^{(r-\delta)h}S \tag{10.7}$$

Thus, when we use p^* to compute the expected stock price, the result is the forward price, $e^{(r-\delta)h}S$.

We will call p^* the **risk-neutral probability** of an increase in the stock price. Equation (10.6) will prove very important and we will discuss risk-neutral pricing more in Chapter 11.

Where Does the Tree Come From?

We now explain the construction of the binomial tree. Recall that the goal of the tree is to characterize future uncertainty about the stock price in an economically reasonable way.

As a starting point in thinking about the construction of a tree, we can ask: What if there were no uncertainty about the future stock price? In the absence of uncertainty, a stock must appreciate at the risk-free rate less the dividend yield. Thus, from time t to time $t + h$, we have

$$S_{t+h} = S_t e^{(r-\delta)h} = F_{t,t+h}$$

The price next period equals the forward price.

Now we generalize this to permit uncertainty. A natural way to proceed is by adding uncertainty to the forward price. If σ is the annualized standard deviation of the continuously compounded return, the standard deviation over a period of length h is $\sigma \sqrt{h}$. (Section 11.3 explains why this is so.) We then model the stock price evolution as

$$\begin{aligned} u S_t &= F_{t,t+h} e^{+\sigma \sqrt{h}} \\ d S_t &= F_{t,t+h} e^{-\sigma \sqrt{h}} \end{aligned} \qquad (10.8)$$

Or we can rewrite this as

$$\begin{aligned} u &= e^{(r-\delta)h + \sigma \sqrt{h}} \\ d &= e^{(r-\delta)h - \sigma \sqrt{h}} \end{aligned} \qquad (10.9)$$

Note that if we set volatility equal to zero (i.e., $\sigma = 0$), we will have $u S_t = d S_t = F_{t,t+h}$. Thus, the price can still rise over time in accord with the forward curve. Zero volatility does not mean that prices are *fixed;* it means that prices are *known in advance.*

Example 10.2 Figure 10.1 represented the tree for a stock with $h = 1$, $r = 0.08$, $\delta = 0$, and $\sigma = 0.3$, which was used in Section 10.1. Using equation (10.9), we get

$$uS = \$41 e^{(0.08-0) \times 1 + 0.3 \times \sqrt{1}} = \$59.954$$

$$dS = \$41 e^{(0.08-0) \times 1 - 0.3 \times \sqrt{1}} = \$32.903 \qquad ❦$$

We will refer to a tree constructed using equation (10.9) as a "forward tree." In Section 11.3 we will discuss alternative ways to construct a tree, including the Cox-Ross-Rubinstein tree.

Summary

We have covered a great deal of ground in this section, so we pause for a moment to review the main points:

- In order to price an option, we need to know the stock price, the strike price, the standard deviation of returns on the stock (in order to compute u and d), the dividend yield, and the risk-free rate.

- Using the risk-free rate, dividend yield, and σ, we can approximate the future distribution of the stock by creating a binomial tree using equation (10.9).

- Once we have the binomial tree, it is possible to price the option using equation (10.3). The solution also provides the recipe for synthetically creating the option: Buy Δ shares of stock (equation (10.1)) and borrow B (equation (10.2)).

- The formula for the option price, equation (10.3), can be written so that it has the appearance of a discounted expected value.

There are still many issues we have to deal with. The simple binomial tree does not look realistic; it seems too simple to provide an accurate option price. Other questions include how to handle more than one binomial period, how to price put options, how to price American options, etc. With the basic binomial formula in hand we can now turn to those questions.

10.2 TWO OR MORE BINOMIAL PERIODS

We now see how to extend the binomial tree to more than one period.

A Two-Period European Call

We begin first by adding a single period to the tree in Figure 10.1; the result is displayed in Figure 10.4. We can use that tree to price a 2-year option with a $40 strike when the current stock price is $41, assuming all inputs are the same as before.

Since we are increasing the time to maturity for a call option on a nondividend-paying stock, then based on the discussion in Section 9.3 we expect the option premium to increase. In this example the two-period tree will give us a price of $10.737, compared to $7.839 in Figure 10.2.

Constructing the tree   To see how to construct the tree, suppose that we move up in year 1, to $S_u = \$59.954$. If we reach this price, then we can move further up or down according to equation (10.8). We get

$$S_{uu} = \$59.954e^{0.08+0.3} = \$87.669$$

and

$$S_{ud} = \$59.954e^{0.08-0.3} = \$48.114$$

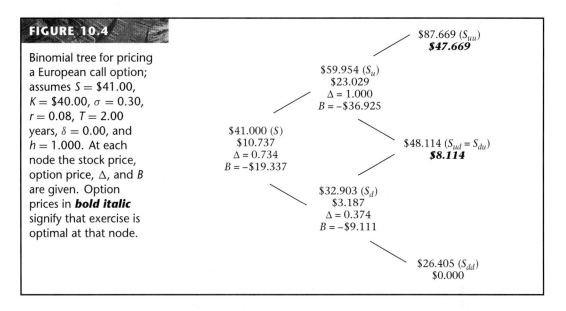

FIGURE 10.4

Binomial tree for pricing a European call option; assumes $S = \$41.00$, $K = \$40.00$, $\sigma = 0.30$, $r = 0.08$, $T = 2.00$ years, $\delta = 0.00$, and $h = 1.000$. At each node the stock price, option price, Δ, and B are given. Option prices in **bold italic** signify that exercise is optimal at that node.

The subscript *uu* means that the stock has gone up twice in a row and the subscript *ud* means that the stock has gone up once and then down.

Similarly if the price in one year is $S_d = \$32.903$, we have

$$S_{du} = \$32.903 e^{0.08+0.3} = \$48.114$$

and

$$S_{dd} = \$32.903 e^{0.08-0.3} = \$26.405$$

Note that an up move followed by a down move (S_{ud}) generates the same stock price as a down move followed by an up move (S_{du}). This is called a **recombining tree.** If an up move followed by a down move led to a different price than a down move followed by an up move, we would have a **nonrecombining tree.**[2] A recombining tree has fewer nodes, which means less computation is required to compute an option price. We will see examples of nonrecombining trees in Sections 11.5 and 23.3.

We also could have used equation (10.9) directly to compute the year-2 stock prices. Recall that $u = e^{0.08+0.3} = 1.462$ and $d = e^{0.08-0.3} = 0.803$. We have

$$S_{uu} = u^2 \times \$41 = e^{2 \times (0.08+0.3)} \times \$41 = \$87.669$$

$$S_{ud} = S_{du} = u \times d \times \$41 = e^{(0.08+0.3)} \times e^{(0.08-0.3)} \times \$41 = \$48.114$$

$$S_{dd} = d^2 \times \$41 = e^{2 \times (0.08-0.3)} \times \$41 = \$26.405$$

---

[2] In cases where the tree recombines, the representation of stock price movements is also (and, some argue, more properly) called a *lattice*. The term *tree* would then be reserved for nonrecombining stock movements.

Pricing the call option   How do we price the option when we have two binomial periods? The key insight is that we work *backward* through the binomial tree. In order to use equation (10.3), we need to know the option prices resulting from up and down moves in the subsequent period. At the outset, the only period where we know the option price is at expiration.

Knowing the price at expiration, we can determine the price in period 1. Having determined that price, we can work back to period 0.

Figure 10.4 exhibits the option price at each node as well as the details of the replicating portfolio at each node. Remember, however, when we use equation (10.3), it is not necessary to compute Δ and B in order to derive the option price.[3] Here are details of the solution:

Year 2, Stock Price = $87.669   Since we are at expiration, the option value is $max(0, S - K) = \$47.669$.

Year 2, Stock Price = $48.114   Again we are at expiration, so the option value is $8.114.

Year 2, Stock Price = $26.405   Since the option is out of the money, the value is 0.

Year 1, Stock Price = $59.954   At this node we use equation (10.3) to compute the option value. (Note that once we are at this node, the "up" stock price, uS, is $87.669, and the "down" stock price, dS, is $48.114.)

$$e^{-0.08} \left(\$47.669 \times \frac{e^{0.08} - 0.803}{1.462 - 0.803} + \$8.114 \times \frac{1.462 - e^{0.08}}{1.462 - 0.803} \right) = \$23.029$$

Year 1, Stock Price = $32.903   Again we use equation (10.3) to compute the option value:

$$e^{-0.08} \left(\$8.114 \times \frac{e^{0.08} - 0.803}{1.462 - 0.803} + \$0 \times \frac{1.462 - e^{0.08}}{1.462 - 0.803} \right) = \$3.187$$

Year 0, Stock Price = $41   Again using equation (10.3):

$$e^{-0.08} \left(\$23.029 \times \frac{e^{0.08} - 0.803}{1.462 - 0.803} + \$3.187 \times \frac{1.462 - e^{0.08}}{1.462 - 0.803} \right) = \$10.737$$

Notice that:

- The option price is greater for the 2-year than for the 1-year option, as we would expect.

- We priced the option by working backward through the tree, starting at the end and working back to the first period.

....

[3]As an exercise you can verify the Δ and B at each node.

- The option's Δ and B are different at different nodes. In particular, at a given point in time, Δ increases to 1 as we go further into the money.

- We priced a European option, so early exercise was not permitted. However, permitting early exercise would have made no difference. At every node prior to expiration, the option price is greater than $S - K$; hence we would not have exercised even if the option had been American.

- Once we understand the two-period option it is straightforward to value an option using more than two binomial periods. The important principle is to work backward through the tree.

Many Binomial Periods

The generalization to many binomial periods is straightforward. We can represent only a small number of binomial periods here, but a spreadsheet or computer program can handle a very large number of binomial nodes.

An obvious objection to the binomial calculations thus far is that the stock can only have two or three different values at expiration. It seems unlikely that the option price calculation will be accurate. The solution to this problem is to divide the time to expiration into more periods, generating a more realistic tree.

To illustrate how to do this, at the same time illustrating a tree with more than two periods, we will re-examine the 1-year European call option in Figure 10.2, which has a $40 strike and initial stock price of $41. Let there be three binomial periods. Since it is a 1-year call, this means that the length of a period is $h = \frac{1}{3}$. We will assume that other inputs stay the same, so $r = 0.08$ and $\sigma = 0.3$.

Figure 10.5 depicts the stock price and option price tree for this option. The option price is $7.074, as opposed to $7.839 in Figure 10.1. The difference occurs because the numerical approximation is different; it is quite common to see large changes in a binomial price when the number of periods, n, is changed, particularly when n is small.

Since the length of the binomial period is shorter, u and d are smaller than before (1.2212 and 0.8637 as opposed to 1.462 and 0.803 with $h = 1$). Just to be clear about the procedure, here is how the second-period nodes are computed:

$$S_u = \$41e^{0.08 \times 1/3 + 0.3\sqrt{1/3}} = \$50.071$$
$$S_d = \$41e^{0.08 \times 1/3 - 0.3\sqrt{1/3}} = \$35.411$$

The remaining nodes are computed similarly.

The option price is computed by working backward. The risk-neutral probability of the stock price going up in a period is

$$\frac{e^{0.08 \times 1/3} - 0.8637}{1.2212 - 0.8637} = 0.4568$$

The option price at the node where $S = \$43.246$, for example, is then given by

$$e^{-0.08 \times 1/3} \left([\$12.814 \times 0.4568] + [\$0 \times (1 - 0.4568)] \right) = \$5.700$$

Option prices at the remaining nodes are priced similarly.

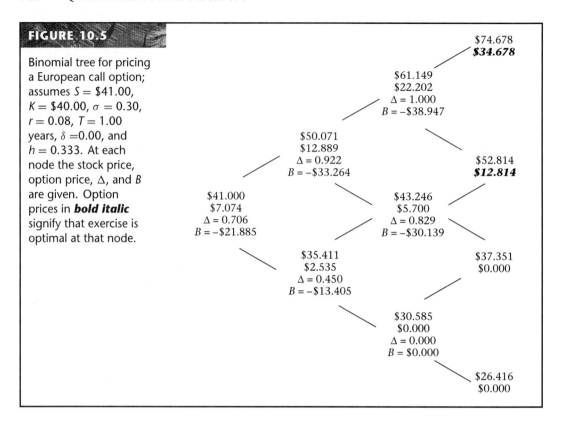

FIGURE 10.5

Binomial tree for pricing a European call option; assumes $S = \$41.00$, $K = \$40.00$, $\sigma = 0.30$, $r = 0.08$, $T = 1.00$ years, $\delta = 0.00$, and $h = 0.333$. At each node the stock price, option price, Δ, and B are given. Option prices in **bold italic** signify that exercise is optimal at that node.

$41.000
$7.074
$\Delta = 0.706$
$B = -\$21.885$

$50.071
$12.889
$\Delta = 0.922$
$B = -\$33.264$

$35.411
$2.535
$\Delta = 0.450$
$B = -\$13.405$

$61.149
$22.202
$\Delta = 1.000$
$B = -\$38.947$

$43.246
$5.700
$\Delta = 0.829$
$B = -\$30.139$

$30.585
$0.000
$\Delta = 0.000$
$B = \$0.000$

$74.678
$34.678

$52.814
$12.814

$37.351
$0.000

$26.416
$0.000

10.3 Put Options

Thus far we have priced only call options. The binomial method easily accommodates put options also, as well as other derivatives. We compute put option prices using the same stock price tree and in almost the same way as call option prices; the only difference with a European put option occurs at expiration: Instead of computing the price as $max(0, S - K)$, we use $max(0, K - S)$.

Figure 10.6 shows the binomial tree for a European put option with 1 year to expiration and a strike of $40 when the stock price is $41. This is the same stock price tree as in Figure 10.5.

To illustrate the calculations, consider the option price at the node where the stock price is $35.411. The option price at that node is computed as

$$e^{-0.08 \times 1/3} \left(\$1.401 \times \frac{e^{0.08 \times 1/3} - 0.8637}{1.2212 - 0.8637} + \$8.363 \times \frac{1.2212 - e^{0.08 \times 1/3}}{1.2212 - 0.8637} \right) = \$5.046$$

Figure 10.6 does raise one issue that we have not previously had to consider. Notice that at the node where the stock price is $30.585, the option price is $8.363. If this option were American, it would make sense to exercise at that node. The option

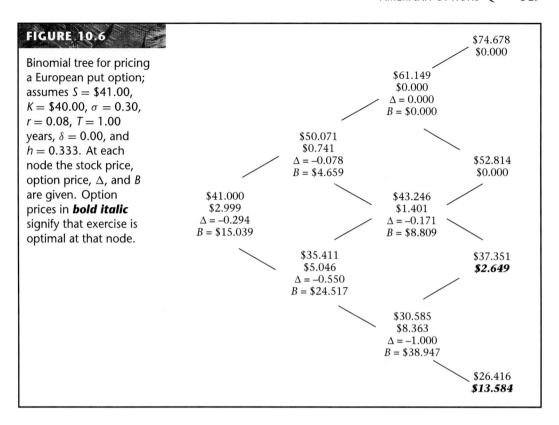

FIGURE 10.6

Binomial tree for pricing a European put option; assumes $S = \$41.00$, $K = \$40.00$, $\sigma = 0.30$, $r = 0.08$, $T = 1.00$ years, $\delta = 0.00$, and $h = 0.333$. At each node the stock price, option price, Δ, and B are given. Option prices in **bold italic** signify that exercise is optimal at that node.

$41.000
$2.999
$\Delta = -0.294$
$B = \$15.039$

$50.071
$0.741
$\Delta = -0.078$
$B = \$4.659$

$35.411
$5.046
$\Delta = -0.550$
$B = \$24.517$

$61.149
$0.000
$\Delta = 0.000$
$B = \$0.000$

$43.246
$1.401
$\Delta = -0.171$
$B = \$8.809$

$30.585
$8.363
$\Delta = -1.000$
$B = \$38.947$

$74.678
$0.000

$52.814
$0.000

$37.351
$2.649

$26.416
$13.584

is worth $8.363 when held until expiration, but it would be worth $40 − \$30.585 = \$9.415$ if exercised at that node. Thus, in this case the American option should be more valuable than the otherwise equivalent European option. We will now see how to use the binomial approach to value American options.

10.4 AMERICAN OPTIONS

Since it is easy to check at each node whether early exercise is optimal, the binomial method is well-suited to valuing American options. The value of the option if it is left "alive" (i.e., unexercised) is given by the value of holding it for another period, equation (10.3). The value of the option if it is exercised is given by $max(0, S − K)$ if it is a call and $max(0, K − S)$ if it is a put.

Thus, for an American put, the value of the option at a node is given by

$$P(S, K, t) = max\left(K - S, e^{-rh}\left[P(uS, K, t + h)p^* + P(dS, K, t + h)(1 - p^*)\right]\right) \quad (10.10)$$

where, as in equation (10.5),

$$p^* = \frac{e^{(r-\delta)h} - d}{u - d}$$

Figure 10.7 presents the binomial tree for the American version of the put option valued in Figure 10.6. The only difference in the trees occurs at the node where the stock price is $30.585. The American option at that point is worth $9.415, its early-exercise value. We have just seen in the previous section that the value of the option if unexercised is $8.363.

The greater value of the option at that node ripples back through the tree. When the option price is computed at the node where the stock price is $35.411, the value is greater in Figure 10.7 than in Figure 10.6; the reason is that the price is greater at the subsequent node S_{dd} due to early exercise.

The initial option price is $3.293, greater than the value of $2.999 for the European option. This increase in value is due entirely to early exercise at the S_{dd} node.

In general the valuation of American options proceeds as in this example. At each node we check for early exercise. If the value of the option is greater when exercised, we

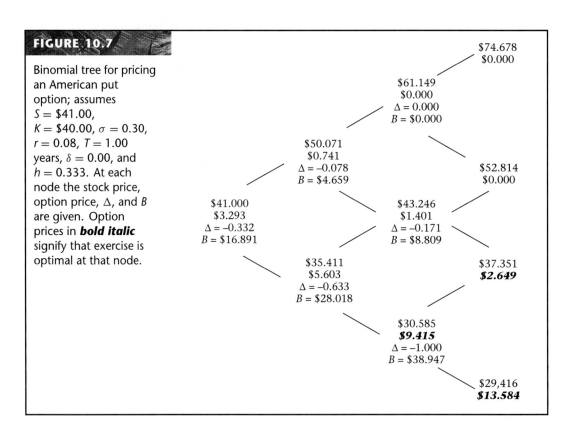

FIGURE 10.7

Binomial tree for pricing an American put option; assumes $S = \$41.00$, $K = \$40.00$, $\sigma = 0.30$, $r = 0.08$, $T = 1.00$ years, $\delta = 0.00$, and $h = 0.333$. At each node the stock price, option price, Δ, and B are given. Option prices in **bold italic** signify that exercise is optimal at that node.

$41.000
$3.293
$\Delta = -0.332$
$B = \$16.891$

$50.071
$0.741
$\Delta = -0.078$
$B = \$4.659$

$35.411
$5.603
$\Delta = -0.633$
$B = \$28.018$

$61.149
$0.000
$\Delta = 0.000$
$B = \$0.000$

$43.246
$1.401
$\Delta = -0.171$
$B = \$8.809$

$30.585
$9.415
$\Delta = -1.000$
$B = \$38.947$

$74.678
$0.000

$52.814
$0.000

$37.351
$2.649

$29,416
$13.584

assign that value to the node. Otherwise, we assign the value of the option unexercised. We work backward through the tree as usual.

10.5 OPTIONS ON OTHER ASSETS

The model developed thus far can be modified easily to price options on underlying assets other than nondividend-paying stocks. In this section we present examples of how to do so. We examine options on stock indexes, currencies, and futures contracts. In every case the general procedure is the same: We compute the option price using equation (10.6). The difference for different underlying assets will be the construction of the binomial tree and the risk-neutral probability.

The valuation of an option on a stock that pays discrete dividends is more involved and is covered in Chapter 11.

Option on a Stock Index

Suppose a stock index pays continuous dividends at the rate δ. This type of option has in fact already been covered by our derivation in Section 10.1. The up and down index moves are given by equation (10.9), the replicating portfolio by equations (10.1) and (10.2), and the option price by equation (10.3). The risk-neutral probability is given by equation (10.5).[4]

Figure 10.8 displays a binomial tree for an American call option on a stock index. Note that because of dividends, early exercise is optimal at the node where the stock price is \$157.101. Given these parameters, we have $p^* = 0.457$; hence, the value of the option unexercised is

$$e^{-0.05 \times 1/3} \left[0.457 \times \$87.747 + (1 - 0.457) \times \$32.779 \right] = \$56.942$$

Since $57.101 > 56.942$, we exercise the option at that node.

Options on Currencies

With a currency with spot price x_0, the forward price is $F_{0,h} = x_0 e^{(r-r_f)h}$, where r_f is the foreign interest rate. Thus, we construct the binomial tree using

$$ux = xe^{(r-r_f)h+\sigma\sqrt{h}}$$

$$dx = xe^{(r-r_f)h-\sigma\sqrt{h}}$$

There is one subtlety in creating the replicating portfolio: Investing in a "currency" means investing in a money-market fund or fixed income obligation denominated in

----

[4]Intuitively, dividends can be taken into account either by (1) appropriately lowering the nodes on the tree and leaving risk-neutral probabilities unchanged, or (2) by reducing the risk-neutral probability and leaving the tree unchanged. The forward tree adopts the first approach.

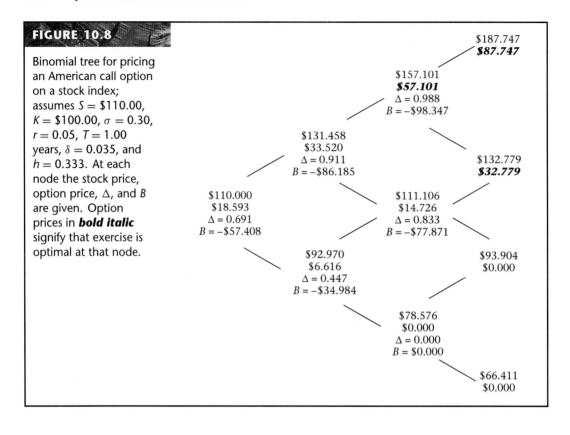

FIGURE 10.8

Binomial tree for pricing an American call option on a stock index; assumes $S = \$110.00$, $K = \$100.00$, $\sigma = 0.30$, $r = 0.05$, $T = 1.00$ years, $\delta = 0.035$, and $h = 0.333$. At each node the stock price, option price, Δ, and B are given. Option prices in **bold italic** signify that exercise is optimal at that node.

$187.747
$87.747

$157.101
$57.101
$\Delta = 0.988$
$B = -\$98.347$

$131.458
$33.520
$\Delta = 0.911$
$B = -\$86.185$

$132.779
$32.779

$110.000
$18.593
$\Delta = 0.691$
$B = -\$57.408$

$111.106
$14.726
$\Delta = 0.833$
$B = -\$77.871$

$92.970
$6.616
$\Delta = 0.447$
$B = -\$34.984$

$93.904
$0.000

$78.576
$0.000
$\Delta = 0.000$
$B = \$0.000$

$66.411
$0.000

that currency. (We encountered this idea previously in Chapter 5.) Taking into account interest on the foreign-currency-denominated obligation, the two equations are

$$\Delta \times dxe^{r_f h} + e^{rh} \times B = C_d$$
$$\Delta \times uxe^{r_f h} + e^{rh} \times B = C_u$$

The risk-neutral probability of an up move in this case is given by

$$p^* = \frac{e^{(r-r_f)h} - d}{u - d} \tag{10.11}$$

Notice that if we think of r_f as the dividend yield on the foreign currency, these two equations look exactly like those for an index option. In fact the solution is the same as for an option on an index: Set the dividend yield equal to the foreign risk-free rate and the current value of the index equal to the spot exchange rate.

Figure 10.9 prices a dollar-denominated American put option on the euro. The current exchange rate is assumed to be $1.05/€ and the strike is $1.10/€. The euro-denominated interest rate is 3.1%, and the dollar-denominated rate is 5.5%.

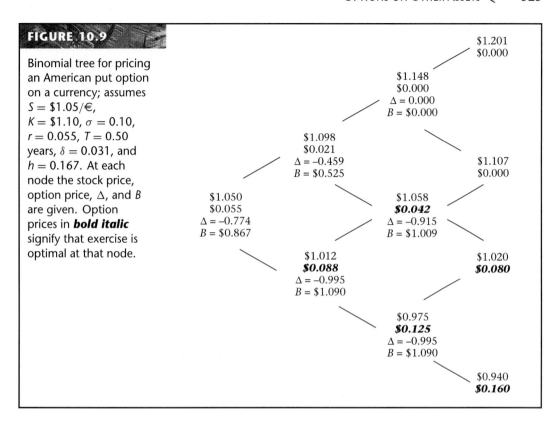

FIGURE 10.9

Binomial tree for pricing an American put option on a currency; assumes $S = \$1.05/€$, $K = \$1.10$, $\sigma = 0.10$, $r = 0.055$, $T = 0.50$ years, $\delta = 0.031$, and $h = 0.167$. At each node the stock price, option price, Δ, and B are given. Option prices in **bold italic** signify that exercise is optimal at that node.

$1.050
$0.055
$\Delta = -0.774$
$B = \$0.867$

$1.098
$0.021
$\Delta = -0.459$
$B = \$0.525$

$1.012
$0.088
$\Delta = -0.995$
$B = \$1.090$

$1.148
$0.000
$\Delta = 0.000$
$B = \$0.000$

$1.058
$0.042
$\Delta = -0.915$
$B = \$1.009$

$0.975
$0.125
$\Delta = -0.995$
$B = \$1.090$

$1.201
$0.000

$1.107
$0.000

$1.020
$0.080

$0.940
$0.160

Because volatility is low and the option is in-the-money, early exercise is optimal at three nodes prior to expiration.

Options on Futures Contracts

We now consider options on futures contracts. We assume the forward price is the same as the futures price. Since we build the tree based on the forward price, we simply add up and down movements around the current price. Thus, the nodes are constructed as

$$u = e^{\sigma\sqrt{h}}$$
$$d = e^{-\sigma\sqrt{h}}$$

Note that this solution for u and d is exactly what we would get for an option on a stock index if Δ, the dividend yield, were equal to the risk-free rate.

In constructing the replicating portfolio, recall that in each period a futures contract pays the change in the futures price, and there is no investment required to enter a futures contract. The problem is to find the number of futures contracts, Δ, and the lending, B, that replicates the option. We have

$$\Delta \times (dF - F) + e^{rh} \times B = C_d$$
$$\Delta \times (uF - F) + e^{rh} \times B = C_u$$

Solving gives[5]

$$\Delta = \frac{C_u - C_d}{F(u - d)}$$

$$B = e^{-rh}\left(C_u \frac{1-d}{u-d} + C_d \frac{u-1}{u-d} \right)$$

While Δ tells us how many futures contracts to hold to hedge the option, the value of the option in this case is simply B. The reason is that the futures contract requires no investment, so the only investment is that made in the bond. We can again price the option using equation (10.3).

The risk-neutral probability of an up move is given by

$$p^* = \frac{1 - d}{u - d} \tag{10.12}$$

Figure 10.10 shows a tree for pricing an American call option on a gold futures contract. Early exercise is optimal when the price is $336.720. The intuition for early exercise is that when an option on a futures contract is exercised, the option holder pays nothing, is entered into a futures contract, and receives mark-to-market proceeds of the difference between the strike price and the futures price. The motive for exercise is the ability to earn interest on the mark-to-market proceeds.

....

[5]The interpretation of Δ here is the number of futures contracts in the replicating portfolio. Another interpretation of Δ is the price sensitivity of the option when the price of the underlying asset changes. These two interpretations usually coincide, but not in the case of options on futures. The reason is that the futures price at time t reflects a price denominated in future dollars. The effect on the option price of a futures price change today is given by $e^{-rh} \Delta$. To see this, consider an option that is one binomial period from expiration and for which $uF > dF > K$. Then

$$\Delta = \frac{uF - K - (dF - K)}{F(u - d)} = 1$$

But we also have

$$B = e^{-rh}\left[(uF - K)\frac{1-d}{u-d} + (dF - K)\frac{u-1}{u-d} \right]$$
$$= e^{-rh}(F - K)$$

From the second expression, you can see that if the futures price changes by $1, the option price changes by e^{-rh}.

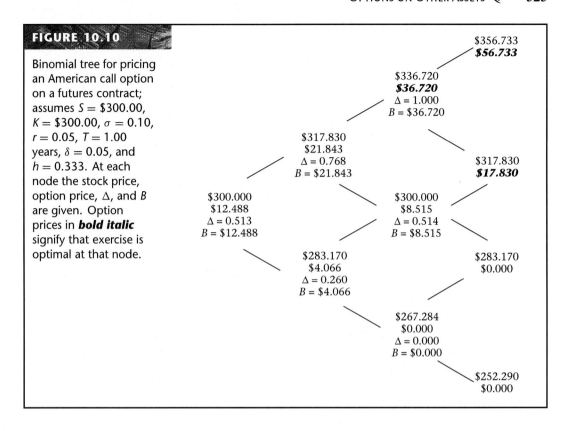

FIGURE 10.10

Binomial tree for pricing an American call option on a futures contract; assumes $S = \$300.00$, $K = \$300.00$, $\sigma = 0.10$, $r = 0.05$, $T = 1.00$ years, $\delta = 0.05$, and $h = 0.333$. At each node the stock price, option price, Δ, and B are given. Option prices in **bold italic** signify that exercise is optimal at that node.

$300.000
$12.488
$\Delta = 0.513$
$B = \$12.488$

$317.830
$21.843
$\Delta = 0.768$
$B = \$21.843$

$283.170
$4.066
$\Delta = 0.260$
$B = \$4.066$

$336.720
$36.720
$\Delta = 1.000$
$B = \$36.720$

$300.000
$8.515
$\Delta = 0.514$
$B = \$8.515$

$267.284
$0.000
$\Delta = 0.000$
$B = \$0.000$

$356.733
$56.733

$317.830
$17.830

$283.170
$0.000

$252.290
$0.000

Options on Commodities

Many options exist on commodity futures contracts. However, it is also possible to have options on the physical commodity. If there is a market for lending and borrowing the commodity, then, in theory, pricing such an option is straightforward.

Recall from Chapter 6 that the *lease rate* for a commodity is conceptually similar to a dividend yield. If you borrow the commodity, you pay the lease rate. If you buy the commodity and lend it, you receive the lease rate. Thus, from the perspective of someone synthetically creating the option, the commodity is like a stock index, with the lease rate equal to the dividend yield.

Because this is conceptually the same as the pricing exercise in Figure 10.8 (imagine a commodity with a price of $110, a lease rate of 3.5%, and a volatility of 30%), we do not present a pricing example.

In practice, pricing and hedging an option based on the physical commodity can be problematic. If an appropriate futures contract exists, a market-maker could use it to hedge a commodity option. Otherwise, transactions in physical commodities often have greater transaction costs than for financial assets. Short-selling a commodity may not be possible, for reasons discussed in Chapter 6. Market-making is then difficult.

Options on Bonds

Finally, we will briefly discuss options on bonds. We devote a separate chapter later to discussing fixed-income derivatives, but it is useful to understand at this point some of the issues in pricing options on bonds. As a first approximation we could just say that bonds are like stocks that pay a discrete dividend (a coupon), and price bond options using the binomial model.

However, bonds differ from the assets we have been discussing in two important respects.

1. The volatility of a bond decreases over time as the bond approaches maturity. The prices of 30-day Treasury bills, for example, are much less volatile than the prices of 30-year Treasury bonds. The reason is that a given change in the interest rate, other things equal, changes the price of a shorter-lived bond by less.

2. We have been assuming in all our calculations that interest rates are the same for all maturities and do not change over time. While these assumptions may be good enough for pricing options on stocks, they are logically inconsistent for pricing options on bonds: If interest rates do not change, neither do bond prices.

In some cases, it may be reasonable to price bond options using the simple binomial model in this chapter. For example, consider a 6-month option on a 29-year bond. The underlying asset in this case is a 29.5-year bond. As a practical matter, the volatility difference between a 29.5- and a 29-year bond is likely to be very small. Also, because it is short-lived, this option will not be particularly sensitive to the short-term interest rate, so the correlation of the bond price and the 6-month interest rate will not matter much.

On the other hand, if we have a 3-year option to buy a 5-year bond, these issues might be quite important. Another issue is that bond coupon payments are discrete, so the assumption of a continuous dividend is an approximation.

In general, the conceptual and practical issues with bonds are different enough that bonds warrant a separate treatment. We will return to bonds in Chapter 23.

Summary

Here is the general procedure covering the other assets discussed in this section.

- Construct the binomial tree for the price of the underlying asset using

$$uS_t = F_{t,t+h}e^{+\sigma\sqrt{h}} \qquad \text{or} \qquad u = \frac{F_{t,t+h}}{S_t}e^{+\sigma\sqrt{h}}$$

$$dS_t = F_{t,t+h}e^{-\sigma\sqrt{h}} \qquad \text{or} \qquad d = \frac{F_{t,t+h}}{S_t}e^{-\sigma\sqrt{h}}$$

(10.13)

	Substitutions for pricing options on assets other than a stock index.

TABLE 10.1

Underlying Asset	Interest Rate	Dividend Yield
Stock Index	Domestic Risk-Free Rate	Dividend Yield
Currency	Domestic Risk-Free Rate	Foreign Risk-Free Rate
Futures Contract	Domestic Risk-Free Rate	Domestic Risk-Free Rate
Commodity	Domestic Risk-Free Rate	Commodity Lease Rate
Coupon Bond	Domestic Risk-Free Rate	Yield on Bond

Since different underlying assets will have different forward price formulas, the tree will be different for different underlying assets.

- The option price at each node, if the option is unexercised, can then be computed as follows:

$$p^* = \frac{F_{t,t+h}/S_t - d}{u - d}$$
$$= \frac{e^{(r-\delta)h} - d}{u - d} \tag{10.14}$$

and, as before,

$$C = e^{-rh}\left(p^*C_u + (1 - p^*)C_d\right) \tag{10.15}$$

where C_u and C_d are the up and down nodes relative to the current node. For an American option, at each node take the greater of this value and the value if exercised.

Pricing options with different underlying assets requires adjusting the risk-neutral probability for the borrowing cost or lease rate of the underlying asset. Mechnanically, this means that we can use the formula for pricing an option on a stock index with an appropriate substitution for the dividend yield. Table 10.1 summarizes the substitutions.

CHAPTER SUMMARY

In order to price options, we must make an assumption about the probability distribution of the underlying asset. The binomial distribution provides a particularly simple stock price distribution: At any point in time, the stock price can go from S up to uS or down to dS, where the movement factors u and d are given by equation (10.9).

Given binomial stock price movements, the option can be replicated by holding Δ shares of stock and B bonds. The option price is the cost of this replicating portfolio,

$\Delta S + B$. For a call option, $\Delta > 0$ and $B < 0$, so the option is replicated by borrowing to buy shares. For a put, $\Delta < 0$ and $B > 0$. If the option price does not equal this theoretical price, arbitrage is possible. The replicating portfolio is dynamic, changing as the stock price moves up or down. Thus it is unlike the replicating portfolio for a forward contract, which is fixed.

The binomial option pricing formula has an interpretation as a discounted expected value, with the risk-neutral probability (equation (10.5)) used to compute the expected payoff to the option and the risk-free rate used to discount the expected payoff. This is known as risk-neutral pricing.

The binomial model can be used to price American and European calls and puts on a variety of underlying assets, including stocks, indexes, futures, currencies, commodities, and bonds.

FURTHER READING

This chapter has focused on the *mechanics* of binomial option pricing. Some of the underlying concepts will be discussed in more detail in Chapter 11. There we will have more to say about risk-neutral pricing, the link between the binomial tree and the assumed stock price distribution, how to estimate volatility, and how to price options when the stock pays a discrete dividend.

The binomial model provides a foundation for much of what we will do in later chapters. We will see in Chapter 12, for example, that the binomial option pricing formula gives results equivalent to the Black-Scholes formula when h becomes small. Consequently, if you thoroughly understand binomial pricing, you also understand the Black-Scholes formula. In Chapter 22, we will see how to generalize binomial trees to handle two sources of uncertainty.

In addition to the original papers by Cox et al. (1979) and Rendleman and Bartter (1979), Cox and Rubinstein (1985) provides an excellent exposition of the binomial model.

PROBLEMS

In these problems, n refers to the number of binomial periods. Assume all rates are continuously compounded unless the problem explicitly states otherwise.

10.1. Let $S = \$100$, $K = \$105$, $r = 8\%$, $T = 0.5$, and $\delta = 0$. Let $u = 1.3$, $d = 0.8$, and $n = 1$.

    a. What are the premium, Δ, and B for a European call?

    b. What are the premium, Δ, and B for a European put?

10.2. Let $S = \$100$, $K = \$95$, $r = 8\%$, $T = 0.5$, and $\delta = 0$. Let $u = 1.3$, $d = 0.8$, and $n = 1$.

    a. Verify that the price of a European call is $16.196.

b. Suppose you observe a call price of $17. What is the arbitrage?

c. Suppose you observe a call price of $15.50. What is the arbitrage?

10.3. Let $S = \$100$, $K = \$95$, $r = 8\%$, $T = 0.5$, and $\delta = 0$. Let $u = 1.3$, $d = 0.8$, and $n = 1$.

    a. Verify that the price of a European put is $7.471.

    b. Suppose you observe a put price of $8. What is the arbitrage?

    c. Suppose you observe a put price of $6. What is the arbitrage?

10.4. Let $S = \$100$, $K = \$95$, $\sigma = 30\%$, $r = 8\%$, $T = 1$, and $\delta = 0$. Let $u = 1.3$, $d = 0.8$, and $n = 2$. Construct the binomial tree for a call option. At each node provide the premium, Δ, and B.

10.5. Repeat the option price calculation in the previous question for stock prices of $80, $90, $110, $120, and $130, keeping everything else fixed. What happens to the initial option Δ as the stock price increases?

10.6. Let $S = \$100$, $K = \$95$, $\sigma = 30\%$, $r = 8\%$, $T = 1$, and $\delta = 0$. Let $u = 1.3$, $d = 0.8$, and $n = 2$. Construct the binomial tree for a European put option. At each node provide the premium, Δ, and B.

10.7. Repeat the option price calculation in the previous question for stock prices of $80, $90, $110, $120, and $130, keeping everything else fixed. What happens to the inital put Δ as the stock price increases?

10.8. Let $S = \$100$, $K = \$95$, $\sigma = 30\%$, $r = 8\%$, $T = 1$, and $\delta = 0$. Let $u = 1.3$, $d = 0.8$, and $n = 2$. Construct the binomial tree for an American put option. At each node provide the premium, Δ, and B.

10.9. Suppose $S_0 = \$100$, $K = \$50$, $r = 7.696\%$ (continuously compounded), $\delta = 0$, and $T = 1$.

    a. Suppose that for $h = 1$, we have $u = 1.2$ and $d = 1.05$. What is the binomial option price for a call option that lives one period? Is there any problem with having $d > 1$?

    b. Suppose now that $u = 1.4$ and $d = 0.6$. Before computing the option price, what is your guess about how it will change from your previous answer? Does it change? How do you account for the result? Interpret your answer using put-call parity.

    c. Now let $u = 1.4$ and $d = 0.4$. How do you think the call option price will change from (a)? How does it change? How do you account for this? Use put-call parity to explain your answer.

10.10. Let $S = \$100$, $K = \$95$, $r = 8\%$ (continuously compounded), $\sigma = 30\%$, $\delta = 0$, $T = 1$ year, and $n = 3$.

a. Verify that the binomial option price for an American call option is $18.283. Verify that there is never early exercise; hence, a European call would have the same price.

b. Show that the binomial option price for a European put option is $5.979. Verify that put-call parity is satisfied.

c. Verify that the price of an American put is $6.678.

10.11. Repeat the previous problem assuming that the stock pays a continuous dividend of 8% per year (continuously compounded). Calculate the prices of the American and European puts and calls. Which options are early-exercised?

10.12. Let $S = \$40$, $K = \$40$, $r = 8\%$ (continuously compounded), $\sigma = 30\%$, $\delta = 0$, $T = 0.5$ year, and $n = 2$.

a. Construct the binomial tree for the stock. What are u and d?

b. Show that the call price is $4.110.

c. Compute the prices of American and European puts.

10.13. Use the same data as in the previous problem, only suppose that the call price is $5 instead of $4.110.

a. At time 0, assume you write the option and form the replicating portfolio to offset the written option. What is the replicating portfolio and what are the net cash flows from selling the overpriced call and buying the synthetic equivalent?

b. What are the cash flows in the next binomial period (three months later) if the call at that time is fairly priced and you liquidate the position? What would you do if the option continues to be overpriced the next period?

c. What would you do if the option is underpriced the next period?

10.14. Suppose that the exchange rate is $0.92/€. Let $r_\$ = 4\%$, and $r_€ = 3\%$, $u = 1.2$, $d = 0.9$, $T = 0.75$, $n = 3$, and $K = \$0.85$.

a. What is the price of a 9-month European call?

b. What is the price of a 9-month American call?

10.15. Use the same inputs as in the previous problem, except that $K = \$1.00$.

a. What is the price of a 9-month European put?

b. What is the price of a 9-month American put?

10.16. Suppose that the exchange rate is 1 dollar for 120 yen. The dollar interest rate is 5% (continuously compounded) and the yen rate is 1% (continuously compounded). Consider an at-the-money American dollar call that is yen-denominated (i.e., the call permits you to buy 1 dollar for 120 yen). The option has 1 year to expiration and the exchange rate volatility is 10%. Let $n = 3$.

    a. What is the price of a European call? An American call?

    b. What is the price of a European put? An American put?

    c. How do you account for the pattern of early exercise across the two options?

10.17. An option has a gold futures contract as the underlying asset. The current 1-year gold futures price is \$300/oz., the strike price is \$290, the risk-free rate is 6%, volatility is 10%, and time to expiration is 1 year. Suppose $n = 1$. What is the price of a call option on gold? What is the replicating portfolio for the call option? Evaluate the statement: "Replicating a call option always entails borrowing to buy the underlying asset."

10.18. Suppose the S&P 500 futures price is 1000, $\sigma = 30\%$, $r = 5\%$, $\delta = 5\%$, $T = 1$, and $n = 3$.

    a. What are the prices of European calls and puts for $K = \$1000$? Why do you find the prices to be equal?

    b. What are the prices of American calls and puts for $K = \$1000$?

    c. What are the time-0 replicating portfolios for the European call and put?

10.19. For a stock index, $S = \$100$, $\sigma = 30\%$, $r = 5\%$, $\delta = 3\%$, and $T = 3$. Let $n = 3$.

    a. What is the price of a European call option with a strike of \$95?

    b. What is the price of a European put option with a strike of \$95?

    c. Now let $S = \$95$, $K = \$100$, $\sigma = 30\%$, $r = 3\%$, and $\delta = 5\%$. (You have exchanged values for the stock price and strike price and for the interest rate and dividend yield.) Value both options again. What do you notice?

10.20. Repeat the previous problem calculating prices for American options instead of European. What happens?

10.21. Suppose that $u < e^{(r-\delta)h}$. Show that there is an arbitrage opportunity. Now suppose that $d > e^{(r-\delta)h}$. Show again that there is an arbitrage opportunity.

APPENDIX 10.A: USING THE SPREADSHEET FUNCTIONS *BINOMCALL* AND *BINOMPUT*

The function *BinomCall* in the option spreadsheets implements the binomial calculation we have been describing. BinomCall has the following arguments:

$$BinomCall(S, K, \sigma, r, T, \delta, OpType, n) \tag{10.16}$$

The parameter "*OpType*" equals 0 for a European option and 1 for an American option. The length of the binomial period, h, is calculated internally in the function as T/n.

To duplicate the option price in Figure 10.4, we enter

$$BinomCall(41, 40, 0.3, 0.8, 2, 0, 0, 2) = 10.737$$

To duplicate the option price in Figure 10.5, enter

$$BinomCall(41, 40, 0.3, 0.8, 1, 0, 0, 3) = 7.074$$

APPENDIX 10.B: TAXES AND OPTION PRICES

It is possible to solve for a binomial price when there are taxes. Suppose that each form of income is taxed at a different rate: Interest at the rate τ_i, capital gains on a stock at the rate τ_g, capital gains on options at the rate τ_O, and dividends at the rate τ_d. We assume that taxes on all forms of income are paid on an accrual basis, and that there is no limit on the ability to deduct losses or to offset losses on one form of income against gains on another form of income.

We then choose Δ_t and B_t by requiring that the *after-tax* return on the stock/bond portfolio equal the *after-tax* return on the option in both the up and down states. Thus we require that

$$\left[S_{t+h} - \tau_g(S_{t+h} - S_t) + \delta S_t(1 - \tau_d) \right] \Delta_t + [1 + r_h(1 - \tau)] B_t$$
$$= \phi_{t+h}(S_{t+h}) - \tau_O \left[\phi_{t+h}(S_{t+h}) - \phi_t(S_t) \right] \tag{10.17}$$

The solutions for Δ and B are then

$$\Delta = \frac{1 - \tau_O}{1 - \tau_g} \frac{\phi_1(S_1^+) - \phi_1(S_1^-)}{S_1^+ - S_1^-}$$

$$B = \frac{1}{1 + r_h \frac{1 - \tau_i}{1 - \tau_O}} \left(\frac{u\phi_1(S_1^-) - d\phi_1(S_1^+)}{u - d} - \frac{\Delta}{1 - \tau_O} S_0 \left[\frac{\tau_g - \tau_O}{1 - \tau_g} + \delta(1 - \tau_d) \right] \right)$$

This gives an option price of

$$\phi_t = \frac{1}{1 + r_h \frac{1 - \tau_i}{1 - \tau_O}} \left[p^* \phi_{t+h}(S_{t+h}^+) + (1 - p^*)\phi_{t+h}(S_{t+h}^-) \right] \tag{10.18}$$

where

$$p^* = \frac{1 + r_h \frac{1 - \tau_i}{1 - \tau_g} - \delta \frac{1 - \tau_d}{1 - \tau_O} - d}{u - d} \tag{10.19}$$

As in Appendix 5.A, assume that broker-dealers are marked-to-market for tax purposes and face the same tax rate on all forms of income. Then taxes drop out of all the option-pricing expressions.

Chapter 11

Binomial Option Pricing: II

hapter 10 introduced binomial option pricing, focusing on how the model can be used to compute European and American option prices for a variety of underlying assets. In this chapter we continue the discussion of binomial pricing, delving more deeply into the economics of the model and its underlying assumptions.

First, the binomial model can value options that may be early-exercised. We will examine early exercise in more detail, and see that the option pricing calculation reflects the economic determinants of early exercise discussed in Chapter 9.

Second, the binomial option pricing formula can be interpreted as the expected option payoff one period, hence, discounted at the risk-free rate. In Chapter 10 we referred to this calculation as *risk-neutral pricing*. This calculation appears to be inconsistent with standard discounted cash flow valuation, in which expected cash flows are discounted at a risk-adjusted rate, not the risk-free rate. We show that, in fact, the binomial pricing formula (and, hence, risk-neutral valuation) is consistent with option valuation using standard discounted cash flow techniques.

Third, we modeled the stock price by using volatility (σ) to determine the magnitude of the up and down stock price movements. In this chapter we explain this calculation in more detail. What is the economic meaning of this assumption? In constructing the binomial tree, why is volatility multiplied by the square root of time ($\sigma \sqrt{h}$). How should we estimate volatility?

Finally, we saw how to price options on stock indices where the dividend is continuous. In this chapter we adapt the binomial model to price options on stocks that pay discrete dividends.

11.1 UNDERSTANDING EARLY EXERCISE

In deciding whether to early-exercise an option, the option holder compares the value of exercising immediately with the value of continuing to hold the option, and exercises if immediate exercise is more valuable. This is the comparison we performed at each binomial node when we valued American options in Chapter 10.

We obtain an economic perspective on the early-exercise decision by considering the costs and benefits of early exercise. As discussed in Section 9.3, there are three economic considerations governing the decision to exercise early. By exercising, the option holder

- Receives the stock and thus receives dividends,
- Pays the strike price prior to expiration (this has an interest cost), and

- Loses the insurance implicit in the call. By holding the call instead of exercising, the option holder is protected against the possibility that the stock price will be less than the strike price at expiration. Once the option is exercised, this protection no longer exists.

Consider an example where a call option has a strike price of $100, the interest rate is 5%, and the stock pays continuous dividends of 5%. If the stock price is $200, the net effect of dividends and interest encourages early exercise. Annual dividends are approximately 5% of $200, or $0.05 \times \$200 = \$10$. The annual interest saved by deferring exercise is approximately $0.05 \times \$100 = \$5$. Thus, for a stock price of $200 (indeed, for any stock price above $100) dividends lost by not exercising exceed interest saved by deferring exercise.

The only reason in this case not to exercise early is the implicit insurance the option owner loses by exercising. This implicit insurance arises from the fact that the option holder could exercise and then the stock price could fall below the strike price of $100. Leaving the option unexercised protects against this scenario. The early-exercise calculation for a call therefore implicitly weighs dividends, which encourage early exercise, against interest and insurance, which discourage early exercise.

If volatility is zero, then the value of insurance is zero, and it is simple to find the optimal exercise policy as long as r and δ are constant. It is optimal to defer exercise as long as interest savings on the strike exceed dividends lost, or

$$rK > \delta S$$

It is optimal to exercise when this is not true, or

$$S > \frac{rK}{\delta}$$

In the special case when $r = \delta$ and $\sigma = 0$, any in-the-money option should be exercised immediately. If $\delta = 0.5r$, then we exercise when the stock price is twice the exercise price.

The decision to exercise is more complicated when volatility is positive. In this case the implicit insurance has value, and the value varies with time to expiration. Figure 11.1 displays the price above which early exercise is optimal for a 5-year option with $K = \$100$, $r = 5\%$, and $\delta = 5\%$, for three different volatilities, computed using 500 binomial steps. Recall from Chapter 9 that if it is optimal to exercise a call at a given stock price, then it is optimal to exercise at all higher stock prices. Figure 11.1 thus shows the *lowest* stock price at which exercise is optimal. The oscillation in this lowest price, which is evident in the figure, is due to the up and down binomial movements that approximate the behavior of the stock; with an infinite number of binomial steps the early-exercise schedule would be smooth and continuously decreasing. Comparing the three lines, we observe a significant volatility effect. A 5-year option with a volatility of 50% should only be exercised if the stock price exceeds about $360. If volatility is 10%, the boundary drops to $130. This volatility effect stems from the fact that the insurance value lost by early-exercising is greater when volatility is greater.

Figure 11.2 performs the same experiment for put options with the same inputs. The picture is similar, as is the logic: The advantage of early exercise is receiving the

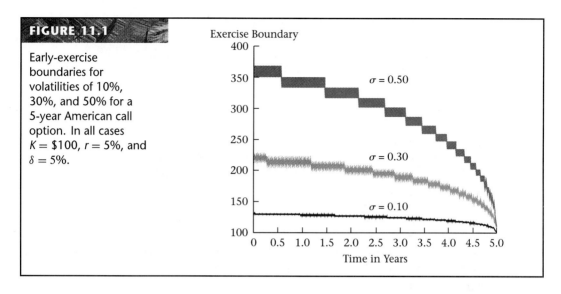

FIGURE 11.1

Early-exercise boundaries for volatilities of 10%, 30%, and 50% for a 5-year American call option. In all cases $K = \$100$, $r = 5\%$, and $\delta = 5\%$.

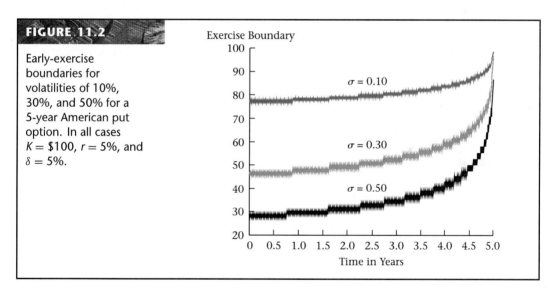

FIGURE 11.2

Early-exercise boundaries for volatilities of 10%, 30%, and 50% for a 5-year American put option. In all cases $K = \$100$, $r = 5\%$, and $\delta = 5\%$.

strike price sooner rather than later. The disadvantages are the dividends lost by giving up the stock, and the loss of insurance against the stock price exceeding the strike price.

Figures 11.1 and 11.2 also show that, other things equal, early-exercise criteria become less stringent closer to expiration. This occurs because the value of insurance diminishes as the options approach expiration.

While these pictures are constructed for the special case where $\delta = r$, the overall conclusion holds generally.

11.2 Understanding Risk-Neutral Pricing

In Chapter 10, we saw that the binomial option pricing formula can be written

$$C = e^{-rh}[p^*C_u + (1 - p^*)C_d] \qquad (11.1)$$

where

$$p^* = \frac{e^{(r-\delta)h} - d}{u - d} \qquad (11.2)$$

We labeled p^* the *risk-neutral probability* that the stock will go up. Equation (11.1) has the appearance of a discounted expected value, where the expected value calculation uses p^* and discounting is done at the risk-free rate.

The idea that an option price is the result of a present value calculation is reassuring, but at the same time equation (11.1) is puzzling. A standard discounted cash flow calculation would require computing an expected value using the true probability that the stock price would go up. Discounting would then be done using the expected return on an asset of equivalent risk, not the risk-free rate. Moreover, what is p^*? Is it really a probability?

We will begin our exploration of risk-neutral pricing by interpreting p^*, showing that it is not the true probability that the stock goes up, but rather the probability that gives the stock an expected rate of return equal to the risk-free rate. We will then show that it *is* possible to compute an option price using standard discounted cash flow calculations using the true probability that the stock goes up, but that doing so is cumbersome.

The Risk-Neutral Probability

It is common in finance to emphasize that investors are risk averse. To see what risk aversion means, suppose you are offered either (a) $1000, or (b) $2000 with probability 0.5, and $0 with probability 0.5. A **risk-averse** investor prefers (a), since alternative (b) is risky and has the same expected value as (a). This kind of investor will require a premium to bear risk when expected values are equal.

A **risk-neutral** investor is indifferent between a sure thing and a risky bet with an expected payoff equal to the value of the sure thing. A risk-neutral investor, for example, will be equally happy with alternative (a) or (b).

Before proceeding, we need to emphasize that *at no point are we assuming that investors are risk-neutral. Now and throughout the book, the pricing calculations are consistent with investors being risk-averse.*

Having said this, let's consider what an imaginary world populated by risk-neutral investors would be like. In such a world, investors care only about expected returns and not about riskiness. Assets would have no risk premium since investors would be willing to hold assets with an expected return equal to the risk-free rate.

In this hypothetical risk-neutral world, we can solve for the probability of the stock going up, p^*, such that the stock is expected to earn the risk-free rate. In the binomial model we assume that the stock can go up to uS or down to dS. If the stock is to earn the risk-free return on average, then the probability that the stock will go up, p^*, must satisfy

$$p^*uSe^{\delta h} + (1 - p^*)dSe^{\delta h} = e^{rh}S$$

Solving for p^* gives

$$p^* = \frac{e^{(r-\delta)h} - d}{u - d}$$

This is exactly the definition of p^* in equation (11.2). This is why we refer to p^* as the *risk-neutral probability that the stock price will go up.* It is the probability that the stock price would increase in a risk-neutral world.

Not only would the risk-neutral probability, equation (11.2), be used in a risk-neutral world, but also all discounting would take place at the risk-free rate. Thus, the option pricing formula, equation (11.1), can be said to price options *as if* investors are risk-neutral. At the risk of being repetitious, we are not assuming that investors are actually risk-neutral, and we are not assuming that risky assets are actually expected to earn the risk-free rate of return. Rather, *risk-neutral pricing is an* interpretation *of the formulas above.* Those formulas in turn arise from finding the cost of the portfolio that replicates the option payoff.

Interestingly, this interpretation of the option-pricing procedure has great practical importance; risk-neutral pricing can sometimes be used where other pricing methods are too difficult. We will see in Chapter 19 that risk-neutral pricing is the basis for Monte Carlo valuation, in which asset prices are simulated under the assumption that assets earn the risk-free rate, and these simulated prices are used to value the option.

Pricing an Option Using Real Probabilities

We are left with the question: Is option pricing consistent with standard discounted cash flow calculations? The answer is yes. We can use the true distribution for the future stock price in computing the expected payoff to the option. This expected payoff can then be discounted with a rate based on the stock's required return.

Discounted cash flow is not used in practice to price options because there is no reason to do so: It is necessary to compute the option price in order to compute the correct discount rate. However, we present two examples of valuing an option using real probabilities to see the difficulty in using real probabilities, and also to understand how to determine the risk of an option.

Suppose that the continuously compounded expected return on the stock is α and that the stock does not pay dividends. Then if p is the true probability of the stock going up, p must be consistent with u, d, and α:

$$puS + (1 - p)dS = e^{\alpha h}S \tag{11.3}$$

Solving for p gives us

$$p = \frac{e^{\alpha h} - d}{u - d} \tag{11.4}$$

For probabilities to be between 0 and 1, we must have $u > e^{\alpha h} > d$. Using p, the actual expected payoff to the option one period hence is

$$pC_u + (1 - p)C_d = \frac{e^{\alpha h} - d}{u - d}C_u + \frac{u - e^{\alpha h}}{u - d}C_d \tag{11.5}$$

Now we face the problem with using real as opposed to risk-neutral probabilities: At what rate do we discount this expected payoff? It is not correct to discount the option at the expected return on the stock, α, because the option is equivalent to a leveraged investment in the stock and, hence, is riskier than the stock.

Denote the appropriate per-period discount rate for the option as γ. To compute γ, we can use the fact that the required return on any portfolio is the weighted average of the returns on the assets in the portfolio.[1] In Chapter 10, we saw that an option is equivalent to holding a portfolio consisting of Δ shares of stock and B bonds. The expected return on this portfolio is

$$e^{\gamma h} = \frac{S\Delta}{S\Delta + B}e^{\alpha h} + \frac{B}{S\Delta + B}e^{rh} \tag{11.6}$$

We can now compute the option price as the expected option payoff, equation (11.5), discounted at the appropriate discount rate, given by equation (11.6). This gives

$$e^{-\gamma h}\left[\frac{e^{\alpha h} - d}{u - d}C_u + \frac{u - e^{\alpha h}}{u - d}C_d\right] \tag{11.7}$$

It turns out that *this gives us the same option price as performing the risk-neutral calculation*. Appendix 11.A demonstrates algebraically that equation (11.7) is equivalent to the risk-neutral calculation, equation (11.1).

The calculations leading to equation (11.7) started with the assumption that the expected return on the stock is α. We then derived a consistent probability, p, and discount rate for the option, γ. You may be wondering if it matters whether we have the "correct" value of α to start with. The answer is that it does not matter: *Any* consistent pair of α and γ will give the same option price. Risk-neutral pricing is valuable because setting $\alpha = r$ results in the *simplest* pricing procedure.

A one-period example   To see how to value an option using true probabilities, we will compute two examples. First, consider the one-period binomial example in Figure 11.3. Suppose that the continuously compounded expected return on XYZ is $\alpha = 15\%$. Then the true probability of the stock going up, from equation (11.4), is

$$p = \frac{e^{0.15} - 0.8025}{1.4623 - 0.8025} = 0.5446$$

The expected payoff to the option in one period, from equation (11.5) is

$$0.5446 \times \$19.954 + (1 - 0.5446) \times \$0 = \$10.867$$

[1] See, for example, Brealey and Myers (2000, Chapter 9).

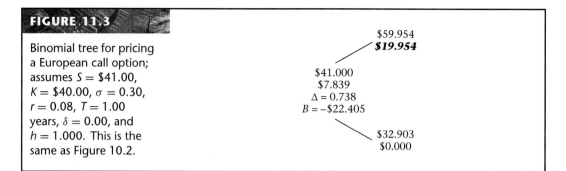

FIGURE 11.3

Binomial tree for pricing
a European call option;
assumes $S = \$41.00$,
$K = \$40.00$, $\sigma = 0.30$,
$r = 0.08$, $T = 1.00$
years, $\delta = 0.00$, and
$h = 1.000$. This is the
same as Figure 10.2.

$59.954
$19.954

$41.000
$7.839
$\Delta = 0.738$
$B = -\$22.405$

$32.903
$0.000

The replicating portfolio, Δ and B, does not depend on p or α. In this example, $\Delta = 0.738$ and $B = -\$22.405$. The discount rate, γ, from equation (11.6) is given by

$$e^{\gamma h} = \frac{0.738 \times \$41}{0.738 \times \$41 - \$22.405}e^{0.15} + \frac{-\$22.405}{0.738 \times \$41 - \$22.405}e^{0.08}$$
$$= 1.386$$

Thus, $\gamma = ln(1.386) = 32.64\%$. The option price is then given by equation (11.7):

$$e^{-0.3264} \times \$10.867 = \$7.839$$

This is exactly the price we obtained before.

Notice that in order to compute the discount rate, we first had to compute Δ and B. But once we have computed Δ and B, we can simply compute the option price as $\Delta S + B$. There is no need for further computations. It can be helpful to know the actual expected return on an option, but for valuation it is pointless.

A multi-period example   To demonstrate that this method of valuation works over multiple periods, Figure 11.4 presents the same binomial tree as Figure 10.5, with the addition that the true discount factor for the option, γ, is reported at each node. Given the 15% continuously compounded discount rate, the true probability of an up move in Figure 11.4 is

$$\frac{e^{0.15 \times 1/3} - 0.8637}{1.2212 - 0.8637} = 0.5247$$

To compute the price at the node where the stock price is $61.149, we discount the expected option price the next period at 26.9%. This gives

$$e^{-0.269 \times 1/3}\left[0.5247 \times \$34.678 + (1 - 0.5247) \times \$12.814\right] = \$22.202$$

When the stock price is $43.246, the discount rate is 49.5%, and the the option price is

$$e^{-0.495 \times 1/3}\left[0.5247 \times \$12.814 + (1 - 0.5247) \times \$0\right] = \$5.700$$

These are both the same option prices as in Figure 10.5, where we used risk-neutral pricing.

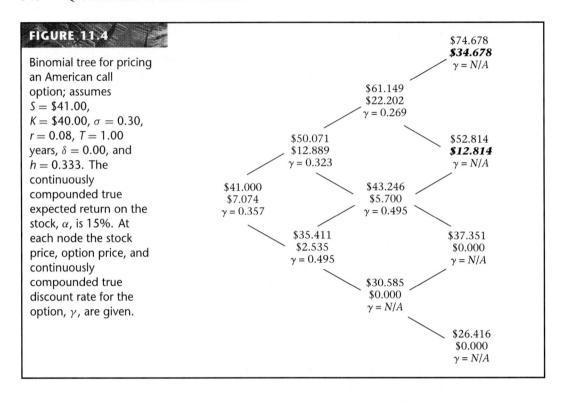

FIGURE 11.4

Binomial tree for pricing an American call option; assumes $S = \$41.00$, $K = \$40.00$, $\sigma = 0.30$, $r = 0.08$, $T = 1.00$ years, $\delta = 0.00$, and $h = 0.333$. The continuously compounded true expected return on the stock, α, is 15%. At each node the stock price, option price, and continuously compounded true discount rate for the option, γ, are given.

$41.000
$7.074
$\gamma = 0.357$

$50.071
$12.889
$\gamma = 0.323$

$35.411
$2.535
$\gamma = 0.495$

$61.149
$22.202
$\gamma = 0.269$

$43.246
$5.700
$\gamma = 0.495$

$30.585
$0.000
$\gamma = N/A$

$74.678
$34.678
$\gamma = N/A$

$52.814
$12.814
$\gamma = N/A$

$37.351
$0.000
$\gamma = N/A$

$26.416
$0.000
$\gamma = N/A$

We continue by working back through the tree. To compute the price at the node where the stock price is \$50.071, we discount the expected option price the next period at 32.3%. Thus,

$$e^{-0.323 \times 1/3} \left[0.5247 \times \$22.202 + (1 - 0.5247) \times \$5.700 \right] = \$12.889$$

Again, this is the same price at this node as in Figure 10.5.

The actual discount rate for the option changes as we move down the tree at a point in time and also over time. The required return on the option is less when the stock price is \$61.149 (26.9%) than when it is \$43.246 (49.5%). The discount rate increases as the stock price decreases because the option is equivalent to a leveraged position in the stock, and the degree of leverage increases as the option moves out of the money.

These examples illustrate that it is possible to obtain option prices using standard discounted-cash-flow techniques. Generally, however, there is no reason to do so. Moreover, the fact that risk-neutral pricing works means that it is not necessary to estimate α, the expected return on the stock, when pricing an option. Since expected returns are hard to estimate precisely, this makes option pricing a great deal easier.

Appendix 11.B goes into more detail about risk-neutral pricing.

11.3 THE BINOMIAL TREE AND LOGNORMALITY

The usefulness of the binomial pricing model hinges on the binomial tree providing a reasonable representation of the stock price distribution. In this section we discuss the motivation for and plausibility of the binomial tree. We will define a lognormal distribution and see that the binomial tree approximates this distribution.

The Random Walk Model

It is often said that stock prices follow a random walk. In this section we will explain what a random walk is. In the next section we will apply the random walk model to stock prices.

To understand a random walk, imagine that we flip a coin repeatedly. Let the random variable Y denote the outcome of the flip. If the coin lands displaying a head, $Y = 1$. If the coin lands displaying a tail, $Y = -1$. If the probability of a head is 50%, we say the coin is fair. After n flips, with the ith flip denoted Y_i, the cumulative total, Z_n, is

$$Z_n = \sum_{i=1}^{n} Y_i \tag{11.8}$$

It turns out that the more times we flip, on average, the farther we will move from where we start. We can understand intuitively why with more flips the average distance from the starting point increases. Think about the first flip and imagine you get a head. You move to +1, and as far as the remaining flips are concerned, *this is your new starting point*. After the second flip, you will either be at 0 or +2. If you are at zero, it is as if you started over; however if you are at +2 you are starting at +2. Continuing in this way your average distance from the starting increases with the number of flips.[2]

Another way to represent the process followed by Z_n is in terms of the *change* in Z_n:

$$Z_n - Z_{n-1} = Y_n$$

We can rewrite this more explicitly as

....

[2] After n flips, the average squared distance from the starting point will be n. Conditional on the first flip being a head, your average squared distance is $0.5 \times 0 + 0.5 \times 2^2 = 2$. If your first flip had been a tail, your average squared distance after two moves would also be 2. Thus, the unconditional average squared distance is 2 after 2 flips. If D_n^2 represents your squared distance from the starting point, then

$$D_n^2 = 0.5 \times (D_{n-1} + 1)^2 + 0.5 \times (D_{n-1} - 1)^2 = D_{n-1}^2 + 1$$

Since $D_0^2 = 0$, this implies that $D_n^2 = n$. This idea that with a random walk you drift increasingly farther from the starting point is critical later in the book to understanding option pricing.

$$\text{Heads:} \quad Z_n - Z_{n-1} = +1 \qquad\qquad (11.9)$$

$$\text{Tails:} \quad Z_n - Z_{n-1} = -1 \qquad\qquad (11.10)$$

With heads, the *change* in Z is 1, and with tails, the change in Z is -1. This random walk is illustrated in Figure 11.5.

The idea that asset prices should follow a random walk was articulated in Samuelson (1965). In efficient markets, an asset price should reflect all available information. By definition, new information is a surprise. In response to new information the price is equally likely to move up or down, as with the coin flip. The price after a period of time is the initial price plus the cumulative up and down movements due to informational surprises.

Modeling Stock Prices as a Random Walk

The idea that stock prices move up or down randomly makes sense; however, the description of a random walk in the previous section is not a satisfactory description of stock price movements. Suppose we take the random walk model in Figure 11.5 literally. Assume the beginning stock price is $100, and the stock price will move up or down $1 each time we flip the coin. There are at least three problems with this model:

1. If by chance we get enough cumulative down movements, the stock price will become negative. Because stockholders have limited liability (they can walk away from a bankrupt firm), a stock price will never be negative.

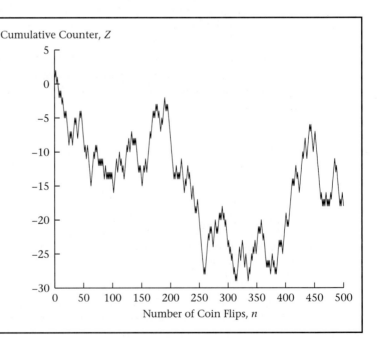

FIGURE 11.5

Illustration of a random walk, where the counter, Z, increases by one when a fair coin flip comes up heads, and decreases by one with tails.

2. The magnitude of the move ($1) should depend upon how quickly the coin flips occur and the level of the stock price. If we flip coins once a second, $1 moves are excessive; in real life, a $100 stock will not typically have 60 $1 up or down movements in one minute. Also, if a $1 move is appropriate for a $100 stock, it likely isn't appropriate for a $5 stock.

3. The stock on average should have a positive return. The random walk model taken literally does not permit this.

It turns out that the binomial model is a variant of the random walk model that solves all of these problems at once. The binomial model assumes that *continuously compounded returns are a random walk*. Thus, before proceeding, we first review some properties of continuously compounded returns.

Continuously Compounded Returns

Here is a summary of the important properties of continuously compounded returns. (See also Appendix 11.B.)

The logarithmic function computes returns from prices   Let S_t and S_{t+h} be stock prices at times t and $t + h$. The continuously compounded return between t and $t + h$, $r_{t,t+h}$ is then

$$r_{t,t+h} = ln(S_{t+h}/S_t) \tag{11.11}$$

The exponential function computes prices from returns   If we know the continuously compounded return, we can obtain S_{t+h} by exponentiating both sides of equation (11.11). This gives

$$S_{t+h} = S_t e^{r_{t,t+h}} \tag{11.12}$$

Continuously compounded returns are additive   Suppose we have continuously compounded returns over a number of periods, for example $r_{t,t+h}$, $r_{t+h,t+2h}$, etc. The continuously compounded return over a long period is the *sum* of continuously compounded returns over the shorter periods, i.e.,

$$r_{t,t+nh} = \sum_{i=1}^{n} r_{t+(i-1)h,t+ih} \tag{11.13}$$

Continuously compounded returns can be less than −100%   A continuously compounded return that is a large negative number still gives a positive stock price. The reason is that e^r is positive for any r. Thus, if the log of the stock price follows a random walk, the stock price cannot become negative.

Here are some examples illustrating these statements.

Example 11.1   Suppose the stock price on four consecutive days is $100, $103, $97, and $98. The daily continuously compounded returns are

$$ln(103/100) = 0.02956; \quad ln(97/103) = -0.06002; \quad ln(98/97) = 0.01026$$

The continuously compounded return from day 1 to day 4 is $ln(98/100) = -0.0202$. This is also the sum of the daily continuously compounded returns:

$$r_{1,2} + r_{2,3} + r_{3,4} = 0.02956 + (-0.06002) + 0.01026 = -0.0202 \qquad ❧$$

Example 11.2 Suppose that the stock price today is $100 and that 1 year from today it is $10. The percentage return is $(10 - 100)/100 = -0.9 = -90\%$. However, the continuously compounded return is $ln(10/100) = -2.30$, a continuously compounded return of -230%. ❧

Example 11.3 Suppose that the stock price today is $100 and that over 1 year the continuously compounded return is -500%. Using equation (11.12), the end-of-year price will be small but positive: $S_1 = 100e^{-5.00} = \$0.6738$. The percentage return is $0.6738/100 - 1 = -99.326\%$. ❧

The Standard Deviation of Returns

Suppose the continuously compounded return over month i is $r_{\text{monthly},i}$. From equation (11.13), we can sum continuously compounded returns. Thus, the annual return is

$$r_{\text{annual}} = \sum_{i=1}^{12} r_{\text{monthly},i}$$

The variance of the annual return is therefore

$$Var(r_{\text{annual}}) = Var\left(\sum_{i=1}^{12} r_{\text{monthly},i} \right) \qquad (11.14)$$

Now suppose that returns are uncorrelated over time; that is, the realization of the return in one period does not affect the expected returns in subsequent periods. With this assumption, the variance of a sum is the sum of the variances. Also suppose that each month has the same variance of returns. If we let σ^2 denote the annual variance, then from equation (11.14) we have

$$\sigma^2 = 12 \times \sigma^2_{\text{monthly}}$$

Taking the square root of both sides and rearranging, we can express the monthly standard deviation in terms of the annual standard deviation:

$$\sigma_{\text{monthly}} = \frac{\sigma}{\sqrt{12}}$$

If we split the year into n periods of length h (so that $h = 1/n$), the standard deviation over the period of length h, σ_h, is

$$\boxed{\sigma_h = \sigma \sqrt{h}} \qquad (11.15)$$

The standard deviation therefore scales with the square root of time. This is why $\sigma \sqrt{h}$ appears in the binomial pricing model.

The Binomial Model

We are now in a position to better understand the binomial model, which is

$$S_{t+h} = S_t e^{(r-\delta)h \pm \sigma \sqrt{h}}$$

Taking logs, we obtain

$$ln(S_{t+h}/S_t) = (r-\delta)h \pm \sigma \sqrt{h} \qquad (11.16)$$

Since $ln(S_{t+h}/S_t)$ is the continuously compounded return from t to $t+h$, $r_{t,t+h}$, the binomial model is simply a particular way to model the continuously compounded return. That return has two parts, one of which is certain [$(r-\delta)h$], and the other of which is uncertain and generates the up and down stock price moves ($\pm \sigma \sqrt{h}$).

Let's see how equation (11.16) solves the three problems in the random walk discussed earlier:

1. The stock price cannot become negative. Even if we move down the binomial tree many times in a row, the resulting large, negative, continuously compounded return will give us a positive price.

2. As h gets smaller, up and down moves get smaller. By construction, annual volatility is the same no matter how many binomial periods there are. Since returns follow a random walk, the percentage price change is the same whether the stock price is $100 or $5.

3. There is a $(r-\delta)h$ term, and we can choose the probability of an up move, so we can guarantee that the expected change in the stock price is positive.

To illustrate that the binomial tree can be thought of as a random walk, Figure 11.6 illustrates the stock price that results when the continuously compounded return follows a random walk. The figure is one particular path through a 500-step binomial tree, with the particular path generated by the same sequence of coin flips as in Figure 11.5.

Lognormality and the Binomial Model

The binomial tree approximates a lognormal distribution, which is commonly used to model stock prices.

First, what is the lognormal distribution? The lognormal distribution is the probability distribution that arises from the assumption that *continuously compounded returns on the stock are normally distributed*. When we traverse the binomial tree, we are implicitly adding up binomial random return components of $(r-\delta)h \pm \sigma \sqrt{h}$. In the limit

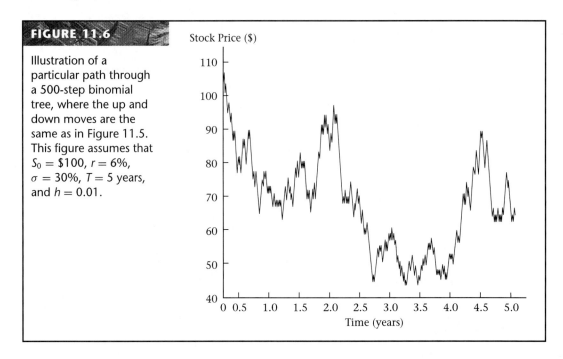

FIGURE 11.6

Illustration of a particular path through a 500-step binomial tree, where the up and down moves are the same as in Figure 11.5. This figure assumes that $S_0 = \$100$, $r = 6\%$, $\sigma = 30\%$, $T = 5$ years, and $h = 0.01$.

(as $n \to \infty$ or $h \to 0$), the sum of binomial random variables is normally distributed. Thus, continuously compounded returns in a binomial tree are (approximately) normally distributed, which means that the stock is lognormally distributed. We defer a more complete discussion of this to Chapters 18 and 20, but we can see with an example how it works.

The binomial model implicitly assigns probabilities to the various nodes. Figure 11.7 depicts the construction of a tree for three binomial periods, along with the risk-neutral probability of reaching each final period node. There is only one path—sequence of up and down moves—reaching the top or bottom node (uuu or ddd), but there are three paths reaching each intermediate node. For example, the first node below the top (S_0u^2d) can be reached by the sequences uud, udu, or duu. Thus, there are more paths that reach the intermediate nodes than the extreme nodes.

We can take the probabilities and outcomes from the binomial tree and plot them against a lognormal distribution with the same parameters. Figure 11.8 compares a three-period binomial approximation with a lognormal distribution assuming that the initial stock price is $100, volatility is 30%, the expected return on the stock is 10%, and the time horizon is 1 year. Because we need different scales for the discrete and continuous distributions, lognormal probabilities are graphed on the left vertical axis and binomial probabilities on the right vertical axis.

Suppose that a binomial tree has n periods and the risk-neutral probability of an up move is p^*. To reach the top node, we must go up n times in a row, which occurs with a probability of $(p^*)^n$. The price at the top node is Su^n. There is only one path through

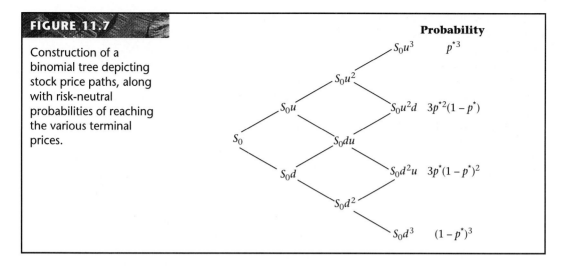

FIGURE 11.7

Construction of a binomial tree depicting stock price paths, along with risk-neutral probabilities of reaching the various terminal prices.

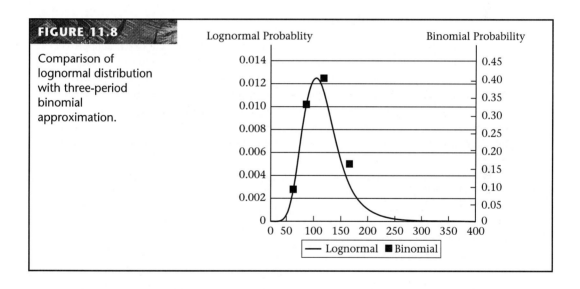

FIGURE 11.8

Comparison of lognormal distribution with three-period binomial approximation.

the tree by which we can reach the top node. To reach the first node below the top node, we must go up $n - 1$ times and down once, for a probability of $(p^*)^{n-1} \times (1 - p^*)$. The price at that node is $Su^{n-1}d$. Since the single down move can occur in any of the n periods, there are n ways this can happen. The probability of reaching the ith node below the top is $(p^*)^{n-i} \times (1 - p^*)^i$. The price at this node is $Su^{n-i}d^i$. The number of ways to reach this node is

$$\text{Number of ways to reach } i^{th} \text{ node} = \frac{n!}{(n - i)! \, i!} = \binom{n}{i}$$

where $n! = n \times (n-1) \times \cdots \times 1$. The expression $\binom{n}{i}$ can be computed in Excel using the combinatorial function, $Combin(n, i)$.

We can construct the implied probability distribution in the binomial tree by plotting the stock price at each final period node, $Su^{n-i}d^i$, against the probability of reaching that node. The probability of reaching any given node is the probability of one path reaching that node times the number of paths reaching that node:

$$\text{Probability of reaching } i^{\text{th}} \text{ node} = p^{*n-i}(1-p^*)^i \frac{n!}{(n-i)! \, i!} \qquad (11.17)$$

Figure 11.9 compares the probability distribution for a 25-period binomial tree with the corresponding lognormal distribution. The two distributions appear close; as a practical matter, a 25-period approximation works fairly well for an option expiring in a few months.

Figures 11.8 and 11.9 show you what the lognormal distribution for the stock price looks like. The stock price is positive, and the distribution is skewed to the right; that is, there is a chance of extremely high stock prices.

Alternative Binomial Trees

There are other ways besides equation (11.16) to construct a binomial tree that approximates a lognormal distribution. An acceptable tree must match the standard deviation of the continuously compounded return on the asset and must generate an appropriate distribution as the length of the binomial period, h, goes to 0. Different methods of constructing the binomial tree will result in different u and d stock movements. No matter how we construct the tree, however, we use equation (10.5) to determine the risk-neutral probability and equation (10.6) to determine the option value.

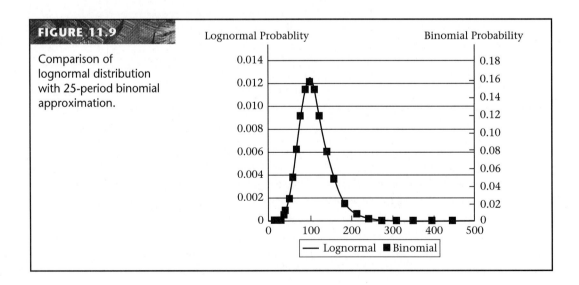

FIGURE 11.9

Comparison of lognormal distribution with 25-period binomial approximation.

The Cox-Ross-Rubinstein binomial tree   The best-known way to construct a binomial tree is that in Cox et al. (1979), in which the tree is constructed as

$$u = e^{\sigma\sqrt{h}}$$
$$d = e^{-\sigma\sqrt{h}}$$

(11.18)

The Cox-Ross-Rubinstein approach is often used in practice. A problem with this approach, however, is that if h is large or σ is small, it is possible that $e^{rh} > e^{\sigma\sqrt{h}}$, in which case the binomial tree violates the restriction in equation (10.4). In real applications h would be small, so this problem does not occur. In any event, the tree based on the forward price never violates equation (10.4).

The lognormal tree   Another alternative is to construct the tree using

$$u = e^{(r-\delta-0.5\sigma^2)h+\sigma\sqrt{h}}$$
$$d = e^{(r-\delta-0.5\sigma^2)h-\sigma\sqrt{h}}$$

(11.19)

This procedure for generating a tree has a very natural motivation that we will understand when we discuss lognormality in Chapter 18. You will find in computing equation (10.5) that the risk-neutral probability of an up-move is generally about 0.5 for this tree.

Notice that for all different ways to construct a binomial tree, up and down movements are generated by the term $\pm\sigma\sqrt{h}$.

Although the three different binomial models give different option prices for finite n, as $n \to \infty$ all three binomial trees approach the same price.

Is the Binomial Model Realistic?

Any option pricing model relies on an assumption about the behavior of stock prices. As we have seen in this section, the binomial model is a form of the random walk model, adapted to modeling stock prices. The lognormal random walk model in this section assumes, among other things, that volatility is constant, that "large" stock price movements do not occur, and that returns are independent over time. All of these assumptions appear to be violated in the data.

We will discuss the behavior of volatility in Chapters 18 and 24. However, there is evidence that volatility changes over time (see Bollerslev et al., 1994). It also appears that on occasion stocks move by a large amount. The binomial model has the property that stock price movements become smaller as the period length, h, becomes smaller. Occasional large price movements—"jumps"— are therefore a feature of the data inconsistent with the binomial model. We will also discuss such moves in Chapters 19 and 21. Finally, there is some evidence that stock returns are correlated across time, with positive correlations at the short to medium term and negative correlation at long horizons (see Campbell et al., 1997b, Chapter 2).

The random walk model is a useful starting point for thinking about stock price behavior, and it is widely used because of its elegant simplicity. However, it is not sacrosanct.

11.4 ESTIMATING VOLATILITY

In practice we need to figure out what parameters to use in the binomial model. The most important decision is the value we assign to σ, which we cannot observe directly. One possibility is to measure σ by computing the standard deviation of continuously compounded historical returns. Volatility computed from historical stock returns is **historical volatility.**

Table 11.1 lists 13 weeks of Wednesday closing prices for the S&P 500 composite index and for IBM, along with the standard deviation of the continuously compounded returns, computed using the *StDev* function in Excel.[3]

TABLE 11.1					Weekly prices and continuously compounded returns for the S&P 500 index and IBM, from 3/5/97 to 5/28/97.

Date	S&P 500		IBM	
	Price	$ln(S_t/S_{t-1})$	Price	$ln(S_t/S_{t-1})$
3/5/97	801.99	—	100.88	—
3/12/97	804.26	0.0028	98.75	−0.0213
3/19/97	785.77	−0.0233	96.75	−0.0205
3/26/97	790.50	0.0060	94.25	−0.0262
4/2/97	750.11	−0.0524	92.00	−0.0242
4/9/97	760.60	0.0139	98.00	0.0632
4/16/97	763.53	0.0038	98.25	0.0025
4/23/97	773.64	0.0132	115.13	0.1585
4/30/97	801.34	0.0352	121.50	0.0539
5/7/97	815.62	0.0177	115.50	−0.0506
5/14/97	836.04	0.0247	115.88	0.0033
5/21/97	839.35	0.0040	120.38	0.0381
5/28/97	847.21	0.0093	125.88	0.0447
Std. Deviation		0.0228	—	0.0573
Std. Deviation $\times \sqrt{52}$		0.1646	—	0.4132

....

[3]We use weekly rather than daily data because computing daily statistics is complicated by weekends and holidays. In theory the standard deviation over the 3 days from Friday to Monday should be greater than over the 1 day from Monday to Tuesday. Using weekly data avoids this kind of complication. Further, using Wednesdays avoids most holidays.

Over the 13-week period in the table, the weekly standard deviation was 0.0228 and 0.0573 for the S&P 500 index and IBM, respectively. These are weekly standard deviations since they are computed from weekly returns; they therefore measure the variability in weekly returns. We obtain annualized standard deviations by multiplying the weekly standard deviations by $\sqrt{52}$, giving annual standard deviations of 16.46% for the S&P 500 index and 41.32% for IBM.

We can now use these annualized standard deviations to construct binomial trees with the binomial period, h, set to whatever is appropriate. Don't be misled by the fact that the standard deviations were estimated with weekly data. Once we annualize the estimated standard deviations by multiplying by $\sqrt{52}$, we can then multiply again by $\sqrt{h}$ to adapt the annual standard deviation to any size binomial step.

The procedure outlined above is a reasonable way to estimate volatility when continuously compounded returns are independent and identically distributed, as in the logarithmic random walk model in Section 11.3. However, if returns are not independent—as with some commodities, for example—volatility estimation becomes more complicated. If a high price of oil today leads to decreased demand and increased supply, we would expect prices in the future to come down. In this case, the volatility over T years will be less than $\sigma \sqrt{T}$, reflecting the tendency of prices to revert from extreme values. Extra care is required with volatility if the random walk model is not a plausible economic model of the asset's price behavior.

11.5 STOCKS PAYING DISCRETE DIVIDENDS

Although it may be reasonable to assume that a stock index pays dividends continuously, individual stocks pay dividends in discrete lumps, quarterly or annually. In addition, over short horizons it is frequently possible to predict the amount of the dividend. How should we price an option when the stock will pay a known dollar dividend during the life of the option? The procedure we have already developed for creating a binomial tree can accommodate this case. However, we will also discuss a preferable alternative due to Schroder (1988).

Modeling Discrete Dividends

When no dividend will be paid between time t and $t + h$, we create the binomial tree as in Chapter 10. Suppose that a dividend will be paid between times t and $t + h$ and that its future value at time $t + h$ is D. The time t forward price for delivery at $t + h$ is then

$$F_{t,t+h} = S_t e^{rh} - D$$

Since the stock price at time $t + h$ will be ex-dividend, we create the up and down moves based on the ex-dividend stock price:

$$\begin{aligned} S_t^u &= \left(S_t e^{rh} - D \right) e^{\sigma \sqrt{h}} \\ S_t^d &= \left(S_t e^{rh} - D \right) e^{-\sigma \sqrt{h}} \end{aligned} \tag{11.20}$$

How does option replication work when a dividend is imminent? When a dividend is paid, we have to account for the fact that the stock earns the dividend. Thus, we have

$$\left(S_t^u + D\right) \Delta + e^{rh} B = C_u$$
$$\left(S_t^d + D\right) \Delta + e^{rh} B = C_d$$

The solution is

$$\Delta = \frac{C_u - C_d}{S_t^u - S_t^d}$$

$$B = e^{-rh} \left[\frac{S_t^u C_d - S_t^d C_u}{S_t^u - S_t^d} \right] - \Delta D e^{-rh}$$

Because the dividend is known, we decrease the bond position by the present value of the certain dividend. (When the dividend is proportional to the stock price, as with a stock index, we reduce the stock position, equation (10.1).) The expression for the option price is given by equation (10.15).

Problems with the Discrete Dividend Tree

The practical problem with this procedure is that the tree does not completely recombine after a discrete dividend. In all previous cases we have examined, we reached the same price after a given number of up and down movements, regardless of the order of the movements.

Figure 11.10, in which a dividend with a period-2 value of $5 is paid between periods 1 and 2, demonstrates that with a discrete dividend, the order of up and down movements affects the price. In the third binomial period there are six rather than four possible stock prices.

To see how the tree is constructed, period-1 prices are

$$\$41 e^{0.08 \times 1/3 + 0.3 \times \sqrt{1/3}} = \$50.071$$
$$\$41 e^{0.08 \times 1/3 - 0.3 \times \sqrt{1/3}} = \$35.411$$

The period-2 prices from the $50.071 node are

$$(\$50.071 e^{0.08 \times 1/3} - 5) \times e^{0.3 \times \sqrt{1/3}} = \$55.203$$
$$(\$50.071 e^{0.08 \times 1/3} - 5) \times e^{-0.3 \times \sqrt{1/3}} = \$39.041$$

Repeating this procedure for the node $S = \$35.411$ gives prices of $37.300 and $26.380. You can see that there are now four prices instead of three after two binomial steps: The ud and du nodes do not recombine. There are six distinct prices in the final period as each set of ex-dividend prices generates a distinct tree (three prices arise from the top two prices in period 2 and three prices arise from the bottom two prices in period 2). Each discrete dividend causes the tree to bifurcate.

There is also a conceptual problem with equation (11.20). Since the amount of the dividend is fixed, the stock price could in principle become negative if there have been large downward moves in the stock prior to the dividend.

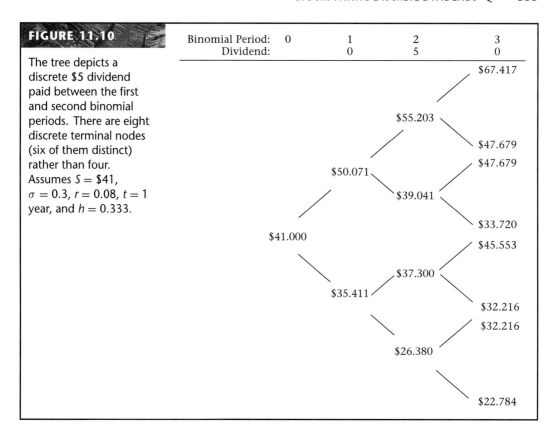

FIGURE 11.10

The tree depicts a discrete $5 dividend paid between the first and second binomial periods. There are eight discrete terminal nodes (six of them distinct) rather than four. Assumes $S = \$41$, $\sigma = 0.3$, $r = 0.08$, $t = 1$ year, and $h = 0.333$.

Binomial Period:	0	1	2	3
Dividend:		0	5	0

$67.417

$55.203

$47.679

$47.679

$50.071

$39.041

$33.720

$41.000

$45.553

$37.300

$35.411

$32.216

$32.216

$26.380

$22.784

This example demonstrates that handling fixed dividends requires care. We now turn to a method that is computationally easier than constructing a tree using equation (11.20) and that will not generate negative stock prices.

A Binomial Tree Using the Prepaid Forward

Schroder (1988) presents an elegant method of constructing a tree for a dividend-paying stock that solves both problems encountered with the method in Figure 11.10. The key insight for this method is that if we know for certain that a stock will pay a fixed dividend, then we can view the stock price as being the sum of two components: The dividend, which is like a zero-coupon bond with zero volatility, and the present value of the ex-dividend value of the stock—in other words, the prepaid forward price. Since the dividend is known, all volatility is attributed to the prepaid forward component of the stock price.

Suppose we know that a stock will pay a dividend D at time $T_D < T$, where T is the expiration date of the option. Then we base stock price movements on the prepaid forward price, $F_{t,T}^P = S_t - De^{-r(T_D-t)}$. The one-period forward price for the prepaid forward is of course $F_{t,t+h} = F_{t,T}^P e^{rh}$. As before, this gives us up and down movements of

$$u = e^{rh+\sigma\sqrt{h}} \qquad d = e^{rh-\sigma\sqrt{h}}$$

However, the actual stock price at each node is given by $S_t = F_{t,T}^P + De^{-r(T_D-t)}$.

Figure 11.11 shows the construction of the binomial tree for this case. Both the observed stock price and the stock price less the present value of dividends (the prepaid forward price) are included in the figure. Note that the volatility is 0.3392 rather than 0.3 as in Figure 10.5. The reason for this difference is that the random walk is assumed to apply to the prepaid forward price. If the actual stock price is observed to have a volatility of 30%, then the prepaid forward price, which is less than the stock price, must have a greater volatility. We use the approximate correction

$$\sigma_F = \sigma_S \times \frac{S}{F^P}$$

$$= 0.3 \times \frac{\$41}{\$36.26} = 0.3392$$

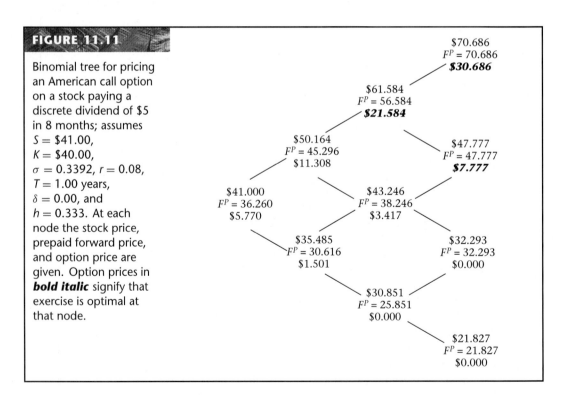

FIGURE 11.11

Binomial tree for pricing an American call option on a stock paying a discrete dividend of $5 in 8 months; assumes $S = \$41.00$, $K = \$40.00$, $\sigma = 0.3392$, $r = 0.08$, $T = 1.00$ years, $\delta = 0.00$, and $h = 0.333$. At each node the stock price, prepaid forward price, and option price are given. Option prices in **bold italic** signify that exercise is optimal at that node.

$70.686
$F^P = 70.686$
$30.686

$61.584
$F^P = 56.584$
$21.584

$50.164
$F^P = 45.296$
$11.308

$47.777
$F^P = 47.777$
$7.777

$41.000
$F^P = 36.260$
$5.770

$43.246
$F^P = 38.246$
$3.417

$35.485
$F^P = 30.616$
$1.501

$32.293
$F^P = 32.293$
$0.000

$30.851
$F^P = 25.851$
$0.000

$21.827
$F^P = 21.827$
$0.000

CHAPTER SUMMARY

Both call and put options may be rationally exercised prior to expiration. The early-exercise decision weighs three considerations: Dividends on the underlying asset, interest on the strike price, and the insurance value of keeping the option alive. Calls will be early-exercised in order to capture dividends on the underlying stock; interest and insurance weigh against early exercise. Puts will be early-exercised in order to capture interest on the strike price; dividends and insurance weigh against early exercise. For both calls and puts, the early-exercise criterion becomes less stringent as the option has less time to maturity.

Risk-neutral option valuation is consistent with valuation using more traditional discounted cash flow methods. With risk-neutral pricing it is not necessary to estimate the expected return on the stock in order to price an option. With traditional discounted cash flow methods, the correct discount rate for the option varies along the binomial tree; thus, valuation is considerably more complicated than with risk-neutral pricing.

The binomial model, which approximates the lognormal distribution, is a random walk model adapted to modeling stock prices. The model assumes that the continuously compounded return on the stock follows a random walk. The volatility needed for the binomial model can be estimated by computing the standard deviation of continuously compounded returns and annualizing the result.

The binomial model can be adapted to price options on a stock that pays discrete dividends. Discrete dividends can lead to a nonrecombining binomial tree. If we assume that the prepaid forward price follows a binomial process instead of the stock price, the tree becomes recombining.

FURTHER READING

The binomial model can be used to derive the Black-Scholes model, which we discuss in Chapter 12. The practical importance of risk-neutral pricing will become evident in Chapter 19, when we see that Monte Carlo valuation hinges upon risk-neutral pricing. In that chapter we will also reexamine Figure 11.4 and show how the option price may be computed as an expected value using only stock prices in the final period.

The issue of how the stock price is distributed will also arise frequently in later chapters. Chapter 18 discusses lognormality in more detail and presents evidence that stock prices are not exactly lognormally distributed. Chapter 20 will examine in more detail the question of how the stock price moves, in particular what happens when h gets very small in the binomial model.

We will return to the determinants of early exercise in Chapter 17, when we discuss real options.

The literature on risk-neutral pricing is fairly technical. Cox and Ross (1976) was the first paper to use risk-neutral pricing and Harrison and Kreps (1979) studied the economic underpinnings. Two good treatments of risk-neutral pricing this topic are

Huang and Litzenberger (1988, Chapter 8; their treatment inspired Appendix 11.B) and Baxter and Rennie (1996).

Campbell et al. (1997b) and Cochrane (2001) summarize evidence on the distribution of stock prices. The original Samuelson work on asset prices following a random walk (Samuelson, 1965) remains a classic, modern empirical evidence notwithstanding.

Broadie and Detemple (1996) discuss the computation of American option prices, and also discuss alternative binomial approaches and their relative numerical efficiency.

PROBLEMS

Many (but not all) of these questions can be answered with the help of the *BinomCall* and *BinomPut* functions available on the spreadsheets accompanying this book.

11.1. Consider a one-period binomial model with $h = 1$, where $S = \$100$, $r = 0$, $\sigma = 30\%$, and $\delta = 0.08$. Compute American call option prices for $K = \$70$, $\$80$, $\$90$, and $\$100$.

    a. At which strike(s) does early exercise occur?

    b. Use put-call parity to explain why early exercise does not occur at the higher strikes.

    c. Use put-call parity to explain why early exercise is sure to occur for all lower strikes than that in your answer to (a).

11.2. Repeat Problem 1, only assume that $r = 0.08$. What is the greatest strike price at which early exercise will occur? What condition related to put-call parity is satisfied at this strike price?

11.3. Repeat Problem 1, only assume that $r = 0.08$ and $\delta = 0$. Will early exercise ever occur? Why?

11.4. Consider a one-period binomial model with $h = 1$, where $S = \$100$, $r = 0.08$, $\sigma = 30\%$, and $\delta = 0$. Compute American put option prices for $K = \$100$, $\$110$, $\$120$, and $\$130$.

    a. At which strike(s) does early exercise occur?

    b. Use put-call parity to explain why early exercise does not occur at the other strikes.

    c. Use put-call parity to explain why early exercise is sure to occur for all strikes greater than that in your answer to (a).

11.5. Repeat Problem 4, only set $\delta = 0.08$. What is the lowest strike price at which early exercise will occur? What condition related to put-call parity is satisfied at this strike price?

11.6. Repeat Problem 4, only set $r = 0$ and $\delta = 0.08$. What is the lowest strike price (if there is one) at which early exercise will occur? If early exercise never occurs, explain why not.

For the following problems, note that the *BinomCall* and *BinomPut* functions are array functions that return the option delta (Δ) as well as the price. If you know Δ, you can compute B as $C - S\Delta$.

11.7. Let $S = \$100$, $K = \$100$, $\sigma = 30\%$, $r = 0.08$, $t = 1$, and $\delta = 0$. Let $n = 10$. Suppose the stock has an expected return of 15%.

> **a.** What is the expected return on a European call option? A European put option?
>
> **b.** What happens to the expected return if you increase the volatility to 50%?

11.8. Let $S = \$100$, $\sigma = 30\%$, $r = 0.08$, $t = 1$, and $\delta = 0$. Suppose the true expected return on the stock is 15%. Set $n = 10$. Compute European call prices, Δ, and B for strikes of $70, \$80, \$90, \$100, \$110, \$120$, and $\$130$. For each strike, compute the expected return on the option. What effect does the strike have on the option's expected return?

11.9. Repeat the previous problem, except that for each strike price, compute the expected return on the option for times to expiration of 3 months, 6 months, 1 year, and 2 years. What effect does time to maturity have on the option's expected return?

11.10. Let $S = \$100$, $\sigma = 30\%$, $r = 0.08$, $t = 1$, and $\delta = 0$. Suppose the true expected return on the stock is 15%. Set $n = 10$. Compute European put prices, Δ, and B for strikes of $70, \$80, \$90, \$100, \$110, \$120$, and $\$130$. For each strike, compute the expected return on the option. What effect does the strike have on the option's expected return?

11.11. Repeat the previous problem, except that for each strike price, compute the expected return on the option for times to expiration of 3 months, 6 months, 1 year, and 2 years. What effect does time to maturity have on the option's expected return?

11.12. Let $S = \$100$, $\sigma = 0.30$, $r = 0.08$, $t = 1$, and $\delta = 0$. Using equation (11.17) to compute the probability of reaching a terminal node and $S u^i d^{n-i}$ to compute the price at that node, plot the risk-neutral distribution of year-1 stock prices as in Figures 11.8 and 11.9 for $n = 3$ and $n = 10$.

11.13. Repeat the previous problem for $n = 50$. What is the risk-neutral probability that $S_1 < \$80$? $S_1 > \$120$?

11.14. We saw in Section 10.1 that the undiscounted risk-neutral expected stock price equals the forward price. We will verify this using the binomial tree in Figure 11.4.

> **a.** Using $S = \$100$, $r = 0.08$, and $\delta = 0$, what are the 4-month, 8-month, and 1-year forward prices?

b. Verify your answers in (a) by computing the risk-neutral expected stock price in the first, second, and third binomial period. Use equation (11.17) to determine the probability of reaching each node.

11.15. Compute the 1-year forward price using the 50-step binomial tree in Problem 13.

11.16. Suppose $S = \$100$, $K = \$95$, $r = 8\%$ (continuously compounded), $t = 1$, $\sigma = 30\%$, and $\delta = 5\%$. Explicitly construct an 8-period binomial tree using the Cox-Ross-Rubinstein expressions for u and d:

$$u = e^{\sigma\sqrt{h}} \qquad d = e^{-\sigma\sqrt{h}}$$

Compute the prices of European and American calls and puts.

11.17. Suppose $S = \$100$, $K = \$95$, $r = 8\%$ (continuously compounded), $t = 1$, $\sigma = 30\%$, and $\delta = 5\%$. Explicitly construct an 8-period binomial tree using the lognormal expressions for u and d:

$$u = e^{(r-\delta-.5\sigma^2)h+\sigma\sqrt{h}} \qquad d = e^{(r-\delta-.5\sigma^2)h-\sigma\sqrt{h}}$$

Compute the prices of European and American calls and puts.

11.18. Obtain at least 5 years' worth of daily or weekly stock price data for a stock of your choice.

a. Compute annual volatility using all the data.

b. Compute annual volatility for each calendar year in your data. How does volatility vary over time?

c. Compute annual volatility for the first and second half of each year in your data. How much variation is there in your estimate?

11.19. Obtain at least 5 years of daily data for at least 3 stocks and, if you can, one currency. Estimate annual volatility for each year for each asset in your data. What do you observe about the pattern of historical volatility over time? Does historical volatility move in tandem for different assets?

11.20. Suppose that $S = \$50$, $K = \$45$, $\sigma = 0.30$, $r = 0.08$, and $t = 1$. The stock will pay a $4 dividend in exactly 3 months. Compute the price of European and American call options using a 4-step binomial tree.

APPENDIX 11.A: PRICING OPTIONS WITH TRUE PROBABILITIES

In this appendix we demonstrate algebraically that computing the option price in a consistent way using α as the expected return on the stock gives the correct option price. Using the definition of γ, equation (11.6), we can rewrite equation (11.7) as

$$(\Delta S + B)\left(\frac{1}{e^{\alpha h}\Delta S + e^{rh}B}\left[\frac{e^{rh}-d}{u-d}C_u + \frac{u-e^{rh}}{u-d}C_d + \frac{e^{\alpha h}-e^{rh}}{u-d}(C_u-C_d)\right]\right)$$

Since $\Delta S + B$ is the call price, we need only show that the expression in large parentheses is equal to one. From the definitions of Δ and B we have

$$\frac{e^{rh} - d}{u - d} C_u + \frac{u - e^{rh}}{u - d} C_d = e^{rh}(\Delta S + B)$$

We can rewrite (11.4) as

$$(\Delta S + B)\left(\frac{1}{e^{\alpha h}\Delta S + e^{rh}B}\left[e^{rh}(\Delta S + B) + (e^{\alpha h} - e^{rh})\Delta S\right]\right) = \Delta S + B$$

This follows since the expression in large parentheses equals one.

APPENDIX 11.B: WHY DOES RISK-NEUTRAL PRICING WORK?

There is a large and highly technical literature on risk-neutral pricing. The underlying economic idea is fairly easy to understand, however.

Utility-Based Valuation

The starting point is that the well-being of investors is not measured in dollars, but in *utility*. Utility is a measure of satisfaction. Economists say that investors exhibit *declining marginal utility*: Starting from a given level of wealth, the utility gained from adding $1 to wealth is less than the utility lost from taking $1 away from wealth. Thus, we expect that more dollars will make an investor happier, but that if we keep adding dollars, each additional dollar will make the investor less happy than the previous dollars.

Declining marginal utility implies that investors are risk-averse, which means that an investor will prefer a safer investment to a riskier investment that has the same expected return. Since losses are more costly than gains are beneficial, a risk-averse investor will avoid a fair bet, which by definition has equal expected gains and losses.[4]

To illustrate risk-neutral pricing, we imagine a world where there are two assets, a risky stock and a risk-free bond. Investors are risk-averse. Suppose the economy in one period will be in one of two states, a high state and a low state. How do we value assets in such a world? We need to know three things:

1. What utility value, expressed in terms of dollars today, does an investor attach to the marginal dollar received in each state in the future? Denote the values of $1 received

---

[4]This is an example of *Jensen's Inequality* (see Appendix C at the end of this book). A risk-averse investor has a concave utility function, which implies that

$$E[U(x)] < U[E(x)]$$

The expected utility associated with a gamble, $E[U(x)]$, is less than the utility from receiving the expected value of the gamble for sure, $U[E(x)]$.

in the high and low states as U_H and U_L, respectively.[5] Because the investor is risk-averse, \$1 received in the high state is worth less than \$1 received in the low state, hence, $U_H < U_L$.

2. How many dollars will an asset pay in each state? Denote the payoffs to the risky stock in each state C_H and C_L.

3. What is the probability of each state occurring? Denote the probability of the high state as p.

We begin by defining a state price as the price of a security that pays \$1 only when a particular state occurs. Let Q_H be the price of a security that pays \$1 when the high state occurs, and Q_L the price of a security paying \$1 when the low state occurs.[6] Since U_H and U_L are the value today of \$1 in each state, the price we would pay is just the value times the probability that state is reached:

$$Q_H = p \times U_H$$
$$Q_L = (1 - p) \times U_L \tag{11.21}$$

Since there are only two possible states, we can value any future cash flow using these state prices.

The price of the risky stock, S_0 is

$$\text{Price of stock} = Q_H \times C_H + Q_L \times C_L \tag{11.22}$$

Since the risk-free bond pays \$1 in each state, we have

$$\text{Price of bond} = Q_H \times 1 + Q_L \times 1 \tag{11.23}$$

We can calculate rates of return by dividing expected cash flows by the price. Thus, the risk-free rate is

$$1 + r = \frac{1}{\text{Price of bond}}$$
$$= \frac{1}{Q_H + Q_L} \tag{11.24}$$

The expected return on the stock is

$$1 + \alpha = \frac{p \times C_H + (1 - p)C_L}{\text{Price of stock}}$$
$$= \frac{p \times C_H + (1 - p)C_L}{Q_H \times C_H + Q_L \times C_L} \tag{11.25}$$

---

[5]Technically U_H and U_L are ratios of marginal utilities, discounted by the rate of time preference. However, you can think of them as simply converting future dollars in a particular state into dollars today.

[6]These are often called "Arrow-Debreu" securities, named after Nobel-prize–winning economists Kenneth Arrow and Gerard Debreu.

Standard Discounted Cash Flow

The standard discounted cash flow calculation entails computing the security price by discounting the expected cash flow at the expected rate of return. In the case of the stock, this gives us

$$\frac{p \times C_H + (1-p)C_L}{1+\alpha} = \text{Price of stock}$$

This is simply a rewriting of equation (11.25); hence, it is obviously correct. Similarly, the bond price is

$$\frac{1}{1+r} = \text{Price of bond}$$

Risk-Neutral Pricing

The point of risk-neutral pricing is to sidestep the utility calculations above. We are looking for probabilities such that when we use those probabilities to compute expected cash flows *without* explicit utility adjustments, and discount that expectation at the risk-free rate, then we will get the correct answer.

The trick is the following: Instead of utility-weighting the cash flows and computing expectations, *we utility-weight the probabilities*, creating new "risk-neutral" probabilities. Now we will see how to perform risk-neutral pricing in this context. Use the state prices in equation (11.21) to define the risk-neutral probability of the high state, p^*, as

$$p^* = \frac{p \times U_H}{p \times U_H + (1-p) \times U_L} = \frac{Q_H}{Q_H + Q_L}$$

Now we compute the stock price by using the risk-neutral probabilities to compute expected cash flow, and then discounting at the risk-free rate. We have

$$\frac{p^* C_H + (1-p^*)C_L}{1+r} = \frac{\frac{Q_H}{Q_H+Q_L}C_H + \frac{Q_L}{Q_H+Q_L}C_L}{1+r}$$

$$= \frac{Q_H C_H + Q_L C_L}{(Q_H + Q_L)(1+r)}$$

$$= Q_H C_H + Q_L C_L$$

which is the price of stock, from equation (11.22). This shows that we can construct risk-neutral probabilities and use them to price risky assets.

Example

Table 11.2 contains assumptions for a numerical example.

State prices Using equation 11.21, the state prices are $Q_H = 0.52 \times \$0.87 = \$0.4524$, and $Q_L = 0.48 \times \$0.98 = \$0.4704$.

	High State	**Low State**

TABLE 11.2 Probabilities, utility weights, and equity cash flows in high and low states of the economy.

	High State	**Low State**
Cash Flow to Risk-Free Bond	$C_H = \$1$	$C_L = \$1$
Cash Flow to Stock	$C_H = \$180$	$C_L = \$30$
Probability	$p = 0.52$	$p = 0.48$
Value of $1	$U_H = \$0.87$	$U_L = \$0.98$

Valuing the risk-free bond   The risk-free bond pays $1 in each state. Thus, using equation (11.23) the risk-free bond price, B_0, is

$$B_0 = Q_H + Q_L = \$0.4524 + \$0.4704 = \$0.9228 \qquad (11.26)$$

The risk-free rate is

$$r = \frac{1}{0.9228} - 1 = 8.366\%$$

Valuing the risky stock using real probabilities   Using equation (11.22) the price of the stock is

$$S_0 = 0.4524 \times \$180 + 0.4704 \times \$30 = \$95.544 \qquad (11.27)$$

The expected cash flow on the stock in one period is

$$E(S_1) = 0.52 \times \$180 + 0.48 \times \$30 = \$108$$

The expected return on the stock is therefore

$$\alpha = \frac{\$108}{\$95.544} - 1 = 13.037\%$$

By definition, if we discount $E(S_1)$ at the rate 13.037%, we will get the price $95.544.

Risk-neutral valuation of the stock   The risk-neutral probability is

$$p^* = \frac{\$0.4524}{\$0.4524 + \$0.4704}$$

$$= 49.025\%$$

Now we can value the stock using p^* instead of the true probabilities, and discount at the risk-free rate:

$$S_0 = \frac{0.49025 \times \$180 + (1 - 0.49025) \times \$30}{1.08366}$$

$$= \$95.544$$

We can also verify that a call option on the stock can be valued using risk-neutral pricing. Suppose the call has a strike of $130. Then the value computed using true probabilities and utility weights is

$$C = 0.52 \times 0.87 \times max(0, \$180 - \$130) + 0.48 \times 0.98 \times max(0, \$30 - \$130)$$

$$= \$22.62$$

Using risk-neutral pricing, we obtain

$$C = \frac{\left[0.49025 \times max(0, \$180 - \$130) + (1 - 0.49025) \times max(0, \$30 - \$130) \right]}{1.08366}$$

$$= \$22.62$$

Why Risk-Neutral Pricing Works

Risk-neutral pricing works in the above example because the same utility weights and probabilities are used to value both the stock and risk-free bond. As long as this is true, risk-neutral pricing formulas can be obtained simply by rewriting the more complicated valuation formulas that take account of utility.

A basic result from portfolio theory states that as long as investors are optimally choosing their portfolios, they will use the same utility weights for an additional dollar of investment in all assets. Thus, in an economy with well-functioning capital markets, risk-neutral pricing is possible for derivatives on traded assets.

When would risk-neutral pricing not work? Suppose you have an asset you cannot trade or hedge, or you have a nontradable asset with cash flows that cannot be replicated by the cash flows of traded assets. If you cannot trade or offset the risk of the asset, then there is no guarantee that the marginal utility you use to value payoffs from this asset in a given state will be the same as for other assets. In other words, U_H and U_L will differ across assets. If the same U_H and U_L are not used to value the stock and bond, the calculations in this appendix fail. Valuing the nontradable stream of cash flows then requires computing the utility value of the payoffs. The point of risk-neutral pricing is to avoid having to do this.

Chapter 12

The Black-Scholes Formula

In 1973 Fischer Black and Myron Scholes (Black and Scholes 1973) published a formula—the Black-Scholes formula—for computing the theoretical price of a European call option on a stock. Their paper, coupled with closely related work by Robert Merton, revolutionized both the theory and practice of finance. The history of the Black-Scholes formula is discussed in the box on page 366.

In this chapter we present the Black-Scholes formula for pricing European options, explain how it is used for different underlying assets, and discuss the so-called option Greeks—delta, gamma, theta, vega, and rho—which measure the behavior of the option price when inputs to the formula change. We also show how observed option prices can be used to infer the market's estimate of volatility. Finally, while there is in general no simple formula comparable to Black-Scholes for valuing options that may be exercised early, perpetual options are an exception. We present the pricing formulas for perpetual American calls and puts.

12.1 INTRODUCTION TO THE BLACK-SCHOLES FORMULA

To introduce the Black-Scholes formula, we first return to the binomial model, discussed in Chapters 10 and 11. When computing a binomial option price, we can vary the number of binomial steps, holding fixed the time to expiration. Table 12.1 computes binomial call option prices, using the same inputs as in Figure 10.2, and increases the number of steps, n. Changing the number of steps changes the option price, but once the number of steps becomes great enough we appear to approach a limiting value for the price. The last row reports the call option price if we were to use an infinite number of steps. We can't literally have an infinity of steps in a binomial tree, but it is possible to show that as the number of steps approaches infinity, the option price is given by the Black-Scholes formula. Thus, the Black-Scholes formula is a limiting case of the binomial price for a European option.

Call Options

The Black-Scholes formula for a European call option on a stock that pays dividends at the continuous rate δ is

$$C(S, K, \sigma, r, T, \delta) = Se^{-\delta T}N(d_1) - Ke^{-rT}N(d_2) \qquad (12.1)$$

The History of the Black-Scholes Formula

The Black-Scholes formula was first published in the May/June 1973 issue of the *Journal of Political Economy* (*JPE*) (see Black & Scholes 1973). By coincidence, the Chicago Board Options Exchange (CBOE) opened at almost the same time, on April 26, 1973. Initially, the exchange traded call options on just 16 stocks. Puts did not trade until 1977. In 2000, by contrast, the CBOE traded both calls and puts on over 1200 stocks.

Fischer Black told the story of the formula in Black (1989). He and Myron Scholes started working on the option-pricing problem in 1969, when Black was an independent consultant in Boston and Scholes an Assistant Professor at MIT. While working on the problem, they had extensive discussions with Robert Merton of MIT, who was also working on option pricing.

The first version of their paper was dated October 1970 and was rejected for publication by the *JPE* and subsequently by another prominent journal. However, in 1971, Eugene Fama and Merton Miller of the University of Chicago, recognizing the importance of their work, interceded on their behalf with the editors of the *JPE*. Later in 1973 Robert Merton published an important and wide-ranging follow-up paper (Merton, 1973b), which, among other contributions, established the standard no-arbitrage restrictions on option prices discussed in Chapter 9, significantly generalized the Black-Scholes formula and their derivation of the model, and provided formulas for pricing perpetual American puts and down-and-out calls.

In 1997, Robert Merton and Myron Scholes won the Nobel Prize in Economics for their work on option pricing. Fischer Black was ineligible for the Prize, having died in 1995 at the age of 57.

TABLE 12.1 Binomial option prices for different numbers of binomial steps. As in Figure 10.2, all calculations assume that the stock price $S = \$41$, the strike price $K = \$40$, volatility $\sigma = 0.30$, risk-free rate $r = 0.08$, time to expiration $T = 1$, and dividend yield $\delta = 0$.

Number of Steps (*n*)	Binomial Call Price ($)
1	7.839
4	7.160
10	7.065
50	6.969
100	6.966
500	6.960
∞	6.961

where

$$d_1 = \frac{ln(S/K) + (r - \delta + \frac{1}{2}\sigma^2)T}{\sigma\sqrt{T}} \tag{12.2a}$$

$$d_2 = d_1 - \sigma\sqrt{T} \tag{12.2b}$$

As with the binomial model, there are six inputs to the Black-Scholes formula: S, the current price of the stock; K, the strike price of the option; σ, the volatility of the stock; r, the continuously compounded risk-free interest rate; T, the time to expiration; and δ, the dividend yield on the stock.

$N(x)$ in the Black-Scholes formula is the cumulative normal distribution function, which is the probability that a number randomly drawn from a standard normal distribution (i.e., a normal distribution with mean 0 and variance 1) will be less than x. Most spreadsheets have a built-in function for computing $N(x)$. In Excel, the function is "NormSDist." The normal and cumulative normal distributions are illustrated in Figure 18.2 on page 567.

Two of the inputs (K and T) describe characteristics of the option contract. The others describe the stock (S, σ, and δ) and the discount rate for a risk-free investment (r). All of the inputs are self-explanatory with the exception of volatility, which we discussed in Section 11.4. Volatility is the standard deviation of the rate of return on the stock—a measure of the uncertainty about the future return on the stock.

It is important to be clear about units in which inputs are expressed. Several of the inputs in equation (12.1) are expressed per unit time: The interest rate, volatility, and dividend yield are typically expressed on an annual basis. These inputs are all multiplied by time: In equation (12.1), the interest rate, dividend, and volatility appear as $r \times T$, $\delta \times T$, and $\sigma^2 \times T$ (or equivalently, $\sigma \times \sqrt{T}$). Thus, when we enter inputs into the formula, the specific time unit we use is arbitrary as long as we are consistent. If time is measured in years, then r, δ, and σ should be annual. If time is measured in days, then we need to use the daily equivalent of r, σ, and δ, and so forth. We will always assume inputs are per year unless we state otherwise.

Example 12.1 Let $S = \$41$, $K = \$40$, $\sigma = 0.3$, $r = 8\%$, $T = 0.25$ (3 months), and $\delta = 0$. Computing the Black-Scholes call price, we obtain[1]

$$\$41 \times e^{-0 \times 0.25} \times N\left(\frac{ln(\frac{41}{40}) + (0.08 - 0 + \frac{0.3^2}{2}) \times 0.25}{0.3\sqrt{0.25}}\right)$$

$$- \$40 \times e^{-0.08 \times 0.25} \times N\left(\frac{ln(\frac{41}{40}) + (0.08 - 0 - \frac{0.3^2}{2}) \times 0.25}{0.3\sqrt{0.25}}\right) = \$3.399$$

---

[1]The call price here can be computed using the Black-Scholes formula call spreadsheet formula, *BSCall*:

$$BSCall(S, K, \sigma, r, t, \delta) = BSCall(41, 40, 0.08, 0.3, 0.25, 0) = \$3.399$$

There is one input which does *not* appear in the Black-Scholes formula, namely the expected return on the stock. You might guess that stocks with a high beta would have a higher expected return; hence, options on these stocks would have a higher probability of settlement in-the-money. The higher expected return would seem to imply a higher option price. However, as we saw in Section 11.2, a high stock beta implies a high option beta, so the discount rate for the expected payoff to such an option is correspondingly greater. The net result—one of the key insights from the Black-Scholes analysis—is that beta is irrelevant: The larger average payoff to options on high beta stocks is exactly offset by the larger discount rate.

Put Options

The Black-Scholes formula for a European put option is

$$P(S, K, \sigma, r, T, \delta) = Ke^{-rT}N(-d_2) - Se^{-\delta T}N(-d_1) \qquad (12.3)$$

where d_1 and d_2 are given by equations (12.2a) and (12.2b).

Since the Black-Scholes call and put prices, equations (12.1) and (12.3), are for European options, put-call parity must hold:

$$P(S, K, \sigma, r, T, \delta) = C(S, K, \sigma, r, T, \delta) + Ke^{-rT} - Se^{-\delta T} \qquad (12.4)$$

This version of the formula follows from equations (12.1) and (12.3), together with the fact that for any x, $1 - N(x_1) = N(-x)$. (This equation says that the probability of a random draw from the standard normal distribution being above x, $1 - N(x)$, equals the probability of a draw being below $-x$, $N(-x)$.)

Example 12.2 Using the same inputs as in Example 12.1, the put price is $1.607. We can compute the put price in two ways. First, computing it using equation (12.3), we obtain[2]

$$\$40e^{-0.08 \times 0.25} N\left(-\frac{ln(\frac{41}{40}) + (0.08 - 0 - \frac{0.3^2}{2})0.25}{0.3\sqrt{0.25}}\right)$$

$$- \$41e^{-0 \times 0.25} N\left(-\frac{ln(\frac{41}{40}) + (0.08 - 0 + \frac{0.3^2}{2})0.25}{0.3\sqrt{0.25}}\right) = \$1.607$$

Computing the price using put-call parity, equation (12.4), we have

$$P(41, 40, 0.3, 0.08, 0.25, 0) = 3.339 + 40e^{-0.08 \times 0.25} - 41$$

$$= \$1.607$$ ❧

---

[2]The put price here can be computed using the Black-Scholes put spreadsheet formula, *BSPut*:

$$BSPut(S, K, \sigma, r, t, \delta) = BSPut(41, 40, 0.08, 0.3, 0.25, 0) = \$3.399$$

When Is the Black-Scholes Formula Valid?

Derivations of the Black-Scholes formula make a number of assumptions that can be sorted into two groups: Assumptions about how the stock price is distributed, and assumptions about the economic environment. For the version of the formula we have presented, assumptions about the distribution of the stock price include the following:

- Continuously compounded returns on the stock are normally distributed and independent over time. (As discussed in Chapter 11, we assume there are no "jumps" in the stock price.)

- The volatility of continuously compounded returns is known and constant.

- Future dividends are known, either as a dollar amount or as a fixed dividend yield.

Assumptions about the economic environment include these:

- The risk-free rate is known and constant.

- There are no transaction costs or taxes.

- It is possible to short-sell costlessly and to borrow at the risk-free rate.

Many of these assumptions can easily be relaxed. For example, with a small change in the formula, we can permit the volatility and interest rate to vary over time in a known way. In Appendix 10.B we discussed why, even though there are taxes, tax rates do not appear in the binomial formula; the same argument applies to the Black-Scholes formula.

As a practical matter, the first set of assumptions—those about the stock price distribution—are the most crucial. Most academic and practitioner research on option pricing concentrates on relaxing these assumptions. They will also be our focus when we discuss empirical evidence. You should keep in mind that almost *any* valuation procedure, including ordinary discounted cash flow, is based on assumptions that appear strong; the interesting question is how well the procedure works in practice.

12.2 APPLYING THE FORMULA TO OTHER ASSETS

The Black-Scholes formula is often thought of as a formula for pricing European options on stocks. Specifically, equations (12.1) and (12.3) provide the price of a call and put option, respectively, on a stock paying continuous dividends. In practice, we also want to be able to price European options on stocks paying discrete dividends, options on futures, and options on currencies. We have already seen in Chapter 10, Table 10.1, that the binomial model can be adapted to different underlying assets by adjusting the dividend yield. The same adjustments work in the Black-Scholes formula.

We can rewrite d_1 in the Black-Scholes formula, equation (12.2a), as

$$d_1 = \frac{ln(Se^{-\delta t}/Ke^{-rT}) + \frac{1}{2}\sigma^2 T}{\sigma\sqrt{T}}$$

When d_1 is rewritten in this way, it is apparent that the dividend yield enters the formula *only* to discount the stock price, as $Se^{-\delta T}$, and the interest rate enters the formula *only* to discount the strike price, as Ke^{-rT}. Notice also that volatility enters only as $\sigma^2 T$.

The prepaid forward prices for the stock and strike asset are $F^P_{0,T}(S) = Se^{-\delta t}$ and $F^P_{0,T}(K) = Ke^{-rT}$. Then we can write the Black-Scholes formula, equation (12.1), entirely in terms of prepaid forward prices and $\sigma\sqrt{T}$:[3]

$$C(F^P_{0,T}(S), F^P_{0,T}(K), \sigma, T) = F^P_{0,T}(S)N(d_1) - F^P_{0,T}(K)N(d_2) \qquad (12.5)$$

$$d_1 = \frac{ln[F^P_{0,T}(S)/F^P_{0,T}(K)] + \frac{1}{2}\sigma^2 T}{\sigma\sqrt{T}}$$

$$d_2 = d_1 - \sigma\sqrt{T}$$

This version of the formula is interesting because the dividend yield and the interest rate do not appear explicitly; they are implicitly incorporated into the prepaid forward prices.

To price options on underlying assets other than stocks, we can use equation (12.5) in conjunction with the forward price formulas from Chapters 5 and 6. For all of the examples in this chapter, we will have a strike price denominated in cash, so that $F^P_{0,T}(K) = Ke^{-rT}$.

Options on Stocks with Discrete Dividends

When a stock makes discrete dividend payments, the prepaid forward price is

$$F^P_{0,T}(S) = S_0 - PV_{0,T}(Div)$$

where $PV_{0,T}(Div)$ is the present value of dividends payable over the life of the option. Thus, using equation (12.5), we can price a European option with discrete dividends by subtracting the present value of dividends from the stock price, and entering the result into the formula in place of the stock price. The use of the prepaid forward price here should remind you of the approach to pricing options on dividend-paying stocks in Section 11.5.

Example 12.3   Suppose $S = \$41$, $K = \$40$, $\sigma = 0.3$, $r = 8\%$, and $t = 0.25$ (3 months). The stock will pay a \$3 dividend in 1 month, but makes no other payouts over the life of the option (hence, $\delta = 0$). The present value of the dividend is

$$PV(Div) = \$3e^{-0.08 \times 1/12} = \$2.98$$

Setting the stock price in the Black-Scholes formula equal to $\$41 - \$2.98 = \$38.02$, the Black-Scholes call price is \$1.763.   ❦

---

[3]We can also let $V(T) = \sigma\sqrt{T}$ represent total volatility—uncertainty about the relative time-T values of the underlying and strike assets—over the life of the option. The option price can then be written solely in terms of $F^P_{0,T}(S)$, $F^P_{0,T}(K)$, and $V(T)$. This gives us a minimalist version of the Black-Scholes formula: To price an option you need to know the prepaid forward prices of the underlying asset and the strike asset, and the relative volatility of the two.

Compared to the $3.399 price computed in Example 12.1, the dividend reduces the option price by about $1.64, or over half the amount of the dividend. Note that this is the price of a *European* option. An American option might be exercised just prior to the dividend, and hence would have a greater price.

Options on Currencies

We can price an option on a currency by replacing the dividend yield with the foreign interest rate. If the spot exchange rate is x (expressed as domestic currency per unit of foreign currency), and the foreign currency interest rate is r_f, the prepaid forward price for the currency is

$$F_{0,T}^P(x) = x_0 e^{-r_f T}$$

Using equation (12.5), the Black-Scholes formula becomes

$$C(x, K, \sigma, r, T, r_f) = xe^{-r_f T} N(d_1) - Ke^{-rT} N(d_2) \qquad (12.6)$$

$$d_1 = \frac{ln(x/K) + (r - r_f + \frac{1}{2}\sigma^2)T}{\sigma\sqrt{T}}$$

$$d_2 = d_1 - \sigma\sqrt{T}$$

This formula for the price of a European call on currencies is called the "Garman-Kohlhagen" model, after Garman & Kohlhagen (1983).

The price of a European currency put is obtained using parity:

$$P(x, K, \sigma, r, t, r_f) = C(x, K, \sigma, r, t, r_f) + Ke^{-rt} - xe^{-r_f t}$$

Example 12.4 Suppose the spot exchange rate is $x = \$0.92/€$, $K = \$0.9$, $\sigma = 0.10$, $r = 6\%$ (the dollar interest rate), $T = 1$, and $\delta = 3.2\%$ (the euro-denominated interest rate). The price of a dollar-denominated euro call is $0.0606, and the price of a dollar-denominated euro put is $0.0172. ◈

Options on Futures

The prepaid forward price for a futures contract is just the present value of the futures price. Thus, we price a European option on a futures contract by using the futures price as the stock price and setting the dividend yield equal to the risk-free rate. The resulting formula is also known as the **Black formula**:

$$C(F, K, \sigma, r, t, r) = Fe^{-rt} N(d_1) - Ke^{-rt} N(d_2) \qquad (12.7)$$

$$d_1 = \frac{ln(F/K) + \frac{1}{2}\sigma^2 t}{\sigma\sqrt{t}}$$

$$d_2 = d_1 - \sigma\sqrt{t}$$

The put price is obtained using the parity relationship for options on futures:

$$P(F, K, \sigma, r, t, r) = C(F, K, \sigma, r, t, r) + Ke^{-rt} - Fe^{-rt}$$

Example 12.5   Suppose the 1-year futures price for natural gas is \$2.10/MMBtu and the volatility is 0.25. We have $F = \$2.10$, $K = \$2.10$, $\sigma = 0.25$, $r = 0.055$, $T = 1$, and $\delta = 0.055$ (the dividend yield is set to equal the interest rate). The Black-Scholes call price and put price are both \$0.197721.   ❧

12.3 OPTION GREEKS

Option Greeks are formulas that express the change in the option price when an input to the formula changes, taking as fixed all the other inputs.[4] One important use of Greek measures is to assess risk exposure. For example, a market-making bank with a portfolio of options would want to understand its exposure to stock price changes, interest rates, volatility, etc. A portfolio manager wants to know what happens to the value of a portfolio of stock index options if there is a change in the level of the stock index. An options investor would like to know how interest rate changes and volatility changes affect profit and loss.

Keep in mind that the Greek measures by assumption change only *one* input at a time. In real life, we would expect interest rates and the stock prices, for example, to change together. The Greeks just answer the question, what happens when *one and only one* input changes?

The actual formulas for the Greeks appear in Appendix 12.B. Greek measures can be computed for options on any kind of underlying asset, but we will focus here on stock options.

Definition of the Greeks

The units in which changes are measured are a matter of convention. Thus, when we define a Greek measure, we will also provide the assumed unit of change.

Delta (Δ) measures the option price change when the stock price increases by \$1.

Gamma (Γ) measures the change in delta when the stock price increases by \$1.

Vega measures the change in the option price when there is an increase in volatility of one percentage point.[5]

---

[4]The Greek measures discussed here all have corresponding spreadsheet formulas. See Appendix E.

[5]"Vega" is not a Greek letter. "Kappa" and "lambda" are also sometimes used to mean the same thing as "vega."

Theta (θ) measures the change in the option price when there is a decrease in the time to maturity of 1 day.

Rho (ρ) measures the change in the option price when there is an increase in the interest rate of one percentage point (100 basis points).

A useful mnemonic device for remembering some of these is that "vega" and "volatility" share the same first letter, as do "theta" and "time." Also "r" is often used to denote the interest rate and is the first letter in "rho."

We will discuss each Greek measure in turn, assuming for simplicity that we are talking about the Greek for a purchased option. The Greek for a written option is opposite in sign to that for the same purchased option.

Delta We have already encountered delta in Chapter 10, where we defined it as the number of shares in the portfolio that replicates the option. For a call option, delta is positive: As the stock price increases, the call price increases. Delta is also the sensitivity of the option price to a change in the stock price: If an option is replicated with 50 shares, the option should exhibit the price sensitivity of approximately 50 shares. You can think of delta as the *share-equivalent* of the option.

Figure 12.1 represents the behavior of delta for three options with different times to expiration. The figure illustrates that an in-the-money option will be more sensitive to

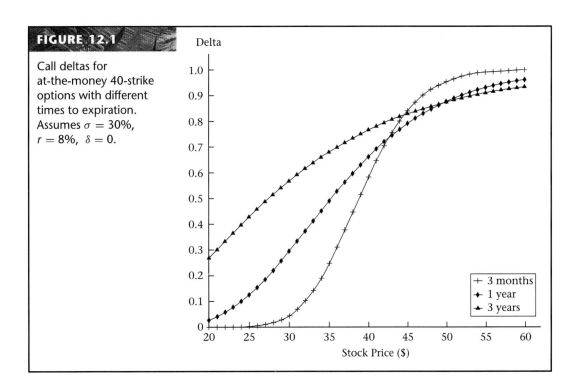

FIGURE 12.1

Call deltas for at-the-money 40-strike options with different times to expiration. Assumes $\sigma = 30\%$, $r = 8\%$, $\delta = 0$.

the stock price than an out-of-the-money option. If an option is deep in-the-money (i.e., the stock price is high relative to the strike price), it is likely to be exercised and hence the option should behave much like a leveraged position in a full share. Delta approaches 1 in this case and the share-equivalent of the option is 1. If the option is out-of-the money, it is unlikely to be exercised and the option has a low price, behaving like a position with very few shares. In this case delta is approximately 0 and the share-equivalent is 0. An at-the-money option may or may not be exercised and, hence, behaves like a position with between 0 and 1 share. This behavior of delta can be seen in Figure 12.1. Note that as time to expiration increases, delta is less at high stock prices and greater at low stock prices. This behavior of delta reflects the fact that, for the depicted options that have greater time to expiration, the likelihood is greater that an out-of-the money option will eventually become in-the-money, and the likelihood is greater that an in-the-money option will eventually become out-of-the-money.

We can use the interpretation of delta as a share-equivalent to interpret the Black-Scholes price. The formula both prices the option and also tells us what position in the stock and borrowing is equivalent to the option. The formula for the call delta is

$$\Delta = e^{-\delta t} N(d_1)$$

If we hold $e^{-\delta t} N(d_1)$ shares and borrow $K e^{-rt} N(d_2)$ dollars, the cost of this portfolio is

$$S e^{-\delta t} N(d_1) - K e^{-rt} N(d_2)$$

This is the Black-Scholes price. Thus, the pieces of the formula tell us what position in the stock and borrowing synthetically recreates the call. Figure 12.1 shows that delta changes with the stock price, so as the stock price moves, the replicating portfolio changes and must be adjusted dynamically. We also saw this in Chapter 10.

Delta for a put option is negative, so a stock price increase reduces the put price. This relationship can be seen in Figure 12.2. Since the put delta is just the call delta minus 1 (from put-call parity), Figure 12.2 behaves similarly to Figure 12.1.

Gamma   Gamma—the change in delta as the stock price changes—is always positive for a purchased call or put. As the stock price increases, delta increases. This behavior can be seen in both Figures 12.1 and 12.2. For a call, delta approaches 1 as the stock price increases. For a put, delta approaches 0 as the stock price increases. Because of put-call parity, gamma is the same for a European call and put with the same strike price and time to expiration.

Figure 12.3 graphs call gammas for options with three different expirations. Deep in-the-money options have a delta of about 1, and, hence, a gamma of about zero. (If delta is 1, it cannot change much as the stock price changes.) Similarly deep out-of-the-money options have a delta of about 0 and, hence, a gamma of about 0. The large gamma for the 3-month option in Figure 12.3 corresponds to the steep increase in delta for the same option in Figure 12.1.

A derivative for which gamma is always positive is said to be *convex*. If gamma is positive, then delta is always increasing, and a graph of the price function will have curvature like that of the cross section of a bowl.

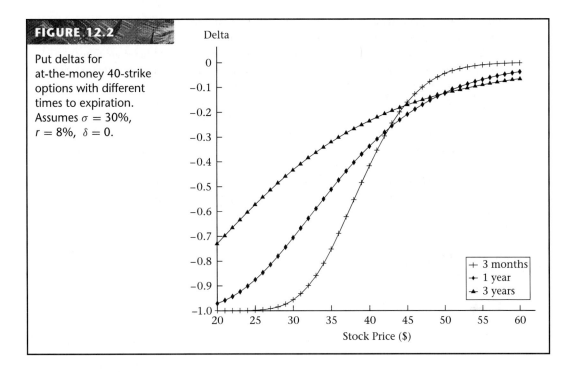

FIGURE 12.2

Put deltas for at-the-money 40-strike options with different times to expiration. Assumes $\sigma = 30\%$, $r = 8\%$, $\delta = 0$.

Delta

Stock Price ($)

+ 3 months
◆ 1 year
▲ 3 years

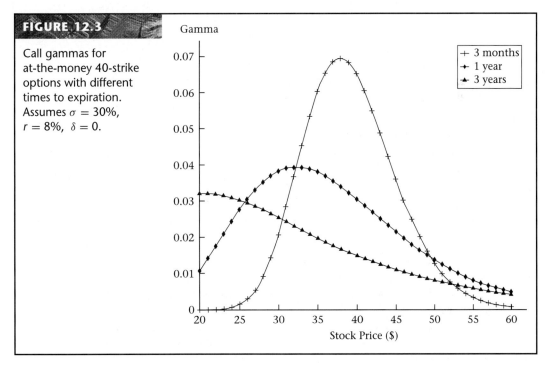

FIGURE 12.3

Call gammas for at-the-money 40-strike options with different times to expiration. Assumes $\sigma = 30\%$, $r = 8\%$, $\delta = 0$.

Gamma

Stock Price ($)

+ 3 months
◆ 1 year
▲ 3 years

Vega An increase in volatility raises the price of a call or put option. Vega measures the sensitivity of the option price to volatility. Figure 12.4 shows that vega tends to be greater for at-the-money options, and greater for options with moderate than with short times to expiration.[6] Because of put-call parity, vega, like gamma, is the same for calls and puts with the same strike price and time to expiration.

When you calculate vega, it is important to be clear about units: How large is the assumed change in volatility? It is common to express vega as the change in option price for a *one percentage point* (0.01) change in volatility.[7] Figure 12.4 follows this convention.

Theta Options generally—but not always—become less valuable as time to expiration decreases. Figure 12.5 depicts the call price for out-of-the-money, at-the-money, and in-the-money options as a function of the time to expiration. For the at-the-money

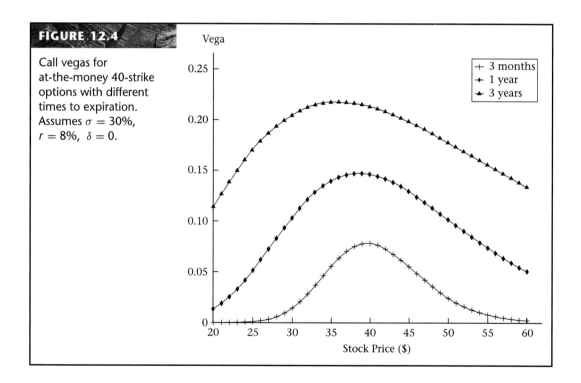

FIGURE 12.4

Call vegas for at-the-money 40-strike options with different times to expiration. Assumes $\sigma = 30\%$, $r = 8\%$, $\delta = 0$.

---

[6]Be aware that neither result is true for very long-lived options. With a 20-year option, for example, vega is greatest for out-of-the-money calls, and lower than that for a 3-year call for the range of prices in the figure.

[7]Vega is the derivative of the option price with respect to σ. Vega is expressed as the result of a percentage point change in volatility by dividing the derivative by 100.

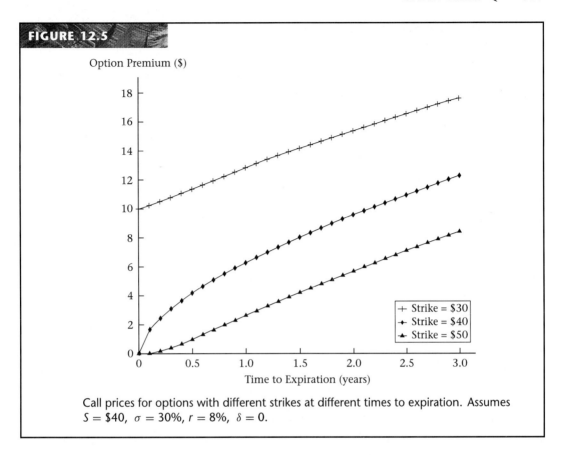

FIGURE 12.5

Option Premium ($)

Call prices for options with different strikes at different times to expiration. Assumes $S = \$40$, $\sigma = 30\%$, $r = 8\%$, $\delta = 0$.

(strike = $40) option, time decay is most rapid at expiration. For the others, time decay is more steady. Figure 12.6 graphs theta explicitly for three different times to expiration, showing that time decay is greatest for the at-the-money short-term option.

Time decay can be positive for European options in some special cases. Deep-in-the-money call options on an asset with a high dividend yield and deep-in-the-money puts are two examples. In both cases we would want to early-exercise the options if possible. Since we cannot, the option effectively becomes a T-bill, appreciating as it gets close to expiration. This effect is evident in Figure 12.7, in which the in-the-money (50-strike) put becomes more valuable, other things equal, as expiration approaches. Figure 12.8 on page 380 graphs the put theta explicitly, illustrating the positive theta.

When interpreting theta we need to know how long is the assumed change in time. Figures 12.6 and 12.8 are computed assuming a *1-day* change in time to expiration. It is also common in practice to compute over longer periods, such as 10 days.

Rho Rho is positive for an ordinary stock call option. Exercising a call entails paying the fixed strike price to receive the stock; a higher interest rate reduces the present value

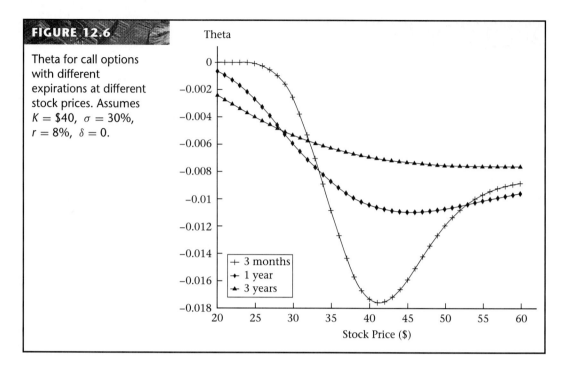

FIGURE 12.6

Theta for call options with different expirations at different stock prices. Assumes $K = \$40$, $\sigma = 30\%$, $r = 8\%$, $\delta = 0$.

of the strike. Similarly, for a put, rho is negative, since the put entitles the owner to receive cash and the present value of this is lower with a higher interest rate. Figure 12.9 shows that as the time to expiration increases and as a call option becomes more in-the-money, rho is greater.

Figure 12.9 assumes a one percentage point (100 basis point) change in the interest rate.

Greek Measures for Portfolios

The Greek measure of a portfolio is the sum of the Greeks of the individual portfolio components. This relationship is important because it means that the risk of complicated option positions is easy to evaluate. For a portfolio containing n options with a single underlying stock, where the quantity of each option is given by ω_i, we have

$$\Delta_{\text{portfolio}} = \sum_{i=1}^{n} \omega_i \Delta_i$$

The same relation holds true for the other Greeks as well.

Example 12.6 Table 12.2 on page 381 lists Greek measures for a 40–45 bull spread. Greeks for the spread are Greeks for the 40-strike call less those for the 45-strike call. ≷

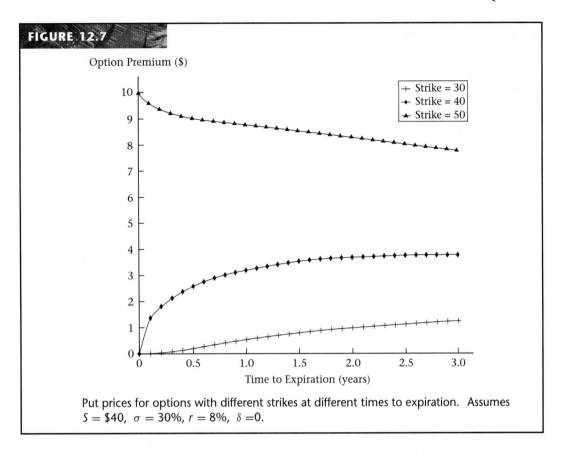

FIGURE 12.7

Put prices for options with different strikes at different times to expiration. Assumes $S = \$40$, $\sigma = 30\%$, $r = 8\%$, $\delta = 0$.

Option Elasticity

An option is an alternative to investing in the stock. Delta tells us the dollar risk of the option relative to the stock: If the stock price changes by $1, how much does the option price change? The option elasticity, by comparison, tells us the risk of the option relative to the stock in percentage terms: If the stock price changes by 1%, what is the percentage change in the value of the option?

Dollar risk of the option   If the stock price changes by ϵ, the change in the option price is

$$\text{Change in option price} = \text{Change in stock price} \times \text{option delta}$$
$$= \epsilon \times \Delta$$

Example 12.7   Suppose that the stock price is $S = \$41$, the strike price is $K = \$40$, volatility is $\sigma = 0.30$, the risk-free rate is $r = 0.08$, the time to expiration is $t = 1$, and the dividend yield is $\delta = 0$. As we saw earlier in the chapter, the option price is $6.961. Delta is 0.6911. If we own options to buy 1000 shares of stock, the delta of

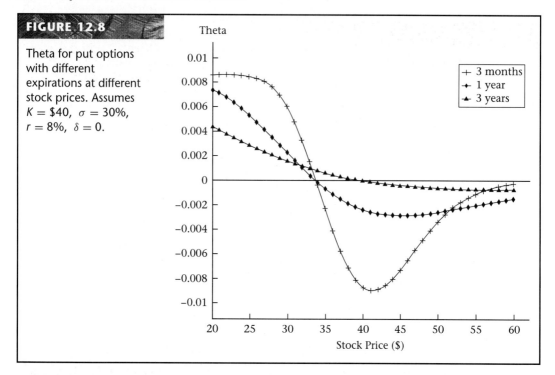

FIGURE 12.8

Theta for put options with different expirations at different stock prices. Assumes $K = \$40$, $\sigma = 30\%$, $r = 8\%$, $\delta = 0$.

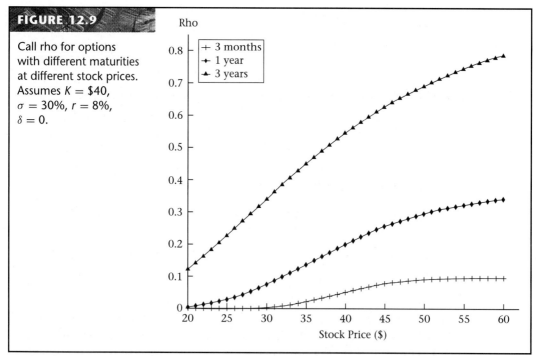

FIGURE 12.9

Call rho for options with different maturities at different stock prices. Assumes $K = \$40$, $\sigma = 30\%$, $r = 8\%$, $\delta = 0$.

		Option 1	Option 2	Combined
TABLE 12.2	Greeks for the bull spread examined in Chapter 3, where $S = \$40$, $\sigma = 0.3$, $r = 0.08$, and $T = 91$ days, with a purchased 40-strike call and a written 45-strike call. The column titled "combined" is the difference between column 1 and column 2.			
	ω_i	1	-1	—
	Price	2.7804	0.9710	1.8094
	Delta	0.5824	0.2815	0.3009
	Gamma	0.0652	0.0563	0.0088
	Vega	0.0780	0.0674	0.0106
	Theta	-0.0173	-0.0134	-0.0040
	Rho	0.0511	0.0257	0.0255

the position is

$$1000 \times \Delta = 691.1 \text{ shares of stock}$$

Thus, the option position at this stock price has a "share-equivalent" of 691 shares. If the stock price changes by $0.50, we expect an option price change of [8]

$$1000 \times \Delta \times \$0.50 = \$345.55$$

Percentage risk of the option   The **option elasticity** computes the percentage change in the option price relative to the percentage change in the stock price. The percentage change in the stock price is simply ϵ/S. The percentage change in the option price is the dollar change in the option price, $\epsilon\Delta$, divided by the option price, C:

$$\frac{\epsilon\Delta}{C}$$

The option elasticity, denoted by Ω, is the ratio of these two:

$$\Omega \equiv \frac{\% \text{ change in option price}}{\% \text{ change in stock price}} = \frac{\frac{\epsilon\Delta}{C}}{\frac{\epsilon}{S}} = \frac{S\Delta}{C} \tag{12.8}$$

The elasticity tells us the percentage change in the option for a 1% change in the stock. It is effectively a measure of the leverage implicit in the option.

---

[8]A more accurate measure of the option price change is obtain by using both delta and gamma. This "delta-gamma approximation" is discussed in Chapter 13.

For a call, $\Omega \geq 1$. We saw in Chapter 10 that a call option is replicated by a levered investment in the stock. A levered position in an asset is always riskier than the underlying asset.[9] Also, the implicit leverage in the option becomes greater as the option is more out-of-the-money. Thus, Ω decreases as the strike price decreases.

For a put, $\Omega \leq 0$. This occurs because the replicating position for a put option involves shorting the stock.

Example 12.8 Suppose $S = \$41$, $K = \$40$, $\sigma = 0.30$, $r = 0.08$, $T = 1$, and $\delta = 0$. The option price is $\$6.961$ and $\Delta = 0.6911$. Hence, the call elasticity is

$$\Omega = \frac{\$41 \times 0.6911}{\$6.961} = 4.071$$

The put has a price of $\$2.886$ and Δ of -0.3089; hence, the elasticity is

$$\Omega = \frac{\$41 \times -0.3089}{\$2.886} = -4.389$$

❦

Figure 12.10 shows the behavior of elasticity for a call, varying both the stock price and time to expiration. The 3-month out-of-the-money calls have elasticities exceeding 8. For longer time-to-expiration options, elasticity is much less sensitive to the moneyness of the option.

The volatility of an option The volatility of an option is the elasticity times the volatility of the stock:

$$\sigma_{option} = \sigma_{stock} \times |\Omega| \tag{12.9}$$

where $|\Omega|$ is the absolute value of Ω. Since elasticity is a measure of leverage, this calculation is analogous to the computation of the standard deviation of levered equity by multiplying the unlevered beta by the ratio of firm value to equity. Based on Figure 12.10, for a stock with a 30% volatility, an at-the-money option could easily have a volatility of 120% or more.

The risk premium of an option Since elasticity measures the percentage sensitivity of the option relative to the stock, it tells us how the risk premium of the option compares to that of the stock. In Section 11.2, we computed the discount rate for an option. We were implicitly using option elasticity to do this.

At a point in time, the option is equivalent to a position in the stock and in bonds; hence, the return on the option is a weighted average of the return on the stock and the

---

[9]Mathematically, this follows since $S\Delta = Se^{-\delta t}N(d_1) > C(S)$.

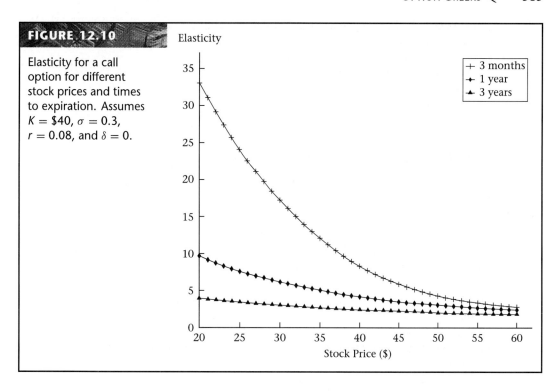

FIGURE 12.10

Elasticity for a call option for different stock prices and times to expiration. Assumes $K = \$40$, $\sigma = 0.3$, $r = 0.08$, and $\delta = 0$.

Elasticity

risk-free rate. Let α denote the expected rate of return on the stock, γ the required return on the option, and r the risk-free rate. We have

$$\gamma = \frac{\Delta S}{C(S)}\alpha + \left(1 - \frac{\Delta S}{C(S)}\right)r$$

Since $\Delta S/C(S)$ is elasticity, this can also be written

$$\gamma = \Omega\alpha + (1 - \Omega)r$$

or

$$\gamma - r = (\alpha - r) \times \Omega \qquad (12.10)$$

Thus, the risk premium on the option equals the risk premium on the stock times Ω.

Using our earlier facts about elasticity, we conclude that if the stock has a positive risk premium, then a call always has an expected return at least as great as the stock and that, other things equal, the expected return on an option goes down as the stock price goes up. In terms of the capital asset pricing model, we would say that the option beta goes down as the option becomes more in-the-money. For puts, we conclude that the put always has an expected return less than that on the stock.

The Sharpe ratio of an option   The Sharpe ratio for any asset is the ratio of the risk premium to volatility:

$$\text{Sharpe ratio} = \frac{\alpha - r}{\sigma} \tag{12.11}$$

Using equations (12.9) and (12.10), the Sharpe ratio for a call is

$$\text{Sharpe ratio for call} = \frac{\Omega(\alpha - r)}{\Omega \sigma} = \frac{\alpha - r}{\sigma} \tag{12.12}$$

Thus, the Sharpe ratio for a call equals the Sharpe ratio for the underlying stock. This equivalence of the Sharpe ratios is obvious once we realize that the option is always equivalent to a levered position in the stock, and that leverage *per se* does not change the Sharpe ratio.[10]

12.4 PROFIT DIAGRAMS BEFORE MATURITY

In order to evaluate investment strategies using options, you would like to be able to answer questions such as: If the stock price in one week is $5 greater than it is today, what will be the change in the price of a call option? What is the profit diagram for an option position in which the options have different times to expiration? Our previous discussion of option strategies in Chapter 3 examined only expiration values. Now we will examine the behavior of option prices *prior* to expiration. To do this we need to use an option pricing formula.

Purchased Call Option

Consider the purchase of a call option. Just as with expiring options, we can ask what the value of the option is at a particular point in time and for a particular stock price. Table 12.3 shows the Black-Scholes value of a call option for five different stock prices at four different times to expiration. By varying the stock price for a given time to expiration, keeping everything else the same, we are able to graph the value of the call.

Figure 12.11 plots Black-Scholes call option prices for stock prices ranging from $20 to $60, including the values in Table 12.3. Notice that the value of the option prior to expiration is a smoothed version of the value of the option at expiration.

---

[10]There is one subtlety: While the Sharpe ratio for the stock and option is the same at every point in time, it is not necessarily the same when measured using realized returns. For example, suppose you perform the experiment of buying a call and holding it for a year, and then evaluate the after-the-fact risk premium and standard deviation using historical returns. A standard way to do this would be to compute the average risk premium on the option and the average volatility and then divide them to create the Sharpe ratio. You would find that the call will have a lower Sharpe ratio than the stock. This is purely a result of dividing one *estimated* statistic by another.

TABLE 12.3

Value of 40-strike call option at different stock prices and times to expiration. Assumes $r = 8\%$, $\sigma = 30\%$, $\delta = 0$.

Stock Price ($)	Time to Expiration			
	12 Months	6 Months	3 Months	0 (Expiration)
36	3.90	2.08	1.00	0
38	5.02	3.02	1.75	0
40	6.28	4.16	2.78	0
42	7.67	5.47	4.07	2
44	9.15	6.95	5.58	4

FIGURE 12.11

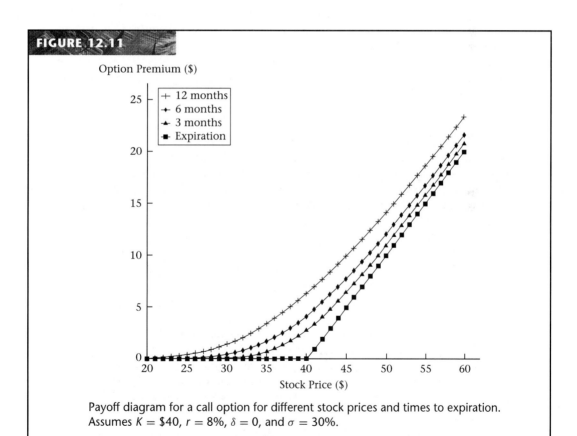

Payoff diagram for a call option for different stock prices and times to expiration. Assumes $K = \$40$, $r = 8\%$, $\delta = 0$, and $\sigma = 30\%$.

The payoff diagram depicted in Figure 12.11 does not show us how the value of the option compares to its original cost. In order to do that, we can subtract the cost of the option, plus interest.[11]

In order to determine profitability, we need to answer two questions that were unnecessary for the payoff diagram: What is the initial cost of the option position, and what is the holding period? To compute the profit, we take the value of the position and subtract the cost of the position, including interest.

Example 12.9 The 1-year option in Table 12.3 costs $6.285 at a stock price of $40. If after 1 day the stock price is still $40, the value of the option will have fallen to $6.274, and the 1-day holding period profit is $6.274 - $6.285 \times e^{0.08/365} = -0.012. This loss reflects the theta of the option. If the stock price were to increase to $42, the option premium would increase to $7.655, and the 1-day holding period profit would be $7.655 - $6.285 \times e^{0.08/365} = 1.369.

After 6 months, the holding period profit at a price of $40 would be $4.155 - $6.285 \times e^{0.08 \times 0.5} = -2.386. Even if the stock price had risen to $42, the holding period return would still be a negative $-$1.068$. These profit calculations are illustrated in Figure 12.12. ❧

The option premium graphs in Figures 12.11 and 12.12 can help us understand the behavior of delta and gamma discussed in Section 12.3. In all cases the slope of the call option graph is positive. This corresponds to a positive delta. In addition, the slope becomes greater as the stock price increases. Delta increasing with the stock price corresponds to a positive gamma. The fact that gamma is always positive implies that the graphs will be curved like the cross section of a bowl, i.e., the option price is *convex*. A positive gamma implies convex curvature. A negative gamma implies the opposite (concave) curvature.

Calendar Spreads

We saw in Chapter 3 that there are a number of option spreads that permit you to speculate on the volatility of a stock, including straddle, strangle, and butterfly spreads. These spreads all contain options with the same time to expiration and different strikes. To speculate on volatility you could also enter into a **calendar spread**, in which the options you buy and sell have different expiration dates.

Suppose you want to speculate that XYZ's stock price will be unchanged over the next 3 months. An alternative to a written straddle or a written butterfly spread is simply to sell a call or put, in the hope that the stock price will remain unchanged and you will

---

[11]As we discussed in Chapter 2, this is like assuming the option is financed by borrowing.

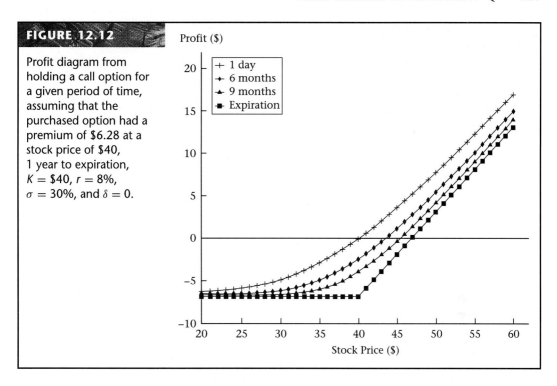

FIGURE 12.12

Profit diagram from holding a call option for a given period of time, assuming that the purchased option had a premium of $6.28 at a stock price of $40, 1 year to expiration, $K = \$40$, $r = 8\%$, $\sigma = 30\%$, and $\delta = 0$.

earn the premium. The potential cost is that if the option does move into the money, you can have a large loss.

To protect against a stock price increase when you sell a call, you can simultaneously buy a call option with the same strike and greater time to expiration. This purchased calendar spread exploits the fact that the written near-to-expiration option exhibits greater time decay than the purchased far-to-expiration option, and therefore is profitable if the stock price does not move. For example, suppose you sell a 40-strike call with 91 days to expiration and buy a 40-strike call with 1 year to expiration. At a stock price of $40, the premiums are $2.78 for the 91-day call and $6.28 for the 1-year call. The profit diagram for this position for holding periods of 1 day, 45 days, and 91 days is displayed in Figure 12.13. You can see that you earn maximum profit over 91 days if the stock price does not change.

We can understand the behavior of profit for this position by considering the theta of the two options. Figure 12.6 shows that theta is more negative for the 91-day call (-0.0173) than for the 1-year call (-0.0104). Thus, if the stock price does not change over the course of 1 day, the position will make money since the written option loses more value than the purchased option. Over 91 days, the written 91-day option will lose its full value (its price declines from $2.78 to 0), while the 1-year option will lose only about $1 (its price declines from $6.28 to $5.28) if the stock price does not change. The difference in the rates of time decay generates profit of approximately $1.78.

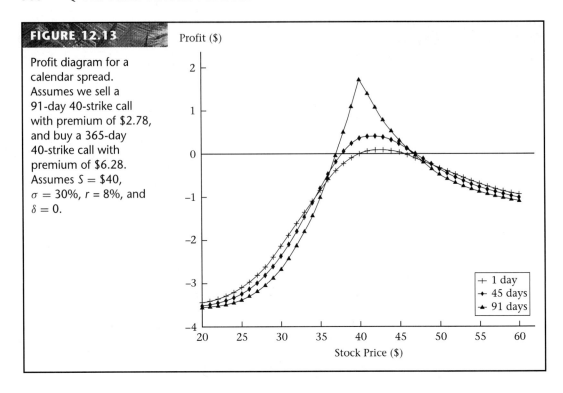

FIGURE 12.13

Profit diagram for a calendar spread. Assumes we sell a 91-day 40-strike call with premium of $2.78, and buy a 365-day 40-strike call with premium of $6.28. Assumes $S = \$40$, $\sigma = 30\%$, $r = 8\%$, and $\delta = 0$.

The profit diagram also illustrates that at a stock price of $40, delta for the position is initially positive. Over 1 day, the maximum profit occurs if the stock price rises by a small amount. This reflects the fact that the delta of the written 91-day call is 0.5825 and that of the purchased 1-year call is 0.6615, for a net positive delta of 0.0790. With the 91-day holding period, the portion of the graph below 40 reflects the purchased 1-year option, which becomes increasingly unprofitable as the stock price falls. Above 40, the gain on the purchased 1-year option is offset by the loss on the expiring 91-day call. Since it is expiring, the delta of the 91-day call is −1 for stock prices above 40, which results in the graph turning back down to a negative slope above 40. As the stock price continues to increase, however, the delta of the purchased 1-year call increases toward 1, so the slope of the net position approaches zero.

12.5 IMPLIED VOLATILITY

Volatility is unobservable; hence, it is the input to the Black-Scholes formula that is hardest to estimate. The history of returns allows us to compute historical volatility (see Section 11.4), but history is not always a guide to the future. Markets have quiet and turbulent periods, and predictable events such as company earnings announcements and Federal Reserve Board Open Market Committee meetings sometimes create periods of greater than normal volatility. This suggests that historical volatility might not always provide the best estimate of *future* volatility. All of the inputs to the Black-Scholes model are observable with the exception of dividends and volatility. Over short horizons dividends are fairly stable. In practice, therefore, it is common to invert the Black-Scholes formula and find the volatility that is consistent with observed option prices. This is called the option's **implied volatility**.[12]

Since implied volatility by definition yields the market price of the option, you might wonder why anyone computes it. There are at least two reasons. First, if you need to price an option for which you *cannot* observe a price, you can use implied volatility to generate a price consistent with prices of traded options. Second, as we will see below, option pricing models implicitly make predictions about implied volatility. For example, *under the Black-Scholes assumptions, implied volatility should be identical for all options on a given underlying asset.* If implied volatilities are not consistent with the model, this tells us something about the model's validity.

Computing Implied Volatility

Note at the outset that computing an implied volatility requires that we (a) observe a market price for an option and (b) have a model with which to infer volatility. Any pricing model can be used to calculate an implied volatility, although Black-Scholes is commonly used. (Someone referring to implied volatility without explanation likely used the Black-Scholes formula.) Assuming that we observe S, K, r, δ, and T, the implied call volatility is the σ that solves

$$\text{Observed option price} = C(S, K, \sigma, r, T, \delta) \qquad (12.13)$$

In practice implied volatilities of in-the-money, at-the-money, and out-of-the-money options are generally different. This is called the **volatility skew**.

Example 12.10 Suppose we observe a 45-strike 6-month European call option with a premium of $8.07. The stock price is $50, the interest rate is 8%, and the dividend yield is zero. We can compute the option price as

$$\$8.07 = BSCall(50, 45, \sigma, 0.08, 0.5, 0).$$

By trial and error (or by using a tool such as Excel's Goalseek), we find that setting $\sigma = 28.7\%$ gives us a call price of $8.07.[13]

----

[12]The Black-Scholes formula is derived assuming that volatility is constant. Thus, strictly speaking we are being internally inconsistent when we use the Black-Scholes model to track changes in implied volatility.

[13]An implied volatility function is available with the spreadsheets accompanying this book. See Appendix E.

Table 12.4 lists European option prices and implied volatilities for the S&P 500 from November 1997. For simplicity we will assume an interest rate of 5.5% and a dividend yield of 2% for all calculations. The implied volatilities are all in the vicinity of 30%, but you can see that implied volatilties are not all the same. The average implied volatility of 30% is substantially higher than the 10-year historical volatility of 12.9% observed in 1997, and also higher than the previous year historical volatility of 14.6%.

When examining implied volatilities you should keep in mind the role of put-call parity. If options are European, then *puts and calls with the same strike and time to expiration must have the same implied volatility.* This must be true since any valid European option pricing formula must satisfy the parity relationship or else there is an arbitrage opportunity. Thus, skew is not related to whether an option is a put or a call, but rather to other differences in option characteristics, such as the strike price. Having said this, transaction costs (including bid-ask spreads) will create a range within which arbitrage will not be profitable. Thus, implied volatilities for puts and calls at a given strike should be close, but need not be exactly the same.

Evidence and Implications

Is the Black-Scholes model "true"? How would we even approach such a question? Because volatility is unobservable, the standard approach to testing the Black-Scholes model is to see whether, for a given underlying asset, implied volatilities are the same at all strike prices. The answer is generally no; there is volatility skew. The existence of volatility skew suggests that the Black-Scholes model and assumptions are not a perfect description of the world.

TABLE 12.4	Implied volatilities for S&P 500 cash options, 11/13/97. Option prices from *Wall Street Journal* of 11/14/97; assumes $S = \$916.66$, $\delta = 2\%$, $r = 5.5\%$.				

Strike ($)	Expiration	Call Price ($)	Implied Volatility	Put Price ($)	Implied Volatility
915	11/21/1997	17.00	0.2922	14.75	0.2943
920	11/21/1997	14.00	0.2820	16.50	0.2795
925	11/21/1997	12.00	0.2856	19.25	0.2785
915	12/19/1997	38.00	0.3111	35.50	0.3313
920	12/19/1997	36.00	0.3149	36.00	0.3134
925	12/19/1997	31.25	0.2938	39.25	0.3187
920	1/16/1998	48.00	0.3076	46.50	0.3128
925	1/16/1998	43.00	0.2902	54.00	0.3449

Bates (2000) examines S&P 500 index futures options over 1988–1993 and finds that out-of-the-money puts (and therefore in-the-money calls) have higher implied volatilities than options at other strikes. He proposes two explanations for this behavior of implied volatility. First is that there is a possibility of large sudden declines (jumps) in the market index price, which would not occur if prices were truly lognormal with constant volatility. An increased probability of large downward moves in stock prices would raise the probability that an out-of-the-money put becomes valuable, and thus would raise their price and implied volatility. A second explanation is that skew is due to volatility changing randomly (a so-called "stochastic volatility" model). Empirically, volatility appears to increase when stock prices decrease; this again would raise the cost of out-of-the-money puts and therefore implied volatilities.

Bates concludes that the jump model does a better job of fitting observed option prices, but that in his sample jumps occur less frequently than option prices would predict. This observation raises the question, which is unresolved, of whether market-makers earn abnormal profits by writing out-of-the-money puts.[14]

Volatility skew is inconsistent with the Black-Scholes assumptions. Does this invalidate the Black-Scholes model? How do we reconcile this with the fact that the Black-Scholes model continues to be widely used? In Chapter 21 we will examine alternative option pricing models, but the important point to keep in mind is that *any* model is an approximation to reality: The question is whether the model is useful, i.e., whether the assumptions are "close enough." Here is the view of Emanuel Derman, a former physicist who has spent years working on Wall Street:

> Models are . . . useful as paradigms. They give you a set of plausible variables to use in describing the world, and a set of relationships between them that people believe are true. . . . Good theories, like Black-Scholes, provide a theoretical laboratory in which you can do *gedanken* experiments to explore possible causes and effects.[15] You cannot prove them "right" by observation, because the parameters in the model have to be estimated. But their values are related to human perceptions, so they keep changing. (Derman 1996, p. 113)

12.6 PERPETUAL AMERICAN OPTIONS

The Black-Scholes formula prices options that are only exercised at expiration. In this section we present formulas, based on Merton (1973), for the prices of calls and puts that never expire. We will call such options **perpetual options**. They are also known as expirationless options.

American options are harder to price than European options because it is difficult to characterize the optimal exercise strategy. Using the binomial model, we saw in Section

---

[14]Coval and Shumulay (2001) examine the empirical returns to option positions.

[15]A *gedanken* experiment in physics is a thought experiment that would be impractical in real life.

11.1 that for a finitely lived call option on a dividend-paying stock, the stock price at which it is optimal to exercise the option declines as the option approaches expiration. It is this changing optimal exercise price that makes it hard to derive a valuation formula.

With perpetual American options it *is* possible to derive a valuation formula because such an option always has the same time to expiration: Infinity. Since time to expiration is constant, the option exercise problem will look the same today, tomorrow, and forever. Thus, the price at which it is optimal to exercise the option is constant. The optimal exercise strategy entails picking the right exercise barrier and exercising the option the first time the stock price reaches that barrier.

Barrier Present Values

As a prelude to valuing a perpetual option, consider computing the present value of $1 payable when the stock price reaches a level, H. We will call H the barrier level and call the value today of $1 paid when the stock price reaches H the "barrier present value." It turns out there is a simple formula for this, which differs depending upon whether H is above or below the current stock value, S.

If H is above S (i.e., S has to rise to reach H), the value today of $1 received when S reaches H—the barrier present value—is

$$\text{Value of \$1 received when } S \text{ first reaches } H \text{ from below} = \left(\frac{S}{H}\right)^{h_1} \qquad (12.14)$$

where

$$h_1 = \frac{1}{2} - \frac{r - \delta}{\sigma^2} + \sqrt{\left(\frac{r - \delta}{\sigma^2} - \frac{1}{2}\right)^2 + \frac{2r}{\sigma^2}}$$

If H is below S (i.e., S has to fall to reach H), the value of $1 received when S reaches H is

$$\text{Value of \$1 received when } S \text{ first reaches } H \text{ from above} = \left(\frac{S}{H}\right)^{h_2} \qquad (12.15)$$

where

$$h_2 = \frac{1}{2} - \frac{r - \delta}{\sigma^2} - \sqrt{\left(\frac{r - \delta}{\sigma^2} - \frac{1}{2}\right)^2 + \frac{2r}{\sigma^2}}$$

Perpetual Calls

Suppose we have a perpetual American call with strike K. If we decide to exercise the option whenever S hits the barrier H, then at exercise we receive $H - K$. From equation (12.14), the value of receiving $H - K$ when S reaches H is

$$(H - K)\left(\frac{S}{H}\right)^{h_1}$$

In order to finish computing the value of the call we need to specify H, the price at which the call should be exercised. We simply need to pick a value for H that makes the value of the call as great as possible. If we make H too small, then we prematurely throw away option value (i.e., protection against a subsequent price decline). If we make H too large, then we forgo dividends for too long while waiting to exercise. It is possible to show that the exercise level H^* that maximizes the value of the call is[16]

$$H^* = K \left(\frac{h_1}{h_1 - 1} \right)$$

Since $h_1 > 1$, we have $H^* > K$. Making this substitution, the value of the perpetual call is

$$\text{Price of perpetual call} = \frac{K}{h_1 - 1} \left(\frac{h_1 - 1}{h_1} \frac{S}{K} \right)^{h_1} \qquad (12.16)$$

If $\delta = 0$, then $H^* = \infty$; i.e., it is never optimal to exercise a call option on a nondividend-paying stock.

Perpetual Puts

For a perpetual put, using equation (12.15), the value if we exercise when $S = H$ is given by

$$(K - H) \left(\frac{S}{H} \right)^{h_2}$$

where

$$h_2 = \frac{1}{2} - \frac{r - \delta}{\sigma^2} - \sqrt{\left(\frac{r - \delta}{\sigma^2} - \frac{1}{2} \right)^2 + \frac{2r}{\sigma^2}}$$

Again selecting the exercise level H^* to maximize the value of the put, we get

$$H^* = K \frac{h_2}{h_2 - 1}$$

which implies that the price of the perpetual put is

$$\text{Price of perpetual put} = \frac{K}{1 - h_2} \left(\frac{h_2 - 1}{h_2} \frac{S}{K} \right)^{h_2} \qquad (12.17)$$

---

[16]This is accomplished by differentiating the expression with respect to H, setting the derivative equal to zero, and solving for H.

Chapter Summary

Under certain assumptions, the Black-Scholes formula provides an exact formula—approximated by the binomial formula—for pricing European options. The inputs to the Black-Scholes formula are the same as for the binomial formula: The stock price, strike price, volatility, interest rate, time to expiration, and dividend yield. As with the binomial formula, the Black-Scholes formula accommodates different underlying assets by changing the dividend yield (see Table 10.1 for a summary).

Option Greeks measure the change in the option price (or other option characteristic) for a change in an option input. Delta, gamma, vega, theta, and rho are widely used in practice to assess the risk of an option position. The option elasticity is the percentage change in the option's price for a 1% change in the stock price. The volatility and beta of an option are the volatility and beta of the stock times the option elasticity. Thus, an option and the underlying stock have the same Sharpe ratio.

Of the inputs to the Black-Scholes formula, volatility is hardest to estimate. In practice it is common to use the formula in backward fashion to infer the market's estimate of volatility from the option price. This implied volatility is computed by finding the volatility for which the formula matches observed market prices for options. In theory, all options of a given maturity should have the same implied volatility. In practice, they do not, a phenomenon known as volatility skew.

Although there is no simple formula for valuing a finitely lived American option, there are simple formulas in the special case of perpetual puts and calls.

Further Reading

Chapter 13 will explore in more detail the market-maker's perspective on options, including how a market-maker uses delta to hedge option positions and the circumstances under which market-makers earn profits or make losses. Chapter 14 extends the discussion in this chapter to include exotic options.

In Chapters 15, 16, and 17, we will use option pricing to explore applications of option pricing, including the creation of structured products, issues in compensation options, capital structure, tax management with options, and real options.

Finally, Chapters 18–21 delve more into the mathematical underpinnings of the Black-Scholes model. The barrier present value calculations will be discussed again in Chapter 22.

The classic early papers on option pricing are Black and Scholes (1973) and Merton (1973). The details of how the binomial model converges to the Black-Scholes model are in Cox et al. (1979). The perpetual put formula is derived in Merton (1973). The link between the perpetual call and put formulas is discussed by McDonald and Siegel (1986).

Problems

In answering many of these problems you can use the functions *BSCall*, *BSPut*, *CallPerpetual*, and *PutPerpetual* and the accompanying functions for the Greeks (see Appendix E).

12.1. Use a spreadsheet to verify the option prices in Examples 12.1 and 12.2.

12.2. Using the *BinomCall* and *BinomPut* functions, compute the binomial approximations for the options in Examples 12.1 and 12.2. Be sure to compute prices for $n = 8, 9, 10, 11$, and 12. What do you observe about the behavior of the binomial approximation?

12.3. Let $S = \$100$, $K = \$120$, $\sigma = 30\%$, $r = 0.08$, and $\delta = 0$.

    a. Compute the Black-Scholes call price for 1 year to maturity and for a variety of very long times to maturity. What happens to the option price as $T \to \infty$?

    b. Set $\delta = 0.001$. Repeat (a). Now what happens to the option price? What accounts for the difference?

12.4. Let $S = \$120$, $K = \$100$, $\sigma = 30\%$, $r = 0$, and $\delta = 0.08$.

    a. Compute the Black-Scholes put price for 1 year to maturity and for a variety of very long times to maturity. What happens to the price as $T \to \infty$?

    b. Set $r = 0.001$. Repeat (a). Now what happens? What accounts for the difference?

12.5. The exchange rate is ¥95/€, the yen-denominated interest rate is 1.5%, the euro-denominated interest rate is 3.5%, and the exchange rate volatility is 10%.

    a. What is the price of a 90-strike yen-denominated euro put with 6 months to expiration?

    b. What is the price of a 1/90-strike euro-denominated yen call with 6 months to expiration?

    c. What is the link between your answer to (a) and your answer to (b), converted to yen?

12.6. Suppose XYZ is a nondividend-paying stock. Suppose $S = \$100$, $\sigma = 40\%$, $\delta = 0$, and $r = 0.06$.

    a. What is the price of a 105-strike call option with 1 year to expiration?

    b. What is the 1-year forward price for the stock?

    c. What is the price of a 1-year 105-strike option, where the underlying asset is a futures contract maturing at the same time as the option?

12.7. Suppose $S = \$100$, $K = \$95$, $\sigma = 30\%$, $r = 0.08$, $\delta = 0.03$, and $T = 0.75$.

    a. Compute the Black-Scholes price of a call.

    b. Compute the Black-Scholes price of a call for which $S = \$100 \times e^{-0.03 \times 0.75}$, $K = \$95 \times e^{-0.08 \times 0.75}$, $\sigma = 0.3$, $T = 0.75$, $\delta = 0$, $r = 0$. How does your answer compare to that for (a)?

12.8. Make the same assumptions as in the previous problem.

    a. What is the 9-month forward price for the stock?

    b. Compute the price of a 95-strike 9-month call option on a futures contract.

    c. What is the relationship between your answer to (b) and the price you computed in the previous question? Why?

12.9. Assume $K = \$40$, $\sigma = 30\%$, $r = 0.08$, $T = 0.5$, and the stock is to pay a single dividend of $2 tomorrow, with no dividends thereafter.

    a. Suppose $S = \$50$. What is the price of a European call option? Consider an otherwise identical American call. What is its price?

    b. Repeat, only suppose $S = \$60$.

    c. Under what circumstance would you not exercise the option today?

12.10. "Time decay is greatest for an option close to expiration." Use the spreadsheet functions to evaluate this statement. Consider both the dollar change in the option value and the percentage change in the option value, and examine both in-the-money and out-of-the-money options.

12.11. In the absence of an explicit formula, we can estimate the change in the option price due to a change in an input—such as σ—by computing the following for a small value of ϵ:

$$\text{Vega} = \frac{BSCall(S, K, \sigma + \epsilon, r, t, \delta) - BSCall(S, K, \sigma - \epsilon, r, t, \delta)}{2\epsilon}.$$

    a. What is the logic behind this calculation? Why does ϵ need to be small?

    b. Compare the results of this calculation with results obtained from *BSCall-Vega*.

12.12. Suppose $S = \$100$, $K = \$95$, $\sigma = 30\%$, $r = 0.08$, $\delta = 0.03$, and $T = 0.75$. Using the technique in the previous problem compute the Greek measure corresponding to a change in the dividend yield. What is the predicted effect of a one-percentage-point change in the dividend yield?

12.13. Consider a bull spread where you buy a 40-strike call and sell a 45-strike call. Suppose $S = \$40$, $\sigma = 0.30$, $r = 0.08$, $\delta = 0$, and $T = 0.5$. Draw a graph with stock prices ranging from $20 to $60 depicting the profit on the bull spread after 1 day, 3 months, and 6 months.

12.14. Consider a bull spread where you buy a 40-strike call and sell a 45-strike call. Suppose $\sigma = 0.30$, $r = 0.08$, $\delta = 0$, and $T = 0.5$.

    a. Suppose $S = \$40$. What are delta, gamma, vega, theta, and rho?

    b. Suppose $S = \$45$. What are delta, gamma, vega, theta, and rho?

    c. Are any of your answers to (a) and (b) different? If so, why?

12.15. Consider a bull spread where you buy a 40-strike put and sell a 45-strike put. Suppose $\sigma = 0.30$, $r = 0.08$, $\delta = 0$, and $T = 0.5$.

    a. Suppose $S = \$40$. What are delta, gamma, vega, theta, and rho?

    b. Suppose $S = \$45$. What are delta, gamma, vega, theta, and rho?

    c. Are any of your answers to (a) and (b) different? If so, why?

    d. Are any of your answers different in this problem from those in Problem 14? If so, why?

12.16. Assume $r = 8\%$, $\sigma = 30\%$, $\delta = 0$. In doing the following calculations, use a stock price range of \$60–\$140, stock price increments of \$5, and two different times to expiration: 1 year and 1 day. Consider purchasing a 100-strike straddle, i.e., buy one 100-strike put and one 100-strike call.

    a. Compute delta, vega, theta, and rho of the call and put separately, for the different stock prices and times to expiration.

    b. Compute delta, vega, theta, and rho of the purchased straddle (do this by adding the Greeks of the individual options). As best you can, explain intuitively the signs of the straddle Greeks.

    c. Graph delta vega, theta, and rho of the straddle with 1 year to expiration as a function of the stock price. In each case explain why the graph looks as it does.

12.17. Assume $r = 8\%$, $\sigma = 30\%$, $\delta = 0$. Using 1-year-to-expiration European options, construct a position where you sell two 80-strike puts, buy one 95-strike put, buy one 105-strike call, and sell two 120-strike calls. For a range of stock prices from \$60 to \$140, compute delta, vega, theta, and rho of this position. As best you can, explain intuitively the signs of the Greeks.

12.18. Consider a perpetual call option with $S = \$50$, $K = \$60$, $r = 0.06$, $\sigma = 0.40$, and $\delta = 0.03$.

    a. What is the price of the option and at what stock price should it be exercised?

    b. Suppose $\delta = 0.04$ with all other inputs the same. What happens to the price and exercise barrier? Why?

    c. Suppose $r = 0.07$ with all other inputs the same. What happens to the price and exercise barrier? Why?

    d. Suppose $\sigma = 50\%$ with all other inputs the same. What happens to the price and exercise barrier? Why?

12.19. Consider a perpetual put option with $S = \$50$, $K = \$60$, $r = 0.06$, $\sigma = 0.40$, and $\delta = 0.03$.

    a. What is the price of the option and at what stock price should it be exercised?

b. Suppose $\delta = 0.04$ with all other inputs the same. What happens to the price and exercise barrier? Why?

c. Suppose $r = 0.07$ with all other inputs the same. What happens to the price and exercise barrier? Why?

d. Suppose $\sigma = 50\%$ with all other inputs the same. What happens to the price and exercise barrier? Why?

12.20. Let $S = \$100$, $K = \$90$, $\sigma = 30\%$, $r = 8\%$, $\delta = 5\%$, and $T = 1$.

a. What is the Black-Scholes call price?

b. Now price a put where $S = \$90$, $K = \$100$, $\sigma = 30\%$, $r = 5\%$, $\delta = 8\%$, and $T = 1$.

c. What is the link between your answers to (a) and (b)? Why?

12.21. Repeat Problem 20, but this time for perpetual options. What do you notice about the prices? What do you notice about the exercise barriers?

APPENDIX 12.A: THE STANDARD NORMAL DISTRIBUTION

The *standard normal probability density function* is given by

$$\phi(x) \equiv \frac{1}{\sqrt{2\pi}} e^{-\frac{1}{2}x^2} \tag{12.18}$$

The *cumulative standard normal distribution function*, evaluated at a point x (for example), tells us the probability that a number randomly drawn from the standard normal distribution will fall below x, or

$$N(x) \equiv \int_{-\infty}^{x} \phi(x)dx \equiv \int_{-\infty}^{x} \frac{1}{\sqrt{2\pi}} e^{-\frac{1}{2}x^2} dx \tag{12.19}$$

Excel computes the cumulative distribution using the built-in function *NORMSDIST*. Note that $N'(x_1) = \phi(x_1)$.

APPENDIX 12.B: FORMULAS FOR OPTION GREEKS

In this section we present formulas for the Greeks for an option on a stock paying continuous dividends.[17] Greek measures in the binomial model are discussed in Appendix 13.B.

---

[17]If you wish to derive any of these formulas for yourself, or if you find that different authors use formulas that appear different, here are two useful things to know. The first is a result of the normal distribution being symmetric around 0:

$$N(x) = 1 - N(-x)$$

Delta (Δ)

Delta is the partial derivative of the option price with respect to the stock price; hence, it measures the change in the option price for a $1 change in the stock price. The delta formulas are

$$\text{Call delta} = e^{-\delta T} N(d_1)$$

$$\text{Put delta} = e^{-\delta T} [N(d_1) - 1]$$

Gamma (Γ)

Gamma is the partial derivative of delta with respect to the stock price, or equivalently the second derivative of the option price with respect to the stock price. The gamma formulas are

$$\text{Call gamma} = \frac{e^{-\delta T} N'(d_1)}{S\sigma\sqrt{T}}$$

$$\text{Put gamma} = \text{Call gamma}$$

The second equation follows from put-call parity.

Theta (θ)

Theta is the partial derivative of the option price with respect to calendar time, holding fixed time to expiration. The theta formulas are

$$\text{Call theta} = \delta e^{-\delta T} SN(d_1) - rKe^{-rT} N(d_2) - \frac{Ke^{-rT} N'(d_2)\sigma}{2\sqrt{T}}$$

$$\text{Put theta} = \text{Call theta} + rKe^{-rT} - \delta Se^{rT}$$

If time to expiration is measured in years, theta will be the *annualized* change in the option value. To obtain a per-day theta, divide by 365.

Vega

Vega is the partial derivative of the option price with respect to volatility. Some writers also use the terms *lambda* or *kappa* to refer to this measure. The formulas are

....

With some effort, the second can be verified algebraically:

$$Se^{-\delta T} N'(d_1) = Ke^{-rT} N'(d_2)$$

$$\text{Call vega} = Se^{-\delta T} N'(d_1)\sqrt{T}$$

$$\text{Call vega} = \text{Put vega}$$

It is common to report vega as the change in the option price *per percentage point* change in the volatility. This requires dividing the vega formula above by 100.

Rho (ρ)

Rho is the partial derivative of the option price with respect to the interest rate. The formulas are

$$\text{Call rho} = TKe^{-rT}N(d_2)$$

$$\text{Put rho} = TKe^{-rT}N(-d_2)$$

These expressions for rho assume a change in r of 1.0. We are typically interested in evaluating the effect of a change of 0.01 (100 basis points) or 0.0001 (one basis point). To report rho as a change per percentage point in the interest rate, divide this measure by 100. To interpret it as a change per basis point, divide by 10,000.

Chapter 13
Market-Making and Delta-Hedging

At least as important as the Black-Scholes *formula* is the Black and Scholes *technique* for deriving the formula. Their approach, which we discuss in this chapter, is not only applicable to pricing call and put options, but provides important insights into derivatives pricing and risk management in general. The discussion in this chapter illustrates the *market-maker* perspective on options. What are the issues confronting the market professionals who supply the options that customers want to buy?

The Black-Scholes approach to deriving the option pricing formula starts by assuming that market-makers are profit-maximizers in a competitive market. As with any other good in a competitive market, the price of an option should equal the cost of producing it. We examine the costs borne by a market-maker who buys and sells options and delta-hedges the resulting exposure to changes in the stock price. Using some of the option Greeks introduced in Chapter 12, we will see how market-making costs are reflected in a fair option price.

The basic idea is like that in Chapter 10: The market-maker can hedge an option position by taking an offsetting position of delta shares of stock. Market-makers face the problem that an option's delta is not constant as the stock price changes. Therefore, market-makers must continually review and modify their hedging decisions. We will see that the costs of carrying a hedged option position can be expressed in terms of delta, gamma, and theta. On average, competitive market-makers should expect to break even by hedging, and under certain assumptions about the behavior of the stock price, the market-maker's break-even price is the Black-Scholes option price.

13.1 WHAT DO MARKET-MAKERS DO?

A **market-maker** stands ready to sell to buyers and to buy from sellers. The owner of an appliance store, for example, is a market-maker. The store owner buys televisions at a low price (the wholesale price) and sells them at cost plus a markup (the retail price), earning the difference. The markup must at a minimum cover the cost of doing business—rent, salaries, utilities, and advertising—so that the retail price covers the cost of acquiring televisions plus all other costs of doing business. In the language of securities markets, we would say that the appliance dealer has both a bid price and an ask price. The **bid price** is the price at which the dealer buys the television, also known as the wholesale price. The **ask price** is the price at which the dealer will sell the television, also known as the retail price.

An appliance seller does not select which models to sell based on personal preference and does not expect to profit by speculating on the price of a television. Rather, the appliance dealer selects inventory based on expected customer demand and earns profit based on the markup. The store maintains an inventory, and the owner is able to satisfy customers who walk in and want to buy a television immediately. Market-makers supply *immediacy*, permitting customers to trade whenever they wish.

Proprietary trading, which is conceptually distinct from market-making, is trading to express an investment strategy. Customers and proprietary traders typically expect their positions to be profitable depending upon whether the market goes up or down. In contrast, market-makers profit by charging the bid-ask spread. The position of a market-maker is the result of whatever order flow arrives from customers.

A difference between appliance sellers and financial market-makers is that an appliance store must possess a physical television in order to sell one. A financial market-maker, by contrast, can supply an asset by short-selling, thereby generating inventory as needed.

In some cases market-makers may trade as customers, but then the market-maker is paying the bid-ask spread and therefore not serving as a market-maker.

13.2 MARKET-MAKER RISK

Without hedging, an active market-maker will have an arbitrary position generated by fulfilling customer orders. An arbitrary portfolio has uncontrolled risk. An adverse price move has the potential to bankrupt the market-maker. Consequently, market-makers attempt to hedge the risk of their positions.

Market-makers can control risk by **delta-hedging**. As in Chapter 10, the market-maker computes the option delta and takes an offsetting position in shares. We say that such a position is *delta-hedged*. In general a delta-hedged position is not a zero-value position: The cost of the shares required to hedge is not the same as the cost of the options. Because of the cost difference the market-maker must invest capital to maintain a delta-hedged position.

A key idea in derivatives is that such a hedged position should earn the risk-free rate: You have money tied up so you should earn a return on it, and you have no risk so you should earn the risk-free rate. We used this argument explicitly in our discussion of forward pricing in Chapter 5, and implicitly in binomial pricing in Chapter 10. The notion that a hedged position earns the risk-free rate is a linchpin of almost all derivative pricing models. It was the fundamental idea exploited by Black and Scholes in their derivation of the option pricing model.

With the help of a simple numerical example, we can understand not only the intuition of the Black-Scholes model, but the mathematics as well. Delta-hedging is key to pricing because it is the technique for offsetting the risk of an option position. If we think of option producers as selling options at cost, then delta-hedging provides us with an understanding of what the cost of the option is when it is replicated. Delta-hedging is thus both a technique widely used in practice, and a key to understanding option pricing.

Option Risk in the Absence of Hedging

If a customer wishes to buy a call option, the market-maker fills this order by selling a call option. To be specific, suppose that $S = \$40$, $K = \$40$, $\sigma = 0.30$, $r = 0.08$ (continuously compounded), and $\delta = 0$. We will let T denote the expiration time of the option and t the present, so time to expiration is $T - t$. Let $T - t = 91/365$. The price, delta, gamma, and theta for this call are listed in Table 13.1.

Because the market-maker has written the option, the sign of the Greek measures for the position is opposite those of a purchased option. In particular, the written option is like shorting shares of stock (negative delta) and the option gains in value over time (positive theta). Because delta is negative, the risk for the market-maker who has written a call is that the stock price will rise.

Suppose that the market-maker does not hedge the written option and the stock price rises to $40.75. We can measure the profit of the market-maker by **marking-to-market** the position. Marking-to-market answers the question, If we liquidated the position today, what would be the gain or loss? In the case of an option price increase, the market-maker would need to buy the option back at a higher price than that at which it was sold, and therefore would lose money. Specifically, at a stock price of $40.75, the call price would increase to $3.2352, so the market-maker profit on a per-share basis would be $2.7804 - \$3.2352 = -\$0.4548$.

Figure 13.1 graphs the overnight profit of the unhedged written call option as a function of the stock price, against the profit of the option at expiration. In computing overnight profit, we are varying the stock price holding fixed all other inputs to the Black-Scholes formula except for time to expiration, which decreases by one day. It is apparent from the graph that the risk for the market-maker is a rise in the stock price. Although it is not obvious from the graph, if the stock price does not change, the market-maker will profit because of time decay: It would be possible to liquidate the option position by buying options at a lower price the next day than the price at which they were sold originally.

TABLE 13.1	Price and Greek information for a call option with $S = \$40$, $K = \$40$, $\sigma = 0.30$, $r = 0.08$ (continuously compounded), $T - t = 91/365$, and $\delta = 0$.

	Purchased	Written
Call Price	2.7804	−2.7804
Delta	0.5824	−0.5824
Gamma	0.0652	−0.0652
Theta	−0.0173	0.0173

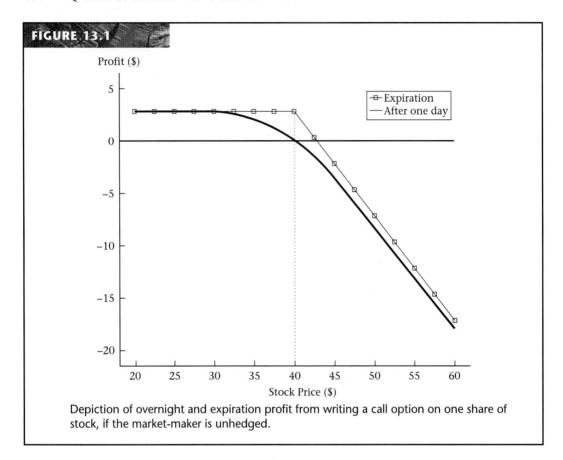

FIGURE 13.1

Depiction of overnight and expiration profit from writing a call option on one share of stock, if the market-maker is unhedged.

Delta and Gamma as Measures of Exposure

Since delta tells us the price sensitivity of the option, it also measures the market-maker's exposure. The delta of the call at a stock price of $40 is 0.5824, which suggests that a $1 increase in the stock price should increase the value of the option by approximately $0.5824. A $0.75 increase in the stock price would therefore increase the option price by $0.75 \times 0.5824 = $0.4368. However, the actual increase in the option's value is $0.4548, greater by $0.0180.

This discrepancy occurs because delta varies with the stock price: As the stock price increases and the option moves more into the money, delta also increases. At a stock price of $40.75, delta is 0.6301. Thus, the delta at $40 will *understate* the actual change in the value of the option due to a price increase.

Similarly, delta will *overstate* the decline in the value of the option due to a stock price decrease. If the stock price had fallen $0.75 to $39.25, the option price would have declined to $2.3622, which would result in a gain of $0.4182 to the market-maker. Using delta we would have predicted a price decline of $-$0.75 \times 0.5824 = -0.4368, which is greater than the actual decline. This occurs because the option delta decreases as the stock price declines. The delta at this new price is 0.5326.

Gamma measures the change in delta when the stock price changes. In the example above, the gamma of 0.0652 means that delta will change by approximately 0.0652 if the stock price moves $1. This is why delta did not accurately predict the change in the option price: The delta itself was changing as the stock price changed. The ultimate change in the option price is a result of the *average* delta during the stock price change, not just the delta at the initial stock price. As you might guess, we can use gamma in addition to delta to better approximate the effect on the value of the option of a change in the stock price. We will discuss this adjustment later.

13.3 DELTA-HEDGING

Suppose a market-maker sells one call option and hedges the position with shares. With the sale of a call, the market-maker is short delta shares. To hedge this position, the market-maker can buy delta shares to delta-hedge the position.

We now will consider the risk of a delta-hedged position by assuming that the market-maker delta-hedges and marks-to-market daily. We first look at numerical examples and then in Section 13.4 explain the results algebraically.

An Example of Delta-Hedging for 2 Days

Day 0   Consider the 40-strike call option described above, written on 100 shares of stock. The market-maker sells the option and receives $278.04. Since $\Delta = 0.5824$, the market-maker also buys 58.24 shares. (We will permit fractional share purchases in this example.) The net investment is

$$(58.24 \times \$40) - \$278.04 = \$2051.56$$

At an 8% interest rate, the market-maker has an overnight financing charge of $2051.56 \times \left(e^{0.08/365} - 1\right) = \$0.45$.

Day 1: Marking-to-market   Without at first worrying about rebalancing the portfolio to maintain delta-neutrality, we can ask whether the market-maker made money or lost money overnight. Suppose the new stock price is $40.50. The new call option price with 1 day less to expiration and at the new stock price is $3.0621. Overnight mark-to-market profit is a gain of $0.50, computed as follows:

Gain on 58.24 shares	$58.24 \times (\$40.50 - \$40)$	=	$29.12
Gain on written call option	$\$278.04 - \$306.21$	=	-$28.17
Interest	$-(e^{0.08/365} - 1) \times \$2051.56$	=	-$0.45
Overnight profit			**$0.50**

Day 1: Rebalancing the portfolio The new delta is 0.6142. Since delta has increased, we must buy $61.42 - 58.24 = 3.18$ additional shares. This transaction requires an investment of $\$40.50 \times 3.18 = \$128.79$. Since the readjustment in the number of shares entails buying at the current market price, it does not affect the mark-to-market profits for that day.

Day 2: Marking-to-market The stock price now falls to $39.25. The market-maker makes money on the written option and loses money on the 61.42 shares. Interest expense has increased over the previous day because additional investment was required for the extra shares. The net result from marking-to-market is a loss of $-\$3.87$:

Gain on 61.42 shares	$61.42 \times (\$39.25 - \$40.50)$	$=$	$-\$76.78$
Gain on written call option	$\$306.21 - \$232.82$	$=$	$\$73.39$
Interest	$-(e^{0.08/365} - 1) \times \$2181.30$	$=$	$-\$0.48$
Overnight profit			$-\mathbf{\$3.87}$

Interpreting the Profit Calculation

At the end of day 1, we show a $0.50 profit from the mark-to-market calculation. Conceptually, we can think of the profit or loss as measuring the extent to which the portfolio requires cash infusions in order to maintain a delta-neutral hedge. When we show a positive profit, as in this case, we can take cash out of the portfolio.

To see that mark-to-market profit measures the net cash infusions required to maintain the delta-neutral position, suppose that a lender is willing at all times to lend us the value of securities in the portfolio. Initially, we buy 58.24 shares of stock, which costs $2329.60, but this amount is offset by the $278.04 option premium, so the net cash we require is $2051.56. This is also the net value of our portfolio (stock less the option), so we can borrow this amount.[1]

As time passes, there are three sources of cash flow into and out of the portfolio:

1. **Borrowing** Our borrowing capacity equals the market value of securities in the portfolio; hence, borrowing capacity changes as the net value of the position changes. On day 0, the net value of our securities was $2051.56. On day 1, the share price rose and we bought additional shares; the market value of the position was $61.42 \times \$40.50 - \$306.21 = \$2181.30$. Thus our borrowing capacity increased by $129.74. The change in the option value changes borrowing capacity, but there is no cash flow since we are not changing the number of options.

2. **Purchase or sale of shares** We buy or sell shares as necessary to maintain delta-neutrality. In the above example, we increased shares in our portfolio from 58.24 to 61.42. The price at the time was $40.50, so we spent $3.18 \times \$40.50 = \$128.79$.

---

[1] In practice we would be able to borrow only part of the funds required to buy securities.

3. Interest We pay interest on the borrowed amount. On day 1 we owed $0.45.

Thus, we need $128.79 to buy more shares and $0.45 to pay interest expense. The change in our borrowing capacity—the extra amount the bank will lend us—is $129.74. The difference between what the bank will lend us on the one hand, and the cost of additional shares plus interest on the other, is

$$\$129.74 - \$128.79 - \$0.45 = \$0.50$$

Since the bank is willing to lend us the value of our securities, we are free to pocket the $0.50 that is left over.

This example demonstrates that the mark-to-market profit equals the net cash flow generated by always borrowing to fully fund the position. Another way to see the equality of mark-to-market profit and net cash flow is by examining the sources and uses of funds, and the extent to which it is necessary to inject additional cash into the position in order to maintain the delta-neutral hedge. We can calculate the net cash flow from the portfolio as

$$
\begin{aligned}
\text{Net cash flow} = {} & \text{Change in borrowing capacity} \\
& - \text{cash used to purchase additional shares} \\
& - \text{interest}
\end{aligned}
$$

Let Δ_i denote the option delta on day i, S_i the stock price, C_i the option price, and MV_i the market value of the portfolio. Borrowing capacity on day i is $MV_i = \Delta_i S_i - C_i$; hence, the change in borrowing capacity is

$$MV_i - MV_{i-1} = \Delta_i S_i - C_i - (\Delta_{i-1} S_{i-1} - C_{i-1})$$

The cost of purchasing additional shares is $S_i(\Delta_i - \Delta_{i-1})$, and interest owed on day i depends on the previous day's borrowing, rMV_i. Thus, on day i we have

$$
\begin{aligned}
\text{Net cash flow} &= MV_i - MV_{i-1} - S_i(\Delta_i - \Delta_{i-1}) - rMV_{i-1} \\
&= \Delta_i S_i - C_i - (\Delta_{i-1} S_{i-1} - C_{i-1}) - S_i(\Delta_i - \Delta_{i-1}) - rMV_{i-1} \\
&= \Delta_{i-1}(S_i - S_{i-1}) - (C_i - C_{i-1}) - rMV_{i-1}
\end{aligned}
$$

The last expression is the overnight gain on shares, less the overnight gain on the option, less interest; this result is identical to the profit calculation we performed above. In the numerical example, we have

$$
\begin{aligned}
MV_1 - MV_0 - S_1(\Delta_1 - \Delta_0) - rMV_0 &= \$2181.30 - \$2051.56 - \$128.79 - \$0.45 \\
&= \$0.50
\end{aligned}
$$

This value is equal to the overnight profit we calculated between day 0 and day 1.

Thus, we can interpret the daily mark-to-market profit or loss as the amount of cash that we can pocket (if there is a profit) or that we must pay (if there is a loss) in order to fund required purchases of new shares and to continue borrowing exactly the amount of our securities. When we have a positive profit, as on day 1, we can take money out of the portfolio, and when we have a negative profit, as on day 2, we must put money into the portfolio.

A hedged portfolio that never requires additional cash investments to remain hedged is **self-financing**. One of the questions we will answer is under what conditions a delta-hedged portfolio is self-financing.

Delta-Hedging for Several Days

We can continue the example by letting the market-maker rebalance the portfolio each day. Table 13.2 summarizes delta and the net investment each day for 5 days. The profit line in the table is *daily* profit, not cumulative profit.

What determines the pattern of gain and loss in the table? There are three effects, attributable to gamma, theta, and the carrying cost of the position.

Gamma   For the largest moves in the stock, the market-maker loses money. For small moves in the stock price, the market-maker makes money. The loss for large moves results from gamma: If the stock price changes, the position becomes unhedged. In this case, since the market-maker is short the option, a large move generates a loss. As the stock price rises, the delta of the call increases and it loses money faster than the stock makes money. As the stock price falls, the delta of the call decreases and it makes money more slowly than the fixed stock position loses money. In effect, the market-maker becomes unhedged net long as the stock price falls and unhedged net short as the stock price rises. The losses on days 2 and 4 are attributable to gamma. For all of the entries in Table 13.2, the gamma of the written call is about -0.06 per share.

Theta   If a day passes with no change in the stock price, the option becomes cheaper. This time decay works to the benefit of the market-maker who could unwind the position more cheaply. Time decay is especially evident in the profit on day 5, but is also responsible for the profit on days 1 and 3.

TABLE 13.2	Daily profit calculation over 5 days for a market-maker who delta-hedges.

| | **Day** | | | | | |
	0	**1**	**2**	**3**	**4**	**5**
Stock ($)	40.00	40.50	39.25	38.75	40.00	40.00
Call ($)	278.04	306.21	232.82	205.46	271.04	269.27
Option Delta	0.5824	0.6142	0.5311	0.4956	0.5806	0.5801
Investment ($)	2,051.58	2,181.30	1,851.65	1,715.12	2,051.35	2,051.29
Interest ($)		−0.45	−0.48	−0.41	−0.38	−0.45
Capital Gain ($)		0.95	−3.39	0.81	−3.62	1.77
Daily Profit ($)		0.50	−3.87	0.40	−4.00	1.32

Interest Cost In order to hedge, the market-maker must purchase stock. The net carrying cost is a component of the overall cost.

Figure 13.2 graphs overnight market-maker profit on day 1 as a function of the stock price on day 1. At a stock price of $40.50, for example, the profit is $0.50, just as in the table. The graph is generated by recomputing the day-1 profit per share for a variety of stock prices between $37 and $43. The graph verifies what is evident in the table: The delta-hedging market-maker who has written a call wants small stock price moves and can suffer a substantial loss with a big move. In fact, should the stock price move to $37.50, for example, the market-maker would lose $20.

If the market-maker had purchased a call and shorted delta shares, every aspect of the profit calculation would be reversed. The market-maker would lose money for small stock price moves and make money with large moves. The profit diagram for such a position would be a mirror image of Figure 13.2.

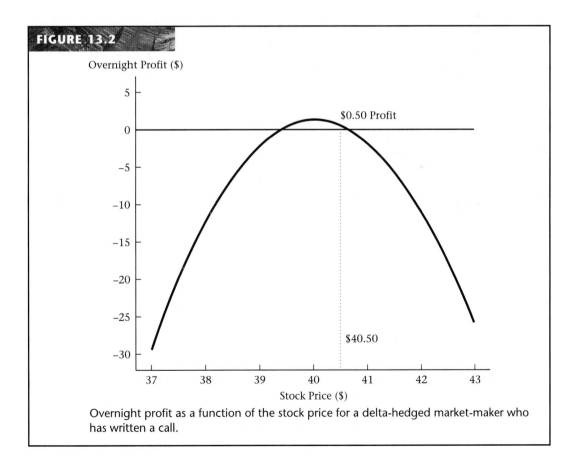

FIGURE 13.2

Overnight profit as a function of the stock price for a delta-hedged market-maker who has written a call.

TABLE 13.3		Daily profit calculation over 5 days for a market-maker who delta-hedges, assuming the stock price moves up or down one σ each day.				

	Day					
	0	**1**	**2**	**3**	**4**	**5**
Stock ($)	40.000	40.642	40.018	39.403	38.797	39.420
Call ($)	278.04	315.00	275.57	239.29	206.14	236.76
Option Delta	0.5824	0.6232	0.5827	0.5408	0.4980	0.5406
Investment ($)	2,051.58	2,217.66	2,056.08	1,891.60	1,725.95	1,894.27
Interest ($)		−0.45	−0.49	−0.45	−0.41	−0.38
Capital Gain ($)		0.43	0.51	0.46	0.42	0.38
Daily Profit ($)		−0.02	0.02	0.01	0.01	0.00

A Self-Financing Portfolio: The Stock Moves One σ

In the previous example, the stock price changes by varying amounts and our daily profit varies substantially. However, in Figure 13.2, there is an up move and a down move for the stock such that the market-maker exactly breaks even in our profit calculations. If the stock always moved by this amount, the portfolio would be self-financing: No cash inflows are required to maintain delta-neutrality. It turns out that the portfolio is self-financing if the stock moves by one standard deviation.

In the binomial option pricing model in Chapter 10, we assumed that the stock moved up to $Se^{rh+\sigma\sqrt{h}}$ or down to $Se^{rh-\sigma\sqrt{h}}$, where $\sigma\sqrt{h}$ is the standard deviation per interval of the rate of return on the stock. Suppose we assume the stock moves up or down according to this binomial model. Table 13.3, which is otherwise the same as the previous example, shows the results of the stock moving up, down three times, and then up. You can see that the market-maker comes close to breaking even each day. If the stock moves according to the binomial model, therefore, the portfolio is approximately self-financing.

13.4 THE MATHEMATICS OF DELTA-HEDGING

Clearly, delta, gamma, and theta all play a role in determining the profit on a delta-hedged position. In this section we examine these relationships more closely in order to better understand the numerical example above. What we do here is a kind of financial forensics: Once we learn how the stock price changed, we seek to discover why we earned the profit we did.

Using Gamma to Better Approximate the Change in the Option Price

Delta alone is an inaccurate predictor of the change in the option price because delta changes with the stock price. When delta is very sensitive to the stock price (gamma is large), the inaccuracy will be relatively great. When delta is not sensitive to the stock price (gamma is small), the inaccuracy will be relatively small. Since gamma measures the change in delta, we can use gamma to develop a better approximation for the change in the option price.

If the stock price were $40.75 instead of $40, the option price would be $3.2352 instead of $2.7804. For the purpose of computing the change in the option price, we want to know the average rate of price increase between $40 and $40.75, which we can approximate by averaging the deltas at $40 and $40.75:

$$\Delta_{\text{Average}} = \frac{\Delta_{40} + \Delta_{40.75}}{2}$$

We could then approximate the option price at $40.75 by computing

$$C(\$40.75) = C(\$40) + 0.75 \times \Delta_{\text{Average}} \tag{13.1}$$

When we average the deltas at $40 and $40.75, we have to compute deltas at two different stock prices. A different approach is to approximate the average delta by using only the delta evaluated at $40 together with gamma. Since gamma measures the change in delta, we can approximate the delta at $40.75 by adding $0.75 \times \Gamma$ to Δ_{40}:

$$\Delta_{40.75} = \Delta_{40} + 0.75 \times \Gamma$$

Using this relationship, the average delta is

$$\Delta_{\text{Average}} = \frac{\Delta_{40} + (\Delta_{40} + 0.75 \times \Gamma)}{2}$$

$$= \Delta_{40} + \frac{1}{2} \times 0.75 \times \Gamma$$

Using equation (13.1), we can then approximate the call price as

$$C(\$40.75) = C(\$40) + 0.75 \times \Delta_{\text{Average}}$$

$$= C(\$40) + 0.75 \times \left(\Delta_{40} + \frac{1}{2} \times 0.75 \times \Gamma \right)$$

$$= C(\$40) + 0.75 \times \Delta_{40} + \frac{1}{2} \times 0.75^2 \times \Gamma \tag{13.2}$$

The use of delta and gamma to approximate the new option price is called a **delta-gamma approximation**.

Example 13.1 If the stock price rises from $40 to $40.75, the option price increases from $2.7804 to $3.2352. Using a delta approximation alone, we would estimate

$C(\$40.75)$ as

$$C(\$40.75) = C(\$40) + 0.75 \times 0.5824 = \$3.2172$$

Using a delta-gamma approximation, we obtain

$$C(\$40.75) = C(\$40) + 0.75 \times 0.5824 + \frac{1}{2} \times 0.75^2 \times 0.0652 = \$3.2355$$

The delta-gamma approximation is significantly closer to the true option price at $40.75 than is the delta approximation.

Similarly, for a stock price decline to $39.25, the true option price is $2.3622. The delta approximation gives

$$C(\$39.25) = C(\$40) - 0.75 \times 0.5824 = \$2.3436$$

The delta-gamma approximation gives

$$C(\$39.25) = C(\$40) - 0.75 \times 0.5824 + \frac{1}{2} \times 0.75^2 \times 0.0652 = \$2.3619$$

Again, the delta-gamma approximation is more accurate.   ❧

Delta-Gamma Approximations

We now repeat the previous arguments using algebra. For a "small" move in the stock price, we know that the rate at which delta changes is given by gamma. Thus, if over a time interval of length h the stock price change is

$$\epsilon = S_{t+h} - S_t$$

then gamma is the change in delta per dollar of stock price change, or

$$\Gamma(S_t) = \frac{\Delta(S_{t+h}) - \Delta(S_t)}{\epsilon}$$

Rewriting this expression, delta will change by approximately the magnitude of the price change, ϵ, times gamma, $\epsilon\Gamma$:

$$\Delta(S_{t+h}) = \Delta(S_t) + \epsilon\Gamma(S_t) \tag{13.3}$$

If the rate at which delta changes is constant (meaning that gamma is constant), this calculation is exact.

How does equation (13.3) help us compute the option price change? If the stock price changes by ϵ, we can compute the option price change if we know the *average* delta over the range S_{t+h} to S_t. If Γ is approximately constant, the average delta is simply the average of $\Delta(S_t)$ and $\Delta(S_{t+h})$, or (using equation (13.3))

$$\frac{\Delta(S_t) + \Delta(S_{t+h})}{2} = \Delta(S_t) + \frac{1}{2}\epsilon\Gamma(S_t) \tag{13.4}$$

The option price at the new stock price is the initial option price, $C(S_t)$, plus the average delta times the change in the stock price, or

$$C(S_{t+h}) = C(S_t) + \epsilon \left[\frac{\Delta(S_t) + \Delta(S_{t+h})}{2} \right]$$

Using equation (13.4), we can rewrite this to express $\Delta(S_{t+h})$ in terms of $\Gamma(S_t)$:

$$C(S_{t+h}) = C(S_t) + \epsilon \Delta(S_t) + \frac{1}{2}\epsilon^2 \Gamma(S_t) \qquad (13.5)$$

The gamma correction is independent of the direction of the change in the stock price because gamma is multiplied by ϵ^2, which is always positive. When the stock price goes up, delta alone predicts too little a change in the call price, and we have to add something to correct the prediction. When the stock price goes down, delta alone predicts too much of a decrease in the option price, and we again have to add something to correct the prediction.

    The new predicted call price is not perfect because gamma changes as the stock price changes. We could add a term correcting for the change in gamma, and a term correcting for the change in the change in gamma, and so forth, but we won't. The important point is that the gamma correction alone dramatically improves the accuracy of the approximation. You might recognize equation (13.5) as a second order (because it uses the first and second derivatives, delta and gamma) *Taylor series approximation* for the change in the call price. Taylor series approximations are discussed in Appendix 13.A.

    Figure 13.3 shows the result of approximating the option price using the delta and delta-gamma approximations. The delta approximation is a straight line tangent to the

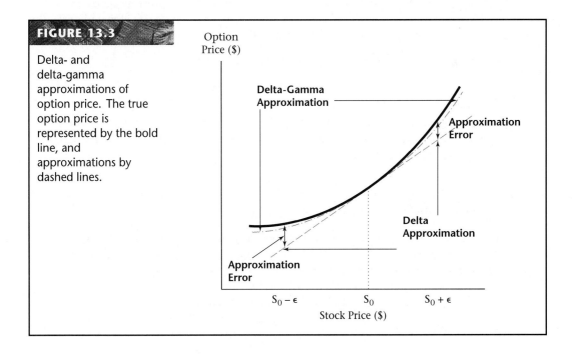

FIGURE 13.3

Delta- and delta-gamma approximations of option price. The true option price is represented by the bold line, and approximations by dashed lines.

option price curve and is always below the option price curve. Because of this, the delta approximation understates the option price, whether the stock price rises or falls. The delta-gamma approximation uses the squared stock price change, which generates a curve more closely approximating the option price curve.

Theta: Accounting for Time

The preceding calculations measured the option risk that arises from price changes alone. Of course as the price changes, time is passing and the option is approaching maturity.

The option's theta (θ) measures the option's change in price due to time passing, holding the stock price fixed. For a period of length h, the change in the option price will be θh. For example, consider the 91-day option in Section 13.3 and consider the effect of a day passing, with no change in the stock price. Since the variables in the option pricing formula are expressed as annual values, a one-unit change in $T - t$ implies a θ of -6.33251. Since h is $1/365$, the implied daily option price change is $-6.33251/365 = -0.01735$.

Adding theta to our previous option price prediction equation, we have

$$
\begin{aligned}
&C(S_{t+h}, T - t - h) \\
&\quad = C(S_t, T - t) + \epsilon \Delta(S_t, T - t) + \frac{1}{2}\epsilon^2 \Gamma(S_t, T - t) + h\theta(S_t, T - t)
\end{aligned}
\tag{13.6}
$$

The experiment reflected in this equation is this: Starting with an option with $T - t$ periods until expiration and a stock price of S_t, we want to express the new option price as a function of the old price and the delta, gamma, and theta evaluated at the original price and time to expiration. This formula is quite accurate for relatively small changes in time and in the stock price.

Example 13.2   Table 13.4 shows the results from using equation (13.6) to predict the option price change when prices move by $0.75 ($\epsilon = \pm 0.75$). In this example, $\Delta = 0.5824$, $\Gamma = 0.0652$, and $h\theta = -0.0173$. Note that in each case the formula slightly overstates the change, but it is close.   ❧

Understanding the Market-Maker's Profit

The calculations in Tables 13.2 and 13.3 use actual option price changes over 1 day, not approximations. However, by using equation (13.6) to approximate the change in the option price we can better understand the profit results in those tables.

The value of the market-maker's investment—long delta shares and short a call—is the value of delta shares of stock less the value of the call, or

$$
\Delta S_t - C(S_t)
$$

TABLE 13.4		Predicted option price over a period of 1 day, assuming stock price move of $0.75, using equation (13.6). Assumes $\sigma = 0.3$, $r = 0.08$, $T - t = 91$ days, $\delta = 0$, and the initial stock price is $40.				
					Option Price 1 Day Later ($h = 1$ day)	
	Starting Price	$\epsilon\Delta$	$\frac{1}{2}\epsilon^2\Gamma$	θh	**Predicted**	**Actual**
$S_{t+h} = \$40.75$	$2.7804	0.4368	0.0183	−0.0173	$3.2182	$3.2176
$S_{t+h} = \$39.25$	$2.7804	−0.4368	0.0183	−0.0173	$2.3446	$2.3452

Suppose that over the time interval h, the stock price changes from S_t to S_{t+h}. The change in the value of the portfolio is the change in the value of the stock and option positions, less interest expense:

$$\underbrace{\Delta(S_{t+h} - S_t)}_{\text{Change in Value of Stock}} \quad - \quad \underbrace{[C(S_{t+h}) - C(S_t)]}_{\text{Change in Value of Option}} \quad - \quad \underbrace{rh[\Delta S_t - C(S_t)]}_{\text{Interest Expense}}$$

Now recall equation (13.6), in which we characterized the change in the option price. Substituting equation (13.6) for $C(S_{t+h}) - C(S_t)$ in this expression tells us

$$\Delta(S_{t+h} - S_t) - [\Delta(S_{t+h} - S_t) + \frac{1}{2}(S_{t+h} - S_t)^2\Gamma + \theta h] - rh[\Delta S_t - C(S_t)]$$

$$= -\left(\frac{1}{2}\epsilon^2\Gamma + \theta h + rh[\Delta S_t - C(S_t)]\right) \quad (13.7)$$

This expression gives us the profit of the market-maker when the stock price changes by ϵ over an interval of length h. It is quite important and variants of it will appear later in the book.

On the right-hand side of equation (13.7) we see the effects of gamma, theta, and interest:

Gamma The effect of gamma is measured by $-\frac{1}{2}\epsilon^2\Gamma$. Since the gamma of the call is positive, by writing the call the market-maker will lose money in proportion to the square of the stock price change. The larger the stock move, the greater is the loss.

Theta The effect of theta is measured by $-\theta h$. Since theta for the call is negative, the option writer benefits from theta.

Interest cost Interest is measured by $-rh[\Delta S_t - C(S_t)]$. The option writer has a net investment because Δ shares are more expensive than one option. Hence, interest is a net cost.

Since θ is negative, time decay benefits the market-maker, whereas interest and gamma work against the market-maker.

Let's examine how ϵ, the change in the stock price, enters equation (13.7). Note first that because we have delta-hedged, ϵ itself does not affect market-maker profit. However, profit *does* depend on the *squared* change in the stock price, ϵ^2. Consequently, as we saw in Table 13.2, it is the magnitude and not the direction of the stock price move that determines profit.

Table 13.5 calculates equation (13.7) for various moves in the stock price. Because equation (13.7) depends only on the *squared* stock price move, the calculation is the same for moves up and down.

If the stock price moves \$0.6281, equation (13.7) is exactly zero. We have already seen in Table 13.3 that the market-maker approximately breaks even for a one-standard-deviation move in the stock. Here we arrive at the same result. Let's explore this idea further.

If σ is measured annually, then a one-standard-deviation move over a period of length h is $\sigma S \sqrt{h}$. Therefore a squared one-standard-deviation move is

$$\epsilon^2 = \sigma^2 S^2 h \tag{13.8}$$

Substituting this expression for ϵ^2, we can rewrite equation (13.7) as

$$\text{Market-maker profit} = -\left(\frac{1}{2}\sigma^2 S_t^2 \Gamma + \theta + r\left[\Delta S_t - C(S_t)\right] \right) h \tag{13.9}$$

This expression gives us market-maker profit when the stock moves one standard deviation. As an example, let $h = 1/365$ and $\sigma = 0.3$. Then $\sigma S \sqrt{h} = \$0.6281$. From Table 13.5, with this stock price move equation (13.9) is *exactly* zero! (Problem 13 asks you to verify this.) It is not an accident that equation (13.9) is zero for this price move. We explain this result in Section 13.5.

In Table 13.5, the loss from a one-dollar move is substantially larger in absolute value than the gain from no move. However, small moves are more probable than big

TABLE 13.5	Predicted effect, using equation (13.7), of different-sized stock price moves on the profit of a delta-hedged market-maker.

Absolute Value of Price Move, $\|\epsilon\|$	$-\frac{1}{2}\epsilon^2 \Gamma - \theta h - rh[\Delta S_t - C(S_t)]$
0.0000	1.283
0.2500	1.080
0.5000	0.470
0.6281	0.000
0.7500	−0.546
1.0000	−1.970
1.5000	−6.036

moves. If we think of returns as being approximately normally distributed, then stock price moves greater than one standard deviation occur about one-third of the time. The market-maker thus expects to make small profits about two-thirds of the time, and larger losses about one-third of the time. On average, the market-maker will break even.

13.5 THE BLACK-SCHOLES ANALYSIS

We have discussed how a market-maker can measure and manage the risk of a portfolio containing options. What is the link to pricing an option?

The Black-Scholes Argument

If a stock moves one standard deviation, then a delta-hedged position will exactly break even, taking into account the cost of funding the position. This finding is not a coincidence; it reflects the arguments Black and Scholes used to derive the option pricing formula.

Imagine, for example, that the stock always moves exactly one standard deviation every minute.[2] A market-maker hedging every minute will be hedged over an hour or over any period of time. Black and Scholes argued that the money invested in this hedged position should earn the risk-free rate since the resulting income stream is risk-free.

Equation (13.9) gives us an expression for market-maker profit when the stock moves one standard deviation. Setting this expression to zero gives

$$-\left(\frac{1}{2}\sigma^2 S^2 \Gamma + \theta + r\left[\Delta S_t - C(S_t)\right]\right)h = 0$$

If we divide by h and rearrange terms, we get

$$\frac{1}{2}\sigma^2 S^2 \Gamma + r S_t \Delta + \theta = r C(S_t) \tag{13.10}$$

This is the equation Black and Scholes used to characterize the behavior of an option. The Greeks Γ, Δ, and θ are partial derivatives of the option price. Equation (13.10) is the well-known Black-Scholes partial differential equation, or just Black-Scholes equation (as opposed to the Black-Scholes *formula* for the price of a European call). We will see in later chapters that this relationship among the Greeks is as fundamental in valuing risky cash flows as is e^{-rT} when valuing risk-free cash flows.

Equation (13.10) embodies numerous assumptions, among them that the underlying asset does not pay a dividend, the option itself does not pay a dividend, the interest rate and volatility are constant, and the stock moves one standard deviation over a small time interval. With these assumptions, equation (13.10) holds for calls, puts, American options, European options, and most of the exotic variants we will consider in Chapter

---

[2]There are $365 \times 24 \times 60 = 525,600$ minutes in a year. Thus, if the stock's annual standard deviation is 30%, the per-minute standard deviation is $0.3/\sqrt{525,600} = 0.04\%$, or \$0.016 for a \$40 stock.

14. With simple modifications, an equation like (13.10) will also hold for options on dividend-paying stocks, currencies, futures, bonds, etc. The link between delta-hedging and pricing is one of the most important ideas in finance.

Delta-Hedging of American Options

Equation (13.10) holds for American options as well as for European options, but it does not hold at times when it is optimal to early-exercise the option. Consider a deep-in-the-money American put option and suppose the option should be exercised early. Since early exercise is optimal, the option price is $K - S$; hence, $\Delta = -1$, $\Gamma = 0$, and $\theta = 0$. In this case, equation (13.10) becomes

$$[r \times (-1) \times S_t] + \left(\frac{1}{2} \times 0 \right) + 0 = r \times (K - S_t)$$

Note that $-rS_t$ appears on both sides of the equation. Thus, we can rewrite the equation as

$$0 = rK$$

Since this equation is false, clearly, something is wrong. We began by assuming that the put was so far in-the-money that it should be early-exercised. From the discussion of early exercise in Chapter 10, this means that interest received on the strike exceeds the loss of the implicit call option. Thus, if the option should be exercised, but you own it, delta-hedge it, and *do not exercise it*, then you lose interest on the strike you are not receiving. Similarly, if you have written the option and delta-hedged, and the owner does not exercise, then you are earning arbitrage profit of rK.

Thus, equation (13.10) is only valid in a region where early exercise is not optimal. If an option should be exercised but is not exercised, then behavior is irrational and there is no reason why a delta-hedged position should earn the risk-free rate and thus no reason that equation (13.10) should hold.

What Is the Advantage to Frequent Re-Hedging?

In practice, because of transaction costs, it is expensive for a market-maker to trade shares for every change in an option delta. Instead, a delta-hedger will wait for the position to become somewhat unhedged before trading to reestablish delta-neutrality. In the binomial model in Chapter 10, and in the preceding discussion, we assumed that market-makers maintain their hedged position and that stock prices move exactly one standard deviation. In real life the stock price will rarely move exactly one standard deviation over the course of a day. What does the market-maker lose by hedging less frequently?

Boyle and Emanuel (1980) considered a market-maker who delta-hedges at set intervals, rather than every time the stock price changes. Let x_i denote the number of standard deviations the stock price moves—we can think of x_i as being drawn randomly from the standard normal distribution. Also let $R_{h,i}$ denote the period-i return to a delta-hedged market-maker who, as in our earlier example, has written a call. Boyle and Emanuel show that this return can be written as[3]

$$R_{h,i} = \frac{1}{2} S^2 \sigma^2 \Gamma (x_i^2 - 1) h \tag{13.11}$$

where Γ is the option's gamma and h is the time interval between hedge readjustments. From Boyle and Emanuel, the variance of $x_i^2 - 1$ is 2; hence,

$$Var(R_{h,i}) = \frac{1}{2} \left(S^2 \sigma^2 \Gamma h \right)^2 \tag{13.12}$$

We assume—as in the binomial model—that the stock return is uncorrelated across time, so that x_i is uncorrelated across time.

Now let's compare hedging once a day against hedging hourly (suppose trading occurs around the clock). The daily variance of the return earned by the market-maker who hedges once a day is given by

$$Var(R_{1/365,1}) = \frac{1}{2} \left(S^2 \sigma^2 \Gamma / 365 \right)^2$$

The daily return of the market-maker who hedges hourly is the sum of the hourly returns. Assuming for the sake of simplicity that S and Γ do not change much, that variance is

$$Var \left(\sum_{i=1}^{24} R_{h,i} \right) = \sum_{i=1}^{24} \frac{1}{2} \left[S^2 \sigma^2 \Gamma / (24 \times 365) \right]^2$$

$$= \frac{1}{24} \times Var(R_{1/365,1})$$

Thus, by hedging hourly instead of daily the market-maker's total return variance is reduced by a factor of 24.

Here is the intuition for this result. Whatever the hedging interval, about two-thirds of the price moves will be less than a single standard deviation, whereas one-third will be greater. Frequent re-hedging does not avoid these large or small moves, since they can occur over any interval. The daily return is the sum of hourly returns. However, frequent hedging does permit better *averaging* of the effects of these moves. Whether you hedge once a day or once an hour, the typical stock price move you encounter will likely not be close to one standard deviation. However, if you hedge every hour, over the course of a day you will have 24 moves and 24 opportunities to re-hedge. The *average* move over this period is likelier to be close to one standard deviation. The gains from

---

[3]This expression can be derived by assuming that the stock price move, ϵ, is normally distributed with variance $S\sigma \sqrt{h}$, and subtracting equation (13.9) from (13.7).

small moves and losses from large moves will tend to average over the course of a day. In effect, the more frequent hedger benefits from diversification over time.[4]

Example 13.3 Using Boyle and Emanuel's formulas to study the market-maker problem in Section 13.3, the standard deviation of profit is about $0.075 for a market-maker who hedges hourly. Since hedging errors are independent from hour to hour, the daily standard deviation for an hourly hedger would be $0.075 \times \sqrt{24} = \$0.37$. If the market-maker were to hedge only daily as in our example, the daily standard deviation would be about $1.82. 🕯

As you would expect, the *mean* return on a delta-hedged position is zero, even if the hedge is not frequently readjusted.

Delta-Hedging in Practice

The Black-Scholes analysis outlined here is the linchpin of modern option pricing theory *and* practice. Market-makers use equation (13.10) to price options, subject to qualifications mentioned above.

Keep in mind, however, that delta-hedging does not eliminate risk. One problem, discussed in the box on page 421, is that firms can unexpectedly change their dividend payments. Another problem, which we emphasized above, is that a delta-hedged portfolio with negative gamma is susceptible to risk from unexpectedly large moves in the price of the underlying asset. Such moves do occur. Consequently, a delta-hedging market-maker needs to worry about gamma. So what should a market-maker do?

There are at least three ways to reduce the risk of extreme price moves, all of which entail using options to hedge options, as opposed to using only stock to hedge options.

First, just as market-makers can adopt a delta-neutral position, they can also adopt a gamma-neutral position. This position cannot be accomplished with the stock alone, since the gamma of the stock is zero. Thus to be gamma-neutral the market-maker must buy or sell options with appropriate gammas so as to offset the existing position.

Second, a market-maker can buy out-of-the-money options. In the example above of delta-neutral hedging of a written option, the market-maker loses money if there are sudden large increases or decreases in the stock price. Consider a strategy of augmenting the portfolio with a deep-out-of-the-money put and a deep-out-of-the-money call. The two options will be relatively inexpensive but will protect against large moves in the stock. As noted before, market-makers would rather not buy options since they then pay

---

[4]This resembles the problem faced by an insurance company. If the company insures one large asset, the standard deviation of the loss is $\sqrt{n}$ greater than if it insures n small assets, with the same total insured value in each case. Similarly, we can view the return over each hedging interval as being an independent draw from a probability distribution.

Dividend Risk

As we have seen, the expected dividend is incorporated into the price of an option. If a firm announces a significant change in dividend policy, delta-hedgers can lose money.

On March 10, 1998, Daimler-Benz stunned option market-makers by announcing a special one-time dividend, payable in May of that year, of approximately 20 Deutschemarks (DM), as opposed to a dividend of several DM that the market had been expecting. The surprise is obvious from a comparison of option prices on March 10 and March 11. Closing Daimler stock prices on March 10 and 11 were DM 163.5 and DM 164.5. Put prices should therefore have gone down from the 10th to the 11th. However, premiums rose: The 150-strike put premium from DM 6 to DM 13.92; the 160-strike put from DM 10.02 to DM 20.94, and the 170-strike put from DM 15.51 to DM 28.98. Put-writing market-makers would have sustained serious losses.

Both Daimler and the Deutsche Terminbörse (the exchange where Daimler options were traded) came under criticism for the surprise and because the exchange did not adjust the terms of traded Daimler options to leave them unaffected by the surprise dividend increase.

rather than receive the spread. But the purchase of a few protective options as part of a large portfolio may be prudent. The problem with this solution is that if investors in the aggregate want to buy out-of-the-money options, the market-making community in the aggregate must sell them.

Third, market-makers can use **static option replication**. The idea is to use options to hedge options where feasible. In the above example, the market-maker might not be able to buy an exactly offsetting call option to hedge the written call, but by selectively setting the bid and ask prices for related options, it might be possible to set the "best" price for options that would help the market-maker hedge. For example, the market-maker could try to sell related calls or to buy a put with a similar strike price. If the market-maker were able to buy a put with the same strike price and maturity as the call (e.g., by setting the bid price to attract any seller of that option), then by buying 100 shares to offset the risk of the position, the market-maker would be delta-hedged and would never need to revise the hedge. In effect the market-maker would use put-call parity to form a hedge that is both gamma- and delta-neutral. More generally, by hedging options with options, the gamma of the portfolio can be under better control.

Gamma-Neutrality

Let's explore gamma-hedging. Suppose we wish to both delta-hedge and gamma-hedge the written option described in Table 13.1. We cannot do this using just the stock, because the gamma of stock is zero. Hence, we must acquire another option in an amount that offsets the gamma of the written call. Table 13.6 presents information for

	40-Strike Call	**45-Strike Call**	**Sell 40-Strike Call, Buy 1.2408 45-Strike Calls**
Price ($)	2.7847	1.3584	−1.0993
Delta	0.5825	0.3285	−0.1749
Gamma	0.0651	0.0524	0.0000
Vega	0.0781	0.0831	0.0250
Theta	−0.0173	−0.0129	0.0013
Rho	0.0513	0.0389	−0.0031

TABLE 13.6 Prices and Greeks for 40-strike call, 45-strike call, and the (gamma-neutral) portfolio resulting from selling the 40-strike call for which $T - t = 0.25$ and buying 1.2408 45-strike calls for which $T - t = 0.33$. By buying 17.49 shares, the market-maker can be both delta- and gamma-neutral. Assumes $S = \$40$, $\sigma = 0.3$, $r = 0.08$, and $\delta = 0$.

the 3-month 40-strike call, and also for a 4-month 45-strike call. We will use the latter to gamma-hedge the former.

The ratio of the gamma of the two options is[5]

$$\frac{\Gamma_{K=40, t=0.25}}{\Gamma_{K=45, t=0.33}} = \frac{0.0651}{0.0524} = 1.2408 \tag{13.13}$$

Thus, we need to buy 1.2408 of the 45-strike 4-month options for every 40-strike 3-month option we have sold. The Greeks resulting from the position are in the last column of Table 13.6. Since delta is −0.1749, we need to buy 17.49 shares of stock to be both delta- and gamma-hedged.

Figure 13.4 compares this delta- and gamma-hedged position to the delta-hedged position, discussed earlier, in which the same call was written. The delta-hedged position has the problem that large moves always cause losses. The gamma-hedged position loses less if there is a large move down, and can make money if the stock price increases. Moreover, as Table 13.6 shows, the gamma-hedged position has a positive vega. Why would anyone *not* gamma-hedge?

There are two reasons. First, as noted already, gamma-hedging requires the use of additional options. The market-maker will have to obtain the required option position

....

[5] The gammas in equation (13.13) are rounded. The actual gammas are 0.065063 and 0.052438, the ratio of which is 1.2408.

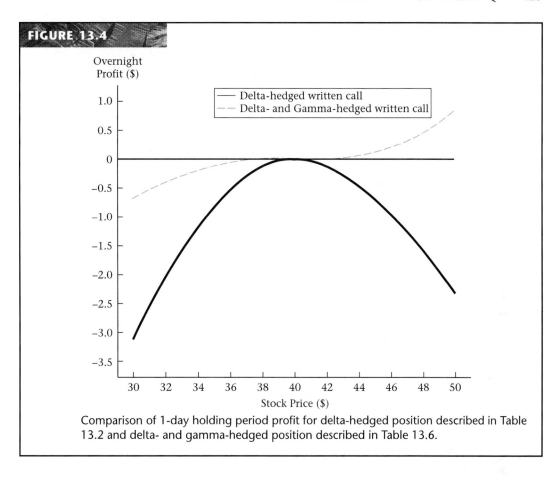

FIGURE 13.4

Comparison of 1-day holding period profit for delta-hedged position described in Table 13.2 and delta- and gamma-hedged position described in Table 13.6.

from another market-maker, paying the bid-ask spread. In this example, all profits earned from writing the 40-strike call will go to pay the market-maker who sells the 45-strike call used in gamma-hedging. Perhaps in a large portfolio, with many options bought and sold, naturally offsetting one another, gamma-hedging the net exposure would not require many option transactions.

The second reason is that if end-users on average buy puts and calls, then in the aggregate they have positive gamma (the end-users "buy gamma," to use market-making parlance). By definition, market-makers in the aggregate must then have negative gamma. Thus, while in principle any one market-maker could gamma-hedge, not all market-makers could be gamma-neutral. If investors want to buy insurance, they will not be gamma-neutral, and, hence, market-makers cannot in the aggregate be gamma-neutral.

While gamma and other risks (such as vega and rho) can be hedged in the same fashion as delta, it is not necessarily feasible.

13.6 MARKET-MAKING AS INSURANCE

The preceding discussion suggests that market-makers who write options can sustain large losses, even if they delta-hedge. This conclusion suggests that option market-making (and derivatives market-making more generally) has more in common with insurance than you might at first think.

Insurance

Insurance companies attempt to pool diversifiable risks. All insured individuals pay an insurance premium. The premiums are then used to compensate those who suffer losses, while those without losses lose the premium. Insurance thereby spreads the pain rather than forcing a few unlucky individuals to bear the brunt of inevitable losses.

In the classic model of an insurance company, risks are independent. Suppose an insurance company provides insurance for a large number of identical households, each of which has an independent 1% chance in any year of losing $100,000 in a fire. The expected loss for each house is $1\% \times \$100,000 = \$1,000$. This is the "actuarially fair" insurance premium, in the sense that if the insurance company collects this amount from each household, it will on average be able to pay annual insurance claims. In general insurance will be priced to cover the expected loss, plus costs of doing business, less interest earned on the premium.

However, even with diversification, there is a chance that actual insurance claims in a particular year will exceed $1000 per insured household, in which case the insurance company will not be able to fulfill its promises unless it has access to additional funds. Thus, the seller of a risk-management product—the insurance company—has a risk-management problem of its own, namely to be sure that it can meet its obligations to customers. Meeting its obligations is not just a matter of conscience for management; if there is a significant chance that the insurance company will be bankrupted by claims, there will be no customers in the first place!

Insurance companies have two primary ways to ensure they meet claims.

Capital   Insurance companies hold capital, i.e., a buffer fund in case there is an unusually large number of claims. Because of diversification, for any given bankruptcy probability insurers can use a smaller reserve fund per insured house as the number of insured houses grows. Capital in the form of reserves has traditionally been an important buffer for insurance companies against unexpectedly large claims.[6]

Reinsurance   There is always the possibility of a loss that can exceed any *fixed* amount of capital. An insurance company can in turn buy insurance against large

---

[6]Estimated capital for the U.S. insurance industry is $250 billion, against $30 trillion in property. Hurricane Andrew in 1992 cost insurers $15.5 billion and losses from the Northridge, California, earthquake in 1994 were $12.5 billion.

losses, in order to be able to make large payouts if necessary. Insurance for insurance companies is called reinsurance. Insurance companies buy insurance from reinsurance firms to cover the event that claims exceed a certain amount. Reinsurance is a put option: The reinsurance claim gives the insurance company the right to sell to the reinsurers claims that have lost money. Reinsurance does not change the aggregate need for capital, but it does permit further diversification.

Market-Makers

Now consider again the role of market-makers. Suppose that investors, fearful of a market crash, wish to buy out-of-the-money puts. Out-of-the-money put writers are selling insurance against large market moves. It is precisely when large market moves occur that delta-hedging breaks down. Just like an insurance company, a market-maker requires capital as a cushion against losses. Since capital has a cost, market-makers may also raise the cost of written options that require a disproportionately large commitment of capital per dollar of premium.

Reinsurance for a market-maker would entail buying out-of-the-money put options to move some risk to another market-maker, but ultimately if the financial industry is a net writer of insurance, there must be capital in the event of losses.

The importance of capital and the analogy to insurance becomes more obvious when we consider new derivatives markets. For example, think about weather derivatives. Financial institutions have hedged ski-resort operators against warm winters, soft-drink manufacturers against cold summers, and lawn sprinkler manufacturers against wet summers. Ultimately, the bank must find a counterparty willing to absorb the risk. If you think about the risks in weather insurance, on a *global* basis they are like traditional insurance. Weather contracts in the United States can be diversified with weather contracts in Asia, and ultimately the global capital committed to insurance absorbs the reinsurance risk. The same is true for earthquake risk (recall the example of the earthquake bond in Chapter 1). Global capital markets broadly defined are thus the natural party to absorb these risks.

Some risk, however, is not globally diversifiable. Consider writing puts on the S&P 500. If the U.S. stock market suffers a large decline, other markets around the world are likely to follow. Ultimately, it is capital that safeguards the financial industry. Delta-hedging plays a key role, but in the end there is always risk that must be absorbed by capital.

CHAPTER SUMMARY

Market-makers buy and sell to satisfy customer demand. A derivatives market-maker can use the underlying stock to delta-hedge the resulting position. By definition, the return on a delta-hedged position does not depend on the *direction* in which the stock price moves, but it does depend on the *magnitude* of the stock price move. If the gamma of the market-maker's position is negative, then, when delta-hedged, the position makes money for small stock price moves and loses money for large stock price moves. If the gamma of the position is positive, then, when delta-hedged, it makes money for large moves and loses money for small moves. Either way, the delta-hedged position breaks even if the stock moves one standard deviation.

Using a delta-gamma-theta approximation to characterize the change in the value of the delta-hedged portfolio, we can demonstrate that there are three factors that explain the profitability of the portfolio. First, gamma measures the tendency of the portfolio to become unhedged as the stock price moves. Second, theta measures the gain or loss on the portfolio due to the passage of time alone. Third, the market-maker will have interest income or expense on the portfolio.

If we assume that the stock price moves one standard deviation and impose the condition that the market-maker earns zero profit, then a fair option price satisfies a particular relationship among delta, gamma, and theta. This relationship, equation (13.10), is the foundation of the Black-Scholes option pricing analysis and applies to derivatives in general, not just to calls and puts.

Ultimately, market-making is risky and requires capital. If customers on average buy puts and calls, and if we think of options as insurance, then market-makers are in the same business as insurance companies. This requires capital, since if an extreme event occurs, delta-hedging will fail.

FURTHER READING

The main example in this chapter assumed that the Black-Scholes formula provided the correct option price and illustrated the behavior of the formula, viewed from the perspective of a delta-hedging market-maker. In Chapters 20 and 21 we will start by building a model of how stock prices behave, and see how the Black-Scholes formula is derived. As in this chapter, we will conclude that equation (13.10) is key to understanding option pricing.

PROBLEMS

In the following problems assume, unless otherwise stated, that $S = \$40$, $\sigma = 30\%$, $r = 8\%$, and $\delta = 0$.

13.1. Suppose you sell a 45-strike call with 91 days to expiration. What is delta? If the option is on 100 shares, what investment is required for a delta-hedged portfolio? What is your overnight profit if the stock tomorrow is $39? What if the stock price is $40.50?

13.2. Suppose you sell a 40-strike put with 91 days to expiration. What is delta? If the option is on 100 shares, what investment is required for a delta-hedged portfolio? What is your overnight profit if the stock price tomorrow is $39? What if it is $40.50?

13.3. Suppose you buy a 40–45 bull spread with 91 days to expiration. If you delta-hedge this position, what investment is required? What is your overnight profit if the stock tomorrow is $39? What if the stock is $40.50?

13.4. Suppose you enter into a put ratio spread where you buy a 45-strike put and sell two 40-strike puts. If you delta-hedge this position, what investment is required? What is your overnight profit if the stock tomorrow is $39? What if the stock is $40.50?

13.5. Reproduce the analysis in Table 13.2 assuming that instead of selling a call you sell a 40-strike put.

13.6. Reproduce the analysis in Table 13.3 assuming that instead of selling a call you sell a 40-strike put.

13.7. Consider a 40-strike 180-day call with $S = \$40$. Compute a delta-gamma-theta approximation for the value of the call after 1, 5, and 25 days. For each day, consider stock prices of $36 to $44.00 in $0.25 increments and compare the actual option premium at each stock price with the predicted premium. Where are the two the same?

13.8. Repeat Problem 7 for a 40-strike 180-day put.

13.9. Consider a 40-strike call with 91 days days to expiration. Graph the results from the following calculations.

    a. Compute the actual price with 90 days to expiration at $1 intervals from $30 to $50.

    b. Compute the estimated price with 90 days to expiration using a delta approximation.

    c. Compute the estimated price with 90 days to expiration using a delta-gamma approximation.

    d. Compute the estimated price with 90 days to expiration using a delta-gamma-theta approximation.

13.10. Consider a 40-strike call with 365 days to expiration. Graph the results from the following calculations.

    a. Compute the actual price with 360 days to expiration at $1 intervals from $30 to $50.

    b. Compute the estimated price with 360 days to expiration using a delta approximation.

    c. Compute the estimated price with 360 days to expiration using a delta-gamma approximation.

    d. Compute the estimated price with 360 days to expiration using a delta-gamma-theta approximation.

13.11. Repeat Problem 9 for a 91-day 40-strike put.

13.12. Repeat Problem 10 for a 365-day 40-strike put.

13.13. Using the parameters in Table 13.1, verify that equation (13.9) is zero.

13.14. Consider a put for which $T = 0.5$ and $K = \$45$. Compute the Greeks and verify that equation (13.9) is zero.

13.15. You own one 45-strike call with 180 days to expiration. Compute and graph the 1-day holding period profit if you delta- and gamma-hedge this position using a 40-strike call with 180 days to expiration.

13.16. You have sold one 45-strike put with 180 days to expiration. Compute and graph the 1-day holding period profit if you delta- and gamma-hedge this position using the stock and a 40-strike call with 180 days to expiration.

13.17. You have written a 35–40–45 butterfly spread with 91 days to expiration. Compute and graph the 1-day holding period profit if you delta- and gamma-hedge this position using the stock and a 40-strike call with 180 days to expiration.

13.18. Suppose you enter into a put ratio spread where you buy a 45-strike put and sell two 40-strike puts, both with 91 days to expiration. Compute and graph the 1-day holding period profit if you delta- and gamma-hedge this position using the stock and a 40-strike call with 180 days to expiration.

13.19. You have purchased a 40-strike call with 91 days to expiration. You wish to delta-hedge, but you are also concerned about changes in volatility; thus, you want to *vega-hedge* your position as well.

    a. Compute and graph the 1-day holding period profit if you delta- and vega-hedge this position using the stock and a 40-strike call with 180 days to expiration.

    b. Compute and graph the 1-day holding period profit if you delta-, gamma-, and vega-hedge this position using the stock, a 40-strike call with 180 days to expiration, and a 45-strike put with 365 days to expiration.

13.20. Repeat Problem 19, except that instead of hedging volatility risk, you wish to hedge interest rate risk, i.e., to *rho-hedge*. In addition to delta-, gamma-, and rho-hedging, can you delta-gamma-rho-vega hedge?

APPENDIX 13.A: TAYLOR SERIES APPROXIMATIONS

We have seen that the change in the option price can be expressed in terms of delta, gamma, and theta. The resulting expression is really just a particular approximation to the option price, called a Taylor series approximation.

Let $G(x, y)$ be a function of two variables. Taylor's theorem says that the value of the function at the point $G(x + \epsilon_x, y + \epsilon_y)$ may be approximated using derivatives of the function, as follows:

$$G(x + \epsilon_x, y + \epsilon_y) =$$

$$G(x, y) + \epsilon_x G_x(x, y) + \epsilon_y G_y(x, y)$$

$$+ \frac{1}{2} \left[\epsilon_x^2 G_{xx}(x, y) + \epsilon_y^2 G_{yy}(x, y) + 2\epsilon_x \epsilon_y G_{x,y}(x, y) \right]$$

$$+ \frac{1}{6} \left[\epsilon_x^3 G_{xxx}(x, y) + 3\epsilon_x^2 \epsilon_y G_{xxy}(x, y) + 3\epsilon_x \epsilon_y^2 G_{xyy}(x, y) + \epsilon_y^3 G_{yyy} G(x, y) \right]$$

$$+ \cdots \tag{13.14}$$

The approximation may be extended indefinitely, using successively higher-order derivatives. The nth term in the expansion is

$$\frac{1}{n!} \sum_{i=0}^{n} \binom{n}{i} \epsilon_x^i \epsilon_y^{n-i} G_{x^i, y^{n-i}}(x, y)$$

where the notation $G_{x^i, y^{n-i}}(x, y)$ means take the ith derivative with respect to x and the $(n-i)^{\text{th}}$ derivative with respect to y. The Taylor series is useful when the approximation is reasonably accurate with not too many terms.

For our purposes, it is enough to note that the delta-gamma approximation, equation (13.6), looks like a Taylor-series approximation that stops with the second derivative. You may wonder, however, why there is no second derivative with respect to time. You may also wonder why the approximation stops with the second derivative. These questions will arise again and be answered in Chapter 20.

Appendix 13.B: Greeks in the Binomial Model

The Black-Scholes Greeks are obtained by differentiating the option price. However, the general binomial option price calculation is not a formula but an algorithm. How can option Greeks be computed using the binomial tree? We can use some of the relations between delta, gamma, and theta discussed in this chapter to compute the binomial Greeks.

From Chapter 10, the option price and stock price for first two time steps in the binomial model can be represented as in Figure 13.5. We saw in Chapter 10 that delta at the initial node is computed using the formula

$$\Delta(S, 0) = e^{-\delta h} \frac{C_u - C_d}{uS - dS} \tag{13.15}$$

Gamma is the change in delta. We cannot compute the change in delta for the time-0 delta, since only one delta at a single stock price is defined at that point. But we can compute the change in delta at time h using the two deltas that are defined there. Thus,

FIGURE 13.5

Option price and stock
price trees, assuming
that the stock can move
up or down u or d each
period.

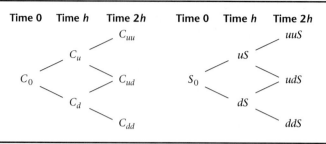

we have

$$\Gamma(S_h, h) = \frac{\Delta(uS, h) - \Delta(dS, h)}{uS - dS} \tag{13.16}$$

This is an approximation since we wish to know gamma at time 0, not at time h, and at the price S_0. However, even with a small number of binomial steps, the approximation works reasonably well.

With theta we are interested in the pure effect on the option price of changing time. We can calculate this using delta and gamma. Define

$$\epsilon = udS - S$$

Using the delta-gamma-theta approximation, equation (13.6), we can write the option price at time $2h$ and node udS as

$$C(udS, 2h) = C(S, 0) + \epsilon\Delta(S, 0) + \frac{1}{2}\epsilon^2\Gamma(S, 0) + 2h\theta(S, 0)$$

Solving for $\theta(S, 0)$ gives

$$\theta(S, 0) = \frac{C(udS, 2h) - \epsilon\Delta(S, 0) - \frac{1}{2}\epsilon^2\Gamma(S, 0) - C(S, 0)}{2h} \tag{13.17}$$

Chapter 14

Exotic Options: I

Thus far we have discussed standard options, futures, and swaps. By altering the terms of standard contracts like these, you obtain a "nonstandard" or "exotic" option. Exotic options can provide precise tailoring of risk exposures, and they permit investment strategies difficult or costly to realize with standard options and securities. In this chapter we discuss some basic kinds of exotic options, including Asian, barrier, compound, gap, and exchange options. In Chapter 22 we will consider other exotic options.

14.1 INTRODUCTION

Imagine that you are discussing currency hedging with Sally Smith, the risk manager of XYZ Corp., a multinational corporation with sizable European operations. XYZ has a large annual inflow of euros that are eventually converted to dollars. XYZ is considering the purchase of 1-year put options as insurance against a fall in the euro but is also interested in exploring alternatives. You have already discussed with Smith the hedging variants from Chapters 2 and 3, including different strike prices, a collar, and a paylater strategy.

Suppose that Smith offhandedly mentions that XYZ receives large euro payments on a monthly basis, amounting to hundreds of millions of dollars per quarter. "Hmm," you think. "A standard 1-year put option would hedge the firm against the level of the euro *on the one day the option expires*. This hedge would have significant basis risk since the price at expiration could be quite different from the average price over the year. Buying a strip of put options in which one option expires every month would have little basis risk but might be expensive. Over the course of the year what really matters is the *average* exchange rate over this period; the ups and downs around the average rate cancel out by definition. I wonder if there is any way to base an option on the *average* of the euro/dollar exchange rate?"

This train of thought leads you to construct a new kind of option—based on the average price, rather than the price at a point in time—that addresses a particular business concern: It provides a more precise hedge against the risk that matters, the average exchange rate. This example demonstrates that exotic options can solve a particular business problem in a way that standard options do not. Generally, an **exotic option** (or **nonstandard option**) is simply an option with some contractual difference from standard options. Although we will focus on hedging examples, these products can also be used to speculate.

431

It is not hard to invent new kinds of options. The challenge is to invent new options that are potentially attractive to buyers (which we did in the preceding example) and that can be priced and hedged without too much difficulty. In Chapters 10 and 13, we saw how a market-maker can delta-hedge an option position. That analysis led us to see how the price of an option is equivalent to the cost of synthetically manufacturing the option. In particular, an option is fairly priced when there is a certain relationship among the Greeks of the option.

The same relationship among the Greeks obtains for exotic options as for ordinary puts and calls; options with exotic features can generally be priced and delta-hedged in the same way as ordinary options.[1] As a consequence, exotic derivative products are quite common in practice and the technology for pricing and hedging them is well understood. In fact, since many such options are in common use, the term "exotic" is an anachronism. We will continue to use it, however.

The goal in this chapter is *not* to master the mathematical details of particular products, but rather to gain an intuitive understanding of the trade-offs in design and pricing. Consequently, most of the formulas appear in the chapter appendix.

Since exotic options are often constructed by tweaking ordinary options in minor ways, ordinary options are useful as benchmarks for exotics. To understand exotic options you should ask questions like these:

- How does the payoff of the exotic compare to that of a standard option?

- Can the exotic option be approximated by some portfolio of other options?

- Is the exotic option cheap or expensive relative to standard options? (Understanding the economics of the option is a critical step in understanding its pricing and use.)

- What is the rationale for the use of the exotic option?

- How easily can the exotic option be hedged? An option may be desirable to a customer, but it will not be sold unless the risk arising from market-making can be controlled.

14.2 ASIAN OPTIONS

An **Asian option** has a payoff that is based on the average price over some period of time. An Asian option is an example of a **path-dependent option,** which means that the value of the option at expiration depends upon the path by which the stock arrived at its final price.[2] Such an option has the potential to solve XYZ's hedging problem.

....

[1] However, as we will see in Chapter 22, there are options that are quite difficult to hedge even though they are easy to price.

[2] You can think of path dependence in the context of a binomial pricing model. In the binomial model of Chapter 10, "udu" and "duu" are a series of up and down stock price moves—paths—occurring in a different order but which lead to the same final stock price. Thus, both yield the same payoff for a European option. However, with a path-dependent option, these two paths would yield different final option payoffs because the intermediate stock prices were different.

There are many practical applications in which we average prices. In addition to cases where the firm cares about the average exchange rate (as with XYZ), averaging is also used when a single price at a point in time might be subject to manipulation or price swings induced by thin markets. Bonds convertible into stock, for example, often base the terms of conversion on the average stock price over a 20-day period at the end of the bond's life. Settlement based on the average is called an **Asian tail,** since the averaging occurs only at the termination of the contract.

As we will see, Asian options are worth less at issuance than otherwise equivalent ordinary options. The reason is that the averaged price of the underlying asset is less volatile than the asset price itself, and an option on a lower volatility asset is worth less.

XYZ's Hedging Problem

Let's think more about XYZ's currency hedging problem. Suppose that XYZ has a monthly euro inflow of €100m, reflecting revenue from selling products in Europe. Its costs, however, are primarily fixed in dollars. Let x_i denote the dollar price of a euro in month i. At the end of the year, the converted amount in dollars is

$$€100\text{m} \times \sum_{i=1}^{12} x_i e^{r(12-i)/12} \tag{14.1}$$

We have numerous strategies available for hedging the end-of-year cash flow. Here are a few obvious ones:

Strip of forward contracts   Sell euro forward contracts maturing each month over the year. The premium of this strategy is zero.

Euro swap   Swap euros for dollars. We saw in Chapter 8 that, except for the timing of cash flows, a swap produces the same result as hedging with the strip of forwards. A swap also has a zero premium.

Strip of puts   Buy twelve put options on €100m, each maturing at the end of a different month. The cost is the twelve option premiums.

As we saw in Chapter 2, the difference between the forward and option strategies is the ability to profit from a euro appreciation, but we pay a premium for the possibility of earning that profit. You can probably think of other strategies as well.

The idea of an Asian option stems from expression (14.1): What we really care about is the future value of the *sum* of the converted cash flows. This in turn depends on the sum of the month-end exchange rates. If for simplicity we ignore interest, what we are trying to hedge is

$$\sum_{i=1}^{12} x_i = 12 \times \left(\frac{\sum_{i=1}^{12} x_i}{12} \right) \tag{14.2}$$

The expression in parentheses is the month-end arithmetic average exchange rate, which motivates the idea of an option on the average.

Options on the Average

As a logical matter there are eight basic kinds of Asian options, depending upon whether the option is a put or a call, whether the average is computed as a geometric or arithmetic average, and whether the average asset price is used in place of the price of the underlying asset or the strike price. Here are details about some of these alternatives.

The definition of the average   It is most common in practice to define the average as an *arithmetic average*. Suppose we record the stock price every h periods from time 0 to T; there are then $N = T/h$ periods. The arithmetic average is defined as

$$A(T) = \frac{1}{N} \sum_{i=1}^{N} S_{ih} \tag{14.3}$$

While arithmetic averages are typically used, they are mathematically inconvenient.[3] It is computationally easier, but less common in practice, to use the *geometric average* stock price, which is defined as

$$G(T) = (S_h \times S_{2h} \times \cdots \times S_{Nh})^{\frac{1}{N}} \tag{14.4}$$

There are easy pricing formulas for options based on the geometric average (see Appendix 14.A).

Whether the average is used as the asset price or the strike   The payoff at maturity can be computed using the average stock price either as the price of the underlying asset or as the strike price. When the average is used as the asset price, the option is called an *average price option*. When the average is used as the strike price, the option is called an *average strike option*. Here are the four variants of options based on the geometric average:

$$\text{Geometric average price call} = max[0, G(T) - K] \tag{14.5}$$

$$\text{Geometric average price put} = max[0, K - G(T)] \tag{14.6}$$

$$\text{Geometric average strike call} = max[0, S_T - G(T)] \tag{14.7}$$

$$\text{Geometric average strike put} = max[0, G(T) - S_T] \tag{14.8}$$

The terms "average price" and "average strike" refer to whether the average is used in place of the asset price or the strike price. In each case the average could also be computed as an arithmetic average, giving us our eight basic kinds of Asian options.

The following example illustrates the difference between an arithmetic and geometric average.

---

[3]Because the sum of lognormal variables is not lognormally distributed, there are no simple pricing formulas for options based on the arithmetic average.

Example 14.1 Suppose that we compute the average based on quarterly stock prices over 1 year. We observe stock prices of $55, $72, $61, and $85. The arithmetic average is

$$\frac{\$55 + \$72 + \$61 + \$85}{4} = \$68.250$$

The geometric average is

$$\left(\$55 \times \$72 \times \$61 \times \$85\right)^{0.25} = \$67.315$$ ❧

The appendix has (relatively simple) formulas for pricing European options based on the geometric average. We further discuss options based on the arithmetic average in Chapter 19.

Comparing Asian Options

Table 14.1 shows values of geometric average price calls and puts. If the number of averages, N, is one, then the average is the final stock price. In that case the average price call is an ordinary call.

Intuitively, averaging reduces the volatility of $G(T)$ relative to the volatility of the stock price at expiration, S_T, and thus we should expect the value of an average price

TABLE 14.1	Premiums of at-the-money geometric average price and geometric average strike calls and puts, for different numbers of prices averaged, N. The case $N = 1$ for the average price options is equivalent to Black-Scholes values. Assumes $S = \$40$, $K = \$40$, $r = 0.08$, $\sigma = 0.3$, $\delta = 0$, and $t = 1$.

| | **Average Price ($)** | | **Average Strike ($)** | |
N	Call	Put	Call	Put
1	6.285	3.209	0.000	0.000
2	4.708	2.645	2.225	1.213
3	4.209	2.445	2.748	1.436
5	3.819	2.281	3.148	1.610
10	3.530	2.155	3.440	1.740
50	3.302	2.052	3.668	1.843
1000	3.248	2.027	3.722	1.868
∞	3.246	2.026	3.725	1.869

option to decrease with the number of stock prices used to compute the average. This is evident in Table 14.1, which shows the decline in value of the average price option as the frequency of averaging increases.

Table 14.1 also shows that, in contrast to average price calls, the price of an average strike call increases with the number of averaging periods. The average of stock prices between time times 0 and T is positively correlated with the stock price at time T, S_T. If $G(T)$ is high, S_T is likely to be high as well. More frequent averaging makes the average strike option more valuable because it reduces the correlation between S_T and $G(T)$. To see this pattern consider what happens if the average is computed only using the final stock price. The value of the call is

$$max[0, S_T - G(T)]$$

If only one stock price observation is used, $G(T) = S_T$, and the value of the option is zero for sure. With more frequent averaging the correlation is reduced and the value of the average strike option increases.

When would an average strike option make sense? Such an option pays off when there is a difference between the average asset price over the life of the option and the asset price at expiration. Such an option could be used for insurance in a situation where we accumulated an asset over a period of time and then sold the entire accumulated position at one price.

An Asian Solution for XYZ

If XYZ receives euros and its costs are fixed in dollars, profits are reduced if the euro depreciates, that is, if the number of dollars received for a euro is lower. We could construct an Asian put option that puts a floor, K, on the average exchange rate received. The per euro payoff of this option would be

$$max\left(0, K - \frac{1}{12}\sum_{i=1}^{12} x_i\right) \tag{14.9}$$

For example, if we wanted to guarantee an average exchange rate of $0.90 per euro, we would set $K = \$0.9$. If the average exchange rate was less than that, we would be paid the difference between $0.9 and the average. Since we repatriate €1.2b over the course of a year, we would buy contracts covering €1.2b.

Do you recognize the kind of option described by equation (14.9)? The averaging is arithmetic, the average is used in place of the asset price, and it is a put. Hence, it is an *arithmetic average price Asian put*.

There are other hedging strategies XYZ could use. Table 14.2 lists premiums for several alternatives. The single put expiring at year-end is the most expensive option. As discussed earlier it has basis risk because the year-end exchange rate could be quite different from the average. Two other strategies have signficantly less basis risk: The strip of European puts expiring monthly, and the arithmetic Asian put. The strip of puts protects against low exchange rates month-by-month, whereas the Asian option protects

Hedge Instrument	Premium ($)
Put Option Expiring in 1 Year	0.2753
Strip of Monthly Put Options	0.2178
Geometric Average Price Put	0.1796
Arithmetic Average Price Put	0.1764

TABLE 14.2 Comparison of costs for alternative hedging strategies for XYZ. The price in the second row is the sum of premiums for puts expiring after 1 month, 2 months, and so forth, out to 12 months. The first, third, and fourth rows premiums are calculated assuming 1 year to maturity, and then multiplied by 12. Assumes the current exchange rate is $0.9/€, option strikes are 0.9, $r_\$ = 6\%$, $r_€ = 3\%$, dollar/euro volatility is 10%.

the 12-month average. The Asian put is cheaper since there will be situations in which some of the individual puts are valuable (for example, if the exchange rate takes a big swing in one month that is reversed subsequently), but the Asian put does not pay off. The geometric option hedges less well than the arithmetic option since the quantity being hedged (equation (14.1)) is an arithmetic, not a geometric, average.

Finally, be aware that this example ignores several subtleties. The option strikes, for example, might be made to vary with the forward curve for the exchange rate. The effect of interest in equation (14.1) could also be taken into account.

14.3 BARRIER OPTIONS

A **barrier option** is an option with a payoff depending upon whether, over the life of the option, the price of the underlying asset reaches a specified level, called the *barrier*. Barrier puts and calls either come into existence or go out of existence the first time the asset price reaches the barrier. If they are in existence at expiration, they are equivalent to ordinary puts and calls. It can be tricky to define what it means for the stock price to reach a barrier. See the box on page 438 for a discussion.

Since barrier puts and calls never pay more than standard puts and calls, they are no more expensive than standard puts and calls. Barrier options are another example of a path-dependent option.

Barrier options are widely used in practice. One appeal of barrier options may be their lower premiums, although of course the lower premium reflects a lower average payoff at expiration.

Types of Barrier Options

There are three basic kinds of barrier options:

Knock-out options   These go out of existence (are "knocked-out") if the asset price reaches the barrier. If the price of the underlying asset has to fall to reach the barrier, the option is a **down-and-out.** If the price of the underlying asset has to rise to reach the barrier, the option is an **up-and-out.**

Knock-in options   These come into existence (are "knocked-in") if the barrier is touched. If the price of the underlying asset has to fall to reach the barrier, the option is a **down-and-in.** If the asset price has to rise to reach the barrier, it is an **up-and-in.**

Rebate options   These make a fixed payment if the asset price reaches the barrier. The payment can occur either at the time the barrier is reached, or at the time the option expires, in which case it is a deferred rebate. Rebate options can be either "up rebates" or "down rebates," depending on whether the barrier is above or below the current price.

Figure 14.1 illustrates how a barrier option works. The stock price starts at around $100, ends at $80, and hits the barrier of $75 about halfway through the year. If the option were a 95-strike down-and-in put, the option would knock in and pay $15 ($95 − $80) at expiration. If the option were a down-and-out put, it would be worthless at expiration.

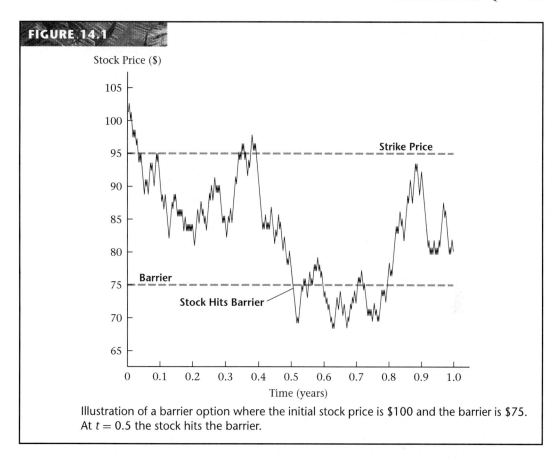

FIGURE 14.1

Illustration of a barrier option where the initial stock price is $100 and the barrier is $75. At $t = 0.5$ the stock hits the barrier.

If the option were a down-and-in call, it would knock-in at $75 but still be worthless at expiration because the stock price is below the strike price.

The formulas for the various kinds of barrier options are in the appendix. Table 14.3 presents the logical possibilities for barrier options, with references to the pricing formulas in the chapter appendix. While we mention rebate options here for completeness, we will discuss them in more detail in Chapter 22.

The important parity relation for barrier options is

$$\boxed{\text{"Knock-in" option} + \text{"Knock-out" option} = \text{Ordinary option}} \qquad (14.10)$$

For example, for otherwise equivalent options, we have

$$\text{Down-and-in call} + \text{Down-and-out call} = \text{Standard call}$$

Since these option premiums cannot be negative, this equation demonstrates directly that barrier options have lower premiums than standard options.

TABLE 14.3	Possible cases for barrier puts and calls, assuming in each instance that the stock price has not yet hit the barrier (thus, for example, for an up-and-in or up-and-out, $S < H$). The Black-Scholes formula for a standard European call is given in equation (12.1), and the put formula is equation (12.4).

| | **Calls** | | **Puts** | |
	$H > K$	$H < K$	$H > K$	$H < K$
Up-and-in	Eq. (14.22)	Black-Scholes	Eq. (14.26)	Eq. (14.26)
Up-and-out	Eq. (14.23)	Worthless	Eq. (14.27)	Eq. (14.27)
Down-and-in	Eq. (14.24)	Eq. (14.24)	Black-Scholes	Eq. (14.28)
Down-and-out	Eq. (14.25)	Eq. (14.25)	Worthless	Eq. (14.29)

Currency Hedging

Consider once again XYZ. Here we will focus on hedging only the cash flow occurring in 6 months to see how barrier puts compare to standard puts.

What kinds of barrier puts make sense in the context of XYZ's hedging problem? We are hedging against a decline in the exchange rate, which makes certain possibilities less attractive. A down-and-out put would be worthless when we needed it. Similarly, an up-and-in put would provide insurance only if, prior to the exchange rate falling below the strike, the exchange rate had risen so the option could knock-in.

This leaves down-and-ins and up-and-outs to consider. Table 14.4 presents prices of standard, down-and-in, and up-and-out puts with different strikes and different barriers. Consider first the row where $K = 0.8$. Notice that all options appear to have the same price. It is a useful exercise in the logic of barrier options to understand why they appear equally priced. In fact, here is an exercise to solve before reading further: Can you deduce which of the six premiums with $K = 0.8$ are exactly equal and which are merely close?

The option prices in Table 14.4 tell us something about the relative likelihood of different scenarios for the exchange rate. The ordinary put premium when the strike is 0.8 reflects the (risk-neutral) probability that the exchange rate will be below 0.8 at maturity. Both of the down-and-ins, having strikes below the starting exchange rate of 0.9 and at least 0.8, will necessarily have knocked-in should the exchange rate fall below 0.8. Described differently, a down-and-in put with a barrier above the strike is equivalent to an ordinary put. Therefore, the first three option premiums in the $K = 0.8$ row are identical.

TABLE 14.4 			Premiums of standard, down-and-in, and up-and-out currency put options with strikes *K*. The column headed "standard" contains prices of ordinary put options. Assumes $x_0 = 0.9$, $\sigma = 0.1$, $r_\$ = 0.06$, $r_\mathfrak{e} = 0.03$, and $t = 0.5$.				

	Standard	**Down-and-In Barrier ($)**		**Up-and-Out Barrier ($)**		
Strike ($)	**($)**	**0.8000**	**0.8500**	**0.9500**	**1.0000**	**1.0500**
$K = 0.8$	0.0007	0.0007	0.0007	0.0007	0.0007	0.0007
$K = 0.9$	0.0188	0.0066	0.0167	0.0174	0.0188	0.0188
$K = 1.0$	0.0870	0.0134	0.0501	0.0633	0.0847	0.0869

Now consider the knock-out puts with $K = 0.8$. The difference between the ordinary put and the up-and-out put with a 0.95 barrier is that sometimes the exchange rate will drift from 0.9 to above 0.95, and then below 0.8. In this case, the ordinary put will have a payoff but the knock-out put will not.

How likely is this scenario? The low premium of 0.0007 for the ordinary put tells us that it is relatively unlikely the exchange rate will drift from 0.9 to 0.8 over 6 months. It is even less likely that the exchange rate will hit 0.95 *in those cases* when it does fall below 0.8. A knock-out may be likely, but it is rare to have a knock-out occur *in those cases when an ordinary put with a strike of 0.8 would pay off.* Thus, the knock-out feature is not subtracting much from the value of the option. This argument is even stronger for the knock-out barriers of 1.0 and 1.05. Nevertheless, since there is a chance these options will knock out and then end up in the money, the premiums are less than for the knock-in puts and are increasing with the barrier. Thus, the up-and-out prices in the $K = 0.8$ row are slightly less than the price of an ordinary put.

When the strike price is 1.0, the up-and-outs with barriers of 1.0 and 1.05 have substantially all the value of the ordinary put with the same strike. The interpretation is that most of the value of the puts comes from scenarios in which the option remains in-the-money; in those scenarios in which the option knocks out, the exchange rate on average does not fall enough for the option to be valuable.

14.4 COMPOUND OPTIONS

A **compound option** is an option to buy an option. If you think of an ordinary option as an asset—analogous to a stock—then a compound option is similar to an ordinary option.

Compound options are a little more complicated than ordinary options because there are two strikes and two expirations, one each for the underlying option and for the compound option. Suppose that the current time is t_0 and that we have a compound option which at time t_1 will give us the right to pay x to buy a European call option with

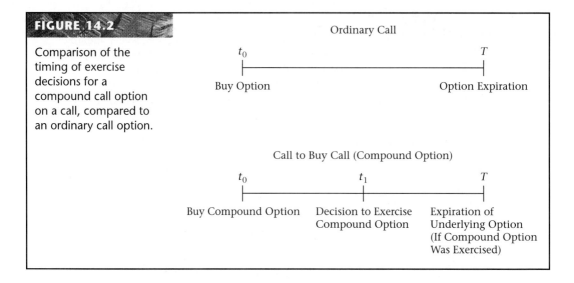

FIGURE 14.2

Comparison of the timing of exercise decisions for a compound call option on a call, compared to an ordinary call option.

strike K. This underlying call will expire at time $T > t_1$. Figure 14.2 compares the timing of the exercise decisions for this compound option with the exercise decision for an ordinary call expiring at time T.

If we exercise the compound call at time t_1, then the price of the option we receive is $C(S, K, T - t_1)$. At time T, this option will have the value $max(0, S_T - K)$, the same as an ordinary call with strike K. At time t_1, when the compound option expires, the value of the compound option is

$$max[C(S_{t_1}, K, T - t_1) - x, 0]$$

We only exercise the compound option if the stock price at time t_1 is sufficiently great that the value of the call exceeds the compound option strike price, x. Let S^* be the critical stock price above which the compound option is exercised. By definition, S^* satisfies

$$C(S^*, K, T - t_1) = x \qquad (14.11)$$

The compound option is exercised for $S_{t_1} > S^*$.

Thus, in order for the compound call to ultimately be valuable, there are two events that must take place. First, at time t_1 we must have $S_{t_1} > S^*$; that is, it must be worthwhile to exercise the compound call. Second, we must have $S_T > K$; that is, it must be profitable to exercise the underlying call. Because two events must occur, the formula for a compound call contains a bivariate cumulative normal distribution, as opposed to the univariate normal distribution in the Black-Scholes formula.

Formulas for the four compound options—a call to buy a call, a put to sell a call, a call to buy a put, and a put to sell a put—are in Appendix 14.A. Valuing a compound option is different from valuing an ordinary option in part for mathematical rather than for conceptual reasons. The Black-Scholes formula assumes that the stock price is lognormally distributed. However, the price of an option—because there is a significant probability that it will be worthless—cannot be lognormally distributed. Thus, while an option on an option is conceptually similar to an option on a stock, it is mathematically different.[4] The difficulty in deriving a formula for the price of a compound option is to value the option based on the value of the stock, which *is* lognormally distributed, rather than the price of the underlying option, which is not lognormally distributed.

Options on Dividend-Paying Stocks

We saw in Chapter 11 that it is possible to price American options on dividend-paying stocks using the binomial model. It turns out that the compound option model also permits us to price an option on a stock that will pay a single discrete dividend prior to expiration.

Suppose that at time t_1 the stock will pay a dividend, D. We have a choice of exercising the option at the cum-dividend price,[5] $S_{t_1} + D$, or holding the call, which will have a value reflecting the ex-dividend price, S_{t_1}. Thus, at t_1, the value of the call option is the greater of its exercise value, $S_{t_1} + D - K$, and the option valued at the ex-dividend price, $C(S_{t_1}, T - t_1)$:

$$max\left[C(S_{t_1}, T - t_1), S_{t_1} + D - K\right] \tag{14.12}$$

By put-call parity, at time t_1 we can write the value of the ex-dividend unexercised call as

$$C(S_{t_1}, T - t_1) = P(S_{t_1}, T - t_1) + S_{t_1} - Ke^{-r(T-t_1)}$$

Making this substitution in equation (14.12) and rewriting the result, we obtain

$$S_{t_1} + D - K + max\left(P[S_{t_1}, T - t_1] - \left[D - K(1 - e^{-r(T-t_1)})\right], 0\right) \tag{14.13}$$

The value of the option is then the present value of this expression.

Equation (14.13) tells us that we can value a call option on a dividend-paying stock as the sum of the following:

1. The stock, with present value S_0. (S_0 is the present value of $S_{t_1} + D$.)

2. Less the present value of the strike price, Ke^{-rt_1}.

3. Plus the value of a compound call option with strike price $D - K(1 - e^{-r(T-t_1)})$ and maturity date t_1, permitting the owner to buy a put option with strike price K and maturity date T. This is a call option on a put option.

In this interpretation, exercising the compound option corresponds to keeping the option unexercised. To see this, notice that if we exercise the compound option in

---

[4]Geske (1979) was the first to derive the formula for a compound option.

[5]The stock is *cum-dividend* if a purchaser of the stock will receive the dividend. Once the stock goes *ex-dividend*, the purchaser will not receive the dividend.

equation (14.13), we give up the dividend and gain interest on the strike in order to acquire the put. The total is

$$S_{t_1} + P(S_{t_1}, T - t_1) - Ke^{-r(T-t_1)}$$

If we do not exercise the compound option, we receive the stock plus dividend, less the strike:

$$S_{t_1} + D - K$$

This valuation exercise provides a way to understand early exercise. We can view exercising an American call as *not* exercising the compound option to buy a put in equation (14.13). The cost of not exercising is that we lose the dividend, less interest on the strike. This is exactly the intuition governing early exercise that we developed in Chapters 9 and 11.

Example 14.2 Suppose a stock with a price of $100 will pay a $5 dividend in 91 days ($t = 0.249$). An option with a strike price of $90 will expire in 152 days ($t = 0.416$). Assume $\sigma = 0.3$ and $r = 0.08$. The value of a European call on the stock is

$$BSCall(\$100 - \$5e^{-(0.08 \times 0.249)}, \$90, 0.3, 0.08, 0.416, 0) = \$11.678$$

The value of an American call is computed using a compound option (call on put) with the exercise price for the compound option equal to $5 - 90(1 - e^{-0.08 \times (0.416 - 0.249)}) = 3.805$, and time to maturity 0.249 for the compound option and 0.416 for the underlying option. The price of the compound option is $0.999; hence, the value of the American option is

$$\$100 - \$90e^{-0.249 \times 0.08} + \$0.999 = \$12.774.$$

Moreover, the option should be exercised if the stock price cum-dividend is above $89.988. ≋

Compound Option Parity

As you might guess, there are parity relationships among the compound option prices. Suppose we buy a call on a call, and sell a put on a call, where both have the same strike, underlying option, and time to maturity. When the compound options expire, we will acquire the underlying option by paying the strike price x. If the stock price is high, we will exercise the compound call, and if the stock price is low, the compound put will be exercised and we will be forced to buy the call. Thus, the difference between the call on call and put on call premiums, plus the present value of x, must equal the premium to acquire the underlying option outright. That is,

$$CallOnCall(S, K, x, \sigma, r, t_1, t_2, \delta) - PutOnCall(S, K, x, \sigma, r, t_1, t_2, \delta) + xe^{-rt_1}$$
$$= BSCall(S, K, \sigma, r, t_2, \delta) \quad (14.14)$$

An analogous relationship holds for puts.

Currency Hedging with Compound Options

Compound options provide yet another variation on possible currency-hedging strategies. Instead of buying a 6-month put option on the euro, we could buy an option to buy an option. In effect, the compound option is giving us the opportunity to wait and see what happens.

Suppose we decide that we will exercise the compound option after 3 months—at that point, we will decide whether to buy the put option. Here is one way to structure such a transaction. We could figure out what premium a 3-month put with a strike of $0.9 would have, if the exchange rate were still at 0.9. The Black-Scholes formula tells us that a 3-month at-the-money option with a strike of $0.9 would have a premium of $0.0146. (This value compares with the premium of $0.0188 for the 6-month option from Table 14.4.)

Now we can use the compound pricing formula to price a call option to buy this put, setting the strike to equal $0.0146. The price of this compound call is $0.0093. So by paying approximately half the premium of the 6-month at-the-money option, we can buy an option that permits us to pay $0.0146 for a 3-month option. By selecting this strike, we have constructed the option so that we will exercise it if the exchange rate is below 0.9. If the exchange rate goes up, we will not exercise the option and save the premium. If the exchange rate goes down, we will acquire an in-the-money option for the price of an at-the-money option. Many other structures are possible.

14.5 GAP OPTIONS

A call option pays $S - K$ when $S > K$. The strike price, K, here serves to determine both when the option makes a payoff (when $S > K$) and also the size of the payoff ($S - K$). However, we could imagine separating these two functions of the strike price. Consider an option that pays $S - 90$ when $S > 100$. Note that there is a difference between the prices that govern when there is a payoff ($100) and the price used to determine the size of the payoff ($90). This difference creates a discontinuity—or gap—in the payoff diagram, which is why the option is called a **gap option**.

Figure 14.3 shows a gap call option with payoff $S - \$90$ when $S > \$100$. The gap in the payoff occurs when the option payoff jumps from $0 to $10 as a result of the stock price changing from $99.99 to $100.01.

Figure 14.4 depicts a gap put that pays $90 - S$ when $S < \$100$. This option demonstrates that a gap option can be structured to require, for some stock prices, a payout from the option holder at expiration. You should compare Figure 14.4 with Figure 4.12—the gap put looks very much like a paylater option. Note that the owner of the put in Figure 14.4 is *required* to exercise the option when $S < \$100$.

The pricing formula for a gap call, which pays $S - K_1$ when $S > K_2$, is obtained by a simple modification of the Black-Scholes formula. Let K_1 be the strike price (the price the option holder pays at expiration to acquire the stock) and K_2 the payment trigger (the price at which payment on the option is triggered). The formula is then

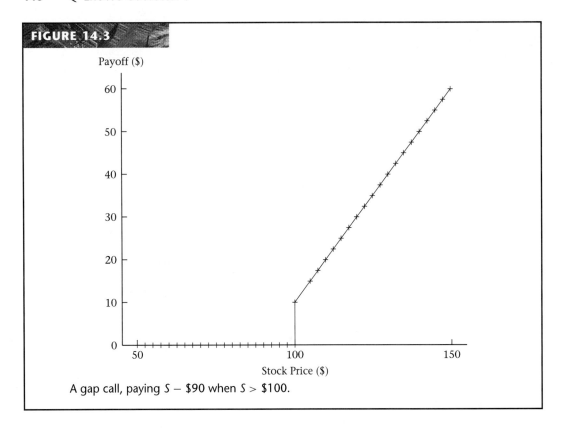

FIGURE 14.3

A gap call, paying $S - \$90$ when $S > \$100$.

$$C(S, K_1, K_2, \sigma, r, t, \delta) = Se^{-\delta t} N(d_1) - K_1 e^{-rt} N(d_2) \qquad (14.15)$$

$$d_1 = \frac{ln(Se^{-\delta t}/K_2 e^{-rt}) + \frac{1}{2}\sigma^2 t}{\sigma \sqrt{t}}$$

$$d_2 = d_1 - \sigma \sqrt{t}$$

The modification to the put formula is similar.[6]

Returning to the XYZ currency hedging example, let's examine the use of gap options as a hedging instrument. The intuitive appeal of a gap option is that we can purchase insurance in which we are fully protected if the loss exceeds a certain amount.

Table 14.5 lists gap put premiums for different strikes and payment triggers. When the strike equals the payment trigger, the premium is the same as for an ordinary put. For a given strike, increasing the payment trigger reduces the premium. The reason is that when the payment trigger is above the strike, the option holder will have to make

---

[6]We will discuss gap and related options more in Chapter 22.

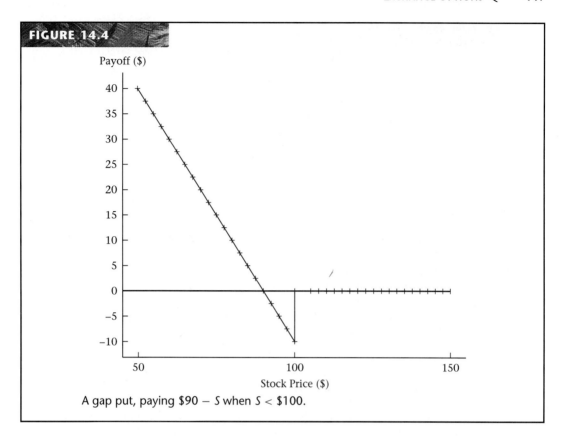

FIGURE 14.4

A gap put, paying $90 - S$ when $S < \$100$.

a payment to the option writer in some cases. For example, consider the case when the strike is $0.8 and the payment trigger is $1. If the exchange rate is 0.95, the gap put holder is obligated to sell euros worth $0.95 for only $0.8, a loss of $0.15. The option premium in this case is −$0.0888, reflecting the possibility that the option buyer will end up making a payment at maturity to the option seller. A hedger believing it highly likely that the exchange rate would be below 0.8 might be willing to receive a premium in exchange for the risk that the exchange rate would end up between 0.8 and 1.0.

Note that for a given strike, K_1, we can always find a trigger, K_2, to make the option premium zero. Thus, gap options permit us to accomplish something similar to the paylater strategy discussed in Section 4.4.

14.6 EXCHANGE OPTIONS

In Chapter 9 we discussed a hypothetical example of Microsoft and AOL compensation options, in which the executives of each company were compensated only if their stock outperformed the other company's stock. An **exchange option**—also called an

TABLE 14.5		Premiums of ordinary and gap put options with strikes K_1 and payment triggers K_2. Assumes $x_0 = 0.9$, $\sigma = 0.1$, $r_\$ = 0.06$, $r_€ = 0.03$, and $t = 0.5$.		
		Payment Trigger (K_2) ($)		
Strike (K_1) ($)	**Put ($)**	**0.8**	**0.9**	**1.0**
0.8000	0.0007	0.0007	−0.0229	−0.0888
0.9000	0.0188	0.0039	0.0188	−0.0009
1.0000	0.0870	0.0070	0.0605	0.0870

outperformance option—pays off only if the underlying asset outperforms some other asset, called the benchmark.

We saw in Section 9.2 that exercising any option entails exchanging one asset for another and that a standard call option is an exchange option in which the stock has to outperform cash in order for the option to pay off. In general, an exchange option provides the owner the right to exchange one asset for another, where both may be risky. The formula for this kind of option is a simple variant of the Black-Scholes formula.

European Exchange Options

Suppose an exchange call maturing t periods from today provides the right to obtain one unit of risky asset 1 in exchange for 1 unit of risky asset 2. (We could think of this as, for example, the right to obtain the Nikkei index by giving up the S&P 500.) Let S_t be the price of risky asset 1 and K_t the price of risky asset 2 at time t, with dividend yields δ_S and δ_K, and volatilities σ_S and σ_K. Let ρ denote the correlation between the continuously compounded returns on the two assets. The payoff to this option is

$$max(0, S_t - K_t)$$

The formula for the price of an exchange option (see Margrabe, 1978) is

$$C(S, K, \sigma, r, t, \delta) = Se^{-\delta_S t} N(d_1) - Ke^{-\delta_K t} N(d_2) \qquad (14.16)$$

where

$$d_1 = \frac{ln(Se^{-\delta_S t}/Ke^{-\delta_K t}) + \frac{1}{2}\sigma^2 t}{\sigma\sqrt{t}}$$

$$d_2 = d_1 - \sigma\sqrt{t}$$

$$\sigma = \sqrt{\sigma_S^2 + \sigma_K^2 - 2\rho\sigma_S\sigma_K} \qquad (14.17)$$

The volatility, σ, is the volatility of $ln(S/K)$ over the life of the option. Since $ln(S/K) = ln(S) - ln(K)$, we have

$$Var[ln(S/K)] = Var[ln(S)] + Var[ln(K)] - 2Cov[ln(S), ln(K)]$$
$$= \sigma_S^2 + \sigma_K^2 - 2\rho\sigma_S\sigma_K$$

The pricing formula for the exchange option turns out to be a simple variant of the Black-Scholes formula: The strike price is replaced by the price of the benchmark asset, the risk-free rate is replaced by the dividend yield on the benchmark asset, and the appropriate volatility is the volatility of the difference between continuously compounded returns on the two assets.

We can also interpret the pricing formula for an exchange option by considering the version of the Black-Scholes formula written in terms of prepaid forward prices, equation (12.5). Equation (14.16) is the same as equation (12.5), except that the volatility of the underlying asset is replaced by the volatility of the difference in continuously compounded returns of the underlying and strike assets. The expression $Ke^{-\delta_K T}$ is the prepaid forward price for the strike asset. The formula for an infinitely lived American exchange option is in Appendix 14.A.

By setting the dividend yields and volatility appropriately, equation (14.16) yields the formulas for ordinary calls and puts:

- With a call, we give up cash to acquire stock. The dividend yield on cash is the interest rate. Thus, if we set $\delta_S = \delta$ (the dividend yield on stock), $\delta_K = r$ (the risk-free rate), and $\sigma_K = 0$ (asset 2 is risk-free), the formula reduces to the standard Black-Scholes formula for a call.

- With a put, we give up stock to acquire cash. Thus, if we set $\delta_S = r$, $\delta_K = \delta$ (the dividend yield on stock), and $\sigma_S = 0$, the formula reduces to the Black-Scholes formula for a put on stock. (Try this to verify that it works.)

Example 14.3 Consider an option to exchange IBM shares for Microsoft shares. On May 30, 1997, the price of IBM was $86.50 and Microsoft was $124. Thus, one share of IBM has the same dollar value as $86.50/124 = 0.6976$ shares of Microsoft. IBM had a history of paying an annual dividend of about 1%, and Microsoft paid no dividend. Their historical volatilities in the previous year had been 31.2% for IBM and 30.0% for Microsoft, with a correlation of 0.4746. Suppose we had an option to exchange IBM for Microsoft, in equal amounts based on the May 30 prices. Then we could exchange 1 share of IBM for 0.6976 shares of Microsoft. The volatility would be

$$\sigma = \sqrt{0.312^2 + 0.300^2 - 2 \times 0.4746 \times 0.312 \times 0.300}$$
$$= 0.3138$$

The price of a 5-year "at-the-money" call would then be

$$BSCall(\$86.50, 0.6976 \times \$124, 0.3138, 0, 5, 0.01) = \$21.095$$

Because Microsoft pays no dividends, the "risk-free rate," which is really the dividend yield on the strike asset, is 0. A plain 5-year at-the-money call on IBM would be worth

$$BSCall(\$86.50, \$86.50, 0.312, 0.055, 5, 0.01) = \$29.467$$

This ordinary option price is greater because the risk-free rate for the ordinary call is positive. It is a coincidence that the volatility for the two options is almost the same.

Problem 14.19 asks you to think about the circumstances under which XYZ might hedge currency risk using exchange options.

CHAPTER SUMMARY

An exotic option is created by altering the contractual terms of a standard option. Exotic options permit hedging solutions tailored to specific problems and speculation tailored to particular views. Examples of exotic options include the following:

- *Asian options* have payoffs that are based on the average price of the underlying asset over the life of the option. The average price can be used in place of either the underlying asset (an *average price* option) or in place of the strike price (an *average strike* option). Averages can be arithmetic or geometric.

- *Barrier options* have payoffs that depend upon whether the price of the underlying asset has reached a barrier over the life of the option. These options can come into existence (*knock-in options*) or go out of existence (*knock-out options*) when the barrier is reached.

- *Compound options* are options on options: Put or call options with put or call options as the underlying asset.

- *Gap options* are options where the option payoff jumps at the price where the option comes into the money.

- *Exchange options* are options that have risky assets as both the underlying asset and the strike asset.

It is helpful in analyzing exotic options to compare them to standard options: In what ways does an exotic option resemble a standard option? How will its price compare to that of an ordinary option? When might someone use the exotic option instead of a standard option?

FURTHER READING

In Chapter 16 we will see some more applications of exotic options. In Chapter 21 we will discuss the underlying logic of pricing exotic options and in Chapter 22 we will discuss additional exotic options.

General books covering exotic options include Briyis and Bellala (1998), Haug (1998), Wilmott (1998), and Zhang (1998). Rubinstein (1991b) discusses exchange options, Rubinstein (1991a) discusses compound options, and Rubinstein and Reiner (1991) discuss barrier options.

PROBLEMS

To answer many of these questions you can use the exotic option functions documented in Appendix E.

14.1. Obtain monthly stock prices for 5 years for three stocks. Compute the arithmetic and geometric average month-end price for each stock. Which is greater?

14.2. Suppose you observe the prices {5, 4, 5, 6, 5}. What are the arithmetic and geometric averages? Now you observe {3, 4, 5, 6, 7}. What are the two averages? What happens to the difference between the two measures of the average as the standard deviation of the observations increases?

14.3. Suppose that $S = \$100$, $K = \$100$, $r = 0.08$, $\sigma = 0.30$, $\delta = 0$, and $T = 1$. Construct a standard two-period binomial stock price tree using the method in Chapter 10.

    a. Consider stock price averages computed by averaging the 6-month and 1-year prices. What are the possible arithmetic and geometric averages after 1 year?

    b. Construct a binomial tree for the *average*. How many nodes does it have after 1 year? (Hint: While the moves *ud* and *du* give the same year-1 price, they do *not* give the same average in year 1.)

    c. What is the price of an Asian arithmetic average price call?

    d. What is the price of an Asian geometric average price call?

14.4. Using the information in Problem 3, compute the prices of

    a. An Asian arithmetic average strike call.

    b. An Asian geometric average strike call.

14.5. Repeat Problem 3, except construct a *three*-period binomial tree. Assume that Asian options are based on averaging the prices every 4 months.

    a. What are the possible geometric and arithmetic averages after 1 year?

    b. What is the price of an Asian arithmetic average price call?

    c. What is the price of an Asian geometric average price call?

14.6. Let $S = \$40$, $K = \$45$, $\sigma = 0.30$, $r = 0.08$, $T = 1$, and $\delta = 0$.

    a. What is the price of a standard call?

    b. What is the price of a knock-in call with a barrier of $44? Why?

    c. What is the price of a knock-out call with a barrier of $44? Why?

14.7. Let $S = \$40$, $K = \$45$, $\sigma = 0.30$, $r = 0.08$, $\delta = 0$, and $T = \{0.25, 0.5, 1, 2, 3, 4, 5, 100\}$.

    a. Compute the prices of knock-out calls with a barrier of $38.

    b. Compute the ratio of the knock-out call prices to the prices of standard calls. Explain the pattern you see.

14.8. Repeat Problem 7 for up-and-out puts assuming a barrier of $44.

14.9. Let $S = \$40$, $K = \$45$, $\sigma = 0.30$, $r = 0.08$, and $\delta = 0$. Compute the value of knock-out calls with a barrier of $60 and times to expiration of 1 month, 2 months, and so on, up to 1 year. As you increase time to expiration, what happens to the price of the knock-out call? What happens to the price of the knock-out call *relative to* the price of an otherwise identical standard call?

14.10. Examine the prices of up-and-out puts with strikes of $0.9 and $1.0 in Table 14.4. With barriers of $1 and $1.05, the .90-strike up-and-outs appear to have the same premium as the ordinary put. However, with a strike of 1.0 and the same barriers, the up-and-outs have lower premiums than the ordinary put. Explain why. What would happen to this pattern if we increased the time to expiration?

14.11. Suppose $S = \$40$, $K = \$40$, $\sigma = 0.30$, $r = 0.08$, and $\delta = 0$.

    a. What is the price of a standard European call with 2 years to expiration?

    b. Suppose you have a compound call giving you the right to pay two dollars 1-year from today to buy the option in part (a). For what stock prices in 1 year will you exercise this option?

    c. What is the price of this compound call?

    d. What is the price of a compound option giving you the right to *sell* the option in part (a) in 1 year for two dollars?

14.12. Make the same assumptions as in Problem 11.

    a. What is the price of a standard European put with 2 years to expiration?

    b. Suppose you have a compound call giving you the right to pay two dollars 1 year from today to buy the option in part (a). For what stock prices in 1 year will you exercise this option?

    c. What is the price of this compound call?

    d. What is the price of a compound option giving you the right to *sell* the option in part (a) in 1 year for two dollars?

14.13. Consider the hedging example using gap options, in particular the assumptions and prices in Table 14.5.

    a. Implement the gap pricing formula. Reproduce the numbers in Table 14.5.

b. Consider the option with $K_1 = \$0.8$ and $K_2 = \$1$. If volatility were zero, what would the price of this option be? What do you think will happen to this premium if the volatility increases? Verify your answer using your pricing model and explain why it happens.

14.14. Problem 12.11 showed how to compute approximate Greek measures for an option. Use this technique to compute delta for the gap option in Figure 14.3, for stock prices ranging from $90 to $110 and for times to expiration of 1 week, 3 months, and 1 year. How easy do you think it would be to hedge a gap call?

14.15. Consider the gap put in Figure 14.4. Using the technique in Problem 12.11, compute vega for this option at stock prices of $90, $95, $99, $101, $105, and $110, and for times to expiration of 1 week, 3 months, and 1 year. Explain the values you compute.

14.16. Let $S = \$40$, $\sigma = 0.30$, $r = 0.08$, $T = 1$, and $\delta = 0$. Also let $Q = \$60$, $\sigma_Q = 0.50$, $\delta_Q = 0.04$, and $\rho = 0.5$. What is the price of a standard 40-strike call with S as the underlying asset? What is the price of an exchange option with S as the underlying asset and $0.667 \times Q$ as the strike price?

14.17. Let $S = \$40$, $\sigma = 0.30$, $r = 0.08$, $T = 1$, and $\delta = 0$. Also let $Q = \$60$, $\sigma_Q = 0.50$, $\delta_Q = 0$, and $\rho = 0.5$. In this problem we will compute prices of exchange calls with S as the price of the underlying asset and Q as the price of the strike asset.

    a. Vary δ from 0 to 0.1. What happens to the price of the call?

    b. Vary δ_Q from 0 to 0.1. What happens to the price of the call?

    c. Vary ρ from -0.5 to 0.5. What happens to the price of the call?

    d. Explain your answers by drawing analogies to the effects of changing inputs in the Black-Scholes call pricing formula.

14.18. Let $S = \$40$, $\sigma = 0.30$, $r = 0.08$, $T = 1$. and $\delta = 0$. Also let $Q = \$40$, $\sigma_Q = 0.30$, $\delta_Q = 0$, and $\rho = 1$. Consider an exchange call with S as the price of the underlying asset and Q as the price of the strike asset.

    a. What is the price of an exchange call with S as the underlying asset and Q as the strike price?

    b. Now suppose $\sigma_Q = 0.40$. What is the price of the exchange call?

    c. Explain your answers to (a) and (b).

14.19. XYZ wants to hedge against depreciations of the euro and is also concerned about the price of oil, which is a significant component of XYZ's costs. However, there is a positive correlation between the euro and the price of oil: The euro appreciates when the price of oil rises. Explain how an exchange option based on oil and the euro might be used to hedge in this case.

14.20. A **chooser option** (also known as an **as-you-like-it option**) becomes a put or call at the discretion of the owner. For example, consider a chooser on the S&R

index for which both the call, with value $C(S_t, K, T - t)$, and the put, with value $P(S_t, K, T - t)$, have a strike price of K. The index pays no dividends. At the choice date, t_1, the payoff of the chooser is

$$max[C(S_{t_1}, K, T - t_1), P(S_{t_1}, K, T - t_1)]$$

a. If the chooser option and the underlying options expire simultaneously, what ordinary option position is this equivalent to?

b. Suppose that the chooser must be exercised at t_1 and that the underlying options expire at T. Show that the chooser is equivalent to a call option with strike price K and maturity T plus $e^{-\delta(T-t_1)}$ put options with strike price $Ke^{-(r-\delta)(T-t_1)}$ and expiration t_1.

14.21. Suppose that $S = \$100$, $\sigma = 30\%$, $r = 8\%$, and $\delta = 0$. Today you buy a contract which, 6 months from today, will give you one 3-month to expiration *at-the-money* call option. (This is called a **forward start** option.) Assume that r, σ, and δ are certain not to change in the next 6 months.

a. Six months from today, what will be the value of the option if the stock price is $100? $50? $200? (Use the Black-Scholes formula to compute the answer.) In each case, what fraction of the stock price does the option cost?

b. What investment *today* would guarantee that you had the money in 6 months to buy an at-the-money option?

c. What would you pay today for the forward start option in this example?

d. How would your answer change if the option were to have a strike price that was 105% of the stock price?

14.22. You wish to insure a portfolio for 1 year. Suppose that $S = \$100$, $\sigma = 30\%$, $r = 8\%$, and $\delta = 0$. You are considering two strategies. The *simple insurance strategy* entails buying one put option with a 1-year maturity at a strike price that is 95% of the stock price. The *rolling insurance strategy* entails buying one 1-month put option each month, with the strike in each case being 95% of the then-current stock price.

a. What is the cost of the simple insurance strategy?

b. What is the cost of the rolling insurance strategy? (Hint: See Problem 21.)

c. Intuitively, what accounts for the cost difference?

Appendix 14.A: Pricing Formulas for Exotic Options

In this appendix we present formulas for options discussed in this chapter.

Asian Options Based on the Geometric Average

The average can be used in place of either the asset price (an average price option) or the strike price (an average strike option).

Average price options Suppose the risk-free rate is r, the stock has a dividend yield δ, and volatility σ. We compute the average using N equally spaced prices from 0 to T, with the first observation at time T/N. A European geometric average price option can then be valued using the Black-Scholes formula for a call by setting the dividend yield and volatility equal to

$$\delta^* = \frac{1}{2}\left[r\frac{N-1}{N} + (\delta + 0.5\sigma^2)\frac{N+1}{N} - \frac{\sigma^2}{N^2}\frac{(N+1)(2N+1)}{6} \right] \qquad (14.18)$$

and

$$\sigma^* = \frac{\sigma}{N}\sqrt{\frac{(N+1)(2N+1)}{6}} \qquad (14.19)$$

With continuous sampling, i.e., $N = \infty$, the formulas reduce to

$$\delta^* = \frac{1}{2}\left(r + \delta + \frac{1}{6}\sigma^2 \right)$$

and

$$\sigma^* = \sigma\sqrt{\frac{1}{3}}$$

Deriving these results is easier than you might guess, but requires some background covered in Chapters 18 and 19. The derivation is in Appendix 19.A.

Average strike options In order to value the geometric average strike option, we need to know the correlation between the average, $G(T)$, and the terminal stock price, S_T. We also need to recognize that the strike asset is the average; hence, we value the option like an exchange option (see Section 14.6), in which we exchange the time-T stock price for its average.

In Appendix 19.A, we show that the average strike option can be valued using the Black-Scholes formula, with the following substitutions:

- Replace the risk-free rate with the "dividend yield," equation (14.18).
- Replace the volatility with

$$\sigma^{**} = \sigma\sqrt{T}\sqrt{1 + \frac{(N+1)(2N+1)}{6N^2} - 2\rho\sqrt{\frac{(N+1)(2N+1)}{6N^2}}}$$

where the correlation between $ln(S_T)$ and $G(T)$ is given by

$$\rho = \frac{1}{2}\sqrt{\frac{6(N+1)}{2N+1}}$$

- Use the current stock price as the strike price.
- The dividend yield remains the same.

Barrier Options

Table 14.6 defines various expressions that are used in barrier option pricing (including the familiar Black-Scholes "d_1" and "d_2").

Since the value of a barrier option depends upon whether the barrier has been hit, we need notation for that occurrence. Suppose the option is issued at time 0 and expires at time T. Let $\overline{S}_t$ denote the greatest stock price between time 0 and t (where $t < T$) and let $\underline{S}_t$ denote the lowest stock price between time 0 and t.

If we have an up-and-in or up-and-out option, we are interested in whether the stock price has exceeded H since the time the option was issued. We say the barrier has been hit if $\overline{S}_t \geq H$. Similarly, if we have a down-and-in or down-and-out, then the barrier has been hit if the lowest price prior to time t was below H. This is denoted as $\underline{S}_t \leq H$.

Ordinary European call and put   From Chapter 12, the formulas for ordinary calls and puts (equations (12.1) and (12.3)) are

$$\text{Call} = Se^{-\delta(T-t)}N(d_1) - Ke^{-r(T-t)}N(d_2) \tag{14.20}$$

$$\text{Put} = -Se^{-\delta(T-t)}N(-d_1) + Ke^{-r(T-t)}N(-d_2) \tag{14.21}$$

Up-and-in call   When $H < K$, the barrier has no effect on the option price; if the option expires in-the-money, the barrier will have been hit for sure. When $H > K$, the value of an up-and-in call is

TABLE 14.6	Definitions of expressions used in barrier option formulas.

$$d_1 = [ln(S/K) + (r - \delta + 0.5\sigma^2)(T - t)]/\sigma\sqrt{T - t}$$

$$d_2 = d_1 - \sigma\sqrt{T - t}$$

$$d_3 = [ln(H^2/SK) + (r - \delta + 0.5\sigma^2)(T - t)]/\sigma\sqrt{T - t}$$

$$d_4 = d_3 - \sigma\sqrt{T - t}$$

$$d_5 = [ln(S/H) + (r - \delta + 0.5\sigma^2)(T - t)]/\sigma\sqrt{T - t}$$

$$d_6 = d_5 - \sigma\sqrt{T - t}$$

$$d_7 = [ln(H/S) + (r - \delta + 0.5\sigma^2)(T - t)]/\sigma\sqrt{T - t}$$

$$d_8 = d_7 - \sigma\sqrt{T - t}$$

$$\text{Up-and-in call} = \begin{cases} Se^{-\delta(T-t)}\left[N(d_5) + \left(\dfrac{H}{S}\right)^{2\frac{r-\delta}{\sigma^2}+1}[N(d_3) - N(d_7)]\right] \\[2em] \quad -Ke^{-r(T-t)}\left[N(d_6) + \left(\dfrac{H}{S}\right)^{2\frac{r-\delta}{\sigma^2}-1}[N(d_4) - N(d_8)]\right] & \overline{S}_t < H \\[2em] Se^{-\delta(T-t)}N(d_1) - Ke^{-r(T-t)}N(d_2) & \overline{S}_t \geq H \end{cases}$$

$$(14.22)$$

Note that when $S > H$, the call has knocked-in, and it is a standard European call (equation (14.20)).

Up-and-out call   The value of an up-and-out call is given by

$$\text{Up-and-out call} = \text{equation (14.20)} - \text{equation (14.22)} \qquad (14.23)$$

Down-and-in call   For a down-and-in call, the relation of the barrier to the strike does not affect the formula. The value of a down-and-in call is

$$\text{Down-and-in call} = \begin{cases} Se^{-\delta(T-t)}\left(\dfrac{H}{S}\right)^{2\frac{r-\delta}{\sigma^2}+1}N(d_3) - \\[2em] \quad Ke^{-r(T-t)}\left(\dfrac{H}{S}\right)^{2\frac{r-\delta}{\sigma^2}-1}N(d_4) & \underline{S}_t > H \\[2em] Se^{-\delta(T-t)}N(d_1) - Ke^{-r(T-t)}N(d_2) & \underline{S}_t \leq H \end{cases}$$

$$(14.24)$$

Down-and-out call

$$\text{Down-and-out call} = \text{Equation (14.20)} - \text{equation (14.24)} \qquad (14.25)$$

Up-and-in put   The value of an up-and-in put does not depend on whether H is greater or less than K.

$$\text{Up-and-in put} = \begin{cases} -Se^{-\delta(T-t)}\left(\dfrac{H}{S}\right)^{2\frac{r-\delta}{\sigma^2}+1}N(-d_3) + \\[2em] \quad Ke^{-r(T-t)}\left(\dfrac{H}{S}\right)^{2\frac{r-\delta}{\sigma^2}-1}N(-d_4) & \overline{S}_t < H \\[2em] -Se^{-\delta(T-t)}N(-d_1) + Ke^{-r(T-t)}N(-d_2) & \overline{S}_t \geq H \end{cases}$$

$$(14.26)$$

Up-and-out put

$$\text{Up-and-out put} = \text{Equation (14.21)} - \text{equation (14.26)} \qquad (14.27)$$

Down-and-in put   When $H > K$, the barrier does not affect the value of a down-and-in put, since in order for the option to have value at expiration ($S < K$), the barrier must have been hit. When $H < K$, the value of a down-and-in put is

$$
\text{Down-and-in put} = \begin{cases} -Se^{-\delta(T-t)}\left[N(-d_5) + \left(\dfrac{H}{S}\right)^{2\frac{r-\delta}{\sigma^2}+1}[N(d_7) - N(d_3)]\right] \\ +Ke^{-r(T-t)}\left[N(-d_6) + \left(\dfrac{H}{S}\right)^{2\frac{r-\delta}{\sigma^2}-1}[N(d_8) - N(d_4)]\right] & \underline{S}_t > H \\ \\ -Se^{-\delta(T-t)}N(-d_1) + Ke^{-r(T-t)}N(-d_2) & \underline{S}_t \leq H \end{cases}
$$

$$(14.28)$$

When $S < H$, the put has knocked-in, and it is a standard European put (equation (14.21)).

Down-and-out put

$$\text{Down-and-out put} = \text{Equation (14.21)} - \text{equation (14.28)} \qquad (14.29)$$

Compound Options

Letting ρ denote the correlation coefficient between normally distributed z_1 and z_2, we denote the cumulative bivariate standard normal distribution as

$$Prob(z_1 < a, z_2 < b; \rho) = NN(a, b; \rho)$$

This function is implemented in the spreadsheets as *BINORMSDIST*.

Suppose we have a compound call option to buy a call option. Let t_1 be the time to maturity of the compound option, and t_2 the time to maturity of the underlying option (obviously, we require that $t_2 > t_1$). Also let K be the strike price on the underlying option and x the strike price on the compound option; i.e., we have the right on date t_1 to pay x to acquire a call option with time to expiration $t_2 - t_1$. Define S^* as in equation (14.11); that is, S^* is the stock price at which the option is worth the strike that must be paid to get it.[7]

The formula for the price of a call option on a call option is

$$CallOnCall(S, K, x, \sigma, r, t_1, t_2, \delta) = Se^{-\delta t_2} NN\left(a_1, d_1; \sqrt{\frac{t_1}{t_2}}\right)$$

$$- Ke^{-rt_2} NN\left(a_2, d_2; \sqrt{\frac{t_1}{t_2}}\right) - xe^{-rt_1}N(a_2) \quad (14.30)$$

....

[7]The spreadsheet function to compute S^* is called *BSCallImpS*, which is similar to the implied volatility function *BSCallImpVol*, except that it computes the stock price consistent with an option price, rather than the volatility.

where

$$a_1 = \frac{ln(S/S^*) + (r - \delta + 0.5\sigma^2)t_1}{\sigma\sqrt{t_1}}$$

$$a_2 = a_1 - \sigma\sqrt{t_1}$$

$$d_1 = \frac{ln(S/K) + (r - \delta + 0.5\sigma^2)t_2}{\sigma\sqrt{t_2}}$$

$$d_2 = d_1 - \sigma\sqrt{t_2}$$

Notice that d_1 and d_2 are identical to the Black-Scholes d_1 and d_2, and relate to ultimate exercise of the underlying option, while a_1 and a_2 differ only in the strike price and time to expiration and relate to exercise of the compound option. The last term in equation (14.30) reflects payment of the compound option strike price and the condition under which it is paid. The sign on the correlation term, $\sqrt{t_1/t_2}$, reflects whether exercise of the compound option is associated with an increase or decrease in the likelihood of exercising the underlying option. (The correlation is positive for a call on a call. For a call on a put, an increase in the stock price reduces the value of the put and also reduces the value of the option to buy the put; hence, the correlation is again positive.)

This discussion suggests that we can guess how the remaining compound option formulas will look. We would like to value puts on calls, calls on puts, and puts on puts.

The put on the call requires a positive sign on Ke^{-rt} and a negative sign on $Se^{-\delta t}$, since the option if ultimately exercised will require the owner to be a call writer. The underlying option is in-the-money if $S > K$; hence, we want positive d_1 and d_2. The compound option will be exercised and the strike x received if $S < S^*$, which requires negative a_1 and a_2 and a positive sign on x. Finally, if the stock price goes up, this increases the value of the call and decreases the value of the put on the call; hence, the correlation must be negatively signed. Thus, the formula is

$$PutOnCall(S, K, x, \sigma, r, t_1, t_2, \delta) = -Se^{-\delta t_2} NN\left(-a_1, d_1; -\sqrt{\frac{t_1}{t_2}}\right)$$

$$+ Ke^{-rt_2} NN\left(-a_2, d_2; -\sqrt{\frac{t_1}{t_2}}\right) + xe^{-rt_1} N(-a_2) \quad (14.31)$$

Similar arguments give us the following formulas:

$$CallOnPut(S, K, x, \sigma, r, t_1, t_2, \delta) = -Se^{-\delta t_2} NN\left(-a_1, -d_1; \sqrt{\frac{t_1}{t_2}}\right)$$

$$+ Ke^{-rt_2} NN\left(-a_2, -d_2; \sqrt{\frac{t_1}{t_2}}\right) - xe^{-rt_1} N(-a_2) \quad (14.32)$$

$$PutOnPut(S, K, x, \sigma, r, t_1, t_2, \delta) = Se^{-\delta t_2} NN\left(a_1, -d_1; -\sqrt{\frac{t_1}{t_2}}\right)$$

$$- Ke^{-rt_2} NN\left(a_2, -d_2; -\sqrt{\frac{t_1}{t_2}}\right) + xe^{-rt_1} N(a_2) \quad (14.33)$$

As an exercise, you can check that as t_1 approaches 0, the compound option formula simplifies to the greater of the value of the underlying option or zero.

Infinitely Lived Exchange Option

The logic of exchange options extends directly to the case of an infinitely lived American option. A key insight is that the optimal exercise level H really depends on the *ratio* of the values of the asset being received to the asset being given up; the absolute level is unimportant. Thus, if it is optimal to exchange stock A for stock B when the price of A is 100 and the price of B is 200, then it will be optimal to exchange A for B when their prices are 1 and 2. We therefore just need to find the *ratio* of prices at which exercise is optimal.

The formula for the infinitely lived option to exchange stock 1 for stock 2 is

$$C^\infty(S_1, S_2, \sigma_1, \sigma_2, \rho, \delta_1, \delta_2) = (s - 1)S_2 \left(\frac{S_1/S_2}{s} \right)^h$$

where δ_i is the dividend yield on asset i, σ_i is the volatility of asset i, ρ is the correlation between stock 1 and stock 2, and

$$s = \frac{h}{1 - h}$$

is the ratio of S_1 to S_2 at which it is optimal to exercise the option. Let $v^2 = \sigma_S^2 + \sigma_2^2 - 2\rho\sigma_S\sigma_2$ and

$$h = \frac{1}{2} - \frac{\delta_2 - \delta_1}{v^2} + \sqrt{\left(\frac{\delta_2 - \delta_1}{v^2} - \frac{1}{2} \right)^2 + \frac{2\delta_2}{v^2}}$$

It is possible to show that if we set $\delta_2 = r$ and $\sigma_2 = 0$, we get the formula for an infinite call, equation (12.16), while if we set $\delta_1 = r$ and $\sigma_1 = 0$, we get the put formula, equation (12.17).

PART 4

FINANCIAL ENGINEERING AND APPLICATIONS

In the preceding chapters we have focused on forwards, swaps, and options (including exotic options) as stand-alone financial claims. In the next three chapters we will see that these claims can be used as financial building blocks to create new claims, and also see that derivatives pricing theory can help us understand corporate financial policy and the valuation of investment projects.

Specifically, in Chapter 15 we see how it is possible to construct and price bonds that make payments that, instead of being denominated in cash, are denominated in stocks, commodities, and different currencies. Such bonds can be structured to contain embedded options. We also see how such claims can be used for risk management and how their issuance can be motivated by tax purposes. Chapter 16 examines some corporate contexts in which derivatives are important, including corporate financial policy, compensation options, and mergers. Chapter 17 examines real options, in which the insights from derivatives pricing are used to value investment projects.

Chapter 15

Financial Engineering and Security Design

Forwards, calls, puts, and common exotic options can be added to bonds or otherwise combined to create new securities. For example, we can view many traded securities as bonds with embedded options. In such cases, individual derivatives become building blocks—ingredients used to construct new kinds of financial products. In this chapter we will see how to assemble the ingredients to create new products. The process of constructing new instruments from these building blocks is called **financial engineering.**

15.1 THE MODIGLIANI-MILLER THEOREM

The starting point for any discussion of modern financial engineering is the analysis of Franco Modigliani and Merton Miller (Modigliani and Miller 1958). Before their work, financial analysts would puzzle over how to compare the values of firms with similar *operating* characteristics but different *financial* characteristics. Modigliani and Miller realized that different financing decisions (for example, the choice of the firm's debt-to-equity ratio) may carve up the firm's cash flows in different ways, but if the *total* cash flows paid to all claimants is unchanged, the total value of all claims would remain the same. They showed that if firms differing only in financial policy differed in market value, profitable arbitrage would exist. Using their famous analogy, the price of whole milk should equal the total prices of the skim milk and butterfat that can be derived from that milk.[1]

The Modigliani-Miller analysis requires numerous assumptions: For example, there are no taxes, no transaction costs, no bankruptcy costs, and no private information. Nevertheless, the basic Modigliani-Miller result provided clarity for a confusing issue, and it created a starting point for thinking about the effects of taxes, transaction costs, and the like, revolutionizing finance.

All of the no-arbitrage pricing arguments we have been using embody the Modigliani-Miller spirit. For example, we saw in Chapter 2 that we could syntheti-cally create a forward contract using options, a call option using a forward contract, bonds, and a put, and so forth. In Chapter 10 we saw that an option could also be

---

[1]A more detailed discussion of the Modigliani-Miller results is in Brealey and Myers (2000, Chapter 17) and Ross et al. (1996, Chapter 15). The original paper (Modigliani and Miller, (1958)) is a classic.

synthetically created from a position in the stock and borrowing or lending. If prices of actual claims differ from their synthetic equivalents, arbitrage is possible.

Financial engineering is an application of the Modigliani-Miller idea. We can combine claims such as stocks, bonds, forwards, and options and assemble them to create new claims. The price for this new security is the sum of the pieces combined to create it. When we create a new instrument in this fashion, the Modigliani-Miller analysis concludes that value is neither created nor destroyed. Thus, financial engineering has no value in a pure Modigliani-Miller world. However, in real life, the new instrument may have different tax, regulatory, or accounting characteristics, or may provide a way for the issuer or buyer to obtain a particular payoff at lower transaction costs than the alternatives. Financial engineering thus provides a way to create instruments that meet specific needs of investors and issuers.

As a starting point, you can ask the following questions when you confront new financial instruments:

- What is the payoff of the instrument?
- Is it possible to synthetically create the same payoffs using some combination of assets, bonds, and options?
- Who might issue or buy such an instrument?
- What problem does the instrument solve?

15.2 PRICING AND DESIGNING STRUCTURED NOTES

We begin by examining structured notes. An ordinary note (or bond) has interest and maturity payments that are fixed at the time of issue. A **structured note** has interest or maturity payments that are not fixed in dollars, but are contingent in some way. Structured notes can make payments based on stock prices, interest rates, commodities, or currencies, and can have options embedded in them. The equity-linked CD discussed in Chapter 2 is an example of a structured note, as it has a maturity payment based upon the performance of the S&P 500 index. The PEPS security discussed in Chapter 3 is also a structured note. In this section we discuss structured notes without options. In the next section we will introduce notes with options.

Zero-Coupon Bonds

The most basic financial instrument is a zero-coupon bond. As in Chapter 7, let $r_s(t_0, t_1)$ represent the annual continuously compounded interest rate prevailing at time $s \le t_0$, for a loan from time t_0 to time t_1. Similarly, the price of a zero-coupon bond purchased at time t_0, maturing at time t_1, and quoted at time s is $P_s(t_0, t_1)$. Thus, we have

$$P_s(t_0, t_1) = e^{-r_s(t_0, t_1)(t_1 - t_0)}$$

When there is no risk of misunderstanding, we will assume that the interest rate is quoted at time $t_0 = 0$, and the bond is also purchased then. We will denote the rate

$r_0(0, t) = r(t)$, and the corresponding bond price P_t. So we will write

$$P_t = e^{-r(t)t}$$

P_t is the current price of a t-period zero-coupon bond.

There are two important, equivalent interpretations of P_t. First, P_t is a discount factor, since it is the price today for \$1 delivered at time t. Second, P_t is the prepaid forward price for \$1 delivered at time t. These are different ways of saying the same thing:

Zero-coupon bond price = Discount factor for \$1 = Prepaid forward price for \$1

Financial valuation entails discounting, which is why zero-coupon bonds are a basic building block. The notion that prepaid forward prices are discount factors will play an important role in this chapter.

Coupon Bonds

Once we have a set of zero-coupon bonds, we can analyze other fixed payment instruments, such as ordinary coupon bonds. Consider a bond that pays the coupon c, n times over the life of the bond, makes the maturity payment M, and matures at time T. We will denote the price of this bond as $B(0, T, c, n, M)$. The time between coupon payments is T/n, and the ith coupon payment occurs at time $t_i = i \times T/n$.

We can value this bond by discounting its payments. To do this, we need to know the price today of \$1 payable in one period, in two periods, and so on to T periods. Zero-coupon bond prices provide discount factors. Thus, this bond would have the value

$$
\begin{aligned}
B(0, T, c, n, M) &= \sum_{i=1}^{n} ce^{-r(t_i)t_i} + Me^{-r(T)T} \\
&= \sum_{i=1}^{n} cP_{t_i} + MP_T
\end{aligned}
$$

(15.1)

Not only do zero-coupon bonds enable us to price the bond, but this valuation equation also shows us how to replicate the coupon bond using zero-coupon bonds. Suppose we buy c zero-coupon bonds maturing in 1 year, c maturing in 2 years, and so on, and $c + M$ zero-coupon bonds maturing in T years. This set of zero-coupon bonds will pay c in 1 year, c in 2 years, and $c + M$ in T years. We can say that the coupon bond is *engineered* from a set of zero-coupon bonds with the same maturities as the cash flows from the bond.

In practice, bonds are usually issued at par, meaning that the bond sells today for its maturity value, M. We can structure the bond to make this happen by setting the coupon so that the price of the bond is M. Using equation (15.1), $B(0, T, c, n, M) = M$

if the coupon is set so that

$$c = M \frac{(1 - P_T)}{\sum_{i=1}^{n} P_{t_i}} \tag{15.2}$$

We have seen this formula before. It appeared in Chapter 7 and it was also the formula for the swap rate, equation (8.3) in Chapter 8. As we mentioned then, the swap rate is the rate on a par bond.

Equity-Linked Bonds

Now we consider a bond that, instead of paying M in cash at maturity, pays *one share* of XYZ stock at maturity. With this change in terms, the bond has an uncertain maturity value. Moreover, this change raises questions. What does it mean for such a bond to sell at par? If there are coupon payments, should they be paid in cash or in shares of XYZ? For regulatory and tax purposes, is this instrument a stock or a bond?

In this section we discuss pricing of various types of equity-linked bonds. In Section 15.5 we discuss why a firm might issue such a security.

Zero-coupon equity-linked bond   Suppose an equity-linked bond pays the bond-holder one share of stock at time T. There are no interim payments. What is a fair price for this bond?

Although the language is now different, this valuation problem is the same as that of valuing a prepaid forward contract, which we analyzed in Chapter 5. In both cases the investor pays today to receive a share of stock at time T. In the context of this chapter, we could also call this instrument a *zero-coupon equity-linked bond*. Recall from Chapter 5 that the prepaid forward price is the present value of the forward price, $F_{0,T}^P = P_T F_{0,T}$. This relationship implies that for a nondividend-paying stock, $F_{0,T}^P = e^{-rT} S_0 e^{(r-\delta)T} = S_0$ since $\delta = 0$. The prepaid forward price is the stock price.

Example 15.1   Suppose XYZ stock has a price of $100, pays no dividends, and the annual continuously compounded interest rate is 6%. *In the absence of dividends, the prepaid forward price equals the stock price.* Thus, we would pay $100 to receive the stock in 5 years. ❧

This example shows that if we issue a bond promising to pay one share of a nondividend-paying stock at maturity, and the bond pays no coupon, then the bond will sell for the current stock price. In general we will say that a bond is at par if the bond price equals the maturity payment of the bond. The bond in Example 15.1 is at par since the bond pays one share of stock at maturity and the price of the note equals the price of one share of stock today.

Instead of denominating the note in dollars, we could denominate it in shares. In this case, we would say that for a nondividend-paying stock, a bond paying one share in the future costs one share today.

Suppose the stock makes discrete dividend payments of D_{t_i}. Then we saw in Chapter 5 that the prepaid forward price is

$$F_{0,T}^P = S_0 - \sum_{i=1}^{n} P_{t_i} D_{t_i} \tag{15.3}$$

If the stock pays dividends and the bond makes no coupon payments, the following example shows that the bond will sell at less than par.

Example 15.2 Suppose the price of XYZ stock is $100, the quarterly dividend is $1.20, and the annual continuously compounded interest rate is 6% (the quarterly interest rate is therefore 1.5%). From equation (15.3), the 5-year prepaid forward price for XYZ is

$$\$100 - \sum_{i=1}^{20} \$1.20e^{-0.015 \times i} = \$79.42$$

Thus, a zero-coupon equity-linked bond promising to pay one share of XYZ in 5 years would have a price of $79.42. ≋

Cash coupon payments We now add cash coupon payments to the bond. Represent the price of a bond paying n coupons of c each and a share at maturity as $B(0, T, c, n, S_T)$. The valuation equation for such a note—the analog of equation (15.1)—is

$$B(0, T, c, n, S_T) = c \sum_{i=1}^{n} P_{t_i} + F_{0,T}^P \tag{15.4}$$

The value today of the maturity payment, which is one share of stock, is the prepaid forward price, $F_{0,T}^P$.

If the stock pays dividends, then in order for the bond to sell at par—the current price of the stock—it must make coupon payments. In particular, if the equity-linked note is to sell for the stock price, *the note must pay coupons with a present value equal to the present value of dividends over the life of the note.* To see this, use equation (15.3) to rewrite equation (15.4):

$$B(0, T, c, n, S_T) = c \sum_{i=1}^{n} P_{t_i} + S_0 - \sum_{i=1}^{n} P_{t_i} D_{t_i}$$

In words: The price of the bond, B, will equal the stock price, S_0, as long as the present value of the bond's coupons (the first term on the right-hand side) equals the present value of the stock dividends (the third term on the right-hand side).

In general, if we wish to price an equity-linked note at par, from equation (15.4), the bond price B will equal the stock price, S_0, if the coupon, c, is set so that

$$c = \frac{S_0 - F_{0,T}^P}{\sum_{i=1}^{n} P_{t_i}} \qquad (15.5)$$

That is, the coupon must amortize the difference between the stock price and the prepaid forward price.

Example 15.3   Consider XYZ stock as in Example 15.2. If the note promised to pay \$1.20 quarterly—a coupon equal to the stock dividend—the note would sell for \$100. ❧

Notice that equation (15.5) is the same as the equation for a par coupon on a cash bond, equation (15.2). Instead of $1 - P_T$ in the numerator, we have $S_0 - F_{0,T}^P$. The former is the difference between the price of \$1 and the prepaid forward price for \$1 delivered at time T. The latter is the difference between the price of one share and the prepaid forward price for one share delivered at time T.

In practice, dividends may change unexpectedly over the life of the note. The note issuer must make an architectural decision: Should the dividend on the note change to match the dividend paid by the stock, or should the dividend on the note be fixed at the outset using equation (15.5)? The price should be the same in either case, but a different party bears dividend risk.

Interest in-kind   An alternative to paying interest in cash is to pay interest in fractional shares. For example, the coupon could be the value of 2% of a share at the time of payment, rather than a fixed \$2. To price such a bond, we represent the number of fractional shares received at each coupon payment as c^*. The value at time 0 of a fractional share received at time t is $F_{0,t}^P$. Thus, the formula for the value of the note at time t_0, V_0 is

$$V_0 = c^* \sum_{i=1}^{n} F_{0,t_i}^P + F_{0,T}^P$$

The number of fractional shares that must be paid each year for the note to be initially priced at par, i.e., for $V_0 = S_0$, is

$$c^* = \frac{S_0 - F_{0,T}^P}{\sum_{i=1}^{n} F_{0,t_i}^P} \qquad (15.6)$$

When we pay coupons as shares rather than cash, the coupons have variable value. Thus, it is appropriate to use the prepaid forward for the stock as a discount factor rather than the prepaid forward for cash.

In the special case of a constant expected continuous dividend yield, δ, this equation becomes

$$c^* = S_0 \frac{1 - e^{-\delta T}}{\sum_{i=1}^{n} e^{-\delta t_i}} \qquad (15.7)$$

We can compare this expression for c^* with that for the coupon on an ordinary cash bond. In the special case of a constant interest rate for a bond with a \$1 par value, equation (15.2) becomes

$$c = M \frac{1 - e^{-rT}}{\sum_{i=1}^{n} e^{-rt_i}} \qquad (15.8)$$

Comparing the equations for c and c^* makes it apparent that the appropriate discount factor for a coupon is determined from the yield on the underlying asset. In the case of a bond denominated in cash, the discount factor is the yield on cash (the interest rate), while in the case of a bond completely denominated in shares, interest is determined by the yield on shares (the dividend yield).

Commodity-Linked Bonds

Now we repeat the analysis of the previous section, except that instead of paying a share of *stock* at maturity, we suppose the note pays one unit of a *commodity*. We ask the same questions about how to structure this note. We will see that the lease rate replaces the dividend yield. A commodity-linked note will pay a coupon if the lease rate is positive, and the present value of coupon payments on the note must equal the present value of the lease payments on the commodity.

Zero-coupon commodity-linked bonds   Suppose we have a note that pays one unit of a commodity in the future, with no interim cash flows. What is the price of the note? Once again, the answer is, by definition, the present value of the forward price, or the prepaid forward price. As we saw in Chapter 6, the difference between the spot price and the prepaid forward price is summarized by the lease rate. Thus, the discount from the spot price on a zero-coupon note reflects the lease rate.

Example 15.4   Suppose the spot price of gold is \$400/oz, the 3-year forward price is \$455/oz, and the 3-year continuously compounded interest rate is 6.25%. Then a zero-coupon note paying 1 ounce of gold in 3 years would sell for

$$F_{0,T}^P = \$455e^{-0.0625 \times 3} = \$377.208$$

This amount is less than the spot price of \$400 because the lease rate is positive.   🎐

Cash interest   Suppose we have a commodity with a current price of S_0 and a forward price of $F_{0,T}$, and we have a commodity-linked note paying a cash coupon. For the note to sell at par, we need to set the coupon so that

$$S_0 = c \sum_{i=1}^{n} P_{t_i} + P_T F_{0,T}$$

Since by definition of the prepaid forward price, $P_T F_{0,T} = F^P_{0,T}$, we have

$$c = \frac{S_0 - F^P_{0,T}}{\sum_{i=1}^{n} P_{t_i}}$$

exactly as with a dividend-paying stock. The coupon serves to amortize the lease rate. Thus, *the lease rate plays the role of a dividend yield in pricing a commodity-linked note.* The present value calculation treats the lease rate exactly as if it were a dividend yield; what matters is that there is a difference between the prepaid forward price and the current spot price.[2]

Example 15.5　Suppose the spot price of gold is \$400/oz, the 3-year forward price is \$455/oz, the 1-year continuously compounded interest rate is 5.5%, the 2-year rate is 6%, and the 3-year rate is 6.25%. The annual coupon is then determined as

$$c = \frac{\$400 - \$377.208}{e^{-0.055} + e^{-0.06 \times 2} + e^{-0.0625 \times 3}} = \$8.561$$

The annual coupon on a 3-year gold-linked note is therefore about 2% of the spot price.　≈

A 2% yield in this example might seem like cheap financing, but this is illusory and stems from denominating the note in terms of gold. Since the implicit yield on gold (the lease rate) is less than the yield on cash (the interest rate), the yield on a gold-denominated note is less than the yield on a dollar-denominated note. This effect is reversed in cases where the interest rate in a particular currency is below the lease rate of gold. In Japan during the late 1990s, the yen-denominated interest rate was close to zero, so the coupon rate on a gold note would be greater than the interest rate on a yen-denominated note.

Interest in-kind　As with stocks, we can pay fractional units of the commodity as a periodic interest payment. The present value of the payment at time t is computed using the prepaid forward price, $F^P_{0,t}$. Thus the value of a commodity-linked note at par is exactly the same as for an equity-linked note paying interest in-kind:

$$S_0 = c^* \sum_{i=1}^{n} F^P_{0,t_i} + F^P_{0,T}$$

The formula for c^* is given by equation (15.6).

---

[2]As we saw in Chapter 6, a lease rate can be negative if there are storage costs. In this case, the holder of a commodity-linked note benefits by not having to pay storage costs associated with the physical commodity, and will therefore pay a price above maturity value (in the case of a zero-coupon note) or else the note must carry a negative dividend, meaning that the holder must make coupon payments to the issuer.

Perpetuities A perpetuity is an infinitely lived coupon bond. We can use equations (15.7) and (15.8) to consider two perpetuities: one that makes annual payments in dollars and another that pays in units of a commodity. Suppose we want the dollar perpetuity to have a price of M and the commodity perpetuity to have a price of S_0. Using standard perpetuity calculations, if we let $T \to \infty$ in equation (15.8) (this also means that $n \to \infty$), the coupon rate on the dollar bond is

$$c = M \frac{1}{\frac{e^{-r}}{1-e^{-r}}} = M(e^r - 1) = \hat{r}M$$

where $\hat{r}$ is the effective annual interest rate. Similarly, for a perpetuity paying a unit of a commodity, equation (15.7) becomes

$$c^* = S_0 \frac{1}{\frac{e^{-\delta}}{1-e^{-\delta}}} = S_0(e^\delta - 1) = \hat{\delta}S_0$$

where $\hat{\delta}$ is the effective annual lease rate. Thus, in order for a commodity perpetuity to be worth one unit of the commodity, it must pay the lease rate in units of the commodity. (For example, if the lease rate is 2%, the bond pays 0.02 units of the commodity per year.)

What if a bond pays one unit of the commodity per year, forever? We know that if it pays $\hat{\delta}S_t$ in perpetuity it is worth S_0. Thus, if it pays S_t it is worth

$$\frac{S_0}{\hat{\delta}} \tag{15.9}$$

This is the commodity equivalent of a perpetuity.

The conclusion of this section is simple: Commodity-linked notes are formally like equity-linked notes, with the lease rate taking the place of the dividend yield.

Currency-Linked Bonds

What happens if we change the currency of denomination of the bond? As you can probably guess by now, the foreign interest rate, being the yield on the foreign currency, takes the place of the dividend yield on the stock.

Suppose that we want to compare issuing a par-coupon bond denominated entirely in dollars and a par-coupon bond denominated entirely in another currency. We will let B^F denote zero-coupon bond prices denominated in the foreign currency, $r_F(t)$ the foreign interest rate, and P_t^F the price of a zero-coupon bond denominated in the foreign currency.

As you would expect, a bond completely denominated in a foreign currency will have a coupon given by the formula

$$c^F = M \frac{1 - P_T^F}{\sum_{i=1}^n P_{t_i}^F}$$

In other words, foreign interest rates are used to compute the coupon.

What happens when the principal, M, is in the domestic currency and the interest payments are in the foreign currency? Once again we just solve for the coupon payment that makes the bond sell at par. There are two ways to do this.

First, we can discount the foreign currency coupon payments using the foreign interest rate, and then translate their value into dollars using the current exchange rate, x_0 (denominated as \$/unit of foreign currency). The value of the ith coupon is $x_0 P_i^F c$, and the value of the bond is

$$B(0, T, c^F, n, M) = x_0 c^F \sum_{i=1}^{n} P_{t_i}^F + M P_T$$

Alternatively, we can translate the future coupon payment into dollars using the forward currency rate, $F_{0,t}$, and then discount back at the dollar-denominated interest rate, P_t. The value of the bond in this case is

$$B(0, T, c^F, n, M) = c^F \sum_{i=1}^{n} F_{0,t_i} P_{t_i} + M P_T$$

The two calculations give the same result since the currency forward rate, from equation (5.19) is given by

$$F_{0,t} = x_0 e^{r(t)t} e^{-r_F(t)t} = x_0 \frac{P_t^F}{P_t}$$

The forward price for foreign exchange is set so that it makes no difference whether we convert the currency and then discount, or discount and then convert the currency.

The coupon on a par bond with foreign interest and dollar principal is given by

$$c^F = M \frac{1 - P_T}{\sum_{i=1}^{n} F_{0,t_i} P_{t_i}} \tag{15.10}$$

The currency formula is the same as that for equities and commodities. If we think of the foreign interest rate as a dividend yield on the foreign currency, equation (15.10) is the same as our previous coupon expressions.

15.3 BONDS WITH EMBEDDED OPTIONS

We now consider the pricing of bonds with embedded options. Such bonds are common.[3] Any option or combination of options can be added to a bond. The option premium (if a purchased option is added to the bond) is amortized and subtracted from the coupon. If the option is written, the amortized premium is added to the coupon.

---

[3] In addition to convertible bonds offered by firms, there are bonds offered under many names for different kinds of equity-linked notes, for example DECS ("Debt Exchangeable for Common Stock"), PEPS ("Premium Equity Participating Shares"), and PERCS ("Preferred Equity Redeemable for Common Stock"), all of which are effectively bonds plus some options position.

Options in Coupon Bonds

One common kind of equity-linked note has a structure where, at maturity, the holder can receive some fraction of the return on the stock but does not suffer a loss of principal if the stock declines. This protection against loss can be accomplished by embedding call options in the note.

Let γ denote the extent to which the note participates in the appreciation of the underlying stock; we will call γ the **price participation** of the note. In general, the value V_0 of a note with fixed maturity payment M, coupon c, maturity T, strike price K, and price participation γ can be written

$$V_0 = MP_T + c\sum_{i=1}^{n} P_{t_i} + \gamma BSCall(S_0, K, \sigma, r, T, \delta) \qquad (15.11)$$

Equation (15.11) assumes that the principal payment is cash. It could just as well be shares. Equation (15.11) also assumes that the note has a single embedded call option.

Given equation (15.11), we could arbitrarily select M, T, c, K, and γ and then value the note, but it is common to structure notes in particular ways. To take one example, suppose that the initial design goals are as follows:

1. The note's initial price should equal the price of a share, i.e., $V_0 = S_0$.

2. The note should guarantee a return of at least zero, i.e., $M = V_0$.

3. The note should pay some fraction of stock appreciation above the initial price, i.e., $K = V_0$.

These conditions imply that $V_0 = S_0 = M = K$, and thus the price of the note satisfies the equation

$$S_0 = c\sum_{i=1}^{n} P_{t_i} + S_0 P_T + \gamma BSCall(S_0, S_0, \sigma, r, T, \delta) \qquad (15.12)$$

Given these constraints, equation (15.12) implies a relationship between the coupon, c, and price participation, γ. Given a coupon, c, we can solve for γ, and vice versa.

Options in Equity-Linked Notes

With an equity-linked note, the maturity value is shares rather than a fixed number of dollars. The price of a note at par paying one unit of a share at expiration is

$$S_0 = c\sum_{i=1}^{n} P_{t_i} + F_{0,T}^P + \gamma BSCall(S, K, \sigma, r, T, \delta) \qquad (15.13)$$

Compare equations (15.12) and (15.13). Instead of paying S_0 dollars at expiration, the equity-linked note pays one share. If the share pays no dividends, then (assuming $\gamma \geq 0$) the equity-linked note can sell at par only if $c = \gamma = 0$. To the extent the share pays dividends, it is necessary for the note to offer either coupons or options.

Valuing and Structuring an Equity-Linked CD

We have already described in Section 2.6 an example of an equity-linked CD, but we did not analyze the pricing. The CD we discussed has a 5.5-year maturity and a return linked to the S&P 500 index.

Pricing the CD   Suppose the S&P index at issue is S_0 and is $S_{5.5}$ at maturity. The CD pays no coupons ($c = 0$), and it gives the investor 0.7 at-the-money calls ($\gamma = 0.7$ and $K = S_0$). After 5.5 years the CD pays

$$S_0 + 0.7 \times max \left(S_{5.5} - S_0, 0 \right) \tag{15.14}$$

Using equation (15.11), the value of this payoff at time 0 is

$$S_0 \times P_{5.5} + 0.7 \times BSCall(S_0, S_0, \sigma, r, 5.5, \delta) \tag{15.15}$$

where $P_{5.5} = e^{-r \times 5.5}$.

To perform this valuation, we need to make assumptions about the interest rate, the volatility, and the dividend yield on the S&P 500 index. Suppose the 5.5-year interest rate is 6%, the 5-year index volatility is 30%, the S&P index is at 1300, and the dividend yield is 1.5%. We have two pieces to value. The zero-coupon bond paying $1300 is worth

$$\$1300 e^{-0.06 \times 5.5} = \$934.60$$

The 0.7 call options have a value of

$$0.7 \times BSCall(\$1300, \$1300, 0.3, 0.06, 5.5, 0.015) = \$309.01$$

The two pieces together, assuming they could be purchased without fees or spreads in the open market, would cost

$$\$934.60 + \$309.01 = \$1243.61$$

This is $56.39 less than the $1300 initial investment. This difference suggests that the sellers earn a 4.3% commission (56.39/1300) for selling the CD. This analysis makes it clear why the CD provides 70% of market appreciation, rather than 100%. At 100%, the value of the CD would exceed $1300, and the bank would lose money by offering it.

The bank offering the CD is serving as a retailer, offering the CD to the public in order to make a profit from it. The bank's position is that has borrowed $934.60 and written 0.7 call options. You can think of equation (15.15) as the *wholesale* cost of the CD—it is the theoretical cost to the bank of this payoff. Thinking of the bank as retailing the CD also reinforces the idea that an issuing bank typically does not accept the market risk of issuing the CD. Banks who offer products like this often hedge the option exposure by buying call options from an investment bank or dealer. Thus the bank itself need not have option expertise in order to offer this kind of product.

Ask yourself what you think the wholesale cost *should* be. The originating bank will hedge the CD, and must either bear the cost and risks of delta-hedging, or else buy the underlying option from another source. The CD is engineered by a bank that wants to earn commissions. Retail customers may have trouble comparing subtly different products offered by different banks. The customers who have not read this book might not understand option pricing, and hence will be unable to calculate the theoretical value of the CD. On balance, it seems reasonable that we would find the value of the CD to be less than its retail cost by at least several percent.

Here are some other considerations:

- It would have been costly for retail customers to duplicate this payoff, particularly since 5-year options were not readily available to public investors at the time of issue.

- Investors buying this product are spared the need to learn as much about options and, for example, taxes on options, as they would were they to replicate this payoff for themselves.

- The price we have just computed is a ballpark approximation: It is not obvious what the appropriate volatility and dividend inputs are for a 5.5-year horizon.

Any specific valuation conclusion obviously depends entirely on the interest rate, volatility, and dividend assumptions. However, Baubonis et al. (1993) suggest that fees in this range are common for equity-linked CD products.

If we allow for issuer profit, α, as a fraction of the issue price, a general expression for the value of a CD issued at par is

$$V(1 - \alpha) = MP_T + c \sum_{i=1}^{n} P_{t_i} + \gamma BSCall(S, K, \sigma, r, T, \delta) \qquad (15.16)$$

In the above example, $\alpha = 0.043$ and $V = 1300$.

The CD versus an index investment A profit comparison between the CD and a straight equity index investment requires that we account for dividends earned on the index but not on the CD. Assuming that dividends paid are reinvested in the index, we will have $e^{0.015 \times 5.5} = 1.086$ units of the index after 5.5 years. The profit on a straight index investment is thus

$$S_T e^{\delta T} - 1300 e^{rT} = S_{5.5} \times 1.086 - 1300 e^{0.06 \times 5.5}$$

The profit on the CD is obtained by subtracting $1300 e^{0.06 \times 5.5}$ from the payoff.

Figure 15.1 compares the two investments. For low index values, the CD outperforms the index because of its built-in insurance. For high index values, the straight equity investment outperforms the CD.

Structuring the product This is a specific example of an equity-linked CD. There are many design questions:

- What index should we link the note to? In addition to the S&P, possibilities include the Dow Jones Industrials, the NYSE, the NASDAQ, sector indexes such as high-tech, and foreign indexes, with or without currency exposure.

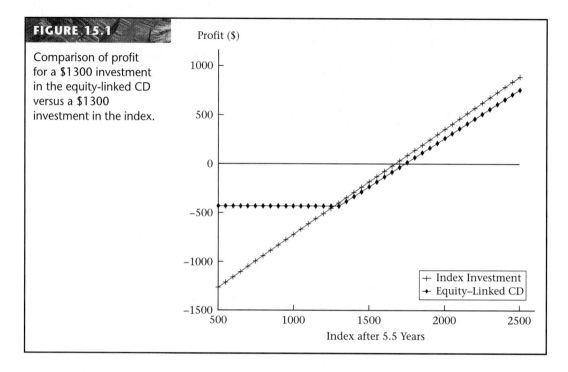

FIGURE 15.1

Comparison of profit for a $1300 investment in the equity-linked CD versus a $1300 investment in the index.

- How much participation in the market should the note provide? The CD we have been discussing provides 70% of the return (if positive) over the life of the CD.

- Should the note make interest payments? (The example CD does not.)

- How much of the original investment should be insured? (The example CD fully insures the investment.)

Alternative Structures

Numerous other variations in the structure of the CD are possible. Some examples follow:

- Use Asian options instead of ordinary options.

- Cap the market participation rate, turning the product into a collar.

- Incorporate a put instead of a call.

- Make the promised payment different from the price.

We will consider the first two alternatives in this section. Problems 15.9 and 15.11 cover the other two.

Asian options The payoff discussed above depends on the simple return over a period of 5.5 years. We could instead compute the return based on the average of year-end prices. As we saw in Chapter 14, an Asian option is worth less than an otherwise equivalent ordinary option. Therefore, when an Asian option is used, the participation rate will be greater than with an ordinary call.

In particular, suppose we base the option on the geometric average price recorded five times over the 5.5-year life of the option, and set the strike price equal to the current index level. The value of this Asian call is $240.97 as opposed to $441.44 for an ordinary call. Assuming the equity-linked note pays no coupon and keeping the present value the same, the participation rate with this geometric-average Asian option is

$$0.7 \times \frac{441.44}{240.97} = 1.28$$

If instead we base the option on the arithmetic average, the option price is $273.12, giving us a participation rate of

$$0.7 \times \frac{441.44}{273.12} = 1.13$$

The arithmetic Asian option has a higher price than one based on the geometric average, hence we get a lower participation rate.

Increasing the number of prices averaged would lower the price of either option, raising the participation rate.

Capped participation Another way to raise the participation rate is to cap the level of participation. For example, suppose we set a cap of y times the initial price. Then the investor writes to the issuer a call with a strike of $y S_0$, and the valuation equation for the CD becomes

$$S_0(1 - \alpha) = S_0 e^{-r \times t} + \gamma \times [BSCall(S_0, S_0, \sigma, r, t, \delta) - BSCall(S_0, y S_0, \sigma, r, t, \delta)]$$

Example 15.6 Suppose we set a cap of a 100% return. Then the investor writes a call with a strike of $2600 to the issuer, and the valuation equation for the CD becomes

$$1300(1 - 0.043) = 1300 e^{-0.06 \times 5.5} + \gamma \times [BSCall(1300, 1300, 0.3, 0.06, 5.5, 0.015)$$

$$-BSCall(1300, 2600, 0.3, 0.06, 5.5, 0.015)]$$

The value of the written 2600-strike call is $162.48. The participation rate implied by this equation is 1.11.   ≷

15.4 ENGINEERED SOLUTIONS FOR GOLDDIGGERS

We now return to the Golddiggers example from Chapter 4 in order to see show how Golddiggers could have used structured notes in place of forwards and options in the hedging scenarios we discussed.

Gold-Linked Notes

A box on page 105 discussed the problems of Ashanti gold. Any hedger using a forward (or futures) contract to hedge faces the risk that the forward contract will suffer a loss prior to expiration of the hedge. That loss generally must be funded when it occurs.[4] This need to fund interim losses arises from the structure of the hedging instrument, in particular the fact that it is a zero-investment contract linked to the price of gold, meant to serve as a hedging instrument and not as a financing instrument.

Instead of shorting a forward contract, Golddiggers could issue a note promising to pay an ounce of gold 1 year from now. Such a note is effectively debt collateralized by future sales of gold. Ordinarily one would think a risky commodity like gold to be poor collateral for a debt issue. But if a *gold-mining firm* issues gold-linked debt, the risk of the bond and the risk of the collateral are the same. Bondholders provide financing as well as absorbing gold price risk.

We begin with the information from Chapter 4: The current price of gold is $405/oz, the forward price is $420, and the effective annual interest rate is 5%. The effective annual lease rate is therefore $0.05 - (420/405 - 1) = 1.296\%$. We wish to construct a debt contract that raises $405 today (the cost of 1 ounce of gold), pays 1 ounce of gold 1 year from today, and if necessary, pays a coupon, c.

We have already seen that the lease rate plays the role of a dividend. Thus, if the bond has a coupon equal to the lease payment on an ounce of gold, it should be priced fairly. A bond with these characteristics should pay a coupon of $1.296\% \times \$405 = \$5.25$.

We can verify that such a bond is fairly priced. The payoff to the bond in 1 year is $5.25 plus 1 ounce of gold. We know we can sell the gold in 1 year for $420 since that is the forward price. The present value of the payoff is therefore the value of the coupon plus the prepaid forward price for gold:

$$\$5.25 \times P_1 + F_{0,1}^P = \frac{\$5.25}{1.05} + \frac{\$420}{1.05} = \$405$$

Because the lease rate is paid as interest, the bond sells at par.

We should verify that the bond serves as an appropriate hedge for Golddiggers. Table 15.1 summarizes the payoffs to Golddiggers and the bondholders at different gold prices in one year. The table assumes that Golddiggers invests the $405 at 5% —this yields the $425.25 that is labeled "FV(gross bond proceeds)." The net cash flow is determined by adding profits without consideration of bond payments (column 2) to the difference between the invested bond proceeds (column 3) and the payment to bond holders (column 4). In this case, issuing the bond achieves the same result as selling a forward contract (compare Table 15.1 and Table 4.2), so Golddiggers is completely hedged.

---

[4]As discussed earlier, forward contracts and swaps typically have collateralization requirements. In practice, a company must have capital to cover a large loss (even if just due to a cash flow mismatch) on a financial contract.

TABLE 15.1		Dollar bond payments and net cash flow to Golddiggers with gold-linked bond paying 1 ounce of gold plus $5.25. The cost of producing 1 ounce of gold is $380.		
Price of Gold ($)	Profit before Bond Flows ($)	FV(Gross Bond Proceeds) ($)	Payment to Bond Holders ($)	Net Cash Flow ($)
350	−30	425.25	−355.25	40
400	20	425.25	−405.25	40
450	70	425.25	−455.25	40
500	120	425.25	−505.25	40

The chief difference between the gold-linked note and the forward contract is that the former provides financing, the latter doesn't. If Golddiggers seeks financing (in order to construct the mine, for example), the issuance of a gold-linked note might be preferable to borrowing and hedging separately.

Notes with Embedded Options

A gold-linked bond leaves bondholders with the risk of a loss should the gold price drop. Golddiggers could instead offer a bond that promises bondholders that they will receive interest plus appreciation of gold above $420, without risk of receiving less than $420.

Such a bond implicitly gives holders a call option on gold with a strike price of $420. From Chapter 2, the cost of this option today is $8.77, with a future value of $8.77 \times 1.05 = $9.21. Let the promised payment on the bond be the $405 issue price plus the coupon, c. In 1 year, the bond is worth

$$\$405 + c + max(0, S_1 - \$420)$$

The valuation equation for the bond is

$$\frac{\$405 + c}{1.05} + \$8.77 = \$405$$

Solving for c gives $c = \$11.04$, which is a yield of 2.726%. Golddiggers thus issues a bond for $405, with a 2.726% coupon, with additional payments to bondholders if the price of gold exceeds $420. The difference between the 2.726% coupon and 5% is due to the cost of the embedded call option.

What is the result for Golddiggers of having issued this bond? If Golddiggers invests at 5% the $405 bond proceeds, then it will have $425.25 cash in 1 year. Recall that costs are $380/oz. If the gold price in 1 year exceeds $420, Golddiggers will show profits of

$$\$420 + \$9.21 - \$380 = \$49.21$$

whereas if gold is less than $420, Golddiggers will make

$$S_1 + \$9.21 - \$380$$

Table 15.2 summarizes the cash flows to bondholders and to Golddiggers from the issuance of this bond. You can verify that this is exactly the same payoff as obtained when Golddiggers hedges by writing a call. The commodity-linked bond achieves the same effect.

Instead of having a low coupon and protection against low gold prices, bondholders might be willing to bear the risk of a decline in the price of gold in exchange for a higher coupon. For example, Golddiggers could issue a bond in which bondholders sell a 420-strike put to Golddiggers. Golddiggers in turn would have to pay greater interest to compensate bondholders for selling the put. The bond would be structured as follows:

- The initial bond price is $405.
- The promised payment on the bond is $434.46, a 7.274% rate of interest.
- If gold sells for less than $420, the payment is reduced by $420 - S_1$.

The bondholders have written a put option to Golddiggers and hence in 1 year receive the future value of the premium. If the price of gold is above $420, Golddiggers makes

$$\$425.25 - \$434.46 + (S_1 - \$380) = S_1 - \$380 - \$9.21$$

If gold is below $420, Golddiggers makes

$$\$425.25 - \$434.46 + (\$420 - S_1) + (S_1 - \$380) = \$30.79$$

With this bond, Golddiggers in effect buys a 420-strike put. Table 15.3 depicts the net cash flow to Golddiggers from issuing this bond. The cash flows are identical to Table 4.3, where Golddiggers purchased a 420-strike put option as insurance against low gold prices.

TABLE 15.2	Dollar bond payments and net cash flow to Golddiggers with gold-linked bond providing gold appreciation to bondholders.			
Price of Gold ($)	Profit before Bond Flows ($)	FV(Gross Bond Proceeds) ($)	Payment to Bond Holders ($)	Net Cash Flow ($)
350	−30	425.25	−416.04	−20.79
400	20	425.25	−416.04	29.21
450	70	425.25	−446.04	49.21
500	120	425.25	−496.04	49.21

TABLE 15.3 Dollar bond payments and net cash flow to Golddiggers with gold-linked bond in which bondholders sell put option to Golddiggers.

Price of Gold ($)	Profit before Bond Flows ($)	FV(Gross Bond Proceeds) ($)	Payment to Bond Holders ($)	Net Cash Flow ($)
350	−30	425.25	−364.46	30.79
400	20	425.25	−414.46	30.79
450	70	425.25	−434.46	60.79
500	120	425.25	−434.46	110.79

15.5 TAX-MOTIVATED STRUCTURES

One common tax-planning goal is to delay paying taxes. A payment of $1 deferred for a year becomes an interest-free loan for that year. Equity-linked notes can be used to defer the payment of capital gains taxes on securities that have appreciated. Although there is some uncertainty about permissible structures, it seems to be generally accepted that equity-linked notes can be used to defer gains. In this section we will look at two examples to see how this is accomplished.

Times Mirror

In April 1995, Times Mirror Co. purchased 1.8m shares of Netscape in a private placement. The price (adjusted for subsequent share splits) was $2/share. As is typical with private placements, the stock was restricted and could not be resold publicly for 2 years even if Netscape were to go public. In order to sell the stock, Times Mirror would have to find a qualified buyer (basically a wealthy or professional investor) and sell the shares in a private placement.[5] In August 1995, Netscape issued shares publicly. In March 1996, Times Mirror wished to sell its position in Netscape. Following the IPO, Netscape's stock price rose as high as $80/share. In early 1996 the price was in the 50s.

    Times Mirror had approximately $85 million in capital gains on the stock. If the shares were to be sold on the open market the tax liability would be approximately $0.35 \times \$85m = \$29.75$ million. Trying to offset or defer capital gains taxes is a standard problem in tax planning. Any sale of shares would trigger the capital gains tax. Thus, the question was whether there was a way for Times Mirror to hedge its holdings of Netscape

---

[5] Stock with these restrictions is called "144A" stock, after the Securities Act section that defined it.

Constructive Sales

In late 1995, Estee Lauder and Ronald Lauder sold 13.8 million shares of Revlon. (See Henriques, 1997.) The capital gains *tax* owed on a direct sale of these shares was estimated at $95 million. The Lauders did not directly sell the shares they owned, however. Instead they borrowed 13.8 million shares from family members, and sold those borrowed shares. Technically they still owned their original shares and owed shares to relatives, but they had received money from selling the borrowed shares. This maneuver is known as "shorting-against-the-box." Clearly shorting-against-the-box has the earmarks of a sale, in that the shareholder has no remaining risk of ownership and has received cash for the stock.

Astounding as it may seem, shorting-against-the-box was for years a well-known and legal strategy for deferring the payment of capital gains taxes. Taxes on the position were not owed until the short position was closed by returning the borrowed shares. Unfortunately for the Lauders, their transaction received publicity, and was widely criticized.

Congress in 1997 passed a tax bill that made a short-against-the-box equivalent to a sale of the stock. The Lauder transaction was believed to be one reason for this tax rule. The idea was that a transaction that was the economic equivalent of a sale would be called a **constructive sale** and taxed like a sale. Facing IRS action, the Lauders in 1997 sold their shares and paid a large tax bill.

A short-against-the-box is a constructive sale because the shareholder has no remaining risk from the shares. What if a hedging transaction leaves some risk? When does a hedge become a constructive sale? The 1997 bill permits shareholders to defer realization if they entered into hedges with sufficient residual risk, such as collars with a large enough difference between the call and put strikes. The bill left it to the Treasury Department to specify the regulations that would codify permissible tax deferral strategies.

without triggering immediate taxation of gains. At this point a little background on the tax issues is helpful.

Times Mirror wanted to sell its Netscape stake in early 1996. The tax environment at the time is described in the box above; the tax community believed that the U.S. Treasury department was scrutinizing tax deferral strategies. Strategies economically similar to short-against-the-box include selling forward (although in that case payment would be deferred), using an equity swap, or using a collar. At the time Congress had not ruled definitively on a change in capital gains tax rules, but the IRS can always challenge a transaction that appears to have no motive other than reducing taxes. Hence, Times Mirror had to be sensitive to the possibility that a transaction intended to defer capital gains would be challenged by the IRS.

A sufficiently wide collar seemed likely to avoid challenge by the IRS. There were still problems, however. Times Mirror's Netscape stake amounted to about a quarter of Netscape's publicly available shares. The required collar position would have been too large to undertake with exchange-traded options. An over-the-counter deal would have left an investment bank with a difficult hedging problem.

Times Mirror elected to use a collar structure, but to issue the collar directly to investors in the form of an equity-linked note. The particular structure, described in Section 3.5, was called a PEPS ("Premium Equity Participating Shares"). Times Mirror's PEPS were issued in March 1996, maturing in March 2001, and were a liability of Times Mirror. They were issued for $39.25 and paid 4.25% interest. The maturity value, described in Table 3.7, was linked to Netscape's stock price in 5 years.[6]

Times Mirror was free to use the cash raised in the PEPS offering for other purposes. Thus, for all practical purposes much of the Netscape holding was sold. The shares were ultimately redeemable in cash or stock, at the discretion of Times Mirror.

The PEPS structure, graphed in Figure 3.16, left Times Mirror imperfectly hedged. If at maturity the Netscape stock price was less than $39.25, Times Mirror would lose the interest payments, hence the net payoff line is below zero. Above $45.14, Times Mirror has the risk of holding 13% of the shares. Note that $39.25 × 1.15 = $45.14, and for the slope, 0.8696 = 1/1.15. Thus the collar width and slope above $45.14 were both determined using 15%.

The PEPS structure thus met the main goals we discussed: Times Mirror effectively sold much of its Netscape position with the risk of the position substantially reduced, and there was at least a 5-year deferral of capital gains tax.

Pricing the PEPS

The structure of the PEPS can be expressed in two ways:

- Buy a 5-year Times Mirror bond.
- Sell 1 Netscape 5-year put with a $39.25 strike.
- Buy 0.8696 Netscape 5-year calls with a $45.14 strike.

  Or equivalently, by put-call parity:

- Buy Netscape stock.[7]
- Sell a 5-year Netscape call with a $39.25 strike.
- Buy 0.8696 Netscape 5-year calls with a $45.14 strike.

Pricing the PEPS requires making an assumption about an appropriate 5-year volatility and dividend yield. The general formula for the PEPS price is familiar, with

---

[6]The share price at maturity was computed based on a 20-day average of Netscape's price prior to the maturity date.

[7]Technically we would want to buy a prepaid forward since we want to acquire Netscape without the dividends. If Netscape is thought unlikely to pay dividends, there is no difference.

the addition of one option:

$$V_0 = S_0 + c \sum_{i=1}^{T} P_{t_i} - BSCall(S, K_1, \sigma, r, T, \delta) + \lambda \times BSCall(S, K_2, \sigma, r, T, \delta)$$

where $c = \$1.67$, $\lambda = 0.8696$, $K_1 = \$39.25$, and $K_2 = \$45.14$. Comparing this case to our earlier discussion of equity-linked notes, if Netscape was not expected to pay dividends, the prepaid forward price equals the stock price. The coupon would have served the sole role of amortizing the net option premium.

Supposing that the price of Netscape is $39.25, Netscape was not expected to pay dividends, the interest rate is 7%, and the 5-year volatility of Netscape is 40%, the cost of the PEPS according to this formula is $42.11.[8]

Cincinnati Bell DECS

A DECS ("Debt Exchangeable for Common Stock") is the same as a PEPS only issued by a different investment bank. In November 1996, Salomon Brothers issued DECS with a maturity payment based on the price of Cincinnati Bell stock. This security paid a quarterly dividend of 6.25%, matured in February 2001, and was noncallable. Let S_{CSN} denote the price of Cincinnati Bell shares. The DECS has the following payment schedule at maturity:[9]

Cincinnati Bell Share Price	Payoff to DECS Holders
$S_{CSN} < \$27.875$	$2 \times S_{CSN}$
$\$27.875 < S_{CSN} < \$33.45$	$\$55.75$
$\$33.45 < S_{CSN}$	$\$55.75 + 1.667 \times (S_{CSN} - \$33.45)$

This is just like the Netscape PEPS, so we will not repeat the analysis of pricing. What is interesting about this issue is that Salomon Brothers, a market-maker, issued it. Why?

The original holder of Cincinnati Bell shares in this case was a subsidiary of Western-Southern Enterprise, a privately held firm. As with Times Mirror, the owner held appreciated stock. The difference here was that Western-Southern was not publicly traded, hence not registered with the SEC. The firm could not issue an equity-linked note to the public without going through the registration process and committing the firm to file quarterly and annual reports.

....

[8]The Netscape PEPS became an AOL PEPS when AOL acquired Netscape.

[9]At issue, the DECS paid the value of one share below $55.75, $55.75 betweeen $55.75 and $66.90, and paid the gain on 0.8333 shares above that price. Cincinnati Bell subsequently split 2 for 1 in June 1997, which changed the cutoffs and conversion ratios proportionately.

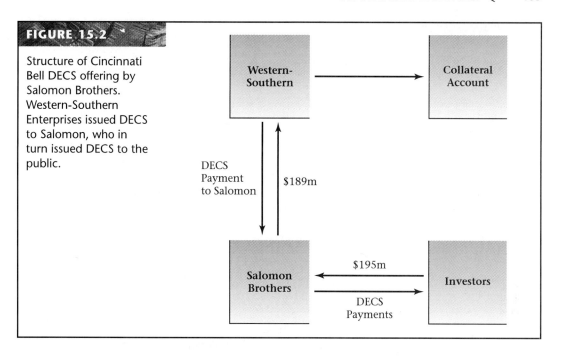

FIGURE 15.2

Structure of Cincinnati Bell DECS offering by Salomon Brothers. Western-Southern Enterprises issued DECS to Salomon, who in turn issued DECS to the public.

The solution was a "parallel DECS" offering, in which Western-Southern issued a privately placed DECS to Salomon; Salomon in turn issued a public DECs. Effectively, Salomon issued the DECS *on behalf of* a client. Western-Southern received the issue proceeds, less a 3% underwriting fee. The DECS offering was a general obligation of Salomon Brothers, backed by an account containing Cincinnati Bell shares as collateral, which was marked to market and maintained at 105% of the value of Cincinnati Bell shares. The structure is illustrated in Figure 15.2.

More General Structures for Equity-Linked Notes

Investment banks frequently construct equity-linked notes with specific characteristics. With both the Times Mirror PEPS and the Cincinnati Bell DECS, the investor was exposed to stock price risk and the credit risk of the issuer. It is possible to create structures in which an investor receives exposure to the equity risk of stock XYZ and exposure to the credit risk of firm ABC. In this case it is possible for an investment bank to use ABC as a *conduit* for the issuance of a structured note that satisfies both criteria.

Suppose, for example, that an investor faces regulatory restrictions against investing in options on XYZ. The investor instead purchases an equity-linked note issued by ABC; this may be called a bond for regulatory purposes. This note has some option-like equity exposure to XYZ embedded in its payments. ABC, having no wish to bear the risk of XYZ exposure, hedges by entering into an option or swap with the bank, which

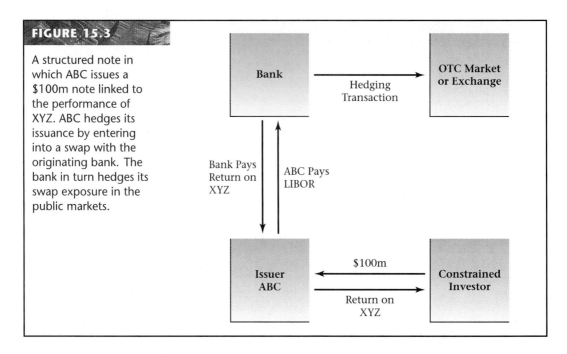

FIGURE 15.3

A structured note in which ABC issues a $100m note linked to the performance of XYZ. ABC hedges its issuance by entering into a swap with the originating bank. The bank in turn hedges its swap exposure in the public markets.

in turn hedges this exposure. A box-and-arrow diagram depicting this structure is in Figure 15.3.

A structure like this has many layers, and hence would entail fees for both the bank and ABC. Thus the investor must either (a) be constrained in some fashion, or it would simply purchase the ordinary notes of ABC and ordinary options on XYZ, or (b) have some unusual desire for a very particular pattern of risk exposure, for which it is willing to pay significant fees.

CHAPTER SUMMARY

Zero-coupon bonds, forwards, calls, and puts serve as building blocks that can be used to engineer new financial products. Fair pricing of a product will depend upon volatility, the dividend or lease rate, and the currency of denomination. Ordinary bonds that are simply denominated in something other than cash follow a simple pricing principle: The lease rate of the underlying asset becomes the coupon rate on the bond.

The specific characteristics of a financial product can be varied, though when one characteristic is changed, another must be changed to keep the value the same. The dials that we can turn include the participation in the underlying asset (via embedded calls and puts), the guaranteed minimum, and the coupon. Pricing theory tells us how to make these tradeoffs.

Instruments can be designed specifically to take advantage of tax rules and regulations. The Netscape PEPS and Cincinnati Bell DECS are examples of this.

FURTHER READING

In this chapter we focused on the creation of engineered instruments using basic building blocks such as assets, bonds, forward contracts, and options. However, using the Black-Scholes technology based on delta-hedging (discussed in Chapter 13), it is possible to engineer more complicated instruments. We will cover the more general approach in Chapter 21 and see some applications in Chapter 22.

Readings about structured products (including some not discussed in this chapter) include Baubonis et al. (1993), McConnell and Schwartz (1992), Arzac (1997), and Crabbe and Argilagos (1994). For more information about Western-Southern, see **http://www.kellogg.northwestern.edu/faculty/petersen/html**.

PROBLEMS

Some of the following problems use this table and the following assumptions:

TABLE 15.4

	Quarter							
	1	**2**	**3**	**4**	**5**	**6**	**7**	**8**
Oil Forward price ($)	21.0	21.1	20.8	20.5	20.2	20.0	19.9	19.8
Zero-Coupon Bond Price ($)	0.9852	0.9701	0.9546	0.9388	0.9231	0.9075	0.8919	0.8763

The spot price of oil is $20.90. Let S_t denote the time price of the S&P 500 index, and assume that the price of the S&P 500 index is $S_0 = \$1200$ and the continuous annual dividend yield on the S&P 500 index is 1.5%.

15.1. Consider a 5-year equity-linked note that pays one share of XYZ at maturity. The price of XYZ today is $100, and XYZ is expected to pay its annual dividend of $1 at the end of this year, increasing by $0.50 each year. The fifth dividend will be paid the day before the note matures. The appropriate discount rate for dividends is a continuously compounded risk-free rate of 6%.

Suppose that the day after the note is issued, XYZ announces a permanent dividend increase of $0.25. What happens to the price of the equity-linked note?

15.2. Suppose the effective semiannual interest rate is 3%.

a. What is the price of a bond that pays one unit of the S&P index in 3 years?

    b. What semiannual dollar coupon is required if the bond is to sell at par?

    c. What semiannual payment of fractional units of the S&P index is required if the bond is to sell at par?

15.3. Use information from Table 15.4.

    a. What is the price of a bond that pays one unit of the S&P index in 2 years?

    b. What quarterly dollar coupon is required if the bond is to sell at par?

    c. What quarterly payment of fractional units of the S&P index is required if the bond is to sell at par?

15.4. Assume that the volatility of the S&P index is 30%.

    a. What is the price of a bond that after 2 years pays $S_2 + max(0, S_2 - S_0)$?

    b. Suppose the bond pays $S_2 + [\lambda \times max(0, S_2 - S_0)]$. For what λ will the bond sell at par?

15.5. Assume that the volatility of the S&P index is 30%.

    a. What is the price of a bond that after 2 years pays $S_0 + max(0, S_2 - S_0)$?

    b. Suppose the bond pays $S_0 + [\lambda \times max(0, S_2 - S_0)]$ in year 2. For what λ will the bond sell at par?

15.6. Assume that the volatility of the S&P index is 30% and consider a bond with the payoff $S_2 + \lambda \times [max(0, S_2 - S_0) - max(0, S_2 - K)]$.

    a. If $\lambda = 1$ and $K = \$1500$, what is the price of the bond?

    b. Suppose $K = \$1500$. For what λ will the bond sell at par?

    c. If $\lambda = 1$, for what K will the bond sell at par?

The next six problems will deal with the equity-linked CD in Section 15.3. If necessary, use the assumptions in that section.

15.7. Explain how to synthetically create the equity-linked CD in Section 15.3 by using a forward contract on the S&P index and a put option instead of a call option. (Hint: Use put-call parity. Remember that the S&P index pays dividends.)

15.8. Consider the equity-linked CD in Section 15.3. Assuming that profit for the issuing bank is zero, draw a graph showing how the participation rate, γ, varies with the coupon, c. Repeat assuming the issuing bank earns profit of 5%.

15.9. Compute the required semiannual cash dividend if the expiration payoff to the CD is $\$1300 - max(0, 1300 - S_{5.5})$ and the initial price is to be $\$1300$.

15.10. Compute λ if the dividend on the CD is 0 and the payoff is $\$1300 - max(0, 1300 - S_{5.5}) + \lambda \times max(0, S_{5.5} - 2600)$ and the initial price is to be $\$1300$.

15.11. Compute λ if the dividend on the CD is 0, the initial price is $\$1300$, and the payoff is $\$1200 + \lambda \times max(0, S_{5.5} - 1300)$.

15.12. Consider the equity-linked CD example in Section 15.3.

  a. What happens to the value of the CD as the interest rate, volatility, and dividend yield change? In particular, consider alternative volatilities of 20% and 40%, interest rates of 0.5% and 7%, and dividend yields of 0.5% and 2.5%.

  b. For each parameter change above, suppose that we want the product to continue to earn a 4.3% commission. What price participation, γ, would the CD need to have in each case to keep the same market value?

15.13. Use the information in Table 15.4.

  a. What is the price of a bond that pays one barrel of oil 2 years from now?

  b. What annual cash payment would the bond have to make in order to sell for $20.90?

15.14. Using the information in Table 15.4, suppose we have a bond that pays one barrel of oil in 2 years.

  a. Suppose the bond pays a fractional barrel of oil as an interest payment after 1 year and after 2 years, in addition to the one barrel after 2 years. What payment would the bond have to make in order to sell for par ($20.90)?

  b. Suppose that the oil payments are quarterly instead of annual. How large would they need to be for the bond to sell at par?

15.15. Using the information in Table 15.4, suppose we have a bond that after 2 years pays one barrel of oil plus $\lambda \times max(0, S_2 - 20.90)$, where S_2 is the year-2 spot price of oil. If the bond is to sell for $20.90 and oil volatility is 15%, what is λ?

15.16. Using the information in Table 15.4, and assuming that the volatility of oil is 15%,

  a. Show that a bond that pays one barrel of oil in 1 year sells today for $19.2454.

  b. Consider a bond that in 1 year has the payoff $S_1 + max(0, K_1 - S_1) - max(0, S_1 - K_2)$. Find the strike prices K_1 and K_2 such that $K_2 - K_1 = \$2$, and the price of the bond is $19.2454. How would you describe this payoff?

  c. Now consider a claim that in 1 year pays $S_1 - \$20.50 + max(0, K_1 - S_1) - max(0, S_1 - K_2)$, where K_1 and K_2 are from the previous answer. What is the value of this claim? What have you constructed?

15.17. Swaps often contain caps or floors. In this problem, you are to construct an oil contract that has the following characteristics: The initial cost is zero. Then in each period, the buyer pays the market price of oil if it is between K_1 and K_2;

otherwise, if $S < K_1$, the buyer pays K_1, and if $S > K_2$, the buyer pays K_2 (there is a floor and a cap). Assume that $K_2 - K_1 = \$2$ and that oil volatility is 15%.

    a. If there is a single settlement date in 1 year, what are K_1 and K_2?

    b. If the swap settles quarterly for eight quarters, what are K_1 and K_2?

15.18. In this problem, you are to construct an oil contract that has the following characteristics: The initial cost is zero. Then in each period, the buyer pays $S - \overline{F}$, with a cap of $\$21.90 - \overline{F}$ and a floor of $\$19.90 - \overline{F}$. Assume oil volatility is 15%. What is $\overline{F}$?

15.19. Using Figure 3.16 on page 82 as the basis for a discussion, under what circumstances might an investor prefer a PEPS to the stock or vice versa?

15.20. Value the Cincinnati Bell DECS assuming that $S = \$26.70$, $\sigma = 35\%$, $r = 9\%$, and $T = 3.3$. Cincinnati Bell pays a quarterly dividend of $\$0.10$.

Chapter 16
Corporate Applications

In this chapter we look at some contexts in which firms issue derivatives, either explicitly or implicitly. First, Black and Scholes (1973) observed that common debt and equity can be viewed as options, with the firm's assets as the underlying asset. We show how this insight can be used to price debt subject to default, as well as the implications for determining how leverage affects the expected return on equity. We also examine warrants and convertible debt as examples of firms issuing securities that explicitly contain options.

Second, many firms grant options as compensation to employees. These options typically cannot be exercised for some period of time and cannot be sold, so they raise interesting valuation issues. In addition, compensation options often have nonstandard features.

Third, merger deals in which firm A offers their own stock to buy firm B sometimes offer price protection to firm B shareholders. This protection can take the form of a collar. We examine one merger—MCI-WorldCom—that used a collar for this purpose.

16.1 EQUITY, DEBT, AND WARRANTS

Firms often issue securities that have derivative components. For example, firms issue options to employees for financing, and convertible debt is a bond coupled with a call option. However, even simple securities, such as ordinary debt and equity, can be viewed as derivatives. In this section we examine both implicit and explicit options issued by firms.

Debt and Equity as Options

Consider a firm with the following very simple capital structure. The firm has nondividend-paying equity outstanding, along with a single zero-coupon debt issue. Represent the time t values of the assets of the firm, the debt, and the equity as A_t, B_t, and E_t. The debt matures at time T and has maturity value $\overline{B}$.

The value of the debt and equity at time T will depend upon the value of the firm's assets. Equity-holders are the legal owners of the firm; in order for them to have unambiguous possession of the firm's assets, they must pay the debt-holders $\overline{B}$ at time T. If $A_T > \overline{B}$, equity-holders will pay $\overline{B}$ to the bondholders since equity will then be worth the value of the assets less the payment to bondholders, or $A_T - \overline{B} > 0$. However, if $A_T < \overline{B}$, equity-holders would have to inject additional funds in order to pay off the debt. In this case equity-holders would declare bankruptcy, permitting the bondholders to take possession of the assets. Therefore, the value of the equity at time T, E_T, is

$$E_T = max(0, A_T - \overline{B}) \tag{16.1}$$

This expression is the payoff to a call option with the assets of the firm as the underlying asset and $\overline{B}$ as the strike price.

Because equity-holders control the firm, bondholders receive the *smallest* payment to which they are legally entitled. If the firm is bankrupt, i.e., if $A_T < \overline{B}$, the bondholders receive A_T. If the firm is solvent, i.e., if $A_T \geq \overline{B}$, the bondholders receive $\overline{B}$. Thus the value of the debt is

$$B_T = min(A_T, \overline{B}) \tag{16.2}$$

This expression can be written[1]

$$B_T = A_T + min(0, \overline{B} - A_T)$$
$$= A_T - max(0, A_T - \overline{B}) \tag{16.3}$$

Equation (16.3) says that the bondholders own the firm, but have written a call option to the equity-holders. This way of expressing the debt value explains where the call option in equation (16.1) comes from. Summing equations (16.1) and (16.2) gives the the total value of the firm—equity plus debt—as A_T.

A different way to write equation (16.2) is the following:

$$B_T = \overline{B} + min(0, A_T - \overline{B})$$
$$= \overline{B} - max(0, \overline{B} - A_T) \tag{16.4}$$

The interpretation of equation (16.4) is that the bondholders own risk-free debt with a payoff equal to $\overline{B}$, but have written a put option on the assets with strike price $\overline{B}$.

Equations (16.3) and (16.4) suggest that we can compute the value of debt and equity prior to time T using option pricing, with the value of assets, A_t, taking the place of the stock price and the face value of the debt taking the place of the strike price. We can value equity at time t, E_t, as a call option on the assets of the firm with strike price $\overline{B}$. The value of the debt is then $B_t = A_t - E_t$.

Example 16.1   Suppose that $\overline{B} = \$100$, $A_0 = \$90$, $r = 6\%$, $\sigma = 25\%$, $\delta = 0$ (the firm makes no payouts), and $T = 5$ years. If we believe that the assets of the firm are lognormally distributed, then the Black-Scholes model can be used to value the debt and equity. Since the firm's assets are the underlying asset, we use asset volatility in the

---

[1]To follow these derivations, note that $min(0, x - y) = -max(0, y - x)$.

pricing formula. We have

$$E_0 = BSCall(\$90, \$100, 0.25, 0.06, 5, 0)$$
$$= \$27.07$$

The value of the debt is

$$B_0 = \$90 - \$27.07$$
$$= \$62.93$$

The debt-to-value ratio of this firm is therefore $\$62.93/\$100 = 0.629$. The yield on the debt, ρ, satisfies $B_0 = \overline{B}e^{-\rho T}$. Thus,

$$\rho = \frac{1}{5}ln(100/62.93)$$

$$= 0.0926$$

The debt yield of 7.16% is 116 basis points greater than the risk-free rate. 🍃

This example illustrates how the model accounts for the possibility of bankruptcy, giving a yield on debt that exceeds the risk-free rate. This model of the firm is very simple, in that there are no coupons or dividends, no refinancings or subsequent debt issues, etc. It is possible to create more complicated models of a firm's capital structure; nevertheless, this model provides a starting point for understanding how leverage affects returns on debt and equity and determines the yield on risky debt.

Leverage and the required return on equity   As leverage increases, equity-holders bear more asset risk per dollar of equity. Thus, if assets have a positive beta, the expected return on equity will increase with leverage. In general, the expected return on assets, r_A, is a weighted average of the expected returns on debt and equity, r_B and r_E:

$$r_A = (\%Equity \times r_E) + (\%Debt \times r_B)$$
$$= \left(\frac{E_t}{E_t + B_t} \times r_E \right) + \left(\frac{B_t}{E_t + B_t} \times r_B \right) \tag{16.5}$$

This relationship requires that r_B represent the *expected return* on debt, not the stated yield on debt. The two are the same only if debt is risk-free and the risk-free rate is constant. If debt is not risk-free, then the stated yield is an upper bound on the return the bondholders can earn; the bondholders earn less if there is a default.

The usual formula relating the expected return on equity to the expected return on assets assumes that debt is risk-free. If debt is risk-free, then $r_B = r$, and we have

$$\hat{r}_E = r + (r_A - r)\frac{1}{\%Equity} \tag{16.6}$$

By viewing debt and equity as options, we can do away with the assumption that debt is risk-free.

Recall from Chapter 12 that the elasticity of an option tells us the relationship between the required return on the underlying asset and that on the option. Using equations (12.8) and (12.10), we can compute the expected return on equity as

$$r_E = r + (r_A - r) \times \frac{A_t \Delta}{E_t} \tag{16.7}$$

where from equation (16.1), E_t is computed as the price of an option and Δ is the delta of that option. As the following example illustrates, equations (16.6) and (16.7) can give very different values for the expected return on equity.

Example 16.2   Use the same assumptions as in Example 16.1, and suppose that the required return on assets, r_A, is 10%. Using equation (16.6), the expected return on equity is

$$\hat{r}_E = 0.06 + \frac{1}{1 - 0.699}(0.1 - 0.06)$$
$$= 19.29\%$$

In order to compute equation (16.7), we can compute the delta of equity as

$$BSCallDelta(90, 100, 0.25, 0.06, 5, 0) = 0.735$$

The expected return on equity is then

$$r_E = 0.06 + (0.1 - 0.06) \times \frac{90 \times 0.735}{27.07}$$
$$= 15.77\%$$

❧

This example shows that the expected return on equity implied by equation (16.7) is less than that implied by equation (16.6). The reason is that equation (16.6) assumes that debt remains risk-free as the firm becomes more levered, so that equity-holders bear all of the risk of the assets. The formula assumes that the delta of equity with respect to the assets is always one.

When bankruptcy is possible, however, debt-holders bear increasing risk as the firm becomes more levered since default becomes more likely. Thus, the risk and risk premium of the assets are absorbed by *both* debt- and equity-holders, with the result that the return on equity increases less than predicted by equation (16.6). In this case the difference is almost four percentage points.

Using equation (16.7), we can examine how the expected return on equity changes as the asset value of the firm changes. Figure 16.1 graphs the debt-to-asset ratio and the expected return on equity as a function of the asset value of the firm, assuming the promised repayment on the debt in 5 years is $100. For very low asset values, the debt-to-asset ratio is almost 1 and the expected return on equity is almost 40%. As the asset value exceeds $200, the expected return on equity is about 12%.

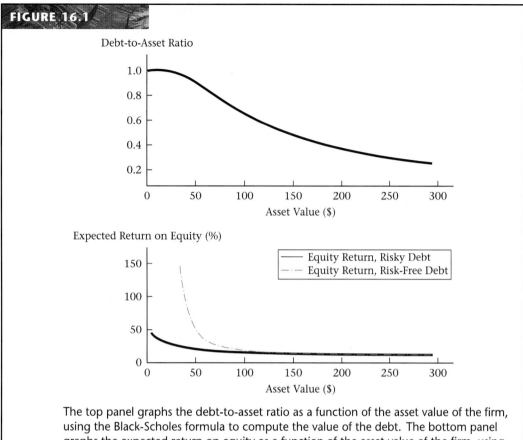

FIGURE 16.1

The top panel graphs the debt-to-asset ratio as a function of the asset value of the firm, using the Black-Scholes formula to compute the value of the debt. The bottom panel graphs the expected return on equity as a function of the asset value of the firm, using equations (16.6) and (16.7). Both graphs assume that there is a single zero-coupon debt issue with maturity value $100 and 5 years to maturity, and also assume that $r = 6\%$, $\sigma = 25\%$ (for the assets), and $\delta = 0$.

For purposes of comparison, Figure 16.1 also graphs the expected return on equity, computed assuming that the debt is risk-free. For asset values close to $200, the difference is less than 20 basis points. For a very highly-levered (low asset value) firm, however, the difference in Figure 16.1 is dramatic.

Conflicts between debt and equity   The idea that equity is a call option on the firm and that corporate bonds are risky provides insights into relations between debt- and equity-holders. Since equity-holders control the firm, bondholders may be concerned that equity-holders will take actions that would harm them, or may fail to take actions that would help them.

There are two decisions equity-holders make that affect the relative value of debt and equity. First, equity-holders can affect the volatility of assets. Equity-holders can increase asset volatility either by increasing the operating risk of existing assets, or by "asset substitution," replacing existing assets with riskier assets. An increase in volatility, other things equal, increases the value of the equity-holder's call option and therefore reduces the value of debt. In Example 16.1, the vega of the equity is 0.66, so an increase in asset volatility of 0.01 leads to an increase in the market value of equity of 0.66, which is $0.66/27.07 = 2.4\%$ of equity value. Debt value would decline by the same amount.

A second decision that equity-holders can make is the size of payouts to share-holders, such as dividends and share repurchases. To see why payouts are a problem for bondholders, suppose that the firm makes a special one-time $1 payout to shareholders. This payout reduces assets by $1. The delta of the equity with respect to assets is less than one, so the value of equity declines by less than $1. Since the value of debt plus equity equals assets, *the value of the debt must decline by one less the delta of the equity.* Unanticipated payouts to equity-holders therefore can hurt bondholders.

Bondholders are well aware of the potentially harmful effects of asset substitution and dividends. Bond covenants (legal restrictions on the firm) often limit the ability of the firm to change assets or pay dividends. Viewing debt and equity as options makes it clear why such restrictions exist.

Bondholders also encounter problems from actions that shareholders fail to take. Suppose the firm has a project worth $2 that requires shareholders to make a $1 investment. If shareholders make the investment, they pay $1, the value of the assets increases by $2 and the value of the shares rises by $2 \times \Delta$. The gain to shareholders is less than the increase in the value of assets. The difference of $2 - 2 \times \Delta$ goes to the bondholders. In making a positive NPV investment, shareholders help bondholders.

The shareholders in this example only will make the investment if the value of shares goes up by more than the $1 they invest, which will only occur if $\Delta > 0.5$. In order for shareholders to be willing to invest, the NPV must be great enough that shareholders gain after allowing for the value increase that is lost to debt-holders.[2] Thus, because of debt, the shareholders may fail to make positive NPV investments. A related problem is asset substitution: Shareholders might make negative NPV investments that increase asset risk, thereby transferring value from bondholders to stockholders.

Multiple Debt Issues

The option-based model of debt accommodates multiple issues of zero-coupon debt with different seniorities, as long as all debt expires on the same date. By definition, more senior debt has priority in the event of bankruptcy. Suppose that there are three debt issues, with maturity values of $30, $30, and $40, ranked in seniority from highest to lowest. We will refer to each distinct level of seniority as a *tranche*. The value of equity

---

[2]The idea that the debt may harm investment incentives is developed in Myers (1977).

| TABLE 16.1 | | | Calculation of market values and yields on three debt tranches. The yield on the senior tranche is computed as $ln(30/22.18)/5 = 6.04\%$, that on the intermediate tranche as $ln(30/20.57)/5 = 7.54\%$, and that on the junior tranche as $ln(40/20.18)/5 = 13.69\%$. | |

Claimant	Owns	Wrote	Total (\$)	Yield
Senior Bonds	Assets	C(30)	$90 - 67.82 = 22.18$	6.04%
Intermediate Bonds	C(30)	C(60)	$67.82 - 47.25 = 20.57$	7.54%
Junior Bonds	C(60)	C(100)	$47.25 - 27.07 = 20.18$	13.69%
Equity	C(100)			

will be the same as in Example 16.1, since it is still necessary for equity-holders to pay \$100 to receive ownership of the assets. However, the option pricing approach permits us to assign appropriate yields to each level of debt.

Senior debt-holders are the first in line to be paid. They own the firm and have written a call option permitting the next set of bondholders to buy the firm from them by paying the maturity value of the senior debt, \$30. Intermediate debt-holders own a call option permitting them to buy the firm for \$30, and have sold a call option permitting the junior bondholders to buy the firm for \$60. Junior bondholders in turn own the call option to buy the firm for \$60, and have written a call option permitting the equity-holders to buy the firm for \$100. The values of these options are

$$BSCall(\$90, \$30, 0.25, 0.06, 5, 0) = \$67.82 \qquad (16.8)$$

$$BSCall(\$90, \$60, 0.25, 0.06, 5, 0) = \$47.25 \qquad (16.9)$$

$$BSCall(\$90, \$100, 0.25, 0.06, 5, 0) = \$27.07 \qquad (16.10)$$

Table 16.1 summarizes the value and yield of each tranche of debt. The junior tranche has a yield to maturity of 13.69%, very close to the required return on equity. The senior tranche, according to the model, is almost risk-free.

In interpreting Table 16.1, it is important to distinguish between two concepts: The yield to maturity on debt and the debt's expected rate of return. The yield is the *greatest* return a bondholder can earn. When bankruptcy is possible, the expected rate of return is less than the yield. In this example, the junior tranche, with a *yield* of 13.69%, has an *expected return* of 10.03%.

This kind of calculation makes it clear why debt cannot be treated as a single homogeneous class when firms with complex capital structures enter bankruptcy. The interests of the most junior debt-holders may well resemble the interests of equity-holders more than those of senior debt-holders.

Warrants

Firms sometimes issue options explicitly. If a firm issues a call option on its own stock, it is known as a **warrant.** (The term "warrant" is used here to denote options on a firm issued by the firm itself, though in practice the term includes traded options issued in fixed supply.) When a warrant is exercised, the warrant-holder pays the firm the strike price, K, and receives a share worth more than K (or else the holder would not have exercised the warrant). Thus, the act of exercise is dilutive to other shareholders in the sense that the firm has sold a share for less than it is worth. Of course, existing shareholders are aware of warrants outstanding and can anticipate this potential exercise. The problem is how to value the warrant, and how to value the equity given the existence of warrants. This valuation problem does not arise with ordinary options, because they are traded by third parties and their exercise has no effect on the firm.

To see how to value a warrant, suppose the firm has n shares outstanding, and that the outstanding warrants are European, on m shares, with strike price K. The asset value is A.

At expiration, if warrant-holders exercise the warrants, they pay K per share and receive m shares. After the warrants are exercised, the firm has assets worth $A + mK$, hence exercised warrants are worth

$$\frac{A + mK}{n + m} - K = \frac{n}{n + m}\left(\frac{A}{n} - K\right) \tag{16.11}$$

The expression A/n is the value of a share of equity in the absence of warrants. Thus, equation (16.11) suggests that we can value a warrant in two steps. First, we compute an option price with A/n as the underlying asset and K as the strike price, ignoring dilution. Second, we multiply the result by a dilution correction factor, $n/(n + m)$. This second step accounts for the fact that warrant exercise changes the number of shares outstanding, with the new shares issued at a "below-market" price of K. The warrant can be valued by using the Black-Scholes formula:

$$\frac{n}{n + m} BSCall\left(\frac{A}{n}, K, \sigma, r, t, \delta\right) \tag{16.12}$$

Convertible Bonds

In addition to issuing warrants directly, firms can issue warrants embedded in bonds. A **convertible bond** is a bond that, at the option of the bondholder, can be exchanged for shares in the issuing company. A simple convertible bond is therefore like the equity-linked notes we studied in Chapter 15, except that the bond is convertible into the company's own shares, rather than the shares of a third party. The call option in the bond gives the bondholder the right to surrender the bond's maturity payment, M, in exchange for q shares. The valuation of a convertible bond entails valuing both debt subject to default and a warrant.

Suppose there are m bonds with maturity payment M, each of which is convertible into q shares. If there are n original shares outstanding, then if the bond is converted, there will be $n + mq$ shares. At expiration, the bondholders will convert if the value of the assets after conversion, $A/(n + mq)$, exceeds the value of the maturity payment per share that would be given up:

$$\frac{A}{n + mq} - \frac{M}{q} > 0$$

or

$$\frac{n}{n + mq} \left(\frac{A}{n} - \frac{M}{q} \frac{n + mq}{n} \right) > 0 \tag{16.13}$$

where A represents the assets of the firm. This expression is different from equation (16.12) for warrants, because rather than injecting new cash into the firm when they convert, the bondholders instead avoid taking cash out of the firm.

Conversion occurs if the assets increase sufficiently in value. If the assets decrease, the firm could default on the promised maturity payment. Assuming the convertible is the only debt issue, bankruptcy occurs if $A/m < M$. Thus, the payoff of the convertible at maturity, time T, is

$$\underbrace{M - max\left(0, M - \frac{A_T}{m}\right)}_{\text{Bond} \quad \text{Written Put}} + \underbrace{q \times \frac{n}{n + mq} \times max\left(0, \frac{A_T}{n} - \frac{M}{q} \frac{n + mq}{n}\right)}_{q \text{ Purchased Warrants}} \tag{16.14}$$

Thus, one convertible can be valued as owning a risk-free bond with maturity payment M, selling a put on $1/m$ of the firm's assets, and buying q warrants with strike $M \frac{1}{q} \frac{n + mq}{n}$.

Example 16.3 A firm with assets of $10,000 has $n = 400$ shares outstanding and $m = 10$ zero-coupon convertible bonds with maturity value $M = \$100$ and $T = 5$ years to maturity, each of which is convertible into $q = 3$ shares. The asset volatility is $\sigma = 30\%$ and the risk-free rate is $r = 6\%$. The firm makes no payouts. Using equation (16.14), the value of one bond is

$$\$100 \times e^{-0.06 \times 5} - BSPut\left(\frac{\$10,000}{10}, \$100, 0.30, 0.06, 5, 0\right)$$

$$+ 3 \times \frac{400}{400 + 3 \times 10} BSCall\left(\frac{\$10,000}{400}, \frac{\$100}{3} \frac{400 + 10 \times 3}{400}, 0.30, 0.06, 5, 0\right)$$

$$= \$90.889$$

Since 10 convertible bonds have the value $908.89, the value of a share is ($10,000 − $908.89)/400 = \$22.728$. The yield on the bond is $ln(\$100/\$90.889)/5 = 0.0191$. The bond has a yield below the risk-free rate because of the conversion option: The bondholders have a call option for which they pay by accepting a lower yield on the debt.

Convertible bonds are typically issued at terms such that a significant increase in the stock price is required for conversion to be worthwhile. In Example 16.3, each bond gives the holder the right to convert into three shares, so the strike price is $100/3 = $33.33. Since the stock price is $22.728, the ratio of the strike price to the stock price, which is called the **conversion premium,** is $33.333/$22.278 = 1.4666.

In practice, valuation of convertible bonds is more complicated than in this example. First, convertible bonds are typically American options, convertible for much of the life of the bond. Second, convertible bonds are typically callable. When the issuer calls a convertible bond, the holder of the bond has the choice of surrendering the bond in exchange for the call price or converting. Generally a bond is noncallable for a period of time, and then once callable, the call price declines over time. Callability is a way for issuers to shorten the life of the bond, forcing holders to convert prior to maturity. Third, interest rates can change, which means that the value of the bond can change for reasons other than stock price changes. Fourth, many companies pay dividends. If the dividends that can be earned by converting the bond into stock exceed the bond coupon, there is a reason for bondholders to exercise. Finally, convertible bonds typically are not zero-coupon. The payment of coupons complicates the analysis because bankruptcy becomes possible at times other than expiration, and the reduction in assets stemming from the payment of the coupon (or any other cash payment to the firm's security-holders) becomes a dividend for purposes of option valuation.

Using the binomial pricing model outlined in Chapters 10 and 11, it is possible to value convertible bonds incorporating early exercise, dividends, and callability. It is also possible to incorporate interest rate risk using techniques described later in the book.

Why do firms issue convertible bonds? One possible explanation is that convertible bonds resolve one of the conflicts between equity- and debt-holders. Shareholders can take value from holders of ordinary bonds by increasing volatility, even if this action has no beneficial effect from the perspective of the firm as a whole. However, convertibles, with a built-in option are harmed less, and may even be helped, by an increase in volatility. This reduces the incentive of shareholders to raise volatility.

Put Warrants

When shares are used to pay employees (as for example with compensation options), there is an increase in the number of shares outstanding. Companies making heavy use of share compensation frequently buy shares back from other shareholders (a *share repurchase*) so there is no net increase in the number of shares outstanding.[3]

Many companies that repurchased shares during the 1990s also sold put options on their own stock; a commonly stated rationale for issuing such put warrants (see, for example, Thatcher et al., 1994) is that the put sales are a hedge against the cost of

---

[3]Corporate finance theory offers no justification for this practice, but firms seem to believe that it is important.

repurchasing shares. Intel, Microsoft, and Dell, for example, all sold significant numbers of puts, with Microsoft alone earning well over $1b in put premiums during the 1990s. Here is a quote from Microsoft's 1999 10-K describing the put program:

> Microsoft enhances its repurchase program by selling put warrants.... On June 30, 1999, 163 million warrants were outstanding with strike prices ranging from $59 to $65 per share. The put warrants expire between September 1999 and March 2002. The outstanding put warrants permit a net-share settlement at the Company's option and do not result in a put warrant liability on the balance sheet.

How do we think about this transaction? If Microsoft repurchases shares, via a written put or by any other means, nonselling shareholders are in effect buying shares from selling shareholders. It is common to say that managers should maximize shareholder value, but which set of shareholders do they care about? Despite this theoretical ambiguity, we will examine the transaction using a standard profit and loss calculation.

Figure 16.2 is a profit diagram for various alternatives. Suppose that the share price today is $100 and the firm will for certain buy one share back in 3 years. The firm has 3 years to earn interest on the $100 it could have spent today. The profit diagram shows that if the price is still $100 in 3 years, the firm has profited by the amount of this interest. The sale of a put expiring in 3 years generates the curve labeled "Written Put."

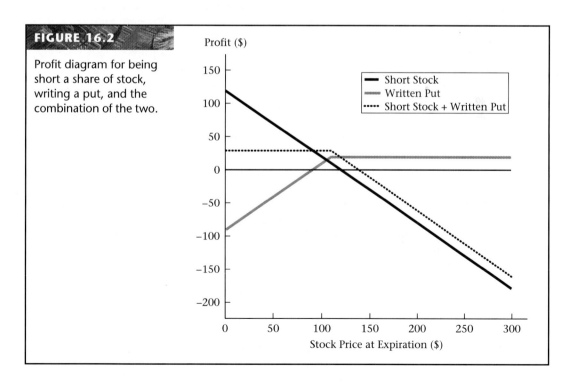

FIGURE 16.2

Profit diagram for being short a share of stock, writing a put, and the combination of the two.

The third curve in Figure 16.2 shows the combined profit and loss for a short share and written put. (By put-call parity, this position looks like a written call.) Should the share price rise, the firm repurchases shares at a higher price but keeps the put premium. If the share price falls, the firm is obligated to pay the strike price to repurchase shares. This transaction is the mirror image of covered call writing, discussed in Chapter 3.

Any transaction by the firm in its own shares, including put-writing, raises the issue of adverse selection: If a seller has private information, buyers taking this into account will be cautious about buying. Presumably a firm's managers have good information about the firm's prospects. Who would want to buy a put sold by Microsoft, for example, given that its managers have private information about the company?

In practice, investment banks have purchased the puts written by firms such as Microsoft, Intel, and Dell. The banks reportedly hold the puts and delta-hedge the position, as in Chapter 13, thus reducing their risk. Moreover, the transactions, including the bank's hedging trades, occur without any public announcement. In effect, put-selling firms transact with shareholders using the investment bank as a conduit. When the share price rises, the delta of the bank's purchased put, which is negative, increases towards zero and the bank sells the shares it had purchased to hedge the put. When the share price falls, delta increases to negative one and the bank buys additional shares to hedge its position. The bank, acting on behalf of the firm, buys as the share price declines and sells as the share price rises.

Problem 16.19 asks you to examine a binomial example of this transaction, showing first that the firm could accomplish the same end as put-writing by transacting directly in its shares. Second, the problem asks you to show how the counterparty bank delta-hedges the transaction.

16.2 COMPENSATION OPTIONS

Many firms compensate executives and other employees with call options on the company's own stock, i.e., warrants. The use of compensation options is common and significant in many companies. Table 16.2, taken from Microsoft's 1999 Annual Report, illustrates Microsoft's use of compensation options over a 3-year period. In June 1999, Microsoft had about 5 billion shares outstanding (not counting compensation options), so compensation options on 766m shares represented about 15% of outstanding shares. This large a use of compensation options is not unusual; Eberhart (2001) finds in a sample of 1800 firms using compensation options in 1999 that options were on average 12% of shares outstanding. Moreover, the use of options is not restricted to executives: Core and Guay (2001) find in a sample of 750 companies that two-thirds of option grants were to nonexecutive employees.

The grant of an option to an employee is obviously costly to shareholders, however, under the accounting treatment as of early 2002, a compensation option is *never* treated as an expense for accounting purposes. The FASB in 1993 proposed treating the grant of options as a compensation expense, but encountered furious corporate and congressional resistance. The box on page 504 discusses some of the history of the battle over compensation options and illustrates some of the absurd claims made by those who oppose treating options as an expense. The compromise rule, FAS 123, requires that

TABLE 16.2		Table from Microsoft's 1999 Annual Report showing the number of compensation option grants (in millions of shares) for 1997–1999, and the range of strike prices at which the options were granted. All prices and shares from previous years are adjusted for splits. The closing stock price on June 30, 1999, was $90\frac{3}{16}$.

| | | **Price per Share** | |
	Shares	**Range ($)**	**Weighted Average ($)**
Balance, June 30, 1996	952	0.28 – 14.74	5.52
Granted	220	13.83 – 29.80	14.58
Exercised	(180)	0.28 – 14.74	3.32
Canceled	(36)	4.25 – 24.29	9.71
Balance, June 30, 1997	956	0.56 – 29.80	7.86
Granted	138	16.56 – 43.63	31.28
Exercised	(176)	0.56 – 31.24	4.64
Canceled	(25)	4.25 – 41.94	14.69
Balance, June 30, 1998	893	0.56 – 43.63	11.94
Granted	78	45.59 – 83.28	54.62
Exercised	(175)	0.56 – 53.63	6.29
Canceled	(30)	4.25 – 74.28	21.06
Balance, June 30, 1999	766	0.56 – 83.28	17.28

companies provide a footnote disclosure of the value of option grants if the value is material. The Black-Scholes formula is acceptable for performing this valuation.

Controversy over option grants may stem from a misunderstanding of options and ignorance about their valuation, and perhaps also from the unwillingness of some executives and companies to acknowledge the value of option grants. Some also fear that once the expense is recognized for accounting purposes, tax law will be changed to require that the grant be taxed.

Any discussion of compensation options is complicated by the fact that there are many special considerations associated with their valuation, the following among them:

- There may be unusual contractual features of the compensation option contract. For example, an industry index may be the strike price.

- Compensation options are intended to motivate employees and tie them to a firm. Therefore options cannot be sold, and typically do not fully vest (i.e., cannot be exercised) for several years.

Accounting for Compensation Options

When a firm issues compensation options, their value is reported in a footnote to the financial statements but not charged against earnings. In 2001 the International Accounting Standards Board proposed reconsidering the accounting treatment of options, a move opposed by Representative Michael G. Oxley (R-Ohio), chairman of the House Committee on Financial Services. *New York Times* columnist Gretchen Morgenson had this comment (*New York Times*, October 21, 2001, Business Section, p. 1):

> After a bruising battle in 1993, the accounting board caved in to corporate lobbyists' demands that stock options, undeniably an employee cost, should not be deducted from revenue as other costs are. Instead, options' costs are relegated to a footnote in company financial statements. That might not be a concern if the largess was not so, well, large. Sanford C. Bernstein & Company, a brokerage firm, estimates that the value of option awards at the nation's 2,000 largest companies was $162 billion last year, up from $50 billion in 1997....
>
> With shares in decline, the tide may finally be turning against stock options. Two of the nation's largest accounting firms, Andersen and Deloitte & Touche, say options should be charged to a company's income statement, and many Wall Street accounting analysts agree. With their options now worthless, some workers are starting to demand cash for their labors.
>
> Still, Mr. Oxley fights on against the evil of truth in financial reporting. He appears to be carrying water for the Financial Executives Institute, a lobbying group. These people love options because they make them rich and because their companies reap enormous tax deductions when their employees exercise options.
>
> The institute argues that the board's proposal "will create a widespread burden on the business environment" and that adding the expense of stock options to a company's results "would throw off their bottom lines and cause an upheaval in the stock market."

Microsoft in 1999 *granted* options worth approximately $20.90 \times 78m = \$1.6\beta$. With 31,000 employees, this is approximately $52,000 per employee in option grants. Elsewhere in the 10-K, Microsoft reports that *outstanding* options had a market value on June 30, 1999, of $69 billion, or $2 million per employee.

- The executive may resign, be fired, die, or become disabled, or the company may be acquired. Any of these may affect the value of the option grant, either by forcing early exercise (as may happen with a death), requiring that the options be forfeited (in the event the executive is fired), or the option contract may be renegotiated (in the event of a takeover).

- The company may reduce the strike price on outstanding options if the stock price drops, a practice known as **repricing.**

- The term of the options can be 10 years or more, which makes volatility and dividend estimates difficult.

- The company may not have a publicly traded stock, in which case the stock price may not even be known.

These considerations make it harder to value compensation options than short-lived exchange-traded options. Some have argued that the difficulty in valuing compensation options means they should not be recognized as an expense.[4] The purpose of this section is to explore some of the issues surrounding compensation options. As you consider the valuation issues, perform the following thought experiment: Imagine that a firm that issues options to employees wants to hedge its compensation obligations. When the firm issues an option, it buys a hedging contract from a third party. Under the terms of this contract, the third party pays the firm the value of the option when the employee exercises it. If the firm does not buy such a contract, it self-insures. Either way, the cost of such insurance is the cost to shareholders of the compensation option. The problem of valuing a compensation option amounts to asking how much it would cost the firm to hedge its commitments in this fashion.

Whose Valuation?

Compensation options cannot be traded. An employee who cannot sell options will typically discount their value. As a result, you can expect that firms and employees will value compensation options differently. In fact, this difference in valuation can occur for any compensation other than immediate cash.

For example, consider membership in a golf club costing $15,000 per year. No one would value the membership at more than $15,000, since it could be purchased for that amount. Moreover, someone who does not play golf might value the membership at zero. Thus, while for one executive the membership might displace $15,000 of salary, for another, it might not displace any salary. Suppose that firms grant this membership as compensation and assume that the nonplaying executive cannot sell the membership for $15,000. However, *the fact that the employee discounts the membership's value does not reduce the cost to the firm.*

For shareholders, the key question is the cost to the company: How should *shareholders* value gold club memberships or option grants, given the behavior of employees?

---

[4]See, for example, "Stock Options Keep the Economy Afloat," by Burton G. Malkiel and William J. Baumol, the *Wall Street Journal*, April 4, 2002. This argument ignores the fact that companies routinely expense hard-to-measure items such as depreciation.

Microsoft

To illustrate a few of the practical issues, we again consider Microsoft. In accord with FAS 123, Microsoft valued its options using Black-Scholes. Here is the discussion from Microsoft's 1999 10-K:

> The weighted average Black-Scholes value of options granted under the stock option plans during 1997, 1998, and 1999 was $5.86, $11.81, and $20.90. Value was estimated using an expected life of 5 years, no dividends, volatility of 0.32 in 1999 and 1998 and 0.30 in 1997, and risk-free interest rates of 6.5%, 5.7%, and 4.9% in 1997, 1998, and 1999.[5]

To understand these values, Table 16.2 shows that the weighted average share price at which options were issued in fiscal 1997 was $14.58. Option grants are approximately at-the-money, so the valuation procedure for options issued in 1997 would be

$$BSCall(\$14.58, \$14.58, 0.3, 0.065, 5, 0) = \$5.68$$

This value is close to the $5.86 reported by Microsoft. Microsoft options vest over $4\frac{1}{2}$ years and expire in 7. Note that the option is worth more than $\frac{1}{3}$ of the stock price.

If Microsoft's options expire in 7 years, why does Microsoft use a 5-year time to expiration to value the options? We saw in Chapter 9 that a publicly traded call option on a nondividend-paying stock is never exercised early since it can be sold for more than its intrinsic value. However, compensation options cannot be sold. Thus, the value of the options *to the holder* may be less than intrinsic value. In this case, employees may exercise the options before expiration.[6] In practice, executives frequently exercise a large fraction of their in-the-money options as soon as they vest.[7] In addition to exercise by continuing employees, options are often canceled due to death, termination, or retirement of the employee. A realistic valuation would account for the likelihood of these various factors. The assumed 5-year life is intended to account for the *expected* life of an option. It is sometimes argued that employees should exercise compensation options early for tax reasons. This argument, which is not valid, is discussed in Appendix 16.A.

Compensation options cannot be exercised until they vest. When companies pay dividends and the options therefore might be exercised early, valuing them requires taking into account their Bermudan exercise style. Fortunately, a Bermudan option is

---

[5]Microsoft does not document how it chose volatilities, but these are close to historical volatilities. Using weekly data, historical volatilities for Microsoft for July to June were 32% for 1996–97, 30% for 1997–98, and 39% for 1998–99.

[6]See Kulatilaka and Marcus (1994) for a discussion of the employee's valuation of options.

[7]Huddart (1998) shows that options are disproportionately exercised on the first through fourth anniversaries of the grant, in blocks of 25% of the grant. Since it is common for grants to vest 25% annually, this finding suggests that many options are being exercised as soon as possible.

easily valued by modifying the binomial formula to not permit exercise until the option is vested.

A firm valuing its option grants faces all the usual issues associated with option valuation, such as how to deal with dividend uncertainty, long-term volatility, and interest rate uncertainty.[8]

Repricing of Compensation Options

Between July and December of 1997, the price of Oracle stock fell from a (split-adjusted) high of almost $14 in August to $7.25 on December 11. On December 12, Oracle's Board of Directors lowered the strike price on a number of Oracle's compensation options. This excerpt is from Oracle's 10-Q issued in January, 1998:

> In December 1997, the Company reduced the exercise price of approximately 20% of the outstanding common stock options held by the Company's employees to the fair market value per share as of the date of the reduction in price. The Company repriced these employee stock options in an effort to retain employees at a time when a significant percentage of employee stock options had exercise prices that were above fair market value. The Company believes that stock options are a valuable tool in compensating and retaining employees. Executive officers and directors were excluded from this repricing.

Reducing the exercise price of compensation options in response to a decline in the stock price is called option repricing. The delta of a deep-out-of-the-money option is low, so that subsequent stock price changes will not have much effect on the value of employee options. Companies in this case often reprice options.[9]

If you know that options will be repriced if the price falls, how valuable is the option grant in the first place?

We can answer this question using barrier options, discussed in Chapter 14. An option that is going to be repriced if the stock price reaches a certain level can be modeled as a knock-out option (the originally granted option vanishes), plus a knock-in option (a new option replaces it) with the same barrier. Specifically, suppose that the option strike is K, and that at the barrier, H, a new at-the-money option will be issued in place of the original option. A repriceable option is then worth

$$CallDownOut(S, K, \sigma, r, T, \delta, H) + CallDownIn(S, H, \sigma, r, T, \delta, H) \qquad (16.15)$$

The second term reflects the knock-in call being at-the-money when it knocks in.

....

[8]Since dividends reduce the value of an option, it is possible that widespread use of compensation options has resulted in a reduction in corporate dividends.

[9]Morgenson (1998) reported that in addition to Oracle, option repricing occurred at Netscape Communications, Apple Computer, Bay Networks, Best Buy, and Oxford Health Plans, among others.

Example 16.4 Suppose $S = \$100$, $\sigma = 0.4$, $r = 0.06$, $t = 10$, $\delta = 0.01$, and that options will be repriced if the stock price hits $60. The value of an option that will *not* be repriced is

$$BSCall(\$100, \$100, 0.4, 0.06, 10, 0.01) = \$54.43$$

The value of an otherwise equivalent option that will be repriced at $60 is

$$CallDownOut(\$100, \$100, 0.4, 0.06, 10, 0.01, 60)$$
$$+ CallDownIn(\$100, \$60, 0.4, 0.06, 10, 0.01, 60) = \$41.11 + \$20.30 = \$61.41$$

Thus, the possibility of repricing increases the value of the option by 13%. 🌿

Reload Options

A **reload option** gives the option-holder new call options when existing call options are exercised. The idea is that the option-holder uses shares to pay for exercise, and new at-the-money options are granted for each share given up in this fashion. This type of option is best explained with an example. Suppose a 10-year option grant for 1000 shares with a strike price of $100 permits a single reload. Suppose the option is exercised when the stock price is $250, with 4 years of option life remaining. The exercise price requires a payment of $100 × 1000 = $100,000. This amount can be paid in cash or by surrendering $100,000/$250 = 400 shares. An executive paying the strike price by surrendering shares receives 400 new at-the-money options with 4 years to expiration.

Arnason and Jagannathan (1994) pointed out that there are two important characteristics of reload options. First, the reload feature is valuable: A reload option can be worth as much as 30% more than an otherwise equivalent option without the reload feature. Second, reload options cannot be valued using the Black-Scholes formula because reload options may be early-exercised. However, they can be valued using the binomial option pricing model.

Reload options might seem esoteric, but Saly et al. (1999) show that in 1997, 1,135 reload options were granted, out of a total of 9,673 grants reported in the S&P Execucomp database.

Reload options can be valued binomially. This is accomplished by replacing the exercise amount at the time of exercise, $S - K$, with the value of a new reload option. We will illustrate this in the simplest possible fashion, with a two-period binomial example.

Figure 16.3 shows the binomial valuation of an ordinary option and a reload option with a single reload. The binomial price for an option without a reload provision is $38.28. (The Black-Scholes price for this option is $36.76.) The reload price, by contrast, is $42.25, and a reload optimally occurs in the second binomial period. Let's examine how this works.

First, consider the valuation without a reload. When $S = \$179.37$ in period 1, the value of the option left alive is $94.153, while the value exercised is $79.37. As we would expect since there are no dividends, the option is not exercised early; the value in period 0 is $38.28.

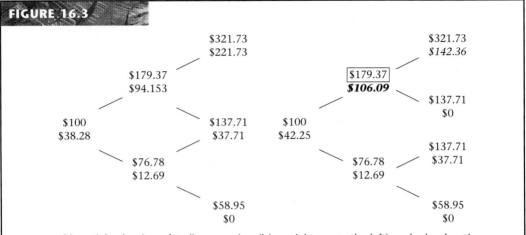

FIGURE 16.3

Binomial valuation of ordinary option (binomial tree on the left) and reload option (binomial tree on the right). The calculations assume that $S = \$100$, $K = \$100$, $\sigma = 0.3$, $r = 0.08$, $\delta = 0$, $T = 4$, $h = 2$, and that there is a single reload. Stock prices and option prices are shown at each node, with the reload value in italics. A reload occurs at the boxed stock price. In this example, we have $u = 1.794$, $d = 0.768$, and $p = 0.395$.

When a reload is permitted, the one candidate node for a reload is when $S = \$179.37$. (A reload would have no value at $S = \$100$ or in the final period.) If a reload occurs, the option holder receives \$79.37 for exercising the option, and 100/179.37 options are issued with a strike price of \$179.37 and 2 years to maturity. Thus, we calculate the value of the option at this node as

$$\$79.37 + \frac{100}{179.37}e^{-0.08\times2}\left(0.395 \times \$142.36 + 0.605 \times \$0\right) = \$106.09 \qquad (16.16)$$

From Figure 16.3, the value of the reload option is \$42.25, 10.5% greater than in the absence of the reload.

In general, we can compute the value of the reload at every node by solving another binomial pricing problem valuing the appropriate number of newly issued options. The option holder reloads if doing so is more valuable than not doing so, just like the exercise decision for an American option.[10]

The rationale for reloads is not obvious. The FASB deemed the reload feature too complicated to value, so it is generally ignored when companies value options under

---

[10]When n reloads are permitted, the problem can be solved by having the binomial pricing function call itself, along with the information that one less reload remains. This is simple to program, but computationally very slow because of the large number of binomial valuations. See Saly et al. (1999) for a discussion.

FAS 123. Saly et al. (1999) suggest that reload options may be a way to give management undisclosed compensation.

Level 3 Communications

Options granted by Level 3 Communications illustrate the complexity that can occur in option grants. In a June 1998 proxy statement, Level 3 described its "outperform stock options" (OSO), granted to employees. This is how they are described in the proxy:

> Participants in the OSO Program do not realize any value from awards unless the Level 3 Common Stock . . . outperforms the Standard & Poor's 500 Index. When the stock price gain is greater than the corresponding gain on the Standard & Poor's 500 Index, the value received for awards under the OSO Program is based on a formula involving a Multiplier related to how much the Common Stock outperforms the Standard & Poor's 500 Index.

The multiplier is then described as follows:

> The Multiplier shall be based on the "Outperform Percentage" . . . for the Period, determined on the date of exercise. The Outperform Percentage shall be the excess of the annualized percentage change . . . in the Fair Market Value of the Common Stock over the Period . . . over the annualized percentage increase or decrease . . . in the Standard & Poor's 500 Index over the Period. . . .

The multiplier is computed based on the outperform percentage as follows:

Outperform Percentage	Multiplier
$x \leq 0$	0
$0 < x \leq 11\%$	$x \times \frac{8}{11} \times 100$
$x > 11\%$	8.0

The multiplier does the following: If Level 3 outperforms the S&P 500 index by at least an annual average of 11%, the option recipient will have the payoff of eight options. The options have a 4-year maturity and are exercisable and fully vested after 2 years.

Example 16.5   Suppose that at the grant of an option, the price of Level 3 is $100, and the S&P 500 index is at 1300. After 4 years, the price of Level 3 is $185, and the S&P 500 index is at 1950. A "non-multiplied" outperformance option would have had a payoff of

$$\$185 - \$100 \times \frac{1950}{1300} = \$35$$

The (nonannualized) returns on Level 3 and the S&P 500 index are 85% and 50%. The outperform percentage is

$$1.85^{0.25} - 1.50^{0.25} = 5.957\%$$

The multiplier is therefore

$$0.05957 \times \frac{8}{11} \times 100 = 4.332$$

The payment on the option is

$$\left(\$185 - \$100 \times \frac{1950}{1300} \right) \times 4.332 = \$151.64$$ ⚡

This option is worth between 0 and 8 times as much as an ordinary option. How can we get an intuitive sense for the value of the difference? We will first examine the effect of the outperformance feature, and then consider the effect of the multiplier.

Valuing the outperformance feature   First, what would be the value of an ordinary 4-year-to-maturity at-the-money call? Using a volatility of 25% (which Level 3 says in its 1999 Annual Report is the "expected volatility" of its common stock), and a risk-free rate of 6%, we obtain an option price of

$$BSCall(\$100, \$100, 0.25, 0.06, 4, 0) = \$30.24$$

The Level 3 1999 Annual Report discusses the valuation of the outperformance option as follows:

> The fair value of the options granted was calculated by applying the Black-Scholes method with an S&P 500 expected dividend yield rate of 1.8% and an expected life of 2.5 years. The Company used a blended volatility rate of 24% between the S&P 500 expected volatility rate of 16% and the Level 3 Common Stock expected volatility rate of 25%. The expected correlation factor of 0.4 was used to measure the movement of Level 3 stock relative the S&P 500.

We saw in Section 14.6 that to value an outperformance option, we use the Black-Scholes formula but make the following substitutions:

$$\sigma_{Level\ 3} \quad \rightarrow \quad \hat{\sigma} = \sqrt{\sigma_{Level\ 3}^2 + \sigma_{S\&P}^2 - 2\rho\sigma_{Level\ 3}\sigma_{S\&P}}$$
$$r \quad \rightarrow \quad \delta_{S\&P}$$

where ρ is the correlation between Level 3 and S&P 500 returns and r is the risk-free rate. The net effect on value of granting an outperformance call depends upon the effect of these substitutions. The "blended" volatility, $\hat{\sigma}$, can be greater or less than $\sigma_{Level\ 3}$. In recent years, $\delta_{S\&P}$ has been less than r. The calculation Level 3 makes for the blended volatility is

$$\hat{\sigma} = \sqrt{0.25^2 + 0.16^2 - 2 \times 0.4 \times 0.25 \times 0.16}$$
$$= 0.2368$$

which is rounded to 24%. The price of the outperformance option is therefore

$$BSCall(\$100, \$100, 0.2368, 0.018, 4, 0) = \$21.75$$

This is about $\frac{2}{3}$ the value of the ordinary option. This reduction in value is primarily due to replacing the 6% interest rate with a 1.8% dividend yield. The volatility reduction by itself lowers the option price only to $29.44.

Adding the multiplier   Now consider the effect of the multiplier. We can approximate the value of the multiplied option using gap options (described in Section 14.5). We can think about the multiplier as providing additional options as outperformance increases. For every $\frac{11}{8} = 1\frac{3}{8}\%$ per year by which Level 3 outperforms the S&P 500, the multiplier increases by 1. Thus, we can approximate the effect of the multiplier by valuing a strip of gap outperformance options.

For example, the multiplier is 2 if over 4 years, Level 3 outperforms the S&P 500 by a factor of $1.0275^4 = 1.1146$, nonannualized. To approximate the value of the option we could assume that if outperformance is between 0 and 1.375% per year, the option-holder receives nothing. Between 1.375% and 2.75%, the option-holder receives one option. At 2.75% per year, the option-holder receives a second option, etc. Above 11% per year, the option holder receives eight options. Each additional option can be valued as a gap option. For example, the option received if performance is above 2.75% per year would pay $S_{Level3} - S_{S\&P}$ if $S_{Level3} > 1.0275^4 \times S_{S\&P}$.

Figure 16.4 shows the payoff of a single nonmultiplied option, plotted against the exact payoff and the payoff approximated by gap options. Note that the exact and gap approximation are not identical, but are quite close.

Table 16.3 shows that, using the gap option approximation, the value of the compensation option is about 7 times the value of a single option. A more precise binomial valuation using 100 binomial steps gives a value for the option of $156.25, so the gap approximation of $153 is quite close.

As a final point, it may be rational to exercise the Level 3 option early even in the absence of dividends! Suppose it is close to expiration and the outperformance percentage is slightly above 11%. If the holder exercises, the multiplier is 8. If the share price rises further, the multiplier remains 8. However, if the share price falls, the multiplier falls; by waiting to exercise, the option-holder can lose options. This extra loss from a share price decline can provide an incentive to exercise early. For very high prices, there is no incentive to exercise early since the multiplier remains constant. For low prices, the potential increase in the multiplier offsets the potential reduction in the multiplier. Thus, early exercise is potentially optimal only for intermediate prices and close to expiration.

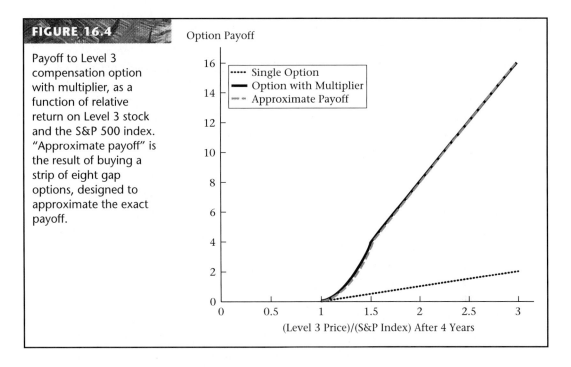

FIGURE 16.4

Payoff to Level 3 compensation option with multiplier, as a function of relative return on Level 3 stock and the S&P 500 index. "Approximate payoff" is the result of buying a strip of eight gap options, designed to approximate the exact payoff.

Option Payoff

Legend:
- ····· Single Option
- —— Option with Multiplier
- —— Approximate Payoff

(Level 3 Price)/(S&P Index) After 4 Years

TABLE 16.3

Valuation of Level 3 option approximated as sum of gap options. For each row, the option value is computed as a gap call option (equation (14.15)), where $S = \$100$, $K_1 = \$100$, $K_2 = \$100\alpha$, $r = 0.018$, $\sigma = 0.2368$, $T = 4$, and $\delta = 0$.

Multiplier	Outperformance (α)	Gap Option Value ($)
1	1.056	21.63
2	1.115	21.28
3	1.175	20.72
4	1.239	19.96
5	1.305	19.04
6	1.373	17.98
7	1.444	16.81
8	1.518	15.58
Total		153.00

16.3 THE USE OF COLLARS IN ACQUISITIONS

When firm A buys firm B, it can pay cash to B's shareholders or it can pay shares, exchanging A shares for B shares. Suppose that Company A offers x shares of Company A in exchange for each share of Company B. Once Company B accepts the offer, the acquisition will take time to complete. Company B shareholders will be concerned that company A's stock may drop before the merger is completed. There are four common ways to structure an offer:[11]

- **Fixed stock offer** A offers to pay B a fixed number of A shares per B share.

- **Floating stock offer** A offers to pay B however many shares have a given dollar value, based on A's share price just before the merger is completed.

- **Fixed collar offer** There is a range for A's share price within which the offer is a fixed stock offer. Outside this range the deal can become a floating stock offer or may be subject to cancellation.

- **Floating collar offer** There is a range for A's share price within which the offer is a floating stock offer. Outside this range the deal can become a fixed stock offer or may be subject to cancellation.

As this list suggests, there are two choices in structuring a stock offer: Which company bears the risk of a change in the stock price of company A, and the magnitude of this exposure. In this section we examine WorldCom's 1997 bid for MCI as an example of a merger with a collar.

WorldCom Bids for MCI

On October 1, 1997, WorldCom Inc. offered to buy MCI Communications Corp., with payment to MCI shareholders to take the form of WorldCom shares. Here is the precise statement of the offer from Bernard Ebbers, President and CEO of WorldCom, to Bert Roberts, Chairman and CEO of MCI:

> I am writing to inform you that this morning WorldCom is publicly announcing that it will be commencing an offer to acquire all the outstanding shares of MCI for $41.50 of WorldCom common stock per MCI share. The actual number of shares of WorldCom common stock to be exchanged for each MCI share in the exchange offer will be determined by dividing $41.50 by the 20-day average of the high and low sales prices for WorldCom common stock prior to the closing of the exchange offer, but will not be less than 1.0375 shares (if WorldCom's average stock price exceeds $40) or

---

[11] These descriptions are based on Petrie (2000), who discusses the kinds of offers and the motives for using alternative kinds of collars.

more than 1.2206 shares (if WorldCom's average stock price is less than $34).[12]

Suppose that MCI's board and shareholders immediately approved the WorldCom offer. The actual acquisition would not occur for several months at the earliest, because it would be necessary for WorldCom to obtain regulatory approval and antitrust approval in addition to shareholder approval.[13] Thus, MCI shareholders have to ascertain the value of the WorldCom offer *today*, given that the transaction will not be consummated for several months at the earliest.

Consider the possible outcomes for WorldCom stock. If WorldCom were to rise above $40, MCI shareholders would benefit from a fixed 1.0375 exchange ratio, gaining $1.0375 per dollar rise in WorldCom. If WorldCom stock were to fall below $34, MCI shareholders would lose at the rate of $1.2206 per dollar drop in WorldCom stock. Anywhere between $34 and $40, the offer is constructed to be worth $41.50. This is a floating collar offer.

The issue of the precise value of the offer became crucial when, 2 weeks later on October 15, GTE bid for MCI, offering $40 in cash. Which offer was more valuable, WorldCom's stock offer or GTE's cash offer? The press portrayed the contest as $41.50 in stock versus $40 in cash, with the implication that a stock offer was somehow worth less, other things equal. WorldCom portrayed the issue as one of which stock (WorldCom or GTE) would provide the better long-term performance for MCI shareholders. However, since shares can be bought and sold at any time, for MCI shareholders the real issue should have been which offer was worth more.[14]

Valuing the WorldCom Offer

WorldCom offered to MCI shareholders the following exchange schedule:

WorldCom Share Price	Payment to MCI shareholders
$S_{WorldCom} < \$34$	$1.2206 \times S_{WorldCom}$
$\$34 \leq S_{WorldCom} \leq \$40$	$\$41.50$
$\$40 < S_{WorldCom}$	$1.0375 \times S_{WorldCom}$

Figure 16.5 graphs this payment schedule. The slope above $40 is 1.0375 and the slope below $34 is 1.2206. There are several equivalent ways to value this offer. One

---

[12]Letter from Ebbers to Roberts, October 1, 1997, from WorldCom press release.

[13]As an example of how complicated these situations can become, Boeing's acquisition of McDonnell-Douglas was almost derailed by European opposition, even though both are U.S. companies. Of course, Boeing does business in Europe so European opposition mattered. To obtain European approval, Boeing had to modify existing contracts with airlines that had agreed to buy from Boeing exclusively.

[14]For some shareholders, there would also have been differing tax consequences of the two offers, an issue we ignore.

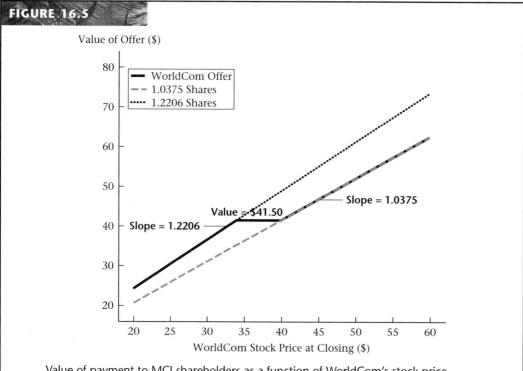

FIGURE 16.5

Value of payment to MCI shareholders as a function of WorldCom's stock price. Between $34 and $40, the value of the offer is $41.50. The graph also shows the value of offers of 1.0375 shares and 1.2206 shares, which bracket the actual offer.

way is to note that it is equivalent to owning 1.0375 WorldCom shares, buying 1.0375 40-strike put options, and selling 1.2206 34-strike put options. You should verify that this position generates the payoff diagram in Figure 16.5.

On October 15, 1997, WorldCom closed at $35\frac{7}{16}$. Suppose that if WorldCom's offer were accepted, the acquisition would be expected to close in 120 days (midway through the first quarter of 1998). The problem for MCI shareholders is that the WorldCom share price could fall during that time. Option pricing allows us to assign a value to possibility that WorldCom is below $34 or above $40. We can value the deal as being worth today

$$1.0375 \times BSPut(S_{WorldCom}, \$40, \sigma, r, 0.33, 0)$$
$$- 1.2206 \times BSPut(S_{WorldCom}, \$34, \sigma, r, 0.33, 0) + 1.0375 \times S_{WorldCom} \tag{16.17}$$

We assume that WorldCom pays no dividends and that the deal will close in 120 days (0.33 of a year). We use a risk-free rate of 5.5% (between the 4-month T-bill rate of 5% and LIBOR of 5.82%). What volatility should we use?

Using a historical volatility might be problematic. WorldCom had just made an offer for MCI, and prior to that had participated in the America Online acquisition of Compuserve, agreeing to buy certain assets of Compuserve. We might not expect the next 4 months to have the same volatility as the previous 4 months. Fortunately we can compute an implied volatility using exchange-traded options on WorldCom.

Table 16.4 reports October 15 implied volatilities for WorldCom options expiring in December and March. Since Table 16.4 uses newspaper price quotes, the reported prices—for example that of the 32.5-strike December put—might be stale. However, a volatility in the range of 38–40% is plausible. Table 16.5 shows values of the WorldCom offer, equation (16.17), computed for various parameters. The goal of Table 16.5 is to see whether small changes in the volatility and interest rate (which might result from estimation error) and large changes in time to expiration (which might result from regulatory holdups) affect the value of the deal. A reasonable conclusion is that the significant uncertainty in the deal results from the behavior of WorldCom's stock price, not from the other inputs to the model.

Several points are evident from Table 16.5. First, changes in the assumptions do not make a large difference in the value of the offer—the difference between the largest and smallest values in the table is less than one dollar. Second, the offer is worth more if it can be closed more quickly because there is less time for the stock to move below $34. For the same reason, the deal is worth more if the volatility is believed to be low. Finally, the risk-free rate matters very little—holding fixed the other assumptions, a 50-basis-point change in the risk-free rate changes the value of the deal by at most 2 cents.

Finally, we can examine the value of the WorldCom offer at different current stock prices by varying the stock price in equation (16.17). The results are the lower two lines in Figure 16.6, where the payoff at expiration (from Figure 16.5) is also graphed.

TABLE 16.4		Implied volatilities for the December (65 days to expiration) and March (157 days to expiration) options. Assumes WorldCom price is $35\frac{7}{16}$, $r = 5.5\%$.			
		Call		**Put**	
Strike ($)	**Expiration (days)**	**Premium ($)**	**Implied Vol. (%)**	**Premium ($)**	**Implied Vol. (%)**
32.5	65	4.000	34.48	1.3125	46.26
35	65	2.875	41.89	2.000	40.23
40	65	0.875	38.23	5.000	37.25
35	157	4.125	38.08	3.000	39.55
40	157	2.000	36.21	—	—

Source for option prices: Wall Street Journal, October 16, 1997.

TABLE 16.5	Value ($) of WorldCom offer for MCI, using equation (16.17). Base case is $S = 35\frac{7}{16}$, $r = 5.5\%$, $\sigma = 38\%$, $t = 120$ days (0.33), $\delta = 0$.

		Expiration (days)			
		90	**120**	**150**	**365**
	0.36	40.123	39.989	39.883	39.430
Volatility	0.38	40.094	39.962	39.858	39.411
	0.40	40.065	39.936	39.833	39.391
	0.0525	40.102	39.971	39.869	39.427
Risk-Free Rate	0.0550	40.094	39.962	39.858	39.411
	0.0575	40.086	39.952	39.847	39.394

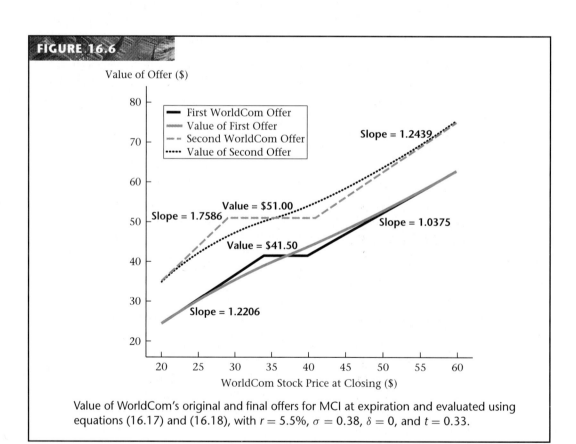

FIGURE 16.6

Value of WorldCom's original and final offers for MCI at expiration and evaluated using equations (16.17) and (16.18), with $r = 5.5\%$, $\sigma = 0.38$, $\delta = 0$, and $t = 0.33$.

GTE Thrusts, WorldCom Parries

On October 15, 1997, GTE made a $40 cash offer for MCI. The preceding analysis suggests ways for WorldCom to sweeten its offer without necessarily increasing the number of shares it was offering to exchange. For example, using the base case above ($\sigma = 38\%$, $r = 5.5\%$, and $t = 120$ days), a change in the lower strike price on the collar from $34 to $30 would increase the value of the offer from $39.96 to $41.53, compared to GTE's $40 cash offer. If WorldCom executives held firmly to the view that WorldCom shares were going to rise, this change in the offer could be viewed as "free." Of course, this change is not free, conditional on publicly available information. Other modifications to the deal might include linking the WorldCom collar to the general level of the market, thereby protecting shareholders against a specific decline in the value of WorldCom stock, but not necessarily against a decline in the value of the market as a whole.

In response to the GTE cash offer, WorldCom both widened the collar and raised the number of shares they were offering. On November 10, 1997, WorldCom and MCI announced an agreement in which WorldCom would pay $37 billion for MCI, or "$51 per share." Here is how the actual final deal was structured:

WorldCom Share Price	Payment to MCI Shareholders
$S_{WorldCom} < \$29$	$1.7586 \times S_{WorldCom}$
$\$29 \leq S_{WorldCom} \leq \$41$	$51
$\$41 < S_{WorldCom}$	$1.2439 \times S_{WorldCom}$

The valuation equation for this offer is analogous to equation (16.17):

$$1.2439 \times BSPut(S_{WorldCom}, \$41, \sigma, r, 0.33, 0)$$
$$- 1.7586 \times BSPut(S_{WorldCom}, \$29, \sigma, r, 0.33, 0) + 1.2439 \times S_{WorldCom} \tag{16.18}$$

Figure 16.6 compares the original and final offers for a variety of stock prices. WorldCom's share price dropped below $29 on several occasions following MCI's acceptance of this offer. However, following regulatory approval, WorldCom's offer for MCI was completed on September 14, 1998, at a stock price of $47.75. This meant that MCI shareholders ultimately received WorldCom shares worth $1.2439 \times \$47.75 = \$59.40$ per share.

MCI's Stock Price Behavior

Finally, Figure 16.7 shows the behavior over time of WorldCom stock, MCI stock, and the value of the WorldCom offer. Following November 10, 1997, the three move together, although the MCI share price is consistently below the offer by $4–$5, and as much as $7 in April and May. Presumably this discount reflected uncertainty (for regulatory and other reasons) that the merger would actually occur. After early July 1998, the difference narrowed to about $2. (On July 8, 1998, the European Commission and on July 15, 1998, the U.S. Department of Justice announced that they would not

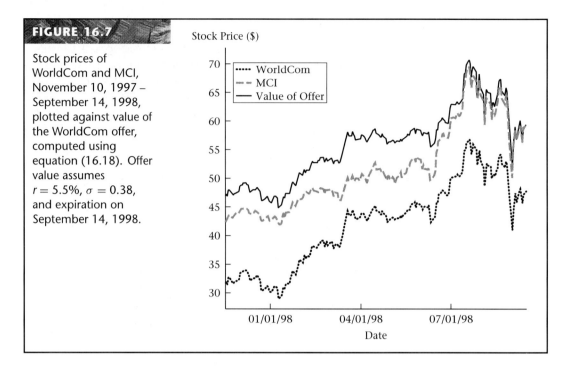

FIGURE 16.7

Stock prices of WorldCom and MCI, November 10, 1997 – September 14, 1998, plotted against value of the WorldCom offer, computed using equation (16.18). Offer value assumes $r = 5.5\%$, $\sigma = 0.38$, and expiration on September 14, 1998.

oppose the acquisition.) After September 1, 1998, the difference between MCI's price and the offer value was more than $1 only once. On September 14, 1998, the merger was consummated.

CHAPTER SUMMARY

Three corporate contexts in which options appear, either explicitly or implicitly, are capital structure (debt, equity, and warrants), compensation, and acquisitions.

If we view the assets of the firm as being like a stock, then debt and equity can be valued as options with the assets of the firm as the underlying asset. Viewing corporate securities as options provides a natural way to measure bankruptcy risk, and illuminates conflicts between bondholders and stockholders.

Compensation options are an explicit use of options by corporations. They exhibit a variety of complications, some naturally occurring (early exercise decisions by risk-averse employees) and some created by the issuer (repricing, reloads, outperformance, and multipliers). For this reason they provide an interesting context in which to use the exotic pricing formulas from Chapter 14.

Offers by one firm to purchase another sometimes have embedded collars. The WorldCom offer to buy MCI was an example of this.

FURTHER READING

The idea that debt and equity are options was first pointed out by Black and Scholes (1973). Merton (1974) and Merton (1977) analyzed the pricing of perpetual debt and demonstrated that the Modigliani-Miller theorem holds even with (costless) bankruptcy. Two principal applications of this idea are the determination of the fair yield on risky debt and the assessment of bankruptcy probabilities. Galai and Masulius (1976) derived the link between the return on assets and the return on the firm's stock.

The discussion of warrants and convertible bonds in this chapter assumes that the options are European. With American warrants the optimal exercise strategy can be more complicated than with European options. The reason is that exercise alters the assets of the firm. The problem of optimal American warrant exercise is studied by Emanuel (1983), Constantinides (1984), and Spatt and Sterbenz (1988). McDonald (2002) examines the tax implications of warrant issues, including put warrants. Complications also arise with convertible bonds, which in practice are almost always callable. Thus, valuing a convertible bond requires understanding the call strategy. Classic papers studying the pricing of convertibles include Brennan and Schwartz (1977) and Ingersoll (1977). Harris and Raviv (1985) discuss how asymmetric information affects the decision to call the bond, and Stein (1992) discusses the decision to issue convertibles in the first place. Finally, there is a large empirical literature on the convertible call decision; for example, see Asquith (1995).

Papers on compensation options include Saly et al. (1999), Johnson and Tian (2000a), and Johnson and Tian (2000). Repricing is studied by Chance et al. (2000) and Acharya et al. (2000). Petrie (2000) examines the use of collars in acquisitions.

PROBLEMS

For all problems, unless otherwise stated assume that the firm has assets worth $A = \$100$, and that $\sigma = 30\%$, $r = 8\%$, and the firm makes no payouts prior to the maturity date of the debt.

16.1. There is a single debt issue with a maturity value of $120. Compute the yield on this debt assuming that it matures in 1 year, 2 years, 5 years, or 10 years. What debt-to-equity ratio do you observe in each case?

16.2. There is a single debt issue. Compute the yield on this debt assuming that it matures in 1 year and has a maturity value of $127.42, 2 years with a maturity value of $135.30, 5 years with a maturity value of $161.98, or 10 years with a maturity value of $218.65. (The maturity value increases with maturity at a 6% rate.) What debt-to-equity ratio do you observe in each case?

16.3. There are four debt issues with different priorities, each promising $30 at maturity.

    a. Compute the yield on each debt issue assuming that all four mature in 1 year, 2 years, 5 years, or 10 years.

b. Assuming that each debt issue matures in 5 years, what happens to the yield on each when you vary σ? r?

16.4. Suppose there is a single 5-year zero-coupon debt issue with a maturity value of $120. The expected return on assets is 12%. What is the expected return on equity? The volatility of equity? What happens to the expected return on equity as you vary A, σ and r?

16.5. Repeat the previous problem for debt instead of equity.

16.6. In this problem we examine the effect of changing the assumptions in Example 16.1.

> **a.** Compute the yield on debt for asset values of $50, $100, $150, $200, and $500. How does the yield on debt change with the value of assets?

> **b.** Compute the yield on debt for asset volatilities of 10% through 100%, in increments of 5%.

For the next three problems, assume that a firm has assets of $100 and 5-year-to-maturity zero-coupon debt with a face value of $150. Assume that investment projects have the same volatility as existing assets.

16.7. The firm is considering an investment project costing $1. What is the amount by which the project's value must exceed its cost in order for shareholders to be willing to pay for it? Repeat for project values of $10 and $25.

16.8. Now suppose the firm finances the project by issuing debt that has *lower* priority than existing debt. How much must a $1, $10, or $25 project be worth if the shareholders are willing to fund it?

16.9. Now suppose the firm finances the project by issuing debt that has *higher* priority than existing debt. How much must a $10 or $25 project be worth if the shareholders are willing to fund it?

16.10. Assume there are 20 shares outstanding. Compute the value of the warrant and the share price for each of the following situations.

> **a.** Warrants for 2 shares expire in 5 years and have a strike price of $15.

> **b.** Warrants for 15 shares expire in 10 years and have a strike of $20.

16.11. A firm has outstanding a bond with a 5-year maturity and maturity value of $50, convertible into 10 shares. There are also 20 shares outstanding. What is the price of the warrant? The share price? Suppose you were to compute the value of the convertible as a risk-free bond plus an option, valued using the Black-Scholes formula and the share price you computed. How accurate is this?

16.12. Suppose a firm has 20 shares of equity, a 10-year zero-coupon debt with a maturity value of $200, and warrants for 8 shares with a strike price of $25. What is the value of the debt, the share price, and the price of the warrant?

16.13. Suppose a firm has 20 shares of equity and a 10-year zero-coupon convertible bond with a maturity value of $200, convertible into 8 shares. What is the value of the debt, the share price, and the price of the warrant?

16.14. Using the assumptions of Example 16.3, suppose you were to perform a "naive" valuation of the convertible as a risk-free bond plus three call options on the stock. How does the price you compute compare with that computed in the Example?

16.15. As discussed in the text, compensation options are prematurely exercised or canceled for a variety of reasons. Suppose that compensation options both vest and expire in 3 years and that the probability is 10% that the executive will die in year 1 and 10% in year 2. Thus, the probability that the executive lives to expiration is 80%. Suppose that the stock price is $100, the interest rate is 8%, the volatility is 30%, and the dividend yield is 0.

  a. Value the option by computing the expected time to exercise and plugging this into the Black-Scholes formula as time to maturity.

  b. Compute the expected value of the option given the different possible times until exercise.

  c. Why are the answers for the two calculations different?

16.16. Obtain stock price information for Microsoft and Level 3 Communications. Compute historical annual volatilities for the past several years. What do you think of the volatilities assumed by each company in their 10-Ks?

16.17. XYZ Corp. compensates executives with 10-year European call options, granted at the money. If there is a significant drop in the share price, the company's board will reset the strike price of the options to equal the new share price. The maturity of the repriced option will equal the remaining maturity of the original option. Suppose that $\sigma = 30\%$, $r = 6\%$, $\delta = 0$, and that the original share price is $100.

  a. What is the value at grant of an option that will not be repriced?

  b. What is the value at grant of an option that is repriced when the share price reaches $60?

  c. What repricing trigger maximizes the initial value of the option?

16.18. Suppose that top executives of XYZ are told they will receive at-the-money call options on 10,000 shares each year for the next 3 years. When granted, the options have 5 years to maturity. XYZ's stock price is $100, volatility is 30%, and $r = 8\%$. Estimate the value of this promise. (Hint: See Problem 14.21.)

16.19. Suppose that $S = \$100$, $\sigma = 30\%$, $r = 6\%$, $t = 1$, and $\delta = 0$. XYZ writes a European put option on one share with strike price $K = \$90$.

  a. Construct a two-period binomial tree for the stock and price the put. Compute the replicating portfolio at each node.

b. If the firm were synthetically creating the put (i.e., trading to obtain the same cash flows as if it issued the put), what transactions would it undertake?

c. Consider the bank that buys the put. What transactions does it undertake to hedge the transaction?

d. Why might a firm prefer to issue the put warrant instead of borrowing and repurchasing shares?

16.20. Firm A has a stock price of $40, and has made an offer for firm B where A promises to pay $60/share for B, as long as A's stock price remains between $35 and $45. If the price of A is below $35, A will pay 1.714 shares, and if the price of A is above $45, A will pay 1.333 shares. The deal is expected to close in 9 months. Assume $\sigma = 40\%$, $r = 6\%$, and $\delta = 0$.

a. How are the values 1.714 and 1.333 arrived at?

b. What is the value of the offer?

c. How sensitive is the value of the offer to the volatility of A's stock?

16.21. Firm A has a stock price of $40, and has made an offer for firm B where A promises to pay 1.5 shares for each share of B, as long as A's stock price remains between $35 and $45. If the price of A is below $35, A will pay $52.50/share, and if the price of A is above $45, A will pay $67.50/share. The deal is expected to close in 9 months. Assume $\sigma = 40\%$, $r = 6\%$, and $\delta = 0$.

a. How are the values $52.50 and $67.50 arrived at?

b. What is the value of the offer?

c. How does the value of this offer compare with that in Problem 16.20?

APPENDIX 16.A: DO TAXES INDUCE EARLY EXERCISE OF COMPENSATION OPTIONS?

It is sometimes argued that taxes are a reason to exercise compensation options before expiration. The argument for tax-induced exercise hinges on the taxation of nonqualified options. Suppose the option is issued at time 0, exercised at time t and expires at time $T > t$. The option-holder is taxed at the ordinary income rate, τ, on $S_t - K$. Assume that subsequent gains are capital gains, taxed at the rate $g < \tau$. One might guess that since subsequent gains are taxed at the lower capital gains rate, g, early exercise minimizes the amount of income that is taxed at the high rate, τ.

This logic is incorrect; *taxes alone do not provide a reason to exercise a compensation option prior to expiration.*

We prove this by showing that the option holder who waits until T to make an exercise decision, employee B, can always obtain a higher payoff than the option holder who exercises at t and sells at T, employee A.

Exercise at time *t*, ultimate sale at time *T* Suppose A exercises the option at time t. Exercise creates a tax liability of $\tau(S_t - K)$; we suppose A borrows this amount. If r is the after-tax interest rate, the time T payoff is

$$S_T - g(S_T - S_t) - Ke^{r(T-t)} - \tau(S_t - K)e^{r(T-t)}$$

This can be rewritten as

$$S_T(1 - g) + S_t\left(g - \tau e^{r(T-t)}\right) - (1 - \tau)Ke^{r(T-t)} \tag{16.19}$$

Exercise at time *T* If B waits until T to decide whether to exercise, the payoff is

$$(1 - \tau)Max(0, S_T - K) \tag{16.20}$$

It is difficult to compare the payoffs in equations (16.19) and (16.20). In order to make the comparision, we assume that if A exercises at t, then B simultaneously borrows to buy $(\tau - g)/(1 - g)$ shares. Borrowing to buy shares is a feasible zero-investment transaction that facilitates the comparison of payoffs. Assuming $S_T > K$, the total after-tax payoff from option exercise plus the shares and borrowing is

$$(1 - \tau)(S_T - K) + \frac{\tau - g}{1 - g}[S_T(1 - g) + gS_t] - \frac{\tau - g}{1 - g}S_t e^{r(T-t)}$$

This can be rewritten as

$$S_T(1 - g) + S_t\frac{\tau - g}{1 - g}\left(g - e^{r(T-t)}\right) - (1 - \tau)K \tag{16.21}$$

It is possible to show that

$$\frac{\tau - g}{1 - g}\left(g - e^{r(T-t)}\right) > \left(g - \tau e^{r(T-t)}\right)$$

Thus, if you compare equation (16.21) with equation (16.19), you will see that every term in equation (16.21) is at least as great as the corresponding term in equation (16.19). (You can also show this when $S_T < K$.) This demonstrates that the investor who borrows to buy shares at t and waits until time T to make an exercise decision has a higher payoff than the investor who exercises at t.

Chapter 17

Real Options

T hus far we have primarily discussed financial assets, but many of the most important decisions that firms make concern *real assets*, a term that broadly encompasses factories, mines, office buildings, research and development, and other nonfinancial firm assets. In this chapter we will see that it is possible to analyze investment and operating decisions for real assets using pricing models we have developed for financial options.

To illustrate how it can be possible to evaluate an investment decision as an option, consider a firm that is deciding whether or not to build a factory. Compare the following two descriptions:

- A *call option* is the right to pay a *strike price* to receive the present value of a stream of future cash flows (represented by the *price of the underlying asset*).

- An *investment project* is the right to pay an *investment cost* to receive the present value of a stream of future cash flows (represented by the *present value of the project*).

Do you notice the similarities in these two statements? We have

Investment Project		Call Option
Investment Cost	=	Strike Price
Present Value of Project	=	Price of Underlying Asset

This comparison suggests that we can view any investment project as a call option, with the investment cost equal to the strike price and the present value of cash flows equal to the asset price. The exploitation of this and other analogies between real investment projects and financial options has come to be called **real options**, which we define as the application of derivatives theory to the operation and valuation of real investment projects. Note the phrase "operation *and* valuation." We will see in this chapter that you cannot value a real asset without also understanding how you will operate it. We have encountered this link before: You cannot value any option without understanding when you will exercise it.

17.1 INVESTMENT AND THE NPV RULE

We first consider a simple investment decision of the sort you would encounter in a basic finance course when studying net present value (NPV). Despite its simplicity, the example illustrates the issues that will arise again later in this chapter.

527

Suppose we can invest in a machine, costing $10, that will produce one widget a year forever. In addition, each widget costs $0.90 to produce. The price of widgets will be $0.55 next year and will increase at 4% per year. The effective annual risk-free rate is 5% per year. We can invest, at any time, in one such machine. There is no uncertainty.

Before reading further, try to answer this question: What is the most you would pay to acquire the rights to this project?

Static NPV

A natural first step is to compute the NPV if we invested in the project today. We obtain

$$NPV_{Invest\ today} \hspace{6cm} (17.1)$$

$$= \$0.55 \times \left(\frac{1}{1.05} + \frac{1.04}{1.05^2} + \frac{1.04^2}{1.05^3} + \cdots \right)$$

$$- \$0.9 \times \left(\frac{1}{1.05} + \frac{1}{1.05^2} + \frac{1}{1.05^3} + \cdots \right) - \$10$$

$$= \frac{\$0.55}{1.04} \times \left(\frac{1}{\frac{1.05}{1.04} - 1} \right) - \frac{\$0.9}{0.05} - \$10 = \frac{\$0.55}{0.01} - \$28 = \$27$$

This calculation tells us that if widget production were to start next year, we would pay $27 for the project. For reasons that will become obvious, we call this the project's **static NPV**.

If we delay investment, the project is worth more than $27. In the early years, the project has an operating loss. If we activate the project today, then next year we will have negative operating cash flows, spending $0.90 to produce a $0.55 widget. In addition, at a 5% rate of interest, the opportunity cost of the $10 investment is $0.50/year.

Why is NPV positive if we will be producing at a loss? Although the initial cash flows are negative, the widget price is growing. The project *will become* profitable in the future. This eventual profitability is why NPV is positive. This analysis suggests that we might consider waiting until later to invest.

Suppose we wait 5 years to invest instead of investing immediately. NPV is then

$$NPV_{wait\ 5\ years} = \frac{1}{1.05^5} \left[(1.04)^5 \frac{\$0.55}{0.01} - \$28 \right]$$

$$= \$30.49$$

Thus, it is better to wait 5 years than to invest today. What is the maximum NPV we can attain?

Common sense points to an approximate answer: We should not invest until annual widget revenue covers marginal production cost ($0.90) plus the opportunity cost of the project ($0.50); i.e., cost is at least $1.40. The widget price will be $1.40 when n satisfies

$$(1 + .04)^n 0.55 = 1.40$$

Solving for n gives us $n = 23.82$.[1] After 23.82 years, the widget price will have reached a break-even level. The value today of waiting that long to invest in the project is

$$\left[\frac{(1.04)^{23.82}\$0.55}{0.01} - \frac{\$0.90}{0.05} - \$10\right]\frac{1}{(1+0.05)^{23.82}} = \$35.03$$

Problem 17.4 asks you to verify this result. You will discover that 23.82 years is not exactly optimal. Rather, waiting approximately 24.32 years—not 23.82 years—maximizes NPV. At this point the widget price will be about $1.43.

We will see the reason for this slight difference in Section 17.4. It occurs because the effective annual interest and growth rates of 5% and 4% are not the relevant rates since the decision to put off the investment is made on a day-to-day basis. It is instead the equivalent *continuously compounded* rates that matter.

This example demonstrates the important point that making an investment decision requires thinking carefully about alternatives, even under certainty.

We are left with (at least) two questions:

- How do we approach this kind of problem in general?
- Why didn't the NPV rule work? Or did it?

The Correct Use of NPV

The NPV rule worked correctly in the above example. The NPV rule for making investment decisions entails two steps:

1. Compute NPV by discounting expected cash flows at the opportunity cost of capital.

2. Accept a project if and only if its NPV is positive *and it exceeds the NPV of all mutually exclusive alternative projects.*[2]

When we computed the widget machine's NPV in equation (17.1), we neglected to take into account the NPV of alternative mutually exclusive projects, namely investing in the project tomorrow or at some other future date. Static NPV—NPV if we accept the project today—ignores project delay. Because static NPV measures the value of an action we could take, namely investing today, it at least provides a lower bound on the value of the project.

In this example it would be correct to invest in the project today *if not activating the project today meant that we would lose it forever.* Under this assumption, the mutually exclusive alternative (never taking the project) has a value of 0, so taking it today would be correct.

....

[1] The price must increase by a factor of 1.40/0.55 to reach $1.40, so we have $ln(1.40/.55)/ln(1.04) = 23.82$.

[2] Introductory finance textbooks state the NPV rule correctly, but in casual discussions it is sometimes stated incorrectly.

To decide whether and when to invest in an arbitrary project, we need to be able to compute the value of delaying that investment. As suggested at the start of the chapter, option pricing theory can help us to value delay.

The Project as an Option

The decision to invest in the project involves a comparison of net present values; in what sense is this an option? As suggested earlier, we can view the investment cost as an exercise price and the value of the project as the underlying asset.

Recall the discussion in Sections 9.3 and 11.1 about the factors governing early exercise. The decision to exercise an option prior to expiration involves an implicit comparison of three factors: The dividends forgone by not acquiring the asset today; the interest saved by deferring the payment of the strike price; and the value of the insurance that is lost by exercising the option. It turns out that the same three considerations govern the decision to invest in a project.

In the widget project, there is no uncertainty and, hence, no insurance value. However, there are interest and forgone dividends.

Once we begin widget production, we are committed to spending the present value of the marginal widget cost, \$18, along with the \$10 initial investment. The value of delaying investment is interest on the total investment cost, or $0.05 \times \$28 = \$1.40$ per year.

In delaying investment, we lose the cash flow from selling widgets. This forgone cash flow is analogous to a stock dividend not received. The lost cash flow is initially \$0.55. The present value of future cash flows is $\$0.55/0.01 = \$55$. Thus, the dividend yield is approximately 1%. (We can also think of the dividend yield as the difference between the discount rate [5%] and the growth rate of the cash flows [4%].)

We can compute the value of the widget project option using the perpetual call calculation discussed in Section 12.6. The formula assumes continuously compounded rates, so for the interest rate we use $ln(1.05) = 4.879\%$, and for the dividend yield we use the difference between the continuously compounded interest rate and growth rate, or $ln(1.05) - ln(1.04) = 0.9569\%$.

With $S = \$55$ (the present value of revenue), $K = \$28$ (the present value of costs), $r = 0.04879$, $\sigma = 0$,[3] and $\delta = 0.009569$, equation (12.16) gives an option price of \$35.03 and investment when the widget price equals \$1.4276. We will call this price the **investment trigger price.** We reach this price after about 24.32 years, which verifies the answer we discussed earlier.

The example in this section illustrates the importance of thinking dynamically about a project and shows how this specific problem can be modeled as an option.

----

[3] It is necessary to set σ to a small positive number such as 0.00001 to avoid a zero-divide error.

17.2 INVESTMENT UNDER UNCERTAINTY

With the widget project, waiting to invest was optimal because project dividends were initially less than the interest gained from deferring the project. If we add uncertainty about project cash flows, the value of insurance (the implicit put option) also influences the decision to delay the project. In this section we show how we can use a binomial tree to value a project with uncertain cash flows. In such a case, waiting to invest provides information about the value of the project. As before, the decision to invest in such a project is like exercising an American option: We pay the investment cost (strike price) to receive the asset (present value of future cash flows).

Suppose a project costs $100 and begins producing an infinite stream of cash flows 1 year after investment. Expected annual cash flows for the first year are $18, and are expected to grow annually at a rate of 3%. Suppose further that the risk-free rate is 7%, the risk premium on the market is 6%, and the beta of the project is 1.33. Using the Capital Asset Pricing Model (CAPM), we compute the discount rate for the project in the usual way:

$$r_{project} = r_{risk\text{-}free} + \beta(r_{market} - r_{risk\text{-}free})$$
$$= 0.07 + 1.33(0.06)$$
$$= 0.15$$

To value the project, we perform a standard discounted cash flow calculation. Since the project lives forever, we treat it as a perpetual growing annuity. The present value is

$$PV = \frac{E(CF_1)}{r_{project} - \text{growth rate}}$$
$$= \frac{\$18}{0.15 - 0.03}$$
$$= \$150$$

Static NPV is therefore $150 − $100 = $50.

Evaluating the Project with a 2-Year Investment Horizon

Suppose we have 2 years in which to decide whether to accept the project; at the end of that time, we either invest in the project or lose it. (Imagine, for example, that the licensing rights for a technology will revert at that time to the original owner). The static NPV rule will apply after two years because further deferral is not possible. However, at time 0, we must evaluate the option to wait.

The forgone initial cash flow (the dividend on the project) is $18 and the interest saving is $7 (7% × 100). Thus, considering only dividends and interest, it makes sense to start the project immediately. However, the project also has implicit insurance that we lose by investing in the project. To value the insurance we need to know the project volatility.

A tree for project value   Suppose that cash flows are lognormally distributed with a 50% volatility. Figure 17.1 uses the Cox-Ross-Rubinstein approach to construct a binomial tree for the evolution of cash flows with a binomial period of 1 year. If we wait to take the project, initial cash flows in 1 year will be either $\$18e^{0.5} = \$29.677$ or $\$18e^{-0.5} = \$10.918$. Since the project value is proportional to cash flows, the value of the project is also lognormally distributed with a 50% volatility.

In 1 year, project value will be either $\$29.677/(0.15 - 0.03) = \$247.31$ or $\$10.918/(0.15 - 0.03) = \$91$. If we will continue to learn about the project at the same rate over time, we can build a binomial tree with constant volatility that shows the evolution of project value. This tree, constructed by discounting at each node the cash flows in Figure 17.1, is in Figure 17.2.

Since the act of investing creates the project, the value at each node in Figure 17.2 is the value of the project *if we were to invest at that node*. The project does not exist prior to investment, but this is the information we need in order to decide whether to invest. The tree in Figure 17.2 is exactly the same tree we would construct for a stock that had a price of $150 and a 50% volatility. Even though the project does not exist, *if it did* exist, the tree would represent the stock price of a company that had the project as its only asset.

Because it looks like a binomial tree for a dividend-paying stock, Figure 17.2 represents the **twin security** or the **traded present value** of the project. If there *were* a stock that paid dividends equal to the cash flow of the project, that stock would evolve according to the same tree. It may trouble you that in valuing this project, option pricing formulas are being used in a context where literal replication of the option is not possible because the twin security does not exist. As we saw in Chapter 11, however, *the binomial procedure also works in a setting where we perform valuation using the CAPM or other pricing model.* Thus, we are using option pricing formulas to create *fair prices*, not *arbitrage-free* prices.

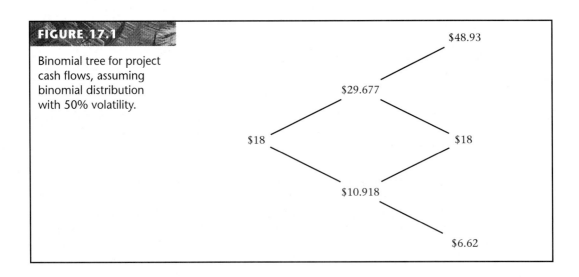

FIGURE 17.1

Binomial tree for project cash flows, assuming binomial distribution with 50% volatility.

$18 $29.677 $48.93 $18 $10.918 $6.62

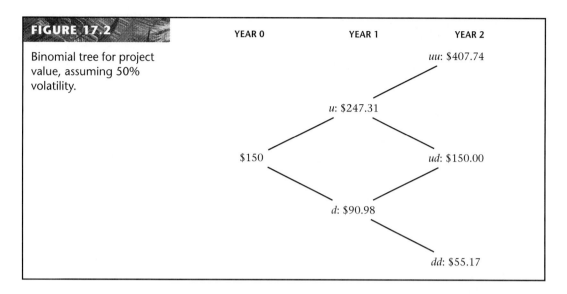

FIGURE 17.2

Binomial tree for project value, assuming 50% volatility.

YEAR 0	YEAR 1	YEAR 2
		uu: $407.74
	u: $247.31	
$150		*ud*: $150.00
	d: $90.98	
		dd: $55.17

Solving for the optimal investment decision   We can use Figure 17.2 to solve the investment problem exactly as we would use it in a binomial option pricing problem. The inputs are initial project value, $S = \$150$; investment cost, $K = \$100$; continuously compounded risk-free rate, $r = ln(1.07) = 6.766\%$; volatility, $\sigma = 0.50$; and time to expiration, $t = 2$ years. Since the market value of the project today is $150 and the cash flow in a year would be $18 if the project were developed, the dividend yield is 12% ($18/$150). Since project value is proportional to next year's cash flow, the dividend yield never changes. The continuously compounded dividend yield is $\delta = ln(1.12) = 0.1133$.

The up and down moves can be modeled using any of the binomial trees from Chapter 10. We can then solve for the value of the investment option just as we solve for the price of an American call option. The risk-neutral probability of the project value increasing in any period, p^*, is given by:

$$p^* = \frac{e^{0.0676-0.1133} - e^{-0.5}}{e^{0.5} - e^{-0.5}} = 0.335$$

Using p^*, we work backward through the tree as in Chapter 10. The results are in Figure 17.3. Notice that the initial value of the project option is $55.80, which is greater than the static NPV of $50. Problem 17.9 asks you to verify these calculations.

In practice, decision trees are often used to analyze this kind of problem. Figure 17.3—like any binomial option problem—*is* a decision tree, albeit with probabilities and nodes constructed in a very particular way. Analysts using a decision tree often use true (not risk-neutral) probabilities and a constant discount rate along the tree. We saw in Section 11.2 that if the discount rate applicable to the underlying asset is constant, then when valuing an option using true probabilities, the correct discount rate varies across the nodes of the tree. Keep in mind, however, that in many cases the tree in

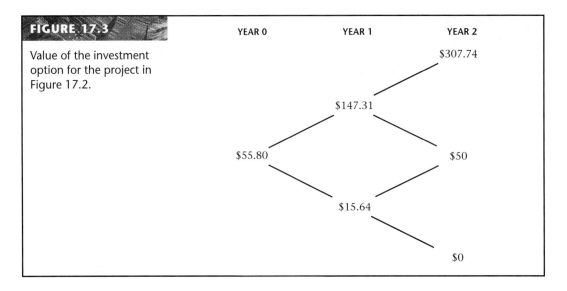

FIGURE 17.3

Value of the investment option for the project in Figure 17.2.

Figure 17.2 is derived from forecasts. In practice we estimate cash flow volatility, the expected growth of earnings, and the project beta, and it is common to assume that the project discount rate and volatility are constant. A tree like that in Figure 17.2 is really an educated guess. Given the uncertainty in characterizing the problem in the first place, it is hard to say whether efforts to precisely mimic a stock option valuation improve accuracy. Nevertheless, binomial option pricing tells us how to perform the valuation so that the assumptions about the project and the assumptions about the tree are consistent with each other.

Evaluating the Project with an Infinite Investment Horizon

The above example assumes that we must start the project by year 2 and that we evaluate it annually. Suppose instead that the project can be started at any time and then will live forever. The project is then a perpetual call option that we can evaluate using the perpetual option pricing formula. Using continuously compounded inputs, we compute

$$CallPerpetual(\$150, \$100, 0.50, 0.0676, 0.1133) = \{\$63.396, \$245.71\}$$

When the project value is $150, the option value is $63.396 and the optimal investment trigger is $245.71. In other words, we invest when the project is worth $245.71, more than twice the investment cost. If we invest immediately, the project is worth $50. The ability to wait increases that value by $13.396.

17.3 REAL OPTIONS IN PRACTICE

Real investment decisions often have option-like features. Consider the following:

1. The decision about whether and when to invest in investment projects.

2. The ability to shut down, restart, and permanently abandon projects.

3. The ability to invest in projects that may give rise to future options.

4. The ability to be flexible in the future about the choice of inputs, outputs, or production technologies.

We have already discussed the first—an investment project is a call option. We can view the ability to shut down a money-losing project (item 2 in the list above) as having the project plus a put option—an insurance policy to protect against even greater losses. The ability to invest in a way that gives rise to future investment options (item 3, sometimes called "strategic options") should remind you of a compound option (an option to buy an option). So-called "flexibility options" (item 4) are analogous to a type of exotic option called a rainbow option, which we will discuss in Chapter 22.

Despite the many similarities between real options and financial options, there is usually no simple and straightforward way to make real-life investment problems fit an option pricing formula. As with any valuation problem, it is necessary to analyze the specific problem. In this section, we look at two examples that use option analysis to value assets: Peak-load electricity generation and pharmaceutical research and development. The box on page 536 describes an investment problem at Intel which was similar to a peak-load problem.

Peak-Load Electricity Generation[4]

In Chapter 6 we explained that electricity forward prices can vary over the course of a day. They also vary seasonally: In the United States, electricity forward prices are high in the summer and low in the winter. In addition to this predictable variation, electricity prices can be volatile. On extremely hot days, for example, prices can spike to 100 times their average price.

A peak-load plant, as the name suggests, produces only when it is profitable to do so, exploiting spikes in the price of electricity. Such plants are designed so that they can be idled when the price of electricity is less than the cost of fuel, but they can be quickly brought online to produce power when the price of electricity is high or when the price of fuel declines. Because it is turned on only when profitable, owning a peak-load plant is like owning a strip of call options, with options maturing daily.[5] The underlying asset is

---

[4]I thank David Moore of El Paso Corporation for helpful discussions and for providing representative data.

[5]Operators will think not only about day-to-day operations, but hour-to-hour as well, since a plant may be operated during the day and not at night.

Peak-Load Manufacturing at Intel

Manufacturers investing in production capacity and facing uncertain demand experience the same peak-load production problem as electricity producers. Consider a manufacturer investing in production capacity and facing uncertain demand. How should the manufacturer choose plant capacity? Consider choosing the plant's capacity to meet expected demand. If demand turns out to be less than forecast, the firm will either produce at a loss or have an idle plant. If demand is greater, the firm will forgo revenue. If it is necessary to produce whether demand is high or low, then extra capacity has no option value. However, if it is possible to idle an unused plant when demand is low, then *extra production capacity is like a peak-load facility*. The extra capacity gives the firm a call option.

Intel in 1997 had to decide upon the capacity of a new plant. Semiconductor fabrication facilities ("fabs") cost about

$2 billion and take 2 years to construct, 1 year for the shell—the building—and 1 year for the equipment. The shell cost was about $350 million, with the rest reflecting equipment cost.

Intel analysts proposed building a shell 1 year ahead of schedule. If demand were high, the firm would be able to install equipment a year early and earn an extra year of revenue. If demand were low, the firm would maintain the building until needed, which was relatively inexpensive.

The planners sought to persuade senior management that early construction of a shell provided benefits. Intel analysts developed a simple binomial model that illustrated the costs and benefits of early construction. They verified that the Black-Scholes formula gave approximately the same option value. Intel then built the shell 1 year early.

electricity. The strike price is the cost of inputs required to produce a unit of electricity, including the cost of the fuel—typically natural gas—and other variable costs associated with operating the plant.[6] The **heat rate, H,** of a plant is the efficiency with which it turns gas into electricity (the number of MMBtus required to produce a megawatt hour (MWh)).[7]

For the moment, let's consider only electricity and gas prices, and assume that we can ignore distribution costs and marginal operating, maintenance, and other costs. Then the profit of the plant is

$$\text{Profit} = max(S_{elec} - H \times S_{gas}, 0)$$

....

[6] In practice, the term "strike price" is sometimes used to refer only to nongas variable costs.

[7] The definition of heat rate is the number of BTUs required to produce one kilowatt/hour of electricity. The heat rate times 1000 is the number of British Thermal Units (BTUs) to produce one MWh. For example, if the heat rate is 9000, then $9000 \times 1000 = 9m$ BTUs is required to produce one megawatt/hour of electricity. If the price of natural gas is $3/MMBtu, then the gas cost of producing one MWh of electricity is $27.

This is the payoff to a European exchange option (see Section 14.6). The difference between the price of electricity and the cost of generation, $S_{elec} - H \times S_{gas}$, is called the **spark spread.** There are operating costs besides gas, but the spark spread is the variable component of marginal profit.

In order to value the option we need forward prices and volatilities for electricity and gas and the correlation between the two. The top panel in Figure 17.4 shows representative forward curves for electricity and gas. The price curve for gas has a shape familiar from Section 6.9, exhibiting seasonal winter peaks. The electricity curve, by contrast, exhibits summer peaks. The bottom panel shows the spark spread implied by the prices in the first panel.

The value of a plant is the sum of the operating options it provides. Let F_{E,t_i} and F_{G,t_i} represent the time 0 forward prices for electricity and gas delivered at time t_i. If we ignore other marginal operating costs, then the value of the operating plant is[8]

$$\text{Value of Plant} = \sum_{i=1}^{n} BSCall(F_{E,t_i}, H \times F_{G,t_i}, \hat{\sigma}_{t_i}, r, t_i, r) \tag{17.2}$$

where $\hat{\sigma}_{t_i}^2 = \sigma_{E,t_i}^2 + H^2 \times \sigma_{G,t_i}^2 - 2\rho H \sigma_{E,t_i} \sigma_{G,t_i}$. Because volatility changes with the time horizon in Figure 17.4, volatility in expression 17.2 has a time subscript. Equation (17.2) provides the value of the plant taking account of optionality. We could also value the plant assuming operation at all times; this would be a static NPV calculation. We can see how the static value relates to the true value by using put-call parity to rewrite equation (17.2):

$$\sum_{i=1}^{n} \left[e^{-rt_i} (F_{E,t_i} - H \times F_{G,t_i}) + BSPut(F_{E,t_i}, H \times F_{G,t_i}, \hat{\sigma}_{t_i}, r, t_i, r) \right]$$

$$= \underbrace{\sum_{i=1}^{n} e^{-rt_i} (F_{E,t_i} - H \times F_{G,t_i})}_{\text{Static NPV}} + \underbrace{\sum_{i=1}^{n} BSPut(F_{E,t_i}, H \times F_{G,t_i}, \hat{\sigma}_{t_i}, r, t_i, r)}_{\text{Option Not to Operate}} \tag{17.3}$$

This way of writing the plant's value makes apparent the difference between a static NPV calculation and the real options valuation. The static calculation assumes operation at all times; we can value the plant by simply discounting the spark spread computed using forward prices. Equation (17.2) also makes it clear that *the value of a peak-load plant does not stem from operating when prices are high—all plants operate when prices are high—but rather from* shutting down *when prices are low.*

In reality, equation (17.3) is overly simplified. There are marginal distribution, operation, and maintenance costs associated with an operating plant. Represent these

---

[8]Because the underlying asset is a forward price, the risk-free rate, r, is used as the dividend yield. This is the Black formula, equation (12.7).

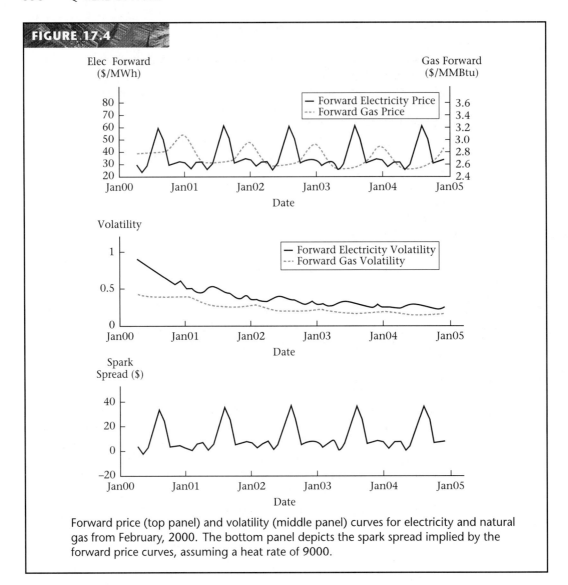

FIGURE 17.4

Forward price (top panel) and volatility (middle panel) curves for electricity and natural gas from February, 2000. The bottom panel depicts the spark spread implied by the forward price curves, assuming a heat rate of 9000.

costs as c. When we take these into account, marginal profit is

$$\text{Profit} = max(S_{elec} - (H \times S_{gas} + c), 0)$$

This payoff is that of a **spread option,** since the payoff is positive if the spread $S_{elec} - H \times S_{gas}$ exceeds c. An option with this payoff cannot be valued using the Black-Scholes formula because neither $S_{elec} - H \times S_{gas}$ nor $H \times S_{gas} + c$ is lognormally distributed.

Equation (17.2) is therefore an approximation once nonfuel costs are added to the strike price.[9]

When we include other costs, the static NPV of a peak-load plant is typically negative. Adding the shutdown option, however, makes NPV positive. One implication is that, in equilibrium, after the optimal number of peak-load plants have been constructed, electricity prices will continue to be variable. Otherwise, the marginal peak-load plant would have negative NPV. Thus, *the existence of peak-load technology will not eliminate equilibrium variability in electricity prices.*

As a final point, note that the volatility curves in Figure 17.4 are declining over time. From the standpoint of February 2000, a 2-year volatility is less than a 1-year volatility. This is in contrast with stocks, for which we typically assume volatility is constant over time.

To understand the behavior of volatility for electricity, recall the discussion of stock prices in Section 11.3. The assumption that a stock price follows a random walk implies that volatility increases with the square root of time. Thus, volatility enters the Black-Scholes model as $\sigma \sqrt{T - t}$; this expression measures the volatility of the stock price over the horizon from t to T. By contrast, we do not expect electricity prices to follow a random walk. When the electricity price is high, users consume less electricity and producers increase production. When prices are low, users consume more and producers produce less. Thus, the price of electricity reverts to a level reflecting the cost of production. When prices revert in this fashion, *volatility grows with T at a rate less than $\sqrt{T - t}$.*

To consider a specific example, suppose it is January. From this perspective, the July price this year and the July price next year have similar distributions; we won't learn much about the July price this year or next until we approach July. (This is not strictly true because economic activity and even weather can follow long-term cycles, but suppose that it is a good approximation.) To compute an option price, we require *annualized* volatility, σ, which the option pricing formula transforms into volatility over the life of the option, $\sigma \sqrt{T - t}$. If you believe the uncertainty this July and next July is the same, the annualized volatility will be lower for next July since a given amount of uncertainty is, when annualized, spread across a greater period of time. If $\sigma \sqrt{T_i - t}$ is the same for two different T_is, the σs will be different and the volatility curve will decline with horizon.

Research and Development

Research and development is a capital expenditure like any other, in that it involves paying R&D costs today to receive cash flows later. If R&D is successful, a project using the new technology can be undertaken if its NPV is positive. This final option is a call option, just like the other projects we have analyzed. The R&D leading up to this

---

[9]Haug (1998, p. 59) discusses approximations that can be used to value spread options.

project is therefore like an option premium: We pay R&D costs to acquire the project. R&D can be thought of as acquiring future investment options.

Drug development by pharmaceutical firms provides a particularly clear example of the options in R&D since the drug development process has clearly delineated points at which there is a decision to abandon or continue development. Figure 17.5, based on a description in Schwartz and Moon (2000), summarizes the process, along with the probabilities of progressing from one stage to the next. In practice, stages sometimes run together, but Figure 17.5 reflects a standard description of the process.

As R&D costs are paid over time, pharmaceutical firms are able to resolve uncertainties about their technical ability to produce and market the product. Specifically, they answer the questions: Will the project work, and, if it works, will anyone want it? At all times, project managers have the option to continue or stop the research. In effect, each ongoing investment purchases an option to continue development.

Figure 17.5 shows that most potential drugs are abandoned before Phase I trials. As with peak-load electricity generation, value arises from what is not done. A pharmaceutical company that pursued all potential drugs, no matter how unpromising, would reap full rewards from successful drugs but would be bankrupted by the unsuccessful drugs. The put option to abandon a drug is what creates value for the firm.

How do we evaluate pharmaceutical investments? The underlying asset is the value of the drug if brought to market. How do we find the value of this asset? With the peak-load electricity plant, we have forward prices for both the input (natural gas) and the output (electricity). We can estimate volatilities from market prices. However, in pharmaceuticals, we must estimate development costs, potential revenues, volatilities, and correlations without the benefit of observing market prices. Project payoffs will vary with the state of the economy and, hence, have systematic risk, which must also be estimated.

Assuming that all of these inputs are known, we can evaluate the sequential investment as in Figure 17.6. The figure presents an example in which, in each period,

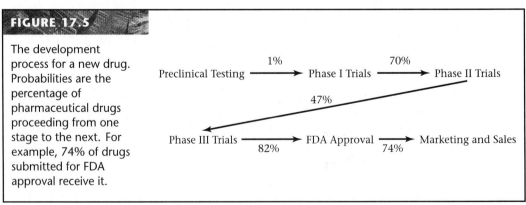

FIGURE 17.5

The development process for a new drug. Probabilities are the percentage of pharmaceutical drugs proceeding from one stage to the next. For example, 74% of drugs submitted for FDA approval receive it.

Source: Schwartz and Moon (2000).

FIGURE 17.6

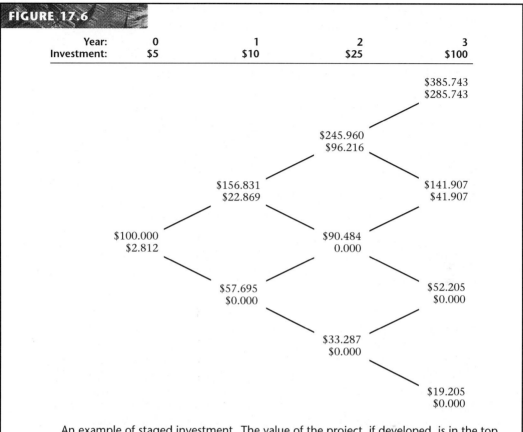

Year:	0	1	2	3
Investment:	$5	$10	$25	$100

An example of staged investment. The value of the project, if developed, is in the top line at each node. The value of the option to develop the project is shown below the value of the project. In each year, it is necessary to pay the amount in the Investment row to keep the project alive in the next period. The tree is generated as a forward tree assuming $S_0 = \$100$, $\sigma = 0.50$, $r = 0.10$, and $\delta = 0.15$.

it is necessary to pay an investment cost (shown in the "investment" row) to keep the project alive for another period. The static NPV of the project is negative, since the initial value of the developed investment is $100, but the present value of the investment costs at a 10% rate of interest is $108.60. This static calculation ignores the staging of the investment, which permits making later-year investment costs only if the project shows promise. With staging, the value of the development option is $2.812. Schwartz and Moon (2000), building on work by Pindyck (1993), developed a general valuation model, with staging, which is applicable to pharmaceutical R&D.

Peak-load pricing and research and development are examples of how option techniques are used in making investment decisions. In the next two sections we develop an extended example of commodity extraction, which is yet another area in which real option considerations are essential.

17.4 COMMODITY EXTRACTION AS AN OPTION

Natural resources investments are an important application of option techniques to investment decisions.[10] The extraction of a resource from the ground exhibits many similarities to the exercise of a financial option. The resource has a value that can be realized by paying an extraction cost. The market for the resource is typically competitive so that the behavior of one producer does not affect the price.

In this section we will consider the problem of extracting oil from the ground. There is an initial cost to sink a well to commence production, after which we assume we keep producing forever. In Section 17.5 we introduce the possibility of shutting down production when it is unprofitable.

Our goal in studying the oil extraction problem will be to understand the *economics* of this problem. The analysis is an example illustrating the costs and benefits of deferring investment and stopping and starting production. The specific formulas do not apply in every situation.

Single-Barrel Extraction under Certainty

Suppose there is a plot of land that contains one barrel of oil. The current price of a barrel of oil is $15, the oil forward curve is such that the effective annual lease rate, δ, is 4% (constant over time and across maturities at a point in time), and the effective annual risk-free rate, r, is 5% (also constant over time). There is no uncertainty about the future price of oil. The barrel can be extracted at any time by paying $13.60, which we denote X. Finally, to make matters simple, suppose that the land is completely worthless once the oil is extracted.

If the price of oil at time 0 is S_t, the time 0 forward price for delivery at time T is given by

$$F_{0,T} = S_0 \left(\frac{1+r}{1+\delta} \right)^T \tag{17.4}$$

Since prices are certain, the future spot price will equal the forward price; hence, the spot price of oil will grow forever at the rate $(1+r)/(1+\delta) - 1 = 1.05/1.04 - 1 = 0.9615\%$ per year.

How much would you pay for this plot of land? The obvious answer—a bid of $1.40 (= $15 − $13.60)—ignores real options considerations. As with the widget project, *you cannot value the land without first deciding under what circumstances you*

[10]See in particular Brennan and Schwartz (1985), McDonald and Siegel (1986), and Paddock et al. (1988).

will extract oil from the ground. A bid of $1.40 is too low. The correct answer is to select T to maximize the present value of net extraction revenue,

$$\frac{S_T - x}{(1tr)^T} \tag{17.5}$$

Using equation (17.4) to model the change in the oil price over time, we can mechanically find the T that maximizes expression (17.5). However, we want to discuss the reasons for this decision.

Optimal extraction   The costs and benefits of extraction are probably familiar by now. If we delay extraction, the barrel of oil in the ground appreciates at 0.9615% per year, less than the risk-free rate. We lose 4% per year—the lease rate—on the value of the barrel. However, extracting the barrel costs $13.60. By delaying extraction 1 year we earn another year's interest on this amount.

Thinking about costs and benefits in this way suggests a simple decision rule, familiar from the widget project: Delay extraction as long as the cost exceeds the benefit. The benefit in this case is constant from year to year since the extraction cost is constant, but the cost of delaying extraction—the forgone dollar lease payment—grows with the oil price. This comparison of costs and benefits should remind you of the widget problem.

This line of thinking leads to a back-of-the-envelope extraction rule. Since the interest rate (5%) is 25% greater than the dividend yield (4%), the dividend yield lost by not investing will equal the interest saved when $S = 1.25 \times \$13.60 = \$17$. Thus, we should expect it to be optimal to extract the oil when $S \approx \$17$.

A more precise calculation is to compare the NPV of investing today with that of investing tomorrow. At a minimum, if we are to invest, we must decide that the NPV of investing today exceeds that of waiting until tomorrow to invest. If we let r_d and δ_d represent the daily interest rate and lease rate, then we defer investing as long as the present value of producing tomorrow exceeds the value of producing today. Since tomorrow's oil price is today's oil price times $(1 + r_d)/(1 + \delta_d)$, we delay investing as long as

$$\frac{1}{1 + r_d}\left(S\frac{1 + r_d}{1 + \delta_d} - X\right) > S - X$$

This expression shows that we defer investment as long as

$$\frac{S}{X} < \frac{\frac{r_d}{1+r_d}}{\frac{\delta_d}{1+\delta_d}} \tag{17.6}$$

In this case we have $r_d = 1.05^{1/365} - 1 = 0.013368\%$, with the daily lease rate $\delta_d = 0.010746\%$. The trigger price, at which $S = X\frac{r_d}{\delta_d}\left(\frac{1+\delta_d}{1+r_d}\right)$, is $16.918.

Note that, since daily rates are essentially the same as continuously compounded rates, we get the same answer by using continuous compounding. We invest when:

$$S_t = \frac{ln(1.05)}{ln(1.04)} \times \$13.60 = \$16.918$$

This shows why our back-of-the-envelope answer of $17 is not exactly right. Instead of computing the ratio of effective annual rates (5%/4%), we want to compute the ratio of continuously compounded rates ($ln(1.05)/ln(1.04)$).

Value and appreciation of the land   We know that we will extract when oil reaches a price of $16.918/barrel. How long will this take? The annual growth rate of the price of oil is $1.05/1.04 - 1 = 0.9615\%$. We have to find the t such that $\$15 \times (1.009615)^t = \$16.918$. Solving gives us $t = 12.575$ years. At that point the value of extraction will be $16.918 - $13.60. Hence, NPV today is

$$\frac{\$16.918 - \$13.60}{1.05^{12.575}} = \$1.796$$

This is what we would pay for the land today. This substantially exceeds the value of $1.40 were we to extract the oil immediately.

At what rate does the land appreciate? The oil in the land is appreciating at 0.9615% per year; nevertheless, *the land itself appreciates at 5%.* If the land appreciated at less than 5%, no one would be willing to own it since bonds would earn a higher return. In fact, our valuation procedure ensures that the land earns 5% since that is the rate at which we discount the future payoff. *The properly operated oil reserve, whether producing or not, must at all times pay the owner a fair return (in this case, 5%).*

Using the option pricing formula   This problem is equivalent to deciding when to exercise a call option. By paying the extraction cost (the strike price), we can receive oil (the stock). As with a financial call, early exercise is a trade-off between interest saved by delaying exercise and dividends forgone. Once we have possession of the oil, we can lease it; hence, oil's lease rate is the dividend yield. We can verify our answers by using the formula for a perpetual call option, *CallPerpetual*, discussed in Chapter 12. Set $S = \$15$, $K = \$13.60$, $\sigma = 0.0001$, $r = ln(1.05)$, and $\delta = ln(1.04)$.[11] We get

$$CallPerpetual(\$15, \$13.60, 0.0001, ln(1.05), ln(1.04)) = \{\$1.796, \$16.918\}$$

The option price is $1.796 and the optimal decision is to exercise when the oil price reaches $16.918, exactly the answer we just obtained. The option formula implicitly makes the same calculations.

Like the widget example, this situation illustrates the similarity between the exercise of a financial and a real option.

Changing extraction costs   What if the cost of extraction, X, changes over time? Inflation might cause X to grow, while technological progress might cause X to decline. Intuitively, real growth in the extraction cost will accelerate investment. The reason is that the benefit from delaying investment is less: We earn interest on money set aside

---

[11] To use equation (12.16), we must convert the interest rate and dividend yield to continuously compounded rates.

to fund extraction, but some of that money has to be reinvested to fund the growth in extraction cost. Thus, if g is the growth rate of the extraction cost, our benefit from delay is $r - g$ instead of r.

If we view the option to extract oil as a general option to exchange one asset (cash) for another (oil), our willingness to make the exchange depends on the relative dividend yields of the two assets. The option is equivalent to being long the underlying asset without receiving its dividend, and short the strike asset without having to pay its dividend. A high dividend yield on the asset we are giving up (the strike asset) makes us less willing to make the exchange, other things equal. Positive growth in the extraction cost reduces the dividend yield on the asset we are giving up, making us more anxious to give it up; hence, there is a lower trigger price.

In the example, if the growth rate of the extraction cost is 0.5% per annum (effective annual), then we would invest when, using continuously compounded rates,

$$S = \frac{r - g}{\delta} X = \frac{0.04879 - 0.00498}{0.03922} \$13.60 = \$15.19$$

It will take 1.32 years to reach this price, and the land would therefore be worth

$$(\$15.19 - \$13.60 \times (1.005)^{1.32})/1.05^{1.32} = \$1.407.$$

Growth in the extraction cost hastens extraction and lowers the value of the property.

Gold extraction revisited   In Section 6.7 we saw that the lease rate of gold is positive. We can now see that if the lease rate of gold were zero, it would never be optimal to mine gold.[12] If a commodity has a zero lease rate, then the cost of delaying extraction is zero: It is always preferable to wait to extract.

To see why a zero lease rate implies that we would never extract gold, think about the comparison we have just made between extracting oil today or tomorrow. If oil had had a zero lease rate, then by definition the forward curve would be growing at the risk-free rate. The present value of oil tomorrow would be the value of oil today; nothing is lost by leaving it in the ground. The gain to deferral, however, would be interest saved on the extraction cost. Thus there would have been no reason ever to extract the oil. In effect, oil in the ground is worth as much as oil out of the ground, so why pay the extraction cost? Equation (17.6) and the option pricing formula give the same answer, with the extraction barrier approaching infinity as the lease rate approaches zero. Thus, *gold, or any extractive resource, will never be extracted if the lease rate is zero.*

This discussion provides an answer to the question of why gold has a positive lease rate. Investors hold a large stock of gold above ground *despite* the positive lease rate. The lease rate must therefore reflect a convenience yield earned by gold investors. This convenience yield is reflected in the forward curve as a positive lease rate. The positive lease rate in turn makes producers willing to extract new gold.

....

[12]This also assumes that extraction cost grows less than the risk-free rate.

Single-Barrel Extraction under Uncertainty

Now we consider the effects of uncertainty on the oil extraction decision. Before proceeding, try to answer this question: If we keep all variables unchanged (the lease rate, extraction cost, and so forth), except that the oil price is uncertain, how do the extraction trigger price and the value of the undeveloped land change?

Option reasoning gives unambiguous answers to this question: The extraction trigger price goes up and the land becomes more valuable. The comparison of dividends (the lease rate) to interest savings in the previous example captures two of the three reasons for early exercise. The third is insurance that results from the ability to delay taking the project. With uncertainty the insurance has value, which increases the value of delay. The forgone dividend has to be greater before it is worth giving up the implicit insurance. Another way to think about the investment decision is that by deferring extraction of the oil, we have more time to see if the oil price will decline or rise further. This effect induces additional delay, in the sense that we will optimally invest at a higher price.

If we decide to extract the oil when the price is $\overline{S}$, we will receive $\overline{S} - X$ when S reaches $\overline{S}$. From our discussion of barrier present values in Chapter 12, we know how to value a payoff of $\overline{S} - X$ when the price $\overline{S}$ is reached. Using the contingent present value formula defined by equation (12.14), the value of the extraction option is

$$(\overline{S} - \$13.60) \left(\frac{S}{\overline{S}} \right)^{h_1}$$

where

$$h_1 = \frac{1}{2} - \frac{r - \delta}{\sigma^2} + \sqrt{\left(\frac{r - \delta}{\sigma^2} - \frac{1}{2} \right)^2 + \frac{2r}{\sigma^2}}$$

This is the present value of our investment strategy.

By varying $\overline{S}$, we can see how the present value of the project is affected by different extraction trigger prices. Figure 17.7 compares the value of the land under different rules about when to pay $13.60 and extract the oil. When oil price volatility is 15%, the trigger price is higher and the land is more valuable. The trigger price that maximizes the value of the land is $\overline{S} = 25.3388$. At this price, we have a project value of

$$(\$25.3388 - \$13.60) \left(\frac{\$15}{25.3388} \right)^{h_1} = \$3.7856$$

We can verify this calculation by exploiting the insight that for option pricing purposes the lease rate is the dividend yield, and use the perpetual call formula:

CallPerpetual[$15, $13.60, 0.15, *ln*(1.05), *ln*(1.04)] = {$3.7856, 25.3388}

The perpetual call calculation also gives $\overline{S} = \$25.3388$ as the price at which exercise should occur.

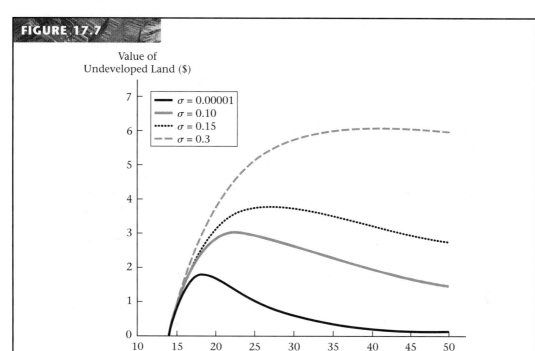

Value of land containing one barrel of oil as a function of the trigger extraction price, $\bar{S}$, for four different oil volatilities. For the curve where $\sigma = 0.00001$, the maximum is attained at $\bar{S} = \$16.918$ with a corresponding value of $\$1.796$. For the curve where $\sigma = 0.15$, the maximum is attained at $\bar{S} = \$25.3388$ with a corresponding value of $\$3.786$.

Valuing an Infinite Oil Reserve

Now suppose that the land contains an infinite number of barrels of oil that can be extracted at the rate of one barrel per year. We will assume that the firm can at any time invest I in order to turn the undeveloped reserve into a developed reserve. Exactly 1 year after that, the reserve will begin to produce one barrel of oil a year forever at a cost c per barrel. We solve this problem by working backward. We first compute the value of the firm supposing that it is already producing, and we then study the decision about when to invest.

Valuing the producing firm   Once the firm has invested, it will continue producing forever since the price of oil is always rising. Recall from our discussion of commodity forwards in Chapter 6 that the lease rate is the discount rate linking the future commodity price with the current commodity price. Thus, the time t value of a barrel received at time T is $PV_t(F_{t,T}) = F_{t,T}/(1+r)^{T-t} = S_t/(1+\delta)^{T-t}$. The value of the producing firm at time 0 is therefore

$$\sum_{i=1}^{\infty} \frac{F_{0,i} - c}{(1+r)^i} = \sum_{i=1}^{\infty} \left(\frac{S_0}{(1+\delta)^i} - \frac{c}{(1+r)^i} \right)$$

$$= \frac{S_0}{\delta} - \frac{c}{r}$$

(17.7)

You might wonder why the present value of a barrel of oil a year forever is S_0/δ. We know that a perpetual-coupon bond paying c/year is worth c/r (the second term on the right in equation (17.7)). We saw in Chapter 15 that the lease rate on a commodity bond is analogous to the interest rate on a cash bond. The operating well is like a bond paying one unit of the commodity forever, so the lease rate δ is the appropriate interest rate for a bond denominated in a commodity, and S_0/δ is the value of the well.

Valuing the option to invest   If the firm invests at the price S_T, the value of the land at that time is the value of the producing well less the investment cost, I, or $S_T/\delta - c/r - I$. The value of the land today is

$$\frac{1}{(T+r)^T} \left(\frac{S_T}{\delta} - \frac{c}{r} - I \right) = \frac{1}{(T+r)^T} \frac{1}{\delta} \left(S_T - \delta \left[\frac{c}{r} + I \right] \right)$$

(17.8)

This is the value of the *undeveloped* oil reserve. Note the similarity with equation (17.5). If in equation (17.5) we replace S_T with the present value of oil extracted, S_T/δ, and replace the extraction cost, X, with the present value of all extraction costs, $c/r + I$, then we have a problem that appears the same as in the single-barrel case. We want to select T to maximize equation (17.8). The right-hand side of equation (17.8) expresses the value on a per-barrel basis, times $1/\delta$. Having multiple barrels in the ground does not change anything fundamental about the problem if there is certainty and the oil price grows indefinitely.

Example 17.1   Suppose $S_0 = \$15$, $r = 5\%$, $\delta = 4\%$, $c = \$8$, and the value of the producing well is $\$15/0.04 - \$8/0.05 = \$215$. If the investment cost, I, is $\$180$, then the *per-barrel* extraction cost is $\delta(c/r + I) = 0.04 \times (\$8/0.05 + \$180) = \$13.60$. The problem is the same as having $1/\delta$ options to extract at a cost of $\$13.60$; hence, the solution is exactly the same as in the single-barrel case. To appreciate the similarity, use the option pricing formula:

$$CallPerpetual \left[\frac{\$15}{0.04}, \frac{\$8}{0.05} + 180, 0.000001, ln(1.05), ln(1.04) \right]$$

$$= \{\$44.914, \$422.956\}$$

The value of the well at which extraction occurs is $\$422.956$. Thus, extraction occurs when $S = 0.04 \times \$422.956 = \$16.918$.   ❧

With uncertainty, we could have the ability to shut a producing well. We will assume for the moment that production continues forever. In that case, the problem is the same as in the single-barrel case.

Example 17.2 Make the same assumptions as in Example 17.1, except suppose that the price of oil is lognormally distributed with a constant lease rate and volatility is $\sigma = 0.15$. The land value and optimal extraction decision is given by

$$CallPerpetual\left[\frac{\$15}{0.04}, \frac{\$8}{0.05} + \$180, 0.15, ln(1.05), ln(1.04)\right] = \{\$94.639, \$633.469\}$$

The well is worth \$94.639 and we invest when it is worth $S/0.04 = \$633.469$, or when $S = \$25.3388$. On a per-barrel basis, the well is worth $0.04 \times \$94.639 = \$3.7856$. With these assumptions, the solution is the same as in the single-barrel case. ≷

In the absence of any shutdown options, the single- and infinite-barrel cases differ only in scale. The interesting difference arises when it is possible to avoid operating losses by shutting down, which matters only in the multiple-barrel case.

17.5 COMMODITY EXTRACTION WITH SHUT DOWN AND RESTART OPTIONS

With production occurring over time and uncertainty about the price of oil, we face two new operating decisions: Whether to keep the well operating, or, if it has been shut down, whether to reopen it. There are thus three stages of production:

Initial investment in the well We begin with an empty field containing oil. This is an undeveloped well. At what point do we drill the well and begin extraction? We answered this question in Section 17.4, assuming that the well operates until the resource is exhausted.

Continuing to produce Once we have made the investment in an oil well, we say that the property is *developed*. However, a developed well may or may not be producing. If we are extracting oil from the ground, we have a *developed and producing* well. However, if the oil price drops below extraction cost, it may make sense to pay a cost in order to shut down the well and avoid future operating losses. Then it is a *shutdown* well.

Restarting an operating well Having shut down the well, if the oil price rises again, it may be possible to pay a cost and *restart* the well, turning it back into a producing well.

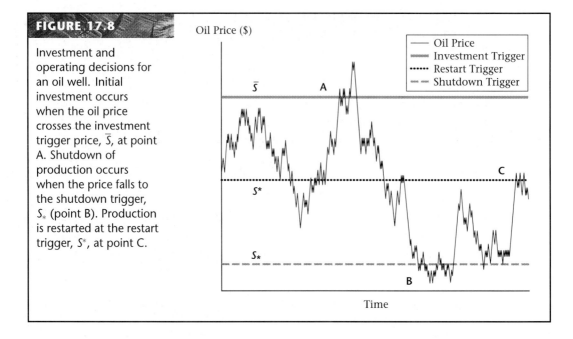

FIGURE 17.8

Investment and operating decisions for an oil well. Initial investment occurs when the oil price crosses the investment trigger price, $\overline{S}$, at point A. Shutdown of production occurs when the price falls to the shutdown trigger, S_* (point B). Production is restarted at the restart trigger, S^*, at point C.

Thus, the well can be in one of three states: Undeveloped, producing, and shutdown (developed but not producing). Figure 17.8 shows a hypothetical price path of oil over time and possible operating rules. Investment occurs the first time the oil price reaches the investment trigger price, $\overline{S}$. Production is shut down at the shutdown trigger price, S_*, and restarted at the restart trigger price, S^*. Thus, before point A the well is undeveloped. Between points A and B, and after C, the well is producing. Between B and C the well is shutdown. Key questions are: How do we determine the investment, shutdown, and restart triggers, $\overline{S}$, S_*, and S^*, and what is the value of the land on which the oil is located?

Once again, we have to work backward, as in the binomial valuation of a stock option. Before we can decide the rule for investing (determining $\overline{S}$), we have to determine the value of a producing well (this is the present value of future cash flows at the point we invest). In order to value a producing well, we need to understand operating decisions, specifically how S_*, and S^* are determined.

It is helpful to analyze shutting down and restarting by considering three separate cases:

1. Production can be shut down once permanently. After the well has been shut, the land has no additional value.

2. Production can be shut down once, then restarted once, this time permanently.

3. Production can be shut down and restarted an infinite number of times.[13]

Each case layers a new option on the previous case. In addition to allowing additional shutting down and restarting, we can impose costs of doing so. We focus in this section on the case where the well can be shut down never or once after the initial investment. Appendix 17.B adds restarting to the analysis.

Permanent Shutting Down

Suppose that we are operating the well. If the current price is S and we ignore shutting down, the value of the operating well is simply

$$V_{operating,\ no\ shutdown} = \frac{S}{\delta} - \frac{c}{r} \tag{17.9}$$

Suppose that we can at any time pay a cost of k_s, abandon the well, and never produce again. S_* is the price at which we shut down.

What is the value of shutting down? There are three considerations:

1. Once we shut down, we no longer sell oil. Thus, we give up the revenue stream with present value S/δ.

2. We no longer pay the extraction cost, so we gain the present value c/r.

3. We give up k_s, the shutdown cost.

Thus, the value of shutting down at price S_* at a cost of k_s is

$$-\frac{S_*}{\delta} + \frac{c}{r} - k_s = \left(\frac{c}{r} - k_s\right) - \frac{S_*}{\delta} \tag{17.10}$$

This is the payoff to a put option with strike price $c/r - k_s$ and asset price S_*/δ. If we are operating and the price is S, we can value this put to determine the value of the option to shut down, as well as the trigger price, S_*, for shutting down.

Example 17.3 Suppose the oil well is operating and the oil price is $S = \$10$. We also have $c = \$8$, $\sigma = 0.15$, and effective annual r and δ are 5% and 4%, respectively. If $k_s = \$0$, the value of the option to shut down is

   PutPerpetual[$\$10/0.04, \$8/0.05, 0.15, ln(1.05), ln(1.04)$] = {$\$9.633, \$106.830$}

Thus, we shut down production when $S/\delta = \$106.83$ or when $S = 0.04 \times \$106.83 = \$4.273$. At this point, the present value of continuing to produce is

---

[13]The model with infinite shutdown and restart was first analyzed in Brennan and Schwartz (1985) and subsequently by Dixit (1989).

$$\frac{\$4.273}{0.04} - \frac{\$8.00}{0.05} = -\$53.17$$

By shutting down production, we avoid losses of $53.17.

When $k_s = \$25$, the shutdown solution is

$$PutPerpetual(\$10/0.04, \$8/0.05 - 25, 0.15, 0.04879, 0.03922) = \{\$5.778, \$90.137\}$$

The shutdown trigger is then $S = 0.04 \times \$90.137 = \$3.605$. We pay $25 to avoid losses with a present value of $-\$69.863$.   ≈

To interpret the shutdown results, there are two natural benchmark prices to consider. The first is the price at which the NPV of the operating well becomes zero, which occurs when $S = \delta \times c/r = \$6.40$. If shutdown is permanent, it makes no sense to shut a well if the present value of future cash flows is positive, so we would never shut down for $S > \$6.40$. The second benchmark is the marginal cost of production, $c = \$8$. As long as we are making money by operating ($S > c$), we will not shut down. (The initial investment is sunk and, hence, irrelevant.) However, for $S < c$, the firm is losing money if it continues to operate, and it makes sense to consider shutting down.

In Example 17.3, shutdown is permanent so the zero NPV price ($S = \$6.40$) is the natural benchmark. The usual option exercise logic applies: We won't shut down as soon as present value is negative, because the decision is irreversible. In fact, we wait until the price is below $5. The price *might* subsequently increase; by shutting down we are unable to benefit from this reversal. This is the counterpart to not investing as soon as NPV is positive.

The value of the producing well   Given that shutdown is possible, what is the value of a producing well? The answer is that the value of the well is the value of the perpetually producing well plus the value of the shutdown option:

$$V_{operating}(S) = V_{no\ shutdown}(S) + V_{shutdown\ option}(S)$$

(17.11)

$$= \frac{S}{\delta} - \frac{c}{r} + PutPerpetual\left[\frac{S}{\delta}, \frac{c}{r} - k_s, \sigma, ln(1+r), ln(1+\delta)\right]$$

Figure 17.9 graphs equation (17.11) for a range of oil prices and four different volatilities, along with the value of the well without a shutdown option. Without the shutdown option, the value of the well is like a stock and declines to $-c/r = -\$160$ when $S = 0$. With the option, the well is worth zero once it is shut. (Recall that once the well has been shut, the land has no additional value.)

When the oil price is significantly above the shutdown price, the shutdown option is worth little and the value of the well changes by $1/\delta$ for each $1 change in the oil price. (The Δ of the well is $1/\delta$.) Close to the shutdown price, however, the value of the well becomes less sensitive to the oil price, because the shutdown option is increasing in value to absorb the effect of declines in the oil price. In each case, the value of the well smoothly approaches zero as we approach the shutdown price.

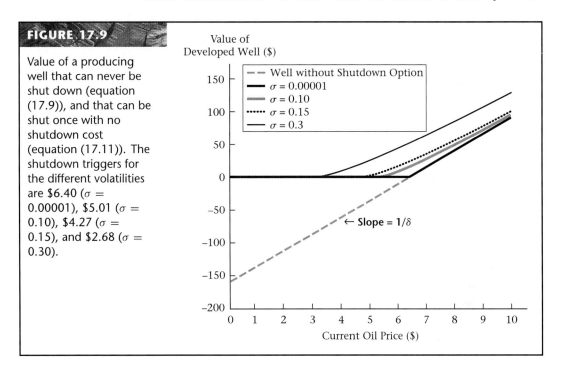

FIGURE 17.9

Value of a producing well that can never be shut down (equation (17.9)), and that can be shut once with no shutdown cost (equation (17.11)). The shutdown triggers for the different volatilities are $6.40 ($\sigma = 0.00001$), $5.01 ($\sigma = 0.10$), $4.27 ($\sigma = 0.15$), and $2.68 ($\sigma = 0.30$).

This example illustrates how the shutdown option affects valuation of an operating well. The next question is how the shutdown option affects the decision to invest in the well in the first place.

Investing When Shutdown Is Possible

How does the ability to shut the well affect the initial investment decision? Once we drill the well, the maximum potential loss is less because of the shutdown option. The ability to shut down makes us willing to invest sooner.

To account for the value of the shutdown option we work backward. Equation (17.11) gives the value of a producing well. Call this $V_p(S)$. If we invest at the price $\bar{S}$, paying an investment cost of I, then the value *at the time we invest* is

Value of well at time of investment $= V_p(\bar{S}) - I$

$$= \frac{\bar{S}}{\delta} - \frac{c}{r} + PutPerpetual\left[\frac{\bar{S}}{\delta}, \frac{c}{r} - k_s, \sigma, ln(1+r), ln(1+\delta)\right] - I \quad (17.12)$$

To solve for $\bar{S}$, we need to find the *present value* of equation (17.12), and then choose $\bar{S}$ to maximize this present value. For a given $\bar{S}$, equation (17.12) tells us the value of investing when $S = \overline{S}$. If the oil price today is $S < \overline{S}$, we can compute the present value of equation (17.12) using equation (12.14). The value will depend upon the current oil price (the lower the price, the longer it will take to hit $\overline{S}$), so we denote it as $V_{Invest}(S; \overline{S})$. This present value is

$$V_{Invest}(S; \overline{S}) = \left(\frac{S}{\overline{S}}\right)^{h_1}$$

$$\times \left(\frac{\overline{S}}{\delta} - \frac{c}{r} + PutPerpetual\left[\frac{\overline{S}}{\delta}, \frac{c}{r} - k_s, \sigma, ln(1+r), ln(1+\delta)\right] - I\right)$$

(17.13)

Equation (17.13) can be maximized with respect to $\overline{S}$ using a spreadsheet or other numerical program.

Example 17.4   Suppose $\delta = 0.04$, $r = 0.05$, $\sigma = 0.15$, $c = \$8$, $k_s = \$0$, and $I = \$180$. If the current oil price, S, is $\$15$, then the value of $\overline{S}$ that maximizes equation (17.13) is $\$25.12$, and the value of the undeveloped well is $V_{Invest}(\$15, \$25.12) = \$95.13$. If $k_s = \$25$, then $\overline{S} = \$25.21$ and the value of the undeveloped well is $\$94.93$.

If we increase the current oil price to $S = \$20$, then the value of the undeveloped well increases to $\$177.01$ when $k_s = \$0$ and $\$176.64$ when $k_s = \$25$. $\overline{S}$ is the same as when $S = \$15$.   ≷

This example illustrates some key points. First, as discussed earlier, the ability to shut down reduces the investment trigger, from $\$25.34$ with no shutting down, to $\$25.12$ with shutting down. Second, if there is a cost of shutting down, shutting down occurs at a lower price and provides less protection. This mitigates the benefit of shutting down, raising the shutdown trigger to $\$25.21$. Finally, a point that may be obvious but is important to understand: The investment trigger implied by maximizing equation (17.13) is independent of S, the current oil price. To see why, suppose that $\overline{S} = \$25$. If $S = \$15$, it must pass $\$20$ before reaching $\$25$. Thus, if we evaluate the option when $S = \$20$, we must obtain the same $\overline{S}$ as when $S = \$15$. Thus, $\overline{S}$ is independent of S.

Restarting Production

The preceding example assumed that the firm could never restart once it had shut down. In this section we examine the restart strategy if the firm could restart after it permanently had shut down.

Suppose the firm can pay k_r to restart production. The ability to restart is a call option in which the firm receives S/δ by paying $c/r + k_r$, future production costs plus the restart cost.

Example 17.5   The value of a shutdown well is

$$CallPerpetual\left[\frac{S}{\delta}, \frac{c}{r} + k_r, \sigma, log(1+r), log(1+\delta)\right]$$

Assuming that $S = \$10$, $\delta = 0.04$, $r = 0.05$, $\sigma = 0.15$, $c = \$8$, and $k_r = \$0$, the option pricing formula gives us the value of the well as $94.46 and $11.92 as the price at which to restart.   ❧

The ability to restart affects the decision to shut down. When we shut down, we not only cut off future losses but *we also acquire a call option to restart*. In equation (17.13) we acquired a put option when we invested, so in this case we acquire a call option when we exercise the put option! And when we invest in the first place, we acquire the put option to shut down, but the value of that put now implicitly contains the call option to restart. The solution for this problem appears in Appendix 17.B.

Additional Options

The firm might be able to restart and shut down production many times. We can determine triggers and solve for the value of the well by following the strategy in the previous sections. Details of the solution are in Appendix 17.B.

Table 17.1 summarizes the price triggers for several different cases. The qualitative results are intuitive. As with any American option, we require that the oil well have positive NPV before we invest—we are reluctant to kill the put option implicit in the option to take the project. If shutting down in the future is possible, there is an additional put option available besides that from deferring investment, and we are willing to invest at a lower price. The addition of an option to restart once we have shut down makes us more willing to shut down, and, hence, more willing to invest. Adding costs to restarting and shutting down makes us more reluctant to restart, to shutdown, and, hence, to invest initially. More options generally mean more value and investment at a lower price; greater costs mean lower value and investment at a higher price.

The results in Table 17.1 illustrate a phenomenon called **hysteresis**, which Dixit (1989, p. 622) defines as "the failure of an effect to reverse itself as the underlying cause is reversed." Suppose that all oil producers have a marginal extraction cost of $8. The current oil price is $7, following a period in which it was $30, and there is a shutdown cost. Oil production is currently unprofitable, and we would not invest in new capacity at this price, but production from existing wells is not unprofitable enough to shut down production. We are in a situation where the cause (the oil price) reversed itself, but the effect (the creation of an oil well) did not. Oil producers lose money on an operating basis, but are not losing enough to shut down production.

Real-life investment decisions exhibit hysteresis. To illustrate hysteresis in a different context, Dixit (1989) considers investment decisions of a manufacturer with operations in a foreign country. Exchange rate fluctuations will change the profitability of the foreign investment. However, since investing and disinvesting are costly, it will

| TABLE 17.1 | Comparison of investment ($\bar{S}$), shutdown (S_*), and restart (S^*) triggers under different assumptions. k_s is the cost of shutting down the well and k_r is the cost of restarting once it is shut. In all cases, $r = 5\%$ and the lease rate is $\delta = 4\%$. |

Parameters			Number of Times		Triggers		
σ	k_s	k_r	Shutdown	Restart	$\bar{S}$	S_*	S^*
0.0	—	—	0	0	16.92	—	—
0.15	—	—	0	0	25.34	—	—
0.15	0	—	1	0	25.12	4.27	—
0.15	25	—	1	0	25.14	3.60	—
0.15	0	0	1	1	25.00	6.03	11.92
0.15	25	25	1	1	25.17	4.33	13.79
0.15	25	25	∞	∞	25.17	4.37	13.18

be optimal to wait until the investment is suffciently profitable before investing, and sufficiently unprofitable before disinvesting. What appear to be sluggish investment decisions may simply result from costs of undoing what has been done.

CHAPTER SUMMARY

Real options is the analysis of investment decisions taking into account the ability to revise future operating decisions. Examples of real options include timing options (the ability to choose when to make an investment), shutdown options (the ability to stop production in order to avoid losses), sequential investments where the decision to make later investments depends on the outcome of earlier investments (common in R&D), and natural resource extraction. Investment decisions in which such options are present can be analyzed using pricing tools from earlier chapters, such as the Black-Scholes model, perpetual options, binomial trees, and barrier present value calculations. In some cases the optimal decision is equivalent to the problem of when to exercise an American option. In general, however, as illustrated by the oil extraction problem, a simple option formulation is just a starting point for analysis.

Even when standard option pricing models are not directly applicable, understanding the economics of derivatives is helpful in understanding the economics of investment and operation decisions.

FURTHER READING

In later chapters we will encounter more general pricing techniques that expand our ability to solve real options problems. Early papers that used techniques from financial options to analyze real assets include Brennan and Schwartz (1985), McDonald and Siegel (1985), and McDonald and Siegel (1986). These papers study investment timing and the option to shut down and restart. Brennan (2000) insightfully summarizes the literature since then. There are several valuable books on real options, including Dixit and Pindyck (1994) and Trigeorgis (1996).

A number of papers have applied real options to understanding the real estate market. These include Titman (1985), Grenadier (1996), and Grenadier (1999).

Many firms use capital budgeting techniques more sophisticated than simple discounted cash flow. Triantis and Borison (2001) survey managers on their use of real options, identifying three categories of real options usage: As an analytical tool, as a language and framing device for investment problems, and as an organizational process. McDonald (2000) argues that the use of high hurdle rates in capital budgeting could be an approximate way to account for real options.

An excellent real options resource on the Web is **http://www.mbs.umd.edu/finance/atriantis/RealOptions.html.**

PROBLEMS

17.1. Suppose you have a project that will produce a single widget. Widgets today cost $1 and the project costs $0.90. The risk-free rate is 5%. Under what circumstances would you invest immediately in the project? What conditions would lead you to delay the project?

17.2. You have a project costing $1.50 that will produce *two* widgets, one each the first and second years after project completion. Widgets today cost $0.80 each, with the price growing at 2% per year. The effective annual interest rate is 5%. When will you invest? What is the value today of the project?

17.3. Consider again the project in Problem 2, only suppose that the widget price is unchanging and the cost of investment is declining at 2% per year. When will you invest? What is the value today of the project?

17.4. Consider the widget investment problem outlined in Section 17.1. Show the following in a spreadsheet.

    a. Compute annual widget prices for the next 50 years.

    b. For each year, compute the net present value of investing in that year.

    c. Discount the net present value for each year back to the present. Verify that investing when the widget price reaches $1.43 is optimal.

17.5. Again consider the widget investment problem in Section 17.1. Verify that with $S = \$50$, $K = \$30$, $r = 0.04879$, $\sigma = 0$, and $\delta = 0.009569$, the perpetual call price is $30.597 and exercise optimally occurs when the present value of cash flows is $152.957. What happens to the value of the project and the investment trigger when you change S? Why? What happens to the value of the project and the investment trigger when you increase volatility? Why?

17.6. The stock price of XYZ is $100. One million shares of XYZ (a negligible fraction of the shares outstanding) are buried on a tiny, otherwise worthless plot of land in a vault that would cost $50 million to excavate. If XYZ pays a dividend, you will have to dig up the shares to collect the dividend.

    a. If you believe that XYZ will never pay a dividend, what would you pay for the land?

    b. If you believe that XYZ will pay a liquidating dividend in 10 years, and the continuously compounded risk-free rate is 5%, what would you pay for the land?

    c. Suppose that XYZ has a 1% dividend yield and a volatility of 0.3. At what price would you excavate and what would you pay for the land?

17.7. Repeat Problem 6, only assume that after the stock is excavated, the land has an alternative use and can be sold for $30m.

17.8. Consider the widget investment problem of Section 17.1 with the following modification. The expected growth rate of the widget price is zero. (This means there is no reason to consider project delay.) Each period, the widget price will be $0.25 with probability 0.5 or $2.25 with probability 0.5. Each widget costs $1 to produce.

    a. What is the expected widget price?

    b. If the firm produces a widget each period, regardless of the price, what is the NPV of the widget project?

    c. If the firm can choose to produce widgets only when the widget price is greater than $1, what is the NPV?

    d. What happens to the NPV if widgets can cost $0.10 or $2.40 with equal probability?

17.9. Verify the binomial calculations in Figure 17.3.

17.10. A project costing $100 will produce perpetual net cash flows that have an annual volatility of 35% with no expected growth. If the project existed, net cash flows today would be $8. The project beta is 0.5, the effective annual risk-free rate is 5%, and the effective annual risk premium on the market is 8%. What is the static NPV of the project? What would you pay to acquire the rights to this project if investment rights lasted only 3 years? What would you pay to acquire perpetual investment rights?

17.11. A project has certain cash flows today of $1, growing at 5% per year for 10 years, after which the cash flow is constant. The risk-free rate is 5%. The project costs

$20 and cash flows begin 1 year after the project is started. When should you invest and what is the value of the option to invest?

17.12. Consider the oil project with a single barrel, in which $S = \$15, r = 5\%, \delta = 4\%$, and $X = \$13.60$. Suppose that, in addition, the land can be sold for the residual value of $R = \$1$ after the barrel of oil is extracted. What is the value of the land?

17.13. Verify in Figure 17.2 that if volatility were 30% instead of 50%, immediate exercise would be optimal.

17.14. Consider the last row of Table 17.1. What is the solution for S_* and S^* when $k_s = k_r = 0$? (This answer does not require calculation.)

In the following five problems, assume that the spot price of gold is \$300/oz, the effective annual lease rate is 3%, and the effective annual risk-free rate is 5%.

17.15. A mine costing \$275 will produce 1 ounce of gold on the day the cost is paid. Gold volatility is zero. What is the value of the mine?

17.16. A mine costing \$1000 will produce 1 ounce of gold per year forever at a marginal extraction cost of \$250, with production commencing 1 year after the mine opens. Gold volatility is zero. What is the value of the mine?

17.17. Repeat Problems 15 and 16 assuming that the annual volatility of gold is 20%.

17.18. Repeat Problem 16 assuming that the volatility of gold is 20% and that once opened, the mine can be costlessly shut down forever. What is the value of the mine? What is the price at which the mine will be shut down?

17.19. Repeat Problem 16 assuming that the volatility of gold is 20% and that once opened, the mine can be costlessly shut down once, and then costlessly reopened once. What is the value of the mine? What are the prices at which the mine will be shut down and reopened?

APPENDIX 17.A: CALCULATION OF OPTIMAL TIME TO DRILL AN OIL WELL

Single-Barrel Solution

It is optimal to defer investing as long as

$$\left(\frac{1}{1+r}\right)^h \left[S\left(\frac{1+r}{1+\delta}\right)^h - X \right] > S - X$$

which can be rewritten

$$\frac{S}{X} < \frac{1 - \left(\frac{1}{1+r}\right)^h}{1 - \left(\frac{1}{1+\delta}\right)^h}$$

The optimal solution entails taking the limit as $h \to 0$. Using L'Hôspital's rule we can show that $\lim_{h \to \infty} \frac{1-(1+r)^{-h}}{h} = ln(1+r)$. Hence,

$$\frac{1 - \left(\frac{1}{1+r}\right)^h}{1 - \left(\frac{1}{1+\delta}\right)^h} \to \frac{ln(1+r)}{ln(1+\delta)}$$

Thus, we defer investing as long as

$$\frac{S}{X} < \frac{ln(1+r)}{ln(1+\delta)}$$

In the text example this calculation gives \$16.918.

APPENDIX 17.B: THE SOLUTION WITH SHUTTING DOWN AND RESTARTING

In this appendix we explain the solution of two problems: Investing and operating (1) when it is possible to shut down once and restart once, permanently; and (2) when it is possible to shut down and restart an infinite number of times. The solutions here can be implemented numerically.

First we develop some notation. Let $V_U(S, m, n; *)$ represent the value of an undeveloped reserve and $V_O(S, m, n; *)$ and $V_C(S, m, n; *)$ the value of developed operating and developed closed reserves, where it is possible to shut down m times and restart n times. The $*$ denotes a dependence on the prices at which shutting and restarting is optimal. We will be using the formulas given by equations (12.14) and (12.15) for the value of \$1 when S reaches a barrier.

Single Shutdown and Restart

Prior to the final permanent restart at S^*, we have

$$V_C(S, 0, 1; S^*) = \left(\frac{S^*}{\delta} - \frac{c}{r} - k_r\right)\left(\frac{S}{S^*}\right)^{h_1} \tag{17.14}$$

We choose S^* to maximize this expression.

While operating, prior to the shutdown at $S > S_*$, we have

$$
V_O(S, 1, 1; S_*, S^*)
$$
$$
= \frac{S}{\delta} - \frac{c}{r} + \left[\frac{c}{r} - k_s - \frac{S_*}{\delta} + V_C(S_*, 0, 1; S^*)\right]\left(\frac{S}{S_*}\right)^{h_2} \tag{17.15}
$$

We choose S_* to maximize this expression, taking S^* as determined by equation (17.14).

Finally, prior to the original investment decision, which occurs at $\bar{S} > S$, the value of the well is

$$V_U(S, 1, 1; S_*, S^*) = \left[\frac{\bar{S}}{\delta} - \frac{c}{r} - I + V_C(S_*, 1, 1; S_*, S^*)\left(\frac{\bar{S}}{S_*}\right)^{h_2}\right]\left(\frac{S}{\bar{S}}\right)^{h_1} \tag{17.16}$$

We find the $\overline{S}$ that maximizes this equation, taking S_* and S^* as given, determined by maximizing equations (17.14) and (17.15).

Infinite Shutdown and Restart

The solution here is conceptually like that in the single shutdown and restart case, except that when we restart, we receive the option to shut down. Thus, when the well is shut, we have

$$V_C(S, \infty, \infty; S_*, S^*)$$
$$= \left[\frac{S^*}{\delta} - \frac{c}{r} - k_r + V_O(S^*, \infty, \infty; S_*, S^*)\right]\left(\frac{S}{S^*}\right)^{h_1} \tag{17.17}$$

While operating, prior to the shutdown at $S > S_*$, we have

$$V_O(S, \infty, \infty; S_*, S^*)$$
$$= \frac{S}{\delta} - \frac{c}{r} + \left[\frac{c}{r} - k_s - \frac{S_*}{\delta} + V_C(S_*, \infty, \infty; S_*, S^*)\right]\left(\frac{S}{S_*}\right)^{h_2} \tag{17.18}$$

Note that V_C and V_O are defined in terms of each other. We can substitute equation (17.17) into equation (17.18) and set $S = S_*$. This gives

$$V_O(S^*, \infty, \infty; S_*, S^*) = \frac{S^*/\delta - c/r - k_r + (c/r - S_*/\delta - k_s) \times (S^*/S_*)^{h_2}}{1 - (S_*/S^*)^{h_1} \times (S^*/S_*)^{h_2}} \tag{17.19}$$

Given starting values of S^* and S_*, we can evaluate equation (17.19), substituting the answer into equation (17.17) to obtain an estimate of $V_C(S, \infty, \infty; S_*, S^*)$. Then we can maximize equation (17.17) with respect to S^* and equation (17.18) with respect to S_*. This gives us new estimates of $V_C(S_*)$ and $V_O(S^*)$. Iterate until convergence. Once we have computed S^*, S_*, and $V_C(S_*)$, the value of the well is

$$V_U(S, \infty, \infty; S_*, S^*) = \left[\frac{\overline{S}}{\delta} - \frac{c}{r} - I + V_C(S_*, \infty, \infty; S_*, S^*)\left(\frac{\overline{S}}{S_*}\right)^{h_2}\right]\left(\frac{S}{\overline{S}}\right)^{h_1} \tag{17.20}$$

We maximize this with respect to $\overline{S}$ to find the investment trigger and value of the well.

PART 5

ADVANCED PRICING THEORY

This part of the book provides an introduction to the mathematical underpinnings of the Black-Scholes approach to pricing derivatives. The standard derivation of the Black-Scholes model has two components: An assumption about how the stock price behaves, and the idea that prices are determined by competitive delta-hedging market-makers.

Chapter 18 discusses the meaning of lognormality and illustrates how the form of the Black-Scholes model arises from straightforward lognormal probability calculations. Chapter 19 covers the Monte Carlo pricing method, which is a powerful and flexible technique widely used to price derivatives.

Black and Scholes assumed that stocks follow geometric Brownian motion and used a mathematical tool called Itô's Lemma to solve the problem they posed. These are discussed in Chapters 20 and 21. Chapter 21 in particular explains the derivation of the option formula and the sense in which the Black-Scholes approach applies to more than ordinary puts and calls. Chapter 22 continues the discussion of exotic options begun in Chapter 14.

Finally, Chapter 23 explains how the Black-Scholes option pricing methodology can be applied to analyze the pricing of bonds. Chapter 24 discusses the practical problems of measuring the risk of a portfolio containing options and provides an introduction to credit derivatives.

Chapter 18
The Lognormal Distribution

W e have seen that it is common in option pricing to assume the lognormality of asset prices. The purpose of this chapter is to explain the meaning of this assumption. We first review the normal distribution, which gives rise to the lognormal distribution. We then define lognormality and illustrate some common calculations based on lognormality. These calculations result in terms that look much like the parts of the Black-Scholes formula. Finally, we examine stock returns to see whether stock price data seem consistent with lognormality.

We will find that stock prices are not exactly lognormal. Nevertheless, the lognormal assumption is the basis for many frequently used pricing formulas. Moreover, it is difficult to understand more realistic models used in practice without first understanding models based on the lognormal distribution.

18.1 THE NORMAL DISTRIBUTION

A random variable, $\tilde{x}$, obeys the **normal distribution**—or is *normally distributed*—if the probability that $\tilde{x}$ takes on a particular value is described by the normal density function, which we represent by ϕ. The formula for the normal density function is[1]

$$\phi(x; \mu, \sigma) \equiv \frac{1}{\sigma\sqrt{2\pi}} e^{-\frac{1}{2}\left(\frac{x-\mu}{\sigma}\right)^2} \tag{18.1}$$

Notice in equation (18.1) that in order to calculate a value for ϕ, in addition to x, you need to supply two numbers: a mean, μ, and a standard deviation, σ. For this reason, the normal distribution is said to be a *two-parameter distribution*; it is completely described by the mean and the standard deviation.

Figure 18.1 graphs equation (18.1) for two different standard deviations (1 and 1.5), and for the same mean (0). The normal density with $\mu = 0$ and $\sigma = 1$ is called the *standard normal density*. When working with the standard normal density, we will write $\phi(x)$, without a mean and standard deviation.

Compared to the standard normal density, the normal density with $\sigma = 1.5$ assigns lower probabilities to values of x close to 0, and greater probabilities for x farther from 0. Increasing the variance spreads out the distribution. The mean locates the center of

---

[1]You can calculate the normal density in Excel using *NormDist(x,μ,σ,False)*.

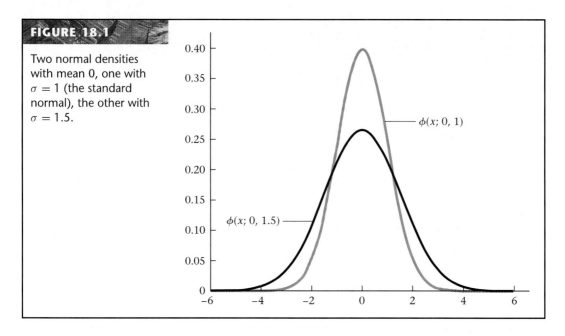

FIGURE 18.1

Two normal densities with mean 0, one with $\sigma = 1$ (the standard normal), the other with $\sigma = 1.5$.

the distribution, and the standard deviation tells you how spread out it is. The normal density is symmetric about the mean, μ, meaning that

$$\phi(\mu + x; \mu, \sigma) = \phi(\mu - x; \mu, \sigma)$$

If a random variable x is normally distributed with mean μ and standard deviation σ, we write this as

$$x \sim \mathcal{N}(\mu, \sigma^2)$$

We will use z to represent a random variable that has the standard normal distribution:

$$z \sim \mathcal{N}(0, 1)$$

We can use the normal distribution to compute the probability of different events, but we have to be careful about what we mean by an event. Since the distribution is continuous, there are an infinite number of events that can occur when we randomly draw a number from the distribution. (This is unlike the binomial distribution, in which an event can have only one of two values.) The probability of any *particular* number being drawn from the normal distribution is zero. Thus, we use the normal distribution to describe the probability that a number randomly selected from the normal distribution will be in a particular *range*.

We could ask, for example, what is the probability that if we draw a number from the standard normal distribution, it will be less than some number a? The area under the curve to the left of a, denoted $N(a)$, equals this probability, $Prob(z < a)$. We call $N(a)$ the **cumulative normal distribution function.** The integral from $-\infty$ to a is the area under the density over that range; it is cumulative in that it sums the probabilities from $-\infty$ to a. Mathematically, this is accomplished by integrating the standard normal density, equation (18.1) with $\mu = 0$ and $\sigma = 1$, from $-\infty$ to a:

$$N(a) \equiv \int_{-\infty}^{a} \frac{1}{\sqrt{2\pi}} e^{-\frac{1}{2}x^2} dx \qquad (18.2)$$

As an example, $N(0.3)$ is shown in Figure 18.2. In the top panel, $N(0.3)$ is the area under the normal density curve between $-\infty$ and 0.3. In the bottom panel, $N(0.3)$ is a point on the cumulative distribution. The range $-\infty$ to $+\infty$ covers all possible outcomes for a single draw from a normal distribution. The probability that a randomly drawn number will be less than ∞ is 1; hence, $N(\infty) = 1$. As you may already have surmised, the $N(a)$ defined above is the same $N(\ )$ used in computing the Black-Scholes formula.

There is no simple formula for the cumulative normal distribution function, equation (18.2), but as we mentioned in Chapter 12, it is a frequent-enough calculation that modern spreadsheets have it as a built-in function. (In Excel the function is called *NormSDist*.) The area under the normal density from $-\infty$ to 0.3 is 0.6179. Thus, if you

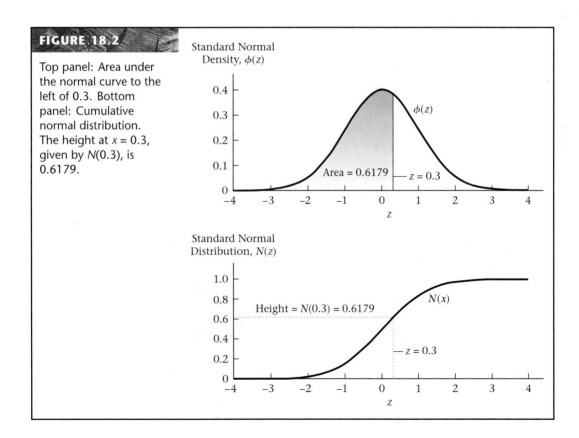

FIGURE 18.2

Top panel: Area under the normal curve to the left of 0.3. Bottom panel: Cumulative normal distribution. The height at $x = 0.3$, given by $N(0.3)$, is 0.6179.

draw a number from the standard normal distribution, 61.79% of the time the number you draw will be less than 0.3.

Suppose that we wish to know the probability that a number drawn from the standard normal distribution will be between a and $-a$. We have

$$Prob(z < -a) = N(-a)$$
$$Prob(z < a) = N(a)$$

These relationships imply that

$$Prob(-a < z < a) = N(a) - N(-a)$$

The area under the curve between $-a$ and a equals the difference between the area below a and the area below $-a$. Since the standard normal distribution is symmetric about 0, the area under the curve *above* a equals the area under the curve *below* $-a$. Thus,

$$N(-a) = 1 - N(a) \qquad (18.3)$$

Example 18.1   The probability that a number drawn from the standard normal distribution will be between -0.3 and $+0.3$ is

$$Prob(-0.3 < z < 0.3) = N(0.3) - N(-0.3)$$

The area under the curve between -0.3 and 0.3 equals the difference between the area below 0.3 and the area below -0.3. We have already seen that the area below 0.3 is 0.6179. Since the area under the entire curve is 1, the area *above* 0.6179 is $1 - 0.6179 = 0.3821$. Since $N(0.3) = 1 - N(-0.3)$, we have

$$Prob(-0.3 < z < 0.3) = N(0.3) - N(-0.3)$$
$$= N(0.3) - [1 - N(0.3)]$$
$$= 2 \times 0.6179 - 1 = 0.2358 \qquad ⬧$$

Finally, if a variable obeys the standard normal distribution, it is extremely unlikely to take on large positive or negative values. The probability that a single draw will be below -3 or above 3 is only 0.0027. If you drew from a standard normal distribution every day, you would draw above 3 or below -3 only about once a year. The probability of being below -4 or above 4 is 0.000063, which, with daily draws, would occur on average about once every 43.25 years.

Converting a Normal Random Variable to Standard Normal

If we have an arbitrary normal random variable, it is easy to convert it to standard normal. Suppose

$$x \sim \mathcal{N}(\mu, \sigma^2)$$

Then we can create a standard normal random variable, z, by subtracting the mean and dividing by the standard deviation:

$$z = \frac{x - \mu}{\sigma} \tag{18.4}$$

Using this fact, we can compute the probability that x is less than some number b:

$$
\begin{aligned}
Prob(x < b) &= Prob\left(\frac{x - \mu}{\sigma} < \frac{b - \mu}{\sigma}\right) \\
&= N\left(\frac{b - \mu}{\sigma}\right)
\end{aligned}
\tag{18.5}
$$

Using equation (18.3), the complementary probability is

$$
\begin{aligned}
Prob(x > b) &= 1 - Prob(x < b) \\
&= 1 - N\left(\frac{b - \mu}{\sigma}\right) \\
&= N\left(\frac{\mu - b}{\sigma}\right)
\end{aligned}
\tag{18.6}
$$

This result will be helpful in interpreting the Black-Scholes formula.

If we have a standard normal random variable z, we can generate a variable $x \sim \mathcal{N}(\mu, \sigma^2)$, using the following:

$$x = \mu + \sigma z \tag{18.7}$$

Example 18.2 Suppose that $x \sim \mathcal{N}(3, 25)$ and $z \sim \mathcal{N}(0, 1)$. Then

$$\frac{x - 3}{5} \sim \mathcal{N}(0, 1),$$

and

$$3 + 5 \times z \sim \mathcal{N}(3, 25) \qquad ❧$$

Sums of Normal Random Variables

Suppose we have n random variables x_i, $i = 1, \ldots, n$, with mean and variance $E(x_i) = \mu_i$, $Var(x_i) = \sigma_i^2$, and covariance $Cov(x_i, x_j) = \sigma_{ij}$. (The covariance between two random variables measures their tendency to move together. We can also write the covariance in terms of ρ_{ij}, the correlation between x_i and x_j: $\sigma_{ij} = \rho_{ij} \sigma_i \sigma_j$.) Then the weighted sum of the n random variables has mean

$$E\left(\sum_{i=1}^{n} \omega_i x_i\right) = \sum_{i=1}^{n} \omega_i \mu_i \tag{18.8}$$

and variance

$$Var\left(\sum_{i=1}^{n}\omega_i x_i\right) = \sum_{i=1}^{n}\sum_{j=1}^{n}\omega_i\omega_j\sigma_{ij} \qquad (18.9)$$

where ω_i and ω_j represent arbitrary weights. These formulas for the mean and variance are true for any distribution of the x_i.

In general, the distribution of the sum of random variables is different from the distribution of the individual random variables. However, the normal distribution is an example of a **stable distribution.** A distribution is stable if sums of random variables have the same distribution as the original random variables. In this case, the sum of normally distributed random variables is normal. Thus, for normally distributed x_i,

$$\sum_{i=1}^{n}\omega_i x_i \sim \mathcal{N}\left(\sum_{i=1}^{n}\omega_i\mu_i, \sum_{i=1}^{n}\sum_{j=1}^{n}\omega_i\omega_j\sigma_{ij}\right) \qquad (18.10)$$

A familiar special case of this occurs with the sum of two random variables:

$$ax_1 + bx_2 \sim \mathcal{N}\left(a\mu_1 + b\mu_2, a^2\sigma_1^2 + b^2\sigma_2^2 + 2ab\rho\sigma_1\sigma_2\right)$$

The central limit theorem   Why does the normal distribution appear in option pricing (and frequently in other contexts)? The normal distribution is important because it arises naturally when random variables are added. The normal distribution was originally discovered by mathematicians studying series of random events, such as gambling outcomes and observational errors.[2] Suppose, for example, that a surveyor is making observations to draft a map. The measurements will always have some error, and the error will differ from measurement to measurement. Errors can arise from observational error, imprecise use of the instruments, or simply from recording the wrong number. Whatever the reason, the errors will in general be accidental and, hence, *uncorrelated.* If you were using such error-prone data, you would like to know the statistical distribution of these errors in order to assess the reliability of your conclusions for a given number of observations, and also to decide how many observations to make to achieve a given degree of reliability. It would seem that the nature of the errors would differ depending on who made them, the kind of equipment used, and so forth. The remarkable result is that sums of such errors are approximately normal.

The normal distribution is therefore not just a convenient, aesthetically pleasing distribution, but it arises in nature when outcomes can be characterized as sums of independent random variables with a finite variance. The distribution of such a sum approaches normality. This result is known as the **central limit theorem.**[3]

---

[2]The history of statistics—including the story of the normal distribution—is entertainingly related in Bernstein (1996).

[3]Most statistics books discuss one or more versions of the central limit theorem. See, for example, DeGroot (1975, pp. 227–231) or Mood et al. (1974, pp. 233–236).

In the context of asset returns, the continuously compounded stock return over a year is the sum of the daily continuously compounded returns. If news and other factors are the shocks that cause asset prices to change, and if these changes are independent, then it is natural to think that longer-period continuously compounded returns are normally distributed. Since the central limit theorem is a theorem about what happens in the limit, sums of just a few random variables may not appear normal. But the normality of continuously compounded returns seems like a reasonable starting point in thinking about stock returns.

18.2 THE LOGNORMAL DISTRIBUTION

A random variable, y, is said to be **lognormally distributed** if $ln(y)$ is normally distributed. Put another way, if x is normally distributed, y is lognormal if it can be written in either of two equivalent ways:

$$ln(y) = x$$

or

$$y = e^x$$

This last equation is the link between normally distributed continuously compounded returns and lognormality of the stock price.

By definition, the continuously compounded return from 0 to t is

$$R(0, t) = ln(S_t/S_0) \tag{18.11}$$

Suppose $R(0, t)$ is normally distributed. By exponentiating both sides, we obtain

$$S_t = S_0 e^{R(0,t)} \tag{18.12}$$

Exponentiation converts the continuously compounded return, $R(0, t)$, into one plus the effective total return from 0 to t, $e^{R(0,t)}$. Notice that because S_t is created by exponentiation of $R(0, t)$, *a lognormal stock price cannot be negative.* Since by assumption $R(0, t)$ in equation (18.11) is normal, S_t in equation (18.12) is lognormal. Saying that continuously compounded returns are normal is *equivalent* to saying that the stock price is lognormal.

We saw that the sum of normal variables is normal. For this reason, the *product* of lognormal random variables is lognormal. If x_1 and x_2 are normal, then $y_1 = e^{x_1}$ and $y_2 = e^{x_2}$ are lognormal. The product of y_1 and y_2 is

$$y_1 \times y_2 = e^{x_1} \times e^{x_2} = e^{x_1+x_2}$$

Since $x_1 + x_2$ is normal, $e^{x_1+x_2}$ is lognormal. Thus, because normality is preserved by addition, lognormality is preserved by multiplication. However, just as the product of normal random variables is not normal, the sum of lognormal random variables is not lognormal.

We saw in Section 11.3 that the binomial model generates a stock price distribution that appears lognormal; this was an example of the central limit theorem. In the binomial model, the continuously compounded stock return is binomially distributed. Sums of binomial random variables approach normality. Thus, in the binomial model, the continuously compounded return approaches normality.

If $ln(y) \sim \mathcal{N}(m, v^2)$, the lognormal density function is given by

$$g(y; m, v) \equiv \frac{1}{yv\sqrt{2\pi}} e^{-\frac{1}{2}\left(\frac{ln(y)-m}{v}\right)^2}$$

One interpretation is that $y = S_t/S_0$ is the effective t-period return, and the continuously compounded return, $ln(S_t/S_0)$, is normally distributed:

$$ln(S_t/S_0) \sim \mathcal{N}(m, v^2)$$

We will interpret S_t as a stock price at some point in the future: a day, a week, or a year. In that context, m and v will be the daily, weekly, or annual mean and standard deviation of the continuously compounded return. This interpretation will become clearer shortly.

Figure 18.3 is a graph of the lognormal distribution as a function of y, assuming $\mu = 0$, and for both $\sigma = 1$ and $\sigma = 1.5$. Notice that the lognormal distribution is non-negative and skewed to the right. Figure 18.3 is based upon exponentiating the distributions in Figure 18.1.

We can compute the mean and variance of a lognormally distributed random variable. If $x \sim \mathcal{N}(m, v^2)$, then the expected value of e^x is given by

$$\boxed{E(e^x) = e^{m+\frac{1}{2}v^2}} \tag{18.13}$$

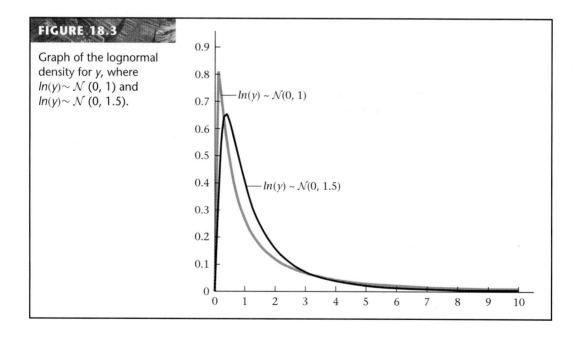

FIGURE 18.3

Graph of the lognormal density for y, where $ln(y) \sim \mathcal{N}(0, 1)$ and $ln(y) \sim \mathcal{N}(0, 1.5)$.

$ln(y) \sim \mathcal{N}(0, 1)$

$ln(y) \sim \mathcal{N}(0, 1.5)$

We prove this in Appendix 18.A, but it is intuitive that the mean of the exponentiated variable will be greater than the exponentiated mean of the underlying normal variable. Exponentiation is asymmetric: A positive random draw generates a bigger increase than an identical negative random draw does a decrease. To see this, consider a mean zero binomial random variable that is 0.5 with probability 0.5 and -0.5 with probability 0.5. You can verify that $e^{0.5} = 1.6487$, which is 0.6487 greater than one, while $e^{-0.5} = 0.6065, 0.3935$ less than one. Thus, $\frac{e^{0.5}+e^{-0.5}}{2} = \frac{1.6487+0.6065}{2} = 1.128$, which is obviously greater than $e^0 = 1$.

This is a specific example of **Jensen's inequality** (see Appendix C): The expectation of a function of a random variable is not generally equal to the function evaluated at the expectation of the random variable. In the context of this example, $E(e^x) \neq e^{E(x)}$. Since the exponential function is convex, Jensen's inequality implies that $E(e^x) > e^{E(x)}$. Derivatives theory is replete with examples of Jensen's inequality.

The variance of a lognormal random variable is

$$Var(e^x) = e^{2m+v^2} \left(e^{v^2} - 1 \right) \tag{18.14}$$

While it is possible to work with the variance of a lognormal variable, y, it is much more convenient to use only the variance of $ln(y)$, which is normal. We will do so exclusively in the rest of this book.

18.3 A LOGNORMAL MODEL OF STOCK PRICES

How do we implement lognormality as a model for the stock price? If the stock price S_t is lognormal, we can write

$$\frac{S_t}{S_0} = e^x$$

where x, the continuously compounded return from 0 to t, is normally distributed. We want to find a specification for x that provides a *useful* way to think about stock prices.

Represent the continuously compounded return from time t to some later time s as $R(t, s)$. Suppose we have times $t_0 < t_1 < t_2$. By the definition of the continuously compounded return, we have

$$S_{t_1} = S_{t_0} e^{R(t_0, t_1)}$$
$$S_{t_2} = S_{t_1} e^{R(t_1, t_2)}$$

The stock price at t_2 can therefore be expressed as

$$S_{t_2} = S_{t_1} e^{R(t_1, t_2)}$$
$$= S_{t_0} e^{R(t_0, t_1)} e^{R(t_1, t_2)}$$
$$= S_{t_0} e^{R(t_0, t_1)+R(t_1, t_2)}$$

Thus, the continuously compounded return from t_0 to t_2, $R(t_0, t_2)$, is the sum of the continuously compounded returns over the shorter periods:

$$R(t_0, t_2) = R(t_0, t_1) + R(t_1, t_2) \tag{18.15}$$

Example 18.3   Suppose the stock price is initially $100 and the continuously compounded return on a stock is 15% one year and 3% the next year. The price after 1 year is $100e^{0.15} = \$116.1834$, and after 2 years is $\$116.1834e^{0.03} = \$119.722$. This equals $100e^{0.15+0.03} = 100e^{0.18}$.   ❧

As we saw in Section 11.3, equation (18.15), together with the assumption that returns are independent and identically distributed over time, implies that the mean and variance of returns over different horizons are proportional to the length of the horizon. Take the period of time from 0 to T and carve it up into n intervals of length h, where $h = T/n$. We can then write the continuously compounded return from 0 to T as the sum of the n returns over the shorter periods:

$$R(0, T) = R(0, h) + R(h, 2h) + \cdots + R[(n-1)h, T]$$

$$= \sum_{i=1}^{n} R[(i-1)h, ih]$$

Let $E(R[(i-1)h, ih]) = \alpha_h$ and $Var(R[(i-1)h, ih]) = \sigma_h^2$. Then over the entire period, the mean and variance are

$$E[R(0, T)] = n\alpha_h \tag{18.16}$$

$$Var[R(0, T)] = n\sigma_h^2 \tag{18.17}$$

Thus, if returns are independent and identically distributed, *the mean and variance of the continuously compounded returns are proportional to time*. This result corresponds with the intuition that both the mean and variance of the return should be greater over long horizons than over short horizons.

Now we have enough background to present an explicit lognormal model of the stock price. Generally we will let t be denominated in years and α and σ be the annual mean and standard deviation, with δ the annual dividend yield on the stock. We will assume that the continuously compounded capital gain from 0 to t, $ln(S_t/S_0)$, is normally distributed with mean $(\alpha - \delta - 0.5\sigma^2)t$ and variance $\sigma^2 t$:

$$\boxed{ln(S_t/S_0) \sim \mathcal{N}[(\alpha - \delta - 0.5\sigma^2)t, \sigma^2 t]} \tag{18.18}$$

This gives us two equivalent ways to write an expression for the stock price.

First, recall from equation (18.7) that we can convert a standard normal random variable, z, into one with an arbitrary mean or variance by multiplying by the standard deviation and adding the mean. We can write

$$ln(S_t/S_0) = (\alpha - \delta - \frac{1}{2}\sigma^2)t + \sigma\sqrt{t}z \tag{18.19}$$

Second, we can exponentiate equation (18.19) to obtain an expression for the stock price:

$$S_t = S_0 e^{(\alpha - \delta - \frac{1}{2}\sigma^2)t + \sigma\sqrt{t}z} \qquad (18.20)$$

We will use equation (18.20) often in what follows.

You may be wondering how to interpret equations (18.18), (18.19), and (18.20). The subtraction of the dividend yield, δ, is necessary since, other things equal, a higher dividend yield means a lower future stock price. But why do we subtract $\frac{1}{2}\sigma^2$ in the mean?

To understand equation (18.20) it helps to compute the expected stock price. We can do this by breaking up the right-hand side of equation (18.20) into two terms, one of which contains the random variable z and the other of which does not:

$$S_t = S_0 e^{(\alpha - \frac{1}{2}\sigma^2)t} e^{\sigma\sqrt{t}z}$$

Next, evaluate the expectation of $e^{\sigma\sqrt{t}z}$ using equation (18.13). Since $z \sim \mathcal{N}(0, 1)$, we have

$$E\left(e^{\sigma\sqrt{t}z}\right) = e^{\frac{1}{2}\sigma^2 t}$$

This gives us

$$E(S_t) = S_0 e^{(\alpha - \delta - \frac{1}{2}\sigma^2)t} e^{\frac{1}{2}\sigma^2 t} \qquad (18.21)$$

or

$$E(S_t) = S_0 e^{(\alpha - \delta)t} \qquad (18.22)$$

The expression $\alpha - \delta$ is the expected continuously compounded rate of appreciation on the stock. If we did not subtract $\frac{1}{2}\sigma^2$ in equation (18.20), then the expected rate of appreciation would be $\alpha - \delta + \frac{1}{2}\sigma^2$. This is fine (we can define things as we like), except that it renders α difficult to interpret.

Thus, the issue is purely one of creating an expression where it is easy to interpret the parameters. If we want $\alpha - \delta$ to have an interpretation as the expected continuously compounded capital gain on the stock, then because of equation (18.13), we need to subtract $\frac{1}{2}\sigma^2$.

The median stock price—the value such that 50% of the time prices will be above or below that value—is obtained by setting $z = 0$ in equation (18.20). The median is thus

$$S_0 e^{(\alpha - \delta - \frac{1}{2}\sigma^2)t} = E(S_t)e^{-\frac{1}{2}\sigma^2 t}$$

This equation demonstrates that the median is below the mean. *More than 50% of the time, a lognormally distributed stock will earn below its expected return.* Perhaps more surprisingly, if σ is large, a lognormally distributed stock will lose money ($S_t < S_0$) more than half the time!

Example 18.4　Suppose that the stock price today is \$100, the expected rate of return on the stock is $\alpha = 10\%/\text{year}$, and the standard deviation (volatility) is $\sigma = 30\%/\text{year}$. If the stock is lognormally distributed, the continuously compounded 2-year return is 20% and the 2-year volatility is $0.30 \times \sqrt{2} = 0.4243$. Thus, we have

$$S_2 = \$100 e^{(0.1-\frac{1}{2}0.3^2)\times 2 + \sigma\sqrt{2}z}$$

The expected value of S_2 is

$$E(S_2) = \$100 e^{(0.1\times 2)} = \$122.14$$

The median stock price is

$$\$100 e^{(0.1-0.5\times 0.3^2)\times 2} = \$111.63$$

If the volatility were 60%, the expected value would still be \$122.14, but the median would be

$$\$100 e^{(0.1-0.5\times 0.6^2)\times 2} = \$85.21$$

Half the time, after 2 years the stock price would be below this value.　❧

We can also address the question of what a "one standard deviation move" in the stock price means. Since z has the standard normal distribution, then if $z = 1$, the continuously compounded stock return is the mean plus one standard deviation, and if $z = -1$, the continuously compounded stock return is the mean minus one standard deviation.

Example 18.5　Using the same assumptions as in Example 18.4, a one standard deviation move up over 2 years is given by

$$S_2 = \$100 e^{(0.1-\frac{1}{2}0.3^2)\times 2 + \sigma\sqrt{2}\times 1} = \$170.62$$

A one standard deviation move down is given by

$$S_2 = \$100 e^{(0.1-\frac{1}{2}0.3^2)\times 2 - \sigma\sqrt{2}\times 1} = \$73.03$$

We can think of these prices as logarithmically centered around the mean price of \$122.14.

This discussion also shows us where the binomial models in Chapter 11 come from. In Section 11.3, we presented three different ways to construct a binomial model. All had up and down stock price moves of the form

$$S_u = S e^{\alpha h + \sigma\sqrt{h}}; \quad S_d = S e^{\alpha h - \sigma\sqrt{h}}$$

where α differed for the three models. In all cases, we generated up and down moves by setting $z = \pm 1$. As $h \to 0$ the three models converge; the effects of the different α's in the three cases are offset by the different risk-neutral probabilities.

18.4 LOGNORMAL PROBABILITY CALCULATIONS

If S_t is lognormally distributed, we can use this fact to compute a number of probabilities and expectations. For example, we can compute the probability that an option will expire in the money, and, given that it expires in the money, the expected stock price. In this section we will present formulas for these calculations.

Probabilities

If the stock price today is S_0, what is the probability that $S_t < K$, where K is some arbitrary number? Note that $S_t < K$ exactly when $ln(S_t) < ln(K)$. Since $ln(S)$ is normally distributed, we can just use the normal calculations we developed above. We have

$$ln(S_t/S_0) \sim \mathcal{N}[(\alpha - \delta - 0.5\sigma^2)t, \sigma^2 t]$$

or, equivalently,

$$ln(S_t) \sim \mathcal{N}\left[ln(S_0) + (\alpha - \delta - 0.5\sigma^2)t, \sigma^2 t\right]$$

We can create a standard normal number random variable, z, by subtracting the mean and dividing by the standard deviation:

$$z = \frac{ln(S_t) - ln(S_0) - (\alpha - \delta - 0.5\sigma^2)t}{\sigma\sqrt{t}}$$

We have $Prob(S_t < K) = Prob[ln(S_t) < ln(K)]$. Subtracting the mean from both $ln(S_t)$ and $ln(K)$ and dividing by the standard deviation, we obtain

$$Prob(S_t < K) =$$
$$Prob\left[\frac{ln(S_t) - ln(S_0) - (\alpha - \delta - 0.5\sigma^2)t}{\sigma\sqrt{t}} < \frac{ln(K) - ln(S_0) - (\alpha - \delta - 0.5\sigma^2)t}{\sigma\sqrt{t}}\right]$$

Since the left-hand side is a standard normal random variable, the probability that $S_t < K$ is

$$Prob(S_t < K) = Prob\left[z < \frac{ln(K) - ln(S_0) - (\alpha - \delta - 0.5\sigma^2)t}{\sigma\sqrt{t}}\right]$$

Since $z \sim \mathcal{N}(0, 1)$, $Prob(S_t < K)$ is

$$Prob(S_t < K) = N\left[\frac{ln(K) - ln(S_0) - (\alpha - \delta - 0.5\sigma^2)t}{\sigma\sqrt{t}}\right]$$

This can also be written

$$Prob(S_t < K) = N(-\hat{d}_2) \tag{18.23}$$

where $\hat{d}_2$ is the standard Black-Scholes argument (see equation (12.1)) with the risk-free rate, r, replaced with the actual expected return on the stock, α. We can also perform the complementary calculation. We have $Prob(S_t > K) = 1 - Prob(S_t < K)$, so

$$Prob(S_t > K) = N(\hat{d}_2) \tag{18.24}$$

The expression $N(\hat{d}_2)$ contains the true expected return on the stock, α. If we replace α with r, the risk-free rate in equations (18.23) and (18.24), we obtain the risk-neutral probabilities that S_t is above or below K. It is exactly these risk-neutral versions of equations (18.23) and (18.24) that appear in the Black-Scholes call and put option pricing formulas.

Lognormal Confidence Intervals

We can ask questions about future prices, such as "what is the range of prices such that there is a 95% probability that the stock price will be in that range 1 year from today?" We can answer this question by computing the 95% confidence interval for a number of different time horizons.

Suppose we would like to know the prices S_t^L and S_t^U such that $Prob(S_t^L < S_t) = p/2$ and $Prob(S_t^U > S_t) = p/2$. If the stock price is S_0, we can generate S_t^L and S_t^U as follows. We know from equation (18.23) that

$$Prob(S < S_t^L) = N(-\hat{d}_2)$$

where

$$\hat{d}_2 = [ln(S_0/S_t^L) + (\alpha - \delta - 0.5\sigma^2)t]/\sigma\sqrt{t}$$

Thus, we want to find the S_t^L such that the probability that S_t is less than S_t^L is $p/2$, or

$$p/2 = N(-\hat{d}_2)$$

In order to do this, we need to invert the cumulative standard normal distribution function, i.e., ask what number $\hat{d}_2$ corresponds to a given probability. We can write this inverse cumulative normal probability function as $N^{-1}(p)$. Then by definition, $N^{-1}[N(x)] = x$. Fortunately, this is a standard calculation, and Excel and other spreadsheets contain a built-in function that does this. (In Excel it is *NormSInv.*) We have

$$N^{-1}(p/2) = -d_2$$

Solving explicity for S_t^L gives us

$$S_t^L = S_0 e^{(\alpha - \delta - \frac{1}{2}\sigma^2)t + \sigma\sqrt{t}N^{-1}(p/2)}$$

Similarly, we solve for the S_t^U such that

$$N^{-1}(p/2) = \hat{d}_2$$

This gives us

$$S_t^U = S_0 e^{(\alpha - \delta - \frac{1}{2}\sigma^2)t - \sigma\sqrt{t}N^{-1}(p/2)}$$

Thus, to generate a confidence interval for a lognormal price, we need only find the values of z corresponding to the same confidence interval for a $N(0, 1)$ variable, and then substitute those values into the expression for the lognormal price.

Example 18.6 If $p = 5\%$, $N^{-1}(0.025) = -1.96$ and $N^{-1}(0.975) = 1.96$. That is, there is a 5% probability that a standard normal random variable will be outside the range $(-1.96, 1.96)$. Thus, if $S_0 = \$100$, $t = 2$, $\alpha = 0.10$, $\delta = 0$, and $\sigma = 0.30$, we have

$$S_t^L = S_0 e^{(\alpha - \delta - \frac{1}{2}\sigma^2)t - \sigma\sqrt{t}1.96}$$

$$= S_0 e^{(0.10 - \frac{1}{2}0.3^2) \times 2 - 0.3 \times \sqrt{2} \times 1.96}$$

$$= \$48.599$$

Similarly, for S_t^U we have

$$S_t^U = S_0 e^{(\alpha - \delta - \frac{1}{2}\sigma^2)t + \sigma\sqrt{t}1.96}$$

$$= \$256.40$$

⚜

Example 18.7 Suppose we have a lognormally distributed \$50 stock with a 15% continuously compounded expected rate of return, a zero dividend yield, and a 30% volatility. Consider a horizon of 1 month ($t = \frac{1}{12}$). The monthly continuously compounded mean return is

$$(\alpha - \delta - \frac{1}{2}\sigma^2)t = \left(0.15 - 0 - \frac{1}{2}0.3^2\right)\frac{1}{12}$$

$$= 0.00875$$

and the monthly standard deviation is

$$\sigma\sqrt{t} = 0.3\sqrt{\frac{1}{12}}$$

$$= .0866$$

For the standard normal distribution, there is a 68.27% probability of drawing a number in the interval $(-1, +1)$, and a 95.45% probability of drawing a number in the interval $(-2, +2)$. Thus, over a 1-month horizon, there is a 68.27% chance that the continuously

| TABLE 18.1 | Stock prices (\$) corresponding to -2, -1, 1, and 2 standard deviations from the inital stock price of 50. | | | | |

Horizon	Fraction of a Year	-2σ	-1σ	$+1\sigma$	$+2\sigma$
1 Day	0.0027	48.47	49.24	50.81	51.61
1 Month	0.0849	42.35	46.22	55.06	60.09
1 Year	1	30.48	41.14	74.97	101.19
2 Years	2	26.40	40.36	94.28	144.11
5 Years	5	22.10	43.22	165.31	323.33

compounded return on the stock will be $0.00875 \pm .0866$ (i.e., the return is between -7.88% and 9.54%), and a 95.45% chance that the return will be $0.00875 \pm 2 \times 0.0866$ (the return will be between -16.44% and 18.19%):

$$-.0788 \quad \le \quad \ln\left(\frac{S_{one\ month}}{50}\right) \le 0.0954 \qquad prob = 68.27\%$$

$$-.1644 \quad \le \quad \ln\left(\frac{S_{one\ month}}{50}\right) \le 0.1819 \qquad prob = 95.45\%$$

Equivalently, by exponentiating all of these terms (for example, $\$50e^{-0.0788} = \$46.22$, $e^{\ln\left(\frac{S_{one\ month}}{50}\right)} = \frac{S_{one\ month}}{50}$, etc.), we can express the confidence interval in terms of prices

$$\$46.22 \le S_{one\ month} \le \$55.06 \qquad prob = 68.27\%$$
$$\$42.35 \le S_{one\ month} \le \$62.09 \qquad prob = 95.45\%$$

Using this same logic, we can compute one standard deviation and two standard deviation intervals over different horizons. This will give us 68.27% and 95.45% confidence intervals over those horizons, which are displayed in Table 18.1.

Notice in Table 18.1 that there is a 95.45% chance over a 1-day horizon that a \$50 stock will be between \$48.47 and \$51.61. Over a 5-year horizon, there is a 95.45% chance that the stock price will be between \$22.10 and \$323.33. The assumption of lognormality implies this kind of band of uncertainty around future stock prices.   ⧧

The calculation in Example 18.7 is often used to compute loss probabilities and risk exposure. We will see in Chapter 24 that this is how value at risk (VaR) is calculated. The idea behind VaR is to assess the magnitude of a possible loss on a position that can occur with a given probability over a given horizon. So, for example, if we examine the 1-day horizon in Table 18.1, there is a 2.275% probability that over a 1-day horizon the stock price will drop below $48.47.[4] In practice, it is common to evaluate the magnitude of moves of 1.96σ since this corresponds to a 5% ("once in 20 days") probability of occurrence.

The box on page 582 illustrates how the probability calculations in this section can be used to analyze the cost of portfolio insurance over time, previously discussed in Chapter 9.

The Conditional Expected Price

Given that an option expires in the money, what is the expected stock price? The answer to this question is the *conditional* expected stock price. For a put with strike price K, we want to calculate $E(S_t | S_t < K)$, the stock price conditional on $S_t < K$. To compute this expectation, we need to take into account only the portion of the probability density representing stock prices below K.

To understand the calculations we are going to perform in this section, consider a binomial model in which the strike price is $50, and the stock price at expiration can be $20, $40, $60, or $80, with probabilities 1/8, 3/8, 3/8, and 1/8. If a put is in the money at expiration, the stock price is either $20 or $40. Suppose that for these two values we sum the stock price times the probability. We obtain

$$\sum_{S_t < 50} Prob(S_t) \times S_t = \left(\frac{1}{8} \times \$20 \right) + \left(\frac{3}{8} \times \$40 \right) = \$17.50 \tag{18.25}$$

The value $17.50 is clearly not an expected stock price since it is below the lowest possible price ($20). We call $17.50 the **partial expectation** of the stock price conditional upon $S_t < \$50$. When we compute a conditional expectation, we are conditioning upon the event $S_t < \$50$, which occurs with probability 0.5. We can convert a partial expectation into a conditional expectation by dividing by the probability of the conditioning event ($S_t < \$50$). Thus, the conditional expectation is

$$\frac{1}{Prob(S_t < 50)} \sum_{S_t < 50} Prob(S_t) \times S_t = \frac{1}{0.5} \left[\left(\frac{1}{8} \times \$20 \right) + \left(\frac{3}{8} \times \$40 \right) \right]$$

$$\tag{18.26}$$

$$= \$35$$

The calculations for a lognormally distributed price are analogous, using integrals rather than summations.

----

[4]You can verify the 2.275% probability by computing $N(-2)$.

Portfolio Insurance for the Long Run, Revisited

In the box on page 289, we discussed the result that the cost of insuring a stock portfolio so that it performs at least as well as a zero-coupon bond is increasing with the time to maturity of the insurance. The demonstration of this in Chapter 9 relies on the absence of arbitrage, which is incontrovertible but does not always provide intuition about the result. Using the results in this section, we can reconcile the historical low probability of stocks underperforming bonds with the increasing cost of insurance as we insure over a longer horizon.

The probability that $S_T < K$ is given by equation (18.23). By setting the strike price to equal the forward price, i.e., $K_T = S_0 e^{rT}$, we can use equation (18.23) to calculate the probability that stocks bought at time 0 will have underperformed bonds at time T. After simplification, equation (18.23) can be written

$$Prob(S_T < K_T) = N \left(\frac{\frac{1}{2}\sigma^2 - (\alpha - r)}{\sigma} \sqrt{T} \right)$$

Thus, if the stock is lognormally distributed, the probability of the stock underperforming a zero-coupon bond depends on the size of the risk premium on stocks, $\alpha - r$, relative to one-half the variance, $\frac{1}{2}\sigma^2$. If the risk premium is high, puts will be increasingly less likely to pay off in the long run, even though the put price is increasing with horizon.

The put price depends in part on the *risk-neutral* probability that the stock will underperform bonds, $Prob^*(S_T < K)$. This is obtained by setting $\alpha = r$, and we then have

$$Prob^*(S_T < K_T) = N \left(\frac{1}{2}\sigma \sqrt{T} \right)$$

The *risk-neutral* probability that the put will pay off is increasing with time. The probability increasing with time does not by itself explain the price of the put increasing with time, since the put price also depends on the conditional expectation of the stock price when the put is in the money. However, this example does illustrate how historical *true* probabilities can mislead about the price of insurance.

The partial expectation of S_t, conditional on $S_t < K$, is

$$\int_0^K S_t g(S_t; S_0) dS_t = S_0 e^{(\alpha - \delta)t} N \left(\frac{ln(K) - [ln(S_0) + (\alpha - \delta + 0.5\sigma^2)t]}{\sigma \sqrt{t}} \right) \quad (18.27)$$

$$= S_0 e^{(\alpha - \delta)t} N(-\hat{d}_1)$$

where $g(S_t; S_0)$ is the probability density of S_t conditional on S_0, and $\hat{d}_1$ is the Black-Scholes d_1 (equation (12.1)) with α replacing r.

The probability that $S_t < K$ is $N(-\hat{d}_2)$. Thus, the expectation of S_t conditional on $S_t < K$ is

$$E(S_t | S_t < K) = Se^{(\alpha-\delta)t} \frac{N(-\hat{d}_1)}{N(-\hat{d}_2)} \qquad (18.28)$$

For a call, we are interested in the expected price conditional on $S > K$. The partial expectation of S_t conditional on $S_t > K$ is

$$\int_K^\infty S_t g(S_t; S_0) dS_t = Se^{(\alpha-\delta)t} N\left(\frac{ln(S_0) - ln(K) + (\alpha - \delta + 0.5\sigma^2)t}{\sigma\sqrt{t}}\right) \qquad (18.29)$$

$$= S_0 e^{(\alpha-\delta)t} N(\hat{d}_1)$$

As before, except for the fact that it contains the expected rate of return on the stock, α, instead of the risk-free rate, the second term is just the Black-Scholes expression, $N(d_1)$. The conditional expectation is

$$E(S_t | S_t > K) = Se^{(\alpha-\delta)t} \frac{N(\hat{d}_1)}{N(\hat{d}_2)} \qquad (18.30)$$

The Black-Scholes Formula

Using equations (18.23), (18.24), (18.28), and (18.30), we can now heuristically derive the Black-Scholes formula. Recall that the Black-Scholes formula can be derived by assuming risk-neutrality. In this case, the expected return on stocks, α, will equal r, the risk-free rate. If we let g^* denote the risk-neutral lognormal probability density, E^* denote the expectation taken with respect to risk-neutral probabilities, and $Prob^*$ denote those probabilities, the price of a European call option on a nondividend-paying stock will be

$$C(S, K, \sigma, r, t, \delta) = e^{-rt} \int_K^\infty (S_t - K) g^*(S_t; S_0) dS_t$$

$$= e^{-rt} E^*(S - K | S > K) \times Prob^*(S > K)$$

We can rewrite this as

$$C(S, K, \sigma, r, t, \delta) = e^{-rt} E^*(S | S > K) \times Prob^*(S > K)$$
$$- e^{-rt} E^*(K | S > K) \times Prob^*(S > K)$$

Using (18.24) and (18.30), with $\alpha = r$, this becomes

$$C(S, K, \sigma, r, t, \delta) = e^{-\delta t} SN(d_1) - Ke^{-rt} N(d_2)$$

which is the Black-Scholes formula.

Similarly, the formula for a European put option on a nondividend-paying stock is derived by computing

$$P(S, K, \sigma, r, t, \delta) = e^{-rt} E^*(K - S | K > S) \times Prob^*(K > S)$$

We can rewrite this as

$$P(S, K, \sigma, r, t, \delta) = e^{-rt} E^*(K|K > S) \times Prob^*(K > S)$$
$$- e^{-rt} E^*(S|K > S) \times Prob^*(K > S)$$

and using (18.23) and (18.28), with $\alpha = r$, this becomes

$$P(S, K, \sigma, r, t, \delta) = Ke^{-rt} N(-d_2) - e^{-\delta t} SN(-d_1)$$

18.5 ESTIMATING THE PARAMETERS OF A LOGNORMAL DISTRIBUTION

In this section we will see how to estimate the mean and variance of lognormally distributed price data. In Section 18.6 we examine the empirical distribution of stock prices. It is easy to estimate parameters and perform statistical inference for normal random variables. So the question is: Are stocks in real life distributed lognormally?

The lognormal model we have described actually has two implications. First, over any horizon the continuously compounded return is normal. Second, the mean and variance of the continuously compounded returns grow proportionally with time.

When stocks are lognormally distributed, a price S_t evolves from the previous price observed at time $t - h$, according to

$$S_t = S_{t-h} e^{(\alpha - \delta - \sigma^2/2)h + \sigma \sqrt{h} z}$$

Suppose we have daily observations. How would we estimate the mean and standard deviation? We have

$$ln(S_t) = ln(S_{t-h}) + (\alpha - \delta - \sigma^2/2)h + \sigma \sqrt{h} z$$

Thus

$$E[ln(S_t/S_{t-h})] = (\alpha - \delta - \sigma^2/2)h$$

$$Var[ln(S_t/S_{t-h})] = \sigma^2 h$$

By using the log ratio of prices at adjacent points in time, we can compute the continuously compounded mean and variance. Note that to estimate α, we have to add $\frac{1}{2}$ the estimate of the variance to the estimate of the mean.

Example 18.8 Table 18.2 contains seven weekly stock price observations along with continuously compounded returns computed from those observations. You can compute the mean and standard deviation of the values in the third column (for example, using the *Average* and *Stdev* functions in Excel). Since these are weekly observations, we are estimating the *weekly* mean of the log price ratio and the *weekly* standard deviation. Here are the results:

TABLE 18.2   Hypothetical weekly stock price observations and corresponding weekly continuously compounded returns, $ln(S_t/S_t - 1)$.

Week	Price ($)	$ln(S_t/S_{t-1})$
1	100	—
2	105.04	0.0492
3	105.76	0.0068
4	108.93	0.0295
5	102.50	−0.0608
6	104.80	0.0222
7	104.13	−0.0064

	Result	×52	×$\sqrt{52}$	+$0.5\sigma^2$	Annualized
Mean	0.006745	0.3507	—	0.3887	38.87%
Std. Dev.	0.038208	—	0.2755	—	27.55%

The prices were actually generated randomly assuming using a standard deviation of 30% and a mean of 10%. Despite having only six observations, the standard deviation estimate is quite close to the true value of 30%. The estimated mean, however, is quite far off. ✿

We used hypothetical data in this example in order to compare the estimates to the true underlying parameters, something we cannot do with real data. As this example illustrates, mean returns are hard to estimate precisely because the mean is determined by the difference between where you start and where you end. If you start at a price of $100 and end at a price of $104, the in-between prices are irrelevant: If you had a big negative weekly return (say −20%) it must have been offset by a big positive return (on the order of +20%), or you would not have ended up at 104! Having many observations is not helpful in estimating means. What is helpful is having a long time interval, and seven weeks is not long.

Statistical theory tells us the precision of our estimate of the mean. With a normally distributed random variable, the standard deviation of the estimated mean is the standard deviation of the variable divided by the square root of the number of observations. The data in this example were generated using an actual weekly σ of $0.3/\sqrt{52} = 0.0416$. Divide this by $\sqrt{6}$ (since there are six return observations) to get 0.017. Thus, one standard deviation for our estimate of the mean is 1.7% on a weekly basis, or 12.25% annualized. There is a 68% probability that the annualized continuously compounded mean falls in the range 38% $\pm$ 12.25%! A 95% confidence interval is 38% $\pm$ 24.5%. This is a wide range. Even with 10 years of weekly data, one standard deviation for our estimated annualized mean would be $30\%/\sqrt{520} = 1.3\%$.

When we estimate a standard deviation, we are interested in the movement of the price. The more observations we have, the more precisely we can estimate movement. With six observations, an approximate 95% confidence interval for the standard deviation is approximately ± 18 percentage points.[5] With only 26 weekly observations, the 95% confidence interval shrinks to ± 8 percentage points. Moreover, unlike the mean, we can increase the precision of our estimate of the standard deviation by making more frequent observations. In general, standard deviations are easier to estimate than means.

In this discussion we have assumed that the variance is not changing over time. There is good evidence, however, that the variance does change over time, and sophisticated statistical methods can be used to estimate changing variances.

You should also be aware that, in practice, using data from very tiny intervals (e.g., hourly prices) may not increase precision. Over short time periods, factors such as bid-ask bounce—the movement of the price between the bid and ask spreads due to some orders being sells and others being buys—can introduce into prices noise that is not related to the values we are trying to measure.

18.6 HOW ARE ASSET PRICES DISTRIBUTED?

The lognormal model assumes that stock returns are independent over time (today's return does not affect future returns), that mean and volatility are constant over time, and that the distribution of continuously compounded returns is normal. However, we saw in Chapter 12 that implied volatilities differ for options with different strikes. One possible explanation is that stock prices are not lognormally distributed. How can we tell whether lognormality (or some other particular distribution) is a reasonable approximation for actual stock prices?

----

[5]The variability of the variance estimate is described by the chi-squared distribution. (The chi-squared distribution is the distribution of sums of squared independent standard normal variables; hence, it describes the distribution of the estimated variance when observations are independent.) Suppose we wish to test the null hypothesis that our variance estimate $s^2 = \sigma_0^2$ and that we have n observations. The variable $(n-1)s^2/\sigma_0^2$ has the chi-squared distribution with $n-1$ degrees of freedom. If we wish to perform a two-tailed test when we have six observations, the critical values for 0.975 and 0.025 confidence are 0.831 and 12.832. If our null hypothesis is that $\sigma_0^2 = 0.09$, then the 95% confidence interval is $0.01496 - 0.23097$. This corresponds to a range of standard deviations of $12.23\% - 48.06\%$, or approximately 30% $\pm$ 18%. The calculation for 26 observations is similar.

Histograms

One way to assess lognormality is simply to plot the continuously compounded returns as a histogram and see whether the resulting distribution appears normal. The top row of Figure 18.4 presents histograms for daily returns over a 10-year period for the S&P 500 index and for IBM. The bottom row is histograms for weekly returns. Also plotted on each graph is a normal distribution, computed using the historical mean and standard deviation for each return series.[6] Several observations are pertinent.

None of the histograms appears exactly normal. The shapes are typical for stock returns. All of the histograms exhibit a peak around zero; the presence or absence of this peakedness is referred to as kurtosis (a measure of how "sharp" the peak of the distribution is), and the graph displays "leptokurtosis" (lepto meaning "small, thin, delicate").[7] For a normally distributed random variable, kurtosis is 3. For the data plotted in Figure 18.4, kurtosis for the S&P and IBM are 8.03 and 9.54 for daily returns, and 4.68 and 5.21 for weekly returns. Accompanying the peaks are *fat tails*, large returns that occur more often than would be predicted by the lognormal model.

There are several possible explanations for returns appearing non-normal. One is that stock prices can jump discretely from time to time. We will discuss jumps in subsequent chapters. Another explanation is that returns are normally distributed, but with a variance that changes over time. If actual daily returns are drawn from a distribution that has a 1% volatility half the time and a 2% volatility half the time, the stock price histogram will appear fat-tailed. This blend of two distributions is commonly referred to as a **mixture of normals** model. Long-horizon returns, which result from summing short-horizon returns, will still appear normal.

Normal Probability Plots

Figure 18.5 presents normal probability plots for the same data as Figure 18.4. These plots are an alternative to histograms for assessing normality. We will examine normal probability plots as a tool for assessing normality and also to introduce a technique that we will encounter again in discussing Monte Carlo simulation.

The interpretation of these plots is straightforward: If the data points (plotted with a "+") lie along the straight line in the graph, the data are consistent with a normal distribution. If the data plot is curved, the data are less likely to have come from a normal distribution. In both cases it appears the data are not normal. There are too many points to the left of the line for low values and to the right of the line for high values.

----

[6]An equivalent approach would be to normalize returns by subtracting the estimated mean and dividing by the estimated standard deviation. The resulting series should then be standard normal if returns are truly lognormal.

[7]The kurtosis of a distribution is the fourth central moment (i.e., $E[(x - \mu)^4]$, where μ is the mean) divided by σ^4.

FIGURE 18.4

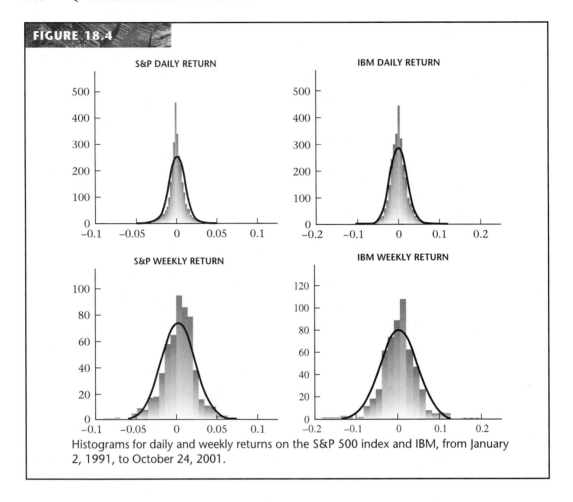

Histograms for daily and weekly returns on the S&P 500 index and IBM, from January 2, 1991, to October 24, 2001.

The interpretation of the plots is that extreme low and high returns occur more often than with a normal distribution.

For both the S&P index and IBM, the weekly returns appear more normal than daily returns, in that the observations more closely resemble the straight line. This is the relationship we would expect from the central limit theorem. Weekly returns are the sum of daily returns. If daily returns are independent and identically distributed, the summed daily returns will tend toward normality.

We will consider a simple example to see how a normal plot is constructed. First we have to define two concepts, *order statistics* and *quantiles*. Suppose that we randomly draw n random variables x_i, $i = 1, \ldots, n$, from some distribution with the cumulative distribution function $F(x)$. (For the normal distribution, $F(x) = N(x)$). If we sort the data in ascending order, the sorted data are called **order statistics.**

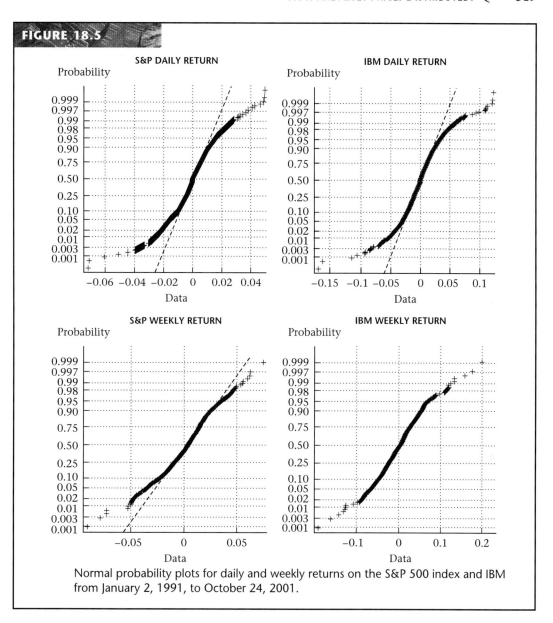

FIGURE 18.5

Normal probability plots for daily and weekly returns on the S&P 500 index and IBM from January 2, 1991, to October 24, 2001.

Example 18.9 Suppose we draw from a distribution five times and obtain the values {7, 3, 11, 5, 4}. The order statistics are {3, 4, 5, 7, 11}. 〰

The qth **quantile** of the distribution F is the smallest value x such that $F(x) \geq q$. In words, the qth quantile is the x such that there is at least probability q of drawing a value from the distribution less than or equal to x.

Example 18.10   Suppose z is standard normal. The 10% quantile is the value such that there is a 10% chance that a draw from the standard normal distribution is less than that number. Using the inverse cumulative distribution, $N^{-1}(0.10) = -1.282$. Thus, the 10% quantile is -1.281. The 30% quantile is $N^{-1}(0.3) = -0.524$.   ❧

The idea of the normal probability plot (which can be done for any distribution, not just normal) is to compare the quantiles of the data with the quantiles of the normal distribution. If they are the same, the normal probability plot is a straight line.

To see how this works, suppose we have the five values in Example 18.9. We want to assign quantiles to the data points, so with five data points we need five quantiles. Divide the range $0 - 100\%$ into $0 - 20\%$, $20\% - 40\%$, and so forth. Assign the order statistics (the ordered data points) to the midpoints of these ranges, so that 3 is assigned a quantile value of 10%, 4 a quantile value of 30%, 5 to 50%, 7 to 70%, and 11 to 90%.[8] The normal probability plot then graphs these points against the points from the corresponding quantiles of the standard normal distribution.

The top left panel of Figure 18.5 presents the normal plot for the data in Example 18.9 with the data points plotted against the corresponding z-values of the standard normal distribution. Appendix 18.B explains the construction of this plot. The top right panel is exactly the same, except that the y-axis is labeled with probabilities corresponding to the z-values. The data do not appear normal, though with only five points there is a large possibility for error.

The bottom row of Figure 18.6 presents normal probability plots with two different y-axes for 1000 randomly generated points from a $\mathcal{N}(0, 1)$ distribution. In this case the data lie along the line and, hence, appear normal. In all of the normal probability plots, the straight line is drawn connecting the 25% and 75% quantiles of the data.[9] In essence, the normal probability plot *changes the scale on the y-axis so the cumulative normal distribution is a straight line rather than an S-shaped curve.*

Volatility over Time

An assumption of the Black-Scholes model is that volatility is constant over time, or at least known in advance. Figure 18.7 displays the historical 40-day volatility for IBM

---

[8]With six data points, we would have assigned quantile ranges of $0 - 16.67$, $16.67 - 33.33$, etc., and the order statistics would then be assigned to the quantiles 8.333, 25, 41.67, etc.

[9]The straight line can be fitted in numerous ways; Matlab connects the quartiles. In the case of the sample data, the 10% and 30% quantiles are 3 and 4, so by interpolation the 25% quantile is 3.75. Similarly, the 70% and 90% quantiles are 7 and 11, so by interpolation the 75% quantile is 8.

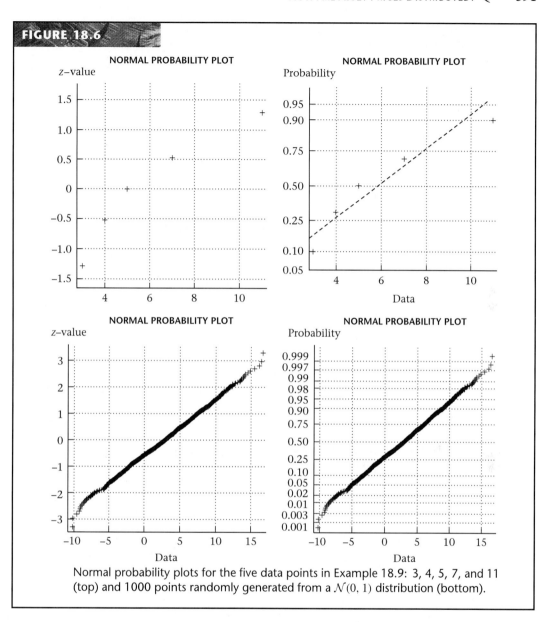

Normal probability plots for the five data points in Example 18.9: 3, 4, 5, 7, and 11 (top) and 1000 points randomly generated from a $\mathcal{N}(0, 1)$ distribution (bottom).

and the S&P 500 index from 1991 to 2001. Each day, the preceding 40 trading days are used to compute volatility. This procedure induces smoothness in the series, since each day shows up in 40 data points. Even so, there is a great deal of variability in the standard deviation, and for both series, volatility appears to have risen toward the end of the 1990s.

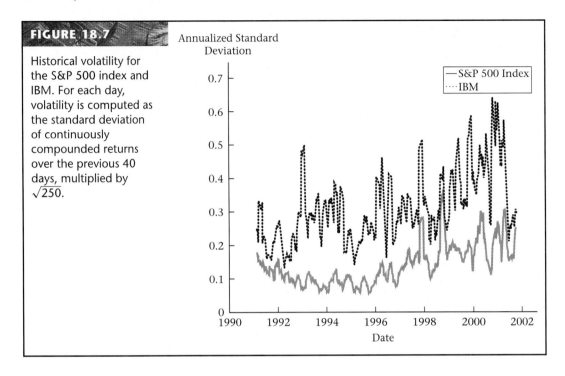

FIGURE 18.7

Historical volatility for the S&P 500 index and IBM. For each day, volatility is computed as the standard deviation of continuously compounded returns over the previous 40 days, multiplied by $\sqrt{250}$.

The variability of volatility creates a problem for the Black-Scholes model, and, as we saw in Chapter 13, a problem for delta-hedging market-makers.

CHAPTER SUMMARY

The normal distribution has these characteristics:

- It is symmetric; i.e., the right and left sides are mirror images of each other.
- It runs to plus and minus infinity, which means it is possible (albeit perhaps unlikely) that *any* number could occur when you draw from the distribution.
- It is unimodal; i.e., it has a single hump, which occurs at the mean.
- Sums of normal random variables are normal.

The lognormal distribution arises from assuming that continuously compounded returns are normally distributed. The lognormal distribution has these characteristics:

- It is skewed to the right.
- It runs from zero to plus infinity, which means that negative outcomes are impossible.
- It is unimodal (i.e., it has a single hump), which occurs to the left of the mean.

- Products of lognormal random variables are lognormal.

The Black-Scholes formula arises from a straightforward lognormal probability calculation using risk-neutral probabilities. The contribution of Black and Scholes was not the particular formula but rather the appearance of the risk-free rate in the formula.

From examining histograms and normal probability plots for daily and weekly continuously compounded returns, we can see that there are too many large returns relative to normally distributed returns. In addition, historical volatility varies over time. Although continuously compounded returns do not appear to be exactly normal, the Black-Scholes model and the accompanying assumption of lognormality is used frequently and we will continue to use and develop this model in the rest of the book. We will also explore extensions that are consistent with departures from normality we have seen in this chapter.

FURTHER READING

In Chapter 19 we will use simulation to price options assuming lognormal stock prices. We will also extend lognormality by allowing stock prices to jump discretely. In Chapter 20 we will introduce the continuous time model of stock returns used by Black and Scholes, which is the basis for modern option pricing and which, with their assumptions, generates lognormal stock prices.

Both the histogram and normal probability plot verify that continuously compounded returns in practice are not normally distributed. The question is whether this matters for pricing, and if so, how to modify the assumed price distributions and pricing formulas to obtain more accurate derivative prices. Two modifications we will examine in later chapters are to allow the stock to jump discretely and to permit volatility to be time varying.

An excellent discussion of the basic characteristics of stock returns is Campbell et al. (1997, Chapters 1 and 2). The history of the normal distribution is entertainingly recounted in Bernstein (1996). (See in particular the accounts of DeMoivre, Gauss, and Galton.)

PROBLEMS

18.1. You draw these five numbers randomly from a normal distribution with mean -8 and variance 15: $\{-7, -11, -3, 2, -15\}$. What are the equivalent draws from a standard normal distribution?

18.2. You draw these five numbers from a standard normal distribution: $\{-1.7, 0.55, -0.3, -0.02, .85\}$. What are the equivalent draws from a normal distribution with mean 0.8 and variance 25?

18.3. Suppose $x_1 \sim \mathcal{N}(1, 5)$ and $x_2 \sim \mathcal{N}(-2, 2)$. The covariance between x_1 and x_2 is 1.3. What is the distribution of $x_1 + x_2$? What is the distribution of $x_1 - x_2$?

18.4. Suppose $x_1 \sim N(2, 0.5)$, and $x_2 \sim N(8, 14)$. The correlation between x_1 and x_2 is -0.3. What is the distribution of $x_1 + x_2$? What is the distribution of $x_1 - x_2$?

18.5. Suppose $x_1 \sim N(1, 5)$, $x_2 \sim N(2, 3)$ and $x_3 \sim N(2.5, 7)$, with correlations $\rho_{1,2} = 0.3$, $\rho_{1,3} = 0.1$, and $\rho_{2,3} = 0.4$. What is the distribution of $x_1 + x_2 + x_3$? $x_1 + (3 \times x_2) + x_3$? $x_1 + x_2 + (0.5 \times x_3)$?

18.6. If $x \sim N(2, 5)$, what is $E(e^x)$? What is the median of e^x?

18.7. Suppose you observe the following month-end stock prices for stocks A and B:

	Day				
	0	**1**	**2**	**3**	**4**
Stock A	100	105	102	97	100
Stock B	100	105	150	97	100

For each stock:

  a. Compute the mean monthly continuously compounded return. What is the annual return?

  b. Compute the mean monthly standard deviation. What is the annual standard deviation?

  c. Evaluate the statement: "The estimate of the mean depends only on the beginning and ending stock prices; the estimate of the standard deviation depends on all prices."

For the following five problems, unless otherwise stated, assume that $S_0 = \$100$, $\alpha = 0.08$, $\sigma = 0.30$, and $\delta = 0$.

18.8. What is $Prob(S_t > \$105)$ for $t = 1$? How does this probability change when you change t? How does it change when you change σ?

18.9. What is $E(S_t | S_t > \$105)$ for $t = 1$? How does this expectation change when you change t, σ, and r?

18.10. What is $Prob(S_t < \$98)$ for $t = 1$? How does this probability change when you change t?

18.11. Let $t = 1$. What is $E(S_t | S_t < \$98)$? What is $E(S_t | S_t < \$120)$? How do both expectations change when you vary t from 0.05 to 5? Let $\sigma = 0.1$. Does either answer change? How?

18.12. Let $K_T = S_0 e^{rT}$. Compute $Prob(S_T < K_T)$ and $Prob(S_T > K_T)$ for a variety of Ts from 0.25 to 25 years. How do the probabilities behave? How do you reconcile your answer with the fact that *both* call and put prices increase with time?

18.13. Consider $Prob(S_t < K)$, equation (18.23), and $E(S_t|S_t < K)$, equation (18.28). Verify that it is possible to pick parameters such that changes in t can have ambiguous effects on $Prob(S_t < K)$ (experiment with very short and long times to maturity, and set $\alpha > 0.5\sigma^2$). Is the effect of t on $E(S_t|S_t < K)$ ambiguous?

18.14. Select a stock or index and obtain at least 5 years of daily or weekly data. Estimate the annualized mean and volatility, using all data and 1 year at a time. Compare the behavior of your estimates of the mean with those of the standard deviation.

18.15. Select a stock that has at least 5 years of daily data. Create data sets consisting of daily data and weekly data, Wednesday to Wednesday. (The *weekday* function in Excel will tell you the day of the week corresponding to a date. Wednesday is 4.) For both data sets, create a histogram of returns and a normal plot. Are the stock prices lognormal?

APPENDIX 18.A: THE EXPECTATION OF A LOGNORMAL VARIABLE

In this appendix we verify equation (18.13). Suppose that $y \sim \mathcal{N}(\mu, \sigma^2)$; hence, e^y is lognormally distributed. The normal distribution is given by

$$\phi(x; \mu, \sigma^2) \equiv \frac{1}{\sigma\sqrt{2\pi}} e^{-\frac{1}{2}\left(\frac{x-\mu}{\sigma}\right)^2}$$

Hence, we can directly compute the expectation:

$$E(e^y) = \int_{-\infty}^{\infty} e^x \frac{1}{\sigma\sqrt{2\pi}} e^{-\frac{1}{2}\left(\frac{x-\mu}{\sigma}\right)^2} dx$$

Collect the exponentiated terms under the integral. This gives us

$$E(e^y) = \int_{-\infty}^{\infty} \frac{1}{\sigma\sqrt{2\pi}} e^{-\frac{1}{2\sigma^2}[(x-\mu)^2 - 2\sigma^2 x]} dx \qquad (18.31)$$

Now focus on the exponentiated term in the square brackets. We have

$$\begin{aligned} (x-\mu)^2 - 2\sigma^2 x &= x^2 + \mu^2 - 2x(\mu + \sigma^2) \\ &= x^2 + (\mu + \sigma^2)^2 - 2x(\mu + \sigma^2) + \mu^2 - (\mu + \sigma^2)^2 \\ &= [x - (\mu + \sigma^2)]^2 - \sigma^4 - 2\mu\sigma^2 \end{aligned}$$

We can now substitute this expression into (18.31), obtaining

$$\begin{aligned} E(e^y) &= \int_{-\infty}^{\infty} \frac{1}{\sigma\sqrt{2\pi}} e^{-\frac{1}{2\sigma^2}([x-(\mu+\sigma^2)]^2 - \sigma^4 - 2\mu\sigma^2)} dx \\ &= e^{\mu + \frac{1}{2}\sigma^2} \int_{-\infty}^{\infty} \frac{1}{\sigma\sqrt{2\pi}} e^{-\frac{1}{2\sigma^2}([x-(\mu+\sigma^2)]^2)} dx \\ &= e^{\mu + \frac{1}{2}\sigma^2} \end{aligned}$$

The last equality follows because the integral expression is one: It is the total area under a normal density with mean $\mu + \sigma^2$ and variance σ^2. Thus we obtain equation (18.13).

Appendix 18.B: Constructing a Normal Probability Plot

This appendix discusses the details of constructing the normal probability plot for the data in Example 18.9. The idea of the normal probability plot is to compare the quantiles of the data with the corresponding quantiles of the normal distribution. Because the shape of the normal distribution is the same whatever the mean and variance, we know that the *relative* distance of normal quantiles will be the same for any normal distribution.[10] For a $\mathcal{N}(0, 1)$ distribution, the cumulative inverse distribution function tells us which x value corresponds to a particular quantile. For example $N^{-1}(0.1) = -1.282$ and $N^{-1}(0.3) = -0.524$. The distance between the x values that give rise to the data quantiles is

$$N^{-1}(0.3) - N^{-1}(0.1) = 0.757$$
$$N^{-1}(0.5) - N^{-1}(0.3) = 0.524$$
$$N^{-1}(0.7) - N^{-1}(0.5) = 0.524$$
$$N^{-1}(0.9) - N^{-1}(0.7) = 0.757$$

The lesser distance between quantiles closer to the median reflects the shape of the normal distribution. If the data come from a normal distribution, the relative distance between data points at these quantiles will have the same *relative* distances.

The procedure in creating Figure 18.6 is to plot the data points on the x-axis against the values from a $\mathcal{N}(0, 1)$ distribution with the same quantiles. Thus, we plot the data point with quantile q against $N^{-1}(q)$. In the case of the five sample data points, we plot the points $(3, -1.282)$, $(4, -.524)$, $(5, 0)$, $(7, 0.524)$ and $(11, 1.282)$. These points are plotted in the top left panel of Figure 18.6. The y-axis is labeled "z-value" since these are values from a standard normal distribution. The top right panel is exactly the same, except that the y-axis is labeled with probabilities corresponding to the z-values. The data do not appear normal, though with only five points there is a large possibility for error.

---

[10]For distributions with variable shapes, the relative distance between quantiles can vary with the parameters of the distribution. For this reason, probability plots work best for distributions where the shape is always the same but location (mean) and scale (variance) can vary.

Chapter 19

Monte Carlo Valuation

So far we have primarily discussed derivatives for which there is a (relatively simple) valuation formula, or which can be valued binomially. Another valuation technique in common use is **Monte Carlo valuation.** In Monte Carlo valuation we simulate future stock prices and then use these simulated prices to compute the discounted expected payoff of the option. The idea that an option price is a discounted expected value is familiar from our discussion of the binomial model in Chapter 11 and the Black-Scholes formula in Chapter 18.

Monte Carlo valuation is performed using the risk-neutral distribution, meaning that we assume assets earn the risk-free rate on average, and we then discount the expected payoff using the risk-free rate. We will see in this chapter that risk-neutral pricing is a cornerstone of Monte Carlo valuation; using the actual distribution instead would create a complicated discounting problem.

Since with Monte Carlo you simulate the possible future values of the security, as a byproduct you generate the *distribution* of payoffs. The distribution can be extremely useful when you want to compare two investment strategies that have different distributions of outcomes. Computing value-at-risk for complicated portfolios is a common use of Monte Carlo.

In this chapter we will see why risk-neutral valuation is important for Monte Carlo, see how to produce normal random numbers, discuss the speed of Monte Carlo, introduce the Poisson distribution to help account for nonlognormal patterns in the data, and see how to create correlated random stock prices.

19.1 COMPUTING THE OPTION PRICE AS A DISCOUNTED EXPECTED VALUE

The concept of risk-neutral valuation is familiar from the discussion of the binomial model in Chapters 10 and 11. We saw that option valuation can be performed *as if* all assets earned the risk-free rate of return and investors performed all discounting at this rate. Monte Carlo valuation exploits this insight. We *assume* that assets earn the risk-free rate of return and simulate their returns. For example, for any given stock price 3 months from now, we can compute the payoff on a call. We perform the simulation many times and average the outcomes. Since we use risk-neutral valuation, we then discount the average payoff at the risk-free rate in order to arrive at the price.

As a practical matter, Monte Carlo valuation depends critically on risk-neutral valuation. In order to see why this is so, we will compute an option price as an expected value with both risk-neutral and true probabilities, using an example we discussed in Chapters 10 and 11.

Figure 19.1 displays a binomial tree from Chapter 10. We saw in Chapter 18 that the Black-Scholes formula can be derived as an expected value using lognormal probability calculations; we can do the same thing with a binomial tree, using either risk-neutral or true probabilities. With the risk-neutral tree, we compute the expected value at expiration and then discount the average payoff using the risk-free rate. However, when we use

FIGURE 19.1

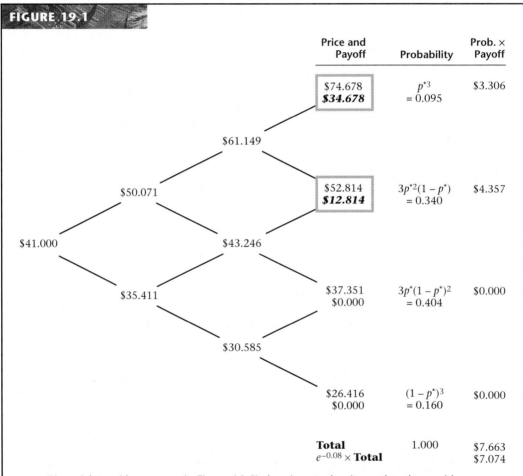

	Price and Payoff	Probability	Prob. × Payoff
	$74.678 $34.678	p^{*3} = 0.095	$3.306
	$52.814 $12.814	$3p^{*2}(1-p^*)$ = 0.340	$4.357
	$37.351 $0.000	$3p^*(1-p^*)^2$ = 0.404	$0.000
	$26.416 $0.000	$(1-p^*)^3$ = 0.160	$0.000
	Total	1.000	$7.663
	$e^{-0.08} \times$ **Total**		$7.074

Binomial tree (the same as in Figure 10.5) showing stock price paths, along with risk-neutral probabilities of reaching the various terminal prices. Assumes $S = \$41.00$, $K = \$40.00$, $\sigma = 0.30$, $r = 0.08$, $t = 1.00$ years, $\delta = 0.00$, and $h = 0.333$. The risk-neutral probability of going up is $p^* = 0.4568$. At the final node the stock price and terminal option payoff (beneath the price) are given.

true probabilties, what is the correct discount rate? We will see that the solution with true probabilities is somewhat involved, which is why the risk-neutral distribution is used when pricing derivatives as an expected value.

Valuation with Risk-Neutral Probabilities

We saw in equation (10.6) that we can interpret the one-period binomial option pricing calculation as an expected value, in which the expectation is computed using the risk-neutral probability p^*, and discounting is at the risk-free rate.

In a multi-period tree, we repeat this process at each node. For a European option, the result obtained by working backward through the tree is equivalent to computing the expected option price in the final period, and discounting at the risk-free rate.

If there are n binomial periods, equation (11.17) gives the probability of reaching any given stock price at expiration. Let n represent the number of binomial steps and i the number of stock price down moves. We can value a European call option by computing the expected option payoff at the final node of the binomial tree and then discounting at the risk-free rate. For example, for a European call,

European call price =

$$
e^{-rT} \sum_{i=1}^{n} max[0, Su^{n-i}d^i - K](p^*)^{n-i}(1 - p^*)^i \frac{n!}{(n-i)!\, i!} \quad (19.1)
$$

To illustrate this calculation, Figure 19.1 shows the stock price tree from Figure 10.5, with the addition of the total risk-neutral probabilities of reaching each of the terminal nodes. Figure 19.1 demonstrates that the option can be priced by computing the expected payoff at expiration using the probability of reaching each final node, and then discounting at the risk-free rate. You can verify that the option price in Figure 19.1 is the same as that in Figure 10.5.

Valuation with True Probabilities

The simple procedure we used to discount payoffs for the risk-neutral tree in Figure 19.1 *does not work* when we use actual probabilities. We analyzed the pricing of this option using true probabilities in Chapter 11, in Figure 11.4. We saw there that when using true probabilities to evaluate the option, the discount rate is different at different nodes on the tree. If we are to compute an option price as an expected value using true probabilities, we need to compute the discount rate *for each path*. There are eight possible paths for the stock price, four of which result in a positive option payoff. All of these paths have a first-period annualized continuously compounded discount rate of 35.7%. The subsequent discount rates depend on the path the stock takes. Table 19.1 verifies that discounting payoffs at path-dependent discount rates gives the correct option price. To take just the first row, the discounted expected option payoff for that row is computed

	TABLE 19.1	Computation of option price using expected value calculation and true probabilities. The stock price tree and parameters are the same as in Figure 11.4. The column entitled "Discount Rates along Path" reports the node-specific true annualized continuously compounded discount rates from that figure. "Discount Rate for Path" is the compound annualized discount rate for the entire path. "Prob. of Path" is the probability that the particular path will occur, computed using the true probability of an up move (52.46%). The last column is the probability times the payoff, discounted at the continuously compounded rate for the path.

Path	Discount Rates along Path			Discount Rate for Path	Prob. of Path	Payoff ($)	Discounted ($) (Prob. × Payoff)
uuu	35.7%	32.3%	26.9%	31.64%	0.1444	34.678	3.649
uud	35.7%	32.3%	26.9%	31.64%	0.1308	12.814	1.222
udu	35.7%	32.3%	49.5%	39.18%	0.1308	12.814	1.133
duu	35.7%	49.5%	49.5%	44.91%	0.1308	12.814	1.070
udd	—	—	—	—	—	0	0
dud	—	—	—	—	—	0	0
ddu	—	—	—	—	—	0	0
ddd	—	—	—	—	—	0	0
					Sum		7.074

as follows:

$$e^{-(0.357 \times \frac{1}{3} + 0.323 \times \frac{1}{3} + 0.269 \times \frac{1}{3})} \times (0.5246)^3 \times (\$74.678 - \$40) = \$3.649$$

This calculation uses the fact that the actual probability that the stock price will move up in any period is 52.46%.

As Table 19.1 illustrates, it is necessary to have a different cumulative discount rate along each *path* the stock can take. A call option is a high-beta security when it is out-of-the-money and it has a lower beta (but still higher than the stock) when it is in-the-money. This variation in the discount rate complicates discounting if we are using the true distribution of stock prices.[1]

....

[1] Here is why a single discount rate does not work. Suppose we represent the terminal option price associated with a particular pattern of stock price up and down movements by $C_i(T)$ and the compound discount factor for that path by β_i. Since both the payoff and the discount rates are uncertain, we need

Risk-neutral valuation neatly sidesteps the hardest problem about using discounted cash flow valuation techniques with an option. While it is easy to compute the expected payoff of an option if the stock is lognormally distributed, it is hard to compute the discount rate. If we value options *as if* the world were risk-neutral, this complication is avoided.

19.2 COMPUTING RANDOM NUMBERS

In this section we discuss how to compute the normally distributed random numbers required for Monte Carlo valuation. We will take for granted that you can compute a uniformly distributed random number between 0 and 1. The uniform distribution is defined on a specified range, over which the probability is 1, and assigns equal probabilities to every interval of equal length on that range. A random variable, u, that is uniformly distributed on the interval (a, b), has the distribution $\mathcal{U}(a, b)$. The uniform probability density, $f(x; a, b)$, is defined as

$$f(x; a, b) = \frac{1}{b - a}; a \leq x \leq b \qquad (19.2)$$

and is 0 otherwise. When $a = 0$ and $b = 1$, the uniform distribution is a flat line at a height of 1 over the range 0 to 1.

Drawing uniformly distributed random variables is very common; virtually all programming languages and spreadsheets have a way to do this.[2] The *Rand* built-in function in Excel does this, for example. It turns out that once we have a way to compute uniformly distributed random variables, there are two common ways to compute a normally distributed random variable. Many programs also have functions to compute normal random numbers directly, in which case it is not necessary to use these methods. However, the second method we will discuss can be used to compute random numbers drawn from *any* distribution.

Using Sums of Uniformly Distributed Random Variables

One standard technique to compute normally distributed random variables is to sum 12 uniform (0,1) random variables and subtract 6. Thus, we compute the $\mathcal{N}(0, 1)$ random variable $\tilde{Z}$ as

---

to compute $E[C_i(T)/(1 + \beta_i)]$. However, if we average the payoff and then separately average the discount factors, we are computing the ratio of the averages, $E[C_i(T)]/E[(1 + \beta_i)]$, rather than the average of the ratios. Jensen's inequality tells us that these are not the same calculation.

[2]Since computers are ultimately deterministic devices, it is virtually impossible to compute "true" random numbers. See Judd (1998, pp. 285–287) for a discussion and additional references.

$$\tilde{Z} = \sum_{i=1}^{12} u_i - 6$$

where the u_i are distributed uniformly on (0,1).

This technique works because the variance of a variable that is uniformly distributed between 0 and 1 is 1/12 and the mean is 1/2. Thus, if you sum 12 uniformly distributed random variables and subtract 6, you get a random variable with a variance of 1 and a mean of 0.

The sum of 12 uniform variables is not precisely normal, but it is close. To see this, you can draw many sets of 12 uniform random variables and perform a frequency count on the outcome, comparing it to the actual standard normal distribution. With 1000 iterations, for example, the frequency distributions are remarkably close. This technique is an application of the central limit theorem.

It is also possible to draw a *single* uniformly distributed random number and convert it to a normally distributed random number. Suppose that $u \sim \mathcal{U}(0, 1)$ and $z \sim \mathcal{N}(0, 1)$. As we saw in Chapter 18, the *cumulative distribution function*, denoted $U(w)$ for the uniform and $N(y)$ for the normal, is the probability that $u < w$ or $z < y$, i.e.,

$$U(w) = Prob(u \leq w)$$
$$N(y) = Prob(z \leq y)$$

As discussed in Chapter 18, w is the $U(w)$ quantile and y is the $N(y)$ quantile of the two distributions. If we randomly draw a uniform number u, how can we use u to construct a corresponding normal random number, z?

It turns out that the same idea we used to construct normal plots in Section 18.6 permits us to generate a normal random number from a uniform random number. Instead of interpreting a random draw from the uniform distribution as a *number*, we interpret it as a *quantile*. So, for example, if we draw 0.7 from a $\mathcal{U}(0, 1)$ distribution, we interpret this as a draw corresponding to the 70% quantile. We then use the inverse distribution function, $N^{-1}(u)$, to find the value from the normal distribution corresponding to that quantile.[3] This technique works because, for any distribution, quantiles are uniformly distributed: If you draw from a distribution, by definition any quantile is equally likely to be drawn.

The algorithm is therefore as follows:

1. Generate a uniformly distributed random number between 0 and 1. Say this is 0.7.

....

[3]The Excel function *NormSInv* computes the inverse cumulative normal distribution. Unfortunately, there is a serious bug in this function in Office 97 and Office 2000. In both versions of Excel, *NormSInv*(0.9999996) = 5.066, and *NormSInv*(0.9999997) = 5,000,000. Because of this, Excel will on occasion produce a randomly drawn normal value of 5,000,000, which ruins a Monte Carlo valuation. I thank Mark Broadie for pointing out this problem with using Excel to produce random normal numbers.

2. Ask: What is the value of z such that $N(z) = 0.7$? The answer to this question is computed using the *inverse cumulative distribution function*. In this case we have $N^{-1}(0.7) = 0.5244$. This value is a single draw of a standard normal random variable (0.5244).

3. Repeat.

This procedure simulates draws from a normal distribution. To simulate a log-normal random variable, simulate a normal random variable and exponentiate the draws.

This procedure of using the inverse cumulative probability distribution is valuable because it works for any distribution for which you can compute the inverse cumulative distribution.

19.3 SIMULATING LOGNORMAL STOCK PRICES

Recall from Chapter 18 that if $Z \sim \mathcal{N}(0, 1)$, a lognormal stock price can be written

$$S_T = S_0 e^{(\alpha - \frac{1}{2}\sigma^2)T + \sigma\sqrt{T}Z} \tag{19.3}$$

Suppose we wish to draw random stock prices for 2 years from today. From equation (19.3), the stock price is driven by the normally distributed random variable Z. Set $T = 2$, $\alpha = 0.10$, and $\sigma = 0.30$. If we then randomly draw a set of standard normal Z's and substitute the results into equation (19.3), the result is a random set of lognormally distributed S_2's. The continuously compounded mean return will be 20% (10% per year) and the continuously compounded standard deviation of $ln(S_2)$ will be $0.3 \times \sqrt{2} = 42.43\%$.

Simulating a Sequence of Stock Prices

There is another way to create a random set of prices 2 years from now. We can also generate *annual* random prices and compound these to get a 2-year price. This will give us exactly the same distribution for 2-year prices. Here is how to do it:

- Compute the 1-year price, S_1 as

$$S_1 = S_0 e^{(0.1 - \frac{1}{2}0.3^2) \times 1 + \sigma\sqrt{1}Z(1)}$$

- Using this S_1 as the starting price, compute S_2:

$$S_2 = S_1 e^{(0.1 - \frac{1}{2}0.3^2) \times 1 + 0.3\sqrt{1}Z(2)}$$

In these expressions, $Z(1)$ and $Z(2)$ are two draws from the standard normal distribution. If we substitute the expression for S_1 into S_2, we get

$$S_2 = S_0 e^{(0.1 - \frac{1}{2}0.3^2) \times 2 + 0.3\sqrt{1}[Z(1) + Z(2)]} \tag{19.4}$$

There are two differences between this expression and equation (19.3). First, instead of the term $\sqrt{2}Z$, we have $[Z(1) + Z(2)]$. Second, the first term in the exponent is multiplied by 2 instead of 1. Note that

$$Var(\sqrt{2}Z) = 2$$

and

$$Var[Z(1) + Z(2)] = 2$$

Therefore, equations (19.3) and (19.4) generate S_2's with the same distribution.

If we really want to simulate a random stock price after 2 years, there is no reason to draw two random variables instead of one. But if we want to simulate the path of the stock price over 2 years, then we can do so by splitting up the 2 years into multiple periods. As we saw in Chapter 14, some exotic options depend on the stock price path.

In general, if we wish to split up a period of length T into intervals of length h, the number of such intervals will be $n = T/h$. We have

$$S_h = S_0 e^{(\alpha - \frac{1}{2}\sigma^2)h + \sigma\sqrt{h}Z(1)}$$
$$S_{2h} = S_h e^{(\alpha - \frac{1}{2}\sigma^2)h + \sigma\sqrt{h}Z(2)}$$

and so on, up to

$$S_{nh} = S_{(n-1)h} e^{(\alpha - \frac{1}{2}\sigma^2)h + \sigma\sqrt{h}Z(n)}$$

These n stock prices can be intepreted as equally spaced points on the stock price path between times 0 and T. Note that if we substitute S_n into the expression for S_{2h}, the expression for S_{2h} into that for S_{3h}, and so on, we get

$$
\begin{aligned}
S_T &= S_0 e^{(\alpha - \frac{1}{2}\sigma^2)t + \sigma\sqrt{h}[\sum_{i=1}^{n} Z(i)]} \\
&= S_0 e^{(\alpha - \frac{1}{2}\sigma^2)t + \sigma\sqrt{t}[\frac{1}{\sqrt{n}}\sum_{i=1}^{n} Z(i)]}
\end{aligned}
\tag{19.5}
$$

Since $\frac{1}{\sqrt{n}}\sum_{i=1}^{n} Z(i) \sim \mathcal{N}(0, 1)$, we get the same distribution at time T with equation (19.5) as if we had drawn a single $\mathcal{N}(0, 1)$ random variable, as in equation (19.3). The important difference is that by splitting up the problem into n draws, we simulate the path taken by S. The simulation of a path is useful in computing the value of path-dependent derivatives, such as Asian and barrier options, the value of which depend on the path by which the price arrives at S_T.

19.4 EXAMPLES OF MONTE CARLO VALUATION

In Monte Carlo valuation, we perform a calculation similar to that in equation (19.1). The option payoff at time T is a function of the stock price, S_T. Represent this payoff as $V(S_T, T)$. The time-0 Monte Carlo price, $V(S_0, 0)$, is then

$$\boxed{V(S_0, 0) = \frac{1}{n}e^{-rT}\sum_{i=1}^{n} V(S_T^i, T)} \tag{19.6}$$

where $S_T^1, \ldots, S_T^n$ are n randomly drawn time-T stock prices. For the case of a call option, for example, $V(S_T^i, T) = max(0, S_T^i - K)$.

Both equations (19.1) and (19.6) use approximations to the time-T stock price distribution to compute an option price. Equation (19.1) uses the binomial distribution to approximate the lognormal stock price distribution, while equation (19.6) uses simulated prices to approximate the lognormal stock price distribution.

As an illustration of Monte Carlo techniques, we will first work with a problem for which we already know the answer. Suppose we have a European option that expires in T periods. The underlying asset has volatility σ and the risk-free rate is r. We can use the Black-Scholes option pricing formula to price the option, but we will price the option using *both* Black-Scholes and Monte Carlo so that we can assess the performance of Monte Carlo valuation.

Monte Carlo Valuation of a European Call

We assume that the stock price follows equation (19.3), with $\alpha = r$. We generate random standard normal variables, Z, substitute them into equation (19.3), and generate many random future stock prices. Each Z creates one trial. Suppose we compute N trials. For each trial, i, we compute the value of a call as

$$max(0, S_T^i - K) = max\left(0, S_0 e^{(r-0.5\sigma^2)T+\sigma\sqrt{T}Z_i} - K\right); \quad i = 1, \ldots, N$$

Average the resulting values:

$$\frac{1}{N}\sum_{i=1}^{N} max(0, S_T^i - K)$$

This expression gives us an estimate of the expected option payoff at time T:

$$E_0[max(0, S_T - K)]$$

We discount the average payoff back at the risk-free rate in order to get an estimate of the option value:

$$\overline{C} = e^{-rT}\frac{1}{N}\sum_{i=1}^{N} max(0, S_T^i - K)$$

Example 19.1 Suppose we wish to value a 3-month European call option where the stock price is $40, the strike price is $40, the risk-free rate is 8%, and the volatility is 30%. We draw random 3-month stock prices by using the expression

$$S_{3\,months} = S_0 e^{(0.08-0.3^2/2)\times0.25+0.3\sqrt{0.25}Z}$$

For each stock price, we compute

$$\text{Option payoff} = max(0, S_{3\,months} - \$40)$$

We repeat this procedure many times, average the resulting option payoffs, and discount the average back 3 months at the risk-free rate. With a single estimate using 2500 draws, we get an answer of $2.804 (see Table 19.2), close to the true value of $2.78. ❦

TABLE 19.2	Results of Monte Carlo valuation of European call with $S = \$40$, $K = \$40$, $\sigma = 30\%$, $r = 8\%$, $t = 91$ days, and $\delta = 0$. The Black-Scholes price is \$2.78. Each trial uses 500 random draws.

Trial	Computed Price ($)
1	2.98
2	2.75
3	2.63
4	2.75
5	2.91
Average	2.804

In this example we priced a European-style option. What about American options? The Monte Carlo technique entails simulating stock price paths *forward*, then averaging and discounting the payoffs when the option is exercised. An American option valuation requires working *backward* to determine the times at which an American option should be exercised. Thus, Monte Carlo valuation cannot easily handle the pricing of American options. Recently, however, Broadie and Glasserman (1997) and Longstaff and Schwartz (2001) have demonstrated methods for using Monte Carlo to value American options.

Accuracy of Monte Carlo

There is no need to value a European call using Monte Carlo methods, but doing so allows us to assess the accuracy of Monte Carlo valuation for a given number of simulated stock price paths. The key question is how many simulated stock prices suffice to value an option to a desired degree of accuracy. Monte Carlo valuation is simple but relatively inefficient. There are methods that improve the efficiency of Monte Carlo; we discuss several of these in Section 19.5.

To assess the accuracy of a Monte Carlo estimate, we can run the simulation different times and see how much variability there is in the results. Of course in this case, we also know that the Black-Scholes solution is $2.78.

Table 19.2 shows the results from running five Monte Carlo valuations, each containing 500 random stock price draws. The result of 2500 simulations is close to the correct answer ($2.804 is close to $2.78). However, there is considerable variation among the individual trials of 500 simulations.

To assess accuracy we need to know the standard deviation of the estimate. The Monte Carlo estimate is the mean of a distribution of prices generated from random numbers. Let $C(\tilde{S}_i)$ be the call price generated from the randomly drawn $\tilde{S}_i$. If there are

n trials, the Monte Carlo estimate is

$$\overline{C}_n = \frac{1}{n} \sum_{i=1}^{n} C(\tilde{S}_i)$$

Let σ_C denote the standard deviation of one draw and σ_n the standard deviation of n draws. The variance of a mean, given independent and identically distributed $\tilde{S}_i$'s, is

$$\sigma_n^2 = \frac{1}{n}\sigma_C^2$$

or

$$\sigma_n = \frac{1}{\sqrt{n}}\sigma_C$$

Thus, the standard deviation of the Monte Carlo estimate is inversely proportional to the square root of the number of draws.

In the Monte Carlo results reported in Table 19.2, the standard deviation of a draw is about \$4.05. (This value is computed by taking the standard deviation of the 2500 price estimates used to compute the average.) For 500 draws, the standard deviation is

$$\frac{\$4.05}{\sqrt{500}} = \$0.18$$

Given that the correct price is \$2.78, a \$0.18 standard deviation is substantial (6.5%). With 2500 observations, the standard deviation is cut to \$0.08, suggesting that the \$2.80 estimate from averaging the five answers was only accidentally close to the correct answer. In order to have a 1% (\$0.028) standard deviation, we would need to have 21,000 trials.

Arithmetic Asian Option

In the previous example of Monte Carlo valuation we valued an option that we already could value with the Black-Scholes formula. In practice, Monte Carlo valuation is useful under these conditions:

- Where the number of random elements in the option valuation problem is too great to permit direct numerical solution.

- Where underlying variables are distributed in such a way that direct solutions are difficult.

- Where options are path-dependent, i.e., the payoff at expiration depends upon the path of the underlying asset price.

For the case of a path-dependent option, the use of Monte Carlo estimation is straightforward. As discussed above, we can simulate the path of the stock as well as its terminal value. For example, consider the valuation of a security that at the end of 3 months makes a payment based on the arithmetic average of the stock price at the end of months 1, 2, and 3. As discussed in Chapter 14, this is an arithmetic average price Asian option: "Asian" because the payoff is based on an average, and "arithmetic average price" because the arithmetic average stock price replaces the actual stock price at expiration.

How will the value of an option on the average compare with an option that settles based on the actual expiration-day stock price? Intuitively, averaging should reduce the likelihood of large gains and losses. Any time the stock ends up high (in which case the call will have a high value at expiration), it will have traversed intermediate stock prices in the process of reaching a high value. The payoff to the Asian option will reflect these lower intermediate prices, and, hence, large payoffs will be much less likely.

We compute the 1-month, 2-month, and 3-month stock prices as follows:

$$S_1 = 40e^{(r-\sigma^2/2)T/3 + \sigma\sqrt{T/3}Z(1)}$$

$$S_2 = S_1 e^{(r-\sigma^2/2)T/3 + \sigma\sqrt{T/3}Z(2)}$$

$$S_3 = S_2 e^{(r-\sigma^2/2)T/3 + \sigma\sqrt{T/3}Z(3)}$$

where $Z(1)$, $Z(2)$, and $Z(3)$ are independent draws from a standard normal distribution. We repeat the trial many times and draw many Z_i's. The value of the security is then computed as

$$C_{Asian} = e^{-rT} E\left(max[(S_1 + S_2 + S_3)/3 - K, 0]\right) \tag{19.7}$$

Example 19.2 Let r = 8%, $\sigma = 0.3$, and suppose that the initial stock price is $40. Figure 19.2 compares histograms for the actual risk-neutral stock price distribution after 3 months and that for the average stock price created by averaging the three month-end prices. As expected, the nonaveraged distribution has significantly higher tail probabilities and a lower probability of being close to the initial stock price of $40. ⚞

Table 19.3 lists prices of Asian options computed using 10,000 Monte Carlo trials each.[4] The first row (where a single terminal price is averaged) represents the price of an ordinary call option with 3 months to expiration. The others represent more frequent averaging. The Asian price declines as the averaging frequency increases, with the largest price decline obtained by moving from no averaging (the first row in Table 19.3 to monthly averaging (the second row of Table 19.3).

Note also in Table 19.3 that, in any row, the arithmetic average price is always above the geometric average price. This is Jensen's inequality at work: Geometric

---

[4]A trial in this case means the computation of a single option price at expiration. When 40 prices are averaged over three months, each trial consists of drawing 40 random numbers; hence, 400,000 random numbers are drawn in order to compute the price.

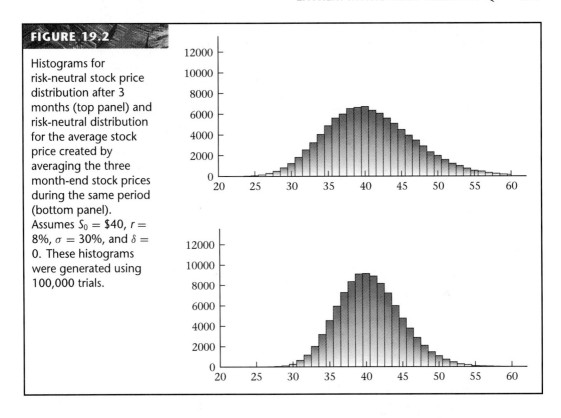

FIGURE 19.2

Histograms for risk-neutral stock price distribution after 3 months (top panel) and risk-neutral distribution for the average stock price created by averaging the three month-end stock prices during the same period (bottom panel). Assumes $S_0 = \$40$, $r = 8\%$, $\sigma = 30\%$, and $\delta = 0$. These histograms were generated using 100,000 trials.

averaging produces a lower average stock price than arithmetic averaging, and hence a lower option price.

19.5 EFFICIENT MONTE CARLO VALUATION

We have been describing what might be called "naive" Monte Carlo, making no attempt to reduce the variance of the simulated answer for a given number of trials. There are a number of methods to achieve faster Monte Carlo valuations.[5]

Control Variate Method

We have seen that naive Monte Carlo estimation of an arithmetic Asian option requires many simulations. In Table 19.3, even with 10,000 simulations, there is still a standard deviation of several percent in the option price.

....

[5] An excellent overview is Boyle et al. (1997). See also Judd (1998, Chapter 8), which in turn contains other references, and Campbell et al. (1997, Chapter 9).

TABLE 19.3	Prices of arithmetic average-price Asian options estimated using Monte Carlo and exact prices of geometric average price options. Assumes option has 3 months to expiration and average is computed using equal intervals over the period. Each price is computed using 10,000 trials, assuming $S = \$40$, $K = \$40$, $\sigma = 30\%$, $r = 8\%$, $T = 0.25$, $\delta = 0$. In each row, the same random numbers were used to compute both the geometric and arithmetic average price options. σ_n is the standard deviation of the estimated prices, divided by $\sqrt{10,000}$.

| Number of | Monte Carlo Prices ($) | | Exact | |
Averages	Arithmetic	Geometric	Geometric Price ($)	σ_n
1	2.79	2.79	2.78	0.0408
3	2.03	1.99	1.94	0.0291
5	1.78	1.74	1.77	0.0259
10	1.70	1.66	1.65	0.0241
20	1.66	1.61	1.59	0.0231
40	1.63	1.58	1.56	0.0226

In each row of Table 19.3, the same random numbers are used to estimate the option price. As a result, the errors in the estimated arithmetic and geometric prices are correlated: When the estimated price for the geometric option is high, this occurs because we have had high returns in the stock price simulation. This should result in a high arithmetic price as well.

This observation suggests the **control variate method** to increase Monte Carlo accuracy. The idea underlying this method is to estimate the error on each trial by using the price of a related option that does have a pricing formula. The error estimate obtained from this control price can be used to improve the accuracy of the Monte Carlo price on each trial.

Asian options provide an effective illustration of this idea.[6] Because we have a formula for the price of a geometric Asian option (see Section 14.2), we know whether the geometric price from a Monte Carlo valuation is too high or too low. For a given set of random stock prices, the arithmetic and geometric prices will typically be too high or too low in tandem, so we can use information on the error in the geometric price to adjust our estimate of the arithmetic price, for which there is no formula.

---

[6]This example follows Kenna and Vorst (1990), who used the control variate method to price arithmetic Asian options.

To be specific, we use simulation to estimate the arithmetic price, $\overline{A}$, and the geometric price, $\overline{G}$. Let G and A represent the true geometric and arithmetic prices. The error for the Monte Carlo estimate of the geometric price is $(G - \overline{G})$. We want to use this error to improve our estimate of the arithmetic price.

Consider calculating

$$A^* = \overline{A} + \left(G - \overline{G}\right) \tag{19.8}$$

This is the control variate estimate. Since Monte Carlo provides an unbiased estimate, $E(\overline{G}) = G$. Hence, $E(A^*) = E(\overline{A}) = A$. Moreover, the variance of A^* is

$$Var(A^*) = Var(\overline{A}) + Var(\overline{G}) - 2Cov(\overline{A}, \overline{G}) \tag{19.9}$$

As long as the estimate $\overline{G}$ is highly correlated with the estimate $\overline{A}$, the variance of the estimate A^* can be less than the variance of $\overline{A}$.

In practice, the variance reduction from the control variate method can be dramatic. Figure 19.3 graphs the results from the first 200 simulations in pricing an arithmetic Asian option. The control variate estimate converges in just a few trials to the correct

FIGURE 19.3

Comparison of "naive" Monte Carlo estimate of arithmetic average option price with control variate method. Graph depicts first 200 simulations for an option with $S = \$40$, $K = \$40$, $\sigma = 0.3$, $r = 0.08$, $T = 0.25$, $\delta = 0$, and the final price computed with three averages.

value of about $1.98. For example, the very first draw in the graphed simulation gave an arithmetic option price of $0.80 and a geometric price—using the same random prices—of $0.75. The correct geometric price is $1.94. Correcting the estimate gives a price of

$$\text{Control variate price} = \$0.80 + (\$1.94 - \$0.75) = \$1.99$$

This example illustrates that if the correlation between the two estimates is high, the control variate method works very well.

Boyle et al. (1997) point out that equation (19.8) does not in general provide the minimum variance Monte Carlo estimate, and in some cases can even increase the variance of the estimate. They suggest that instead of estimating equation (19.8), you estimate

$$A^* = \overline{A} + \beta \left(G - \overline{G} \right) \tag{19.10}$$

The variance of this estimate is

$$Var(A^*) = Var(\overline{A}) + \beta^2 Var(\overline{G}) - 2\beta Cov(\overline{A}, \overline{G}) \tag{19.11}$$

The variance $Var(A^*)$ is minimized by setting $\beta = Cov(\overline{A}, \overline{G})/Var(\overline{G})$. One way to obtain β is to perform a small number of Monte Carlo trials, run a regression of equation (19.10) to obtain $\hat{\beta}$, and then use $\hat{\beta}$ for the remaining trials. The optimal value of β will vary depending on the application.

Other Monte Carlo Methods

The control variate example is just one method for improving the efficiency of Monte Carlo valuation. The **antithetic variate method** uses the insight that for every simulated realization, there is an opposite and equally likely realization. For example, if we draw a random normal number of 0.5, we could just as well have drawn −0.5. By using the opposite of each normal draw we can get two simulated outcomes for each random path we draw. This seems as if it would help, since it doubles the number of draws. But drawing a random number is often not the time-consuming part of a Monte Carlo calculation.

There can be an efficiency gain because the two estimates are negatively correlated; adding them reduces the variance of the estimate. In practical terms, this means that if you draw an extreme estimate from one tail of the distribution, you will also draw an extreme estimate from the other tail, balancing the effect of the first draw. Boyle et al. (1997) find modest benefits from using the antithetic variate method.

Another important class of methods controls the region in which random numbers are generated. **Stratified sampling** is an example of this kind of method. Suppose you have 100 uniform random numbers, $u_i, i = 1, \ldots, 100$. With naive Monte Carlo you would compute $z_i = N^{-1}(u_i)$. This calculation treats each random number as representing a random draw from the cumulative distribution. However, because of random variation, 100 uniform random numbers will not be exactly uniformly distributed and therefore the z_i will not be exactly normal. We can improve the distribution of the u_i, and therefore of the z_i, if we treat each number *as a random draw from each percentile* *of the uniform distribution.* Thus, take the first draw, u_1, and divide it by 100. The resulting $\hat{u}_1$ is now uniformly distribtuted over [0,0.01]. Take the second draw, divide it by 100, and add 0.01. The resulting $\hat{u}_2$ is uniformly distributed over (0.01,0.02). For the ith draw, compute $\hat{u}_i = (i - 1 + u_i)/100$. This value is uniformly distributed over the ith percentile. Proceeding in this way we are guaranteed to generate a random number for each percentile of the normal distribution. You can select a number of intervals different from 100, and you can repeat the simulation multiple times. A generalization of this technique when the payoff depends on more than one random variable is *Latin hypercube sampling,* discussed by Boyle et al. (1997).

There are other techniques for improving the efficiency of Monte Carlo. The approach called *importance sampling* concentrates the generation of random numbers where they have the most value for pricing a particular claim. *Low discrepancy sequences* use carefully selected deterministic points to create more uniform coverage of the distribution. Boyle et al. (1997) provide an excellent summary and comparison of the different methods.

If you are performing a one-time calculation, the simplicity of naive Monte Carlo is appealing. However, if you are performing a Monte Carlo valuation repeatedly, you may achieve large efficiency gains by analyzing the problem and using one or more variance reduction techniques to increase efficiency.

19.6 THE POISSON DISTRIBUTION

We have seen that the lognormal distribution assigns a low probability to large stock price moves. One approach to generating a more realistic stock price distribution is to permit large stock price moves to occur randomly. Occasional large price moves can generate the fat tails observed in the data in Section 18.6.

The **Poisson distribution** is a discrete probability distribution that counts the number of events—such as large stock price moves—that occur over a period of time. The Poisson distribution is summarized by the parameter λ, where λh is the probability that one event occurs over the short interval h. A Poisson-distributed event is very unlikely to occur more than once over a sufficiently short interval. Thus, λ is like an annualized probability of the event occurring over a short interval.

Over a longer period of time, t, the probability that the event occurs exactly m times is given by

$$p(m, \lambda t) = \frac{e^{-\lambda t}(\lambda t)^m}{m!}$$

The cumulative Poisson distribution is then the probability that there are m or fewer events from 0 to t.[7]

[7]In Excel, you can compute $p(m, \lambda t)$ as *Poisson$(m, \lambda t, false)$*, and the cumulative distribution, $\mathcal{P}(m, \lambda t)$, as *Poisson$(m, \lambda t, true)$*.

$$P(m, \lambda t) = Prob(x \leq m; \lambda t) = \sum_{i=0}^{m} \frac{e^{-\lambda t}(\lambda t)^i}{i!}$$

Given an expected number of events, the Poisson distribution tells us the probability that we will see a particular number of the events over a given period of time.[8] The mean of the Poisson distribution is λt.

Example 19.3   Suppose the probability of a market crash is $\lambda = 2\%$ per year. Then the probability of seeing no market crashes in any given year can be computed as $p(0, 0.02 \times 1) = 0.9802$. The probability of seeing no crashes over a 10-year period would be $p(0, 0.02 \times 10) = 0.8187$. The probability of seeing exactly two crashes over a 10-year period would be $p(2, 0.02 \times 10) = 0.0164$.   ❧

Figure 19.4 graphs the Poisson distribution for three values of the Poisson parameter, λt. Suppose we are interested in the number of times an event will occur over a 10-year period. Figure 19.4 shows us the distribution for $t = 10$ and $\lambda = 0.01$ (1% per year), $\lambda = 0.025$ (2.5% per year), and $\lambda = 0.05$ (5% per year). The likeliest occurrence in all three scenarios is that no events occur. It is also extremely unlikely that four or more events occur.

The Poisson distribution only counts the number of events. If an event occurs, we need to determine the magnitude of the jump as an independent draw from some other density; the lognormal is frequently used. Thus, in those periods when a Poisson event occurs, we would draw a separate random variable to determine the magnitude of the jump.

Using the inverse cumulative distribution function for a Poisson random variable, it is easy to generate a Poisson-distributed random variable. Even without the inverse cumulative distribution function (which Excel does not provide), we can construct the inverse distribution function from the cumulative distribution function.

Table 19.4 calculates the Poisson distribution for a mean of 0.8. Using this table we can easily see how to randomly draw a Poisson event. First we draw a uniform (0,1) random variable. Then we use the values in the table to decide how many events occur. If the uniform random variable is less than 0.4493, for example, we say that no events occur. If the value is between 0.4493 and 0.8088, we say that one event occurs, and so forth.

---

[8]The probability that no event occurs between time 0 and time t is $p(0, \lambda t) = e^{-\lambda t}$. The probability that one or more events occurs between 0 and t is therefore $1 - e^{-\lambda t}$. This expression is also the cumulative distribution of the **exponential distribution,** which models the time until the first event. The density function of the exponential distribution is $f(t, \lambda) = \lambda e^{-\lambda t}$.

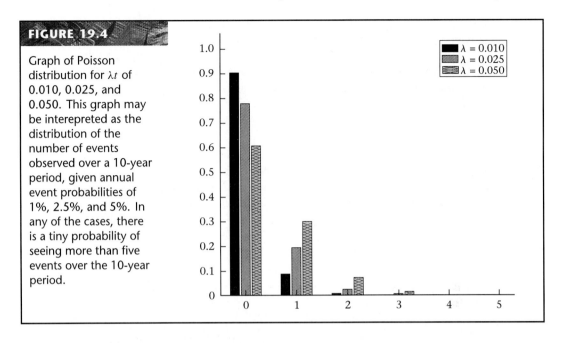

FIGURE 19.4

Graph of Poisson distribution for λt of 0.010, 0.025, and 0.050. This graph may be interepreted as the distribution of the number of events observed over a 10-year period, given annual event probabilities of 1%, 2.5%, and 5%. In any of the cases, there is a tiny probability of seeing more than five events over the 10-year period.

TABLE 19.4 Values of Poisson distribution and cumulative Poisson distribution with mean $(\lambda t) = 0.8$.

Number of Events	Probability	Cumulative Probability
0	0.4493	0.4493
1	0.3595	0.8088
2	0.1438	0.9526
3	0.0383	0.9909

19.7 SIMULATING JUMPS WITH THE POISSON DISTRIBUTION

As we discussed, stock prices sometimes move more than would be expected from a lognormal distribution. If market volatility is 20% and the expected return is 15%, a one-day 5% drop in the market occurs about once every 2.5 million days. (See Problem 19.8.) A 20% one-day drop (as in October 1987) is virtually impossible if prices are lognormally distributed with a reasonable volatility.

Merton (1976) introduced the use of the Poisson distribution in an option pricing context. The Poisson distribution counts the number of events that occur in a given period of time. If each event is a jump in the price, we can then use the lognormal (or other) distribution to compute the size of the jump. This Poisson-lognormal model assumes that jumps are independent.[9] In addition to independence, we will assume that jumps are idiosyncratic, meaning that jumps can be diversified. In this case, the possibility of a jump does not affect the risk premium of the asset. (This is a common assumption made for tractability, but it is not always appropriate. While some jumps are idiosyncratic, a large market move is by definition systematic.)

Let the lognormally distributed jump magnitude Y be given by

$$Y = e^{\alpha_J - 0.5\sigma_J^2 + \sigma_J W}$$

Using the calculations in Chapter 18, e^{α_J} is the expected jump and σ_J is the standard deviation of the log of the jump. W is a standard normal variable. When a jump occurs, if the pre-jump price is S, the post-jump price is YS. For future reference, let

$$k = e^{\alpha_J} - 1 \tag{19.12}$$

be the expected percentage jump.

Simulating the Stock Price with Jumps

To simulate the stock price over a period of time h, we first pick two uniform random variables to determine the number of jumps and the ordinary (nonjump) lognormal return. If there are m jumps, we must then pick m additional random variables to determine the magnitudes of the jumps. Each jump has a multiplicative effect on the stock price.

Specifically, suppose the stock price is S_t. If a stock cannot jump, its price at time $t + h$ is

$$S_{t+h} = S_t e^{(\alpha - \delta - 0.5\sigma^2)h + \sigma\sqrt{h}Z}$$

where α is the expected return.

Now consider an otherwise identical stock that can jump, with price $\hat{S}_t$. The stock price will have two components, one with and one without jumps. The no-jump lognormal component is

$$S_t e^{(\hat{\alpha} - \delta - 0.5\sigma^2)h + \sigma\sqrt{h}Z}$$

where the expected stock return, conditional on no jump, is $\hat{\alpha}$. We will see in a moment why we use a different notation for the expected return in this expression. If the stock

---

[9]By definition, the number of occurrences of an event is Poisson-distributed if three assumptions are satisfied:

1. The probability that one event will occur in a small interval h is proportional to the length of the interval.

2. The probability that more than one event will occur in a small interval h is substantially smaller than the probability that a single event will occur.

3. The number of events in nonoverlapping time intervals is independent.

The Poisson distribution can be derived from these three assumptions. See Mood et al. (1974, p. 95).

jumps m times between t and $t + h$, each jump changes the price by a factor of

$$Y_i = e^{\alpha_J - 0.5\sigma_J^2 + \sigma_J W(i)}$$

Where Z and $W(i)$, $i = 1, \ldots, m$ are standard normal random variables. The cumulative jump is the product of the Y_i's, or

$$\prod_{i=1}^{m} Y_i = e^{m(\alpha_J - 0.5\sigma_J^2) + \sigma_J \Sigma_{i=1}^{m} W(i)}$$

Notice that the cumulative jump is lognormal, since it is the product of lognormal random variables. The stock price at time $t + h$, taking account of both the normal lognormal return and jumps, is then

$$\hat{S}_{t+h} = \hat{S}_t e^{(\hat{\alpha} - \delta - 0.5\sigma^2)h + \sigma\sqrt{h}Z} \times e^{m(\alpha_J - 0.5\sigma_J^2) + \sigma_J \Sigma_{i=1}^{m} W(i)} \tag{19.13}$$

It is possible to simulate $\hat{S}_{t+h}$ using this expression. There are three steps:

1. Select a standard normal Z.

2. Select m from the Poisson distribution.

3. Select m draws, $W(i)$, $i = 1, \ldots, m$, from the standard normal distribution.

By inserting these values into equation (19.13), we generate $\hat{S}_{t+h}$, which is lognormal since it is a product of lognormal expressions.

We have not answered the question: What is $\hat{\alpha}$? There is a subtlety associated with modeling jumps. When a jump occurs, the expected percentage change in the stock price is $e^{\alpha_J} - 1$. If $\alpha_J \neq 0$, jumps will induce average up or down movement in the stock, depending upon whether $\alpha_J > 0$ or $\alpha_J < 0$. Recall, however, that we assumed jumps are idiosyncratic. Therefore, *the unconditional (meaning that we do not know whether jumps will occur) expected return for a stock that does not jump should be the same as the unconditional expected return for an otherwise identical stock that does jump.* When jumps have no systematic risk, the jump does not affect the stock's expected return. We have to adjust the nonjump expected return, $\hat{\alpha}$, in order for jumps not to affect the expected return. For example, if the average jump return is -10%, then over time the stock price will drift down on average due to jumps. In equilibrium, the stock must appreciate when not jumping in order to give the owner a fair return unconditionally. If $\alpha_J = -10\%$, we would need to raise the average expected return on the stock in order for it to earn a fair rate of return on average.

We adjust for α_J by subtracting λk from the no-jump expected return, where λ is the Poisson parameter and k is given by equation (19.12). Thus,

$$\hat{\alpha} = \alpha - \lambda k \tag{19.14}$$

With this correction, if the expected jump is positive, we lower the expected return on the stock when it is not jumping, and vice versa for a negative expected jump.

The final expression for the stock price is thus

$$\hat{S}_{t+h} = \hat{S}_t e^{(\alpha-\delta-\lambda k-0.5\sigma^2)h+\sigma\sqrt{h}Z} \prod_{i=0}^{m} e^{\alpha_J-0.5\sigma_J^2+\sigma_J W_i}$$

$$= \hat{S}_t e^{(\alpha-\delta-\lambda k-0.5\sigma^2)h+\sigma\sqrt{h}Z} e^{m(\alpha_J-0.5\sigma_J^2)+\sigma_J \Sigma_{i=0}^{m} W_i}$$

(19.15)

where α_J and σ_J are the mean and standard deviation of the jump magnitude and Z and W_i are random standard normal variables. A similar expression appears in Merton (1976).

Figure 19.5 displays two simulated stock price series, one for which jumps do not occur, and one generated using equation (19.15). In the absence of jumps, the stock price is assumed to follow a lognormal process with $\alpha = 8\%$ and $\sigma = 30\%$. For the jump component, we assume $\lambda = 3$ (an average of three jumps per year), $\alpha_J = -2\%$, and $\sigma_J = 5\%$. In the figure, we can detect jumps because the no-jump series is drawn using the same random Z's. Some of the disparity, for example between days 1000 and 1500, is due to the approximate extra 6% return (λk) that is added to the stock when it does not jump.

What happens if we apply the normality tests from Chapter 18 to the stock price series in Figure 19.5? Figure 19.6 displays histograms and normal probability plots for the two series. Without jumps, continuously compounded returns look normal. With jumps, the data look non-normal and resemble Figures 18.4 and 18.5. The price $\hat{S}$ is

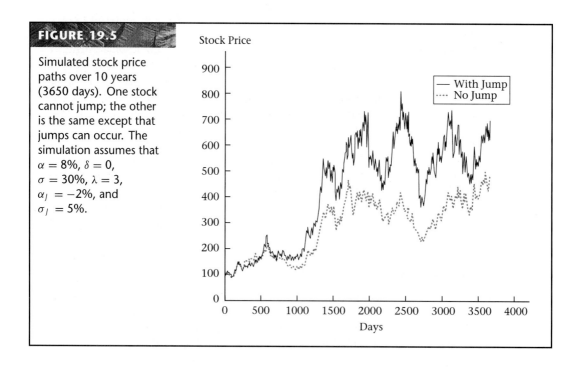

FIGURE 19.5

Simulated stock price paths over 10 years (3650 days). One stock cannot jump; the other is the same except that jumps can occur. The simulation assumes that $\alpha = 8\%$, $\delta = 0$, $\sigma = 30\%$, $\lambda = 3$, $\alpha_J = -2\%$, and $\sigma_J = 5\%$.

FIGURE 19.6

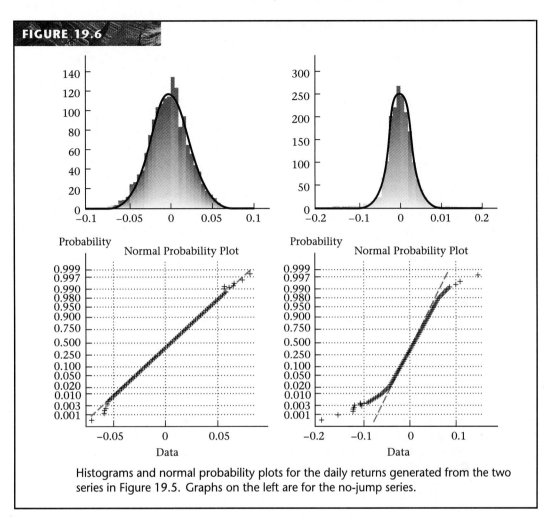

Histograms and normal probability plots for the daily returns generated from the two series in Figure 19.5. Graphs on the left are for the no-jump series.

lognormal, but it is not drawn from a single distribution; it is a mix of two lognormals with the second lognormal induced by the Poisson process. This results in data that do not look normal. The kurtosis of the continuously compounded returns without jumps is 2.93, very close to the value of 3 expected for a normal distribution. With jumps, kurtosis is 7.40.

Multiple Jumps

When we assume lognormal moves of the stock conditional on a single jump event, we can only get large up *and* down moves by assuming a large standard deviation of the jump move. The reason is that we are drawing from a single lognormal distribution, conditional on the Poisson event. An alternative is to assume there are *two* (or more)

Poisson variables, one controlling up jumps and one controlling down jumps. The lognormal moves associated with each can have different means and standard deviations. This obviously provides for a richer and potentially more realistic set of outcomes.

19.8 SIMULATING CORRELATED STOCK PRICES

Suppose that S and Q are both lognormally distributed stock prices such that

$$ln(S_t) = ln(S_0) + (\alpha_S - 0.5\sigma_S^2)t + \sigma_S\sqrt{t}W$$

$$ln(Q_t) = ln(Q_0) + (\alpha_Q - 0.5\sigma_Q^2)t + \sigma_Q\sqrt{t}Z$$

If S and Q are uncorrelated, then we can simulate both prices by drawing independent W and Z. However, suppose that the correlation between S and Q is ρ. We would like to be able to simulate these two random variables taking account of their correlation. Here is how to do so.

Let ϵ_1 and ϵ_2 be independent and distributed as $\mathcal{N}(0, 1)$. Let

$$W = \epsilon_1$$
$$Z = \rho\epsilon_1 + \epsilon_2\sqrt{1 - \rho^2}$$

(19.16)

Then $Corr(Z, W) = \rho$, and Z is distributed $\mathcal{N}(0, 1)$.

To see this, note first that Z and W both have zero mean. Compute the covariance between Z and W and the variance of Z:

$$E(WZ) = E[\epsilon_1(\rho\epsilon_1 + \epsilon_2\sqrt{1 - \rho^2})] = \rho E(\epsilon_1^2) = \rho$$
$$E(Z^2) = E[(\rho\epsilon_1 + \epsilon_2\sqrt{1 - \rho^2})^2] = \rho^2 + 1 - \rho^2 = 1$$

Thus, W and Z are both $\mathcal{N}(0, 1)$ and have a correlation coefficient of ρ.

Now we will check that the continuously compounded returns of S and Q have correlation ρ. The covariance between $ln(S_t)$ and $ln(Q_t)$ is

$$E\left[(ln(S_t) - E[ln(S_t)])(ln(Q_t) - E[ln(Q_t)])\right] = E\left(\sigma_S W\sqrt{t}\sigma_Q Z\sqrt{t}\right)$$

$$= \sigma_S\sigma_Q\rho t$$

The correlation coefficient is

$$\text{Correlation} = \frac{\sigma_S\sigma_Q\rho t}{\sigma_S\sqrt{t}\sigma_Q\sqrt{t}} = \rho$$

Thus, if W and Z have correlation ρ, so will the continuously compounded returns of S and Q.

Generating n Correlated Lognormal Random Variables

Suppose we have n correlated lognormal variables. The question we address here is how to generalize the previous analysis. The first of the n random variables will have $n - 1$ pairwise correlations with the others. The second will have $n - 2$ (not counting its correlation with the first, which we have already counted). Continuing in this way, we will have

$$n - 1 + n - 2 + \cdots + 1 = \frac{1}{2}n(n-1)$$

pairwise correlations we have to take into account. We will denote the correlation between variables i and j as $\rho_{i,j}$.

We denote the original uncorrelated random $\mathcal{N}(0, 1)$ variables as $\epsilon_1, \epsilon_2, \ldots, \epsilon_n$. The correlated random variables are $Z(1), Z(2), \ldots, Z(n)$, with

$$E[Z(i)Z(j)] = \rho_{i,j}$$

We can generate the $Z(i)$ as

$$Z(i) = \sum_{j=1}^{i} a_{i,j}\epsilon_j$$

where the $a_{i,j}$ are coefficients selected to make sure the pairwise correlations are correct.

Creating the coefficients $a_{i,j}$ has a recursive solution. That is, we construct $Z(1)$, then $Z(2)$ using the solution to $Z(1)$, and so on. The formula for the $a_{i,j}$ is

$$a_{i,j} = \frac{1}{a_{j,j}}\left[\rho_{i,j} - \sum_{k=1}^{j-1} a_{j,k}a_{i,k}\right] \quad i > j$$

$$\tag{19.17}$$

$$a_{i,i} = \sqrt{1 - \sum_{k=1}^{i-1} a_{i,k}^2}$$

For the case of two random variables, this reduces to equation (19.16).

The matrix of $a_{i,j}$'s is called the **Cholesky decomposition** of the original correlation matrix. In order for equation (19.17) to give correct coefficients, the set of correlations must be **positive-definite,** which means that the correlations must be such that there is no way to sum random variables and compute a negative variance. This is *not* an arbitrary condition: If this condition is not satisfied, the set of correlations is not valid.[10]

---

[10] Suppose there are three random variables, a, b, and c, each with a variance of 1. Suppose that a is perfectly correlated with b ($\rho_{a,b} = 1$) and b is perfectly correlated with c ($\rho_{b,c} = 1$). It must then be the case that c is perfectly correlated with a. If $\rho_{a,c} \neq 1$, the matrix of correlations is not positive-definite.

To see this, suppose that $\rho_{a,c} = 0$, then compute $Var(a - b + c)$. You will find that the variance is -1, which is impossible. To take a different example, suppose $\rho_{a,c} = 0.9$. You will then find that $Var(a - 2b + c) = -0.2$, which is again impossible.

If a matrix of correlations is not positive-definite, it means that there is some combination of the random variables for which you will compute a negative variance. (For many combinations the variance will still be positive.) The interpretation of a negative variance is that you had an invalid correlation matrix to start with.

The point—and the reason for mentioning this—is that correlations and covariances cannot be arbitrary. In practice, depending upon how a covariance matrix is estimated, this can be an important concern. The *true* covariances among hundreds of bonds, stocks, currencies, and commodities *must* create a positive-definite covariance matrix. However, *estimated* covariances might not be positive-definite. If there are m assets and $n > m$ observations, the covariance matrix estimated from these data will be positive-definite. However, if different covariances are estimated from different data sets, positive-definiteness is not assured. The results of a simulation based on such covariances may produce nonsensical results.

CHAPTER SUMMARY

Monte Carlo methods entail simulating asset returns in order to obtain a future distribution for prices. This distribution can then be used to price claims on the asset (for example, Asian options) or to assess the risk of the asset (we will focus on such uses in Chapter 24). Performing simulations requires that we draw random numbers from an appropriate distribution (for example, the normal) in order to generate future asset prices. There are adjustments, such as the control variate method, which can dramatically increase the speed with which Monte Carlo estimates converge to the correct price.

It is possible to incorporate jumps in the price by mixing Poisson and log-normal random variables. Simulated correlated random variables can be created using the Cholesky decomposition.

FURTHER READING

The first use of Monte Carlo methods to price options was Boyle (1977) and the technique is now quite widespread. An excellent survey of the use of Monte Carlo in valuing derivatives is Boyle et al. (1997). We will see how Monte Carlo is used in value-at-risk calculations in Chapter 24. Bodie and Crane (1999) use Monte Carlo to analyze retirement investment products. Schwartz and Moon (2000) use Monte Carlo to value Internet firms by simulating future cash flows.

Broadie and Glasserman (1997) and Longstaff and Schwartz (2001) have recently demonstrated techniques for using Monte Carlo to value American-style options.

Merton (1976) derived an option pricing formula in the presence of idiosyncratic jumps. Naik and Lee (1990) illustrate option pricing in the presence of systematic jumps. Risk aversion affects the option price in such cases.

PROBLEMS

19.1. Let $u_i \sim \mathcal{U}(0, 1)$. Draw 1000 random u_i and construct a histogram of the results. What are the mean and standard deviation?

19.2. Let $u_i \sim \mathcal{U}(0, 1)$. Compute $\sum_{i=1}^{12} u_i - 6$, 1000 times. (This will use 12,000 random numbers.) Construct a histogram and compare it to a theoretical standard normal density. What are the mean and standard deviation?

19.3. Suppose that $x_1 \sim \mathcal{N}(0, 1)$ and $x_2 \sim \mathcal{N}(0.7, 3)$. Compute 2000 random draws of e^{x_1} and e^{x_2}.

    a. What are the means of e^{x_1} and e^{x_2}? Why?

    b. Create a graph that displays a frequency distribution in each case

19.4. The Black-Scholes price for a European put option with $S = \$40$, $K = \$40$, $\sigma = 0.30$, $r = 0.08$, $\delta = 0$, and $t = 0.25$ is \$1.99. Use Monte Carlo to compute this price. Compute the standard deviation of your estimates. How many trials do you need to achieve a standard deviation of \$0.01 for your estimates?

19.5. Let $r = 0.08$, $S = \$100$, $\delta = 0$, and $\sigma = 0.30$. Using the risk-neutral distribution, simulate $1/S_1$. What is $E(1/S_1)$? What is the forward price for a contract paying $1/S_1$?

19.6. Suppose $S_0 = 100$, $r = 0.06$, $\sigma_S = 0.4$ and $\delta = 0$. Use Monte Carlo to compute prices for claims that pay the following:

    a. S_1^2

    b. $\sqrt{S_1}$

    c. S_1^{-2}

19.7. Suppose that $ln(S)$ and $ln(Q)$ have correlation $\rho = -0.3$ and that $S_0 = \$100$, $Q_0 = \$100$, $r = 0.06$, $\sigma_S = 0.4$ and $\sigma_Q = 0.2$. Neither stock pays dividends. Use Monte Carlo to find the price today of claims that pay

    a. $S_1 Q_1$

    b. S_1/Q_1

    c. $\sqrt{S_1 Q_1}$

    d. $1/(S_1 Q_1)$

    e. $S_1^2 Q_1$

19.8. Assume that the market index is 100. Show that if the expected return on the market is 15%, the dividend yield is zero, and volatility is 20%, the probability of the index falling below 95 over a 1-day horizon is approximately 0.0000004.

19.9. Suppose that on any given day the annualized continuously compounded stock return has a volatility of either 15%, with a probability of 80%, or 30%, with a probability of 20%. This is a **mixture of normals** model. Simulate the daily stock return and construct a histogram and normal plot. What happens to the normal plot as you vary the probability of the high volatility distribution?

19.10. For stocks 1 and 2, $S_1 = \$40$, $S_2 = \$100$, and the return correlation is 0.45. Let $r = 0.08$, $\sigma_1 = 0.30$, $\sigma_2 = 0.50$, and $\delta_1 = \delta_2 = 0$. Generate 1000

1-month prices for the two stocks. For each stock, compute the mean and standard deviation of the continuously compounded return. Also compute the return correlation.

19.11. Assume $S_0 = \$100$, $r = 0.05$, $\sigma = 0.25$, $\delta = 0$, and $T = 1$. Use Monte Carlo valuation to compute the price of a claim that pays $1 if $S_T > \$100$, and 0 otherwise. (This is called a *cash-or-nothing call* and will be further discussed in Chapter 22. The actual price of this claim is $0.5040.)

    a. Running 1000 simulations, what is the estimated price of the contract? How close is it to $0.5040?

    b. What is the standard deviation of your Monte Carlo estimate? What is the 95% confidence interval for your estimate?

    c. Use a 1-year at-the-money call as a control variate and compute a price using equation (19.8).

    d. Again use a 1-year at-the-money call as a control variate, only this time use equation (19.10). What is the standard deviation of your estimate?

For the following three problems, assume that $S_0 = \$100$, $r = 0.08$, $\alpha = 0.20$, $\sigma = 0.30$, and $\delta = 0$. Perform 2000 simulations. Note that most spreadsheets have built-in functions to compute skewness and kurtosis. (In Excel, the functions are *Skew* and *Kurt*.) For the normal distribution, skewness, which measures asymmetry, is zero. Kurtosis, discussed in Chapter 18, equals 3.

19.12. Let $h = 1/52$. Simulate both the continuously compounded actual return and the actual stock price, S_{t+h}. What are the mean, standard deviation, skewness, and kurtosis of both the continuously compounded return on the stock and the stock price? Use the same random normal numbers and repeat for $h = 1$. Do any of your answers change? Why?

19.13. An options trader purchases 1000 1-year at-the-money calls on a nondividend-paying stock with $S_0 = \$100$, $\alpha = 0.20$, and $\sigma = 0.25$. Assume the options are priced according to the Black-Scholes formula and $r = 0.05$.

    a. Use Monte Carlo (with 1000 simulations) to estimate the expected return, standard deviation, skewness, and kurtosis of the return on the call when it is held until expiration. Interpret your answers.

    b. Repeat for an at-the-money put.

19.14. Repeat the previous problem, only assume that the options trader purchases 1000 1-year at-the-money *straddles*.

19.15. Assume $S_0 = \$50$, $r = 0.05$, $\sigma = 0.50$, and $\delta = 0$. The Black-Scholes price for a 2-year at-the-money put is $10.906. Suppose that the stock price is lognormal but can also jump, with the number of jumps Poisson-distributed. Assume $\alpha = 0.05$ (the expected return to the stock is equal to the risk-free rate), $\sigma = 0.50$, $\lambda = 2$, $\alpha_J = -0.04$, $\sigma_J = 0.08$.

a. Using 2000 simulations incorporating jumps, simulate the 2-year price and draw a histogram of continuously compounded returns.

b. Using Monte Carlo incorporating jumps, value a 2-year at-the-money put. Is this value significantly different from the Black-Scholes value?

APPENDIX 19.A: FORMULAS FOR GEOMETRIC AVERAGE OPTIONS

The discussion of Monte Carlo valuation of geometrically averaged Asian options enables us to understand the formulas for geometrically averaged Asian options, described in Appendix 14.A. If we sample the stock price N times from time 0 to T, with the distance between samples $h = T/N$ and the first sample occurring at time h, the log of the geometric average is

$$\frac{1}{N}\sum_{i=1}^{N}\ln(S_{ih}) = \frac{1}{N}\left[\sum_{i=1}^{N}\left(\ln(S_0) + (r - \delta - 0.5\sigma^2)ih + \sigma\sum_{j=1}^{i}Z_j\sqrt{h}\right)\right]$$

$$\tag{19.18}$$

$$= \ln(S_0) + (r - \delta - 0.5\sigma^2)\frac{h}{N}\sum_{i=1}^{N}i + \frac{\sigma\sqrt{h}}{N}\sum_{i=1}^{N}\sum_{j=1}^{i}Z_j$$

where $Z_j \sim \mathcal{N}(0, 1)$ and Z_i and Z_j are independent.

The last double summation can be rewritten as

$$\sum_{i=1}^{N}\sum_{j=1}^{i}Z_j = NZ_1 + (N-1)Z_2 + \cdots + Z_N$$

Thus we have

$$E\left[\frac{1}{N}\sum_{i=1}^{N}\ln(S_{ih})\right] = \ln(S_0) + (r - \delta - 0.5\sigma^2)\frac{h}{N}\frac{N(N+1)}{2}$$

$$= \ln(S_0) + (r - \delta - 0.5\sigma^2)T\frac{N+1}{2N}$$

where we have used the fact that

$$\sum_{i=1}^{N}i = \frac{N(N+1)}{2}$$

The variance is

$$Var\left[\frac{1}{N}\sum_{i=1}^{N}\ln(S_{ih})\right] = \frac{\sigma^2 h}{N^2}\left(N^2 + (N-1)^2 + \cdots + 1\right)$$

$$= \sigma^2 T\frac{N(N+1)(2N+1)}{6N^3}$$

where we have used the fact that

$$\sum_{i=1}^{N} i^2 = \frac{N(N+1)(2N+1)}{6}$$

These calculations tell us that the average price, $G(T)$, can be written as a lognormal process,

$$G(T) = S_0 e^{\left[(r-\delta-0.5\sigma^2)\frac{T}{2}\frac{N+1}{N} + \sigma\sqrt{T}\sqrt{\frac{(N+1)(2N+1)}{6N^2}}Z\right]}$$

where $Z \sim \mathcal{N}(0, 1)$. Using equation (18.13), we have

$$E[G(T)] = S_0 e^{\left[(r-\delta-0.5\sigma^2)\frac{N+1}{N} + \sigma^2\frac{(N+1)(2N+1)}{6N^2}\right]\frac{1}{2}T}$$

The prepaid forward price for the average is

$$e^{-rT} E[G(T)] = S_0 e^{-\left[r\frac{N-1}{N} + (\delta+0.5\sigma^2)\frac{N+1}{N} - \sigma^2\frac{(N+1)(2N+1)}{6N^2}\right]\frac{1}{2}T}$$

Thus, we can price an option on the geometric average by setting the dividend yield for the average, δ^*, equal to

$$\delta^* = \frac{1}{2}\left[r\frac{N-1}{N} + (\delta+0.5\sigma^2)\frac{N+1}{N} - \sigma^2\frac{(N+1)(2N+1)}{6N^2}\right]$$

and the volatility of the average, σ^*, equal to

$$\sigma^* = \frac{\sigma}{N}\sqrt{\frac{(N+1)(2N+1)}{6}}$$

If we take the limit as $N \to \infty$, we have

$$\delta^* = \frac{1}{2}\left(r + \delta + \frac{1}{6}\sigma^2\right)$$

$$\sigma^* = \sigma\sqrt{\frac{1}{3}}$$

Average Price Options

Geometric average price options, for which the geometric average replaces the stock price, are priced by substituting δ^* and σ^* for δ and σ in the Black-Scholes formula.

Average Strike Options

With geometric average strike options, the average replaces the strike price. Thus, we replace the risk-free rate with δ^* and the strike price with S_0. However, we also need to compute the volatility of the *difference* between $ln(S_T)$ and $ln(A(T))$,

$$\sigma^{**2} = Var[ln(S_T) - ln(A_T)]$$

We can write

$$ln(S_T) = ln(S_0) + (r - \delta - 0.5\sigma^2)T + \sigma \sum_{i=1}^{N} Z_i \sqrt{h}$$

Using equation (19.18), the covariance between $ln(S_T)$ and $ln(A_T)$ is

$$E\left[\left(\sigma\sqrt{h}\sum_{i=1}^{N} Z_i\right)\left(\frac{\sigma\sqrt{h}}{N}\sum_{i=1}^{N}\sum_{j=1}^{i} Z_j\right)\right] = \frac{\sigma^2 h}{N}\left(\sum_{i=1}^{N} Z_i\right)\left(\sum_{i=1}^{N}\sum_{j=1}^{i} Z_j\right)$$

$$= \frac{\sigma^2 h}{N}(N + (N-1) + \cdots + 1)$$

$$= \frac{\sigma^2 h}{2}(N+1)$$

The correlation coefficient, ρ, is therefore

$$\rho = \frac{\frac{\sigma^2 h}{2}(N+1)}{\left(\sigma\sqrt{T}\right)\left(\sigma\sqrt{T}\frac{1}{N}\sqrt{\frac{(N+1)(2N+1)}{6}}\right)}$$

$$= \frac{1}{2}\sqrt{\frac{6(N+1)}{2N+1}}$$

Note that when $N = 1$, $\rho = 1$, and as $N \to \infty$, $\rho = \sqrt{3}/2$.

Using this expression for ρ, we have

$$\sigma^{**2} = \sigma^2 T + \sigma^2 T\frac{(N+1)(2N+1)}{6N^2} - 2\rho\sigma^2 T\frac{1}{N}\sqrt{\frac{(N+1)(2N+1)}{6}}$$

Thus, to value an average strike option we substitute σ^{**} for the volatility and δ^* for the interest rate. The dividend yield on the underlying asset remains the same.

Chapter 20

Brownian Motion and Itô's Lemma

This chapter addresses two important topics. First, in the study of derivatives, stock and other asset prices are commonly assumed to follow a stochastic process called geometric Brownian motion. This chapter explains what this means and develops the notation and assumptions underlying the Black-Scholes model.

Second, given that a stock price follows geometric Brownian motion, we want to characterize the behavior of a claim—such as an option—that has a payoff dependent upon the stock price. In this chapter we discuss Itô's Lemma, which permits us to study the process followed by a claim that is a function of the stock price.

This material is mathematically more challenging than the material in earlier chapters, but it provides the foundation for everything that comes later, as well as much of what has come before. Both academic researchers on options and practitioners rely on the concepts and techniques discussed in this chapter.

20.1 THE BLACK-SCHOLES ASSUMPTION ABOUT STOCK PRICES

The vast majority of technical option pricing discussions, including the original paper by Black and Scholes, begin by assuming that the price of the underlying asset follows a process like the following:

$$\frac{dS(t)}{S(t)} = \alpha dt + \sigma dZ(t) \tag{20.1}$$

$S(t)$ is the stock price, $dS(t)$ is the instantaneous change in the stock price, α is the continuously compounded expected return on the stock, σ is the continuously compounded standard deviation (volatility), and $Z(t)$ is a normally distributed random variable that follows a process called Brownian motion. The variable $dZ(t)$ represents the change in $Z(t)$ over a short period of time. A stock obeying equation (20.1) is said to follow a process called **geometric Brownian motion.** Expressions like equation (20.1) are called *stochastic differential equations.*

One main purpose of this chapter is to understand the meaning of equations like (20.1). For our purposes, there are two important implications of equation (20.1):

1. Suppose the stock price now is $S(0)$. If the stock price follows equation (20.1), the distribution of $S(T)$ is lognormal, i.e.

$$ln[S(T)] \sim \mathcal{N}(ln[S(0)] + [\alpha - 0.5\sigma^2]T, \sigma^2 T)$$

The assumption that the stock follows geometric Brownian motion thus provides a foundation for our assumption that the stock price is lognormally distributed.

2. Lognormality tells us about the distribution of the stock price at a point in time. For many purposes, however, we are interested not just in the distribution at a terminal point but also the *path* the stock price takes in getting to that terminal point. With barrier options, for example, the price of the option depends upon the probability that the asset price reaches the barrier. Geometric Brownian motion allows us to describe this path.

Our goal is to provide a heuristic, rather than technical, understanding of equations like (20.1).

20.2 A DESCRIPTION OF STOCK PRICE BEHAVIOR

As discussed in Chapter 18, the normal distribution provides an unrealistic description of the stock price, since normally distributed prices—unlike real stock prices—could become negative. However, normality can be a plausible description of continuously compounded returns since continuously compounded returns can become negative while the stock price remains positive. If the continuously compounded return is $R(0, T)$, the price is $S(0)e^{R(0,T)}$, which is always positive.

If we are talking about very short periods of time, it can be reasonable to assume that effective stock returns, $S(t + h)/S(t)$, are normally distributed. Suppose that h is small and that the return on the stock, r_h, is normally distributed with mean and variance of αh and $\sigma^2 h$. Thus,

$$S(t + h) = S(t)(1 + r_h) \qquad (20.2)$$

with

$$r_h \sim \mathcal{N}(\alpha h, \sigma^2 h)$$

If r_h is normally distributed, it appears that there is a possibility that $S(t)r_h$ can become negative. In particular, if r_h is less than -1 (i.e., the return is less than -100%), then from equation (20.2), the stock price, $S(t + h)$, would be negative. However, as h becomes smaller, the probability that r_h is less than -1 becomes smaller. In fact, for small h, it becomes almost impossible that r_h would be less than -1.

Suppose, for example, that $\alpha = 0.15$, $\sigma = 0.3$ and $h = 1/365$. Under the assumption of normally distributed returns, the 1-day expected return is $0.15/365 = 0.00041$ and the 1-day variance is $0.3^2/365 = 0.000247$. Thus,

$$r_h \sim \mathcal{N}(0.00041, 0.000247)$$

For this distribution a negative stock price is logically possible but almost impossible as a practical matter. In order to have a 1-day return less than -100%, we would need to draw from a standard normal distribution a value less than

$$\frac{-1 - 0.00041}{\sqrt{0.000247}} = -63.71$$

The probability of drawing -63.71 or less from a standard normal distribution is astronomically tiny. And since it is the stock's *rate of return* that we assume to be normally distributed, this probability is independent of the stock price. Whether the stock sells for \$1 or \$1000, over a period of 1 day there is virtually no chance of a negative price. If the period is 1 hour or even less, the probability of a negative realization is lower still.

The stock price T periods from now is the *product* of 1 plus the returns over n shorter periods of length $h = T/n$. Because normality is not preserved under multiplication, the stock price n periods in the future will *not* be normally distributed. Over n periods we have

$$S(T) = S(0) \times (1 + r_h) \times (1 + r_{2h}) \times \cdots \times (1 + r_{nh}) \equiv S(0) \prod_{i=1}^{n}(1 + r_{ih})$$

This expression is a compound interest calculation, in which returns are being earned on previous returns every h periods.

The continuously compounded return from 0 to T, $ln(S(T)/S(0))$, is

$$ln[S(T)/S(0)] = \sum_{i=1}^{n} ln(1 + r_{ih})$$

The logarithm of a normal random variable is not normal. However, by the central limit theorem, the sum of many such terms tends toward normality. Thus, as $n \to \infty$ (or $h \to 0$), the continuously compounded return from 0 to T is normal. Consequently $S(T)$ tends toward lognormality.

Intuitively, $S(T)$ will have the following properties:

- If the time interval h is short, each one-period return, r_i, will have a very low probability of being less than -100%. If the r_i is never less than -100%, $S(T)$ represents the product of positive numbers. Hence, $S(T)$ will not be negative.

- $S(T)$ is modeled as the product of returns times the initial starting price, $S(0)$. Therefore the variance and mean of the *percentage* return will be independent of the level of the price. The variance and mean of *dollar* returns will increase with the level of the price.

- $S(T)/S(0)$ will not be symmetrically distributed but will be skewed to the right. The reason is that if percentage returns are the same for any stock price, then high dollar returns follow a price increase and low dollar returns follow a price decrease.

- As discussed above, the compounding of many short-period, normally distributed returns gives rise to a lognormally distributed stock price.

In the next two sections we will construct a model that resembles equation (20.2) and that generates lognormal stock prices.

20.3 BROWNIAN MOTION

Brownian motion is a random walk occurring in continuous time, with movements that are continuous rather than discrete.[1] A random walk can be generated by flipping a coin each period and moving one step, with the direction determined by whether the coin is heads or tails. To generate Brownian motion, we would flip the coins infinitely fast and take infinitesimally small steps at each point. Since all steps are infinitely small, movements are continuous. (This description is abstract; being precise requires mathematics beyond the scope and purpose of this book.)

Let $Z(t)$ represent the value of the random walk—the cumulative sum of all the moves—after t periods. (Whatever t is, there has been an infinite number of moves.) Technically, **Brownian motion** is a random walk with specific characteristics:

- $Z(0) = 0$.
- $Z(t + s) - Z(t)$ is normally distributed with mean 0 and variance s.
- $Z(t + s_1) - Z(t)$ is independent of $Z(t) - Z(t - s_2)$, where $s_1, s_2 > 0$. In other words, nonoverlapping increments are independently distributed.
- $Z(t)$ is continuous (you can draw a picture of Brownian motion without lifting your pencil).

How do we represent this process mathematically? We can focus on the *change* in $Z(t)$, which we model as binomial, times a scale factor that makes the change in $Z(t)$ small over a small period of time. Denote the short period of time as h, and again let $Y(t)$ be a random draw from a binomial distribution, where $Y(t)$ is ± 1 with probability 50%. Note that $E(Y(t)) = 0$ and $Var(Y(t)) = 1$. We can write

$$Z(t + h) - Z(t) = Y(t + h)\sqrt{h} \tag{20.3}$$

Over any period of time longer than h, Z will be the sum of the binomial increments specified in equation (20.3). Consider the distribution of $Z(T)$, taking $Z(0)$ as a given starting value. Let $n = T/h$ be the number of intervals of length h between 0 and T. We can write $Z(T) - Z(0)$ as the sum of the increments to Z from time 0 to T. Thus,

$$Z(T) - Z(0) = \sum_{i=1}^{n} (Z(ih) - Z[(i - 1)h]) = \sum_{i=1}^{n} Y(ih)\sqrt{h}$$

Since $h = T/n$, we can also write this as

$$Z(T) - Z(0) = \sqrt{T} \left[\frac{1}{\sqrt{n}} \sum_{i=1}^{n} Y(ih) \right] \tag{20.4}$$

---

[1]The development in this section draws heavily on Cox and Miller (1965, Chapter 5) and Merton (1990).

Since $E(Y(ih)) = 0$, we have

$$E[Z(T) - Z(0)] = 0$$

Also, since $Var(Y(ih)) = 1$, and the Y's are independent, we have

$$Var[Z(T) - Z(0)] = T \left[\frac{1}{n} \sum_{i=1}^{n} Var(Y(ih)) \right] = T$$

The term in square brackets has mean 0 and variance 1, since it is the sum of n independent random variables with mean 0 and variance 1, divided by $\sqrt{n}$. By the Central Limit Theorem, the distribution of the sum of independent binomial random variables approaches normality. We have

$$\lim_{n \to \infty} \frac{1}{\sqrt{n}} \sum_{i=1}^{n} Y(ih) \sim \mathcal{N}(0, 1)$$

We need to divide by $\sqrt{n}$ in this expression to prevent the variance from going to infinity as n goes to infinity.

Returning to equation (20.4), in the limit we have

$$Z(T) - Z(0) \to \mathcal{N}(0, T)$$

To summarize, we can think of Brownian motion being approximately generated from the sum of independent binomial draws with mean 0 and variance h. However, $Z(T)$ defined in equation (20.4) is not true Brownian motion because it is not a continuous process—since h is positive, movements in Z are discrete.

In order to attain continuity we would like to let h get arbitrarily small. Informally, we can just say that h becomes small, and rename h as dt. This notation is intended to convey that the change in time is infinitesimally small. Denote the change in Z as $dZ(t)$, and write

$$dZ(t) = Y(t)\sqrt{dt} \tag{20.5}$$

Equation (20.5) is just like equation (20.3), except that $Z(t + h) - Z(t)$ is now called $dZ(t)$, and $\sqrt{h}$ is now $\sqrt{dt}$. Should we think of $Y(t)$ as being binomially or normally distributed? For any t and ϵ, $Z(t + \epsilon) - Z(t)$ is the sum of infinitely many $dZ(t)$'s. Therefore, we can think of $Y(t)$ as binomial or normal; either way, $Z(t)$ is normal for any finite interval.

The expression for the change in the value of a Brownian process, equation (20.5), *is fundamental in the derivatives literature.* It is a mathematical way to say: "Over small periods of time, changes in the value of the process are normally distributed with a variance that is proportional to the length of the time period."

Expression (20.5) has an integral counterpart. Since $Z(T)$ is the sum of individual $dZ(t)$'s, it is natural to write

$$Z(T) = Z(0) + \int_0^T dZ(t) \tag{20.6}$$

This is equivalent to expression (20.5). The integral in equation (20.6) is called a stochastic integral.[2] The process $Z(t)$ is also called a **diffusion process.**

The value for $Z(t)$ at any point in time is the cumulative effect of infinitely many up and down moves, each infinitely small. As you might guess from this description, the mathematical properties of Brownian motion can be bewildering to contemplate. Two of the least intuitive are known as the "infinite-crossing property" and "infinite variation."

To illustrate the first, imagine that you take the starting point for a Brownian process and let it run for a second (or any length of time). Within that period of time, the Brownian process will have moved back and forth across the starting point an infinite number of times!

The second property is closely related to the first. "Infinite variation" means that if you could take the path of the Brownian process that ran for a second, pick it up by its beginning and ending points, and stretch it out fully, you would have a line of infinite length.

Arithmetic Brownian Motion

The Brownian motion process described above is a building block for more elaborate and realistic processes. With pure Brownian motion, the expected change in Z is 0, and the variance per unit time is 1. We can generalize this to allow an arbitrary variance and a nonzero mean. To make this generalization, we can write

$$X(t + h) - X(t) = \alpha h + \sigma Y(t + h)\sqrt{h}$$

This equation implies that $X(T)$ is normally distributed. Since $h = T/n$, we have

$$X(T) - X(0) = \sum_{i=1}^{n} \left(\alpha \frac{T}{n} + \sigma Y(ih)\sqrt{\frac{T}{n}} \right)$$

$$= \alpha T + \sigma \left(\sqrt{T} \sum_{i=1}^{n} \frac{Y(ih)}{\sqrt{n}} \right)$$

We have seen that as $n \to \infty$, the term in parentheses on the right-hand side has the distribution $\mathcal{N}(0, T)$. We can write

$$X(T) - X(0) = \alpha T + \sigma Z(T) \tag{20.7}$$

The differential form of this expression is

$$dX(t) = \alpha dt + \sigma dZ(t) \tag{20.8}$$

This process is called **arithmetic Brownian motion.** We say that α is the instantaneous mean per unit time and σ^2 is the instantaneous variance per unit time. The variable $X(t)$

---

[2]Because $dZ(t)$ is a random variable, some care is required in defining equation (20.6). See Neftci (2000, Chapter 9) for a discussion of stochastic integration. Karatzas and Shreve (1991) provide a more advanced treatment.

is the sum of the individual changes dX. An implication of equation (20.8) is that $X(T)$ is normally distributed, or

$$X(T) - X(0) \sim \mathcal{N}(\alpha T, \sigma^2 T)$$

Since equation (20.8) describes the change in the level of X, not a rate of return on X, this process *does not* exhibit the compounding of normal returns we discussed above.

As before, there is an integral representation of equation (20.8):

$$X(T) = X(0) + \int_0^T \alpha dt + \int_0^T \sigma dZ(t)$$

This expression is equivalent to equation (20.7).

Here are some of the properties of the process in equation (20.8):

- $X(t)$ is normally distributed because it is created by adding together many normally distributed dX's.

- The random term has been multiplied by a scale factor that enables us to change variance. Since $dZ(t)$ has a variance of 1 per unit time, $\sigma dZ(t)$ will have a variance of σ^2 per unit time.

- The αdt term introduces a nonrandom *drift* into the process. Adding αdt has the effect of adding α per unit time to $X(0)$.

Being able to adjust the drift and variance is a big step toward a more useful model, but arithmetic Brownian motion has several drawbacks:

- There is nothing to prevent X from becoming negative, so it is a poor model for stock prices.

- The mean and variance of changes in dollar terms are independent of the level of the stock price. In practice if a stock doubles, we would expect both the dollar expected return and the dollar standard deviation of returns to approximately double.

We will eliminate both of these criticisms with geometric Brownian motion, which we consider in Section 20.4.

The Ornstein-Uhlenbeck Process

Another modification of the arithmetic Brownian process permits mean reversion. It is natural to consider mean reversion when modeling commodity prices or interest rates. For example, if the interest rate becomes sufficiently high, it is likely to fall, and if the value is sufficiently low, it is likely to rise. Commodity prices may also exhibit this tendency to revert to the mean. We can incorporate mean reversion by modifying the drift term:

$$dX(t) = \lambda[\alpha - X(t)]dt + \sigma dZ(t) \tag{20.9}$$

When $\alpha = 0$, equation (20.9) is called an **Ornstein-Uhlenbeck process.**

Equation (20.9) has the implication that if X rises above α, the drift, $\lambda[\alpha - X(t)]$, will become negative. If X falls below α, the drift becomes positive. The parameter λ measures the speed of the reversion: If λ is large, reversion happens more quickly. In the long run, we expect X to revert toward α. As with arithmetic Brownian motion, X can still become negative.

20.4 Geometric Brownian Motion

In general we can write both the drift and volatility as functions of X (or other variables):

$$dX(t) = \alpha[X(t)]dt + \sigma[X(t)]dZ(t) \qquad (20.10)$$

This equation, in which the drift, α, and volatility, σ, depend on the stock price, is called an **Itô process.**

Suppose we modify arithmetic Brownian motion to make the instantaneous mean and standard deviation proportional to $X(t)$:

$$dX(t) = \alpha X(t)dt + \sigma X(t)dZ(t)$$

This is an Itô process that can also be written

$$\frac{dX(t)}{X(t)} = \alpha dt + \sigma dZ(t) \qquad (20.11)$$

This equation says that the dollar mean and standard deviation of the stock price change are $\alpha X(t)$ and $\sigma X(t)$, and they are proportional to the level of the stock price. Thus, *the percentage change in the asset value is normally distributed with instantaneous mean α and instantaneous variance σ^2.* The process in equation (20.11) is known as **geometric Brownian motion.** For the rest of the book, we will frequently assume that prices of stocks and other assets follow equation (20.11).

The integral representation for equation (20.11) is

$$X(T) - X(0) = \int_0^T \alpha X(t)dt + \int_0^T \sigma X(t)dZ(t)$$

Lognormality

We now circle back to our discussion of lognormality because of this fact: A variable that follows geometric Brownian is lognormally distributed. Suppose we start a process at $X(0)$ and it follows geometric Brownian motion. Because the mean and variance at time t are proportional to $X(t)$, the evolution of X implied by equation (20.11) generates compounding (the change in X is proportional to X) and, hence, non-normality.

However, while X is not normal, $ln[X(t)]$ is normally distributed:

$$ln[X(t)] \sim \mathcal{N}(ln[X(0)] + (\alpha - 0.5\sigma^2)t, \sigma^2 t) \qquad (20.12)$$

As a result, we can write

$$X(t) = X(0)e^{(\alpha - 0.5\sigma^2)t + \sigma\sqrt{t}Z} \qquad (20.13)$$

where $Z \sim \mathcal{N}(0, 1)$. This is the link between Brownian motion and lognormality. If a variable is distributed in such a way that instantaneous percentage changes follow geometric Brownian motion, then over discrete periods of time, the variable is lognormally distributed.

Given that X follows (20.11), we can compute the expected value of X at a point in the future. It follows from the discussion in Section 18.2 that

$$\begin{aligned} E[X(t)] &= X(0)e^{(\alpha-0.5\sigma^2)t} E_0(e^{\sigma\sqrt{t}Z}) \\ &= X(0)e^{(\alpha-0.5\sigma^2)t} e^{0.5\sigma^2 t} \qquad\qquad (20.14) \\ &= X(0)e^{\alpha t} \end{aligned}$$

Thus, α in equation (20.11) is the expected, continuously compounded return on X.

Relative Importance of the Drift and Noise Terms

Consider the discrete counterpart for geometric Brownian motion:

$$X(t+h) - X(t) = \alpha X(t)h + \sigma X(t)Y(t)\sqrt{h}$$

Over a short interval of time, there are two components to the change in X: A deterministic component, $\alpha X(t)h$, and a random component, $\sigma X(t)Y_t\sqrt{h}$. An important fact is that *over short periods of time, the character of the Brownian process is determined almost entirely by the random component*. The drift can be undetectable amid all the up and down movement due to the random term.

To understand why the random term is important over short horizons, consider the ratio of the standard deviation to the drift:

$$\frac{\sigma X(t)\sqrt{h}}{\alpha X(t)h} = \frac{\sigma}{\alpha\sqrt{h}}$$

This ratio becomes infinite as h approaches dt.

A numerical example shows this more concretely. Suppose $\alpha = 10\%$ and $\sigma = 10\%$. Over a year, the mean and standard deviations are the same. Table 20.1 shows that the ratio increases as the time interval becomes smaller. Over a period of 1 day, the standard deviation is 19 times larger than the mean. This is important in practice since it means that when you look at daily returns, you are primarily seeing the movement of a random variable following pure Brownian motion.[3] The deterministic drift (the expected return) is virtually undetectable.

As the time interval becomes longer than a year, the reverse happens: The mean becomes more important than the standard deviation. Since the mean is proportional to h while the standard deviation is proportional to $\sqrt{h}$, the mean comes to dominate over

---

[3]There are other considerations when you look at prices over short periods of time, including the bouncing of prices between the bid and the ask, and the effects of trades such as large blocks that may temporarily depress prices. Brownian motion implies that even in the absence of these effects, prices would still bounce around significantly.

				$\dfrac{\sigma\sqrt{h}}{\alpha h}$
Period Length	**h**	**αh**	**σ√h**	
Five Years	5	0.5	0.2236	0.447
One Year	1	0.10	0.10	1.00
One Month	0.0833	0.0083	0.0289	3.464
One Day	0.0027	0.00027	0.0052	19.105
One Minute	0.000002	0.0000002	0.00014	724.98

TABLE 20.1 The last column computes the ratio of the per-period standard deviation to the per-period mean for different time intervals. The ratio becomes infinite as the time interval goes to zero.

longer horizons. Since we take the ratio of the instantaneous standard deviation to the instantaneous mean, Table 20.1 also holds for arithmetic Brownian motion.

Correlated Itô Processes

Suppose that we have the Itô process

$$dQ(t) = \alpha_Q[Q(t)]dt + \sigma_Q[Q(t)]dZ'(t) \tag{20.15}$$

where $Z'(t)$ is a Brownian motion. The Brownian motion $Z(t)$ in equation (20.10) can be correlated with $Z'(t)$ in equation (20.15). In many applications with multiple variables we would expect the variables to be correlated. For example, if X and Q represent stock prices, X and Q will typically be correlated. Let $W_1(t)$ and $W_2(t)$ be independent Brownian motions. Then we can write

$$Z(t) = W_1(t)$$
$$Z'(t) = \rho W_1(t) + \sqrt{1 - \rho^2}W_2(t) \tag{20.16}$$

You may recognize this is as the Cholesky decomposition, which we discussed in Section 19.8. Using equation (20.16), the correlation between $Z(t)$ and $Z'(t)$ is

$$E[Z(t)Z'(t)] = \rho E[W_1(t)^2] + \sqrt{1 - \rho^2}E[W_1(t)W_2(t)]$$
$$= \rho t + 0$$

The second term on the right-hand side is zero because $W_1(t)$ and $W_2(t)$ are independent. We then say the correlation between dZ and dZ' is ρdt.

Multiplication Rules

The dominance of the noise term over short intervals has another implication. Since the behavior of dX is dominated by the noise term, the squared return, $(dX)^2$, reflects primarily the noise term. We have

$$[X(t+h) - X(t)]^2 = \left[\alpha X(t)h + \sigma X(t)Y(t)\sqrt{h}\right]^2$$

Expanding this expression and simplifying, we have

$$[X(t+h) - X(t)]^2 = \alpha^2 X(t)^2 h^2 + 2\alpha\sigma X(t)^2 Y(t)^2 h^{1.5} + \sigma^2 X(t)^2 Y(t)^2 h$$

Suppose that h is 1 day. Then $h = 0.00274$, $h^{1.5} = 0.000143$, and $h^2 = 0.0000075$. If h is 1 hour, then $h = 0.000114$, $h^{1.5} = 0.0000012$, and $h^2 = 0.00000001$. Clearly, the relative magnitude of the term multiplied by h is much greater than the other terms as h becomes very small. In addition, if we think of Y as binomial, then $Y(t)^2 = 1$. This leads us to write

$$[X(t+h) - X(t)]^2 \approx \sigma^2 X(t)^2 h$$

or

$$[dX(t)]^2 = \sigma^2 X(t)^2 dt$$

essentially ignoring all terms that are higher powers of h. This equation tells you that if you look at the squared stock price change over a small interval, all you are seeing is the effect of the variance.

We can also consider terms like

$$[X(t+h) - X(t)]h$$

Rewriting this expression gives us

$$\left[\alpha X(t)h + \sigma X(t)Y(t)\sqrt{h}\right]h = \alpha X(t)h^2 + \sigma X(t)Y(t)h^{1.5}$$

Since the smallest power of h is 1.5, this entire term vanishes relative to h as h goes to zero.

Suppose we have two different Itô processes such as equations (20.10) and (20.15). We can write $dZ'(t) = Y'\sqrt{dt}$ where $E[Y(t)Y'(t)] = \rho$. Thus, ρ is the correlation between $Y(t)$ and $Y'(t)$. We have

$$E\left([X(t+h) - X(t)][Q(t+h) - Q(t)]\right)$$
$$= E\left([\alpha X(t)h + \sigma X(t)Y(t+h)\sqrt{h}][\alpha_Q Q(t)h + \sigma_Q Q(t)Y'(t+h)\sqrt{h}]\right)$$
$$= \sigma\sigma_Q \rho X(t)Q(t)h + \text{terms with power} \geq \tfrac{3}{2}$$

One way to make these calculations mechanical is to use the following so-called "multiplication rules" for terms containing dt and dZ:

$$dt \times dZ = 0 \qquad (20.17a)$$
$$(dt)^2 = 0 \qquad (20.17b)$$

$$(dZ)^2 = dt \qquad (20.17c)$$

$$dZ \times dZ' = \rho dt \qquad (20.17d)$$

The reasoning behind these multiplication rules is that the multiplications resulting in powers of dt greater than 1 vanish, relatively speaking.

20.5 THE SHARPE RATIO

If asset i has expected return α_i, the risk premium is defined as

$$\text{Risk premium}_i = \alpha_i - r$$

where r is the risk-free rate. A basic idea in finance is that the return on an asset is linked to its risk, where risk is measured as the covariance between the return on the asset and investor utility.[4] In the Capital Asset Pricing Model (CAPM), the risk that matters is the covariance between a stock and the market return since investor utility depends on the market return. There are other models of risk, but for our purposes we need not take a stand on a particular model.

The **Sharpe ratio** for asset i is the risk premium, $\alpha_i - r$, per unit of volatility, σ_i:

$$\text{Sharpe ratio}_i = \frac{\alpha_i - r}{\sigma_i} \qquad (20.18)$$

The Sharpe ratio is commonly used to compare well-diversified portfolios and is not intended to compare individual assets. In particular, if diversifiable risk is different, two assets with the same σ can have different risk premiums (and hence different Sharpe ratios) if they have different covariances with the market. However, we *can* use the Sharpe ratio to compare two perfectly correlated claims, such as a derivative and its underlying asset. The main point of this section is that two assets that are perfectly correlated will have the same Sharpe ratio.

To see that two perfectly-correlated assets must have the same Sharpe ratio, consider the processes for two non-dividend paying stocks:

$$dS_1 = \alpha_1 S_1 dt + \sigma_1 S_1 dZ \qquad (20.19)$$

$$dS_2 = \alpha_2 S_2 dt + \sigma_2 S_2 dZ \qquad (20.20)$$

Because the two stock prices are driven by the same dZ, it must be the case that $(\alpha_1 - r)/\sigma_1 = (\alpha_2 - r)/\sigma_2$, or else there will be an arbitrage opportunity.

Before we examine the arbitrage, let's explore the intuition. For example, in the Capital Asset Pricing Model (CAPM), the risk premium of asset i, $\alpha_i - r$, is

$$\alpha_i - r = \beta_i(\alpha_M - r) \qquad (20.21)$$

---

[4] See Appendix 11.B.

where α_M is the expected return on the market portfolio. The beta of asset i is

$$\beta_i = \frac{\rho_{i,M}\sigma_i}{\sigma_M} \tag{20.22}$$

where $\rho_{i,M}$ is the correlation of asset i with the market, σ_i is the volatility of the asset, and σ_M is the market volatility. Using equation (20.22), we can rewrite equation (20.21) as

$$\frac{\alpha_i - r}{\sigma_i} = \rho_{i,M}\frac{\alpha_M - r}{\sigma_M} \tag{20.23}$$

Thus, if two assets have the same correlation with the market ($\rho_{i,M}$), they will have the same Sharpe ratios. In equations (20.19) and (20.20), the fundamental uncertainty driving the processes for both S_1 and S_2 is dZ. Thus, both assets have the same correlation with the market, and in the CAPM would have equal Sharpe ratios.

We will now demonstrate an arbitrage if the Sharpe ratios in equations (20.19) and (20.20) are different. Suppose that the Sharpe ratio for asset 1 is greater than that for asset 2. We then buy $1/(\sigma_1 S_1)$ shares of asset 1 and short $1/(\sigma_2 S_2)$ shares of asset 2. These two positions will generally have different costs, so we invest (or borrow) the cost difference, $1/\sigma_1 - 1/\sigma_2$, by buying (or borrowing) the risk-free bond, which has the rate of return rdt. The return on the two assets and the risk-free bond is

$$\frac{1}{\sigma_1 S_1}dS_1 - \frac{1}{\sigma_2 S_2}dS_2 + \left(\frac{1}{\sigma_2} - \frac{1}{\sigma_1}\right)rdt = \left(\frac{\alpha_1 - r}{\sigma_1} - \frac{\alpha_2 - r}{\sigma_2}\right)dt \tag{20.24}$$

This demonstrates that if the Sharpe ratio of asset 1 is greater than that of asset 2, we can construct a zero-investment portfolio with a positive risk-free return. Therefore, to preclude arbitrage assets 1 and 2 must have the same Sharpe ratio.[5]

This link between volatility and risk premiums for perfectly correlated assets arose in Chapter 12 when we discussed option elasticity. There we saw that the Sharpe ratio for a stock and an option on the stock are the same. The reason is that the stock and option have the same underlying source of risk—the same dZ. They do not have the same volatility—the volatility of a call option is greater than that of the stock—and, hence, they do not have the same risk premium, but they do have the same Sharpe ratio.

The Risk-Neutral Process

We saw in discussing the binomial model in Chapters 10 and 11 that we could interpret the model either as risk-neutral, in which case we set probabilities so that assets earn the risk-free rate and we discount at the risk-free rate, or as representing the true stock price process, in which case we use true probabilities and discount at an appropriate (not risk-free) interest rate. In valuing options using Monte Carlo simulation in Chapter 19, we again used the risk-neutral approach, assuming that stocks on average earn the risk-free rate and discounting expected payoffs at that rate.

----

[5]Problem 20.12 asks you to consider the case where two assets are perfectly *negatively* correlated.

We can do something comparable with Itô processes. Suppose the true price process is

$$\frac{dS(t)}{S(t)} = (\alpha - \delta)dt + \sigma dZ(t)$$

where δ is the dividend yield on the stock. We can write a risk-neutral version of this process by subtracting the risk premium, $\alpha - r$, from the drift, $\alpha - \delta$. This gives

$$\frac{dS(t)}{S(t)} = (r - \delta)dt + \sigma dZ^*(t) \tag{20.25}$$

In the second equation, we not only subtract $\alpha - r$ from the drift $\alpha - \delta$, we also replace $dZ(t)$ with $dZ^*(t)$. As in the binomial model, when we replace α with r, we must also modify the probabilities associated with stock price movements. In effect, when we take expectations of the future stock price, we use a distribution with a mean that differs depending upon whether we are using the true or risk-neutral distribution. The probability distribution associated with the risk-neutral process is said to be the **risk-neutral measure.**[6] When we perform risk-neutral pricing, we will implicitly assume that we are using the risk-neutral measure.

An important point, both here and in the binomial model, is that when we switch to the risk-neutral process, the volatility remains the same.

20.6 ITÔ'S LEMMA

Suppose a stock with an expected instantaneous return of α, dividend yield of δ, and instantaneous volatility σ follows geometric Brownian motion:

$$dS(t) = (\alpha - \delta)S(t)dt + \sigma S(t)dZ(t) \tag{20.26}$$

In this equation, α, δ, and σ can be functions of the stock price. Now suppose that we also have a derivative claim that is a function of the stock price. Express the value of this claim as $V[S(t), t]$. Given that we know how the stock behaves, how does the claim behave? In particular, how can we describe the behavior of the claim in terms of the behavior of S?

Functions of an Itô Process

Recall that dS is a geometric random walk with drift. Suppose for a moment that the drift is zero, in which case S obeys a geometric random walk with equal probabilities of up and down moves.

Now look at Figure 20.1. Notice that equal changes up and down in S do not give rise to equal changes in $V(S, t)$. Since V is an increasing convex function of S, a change

---

[6]The technical result underlying this discussion is called **Girsanov's theorem.** Two good references on this topic are Baxter and Rennie (1996) and Neftci (2000, Chapter 14).

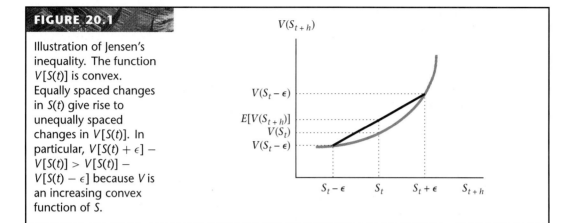

FIGURE 20.1

Illustration of Jensen's inequality. The function $V[S(t)]$ is convex. Equally spaced changes in $S(t)$ give rise to unequally spaced changes in $V[S(t)]$. In particular, $V[S(t) + \epsilon] - V[S(t)] > V[S(t)] - V[S(t) - \epsilon]$ because V is an increasing convex function of S.

to $S + \epsilon$ increases V by more than a change to $S - \epsilon$ decreases V. Thus, if the expected change in S is zero, the expected change in V will not be zero. The actual expected change will depend on the curvature of V and the probability distribution of S, which tells us the expected size of the up and down moves.

In Figure 20.1, the second derivative is positive; i.e., the slope of V becomes greater as S increases. As is evident in the figure, the expected change in V will then be positive. The figure illustrates Jensen's inequality: $V[E(S)] \leq E[V(S)]$ if V is convex (see Appendix C).

Using a Taylor series expansion (see Appendix 13.A), we can see how V depends on S. We have

$$V(S + dS, t + dt) = V(S, t) + V_S dS + V_t dt$$
$$+ \tfrac{1}{2} V_{SS} (dS)^2 + \tfrac{1}{2} V_{tt} (dt)^2 + V_{St} dS dt$$
$$+ \text{ terms in } (dt)^{3/2} \text{ and higher}$$

The multiplication rules already discussed in Section 20.4 tell us that since S is an Itô process, the terms $(dt)^2$ and $dS \times dt$ vanish, along with all higher-order terms. The reason is that since the interval of time is short, the noise term dominates, and the squared noise term is the same order of magnitude as the drift.[7] This calculation is the basis for Itô's Lemma.

Proposition 20.1 (Itô's Lemma)   Let the change in the stock price be given by equation (20.26). If $C[S(t), t]$ is a twice-differentiable function of $S(t)$, then the change

---

[7]You can consult Arnold (1974) or Merton (1990) for more details.

in C, $dC[S(t), t]$, is

$$dC(S, t) = C_S dS + \tfrac{1}{2} C_{SS}(dS)^2 + C_t dt \tag{20.27}$$

$$= \left[(\alpha - \delta)SC_S + \tfrac{1}{2}\sigma^2 S^2 C_{SS} + C_t\right] dt + \sigma S C_S dZ$$

(We use the notation $C_S = \partial C / \partial S$, $C_{SS} = \partial^2 C / \partial S^2$, and $C_t = \partial C / \partial t$.) The terms in square brackets are the expected change in the option price. ❧

If there is no uncertainty, that is if $\sigma = 0$, then Itô's Lemma reduces to the calculation of a total derivative familiar from ordinary calculus:

$$dC(S, t) = C_S dS + C_t dt$$

The extra term involving the variance arises from $(dS)^2$ and is the Jensen's inequality correction due to the uncertainty of the stochastic process.

We encountered Itô's Lemma—without naming it—when we discussed delta-gamma approximations in Chapter 13. Equation (13.6) stated

$$C[S(t + h), t + h] - C[S(t), t] \approx [S(t + h) - S(t)]\Delta[S(t), t]$$
$$+ \tfrac{1}{2}[S(t + h) - S(t)]^2 \Gamma[S(t), t] + \Theta[S(t), t]h$$

Make the substitutions $h \to dt$ and $S(t + h) - S(t) \to dS$, and recall that Γ, Δ, and Θ are just partial derivatives of the option price:

$$\Delta \equiv C_S; \quad \Gamma \equiv C_{SS}; \quad \Theta = C_t$$

The delta-gamma approximation over a very short period of time is Itô's Lemma.

We can use Itô's Lemma to verify that the expression for a lognormal stock price satisfies the equation for geometric Brownian motion, equation (20.26).

Example 20.1 The expression for a lognormal stock price is

$$S(t) = S(0)e^{(\alpha - \delta - \frac{1}{2}\sigma^2)t + \sigma Z(t)} \tag{20.28}$$

Although we did not write it explicitly, the stock price is a function of the Brownian process $Z(t)$. We can use Itô's Lemma to characterize the behavior of the stock as a function of $Z(t)$. We have

$$\frac{\partial S(t)}{\partial t} = \left(\alpha - \delta - \frac{1}{2}\sigma^2\right) S(t); \quad \frac{\partial S(t)}{\partial Z(t)} = \sigma S(t); \quad \frac{\partial^2 S(t)}{\partial Z(t)^2} = \sigma^2 S(t)$$

Itô's Lemma states that $dS(t)$ is given as

$$dS(t) = \frac{\partial S(t)}{\partial t}dt + \frac{\partial S(t)}{\partial Z(t)}dZ(t) + \frac{1}{2}\frac{\partial^2 S(t)}{\partial Z(t)^2}[dZ(t)]^2$$

$$= \left(\alpha - \delta - \frac{1}{2}\sigma^2\right)S(t)dt + \sigma S(t)dZ(t) + \frac{1}{2}\sigma^2 S(t)dt$$

$$= (\alpha - \delta)S(t)dt + \sigma S(t)dZ(t)$$

In going from the second line to the third we have used the fact that $dZ(t)^2 = dt$. This calculation demonstrates that by using Ito's Lemma to differentiate equation (20.28), we recover equation (20.26). ⟩

Multivariate Itô's Lemma

So far we have considered the case where the value of an option depends on a single Itô process. A derivative may have a value depending on more than one price, in which case we can use a multivariate generalization of Itô's Lemma.

Proposition 20.2 (Multivariate Itô's Lemma)   Suppose we have n correlated Itô processes:

$$\frac{dS_i(t)}{S_i(t)} = \alpha_i dt + \sigma_i dz_i, \qquad i = 1, \ldots, n$$

Denote the pairwise correlations as $E(dz_i \times dz_j) = \rho_{i,j}dt$. If $C(S_1, \ldots, S_n, t)$ is a twice-differentiable function of the S_i's, we have

$$dC(S_1, \ldots, S_n, t) = \sum_{i=1}^{n} C_{S_i} dS_i + \frac{1}{2}\sum_{i=1}^{n}\sum_{j=1}^{n} dS_i dS_j C_{S_i S_j} + C_t dt$$

The expected change in C per unit time is

$$\frac{1}{dt}E\left[dC(S_1, \ldots, S_n, t)\right] = \sum_{i=1}^{n} \alpha_i S_i C_{S_i} + \frac{1}{2}\sum_{i=1}^{n}\sum_{j=1}^{n} \sigma_i \sigma_j \rho_{ij} S_i S_j C_{S_i S_j} + C_t$$

⟩

Example 20.2   Suppose $C(S_1, S_2) = S_1 S_2$. Then by Itô's Lemma we have

$$d(S_1 S_2) = S_2 dS_1 + S_1 dS_2 + dS_1 dS_2$$

This implies that

$$\frac{1}{dt}E(dC) = (\alpha_1 + \alpha_2 + \rho\sigma_1\sigma_2)S_1 S_2$$

Note that since $C(S_1, S_2)$ does not depend explicitly on time, $C_t = 0$. ⟩

Example 20.2 is interesting because we know that the product of lognormal variables is lognormal. Hence, we might expect that the drift for the product of two lognormal variables would just be the sum of the drifts. However, Example 20.2 shows that the drift has an extra term, stemming from the term $dS_1 dS_2$, due to the covariation between the two variables. The intuition for this result will be explored further in the discussion of quantos in Chapter 22.

20.7 Valuing a Claim on S^a

Suppose we have a claim with a payoff depending on S raised to some power. For example, we may have a claim that pays $S(T)^2$ at time T. In this section we examine this claim with two goals. First, we want to compute the price of such a claim. Second, we want to understand the different ways to approach the problem.

The following proposition gives us the forward and prepaid forward prices for this claim.

Proposition 20.3 Suppose S follows the process given by equation (20.26). The value at time 0 of a claim paying $S(T)^a$—the prepaid forward price—is

$$F_{0,T}^P[S(T)^a] = e^{-rT} S(0)^a e^{[a(r-\delta)+\frac{1}{2}a(a-1)\sigma^2]T} \qquad (20.29)$$

The forward price for $S(T)^a$ is

$$F_{0,T}[S(T)^a] = S(0)^a e^{[a(r-\delta)+\frac{1}{2}a(a-1)\sigma^2]T} \qquad (20.30)$$

The lease rate for a claim paying S^a is $\delta^* = r - a(r - \delta) - \frac{1}{2}a(a - 1)\sigma^2$. ❧

To prove this proposition, we will first use Itô's Lemma to determine the process followed by S^a. We will then use three different arguments to obtain the pricing formula, equation (20.29).

The Process Followed by S^a

Consider a claim maturing at time T that pays $C[S(T), T] = S(T)^a$. If S follows equation (20.26), then we can use Ito's Lemma to determine the process followed by S^a. We obtain

$$dS^a = aS^{a-1}dS + \frac{1}{2}a(a - 1)S^{a-2}(\sigma S)^2 dt$$
$$= aS^a \frac{dS}{S} + \frac{1}{2}a(a - 1)S^a\sigma^2 dt$$

Dividing by S^a, we get

$$\frac{dS^a}{S^a} = \left[a(\alpha - \delta) + \frac{1}{2}a(a - 1)\sigma^2\right]dt + a\sigma dZ \qquad (20.31)$$

Thus, S^a follows geometric Brownian motion with drift $a(\alpha - \delta) + \frac{1}{2}a(a - 1)\sigma^2$ and risk $a\sigma dZ$. Hence, if α is the expected return for S, the expected return of a claim with price S^a will be

$$a(\alpha - r) + r \tag{20.32}$$

Thus, the risk premium is $a(\alpha - r)$.

There is another way to obtain the drift term in equation (20.31) that does not require the use of Itô's Lemma. We can write

$$S(T)^a = S(0)^a e^{a(\alpha - \delta - 0.5\sigma^2)T + a\sigma Z(T)}$$

Using equation (18.13) to compute the expectation of a lognormal variable, we have

$$E[S(T)^a] = S(0)^a e^{a(\alpha - \delta - 0.5\sigma^2)T + 0.5a^2\sigma^2 T}$$
$$= S(0)^a e^{[a(\alpha - \delta) + 0.5a(a-1)\sigma^2]T}$$

Thus, the expected continuously compounded return on S^a is $a(\alpha - \delta) + 0.5a(a - 1)\sigma^2$, as in equation (20.31).

Proving the Proposition

Given equations (20.31) and (20.32), there are three arguments we can use to compute the time-0 value of a claim that pays $S(T)^a$ at time T. All three methods will confirm Proposition 20.3.

Risk-neutral pricing First we use risk-neutral pricing. Subtract the risk premium, $a(\alpha - r)$, from the drift, $a(\alpha - \delta)$, to obtain the following as the risk-neutral process for dS^a:

$$\frac{dS^a}{S^a} = \left[a(r - \delta) + \frac{1}{2}a(a - 1)\sigma^2 \right] dt + a\sigma dZ^* \tag{20.33}$$

Using the drift term in equation (20.33), the expected value of the claim at time T under the risk-neutral measure, which we denote E^*, is

$$E_0^*[S(T)^a] = S(0)^a e^{[a(r - \delta) + \frac{1}{2}a(a-1)\sigma^2]T} \tag{20.34}$$

We saw in Section 10.1 that the expected price under the risk-neutral measure is the forward price. Thus, equation (20.34) gives the forward price. Discounting this expression at the risk-free rate gives us the prepaid forward price, equation (20.29).

Discounted cash flow We can also value the claim on S^a by discounting the true (nonrisk-neutral) expected value. To do this we must compute the expected value of the claim and discount the expected payoff appropriately. From equation (20.14), the expected value of $S(T)^a$ is

$$E_0[S(T)^a] = S(0)^a e^{[a(\alpha - \delta) + \frac{1}{2}a(a-1)\sigma^2]T}$$

The discount rate is expression (20.32). The price at time 0 of a claim paying $S(T)^a$ at time T is the prepaid forward price, which we will denote $F_{0,T}^P(S^a)$:

$$F_{0,T}^P(S^a) = e^{-[r+a(\alpha-r)]T} E(S(T)^a)$$
$$= e^{-[r+a(\alpha-r)]T} S(0)^a e^{[a(\alpha-\delta)+\frac{1}{2}a(a-1)\sigma^2]T}$$
$$= S(0)^a e^{-rT} e^{[a(r-\delta)+\frac{1}{2}a(a-1)\sigma^2]T}$$

Note that the risk premium on the stock, $\alpha - r$, drops out. The forward price for S^a, which we will denote $F_{0,T}(S^a)$, is just the future value of the prepaid forward:

$$F_{0,T}(S^a) = e^{rT} F_{0,T}^P(S^a)$$
$$= S(0)^a e^{[a(r-\delta)+\frac{1}{2}a(a-1)\sigma^2]T}$$

The use of a single discount rate works in this case because the payoff to the claim is simple. In general, computing a price as a nonrisk-neutral discounted expected value is more difficult than this.

Finding the lease rate Finally, we value the claim by finding its lease rate. We ask what cash payment the claim would have to make in order for us to willingly hold it, or equivalently, what payment we would have to make to short-sell it. We can then treat the lease rate as the dividend yield and compute the forward price.

From equation (20.31), the claim has risk $a\sigma dZ$ and so must be expected to earn a rate of return of $a(\alpha - r) + r$. Equation (20.31) also tells us that the actual expected capital gain on this security is $a(\alpha - \delta) + \frac{1}{2}a(a - 1)\sigma^2$.

In order to hold the security, we would need to earn the difference between the expected return and expected capital gain as a cash payment. Thus, the payment would have to be

$$\delta^* = a(\alpha - r) + r - \left[a(\alpha - \delta) + \tfrac{1}{2}a(a - 1)\sigma^2\right]$$
$$= r - a(r - \delta) - \tfrac{1}{2}a(a - 1)\sigma^2$$

The value δ^* is the lease rate of the claim paying S^a. The prepaid forward price is then

$$F_{0,T}^P(S^a) = S(0)^a e^{-\delta^* T}$$
$$= S(0)^a e^{[-r+a(r-\delta)+\frac{1}{2}a(a-1)\sigma^2]T}$$

This is the same as equation (20.29).

Specific Examples

We now examine four special cases of equations (20.29) and (20.30): $a = -1, 0, 1$, and 2.

Claims on S First, suppose $a = 1$. Equation (20.29) then gives us

$$V(0) = S(0)e^{-\delta T}$$

This equation is just the prepaid forward price on a stock.

Claims on S^0 If $a = 0$, the claim does not depend on the stock price; rather since $S^0 = 1$, it is a bond. Setting $a = 0$ gives us

$$V(0) = e^{-rT}$$

which is the price of a T-period pure discount bond.

Claims on S^2 When $a = 2$ the claim pays $S(T)^2$. From equation (20.30), the forward price is

$$\begin{aligned}
F_{0,T}(S^2) &= e^{rT}S(0)^2 e^{-[-r+2\delta-\sigma^2]T} \\
&= S(0)^2 e^{2(r-\delta)T} e^{\sigma^2 T} \quad\quad\quad (20.35) \\
&= \left[F_{0,T}(S)\right]^2 e^{\sigma^2 T}
\end{aligned}$$

Thus, the forward price on the squared stock price is the squared forward price times a variance term. The squared forward price is intuitive, but the variance term requires some discussion.

One way to think about equation (20.35) is to perform the following thought experiment. Suppose that we have an ordinary stock with a price denominated in dollars. Now imagine that we have a second stock that is identical to the first *except* that instead of receiving dollars when we sell the stock, we receive one share of ordinary stock for each dollar in the quoted price of the second stock. This conversion from dollars to shares is what it means to have a squared security.

With the squared stock, when the stock price goes up, we not only receive the extra dollars a share of stock is worth, but we also receive the appreciated value of each share we receive in lieu of dollars. We therefore receive an extra gain when the stock price goes up.

The effect works in reverse when the price goes down. In that case, we receive fewer dollars per share, and each share received in lieu of dollars is worth less as well. However, the lower price per share hurts us less because we receive fewer shares! Thus, on average, the extra we receive when the price goes up exceeds the loss when the price goes down. This effect becomes more important as the variance is greater, since large losses and large gains become more likely.

The result is that we will pay extra for the security, and the extra amount we pay is positively related to the variance. This example provides another illustration of Jensen's inequality.

Claims on 1/S Finally, let $a = -1$, so the claim pays $1/S$. Using equation (20.30) with $a = -1$, we get

$$F_{0,T}(1/S) = [1/S(0)] \, e^{(\delta-r)T} e^{\sigma^2 T}$$
$$= F_{0,T}^{-1} e^{\sigma^2 T}$$

As with the squared security, the forward price is increasing in volatility.

The payoffs for both the S^2 and $1/S$ securities are convex; hence, Jensen's inequality tells us that the price is higher when the asset price is risky than when it is certain. In both cases the forward price contains a volatility term, and in both cases the price is increasing in volatility. If we considered a concave claim, for example $\sqrt{S}$, the effect of increased volatility would be to lower the value of the claim. See the end-of-chapter problems for an example.

Valuing a Claim on $S^a Q^b$

Now we generalize the previous example by having two prices. Consider a claim paying $S(T)^a Q(T)^b$ where S follows

$$\frac{dS}{S} = (\alpha_S - \delta_S)dt + \sigma_S dZ_S \tag{20.36}$$

and Q follows

$$\frac{dQ}{Q} = (\alpha_Q - \delta_Q)dt + \sigma_Q dZ_Q \tag{20.37}$$

where

$$dZ_S dZ_Q = \rho dt$$

Using multivariate Ito's Lemma, we have

$$dS^a Q^b = aS^{a-1} Q^b dS + bS^a Q^{b-1} dQ + \tfrac{1}{2} \big[a(a-1)S^{a-2} Q^b \, (dS)^2$$
$$+ b(b-1)S^a Q^{b-2} \, (dQ)^2 + 2ab S^{a-1} Q^{b-1} dS dQ \big]$$
$$= S^a Q^b \left(a\frac{dS}{S} + b\frac{dQ}{Q} + \tfrac{1}{2} \big[a(a-1)\sigma_S^2 + b(b-1)\sigma_Q^2 + 2ab\rho\sigma_S\sigma_Q \big] dt \right)$$

The process for $S^a Q^b$ is therefore

$$\frac{d\left(S^a Q^b\right)}{S^a Q^b} = \big[a(\alpha_S - \delta_S) + b(\alpha_Q - \delta_Q) + \tfrac{1}{2}a(a-1)\sigma_S^2 + \tfrac{1}{2}b(b-1)\sigma_Q^2$$
$$+ ab\rho\sigma_S\sigma_Q \big] dt + a\sigma_S dZ_S + b\sigma_Q dZ_Q \tag{20.38}$$

The expected return on this claim depends on the risk premiums for both S and Q:[8]

$$r + a(\alpha_S - r) + b(\alpha_Q - r)$$

----

[8] Problem 20.11 asks you to verify that this expression gives the expected return.

As before, there are three ways to find the price of a prepaid forward on this claim. Here we use risk-neutral pricing. Problem 20.13 asks you to use the discounting and lease-rate methods to find the answer.

The risk-neutral process for $dS^a Q^b$ is obtained by subtracting the risk premium, $a(\alpha_S - r) + b(\alpha_Q - r)$, from the drift in equation (20.38). This gives

$$\frac{d\left(S^a Q^b\right)}{S^a Q^b} = \left[a(r - \delta_S) + b(r - \delta_Q) + \tfrac{1}{2}a(a-1)\sigma_S^2 + \tfrac{1}{2}b(b-1)\sigma_Q^2 \right.$$
$$\left. + ab\rho\sigma_S\sigma_Q \right] dt + a\sigma_S dZ_S^* + b\sigma_Q dZ_Q^*$$

The expected time-T value of $S^a Q^b$ under the risk-neutral measure is

$$E^*[S(T)^a Q(T)^b] = S(0)^a Q(0)^b e^{[a(r-\delta_S)+b(r-\delta_Q)+\frac{1}{2}a(a-1)\sigma_S^2+\frac{1}{2}b(b-1)\sigma_Q^2+ab\rho\sigma_S\sigma_Q]T}$$

Using Proposition 20.3, in particular equation (20.30), this expression can be rewritten as

$$F_{0,T}(S^a Q^b) = F_{0,T}(S^a) F_{0,T}(Q^b) e^{ab\rho\sigma_S\sigma_Q T} \tag{20.39}$$

The expression on the right is the product of the forward prices times a factor that accounts for the covariance between the two assets.

This is an important result: The price that results when we multiply two prices together requires a correction for the covariance. We will see this result again in Chapters 21 and 22. The following proposition summarizes this result.

Proposition 20.4 Suppose that S and Q follow the processes given by equations (20.36) and (20.37). The forward prices for S^a and Q^b are given by Proposition 20.3. The forward price for $S^a Q^b$ is the product of those two forward prices times a covariance correction factor:

$$F_{t,T}(S^a Q^b) = F_{t,T}(S^a) F_{t,T}(Q^b) e^{ab\rho\sigma_S\sigma_Q(T-t)}$$

The variance of $S^a Q^b$ is given by

$$a^2\sigma_S^2 + b^2\sigma_Q^2 + 2ab\rho\sigma_S\sigma_Q \qquad ⬧$$

Incidentally, the squared security, S^2, is a special case of Proposition 20.4. When $S = Q$, $a = b = 1$, and $\rho = 1$ (since a variable is perfectly correlated with itself) the covariance term becomes

$$ab\rho\sigma_S\sigma_Q = \sigma_S^2$$

This gives us the same result as equation (20.35) for the forward price for a squared stock.

Proposition 20.4 can be generalized. Suppose there are n stocks, each of which follows the process

$$\frac{dS_i}{S_i} = (\alpha_i - \delta_i)dt + \sigma_i dz_i \tag{20.40}$$

where $dz_i dz_j = \rho_{ij} dt$. Let

$$V(t) = \prod_{i=1}^{n} S_i^{a_i} \tag{20.41}$$

The forward price for V is then

$$F_{0,T}(V) = \prod_{i=1}^{n} [F_{0,T}(S_i)]^{a_i} e^{\sum_{i=1}^{n-1} \sum_{j=i+1}^{n} \rho_{ij}\sigma_i\sigma_j a_i a_j T} \tag{20.42}$$

20.8 JUMPS IN THE STOCK PRICE[9]

A practical objection to the Brownian process as a model of the stock price is that Brownian paths are continuous—there are no discrete jumps in the stock price. In practice, asset prices occasionally do seem to jump; a famous example is October 19, 1987, when the Dow Jones index fell 22% in one day. A move of this size is exceedingly unlikely in the lognormal model. On a smaller scale, consider the stock price of a company that reports unexpectedly favorable earnings. To account for such nonlognormal behavior, Merton (1976) proposed modeling the stock price as lognormal with an occasional discrete jump. One way to model such jumps is by using the Poisson distribution mixed with a standard Brownian process, as we did in Chapter 19.

As discussed in Chapter 19, the Poisson distribution counts the number of jumps that occur in any interval. Conditional on a jump occurring, we assign some distribution to the change in the stock price. It is convenient to use the lognormal density to compute the price change if the jump occurs.

We can write a stock price process with jumps as follows. With the Poisson process, the probability of a jump event is proportional to the length of time. Furthermore, for an infinitesimal interval dt, the probability of more than a single jump is zero (this is part of the definition of the Poisson process). Let $q(t)$ represent the cumulative jump and dq the change in the cumulative jump. Most of the time, there is no jump and $dq = 0$. When there is a jump, we let the random variable Y denote the magnitude of the jump, and $k = E(Y) - 1$ is then the expected percentage change in the stock price. If λ is the expected number of jumps per unit time over an interval dt, then

$$Prob(\text{jump}) = \lambda dt$$

$$Prob(\text{no jump}) = 1 - \lambda dt$$

---

[9]This section follows Merton (1976).

We can then write the stock price process as

$$dS(t)/S(t) = (\alpha - \lambda k)dt + \sigma dZ + dq \qquad (20.43)$$

where

$$dq = \begin{cases} 0 & \text{if there is no jump} \\ Y - 1 & \text{if there is a jump} \end{cases}$$

and $E(dq) = \lambda k dt$. The drift term contains $-\lambda k dt$ for the reason discussed in Chapter 19: The dq term has a nonzero expectation, so we subtract $\lambda k dt$ in order to preserve the interpretation of α as the expected return on the stock. We have

$$E(dS/S) = (\alpha - \lambda k)dt + E(\sigma dZ) + E(dq) = \alpha dt$$

Thus, for example, if there is on average a downward jump, then $k < 0$, and, when no jump is occurring, we need extra drift of $-\lambda k dt > 0$ to compensate for the occasional bad times due to the jump.

The upshot of this model is that when no jump is occurring, the stock price S evolves as geometric Brownian motion. When the jump occurs, the new stock price is YS. The fact that it is straightforward to model jumps does not necessarily mean that it is easy to price options when there are jumps. We will discuss this further in Chapter 21.

Proposition 20.5 Suppose an asset follows equation (20.43). If $C(S, t)$ is a twice continuously differentiable function of the stock price, the process followed by C is

$$dC(S, t) = C_S dS + \tfrac{1}{2} C_{SS} \sigma^2 S^2 dt + C_t dt + \lambda E_Y[C(SY, t) - C(S, t)] \qquad (20.44)$$

The last term in equation (20.44) is the expected change in the option price conditional on the jump times the probability of the jump. 🔖

The last term in equation (20.44) accounts for the jump. That term is not present in the version of Itô's Lemma for a stock that cannot jump, equation (20.27).

CHAPTER SUMMARY

A stochastic process $Z(t)$ is a Brownian motion if it is normally distributed, changes independently over time, has variance proportional to time, and is continuous. The change in Brownian motion is denoted $dZ(t)$. The process $Z(t)$ and its change $dZ(t)$ provide the foundation for modern derivatives pricing models. The Brownian process $Z(t)$ by itself would be a poor model of an asset price, but its change, $dZ(t)$, provides a model for asset risk. By multiplying $dZ(t)$ by a scale factor and adding a drift term, we can control the variance and mean, and thereby construct more realistic processes. Such processes are called Itô processes or diffusion processes. Black and Scholes used just such a process in their original derivation of the option pricing model.

Given that a stock follows a particular Itô process, Itô's Lemma permits us to compute the process followed by an option or other claim on the stock. The pricing of claims with payoffs S^a and $S^a Q^b$, where S and Q follow geometric Brownian motion, illustrates the use of Itô's Lemma.

An important objection to Brownian motion as a driving process for a stock is the continuity of its path. It is possible to add jumps to a Brownian process, and there is a version of Itô's Lemma for such cases.

FURTHER READING

We will use the concepts in this chapter throughout the rest of the book. In the next chapter we will directly apply the concepts of this chapter, in particular Itô's Lemma, showing that prices of derivatives must satisfy a particular partial differential equation. In later chapters we will use these concepts to discuss the pricing of exotic options (Chapter 22), options based on interest rates (Chapter 23), and risk assessment (Chapter 24).

Many books cover the material in this chapter at a more advanced level. Merton (1990) in particular is an outstanding introduction. Other good sources include Neftci (2000), Duffie (1996a), Wilmott (1998), Karatzas and Shreve (1991), and Baxter and Rennie (1996).

PROBLEMS

For the following four problems, use Itô's Lemma to determine the process followed by the specified equation, assuming that $S(t)$ follows (a) arithmetic Brownian motion, equation (20.8); (b) a mean reverting process, equation (20.9); and (c) geometric Brownian motion, equation (20.26).

20.1. Use Itô's Lemma to evaluate $d[ln(S)]$.

20.2. Use Itô's Lemma to evaluate dS^2.

20.3. Use Itô's Lemma to evaluate dS^{-1}.

20.4. Use Itô's Lemma to evaluate $d(\sqrt{S})$.

20.5. Suppose that S follows equation (20.36) and Q follows equation (20.37). Use Itô's Lemma to find the process followed by $S^2 Q^{0.5}$.

20.6. Suppose that S follows equation (20.36) and Q follows equation (20.37). Use Itô's Lemma to find the process followed by $ln(SQ)$.

20.7. Suppose $S(0) = \$100$, $r = 0.06$, $\sigma_S = 0.4$ and $\delta = 0$. Use equation (20.29) to compute prices for claims that pay the following:

a. S^2

b. $\sqrt{S}$

c. S^{-2}

Compare your answers to the answers you obtained to Problem 19.6.

20.8. Suppose that $ln(S)$ and $ln(Q)$ have correlation $\rho = -0.3$ and that $S(0) = \$100$, $Q(0) = \$100$, $r = 0.06$, $\sigma_S = 0.4$ and $\sigma_Q = 0.2$. Neither stock pays dividends. Use equation (20.39) to find the price today of claims that pay

a. SQ

b. S/Q

c. $\sqrt{SQ}$

d. $1/(SQ)$

e. S^2Q

Compare your answers to the answers you obtained to Problem 19.7.

20.9. Suppose that $X(t)$ follows equation (20.9). Use Itô's Lemma to verify that a solution to this differential equation is

$$X_t = X(0)e^{-\lambda t} + \alpha\left(1 - e^{-\lambda t}\right) + \sigma \int_0^t e^{\lambda(s-t)}dZ_s$$

(Hint: Note that when t increases by a small amount, the integral term changes by $dZ(t)$.)

20.10. The formula for an infinitely lived call is given in equation (12.16). Suppose that S follows equation (20.26), with α replaced by r and that $E^*(dV) = rVdt$. Use Itô's Lemma to verify that the value of the call, $V(S)$, satisfies this equation:

$$\tfrac{1}{2}\sigma^2 S^2 V_{SS} + (r - \delta)SV_S - rV = 0$$

20.11. Suppose that the processes for S_1 and S_2 are given by these two equations:

$$dS_1 = \alpha_1 S_1 dt + \sigma_1 S_1 dZ_1$$
$$dS_2 = \alpha_2 S_2 dt + \sigma_2 S_2 dZ_2$$

Note that the diffusions dZ_1 and dZ_2 are different. In this problem we want to find the expected return on Q, α_Q, where Q follows the process

$$dQ = \alpha_Q Qdt + Q\left(\eta_1 dZ_1 + \eta_2 dZ_2\right)$$

Show that, to avoid arbitrage,

$$\alpha_Q - r = \frac{\eta_1}{\sigma_1}(\alpha_1 - r) + \frac{\eta_2}{\sigma_2}(\alpha_2 - r)$$

(Hint: Consider the strategy of buying one unit of Q and shorting $Q\eta_1/S_1\sigma_1$ units of S_1 and $Q\eta_2/S_2\sigma_2$ units of S_2. Finance any net cost using risk-free bonds.)

20.12. Suppose that S follows equation (20.26) with $\delta = 0$. Consider an asset that follows the process

$$dQ/Q = \alpha_Q dt - \eta dZ$$

What is α_Q, expressed in terms of α? (Hint: Find a zero-investment position in S and Q that eliminates risk.)

20.13. Suppose that S and Q follow equations (20.36) and (20.37). Derive the value of a claim paying $S(T)^a Q(T)^b$ by each of the following methods:

    a. Computing the expected value of the claim and discounting at an appropriate rate. (Hint: The expected return on the claim can be derived using the result of Problem 11.)

    b. Computing the lease rate and substituting this into the formula for the forward price.

20.14. Assume that one stock follows the process

$$dS/S = \alpha dt + \sigma dZ \qquad (20.45)$$

Another stock follows the process

$$dQ/Q = \alpha_Q dt + \sigma dZ + dq_1 + dq_2 \qquad (20.46)$$

(Note that the σdZ terms for S and Q are identical.) Neither stock pays dividends. dq_1 and dq_2 are both Poisson jump processes with Poisson parameters λ_1 and λ_2. Conditional on either jump occurring the percentage change in the stock price is $Y_1 - 1$ or $Y_2 - 1$.

    Consider the two stock price processes, equations (20.45) and (20.46).

    a. If there were no jump terms (i.e., $\lambda_1 = \lambda_2 = 0$), what would be the relation between α and α_Q?

    b. Suppose there is just one jump term ($\lambda_2 = 0$) and that $Y_1 > 1$. In words, what does it mean to have $Y_1 > 1$? What can you say about the relation between α and α_Q?

    c. Write an expression for α_Q when both jump terms are nonzero. Explain intuitively why α_Q might be greater or less than α.

Chapter 21
The Black-Scholes Equation

In deriving the option pricing formula, Black and Scholes studied the problem faced by a delta-hedging market-maker. As we saw in Chapter 13, the market-maker who sells a call option then buys shares to offset the risk of the written call. To analyze this situation it is necessary to characterize the risk of the position as a function of the share price. Itô's Lemma, discussed in Chapter 20, provides a tool that permits us to see how the option price changes in response to the stock price.

Black and Scholes assumed that the stock follows geometric Brownian motion and used Itô's Lemma to describe the behavior of the option price. Their analysis yields a partial differential equation, which the correct option pricing formula must satisfy.

In this chapter we study the Black-Scholes approach to pricing options. This methodology is important not only for pricing European call options; it provides the intellectual foundation for pricing virtually all derivatives, and also underpins the risk-management practices of modern financial institutions.

21.1 DIFFERENTIAL EQUATIONS AND VALUATION UNDER CERTAINTY

The end result of the Black-Scholes derivation is that there is a partial differential equation that describes the price of an option. At first glance the idea of using a differential equation to perform valuation may seem perplexing and special to options. However, differential equations can also be used to motivate even very simple calculations that appear in an elementary finance course. The valuation of stocks and bonds when payouts are known provides simple examples. We will demonstrate this in order to provide some context for the discussion of the Black-Scholes model.

The Valuation Equation

A familiar equation from introductory finance is the following:

$$S(t) = \frac{D(t+h)h + S(t+h)}{(1+r_h)} \tag{21.1}$$

This equation says that the stock price today, $S(t)$, is the discounted value of the future stock price, $S(t+h)$, plus dividends paid over the period of length h, $D(t+h)h$. The discount rate over a period of length h is r_h. We can also interpret $S(t)$ as the price of a bond and $D(t)$ as the coupon payment.

Whatever the interpretation, we can rewrite equation (21.1) as

$$\underbrace{S(t+h) - S(t)}_{\text{Change in Stock Price}} + \underbrace{D(t+h)h}_{\text{Cash Payout}} = \underbrace{r_h S(t)}_{\text{Return on Stock}} \qquad (21.2)$$

Written in this form, the equation says that the change in the stock price plus dividends equals the expected return on the stock. Equation (21.2) is written to emphasize how the stock price should *evolve* over time, rather than the value of the stock at a point in time.

Dividing by h and letting $h \to 0$ in equation (21.2), we obtain

$$\frac{dS(t)}{dt} + D(t) = rS(t) \qquad (21.3)$$

Equation (21.3) is a differential equation stating the condition that the stock must appreciate to earn an appropriate rate of return. The transformation from equation (21.1) to equation (21.3) illustrates the sense in which an equation describing the evolution of the price is linked to valuation.

Bonds

Let $S(t)$ represent the price of a zero-coupon bond that pays \$1 at time T. Since the bond makes no payouts, the evolution of the bond price satisfies equation (21.3) with $D = 0$. The interpretation is that at every time, t, the percentage change in the price of the bond $[\frac{dS(t)}{dt}/S(t)]$ equals the interest rate. This is a familiar condition that the bond should satisfy if it is fairly priced. The general solution to this equation is[1]

$$S(t) = Ae^{-r(T-t)} \qquad (21.4)$$

where A can be any number. You can check that this is in fact a solution by differentiating it to be sure that it satisfies the differential equation.

The differential equation describes the bond's behavior over time but does not tell us what A is. In order to price the bond we also need to know the bond price at some particular point in time. This price is called a **boundary condition.** If the bond is worth \$1 at maturity, we have the boundary condition $S(T) = \$1$. Examining equation (21.4) shows that $S(T)$ can equal \$1 only if $A = \$1$. Thus, the bond price is

$$S(t) = e^{-r(T-t)}$$

The condition $S(T) = \$1$ is called a terminal boundary condition because it sets the bond price at its maturity date. If instead we knew the bond price today, say $P(0)$, we could set A so that the equation gave the correct value for $P(0)$. That value would be an initial boundary condition.

The solution confirms what you already know: The price of the bond is the present value of \$1.

---

[1] You might wish to verify that $S(t) = Ae^{-r(T-t)} + a$ satisifies the differential equation only if $a = 0$.

Dividend-Paying Stocks

We can interpret $S(t)$ as the price of a risk-free stock that pays a continuous fixed dividend of D and has a price of $\bar{S}$ at time T. Equation (21.3) then says that at every time, t, dividends plus capital gains on the stock provide the risk-free rate of return.

Since we know the value at time T will be $\bar{S}$, we also have the boundary condition

$$S(T) = \bar{S}$$

Equation (21.3) with this boundary condition has the solution

$$S(t) = \int_t^T De^{-r(s-t)}ds + \bar{S}e^{-r(T-t)}$$

The stock price today is the discounted value of dividends to be paid between now and time T, plus the present value of the stock at time T. Again, the discrete time version of this equation is the standard present value formula taught in every introductory finance class.

The General Structure

Under certainty a bond or stock will be priced so that the owner receives a risk-free return. The differential equation in these examples describes how the security *changes* from a given point. The boundary condition describes the price at some point in the security's life (such as at a bond's maturity date). By combining the differential equation and the boundary condition, we can determine the price of the bond at any point in time.

By analogy, if at every point you know an automobile's speed and direction, and if you know where it stops, you can work backward to figure out where it started. Essentially the same idea is used to price options: We know the price of the option at maturity (for a call it is $max[0, S - K]$), and we then need to know how the option price changes over time.

21.2 THE BLACK-SCHOLES EQUATION

Consider the problem of owning an option and buying or selling enough shares to create a riskless position. Assume that the stock price follows geometric Brownian motion:

$$\frac{dS}{S} = (\alpha - \delta)dt + \sigma dZ \tag{21.5}$$

where α is the expected return on the stock, σ is the stock's volatility, and δ is the continuous dividend yield on the stock. The option value depends on the stock price, $S(t)$, and time, t, so we write it as $V[S(t), t]$. Also suppose there are risk-free bonds that pay the return r. If we invest W in these bonds, the change in the value of the bond position is

$$dW = rWdt \tag{21.6}$$

Let I denote the total investment in the option, stocks, and the risk-free bond. Suppose that we buy N shares of stock to hedge the option and invest W in risk-free bonds so that our total investment is zero. Then we have

$$I = V(S, t) + NS + W = 0 \qquad (21.7)$$

The zero-investment condition ensures that we keep track of financing costs. It imposes the requirement that in order to buy more of one asset we have to sell something else. To buy stock, for example, we can short-sell bonds.

Applying Itô's Lemma to equation (21.7), we have

$$\begin{aligned} dI &= dV + N(dS + \delta S dt) + dW \\ &= V_t dt + V_S dS + \tfrac{1}{2}\sigma^2 S^2 V_{SS} dt + N(dS + \delta S dt) + rW dt \end{aligned} \qquad (21.8)$$

If we own the physical stock, we receive dividends; this accounts for the $N\delta S dt$ term.[2]

As in Chapter 13, we delta-hedge the position to eliminate risk. The option's delta (Δ) is V_S. We delta-hedge by setting

$$N = -V_S$$

Holding this number of shares has two results. First, the dS and, hence, dZ terms in equation (21.8) vanish, so the portfolio is no longer affected by changes in the stock price—the portfolio is risk-free. Second, because we are also maintaining zero investment (equation (21.7)), our holding of bonds is whatever is necessary to finance the net purchase or sale of the option and the hedging position in stock:

$$W = V_S S - V \qquad (21.9)$$

Substituting $N = -V_S$ and this expression for W into equation (21.8) gives

$$dI = V_t dt + \tfrac{1}{2}\sigma^2 S^2 V_{SS} dt - V_S \delta S dt + r(V_S S - V) dt \qquad (21.10)$$

With a zero-investment, zero-risk portfolio, we should expect to earn a zero return or else there is arbitrage, so that $dI = 0$. Imposing this condition in equation (21.10) and dividing by dt gives

$$\boxed{V_t + \tfrac{1}{2}\sigma^2 S^2 V_{SS} + (r - \delta)SV_S - rV = 0} \qquad (21.11)$$

This is the famous Black-Scholes partial differential equation (PDE), which we will call the Black-Scholes *equation*. (We will refer to the formula giving us the price of a European call as the Black-Scholes *formula*.) Appendix 21.A derives the generalization of equation (21.11) when the value of V depends on more than one underlying asset.

The significance of equation (21.11) is that the price of an option must satisfy this equation, or else there is an arbitrage opportunity. In fact you may recall this equation

---

[2] Similarly, if we short the stock we have to pay the dividends.

from Chapter 13. There we examined delta-hedging and saw that the delta, gamma, and theta of a fairly priced option had to be related in a certain way. Since V_{SS} is the option's gamma, V_S the option's delta, and V_t the option's theta, equation (21.11) describes the same relationship among the Greeks.

We started this discussion by supposing that we owned an option that we wished to delta-hedge. Nothing in the derivation uses the fact that V is the price of a call option or indeed any particular kind of option at all. Thus, equation (21.11) *describes the change in value of any contingent claim for which the underlying assumptions are met*.[3] To be sure, we have assumed a great deal: That (a) the underlying asset follows geometric Brownian motion with constant volatility, (b) the underlying asset pays a continuous proportional dividend at the rate δ (this can be zero), (c) the contingent claim itself pays no dividend and has a payoff depending on S, (d) the interest rate is fixed, with equal borrowing and lending rates, and (e) there are no transaction costs.

These assumptions are unquestionably violated in practice. There are transaction costs, volatility and interest rates change over time, asset prices can jump, etc. However, our goal is to have a thorough understanding of how derivatives pricing and hedging works in this basic setting. This is a starting point for developing more realistic models.

Verifying the Formula for a Derivative

We can now answer the main question of option pricing: Given that asset prices follow geometric Brownian motion (equation (21.5)) what is the correct formula for the price of an option? As discussed in Section 21.1, there are two conditions. The pricing formula must satisfy the Black-Scholes equation, (21.11), and must also satisfy the appropriate boundary conditions for the option. If we satisfy both conditions, we have the correct option price.

Almost all of the nonstandard option formulas we looked at in Chapter 14 solve the Black-Scholes equation.[4] The pricing formulas seem different, but they differ only in the boundary conditions. Appendix 21.C discusses a general set of solutions. Here, we discuss several particular solutions in order to convey the basic idea of how the Black-Scholes equation works.

Simple present value calculations   Let's begin by considering two familiar calculations: The price of a zero-coupon bond and the prepaid forward contract for a stock.

Suppose the bond matures at time T and pays \$1. The boundary condition is that it must be worth \$1 at time T. In addition it must satisfy the Black-Scholes equation, equation (21.11). Consider this formula for the price of the bond:

$$V^1(t, T) = e^{-r(T-t)} \tag{21.12}$$

----

[3]Equation (21.11) holds for unexercised American options as well as for European options.

[4]The exception is Asian options. Since the Asian option payoff is based on the average stock price, prices of those options solve a different partial differential equation, in which there is a term reflecting the evolution of the average.

First, this satisfies the boundary condition since $V^1(T, T) = \$1$. Second, the price of the bond does not depend on the price of a stock. Thus, $V_S = 0$ and $V_{SS} = 0$. Equation (21.11) then becomes

$$V_t^1 = rV^1$$

Equation (21.12) satisfies this equation, with the boundary condition $V^1(T, T) = \$1$.

Now consider the prepaid forward contract for a share of stock. We know the value is

$$V^2[S(t), t] = S(t)e^{-\delta(T-t)} \tag{21.13}$$

Since this contract pays a share at maturity, the boundary condition is that it is worth a share at maturity:

$$V^2[S(T), T] = S(T)$$

We will verify that equation (21.13) solves the Black-Scholes equation. We have

$$V_S^2 = e^{-\delta(T-t)}$$
$$V_{SS}^2 = 0$$
$$V_t^2 = \delta S(t)e^{-\delta(T-t)}$$

Substituting these into the Black-Scholes equation gives

$$\tfrac{1}{2}\sigma^2 S(t)^2 \times 0 + (r - \delta)S(t) \times e^{-\delta(T-t)} + \delta S(t)e^{-\delta(T-t)} - rS(t)e^{-\delta(T-t)} = 0$$

Equation (21.13) thus satisfies the Black-Scholes equation and the boundary condition.

Notice that for both claims, $V_{SS} = 0$; their gamma is zero. We already saw in Chapter 5 that we can replicate a prepaid forward by buying a tailed position in the stock. No further trading is necessary. This static hedging strategy works because gamma is zero.

Call option A European call option has the boundary condition

$$V[S(T), T] = max[0, S(T) - K] \tag{21.14}$$

Let's verify that the Black-Scholes formula does satisfy the boundary condition. We can examine the behavior of the formula as t approaches T, the option expiration date. From equation (12.1), the value of the call is

$$Se^{-\delta(T-t)}N(d_1) - Ke^{-r(T-t)}N(d_2)$$

For an option at expiration, since $t = T$, the terms $e^{-\delta(T-t)}$ and $e^{-r(T-t)}$ are both equal to 1. What happens to $N(d_1)$ and $N(d_2)$?

We will rewrite slightly the definitions of d_1 and d_2:

$$d_1 = \frac{ln(S/K)}{\sigma\sqrt{T-t}} + \left(r - \delta + \tfrac{1}{2}\sigma^2\right)\frac{\sqrt{T-t}}{\sigma}$$

$$d_2 = d_1 - \sigma\sqrt{T-t}$$

As t approaches T, the difference between d_1 and d_2 goes to zero, since the term $-\sigma\sqrt{T-t}$ goes to zero. Moreover, the term $(r-\delta+\frac{1}{2}\sigma^2)\sqrt{T-t}$ also goes to zero. Thus, both d_1 and d_2 are governed by the term $ln(S/K)/\sigma\sqrt{T-t}$.

If $S > K$, then the option is in-the-money and $ln(S/K) > 0$. If $S < K$, the option is out-of-the-money and $ln(S/K) < 0$. Thus, as $t \to T$, we have

$$S > K \quad \Rightarrow \quad ln(S/K) > 0 \quad \Rightarrow \quad \frac{ln(S/K)}{\sigma\sqrt{T-t}} \to +\infty \quad \Rightarrow \quad N(d_1) = N(d_2) = 1$$

$$S < K \quad \Rightarrow \quad ln(S/K) < 0 \quad \Rightarrow \quad \frac{ln(S/K)}{\sigma\sqrt{T-t}} \to -\infty \quad \Rightarrow \quad N(d_1) = N(d_2) = 0$$

Thus, at expiration the Black-Scholes formula for a call evaluates to $S - K$ if $S > K$, and 0 if $S < K$, so it satisfies the boundary condition, equation (21.14). The call formula also satisfies equation (21.11), but we will not verify that here.

Puts can be analyzed just like calls. European puts have the boundary condition

$$V[S(T), T] = max[0, K - S(T)]$$

The put formula contains $N(-d_1)$ and $N(-d_2)$; as a result, the $N()$ expressions at maturity equal 1 when $S < K$, and 0 when $S > K$.

All-or-nothing options It turns out that both terms in the Black-Scholes formula *individually* satisfy the Black-Scholes equation. Consequently, each of the two expressions

$$V^3[S(t), t] = e^{-\delta(T-t)} S \times N\left(\frac{ln[S(t)/K] + [r - \delta + 0.5\sigma^2][T-t]}{\sigma\sqrt{T-t}}\right) \qquad (21.15)$$

$$V^4[S(t), t] = e^{-r(T-t)} \times N\left(\frac{ln[S(t)/K] + [r - \delta - 0.5\sigma^2][T-t]}{\sigma\sqrt{T-t}}\right) \qquad (21.16)$$

on its own is a legitimate price of a derivative. What are they the prices of?

Suppose we have a claim called an **asset-or-nothing option,** which pays one share of stock if $S(T) > K$, and nothing otherwise.[5] Examine V^3 closely. We have $V^3[S(T), T] = 0$ if $S(T) < K$, and $V^3[S(T), T] = S(T)$ if $S(T) > K$. Thus, at time T, V^3 has the same value as an asset-or-nothing option. Moreover, because V^3 satisfies the Black-Scholes equation, it gives the correct value at time t for this payoff. Thus, V^3 is the value of an asset-or-nothing option.

Now suppose we have a claim that pays $1 at time T if $S(T) > K$, and nothing otherwise. Call this claim a **cash-or-nothing option.**[6] Equation (21.16) has the same value at maturity as a cash-or-nothing option and satisifies the Black-Scholes equation.

---

[5]This claim is also called a **digital share.**

[6]This claim is also called **digital cash.**

Thus, equation (21.16) gives us the time-t value of a cash-or-nothing option. Both asset-or-nothing and cash-or-nothing options are examples of all-or-nothing options, which pay a discrete amount or nothing.

A European call option is equivalent to buying one asset-or-nothing option and selling K cash-or-nothing options, both maturing at time T. The price of a European call is the cost of this strategy:

$$V^3[S(t), t] - K \times V^4[S(t), t]$$

You should verify that this is in fact the Black-Scholes formula. (See Problem 21.7.)

The fact that V^3 and V^4 solve the Black-Scholes equation gives us pricing formulas for two new derivatives, asset-or-nothing and cash-or-nothing options. Also, however, because V^4 by itself solves the Black-Scholes equation, we could have sold any number of cash-or-nothing options and still had a valid price for a derivative claim. In order to create a standard call, we buy one asset-or-nothing option and sell K cash-or-nothing options. However, suppose we had instead sold $0.5K$ cash-or-nothing options. The resulting claim would have paid $S(T) - 0.5K$ if $S(T) > K$ and 0 otherwise. This is a *gap option*, discussed in Chapter 14. This analysis verifies that equation (14.15) gives the correct price for a European gap call.[7]

The boundary conditions we have considered thus far are all *terminal* boundary conditions, meaning that they are satisfied by an option at expiration. American options and some nonstandard options have a boundary condition that must be satisfied prior to expiration. For example, barrier options have boundary conditions prior to expiration related to knocking in or out. Nevertheless, their price still solves equation (21.11).

The Black-Scholes Equation and Equilibrium Returns

In the foregoing derivation of the option pricing formula we required that a delta-hedged position earn the risk-free rate of return. A different approach to pricing an option is to impose the condition that the actual expected return on the option must equal the equilibrium expected return.[8] As we saw in Section 11.2 in the context of the binomial model, we have to deal with the change in leverage as the option moves into or out of the money.

As we saw in Section 12.3, at any point in time, the ratio of the risk of the option to that of the stock is given by the option elasticity, Ω, where

$$\Omega = \frac{SV_S}{V} \tag{21.17}$$

---

[7] In practice, all-or-nothing and gap options are difficult to delta-hedge. We will discuss this further in Chapter 22.

[8] Black and Scholes also used this method to solve for the option price in their original paper.

If the stock has an expected rate of return of α, then the risk premium on the option is then given by $\Omega(\alpha - r)$. The expected return on the option is the risk premium plus the risk-free rate, or

$$\alpha_{option} = r + \frac{SV_S}{V}(\alpha - r) \tag{21.18}$$

Using Itô's Lemma, the actual instantaneous expected return on the option, per unit time, is

$$\frac{1}{dt}\frac{E(dV)}{V} = \frac{1}{dt}\frac{\left[V_t dt + \frac{1}{2}\sigma^2 S^2 V_{SS} dt + (\alpha - \delta)SV_S dt\right]}{V} \tag{21.19}$$

If the option is fairly priced, the actual drift on the option, given by equation (21.19), must equal the expected return on the option, given by equation (21.18). This gives us the following equation:

$$r + \frac{SV_S}{V}(\alpha - r) = \frac{V_t + \frac{1}{2}\sigma^2 S^2 V_{SS} + (\alpha - \delta)SV_S}{V} \tag{21.20}$$

When we multiply both sides by V and rearrange terms, the expected return on the stock, α, vanishes: We once again obtain the Black-Scholes PDE, equation (21.11). Thus, an interpretation of the Black-Scholes equation is that the option is priced so as to earn its equilibrium expected return.

A different way to understand the requirement that the option earn an appropriate expected return is to use the result from Chapter 20 that two perfectly correlated assets must have the same Sharpe ratio. For the stock and option we then have

$$\frac{\alpha - r}{\sigma} = \frac{\alpha_{option} - r}{\sigma_{option}} \tag{21.21}$$

Since $\sigma_{option} = \Omega\sigma$, this is equivalent to

$$\frac{\alpha - r}{\sigma} = \frac{\frac{1}{V}\left[V_t dt + \frac{1}{2}\sigma^2 S^2 V_{SS} dt + (\alpha - \delta)SV_S dt\right] - r}{\frac{SV_S}{V}\sigma}$$

Rewriting this equation also gives us the Black-Scholes PDE, equation (21.11).

When we equate expected and actual returns, we can interpret the result as giving us a *fair* price for the option, as opposed to a no-arbitrage price. This is *equilibrium* pricing. The no-arbitrage and equilibrium prices are the same. The equilibrium approach makes clear that determining a fair price for the option using the Black-Scholes equation does not depend upon the assumption that hedging is actually possible.

What If the Underlying Asset Is Not an Investment Asset?

So far we have been discussing option pricing when the underlying asset is an investment asset, meaning that the asset is priced so as to be held by investors. Stocks and bonds are investment assets. Many commodities are not (see Chapter 6, especially Sections

6.3 and 6.4). Suppose that the price of widgets, S, follows the process

$$\frac{dS}{S} = \mu dt + \sigma dZ \qquad (21.22)$$

From this equation, widget price risk is generated by the term dZ. Let ϕ represent the Sharpe ratio associated with dZ and let $\hat{\alpha}$ represent the expected return for an asset with this risk. Since the Sharpe ratio is $\phi = (\hat{\alpha} - r)/\sigma$, we have

$$\hat{\alpha} = r + \sigma\phi$$

The important characteristic of an investment asset is that $\mu = \hat{\alpha}$. What happens if an asset is not an investment asset and $\mu < \hat{\alpha}$?

Consider again equation (21.20), which says that the expected return on the option equals the actual return on the option. When we derive this equation again using $\hat{\alpha}$ as the equilibrium expected return for an asset with risk dZ and μ as the actual expected return for widgets, we obtain

$$r + \frac{SV_S}{V}(\hat{\alpha} - r) = \frac{V_t + \frac{1}{2}\sigma^2 S^2 V_{SS} + \mu SV_S}{V} \qquad (21.23)$$

Rearranging this equation, we obtain

$$\boxed{V_t + \frac{1}{2}\sigma^2 S^2 V_{SS} + [r - (\hat{\alpha} - \mu)]SV_S - rV = 0} \qquad (21.24)$$

If you compare equation (21.24) with (21.11), the dividend yield, δ, has been replaced with $\hat{\alpha} - \mu$, the difference between the equilibrium expected return and the actual expected return on noninvestment widgets.[9]

Let $\hat{\delta} = \hat{\alpha} - \mu$. We can interpret $\hat{\delta}$ as follows: μ is the return you get from holding a widget and $\hat{\alpha}$ is the return you must expect if you are to voluntarily hold a widget. Thus, in order for you to hold a widget you would need an additional return of $\hat{\delta} = \hat{\alpha} - \mu$. Given the expected widget price change, μ, the only way to receive the extra return is through a dividend. This is the reason that $\hat{\alpha} - \mu$ replaces the dividend yield in the Black-Scholes equation.

We have encountered this concept before: $\hat{\delta}$ is the *lease rate* for the widget, or more generally the lease rate for an asset with expected capital gain μ and risk σdZ. When you lend a commodity, you receive its capital gains. The lease rate is the extra income you need to make you willing to buy and lend the asset. In the same way, $\hat{\delta}$ is the extra income you need to make you willing to hold a widget as an investment asset.

In practice, a widget-linked bond could be used to hedge the risk of a widget option. If the widget bond were constructed so that its price equalled the widget price today and at maturity, we saw in Chapter 15 that the bond would pay the widget lease

----

[9]This modification to the Black-Scholes equation is discussed in Constantinides (1978) and McDonald and Siegel (1984).

rate as a coupon. This coupon, being a cash payment on the underlying asset, would play the role in the option pricing formula of a dividend on the underlying asset. This idea of a hypothetical lease-rate-paying, widget-linked security is also like the *twin security* mentioned in Chapter 17. It provides an investment vehicle for owning the risk dZ. If such a twin security existed, we could use it to hedge the risk of the option, and its dividend yield, $\hat{\delta}$, would appear in the option price.

An equivalent way to write equation (21.24) is to replace $\hat{\alpha}$ with $r + \phi\sigma$. We then obtain

$$V_t + \tfrac{1}{2}\sigma^2 S^2 V_{SS} + (\mu - \phi\sigma)SV_S - rV = 0 \qquad (21.25)$$

In this version, the coefficient on the SV_S term is the drift on the widget less the risk premium appropriate for widgets.

Note that when the asset is an investment asset, $\hat{\alpha} = \alpha$ and $\mu = \alpha - \delta = r + \phi\sigma - \delta$. Both equations (21.24) and (21.25) reduce to equation (21.11).

To summarize, the Black-Scholes PDE, equation (21.11), also characterizes derivative prices for assets that are not investment assets. In the case of an asset that is not an investment asset, the dividend yield, δ, is replaced with the lease rate of the asset, $\hat{\delta}$.

Example 21.1 To see how to use equation (21.24), suppose we have an option for which the maturity payoff is based upon the stock price raised to a power, S^a. This type of option is called a **power option.** For example, we could have a call option with a payoff of

$$max(S^a - K^a, 0)$$

We have already seen in Proposition 20.3 that the lease rate on an asset paying S^a is $\delta^* = r - a(r - \delta) - \tfrac{1}{2}a(a - 1)\sigma^2$. From Itô's Lemma the volatility is $a\sigma$. Thus, using equation (21.24), we can price the option by using S^a as the stock price, K^a as the strike price, δ^* as the dividend yield, and $a\sigma$ as the volatility.

21.3 RISK-NEUTRAL PRICING

The expected return on the stock, α, does not appear in the Black-Scholes equation, equation (21.11). Thus, when pricing derivatives on investment assets, only the risk-free rate matters; the actual expected return on a stock is irrelevant for pricing an option on the stock. The binomial pricing formula (see Chapter 10) also depends only on the risk-free rate.

This observation led Cox and Ross (1976) to the following important conclusion: Since only the risk-free rate appears in the Black-Scholes PDE, it must be consistent with any possible world in which there is no arbitrage. If we are trying to value an option, we can assume that we are in the world in which it is easiest to value the option. Valuation will be easiest in a risk-neutral world, in which (if it actually existed) all assets would earn the risk-free rate of return and we would discount expected future cash flows at the risk-free rate. Thus, we can value options and other derivative claims by *assuming* that the stock earns the risk-free rate of return and calculate values based on that premise. We assume that the stock in this world follows the process

$$\frac{dS}{S} = (r - \delta)dt + \sigma dZ^* \tag{21.26}$$

As we keep emphasizing, the risk-neutral distribution is *not* an assumption about investor risk preferences. It is a device that can be used when pricing by arbitrage is possible (see Appendix 11.B for a discussion).

Interpreting the Black-Scholes Equation

The actual expected change in the option price is given by

$$\frac{1}{dt}E(dV) = V_t + \tfrac{1}{2}\sigma^2 S^2 V_{SS} + (\alpha - \delta)SV_S \tag{21.27}$$

Let E^* represent the expectation with respect to the risk-neutral distribution. Under the risk-neutral distribution, the expected change in the stock price is $E^*(dS) = (r - \delta)dt$. The drift in the option price can thus be written

$$\frac{1}{dt}E^*(dV) = V_t + \tfrac{1}{2}\sigma^2 S^2 V_{SS} + (r - \delta)SV_S \tag{21.28}$$

The Black-Scholes equation, (21.11), can therefore be rewritten as

$$\frac{1}{dt}E^*(dV) = rV \tag{21.29}$$

Under the risk-neutral process, the option appreciates on average at the risk-free rate.

The Backward Equation

Closely related to equation (21.29) are the following equations, which characterize both the actual and risk-neutral probability distributions:

$$\frac{1}{dt}E(dV) = 0 \tag{21.30}$$

$$\frac{1}{dt}E^*(dV) = 0 \tag{21.31}$$

For the risk-neutral process, equation (21.31) is

$$\boxed{V_t + \tfrac{1}{2}\sigma^2 S^2 V_{SS} + (r - \delta)SV_S = 0} \tag{21.32}$$

Equation (21.32) is called the **Kolmogorov backward equation** for the geometric Brownian motion process given by equation (21.26). Whereas the Black-Scholes PDE characterizes prices, the backward equation characterizes probabilities. The backward equation is just like the Black-Scholes PDE except that there is no rV term.[10]

The Black-Scholes equation can be interpreted as saying that the expected return on the option must equal the risk-free rate. The backward equation pertains to probabilities of events, such as the probability that an option will expire in-the-money. To understand how such probabilities should behave, suppose we decide that the probability is 0.65 that the stock price 1 year from today will be greater than $100. We know today that if the stock price goes up tomorrow, we will then assign a greater probability to the event that the stock price exceeds $100 in 1 year. If the stock price goes down tomorrow, our estimate of the probability will go down. However, we should not expect our estimate of the probability to change: Our expectation *today*, of *tomorrow's* probability, must also be 0.65. If today's estimate of tomorrow's probability were not 0.65, then 0.65 could not have been the correct probability today.

Thus, whereas the price of a financial asset is expected to change over time, the expected change in the probability of an event is zero. This is why the backward equation does not have the rV term.

If $f(S_T; S_t)$ is the probability density for S_T given that the price today is S_t, both of these expressions would satisfy the backward equation:

$$\int_K^\infty f(S_T; S_t)dS_T$$

$$\int_K^\infty S_T f(S_T; S_t)dS_T$$

The first is the *probability* a call is in-the-money at time T. The second is the *partial expectation* of the stock price, conditional on $S_T > K$. Both are undiscounted. The backward equation holds for both the true and risk-neutral distributions generated by Itô processes.

Derivative Prices as Discounted Expected Cash Flows

The solution to equation (21.29) is equivalent to computing an expected value of the derivative payoff under the risk-neutral probability distribution and discounting at the risk-free rate. The specific form of the integral depends upon boundary conditions and payouts. We can see how this works with our assumptions (in particular a constant risk-free interest rate) by considering a simple European call option on a stock that pays continuous dividends at the rate δ. In that case, equation (21.11), along with the boundary condition that the option at expiration is worth $max[0, S(T) - K]$, is equivalent to the

[10]The backward equation is covered in detail in standard texts (see, for example, Cox and Miller, 1965, and Karlin and Taylor, 1981). Wilmott (1998, Chapter 10) contains a particularly clear heuristic derivation of equation (21.32).

discounted expectation

$$C[S(t), K, \sigma, r, T - t, \delta] = e^{-r(T-t)} \int_K^\infty [S(T) - K] f^*[S(T), \sigma, r, \delta; S(t)] dS(T)$$

where $f^*[S(T), \sigma, r, \delta; S(t)]$ is the *risk-neutral* probability density for $S(T)$, conditional on the time-t price being $S(t)$. In general it is possible to write the solution to equation (21.11), with appropriate boundary conditions, as an explicit integral.[11]

If a probability $W(S, t)$ satisifies the backward equation under the risk-neutral distribution, expression (21.31), then $V(S, t) = e^{-r(T-t)} W(S, t)$, the present value of $W(S, t)$, will satisfy the Black-Scholes equation, equation (21.29). To see this, suppose that $W(S, t)$ satisfies the backward equation, i.e.,

$$\frac{1}{dt} E^* [dW(S, t)] = 0$$

Now we have

$$\frac{1}{dt} E^* [dV(S, t)] = \frac{1}{dt} E^* \left\{ d \left[e^{-r(T-t)} W(S, t) \right] \right\}$$

$$= rV + e^{-r(T-t)} \frac{1}{dt} E^* [dW(S, t)]$$

$$= rV$$

This is the Black-Scholes PDE, equation (21.11).

This result means that *discounted risk-neutral probabilities and partial expectations* are prices of derivatives. Thus, any risk-neutral probability or partial expectation also has a corresponding derivative price. As an example of this, we saw in Chapter 18 that the Black-Scholes term $N(d_2)$ is the risk-neutral probability that an option is in-the-money at expiration. The discounted probability, $e^{-r(T-t)} N(d_2)$, is therefore the price of a derivative that pays $1 if the option is in-the-money at expiration.

21.4 CHANGING THE NUMERAIRE

Now we consider what happens when the number of options (or other derivative contracts) that we receive at expiration is random, determined by some asset price. This odd-sounding payoff is common. Consider the following example.

Example 21.2 The price today of a nondividend-paying stock is $100, and the forward price is $106.184. Joe bets Sarah that in 1 year the stock price will be greater

---

[11] See for example Cox et al. (1985, Lemma 4). The integral form of the Black-Scholes equation is also called the Feynman-Kac solution. See Karlin and Taylor (1981, pp. 222–224) and Duffie (1996, Chapter 5).

than \$106.184. Joe wants the loser to pay one share to the winner. Sarah wants the loser to pay \$106.184 to the winner.

The share received by Joe would be worth more than \$106.184 if he wins. Similarly, Sarah's desired payoff of \$106.184 is worth more than one share if she wins. Are either of these fair bets? If not, who has the more valuable side of the bet in each case?

🎐

If Sarah wins (i.e., the share price is below \$106.184), a payment of \$106.184 will exceed the value of one share. If Joe wins (i.e., the share price is greater than \$106.184), a payment of one share will be worth more than \$106.184. However, what is not obvious is which bet has a greater fair value if the stock price is \$100. Assuming no inside information about the stock, would an investor pay a greater price for Joe's desired bet or Sarah's desired bet?

We can describe these two forms of the bet as each having a different **numeraire** or *unit of denomination*. Joe's desired bet is denominated in shares, whereas Sarah's desired bet is denominated in dollars. You can interpret the share-denominated bet as paying either a fixed number of shares (one) or a variable number of dollars (the dollar price of one share). The dollar-denominated bet pays a fixed number of dollars (\$106.184) or a variable number of shares (the number of shares with the value \$106.184). The general question we want to answer is how a change in the numeraire (unit of denomination) for a derivative changes the price of the derivative.

Here are some other examples where a change of denomination is relevant:

- **Currency translation** A cash flow originating in yen (for example) can be valued in yen, or in some other currency. We will discuss this example in depth in Chapter 22.

- **Quantity uncertainty** An agricultural producer who wants to insure production of an entire field must hedge total revenue—the product of price and quantity—rather than quantity alone.

- **All-or-nothing options** All-or-nothing options, which we briefly discussed earlier, can be structured either to pay cash if a certain event occurs (such as the stock price exceeding the strike) or shares. The payoffs to the stock price bets above are in fact all-or-nothing payoffs; thus, the bets can be valued as all-or-nothing options.

To see what happens when we change the denomination of an option, suppose Q is the price of an asset that follows

$$\frac{dQ}{Q} = (\alpha_Q - \delta_Q)dt + \sigma_Q dZ_Q \tag{21.33}$$

Let $V(S, t)$ represent the price of an option denominated in cash, where S follows the process in equation (21.5). The correlation between dZ_Q and dZ is ρ. Suppose we receive the time-T payoff

$$Y[Q(T), S(T), T] = Q(T)^b V[S(T), K, \sigma, r, T, \delta] \tag{21.34}$$

Equation (21.34) represents a random number, Q^b, of claims, V. The value of this payoff is given in the following proposition.

Proposition 21.1 Suppose the process for S is given by equation (21.5) and the process for Q by equation (21.33), with ρ the correlation between dS and dQ. Let $V(S, K, \sigma_S, r, T-t, \delta_S)$ represent the price of a European derivative claim on S expiring at time T. The price of a claim paying $Q^b V$ is given by

$$Q(t)^b e^{(r-\delta^*)(T-t)} V[S(t), K, \sigma_S, r, T-t, \eta] \tag{21.35}$$

where $\eta = \delta - b\rho\sigma\sigma_Q$ and $\delta^* = r - b(r - \delta_Q) - \frac{1}{2}b(b-1)\sigma_Q^2$. In other words, to value Q^b claims, each with value V, we replace the dividend yield on S, δ, by η, and multiply the resulting price by $Q(t)^b e^{(r-\delta^*)(T-t)}$. ❧

The proof is in Appendix 21.B. Equation (21.35) deserves further comment. We encountered δ^* in Section 20.7, in Proposition 20.3; it is the lease rate for Q^b. Thus $Q(t)^b e^{(r-\delta^*)(T-t)}$ is the forward price for a claim paying Q^b. The value of a claim paying $Q^b V$ is thus the forward price for Q^b times V evaluated at a modified dividend yield. We know from Section 20.7 that if Q and S are correlated (in which case Q and V are correlated), there must also be a covariance term. The term η replaces the dividend yield δ to account for this covariance.

Example 21.3 Consider the share-price bet described in Example 21.2. Let V denote the value of the cash bet expiring at time T, with today being time 0. A cash bet that pays \$1 when $S(T) > K$ has the value

$$V[S(0), K, \sigma, r, T, \delta] = e^{-rT} N\left(\frac{ln[S(0)/K] + [r - \delta - 0.5\sigma^2]T}{\sigma\sqrt{T}}\right)$$

This is the value of a cash-or-nothing option, equation (21.16), and is the second term in the Black-Scholes formula. It is also the discounted risk-neutral probability that the bet pays off. The value of the bet paying \$1 when $S(T) < K$ is $e^{-rT} - V$.

The share bet pays one share when $S(T) > K$, and therefore is like having a random number, S, of cash bets.[12] By Proposition 21.1, the value of the share bet is obtained by multiplying V by the forward price for S, and replacing δ with $\delta - \sigma^2$ (we have $b = 1$ and $\rho = 1$ since S multiplies a claim based on S). Making these substitutions,

---

[12]This argument linking the two terms in the Black-Scholes equation by changing the units of denomination is due to German et al. (1995).

the value of the share bet is $S(0)e^{(r-\delta)T} V[S(0), K, \sigma, r, T, \delta - \sigma^2]$, or

$$Y[S(0), K, \sigma, r, T, \delta] = S(0)e^{-\delta T} N\left(\frac{ln[S(0)/K] + [r - \delta + 0.5\sigma^2]T}{\sigma\sqrt{T}}\right)$$

This is the value of an asset-or-nothing option, equation (21.15), and is the first term in the Black-Scholes formula. Thus, we can view the first Black-Scholes term as a discounted risk-neutral probability with a change of numeraire.

In the case of Joe and Sarah's bet, suppose that the share-price volatility is 30%, the continuously compounded risk-free rate is 6%, the time to expiration is 1 year, and the share pays no dividends. The cash bet will have the winner receive $106.184 (which, incidentally, is the forward price). Joe bets that the share price will be above $106.184. A bet that paid $106.184 if the price were **above** $106.184 would have the value

$$\$106.184 \times V(\$100, \$106.184, 0.3, 0.06, 1, 0) = \$44.038$$

The value of this bet plus the value of the bet paying $106.184 if the share price is below $106.184 (Sarah's desired bet) must sum to the present value of $106.184 (this is because if you make both bets, you receive $106.184 for sure). Thus, the value of Sarah's bet is

$$\$106.184 \times e^{-0.06} - \$44.038 = \$55.962$$

When the bet pays one share, the value of Joe's bet is

$$Y(\$100, \$106.184, 0.3, 0.06, 1, 0) = \$55.962$$

Sarah's side of this bet is

$$\$100 - \$55.962 = \$44.038$$

Thus, both Sarah and Joe wish to denominate the bet in their favor. Moreover, Sarah and Joe's bets have the same value! ⚓

Problem 21.8 asks you to find the strike prices such that the cash and share-denominated bets have equal value. We will return to changes in the unit of denomination in Chapter 22 when we discuss more nonstandard options.

21.5 OPTION PRICING WHEN THE STOCK PRICE CAN JUMP

We discussed jumps in the stock price in Chapters 19 and 20. Jumps pose a serious problem for the Black-Scholes option pricing methodology. When the stock price can jump discretely as well as move continuously, a position that hedges against small moves will not also hedge against big moves. As we saw in Chapter 13, large moves in the stock typically cannot be hedged.

The fact that jumps cannot be hedged does not mean that option pricing is impossible; rather, it means that *risk-neutral* option pricing may be impossible. When moves in the option price cannot be hedged, we can still price the option by computing discounted expected payoffs using the actual probability density rather than the risk-neutral probability density. The problem is that the option has the risk of a leveraged position in the stock, and we do not know what discount rate is appropriate. Some assumption about appropriate discount rates (which is really an assumption about investor preferences) will then be necessary to price an option.

Merton (1976) derived an option pricing formula when the stock price can jump by assuming that the jump risk is diversifiable. This assumption neatly sidesteps the discounting issue since diversifiable risk does not affect expected returns. While jump risk for a broad index is not diversifiable, arguably many of the discrete moves for individual stocks are. In that case, by holding a portfolio of delta-hedged positions, the market-maker can diversify the effects of jump risk.

Ultimately, the importance of jumps and their systematic component is an empirical issue. Nevertheless, Merton's formulas provide useful insights into the effects of jumps.

The Black-Scholes Solution for Diversifiable Jumps

Merton (1976) shows that with diversifiable jumps, the Black-Scholes PDE becomes

$$V_t + \tfrac{1}{2}V_{SS}\sigma^2 S^2 + V_S(r - \delta - \lambda k)S + \lambda E_Y[V(SY, t) - V(S, t)] = rV \qquad (21.36)$$

As in Chapter 20, λdt is the probability of a jump over the small interval dt, $Y - 1$ is the percentage change in the stock price due to the jump, and $k = E(Y - 1)$ is the expected percentage jump.

Merton (1976) discusses the general solution to this equation for calls and puts. One interesting special case occurs when the only jump that can occur is a jump of the stock price to zero, i.e., $Y = 0$. If the stock jumps to zero, a call option becomes worthless: $V(SY, t) = 0$, and $\lambda k = -\lambda$. Hence, with a jump to zero, the PDE for a call becomes

$$V_t + \tfrac{1}{2}V_{SS}\sigma^2 S^2 + V_S(r + \lambda - \delta)S = (r + \lambda)V$$

Every occurrence of r is replaced by $r + \lambda$; hence, the Black-Scholes formula for a call becomes

$$C(S, K, \sigma, r, T - t, \delta, \lambda) = Se^{-\delta(T-t)}N(d_1) + Ke^{-(r+\lambda)(T-t)}N(d_2) \qquad (21.37)$$

$$d_1 = \frac{ln(S/K) + (r + \lambda - \delta + \tfrac{1}{2}\sigma^2)(T - t)}{\sigma\sqrt{T - t}}$$

$$d_2 = d_1 - \sigma\sqrt{T - t}$$

	Call Price				**Jump-**
Strike ($)	**Jump**	**No Jump**	**Difference ($)**	**Call Vega**	**Implied σ**
40	2.8104	2.7847	0.0257	0.0781	0.303
35	6.1704	6.1348	0.0356	0.0436	0.308
30	10.6679	10.6320	0.0359	0.0083	0.334

TABLE 21.1 Option prices when the stock can and cannot jump. Assumes $S = \$40$, $\sigma = 30\%$, $r = 8\%$, $\delta = 0$, $\lambda = 0.5\%$, and $T - t = 0.25$.

The formula for a put is then obtained by put-call parity:[13]

$$P(S, K, \sigma, r, T - t, \delta, \lambda) = C(S, K, \sigma, r, T - t, \delta, \lambda) - Se^{-\delta(T-t)} + Ke^{-r(T-t)}$$

Jump Risk and Implied Volatility

This particular jump risk model oversimplifies reality, but it can illustrate the effect of jumps on option prices. In particular, the possibility that prices can jump is consistent with a volatility skew, discussed in Chapter 12, where options with different strike prices have different implied volatilities.[14]

Suppose that option prices are generated by a jump-diffusion, where the jump can be only to zero and occurs with 0.5% probability per year. If we let $S = \$40$, $K = \$40$, $\sigma = 30\%$, $r = 8\%$, $T - t = 0.25$, and $\delta = 0$, then we have call and put prices of $2.81 and $2.02, compared to the no-jump prices of $2.78 and $1.99. Now we do the following experiment: Generate "correct" option prices, i.e., prices properly accounting for the jump, for a variety of strikes and different times to maturity. We then ask what implied volatility we would compute for these options using the ordinary Black-Scholes formula. Table 21.1 shows the jump and no-jump prices for options at three different strike prices, along with the option vegas. The results are also graphed in Figure 21.1. Because of parity, puts and calls have the same implied volatility, so we need graph only one of them.

In every case, out-of-the money puts (in-the-money calls) have higher implied volatilities than at-the-money options. We can see why this is happening by examining

---

[13]For a put option, the solution does *not* entail replacing every occurrence of r with $r + \lambda$. The reason is that the PDE for the put option is different from the PDE for the call option in the case of a jump. In particular we have

$$P(SY, t) = Ke^{-rT}$$

rather than 0 in the case of a call.

[14]The implied volatility pattern is also sometimes called a **volatility smile,** when a plot of implied volatility against strike prices looks like a smile. Volatility *frowns* and *smirks* are also observed.

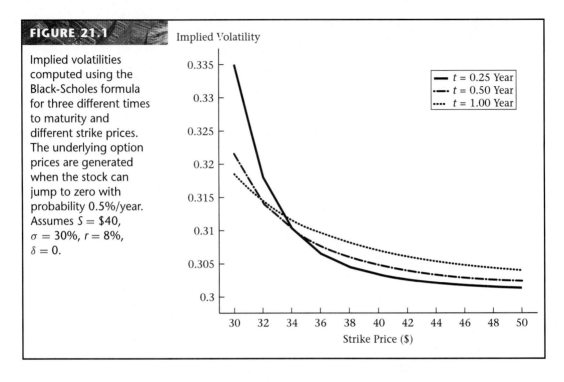

FIGURE 21.1

Implied volatilities computed using the Black-Scholes formula for three different times to maturity and different strike prices. The underlying option prices are generated when the stock can jump to zero with probability 0.5%/year. Assumes $S = \$40$, $\sigma = 30\%$, $r = 8\%$, $\delta = 0$.

the numbers more closely. The small possibility of a jump causes all the option prices to increase about 2.5–3.5 cents. The standard implied volatility calculation uses the Black-Scholes formula without a jump adjustment to compute the implied volatility. The no-jump prices all have implied volatilities of 30%. What volatility in the no-jump model is required to generate the prices in the jump column? For the 40-strike option, vega is 0.0781, so a change in volatility of approximately $0.0257/0.0781 = 0.323$ percentage points, or a volatility of 0.30323, will generate the higher price of $2.81. For the 30-strike option, however, vega is only 0.0083. Thus, a change in volatility of approximately $0.0359/0.0083 = 4.3$ percentage points is required in order for the no-jump Black-Scholes model to explain the price of $10.6679. The actual implied volatility in this case is 0.334. When vega is lower, a larger change in volatility is required to explain a given change in the option price.

This example is at most suggestive. In practice, jumps can be positive or negative and of uncertain magnitude. If jumps can occur in both directions, then we would expect to see higher implied volatilities for both in-the-money and out-of-the-money options. Furthermore, jump risk is unlikely to be purely diversifiable since there can be market-wide moves. The example does, however, illustrate important intuition for why jumps can generate volatility smiles.

21.6 STOCHASTIC VOLATILITY

As we saw in Chapter 18 (see Figure 18.7), volatility appears to vary over time. In this section we see how to price options when volatility can follow an Itô process.

Let $v(t)$ be the instantaneous stock return variance; hence, $\sqrt{v(t)}$ is the volatility. Suppose that the stock follows the process

$$\frac{dS}{S} = (\alpha - \delta)dt + \sqrt{v(t)}dZ_1 \tag{21.38}$$

Assume that the variance, $v(t)$, follows the mean-reverting process

$$dv(t) = \kappa[\bar{v} - v(t)]dt + \sigma_v\sqrt{v(t)}dZ_2 \tag{21.39}$$

We assume that $E(dZ_1 dZ_2) = \rho dt$.

The interpretation of equations (21.38) and (21.39) is familiar. Equation (21.38) for the stock is the same as equation (21.5) except that the volatility, $\sqrt{v(t)}$, is random. The equation for volatility, equation (21.39), has two noteworthy characteristics. First, the instantaneous variance, $v(t)$, is mean-reverting, tending toward the value $\bar{v}$, with a speed of adjustment given by κ. Second, the volatility of variance, $\sigma_v\sqrt{v(t)}$, depends on the square root of $v(t)$, and variance is therefore said to follow a *square root process*.

Suppose that the risk premium for the risk $\sigma_v\sqrt{v(t)}dZ_2$ can be written as $v(t)\beta_v$, where we assume β_v is constant. This assumption that the risk premium is proportional to the level of the variance is analytically convenient. Given this assumption about the risk premium, the risk-neutral volatility process is

$$
\begin{aligned}
dv(t) &= \left\{\kappa[\bar{v} - v(t)] - v(t)\beta_v\right\}dt + \sigma_v\sqrt{v(t)}dZ_2^* \\
&= \kappa^*\left[\bar{v}^* - v(t)\right] + \sigma_v\sqrt{v(t)}dZ_2^*
\end{aligned} \tag{21.40}
$$

where $\kappa^* = \kappa + \beta_v$ and $\bar{v}^* = \bar{v}\kappa/(\kappa + \beta_v)$. This model of stochastic volatility is called the **Heston model** (Heston, 1993).

Let $V[S(t), v(t), t]$ represent the price of a derivative on the stock when the stock price and volatility are given by equations (21.38) and (21.39). Suppose we proceed with the Black-Scholes derivation, in which we hold the option and try to hedge the resulting risk. We immediately encounter the problem that there are *two* sources of risk, dZ_1 and dZ_2. A position in the stock will hedge dZ_1, but what can we use to hedge risk resulting from stochastic volatility? Apart from other options, there will typically be no asset that is a perfect hedge for volatility.[15] In that case, we rely on the equilibrium approach to pricing the option. The PDE for the derivative $V[S(t), v(t), t]$ is then:

---

[15] It might be possible to use other options on the same stock to hedge volatility, but the option would then be priced *relative* to the price of the option used as a hedge.

$$\tfrac{1}{2}v(t)S^2 V_{SS} + \tfrac{1}{2}\sigma_v^2 v(t)V_{vv} + \rho v(t)\sigma_v S V_{Sv}$$
$$+ (r - \delta)SV_S + \left\{\kappa[\bar{v} - v(t)] - v(t)\beta_v\right\} V_v + V_t = rV \tag{21.41}$$

This equation is the multivariate Black-Scholes equation, described in Appendix 21.A. The third term is due to the covariance between the stock return and volatility. Since there is no asset to hedge volatility, the coefficient on the V_v term has a correction for the risk premium associated with volatility.

Heston (1993) shows that equation (21.41) has an integral solution that can be evaluated numerically. Given this solution, we can see how implied volatility behaves when volatility is stochastic. Similar to the analysis of jumps in Section 21.5, we price options for different strikes and expirations under the stochastic volatility model, and then use Black-Scholes to compute implied volatilities. We assume that the stock price is \$40, and compute implied volatilities for options with strike prices ranging from \$30 to \$50, and with maturities from 3 months to 1 year.

Figure 21.2 shows the result of this experiment for two different values of σ_v and ρ. In the figure the long-run volatility, $\bar{v}^*$, is 25%, less than the current volatility, 32%. Because volatility reverts to the mean, implied volatility decreases with time to maturity in every case. In the panel where $\sigma_v = 0.10$ and $\rho = 0$, there is almost no skew, although the mean reversion in volatility is apparent. When $\sigma_v = 50\%$ and $\rho = 0$, the figure exhibits both symmetric skew and mean reversion. The asymmetric skew in both right-hand panels of Figure 21.2 arises from assuming a negative correlation between volatility and the stock price.

Empirical studies of option pricing typically ask whether a pricing model can be constructed to match the observed volatility skew.[16] Bakshi et al. (1997) and Bates (2000) both asked whether option pricing models incorporating jumps and stochastic volatility can generate realistic volatility skew for S&P index options. Both studies find greater volatility skew at short maturities. If you compare Figures 21.1 and 21.2, you can see that this pattern is generated by the jump model. This explains why, although Bakshi et al. (1997) found that the stochastic volatility model provided the best overall explanation of prices, they added jumps to account for skew at short maturities. They also found that permitting stochastic interest rates (which can be added in the same fashion as stochastic volatility) helped explain prices at longer maturities. Bates (2000) also found that jump models (as in Figure 21.1) fit near-term option prices better but found that the stock price itself did not appear to jump as often as implied by the model. Bates also concluded that in order for the stochastic volatility model to explain skew, the volatility of volatility had to be implausibly large.

---

[16]The true model should give equal implied volatilities for options at different strikes and maturities. For example, if the stochastic volatility model were true and option prices were consistent with equation (21.41), then Black-Scholes implied volatilities would exhibit skew, but if the Heston model were used, the options in Figure 21.2 would all have implied volatilities of 32%.

FIGURE 21.2

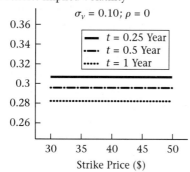

Black-Scholes Implied Volatility

$\sigma_v = 0.10; \rho = 0$

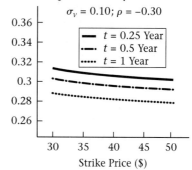

Black-Scholes Implied Volatility

$\sigma_v = 0.10; \rho = -0.30$

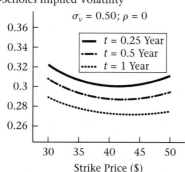

Black-Scholes Implied Volatility

$\sigma_v = 0.50; \rho = 0$

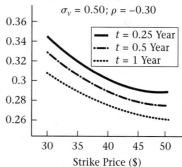

Black-Scholes Implied Volatility

$\sigma_v = 0.50; \rho = -0.30$

Implied volatilities computed using the Black-Scholes formula when prices are computed using the Heston model for three different times to maturity, different strike prices, and two different volatilities of volatility, σ_v. The top panel assumes that $\sigma_v = 0.10$, while the bottom panel assumes that $\sigma_v = 0.5$. In both panels, $\kappa^* = 2.0$, $v(t) = 0.32$, $\bar{v}^* = 0.25$, $r = 8\%$, and $\delta = 0$.

CHAPTER SUMMARY

The Black-Scholes equation, equation (21.11), characterizes the behavior of a derivative as a function of the price of one or more underlying assets. (The Black-Scholes equation also appeared in Chapter 13 as a break-even condition for delta-hedging market-makers.) We can interpret the Black-Scholes equation as requiring that a derivative earn an appropriate rate of return, which occurs when the delta, gamma, and theta of an asset satisfy a particular relationship. The Black-Scholes equation is thus a generalization of the idea, familiar from introductory finance, that zero-coupon bonds appreciate at the risk-free rate. Probabilities and partial expectations satisfy a related condition known as the backward equation. Along with the Black-Scholes equation, a derivative must satisfy an appropriate boundary condition.

A change of the units of an option payoff is called a change of numeraire. Proposition 21.1 shows that the price effect of a change of numeraire is accounted for with a simple transformation of the pricing formula.

The Black-Scholes model does not perfectly explain observed option prices; there is volatility skew, which means that implied volatility varies with the strike price and time to expiration. Two modifications to the model are to permit jumps in the stock price and to allow volatility to be stochastic. Both changes generate option prices that exhibit volatility skew and that better fit the data than the unmodified Black-Scholes model.

FURTHER READING

In Chapter 22, we extend the Black-Scholes analysis to exotic options and in Chapter 23 to studying interest rates.

Two classic papers on option pricing are Black and Scholes (1973) and Merton (1973b). Merton (1976) extends the Black-Scholes model to allow diversifiable jumps in the stock price, and Naik and Lee (1990) develop a model to price options when jumps are systematic. The Heston model is described in Heston (1993). In addition to Bakshi et al. (1997) and Bates (2000), recent empirical studies of volatility skew include Benzoni (2001), Andersen et al. (2002), Eraker (2001), and Pan (2002).

Cox and Miller (1965) and Wilmott (1998, Chapter 10) discuss the backward equation and its counterpart, the forward equation, which characterizes the probability density for S_t, conditional on S_T. German et al. (1995) studied the role of changing the numeraire as a pricing technique. Schroder (1999) extends their results, including examples with stochastic volatility and jump-diffusion models. Ingersoll (2000) provides some additional examples of the use of this technique. Marcus and Modest (1984, 1986) examine quantity uncertainty in agricultural production.

An alternative approach to modeling volatility is to calibrate a binomial tree to match the observed volatility skew. This approach is explored in Derman and Kani (1994), Rubinstein (1994), and Shimko (1993).

PROBLEMS

21.1. Verify that equation (21.12) satisfies the Black-Scholes equation. What is the boundary condition for which this is a solution?

21.2. Verify that $A S^a e^{\gamma t}$ satisfies the Black-Scholes PDE for

$$a = \left(\frac{1}{2} - \frac{r - \delta}{\sigma^2} \right) \pm \sqrt{ \left(\frac{r - \delta}{\sigma^2} - \frac{1}{2} \right)^2 + \frac{2(r - \gamma)}{\sigma^2} }$$

21.3. Use the Black-Scholes equation to verify the solution in Chapter 20, given by Proposition 20.3, for the value of a claim paying S^a.

21.4. Assuming that the stock price satisfies equation (20.26), verify that $Ke^{-r(T-t)} + S(t)e^{-\delta(T-t)}$ satisfies the Black-Scholes equation, where K is a constant. What is the boundary condition for which this is a solution?

21.5. Verify that $S(t)e^{-\delta(T-t)}N(d_1)$ satisfies the Black-Scholes equation.

21.6. Verify that $e^{-r(T-t)}N(d_2)$ satisfies the Black-Scholes equation.

21.7. Use the answers to Problems 5 and 6 to verify that the Black-Scholes formula, equation (12.1), satisfies the Black-Scholes equation. Verify that the boundary condition $V[S(T), T] = max[0, S(T) - K]$ is satisfied.

21.8. Consider the bet in Example 21.3.

    a. Consider Joe and Sarah's bet in Examples 21.2 and 21.3. Note that $106.184 is the forward price. A bet paying $1 if the share price is above the forward price is worth less than a bet paying $1 if the share price is below the forward price. Why?

    b. Suppose the bet were to be denominated in cash. If we want the bet to pay x if $S > x$, what would x have to be in order to make the bet fair?

    c. Now suppose that we pay one share if $S > x$. What would x have to be in this case to make the bet fair?

21.9. Consider again the bet in Example 21.3. Suppose the bet is $S - \$106.184$ if the price is above $106.184, and $\$106.184 - S$ if the price is below $106.184. What is the value of this bet to each party? Why?

21.10. Suppose that a derivative claim makes continuous payments at the rate Γ. Show that the Black-Scholes equation becomes

$$V_t + \frac{1}{2}\sigma^2 S^2 V_{SS} + (r - \delta)SV_S + \Gamma - rV = 0$$

For the following four problems assume that S follows equation (21.5) and Q follows equation (21.33). Suppose $S_0 = \$50$, $Q_0 = \$90$, $T = 2$, $r = 0.06$, $\delta = 0.02$, $\delta_Q = 0.01$, $\sigma = 0.3$, $\sigma_Q = 0.5$, and $\rho = -0.2$. Use Proposition 21.1 to find solutions to the problems. Optional: For each problem, verify the solution using Monte Carlo.

21.11. What is the value of a claim paying $Q(T)^2 S(T)$? Check your answer using Proposition 20.4.

21.12. What is the value of a claim paying $Q(T)^{-1}S(T)$? Check your answer using Proposition 20.4.

21.13. You are offered the opportunity to receive for free the payoff

$$[Q(T) - F_{0,T}(Q)] \times max[0, S(T) - K]$$

(Note that this payoff can be negative.) Should you accept the offer?

21.14. An agricultural producer wishes to insure the value of a crop. Let Q represent the quantity of production in bushels and S the price of a bushel. The insurance payoff is therefore $Q(T) \times V[S(T), T]$, where V is the price of a put. What is the cost of insurance?

APPENDIX 21.A: MULTIVARIATE BLACK-SCHOLES ANALYSIS

Consider a claim for which the payoff depends on the n asset prices, $S_1, S_2, \ldots, S_n$, where

$$\frac{dS_i}{S_i} = (\alpha_i - \delta_i)dt + \sigma_i dZ_i \tag{21.42}$$

The pairwise correlation between S_i and S_j is ρ_{ij}. Let $V(S_1, S_2, \ldots, S_n, t, T)$ be the value of this claim. Consider a portfolio consisting of the claim, the n assets, and bonds, W, such that

$$I = V + \sum_{i=1}^{n} N_i S_i + W$$

Using the multivariate version of Itô's Lemma (Proposition 20.2 (Multivariate Itô's Lemma)), the change in the value of the portfolio is

$$dI = V_t dt + \sum_{i=1}^{n} V_{S_i} dS_i + \frac{1}{2} \sum_{i=1}^{n} \sum_{j=1}^{n} dS_i dS_j V_{S_i S_j} dt + \sum_{i=1}^{n} N_i dS_i + dW$$

In order to delta-hedge V, set $N_i = -V_{S_i}$. Hold bonds to finance the residual such that $I = 0$. The same analysis used to derive equation (21.11) leads to the following PDE for V:

$$V_t + \sum_{i=1}^{n}(r - \delta_i)S_i V_{S_i} + \frac{1}{2} \sum_{i=1}^{n} \sum_{j=1}^{n} \sigma_i \sigma_j \rho_{i,j} S_i S_j V_{S_i S_j} = rV \tag{21.43}$$

APPENDIX 21.B: PROOF OF PROPOSITION 21.1

In this section we will verify the solution in Proposition 21.1. We begin by assuming that we have a derivative price $V(S, \sigma, r, T - t, \delta)$, that satisfies

$$V_t + (r - \delta)SV_S + \frac{1}{2}\sigma^2 S^2 V_{SS} = rV \tag{21.44}$$

By the multivariate Black-Scholes equation described in Appendix 21.2, the claim $Y(S, Q, t)$ must satisfy

$$Y_t + (r - \delta)SY_S + (r - \delta_Q)QY_Q + \frac{1}{2}\left(\sigma^2 S^2 Y_{SS} + \sigma_Q^2 Q^2 Y_{QQ} + 2\rho\sigma\sigma_Q SQY_{SQ}\right) = rY$$

Guess the solution $Y = Ae^{-(r-\delta^*)t}Q^b W$, where A is determined by boundary conditions, δ^* is to be determined, and W satisfies the same boundary condition as V. Compute the derivatives of this guess and substitute them into equation (21.43). After simplification (in particular, the Y multiplying every term divides out), this yields

$$\delta^* - r + b(r - \delta_Q) + \tfrac{1}{2}\sigma_Q^2 b(b-1)$$
$$+ \frac{1}{W}\left\{W_t + [r - (\delta - b\rho\sigma\sigma_Q)]SW_S + \tfrac{1}{2}\sigma^2 S^2 W_{SS}\right\} = r \quad (21.45)$$

The term in braces is the same as equation (21.44), except that δ is replaced with $\eta = \delta - b\rho\sigma\sigma_Q$. Thus, W is the same as V except that δ is replaced by η. With this replacement, from equation (21.44), the term in parentheses equals $r\,W$. Equation (21.45) becomes

$$\delta^* - r + b(r - \delta_Q) + \tfrac{1}{2}\sigma_Q^2 b(b-1) + \frac{r\,W}{W} = r$$

This equation is satisfied if $\delta^* = r - b(r - \delta_Q) - \tfrac{1}{2}\sigma_Q^2 b(b-1)$. Thus, with the η and δ^* in Proposition 21.1, the candidate solution solves equation (21.43). The parameter A is set so, at the point the option is exercised, $A = e^{(r-\delta^*)t}$. For a European option, set $A = e^{(r-\delta^*)T}$ to solve the terminal boundary condition.

APPENDIX 21.C: SOLUTIONS FOR PRICES AND PROBABILITIES

The Black-Scholes partial differential equation has the form:

$$V_t + \tfrac{1}{2}\sigma^2 S^2 V_{SS} + \eta S V_S = \beta V \qquad (21.46)$$

In equation (21.11), we have $\eta = r - \delta$ and $\beta = r$. When $\beta = 0$, equation (21.46) is the backward equation, equation (21.31).

Suppose we guess the following general solution to equation (21.46):

$$V(S, t) = A e^{\gamma t} S^a N(x)^y \qquad (21.47)$$
$$x = \frac{\ln[S(t)] + f + g(T - t)}{\sigma\sqrt{T - t}}$$

where A, a, f, g, and γ are constants to be determined, and σ and y are parameters. $N(x)$ is the cumulative standard normal distribution. We will consider the cases $y = \{0, 1\}$. Note that sums of solutions are also solutions.

Computing the various derivatives of this guessed solution, substituting them into equation (21.46), and simplifying, gives

$$0 = \left[\tfrac{1}{2}\sigma^2 a^2 + a\left(\eta - \tfrac{1}{2}\sigma^2\right) + \gamma - \beta\right]$$
$$+ y N(x)^{-1} N'(x)\left[\frac{\sigma^2\left(a - \tfrac{1}{2}\right) + \eta - g}{\sigma\sqrt{T - t}}\right] \qquad (21.48)$$

The parameters A and f are not in any way determined by this equation; hence, they are solely determined by boundary conditions. Equation (21.48) is satisfied for

$$a = \left(\tfrac{1}{2} - \tfrac{\eta}{\sigma^2}\right) \pm \sqrt{\left(\tfrac{\eta}{\sigma^2} - \tfrac{1}{2}\right)^2 + 2\frac{\beta - \gamma}{\sigma^2}} \tag{21.49}$$

and

$$g = \sigma^2 \left(a - \tfrac{1}{2}\right) + \eta \tag{21.50}$$

The first term in square brackets stems from differentiating $Ae^{\gamma t} S^a$, while the second bracketed term stems from differentiating $N(x)$. We will examine only a few of the commonly occurring solutions. Since $Ae^{-\gamma(T-t)} S^a N(x)$ and $Ae^{-\gamma(T-t)} S^a$ both solve the PDE, and since sums of solutions are also solutions, then

$$Ae^{-\gamma(T-t)} S^a [N(x) - 1] = Ae^{-\gamma(T-t)} S^a N(-x)$$

is also a solution.

Solutions to the Black-Scholes Equation

The parameters η and β are determined by the PDE that arises in solving a particular problem. In the standard Black-Scholes equation, $\eta = r - \delta$ and $\beta = r$; this is the case we will consider. Let a^+ denote the positive root in equation (21.49), and a^- the negative root. Since g is defined in terms of a, for any given γ, there are two matched $\{a, g\}$ pairs.

If we pick γ, the rest of the solution is determined by equations (21.49) and (21.50) in conjunction with boundary conditions. Two obvious choices are $\gamma = r$ and $\gamma = \delta$. If $\gamma = r$, then $\{a^+, g^+\} = \{0, r - \delta - \tfrac{1}{2}\sigma^2\}$ and $\{a^-, g^-\} = \left\{1 - 2\frac{r-\delta}{\sigma^2}, -\left(r - \delta - \tfrac{1}{2}\sigma^2\right)\right\}$. The positive roots here, together with appropriate boundary conditions, generate the price of a cash-or-nothing option, equation (21.16). If $\gamma = \beta - \eta = \delta$, then $\{a^+, g^+\} = \{1, r - \delta + \tfrac{1}{2}\sigma^2\}$ and $\{a^-, g^-\} = \left\{-2\frac{r-\delta}{\sigma^2}, -\left(r - \delta + \tfrac{1}{2}\sigma^2\right)\right\}$. The positive roots here, together with boundary conditions, generate the price of an asset-or-nothing option, equation (21.15).

The following expressions all satisfy the Black-Scholes PDE:

$$V^5[S(t), t] = e^{-\delta(T-t)} S^{-a_3} \times N\left(\frac{ln[S(t)] + f - [r - \delta + 0.5\sigma^2][T - t]}{\sigma\sqrt{T - t}}\right) \tag{21.51}$$

$$V^6[S(t), t] = e^{-r(T-t)} S^{1-a_3} \times N\left(\frac{ln[S(t)] + f - [r - \delta - 0.5\sigma^2][T - t]}{\sigma\sqrt{T - t}}\right) \tag{21.52}$$

$$V^7[S(t), t] = AS(t)^{a_1} \tag{21.53}$$

$$V^8[S(t), t] = AS(t)^{a_2} \tag{21.54}$$

TABLE 21.2		Parameters generating the solutions to the Black-Scholes PDE for the indicated equation.	

Equation	y	γ	a (Equation (21.49))
(21.12)	0	r	$a^+ = 0$
(21.13)	0	δ	$a^+ = 1$
(21.15)	1	δ	$a^+ = 1$
(21.16)	1	δ	$a^- = -2\frac{r-\delta}{\sigma^2}$
(21.51)	1	r	$a^+ = 0$
(21.52)	1	r	$a^- = 1 - 2\frac{r-\delta}{\sigma^2}$
(21.53)	0	0	a^+
(21.54)	0	0	a^-

where:

$$a_1 = \left(\frac{1}{2} - \frac{r-\delta}{\sigma^2}\right) + \sqrt{\left(\frac{r-\delta}{\sigma^2} - \frac{1}{2}\right)^2 + \frac{2r}{\sigma^2}}$$

$$a_2 = \left(\frac{1}{2} - \frac{r-\delta}{\sigma^2}\right) - \sqrt{\left(\frac{r-\delta}{\sigma^2} - \frac{1}{2}\right)^2 + \frac{2r}{\sigma^2}}$$

$$a_3 = \frac{2(r-\delta)}{\sigma^2}$$

With appropriate choice of A, equations (21.53) and (21.54) are the formulas for infinitely lived options. We will see in Chapter 22 that equations (21.51) and (21.52) play a role in pricing barrier options.

The solutions to the equations in Table 21.2 are obtained by choosing the parameters listed there. These equations also satisfy specific boundary conditions.

Solutions to the Backward Equation

For a stock following geometric Brownian motion, the backward equation is satisfied if $\beta = 0$. It turns out that $\gamma = 0$ is frequently the solution of interest. For example, the Black-Scholes term $N(d_2)$, without a discount factor, is the risk-neutral probability that $S(T) > K$, and is a solution to the forward equation.

Consider these (undiscounted) variants of equations (21.51) and (21.52):

$$e^{r(T-t)}V^5[S(t), t] = e^{(r-\delta)(T-t)}S(t)^{-a_3}N\left(\frac{\ln[S(t)] + f - [r - \delta + 0.5\sigma^2][T - t]}{\sigma\sqrt{T-t}}\right)$$

$$(21.55)$$

$$e^{r(T-t)}V^6[S(t), t] = S^{1-a_3} N\left(\frac{ln[S(t)] + f - [r - \delta - 0.5\sigma^2][T - t]}{\sigma\sqrt{T-t}}\right) \quad (21.56)$$

You can verify that equations (21.55) and (21.56) obey equation (21.32). With an appropriate scale factor and choice of f, equation (21.56) will appear in Chapter 22 as the risk-neutral probability that the stock price hits a barrier and exceeds a terminal strike price.

Finally, note that you can use Proposition 21.1 to obtain equation (21.55) from equation (21.56).

Chapter 22

Exotic Options: II

Chapter 14 introduced exotic (or nonstandard) options, including barrier, gap, and outperformance options. In this chapter, we continue our study of exotic options. There are two main themes in this chapter. First, we introduce a variety of simple options such as all-or-nothing options that can be used as components for building more complex options. Second, we will examine options that depend on prices of more than one asset, such as quantos and rainbow options. The discussion in this chapter relies on material in Chapters 20 and 21.

Throughout this chapter, we will assume that there are two assets that follow the processes

$$\frac{dS}{S} = (\alpha - \delta)dt + \sigma dZ \tag{22.1}$$

$$\frac{dQ}{Q} = (\alpha_Q - \delta_Q)dt + \sigma_Q dZ_Q \tag{22.2}$$

The correlation between dZ and dZ_Q is ρ.

22.1 ALL-OR-NOTHING OPTIONS

We begin with a discussion of simple all-or-nothing options, which pay the holder a discrete amount of cash or a share if some particular event occurs. These are described as all-or-nothing (also called *binary* or *digital* options) because the payoff can be thought of as 0 or 1: Either you receive the cash or share, or you do not.

Terminology

There are many different kinds of all-or-nothing options; payoffs can be contingent on the stock price at expiration, as well as on whether the stock price has hit a barrier over the life of the option. We are interested in these options in and of themselves, and also because they are building blocks, useful for constructing variants of ordinary puts and calls as well as barrier options.

Naming all of these options can be a complex task. Table 22.1 describes the naming scheme we will use. The terminology will make sense as we introduce the various claims.

To see how the naming scheme works, consider the cash-or-nothing option, a claim that we introduced in Chapter 21. One kind of cash-or-nothing option pays the holder

TABLE 22.1	Option nomenclature used in this chapter.

Notation	Meaning
Asset	Payment at expiration is one unit of the asset
Cash	Payment at expiration is $1
Call	Payment received if $S_T > K$
Put	Payment received if $S_T < K$
UI	Up and in: Payment received only if barrier $H > S_0$ is hit
DI	Down and in: Payment received only if barrier $H < S_0$ is hit
UO	Up and out: Payment received only if barrier $H > S_0$ is not hit
DO	Down and out: Payment received only if barrier $H < S_0$ is not hit
UR	Up rebate: Rebate received at the time the barrier, $H > S_0$, is hit
DR	Down rebate: Rebate received at the time the barrier, $H < S_0$, is hit
URDeferred	Same as UR, except $1 paid at expiration
DRDeferred	Same as DR, except $1 paid at expiration

$1 at time T if the stock price is greater than K. The condition under which it pays off, $S_T > K$, is like that for an ordinary call option, but it is not an ordinary call because it pays $1 instead of $S_T - K$. We will identify an option like this as a "cash call" (*CashCall*), i.e., a contract that pays cash under the same condition as a call—when $S_T > K$.

Some options make payments only if multiple events occur. For example, consider a cash-or-nothing call that pays $1 only if $S_T > K$ and the barrier $H > S_0$ has not been hit. We will refer to this as a "cash up and out call" (*CashUOCall*): "Cash" because it pays $1, "up and out" because payment does not occur if the stock price rises to the barrier, and "call" because payment requires $S_T > K$. Similarly we will use the terms "asset" to refer to options that pay off in shares and "put" to refer to options that pay off only when $S_T < K$. To simplify the formulas in this chapter, we will use the notation in Table 22.2.

Cash-or-Nothing Options

Recall from Chapter 18 that the risk-neutral probability that $S_T > K$ is given by $N(d_2)$ from the Black-Scholes formula. We know from Chapter 21 that discounted risk-neutral probabilities are prices of derivatives. Thus, the price for a **cash-or-nothing call**—which pays $1 if $S_T > K$ and zero otherwise—is

$$CashCall(S, K, \sigma, r, T - t, \delta) = e^{-r(T-t)} N(d_2) \qquad (22.3)$$

where d_2 is defined in Table 22.2. Equation (22.3), multiplied by the strike price, K, is the second term in the Black-Scholes formula for a call option. If you were to be paid x

| TABLE 22.2 | Definitions of expressions used in pricing formulas in this chapter. |

$$d_1 = [ln(S_t/K) + (r - \delta + 0.5\sigma^2)(T - t)]/\sigma\sqrt{T - t}$$

$$d_2 = d_1 - \sigma\sqrt{T - t}$$

$$d_3 = [ln(H^2/S_t K) + (r - \delta + 0.5\sigma^2)(T - t)]/\sigma\sqrt{T - t}$$

$$d_4 = d_3 - \sigma\sqrt{T - t}$$

$$d_5 = [ln(S_t/H) + (r - \delta + 0.5\sigma^2)(T - t)]/\sigma\sqrt{T - t}$$

$$d_6 = d_5 - \sigma\sqrt{T - t}$$

$$d_7 = [ln(H/S_t) + (r - \delta + 0.5\sigma^2)(T - t)]/\sigma\sqrt{T - t}$$

$$d_8 = d_7 - \sigma\sqrt{T - t}$$

if $S > K$, you could value this as x cash-or-nothing options:

$$xe^{-r(T-t)}N(d_2)$$

You could also have a security that pays \$1 if S is *less than* K. This is equivalent to a security that pays \$1, less a security that pays \$1 if S_T is greater than K. Such an option is called a **cash-or-nothing put.** The value is

$$CashPut(S, K, \sigma, r, T - t, \delta) = e^{-r(T-t)} - e^{-r(T-t)}N(d_2)$$
$$= e^{-r(T-t)}N(-d_2) \tag{22.4}$$

Example 22.1 Suppose $S = \$40$, $K = \$40$, $\sigma = 0.3$, $r = 0.08$, $T - t = 0.25$, and $\delta = 0$. The value of a claim that pays \$1 if $S > K$ in 3 months is \$0.5129, computed using equation (22.3). The value of a claim that pays \$1 if $S < K$ is \$0.4673, using equation (22.4). The combined value of the two claims is $e^{-0.08\times0.25} = \$0.9802$.

We know that equations (22.3) and (22.4) are correct since, as discussed in Chapter 21, both formulas satisfy the Black-Scholes equation (equation (21.11)) and the appropriate boundary conditions.

Asset-or-Nothing Options

An **asset-or-nothing call** is an option that gives the owner a unit of the underlying asset if the asset price exceeds a certain level and zero otherwise. As discussed in Chapter 21, Propostion 21.1, the price of an asset-or-nothing call is obtained from the price of a cash-or-nothing by replacing the dividend yield, δ, in the cash-or-nothing formula with $\delta - \sigma^2$, and multiplying the result by the forward price for the stock. The result is

$$Se^{(r-\delta)(T-t)}e^{-r(T-t)}N\left(\frac{ln[S_t/K] + [r - (\delta - \sigma^2) - 0.5\sigma^2][T-t]}{\sigma\sqrt{T-t}}\right)$$
$$= Se^{-\delta(T-t)}N(d_1)$$

This is the first term in the Black-Scholes formula.

Thus, the formula for an asset-or-nothing call that pays one unit of stock is

$$AssetCall(S, K, \sigma, r, T - t, \delta) = e^{-\delta(T-t)}SN(d_1) \tag{22.5}$$

We could also have an option in which we receive the stock if $S_T < K$, in which case the value is

$$Se^{-\delta(T-t)} - Se^{-\delta(T-t)}N(d_1) = Se^{-\delta(T-t)}N(-d_1)$$

Thus, the value of the asset-or-nothing put is

$$AssetPut(S, K, \sigma, r, T - t, \delta) = e^{-\delta(T-t)}SN(-d_1)$$

Example 22.2   Suppose $S = \$40$, $K = \$40$, $\sigma = 0.3$, $r = 0.08$, $T - t = 0.25$, and $\delta = 0$. The value of a claim that pays one share if $S > K$ in 3 months is $23.30, computed using equation (22.5). The value of a claim that pays one share if $S < K$ is $16.70. The combined value of the two claims is $40.   ❦

Figure 22.1 graphs the maturity payoffs of cash and asset calls.

Ordinary Options and Gap Options

We can construct an ordinary call by buying a European asset-or-nothing call with strike price K and selling K European cash-or-nothing calls with strike price K. That is,

$$BSCall(S, K, \sigma, r, T - t, \delta)$$
$$= AssetCall(S, K, \sigma, r, T - t, \delta) - K \times CashCall(S, K, \sigma, r, T - t, \delta)$$
$$= Se^{-\delta(T-t)}N(d_1) - Ke^{-r(T-t)}N(d_2)$$

This is the Black-Scholes formula.

Similarly, we can construct a put:

$$BSPut(S, K, \sigma, r, T - t, \delta)$$
$$= K \times CashPut(S, K, \sigma, r, T - t, \delta) - AssetPut(S, K, \sigma, r, T - t, \delta)$$

Finally, we can construct a gap option using asset-or-nothing options. Consider a call option that pays $S - K_1$ if $S > K_2$. The value of this is

$$AssetCall(S, K_2, \sigma, T - t, r, \delta) - K_1 \times CashCall(S, K_2, \sigma, T - t, r, \delta)$$

We buy an asset call and sell K_1 cash calls, both with the strike price K_2.

FIGURE 22.1

Payoff at maturity to one asset call and 40 cash calls. Assumes $K = \$40$, $\sigma = 0.30$, $r = 0.08$, and $\delta = 0$. The payoff to both is zero for $S < \$40$.

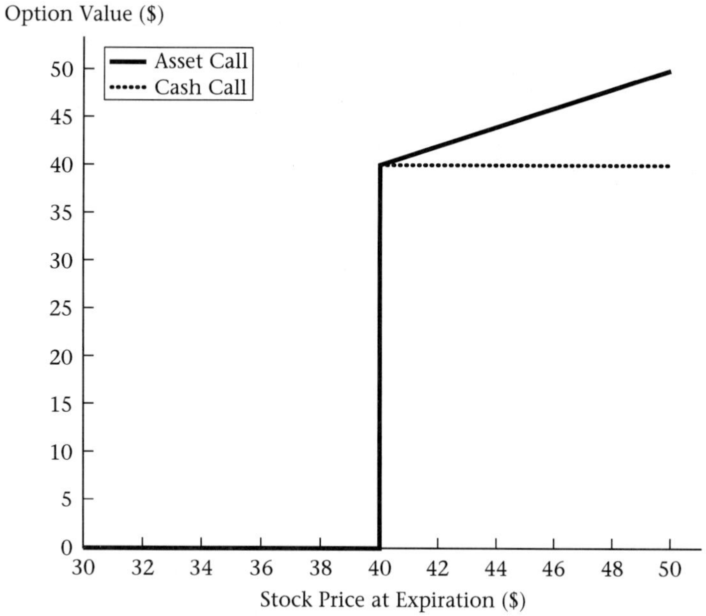

Option Value ($)

Stock Price at Expiration ($)

Example 22.3 Suppose $S = \$40$, $K = \$40$, $\sigma = 0.3$, $r = 0.08$, $T - t = 0.25$, and $\delta = 0$. The price of an ordinary call is an asset call less 40 cash calls. Using results in Examples 22.1 and 22.2, the price of the ordinary call is $\$23.30 - 40 \times \$0.5129 = \$2.7848$.

The price of a gap call in which the owner pays $20 ($K_1$) if the stock is greater than $40 ($K_2$) at expiration is $\$23.20 - 20 \times \$0.5129 = \$13.0427$. ≷

Delta-Hedging All-or-Nothing Options

All-or-nothing options appear frequently in writings about options, but they are relatively rare in practice. The reason is that they are easy to price but hard to hedge. To understand why, think about the position of a market-maker when such an option is close to expiration. The nightmare scenario for a market-maker is that the option is close to expiration *and* close to the strike price. In this case a small swing in the stock price can determine whether the option is in- or out-of-the-money, with the payoff changing discretely. This potential for a small price change to have a large effect on the option value is evident in Figure 22.1.

To assess hedging difficulty, Figure 22.2 graphs the price and delta of cash calls paying $1 with 3 months to expiration and two minutes to expiration. With 3 months to go, hedging is straightforward and delta is well-behaved. However, with 2 minutes to go until expiration, the cash call delta at $40 is 15. For the at-the-money option, delta and

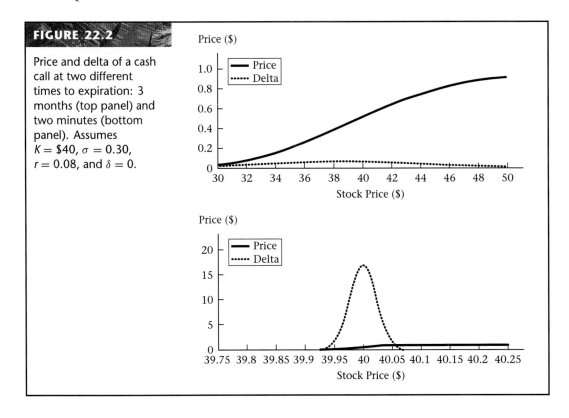

FIGURE 22.2

Price and delta of a cash call at two different times to expiration: 3 months (top panel) and two minutes (bottom panel). Assumes $K = \$40$, $\sigma = 0.30$, $r = 0.08$, and $\delta = 0$.

gamma approach infinity at expiration because an arbitrarily small change in the price can result in a $1 change in the option's value.

An ordinary call or put is easier to hedge because the payoff is continuous—there is no discrete jump at the strike price as the option approaches expiration.

22.2 ALL-OR-NOTHING BARRIER OPTIONS

Barrier options, introduced in Chapter 14, are options in which the option comes into or goes out of existence if the price of the underlying asset hits a barrier.[1] There are down-and-out options, which become worthless if the stock price hits a barrier price below the initial stock price, as well as up-and-out, down-and-in, and up-and-in options. We can construct options such as these using *all-or-nothing barrier options.*

Suppose we take a cash-or-nothing call paying $1 if $S_T > K$, but modify it by adding the additional requirement that it will only pay $1 at expiration if the stock has

---

[1] Three comprehensive discussions of barrier options are Rubinstein and Reiner (1991a), Rubinstein and Reiner (1991b), and Derman and Kani (1993).

also hit the barrier H sometime during the life of the option. If $H < S(0)$, this is a down-and-in cash call. Using the notation in Table 22.1, this would be a *CashDICall*. Just as we were able to construct ordinary options from digital options, we will also be able to construct barrier options from digital barrier options.

We will examine three different kinds of barrier options:

- A contract that pays $1 contingent on either a barrier having or not having been reached (*cash-or-nothing barrier options*).

- A contract that pays a share of stock worth S contingent on either a barrier having or not having been reached (*asset-or-nothing barrier options*).

- A contract that pays $1 at the time a barrier is reached (*rebate options*) or that pays $1 at expiration as long as the barrier has been reached during the life of the option (*deferred rebate options*).

By valuing these pieces and adding them together we can price any standard barrier option. The assumption that the stock follows geometric Brownian motion makes it possible to derive relatively simple formulas for these options.

There are 16 basic kinds of all-or-nothing barrier options. First, consider cash-or-nothing barrier options that pay $1 at expiration. Such options can knock-in or knock-out; they can be calls (pay cash if $S_T > K$) or puts (pay cash if $S_T < K$); and the barrier event can occur if the barrier is above the price (up-and-ins or up-and-outs) or below the price (down-and-ins or down-and-outs). This gives us $2^3 = 8$ basic cash-or-nothing barrier options to value. By the same reasoning there are also 8 basic asset-or-nothing barrier options, for a total of 16 all-or-nothing barrier options.

Cash-or-Nothing Barrier Options

We first consider the valuation of barrier cash-or-nothing options. To anticipate the results in this section, we will first see how to value one particular barrier cash-or-nothing option, a down-and-in cash call. From this one formula we will be able to value the remaining seven cash-or-nothing options and deferred rebate options.

Assume that the option is issued at time 0 and expires at time T. Let $\overline{S}_t$ denote the greatest stock price between times 0 and t (where $t \leq T$) and let $\underline{S}_t$ denote the lowest stock price between times 0 and t. Suppose the barrier is below the initial stock price, i.e., $H < S_0$. A cash down-and-in call (*CashDICall*) is an option that pays $1 if two conditions are satisfied. First, at some point prior to maturity, the stock price drops to reach H, i.e., $\underline{S}_T \leq H$. Second, at expiration, the stock price is greater than the strike price, K.

We can analyze this option by first examining the risk-neutral probability that this joint event ($\underline{S}_T \leq H$ and $S_T \geq K$) occurs. This probability should satisfy three conditions:

1. Once the barrier has been hit ($\underline{S}_t \leq H$) the probability equals the probability that $S_T \geq K$ (the barrier at this point is irrelevant).

2. If at time T, $\underline{S}_T \leq H$ and $S_T \geq K$, the probability equals 1.

3. If at time T, $\underline{S}_T > H$ or $S_T < K$, the probability equals 0.

Assume that $H \leq K$, and consider this expression:

$$Prob(\underline{S}_T \leq H \text{ and } S_T > K) = \left(\frac{H}{S}\right)^{2\frac{r-\delta}{\sigma^2}-1} N(d_4) \qquad (22.6)$$

The terms d_1 through d_8 are defined in Table 22.2. In Appendix 21.C, we saw that an expression of this form solves the backward equation. We also want to verify that it satisfies the three boundary conditions described above.

First, at the point where $S_t = H$, equation (22.6) collapses to $N(d_2)$, which is the risk-neutral probability that $S_T > K$. (This occurs because when $H = S_t$, $d_1 = d_3$. You should examine equation (22.6) to verify that this happens.) Thus, once we hit the barrier, the barrier value H drops out of the expression because it is irrelevant. Second, if at expiration $\underline{S}_T \leq H$ and $S_T > K$, then equation (22.6) equals 1. The reason is that the probability equals $N(d_2)$ once the barrier is hit, and if $S_T > K$, $N(d_2) = 1$. Finally, if $\underline{S}_T > H$, i.e., S_t never reaches H, then at expiration $H^2 < S_T K$ (recall that $H \leq K$) and equation (22.6) collapses to 0. Thus, equation (22.6) both satisfies the backward equation and obeys the appropriate boundary conditions.

Equation (22.6) assumes that $H \leq K$. Why is this important? The answer is that if $H > K$, the boundary conditions may be violated. Consider the case where at expiration $S_T = \$55$, $K = \$45$, and $H = \$54$ (thus violating the condition $H \leq K$), and the boundary has not been hit. In this case a correct expression for the probability will evaluate to zero at expiration. However, $ln(H^2/S_T K) = ln(54^2/45 \times 55) = 0.164$, so equation (22.6) at maturity will equal 1 when the event has not occurred.

As a final comment on equation (22.6), you might ask why it is necessary to multiply $N(d_4)$ by the term $(H/S)^{2(r-\delta)/\sigma^2-1}$. The answer is simply that $N(d_4)$ by itself does not solve the backward equation, whereas equation (22.6) *does* solve the backward equation.

To handle the case where $H > K$ we need a more complicated version of equation (22.6). When $H > K$, we have

$$Prob(\underline{S}_T \leq H \text{ and } S_T > K) = N(d_2) - N(d_6) + \left(\frac{H}{S}\right)^{2\frac{r-\delta}{\sigma^2}-1} N(d_8) \qquad (22.7)$$

Problem 22.3 asks you to verify that this equation satisfies the boundary conditions. Note that when $S = H$, $N(d_6) = N(d_8)$; the formula again reduces to $N(d_2)$.

Down-and-in cash call   Equations (22.6) and (22.7) give us expressions for the probability that the barrier is hit and $S_T > K$. What is the value of a claim that pays \$1 when this event occurs? To answer this question we can use the result from Chapter 21 that discounted risk-neutral probabilities are prices of derivative claims. Discounting equations (22.6) and (22.7), we have

$$CashDICall(S, K, \sigma, r, T - t, \delta, H) =$$

$$
\begin{cases}
e^{-r(T-t)} \left(\frac{H}{S}\right)^{2\frac{r-\delta}{\sigma^2}-1} N(d_4) & H \leq K \\
e^{-r(T-t)} \left[N(d_2) - N(d_6) + \left(\frac{H}{S}\right)^{2\frac{r-\delta}{\sigma^2}-1} N(d_8)\right] & H > K
\end{cases}
\tag{22.8}
$$

Equation (22.8) gives us the value for a cash down-and-in call when $S_0 > H$. There are three closely related options we can now price: Cash down-and-out calls (*CashDO-Call*), cash down-and-in puts (*CashDIPut*), and cash down-and-out puts (*CashDOPut*). We can value each of these using only the formula for the cash down-and-in call, equation (22.8). In addition, we can value a deferred down rebate option.

Deferred down rebate option We first value a deferred down rebate, which is a claim that pays \$1 at time T as long as the barrier has been hit over the life of the option. The payoff to this claim does not depend on a strike price: It pays \$1 as long as the barrier has been hit. We will call this claim a **deferred down rebate.** It is a "down rebate" because it pays \$1 if we reach the barrier, and it is "deferred" because the payment is at expiration rather than at the time we reach the barrier. We obtain the value of this claim by setting $K = \$0$ in equation (22.8). Since we always have $S_T > 0$, the result is a claim that pays \$1 at T as long as $S_T \leq H$. Thus, we have[2]

$$DRDeferred(S, \sigma, r, T - t, \delta, H) = CashDICall(S, 0, \sigma, r, T - t, \delta, H) \tag{22.9}$$

Note that since we set $K = 0$, the value of the deferred down rebate does not depend on the strike price.

Now we can compute the value of the remaining three options.

Down-and-out cash call We can create a synthetic cash call by buying down-and-in and down-and-out cash calls with the same barrier; this combination is guaranteed to pay \$1 if $S_T > K$. Thus, the value of a down-and-out cash call is

$$
\begin{aligned}
CashDOCall(S, K, \sigma, r, T - t, \delta, H) &= CashCall(S, K, \sigma, r, T - t, \delta) \\
&\quad - CashDICall(S, K, \sigma, r, T - t, \delta, H)
\end{aligned}
\tag{22.10}
$$

Down-and-in cash put If you buy a down-and-in cash put with strike price K, you receive \$1 if the barrier is reached and $S_T < K$. If you buy a down-and-in cash call, you receive \$1 if the barrier is reached and $S_T \geq K$. Thus, if you buy *both* a down-and-in call and put, you receive \$1 as long as the barrier is hit. This is the same payoff as a deferred rebate; thus, we have

$$
\begin{aligned}
CashDIPut(S, K, \sigma, r, T - t, \delta, H) &= DRDeferred(S, \sigma, r, T - t, \delta, H) \\
&\quad - CashDICall(S, K, \sigma, r, T - t, \delta, H)
\end{aligned}
\tag{22.11}
$$

....

[2] In peforming this calculation, to avoid a zero-divide error it is necessary to set K to be small, such as $K = \$0.000001$, rather than exactly \$0.

Down-and-out cash put   Buying down-and-in and down-and-out cash puts creates an ordinary cash put. Thus, the value of the down-and-out put is

$$CashDOPut(S, K, \sigma, r, T - t, \delta, H) = CashPut(S, K, \sigma, r, T - t, \delta)$$
$$- CashDIPut(S, K, \sigma, r, T - t, \delta, H) \tag{22.12}$$

As a final point we can compute the risk-neutral probability that we reach the barrier. The deferred down rebate option pays $1 at expiration as long as the barrier is hit. Thus the price of this option is the present value of the risk-neutral probability that the barrier is reached. Therefore,

$$e^{r(T-t)} DRDeferred(S, 0, \sigma, r, T - t, \delta) \tag{22.13}$$

is the risk-neutral probability that the barrier is reached during the life of the option.

Example 22.4   Suppose $S = \$40$, $\sigma = 0.3$, $r = 0.08$, $\delta = 0$, and $T - t = 1$. The value of a claim that pays $1 if the stock hits the barrier $H = \$35$ over the next year is computed by setting $K = \$0$ in equation (22.8):

$$CashDICall(\$40, \$0.0000001, 0.3, 0.08, 1, 0, \$35) =$$

$$e^{-r(T-t)} \left[1 - N(d_6) + \left(\frac{H}{S} \right)^{2(r-\delta)/\sigma^2 - 1} N(d_8) \right] = \$0.574$$

The risk-neutral probability that the stock will hit the barrier is the undiscounted value of this claim, or $0.574 \times e^{0.08} = 0.622$.

The value of a claim that pays $1 if the stock hits the barrier, $35, and then is also greater than $K = \$35$ at the end of the year is

$$e^{-r(T-t)} \left(\frac{H}{S} \right)^{2(r-\delta)/\sigma^2 - 1} N(d_4) = \$0.309$$

This is the value of $CashDICall(\$40, \$35, 0.3, 0.08, 1, 0, \$35)$. The risk-neutral probability of hitting the barrier and being above $35 is $0.309 \times e^{0.08} = 0.335$.   ⚞

This example illustrates an interesting point. The value of the claim that pays $1 at expiration when the stock at expiration is greater than $35 and has hit the $35 barrier ($0.309), is approximately one-half the value of the claim that pays $1 at expiration as long as the stock has hit the $35 barrier ($0.574). The reason is that once the stock has hit $35, it subsequently has about a 50% chance of being above or below that value. This observation suggests that the probability of being above $35 conditional upon having hit $35 is $0.5 \times 0.622 = 0.311$. The actual probability is greater than that, however. The reason is that the lognormal drift is $r - 0.5\sigma^2 = 0.035$, which is positive. Thus, after having hit $35, the stock on average drifts higher.

To verify this intuition, suppose we set the lognormal drift equal to zero. We can do this by setting the risk-free rate to 0.045, which gives us $r - 0.5\sigma^2 = 0.045 - 0.5 \times$

$0.3^2 = 0$. We expect that the value of a claim paying \$1 at T if the barrier is hit is exactly one-half the value of a claim paying \$1 at T if the barrier is hit and the stock price at expiration is greater than the barrier. Put differently, when $r = 0.5\sigma^2$, the probability of hitting and ending up above \$35 is half the unconditional probability of hitting \$35. The next example shows that this intuition works.

Example 22.5   Suppose $S = \$40$, $\sigma = 0.3$, $r = 0.045$, $\delta = 0$, and $T - t = 1$. The value of a claim paying \$1 if the stock hits the barrier $H = \$35$ over the next year is

$$e^{-r(T-t)} \left[1 - N(d_6) + \left(\frac{H}{S} \right)^{2(r-\delta)/\sigma^2 - 1} N(d_8) \right] = \$0.6274$$

The corresponding risk-neutral probability is $e^{0.045} \times 0.6274 = 0.6562$.

The value of a claim paying \$1 if the stock hits the barrier and is then greater than $K = \$35$ at the end of the year is

$$e^{-r(T-t)} \left(\frac{H}{S} \right)^{2(r-\delta)/\sigma^2 - 1} N(d_4) = \$0.3137$$

This is one-half of \$0.6274. The corresponding risk-neutral probability is $e^{0.045} \times 0.3137 = 0.3281$. ❦

Up-and-in cash put   Now we consider cash-or-nothing options when the barrier is *above* the current stock price. First, consider the following formula for an up-and-in cash put, which pays \$1 when $\overline{S}_T > H$ and $S_T < K$:

$$CashUIPut(S, K, \sigma, r, T - t, \delta, H) =$$

$$\begin{cases} e^{-r(T-t)} \left(\frac{H}{S} \right)^{2\frac{r-\delta}{\sigma^2} - 1} N(-d_4) & H \geq K \\ e^{-r(T-t)} \left[N(-d_2) - N(-d_6) + \left(\frac{H}{S} \right)^{2\frac{r-\delta}{\sigma^2} - 1} N(-d_8) \right] & H < K \end{cases} \quad (22.14)$$

If you compare this formula to equation (22.8), you will see that $N(d_2)$ is replaced with $N(-d_2)$, $N(d_4)$ with $N(-d_4)$, and so forth. We know from Appendix 21.C that these terms also solve the Black-Scholes equation. The effect of these changes is to reverse the effect of the d_i terms. As a consequence, equation (22.8), which prices a down-and-in cash call, is transformed into an equation pricing an up-and-in cash put. Problem 22.4 asks you to verify that equation (22.14) solves the appropriate boundary conditions for an up-and-in cash put.

Deferred up rebate   Given equation (22.14), the procedure for obtaining the prices of the other three cash-or-nothing options when $H > S_0$ is analogous to that before. First, by setting $K = \infty$ in equation (22.14), we obtain the price of a claim paying \$1 at expiration as long as the barrier is reached:[3]

$$URDeferred(S, \sigma, r, T - t, \delta, H) = CashUIPut(S, \infty, \sigma, r, T - t, \delta, H) \quad (22.15)$$

With this equation, we can solve for the price of the other cash-or-nothing options.

Up-and-out cash put Buying up-and-in and up-and-out cash puts gives an ordinary cash put; hence,

$$\begin{aligned} CashUOPut(S, K, \sigma, r, T - t, \delta, H) = {} & CashPut(S, K, \sigma, r, T - t, \delta) \\ & - CashUIPut(S, K, \sigma, r, T - t, \delta, H) \end{aligned} \quad (22.16)$$

Up-and-in cash call Buying an up-and-in cash call and an up-and-in cash put yields the same payoff as a deferred up rebate. Thus, we have

$$\begin{aligned} CashUICall(S, K, \sigma, r, T - t, \delta, H) = {} & URDeferred(S, \sigma, r, T - t, \delta, H) \\ & - CashUIPut(S, K, \sigma, r, T - t, \delta, H) \end{aligned} \quad (22.17)$$

Up-and-out cash call Buying up-and-in and up-and-out cash calls gives an ordinary cash call; hence,

$$\begin{aligned} CashUOCall(S, K, \sigma, r, T - t, \delta, H) = {} & CashCall(S, K, \sigma, r, T - t, \delta) \\ & - CashUICall(S, K, \sigma, r, T - t, \delta, H) \end{aligned} \quad (22.18)$$

Asset-or-Nothing Barrier Options

We now wish to find the eight pricing formulas for asset-or-nothing options corresponding to those for the eight cash-or-nothing options. Fortunately, there is a simple way to do this. If we view asset-or-nothing options as cash-or-nothing options denominated in shares rather than cash, we can use Proposition 21.1, dealing with a change of numeraire, to transform the pricing formulas for cash-or-nothing options into formulas for asset-or-nothing options. In each case, we replace δ by $\delta - \sigma^2$, and we multiply the cash-or-nothing formula by $S_0 e^{(r-\delta)(T-t)}$, the forward price for the stock. For example, we have

$$\begin{aligned} AssetDICall(S, K, \sigma, r, T - t, \delta, H) \\ = Se^{(r-\delta)(T-t)} CashDICall(S, K, \sigma, r, T - t, \delta - \sigma^2, H) \end{aligned} \quad (22.19)$$

The other seven asset-or-nothing pricing formulas—*AssetDOCall, AssetDIPut, AssetDOPut, AssetUICall, AssetUOCall, AssetUIPut,* and *AssetUOP*—can be created in exactly the same way.

---

[3]To evaluate equation (22.14) at $K = \infty$, we simply set $N(-d_2) = 1$.

Rebate Options

Rebate options pay $1 if the barrier is hit. We have already seen how to price deferred rebate options, which pay the $1 at expiration of the option. If the option pays at the time the barrier is hit, we will call the claim a **rebate option** (or *immediate rebate option*).

We have already seen in equations (22.9) and (22.15) how to price deferred rebates. The formulas for rebates paid when the barrier is hit are more complicated because the discount factor for the $1 payment depends on the time at which the barrier is hit. In effect there is a random discount factor.

The formula for the price of a down rebate when $S > H$ is

$$DR(S, \sigma, r, T - t, \delta, H) = \left(\frac{H}{S}\right)^{h_1} N(Z_1) + \left(\frac{H}{S}\right)^{h_2} N(Z_2) \qquad (22.20)$$

where, letting

$$g = \sqrt{\left(r - \delta - \frac{1}{2}\sigma^2\right)^2 + 2r\sigma^2}$$

then

$$Z_1 = [ln(H/S) + g(T - t)]/\sigma\sqrt{T - t}$$
$$Z_2 = [ln(H/S) - g(T - t)]/\sigma\sqrt{T - t}$$
$$h_1 = \left(\frac{r - \delta}{\sigma^2} - \frac{1}{2}\right) + \sqrt{\left(\frac{r - \delta}{\sigma^2} - \frac{1}{2}\right)^2 + \frac{2r}{\sigma^2}}$$
$$h_2 = \left(\frac{r - \delta}{\sigma^2} - \frac{1}{2}\right) - \sqrt{\left(\frac{r - \delta}{\sigma^2} - \frac{1}{2}\right)^2 + \frac{2r}{\sigma^2}}$$

This formula satisfies (as it must) both the Black-Scholes equation and the boundary conditions for a rebate option. Suppose that the barrier is not hit over the life of the option. Then $H < S$ and both terms go to 0 as $t \to T$. At the point when the barrier is hit, $H = S$ and $ln(H/S) = 0$. Because the normal distribution is symmetric around 0,

$$N\left[\frac{g(T - t)}{\sigma\sqrt{T - t}}\right] + N\left[\frac{-g(T - t)}{\sigma\sqrt{T - t}}\right] = 1$$

Thus, the formula evaluates to 1 when the barrier is hit.

The up-rebate formula is symmetric:

$$UR(S, \sigma, r, T - t, \delta, H) = \left(\frac{H}{S}\right)^{h_1} N(-Z_1) + \left(\frac{H}{S}\right)^{h_2} N(-Z_2) \qquad (22.21)$$

where all variables are defined as above for the down rebate.

If we let $T \to \infty$, the formulas for up and down rebates become the barrier present value formulas, equations (12.14) and (12.15), discussed in Chapter 12. (Problem 22.5 asks you to verify this.) The rebate formulas provide the value of $1 when the stock price hits a barrier, and this is exactly the calculation performed by barrier present value calculations, only for the case of infinitely lived claims.

22.3 BARRIER OPTIONS

At this point it is easy to construct the barrier option formulas from Chapter 14 using the preceding formulas. A down-and-out call, for example, can be valued as

$$CallDownOut(S, K, \sigma, r, T - t, \delta, H) = AssetDOCall(S, K, \sigma, r, T - t, \delta, H)$$
$$- K \times CashDOCall(S, K, \sigma, r, T - t, \delta, H)$$

Up-and-outs, down-and-ins, and so forth are all constructed analogously.

Barrier puts are constructed similarly. An up-and-in put, for example, would be

$$PutUpIn(S, K, \sigma, r, T - t, \delta, H) = K \times CashUIPut(S, K, \sigma, r, T - t, \delta, H)$$
$$- AssetUIPut(S, K, \sigma, r, T - t, \delta, H)$$

As another example of the use of all-or-nothing options as building blocks, **capped options** are single options that have the payoff of bull spreads, except that the option is exercised the first time the stock price reaches the upper strike price. An example of an American capped option is an option with a strike price of $100 and a cap of $120. When the stock hits $120, the option pays $20. If the option expires without the stock having hit $120, then the payoff is $max(S_T - 100, 0)$. This option can be priced as the sum of the following two options:

- A rebate call, which pays the $20 when the stock hits $120 prior to expiration.

- A knock-out call with a strike of $100, which knocks out at $120.

If the stock reaches $120 prior to expiration, the rebate is triggered and the call knocks out. If the stock has not hit $120 prior to expiration but is above $100, the knock-out call pays $S - $100. The following table illustrates the payoffs, assuming that the option strike is K, the cap is H, and the option expires at T:

	H Hit	*H* Not Hit
Purchased Knock-Out	0	$max(0, S_T - K)$
Rebate	$H - K$ at Hit	0
Total	$H - K$ at Hit	$max(0, S_T - K)$

The table shows that we can price the American capped option above as a straight application of the rebate formula together with a knock-out. The holder owns a 100-strike call with a knock-out of $120, and a rebate call with a $20 rebate payable at $120. Note that a European capped option is much simpler to price. Since the payoff does not occur until expiration, this option is just an ordinary vertical spread (buy a 100-strike call and sell a 120-strike European call with the same times to expiration).

Example 22.6 Consider the capped call discussed in the text above and suppose that $S = \$100$, $\sigma = 0.3$, $r = 0.08$, $T - t = 1$, and $\delta = 0$. We can compute the price of an up-and-out call as

$$CallUpOut(S, K, \sigma, r, T - t, \delta, H) = AssetUOCall(S, K, \sigma, r, T - t, \delta, H)$$
$$- K \times CashUOCall(S, K, \sigma, r, T - t, \delta, H)$$

The price of the capped call is

$$20 \times UR(\$100, 0.3, 0.08, 1, 0, \$120) + CallUpOut(\$100, \$100, 0.3, 0.08, 1, 0, \$120)$$
$$= 20 \times \$0.5649 + \$0.4298 = \$11.73$$

The price of a European bull spread for the same parameters would be

$$BSCall(\$100, \$100, 0.3, 0.08, 1, 0) - BSCall(\$100, \$120, 0.3, 0.08, 1, 0)$$
$$= \$15.7113 - \$7.8966 = \$7.8147$$

The capped call is more expensive because all of the stock price paths that cross \$120 and end up lower result in the maximum payout on the capped call but a lower payout on the bull spread. ✎

22.4 QUANTOS

A U.S. investor wishing to invest in a foreign stock index can purchase the foreign index directly or hold futures based on that index. However, the investor then bears two risks: The risk of the foreign index and currency (exchange rate) risk.

For example, suppose that a U.S. investor wishes to invest in the Nikkei 225 index, expecting that it will increase over the next month. The investor can take a position in the Nikkei by directly investing in the cash Nikkei index or by investing in yen-denominated futures, such as a Nikkei futures contract trading in Japan. Both strategies have a payoff denominated in yen. If the Nikkei appreciates but the yen depreciates, *the investor can lose money despite being correct about the movement of the Nikkei.*

You could try to reduce the problem of exchange rate risk by hedging the Nikkei investment using currency futures. However, the quantity of yen to be exchanged is high when the index has a high return and low when the index has a low return. Thus, *there is no way to know in advance how many yen to short.* This price uncertainty creates quantity uncertainty with respect to the yen exposure.

We could imagine a synthetic Nikkei investment in which the quantity of currency forwards depended upon the Nikkei's yen return. Such a contract would permit an investor in one currency to hold an asset denominated in another currency, without exchange rate risk. This contract is called an **equity-linked forward,** or **quanto.** For reasons that will become clear below, a quanto is also sometimes defined as a derivative having a payoff that depends on the product or ratio of two prices.

TABLE 22.3	Parameters used in the Nikkei/yen quanto example.		
Dollar-denominated interest rate	r	0.08	
Yen-denominated interest rate	r_f	0.04	
Current Nikkei index	Q_0	¥20,000	
Nikkei dividend yield	δ_Q	0.02	
Nikkei volatility (¥)	σ_Q	0.15	
Current exchange rate ($\$/¥$)	x_0	0.0100	
Exchange rate volatility	s	0.1	
Nikkei-exchange rate ($\$/¥$) correlation	ρ	0.2	
Time to expiration	T	1 year	

The Nikkei 225 index futures contract, traded at the Chicago Mercantile Exchange and discussed in Chapter 5, is an example of a quanto contract. This futures contract is marked-to-market daily in *dollars,* even though it settles based on a yen-denominated price.[4] There is also a yen-denominated Nikkei futures contract that trades in Osaka. Both futures are based on the Nikkei 225 contract, but they differ in currency of denomination. We will see in this section how their pricing differs. The box on page 710 discusses Nikkei put warrants, which were another example of a quanto contract. Table 22.3 lists the symbols and specific numbers used throughout the examples in this section.

The Yen Perspective

The yen-based investor is interested in the yen price of $1 and, hence, faces an exchange rate of $1/x_0 = 100¥/\$$. Because the Nikkei index and the yen price of a dollar are both denominated in yen, we use the usual formulas to find forward prices for the yen and Nikkei. For the Nikkei, we have

$$\text{Nikkei forward (¥): } F_{0,T}(Q) = Q_0 e^{(r_f - \delta_Q)T} \tag{22.22}$$

For the exchange rate, the dollar-denominated interest rate is the yield on dollars, so the forward price is

$$\text{Exchange rate forward (¥/\$): } F_{0,T}(1/x) = \frac{1}{x_0} e^{(r_f - r)T} \tag{22.23}$$

These will be the forward prices observed in Japan.

....

[4]To illustrate dollar settlement, suppose the Nikkei 225 is at 22,000. Under the terms of the CME contract, a one point move corresponds to $5, so the notional value of one contract is $22,000 \times \$5 = \$110,000$. If instead the Nikkei had been 22,100, the notional value of the contract would be $110,500, a difference of $500.

FIGURE 22.3

Binomial trees for the dollar and the Nikkei index from the perspective of a yen-based investor. Both are forward trees constructed using the parameters in Table 22.3. The risk-neutral probabilities of up moves are 0.4750 in the dollar tree and 0.4626 in the Nikkei tree.

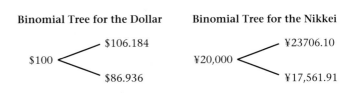

Binomial Tree for the Dollar

Binomial Tree for the Nikkei

A yen-based investor would construct binomial trees for the yen and Nikkei in the usual fashion. Figure 22.3 depicts trees for the dollar and Nikkei. The nodes on the dollar tree are constructed as

$$(1/x_T) = (1/x_0)e^{(r_f-r)T\pm s\sqrt{T}}$$

and on the Nikkei tree as

$$Q_T = Q_0e^{(r_f-\delta_Q)T\pm\sigma_Q\sqrt{T}}$$

Example 22.7 Given the parameters in Table 22.3, the 1-year yen-denominated forward price for the Nikkei index is

$$F_{0,1}(Q) = ¥20,000e^{(0.04-0.02)\times1} = ¥20,404.03$$

and that for the exchange rate is

$$F_{0,1}(1/x) = ¥100e^{(0.04-0.08)\times1} = ¥96.079$$

We can also compute the forward prices on both trees as expected values. For the dollar tree we have

$$F_{0,1}(1/x) = 0.4750 \times \$106.184 + (1 - 0.4750) \times \$86.936 = \$96.079$$

For the Nikkei tree we have[5]

$$F_{0,1}(Q) = ¥0.4626 \times ¥23,706.10 + (1 - 0.4626) \times ¥17,561.91 = ¥20,404.03$$

---

[5]The calculation shown here uses rounded numbers and therefore does not exactly equal ¥20,404.03.

The Dollar Perspective

Now we consider yen and Nikkei investments from the perspective of a dollar-based investor. The yen forward price is given by

$$\text{Exchange rate forward (\$/¥): } F_{0,T}(x) = x_0 e^{(r-r_f)T} \tag{22.24}$$

However, from the dollar perspective, the forward price of the Nikkei is not so straight-forward.

As discussed above, any Nikkei investment entails a combination of currency and index risk. To see why, suppose a dollar-based investor buys $e^{-\delta_Q T}$ units of the Nikkei and holds it for T years. The actual steps in this transaction are as follows:

1. Exchange $Q_0 x_0 e^{-\delta_Q T}$ dollars into yen (this is enough dollars to buy $e^{-\delta_Q T}$ units of the index).

2. Buy $e^{-\delta_Q T}$ units of the Nikkei index and hold for T periods.

3. Dividends are paid continuously over time and reinvested in the index; after T years we have an additional $e^{\delta_Q T}$ shares.

4. After T years sell the index and convert back into dollars.

The time-T value of the investment, denominated in dollars, is

$$Y(T) = x_T Q_T$$

The payoff is a *combination* of yen and Nikkei risk; we will call this investment the **currency-translated index.** Here is a point that is crucial for understanding what follows: *From the perspective of a dollar-based investor, the dollar-translated price of a yen-denominated asset, Y_T, is just like any other dollar-denominated asset.* However, Q_T is *not* the price of an asset for a dollar-based investor, because there is no simple way to obtain the risk of Q without also bearing currency risk.

If you are not convinced that Y_T really is like any other dollar-denominated asset, consider the following thought experiment. Suppose you learn of a new stock, traded on a U.S. exchange, called "As American as Apple Pie, Inc." (AAAPI). The price is in dollars, just like any other domestic stock. You decide to investigate the stock and, to your surprise, you learn that the company is actually an American Depositary Receipt (ADR) for the Nikkei index.[6] The sole asset of this company is shares of the Nikkei, translated into dollars at the current exchange rate, and held in trust. The value at any time is $Y_t = x_t Q_t$ and it has a dividend yield of δ_Q. This ADR trades just like a dollar-denominated stock, because it *is* a dollar-denominated stock. Had you not investigated, you would never have known that you were holding a currency-translated yen-denominated stock.

....

[6] In simplest terms, an ADR is a claim to a trust containing a foreign stock. ADRs are a common means for investors in one country to buy a stock trading in another country.

This thought experiment is important, because it tells us that, for a dollar-based investor, the forward price for Y is given by

$$F_{0,T}(Y) = Y_0 e^{(r-\delta_Q)T} \tag{22.25}$$

Since we can trade shares of AAAPI, we can undertake arbitrage if the forward price is anything other than equation (22.25). Similarly, the prepaid forward price on the currency-translated index is

$$F_{0,T}^P(Y) = x_0 Q_0 e^{-\delta_Q T} \tag{22.26}$$

In order to obtain Nikkei risk without currency risk, we need to combine the dollar-translated Nikkei with a position in forward yen contracts. Intuitively, we want to invest in Y and use currency contracts to hedge exchange rate risk. Let $V_{t,T}(Y_t, x_t; T)$ represent the price of a claim that, at maturity, pays the dollar value of the Nikkei. The boundary condition for this security is

$$V_{T,T}(Y_T, x_T; T) = \bar{x} \frac{Y_T}{x_T} \tag{22.27}$$

where $\bar{x}$ is an arbitrary exchange rate determined in advance. The boundary condition says that we will receive Y_T, the dollar-translated Nikkei, convert it to yen by multiplying by $1/x_T$, and then convert back to dollars at the rate $\bar{x}$. (Since the only purpose of $\bar{x}$ is to convert yen to dollars, the value is arbitrary and we can set it to 1. In practice the contract can call for any fixed exchange rate.) Prior to time T, the market-maker hedges the value of the security using both the dollar-translated Nikkei and exchange rate contracts. Equation (22.27) makes it clear why quantos are said to be derivatives that depend on the ratio or product of two assets.

We can price this contract by using Proposition 21.1. That proposition implies that we obtain the forward price for Y_T/x_T by multiplying the forward price for Y by the forward price for $1/x$, and adjusting the dividend yield to take account of the covariance between x and Y.

To apply Proposition 21.1 we need to know the forward price of $1/x$ for *dollar-denominated* investors. We can obtain the forward price for $1/x$ using Proposition 20.3. This gives[7]

$$F_{t,T}(1/x) = \frac{1}{x_0} e^{(r_f - r + s^2)(T-t)}$$

We also need to know the covariance between x and Y. Using Itô's Lemma, that covariance is

$$\frac{1}{dt}[dx - E(dx)][dY - E(dY)] = \rho s \sigma_Q + s^2 \tag{22.28}$$

---

[7]In this calculation we start with the forward price for x from the dollar perspective and convert it to the forward price for $1/x$. As a result, the forward price for $1/x$ given here is different from that given by equation (22.23), which is the appropriate forward price given a yen perspective.

In applying Proposition 21.1, we have $b = -1$; hence, when we compute the forward price for Q we replace δ_Q with $\delta_Q - (-1)(\rho s \sigma_Q + s^2)$.

Putting this all together, using Proposition 21.1 and with $\bar{x} = 1$ we have

$$
\begin{aligned}
V_{t,T}(Y_t, x_t; T) &= \frac{1}{x_t} e^{(r_f - r + s^2)(T-t)} Q_t x_t e^{(r - \delta_Q - \rho s \sigma_Q - s^2)(T-t)} \\
&= Q_t e^{(r_f - \delta_Q - \rho s \sigma_Q)(T-t)}
\end{aligned}
\tag{22.29}
$$

The dollar-denominated forward price for the Nikkei index is the same as the yen-denominated forward price, with a covariance correction. The prepaid quanto index forward price is thus

$$
F_{0,T}^P(Q) = Q_0 e^{(r_f - \delta_Q - \rho \sigma_Q s - r)T}
\tag{22.30}
$$

The role of the covariance term in equation (22.29) is intuitive. Consider an investor who buys the cash Nikkei index and ultimately converts yen back to dollars. Suppose the index and the exchange rate (measured in dollars/yen) are positively correlated. When the index does well, there are many yen to exchange. If ρ is positive, on average the exchange rate is favorable when there are many yen to exchange. When the index does poorly, there are fewer yen to exchange so the decline in the exchange rate does not matter as much. Thus, other things equal, the positive correlation systematically benefits the unhedged investment in the Nikkei relative to a contract with a fixed exchange rate. Consequently, if the exchange rate is fixed, as in a quanto contract, the price for the index settling in dollars will be lower in order to compensate the buyer for the loss of beneficial correlation between the index and exchange rate.

Example 22.8   Using equation (22.29) and the information in Table 22.3, the yen forward price is

$$
F_{0,1} = x_0 e^{(r - r_f)t} = 0.01\$/¥ e^{(0.08 - 0.04)} = 0.010408\$/¥
$$

The forward price for the currency-translated Nikkei is

$$
F_{0,1} = x_0 Q_0 e^{(r - \delta_Q)t} = 0.01\$/¥ \times ¥20,000 e^{(0.08 - 0.02)} = \$212.367
$$

Finally, using equation (22.29), the quanto forward price is

$$
V_{0,1}(\$200, 0.01\$/¥) = ¥20,000 e^{(0.04 - 0.02 - 0.2 \times 0.1 \times 0.15)}
$$
$$
= ¥20,342.91
$$

This is lower than the yen-denominated Nikkei forward price of ¥20,404 in Example 22.7.   ≹

A Binomial Model for the Dollar-Denominated Investor

As another way to understand quanto pricing, we can construct a binomial tree that simultaneously models the currency-translated index and the exchange rate. In addition to this particular application of two-variable binomial trees, some options have prices that depend on two state variables.

In Figure 22.3 we constructed separate binomial trees for the yen-based investor. For the dollar-based investor we need to construct a tree that takes account of the correlation between the Nikkei and the yen. We can do so by first modeling the behavior of the yen in the usual way, and then, *conditional upon the yen*, model the movement in the Nikkei.[8] Since for each yen move there are two Nikkei moves, the tree will have four binomial nodes. We will denote these as $\{uu, ud, du, dd\}$, with the first letter denoting the yen move and the second the Nikkei move. We have a choice of constructing a joint tree for the yen and Nikkei or the yen and dollar-translated Nikkei, but we obtain the same answer either way. Here we will model the yen and Nikkei. Problem 22.17 asks you to jointly model the yen and dollar-translated Nikkei.

The basic idea underlying the joint binomial model for x and Q is as follows. If x and Q are lognormal, they evolve like this:

$$x_h = x_0 e^{(r-r_f)h+s\sqrt{h}Z_1} \tag{22.31a}$$

$$Q_h = Q_0 e^{(r-\delta_Q)h+\sigma_Q\sqrt{h}Z_2} \tag{22.31b}$$

In the standard binomial model, we simply approximate Z_1 and Z_2 binomially, so that $Z_i = \pm 1$. However, we want to induce correlation between Z_1 and Z_2. We can create correlation by using the Cholesky decomposition discussed in Chapter 19. Begin by rewriting equation (22.31) using equation (19.16):

$$x_h = x_0 e^{(r-r_f)h+s\sqrt{h}\epsilon_1} \tag{22.32a}$$

$$Q_h = Q_0 e^{(r_f-\delta_Q)h+\sigma_Q\sqrt{h}(\epsilon_1\rho+\epsilon_2\sqrt{1-\rho^2})} \tag{22.32b}$$

Thus, $Z_1 = \epsilon_1$ and $Z_2 = \rho\epsilon_1 + \sqrt{1-\rho^2}\epsilon_2$. By construction, this Z_1 and Z_2 have correlation ρ. Now we construct the binomial tree by setting $\epsilon_1 = \pm 1$ (the exchange rate moves up or down) and $\epsilon_2 = \pm 1$ (the index moves up or down). There are four possible outcomes, which we will label A ($\epsilon_1 = 1; \epsilon_2 = 1$), B ($\epsilon_1 = 1; \epsilon_2 = -1$), C ($\epsilon_1 = -1; \epsilon_2 = 1$), and D ($\epsilon_1 = -1; \epsilon_2 = -1$).

For a dollar-based investor, the possible yen moves are

$$x_A = x_B = x_0 e^{(r-r_f)h+s\sqrt{h}} = x_0 u \tag{22.33a}$$

$$x_C = x_D = x_0 e^{(r-r_f)h-s\sqrt{h}} = x_0 d \tag{22.33b}$$

For each yen move, there are two Nikkei moves:

$$Q_A = Q_0 e^{(r_f-\delta_Q)h+\sigma_Q\sqrt{h}(\rho+\sqrt{1-\rho^2})} = Q_0 A \tag{22.34a}$$

$$Q_B = Q_0 e^{(r_f-\delta_Q)h+\sigma_Q\sqrt{h}(\rho-\sqrt{1-\rho^2})} = Q_0 B \tag{22.34b}$$

$$Q_C = Q_0 e^{(r_f-\delta_Q)h+\sigma_Q\sqrt{h}(-\rho+\sqrt{1-\rho^2})} = Q_0 C \tag{22.34c}$$

$$Q_D = Q_0 e^{(r_f-\delta_Q)h+\sigma_Q\sqrt{h}(-\rho-\sqrt{1-\rho^2})} = Q_0 D \tag{22.34d}$$

---

[8]This is similar to the two-variable binomial model in Rubinstein (1994). See also Boyle et al. (1989) for a procedure to generate n-asset binomial trees.

Finally, we have to determine the risk-neutral probabilities associated with the nodes. As in Chapter 10, the risk-neutral probability for an up move of the currency is

$$p = \frac{e^{(r-r_f)h} - d}{u - d} \tag{22.35}$$

where u and d are implied by equation (22.33a and 22.33b). The risk-neutral probability for an up move in the currency is 0.4750.

Recall that the risk-neutral probability arises from the requirement that an investment in the asset earn the risk-free rate. Specifically, for the currency, we consider an investment in the yen-denominated risk-free asset, hedged to remove currency risk when the investment is turned back into dollars. This investment earns the dollar-denominated risk-free return if the probability of an up move is given by equation (22.35).

We need a similar argument for the Nikkei. Since we cannot own the Nikkei index without bearing currency risk, we model an investment in the dollar-translated Nikkei. Let p^* denote the probability of an up move in the Nikkei, conditional on the move in the yen. We require that the dollar-translated Nikkei investment earn the dollar-denominated risk-free rate. This gives us

$$x_u Q_A p p^* + x_u Q_B p(1 - p^*) + x_d Q_C(1 - p)p^*$$
$$+ x_d Q_D(1 - p)(1 - p^*) = x_0 Q_0 e^{(r-\delta_Q)h} \tag{22.36}$$

Solving for p^* gives

$$p^* = \frac{x_0 Q_0 e^{(r-\delta_Q)h} - x_u Q_B p - x_d Q_D(1 - p)}{p x_u(Q_A - Q_B) + (1 - p)x_d(Q_C - Q_D)}$$
$$= \frac{e^{(r-\delta_Q)h} - uBp - dD(1 - p)}{pu(A - B) + (1 - p)d(C - D)} \tag{22.37}$$

This expression is a generalization of the one-variable formula for a risk-neutral probability, taking account of the two up and two down states for Q.

Figure 22.4 depicts the binomial tree constructed using equations (22.33) and (22.34), and probabilties of each node constructed using equations (22.35) and (22.37). The quanto forward price can be constructed as the expectation $E(Y_1/x_1)$.

Example 22.9 Using Figure 22.4 we can compute forward prices for the yen, the dollar-translated Nikkei, and the quanto Nikkei. The risk-neutral probability of an up move in the yen is 0.4750. The yen forward price is

$$F_{0,1}(x) = 0.4750 \times 0.011503\$/¥ + (1 - 0.4750) \times 0.009418\$/¥ = 0.010408\$/¥$$

The forward price for the currency-translated Nikkei is

$$F_{0,1}(xQ) = 0.2194 \times \$272.68 + 0.2556 \times \$214.50$$
$$+ 0.2425 \times \$210.25 + 0.2825 \times \$165.39 = \$212.367$$

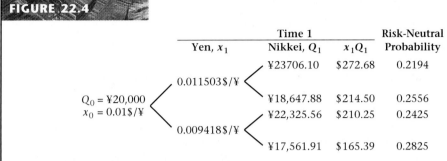

FIGURE 22.4

		Time 1		Risk-Neutral
	Yen, x_1	Nikkei, Q_1	$x_1 Q_1$	Probability
		¥23706.10	$272.68	0.2194
0.011503$/¥				
Q_0 = ¥20,000		¥18,647.88	$214.50	0.2556
x_0 = 0.01$/¥		¥22,325.56	$210.25	0.2425
0.009418$/¥				
		¥17,561.91	$165.39	0.2825

The binomial process for the dollar/yen exchange rate (x) and the Nikkei (Q). The last two columns contain the value of the currency-translated Nikkei and the risk-neutral probability of each node, computed using equations (22.35) and (22.37).

Finally, the quanto forward price is

$$F_{0,1}(Q) = 0.2194 \times \frac{\$272.68}{0.011503\$/¥} + 0.2556 \times \frac{\$214.50}{0.011503\$/¥}$$

$$+0.2425 \times \frac{\$210.25}{0.009418\$/¥} + 0.2825 \times \frac{\$165.39}{0.009418\$/¥} = ¥20,342.91$$

All of the prices computed from the tree match those in Example 22.8.

The tree in Figure 22.4 can be extended to multiple periods. Rubenstein (1994b) shows that in general, with n steps, there are $(n + 1)^2$ nodes; for example, with two steps there are nine nodes. To see why, if we add another binomial period to the tree, there are $4^2 = 16$ combinations of the up-down moves ($AA, AB, \ldots, DD$). The order of the moves is irrelevant, so, for example, $AB = BA$. This equivalence eliminates $n \times (n-1) = 6$ nodes, leaving 10. Further, from equation (22.34), $AB = CD$. Because $n = 2$, this leaves $(n + 1)^2 = 9$ unique nodes.

22.5 CURRENCY-LINKED OPTIONS

There are several common ways to construct options on foreign assets, for which the return has an exchange rate component.[9] The different variants permit investors to assume different amounts of currency and equity risk. In this section we examine four

---

[9]This section draws heavily from Reiner (1992), in particular adopting Reiner's terminology for the different kinds of options.

Nikkei Put Warrants

An example of quanto options is the Nikkei 225 put warrants that traded on the American Stock Exchange beginning in 1990. Ryan and Granovsky (2000) provide an interesting account of the history of these options, in which Nikkei risk was repackaged and transformed several times by various global financial players.

Japanese institutional investors in the late 1980s bought Nikkei bull notes. These were bonds that carried a high coupon and contained an embedded written put spread: The note principal was not paid in full if the Nikkei fell below ¥32,000. The issuer of the notes was a European bank that sold the embedded put spread to an investment bank and entered into a currency swap to achieve dollar-denominated financing without any Nikkei risk. Japanese buyers were willing to pay a price that made it profitable for the European bank to issue the notes and hedge the resulting exposure.

The investment bank, having bought the put spread, had short exposure to the Nikkei. It sold dollar-denominated Nikkei puts to a European sovereign, which in turn sold dollar-denominated Nikkei puts to investors who wanted dollar-denominated Nikkei exposure in the form of SEC-registered securities without investment bank credit risk. (The sovereign issuer bore the investment bank credit risk and the notes carried sovereign risk.)

The net result of this chain of transactions was that Japanese institutional investors were betting—via the bull notes—that the Nikkei would rise. Buyers of the dollar-denominated Nikkei put warrants were betting that the Nikkei would fall. In the end, the Nikkei index suffered a long decline and the put warrant buyers won the bet.

variants and their pricing formulas. We will continue to use the notation and numbers from Table 22.3.

Before we discuss particular currency-linked options, recall the result from Chapter 12, equation (12.5), and Chapter 14, equation (14.16), that an option can be priced using only the prepaid forward prices for the underlying asset and strike asset, and the relative volatility of the two.[10] The intuition for this result is that a market-maker could hedge an option position using the two prepaid forwards, neither of which, by definition, makes any payouts. In the discussions to follow we will use this result to simplify the valuation of seemingly complex options.

----

[10]To convince yourself of this, note that

$$BSCall(S, K, \sigma, r, T, \delta) = BSCall(Se^{-\delta T}, Ke^{-rT}, \sigma, 0, T, 0)$$

This equality will hold for any inputs you try.

Foreign Equity Call Struck in Foreign Currency

If we want to speculate on a foreign index, one possibility is to buy an option completely denominated in a foreign currency. The value of this option at expiration is

$$V(Q_T, T) = max(0, Q_T - K_f)$$

where K_f denotes the strike denominated in the foreign currency.

As an example, we might have a 1-year call option to buy the Nikkei index by paying ¥19,500. An investor based in the foreign currency would use this kind of option; thus, it can be priced using the Black-Scholes formula from the perspective of the foreign currency. Only yen inputs—the yen-denominated interest rate and the Nikkei volatility and dividend yield—enter the pricing formula. The dollar price can be obtained by converting the option price at the current exchange rate.

$$C_¥ = Q_0 e^{-\delta_Q t} N(d_1) - K_f e^{-r_f t} N(d_2) \tag{22.38}$$

$$d_1 = \frac{ln(Q_0 e^{-\delta_Q t} / K_f e^{-r_f t}) + \frac{1}{2}\sigma_Q^2 t}{\sigma_Q \sqrt{t}}$$

$$d_2 = d_1 - \sigma_Q \sqrt{t}$$

Thus, we price this option by using the Black-Scholes formula with inputs appropriate for the asset being denominated in a different currency.

Example 22.10   Using the parameters in Table 22.3 and assuming a strike price of ¥19,500, we price the call by using the Black-Scholes formula and setting $S = ¥20,000$ (the current Nikkei index price), $K = ¥19,500$, $\sigma_Q = 0.15$ (the Nikkei volatility in yen), $r_f = 0.04$, $T - t = 1$, and $\delta_Q = 0.02$ (the dividend yield on the Nikkei). We obtain a call price of $BSCall(¥20,000; ¥19,500; 0.15; 0.04; 1; 0.02) = ¥1632.16$. The dollar price is $16.32. ❦

Foreign Equity Call Struck in Domestic Currency

Suppose we have a call option to buy the Nikkei but we denominate the strike, K, in *dollars*. If we exercise the option, we pay K dollars to acquire the Nikkei, which is worth $x_T Q_T$. Thus, at expiration, the option is worth

$$V(x_T Q_T, T) = max(0, x_T Q_T - K)$$

In order to price this option, recognize that $Y(T) = x_T Q_T$, the currency-translated index, is priced like any domestic asset. The prepaid forward price for the currency-translated index is, from equation (22.26), $x_0 Q_0 e^{-\delta_Q T}$. The prepaid forward price for the strike is $K e^{-rT}$. The value of the option will depend upon the distribution of $x_T Q_T$; thus, the volatility that enters the option pricing formula is that of the currency-translated index.

The volatility of $x_t Q_t$ is

$$v = \sqrt{\sigma_Q^2 + s^2 + 2\rho\sigma_Q s}$$

Using this volatility and the prepaid forward prices we have

$$C = x_0 Q_0 e^{-\delta T} N(d_1) - e^{-rt} K N(d_2) \tag{22.39}$$

$$d_1 = \frac{ln(x_0 Q_0 e^{-\delta T} / e^{-rt} K) + \frac{1}{2} v^2 t}{v\sqrt{t}}$$

$$d_2 = d_1 - v\sqrt{t}$$

You can interpret this formula in terms of prepaid forward prices or as the Black-Scholes formula with $x_0 Q_0$ as the stock price, δ_Q as the dividend yield, v as the volatility, the domestic interest rate r as the risk-free rate, and K as the strike price.

Example 22.11   Using the parameters in Table 22.3, the volatility is

$$v = \sqrt{0.15^2 + 0.1^2 + (2 \times 0.2 \times 0.15 \times 0.1)} = 0.1962$$

and assuming a strike price of $195, we price the call using prepaid forwards as

$$BSCall(x_0 Q_0 e^{-\delta T}, Ke^{-rT}, v, 0, T, 0)$$
$$= BSCall(0.01\$/¥ \times ¥20{,}000 e^{-0.02}, \$195 \times e^{-0.08}, 0.1962, 0, 1, 0) = \$24.0719$$

≋

Fixed Exchange Rate Foreign Equity Call

Suppose we have a foreign equity call denominated in the foreign currency, but with the option proceeds to be repatriated at a predetermined exchange rate. This is a quanto option, analogous to the quanto forward, with the value of the option translated into dollars at a fixed exchange rate. Let $\bar{x}$ represent this rate. The payoff to this option with strike price K_f (denominated in the foreign currency) is

$$V(Q_T, T) = \bar{x} \times max(0, Q_T - K_f)$$
$$= max(0, \bar{x} Q_T - \bar{x} K_f)$$

Once again we can construct the pricing formula by thinking in terms of forward prices for the underlying and strike assets. From a dollar perspective, the underlying asset, $\bar{x} Q_T$, is a quanto index investment. The strike asset is simply a fixed number of dollars, translated at the rate $\bar{x}$. Since $\bar{x}$ is just a scale factor, we can set $\bar{x} = 1$.

Because the exchange rate is fixed, the volatility that affects the value of the option is that of the foreign-currency–denominated foreign index, σ_Q. We can obtain the pricing formula by using the prepaid forwards for the underlying and strike asset:

$$C = F_{0,T}^{P}(Q)N(d_1) - e^{-rT}K_f N(d_2) \qquad (22.40)$$

$$d_1 = \frac{ln[F_{0,t}^{P}(Q)/e^{-rT}K_f] + \frac{1}{2}\sigma_Q^2 T}{\sigma_Q\sqrt{T}}$$

$$d_2 = d_1 - \sigma_Q\sqrt{t}$$

The formula for $F_{0,T}^{P}(Q)$ is given in equation (22.30). Note that all values are dollar-denominated since $\bar{x}$ implicitly multiplies all prices. By substituting for $F_{0,t}^{P}$, equation (22.40) is the Black-Scholes formula with Q_0 as the stock price, $\delta_Q + \rho s\sigma_Q + r - r_f$ as the dividend yield, the domestic interest rate r as the risk-free rate, K_f as the strike, and σ_Q as the volatility.

Example 22.12 Using the parameters in Table 22.3 and assuming a strike price of ¥19,500 with a fixed exchange rate of $\bar{x} = 0.01\$/¥$, we price the call by using the Black-Scholes formula. We obtain

$$BSCall(F_{0,T}^{P}(Q), K_f e^{-rT}, \sigma_Q, 0, T, 0) =$$

$BSCall(0.01\$/¥ \times ¥20,000 \times e^{-(0.02 + 0.2 \times 0.1 \times 0.15 + 0.08 - 0.04)}, 0.01\$/¥ \times ¥19,500 e^{-0.08},$

$$0.15, 0, 1, 0) = \$15.3187$$

Problem 22.6 asks you to verify that you obtain the same answer with $x_0 Q_0$ as the underlying asset and an appropriate choice of the dividend yield. ❧

Equity-Linked Foreign Exchange Call

If we invest in a foreign asset, we might like to insure against low exchange rates when we convert back to the domestic currency, while still having the ability to profit from favorable exchange rates. Buying an exchange rate put is insufficient because the quantity of currency to be exchanged is uncertain. What we want is an option that guarantees a minimum exchange rate *when we convert the asset value back to the domestic currency*. Such an option must therefore protect a variable quantity of currency. This is an *equity-linked foreign exchange option*, which is another example of a quanto option.

Let K be the minimum exchange rate. Then the payoff to such an insured position would be

$$Q_T x_T + Q_T max(0, K - x_T) = Q_T K + Q_T max(0, x_T - K)$$
$$= Q_T K + max(0, Q_T x_T - Q_T K) \qquad (22.41)$$

The expression to the left of the equal sign in equation (22.41) is the unprotected currency-translated Nikkei investment plus Q_T exchange rate puts with strike K. The equivalent expression on the right is a quanto investment with the fixed exchange rate equal to K, plus Q_T exchange rate calls. Either way, the protection entails receiving the payoff to a random number of options. All cash flows are denominated in the home currency.

There are at least two ways to value the payoff in equation (22.41): (1) By using Proposition 21.1 and (2) by using the prepaid forward approach. Using Proposition 21.1, we value $Q_T \times max(0, x_T - K)$ as a currency call with a change of numeraire. We will pursue that approach; Problem 22.7 asks you to derive the same formula using prepaid forward prices.

The forward price for Q_T is the quanto forward price, equation (22.29). The put is a standard currency call denominated in the home currency. Since it is a currency option, the dividend yield is the foreign interest rate. To change the numeraire we subtract $\rho\sigma s$, the covariance between Q and x, from the dividend yield, r_f. Thus, we price the payoff $Q_T \times max(0, x_T - K)$ by multiplying $Q_0 e^{(r_f - \delta_Q - \rho\sigma s)T}$, the quanto forward price, times the Black-Scholes currency call formula with r_f replaced by $r_f - \rho\sigma s$. This gives

$$
\begin{aligned}
C &= Q_0 e^{(r_f - \delta_Q - \rho\sigma s)T} \left[x_0 e^{-(r_f - \rho\sigma s)T} N(d_1) - e^{-rT} K N(d_2) \right] \\
&= x_0 Q_0 e^{-\delta_Q T} N(d_1) - K Q_0 e^{-(r + \delta_Q + \rho\sigma s - r_f)T} N(d_2)
\end{aligned}
\tag{22.42}
$$

$$
d_1 = \frac{ln(x_0/K) + (r - r_f + \rho\sigma s + 0.5s^2)T}{s\sqrt{T}}
$$

$$
d_2 = d_1 - s\sqrt{T}
$$

This is the price of a call option with $x_0 Q_0$ as the stock price, $K Q_0$ as the strike price, $r + \delta_Q + \rho\sigma s - r_f$ as the risk-free rate, δ_Q as the dividend yield, and s as the volatility. It is perhaps surprising that only the volatility of the exchange rate matters. This occurs because the underlying option is a currency option and the change of numeraire does not affect the volatility.

Example 22.13   Using the parameters in Table 22.3 and assuming a strike price of 0.00975$/¥, we price the call by using the Black-Scholes formula. The price of the underlying asset is $x_0 Q_0 = 0.01$/¥ × ¥20,000 = 200, the strike price is 0.00975/¥ × ¥20,000 = 195, the risk-free rate is replaced by $r + \delta_Q + \rho\sigma s - r_f = 0.08 + 0.02 + 0.2 \times 0.15 \times 0.1 - 0.04 = 0.063$, and the dividend yield is $\delta_Q = 0.02$. The value of the option in equation (22.42) is

$$
BSCall(\$200, \$195, 0.10, 0.063, 1, 0.02) = \$15.7287
$$
❧

22.6 OTHER MULTIVARIATE OPTIONS

Quantos are a particular kind of claim with a payoff dependent on the price of two assets. There are many other options for which the payoff depends on two or more assets. In this section we examine several kinds of multivariate options that can be priced either by modifying the Black-Scholes formula or by using the bivariate normal distribution. We will also see how to price some of these options binomially. Throughout this section, we assume that the assets S and Q follow the processes given by equations (22.1) and (22.2).

Exchange Options

We saw in Section 14.6 that exchange options, in which the strike price is the price of a risky asset, can be priced with a simple modification of the Black-Scholes formula. Here we will use a change of numeraire to see why this is so.

At maturity, an exchange option with price $V(S_t, Q_t, t)$ pays

$$V(S_T, Q_T, T) = max(S_T - Q_T, 0)$$
$$= Q_T \times max(S_T/Q_T - 1, 0) \qquad (22.43)$$

This payoff is like receiving a random number, Q_T, of options in which the underlying asset is S_T/Q_T and the strike price is \$1. We can price this option by applying Propositions 20.4 and 21.1.

First, consider the price of an option with S/Q as the underlying asset. We can price this option using the Black-Scholes formula with the lease rate for S/Q in place of the dividend yield and the variance of $ln(S/Q)$ as the variance. Propositions 20.3 and 20.4 imply that the lease rate for S/Q is

$$\delta^* = r + \delta - \delta_Q - \sigma_Q^2 + \rho\sigma\sigma_Q \qquad (22.44)$$

and the variance is

$$\hat{\sigma}^2 = \sigma^2 + \sigma_Q^2 - 2\rho\sigma\sigma_Q \qquad (22.45)$$

Denote the value of this option by $W(S/Q, t)$. Its price is

$$W(S/Q, t) = S/Qe^{-\delta^*(T-t)}N(\hat{d}_1) - e^{-rt}N(\hat{d}_2) \qquad (22.46)$$

$$\hat{d}_1 = \frac{ln(S/Q) + (r - \delta^* + 0.5\hat{\sigma}^2)(T - t)}{\hat{\sigma}\sqrt{T - t}} \qquad (22.47)$$

$$\hat{d}_2 = \hat{d}_1 - \hat{\sigma}\sqrt{T - t} \qquad (22.48)$$

Now we want to value the option with payoff $Q \times W(S/Q, t)$. To do this we apply Proposition 21.1. The covariance between Q and S/Q is $\rho\sigma\sigma_Q - \sigma_Q^2$. Thus, applying Proposition 21.1, we replace δ^* with

$$\delta^* - (\rho\sigma\sigma_Q - \sigma_Q^2) = r + \delta - \delta_Q$$

Finally, multiplying W by $Qe^{(r-\delta_a)(T-t)}$ gives

$$V(S, Q, t) = Se^{-\delta(T-t)}N(\hat{d}_1) - Qe^{-\delta_Q(T-t)}N(\hat{d}_2) \qquad (22.49)$$

$$\hat{d}_1 = \frac{ln(S/Q) + (\delta_Q - \delta + 0.5\hat{\sigma}^2)(T - t)}{\hat{\sigma}\sqrt{T - t}}$$

$$\hat{d}_2 = \hat{d}_1 - \hat{\sigma}\sqrt{T - t}$$

This is the formula for an exchange option from Section 14.6. The risk-free rate is replaced by δ_Q and the volatility by $\hat{\sigma}$.

American exchange options can be valued using a two-state variable binomial tree, as in Section 22.4. However, it is also possible to value an American exchange option using a *one-variable* binomial tree. Rubinstein (1991b) shows that a standard binomial tree can be constructed setting the volatility equal to $\hat{\sigma}$, the dividend yield equal to δ, and the risk-free rate equal to δ_Q. This result can also be demonstrated by using arguments based on Propositions 20.4 and 21.1.

Options on the Best of Two Assets

Suppose an investor allocates a portfolio to both the S&P index and the currency-translated Nikkei. Allocating the portfolio to the index that the investor believes will obtain the highest return is called **market-timing.** A perfect market-timer would invest in the S&P when it outperformed the Nikkei and the Nikkei when it outperformed the S&P. What is the value of being able to infallibly select the portfolio with the superior performance?

We can answer this question by valuing an option giving us the greater of the two returns. This option would have the payoff $max(S_T, Q_T)$, where S is the S&P index and the Q the Nikkei index. Note that

$$max(S_T, Q_T) = Q_T + max(S_T - Q_T, 0)$$

Thus, an option on the best of two assets is the same as owning one asset plus an option to exchange that asset for the other asset. As discussed in Chapter 9, $max(S_T - Q_T, 0)$ can be viewed either as a call on S with strike asset Q, or as a put on Q, with strike asset S.

An investor allocating funds between the S&P index and the Nikkei index might also want to include cash in the comparison, so that there is a guaranteed minimum return. If K represents this minimum return, the payoff for a perfect market-timer is then

$$max(K, S_T, Q_T)$$

This option, called a **rainbow option,** has no simple one-variable solution. Instead, valuing this option requires the use of the bivariate normal distribution.[11] The bivariate normal distribution is defined as

$$Prob(z_1 < a, z_2 < b; \rho) = NN(a, b; \rho) \qquad (22.50)$$

where z_1 and z_2 are standard normal random variables with correlation coefficient ρ. You may recall that we used the bivariate normal distribution in Chapter 14 to value compound options.

The formula for a rainbow option is

$$
\begin{aligned}
RainbowCall&(S, Q, K, \sigma, s, \rho, \delta, \delta_Q, T - t) \\
&= Se^{-\delta(T-t)} \left\{ N(d_{SQ}) - NN[-d_1(S), d_{SQ}, (\rho\sigma_Q - \sigma)/\hat{\sigma}] \right\} \\
&+ Qe^{-\delta_Q(T-t)} \left\{ N(d_{QS}) - NN[-d_1(Q), d_{QS}, (\rho\sigma - \sigma_Q)/\hat{\sigma}] \right\} \\
&+ Ke^{-r(T-t)} NN[-d_2(S), -d_2(Q), \rho]
\end{aligned}
\qquad (22.51)
$$

---

[11] Stulz (1982) first valued a rainbow option. See also Rubinstein (1991c) for a discussion.

where

$$d_1(S) = \frac{ln(S/K) + (r - \delta + 0.5\sigma^2)(T - t)}{\sigma\sqrt{T - t}}$$

$$d_1(Q) = \frac{ln(Q/K) + (r - \delta_Q + 0.5\sigma_Q^2)(T - t)}{\sigma_Q\sqrt{T - t}}$$

$$d_2(S) = d_1(S) - \sigma\sqrt{T - t}$$

$$d_2(Q) = d_1(Q) - \sigma_Q\sqrt{T - t}$$

$$d_{SQ} = \frac{ln(S/Q) + (\delta_Q - \delta + 0.5\hat{\sigma}^2)(T - t)}{\hat{\sigma}\sqrt{T - t}}$$

$$d_{QS} = \frac{ln(Q/S) + (\delta - \delta_Q + 0.5\hat{\sigma}^2)(T - t)}{\hat{\sigma}\sqrt{T - t}}$$

$$\hat{\sigma} = \sqrt{\sigma^2 + \sigma_Q^2 - 2\rho\sigma\sigma_Q}$$

You can understand this daunting formula by recognizing that, at maturity, the option must be worth either S, Q, or K. By setting $t = T$, you can verify that the formula satisfies this boundary condition. The formula for an option that pays $min(S, Q, K)$—a rainbow put—is obtained by putting a minus sign in front of each "d" argument in the normal and bivariate normal functions.

Certain related options can be valued using the rainbow option formula.[12] For example, consider an option on the maximum of two assets with the payoff

$$max[0, max(S, Q) - K]$$

This is equal to $max(S, Q, K) - K$, which has the value

$$RainbowCall(S, Q, K, \sigma, \sigma_Q, \rho, \delta, \delta_Q, r, T - t) - Ke^{-r(T-t)}$$

Some options that seem as if they might be valued using the rainbow option formula, however, cannot be. For example, in Chapter 17 we discussed the valuation of peak-load electricity plants and encountered spread options, which have the payoff

$$max(0, S - Q - K)$$

While there are approximations for valuing such an option (see Haug, 1998, pp. 59–61), more exact solutions require Monte Carlo or two-state binomial trees.

Basket Options

Basket options have payoffs that depend upon the average of two or more asset prices. Basket options are frequently used in currency hedging. A multinational firm dealing in multiple currencies, for example, might care only about hedging the average exchange

---

[12]Rubinstein (1991c) provides a thorough discussion of these related options, as well as discussing which options *cannot* be valued as rainbow options.

rate, rather than each exchange rate individually. As another example, an option on the S&P index might pay off only if the S&P outperforms an average of the currency-translated Nikkei and Dax (German stock) indices. With equal weights on the Nikkei and Dax, the payoff to such an option would be

$$max[0, S_{S\&P} - 0.5 \times (S_{Nikkei} + S_{Dax})]$$

You may be able to guess the problem with deriving a simple formula to value such a payoff. The arithmetic average of two indices does not follow geometric Brownian motion. (In fact, if an index is an arithmetic average of stocks, the index itself does not follow geometric Brownian motion. We have been making the common, yet inconsistent, assumption that both stocks and indices containing those stocks follow geometric Brownian motion.)

Because the payoff can depend on many random variables and there is no easy formula, Monte Carlo is a natural technique for valuing basket options. Moreover, basket options provide a natural application for the control variate method to speed up Monte Carlo. A basket option based on the geometric average can be valued using Black-Scholes with appropriate adjustments to the volatility and dividend yield. This price can then serve as a control variate for the more conventional basket option based on an arithmetic average.

CHAPTER SUMMARY

It is possible to build new derivative claims by using simpler claims as building blocks. Important building blocks include all-or-nothing options, which pay either cash or an asset under certain conditions. Assuming that prices are lognormal with constant volatility, it is straightforward to value cash-or-nothing and asset-or-nothing options both with and without barriers. Cash-or-nothing claims can be priced as discounted risk-neutral probabilities, and a change of numeraire can then be used to price asset-or-nothing options. These claims can be used to create, among other things, ordinary options, gap options, and barrier options. While these options are straightforward to price, they may be quite difficult to hedge because of discontinuities in the payoff created by the all-or-nothing characteristic.

Quantos are claims for which the payoff depends on the product or quotient of two prices. They can be priced using arguments developed in Chapters 20 and 21. Quantos can be used to remove the currency risk from an investment in a foreign stock index and thus are used in international investing. It is possible to construct bivariate binomial trees to price quantos. International investors can also use currency-linked options to tailor their exposure to currency. The standard currency options can be priced using prepaid forwards and change of numeraire.

Other options, such as rainbow and basket options, have payoffs depending on two or more asset prices. Some of these options have simple pricing formulas; others must be valued binomially, using Monte Carlo, or in some other way.

FURTHER READING

Mark Rubinstein and Eric Reiner published a series of papers on exotic options in *Risk* magazine in the early 1990s. These provide a comprehensive discussion of pricing formulas on a wide variety of options. Some of the material in this chapter is based directly on those papers, which can be hard to obtain but are available on Mark Rubinstein's website (**http://www.in-the-money.com**). Ingersoll (2000) also provides examples of the use of all-or-nothing options as building blocks. An alternative approach to two-state binomial pricing is detailed in Boyle et al. (1989).

If you are interested in more pricing formulas, Haug (1998) presents numerous formulas and discusses approximations when those simple formulas are not available. Wilmott (1998) also has a comprehensive discussion emphasizing the use of partial differential equations (which, as we have seen, underlie all derivatives pricing). Zhang (1998) and Briys and Bellala (1998) discuss exotic options, including many not discussed in this chapter. In practice, the hitting of a barrier is often determined on a daily or other periodic basis. Broadie et al. (1997) provide a simple correction term that makes the barrier pricing formulas more accurate when monitoring of the barrier is not continuous. One class of options we have not discussed is lookback options, which pay out based on the highest (or lowest) price over the life of the option. These are discussed in Goldman, Sosin, and Gatto (1979) and Goldman, Sosin, and Shepp (1979) and are covered in Problems 22.13 and 22.14.

PROBLEMS

22.1. A **collect-on-delivery call** (COD) costs zero initially, with the payoff at expiration being 0 if $S < K$, and $S - K - P$ if $S \geq K$. The problem in valuing the option is to determine P, the amount the option-holder pays if the option is in-the-money at expiration. The premium P is determined once and for all when the option is created. Let $S = \$100$, $K = \$100$, $r = 5\%$, $\sigma = 20\%$, $T - t = 1$ year, and $\delta = 0$.

    a. Value a European COD call option with the above inputs. (Hint: Recognize that you can construct the COD payoff by combining an ordinary call option and a cash-or-nothing call.)

    b. Compute delta and gamma for a COD option (you may do this by computing the value of the option at slightly different prices and calculating delta and gamma directly, rather than by using a formula). Consider different stock prices and times to expiration, in particular setting t close to T.

    c. How hard is it to hedge a COD option?

22.2. A **barrier COD** option is like a COD except that payment for the option occurs whenever a barrier is struck. Price a barrier COD put for the same values as in Problem 1, with a barrier of $95 and a strike of $90. Compute the delta and gamma for the paylater put. Compare the behavior of delta and gamma with that for a COD. Explain the differences, if any.

22.3. Verify that equation (22.7) satisfies the appropriate boundary conditions for $Prob(\underline{S}_T \leq H$ and $S_T > K)$.

22.4. Verify that equation (22.14) (for both cases $K > H$ and $K < H$) solves the boundary conditions for an up-and-in cash put.

22.5. Verify that as $T \to \infty$ in equations (22.20) and (22.21) you obtain equations (12.14) and (12.15), discussed in Chapter 12.

22.6. Verify in Example 22.12 that you obtain the same answer if you use $x_0 Q_0$ as the stock price, $\delta_Q + \rho s \sigma_Q + r - r_f$ as the dividend yield, r as the interest rate, and σ_Q as the volatility.

22.7. Consider the equity-linked foreign exchange call in equation (22.42). In this problem we want to derive the formula for an option with the payoff $max(0, Q_T x_T - Q_T K)$.

   a. What is the prepaid forward price for $Q_T x_T$?

   b. What is the prepaid forward price for $Q_T K$, where K is a dollar amount?

   c. What is the formula for the price of the option with the payoff $max(0, Q_T x_T - Q_T K)$? Verify that your answer is the same as equation (22.43).

22.8. The quanto forward price can be computed using the risk-neutral distribution as $E(Yx^{-1})$. Use Proposition 20.4 to derive the quanto forward price given by equation (22.29).

22.9. In this problem we use the lognormal approximation (see equation (11.19)) to draw one-step binomial trees from the perspective of a yen-based investor. Use the information in Table 22.3.

   a. Construct a one-step tree for the Nikkei index.

   b. Construct a one-step tree for the exchange rate (yen/dollars).

   c. Use the trees to price Nikkei and dollar forwards. Compare your answers to those in Example 22.7.

22.10. Suppose an option knocks in at $H_1 > S$, and knocks out at $H_2 > H_1$. Suppose that $K < H_2$ and the option expires at T. Call this a "knock-in, knock-out" option. Here is a table summarizing the payoff to this option (note that because $H_2 > H_1$ it is not possible to hit H_2 without hitting H_1):

H_1 **Not Hit**	H_1 **Hit**	
	H_2 **Not Hit**	H_2 **Hit**
0	$max(0, S_T - K)$	0

What is the value of this option?

22.11. Suppose the stock price is $50, but that we plan to buy 100 shares if and when the stock reaches $45. Suppose further that $\sigma = 0.3$, $r = 0.08$, $T - t = 1$, and $\delta = 0$. This is a noncancellable limit order.

    a. What transaction could you undertake to offset the risk of this obligation?

    b. You can view this limit order as a liability. What is its value?

22.12. Covered call writers often plan to buy back the written call if the stock price drops sufficiently. The logic is that the written call at that point has little "upside," and, if the stock recovers, the position could sustain a loss from the written call.

    a. Explain in general how this buy-back strategy could be implemented using barrier options.

    b. Suppose $S = \$50$, $\sigma = 0.3$, $r = 0.08$, $t = 1$, and $\delta = 0$. The premium of a written call with a $50 strike is 7.856. We intend to buy the option back if the stock hits $45. What is the net premium of this strategy?

A European **lookback call** at maturity pays $S_T - \underline{S}_T$. A European **lookback put** at maturity pays $\overline{S}_T - S_T$. (Recall that $\overline{S}_T$ and $\underline{S}_T$ are the maximum and minimum prices over the life of the option.) Here is a formula that can be used to value both options:

$$W(S_t, \tilde{S}_t, \sigma, r, T - t, \delta, \omega) = \omega S_t e^{-\delta(T-t)} \left[N(\omega d_5') - \frac{\sigma^2}{2(r - \delta)} N(-\omega d_5') \right]$$
$$- \omega \tilde{S}_t e^{-r(T-t)} \left[N(\omega d_6') - \frac{\sigma^2}{2(r - \delta)} \left(\frac{S_t}{\tilde{S}_t} \right)^{1 - 2\frac{r - \delta}{\sigma^2}} N(\omega d_8') \right] \quad (22.52)$$

where

$$d_5' = [ln(S_t/\tilde{S}_t) + (r - \delta + 0.5\sigma^2)(T - t)]/\sigma\sqrt{T - t}$$
$$d_6' = d_5' - \sigma\sqrt{T - t}$$
$$d_7' = [ln(\tilde{S}_t/S_t) + (r - \delta + 0.5\sigma^2)(T - t)]/\sigma\sqrt{T - t}$$
$$d_8' = d_7' - \sigma\sqrt{T - t}$$

The value of a lookback call is obtained by setting $\tilde{S}_t = \underline{S}_t$ and $\omega = 1$. The value of a lookback put is obtained by setting $\tilde{S}_t = \overline{S}_t$ and $\omega = -1$.

22.13. For the lookback call:

    a. What is the value of a lookback call as S_t approaches 0? Verify that the formula gives you the same answer.

    b. Verify that at maturity the value of the call is $S_T - \underline{S}_T$.

22.14. For the lookback put:

    a. What is the value of a lookback put if $S_t = 0$? Verify that the formula gives you the same answer.

b. Verify that at maturity the value of the put is $\overline{S}_T - S_T$.

22.15. A European **shout option** is an option for which the payoff at expiration is $max(0, S - K, G - K)$, where G is the price at which you shouted. (Suppose you have an XYZ shout call with a strike price of $100. Today XYZ is $130. If you shout at $130, you are guaranteed a payoff of $max(\$30, S_T - \$130)$ at expiration.) You can only shout once, irrevocably.

   a. Demonstrate that shouting at some arbitrary price $G > K$ is better than never shouting.

   b. Compare qualitatively the value of a shout option to (i) a lookback option (which pays $max[0, \overline{S}_T - K]$, where $\overline{S}_T$ is the greatest stock price over the life of the option) and (ii) a **ladder option** (which pays $max(0, S - K, L - K)$ if the underlying hits the value L at some point over the life of the option).

   c. Explain how to value this option binomially. (Hint: Think about how you would compute the value of the option at the moment you shout.)

22.16. Consider the Level 3 outperformance option with a multiplier, discussed in Section 16.2. This can be valued binomially using the single state variable $S_{Level3}/S_{S\&P}$, and multiplying the resulting value by $S_{S\&P}$.

   a. Compute the value of this option if it were European, assuming the Level 3 stock price is $100, the S&P index is 1300, and the volatilities and dividend yields are 25% and 0 for the Level 3 and 16% and 1.8% for the S&P. The Level 3–S&P correlation is 0.4 and the option has 4 years to expiration.

   b. Repeat the valuation assuming the option is American.

   c. In the absence of a multiplier, would you expect the option ever to be early-exercised? Under what circumstances does early exercise occur with the multiplier?

22.17. Consider AAAPI, the Nikkei ADR in disguise. To answer this question, use the information in Table 22.3.

   a. What is the volatility of Y, the price of AAAPI?

   b. What is the covariance between Y and x, the dollar-yen exchange rate?

   c. What is the correlation between Y and x, the dollar-yen exchange rate?

   d. Using this information on the volatility of Y and the correlation between Y and x, construct a joint binomial tree for x and Y. Use this tree to price a Nikkei quanto forward.

Chapter 23

Interest Rate Models

O ur goal in this chapter is to understand how to price derivatives that have bonds and interest rates, rather than stocks, as the underlying asset. We begin by pricing bond and interest rate options using the Black model (the name for the version of the Black-Scholes model for which the underlying asset is a futures contract). The Black model assumes that forward interest rates are lognormally distributed and can be be used to price interest rate caps as well as bonds. Next we see how the Black-Scholes approach to option pricing, discussed in Chapter 21, applies to bonds. As with stocks, there is a partial differential equation that characterizes the behavior of bond prices and other functions of interest rates. The Vasicek and Cox-Ingersoll-Ross models illustrate the procedure for deriving bond prices from an assumed model of the short-term interest rate. Finally we examine binomial interest rate models, in particular the Black-Derman-Toy model.

23.1 BOND OPTIONS, CAPS, AND THE BLACK MODEL

We encountered the Black formula for pricing options on futures in Chapter 12. In this section we see how to use the Black model to price interest rate and bond options. The idea behind using the Black model in this context is that the forward price for a bond is the underlying asset, and we assume that this forward price is lognormally distributed.

We will begin by seeing how the Black model can be used to price an option on a zero-coupon bond. As in Chapter 7, let $P_t(T, T + s)$ denote the time-t price of a zero-coupon bond purchased at T and paying \$1 at time $T + s$. If $t = T$, then $P_T(T, T+s)$ is the spot price of the bond and we will write $P(T, T + s)$ without a subscript. If $t < T$, then $P_t(T, T + s)$ is a forward price, which we will also represent as $F_{t,T}[P(T, T+s)]$.

Consider a call option with strike price K, expiring at time T, on a zero-coupon bond paying \$1 at time $T + s$. The payoff of this option at time T is

$$\text{Call option payoff} = max[0, P(T, T + s) - K] \qquad (23.1)$$

We can price this option as an exchange option (see Sections 14.6 and 22.6). Recall that the time-t forward price of the bond deliverable at T is

$$F_{t,T}[P(T, T + s)] = P(t, T + s)/P(t, T) \qquad (23.2)$$

The prepaid forward price of this bond at time t is $F_{t,T}[P(T, T + s)] \times P(t, T) = P(t, T + s)$, which is just the time-t price of the $T + s$ maturity bond. The time-t prepaid forward for the strike price is $KP(t, T)$.

The appropriate volatility for pricing this exchange option is the volatility of the ratio of the prepaid forward prices for the underlying asset and strike asset:

$$Var(ln[P(t, T + s)/KP(t, T)]) = Var(ln[P(t, T + s)/P(t, T)]$$
$$= Var(ln(F_{t,T}[P(T, T + s)]))$$

That is, the volatility that enters the pricing formula is the volatility of the forward price for the bond, where the forward contract calls for time-T delivery of the bond maturing at $T + s$.

If we assume that the bond forward price is lognormally distributed with constant volatility σ, we obtain the Black formula for a bond option:[1]

$$\boxed{C[F, P(0, T), \sigma, T] = P(0, T)[FN(d_1) - KN(d_2)]} \qquad (23.3)$$

where

$$d_1 = \frac{ln(F/K) + 0.5\sigma^2 T}{\sigma\sqrt{T}}$$

$$d_2 = d_1 - \sigma\sqrt{T}$$

and where F is an abbreviation for the bond forward price $F_{0,T}[P(T, T + s)]$. Since $P(0, T)F = P(0, T + s)$, this formula simply uses the price of the $T + s$ bond as the underlying asset. The formula for a put can be obtained by put-call parity.

This use of the Black formula to price bond options is intuitively reasonable. The price of any particular bond varies over time. However, the value of a bond option depends upon the volatility of the *ratio* in the prices of bonds with different maturities. If today is time t and the option expires at time T, the interest rate from time t to time T affects the discounting of *both* the underlying asset (the bond maturing at time $T + s$) and the strike price (from time t to time T). Since the option price depends on $ln[P(t, T + s)/P(t, T)]$, only the volatility of the bond forward price affects the price of the option.

The Black formula can be extended to price options on interest rates. Imagine that a floating rate borrower wishes to hedge the interest rate at time T for a loan with time to maturity s (therefore maturing at time $T + s$). We saw in Chapter 7 that the forward interest rate from time T to time $T + s$, $R_0(T, T + s)$, is

$$R_0(T, T + s) = \frac{P(0, T)}{P(0, T + s)} - 1 \qquad (23.4)$$

Notice that in equation (23.4), R is not annualized. If you invest \$1 at time T at the forward rate, after s periods you will have $1 + R_0(T, T + s)$.

---

[1]Note that we can write the option in terms of the bond prices as $P(0, T + s)N(d_1) - KP(0, T)N(d_2)$, where $d_1 = (ln[P(0, T + s)/KP(0, T)] + 0.5\sigma^2 T)/\sigma\sqrt{T}$. Writing the formula as in equation (23.3) emphasizes that the relevant volatility is that of the forward bond price.

One way for the borrower to hedge interest rate risk is by entering into a forward rate agreement (FRA), receiving at time $T + s$ the difference between the spot s-period rate, $R_T(T, T + s)$, and the forward rate, $R_0(T, T + s)$:

$$\text{Payoff to FRA} = R_T(T, T + s) - R_0(T, T + s)$$

As an alternative to hedging with an FRA, the borrower could enter into a call option on an FRA, with strike price K_R. This option, which is also called a **caplet**, at time $T + s$ pays

$$\text{Payoff to caplet} = max[0, R_T(T, T + s) - K_R] \qquad (23.5)$$

The caplet permits the borrower to pay the time-T market interest rate if it is below K_R, but receive a payment for the difference in rates if the rate is above K_R. If settled at time T, the option would pay

$$\frac{1}{1 + R_T(T, T + s)} \, max[0, R_T(T, T + s) - K_R] \qquad (23.6)$$

Let R_T be shorthand for $R_T(T, T + s)$. We can rewrite equation (23.6) as

$$(1 + K_R)max\left[0, \frac{R_T - K_R}{(1 + R_T)(1 + K_R)}\right]$$

$$= (1 + K_R)max\left[0, \frac{1}{1 + K_R} - \frac{1}{1 + R_T}\right] \qquad (23.7)$$

Note that $1/(1 + R_T)$ is the time-T price of a bond paying \$1 at time $T + s$. The expression on the right-hand side of equation (23.7) is therefore the expiration payoff to $1 + K_R$ bond put options with strike price $1/(1 + K_R)$. The bond option model, equation (23.3), can therefore be used to price caplets.

An interest rate **cap** is a collection of caplets. Suppose a borrower has a floating rate loan with interest payments at times $t_i, i = 1, \ldots, n$. A cap would make the series of payments

$$\text{Cap payment at time } t_{i+1} = max[0, R_{t_i}(t_i, t_{i+1}) - K_R] \qquad (23.8)$$

The value of the cap is the summed value of the individual caplets.

Example 23.1 One-year and 2-year zero-coupon bonds with a \$1 maturity value have prices of \$0.9091 and \$0.8116. The 1-year implied forward 1-year bond price is therefore \$0.8116/\$0.9091 = \$0.8928, with an implied forward rate of 12.01%. Suppose the volatility of the forward bond price is 10%. The price of a 1-year put option to sell the 1-year bond for a price of \$0.88 is

$$BSPut(\$0.8116, \$0.9091 \times \$0.88, 0.1, 0, 1, 0) = \$0.0267 \qquad \text{≷}$$

23.2 MARKET-MAKING AND BOND PRICING

In this section we examine market-making in bonds in order to better understand how the Black-Scholes option pricing framework applies to bonds. We begin by examining the hedging of one bond with another.

The Black-Scholes derivation of the option pricing model characterizes the fair option price for a delta-hedging market-maker. Vasicek (1977) used the same approach for pricing bonds. Consider a delta-hedging bond portfolio manager, like the market-maker who delta-hedged options in Chapters 13 and 21. Specifically, suppose the manager owns one bond with maturity T_2 and hedges this bond by buying N bonds with maturity T_1 (N can be negative). The position is financed using short-term bonds paying r. Hedging one bond with another is often called duration-hedging rather than delta-hedging. The intent of duration- and delta-hedging is the same, but as we will see, the two are generally *not* the same if we use the standard definition of duration from Section 7.8.

The logic of the Vasicek approach to pricing bonds is identical to the Black-Scholes approach to analyzing options: We think about the problem faced by a market-maker and see what it tells us about bond price behavior. We will focus on pricing zero-coupon bonds since, as discussed in Chapter 7, they are a building block for all fixed-income products.

The Behavior of Bonds and Interest Rates

Before discussing how a bond market-maker would delta-hedge, we first need to specify how bonds behave. Suppose we try to model a zero-coupon bond the same way we model a stock, by assuming that the bond price, $P(t, T)$ follows an Itô process:

$$\frac{dP}{P} = \alpha(r, t)dt + q(r, t)dZ \tag{23.9}$$

In this equation, the coefficients α and q cannot be constants and in fact must be modeled rather carefully to ensure that the bond satisfies its boundary conditions. For example, the bond must be worth \$1 at maturity. Also, the volatility of the bond price should decrease as the bond approaches maturity—a given change in interest rates affects the price of a long-lived bond more than the price of a short-lived bond. Neither of these restrictions is automatically reflected in equation (23.9). In order to accommodate such behavior α and q must be functions of the interest rate and time.

An alternative to beginning with equation (23.9) is to model the behavior of the interest rate and *solve* for the bond price. If we follow this approach, the bond price will *automatically* behave in an appropriate way, as long as the interest rate process is reasonable.

Suppose we assume that the short-term interest rate follows the Itô process

$$dr = a(r)dt + \sigma(r)dZ \tag{23.10}$$

This equation for the behavior of the interest rate is general, in that the drift and standard deviation are functions of r. Given equation (23.10), what is the bond price? We will see that different bond price models arise from different versions of this interest rate process.

An Impossible Bond Pricing Model

We will first look at a bond pricing model that is intuitive, appealing in its simplicity, and widely used informally as a way to think about bonds. We will assume that the yield curve is flat; that is, at any point in time, zero-coupon bonds at all maturities have the same yield to maturity. If the interest rate changes, yields for all bonds change uniformly so that the yield curve remains flat. Unfortunately, this model of the yield curve gives rise to arbitrage opportunities. It can be instructive, however, to see what doesn't work in order to better appreciate what does.

To analyze the flat-yield curve assumption, we assume that the interest rate follows equation (23.10). The price of zero-coupon bonds is given by

$$P(t, T) = e^{-r(T-t)} \tag{23.11}$$

In this specification, every bond has yield to maturity r.

We now analyze the delta-hedging problem. If we buy one bond maturing at time T_2, hedge by buying N bonds maturing at time T_1, and finance the difference at the short-term interest rate, the bond portfolio has value

$$I = NP(t, T_1) + P(t, T_2) + W = 0 \tag{23.12}$$

Since W is invested in short-term bonds, we have

$$dW = rWdt \tag{23.13}$$

By Itô's Lemma, and using the formula for the bond price, equation (23.11), the change in the value of the portfolio is

$$dI = NdP(t, T_1) + dP(t, T_2) + dW$$
$$= N\left(-(T_1 - t)P(t, T_1)dr + \frac{1}{2}(T_1 - t)^2\sigma^2 P(t, T_1)dt + rP(t, T_1)dt\right) \tag{23.14}$$
$$+ \left(-(T_2 - t)P(t, T_2)dr + \frac{1}{2}(T_2 - t)^2\sigma^2 P(t, T_2)dt + rP(t, T_2)dt\right) + rWdt$$

We pick N to eliminate the effect of interest rate changes, dr, on the value of the portfolio. Thus, we set

$$N = -\frac{(T_2 - t)P(t, T_2)}{(T_1 - t)P(t, T_1)} \tag{23.15}$$

The delta-hedged portfolio has no risk and no investment; it should therefore earn zero:

$$dI = 0 \tag{23.16}$$

Combining equations (23.12), (23.14), (23.15), and (23.16), and then simplifying, gives us

$$\tfrac{1}{2}(T_2 - T_1)\sigma^2 = 0 \tag{23.17}$$

This equation cannot hold unless $T_1 = T_2$. Thus, we conclude that *the bond valuation model implied by equations (23.10) and (23.11) is impossible*, in the sense that arbitrage is possible if the yield curve is stochastic and always flat.

This example demonstrates the difficulties of bond pricing: A casually specified model may give rise to arbitrage opportunities. A crucial feature of bond prices is the nonlinearity of prices as a function of interest rates, a characteristic ignored in equation (23.11). The same issue arises in pricing stock options: The nonlinearity of the option price with respect to the stock price is critical in pricing options. This is another example of Jensen's inequality.

The example also illustrates that, in general, *hedging a bond portfolio based on duration does not result in a perfect hedge*. Recall that the duration of a zero-coupon bond is the bond's time to maturity. The hedge ratio, equation (23.15), is *exactly* the same as equation (7.13) in Chapter 7. The use of duration to compute hedge ratios assumes that the yield to maturity of all bonds shifts by the same amount, which is what we assumed in equation (23.11). However, this assumption gives rise to arbitrage opportunities. The use of duration to compute hedge ratios can be a useful approximation; however, bonds in equilibrium *must* be priced in such a way that duration-based hedging does not work exactly.

An Equilibrium Equation for Bonds

Let's consider again the bond-hedging problem, only this time we will not assume a particular bond pricing model. Instead we view the bond as a general function of the short-term interest rate, r, which follows equation (23.10).[2]

First, let's see how the bond behaves. From Itô's Lemma, the bond, which is a function of the interest rate and time, follows the process

$$
\begin{aligned}
dP(r, t, T) &= \frac{\partial P}{\partial r} dr + \frac{1}{2} \frac{\partial^2 P}{\partial r^2} (dr)^2 + \frac{\partial P}{\partial t} dt \\
&= \left[a(r) \frac{\partial P}{\partial r} + \frac{1}{2} \frac{\partial^2 P}{\partial r^2} \sigma(r)^2 + \frac{\partial P}{\partial t} \right] dt + \frac{\partial P}{\partial r} \sigma(r) dZ
\end{aligned}
\tag{23.18}
$$

This equation does not look like equation (23.9), but we can define terms so that it does. Let

$$
\alpha(r, t, T) = \frac{1}{P(r, t, T)} \left[a(r) \frac{\partial P}{\partial r} + \frac{1}{2} \frac{\partial^2 P}{\partial r^2} \sigma(r)^2 + \frac{\partial P}{\partial t} \right]
\tag{23.19}
$$

$$
q(r, t, T) = \frac{1}{P(r, t, T)} \frac{\partial P}{\partial r} \sigma(r)
\tag{23.20}
$$

---

[2] The discussion in this section follows Vasicek (1977).

We can now rewrite equation (23.18) as

$$\frac{dP(r, t, T)}{P(r, t, T)} = \alpha(r, t, T)dt + q(r, t, T)dZ \tag{23.21}$$

By using equations (23.19) and (23.20) to define α and q, equations (23.9) and (23.21) are the same. Note that α and q depend on both the interest rate and on the time to maturity of the bond.

Now we consider again the delta-hedged bond portfolio, the value of which is given by equation (23.12). From Itô's Lemma, we have

$$dI = N\left[\alpha(r, t, T_1)dt + q(r, t, T_1)dZ\right] P(r, t, T_1)$$
$$+ \left[\alpha(r, t, T_2)dt + q(r, t, T_2)dZ\right] P(r, t, T_2) + rWdt \tag{23.22}$$

In order to eliminate interest rate risk, we set

$$N = -\frac{P(r, t, T_2)}{P(r, t, T_1)} \frac{q(r, t, T_2)}{q(r, t, T_1)} \tag{23.23}$$

Note that by using the definition of q, equation (23.20), this can be rewritten

$$N = -\frac{P_r(r, t, T_2)}{P_r(r, t, T_1)}$$

If you compare this expression to equation (7.13), you will see that $P_r(r, t, T)$ replaces duration when computing the hedge ratio, N.

Substituting equation (23.25) into equation (23.22), and setting $dI = 0$ (equation (23.16)), we obtain

$$\frac{\alpha(r, t, T_1) - r}{q(r, t, T_1)} = \frac{\alpha(r, t, T_2) - r}{q(r, t, T_2)} \tag{23.24}$$

This equation says that *the Sharpe ratio for the two bonds is equal.* Since both bond prices are driven by the same random term, dZ, they must have the same Sharpe ratio if they are fairly priced. Similarly, we saw in Chapter 21 that a stock and an option on the stock have the same Sharpe ratios.

Denote the Sharpe ratio for dZ as $\phi(r, t)$. For any bond we then have

$$\frac{\alpha(r, t, T) - r}{q(r, t, T)} = \phi(r, t) \tag{23.25}$$

Substituting equations (23.19) and (23.20) for α and q then gives us

$$\boxed{\frac{1}{2}\sigma(r)^2\frac{\partial^2 P}{\partial r^2} + [a(r) - \sigma(r)\phi(r, t)]\frac{\partial P}{\partial r} + \frac{\partial P}{\partial t} - rP = 0} \tag{23.26}$$

When the short-term interest rate is the only source of uncertainty, *this partial differential equation must be satisfied by any zero-coupon bond.* Different bonds will have different maturity dates and therefore different boundary conditions. All bonds solve the same PDE, however. The Black-Scholes equation, equation (21.11), characterizes claims that are a function of the stock price. Equation (23.26) is the analogous equation for derivative claims that are a function of the interest rate.

A difference between equation (23.26) and equation (21.11) is the explicit appearance of the risk premium, $\sigma(r, t)\phi(r, t)$, in the bond equation. Let's talk about why that happens.

In the context of stock options, the Black-Scholes problem entails hedging an option with a stock, which is an investment asset. The stock is expected to earn its risk premium, which we will call $\phi'\sigma$. Thus, for the stock, the drift term, which is analogous to $a(r)$, equals $r + \phi'\sigma$. The Black-Scholes delta-hedging procedure eliminates the risk premium on the stock. By subtracting the risk premium, we are left with the risk-free rate, r, as a coefficient on the $\partial V / \partial S$ term in equation (21.11).

The interest rate, by contrast, is not the price of an investment asset. The interest rate is a *characteristic* of an asset, not an asset by itself. The risk-neutral process for the interest rate is obtained by subtracting the risk premium from the drift. The risk-neutral process for the interest rate is therefore

$$dr = [a(r) - \sigma(r)\phi(r, t)]dt + \sigma(r)dZ \tag{23.27}$$

The drift in this equation is what appears in equation (23.26). You can also confirm that equation (23.26) is the same as equation (21.25).

Given a zero-coupon bond (which has a terminal boundary condition that the bond is worth \$1 at maturity), Cox et al. (1985) show that the solution to equation (23.26) is

$$P[t, T, r(t)] = E_t^* \left[e^{-R(t,T)} \right] \tag{23.28}$$

where E^* represents the expectation taken with respect to risk-neutral probabilities and $R(t, T)$ is the random variable representing the cumulative interest rate over time:

$$R(t, T) = \int_t^T r(s)ds \tag{23.29}$$

Thus, to value a zero-coupon bond, we take the expectation over all the discount factors implied by these paths. We will see the discrete time analogue of this equation when we examine binomial models.

Keep in mind that it is *not* correct to value the bond by discounting the bond payoff by the average interest rate, $\bar{R} = E^*[R(t, T)]$:

$$P(t, T, r) \neq e^{-\bar{R}}$$

Because of Jensen's inequality, this seemingly reasonable procedure gives a different bond price than equation (23.28).

Different bond price models solve equation (23.28), differing only in the details of how r behaves and the modeling of the risk premium.

To summarize, a consistent approach to modeling bonds is to begin with a model of the interest rate and then use equation (23.26) to obtain a partial differential equation that describes the bond price (this equation is really the same as the Black-Scholes equation), but with a time-varying interest rate. Using the PDE together with boundary conditions, we can determine the price of the bond. If this seems familiar, it should: It is *exactly* the procedure we used to price options on stock.

The derivation of equation (23.26) assumes that bond prices are a function of a single state variable, the short-term interest rate r. It is possible to allow bond prices to depend on additional state variables, and there is empirical support for having bond prices depend on more than one state variable. Litterman and Scheinkman (1991) estimate a factor model for Treasury bond returns and find that a three-factor model typically explains more than 95% of the variability in a bond's return. They identify the three factors as level, steepness, and curvature of the yield curve. The single most important factor, the level of interest rates, accounts for almost 90% of the movement in bond returns. The overwhelming importance of the level of interest rates explains why duration-based hedging, despite its conceptual problems, is widely used. We will focus on single-variable models in this chapter.

Delta-Gamma Approximations for Bonds

One interpretation of equation (23.26) is familiar from Chapter 21. Using Itô's Lemma, the expected change in the bond price under the risk-neutral distribtion of the interest rate, equation (23.27), is

$$\frac{1}{dt}E^*(dP) = \frac{1}{2}\sigma(r)^2\frac{\partial^2 P}{\partial r^2} + [a(r) - \sigma(r)\phi(r, t)]\frac{\partial P}{\partial r} + \frac{\partial P}{\partial t}$$

Equation (23.26) therefore says that

$$\frac{1}{dt}E^*(dP) = rP \tag{23.30}$$

This is the same as equation (21.29) for options: Using the risk-neutral distribution, bonds are priced to earn the risk-free rate.

The fact that bonds satisfy equation (23.30) means that, as in Chapter 13, *the delta-gamma-theta approximation for the change in a bond price holds exactly if the interest rate moves one standard deviation.* However, the Greeks for a bond are not exactly the same as duration and convexity.

We discussed bond duration in Chapter 7. If y is the bond's yield to maturity, **convexity** is the scaled second derivative of the bond price with respect to the yield, P_{yy}/P. For a zero-coupon bond, duration is time to maturity and convexity is squared time to maturity. Conceptually it seems as if duration should be the delta of a bond and convexity should be gamma. However, this is true only in the "impossible" bond pricing model of equation (23.11). For any correct bond pricing model, duration and convexity will be different than P_r/P and P_{rr}/P. We will see examples of this in the next section.

23.3 EQUILIBRIUM SHORT-RATE BOND PRICE MODELS

In this section we discuss several bond pricing models based on equation (23.26), in which all bond prices are driven by the short-term interest rate, r. The three pricing models we discuss—Rendleman-Bartter, Vasicek, and Cox-Ingersoll-Ross—differ in their specification of $\alpha(r)$, $\sigma(r)$, and $\phi(r)$. These differences can result in very different pricing implications.

The Rendelman-Bartter Model

The simplest models of the short-term interest rate are those in which the interest rate follows arithmetic or geometric Brownian motion. For example, we could write

$$dr = adt + \sigma dZ \tag{23.31}$$

In this specification, the short-rate is normally distributed with mean $r_0 + at$ and variance $\sigma^2 t$. There are several objections to this model:

- The short-rate can be negative. It is not reasonable to think the *nominal* short-rate can be negative, since if it were, investors would prefer holding cash under a mattress to holding bonds.

- The drift in the short-rate is constant. If $a > 0$, for example, the short-rate will drift up over time forever. In practice if the short-rate rises, we expect it to fall; i.e., it is *mean-reverting*.

- The volatility of the short-rate is the same whether the rate is high or low. In practice, we expect the short-rate to be more volatile if rates are high.

The Rendleman and Bartter (1980) model, by contrast, assumes that the short-rate follows geometric Brownian motion:

$$dr = ardt + \sigma rdz \tag{23.32}$$

While interest rates can never be negative in this model, one objection to equation (23.32) is that interest rates can be arbitrarily high. In practice we would expect rates to exhibit mean reversion; if rates are high, we expect them on average to decrease. The Rendleman-Bartter model, on the other hand, says that the probability of rates going up or down is the same whether rates are 100% or 1%.

The Vasicek Model

The Vasicek model incorporates mean reversion:

$$\boxed{dr = a(b - r)dt + \sigma dz} \tag{23.33}$$

This is an Ornstein-Uhlenbeck process (see Chapter 20). The $a(b - r)dt$ term induces mean reversion. Suppose we set $a = 20\%$, $b = 10\%$, and $\sigma = 1\%$. These parameters imply that a one-standard-deviation move for the short-rate is 100 basis points. The parameter b is the level to which short-term interest rates revert. If $r > b$, the short-rate is expected to decrease. If $r < b$, the short-rate is expected to rise. Table 23.1 illustrates mean reversion.

The parameter a reflects the speed with which the interest rate adjusts to b. If $a = 0$, then the short-rate is a random walk. If $a = 1$, the gap between the short-rate and b is expected to be closed in a year. If $a = 20\%$, we expect the rate to decrease in the first year by 20% of the gap.

TABLE 23.1	Expected change in the interest rate in the Vasicek model. Assumes $a = 0.2$, $b = 0.1$, and $\sigma = 0.01$.

Short-Rate	Expected Change in Short-Rate
5%	0.01
10%	0
15%	−0.01
20%	−0.02

Note also that the term multiplying dz is simply σ, independent of the level of the interest rate. This formulation implies that it is possible for interest rates to become negative and that the variability of interest rates is independent of the level of rates.

In the Rendleman-Bartter model, interest rates could not be negative because both the mean and variance in that model are proportional to the level of the interest rate. Thus, as the short-rate approaches zero, both the mean and variance also approach zero, and it is never possible for the rate to fall below zero. In the Vasicek model, by contrast, rates can become negative because the variance does not vanish as r approaches zero.

Why would anyone construct a model that permitted negative interest rates? Vasicek used equation (23.33) to illustrate the more general pricing methodology outlined in Section 23.2, not because it was a compelling empirical description of interest rates. The Vasicek model does in fact have some unreasonable pricing implications, in particular negative yields for long-term bonds.

We can solve for the price of a pure discount bond in the Vasicek model. Let the Sharpe ratio for interest rate risk be ϕ. With the Vasicek interest rate dynamics, equation (23.33), equation (23.26) becomes

$$\frac{1}{2}\sigma^2\frac{\partial^2 P}{\partial r^2} + [a(b-r) - \sigma\phi]\frac{\partial P}{\partial r} + \frac{\partial P}{\partial t} - rP = 0$$

The bond price formula that solves this equation subject to the boundary condition $P(T, T, r) = 1$, and assuming $a \neq 0$, is[3]

$$P[t, T, r(t)] = A(t, T)e^{-B(t,T)r(t)} \tag{23.34}$$

....

[3]When $a = 0$, the solution is equation (23.34), with

$$A = e^{0.5\sigma\phi(T-t)^2 + \sigma^2(T-t)^3/6}$$

$$B = T - t$$

When $a = 0$ the interest rate follows a random walk; therefore, $\bar{r}$ is undefined.

where

$$A(t, T) = e^{\bar{r}(B(t,T)+t-T)-B^2\sigma^2/4a}$$

$$B(t, T) = (1 - e^{-a(T-t)})/a$$

$$\bar{r} = b + \sigma\phi/a - 0.5\sigma^2/a^2$$

with $\bar{r}$ being the yield to maturity on an infinitely lived bond.

The Cox-Ingersoll-Ross Model

Cox et al. (1985b) (CIR) assume a short-term interest rate model of the form

$$dr = a(b - r)dt + \sigma\sqrt{r}dz \tag{23.35}$$

The variance of the interest rate is proportional to the square root of the interest rate, instead of being constant as in the Vasicek model. Because of this subtle difference, the CIR model satisfies all the objections to the earlier models:

- It is impossible for interest rates to be negative. If $r = 0$, the drift in the rate is positive and the variance is zero, so the rate will become positive.

- As the short-rate rises, the volatility of the short-rate also rises.

- The short-rate exhibits mean reversion.

The assumption that the variance is proportional to $\sqrt{r}$ also turns out to be convenient analytically—Cox, Ingersoll, and Ross derive bond and option pricing formulas using this model. The risk premium in the (CIR) model takes the form

$$\phi(r, t) = \bar{\phi}\sqrt{r}/\sigma \tag{23.36}$$

With this specification for the risk premium and equation (23.35), the CIR interest rate dynamics, the partial differential equation for the bond price is

$$\frac{1}{2}\sigma^2 r \frac{\partial^2 P}{\partial r^2} + [a(b - r) - r\bar{\phi}]\frac{\partial P}{\partial r} + \frac{\partial P}{\partial t} - rP = 0$$

The CIR bond price looks similar to that for the Vasicek dynamics, equation (23.34), but with $A(t, T)$ and $B(t, T)$ defined differently:

$$P[t, T, r(t)] = A(t, T)e^{-B(t,T)r(t)} \tag{23.37}$$

where

$$A(t, T) = \left[\frac{2\gamma e^{(a+\bar{\phi}+\gamma)(T-t)/2}}{(a + \bar{\phi} + \gamma)(e^{\gamma(T-t)} - 1) + 2\gamma}\right]^{2ab/\sigma^2}$$

$$B(t, T) = \frac{2(e^{\gamma(T-t)} - 1)}{(a + \bar{\phi} + \gamma)(e^{\gamma(T-t)} - 1) + 2\gamma}$$

$$\gamma = \sqrt{(a + \bar{\phi})^2 + 2\sigma^2}$$

With the CIR process, the yield on a long-term bond approaches the value $\bar{r} = 2ab/(a + \bar{\phi} + \gamma)$ as time to maturity goes to infinity.

Comparing Vasicek and CIR

How different are the prices generated by the CIR and Vasicek models? What is the role of the different variance specifications in the two models?

Figure 23.1 illustrates the yield curves generated by the Vasicek and by the CIR models, assuming that the current short-term rate, r, is 5%, $a = 0.2$ and $b = 10\%$. Volatility in the Vasicek model is 2% in the top panel and 10% in the bottom panel. The volatility, σ, has a different interpretation in each model. In the Vasicek model, volatility is absolute, whereas in the CIR model, volatility is scaled by the square root of the current interest rate. To make the CIR volatility comparable at the initial interest rate, it is set so that $\sigma_{CIR}\sqrt{r} = \sigma_{Vasicek}$, or 0.0894 in the top panel and 0.447 in the bottom panel. The interest rate risk premium is assumed to be zero.

The two models can exhibit very different behavior. The bottom panel has a relatively high volatility. For short-term bonds—with a maturity extending to about 2.5 years—the yield curves look similar. This is a result of setting the CIR volatility to match the Vasicek volatility. Beyond that point the two diverge, with Vasicek yields below CIR yields. The long-run interest rate in the Vasicek model is −0.025, whereas

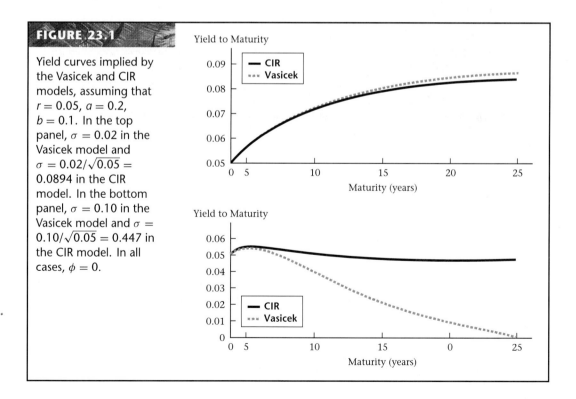

FIGURE 23.1

Yield curves implied by the Vasicek and CIR models, assuming that $r = 0.05$, $a = 0.2$, $b = 0.1$. In the top panel, $\sigma = 0.02$ in the Vasicek model and $\sigma = 0.02/\sqrt{0.05} = 0.0894$ in the CIR model. In the bottom panel, $\sigma = 0.10$ in the Vasicek model and $\sigma = 0.10/\sqrt{0.05} = 0.447$ in the CIR model. In all cases, $\phi = 0$.

that in the CIR model is 0.0463. This difference is evident in Figure 23.1 as the Vasicek yields approach zero (in the long run approaching -0.025).

What accounts for the difference in medium to long-term bonds? As discussed earlier, the pricing formulas are based on *averages* of interest rate paths, as in equation (23.28). Some of the interest paths in the Vasicek model will be negative. Although the *typical* path will be positive because of mean reversion—rates will be pulled toward 10%—there will be paths on which rates are negative. Because of Jensen's inequality, these paths will be disproportionately important. Over sufficiently long horizons, large negative interest rates become more likely and this leads to negative yields. In the CIR model, this effect results in the long-run yield decreasing with volatility. Negative yields are impossible in the CIR model, however, since the short-term interest rate can never become negative.

In the top panel, with relatively low volatility, both yield curves are upward sloping. The effect of mean reversion outweighs that of volatility. In the long run, the Vasicek yield exceeds the CIR yield because volatility increases with the level of the interest rate in the CIR model. Consequently, the Jensen's inequality effect is more pronounced in the CIR model than in the Vasicek model.

We mentioned earlier that hedging in the context of this kind of interest rate model is different from duration hedging. In the CIR and Vasicek models, delta and gamma for a zero-coupon bond are based on the change in the short-term rate. The following example illustrates that the resulting hedge ratios can differ from duration and convexity as traditionally measured.

Example 23.2 Consider a 5-year zero-coupon bond priced using the CIR model, and suppose that $a = 0.2$, $b = 0.1$, $r = 0.08$, $\bar{\phi} = 0$, and $\sigma = 0.2$. The bond price is $0.667. Because it is a 5-year zero-coupon bond, duration is 5 and convexity is 25. However, in the CIR model with these parameters, $P_r = -1.918$ and $P_{rr} = 5.518$. The implied sensitivities to the short-term rate are $-P_r/P = 2.876$ (instead of 5) and $P_{rr}/P = 8.273$ (instead of 25). 🦢

23.4 A BINOMIAL INTEREST RATE MODEL

We now examine binomial interest rate models, which permit the interest rate to move randomly over time. One approach is to model the short-term rate, where the definition of short-term is h, the length of the binomial period. In this example we will model the 1-year rate; hence, a period is 1 year and $h = 1$.

To construct a binomial tree of the 1-year rate, note that we can observe today's 1-year rate. We assume the 1-year rate moves up or down the second year, and again the third year. This behavior gives us the tree in Figure 23.2, which is drawn so that it need not recombine.

The notation required for interest rate trees is a bit more complicated than the interest rate notation we have been using. We have $r_{t_0}(t, T)$ as the forward interest rate

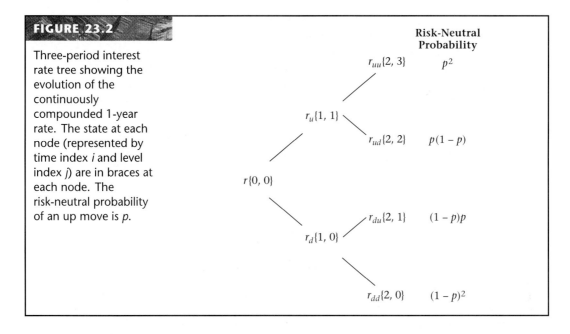

FIGURE 23.2

Three-period interest rate tree showing the evolution of the continuously compounded 1-year rate. The state at each node (represented by time index i and level index j) are in braces at each node. The risk-neutral probability of an up move is p.

Risk-Neutral Probability

$r_{uu}\{2, 3\}$ p^2

$r_u\{1, 1\}$

$r_{ud}\{2, 2\}$ $p(1-p)$

$r\{0, 0\}$

$r_{du}\{2, 1\}$ $(1-p)p$

$r_d\{1, 0\}$

$r_{dd}\{2, 0\}$ $(1-p)^2$

at time t_0 for time t to time T. This notation accounts for the fact that at a point in time, there is a set of forward interest rates at different future times (t) and covering different times to maturity ($T - t$). When $t_0 = t$, $r_t(t, T)$ is the set of current spot interest rates for different times to maturity.

When we have a binomial tree as in Figure 23.2, *at each node* we have this large set of spot interest rates with different maturities, as well as forward rates. Thus, we need to expand the notation to identify the node under discussion. We will let $r_{t_0}(t, T; j)$ represent the interest rate prevailing from t to T, where the rate is quoted at time $t_0 < t$ and the state is j. Since t_0 tells us the binomial period at which the rate is quoted, you can think of j as telling us the height along the tree at time t_0. Similarly, at any point in time t_0, there is a set of both spot and implied forward zero-coupon bond prices, $P_{t_0}(t, T; j)$.

Using this notation, the one-period rate at the ith time and level j is $r_i(i, i+1; j)$.[4] In Figure 23.2 the initial one-period rate is $r_0(0, 1; 0)$ and the rate r_{du}, for example, is $r_2(2, 3; 1)$. The timing is such that the final nodes represent one-period rates observed

....

[4]Any interest rate is reached by one (or more, if the tree is recombining) combination of up and down movements. One convenient way to characterize a node is by numbering the nodes at a given point in time, beginning with 0 at the bottom node. If we are at node j in period i, then we can move to either node $2 \times j$ or $2 \times j + 1$ in period $i + 1$. For example, if we are at node 1 in period 1, then we can move to node 2 (2×1) or 3 ($2 \times 1 + 1$) in period 2. It is also possible to use this scheme to assign to each node the number $2^i + j$. Thus, the $\{0, 0\}$ node is numbered 1 ($2^0 + 0$), the $\{1, 0\}$ node is numbered 2 ($2^1 + 0$), and so on. In effect this uses a binary representation to number the nodes. A similar scheme is suggested in Rendleman (2002).

two periods from today. Thus, the tree in Figure 23.2 can price bonds up to 3 years in maturity. Let p denote the risk-neutral probability of an up move. We will assume that rates are continuously compounded in this example.

Zero-Coupon Bond Prices

At time 0 we can determine a bond price on the binomial tree in much the same way we determined option prices in a binomial stock-price tree. The one-period bond price at any time is determined by discounting at the current one-period rate, which is given at each node:

$$P_i(i, i+1; j) = e^{-r_i(i,i+1;j)h} \tag{23.38}$$

We can value a two-period bond by discounting the expected one-period bond price, one period hence. At any node we can value an n-period zero-coupon bond by proceeding in this way recursively. Beginning in period $i + n$, we value one-period bonds, then in period $i + n - 1$ we have two-period bond values, and so forth.

Because the tree can be used at any node to value zero-coupon bonds of any maturity (up to the remaining size of the tree), the tree also generates implied forward interest rates of all maturities and *volatilities* of implied forward rates. Thus, we can equivalently specify a binomial interest rate tree in terms of interest rates, zero-coupon bond prices, or volatilities of implied forward interest rates.[5]

Using the tree in Figure 23.2, we obtain the following valuation equations. For the one-period bond we have

$$P_0(0, 1; 0) = e^{-rh} \tag{23.39}$$

The two-year bond is priced by working backward along the tree. In the second period, the price of the bond is $1. One year from today, the bond will have the price e^{-r_u} with probability p or e^{-r_d} with probability $1 - p$. The price of the bond is therefore

$$P_0(0, 2; 0) = e^{-rh} \left(p e^{-r_u h} + (1 - p) e^{-r_d h} \right) \tag{23.40}$$

$$= e^{-rh} \left[p P_1(1, 2; 1) + (1 - p) P_1(1, 2; 0) \right] \tag{23.41}$$

Thus, we can price the 2-year bond using either the interest rate tree or the implied bond prices.

Finally, the 3-year bond is again priced by traversing the entire tree. The price is $1 after 3 years. After 2 years, the price will be $1 discounted at r_{uu}, r_{ud}, r_{du}, or r_{dd}. Continuing in this way, the price is

$$P_0(0, 3; 0) = e^{-r} \left[p e^{-r_u} \left(p e^{-r_{uu}} + (1 - p) e^{-r_{ud}} \right) \right.$$
$$\left. + (1 - p) e^{-r_d} \left(p e^{-r_{du}} + (1 - p) e^{-r_{dd}} \right) \right] \tag{23.42}$$

---

[5]The central role of volatility in a term structure model is emphasized by Heath et al. (1992). Their model is discussed in Appendix 23.A.

The 3-year bond calculation can be written differently. By collecting terms in equation (23.42), we can rewrite it as

$$P_0(0, 3; 0) = p^2 e^{-(r+r_u+r_{uu})} + p(1 - p)e^{-(r+r_u+r_{ud})}$$
$$+ (1 - p)pe^{-(r+r_d+r_{du})} + (1 - p)^2 e^{-(r+r_d+r_{dd})} \qquad (23.43)$$

This version of equation (23.42) makes clear that we can value the bond by considering separately each *path* the interest rate can take. Each path implies a realized discount factor. We then compute the expected discount factor, using risk-neutral probabilities. Denoting this expectation as E^*, the value of the zero-coupon bond is

$$E^* \left(e^{-(r_0+r_1+r_2)h} \right)$$

More generally, letting r_i represent the time-i rate, we have

$$\boxed{E^* \left(e^{-\sum_{i=0}^n r_i h} \right)} \qquad (23.44)$$

All bond valuation models implicitly calculate equation (23.44).

Example 23.3   Figure 23.2 constructs an interest rate tree assuming that the current 1-year rate is 10% and that each year the 1-year rate moves up or down 4%, with probability $p = 0.5$. We can use this tree to price 1-, 2-, and 3-year zero-coupon default-free bonds.

One-year bond   From equation (23.39), the price of the 1-year bond is

$$P(0, h) = e^{-0.10} = \$0.9048 \qquad (23.45)$$

Two-year bond   From equation (23.40), the two-period bond price is

$$P(0, 2) = e^{-0.10} \left(0.5e^{-0.14} + 0.5e^{-0.06} \right)$$
$$= \$0.8194$$

Three-year bond   Finally, from equation (23.42), the price of the 3-year bond is

$$P(0, 3) = e^{-0.10} \left[0.5e^{-0.14} \left(0.5e^{-0.18} + 0.5e^{-0.10} \right) + 0.5e^{-0.06} \left(0.5e^{-0.10} + 0.5e^{-0.02} \right) \right]$$
$$= \$0.7438$$

Equation (23.44) also gives \$0.7438 as the price of the three-period zero-coupon bond.

We should note that the volatility of the bond price implied by Figure 23.3 is different from the behavior of a stock. With a stock, uncertainty about the future stock price increases with horizon due to the fact that the volatility of the continuously compounded return grows with the square root of time. With a bond, the volatility of the bond price

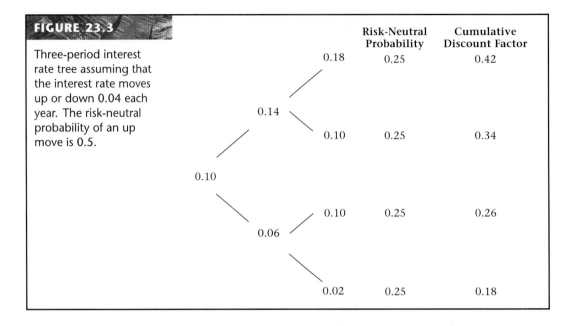

FIGURE 23.3

Three-period interest rate tree assuming that the interest rate moves up or down 0.04 each year. The risk-neutral probability of an up move is 0.5.

	Risk-Neutral Probability	Cumulative Discount Factor
0.18	0.25	0.42
0.14		
0.10	0.25	0.34
0.10		
0.10	0.25	0.26
0.06		
0.02	0.25	0.18

initially grows with time. However, as the bond approaches maturity, volatility declines because of the boundary condition that the bond price approaches $1. Just before maturity, volatility of the price must be essentially zero for a default-free bond. The binomial model in Figure 23.3 produces this behavior of volatility as a matter of course since it models the interest rate, not the bond price.

Yields and Expected Interest Rates

In Figure 23.3, we assume that $p = 0.5$ and the up and down moves are symmetric—the interest rate follows a random walk. Consequently, the expected interest rate at each node is 10%. The yields on the two- and three-period bonds, however, are *not* 10%. The yield on the two-period bond is

$$-ln[P(0, 2)]/2 = -ln(0.8194)/2 = 0.0996$$

The yield on the three-period bond is

$$-ln[P(0, 3)]/3 = -ln(0.7438)/3 = 0.0987$$

Yields are less than 10% on the two- and three-period bonds because of Jensen's inequality: The average of the exponentiated interest rates is less than the exponentiated average. Thus, as we discussed earlier, we cannot price a bond by using the expected interest rate. *Uncertainty causes bond yields to be lower than the expected average interest rate.* The discrepancy between yields and average interest rates increases with volatility. (Problem 23.7 asks you to verify this relationship by constructing a different interest rate tree and repeating the bond valuation.) This is another illustration of the effect of Jensen's inequality that was evident in the Vasicek–CIR comparison.

Option Pricing

Using the binomial tree to price a bond option works the same way as bond pricing. Suppose we have a call option with strike price K on a $(T - t)$-year zero-coupon bond, with the option expiring in $t - t_0$ periods. The expiration value of the option is

$$O(t, j) = max[0, P_t(t, T; j) - K] \tag{23.46}$$

To price the option we can work recursively backward through the tree using risk-neutral pricing, as with an option on a stock. The value one period earlier at the node j' is

$$O(t - h, j') = P_{t-h}(t - h, t; j')$$
$$\times \left[p \times O(t, 2 \times j' + 1) + (1 - p) \times O(m, 2 \times j') \right] \tag{23.47}$$

The calculation here assumes there is a nonrecombining tree. Since each node generates two new nodes, if there are J nodes in one period, there will be $2 \times J$ nodes the next period. Thus, if we are at node j, we can potentially move to node $2 \times j$ or $(2 \times j) + 1$ in one period.[6] We continue in this way to obtain the option value in period 0. In the same way, we can value an option on a yield, or an option on any instrument that is a function of the interest rate.

Delta-hedging works for the bond option just as for a stock option. In this case the underlying asset is a zero-coupon bond maturing at T, since that will be a $(T - t)$-period bond in period t. Each period, the delta-hedged portfolio of the option and underlying asset (the bond with $T - t_0$ to expiration) is financed by the short-term bond, paying whatever one-period interest rate prevails at that node.

Example 23.4 Suppose we have a two-year put on a 1-year zero-coupon bond and the strike price is $0.88. The payoff in year 2 is

$$max[0, \$0.88 - P(2, 3; 2, j)]$$

The option price is computed based on the 1-year bond price in year 2.

From Figure 23.3, there is only one node at which the put will be exercised, namely that where the interest rate is 0.18 and, hence, the bond price is $e^{-0.18} = \$0.8353$. Using the interest rates along the tree, and accounting for the 0.25 risk-neutral probability of reaching that one node, we obtain an option price of

$$(\$0.88 - \$0.8353)e^{-(0.14+0.10)} \times 0.25 = \$0.0088 \qquad ≸$$

---

[6]For example, from node 0, we move to node 0 or 1; from node 1, to node 2 or 3, and so forth.

23.5 THE BLACK-DERMAN-TOY MODEL

At any point in time we can observe the yield curve and the volatilities of bond options. Thus far we have ignored the important practical question of whether a particular interest rate model fits these data. For example, for any interest rate model, we can ask whether it correctly prices zero-coupon bonds (in which case it will correctly price forwards and swaps) and selected options. Matching a model to fit the data is called *calibration*.

Yield curves can have various shapes. The models we have examined, however, are not particularly flexible. For example, the binomial random walk model has two parameters: The starting interest rate and the volatility generating up and down moves. The CIR and Vasicek models have four parameters (a, b, r, and σ) and generate yield curves with particular stylized shapes that may not match the data. These models are arbitrage-free in a world consistent with their assumptions. In the real world, however, they will generate *apparent* arbitrage opportunities, in the sense that observed prices will not match theoretical prices. We then have a choice of concluding either that zero-coupon bonds are priced incorrectly or that the models are not accurate enough to capture reality.

Some models attempt to provide a rich characterization of the yield curve and the yield curve volatility. Notable papers describing these models include Ho and Lee (1986), Black et al. (1990), and Heath et al. (1992). We will focus primarily on the Black-Derman-Toy (BDT) model to illustrate how calibration works.

The basic idea of the Black-Derman-Toy model is to compute a binomial tree of short-term interest rates, with a flexible enough structure to match the data. We will begin with sample data and demonstrate that a particular tree matches these data. We will then explain how to construct the tree. We assume in this discussion that the length of a binomial period is 1 year, although that is arbitrary.

Table 23.2 lists market information about bonds that we would like to match. We follow the Black-Derman-Toy paper in using effective annual yields rather than

TABLE 23.2	Hypothetical bond-market data. Bond prices and yields are the observed prices and effective annual yields for zero-coupon bonds with the indicated maturity. Volatility refers to the volatility of the bond price 1 year from today.		
Maturity (years)	**Yield to Maturity**	**Bond Price ($)**	**Volatility in Year 1**
1	10%	0.9091	N/A
2	11%	0.8116	10%
3	12%	0.7118	15%
4	12.5%	0.6243	14%

continuously compounded yields. Since the table contains prices of zero-coupon bonds, we can infer the term structure of implied forward interest rates. There is also information about the volatility of interest rates. The column headed "Volatility in Year 1" is the standard deviation of the natural log of the *yield* for that bond 1 year hence. (We could, if we wished, convert this into a standard deviation of the bond price in a year.) The volatility for the *n*-year bond tells us the uncertainty about the year-1 yield on an $(n-1)$-year bond. The volatility in year 1 of the 2-year bond is 10%; this tells us that the 1-year yield in year 1 will have a 10% volatility. Similarly, the volatility in year 1 of the 4-year bond (which will be a 3-year bond in year 1) is 14%. While the tree matches observed yields and volatilities, it makes no attempt to capture the evolution of the yield curve over time. The yield curve evolution is of course implicit in the tree, but the tree is not calibrated with this in mind.

The BDT approach provides enough flexibility to match this data. Black, Derman, and Toy describe their tree as driven by the short-term rate, which they assume is log-normally distributed. The general structure of the resulting tree is illustrated in Figure 23.4. We assume that the risk-neutral probability of an up move in the interest rate is 50%.

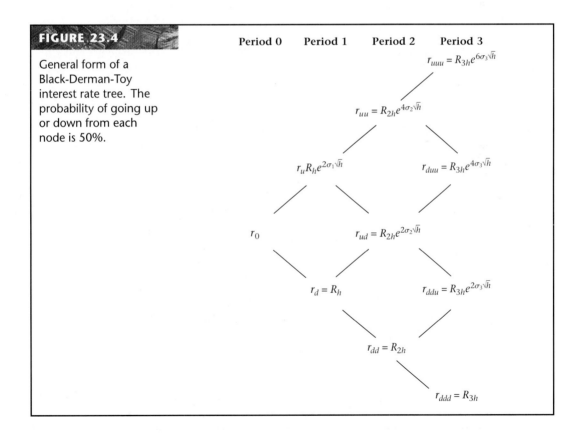

FIGURE 23.4

General form of a Black-Derman-Toy interest rate tree. The probability of going up or down from each node is 50%.

Period 0	Period 1	Period 2	Period 3

$r_{uuu} = R_{3h}e^{6\sigma_3\sqrt{h}}$

$r_{uu} = R_{2h}e^{4\sigma_2\sqrt{h}}$

$r_u R_h e^{2\sigma_1\sqrt{h}}$

$r_{duu} = R_{3h}e^{4\sigma_3\sqrt{h}}$

r_0

$r_{ud} = R_{2h}e^{2\sigma_2\sqrt{h}}$

$r_d = R_h$

$r_{ddu} = R_{3h}e^{2\sigma_3\sqrt{h}}$

$r_{dd} = R_{2h}$

$r_{ddd} = R_{3h}$

For each period in the tree there are two parameters. R_{ih} can be thought of as a rate level parameter at a given time and σ_i as a volatility parameter. These parameters can be used to match the tree with the data. In an ordinary lognormal stock-price tree, the ratio of the up node to the down node is $Ae^{\sigma\sqrt{h}}/Ae^{-\sigma\sqrt{h}} = e^{2\sigma\sqrt{h}}$. The ratio between adjacent nodes is the same in Figure 23.4.

The volatilities in Table 23.2 are measured in the tree as follows. Let the time-h price of a zero-coupon bond maturing at T when the time-t short-term rate is $r(h)$ be $P[h, T, r(h)]$. The yield of the bond is

$$y[h, T, r(h)] = P[h, T, r(h)]^{-1/(T-h)} - 1$$

At time h the short-term rate can take on the two values r_u or r_d. The annualized lognormal yield volatility is then

$$\text{Yield volatility} = 0.5 \times ln\left[\frac{y(h, T, r_u)}{y(h, T, r_d)}\right] \tag{23.48}$$

We multiply by 0.5 since the distance between nodes is twice the exponentiated volatility.

The tree in Figure 23.5, which depicts 1-year effective annual rates, was constructed using the data in Table 23.2. The tree behaves differently from binomial trees we have seen thus far. Unlike a stock-price tree, the nodes are not necessarily centered

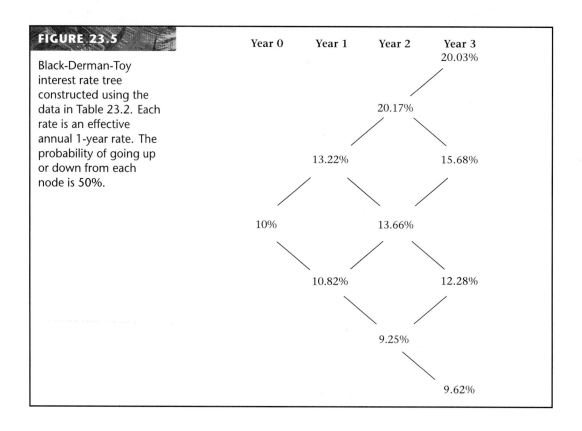

FIGURE 23.5

Black-Derman-Toy interest rate tree constructed using the data in Table 23.2. Each rate is an effective annual 1-year rate. The probability of going up or down from each node is 50%.

Year 0	Year 1	Year 2	Year 3
			20.03%
		20.17%	
	13.22%		15.68%
10%		13.66%	
	10.82%		12.28%
		9.25%	
			9.62%

on the previous period's nodes. For example, in year 1, the lowest interest rate node is above the year-0 interest rate. If we track the minimum interest rate along the bottom of the tree, it increases, then decreases, then increases again. The maximum interest rate in year 3 is below the maximum rate in year 2.

These oddities arise because we constructed the tree to match the data in Table 23.2. Although bond yields steadily increase with maturity, volatilities do not. In order to match the pattern of volatilities given the structure of the BDT tree, rates must behave in what seems like an unusual fashion. Notice that in periods 2 and 3 the ratio of adjacent nodes in the same period is the same. For example, $r_{uuu}/r_{duu} = 20.03/15.68 = 15.68/12.28 = r_{duu}/r_{ddu}$.

Now let's verify that the tree in Figure 23.5 matches the data in Table 23.2. To verify that the tree matches the yield curve, we need to compute the prices of zero-coupon bonds with maturities of 1, 2, 3, and 4 years. To verify the volatilities, we need to compute the prices of 1-, 2-, and 3-year zero-coupon bonds at year 1, and then compute the yield volatilities of those bonds.

Verifying Yields

The rate at the first node is 10%, which corresponds to the current 1-year yield.

We can compute the price (and thus yield) of the 2-year zero-coupon bond by starting in year 2 and working backward. It is slightly more convenient to use the tree of 1-year bond prices in Figure 23.6. In year 1, the 2-year bond will be worth either $0.8832 (a yield of 13.22%) or $0.9023 (a yield of 10.82%). Thus, the discounted expected price at time 0 is

$$\$0.9091 \times (0.5 \times \$0.8832 + 0.5 \times \$0.9023) = \$0.8116$$

Figure 23.7 illustrates the tree corresponding to this calculation.

The price of the 3-year zero is computed in a similar way. Working backwards from the year-3 nodes we have

$$\$0.9091 \times [0.5 \times \$0.8832 \times (0.5 \times \$0.8321 + 0.5 \times \$0.8798)$$
$$+ 0.5 \times \$0.9023 \times (0.5 \times \$0.8798 + 0.5 \times \$0.9153)] = \$0.7118$$

Figure 23.8 illustrates the tree showing the evolution of the 3-year bond. Problem 23.8 asks you to verify that the tree in Figure 23.6 generates the correct 4-year zero-coupon bond price.

Verifying Volatilities

Now we want to see what volatilities are implied by the tree. The volatilities in Table 23.2 are *yield* volatilities. Thus, for each bond, we need to compute implied bond yields in year 1 and then compute the volatility.

For the 2-year bond (1-year bond in year 1), the yield volatility using equation (23.48) is

$$0.5 \times ln \left(\frac{0.8832^{-1} - 1}{0.9023^{-1} - 1} \right) = 0.1$$

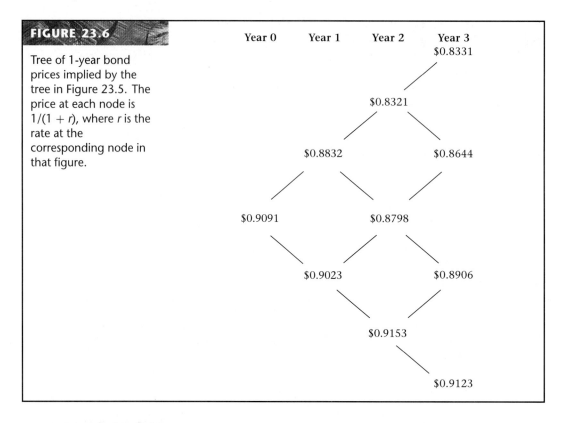

FIGURE 23.6

Tree of 1-year bond prices implied by the tree in Figure 23.5. The price at each node is $1/(1 + r)$, where r is the rate at the corresponding node in that figure.

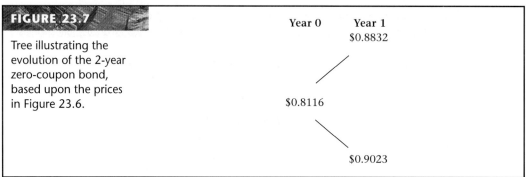

FIGURE 23.7

Tree illustrating the evolution of the 2-year zero-coupon bond, based upon the prices in Figure 23.6.

From Figure 23.8, the 3-year bond in year 1 (which will be a 2-year bond) will be worth either $0.7560, with a yield of $0.7560^{-1/2} - 1 = 0.1501$ or $0.8099^{-1/2} - 1 = 0.1112$. The yield volatility is then

$$0.5 \times ln\left(\frac{0.1501}{0.1112}\right) = 0.15$$

Both yields match the inputs in Table 23.2.

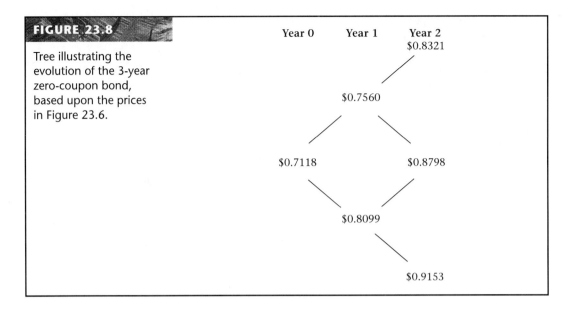

FIGURE 23.8

Tree illustrating the evolution of the 3-year zero-coupon bond, based upon the prices in Figure 23.6.

Year 0   Year 1   Year 2

$0.8321

$0.7560

$0.7118

$0.8798

$0.8099

$0.9153

Problem 23.9 asks you to verify that the tree generates the correct 4-year yield volatility.

Constructing a Black-Derman-Toy Tree

We have verified that the tree in Figure 23.5 is consistent with the data in Table 23.2. Now we turn the question around: Given the data, how did we generate the tree in the first place? The answer is that we started at early nodes and worked to the later nodes, building the tree outward.

The first node is given by the prevailing 1-year rate. Therefore the 1-year bond price is

$$\$0.9091 = \frac{1}{1 + R_0} \tag{23.49}$$

Thus, $R_0 = 0.10$.

For the second node, the year-1 price of a 1-year bond is $P(1, 2, r_u)$ or $P(1, 2, r_d)$. We require that two conditions be satisfied:

$$\$0.8116 = \frac{1}{1 + 0.10} [0.5 \times P(1, 2, r_u) + 0.5 \times P(1, 2, r_d)]$$

$$= \frac{1}{1 + 0.10} \left(0.5 \times \frac{1}{1 + R_1 e^{2\sigma_1}} + 0.5 \times \frac{1}{1 + R_1} \right) \tag{23.50}$$

$$0.10 = 0.5 \times ln([P(1, 2, r_u)^{-1} - 1]/[P(1, 2, r_d)^{-1} - 1])$$

$$= 0.5 \times ln(R_1 e^{2\sigma}/R_1) \tag{23.51}$$

The second equation gives us $\sigma = 0.1$ and this value enables us to solve the first equation to obtain $R_1 = 0.1082$.

It is a bit messier to solve for the next set of conditions, but conceptually we are still fitting two parameters (R_2 and σ_2) to match two inputs (the 3-year yield and the 2-year yield volatility 1 year hence). The possible prices of a 2-year bond at the two nodes in year 1 are $P(1, 3, r_u)$ and $P(1, 3, r_d)$. Thus, we have the two conditions

$$\$0.7118 = \frac{1}{1+0.10} [0.5 \times P(1, 3, r_u) + 0.5 \times P(1, 3, r_d)]$$

$$= \frac{1}{1+0.10} \left[0.5 \times \frac{1}{1.1322} \left(0.5 \times \frac{1}{1 + R_2 e^{4\sigma_2}} + 0.5 \times \frac{1}{1 + R_2 e^{2\sigma_2}} \right) \right.$$

$$\left. + 0.5 \times \frac{1}{1.1082} \left(0.5 \times \frac{1}{1 + R_2 e^{2\sigma_2}} + 0.5 \times \frac{1}{1 + R_2} \right) \right] \tag{23.52}$$

$$0.15 = 0.5 \times ln([P(1, 3, r_u)^{-1/2} - 1]/[P(1, 3, r_d)^{-1/2} - 1]) \tag{23.53}$$

By iterating, it is possible to solve R_2 and σ_2. In the same way, it is possible to solve for the parameters for each subsequent period.

Black-Derman-Toy Examples

In this section we use the interest rate tree in Figure 23.5 to compute several examples.

Caplets and caps   As discussed in Section 23.1, an interest rate cap pays the difference between the realized interest rate in a period and the interest cap rate, if the difference is positive. To illustrate the workings of a cap, Figure 23.9 computes the cap payments on a \$100 3-year loan with annual interest payments, assuming a 12% cap settled annually. The payments in the figure are the *present value* of the cap payments for the interest rate at that node. For example, consider the topmost node in year 2. The realized interest rate is 20.173%. The cap payment made at the node, 2 years from today, is therefore

$$\text{Cap payment} = \frac{\$100 \times (0.2017 - 0.12)}{1 + 0.2017} = \$6.799$$

Since 20.17% is the observed 1-year rate 2 years from today, 3 years from today the borrower will owe an interest payment of \$20.17. The \$6.799 payment can be invested at the rate of 20.17%, so the net interest payment will be

$$\$20.17 - (\$6.799 \times 1.2017) = \$12.00$$

In the same way, we can compute the cap payment at the middle node in year 2, \$1.463. The payment at the bottom node is zero since 9.254% is below the 12% cap.

We can value the year-2 caplet binomially by working back through the tree in the usual way. The calculation is

Value of year-2 cap payment $= \$0.9091 \times [0.5 \times \$0.8832 \times (0.5 \times \$6.799$

$+ 0.5 \times \$1.463) + 0.5 \times \$0.9023 \times (0.5 \times 1.463 + 0.5 \times 0)] = \$1.958$

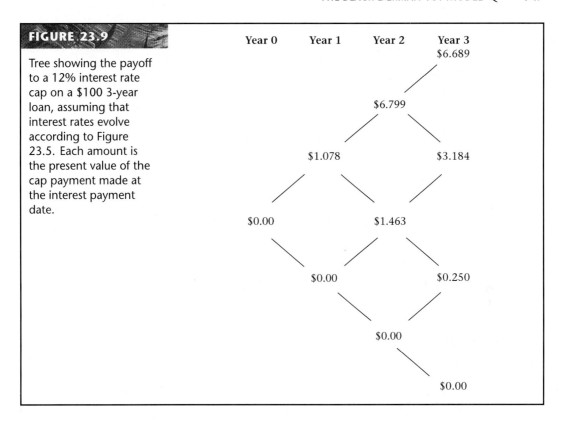

FIGURE 23.9

Tree showing the payoff to a 12% interest rate cap on a $100 3-year loan, assuming that interest rates evolve according to Figure 23.5. Each amount is the present value of the cap payment made at the interest payment date.

	Year 0	Year 1	Year 2	Year 3

The value of the cap is the value of the sum of the caplets. Problem 23.10 asks you to verify that the value of the cap is $3.909.

Forward rate agreements We discussed in Chapter 7 two different styles of settlement for a forward contract based on interest rates. The standard FRA calls for settlement at maturity of the loan, when the interest payment is made. (Equivalently, the FRA can be settled to pay the present value of this amount when the loan is made, with the present value computed using the prevailing interest rate.) Eurodollar-style settlement, by contrast, calls for payment at the time the loan is made. As we discussed in Chapter 7, the two settlement procedures generate different fair forward interest rates.

We can illustrate this difference with a simple example. Consider two contracts. Contract A is a standard forward rate agreement as described in Section 7.2. If $r(3, 4)$ is the 1-year rate in year 3, the payoff to contract A 4 years from today is

$$\text{Contract A payoff in year } 4 = r(3, 4) - \bar{r}_A \qquad (23.54)$$

This is a forward rate agreement settled at maturity. We can compute $\bar{r}_A$ by taking the discounted expectation along a binomial tree of $r(3, 4)$ paid in year 4 and dividing by $P(0, 4)$. Since it is an implied forward rate, we can also value $\bar{r}_A$ as $P(0, 3)/P(0, 4) - 1$.

Contract B is a forward agreement that settles on the borrowing date in year 3:

$$\text{Contract B payoff in year } 3 = r(3, 4) - \bar{r}_B \qquad (23.55)$$

This second contract resembles a Eurodollar futures contract. There is no marking-to-market prior to settlement, which would occur with a real futures contract, but the timing of settlement is mismatched with the timing of interest payments. The correlation between the contract payment and the interest rate discussed above and in Section 7.2 is therefore present in contract B. We can compute $\bar{r}_B$ by taking the discounted expectation along a binomial tree of $r(3, 4)$ paid in year 3, and dividing by $P(0, 3)$.

Example 23.5 We can value both contracts A and B using the interest rate tree in Figure 23.5. The rate on contract A is $\bar{r}_A = P(0, 3)/P(0, 4) - 1 = 0.7118/0.6243 - 1 = 0.140134$.

Contract B can be valued as follows. Suppose the forward rate on B is $\bar{r}_B$. In year 3, B makes the payment $r(3, 4) - \bar{r}_B$. We can value on the tree the payment $r(3, 4)$; the time $= 0$ value of $\bar{r}_B$ is simply $\bar{r}_B \times P(0, 3)$. Figure 23.10 depicts

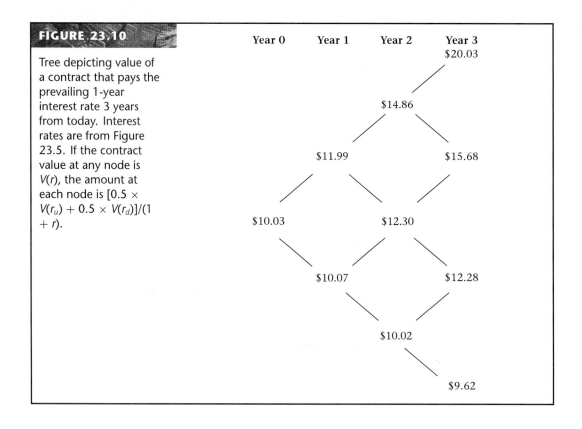

FIGURE 23.10

Tree depicting value of a contract that pays the prevailing 1-year interest rate 3 years from today. Interest rates are from Figure 23.5. If the contract value at any node is $V(r)$, the amount at each node is $[0.5 \times V(r_u) + 0.5 \times V(r_d)]/(1 + r)$.

	Year 0	Year 1	Year 2	Year 3
				$20.03
			$14.86	
		$11.99		$15.68
	$10.03		$12.30	
		$10.07		$12.28
			$10.02	
				$9.62

the payment for a $100 notional amount. In the final period, we receive the prevailing 1-year rate times $100. We then discount this payment back through the tree. The time-0 value is $10.03. The implied rate is $10.03/P(0, 3) = $10.03/$71.18 = 0.1409.

Thus, Eurodollar-style settlement in year 3 raises the forward rate from 14.01% to 14.09%. Problem 23.11 asks you to verify using the binomial tree that $\bar{r}_A = 14.0134\%$.

CHAPTER SUMMARY

Under the assumption that the forward price for a bond is lognormally distributed, the Black model can be used to price bond and interest rate options, and therefore interest rate caps.

Derivatives that are functions of interest rates can be priced and hedged in the same way as options. As with derivatives on stocks, prices of interest rate derivatives are characterized by a partial differential equation that is essentially the same as the Black-Scholes equation. The Vasicek and Cox-Ingersoll-Ross interest rate models are derived using this equation by assuming that the short-term interest rate follows particular means-reverting processes. These models generate theoretical yield curves but are too restrictive to match observed yield curves.

The Black-Derman-Toy tree is a binomial interest rate tree calibrated to match zero-coupon yields and a particular set of volatilities. This calibration ensures that it matches a set of observed market prices (for example the swap curve) but not necessarily the evolution of the yield curve. Valution of interest rate claims on a binomial interest rate tree is much like that on a stock-price tree.

FURTHER READING

Classic treatments of bond pricing with interest rate uncertainty are Vasicek (1977) and Cox et al. (1985b).

Binomial treatments include Rendleman and Bartter (1980), Ho and Lee (1986), and Black et al. (1990). Heath et al. (1992) have been extremely influential insofar as they provide an equilibrium characterization of the evolution of forward rates. See also Brace et al. (1997) and Miltersen et al. (1997). More in-depth treatments of interest rate derivatives can be found in Hull (2000, Chapters 20–22), Rebonato (1996), Jarrow (1996), and James and Webber (2001).

Litterman and Scheinkman (1991) is a classic study of factors affecting bond returns. Bliss (1997) surveys this literature.

PROBLEMS

For the first three problems, use the following information:

Bond Maturity (years)	1	2	3	4
Bond Price	0.9259	0.8495	0.7722	0.7020
1-Year Forward Price Volatility		0.1000	0.1050	0.1100

23.1.   **a.** What is the 1-year bond forward price in year 1?

b. What is the price of a call option that expires in 1 year, giving you the right to pay $0.9009 to buy a bond expiring in 1 year?

c. What is the price of an otherwise identical put?

d. What is the price of an interest rate caplet that provides an 11% (effective annual rate) cap on 1-year borrowing 1 year from now?

23.2.   **a.** What is the 2-year forward price for a 1-year bond?

b. What is the price of a call option that expires in 2 years, giving you the right to pay $0.90 to buy a bond expiring in 1 year?

c. What is the price of an otherwise identical put?

d. What is the price of a interest rate caplet that provides an 11% (effective annual rate) cap on 1-year borrowing 2 years from now?

23.3. What is the price of a 3-year interest rate cap with an 11.5% (effective annual) cap rate?

23.4. Suppose the yield curve is flat at 8%. Consider 3- and 6-year zero-coupon bonds. You buy one 3-year bond and sell an appropriate quantity of the 6-year bond to duration-hedge the position. Any additional investment is in short-term (zero-duration) bonds. Suppose the yield curve can move up to 8.25% or down to 7.75% over the course of 1 day. Do you make or lose money on the hedge? What does the result tell you about the (impossible) flat-yield curve model discussed in Section 23.2?

23.5. Suppose the yield curve is flat at 6%. Consider a 4-year 5%-coupon bond and an 8-year 7%-coupon bond. All coupons are annual.

a. What are the prices and durations of both bonds?

b. Consider buying one 4-year bond and duration-hedging by selling an appropriate quantity of the 8-year bond. Any residual is financed with short-term (zero-duration) bonds. Suppose the yield curve can move up to 6.25% or down to 5.75% over the course of 1 day. What are the results from the hedge?

23.6. Consider two zero-coupon bonds with 2 years and 10 years to maturity. Let $a = 0.2, b = 0.1, r = 0.05, \sigma_{Vasicek} = 10\%$, and $\sigma_{CIR} = 44.721\%$. The interest rate risk premium is zero in each case. We will consider a position consisting of one $100 par value 2-year bond, which we will hedge with a position in the 10-year bond.

    a. Compute the prices, deltas, and gammas of the bonds using the CIR and Vasicek models. How do delta and gamma compare to duration and convexity?

    b. Suppose the Vasicek model is true. You wish to hedge the 2-year bond using the 10-year bond. Consider a 1-day holding period and suppose the interest rate moves one standard deviation up or down. What is the return on the duration-hedged position? What is the return on the Vasicek delta-hedged position?

    c. Repeat the previous part, only use the CIR model in place of the Vasicek model.

23.7. Construct a 4-period, 3-step (8 terminal node) binomial interest rate tree where the initial interest rate is 10% and rates can move up or down by 2%; model your tree after that in Figure 23.3. Compute prices and yields for 1-, 2-, 3-, and 4-year bonds. Do yields decline with maturity? Why?

23.8. Verify that the 4-year zero-coupon bond price generated by the tree in Figure 23.6 is $0.6243.

23.9. Verify that the 1-year yield volatility of the 4-year zero-coupon bond price generated by the tree in Figure 23.6 is 0.14.

23.10. Verify that the price of the 12% interest rate cap in Figure 23.9 is $3.909.

23.11. Using a binomial tree like that in Figure 23.10, verify that the 1-year forward rate 3 years hence in Figure 23.5 is 14.0134%.

For the next four problems, here are two BDT interest rate trees with effective annual interest rates at each node.

Tree #1

0.08000	0.07676	0.08170	0.07943	0.07552
	0.10362	0.10635	0.09953	0.09084
		0.13843	0.12473	0.10927
			0.15630	0.13143
				0.15809

Tree #2

0.08000	0.08112	0.08749	0.08261	0.07284
	0.09908	0.10689	0.10096	0.08907
		0.13060	0.12338	0.10891
			0.15078	0.13317
				0.16283

23.12. What are the 1-, 2-, 3-, 4-, and 5-year zero-coupon bond prices implied by the two trees?

23.13. What volatilities were used to construct each tree? (You computed zero-coupon bond prices in the previous problem; now you have to compute the year-1 yield volatility for 1-, 2-, 3-, and 4-year bonds.) Can you unambiguously say that rates in one tree are more volatile than the other?

23.14. For years 2–5, compute the following:

    a. The forward interest rate, r_f, for a forward rate agreement that settles at the time borrowing is repaid. That is, if you borrow at $t - 1$ at the 1-year rate $\tilde{r}$, and repay the loan at t, the contract payoff in year t is

$$(\tilde{r} - r_f)$$

    b. The forward interest rate, r_e, for a Eurodollar-style forward rate agreement that settles at the time borrowing is *initiated*. That is, if you borrow at $t - 1$ at the 1-year rate $\tilde{r}$, and repay the loan at t, the contract payoff in year $t - 1$ is

$$(\tilde{r} - r_e)$$

    c. How is the difference between r_f and r_e affected by volatility (you can compare the two trees) and time to maturity?

23.15. You are going to borrow \$250m at a floating rate for 5 years. You wish to protect yourself against borrowing rates greater than 10.5%. Using each tree, what is the price of a 5-year interest rate cap? (Assume that the cap settles each year at the time you repay the borrowing.)

APPENDIX 23.A: THE HEATH-JARROW-MORTON MODEL

The Black-Derman-Toy model illustrates one particular way to construct a binomial tree from data. There are other ways to construct trees, such as the Ho and Lee (1986) model, which we do not discuss here. The Heath-Jarrow-Morton model (Heath et al., 1992) is notable for proposing a general structure for interest rate models, one which contains other models as a special case. Their basic insight is that no-arbitrage restrictions require that the evolution of forward rates (or equivalently, forward bond prices) hinges in a specific way on bond price volatilities. When you adopt a specific volatility model, you implicitly adopt a specific model for the evolution of forward interest rates.

To understand the link between volatilities and forward rates, suppose the single-state variable is the short-term interest rate, r, and we have two zero-coupon bonds with prices $P(t, T_1, r)$ and $P(t, T_2, r)$ with $T_2 > T_1$. The implied forward zero-coupon bond price between T_1 and T_2 is

$$F(t, T_1, T_2) = \frac{P(t, T_2, r)}{P(t, T_1, r)} \qquad (23.56)$$

Under the risk-neutral distribution, all zero-coupon bond prices follow the equation

$$\frac{dP}{P} = r dt + q(t, T, r) dZ \qquad (23.57)$$

Using Itô's Lemma, this equation implies that the forward bond price follows the process

$$\frac{dF}{F} = [q(t, T_1, r)^2 - q(t, T_1, r) q(t, T_2, r)] dt + [q(t, T_2, r) - q(t, T_1, r)] dZ$$

We can do this same calculation for every possible forward bond price. In every case, *only bond price volatilities affect the evolution of the forward curve.*

We can use equation (23.57) to derive the process that must be followed by forward interest rates. If the forward bond price is $F(t, T_1, T_2)$, then the implied forward interest rate is

$$f(t, T_1, T_2) = -\frac{ln[F(t, T_1, T_2)]}{T_2 - T_1}$$

Using Itô's Lemma to compute df, we obtain

$$
\begin{aligned}
df &= -\frac{1}{T_2 - T_1} \left(\frac{dF}{F} - \frac{1}{2} \frac{(dF)^2}{F^2} \right) \\
&= \frac{\frac{1}{2}[q(t, T_2, r)^2 - q(t, T_1, r)^2]}{T_2 - T_1} dt + \frac{q(t, T_1, r) - q(t, T_2, r)}{T_2 - T_1} dZ
\end{aligned}
\qquad (23.58)
$$

The intuition for the result that the forward rate process depends on volatilities is straightforward. For all bonds, the risk-neutral expected return is the risk-free rate, and in a one-factor world, the prices of all bonds are perfectly correlated. The forward bond price, $P(t, T_2)/P(t, T_1)$, varies *only* because of the volatility differences for the two bonds. Thus, the process for the forward bond price, and, hence, the forward interest rate, depends only on volatilities. This approach is more general than Black-Derman-Toy since a model of the volatility process can potentially be calibrated to the evolution of the yield curve as well as a snapshot at a point in time.

Jarrow (1996), Rebonato (1996), and James and Webber (2001) discuss empirical implementation of the model, which entails assuming and calibrating a model for bond volatilities.

Chapter 24

Risk Assessment

R*isk assessment* is the evaluation of distributions of outcomes, with a focus on the worst that might happen. Insurance companies, for example, are in the business of determining the likelihood of, and loss associated with, an insured event. In this chapter we use the framework and tools developed in this book to understand risk assessment. We first discuss *value at risk*, which is a method of measuring the possible losses on a portfolio of financial assets. We then discuss credit derivatives and models for assessing default risk.

24.1 VALUE AT RISK

A financial institution might have a complex portfolio containing stocks, bonds with different maturities and with various embedded options, and instruments denominated in different currencies. The form of these instruments could be simple notes or complex options. **Value at risk** (VaR) is one way to perform risk assessment for such a portfolio.

With an estimate of the distribution of outcomes we can either ask about the probability of losing a given sum (e.g., what is the chance our loss exceeds $5m?) or ask, for a given probability, how much might we lose (what level of loss do we exceed with a 1% probability)? The idea of value at risk is to estimate the losses on a portfolio that occur with a given probability. For example, a derivatives market-maker could estimate that for a given portfolio there is a 1% chance of losses in excess of $500,000. The amount $500,000 is then the 99% 1-day value at risk.[1] In general, computing value at risk means finding the value of a portfolio such that there is a specified probability that the portfolio will be worth at least this much over a given horizon. The choice of horizon and probability will depend on how VaR is to be used. Regulators have proposed assessing capital at three times the 99% 10-day VaR (see the box on page 759 for more details). "Riskmetrics" (see J. P. Morgan/Reuters, 1996), developed by J. P. Morgan in the mid-1990s, is one comprehensive proposal for a value at risk methodology. Much of the discussion in this section, especially for bonds, follows the Riskmetrics methodology.

Before we discuss how to compute value at risk, recognize that the ideas underlying risk assessment matter in contexts other than measuring the riskiness of bank portfolios. For example, suppose a firm has $10m in capital and can pursue one of two investment

-----

[1]You could also refer to $500,000 as the 1% VaR. Since VaR is always based upon tail probabilities, in practice it will be obvious that a "99% VaR" and a "1% VaR" refer to the same quantity.

opportunities, each costing $10 million. One year, investment A returns $12 million for sure, whereas investment B returns $24 million with probability one-half and $0 with probability one-half. Suppose the risk of investment B is idiosyncratic and the risk-free rate is 10%. Standard investment theory will assess both projects as having the same positive NPV. However, with investment B, half of the time the firm will lose its entire investment and therefore all of its capital. In order to make additional investments, the firm must raise additional capital, a costly process. Once we account for the costs associated with losing all capital, A and B may no longer seem equally attractive. More generally, managers will want to know how much of a firm's capital is at risk with a given project. Risk assessment can therefore affect project selection.[2]

Distributions of outcomes matter at the personal level as well. Suppose you are planning for retirement. You will need to decide both how much to save and how to allocate your savings, as for example between stocks and bonds. For any strategy, a key question is: What is the probability that by following this strategy you will fail to achieve a desired minimum level of retirement savings by the time you retire?[3] This is not the only question to ask, but a strategy with a high probability of leaving you penniless—no matter how desirable on other grounds—should call for careful consideration. We will not discuss personal financial planning in this chapter, but the ideas underlying risk assessment can be used in making personal decisions as well as corporate decisions.

There are at least three uses of value at risk. First, as mentioned, regulators can use VaR to compute capital requirements for financial institutions. Second, managers can use VaR as an input in making risk-taking and risk-management decisions. Third, managers can also use VaR to assess the quality of the bank's models. For example, if the models say that there is a 5% chance that a particular trading operation will lose $1m over a 1-day horizon, then on average once every 20 days (5% of the time) the trading operation *should* lose $1m. If losses of this size occur more frequently, the models are assigning too little risk to the bank's activities. If such losses occur less frequently, the models are assigning too much risk.

Most of the examples in this section use lognormally distributed stocks and linear normal approximations to illustrate VaR calculations. Currencies and commodities can be modeled in this way as well. Although for long horizons it might not be reasonable to treat commodities as lognormally distributed, for short horizons this is generally a reasonable assumption. We ignore the possibility of jumps. We discuss bonds separately.

Value at Risk for One Stock

Suppose $\tilde{x}_h$ is the dollar return on a portfolio over the horizon h, and $f(x, h)$ is the distribution of returns. Define the value at risk of the portfolio as the return, $x_h(c)$, such

---

[2] See Stulz (1996) for a detailed discussion of the link between investment decisions and risk assessment.

[3] Bodie and Crane (1999) for example use Monte Carlo simulation to examine return distributions to assess the suitability of financial products for retirement savings.

VaR and Regulatory Capital

As an example of VaR being used to determine regulatory capital, here is an excerpt of a capital rule proposed jointly in 1996 by the Office of the Comptroller of the Currency, the Federal Reserve Board of Governors, and the Federal Deposit Insurance Corporation:

> The proposed internal models approach requires an institution to employ an internal model to calculate daily value at risk (VaR) measures for each of four risk categories: interest rates, equity prices, foreign exchange rates, and commodity prices, including related options in each category. For regulatory capital purposes, the market risk proposal requires an institution to calibrate VaR measures to a 10-day movement in rates and prices and a 99% confidence level. An institution must base its VaR measures upon rates and prices observed over a period of at least 1 year. In deriving the overall VaR measure, an institution could take into account historical correlations within a risk category (e.g., between interest rates), but not across risk categories (e.g., not between interest rates and equity prices); in other words, the overall VaR measure equals the sum of the VaR measures for each risk category. An institution's capital charge for general market risk equals the greater of (1) the previous day's overall VaR measure, or (2) the average of the preceding 60 days' overall VaR measures multiplied by a factor of three (the multiplication factor). Moreover, the market risk proposal requires an institution to hold additional capital for specific risk associated with debt and equity positions in the trading account to the extent that its internal model does not incorporate that risk. (From the *Federal Register*: September 6, 1996, Volume 61, Number 174, Rules and Regulations, pp. 47357-47378.)

The 99% level in this proposal, multiplied by 3, is intended to ensure that institutions have sufficient capital to cover even rare events. The 10-day horizon would give the institution time to liquidate a position.

that $Prob(\tilde{x}_h \geq x_h(c)) = c$. In other words, $x_h(c)$ is the $1 - c$ quantile of the return distribution over the horizon h.

Notice that the definition of value at risk requires that we specify a horizon, h, and a probability, c. Thus, the value at risk of a position measures the loss that will occur with a given probability over a specified period of time.

Suppose a portfolio consists of a single stock and we wish to compute value at risk over the horizon h. If the distribution of the stock price after h periods, S_h, is lognormal, we have

$$ln(S_h/S_0) \sim \mathcal{N}[(\alpha - \delta - 0.5\sigma^2)h, \sigma^2 h] \tag{24.1}$$

As we saw in Chapter 18, if we pick a stock price $\bar{S}_h$, then the probability that the stock price will exceed $\bar{S}_h$ is

$$Prob(S_h > \bar{S}_h) = N\left(\frac{-ln(\bar{S}_h) + ln(S_0) + (\alpha - \delta - 0.5\sigma^2)h}{\sigma\sqrt{h}}\right) \tag{24.2}$$

The complementary calculation is to compute the $\bar{S}_h(c)$ corresponding to the probability c. Suppose that we want to know the level of the stock price that we will exceed with probability c. We have

$$c = N\left(\frac{-ln(\bar{S}_h(c)) + ln(S_0) + (\alpha - \delta - 0.5\sigma^2)h}{\sigma\sqrt{h}}\right) \tag{24.3}$$

We can solve for $\bar{S}_h(c)$ by using the inverse cumulative probability distribution, N^{-1}. Applying this function to both sides of equation (24.3), we have

$$N^{-1}(c) = \frac{-ln(\bar{S}_h(c)) + ln(S_0) + (\alpha - \delta - 0.5\sigma^2)h}{\sigma\sqrt{h}} \tag{24.4}$$

Solving for $\bar{S}_h(c)$ gives

$$\bar{S}_h(c) = S_0 e^{(\alpha-\delta-0.5\sigma^2)h - \sigma\sqrt{h}N^{-1}(c)} \tag{24.5}$$

This expression should look familiar from Chapters 18. In equation (24.5), $-N^{-1}(c)$ takes the place of a standard normal random variable.

Example 24.1 Suppose we own \$3m worth of stock A, which has an expected return of 15% and a 30% volatility, and pays no dividend. Moreover, assume A is lognormally distributed. The value of the position in 1 week, V, is

$$V = \$3\text{m} \times e^{(0.15-0.5\times0.3^2)\frac{1}{52}+0.3\sqrt{\frac{1}{52}}Z} \tag{24.6}$$

where $Z \sim \mathcal{N}(0, 1)$.

Given this assumed stock price distribution, a 5% loss will occur if Z satisfies

$$\$3\text{m} \times e^{(0.15-0.5\times0.3^2)\frac{1}{52}+0.3\sqrt{\frac{1}{52}}Z} = 0.95 \times \$3\text{m}$$

or

$$Z = \frac{ln(0.95) - (0.15 - 0.5 \times 0.3^2)\frac{1}{52}}{0.3 \times \sqrt{\frac{1}{52}}} = -1.2815$$

We have

$$NormSDist(-1.2815) = 0.1000$$

Thus, we expect that 10% of the time there will be a weekly loss in excess of 5%.

With 95% probability, the value of the portfolio over a 1-week horizon will exceed

$$\$3\text{m} \times e^{(0.15-0.5\times0.3^2)\frac{1}{52}+0.3\sqrt{\frac{1}{52}}\times(-1.645)} = \$2.8072\text{m}$$

where $N^{-1}(0.05) = -1.645$. In this case, we would say the 95% value at risk is $2.8072m - $3m = -$0.1928m. ❧

If the assumption of lognormality is valid and if the inputs are correct, a 1-week loss of this magnitude occurs on average once every 20 weeks.

In practice it is common to simplify the VaR calculation by assuming a normal return rather than a lognormal return. Recall from Chapter 20 that the standard lognormal model is generated by assuming normal returns over very short horizons. We can therefore approximate the exact lognormal result with a normal approximation:

$$S_h = S_0 \left(1 + \alpha h + z\sigma\sqrt{h}\right) \tag{24.7}$$

We could also further simplify by ignoring the mean:

$$S_h = S_0 \left(1 + z\sigma\sqrt{h}\right) \tag{24.8}$$

Both equations (24.7) and (24.8) become less reasonable as h grows.

Example 24.2   Using the same assumptions as in Example 24.1, equation (24.7) gives

$$\$3m \times \left[1 + \frac{0.15}{52} + \left(\frac{0.3}{\sqrt{52}} \times (-1.645)\right)\right] = \$2.8033m$$

VaR is therefore $2.8033m - $3m = -$0.1966m. Ignoring the mean, equation (24.8) gives

$$\$3m \times \left(1 + \frac{0.3}{\sqrt{52}} \times (-1.645)\right) = \$2.7947m$$

VaR is $2.7947m - $3m = -$0.2053m. ❧

Figure 24.1 compares the three models—lognormal, normal with mean, and normal without mean—over horizons of one day to one year. As you would expect, the approximation ignoring the mean (equation (24.8)) is less accurate over longer horizons. In practice the mean is often ignored for two reasons. First, as we saw in Chapter 18, means are hard to estimate precisely. Second, as we saw in Chapter 20, for short horizons the mean is less important than the diffusion term in an Itô process.

Two or More Stocks

When we consider a portfolio having two or more stocks, the distribution of the future portfolio value is the sum of lognormally distributed random variables and is therefore not lognormal. Since the lognormal distribution is no longer exact, we can use the normal approximation.

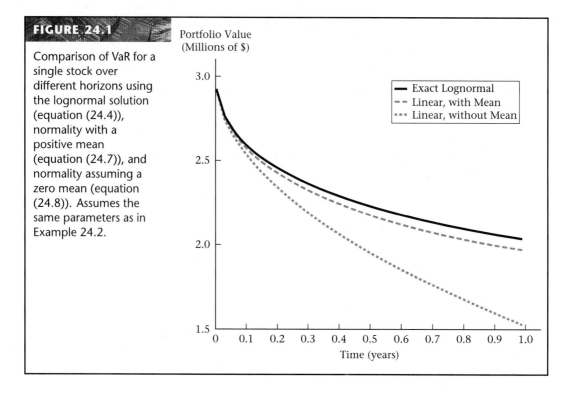

FIGURE 24.1

Comparison of VaR for a single stock over different horizons using the lognormal solution (equation (24.4)), normality with a positive mean (equation (24.7)), and normality assuming a zero mean (equation (24.8)). Assumes the same parameters as in Example 24.2.

Let the annual mean and standard deviation of the realized return on stock i, $\tilde{\alpha}_i$, be α_i and σ_i, with the correlation between stocks i and j being ρ_{ij}. The dollar investment in stock i is W_i. The value of a portfolio containing n stocks is

$$W = \sum_{i=1}^{n} W_i$$

The return on the portfolio over the horizon h, R_h, is

$$\text{Portfolio return} = R_h = \frac{1}{W} \sum_{i=1}^{n} \tilde{\alpha}_{i,h} W_i$$

Assuming normality, the annualized distribution of the portfolio return is

$$R_h \sim \mathcal{N} \left(\frac{1}{W} \sum_{i=1}^{n} \alpha_i h W_i, \ \frac{1}{W^2} \sum_{i=1}^{n} \sum_{j=1}^{n} \sigma_i \sigma_j \rho_{ij} h W_i W_j \right) \qquad (24.9)$$

Example 24.3   Suppose we have $\alpha_1 = 0.15$, $\sigma_1 = 0.3$, $W_1 = \$3m$, $\alpha_2 = 0.18$, $\sigma_2 = 0.45$, $W_2 = \$5m$, and $\rho_{1,2} = 0.4$. The annual mean of the portfolio return is

$$\alpha_p = \frac{W_1 \alpha_1 + W_2 \alpha_2}{W_1 + W_2} = \frac{\$3m \times 0.15 + \$5m \times 0.18}{\$3m + \$5m} = 0.16875$$

The annual standard deviation of the portfolio return, σ_p, is

$$\sigma_p = \frac{\sqrt{W_1^2\sigma_1^2 + W_2^2\sigma_2^2 + 2W_1W_2\sigma_1\sigma_2\rho_{1,2}}}{W_1 + W_2}$$

$$= \frac{\sqrt{(\$3m \times 0.3)^2 + (\$5m \times 0.45)^2 + (2 \times \$3m \times \$5m \times 0.3 \times 0.45 \times 0.4)}}{\$3m + \$5m}$$

$$= 0.34216$$

Using equation (24.7), there is a 95% probability that in 1 week, the value of the porfolio will exceed

$$\$8m \times \left[(1 + \left(0.16875 \times \frac{1}{52}\right) + \left(0.34216 \times \sqrt{\frac{1}{52}} \times (-1.645)\right) \right] = \$7.40154m$$

The 1-week 95% VaR is therefore $\$7.40154m - \$8m = -\$0.5985m$. Using equation (24.8), which ignores the mean, we have a 95% chance that the value of the portfolio will exceed

$$\$8m \times \left(1 + 0.34216 \times \sqrt{\frac{1}{52}} \times (-1.645)\right) = \$7.3756m$$

The 1-week VaR is therefore $\$7.3756m - \$8m = -\$0.6244m$. ✺

This example illustrates the effects of diversification. Although stock 2, which constitutes more than half of the portfolio, has a standard deviation of 45%, the portfolio standard deviation is only about 34%. Problem 24.5 asks you to consider the effects of different correlations.

If there are n assets, the VaR calculation requires that we specify at least the standard deviation (and possibly the mean) for each stock, along with all pairwise correlations.

VaR for Nonlinear Portfolios

If a portfolio contains options as well as stocks, it is more complicated to compute the distribution of returns. Specifically, suppose the portfolio consists of n different stocks with ω_i shares of stock i worth $\omega_i S_i = W_i$. There are also N_i options worth $C(S_i)$ for each stock i. The portfolio value is therefore $W = \sum_{i=1}^{n}[\omega_i S_i + N_i C_i(S_i)]$. We cannot easily compute the exact distribution of this portfolio; not only is the sum of the lognormally distributed stock prices not lognormal, but the option price distribution is also complicated.

We will explore two different approaches to handling nonlinearity. First, we can create a linear approximation to the option price by using the option delta. Second, we can value the option using an appropriate option pricing formula and then perform Monte Carlo simulation to obtain the return distribution.[4]

Delta approximation If the return on stock i is $\tilde{\alpha}_i$, we can approximate the return on the option as $\Delta_i \tilde{\alpha}_i$, where Δ_i is the option delta. The expected annual return on the stock and option portfolio is then

$$R_p = \frac{1}{W} \sum_{i=1}^{n} \alpha_i S_i (\omega_i + N_i \Delta_i) \tag{24.10}$$

The term $\omega_i + N_i \Delta_i$ measures the exposure to stock i. The variance of the return is

$$\sigma_p^2 = \frac{1}{W^2} \sum_{i=1}^{n} \sum_{j=1}^{n} S_i S_j (\omega_i + N_i \Delta_i)(\omega_j + N_j \Delta_j) \sigma_i \sigma_j \rho_{ij} \tag{24.11}$$

With this mean and variance, we can mimic the n-stock analysis. First, however, we will compute an example with a single stock for which we know the exact solution.

Example 24.4   Suppose we own 30,000 shares of a nondividend-paying stock and have sold 105-strike call options, with 1 year to expiration, on 25,000 shares. The stock price is \$100, the stock volatility is 30%, the expected return on the stock is 15%, and the risk-free rate is 8%. The Black-Scholes option price is \$13.3397 and the value of the portfolio is

$$W = 30,000 \times \$100 - 25,000 \times \$13.3397 = \$2,666,507$$

(Since the written options are a liability, we subtract their value in computing the value of the portfolio.) The delta of the option is 0.6003. Using equations (24.10) and (24.11), we obtain $R_p = 0.084343$ and $\sigma_p = 0.16869$. The written options reduce the mean and volatility of the portfolio. Therefore, there is a 95% chance that the value of the portfolio in 1 week will exceed

$$\$2,666,507 \times \left(1 + 0.084343 \times \frac{1}{52} + 0.16869 \times \sqrt{\frac{1}{52}} \times (-1.645)\right)$$

$$= \$2,568,220 \tag{24.12}$$

Value at risk using the delta approximation is therefore $\$2,568,220 - \$2,666,507 = -\$98,287$.

----

[4]A third alternative is to use a delta-gamma approximation, which—as we saw in Chapter 13—is more accurate than a delta approximation. However, because the gamma term depends on the squared change in the stock price, the approximation is harder to implement than the delta approximation. The *Riskmetrics Technical Document* (Morgan/Reuters 1996, pp. 129–133) discusses an approach for implementing the delta-gamma approximation.

We can compute the exact value at risk by first determining the stock price that there is a 95% chance of exceeding, and then computing the exact portfolio value at that price. We are 95% sure to exceed the stock price

$$\$100 \times e^{(0.15-0.5\times0.3^2)\frac{1}{52}+0.3\sqrt{\frac{1}{52}}\times(-1.645)} = \$93.574$$

If this is the stock price 1 week later, the option price will be $9.5913, and the value of the portfolio will be

$$(\$93.574 \times 30,000) - (\$9.5913 \times 25,000) = \$2,576,438$$

The exact 95% value at risk is therefore $2,576,438 - $2,666,507 = -$99,069.

Figure 24.2 compares the exact value of the portfolio as a function of the stock price 7 days later, compared to the value implied by the delta approximation. The delta approximation is close, but the VaR derived using delta is slightly low. The delta approximation also fails to account for theta—the time decay in the option position. Because the option is written, time decay over the 1-week horizon increases the return of the portfolio. This increased return is barely perceptible in Figure 24.2 as the delta approximation lying below the exact portfolio line.

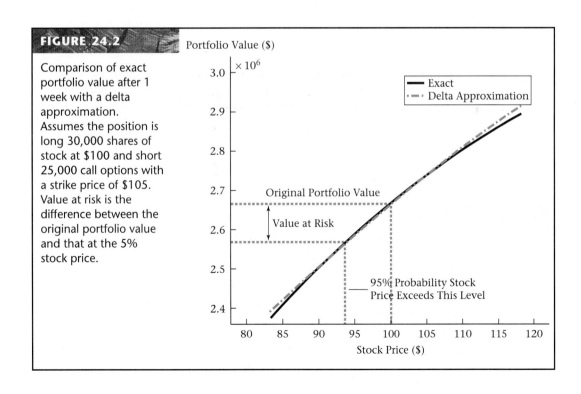

FIGURE 24.2

Comparison of exact portfolio value after 1 week with a delta approximation. Assumes the position is long 30,000 shares of stock at $100 and short 25,000 call options with a strike price of $105. Value at risk is the difference between the original portfolio value and that at the 5% stock price.

Example 24.5   Suppose we have two stocks along with written call options on those stocks. Information for the stocks and options is in Table 24.1. Using this information, we obtain a portfolio value of

$$W = (30{,}000 \times \$100) - (25{,}000 \times \$13.3397)$$
$$+ (50{,}000 \times \$100) - (60{,}000 \times 10.3511) = \$7{,}045{,}440$$

Using equations (24.10) and (24.11), the annual mean and standard deviation are 8.392% and 16.617%. There is a 95% chance that the portfolio value will exceed

$$W \times \left[1 + (R_p \times h) + (\sigma_p \times \sqrt{h} \times z)\right]$$

$$= \$7{,}045{,}440 \times \left[1 + 0.08392 \times \frac{1}{52} + 0.16617 \times \sqrt{\frac{1}{52}} \times (-1.645)\right] = \$6{,}789{,}740$$

The 95% value at risk over a 1-week horizon is therefore

$$\text{VaR} = \$6{,}789{,}740 - \$7{,}045{,}440 = -\$255{,}700$$

Monte Carlo simulation   The delta approximation can work poorly for nonlinear portfolios. For example, consider an at-the-money written straddle (a written call and written put, both with the same strike price). The straddle suffers a loss if the stock price increases or decreases, which is not a situation suited to a linear approximation. Because of losses from stock moves in either direction, we need a two-tailed approach to VaR. Monte Carlo simulation works well in this situation since the simulation produces the distribution of portfolio values.

To use Monte Carlo simulation in the case of a single stock, we randomly draw a set of stock prices as discussed in Chapter 19. For multiple stocks, we can use the appropriate parameters for each stock and use the Cholesky decomposition (see Section 19.8) to ensure the appropriate correlation among stock prices. Once we have the portfolio values corresponding to each draw of random prices, we sort the resulting portfolio values in ascending order. The 5% lower tail of portfolio values, for example, is used to compute the 95% value at risk.

TABLE 24.1   Information about two stocks and call options on those stocks. Assumes the risk-free rate is 8% and that neither stock pays a dividend. The correlation between the stocks is 0.4.

Stock	S	Stock Information # Shares	α	σ	Option Information $C(S)$	Strike	Δ	Expiration	# Shares
# 1	$100	30,000	0.15	0.30	$13.3397	$105	0.6003	1.0	−25,000
# 2	$100	50,000	0.18	0.45	$10.3511	$110	0.4941	0.5	−60,000

We will look at two examples in which we compute VaR for a position using Monte Carlo simulation. First we will examine a straddle on a single stock, and then a straddle-like position that contains a written call on one stock and a written put on the other.

Example 24.6 Consider the 1-week 95% value at risk of an at-the-money written straddle on 100,000 shares of a single stock. Assuming that $S = \$100$, $K = \$100$, $\sigma = 30\%$, $r = 8\%$, $T = 30$ days, and $\delta = 0$, the initial value of the straddle is −$685,776. Because the underlying asset is a single stock, we can compute the VaR of the position directly without Monte Carlo simulation. Figure 24.3 graphs the exact value of the straddle after 1 week, compared with its initial value.[5] The expected return on the stock is 15% in this calculation.

Table 24.2 shows a subset of the values plotted in Figure 24.3. Examine the boxed entries in Table 24.2. If the stock price declines, there is a 0.9% probability that the value of the position will be less than −$942,266. If the stock price rises, there is a 4% chance that the position value will be less than −$942,639. Thus, in total, there

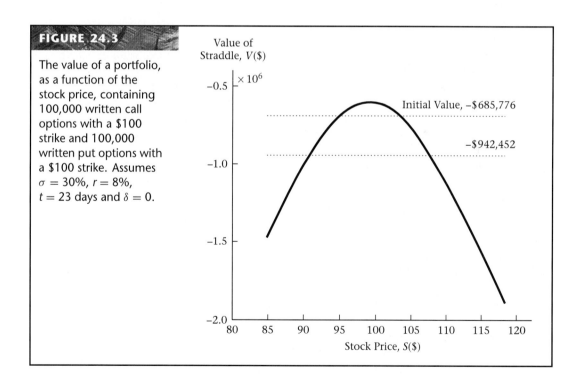

FIGURE 24.3

The value of a portfolio, as a function of the stock price, containing 100,000 written call options with a $100 strike and 100,000 written put options with a $100 strike. Assumes $\sigma = 30\%$, $r = 8\%$, $t = 23$ days and $\delta = 0$.

[5]The increase in value of the straddle if the stock price does not change is due to theta.

TABLE 24.2

Value of written straddle, V, for different stock prices, S. Values in the z column are standard normal values with the corresponding cumulative probabilities in the N(z) column. Over 1 week there is approximately a 5% probability that the stock price will be outside the range $90.87 − $107.77. The option values are computed using the Black-Scholes formula with $\sigma = 30\%$, $r = 8\%$, $t = 23$ days, and $\delta = 0$. The stock price movement assumes $\alpha = 15\%$.

z	S($)	V($)	N(z)	z	S($)	V($)	N(z)
−2.50	90.30	−985970	0.006	1.70	107.55	−926472	0.955
−2.45	90.49	−971234	0.007	1.75	107.77	−942639	0.960
−2.40	90.68	−956663	0.008	1.80	107.99	−959111	0.964
−2.35	90.87	−942266	0.009	1.85	108.22	−975880	0.968
−2.30	91.06	−928050	0.011	1.90	108.44	−992939	0.971
−2.25	91.25	−914023	0.012	1.95	108.67	−1010281	0.974
−2.20	91.44	−900192	0.014	2.00	108.90	−1027900	0.977
−2.15	91.63	−886566	0.016	2.05	109.12	−1045788	0.980
−2.10	91.82	−873152	0.018	2.10	109.35	−1063938	0.982
−2.05	92.01	−859958	0.020	2.15	109.58	−1082345	0.984
−2.00	92.20	−846992	0.023	2.20	109.81	−1101000	0.986
−1.95	92.39	−834263	0.026	2.25	110.03	−1119898	0.988
−1.90	92.59	−821779	0.029	2.30	110.26	−1139031	0.989
−1.85	92.78	−809547	0.032	2.35	110.49	−1158393	0.991
−1.80	92.97	−797576	0.036	2.40	110.72	−1177978	0.992
−1.75	93.17	−785875	0.040	2.45	110.95	−1197780	0.993
−1.70	93.36	−774450	0.045	2.50	111.19	−1217792	0.994

is a 4.9% probability of a loss in excess of about $942,452, which is the average of the boxed numbers. The 1-week 95% VaR is therefore approximately −$942,452 − (−$685,776) = −$256,676. Even in this one-stock example, calculating the VaR for this two-tailed position is not as simple as computing the stock prices that are exceeded with 2.5% probability.

Monte Carlo simulation simplifies the analysis. To use Monte Carlo we randomly draw a set of $z \sim \mathcal{N}(0, 1)$, and construct the stock price as

$$S_h = S_0 e^{(\alpha - \delta - 0.5\sigma^2)h + \sigma\sqrt{h}z} \qquad (24.13)$$

We compute the Black-Scholes call and put prices using each stock price, which gives us a distribution of straddle values. We then sort the resulting straddle values in ascending order. The 5% value is used to compute the 95% value at risk.

Figure 24.4 plots the histogram of values resulting from 100,000 random simulations of the value of the straddle. There is a 95% chance the straddle value will exceed −$943,028; hence, value at risk is −$943,028 − (−$685,776) = −$257,252. This result is very close to the value we inferred from Table 24.2.

As a second example we suppose that instead of the written put and call having the same underyling stock, they have different, correlated underlying stocks.

Example 24.7 Suppose that there are two stocks. Stock 1 is the same as the stock in Example 24.6. Stock 2 has the same parameters and a correlation of 0.40 with stock 1. Because the stocks have the same volatility and dividend yield, the initial option values are the same and the written straddle has an initial value of −$685,776. Based on 100,000 simulated prices for both stocks, the portfolio has a 95% chance of having a value greater than $1,135,421. Hence, the 95% value at risk is −$1,135,421 − (−$685,776) = −$449,645. The histogram for this calculation is in Figure 24.5.

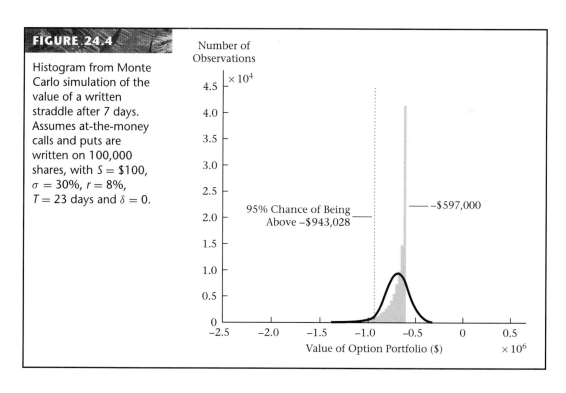

FIGURE 24.4

Histogram from Monte Carlo simulation of the value of a written straddle after 7 days. Assumes at-the-money calls and puts are written on 100,000 shares, with $S = \$100$, $\sigma = 30\%$, $r = 8\%$, $T = 23$ days and $\delta = 0$.

Number of Observations

95% Chance of Being Above −$943,028

−$597,000

Value of Option Portfolio ($)

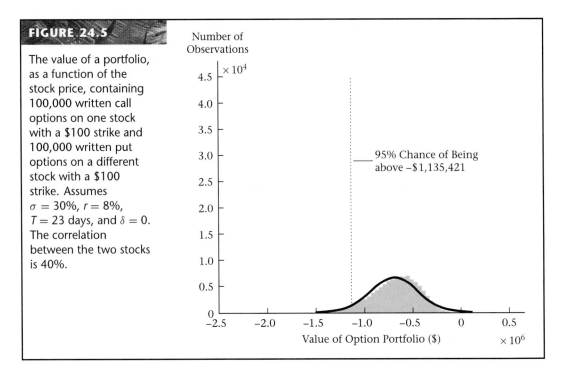

FIGURE 24.5

The value of a portfolio, as a function of the stock price, containing 100,000 written call options on one stock with a $100 strike and 100,000 written put options on a different stock with a $100 strike. Assumes $\sigma = 30\%$, $r = 8\%$, $T = 23$ days, and $\delta = 0$. The correlation between the two stocks is 40%.

Number of Observations

95% Chance of Being above –$1,135,421

Value of Option Portfolio ($)

A comparison of the results in Examples 24.6 and 24.7 shows that writing the straddle on two different stocks increases value at risk. If we examine the distributions in Figures 24.4 and 24.5, we can see why this happens.

Notice first that in Figure 24.4, the value of the portfolio never exceeds about –$597,000. The reason is that, since the call and put are written on the same stock, *stock price moves can never induce the two to appreciate together.* They can appreciate due to theta, but a change in the stock price will induce a gain in one option and a loss in the other. The same effect limits a loss, since the two options can never lose money together.

When the options are written on different stocks, as in Figure 24.5, it is possible for both to gain or lose simultaneously. As a result, the distribution of prices has a greater variance and increased value at risk.

As a final comment, all the value at risk calculations in this section assumed an expected return for the stocks that was positive and different from the risk-free rate. Because the horizon was only 7 days, the results are not too different from those obtained assuming the drift is zero or equal to the risk-free rate. For longer horizons the particular assumption would make more of a difference.

VaR for Bonds

In this section we see how to compute VaR for bonds, using information about the volatilities and correlations of yields for bonds at different maturities.

At any point in time there are numerous interest rate sensitive claims, including bonds, FRAs, and swaps, all of which can have different maturities and be denominated in different currencies. Moreover, bonds and interest rate claims have finite maturity, which means that, for a given claim, the historical volatility of that claim is not necessarily a good measure of prospective volatility. We can simplify the problem of risk modeling for interest-rate sensitive claims by recalling from Chapter 7 that all of these claims can be decomposed into zero-coupon bonds. Thus, the problem of assessing the risk of a bond, FRA, or swap reduces to one of decomposing the claim into its constitutent zero-coupon bonds and assessing the risk of these. The risk of the bond or other claim can then be measured as the risk of a portfolio of zero-coupon bonds.

We begin by seeing how to measure VaR for a zero-coupon bond. Suppose a zero-coupon bond matures at time T, has price $P(T)$, and that the annualized yield volatility of the bond is σ_T. For a zero-coupon bond, duration equals maturity. Thus, if the yield changes by ϵ, the percentage change in the bond price will be approximately ϵT. Using this linear approximation based on duration, and ignoring the mean return on the bond, over the horizon h the bond has a 95% chance of being worth more than

$$P(T)[1 + \sigma_T T \sqrt{h} \times (-1.645)]$$

Example 24.8 Suppose a bond has $T = 10$ years to maturity. Its yield to maturity is 5.5% and the annualized yield volatility is 1%. The one-week VaR on a $10m position in these bonds is

$$\$10\text{m} \times \left[1 + 0.01 \times 10 \times \sqrt{\frac{1}{52}} \times (-1.645) \right] - \$10\text{m} = -\$228,120 \qquad 🎋$$

Now suppose that instead of a single bond we have a portfolio of zero-coupon bonds. In particular, suppose we own W_1 of a bond maturing at T_1 with annualized yield volatility σ_{T_1} and W_2 of a bond maturing at T_2 with annualized yield volatility σ_{T_2}. Let ρ represent the correlation between the yields on the two bonds. (This yield volatility information could be estimated using historical data or using implied volatilities.) As with a portfolio of stocks, we can use the delta approximation, only here instead of two correlated stock returns we have two correlated bond yields.

Example 24.9 Let $T_1 = 10$, $T_2 = 15$, $\sigma_{T_1} = 0.01$, $\sigma_{T_2} = 0.012$ $\rho = 0.985$, $W_1 = \$6\text{m}$ and $W_2 = \$4\text{m}$. Since the portfolio is 60% invested in the 10-year bond and 40% invested in the 15-year bond, the variance of the bond portfolio is

$$(0.6 \times 0.01 \times 10)^2 + (0.4 \times 0.012 \times 15)^2$$

$$+ (2 \times 0.985 \times 0.6 \times 0.4 \times 0.01 \times 10 \times 0.012 \times 15) = 0.01729$$

The volatility is $\sqrt{0.01729} = 0.1315$. The 95% one-week VaR for this portfolio is therefore

$$\$10\text{m} \times [1 + 0.1315\sqrt{1/52} \times (-1.645)] - \$10\text{m} = -\$301,638 \qquad 🎋$$

We discussed in Chapter 23 the shortcomings of duration as a measure of bond price risk, so you might be wondering about the use of duration in these examples. Duration here is used mechanically to compute the price change for a bond for a given change in the bond's own yield. This is a delta approximation to the actual bond price change. The conceptual problem with duration arises when we use duration to compute a hedge ratio for *two* bonds. The hedge ratio calculation assumes that the yield to maturity for the two bonds changes by the same amount. By contrast, in Example 24.9 each bond has a different yield volatility and there is an imperfect correlation between the two yields; thus, we do *not* assume a parallel yield curve shift. (For a parallel yield curve shift we would need each bond to have the same annualized yield volatility and $\rho = 1$.)

In general, if we are analyzing the risk of an instrument with multiple cash flows, the first step is to find the equivalent portfolio of zero-coupon bonds. A 10-year bond with semiannual coupons is equivalent to a portfolio of 20 zero-coupon bonds. Every interest rate claim is decomposed in this way into interest rate "buckets" containing the claim's constituent zero-coupon bonds. A set of bonds and swaps reduces to a portfolio of long and short positions in zero-coupon bonds. We need volatilities and correlations for all these bonds.

As an empirical matter, the movement of a zero-coupon bond at an 8-year maturity, for example, is highly correlated with that of a zero-coupon bond at an 8 1/2-year maturity. Thus, for tractability, volatility and yields are tracked only at certain benchmark maturities: In Riskmetrics, these are 1, 3, 6, and 12 months, and 2, 3, 4, 5, 7, 9, 10, 15, 20, and 30 years. If we have a zero-coupon bond in the portfolio that does not exactly match a benchmark maturity, we want to determine the portfolio of the benchmark zero-coupon bonds that matches the characteristic of the nonbenchmark zero-coupon bond. The goal is to find an interpolation procedure to express any hypothetical zero-coupon bond in terms of the benchmark zero-coupon bonds. This procedure in which cash flows are allocated to benchmark claims (in this case zero-coupon bonds) is called **cash flow mapping.**

Suppose, for example, that we wish to assess the risk of a 12-year zero-coupon bond, given information on the 10-year and 15-year zero-coupon bonds. It is reasonable to use simple linear interpolation to obtain the yield and yield volatility for the 12-year bond from those of the 10-year and 15-year bonds. For example, if the yield and volatility of the t-year bond are y_t and σ_t, linear interpolation gives us

$$y_{12} = (0.6 \times y_{10}) + (0.4 \times y_{15}) \tag{24.14}$$

$$\sigma_{12} = (0.6 \times \sigma_{10}) + (0.4 \times \sigma_{15}) \tag{24.15}$$

These interpolations enable us to determine the price and volatility of $1 paid in year 12. In particular, the price is $e^{-y_{12} \times 12}$. However, we are not finished because these interpolations do *not* provide correlations between the 12-year zero and the adjacent benchmark bonds. We need these correlations because we could have a portfolio containing 10-, 12-, and 15-year bonds.

The next step is to ask what combination of the 10- and 15-year zero-coupon bonds would have the same volatility as the hypothetical 12-year bond. If we let ω equal the fraction allocated to the 10-year bond, we must solve

$$\sigma_{12}^2 = (\omega^2 \sigma_{10}^2) + [(1-\omega)^2 \sigma_{10}^2] + [2\rho_{10,15}\omega(1-\omega)\sigma_{10}\sigma_{15}] \tag{24.16}$$

Since this is a quadratic equation, there are two solutions for ω. Typically, as in the following example, one of the two solutions will be economically appealing and the other will seem unreasonable.

Example 24.10   Suppose we have a $1 cash flow occurring in year 12 and that we wish to map to the 10- and 15-year zero-coupon bonds. Suppose that $y_{10} = 5.5\%$, $y_{15} = 5.75\%$, $\sigma_{10} = 1\%$, $\sigma_{15} = 1.2\%$, and $\rho = 0.985$. The yield and volatility of the hypothetical 12-year zero-coupon bond are

$$y_{12} = (0.6 \times 0.055) + (0.4 \times 0.0575) = 0.056$$
$$\sigma_{12} = (0.6 \times 0.01) + (0.4 \times 0.012) = 0.0108$$

We next need to find the cash flow mapping that matches the volatility. Solving equation (24.16) gives the two solutions $\omega = 6.2097$ and $\omega = 0.5797$. The first solution maps the cash flow by going long 621% of the 10-year bond and short 520% of the 15-year bond. The second, more economically reasonable solution, entails going long 57.97% of the 10-year bond and 42.03% of the 15-year bond.   🌲

Notice that the solution $\omega = 0.5797$ is close to the 60%–40% split you might have guessed at the outset. Given these weights, value at risk for the 12-year bond can be computed in the same way as VaR for the bond portfolio in Example 24.9.

If you find this procedure confusing, recognize that if we had mapped the 12-year bond by assigning 60% of it to the 10-year bond and 40% to the 15-year bond, then *we would not have matched the yield and volatility given by equations (24.14) and (24.15).* Because of the nonlinear relationship between prices and yields, an interpolation based on the yield will give a different cash flow map than an interpolation based on prices.

Although we have discussed cash flow mapping in the context of bonds, mapping can be applied to any claim with multiple cash flows.

Conceptual Problems with VaR

VaR is relatively simple to compute and has a clear interpretation. However, Artzner et al. (1999) point out that there are conceptual problems with VaR. To understand the problems, suppose that the purpose of a risk measure is to decide how much capital is required to support an activity. Artzner et al. argue that a reasonable risk measure should have certain properties, among them **subadditivity.** If $\rho(X)$ is the risk measure associated with activity X (the capital required to support activity X), then ρ is subadditive if for two activities X and Y

$$\rho(X + Y) \le \rho(X) + \rho(Y) \tag{24.17}$$

This simply says that the risk measure for the two activities combined should be less than for the two activities separately. Because of diversification from combining activities, it makes sense that the capital required to support two activities together is less than that required to support the two separately. If capital requirements are imposed using a rule that is not subadditive, then firms can reduce required capital by splitting up activities.

VaR is not subadditive. To show this, Artzner et al. provide an example using out-of-the-money written cash-or-nothing options. Option A, a cash-or-nothing call, pays $1 if $S_T > H$, while option B, a cash-or-nothing put, pays $1 if $S_T < L$. Represent the premiums of the two options as P_A and P_B and suppose that either option has a 0.8% probability of paying off. The probability that either option expires out-of-the-money is 99.2%. Thus, for either option considered alone, 1% VaR is $-P_A$ (for option A) or $-P_B$ (for option B). At the 1% level, VaR is *negative* because there is only a 0.8% probability that the option will be exercised.

Now consider an option writer who sells both options. Because the two written options have the same underlying stock, they are perfectly negatively correlated. Therefore, the probability that one of the two options will be exercised is 0.8%+0.8% = 1.6%. In the lower 1% of the return distribution, one of the two options will be exercised for certain. The 1% VaR for the writer of the two options is therefore $1 - P_A - P_B$. We have

$$\rho(-A - B) = \$1 - P_A - P_B > -P_A - P_B = \rho(-A) + \rho(-B)$$

Since this expression has the opposite inequality as equation (24.17), VaR is not subadditive in this example.

One of the problems with VaR, which this example highlights, is that small changes in the VaR probability can cause VaR to change by a large amount. For the written cash-or-nothing call in this example, a 0.9% VaR is $-P_A$, while the 0.7% VaR is $1 - P_A$. If VaR were being used to determine required capital, you would not want a small change in the VaR probability to radically change the capital requirement from 0 (since the 0.9% VaR is negative) to positive (since the 0.7% VaR is positive).

As a different example that illustrates this point, suppose you are comparing activity C, which generates a $1 loss with a 1.1% probability, with activity D, which generates a $1m loss with a 0.9% probability. Any reasonable rule would require more capital for activity D, but a 1% VaR would be greater for C than for D.

One approach to improving VaR, discussed by Artzner et al., is to compute the average loss conditional upon the VaR loss being exceeded. This is called the **Tail VaR.** Because the Tail VaR takes into account the distribution of losses beyond the VaR level, it does not change abruptly when we change the VaR probability. (For example, the 1% Tail VaR for activity C would be $1, and the 1% Tail VaR for activity D would be $900,000 instead of the VaR of $0.)

We can use calculations from Chapter 18 to compute Tail VaR in the case of a lognormally distributed stock.

Example 24.11   Consider Example 24.1 on page 760, in which we computed the VaR of a stock. The 5% Tail VaR is computed using the conditional expectation of the portfolio value, conditional on the portfolio being worth less than $2.8072m. Using equation (18.28), the expectation of the price at time h, conditional upon S_0 and $S_h < K$ is

$$E(S_h|S_h \leq K) = \frac{S_0 e^{\alpha h} N(-d_1)}{N(-d_2)}$$

where

$$d_1 = \frac{ln(S_0/K) + (\alpha + 0.5\sigma^2)h}{\sigma\sqrt{h}}$$
$$d_2 = d_1 - \sigma\sqrt{h}$$

Using the same values as in Example 24.1, we obtain $E(S_h|S_h \leq K) = \$2.7592m$, for a Tail VaR of $2.7592m − $3m = −$0.2408m. ☙

Estimating Volatility

Volatility is the key input in any VaR calculation. We discussed in Chapter 18 how to estimate volatility given returns from a distribution with constant volatility. However, we also saw evidence in Chapter 18 that volatility is not constant. Volatility estimation is important, both for VaR and for derivative pricing in general. The goal here is to discuss some of the issues that arise in estimating volatility.

In most of the examples in this book, return volatility over the horizon h is $\sigma\sqrt{h}$, with σ constant. In addition to assuming that the volatility, σ, does not change, this calculation assumes that returns are independent over time.

If returns are negatively correlated over time, then high returns are followed by low returns. Other things equal, negative return correlation dampens volatility relative to the independent returns case. If returns are positively correlated, high returns follow high returns, which results in a higher volatility than in the independent returns case.

Assessing return correlation is complicated. To a first approximation, stock returns are independent over time. However, over horizons as short as a day, returns may be negatively correlated due to factors such as bid-ask bounce (if the end-of-day stock price you observed yesterday represented a sale of stock, it will be low because it was a sale; on average the closing price will be higher today since it could be either a purchase or a sale). There is some evidence of negative correlation at longer horizons, though the effect is more subtle.

With commodities, independence may or may not be a reasonable assumption, depending on the horizon. For example, high copper prices lead to increased supply and reduced demand, which eventually induces the price to fall. So return independence is not reasonable for long horizons. However, independence may be reasonable over shorter horizons, where supply and demand responses have not had time to occur.

Implied volatility   Option prices can be used to estimate implied volatility, which has the desirable characteristic of being a forward-looking measure of volatility. However, implied volatility is not readily available for some underlying assets. For VaR calculations we also need to know correlations between assets, for which there is no measure comparable to implied volatility. There is also a conceptual problem posed by volatility skew: If different options give different implied volatilities, which volatility should we use? Even with these caveats, implied volatilities are potentially valuable since, if they are sharply at odds with other volatility measures, this discrepancy is information that should be taken into account.

Historical volatility   Historical volatility estimates are typically used in VaR calculations. Figure 24.6 graphs two rolling 60-day measures of volatility. In the top panel, volatility is measured as

$$V_t = \sqrt{\frac{1}{n}\sum_{i=1}^{n} r_{t-i}^2} \tag{24.18}$$

where r_t is the daily continuously compounded return on day t and $n = 60$. The bottom panel displays a volatility estimate that gives more weight to recent observations:

$$\hat{V}_t = \sqrt{\sum_{i=1}^{n}\left[\frac{(1-\lambda)\lambda^{i-1}}{\sum_{j=1}^{n}(1-\lambda)\lambda^{j-1}}\right] r_{t-i}^2} \tag{24.19}$$

Again, $n = 60$ days. In both cases we ignore the mean, which is small for daily returns. V is the standard estimator for volatility, and $\hat{V}$ is an estimate that gives more weight to recent returns and less to 60-day-old returns. The term in square brackets in equation

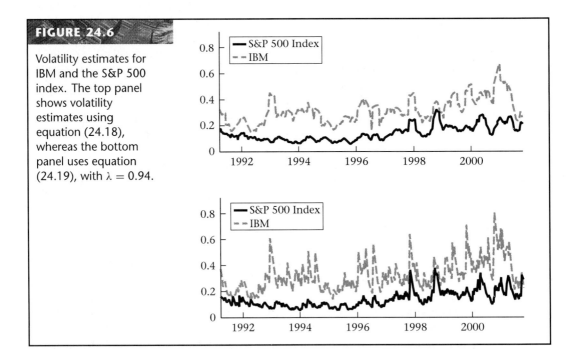

FIGURE 24.6

Volatility estimates for IBM and the S&P 500 index. The top panel shows volatility estimates using equation (24.18), whereas the bottom panel uses equation (24.19), with $\lambda = 0.94$.

(24.19) is the weight applied to historical returns. The weight declines at the rate λ, with the most recent return receiving the greatest weight. The estimator $\hat{V}$ is called an *exponential weighted moving average* (EWMA) estimate of volatility.

Research on the behavior of volatility shows that for many assets, high volatility tends to be followed by high volatility and low volatility by low volatility; there are periods of turbulence and periods of calm. Put differently, during a period when measured volatility is high, the typical day tends to exhibit high volatility. (High volatility could in principle also arise from an increased chance of large but infrequent price moves.) Figure 24.7 displays squared daily returns for the S&P 500 index and IBM. At a casual level, this figure exhibits this effect, with periods in which many of the daily squared returns are large, and periods when many are small.

If volatility is persistent, a volatility measure should weight recent returns more heavily than more distant returns. This difference in weighting is exactly how an EWMA volatility estimate differs from the ordinary equally weighted volatility measure. The different characteristics of equations (24.18) and (24.19) are evident in Figure 24.6. When there is a large return, the EWMA measure, $\hat{V}$, immediately jumps up, reflecting the large weight given to recent shocks (in the figure, $\lambda = 0.94$). The effect then decays. With the ordinary volatility estimator, V, the spikes in measured volatility are

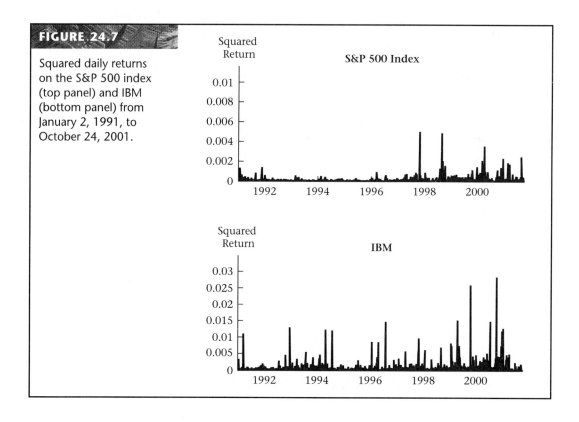

FIGURE 24.7

Squared daily returns on the S&P 500 index (top panel) and IBM (bottom panel) from January 2, 1991, to October 24, 2001.

less pronounced when there is a large return, but when a return drops out of the 60-day window (a 61-day return does not affect either measure), there is a noticeable fall in the volatility measure.

Looking at Figure 24.6, you might think from the number of large temporary spikes in the graph that the EWMA volatility estimator is too sensitive to a large 1-day return. Sometimes such a return does not portend a volatility increase on subsequent days. The search for more subtle and sophisticated volatility models has led to generalizations of the EWMA estimator, with acronyms like ARCH, GARCH, and EGARCH.[6] These models attempt to capture statistically the ebbs and flows of volatility.

Bootstrapping Return Distributions

It is possible to use observed past returns to create an empirical probability distribution of returns that can then be used for simulation. This procedure is called **bootstrapping.** The idea of bootstrapping is to sample, with replacement, from observed historical returns under the assumption that future returns will be drawn from the same distribution. So for example, if the stock price over a 5-day period has returns of $\{-0.02, 0.015, -0.01, 0.10, 0.03\}$, then this distribution can be bootstrapped by randomly selecting one of these returns each time a new 1-day return is needed. In effect, bootstrapping randomly shuffles past returns to create hypothetical future returns.

We have seen how the lognormal model has trouble accounting for events like the 1987 market crash. The advantage of bootstrapping is that, since it is not based on a particular assumed distribution, it is consistent with any distribution of returns. For example, if an event like a significant market crash occurs once every 10 years historically, it will occur on average once every 10 years in the bootstrapped distribution.

The disadvantage of bootstrapping is that key features of the data might be lost when the data are reshuffled. For example, if historical returns exhibit persistence in volatility, randomly reshuffled historical returns will not exhibit such persistence. There is also the question of how to bootstrap multiple series in such a way that correlations are preserved.

24.2 CREDIT RISK

Credit risk is the risk that a counterparty will fail to meet a contractual payment obligation. Most commonly, credit risk is the possibility that a counterparty—such as a bond issuer—will declare bankruptcy. Lenders have always tried to consider the possibility that a borrower will go bankrupt. The classic tools for dealing with bankruptcy include diversification across borrowers, collateral requirements, and statistical tests based on borrower characteristics designed to predict the likelihood of bankruptcy.

....

[6]"ARCH" stands for autoregressive conditional heteroskedasticity, "GARCH" is generalized ARCH, and "EGARCH" is exponential generalized ARCH. Bollerslev et al. (1994) survey the literature on these models.

In recent years there have been two developments that we will discuss in this section. First, there are credit-based derivatives claims, such as credit default swaps, that pay when a firm defaults, and thus effectively permit the trading of default risk. Second, the derivative pricing models we have developed can be adapted for modeling default.

Credit Derivatives

Value at risk is used to evaluate the *market risks* due to price changes in stocks, interest rates, currencies, and commodities. These are risks that generally can be hedged. We saw that an option market-maker, for example, will try to hedge the risk generated by the option positions that result from market-making. Hedging results in a lower value at risk, and thus frees capital for the market-maker to engage in additional transactions.

Many market-making activities also leave a market-maker exposed to credit risk. Credit derivatives, which have been trading since the early 1990s, are intended to allow institutions to hedge credit risk, in much the same way that, for example, gold futures permit the hedging of gold price risk. Credit derivatives are necessarily more complicated than gold futures, however. To understand the reason for this extra complexity, it will help to consider some examples.

The nature of credit risk Consider the credit risk in a standard forward contract. Suppose $S_0 = \$100$ and the effective annual interest rate is 8%. The theoretical forward price for the stock is therefore $108. Both the buyer and the seller have obligations to perform at maturity.

The buyer faces the risk from the seller not delivering, but only cares about a seller default *when the stock price exceeds $108*. If the seller were to default when the price is lower, the buyer would be able to buy the stock at less than the contracted price and thus would reap a windfall. Of course, when the price is lower the seller will deliver the stock as promised since it is worth less than the $108.[7]

The seller also faces risk due to the possibility that the buyer will default. However, the seller only cares about default when the price is below $108. If the buyer defaults at a higher price, the seller has a windfall from selling the stock at more than the contracted price. As before, however, we cannot expect a buyer default when the contract is profitable for the buyer.

Table 24.3 summarizes this discussion. From examining Table 24.3, it is apparent that credit risk on a forward contract is analogous to each party writing an option to the other. Suppose that the two parties enter into a forward contract at a price of $108. If the buyer defaults when the price is less than $108, the loss is as if the seller had written a put option with a strike price of $108. Similarly, if the seller defaults when the price is greater than $108, it is as if the buyer had written a call option at a strike of $108. If

---

[7]Typically a company in default will collect on payments it is owed from in-the-money swaps and forwards.

TABLE 24.3	The credit risks for a forward contract when either party defaults.		
	Stock Price at Maturity		
Occurrence	$S_1 > \$108$	$S_1 < \$108$	**Option Equivalent**
Seller Loss If Buyer Defaults	$0	$\$108 - S_1$	Written Put at $108
Buyer Loss If Seller Defaults	$S_1 - \$108$	$0	Written Call at $108

the loss in default is uncorrelated with the likelihood of default, than the *ex ante* cost of credit risk is the value of the option times the probability that the company defaults.

Suppose that the forward buyer in this example wanted to enter into a derivative that eliminated credit risk—a default option. This derivative would pay $S_1 - \$108$ if the seller defaulted. The buyer would have to pay an option premium to acquire this protection. In practice the premium is often amortized and paid as an annuity. This kind of structure—small periodic payment and potentially large payment if the default occurs—is typical of default swaps.

The structure of a default swap   Default swaps are typically used to protect the owner of a bond against default by the issuer of the bond. Suppose that an investor owns a bond issued by XYZ. A perfect hedge of the bond's credit risk, which is in theory what a default swap accomplishes, would convert the bond into the economic equivalent of a Treasury bond. We will refer to the market-maker providing the default insurance as the *swap writer*. The investor (the owner of the bond) will pay a premium to the swap writer; this premium payment can be a lump sum or amortized. (In practice the premium is usually amortized and the premium payments stop once default occurs.)

Figure 24.8 illustrates the cash flows and parties involved in a credit default swap. Note in particular that there is no connection between XYZ and the swap writer. The default swap must specify a specific XYZ debt issue, called the *reference asset*. The reference asset matters because, for example, senior secured and junior unsecured debt can have different prices after a default.

If there is an actual default, the default swap could settle either financially or physically. In a financial settlement, the swap writer would pay the bondholder the value of the loss on the bond. The bondholder would continue to hold the defaulted bond. In a physical settlement, the swap writer would buy the defaulted bond at the price it would have in the absence of default.

Financial settlement and physical settlement are economically equivalent in theory. However, the market for a defaulted corporate bond may not be liquid, and it may be difficult to determine a fair price upon which to base financial settlement. To avoid this problem, default swaps often call for, or at least permit, physical settlement.

Finally, recognize that there is credit risk in the default swap. The default swap buyer faces the possibility that the swap writer will go bankrupt at the same time as a

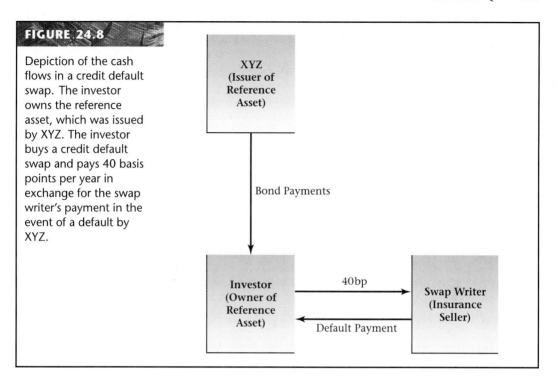

FIGURE 24.8

Depiction of the cash flows in a credit default swap. The investor owns the reference asset, which was issued by XYZ. The investor buys a credit default swap and pays 40 basis points per year in exchange for the swap writer's payment in the event of a default by XYZ.

default occurs on the reference asset. The default swap market does permit investors to trade exposure to particular credits, but there is still default risk.

Credit-linked notes   Banks can issue securities known as credit-linked notes to hedge the credit risk of loans. A **credit-linked note** is a bond issued by one company with payments that depend upon the credit status (for example, bankrupt or not) of a different company. To see how a credit-linked note works, suppose that bank ABC lends money to company XYZ. At the time of the loan, ABC creates a trust that in turn issues notes bought by investors. These notes are the credit-linked notes. The funds raised by the issuance of these notes are invested in bonds with a low probability of default (such as government bonds), which are held in the trust. If XYZ remains solvent, ABC is obligated to pay the notes in full. If XYZ goes bankrupt, the note-holders receive the XYZ loans and become creditors of XYZ. ABC takes possession of the securities in the trust. Thus, the credit-linked note is in effect a bond issued by ABC, which ABC does not need to repay in full if XYZ goes bankrupt.

Because of the trust, the credit-linked notes can be paid in full even if ABC defaults. Thus, even though they are issued by ABC, the interest rate on the notes is determined by the credit risk of XYZ. An arrangement like this was used by Citigroup when it made loans to Enron in 2000 and 2001.[8] When Enron went bankrupt in late 2001, Citigroup avoided losses on over $1 billion in loans because it had hedged the loans by issuing credit-linked notes.

The structure of the credit-linked note might remind you of the Oriental Land Co. earthquake bond, discussed in Chapter 1. In both structures, the issuer is not obligated to repay the bond if a specified event occurs. This structure eliminates a third-party insurance provider.

Pricing a default swap How is the premium on a default swap determined? A simple argument suggests that the default swap premium should equal the difference between the yield on the reference asset and the yield on an otherwise equivalent default-free bond. We will first make this argument and then offer some qualifications.

Suppose the reference asset is at par and pays the coupon rate c, and the default-free interest rate is r. The cash flows from the reference bond are c per period and $1 + c$ at maturity. The default-free bond pays r per period and $1 + r$ at maturity. The difference $c - r$ is called the *credit spread* on the reference asset. Denote the price of the bond out of default as B and in default as B_D. If the bond defaults, the default swap typically pays based on 100% of the value of the bond:

$$\text{Default swap payment} = 1 - B_D \tag{24.20}$$

Let ρ be the per-period premium on the default swap. An investor who buys the reference asset and a credit default swap with the same maturity as the reference asset receives $c - \rho$ each period and $1 + c - \rho$ at maturity. If the bond defaults, the investor can sell the defaulted bond for B_D, receives $1 - B_D$ from the swap, and can buy a default-free bond paying r.

If $\rho = c - r$, i.e., if the swap premium is the credit spread, then an investor is indifferent between buying the default-free bond on the one hand and the reference asset plus a credit default swap. This argument suggests that one way to think about an ordinary bond subject to default is that the investor who owns the bond is receiving the default-free rate plus the credit default swap premium. By holding a defaultable bond without hedging the credit risk, it is as if the investor bought Treasury bonds and wrote a credit default swap.

The idea that the default swap premium should equal the credit spread seems straightforward. Pricing is more complicated than this, however. First, consider a swap writer who wants to hedge the written swap, a situation described by Rooney (1998). The swap writer will buy a synthetic default swap by short-selling the reference asset and buying the equivalent default-free bond. The costs of short-selling, described in Chapter 1, will be reflected in the price of the default swap.

Second, what exactly is an "otherwise equivalent default-free bond"? It seems natural to use government bonds as a benchmark, but government bonds can be unique in certain respects. Prices of government bonds may include a liquidity premium and

....

[8] See "How Citigroup Hedged Bets on Enron" by Daniel Altman, *New York Times*, p. C1, Feb. 8, 2002.

sometimes reflect special tax attributes (for example, in the United States, federal government bonds are exempt from state taxes). Houweling and Vorst (2001) estimate a credit swap pricing model and find that, empirically, credit swap premiums are more related to the interest rate swap curve than to the government bond yield curve. This linkage between credit swaps and interest rate swaps suggests that the yield on an "equivalent default-free bond" is not the government bond curve, and in fact may not be directly observable. Rather the equivalent default-free yield may be inferred from the market for default swaps as the rate on the reference asset less the default swap premium.

This description of pricing takes as given the credit spread on the reference asset. What determines the credit spread? We now turn to that issue.

Credit Pricing Models

We will first discuss the pricing of credit risk at a general level, and then describe two different approaches to implementing credit pricing models.

The starting point for pricing credit risk is understanding what happens when a firm defaults. Consider firm XYZ, which has the following capital structure:

Assets	Liabilities
Assets	Bank Debt
	Senior Secured Debt
	Junior Unsecured Debt
	Equity

Suppose that XYZ declares bankruptcy. The bankruptcy process can proceed in different ways, but ultimately the debt claims are settled, usually for less than the stated amount of the debt. The amount the debt-holders receive as a fraction of what they are owed is called the **recovery value.**

Determining the price of a bond or the terms of a default swap entails modeling the occurrence of bankruptcy (with what probability and at what time the bankruptcy occurs) and the recovery value (how much the bondholder of a bankrupt firm receives).

Ratings transitions   Bond ratings are attempts to assess the probability that a company will default. Ratings are assigned to bonds by ratings agencies such as Moody's and Standard and Poor's. One way to measure bankruptcy probabilities is by looking at the frequency with which bonds experiences a ratings change, also called a **ratings transition.** Table 24.4 summarizes the probability that a firm in a given ratings category will switch to another ratings category over the course of a year.[9] Highly rated firms are unlikely to suffer a default. The default probability increases as the rating decreases.

----

[9]A rating can be withdrawn if the rated obligation has matured or if the ratings agency deems there is insufficient information for a rating.

TABLE 24.4			Moody's average 1-year credit ratings transition matrix, 1920 to 1996. "WR" stands for "withdrawn rating."						
Rating From:	**Aaa**	**Aa**	**A**	**Baa**	**Ba**	**B**	**Caa-C**	**Default**	**WR**
Aaa	88.32%	6.15%	0.99%	0.23%	0.02%	0.00%	0.00%	0.00%	4.29%
Aa	1.21%	86.76%	5.76%	0.66%	0.16%	0.02%	0.00%	0.06%	5.36%
A	0.07%	2.30%	86.09%	4.67%	0.63%	0.10%	0.02%	0.12%	5.99%
Baa	0.03%	0.24%	3.87%	82.52%	4.68%	0.61%	0.06%	0.28%	7.71%
Ba	0.01%	0.08%	0.39%	4.61%	79.03%	4.96%	0.41%	1.11%	9.39%
B	0.00%	0.04%	0.13%	0.60%	5.79%	76.33%	3.08%	3.49%	10.53%
Caa-C	0.00%	0.02%	0.04%	0.34%	1.26%	5.29%	71.87%	12.41%	8.78%

Source: Carty (1997).

Under the assumption that ratings transitions are independent (i.e., the probability of moving from one rating to another in a given year does not depend on the rating in a previous year), we can use Table 24.4 to compute the probability that after s years a firm will transit from one rating to another. Let $p(i, t; j, t + s)$ denote the probability that, over an s-year horizon, a firm will move from the rating in row i to that in column j. The entries in Table 24.4 give us $p(i, t; j, t + 1)$. Suppose there are n ratings. Over 2 years, the probability of moving from rating i to rating j is

$$p(i, t; j, t + 2) = \sum_{k=1}^{n} p(i, t; k, t + 1) \times p(k, t + 1; j, t + 2)$$

From the 2-year transitions we can go to 3 years, and then 4, and so on. Given the $s - 1$-year transition probabilities, the s-year transition probability is

$$p(i, t; j, t + s) = \sum_{k=1}^{n} p(i, t; k, t + s - 1) \times p(k, t + s - 1; j, t + s) \qquad (24.21)$$

Thus, a transition probability matrix can be used to tell us the probability that a firm will go bankrupt after a given period of time.

The Merton default model   The ratings transition approach uses history to model default. Since default is relatively rare, the transition model cannot be expected to provide a model that is attuned to the idiosyncracies of a given firm. A different approach to modeling credit risk is to recognize that market-determined bond and stock prices implicitly reflect the market's belief about the statistical distribution governing the value of the firm. Using option pricing theory, it is possible to extract that implicit distribution from observed prices.

Recall the discussion in Section 16.1, in which we viewed corporate securities as options, and we saw in particular that debt is a put option. If we assume that the assets of the firm are lognormally distributed, then we can use the lognormal probability calculations of Chapter 18 to compute either the risk-neutral or actual probability that the firm will go bankrupt. This approach to bankruptcy modeling has come to be called the Merton model since Merton (1974) used continuous-time methods to provide the first comprehensive model of the credit spread.

Specifically, suppose we assume that the assets of the firm, A, follow the process

$$\frac{dA}{A} = \mu dt + \sigma dZ \tag{24.22}$$

Suppose we assume also that the firm has issued a single zero-coupon bond that matures at time T and makes no payouts. If the promised payment on the bond is $\bar{B}$, then the probability of bankruptcy at time T, conditional on the value of assets at time t, is

$$Prob(A_T < \bar{B}; A_t) = N\left[-\frac{ln(A_t/\bar{B}) + (\mu - \frac{1}{2}\sigma^2)(T-t)}{\sigma\sqrt{T-t}}\right] \tag{24.23}$$

The expected recovery value, conditional on default, is

$$E(A_T|A_T < \bar{B}) = A_t e^{\mu t} \frac{N\left[-\frac{ln(A_t/\bar{B}) + (\mu + \frac{1}{2}\sigma^2)(T-t)}{\sigma\sqrt{T-t}}\right]}{N\left[-\frac{ln(A_t/\bar{B}) + (\mu - \frac{1}{2}\sigma^2)(T-t)}{\sigma\sqrt{T-t}}\right]}$$

This is the same as equation (18.28). In order to use these equations to price credit default swaps, we would replace the actual asset drift, μ, with the risk-free rate, r, and discount at the risk-free rate. For example, if we replace μ with r in equation (24.23), we obtain the risk-neutral probability of default. Discounting this probability at the risk-free rate gives us the value of a security that pays $1 when the firm defaults.

More complex models can permit bankruptcy before maturity. For example, it is possible that bankruptcy will occur if assets fall to a certain level, say $\underline{A}$, prior to maturity. (Black and Cox (1976) refer to this as a "safety covenant.") In this case the equity is a call option that knocks out if $A \leq \underline{A}$.

The information in equation (24.22) is not directly observable, but rather can be inferred from observing the traded assets of the firm, namely the debt and equity. Given the contractual characteristics of the firm's debt issues and a process like that in equation (24.22), we can in theory determine the price and volatility of debt and equity. The volatility of debt and equity, and the debt-equity ratio, are all observable. Thus, we can turn the pricing process around and infer the A and σ that give rise to observed prices.

The difficulty with the Merton model is implementing it for real capital structures and the real default decisions. Firms issue numerous securities, some of which are complex. Also, the decision to default is not mechanical, but results from business judgment, which can be difficult to model.

CHAPTER SUMMARY

Value at risk is used to measure and manage risk, for example, in computing capital requirements. The p-percent n-day value at risk of a portfolio is the level of loss that will be exceeded $1 - p$ percent of the time over a horizon of n days. Computing value at risk requires approximating the return distribution of the portfolio, which in turn requires information on the variance and covariance of assets in the portfolio. When portfolios are simple, for example, containing only stocks, standard portfolio risk calculations can be used to compute VaR. When portfolios contain options and other nonlinear assets, Monte Carlo simulation is commonly used to assess the return distribution of the portfolio. It is possible to construct examples in which VaR is an ill-behaved risk measure. Tail VaR, which takes into account the distribution of losses beyond the VaR level, may provide better alternatives.

VaR deals primarily with so-called "market risks": Price changes of stocks, currencies, interest rates, and commodities. Credit risk is another important source of risk for financial institutions and investors. Credit default swaps permit hedging default risk. One approach to credit risk modeling is based on estimated ratings transition probabilities, together with estimates of recovery values (the fraction of a bond's value that is received by bondholders in a default). Another approach treats a firm's securities as options, with the underlying asset being the assets of the firm. Relative to the ratings transition approach, the option approach has the advantage of using market information about the specific company, and the disadvantage of being difficult to implement.

FURTHER READING

The *Riskmetrics Technical Document* (J. P. Morgan/Reuters, 1996) is available from **www.riskmetrics.com**. It was distributed by J. P. Morgan—and now by Riskmetrics—to explain VaR, illustrate some of the calculations behind VaR, and explain some of the judgments behind the particular set of calculations. The document was influential and remains worth reading. Artzner et al. (1999) offer some important warnings about the use of VaR as a decision-making tool.

Jorion (2001) provides a broad overview of the regulatory, practical, and analytical issues in computing value at risk. Bollerslev et al. (1994) is a fairly technical review of the literature on ARCH-style models.

Sources on credit risk and credit default swaps include Tavakoli (1998), Credit Suisse Financial Products (1997), Morgan (1997), and Rooney (1998). KMV sells credit assessments based on market information about companies and has white papers on their website, **www.kmv.com**. These papers describe the KMV approach, which is a Merton-style approach. A debate between advocates and critics of the KMV approach is in the February 2002 issue of *Risk* (Kealhofer and Kurbat, 2002, and Keenan, 2002).

PROBLEMS

In the following problems, assume that the risk-free rate is 0.08 and that there are three stocks with a price of $100 and the following characteristics:

	α	σ	δ	Correlation with B	Correlation with C
Stock A	0.15	0.30	0.00	0.25	0.20
Stock B	0.18	0.45	0.02	1.00	0.30
Stock C	0.16	0.50	0.00	0.30	1.00

24.1. Consider the expression in equation (24.6). What is the exact probability that, over a 1-day horizon, stock A will have a loss?

24.2. Assuming a $10m investment in one stock, compute the 95% and 99% VaR for stocks A and B over 1-day, 10-day, and 20-day horizons.

24.3. Assuming a $10m investment that is 40% stock A and 60% stock B, compute the 95% and 99% VaR for the position over 1-day, 10-day, and 20-day horizons.

24.4. What are 95% and 99% 1-, 10- and 20-day VaRs for a portfolio that has $4m invested in stock A, $3.5m in stock B, and $2.5m in stock C?

24.5. Using the same assumptions as in example 24.3, compute VaR with and without the mean assuming correlations of $-1, -0.5, 0, 0.5$, and 1. Is risk eliminated with a correlation of -1? If not, why not?

24.6. Using the delta-approximation method and assuming a $10m investment in stock A, compute the 95% and 99% 1-, 10-, and 20-day VaRs for a position consisting of stock A plus one 105-strike put option for each share. Use the same assumptions as in Example 24.4.

24.7. Repeat the previous problem, only use Monte Carlo simulation.

24.8. Compute the 95% 10-day VaR for a written strangle (sell an out-of-the-money call and an out-of-the-money put) on 100,000 shares of stock A. Assume the options have strikes of $90 and $110 and have 1 year to expiration. Use the delta-approximation method and Monte Carlo simulation. What accounts for the difference in your answers?

24.9. Using Monte Carlo, compute the 95% and 99% 1-, 10-, and 20-day Tail VaRs for the position in Problem 2.

24.10. Compute the 95% 10-day Tail VaR for the position in Problem 8.

24.11. Suppose you write a 1-year cash-or-nothing put with a strike of $50 and a 1-year cash-or-nothing call with a strike of $215, both on stock A.

    a. What is the 1-year 99% VaR for each option separately?

    b. What is the 1-year 99% VaR for the two written options together?

    c. What is the 1-year 99% Tail VaR for each option separately and the two together?

24.12. Suppose the 7-year zero-coupon bond has a yield of 6% and yield volatility of 10% and the 10-year zero-coupon bond has a yield of 6.5% and yield volatility of 9.5%. The correlation between the 7-year and 10-year yields is 0.96. What are 95% and 99% 10-day VaRs for an 8-year zero-coupon bond that pays $10m at maturity?

24.13. Using the same assumptions as in Problem 12, compute the 10-day 95% VaR for a claim that pays $3m each year in years 7–10.

For the next two problems, use this information on credit ratings. Suppose there are three credit ratings, F (first-rate), FF (future failure?), and FFF (fading, forlorn, and forsaken). The transition matrix between ratings looks like this:

	Rating To:		
Rating From:	**F**	**FF**	**FFF**
F	.9	.07	.03
FF	.15	.80	.05
FFF	.10	.30	.6

24.14. Consider a firm with an F rating.

    a. What is the probability that after 4 years it will still have an F rating?

    b. What is the probability that after 4 years it will have an FF or FFF rating?

    c. From examining the transition matrix, are firms tending over time to become rated more or less highly? Why?

24.15. Consider two firms, one with an FF rating and one with an FFF rating. What is the probability that after 4 years each will have retained its rating? What is the probability that each will have moved to one of the other two ratings?

24.16. A firm has assets of $100, with $\sigma = 40\%$, $\alpha = 15\%$, and $\delta = 0$. The risk-free rate is 8%. There is a single outstanding debt issue with a promised maturity payment of $120 in 5 years. Assume that banktrupcy occurs if assets in year 5 are less than $120. What is the probability of bankruptcy over the life of the bond? What is the credit spread?

24.17. Make the same assumptions as in Problem 16, except assume that bankruptcy is triggered by assets (which are observable) falling below $40 in value at any time over the life of the bond, or by assets being worth less than $120 at maturity. What is the probability of bankruptcy over the life of the bond? What is the credit spread?

PART 6

APPENDICES

Appendix A

The Greek Alphabet

The use of Greek letters is common in writing about derivatives and mathematics in general. Important concepts in this book are option characteristics that have the names of Greek letters such as "delta" and "gamma."

Table A.1 presents the complete Greek alphabet, including both lowercase and uppercase forms. Some of the letters look like their Roman counterparts. Not all of these symbols will be used in the book.

TABLE A.1   The Greek alphabet.

alpha	α	A	nu	ν	N
beta	β	B	xi	ξ	Ξ
gamma	γ	Γ	omicron	o	O
delta	δ	Δ	pi	π	Π
epsilon	ϵ	E	rho	ρ	P
zeta	ζ	Z	sigma	σ	Σ
eta	η	H	tau	τ	T
theta	θ	Θ	upsilon	υ	Υ
iota	ι	I	phi	ϕ	Φ
kappa	κ	K	chi	χ	X
lambda	λ	Λ	psi	ψ	Ψ
mu	μ	M	omega	ω	Ω

Appendix B

Continuous Compounding

In this book we use both effective annual interest rates and continuously compounded interest rates. These are simply different conventions for expressing the same idea: If you invest $1 today, how much will you have after 1 year? One simple unambiguous way to answer this question is using zero-coupon bonds. If you invest $1 in zero-coupon bonds costing $P(0, T)$ for a $1 maturity payoff at time T, then at time T you will have $1/P(0, T)$ dollars. However, it is more common to answer the question using interest rates rather than zero-coupon bond prices.

Interest rates measure the rate of appreciation of an investment, but there are innumerable ways of quoting interest rates. Continuous compounding turns out to provide a particularly simple quoting convention, though it may not seem so simple at first. Since in practice option pricing formulas and other financial formulas make use of continuous compounding, it is important to be comfortable with it.

You might think that continuous compounding is not much used in the real world and, hence, there is no point in using it when studying derivatives. It is true that an auto dealer is likely to give you a blank stare if you inquire about the continuously compounded loan rate for your new car. However, continuous compounding does have advantages, and it is not often appreciated that almost *all* interest rate quoting conventions are complicated, some devilishly so. (If you doubt this, read Appendix 7.A, especially equation (7.15)).

B.1 THE LANGUAGE OF INTEREST RATES

We begin with definitions. There are two terms that we will use often to refer to interest rates:

Effective annual rate If r is quoted as an **effective annual rate,** this means that if you invest $1, n years later you will have $(1 + r)^n$. If you invest x_0 and earn x_n n years later, then the implied effective annual rate is $(x_n/x_0)^{1/n} - 1$.

Continously compounded rate If r is quoted as an annualized **continuously compounded rate,** this means that if you invest $1, n years later you will have e^{rn}. If you invest x_0 and earn x_n n years later, then the implied annual continuously compounded rate is $ln(x_n/x_0)/n$.

Let's look at this definition in more detail.

B.2 THE LOGARITHMIC AND EXPONENTIAL FUNCTIONS

Interest rates are typically quoted as "$r\%$ per year, compounded n times per year." As every beginning finance student learns, this has the interpretation that you will earn an interest rate of r/n per period for n periods. Thus, if you invest \$1 today, in 1 year you will have

$$\left(1 + \frac{r}{n}\right)^n$$

In T years you will have

$$\left(1 + \frac{r}{n}\right)^{nT} \tag{B.1}$$

What happens if we let n get very large, that is, if interest is compounded many times a year (even daily or hourly)? If, for example, the interest rate is 10%, after 3 years we will have

- $(\$1 + 0.1)^3 = \$1.331$ with annual compounding,

- $(\$1 + 0.1/12)^{36} = \$1.3482$ with monthly compounding,

- $(\$1 + 0.1/365)^{1095} = \$1.34980$ with daily compounding, and

- $(\$1 + 0.1/8760)^{26280} = \$1.349856$ with hourly compounding.

The exponential function, e, is a constant approximately equal to 2.71828. If compounding is *continuous*, that is, if interest accrues every instant, then we can use the exponential function to compute future values. For example, with a 10% continuously compounded rate, after 3 years we will have a future value of

$$e^{0.1 \times 3} = \$1.349859$$

Notice that assuming continuous compounding gives us a result very close to that assuming daily compounding. In Excel, we compute continuously compounded results using the built-in exponential function, *exp*. The above example is computed as exp(0.1 × 3).

Why does the exponential function work? The number e is *defined* as

$$e^{rT} \equiv \lim_{n \to \infty} \left(1 + \frac{r}{n}\right)^{nT} \tag{B.2}$$

Thus, the expression defining e is the same expression used for interest compounding calculations, equation (B.1)! By using e, you can compute a future value.

If you know how much you have earned from a \$1 investment, you can determine the continuously compounded rate of return by using the natural logarithm, *ln*. *Ln* is the *inverse* of the exponential function in that it takes a dollar amount and gives you a rate of return. In other words, if you apply the logarithmic function to the exponential function, you compute the original argument to the exponential function. Here is an example:

$$ln(e^{rt}) = rt$$

Example B.1 Suppose you have a zero-coupon bond that matures in 5 years. The price today is $62.092 for a bond that pays $100. The annually compounded rate of return is

$$(\$100/\$62.092)^{1/5} - 1 = 0.10$$

The continuously compounded rate of return is

$$\frac{ln(\$100/\$62.092)}{5} = \frac{0.47655}{5} = 0.09531$$

The continuously compounded rate of return of 9.53% corresponds to the annually compounded rate of return of 10%. To verify this, observe that

$$e^{0.0953} = 1.10$$

Finally, note that

$$ln(e^{0.0953}) = 0.0953 \qquad ≸$$

Changing Interest Rates

When we multiply exponentials, exponents add. So we have

$$e^x e^y = e^{x+y}$$

Suppose you can invest for 4 years, earning a continuouously compounded return of 5% the first 2 years and 6% the second 2 years. If you invest $1 today, after 4 years you will have

$$e^{2\times0.05} e^{2\times0.06} = e^{0.10+0.12} = \$1.2461$$

We could of course do the same calculation using effective annual rates. For the first 2 years we earn $e^{0.05} - 1 = 5.127\%$, and for the second 2 years, $e^{0.06} = 6.184\%$. The future value of $1 is

$$1.05127^2 1.06184^2 = \$1.2461$$

This calculation gives us the same answer.

What is the average annual rate earned over the 4 years? The average annual continously compounded rate is

$$\frac{1}{4}ln(1.24608) = 0.055$$

which is the average of 5% and 6%.

However, if we express the answer in terms of effective annual rates, we get

$$1.24608^{0.25} - 1 = 5.6541\%$$

This is *not* the average of 5.127% and 6.184%, which is 5.6554. This makes calculations with continuous compounding easier.

Symmetry for Increases and Decreases

On March 4, 1999, the NASDAQ composite index closed at 2292.89. On March 10, 2000, the index closed at 5048.62. On January 2, 2001, the index closed at 2291.86, essentially the same level as in March 1999. The percentage increase from March 1999 to March 2000 was

$$\frac{5048.62}{2292.89} - 1 = 120.19\%$$

The subsequent decrease was

$$\frac{2291.86}{5048.62} - 1 = -54.60\%$$

When computing simple rates of return, a price can have an increase exceeding 100%, but its decrease can never be less than 100%.

We can do the same calculations using continuous compounding. The continuously compounded increase from March 1999 to March 2000 was

$$ln(5043.62/2292.89) = 78.93\%$$

while the subsequent decrease was

$$ln(2291.86/5048.62) = -78.97\%$$

When using continuous compounding, increases and decreases are symmetric.

Moreover, if the index dropped to 1000, the continuously compounded return from the peak would be

$$ln(1000/5048.62) = -161.91\%$$

Continuously compounded returns can be less than -100%.

PROBLEMS

B.1.   **a.** A bond costs $67,032 today and pays $100,000 in 5 years. What is its continuously compounded rate of return?

b. A bond costs $50 today, pays $100 at maturity, and has a continuously compounded annual return of 10%. In how many years does it mature?

c. An investment of $5 today pays a continuously compounded rate of 7.5%/year. How much money will you have after 7 years?

d. A stock selling for $100 is worth $5 1 year later. What is the continuously compounded return over the year? What if the stock price is $4? $3? $2? What would the stock price after 1 year have to be in order for the continuously compounded return to be -500%?

B.2. Suppose that over 1 year a stock price increases from $100 to $200. Over the subsequent year it falls back to $100.

a. What is the arithmetic return [i.e., $(S_{t+1} - S_t)/S_t$] over the first year? What is the continuously compounded return [i.e., $ln(S_{t+1}/S_t)$]?

b. What is the arithmetic return over the second year? The continuously compounded return?

c. What do you notice when you compare the first- and second-year returns computed arithmetically and continuously?

B.3. Here are stock prices on 6 consecutive days: $100, $47, $88, $153, $212, $100. Note that the cumulative return over the 6 days is 0.

   a. What are the arithmetic returns from the first to the second day, the second to the third, and so forth?

   b. What are the continuously compounded returns from the first to the second day, the second to the third, and so forth?

   c. Suppose you want to compute the cumulative return over the 6 days. Suppose you don't know the prices, but only your answers to parts (a) and (b). How would you compute the cumulative return (which is 0) using arithmetic returns and continuously compounded returns?

Appendix C

Jensen's Inequality

The purpose of this appendix is to understand Jensen's inequality, which is a result cited frequently in this book. Suppose that x is a random variable with mean $E(x)$, and $f(x)$ is a convex function of x.

Proposition C.1 *Jensen's inequality* states that if $f(x)$ is convex, then for any probability distribution for x,

$$E[f(x)] \geq f[E(x)] \tag{C.1}$$

If $f(x)$ is concave, the inequality is reversed.

In order to understand this result we first need some definitions. A function is convex if it is curved like the cross-section of a bowl; a function is concave if it is curved like the cross section of an upside-down bowl.[1] We will provide some examples illustrating Jensen's inequality, and then provide a proof (including a more precise definition of convexity).

C.1 EXAMPLE: THE EXPONENTIAL FUNCTION

Figure C.1 shows a graph of the exponential function, $f(x) = e^x$. Note that e^x is convex. Let $x \sim Binomial(-1, 1; 0.5)$. We have

$$E(x) = (0.5 \times -1) + (0.5 \times 1) = 0$$

We also have

$$f(1) = e^1 = 2.7183$$
$$f(-1) = e^{-1} = 0.3679$$

---

[1] A way to remember this is that a convex function has the shape of a "v" while a concave function has the curvature of a **cave**.

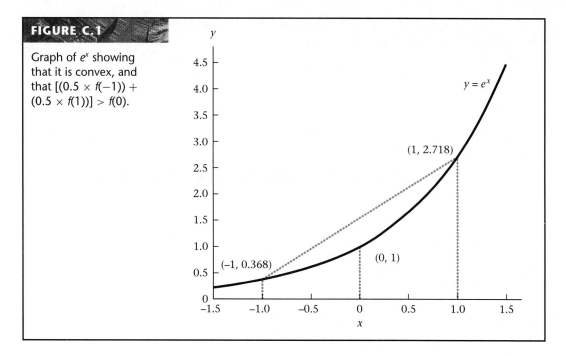

FIGURE C.1

Graph of e^x showing that it is convex, and that $[(0.5 \times f(-1)) + (0.5 \times f(1))] > f(0)$.

Thus,

$$f[E(x)] = e^{E(x)}$$
$$= e^0$$
$$= 1$$

and

$$E[f(x)] = (0.5 \times e^1) + (0.5 \times e^{-1})$$
$$= 1.5431$$

which is consistent with Jensen's inequality.

Graphically, the average of $f(1)$ and $f(-1)$ lies on the chord connecting those points, which is the straight line in Figure C.1. $f(0)$ is below the chord, which is what Jensen's inequality states.

C.2 AN IMPORTANT FACT ABOUT $E(e^x)$

Suppose $x \sim Binomial(-a, a; 0.5)$. Jensen's inequality tells us that in general, $E(e^x) > e^{E(x)}$. However, suppose we adjust the exponential function by subtracting $0.5a^2$ from the exponent. That is, we evaluate

$$g(x) = e^{x - 0.5a^2}$$

The interesting fact is that as a gets small, $E[g(x)]$ approaches 1. For example, suppose $a = 0.1$. Then

$$E[g(x)] = 0.5e^{0.1 - 0.5 \times 0.1^2} + 0.5e^{-0.1 - 0.5 \times 0.1^2}$$
$$= 0.5 \times 1.0997 + 0.5 \times 0.9003$$
$$\approx 1$$

Problem C.3 asks you to verify for a range of a's that $E[g(x)]$ is approximately equal to 1, with the approximation worse as a gets larger. For example, for $a = 1$, $E[g(x)] = 0.9359$.

This is related to the result, proved in Appendix 18.A, that if z is normally distributed with mean 0 and variance 1, i.e. $z \sim \mathcal{N}(0, 1)$, then

$$E\left(e^{\sigma z}\right) = e^{0.5\sigma^2}$$

This gives us the following result:

$$E\left(e^{\mu - 0.5\sigma^2 + \sigma z}\right) = e^{\mu}$$

C.3 EXAMPLE: THE PRICE OF A CALL

Here is another example of Jensen's inequality. Consider a call option with a strike price of \$40. Suppose that x is the stock price, and that $x \sim Binomial(35, 45; 0.5)$. Then

$$E(x) = (0.5 \times 35) + (0.5 \times 45) = 40.$$

Now let $f(x)$ be the value of the call at expiration:

$$f(x) = max(x - K, 0)$$

When we evaluate the call price at the expected stock price, $f[E(x)]$, we have

$$f[E(x)] = max[E(x) - 40, 0]$$
$$= 0$$

And when we evaluate the expected value of the the the call, $E[f(x)]$, we have

$$E[f(x)] = 0.5 \times f(45) + 0.5 \times f(35)$$
$$= 0.5 \times max(45 - 40, 0) + 0.5 \times max(35 - 40, 0)$$
$$= 0.5 \times 5 + 0 = 2.5$$

Since $2.5 > 0$, $E[f(x)] \geq f[E(x)]$, in accord with Jensen's inequality.

Figure C.2 displays this example graphically. The straight line connecting $f(35)$ and $f(45)$ represents $E[f(x)]$; this line always exceeds the payoff to the call option. This example illustrates in a purely mechanical fashion why uncertainty makes an option more valuable.

FIGURE C.2

Illustration of Jensen's inequality with a call option. The line labeled $f(x)$ depicts the call payoff at expiration. The option evaluated at the expected stock price lies on this line. The expected value of the call, on the other hand, lies on the line connecting the points labeled (35,0) and (45,5). That line is always above the call payoff at expiration.

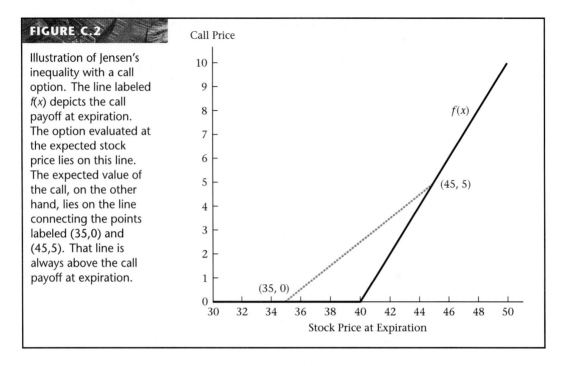

C.4 PROOF OF JENSEN'S INEQUALITY[2]

A mathematical way to state the definition of convexity is that $f(x)$ is convex if for any two points x and y, $0 \leq \lambda \leq 1$, and $z = \lambda x + (1 - \lambda)y$,

$$f(z) \leq \lambda f(x) + (1 - \lambda)f(y) \tag{C.2}$$

If $f(x)$ is convex, then there is a line $L(x)$, running through the point $[z, f(z)]$ such that $L(z) = f(z)$ and for every x, $f(x) \geq L(x)$. Because $L(x)$ is a line, it can be written as $a + bx$, hence $E[L(x)] = L[E(x)]$. Define $L^*(x)$ as the tangent line at the point $\{E(x), f[E(x)]\}$. (In Figure C.1, this line would be the tangent line at the point $x = 0$.)

Now because $f(x) \geq L^*(x)$, we have $E[f(x)] \geq E[L^*(x)] = L^*[E(x)] = f[E(x)]$. (The last step is because we defined $L^*(x)$ to include the point $\{E(x), f[E(x)]\}$.) This proves Jensen's inequality.

PROBLEMS

C.1. The logarithmic function is $f(x) = ln(x)$.

    a. Graph the logarithmic function in a spreadsheet. Observe that it is concave.

....

[2]This proof is from Mood et al. (1974).

   b. Using whatever examples you wish, verify Jensen's inequality for the logarithmic function.

C.2. Do the following in a spreadsheet. Let σ vary from 0.05 to 1 in increments of 0.05, and let h vary from 1 month to 1 year in increments of 1 month.

   a. Compute $0.5(e^{\sigma\sqrt{h}} + e^{-\sigma\sqrt{h}})$

   b. Compute $0.5(e^{-0.5\sigma^2 h + \sigma\sqrt{h}} + e^{-0.5\sigma^2 h - \sigma\sqrt{h}})$

C.3. Let $x \sim Binomial(-a, a; 0.5)$. Using a spreadsheet, evaluate $E(e^{x-0.5a^2})$, for a's ranging from 0.025 to 1, in increments of 0.025.

C.4. Let $x \sim Binomial(-1, 2; 0.67)$. Verify Jensen's inequality for $f(x) = e^x$.

C.5. For the example of the call option in Section C.3, verify with a numerical example that the value of the call is increasing in the spread of the prices around the mean of $40.

C.6. Using the numerical example in Section C.3, verify Jensen's inequality for a put option.

Appendix D

An Introduction to Visual Basic for Applications

Visual Basic for Applications, Excel's powerful built-in programming language, lets you incorporate user-written functions and subroutines into a spreadsheet.[1] You can easily calculate Black-Scholes and binomial option prices, for example. This appendix shows how to create user-written functions using VBA. You need not write complicated programs using VBA in order for it to be useful. At the very least, knowing VBA can make it easier for you to analyze relatively complex problems, and to create better-documented, more reliable spreadsheets.

This appendix presumes that you have a basic knowledge of Excel, including the use of built-in functions and named ranges. It does not presume that you know anything about writing macros or programming. The examples here are mostly related to option pricing, but the principles apply generally to any situation in which you use Excel as a tool for numerical analysis.

All of the examples here are contained in the Excel workbook *VBA_examples.xls*.

D.1 CALCULATIONS WITHOUT VBA

Suppose you wish to compute the Black-Scholes formula in a spreadsheet. Suppose also that you have named cells[2] for the stock price (s), strike price (k), interest rate (r_), time to expiration (t), volatility (v), and dividend yield (d). You could enter the following into a cell:

```
s*Exp(-d*t)*NormSDist((Ln(s/k)+(r_-d+v^2/2)*t)/(v*t^0.5))
 -k*Exp(-r_*t)*NormSDist((Ln(s/k)+(r_-d-v^2 / 2)*t)/(v*t^0.5))
```

Typing this formula is cumbersome, though of course you can copy the formula wherever you would like it to appear. It is possible to use Excel's data table feature to create a table of Black-Scholes prices, but this is cumbersome and inflexible. If you want to calculate option Greeks (e.g., delta and gamma), you must again enter or copy the formulas into each cell where you want a calculation to appear. And if you decide to

---

[1]This appendix is written for the version of VBA in Office 2000. Almost everything works without change in Office 97. However, VBA changed dramatically between Office 95 and Office 97. The general idea has remained the same, but specific keystrokes changed. There are numerous books on VBA. Green (1999) is very useful.

[2]If you do not know what a named cell is, consult Excel's online help.

change some aspect of your formula, you have to hunt down all occurrences and make the changes. When the same formula is copied throughout a worksheet, that worksheet potentially becomes harder to modify safely and reliably. When the worksheet is to be used by others, maintainability becomes even more of a concern.

Spreadsheet construction becomes even harder if you want to, for example, compute a price for a finite-lived American option. There is no way to do this in one cell, so you must compute the binomial tree in a range of cells and copy the appropriate formulas for the stock price and the option price. This is not so difficult with a three-step binomial calculation, but for 100 steps you will spend quite a while setting up the spreadsheet. If you decide you want to set up a binomial tree for pricing put options, it can be time-consuming to edit your call tree to price puts. If you plan ahead, you can make the formulas flexible and general with the use of "if" statements. But things would become much easier if you could create your own formulas within Excel. This is what Visual Basic for Applications permits you to do.

D.2 How to Learn VBA

Before delving into VBA, it is helpful to appreciate what learning VBA will entail. First, you will never learn VBA by reading about it; you must try to use it. Part of the challenge is that if a macro language is so powerful that it enables you to do everything, it is going to be too complex for you to memorize all the commands. A book or tutorial (like this one) will enable you to use VBA to solve specific problems. However, once you want to do more, you will have to become comfortable figuring out VBA by trial and error.

To facilitate learning VBA, you should use the macro recorder in Excel. When you use the macro recorder, the results of your actions will be recorded in VBA. Try this: Select Tools|Macro|Record New Macro in Excel. Then create a simple graph using the graph wizard. Look at the VBA code that Excel creates. (This example is described in more detail on page 824.) The result is daunting when you first look at it, but if you want to use VBA to create graphs, the recorded macro gives you a starting point that you can modify; you need not create the basic code from scratch.

The main objective of this tutorial is to help you create your own functions. While the examples here relate to option pricing, there are many other uses of VBA.

D.3 Calculations with VBA

In this section we will discuss functions and subroutines, which are techniques in VBA for performing calculations or automating actions.

Creating a Simple Function

With VBA, it is a simple matter to create your own function, say BSCall, which will compute a Black-Scholes option price. To do this, you must first create and open a macro module. Here are the steps required to open a new macro module and to create a simple formula:

1. *Open a blank workbook using File|New.*

2. *Select Tools|Macro|Visual Basic Editor from the Excel menu.*

3. *Within the VBA editor, select Insert|Module from the menu. You will find yourself in a new window, in which you can type macro commands.*

4. *Within the newly created macro module, type the following exactly (be sure to include the "_" at the end of the first line):*

```
' Here is a function to add two numbers _
Works well, doesn't it?

Function AddTwo(x, y)
 AddTwo = x + y
End Function
```

5. *Return to Excel. In cell A1 enter*

```
=AddTwo(3, 5)
```

6. *Hit <Enter>. You will see the result "8".*

These steps create an add-in function. Notice the following:

- You need to tell the function what to expect as input, hence, the list "(x, y)" following the name of the function.

- You specify the value of the function with a statement where you set the function name ("AddTwo") equal to a calculation ("x + y").

- An apostrophe denotes a comment, i.e., text that is not interpreted by VBA. You need not write comments, but they are very useful when you return to work you did several months ago.

- VBA is line-oriented. This means that when you start a comment with an apostrophe, if you press <Enter> to go to a new line, you must enter another apostrophe or else—since what you type will almost surely not be a valid command—VBA will report an error. You can continue a line to the next line by typing an underscore, i.e., "_" without the quotes. (You can test this by deleting the "_" in the example above.)

- When you entered the comment and the function, VBA automatically color-coded the text and completed the syntax (the line "End Function" was automatically inserted). Comments are coded green and the reserved words "Function" and "End" were coded in blue and automatically capitalized.

- The function you typed now appears in the function wizard, just as if it were a built-in Excel function. To see this, open the function wizard using Insert|Function. In the left-hand pane ("Function Category"), scroll to and highlight "User Defined". Note that "AddTwo" appears in the right-side pane ("Function Name"). Click on it and Excel pops up a box where you are prompted to enter inputs for the function.

If you use a custom function in a spreadsheet, it will automatically recalculate when the spreadsheet recalculates.

A Simple Example of a Subroutine

A *function* returns a result. A *subroutine* (called a "sub" by VBA) performs an action when invoked. In the above example we used a function, because we wanted to supply two numbers and have VBA add them for us and tell us the sum. While functions recalculate automatically, subroutines are a set of statements that execute when the subroutine is explicitly invoked. Here are the steps to create a subroutine:

1. *Return to the Visual Basic Editor.*

2. *Click on the "Module1" window.*

3. *At the bottom of the module (i.e., below the function we just created) enter the following:*

```
Sub DisplayBox()
 Response = MsgBox("Greetings!")
End Sub
```

4. *Return to Excel.*

5. *Run the subroutine by using Tools|Macro|Macros, then double-clicking on "DisplayBox" out of the list.*

We have just created and run a subroutine. It pops up a dialog box that displays a message. The MsgBox function can be very useful for giving information to the spreadsheet user.

Creating a Button to Invoke a Subroutine

We ran the subroutine by clicking on Tools|Macro|Macros and then double-clicking on the subroutine name. If you are going to run the subroutine often, creating a button in the spreadsheet provides a shortcut to the subroutine. Here is how to create a button:

1. *Move the mouse to the Excel toolbar and right-click once.*

2. *You will see a list of toolbar names. Move the highlight bar down to "Forms" and left-click. A new toolbar will pop up.*

3. *The rectangular icon on this toolbar is the "Button" icon, which looks something like a button (of the software, not the clothing, variety). Click on it.*

4. *The cursor changes to a crosshair. Move the mouse to the spreadsheet, hold down the left mouse button, and drag to create a rectangle. When you lift your finger off the mouse button, a dialog box will pop up. One of the choices will be "DisplayBox". Double click on it.*

5. *Now move the mouse away from the button you've created and click once (this de-selects the button). Move the mouse back to the button you created and left-click once on it. Observe the dialog box that pops up, and click "OK" to get rid of the dialog.*

Some comments:

- This is a trivial example. However, if you have a calculation that is particularly time-consuming (for example, a Monte Carlo calculation), you might want to create a subroutine for it. Creating a button to activate the subroutine would be a natural adjunct.

- There is a more sophisticated version of the MsgBox function that permits you to customize the appearance of the dialog box. It is documented in the online help and an example of its use is contained in DisplayBox2 in the workbook. One nice feature of this more sophisticated version is that within the subroutine, we could have checked the value of the variable *Response* and had the subroutine perform different actions depending upon which button the user clicked. For an example of this, see the example DisplayBox2.[3]

Functions Can Call Functions

Functions can call functions. Here is an example.

1. *Enter this code in the "Module1" window.*

```
Function AddThree(x, y, z)
  AddThree = AddTwo(x, y) + z
End Function
```

2. *Now in cell A2, enter*

```
=AddThree(3, 5, 7)
```

The answer "15" will appear.

Illegal Function Names

Some function names are illegal, which means that you will receive an error message if you try to use them. You cannot use a number as a function name. You cannot use the following characters in a function name: space . , + - : ; " ' ` # $ % / \. If you try to use any of these characters in a name, Visual Basic lets you know immediately that something is wrong. Note that you *can* use an underscore where you would like to have

....

[3]If you have examined the code for DisplayBox2, you may be puzzled by checking to see if *Response* = "vbYes". VbYes is simply an internal constant which VBA uses to check for a "yes" button response to a dialog box. The possible responses—documented in the help file—are vbOK, vbCancel, vbAbort, vbRetry, vbIgnore, vbYes, and vbNo.

a space for readability of the function name. So BS_2, for example, is a legal function name.

Here is a more subtle issue. There are function names that are legal but that you should not use. BS2 is an example. This would be fine as the name of a subroutine, which is not called directly from a cell. But think about what happens if you give this name to a user-defined function. You enter, for example, "BS2(3)", in a cell. How does Excel understand this? The problem is that "BS2" *is also the name of a cell*. So if you try to use it as a function in the spreadsheet, Excel will become confused and return an error. This is why, later in this tutorial, you will see functions named BS_2, BS_3, and so on.

Differences between Functions and Subroutines

Functions and subroutines are *not* interchangeable and do not have the same capabilities. Think of subroutines as code meant to be invoked by a button or otherwise explicitly called, while functions return results and are meant to be inserted into cells (although functions can also be called by subroutines). Because of their different purpose, some VBA capabilities will work in one but not the other.

In a subroutine, for example, you can write to cells of the workbook. With a subroutine you could perform a calculation and have the answer appear in cell A1. However, if you invoke a function from a worksheet by entering it into a cell, you cannot write to cells from within that function. You cannot activate a worksheet or change anything about the display from within such a function. (On the other hand, if the function is invoked by a subroutine, but not invoked from a worksheet, it can do these things.) Subroutines, on the other hand, cannot be called from cells. These restrictions exist because functions and subroutines are intended for different purposes.

D.4 Storing and Retrieving Variables in a Worksheet

Suppose that there is a value in the spreadsheet that you want to include as input to your function or subroutine. (For instance, you might have a variable that determines whether the option to be valued is American or European.) Or suppose you create a subroutine that performs computations. You may want to display the output in the spreadsheet. (For example, you might wish to create a subroutine to draw a binomial tree.) Using VBA, how do you read and write values to the spreadsheet?

If you are going to read and write numbers to specific locations in the spreadsheet, you must identify those locations. The easiest way to identify a location is to use a named range. The alternatives—which we will examine below—require that you "activate" a specific location or worksheet within the workbook, and then read and write within this activated region.

There are at least three ways to read and write to cells:

- Range lets you address cells by name.

- Range().Activate and ActiveCell let you access cells by using traditional cell addresses (e.g., "A1").

- Cell lets you address cells using a row and column numbering scheme.

You may be thinking that it seems redundant to have so many ways to access cells, but each is useful at different times.

Using a Named Range to Read and Write Numbers from the Spreadsheet

1. *Enter the following subroutine in Module1:*

```
Sub ReadVariable()
 x = Range("Test")
 MsgBox (Str(x))
End Sub
```

2. *Select cell A1 in sheet "Sheet2"; then Insert\Name\Define, and type "Test"; then click OK. You have just created a named range.*

3. *Enter the value "5" in the cell you just named "Test".*

4. *Select Tools\Macro\Macros, then double-click on "ReadVariable".*

At this point you have just read from a cell and displayed the result. Note that "x" is a number in this example. Sometimes it is useful to be able to convert a number to its character equivalent (for example the character "7" rather than the number "7.0000000"). You can do this using VBA's built-in "Str" function.[4] It turns out this was not necessary in this example; entering "MsgBox(x)" would have worked as well.

As you might guess, you can use the Range function to write as well as read.

1. *Enter the following subroutine in Module1:*

```
Sub WriteVariable()
 Range("Test2") = Range("Test")
 MsgBox ("Number_copied!")
End Sub
```

2. *Give the name "Test2" to cell Sheet2.B2.*

3. *Enter a number in Sheet2.B2.*

4. *Go to Tools\Macro\Macros; then double-click on "WriteVariable".*

5. *The number from Test is copied to Test2.*

---

[4] You can locate the "Str" function by using the object browser, looking under VBA, then "Conversions".

Reading and Writing to Cells That Are Not Named

You can also access a specific cell directly. In order to do this, you first have to activate the worksheet containing the cell. Here is VBA code to read a variable:

```
Sub ReadVariable2()
  Worksheets("Sheet2").Activate
  Range("A1").Activate
  x = ActiveCell.Value
  MsgBox (Str(x))
End Sub
```

In this subroutine we first activate the worksheet named "Sheet2". Next we activate the cell "A1" within Sheet2. You will see that when you have finished calling this function, the cursor has moved to cell A1 in Sheet2. This is because the "active cell" is whatever cell the cursor happens to be on; the first two lines instruct the cursor to move to Sheet2.A1.

The active cell has properties, such as the font, color of the cell, and formatting. All of these properties may be accessed using the ActiveCell function. For fun, insert the line

```
ActiveCell.Font.Bold=True
```

after the MsgBox function. Then switch to Sheet2, run the subroutine, and watch the change in cell A1.

We can also assign a value to ActiveCell.Value; this is a way to write to a cell. Here is a macro that does this:

```
Sub WriteVariable2()
  Worksheets("Sheet2").Activate
  Range("A1").Activate
  x = ActiveCell.Value
  Range("B1").Activate
  ActiveCell.Value = x
End Sub
```

This subroutine reads the number from Sheet2.A1 and copies it to Sheet2.B1.

Using the Cells Function to Read and Write to Cells

There is yet another way to read and write to cells. The Cells function lets you address cells using a numerical row and column numbering scheme. Here is an example illustrating how Cells works:

```
Sub CellsExample()
  ' Make "Sheet2" the active sheet
  Worksheets("Sheet2").Activate
  ' The first entry is the row, the second is the column
```

```
' Write the number 1 into cell A3
Cells(3, 1) = 1
' Write the number 2 into cell A4
Cells(4, 1) = 2
' Copy the number from cell A3 into cell C3
Cells(3, 3) = Cells(3, 1)
' Copy the number from cell A4 into cell C4
Cells(4, 3) = Cells(4, 1)
End Sub
```

This subroutine reads the numbers 1 and 2 into cells A3 and A4, and it then copies the values into C3 and C4. Later we will use the Cells function to draw a binomial tree.

Reading from within a Function

It is possible to read from a worksheet from within a function. For example, consider these two functions:

```
Function ReadTest1(x, y)
 ReadTest1 = x + y + Range("Read_In_Function!A1").Value
End Function

Function ReadTest2(x, y)
 Application.Volatile
 ReadTest2 = x + y + Range("Read_In_Function!A1").Value
End Function
```

An interesting experiment is to create the sheet named "Read_In_Function", put the number "5" in cell A1, and enter ReadTest1(3,4) and ReadTest2(3,4) in cells A2 and A3. Both functions will return the value "12".

Now change the value in cell A1 to 20. *The function ReadTest2 will properly return the value 27, but ReadTest1 will not change.* Press the F9 key to recalculate the spreadsheet. *ReadTest1 will still not recalculate.* The problem is that Excel has no way of knowing that the value change in A1 affects either function. However, ReadTest2 recalculates because of the Application.Volatile statement at the beginning. This tells ReadTest2 to recalculate anytime *anything* changes. Obviously this will slow the worksheet, but it is necessary in this case.

Reading from the worksheet from within a function is possible, but, other things equal, it is preferable to pass values to the function explicitly as arguments.

D.5 USING EXCEL FUNCTIONS FROM WITHIN VBA

VBA permits you to use most Excel functions within your own custom functions. Since Excel has a large number of built-in functions, this is a powerful feature.

Using VBA to Compute the Black-Scholes Formula

There is only one complicated piece of the Black-Scholes calculation: Computing the cumulative normal distribution (the "$N()$" function in the formula). Based on the example at the start of this appendix, we would like to do something like the following:

```
Function BS(s, k, v, r, t, d)
  BS=s*Exp(-d*t)*NormSDist((Ln(s/k)+(r-d+v^2/2)*t)/(v*t^0.5)) _
  -k*Exp(-r*t)*NormSDist((Ln(s/k)+(r-d-v^2/2)*t)/(v*t^0.5))
End Function
```

Unfortunately, this doesn't work. The reason it doesn't work is that VBA does not understand either "Ln" or "NormSDist". Though these are functions in Excel they are not functions in VBA, even though VBA is part of Excel. Instead of using "Ln", we can use "Log", which is the VBA version of the same function. However, there is no VBA version of NormSDist.

Fortunately, there is a way for you to tell VBA that NormSDist is located inside of Excel. The following example will show you the error you get if you fail to call NormSDist correctly:

1. *Click on the "Module1" tab.*

2. *Enter the following:*

```
Function BS(s, k, v, r, t, d)
  d1 = (Log(s / k) + (r - d + v ^ 2 / 2) * t) / (v * Sqr(t))
  d2 = d1 - v * Sqrt(t)
  BS = s*Exp(-d*t)*normsdist(d1)-k*Exp(-r*t)*NormSDist(d2)
End Function
```

Comment: To save a little typing and to make the function more readable, we are defining the Black-Scholes "d1" and "d2" separately. You will also notice that instead of entering "Ln", we entered "Log", which—as we noted above—is built into VBA.

3. *Enter into the spreadsheet*

```
=BS(40, 40, .3, .08, .25, 0)
```

Hit <Enter>. You will get the error message "sub or function not defined".

This error occurs because there is no version, however spelled, of "NormSDist" that is built in to VBA. Instead, we have to tell VBA where to look for "NormSDist". We do this by typing instead "WorksheetFunction.NormSDist" or "Application.NormSDist".[5]

---

[5] If you are curious about this, do the following: Select View|Object Browser or press F2. Click on the drop-down arrow under "Libraries/Workbooks"; then select "Excel". Under "Objects/Modules" click on "Application"; then under "Methods/Properties" scroll down to "NormSDist". You have now just located "NormSDist" as a method available from the application. If you scroll around a bit, you will see that there is an enormous and overwhelming number of functions available to be called from VBA.

With a correctly referenced NormSDist, the function becomes:

```
Function BS(s, k, v, r, t, d)
 d1 = (Log(s / k) + (r - d + v ^ 2 / 2) * t) / (v * t ^ 0.5)
 d2 = d1 - v * t ^ 0.5
 BS = s*Exp(-d*t)*WorkSheetFunction.NormSDist(d1) _
   -k*Exp(-r*t)*WorkSheetFunction.NormSDist(d2)
End Function
```

The Black-Scholes function will now evaluate correctly to 2.78.

The Object Browser

The previous example illustrates an extremely powerful feature of VBA: It can access the functions built into Excel if you tell it where to find them. The way you locate other functions is to use the *Object Browser*, which is part of VBA. Here is how to use it:

1. *From within a macro module, press the F2 key. This will pop up a dialog box with the title "Object Browser".*

2. *In the top left you will see a drop-down box that says "All Libraries". Click on the down arrow at the right of this line. You will see a drop-down list with, at a minimum, "VBA" and "Excel" as two entries. (There may be other entries, depending upon how you have set up Excel.)*

3. *Click on VBA.*

4. *In the "Classes" list, click on "Math".*

5. *To the right, in the "Members of Math" box, you now have a list of all the math functions that are available in VBA. Note that "Log" is included in this list, but not "Ln" or "NormSDist". If you right-click on "Log" and then click on "Help", you will see that "Log" returns the natural logarithm.*

6. *Return to the top left box, which now says "VBA". Click on the down arrow at the right of this line.*

7. *Click on Excel.*

8. *In the "Classes" list, click on "WorksheetFunction".*

9. *To the right, in the "Members of WorksheetFunction" box, you now have a list of Excel built-in functions that may be called from a macro module by specifying "WorksheetFunction.functionname". Note that both "Ln" and "NormSDist" are*

By the way, you should not make the mistake of thinking that you can call any Excel function simply by prefacing it with "WorksheetFunction". Try it with "Sqrt" and it won't work. While most functions are accessible from VBA, the only way to know for sure which functions you can and can't call is by using the object browser.

included in this list. Note also that "Log" is included in this list, but be aware that Excel's "Log" function is base 10 by default (you can specify a different base), whereas VBA's is base e.[6]

If you create any VBA functions that are even moderately ambitious, you will need to use the object browser. It is the heart and soul of VBA.

D.6 Checking for Conditions

Frequently, you want to perform a calculation only if certain conditions are met. For example, you would not want to calculate an option price with a negative volatility. It makes sense to check to see if your inputs make sense before proceeding with the calculation and aborting—possibly with an error message—if they do not.

The easy way to check if a condition exists is to use the construct *If ... Then ... Else*.[7] Here is an example of its use in checking for a negative volatility in the Black-Scholes formula:[8]

```
Function BS_2(s, k, v, r, t, d)
  If v > 0 Then
   BS_2 = BS(s, k, v, r, t, d)
  Else
   MsgBox ("Negative_volatility!")
   BS_2 = CVErr(xlErrValue)
  End If
End Function
```

This function checks to see if volatility is greater than 0; if it is, the function computes the Black-Scholes formula using the BS function we created earlier. If volatility is not greater than zero, then two things happen: (i) a message box pops up to inform you of the mistake and (ii) the function returns a value indicating that there is an error.

In general you should be cautious about putting message boxes into a function (as opposed to a subroutine), since every time the spreadsheet is recalculated the message box will pop up.

Because error-checking is often critically important (you would not want to quote a client a price on a deal for which you had accidentally entered a negative volatility), it is worth expanding a bit on the use of the CVErr function.

----

[6]Scroll down to the ":Log" entry and then click on the "?" button at the bottom left. If you use "Log" in a spreadsheet, or if you use "WorksheetFunction.log" in a function, you will get the base 10 logarithm. However, if you use "Log" in a function, you will get the base *e* logarithm. Note also that, as mentioned earlier, "Sqrt" is not included and, hence, is not available in VBA.

[7]There is also a *Case ... Select* construct that we will not use but that is documented in VBA's help file.

[8]You need to be aware that VBA will expect the "If Then", "Else", and "End If" pieces to be on separate lines. If you write "Else" on the same line as "If Then", for example, the code will fail.

If the user enters a negative volatility, you *could* just have Excel return a nonsense value for the option, such as −99. This would be a bad idea, however. Suppose you have a complicated worksheet with many option calculations. If you failed to notice the error, the −99 would be treated as a true option value and propagated throughout your calculations.

Alternatively, you could have the function return a string such as "Oops, you entered a negative volatility". Entering a string in a cell when you should have a number could have unpredictable effects on calculations that depend on the cell. It is obvious that an addition between a string and a number will fail. However, suppose you are performing a frequency count. Are you sure what will happen to the calculation if you introduce a string among the numbers in your data?

Excel has built-in error codes that are documented in VBA's online help. For example, xlErrNA returns "#N/A", xlErrRef returns "#REF!", and xlErrValue returns "#VALUE!". By using CVErr along with one of the built-in error codes, you guarantee that your function will return a result that Excel recognizes as a numerical error. Excel programmers have already thought through the issues of how subsequent calculations should respond to a recognized error, and Excel usually does something reasonable in those circumstances.

D.7 ARRAYS

Often you will wish to use a single variable to store many numbers. For example, in a binomial option calculation, you have a stock price tree. After n periods, you have $n + 1$ possible stock prices. It can be useful to write the lowest stock price as $S(0)$, the next as $S(1)$, and the highest as $S(n)$. The variable S is then called an array—it is a single variable that stores more than one number. Each item in the array is called an *element*. Think of an array as a table of numbers. You access a specific element of the array by specifying a row and column number. Figure D.1 provides an example of an array.

Defining Arrays

When you create an array, it is necessary to tell VBA how big the array is going to be. You do this by using the Dim statement ("Dim" is short for "dimension"—the size of the array). Here are some examples of how to use Dim to create a one-dimensional array:

```
Dim P(2) As Double
```

This creates an array of three double-precision real numbers, with the array index running from 0 to 2. (By default, the first subscript in an array in VBA is 0.) If you had written

```
Dim P(3 to 5) As Double
```

you would have created a three-element array with the index running from 3 to 5. In this example we told Excel that the variable is type "Double". This was not necessary—we could have left the type unspecified and permitted Excel to determine the type automatically. It is faster and easier to detect mistakes, however, if we specify the type.

FIGURE D.1

Example of an array
with 3 rows and 5
columns. By default,
VBA numbers rows and
columns start with 0. If
the array is named X,
the number "8" is
retrieved as X(1, 3).

		Column Number				
		0	**1**	**2**	**3**	**4**
Row Number	**0**	12	3.91	−5	23	−33.183
	1	3	−82.5	1	**8**	24
	2	−19.8	44	6	17.2	7

You can also create arrays with multiple dimensions. For example, the following
are valid Dim statements:

```
Dim X(3, 8)
Dim Y(1 to 4, -5 to 3)
Dim Z(1 to 4, -5 to 3, 25)
```

The first statement creates a two-dimensional array that has 4 rows and 9 columns—a
4×9 array. The second also creates a two-dimensional array with 4 rows and 9 columns.
The third creates a three-dimsional array which is $4 \times 9 \times 25$. Since $4 \times 9 \times 25 = 900$,
this last array has 900 spaces, or elements.

Here is a routine that defines a three-element one-dimensional array, reads numbers
into the array, and then writes the array out into dialog boxes:

```
Sub UseArray()
 Dim X(2) As Double
 X(0) = 0
 X(1) = 1
 X(2) = 2
 MsgBox (X(0))
 MsgBox (X(1))
 MsgBox (X(2))
End Sub
```

You should enter this code and execute it to see what happens. The subroutine UseArray
can also be written as follows:

```
Sub UseArray2()
 X = Array(0, 1, 2)
 MsgBox (X(0))
 MsgBox (X(1))
 MsgBox (X(2))
End Sub
```

The difference between UseArray and UseArray2 is the way arrays are declared. In
UseArray, there is a dimension statement, and then array elements are created one by

one. In UseArray2, there is *no* dimension statement, and the Array function (built into VBA) is used to set the initial values of the array elements (this is called *initializing* the array). UseArray will fail without the Dim statement, and UseArray2 will fail *with* the Dim statement.

Finally, notice the repetition in these examples. The statements that put numbers into the array are essentially repeated three times (albeit more compactly in UseArray2), and the statements that read numbers out of the array are repeated three times. If the array had 100 elements, it would take a long time to write the subroutine in this way. Fortunately, we can perform repetitive calculations by iteration.

D.8 ITERATION

Many option calculations are repetitive. For example, when we compute a binomial option price, we generate a stock price tree and then traverse the tree, calculating the option price at each node. Similarly, when we compute an implied volatility, we need to perform a calculation repeatedly until we arrive at the correct volatility. VBA provides us with the ability to write one or more lines of code that can be repeated as many times as we like.

A Simple *for* Loop

Here is an example of a *for* loop. This subroutine does exactly the same thing as the UseArray subroutine:

```
Sub UseArrayLoop()
  Dim X(2) As Double
  For i = 0 To 2
    X(i) = i
  Next i
  For i = 0 To 2
    MsgBox (Str(X(i)))
  Next i
End Sub
```

The following translates the syntax in the first loop above:

`For i = 0 to 2`	Repeat the following statements three times, the first time setting $i = 0$, the next time $i = 1$, and finally $i = 2$.
`X(i) = i`	Set the ith value of X equal to i.
`Next i`	Go back and repeat the statement for the next value of i.

Creating a Binomial Tree

In order to create a binomial tree, we need the following information:

- The initial stock price.
- The number of time periods.
- The magnitudes up and down by which the stock moves.

Suppose we wish to draw a tree where the initial price is \$100, we have 10 binomial periods, and the moves up and down are $u = 1.25$ and $d = 0.8$. Here is a subroutine, complete with comments explaining the code, that will create this tree. You first need to name a worksheet "Output", and then we will write the tree to this worksheet. The number of binomial steps and the magnitude of the moves are read from named cells, which can be in any worksheet. I have placed those named cells in Sheet1 in VBA_examples.xls.

```
Sub DrawBinomialTree()

ReDim Stock(2) ' provide default of 2 steps if no steps specified
Dim i As Integer
Dim t As Integer
n = Range("n") ' number of binomial steps
u = Range("u") ' move up
P0 = Range("P0") ' initial stock price
d = 1 / u ' move down
ReDim Stock(n + 1) ' array of stock prices
Worksheets("Output").Activate
' Erase any previous calculations
Worksheets("Output").Cells.ClearContents
Cells(1, 1) = P0
' We will adopt the convention that the column holds the
' stock prices for a given point in time. The row holds
' stock prices over time. For example, the first row
' holds stock prices resulting from all up moves, the
' second row holds stock prices resulting from a single
' down move, etc.

' The first loop is over time
For t = 2 To n
 Cells(1, t) = Cells(1, t - 1) * u
 ' The second loop is across stock prices at a given time
 For i = 2 To t
  Cells(i, t) = Cells(i - 1, t - 1) * d
 Next i
Next t
End Sub
```

Several comments:

- There is a simple command to clear an entire worksheet, namely: Worksheets(*worksheetname*).Cells.ClearContents.
- The use of the Cells function means that you can perform the calculation exactly as you would if you were writing it down, using subscripts to denote which price

you are dealing with. Think about how much more complicated it would be to use traditional row and column notation (e.g., "A1") to perform the same function.

- This subroutine does not price an option; it merely creates a binomial stock price tree.

Note that this subroutine uses the ReDim command to specify a flexible array size. Sometimes you do not know in advance how big your array is going to be. In this example you are unsure how many binomial periods the subroutine must handle. If you are going to use an array to store the full set of prices at each point in time, this presents a problem—how large do you make the array? You could specify the array to have a very large size, one larger than any user is ever likely to use, but this kind of practice could get you into trouble if memory is limited. Fortunately, with the ReDim statement VBA permits you to specify the size of an array using a variable.

Other Kinds of Loops

Although we will not discuss them, there are other looping constructs available in VBA. The following kinds of loops are available:

- *Do Until . . . Loop and Do . . . Loop Until*
- *Do While . . . Loop and Do . . . Loop While*
- *While . . . Wend*

If you ever think you need them, you can look these up in the online help. There is also a *For Each . . . In . . . Next* construct, which we discuss below.

D.9 READING AND WRITING ARRAYS

A powerful feature of VBA is the ability to read arrays as inputs to a function and also to write functions that return arrays as output.

Arrays as Output

Suppose you would like to create a single function that returns two numbers: The Black-Scholes price of a call option and the option delta. Let's call this function BS_3 and create it by modifying the function BS from Section D.5.

```
Function BS_3(s, k, v, r, t, d)
  d1 = (Log(s / k) + (r - d + 0.5 * v ^ 2) * t) / (v * t ^ 0.5)
  d2 = d1 - v * t ^ 0.5
  nd1 = WorksheetFunction.NormSDist(d1)
  nd2 = WorksheetFunction.NormSDist(d2)
  delta = Exp(-d * t) * nd1
  price = s * delta - k * Exp(-r * t) * nd2
  BS_3 = Array(price, delta)
End Function
```

The key section is the line

```
BS_3 = Array(price, delta)
```

We assign an array as the function output, using the array function introduced in Section D.7.

If you just enter the function BS_3 in your worksheet in the normal way, in a single cell, it will return a single number. In this case, that single number will be the option price, which is the first element of the array. If you want to see both numbers as output from the function, you have to enter BS_3 as an array function spanning multiple cells: Select a range of two cells, enter the formula in the first, and then press Ctrl-Shift-Enter (instead of just Enter).

There is a 50% probability you just discovered a catch. The way we have written BS_3, the array output is *horizontal*. If you enter the array function in cells A1:A2, for example, you will see only the option price. If you enter the function in A1:B1, you will see the price and the delta. What happens if we want vertical output? The answer is that we transpose the array using the Excel function of that name, modifying the last line to read

```
BS_3 = WorksheetFunction.Transpose(Array(price, delta))
```

This will make the output vertical.

There is also a way to make the output *both* horizontal and vertical. We just have to return a 2×2 array. Here is an illustration of how to do that:

```
Function BS_4(s, k, v, r, t, d)
Dim temp(1, 1) As Double
d1 = (Log(s / k) + (r - d + 0.5 * v ^ 2) * t) / (v * t ^ 0.5)
d2 = d1 - v * t ^ 0.5
nd1 = WorksheetFunction.NormSDist(d1)
nd2 = WorksheetFunction.NormSDist(d2)
delta = Exp(-d * t) * nd1
price = s * delta - k * Exp(-r * t) * nd2
temp(0, 0) = price
temp(0, 1) = delta
temp(1, 0) = delta
temp(1, 1) = 0
BS_4 = temp
End Function
```

Now it does not matter whether you select cells A1:A2 or A1:B1; either way, you will see both the price and the delta.[9]

....

[9] What do you see if you select cells A1:B2? What about A1:D4?

Arrays as Inputs

We may wish to write a function that processes many inputs, where we do not know in advance how many inputs there will be. Excel's built-in functions "sum" and "average" are two familiar examples of this. They both can take a *range* of cells as input. For example, you could enter in a worksheet "sum(a1:b8)". It turns out that it is easy to write functions that accept ranges as input. Once in the function, the array of numbers from the range can be manipulated in at least two ways: As a *collection*, or as an actual array with the same dimensions as the range.

The array as a collection   First, here are two examples of how to use a collection. Excel has built-in functions called SumSq and SumProd, which (as the names suggest) sum the squared elements of a range and sum the product of the corresponding elements of two or more arrays. We will see how to implement similar functions in VBA.

SumSq takes a set of numbers, squares each one, and adds them up:

```
Function SumSq(x)
  Sum = 0
  For Each y In x
   Sum = Sum + y ^ 2
  Next
  SumSq = Sum
End Function
```

The function SumSq can take a range (e.g., "A1:A10") as its argument. The *For Each* construct in VBA loops through each element of a collection without our having to know in advance how many elements the collection has.

There is another way to loop through the elements of a collection. The function SumProd takes two equally sized arrays, multiplies them element by element, and returns the sum of the multiplied elements. In this example, because we are working with two collections, we need to use a more standard looping construct. To do this, we need to first count the number of elements in each array. This is done using the Count property of a collection. If there is a different number of elements in each of the two arrays, we exit and return an error code.

```
Function SumProd(x1, x2)
  n1 = x1.Count
  n2 = x2.Count
  If n1 <> n2 Then
   'exit if arrays not equally sized
   SumProd = CVErr(xlErrNum)
  End If
  Sum = 0
  For i = 1 To n1
   Sum = Sum + x1(i) * x2(i)
  Next i
  SumProd = Sum
End Function
```

The array as an array   We can also treat the numbers in the range as an array. The only trick to doing that is that we need to know the dimensions of the array, i.e., how many rows and columns it has. The function RangeTest illustrates how to do this.

```
Function RangeTest(x)
  prod = 1
  r = x.Rows.Count
  c = x.Columns.Count
  For i = 1 To r
   For j = 1 To c
    prod = prod * x(i, j)
   Next j
  Next i
  RangeTest = WorksheetFunction.Transpose(Array(prod, r, c))
End Function
```

This function again multiplies together the cells in the range. It returns not only the product, but also the number of rows and columns.

When x is read into the function, it is considered by VBA to be an array.[10] Rows and Columns are properties of an array. The construct

```
x.Rows.Count
```

tells us the number of rows in the array. With this capability, we could multiply arrays, check to see whether two ranges have the same dimensions, and so on.

D.10 MISCELLANY

In this section we discuss miscellaneous topics.

Getting Excel to Generate Macros for You

Suppose you want to perform a task and you don't know how to program it in VBA. For example, suppose you want to create a subroutine to set up a graph. You can set up a graph manually and tell Excel to record the VBA commands that accomplish the same thing. You then examine the result and see how it works. To do this, select Tools|Macro|Record New Macro. Excel will record all your actions in a new module located at the *end* of your workbook, i.e., following Sheet16. You stop the recording by clicking the Stop button that should have appeared on your spreadsheet when you started recording. Macro recording is an *extremely* useful tool for understanding how Excel and VBA work and interact.

----

[10]You can verify this by using the VBA function IsArray. For example, you could write

```
y = IsArray(x)
```

and y will have the value "true" if x is a range input to the function.

For example, here is the macro code Excel generates if you use the chart wizard to set up a chart using data in the range A2:C4. You can see, among other things, that the selected graph style was the fourth line graph in the graph gallery, and that the chart was titled "Here is the title". Also, each data series is in a column and the first column was used as the x-axis ("CategoryLabels:=1").

```
' Macro1 Macro
' Macro recorded 2/17/99 by Robert McDonald
'
'
Sub Macro1()
Range("A2:C4").Select
ActiveSheet.ChartObjects.Add(196.5, 39, 252.75, 162).Select
Application.CutCopyMode = False
ActiveChart.ChartWizard Source:=Range("A2:C4"), Gallery:=xlLine, _
  Format:=4, PlotBy:=xlColumns, CategoryLabels:=1,SeriesLabels _
  :=0, HasLegend:=1, Title:="Here is the Title", CategoryTitle _
  :="X-Axis", ValueTitle:="Y-Axis", ExtraTitle:=""
End Sub
```

Using Multiple Modules

You can split up your functions and subroutines among as many modules as you like—functions from one module can call another, for example. Using multiple modules is often convenient for clarity.

Recalculation Speed

One unfortunate drawback of VBA—and of most macro code in most applications—is that it is slow. When you are using built-in functions, Excel performs clever internal checking to know whether something requires recalculation (you should be aware that on occasion it appears that this clever checking goes awry and something that should be recalculated isn't). When you write a custom function, however, Excel is not able to perform its checking on your functions, and it therefore tends to recalculate everything. This means that if you have a complicated spreadsheet, you may find *very* slow recalculation times. This is a problem with custom functions and not one you can do anything about.

If your calculation writes to the worksheet, you can significantly speed up your routine by turning off Excel's screen updating. You do this by

```
Application.ScreenUpdating=False
```

If you want to check the progress of your calculations, you can turn ScreenUpdating off at the beginning of your subroutine. Whenever you would like to see your calculation's progress (for example every 100th iteration), you can turn it on and then immediately turn it off again. This will update the display.

Finally, the keystroke Ctrl-Break will (usually) stop a recalculation. Ctrl-Break is more reliable if your macro writes output to the screen or spreadsheet.

Debugging

We will not go into details here, but VBA has sophisticated debugging capabilities. For example, you can set breakpoints (i.e., lines in your routine where Excel will stop calculating to give you a chance to see what is happening) and watches (which means that you can look at the values of variables at different points in the routine). Look up "debugging" in the online help.

Creating an Add-In

Suppose you have written a useful set of option functions and wish to make them broadly available in your spreadsheets. You can make the functions automatically available in *any* spreadsheet your write by creating an add-in. To do this, you simply save the file as an add-in, by selecting File|Save As and then selecting the type of file to be "Microsoft Excel Add-in (*.xla)". Excel will create a file with the .xla extension that contains your functions. You can then make these functions automatically available by Tools|Add-ins and browse to locate your own add-in module if it does not appear on the list. Any functions available through an add-in will automatically appear in the function list under the set of "User Defined" functions.

By default, a user of your add-in module will be able to see the VBA code by using the Visual Basic editor. You can password-protect the code from within the VBA editor by selecting Tools|VBAProject Properties. The protection tab gives you the option to "Lock Project for Viewing", which renders the code invisible.

D.11 A Simulation Example

Suppose you have a large amount of money to invest and at the end of the next 5 years you wish to have it fully invested in stocks. It is often asserted in the popular press that it is preferable to invest it in the market gradually, rather than all at once. In particular, consider the strategy of each quarter taking a pro rata share of what is left and investing it in stocks. So the first quarter invest 1/20th in stocks, the second invest 1/19th of money remaining in stocks, etc. It is obvious that the strategy in which we invest in stocks over time should have a smaller average return and a lower standard deviation than a strategy in which we plunge into stocks, but how much lower and smaller? Monte Carlo simulation is a natural tool to address a question like this. We will first see how to structure the problem and then analyze it in Excel.[11,12] You may not understand the

---

[11]The following example is considerably more complicated than those that precede it. It is designed to illustrate many of the basic concepts in a nontrivial fashion. You may wish to skip it initally and return to it once you have had some experience with VBA.

[12]If you are thinking about option pricing, you might expect this example to be computed using the risk-neutral distribution. Instead, we will compare the actual payoff distributions of the two strategies in order to compare the means and standard deviations. If we wished to value the two strategies, we would substitute the risk-neutral distribution by replacing the 15% expected rate of return with the 10%

details of how the random stock price is generated. That does not matter for purposes of this example; rather, the important thing is to understand how the problem is structured and how that structure is translated into VBA.

What Is the Algorithm?

To begin, we describe the investment strategy and the evolution over time of the portfolio. Suppose we initially have $100 that is invested in bonds and nothing invested in stock. Let the variables *bonds* and *stock* denote the amount invested in each. Let h be the fraction of a year between investments in stock (so for example if h = 0.25, there are four transfers per year from bonds to stock), and let r, mu, and v denote the risk-free rate, the expected return on the stock, and the volatility of the stock, respectively.

Suppose we switch from bonds to stock 20 times, once a quarter for 5 years. Let n = the number of times we will switch. We need to know the stock price each time we switch. Denote these prices by price(0), price(1), price(2), ... , price(20). Now, each period, at the beginning of the period we first switch some funds from bonds to stock. At the end of the period, we figure out how much we earned over the period. If we wish to switch a roughly constant proportion each period, we could switch 1/20 the first period, 1/19 with 19 periods to go, and so forth. This suggests that at the beginning of period j,

```
bonds(j)=bonds(j-1) * (1-1/(n+1-j))
stock(j)=stock(j-1)+bonds(j-1)/(n+1-j)
```

At the end of the period we have

```
stock(j)=stock(j) * price(j)/price(j-1)
bonds(j) = bonds(j) * Exp(r * h)
```

In words, during period j, we earn interest on the bonds and capital gains on the stock. We can think of the *stock(j)* and *bonds(j)* on the right-hand side as denoting beginning-of-period values after we have allocated some dollars from bonds to stock, and the values on the right-hand side as the end-of-period values after we have earned interest and capital gains.

We compute the next period price as

```
price(j) = price(j-1) * Exp((mu - 0.5 * v ^ 2) * h _
   + v * h ^ (0.5) * WorksheetFunction.NormSInv(Rnd()))
```

As mentioned above, it is not important if you do not understand this expression. It is the standard way to create a random lognormally distributed stock price, where the expected return on the stock is mu, the volatility is v, and the length of a period is h. At

risk-free rate. After making this substitution, both strategies would have the same expected payoff of $161 ($100 × 1.15). Since both strategies entail buying assets at a fair price, there is no need to perform a valuation! Both will be worth the initial investment.

the end, j = n, and we will invest all remaining bonds in stock and earn returns for one final period.

This describes the stock and bond calculations for a single set of randomly drawn lognormal prices. Now we want to repeat this process many times. Each time, we will save the results of the trial and use them to compute the distribution.

VBA Code

We will set up the VBA code as a subroutine. The first several lines in the routine simply activate the worksheet where we will write the data and then clear the area. We need two columns: One to store the terminal portfolio value if we invest fully in stock at the outset; the other to store the terminal value if we invest slowly. Note that we have set it up to run 2000 trials, and we also clear 2000 rows. We tell VBA that the variables *bonds, stock,* and *price* are going to be arrays of type double, but we do not yet know what size to make the array. The "Worksheets("InvestOutput").Activate" command makes the "Invest Output" worksheet the default worksheet, so that all reading and writing will be done to it unless another worksheet is specified.

```
Sub Monte_invest()
Dim bonds() As Double
Dim stock() As Double
Dim price() As Double
Worksheets("InvestOutput").Activate
Range("a1..b2000").Select
Selection.Clear
' number of monte carlo trials
iter = 2000
```

Now we set the parameters. The risk-free rate, mean return on the stock, and volatility are all annual numbers. We invest each quarter, so h = 0.25. There are 20 periods to keep track of since we invest each quarter for 5 years. Note that once we specify 20 periods, we can dimension the bonds, stock, and price variables to run from 0 to 20. We do this using the ReDim command.

```
' number of reinvestment periods
n = 20
' Reset the dimension of the bonds and stock variable
ReDim bonds(0 To n), stock(0 To n), price(0 To n)
' length of each period
h = 0.25
' expected return on stock
mu = 0.15
' risk-free interest rate
r = 0.1
' volatility
v = 0.3
```

There will be two loops. The first, or *outer loop*, will perform one simulation. Each time through this outer loop, we have one trial; i.e., we draw a series of 20 random stock prices and we see what the terminal payoff is from our two strategies. Note that before we run through a single trial, we have to initialize our variables: The initial stock price is $100, we have $100 of bonds and no stock, and price(0), which is the intial stock price, is set to 100.

```
' each time through this loop is one complete iteration
For i = 1 To iter
 price(0) = 100
 bonds(0) = 100
 stock(0) = 0
```

The heart of the program is in the *inner loop*. This is where we perform the detailed calculations for one simulation. Each period for 20 periods we perform our allocation as above. Note that we draw a new random stock price using our standard lognormal expression.

```
For j = 1 To n
 ' allocate 1/n of bonds to stock
 stock(j) = stock(j-1) + bonds(j-1) / (n + 1 - j)
 bonds(j) = bonds(j-1) * (1 - 1 / (n + 1 - j))

 ' draw a new lognormal stock price
 price(j) = price(j-1) * Exp((mu - 0.5 * v ^ 2) * h + _
     v * h ^ (0.5) * WorksheetFunction.NormSInv(Rnd()))

 ' earn returns on bonds and stock
 bonds(j) = bonds(j) * Exp(r * h)
 stock(j) = stock(j) * (price(j) / price(j-1))

Next j
```

Once through this loop, all that remains is to write the results to "Sheet1". The following two statements do that, by writing the terminal price to column 1, row i, and the value of the terminal stock position to column 2, row i.

```
ActiveSheet.Cells(i, 1) = price(n)
ActiveSheet.Cells(i, 2) = stock(n)

Next i

End Sub
```

Note that you could also write the data across in columns: You would do this by writing

```
ActiveSheet.Cells(1, i) = price(n)
```

This would write the terminal price across the first row.

A Trick to Speed Up the Calculations

Modify the inner loop by adding the two lines referring to "ScreenUpdating":

```
' each time through this loop is one complete iteration
For i = 1 To iter
  Application.ScreenUpdating = false
  ...
  If (i Mod 100 = 0) Then Application.Screenupdating = true
  ActiveSheet.Cells(i, 1) = price(i)
  ActiveSheet.Cells(i, 2) = stock(i)
Next i
```

The first line prevents Excel from updating the display as the subroutine is run. Excel takes time to redraw the spreadsheet and graphs when numbers are added.

The second line, which is added near the end of the loop, redraws the spreadsheet every 100 iterations. The "mod" function returns the remainder from dividing the first number by the second. Thus,

```
i Mod 100
```

will equal 0 whenever i is evenly divisible by 100. So on iteration numbers 100, 200, etc., the spreadsheet will be redrawn. This cuts the calculation time approximately in half.

A p p e n d i x   E
Option Functions Available in Excel

This appendix defines the option pricing functions available in the spreadsheets accompanying this book. All are user-defined functions in Excel, written in VBA, with the code accessible and modifiable via the Visual Basic editor built into Excel. Please be aware that the spreadsheet functions provided with this book are intended for educational use, namely, to help you learn about derivatives as you read this book. Although we have tried to ensure that the functions are correct, neither the author nor Addison-Wesley claims that these functions are suitable for commercial purposes.

Three spreadsheets come with the book:

OptAll.xls This contains all of the functions and provides examples of most (not all) of the pricing functions described here.

OptBasic.xls This provides basic Black-Scholes and binomial calculations.

VBA_examples.xls This contains the VBA examples from Appendix D.

Some of the functions described here are array functions. This means that the output of the function can be in more than one cell. In order to enter an array function, highlight the output range, press the F2 key to edit the first cell in the range, enter the formula, and then press the control, shift, and enter keys simultaneously. Once an array function is entered, it can only be edited or deleted as a single entity; Excel will prohibit you from editing one cell of an array.

E.1 BLACK-SCHOLES FUNCTIONS

The following symbol definitions are used in this section: "s" = stock price, "k" = strike price, "v" = volatility (annualized), "r" = interest rate (continuously compounded, annualized), "t" = time to expiration (years), and "d" = dividend yield (continuously compounded, annualized).

Prices

Function	Description
BSCall(s, k, v, r, t, d)	*European call option price*
BSPut(s, k, v, r, t, d)	*European put option price*

Greeks

Function	Description
BSCallDelta(s, k, v, r, t, d)	*European call delta*
BSPutDelta(s, k, v, r, t, d)	*European put delta*
BSCallGamma(s, k, v, r, t, d)	*European call gamma*
BSPutGamma(s, k, v, r, t, d)	*European put gamma*
BSCallVega(s, k, v, r, t, d)	*European call vega*
BSPutVega(s, k, v, r, t, d)	*European put vega*
BSCallRho(s, k, v, r, t, d)	*European call rho*
BSPutRho(s, k, v, r, t, d)	*European put rho*
BSCallTheta(s, k, v, r, t, d)	*European call theta*
BSPutTheta(s, k, v, r, t, d)	*European put theta*
BSCallElast(s, k, v, r, t, d)	*European call elasticity*
BSPutElast(s, k, v, r, t, d)	*European put elasticity*
BSCallImpVol(s, k, v, r, t, d, c)	*Implied volatility for European call* The option price is entered as "c"; the volatility entered does not matter.
BSPutImpVol(s, k, v, r, t, d, c)	*Implied volatility for European put* The option price is entered as "c"; the volatility entered does not matter.
BSCallImpS(s, k, v, r, t, d, c)	*Implied stock price for a given European call option price*
BSPutImpS(s, k, v, r, t, d, c)	*Implied stock price for a given European put option price*

Black-Scholes Array Functions

The functions in this section are all array functions (up to 16 × 16) and have an extra string, "x", as a parameter. This parameter controls the output, with a "c" denoting "call" and "p" denoting "put", and "d", "g", "r", "v", "t", and "e" denoting delta, gamma, rho, vega, theta, and elasticity. A "+" means continue placing the output in the same row and a "/" means move to the next row. For example, the string "cp+cd+cg/pp+pd+pg" will output a two-row, three-column array containing a call price, delta, and gamma in the first row, with the same information for a put in the second row.

Function	Description
BS(s,k,v,r,t,d,x)	*Black-Scholes prices and Greeks*
BS_Text(x)	*Array function providing text description of the items in the string "x"*

Perpetual American Options

There is no simple pricing formula for American options except when the options are infinitely lived (see Chapter 12). These functions are array functions, returning the option price and the stock price at which the option should optimally be exercised, in that order. The results may be returned in either a horizontal or vertical array.

Function	Description
CallPerpetual(s, k, v, r, d)	*Perpetual American call*
PutPerpetual(s, k, v, r, d)	*Perpetual American put*

E.2 BINOMIAL FUNCTIONS

The following symbol definitions are used in this section: "s" = stock price, "k" = strike price, "v" = volatility (annualized), "r" = interest rate (continuously compounded, annualized), "t" = time to expiration (years), "d" = dividend yield (continuously compounded, annualized), "N" = number of binomial steps, "opstyle" = option style (0 = European, 1 = American), and "vest" = the period of time during which the option cannot be exercised (after this time, exercise is permitted). If "N", the number of binomial steps, is set less than or equal to 0, then N is internally reset to be 100.

By default, all binomial calculations are done using the forward tree outlined in Chapter 10. There is a constant in the VBA code called "TreeType". If set equal to 0 (the default), all calculations are done with a forward tree. If equal to 1, a CRR tree is used, and if equal to 2, a lognormal tree is used (see Section 11.3).

The functions in this section are all array functions, returning the option price, along with delta, gamma, and theta, in that order. So, for example, if you just enter the BinomCall function in a single cell, it will return the option price. If you enter it as an array function spanning two cells, you will get the price and delta, etc. The array can be entered either horizontally or vertically.

Function	Description
BinomCall(s, k, v, r, t, d, opstyle, N)	*Binomial call*
BinomPut(s, k, v, r, t, d, opstyle, N)	*Binomial put*
BinomCallBermudan(s, k, v, r, t, d, opstyle, N, vest)	*Binomial Bermudan call*
BinomPutBermudan(s, k, v, r, t, d, opstyle, N, vest)	*Binomial Bermudan put*

E.3 EXOTIC OPTIONS

The following symbol definitions are used in this section: "s" = stock price, "k" = strike price, "v" = volatility (annualized), "r" = interest rate (continuously compounded, annualized), "t" = time to expiration (years), "d" = dividend yield (continuously compounded, annualized), "rho" = correlation coefficient, and "h" = barrier.

"Vanilla" Barrier Options

For ordinary barrier puts and calls, the (descriptive) names are of the form

Option Type + Barrier Type

For example, the pricing function for an up-and-in call is "CallUpIn".

Function	Description
CallDownIn(s, k, v, r, t, d, h)	*Down-and-in call*
CallDownOut(s, k, v, r, t, d, h)	*Down-and-out call*
CallUpIn(s, k, v, r, t, d, h)	*Up-and-in call*
CallUpOut(s, k, v, r, t, d, h)	*Up-and-out call*
PutDownIn(s, k, v, r, t, d, h)	*Down-and-in put*
PutDownOut(s, k, v, r, t, d, h)	*Down-and-out put*
PutUpIn(s, k, v, r, t, d, h)	*Up-and-in put*
PutUpOut(s, k, v, r, t, d, h)	*Up-and-out put*

Other Barrier Options

For most other barrier options, the function names are mnemonic, and have three parts:

Payoff Type + Barrier Type + Option Type

In particular,

- The payoff type is one of

    Cash—the payoff is $1.

    Asset—the payoff is one unit of the asset.

- The barrier type is one of

    DI—"down-and-in," in other words the stock price is initially above the barrier, which must be hit in order for the payoff to be received.

    DO—"down-and-out," in other words the stock price is initially above the barrier, which must not be hit in order for the payoff to be received.

    UI—"up-and-in," in other words the stock price is initially below the barrier, which must be hit in order for the payoff to be received.

    UO—"up-and-out," in other words the stock price is initially below the barrier, which must not be hit in order for the payoff to be received.

- The option type is one of

> **Call**—in order for the payoff to be received, the asset price must be above the strike at expiration.
>
> **Put**—in order for the payoff to be received, the asset price must be below the strike at expiration.

For example, an option that pays $1 if the stock price exceeds the strike price at expiration, provided that the barrier, below the inital stock price, has not been hit would have the name

$$\text{CashDOCall} = \underbrace{\text{Cash}}_{\substack{\text{Payoff of \$1}}} + \underbrace{\text{DO}}_{\substack{\text{if the barrier, below} \\ \text{the intial stock price,} \\ \text{has not been hit}}} + \underbrace{\text{Call}}_{\substack{\text{and the stock price} \\ \text{exceeds the strike} \\ \text{at expiration}}}$$

Cash-or-Nothing

Function	Description
CashCall(s, k, v, r, t, d)	*Cash-or-nothing call* Receive $1 if $s_t > k$ at expiration.
CashPut(s, k, v, r, t, d)	*Cash-or-nothing put* Receive $1 if $s_t < k$ at expiration.
CashDICall(s, k, v, r, t, d, h)	*Cash-or-nothing down-and-in call* Receive $1 if $s_t > k$ at expiration and the barrier $h < s$ has been hit.
CashDOCall(s, k, v, r, t, d, h)	*Cash-or-nothing down-and-out call* Receive $1 if $s_t > k$ at expiration and the barrier $h < s$ has not been hit.
CashDOPut(s, k, v, r, t, d, h)	*Cash-or-nothing down-and-out put* Receive $1 if $s_t < k$ at expiration and the barrier $h < s$ has not been hit.
CashDIPut(s, k, v, r, t, d, h)	*Cash-or-nothing down-and-in put* Receive $1 if $s_t < k$ at expiration and the barrier $h < s$ has been hit.
CashUICall(s, k, v, r, t, d, h)	*Cash-or-nothing up-and-in call* Receive $1 if $s_t > k$ at expiration and the barrier $h > s$ has been hit.

CashUOCall(s, k, v, r, t, d, h)	*Cash-or-nothing up-and-out call* Receive $1 if $s_t > k$ at expiration and the barrier $h > s$ has not been hit.
CashUOPut(s, k, v, r, t, d, h)	*Cash-or-nothing up-and-out put* Receive $1 if $s_t < k$ at expiration and the barrier $h > s$ has not been hit.
CashUIPut(s, k, v, r, t, d, h)	*Cash-or-nothing up-and-in put* Receive $1 if $s_t < k$ at expiration and the barrier $h > s$ has been hit.
DR(s, v, r, t, d, h)	*Down rebate* Receive $1 at the time the barrier, $h < s$, is hit.
UR(s, v, r, t, d, h)	*Up rebate* Receive $1 at the time the barrier, $h > s$, is hit.
DRDeferred(s, v, r, t, d, h)	*Deferred down rebate* Receive $1 at expiration if prior to expiration the barrier, $h < s$, is hit.
URDeferred(s, v, r, t, d, h)	*Deferred up rebate* Receive $1 at expiration if prior to expiration the barrier, $h > s$, is hit.

Asset-or-Nothing Note that there is no need for an asset-or-nothing rebate option, because there is no difference between an option that pays h if the share price hits h, and an option that pays a share if the share price hits h.

Function	**Description**
AssetCall(s, k, v, r, t, d)	*Asset-or-nothing call* Receive one unit of the asset if $s_t > k$ at expiration.
AssetPut(s, k, v, r, t, d)	*Asset-or-nothing put* Receive one unit of the asset if $s_t < k$ at expiration.
AssetDICall(s, k, v, r, t, d, h)	*Asset-or-nothing down-and-in call* Receive one unit of the asset if $s_t > k$ at expiration and the barrier $h < s$ has been hit.
AssetDOCall(s, k, v, r, t, d, h)	*Asset-or-nothing down-and-out call* Receive one unit of the asset if $s_t > k$ at expiration and the barrier $h < s$ has not been hit.
AssetDOPut(s, k, v, r, t, d, h)	*Asset-or-nothing down-and-out put* Receive one unit of the asset if $s_t < k$ at expiration and the barrier $h < s$ has not been hit.

`AssetDIPut(s, k, v, r, t, d, h)`	*Asset-or-nothing down-and-in put* Receive one unit of the asset if $s_t < k$ at expiration and the barrier $h < s$ has been hit.
`AssetUICall(s, k, v, r, t, d, h)`	*Asset-or-nothing up-and-in call* Receive one unit of the asset if $s_t > k$ at expiration and the barrier $h > s$ has been hit.
`AssetUOCall(s, k, v, r, t, d, h)`	*Asset-or-nothing up-and-out call* Receive one unit of the asset if $s_t > k$ at expiration and the barrier $h > s$ has not been hit.
`AssetUOPut(s, k, v, r, t, d, h)`	*Asset-or-nothing up-and-out put* Receive one unit of the asset if $s_t < k$ at expiration and the barrier $h > s$ has not been hit.
`AssetUIPut(s, k, v, r, t, d, h)`	*Asset-or-nothing up-and-in put* Receive one unit of the asset if $s_t < k$ at expiration and the barrier $h > s$ has been hit.

Asian Options

There are straightforward closed-form solutions for geometric average European options, but not for arithmetic average options (see Chapter 19). Hence, the only functions implemented in Excel are for options with payoffs based on the geometric average price at expiration, G_t, which is computed over the life of the option.

The geometric average can be computed based on prices sampled N times over the life of the option. If N is not specified, a continuous average is assumed.

Function	Description
`GeomAvgPriceCall(s, k, v,` `r, t, d, Optional N)`	*Geometric average price call* Option with time t payoff $max(0, G_t - k)$.
`GeomAvgPricePut(s, k,` `v, r, t, d, Optional N)`	*Geometric average price put* Option with time t payoff $max(0, k - G_t)$.
`GeomAvgStrikeCall(s, m,` `v, r, t, d, Optional N)`	*Geometric average strike call* Option with time t payoff $max(0, s_t - G_t)$.
`GeomAvgStrikePut(s, m,` `v, r, t, d, Optional N)`	*Geometric average strike put* Option with time t payoff $max(0, G_t - s_t)$.

Compound Options

European compound options are options to buy or sell some other option, and as such have two expiration dates. The first, denoted t1, is the date at which the option to buy or sell an option must be exercised. The second, t2 is the date at which the bought or sold option expires. The strike price for buying or selling the underlying option at date t1 is denoted "x".

Function	Description
CallOnCall(s, k, x, v, r, t1, t2, d)	*Compound call on call* Call option to buy a call option.
PutOnCall(s, k, x, v, r, t1, t2, d)	*Compound put on call* Put option to sell a call option.
CallOnPut(s, k, x, v, r, t1, t2, d)	*Compound call on put* Call option to buy a put option.
PutOnPut(s, k, x, v, r, t1, t2, d)	*Compound put on put* Put option to sell a put option.

Exchange and Rainbow Options

Exchange options and rainbow options have payoffs depending on two or more asset prices. An exchange option is the right to exchange one asset for another (ordinary calls and puts are exchange options where one of the two assets is cash). A rainbow option has the payoff $max(s, q, k)$, where s and q are risky asset prices with dividend yields δ_s and δ_q, volatilities v_s and v_q, and correlation coefficient ρ. For binomial valuation, the number of binomial steps is N and the option style, *OpStyle*, is 0 for a European option and 1 for an American option.

Function	Description
BSCallExchange(s, v_s, δ_s, q, v_q, δ_q, ρ, t)	*European exchange call* Option to acquire s by giving up q.
BSPutExchange(s, v_s, δ_s, q, v_q, δ_q, ρ, t)	*European exchange put* Option to give up s in exchange for q.
BinomCallExchange(s, v_s, δ_s, q, v_q, δ_q, ρ, t, OpStyle, N)	*American exchange call* Option to acquire s by giving up q.
BinomPutExchange(s, v_s, δ_s, q, v_q, δ_q, ρ, t, OpStyle, N)	*American exchange put* Option to give up s in exchange for q.
RainbowCall(s, v_s, δ_s, q, v_q, δ_q, ρ, k, r, t)	*European rainbow call* Option on the maximum of s, q, and k.
RainbowPut(s, v_s, δ_s, q, v_q, δ_q, ρ, k, r, t)	*European rainbow put* Option on the minimum of s, q, and k.

E.4 INTEREST RATE FUNCTIONS

These are array functions that compute prices, yields, delta, and gamma for zero-coupon bonds. These functions assume the short-term interest rate is generated by a process of the form

$$dr = a(b - r)dt + sr^\eta dZ$$

where $\eta = 0$ for the Vasicek formula and $\eta = 0.5$ for the CIR formula. The interest rate risk premium is ϕ.

Function	Description
Vasicek(a, b, ϕ, v, r, T)	*Vasicek interest rate function* Array function that returns the price of a zero-coupon bond paying $1; the long-term yield, delta, and gamma with respect to the interest rate; and the yield to maturity.
CIR(a, b, ϕ, v, r, T)	*Cox-Ingersoll-Ross interest rate function* Array function that returns the price of a zero-coupon bond paying $1; the long-term yield, delta, and gamma with respect to the interest rate; and the yield to maturity.

Glossary

Accreting swap   A swap where the notional amount increases over the life of the swap.

Accrued interest   The pro-rated portion of a bond's coupon since the previous coupon date.

American option   An option that may be exercised at any time during its life.

Amortizing swap   A swap where the notional amount declines over the life of the swap.

Antithetic variate method   A technique used in Monte Carlo valuation, in which each random draw is used to create two simulated prices from opposite tails of the asset price distribution.

Arbitrage   A transaction generating a positive cash flow either today or in the future by simultaneously buying and selling related assets, with no net investment of funds, and with no risk.

Arithmetic Brownian motion   A continuous stochastic process, $x(t)$, in which the increments are given as $dx(t) = \alpha\, dt + \sigma\, dZ$, where dZ is the increment to a Brownian process.

Asian option   An option in which the payoff at maturity depends upon an average of the asset prices over the life of the option.

Asian tail   A reference price that is computed as an average of recent prices. For example, an equity-linked note may have a payoff based on the average daily stock price over the last 20 days (the Asian tail).

Ask price   The price at which a dealer or market-maker offers to sell a security. Also called the *offer price*.

Asset swap   A swap, typically involving a bond, in which fixed bond payments are swapped for payments based on a floating rate.

Asset-or-nothing call   An option that pays a unit of the asset if the asset price exceeds the strike price at expiration or zero otherwise.

Asset-or-nothing option   An option that pays a unit of the asset if the option is in-the-money or zero otherwise.

Asset-or-nothing put   An option that pays a unit of the asset if the asset price is less than the strike price at expiration or zero otherwise.

Asymmetric butterfly spread   A butterfly spread in which the distance between strike prices is not equal.

At-the-money   An option for which the price of the underlying asset approximately equals the strike price.

Back-to-back transaction   A transaction where a dealer enters into offsetting transactions with different parties, effectively serving as a go-between.

Backward equation   See *Kolmogorov backward equation*.

Backwardation   A forward curve in which the futures prices are falling with time to expiration.

Barrier option   An option that has a payoff depending upon whether, at some point during the life of the option, the price of the underlying asset has moved past a reference price (the barrier). Examples are knock-in and knock-out options.

Basis   The difference between the cash price of the underlying asset and the futures price.

Basis point $1/100^{th}$ of one percent, i.e., one ten-thousandth (.0001).

Basis risk   The possibility of unexpected changes in the difference between the price of an asset and the price of the contract hedging the asset.

Bear spread   The sale of a call (or put) together with the purchase of an otherwise identical higher-strike call (or put).

Bermudan option   An option that can only be exercised at specified times during its life.

Bid price   The price at which a dealer or market-maker buys a security.

Bid-ask spread   The difference between the bid price and the ask price.

Binary option   An option that has a payoff that is a discrete amount, for example, $1 or one share. Also called a *digital option*.

Binomial tree   A representation of possible asset price movements over time, in which the asset price is modeled as moving up or down by a given amount each period.

Black formula   A version of the Black-Scholes formula in which the underlying asset is a futures price and the dividend yield is replaced with the risk-free rate. See equation (12.7) (p. 371).

Black-Scholes equation   The partial differential equation, equation (21.11) (p. 660), relating price, delta, gamma, and theta, that must be satisfied by derivatives. The Black-Scholes *formula* solves the Black-Scholes *equation*.

Black-Scholes formula   The formula giving the price of a European call option as a function of the stock price, strike price, time to expiration, interest rate, volatility, and dividend yield. See equation (12.1) (p. 365).

Bootstrapping   This term has two meanings. First, it refers to the procedure where coupon bonds are used to generate the set of zero-coupon bond prices. Second, it means the use of historical returns to create an empirical probability distribution for returns.

Boundary condition   The value of a derivative claim at a certain time, or at a particular price of the underlying asset. For example, a boundary condition for a zero-coupon bond is that the bond at maturity is worth its promised maturity value.

Box spread   An option position in which the stock is synthetically purchased (buy call, sell put) at one price and sold (sell call, buy put) at a different price. When constructed with European options, the box spread is equivalent to a zero-coupon bond.

Brownian motion   A stochastic process in which the random variable moves continuously and follows a random walk with normally distributed, independent increments. Named after the Scottish botanist Robert Brown, who in 1827 noticed that pollen grains suspended in water exhibited continual movement. Brownian motion is also called a *Wiener process*.

Bull spread   The purchase of a call (or put) together with the sale of an otherwise identical higher-strike call (or put).

Butterfly spread   A position created by buying a call, selling two calls at a higher strike price, and buying a fourth call at a still higher strike price, with an equal distance between strike prices. The butterfly spread can also be created using puts alone, or by buying a straddle and insuring it with the purchase of out-of-the-money calls and puts, or in a variety of other ways.

Calendar spread   A spread position in which the bought and sold options or futures have the same underlying asset but different times to maturity.

Call option   A contract giving the buyer the right, but not the obligation, to buy the underlying asset at a prespecified price.

Cap   An options contract that serves as insurance against a high price. (See also *Interest rate cap*.)

Caplet   A contract that insures a borrower against a high interest rate on a single date. A collection of caplets is an *interest rate cap*.

Capped option   An option with a maximum payoff, where the option is automatically exercised if the underlying asset reaches the price at which the maximum payoff is attained.

Carry   Another term for owning an asset, typically used to refer to commodities. (See also *Carry market* and *Cost of carry*).

Carry market   A situation where the forward price is such that the return on a cash-and-carry is the risk-free rate.

Cash flow mapping   A procedure in which the cash flows of a given claim are assigned—or mapped—to a set of benchmark claims. This provides a way to approximate the claim in terms of the benchmark claims.

Cash settlement   A procedure where settlement entails a cash payment from one party to the other, instead of delivery of an asset.

Cash-and-carry   The simultaneous spot purchase and forward sale of an asset or commodity.

Cash-and-carry arbitrage   The use of a cash-and-carry to effect an arbitrage.

Cash-or-nothing call An option that pays a fixed amount of cash if the asset price exceeds the strike price at expiration or zero otherwise.

Cash-or-nothing option An option that pays a fixed amount of cash if the option is in-the-money or zero otherwise.

Cash-or-nothing put An option that pays a fixed amount of cash if the asset price is less than the strike price at expiration or zero otherwise.

Central limit theorem One of the most important results in statistics, which states that the sum of independent and identically distributed random variables has a limiting distribution that is normal.

Cheapest to deliver When a futures contract permits the seller to select the precise asset or commodity to deliver to the buyer, the cheapest to deliver is the asset that is most profitable for the short to deliver.

Cholesky decomposition A formula used to construct a set of correlated random variables from a set of uncorrelated random variables.

Clean price The present value of a bond's future cash flows less accrued interest.

Clearinghouse A financial organization, typically associated with one or more exchanges, that matches the buy and sell orders that take place during the day and keeps track of the obligations and payments required of the members of the clearinghouse.

Collar The purchase of a put and sale of a call at a higher strike price.

Collar width The difference between the strike prices of the two options in a collar.

Collect-on-delivery option An option where the premium is paid only when the option is exercised.

Commodity spread Offsetting long and short positions in closely related commodities. (See also *Crack spread* and *Crush spread*.)

Compound option An option that has an option as the underlying asset.

Concave Shaped like the cross section of an upside-down bowl.

Constructive sale A term in tax law describing the owner of an asset entering into an offsetting position that largely eliminates the risk of holding the asset.

Contango A forward curve in which futures prices are rising with time to expiration.

Continuously compounded interest rate A way of quoting an interest rate such that if $1 is invested at a continuously compounded rate of r, the payoff in one year is e^r.

Control variate method A technique used in Monte Carlo valuation in which simulated asset prices are used to compute two derivatives prices: The price of the derivative that is being valued, and the price of a related derivative for which the value is known. The error in valuing the derivative with a known price is used as a control for that with the unknown price.

Convenience yield A nonmonetary return to ownership of an asset or commodity.

Conversion A risk-free position consisting of an asset, a purchased put, and a written call.

Convertible bond A bond which, at the option of the bondholder, can be surrendered for a specified number of shares of stock.

Convex Shaped like the cross section of a bowl.

Convexity The second derivative of a bond's price with respect to a change in the interest rate, divided by the bond price.

Cost of carry The interest cost of owning an asset, less lease or dividend payments received as a result of ownership; the net cash flow resulting from borrowing to buy an asset.

Covered call A long position in an asset together with a written call on the same asset.

Covered interest arbitrage A zero-investment strategy with simultaneous borrowing in one currency, lending in another, and entering into a forward contract to guarantee the exchange rate when the loans mature.

Covered write A long position in an asset coupled with sale of a call option on the same asset.

Crack spread The difference between the price of crude oil futures and that of equivalent amounts of heating oil and gasoline.

Credit derivative A claim where the payoff depends upon the credit rating or default status of a firm.

Credit risk Risk resulting from the possibility that a counterparty will be financially unable to meet its contractual obligations.

Credit-linked note   A bond that has payments determined at least in part by credit events (e.g., default) at a different firm.

Crush spread   The difference between the price of a quantity of soybeans and that of the soybean meal and oil that can be produced by those soybeans.

Cumulative distribution function   A function giving the probability that a value drawn from a distribution will be less than or equal to some specified value.

Cumulative normal distribution function
The cumulative distribution function for the normal distribution; $N(x)$ in the Black-Scholes equation.

Currency swap   A swap in which the parties make payments based on the difference in debt payments in different currencies.

Currency-translated index   An investment in an index denominated in a foreign currency, where the buyer bears both currency and asset risk.

Debt capacity   The maximum amount of debt that can be issued by a firm or secured by a specific asset.

Default premium   The difference between the yield on a bond and that on an otherwise equivalent default-free bond.

Default swap   A contract in which the swap buyer pays a regular premium; in exchange, if a default in a specified bond occurs, the swap seller pays the buyer the loss due to the default.

Deferred down rebate option   A deferred rebate option for which the current stock price is above the rebate barrier.

Deferred rebate option   A claim that pays $1 at expiration if the price of the underlying asset has reached a barrier prior to expiration.

Deferred swap   A swap with terms specified today, but for which swap payments begin at a later date than for an ordinary swap.

Deferred up rebate option   A deferred rebate option for which the current stock price is below the rebate barrier.

Delivery   The act of the seller (e.g., of a forward contract) supplying the underlying asset to the buyer.

Delta   The change in the price of a derivative due to a change in the price of the underlying asset.

Delta-gamma approximation   A formula using the delta and gamma to approximate the change in the derivative price due to a change in the price of the underlying asset.

Delta-gamma-theta approximation   A formula using the delta, gamma, and theta to approximate the change in the derivative price due to a change in the price of the underlying asset and the passage of time.

Delta-hedging   Hedging a derivative position using the underlying asset, with the amount of the underlying asset determined by the derivative's sensitivity (*delta*) to the price of the underlying asset.

Derivative   A financial instrument that has a value determined by the price of something else.

Diff swap   A swap in which payments are based on the difference in floating interest rates on a given notional amount denominated in a single currency.

Differential equation   An equation relating a variable to its derivatives and one or more independent variables.

Diffusion process   Generally, a continuous stochastic process in which uncertainty increases with time. Also used to describe the Brownian (random) part of an Itô process.

Digital option   Another name for a binary option.

Dirty price   The present value of a bond's future cash flows (this implicitly includes accrued interest).

Diversifiable risk   Risk that is, in the limit, eliminated by combining a large number of assets in a portfolio.

Down-and-in   A knock-in option for which the barrier is less than the current price of the underlying asset.

Down-and-out   A knock-out option for which the barrier is less than the current price of the underlying asset.

Drift   The expected change per unit time in an asset price.

Duration Generally, the weighted average life of the bond, which also provides a measure of the bond's sensitivity to interest rate changes. Two common duration measures are *modified duration* and *Macaulay duration*.

Effective annual interest rate A way of quoting an interest rate such that the quoted rate is the annual percentage increase in an amount invested at this rate. If $1 is invested at an effective annual rate of r, the payoff in one year is $1 + r$.

Elasticity The percent change in an option price for a one-percent change in the price of the underlying asset.

Equity-linked forward A forward contract (e.g., for currency) where the quantity to be bought or sold depends upon the performance of a stock or stock index.

European option An option that can only be exercised at expiration.

Exchange option An option permitting the holder to obtain one asset by giving up another. Standard calls and puts are exchange options in which one of the two assets is cash.

Exercise The exchange of the strike price (or strike asset) for the underlying asset at the terms specified in the option contract.

Exercise price Under the terms of an option contract, the amount that can be exchanged for the underlying asset.

Exercise style The circumstances under which an option holder has the right to exercise an option. "European" and "American" are exercise styles.

Exotic option A derivatives contract in which an ordinary derivative has been altered to change the characteristics of the derivative in a meaningful way. Also called a *nonstandard option*.

Expectations hypothesis A term with multiple meanings, one of which is that the expected future interest rate equals the implied forward rate.

Expiration The date beyond which an unexercised option is worthless.

Fair value Another name for the theoretical forward price: Spot price plus interest less the future value of dividends.

Financial engineering Creating new financial instruments by combining other derivatives, or more generally, by using derivatives pricing techniques.

Floor An option position that guarantees a minimum price.

Forward contract An agreement that sets today the terms—including price and quantity—at which you buy or sell an asset or commodity at a specific time in the future.

Forward curve The set of forward or futures prices with different expiration dates on a given date for a given asset.

Forward premium The annualized percentage difference between the forward price and the spot price.

Forward rate agreement A forward contract for an interest rate.

Forward strip Another name for the *forward curve*.

Futures contract An agreement that is similar to a forward contract except that the buyer and seller post margin and the contract is marked-to-market periodically. Futures are typically exchange-traded.

Futures overlay Converting an investment in asset A into the economic equivalent of an investment in asset B by entering into a short futures position on asset A and a long futures position on asset B.

Gamma The change in delta when the price of the underlying asset changes by one unit.

Gap option An option where the option owner has the right to exercise the option at strike K_1 if the stock price exceeds (or, depending on the option, is less than) the price K_2. For an ordinary option, $K_1 = K_2$.

Geometric Brownian motion A continuous stochastic process, $x(t)$, in which the increments are given as $dx(t)/x(t) = \alpha dt + \sigma dZ$, where dZ is the increment to a Brownian process.

Girsanov's theorem A result that permits a change in the drift of an Itô process accompanied by a change in the Brownian motion driving the process.

Greeks A term generally referring to delta, gamma, vega, theta, and rho, all of which measure the change in the price of a derivative when there is a change in an input to the pricing formula.

Haircut The collateral, over and above the market value of the security, required by the lender when a security is borrowed.

Heat rate A measure of the efficiency with which heat can be used to produce electricity. Specifically, it is the number of British Thermal Units required to produce one kilowatt/hour of electricity.

Hedging An action—such as entering into a derivatives position—that reduces the risk of loss.

Heston model An option pricing model in which the instantaneous variance of the stock return follows a mean-reverting square root process.

Historical volatility The standard deviation of the continuously compounded return on an asset, measured using historical prices.

Hysteresis The failure of an effect to reverse itself as the underlying cause is reversed.

Implied forward rate The forward interest rate between time t_1 and time t_2 ($t_1 < t_2$) that makes an investor indifferent between, on the one hand, buying a bond maturing at t_2, and, on the other hand, buying a bond maturing at t_1 and reinvesting the proceeds at this forward interest rate.

Implied repo rate The rate of return on a cash-and-carry.

Implied volatility The volatility for which the theoretical option price (typically computed using the Black-Scholes formula) equals the observed market price of the option.

Interest rate cap A contract that periodically pays the difference between the market interest rate and a guaranteed rate, if the difference is positive.

In-the-money An option that would have value if exercised. For an in-the-money call, the stock price exceeds the strike price. For an in-the-money put, the stock price is less than the strike price.

Investment trigger price The price of an investment project (or the price of the good to be produced) at which it is optimal to invest in the project.

Itô process A continuous stochastic process that can be written in the form $dX(t) = \alpha[X(t), t] dt + \sigma[X(t), t] dZ(t)$, where $dZ(t)$ is the increment to a Brownian process.

Itô's Lemma If x follows an Itô process, Itô's Lemma describes the process followed by $f(x)$. For example, if x is a stock price and $f(x)$ an option price, Itô's Lemma characterizes the behavior of the option price in terms of the process for the stock.

Jensen's inequality If x is a random variable and $f(x)$ is convex, Jensen's inequality states that $E[f(x)] \geq f[E(x)]$. The inequality is reversed if $f(x)$ is concave.

Jump-diffusion model A process for an asset price in which the asset most of the time follows an Itô process but can also jump discretely, with occurrence of the jump controlled by a Poisson process.

Kappa Another name for *vega*.

Knock-in option An option in which there can only be a final payoff if, during a specified period of time, the price of the underlying asset has reached a specified level.

Knock-out option An option in which there can only be a final payoff if, during a specified period of time, the price of the underlying asset has *not* reached a specified level.

Kolmogorov backward equation A partial differential equation, equation (21.32) (p. 668), that is related to the Black-Scholes equation and that is satisfied by probability distributions for the underlying asset.

Kurtosis A measure of the peakedness of a probability distribution. For a random variable x with mean μ and standard deviation σ, kurtosis is the fourth central moment divided by the squared variance, $E(x - \mu)^4/\sigma^4$. For a normal random variable, kurtosis is 3.

Ladder option If the barrier $L > K$ is reached over the life of the option, a ladder option at expiration pays $max(0, L - K, S_T - K)$. If the barrier is not reached, the option pays $max(0, S_T - K)$.

Lambda   Another name for *vega*.

Lattice   A binomial tree in which an up move followed by a down move leads to the same price as a down move followed by an up move. Also called a *recombining* binomial tree.

Lease rate   The annualized payment required to borrow an asset, or equivalently, the annualized payment received in exchange for lending an asset.

LIBID   London Interbank Bid Rate. See *LIBOR*.

LIBOR   London Interbank Offer Rate. A measure of the borrowing rate for large international banks. The British Banker's Association determines LIBOR daily for different currencies by surveying at least 8 banks, asking at what rate they could borrow, dropping the top and bottom quartiles of the responses, and computing an arithmetic average of the remaining quotes. Since LIBOR is an average, there may be no actual transactions at that rate. Confusingly, LIBOR is also sometimes referred to as a lending rate. This is because a bank serving as a market-maker in the interbank market will offer to lend money at a high interest rate (LIBOR) and borrow money at a low interest rate (LIBID). (The difference between LIBOR and LIBID is the bid-ask spread in the interbank market.) A bank needing to borrow will thus pay LIBOR, and a bank with excess funds will receive LIBID. See also *LIBID*.

Lognormal distribution   A probability distribution in which the natural logarithm of the variable is normally distributed.

Long   A position is long with respect to a price if the position profits from an increase in that price. An owner of a stock profits from an increase in the stock price and, hence, is long the stock. An owner of an option profits from an increase in volatility and, hence, is long volatility.

Long forward   The party to a forward contract who has an obligation to buy the underlying asset.

Lookback call   See *Lookback option*.

Lookback option   An option that, at maturity, pays off based on the maximum ($\overline{S}_T$) or minimum ($\underline{S}_T$) stock price over the life of the option. A *lookback call* has the payoff $S_T - \underline{S}_T$ and a *lookback put* has the payoff $\overline{S}_T - S_T$.

Lookback put   See *Lookback option*.

Macaulay duration   The percent change in a bond's price for a given percent change in one plus the bond's yield. This calculation can be interpreted as the weighted average life of the bond, with the weights being the percentage of the bond's value due to each payment.

Maintenance margin   The level of margin at which the contract holder is required to add cash or securities to the margin account.

Margin   A deposit required for both buyers and sellers of a futures contract, which indemnifies the counterparty against the failure of the buyer or seller to meet the obligations of the contract.

Margin call   The requirement that the owner of a margined position add funds to the margin account. This can result from a loss on the position or an increase in the margin requirement.

Market corner   Owning a large percentage of the available supply of an asset or commodity that is required for delivery under the terms of a derivatives contract.

Market-maker   A trader in an asset, commodity, or derivative who simultaneously offers to buy at one price (the bid price) or to sell at a higher price (the offer price), thereby "making a market."

Market-timing   The allocation of assets between stocks and bonds in an attempt to invest in whichever asset is going to have a higher return.

Mark-to-market   The procedure of revaluing a portfolio or position to reflect current market prices.

Modified duration   The percent change in a bond's price for a unit change in the yield. Modified duration is also Macaulay duration divided by one plus the bond's yield per payment period.

Monte Carlo valuation   A procedure for pricing derivative claims by discounting expected payoffs, where the expected payoff is computed using simulated prices for the underlying asset.

Naked writing   Selling options without an offsetting position in the underlying asset.

Net payoff   Another term for *profit*.

Nondiversifiable risk   Risk that remains after a large number of assets are combined in a portfolio.

Nonrecombining tree   A binomial tree describing asset price moves in which an up move followed by a down move yields a different price than a down move followed by an up move.

Nonstandard option   See *Exotic option*.

Normal distribution   A bell-shaped, symmetric, continuous probability distribution that assigns positive probability to all values from $-\infty$ to $+\infty$. Sometimes called the "bell curve." (See also *Central limit theorem*.)

Notional amount   The dollar amount used as a scale factor in calculating payments for a forward contract, futures contract, or swap.

Notional principal   The notional amount for an interest rate swap.

Numeraire   The units in which a payoff is denominated.

Offer price   The same as the *ask price*.

Off-market forward   A forward contract in which the forward price is set so that the value of the contract is not zero.

Open interest   The quantity of a derivatives contract that is outstanding at a point in time. (One long and one short position count as one unit outstanding.)

Open outcry   A system of trading in which buyers and sellers in one physical location convey offers to buy and sell by gesturing and shouting.

Option elasticity   The percent change in an option price for a one percent change in the price of the underlying asset.

Option overwriting   Selling a call option against a long position in the underlying asset.

Option writer   The party with a short position in the option.

Order statistics   The n draws of a random variable sorted in ascending order.

Out-of-the-money   An option that would be exercised at a loss. An out-of-the-money call has the stock price less than the strike price. An out-of-the-money put has the stock price greater than the strike price.

Outperformance option   An option in which the payoff is determined by the extent to which one asset price is greater than another asset price.

Over-the-counter market   A term used generally to refer to transactions (e.g., purchases and sales of securities or derivatives contracts) that occur without the involvement of a regulated exchange.

Par bond   A bond for which the price at issue equals the maturity value.

Par coupon   The coupon rate on a par bond.

Partial expectation   The sum (or integral) of a set of outcomes times the probability of those outcomes.

Path-dependent   A derivative where the final payoff depends upon the path taken by the stock price, instead of just the final stock price.

Payer swaption   A swaption giving the holder the right to be the fixed-rate payer in a swap.

Paylater strategy   Generally used to refer to option strategies in which the position buyer makes no payments unless the option moves more into the money.

Payoff   The value of a position at a point in time. The term often implicitly refers to a payoff at expiration or maturity.

Payoff diagram   A graph in which the value of a derivative or other claim at a point in time is plotted against the price of the underlying asset.

Perpetual option   An option that never expires.

Poisson distribution   A probability distribution that counts the number of events occurring in an interval of time, assuming that the occurrence of events is independent.

Positive-definite   An $n \times n$ matrix with elements $a_{i,j}$ is positive-definite if, for every $\omega_i \neq 0$, $i = 1, \ldots, n$, $\sum_{i=1}^{n} \sum_{j=1}^{n} \omega_i \omega_j a_{i,j} > 0$. A covariance matrix is positive-definite.

Power option   An option where the payoff is based on the price of an asset raised to a power.

Prepaid forward contract   A contract calling for payment today and delivery of the asset or commodity at a time in the future.

Prepaid forward price   The price the buyer pays today for a prepaid forward contract.

Prepaid swap   A contract calling for payment today and delivery of the asset or commodity at multiple specified times in the future.

Price participation   The extent to which an equity-linked note benefits from an increase in the price of the stock or index to which it is linked.

Price value of a basis point   The change in a bond price due to a one-basis-point change in the yield of the bond. Frequently abbreviated PVBP.

Profit   The payoff less the future value of the original cost to acquire the position.

Profit diagram   A graph plotting the *profit* on a position against a range of prices for the underlying asset.

Proprietary trading   Taking positions in an asset or derivative to express a view, for example, that a stock price will rise or that implied volatility will fall.

Purchased call   A long position in a call.

Purchased put   A long position in a put.

Put option   A contract giving the buyer the right, but not the obligation, to sell the underlying asset at a prespecified price.

Put-call parity   A relationship stating that the difference between the premiums of a call and a put with the same strike price and time to expiration equals the difference between the present value of the forward price and the present value of the strike price.

Quantile   The percentage of data points below a given value.

Quanto   A derivatives contract with a payoff in which foreign-currency-denominated quantities are treated as if they were denominated in the domestic currency.

Quasi-arbitrage   The replacement of one asset or position with another that has equivalent risk and a higher expected rate of return.

Rainbow option   An option that has a payoff based on the maximum or minimum of two (or more) risky assets and cash. For example, the payoff to a rainbow call is $max(S_T, Q_T, K)$, where S_T and Q_T are risky asset prices.

Random walk   A stochastic process, $X(t)$, in which increments, $\epsilon(t)$, are independent and identically distributed: $X(t) = X(t - h) + \epsilon(t)$.

Ratings transition   A change in the credit rating of a bond from one value to another.

Ratio spread   Buying m of an option at one strike and selling n of an otherwise identical option at a different strike.

Real options   The applications of derivatives theory to the operation and valuation of real (physical) investment projects.

Rebate option   A claim that pays $1 at the time the price of the underlying asset reaches a barrier.

Receiver swaption   A swaption giving the holder the right to receive the fixed rate in a swap.

Recombining tree   A binomial tree describing asset price moves in which an up move followed by a down move yields the same price as a down move followed by an up move. Also called a *lattice*.

Recovery value   The percentage of par value received by a bondholder in a bankruptcy.

Reference price   A market price or rate used to determine the payoff on a derivatives contract.

Repo   Another name for a *repurchase agreement*.

Repo rate   The annualized percentage difference between the original sale price and final repurchase price in a repurchase agreement.

Repricing   The replacement of an out-of-the-money compensation option with an at-the-money compensation option.

Repurchase agreement   The sale of a security coupled with an agreement to buy it back at a later date.

Reverse cash-and-carry   The simultaneous short-sale and forward purchase of an asset or commodity.

Reverse conversion   A short position in an asset coupled with a purchased call and written put, both with the same strike price and time to expiration. The position is equivalent to a short bond.

Reverse repo   Another name for *reverse repurchase agreement*.

Reverse repurchase agreement   The purchase of a security coupled with an agreement to sell it at a later date. The opposite of a repurchase agreement.

Rho   The change in value of a derivative due to a change in the interest rate.

Risk averse   A term describing an investor who prefers x to taking a risky bet with an expected value equal to x.

Risk management   The active use of derivatives and other techniques to alter risk and protect profitability.

Risk neutral   A term describing an investor who is indifferent between receiving x and taking a risky bet with an expected value equal to x.

Risk premium   The difference between the expected return on an asset and the risk-free rate; the expected return differential that compensates investors for risk.

Risk-neutral measure   The probability distribution for an asset transformed so that the expected return on the asset is the risk-free rate.

Risk-neutral probability   In the binomial model, the probability of an up move in the asset price such that the expected return on the asset is the risk-free rate.

Self-financing portfolio   A portfolio that retains specified characteristics (e.g., it is zero-investment and risk-free) without the need for additional investments in the portfolio.

Settlement   The time in a transaction at which all obligations of both the buyer and the seller are fulfilled.

Share-equivalent   The position in shares that has equivalent dollar risk to a derivative. (See also *Delta*.)

Sharpe ratio   For an asset, the ratio of the risk premium to the return standard deviation.

Short   A position is short with respect to a price if the position profits from a decrease in that price. A short-seller of a stock profits from a decrease in the stock price and, hence, is short the stock. A seller of an option profits from a decrease in volatility and, hence, is short volatility.

Short call   A call that has been sold.

Short forward   The party to a forward contract who has an obligation to sell the underlying asset.

Short put   A put that has been sold.

Short rebate   The rate of return paid on collateral when shares are borrowed.

Short-against-the-box   The short-sale of a stock that the short-seller owns. The result of a short-against-the-box is that the short-seller has both a long and short position and, hence, bears no risk from the stock yet receives the value of the shares from the short sale.

Short-sale   A transaction in which an investor borrows a security, sells it, and then returns it at a later date to the lender. If the security makes payments, the short-seller must make the same payments to the lender.

Shout option   A shout call option expiring at time T has the payoff $max(0, S_{\hat{t}} - K, S_T - K)$, where $\hat{t}$ is the time and $S_{\hat{t}}$ is the price at which the option holder "shouted," thereby guaranteeing an expiration payoff at least as great as $S_{\hat{t}} - K$.

Skewness   A measure of the symmetry of a probability distribution. For a random variable x with mean μ and standard deviation σ, skewness is the third central moment divided by the cubed standard deviation, $E(x - \mu)^3/\sigma^3$. For a normal variable, skewness is 0. (See also *Volatility skew*.)

Spark spread   The difference between the price of electricity and that of the quantity of natural gas required to produce the electricity.

Spot curve   The set of zero-coupon bond prices with different maturities, usually inferred from government bond prices.

Spot price   The current market price of an asset.

Spread   Simultaneously buying and selling closely related derivatives. A spread in options is a position in which some options are bought and some are sold, and all options in the position are calls or all are puts. (See also *Calendar spread* and *Commodity spread*.)

Spread option   An option with a payoff where a spread (the difference between prices) takes the place the of the underlying asset.

Stable distribution   A probability distribution for which sums of random variables have the same distribution as the original random variable. The normal distribution is stable because sums of normally distributed random variables are normally distributed.

Stack and roll   A hedging strategy in which an existing stack hedge with maturing futures contracts is replaced by a new stack hedge with longer dated futures contracts.

Stack hedge   Hedging a stream of obligations by entering futures contracts with a *single* maturity, with the number of contracts selected so that changes in the *present value* of the future obligations are offset by changes in the value of this "stack" of futures contracts.

Static NPV   The net present value of a project at a point in time, ignoring the possibility of postponing adoption of the project.

Static option replication   The use of options to hedge options, with the goal of creating a hedging portfolio that has a delta that naturally moves in tandem with the delta of the option being hedged.

Stochastic differential equation   An equation characterizing the change in a variable in which one or more of the differential terms are increments to a stochastic process.

Stock index   An average of the prices of a group of stocks. A stock index can be a simple average of stock prices, in which case it is *equally weighted*, or it can be a weighted average, with the weights proportional to market capitalization, in which case it is *value-weighted*.

Straddle   The purchase of a call and a put with the same strike price and time to expiration.

Straddle rules   Tax regulations controlling the circumstances in which a loss on a claim can be realized when a taxpayer continues to own related securities or derivatives.

Strangle   The purchase of a put and a higher-strike call with the same time to expiration.

Stratified sampling   A technique used in Monte Carlo valuation in which random numbers are drawn from each percentile (or other regular interval) of the distribution.

Strike price   Another term for *exercise price*.

Strip hedge   Hedging a stream of obligations by offsetting each individual obligation with a futures contract matching the maturity and quantity of the obligation.

STRIPS   Acronym for *Separate Trading of Registered Interest and Principal of Securities*. STRIPS are the interest and principal payments from Treasury bonds and notes traded as individual securities.

Structured note   A bond that makes payments that, at least in part, are contingent on some variable such as a stock price, interest rates, or exchange rates.

Swap   A contract calling for the exchange of payments over time. Often one payment is fixed in advance and the other is floating, based upon the realization of a price or interest rate.

Swap spread   The difference between the fixed rate on an interest rate swap and the yield on a Treasury bond with the same maturity.

Swap tenor   The lifetime of a swap.

Swap term   Another name for *swap tenor*.

Swaption   An option to enter into a swap.

Tail VaR   The expected loss conditional upon the VaR loss being exceeded.

Tailing   A reduction in the quantity of an asset held in order to offset future income received by the asset.

Tenor   Time to maturity or expiration of a contract, frequently used when referring to swaps.

Term repo   A repurchase agreement lasting for a specified period of time longer than one day.

Theta   The change in the value of a derivative due solely to the passage of time.

Time decay   Another term for *theta*.

Total return swap   A swap in which one party pays the total return (dividends plus capital gains) on a reference asset, and the other party pays a floating rate such as LIBOR.

Traded present value   The value an investment project would have once the investment was made; also called *twin security*.

Twin security   See *Traded present value*.

Underlying asset   The asset whose price determines the profitability of a derivative. For example, the underlying asset for a purchased call is the asset that the call owner can buy by paying the strike price.

Up-and-in   A knock-in option for which the barrier exceeds the current price of the underlying asset.

Up-and-out   A knock-out option for which the barrier exceeds the current price of the underlying asset.

Value at risk   The level of loss that will be exceeded a given percentage of the time over a given horizon.

Vanilla   A standard option or other derivative. For example, ordinary puts and calls are "vanilla" options.

Vega   The change in the price of a derivative due to a change in volatility. Also sometimes called *kappa* or *lambda*.

Vertical spread   The sale of an option at one strike and purchase of an option of the same type (call or put) at a different strike, both having the same underlying asset and time to expiration.

Volatility   The standard deviation of the continuously compounded return on an asset.

Volatility skew   Generally, implied volatility as a function of the strike price. Volatility skew refers to a difference in premiums as reflected in differences in implied volatility. Skew is sometimes used more precisely to refer to a difference in implied volatilities between in-the-money and out-of-the-money options.

Volatility smile   A volatility skew in which both in-the-money and out-of-the-money options have a higher volatility than at-the-money options (i.e., when you plot implied volatility against the strike price, the curve looks like a smile).

Warrant   An option issued by a firm with its own stock as the underlying asset. This term also refers more generally to an option issued in fixed supply.

Wiener process   See *Brownian motion*.

Written call   A call that has been sold; a short call.

Written put   A put that has been sold; a short put.

Written straddle   The simultaneous sale of a call and sale of a put, with the same strike price and time to expiration.

Yield curve   The set of yields to maturity for bonds with different times to maturity.

Yield to maturity   The single discount factor for which the present value of a bond's payments is equal to the observed bond price.

Zero-cost collar   The purchase of a put and sale of a call where the strikes are chosen so that the premiums of the two options are the same.

Zero-coupon bond   A bond that makes only a single payment, at maturity.

Zero-coupon yield curve   The set of yields to maturity for zero-coupon bonds with different times to maturity.

Bibliography

Acharya, V. V., John, K., and Sundaram, R. K., 2000; "On the Optimality of Resetting Executive Stock Options." *Journal of Financial Economics*, 57(1), 65–101.

Allayannis, G. and Weston, J., 2001; "The Use of Foreign Currency Derivatives and Firm Market Value." *Review of Financial Studies*, 14(1), 243–276.

Andersen, T., Benzoni, L., and Lund, J., 2002; "An Empirical Investigation of Continuous-Time Equity Return Models." *Journal of Finance*, 57(3), 1239–1284.

Arnason, S. T. and Jagannathan, R., 1994; "Evaluating Executive Stock Options Using the Binomial Pricing Model." Working Paper, Carlson School of Management, University of Minnesota.

Arnold, L., 1974; *Stochastic Differential Equations: Theory and Applications.* John Wiley & Sons, New York.

Artzner, P., Delbaen, F., Eber, J.-M., and Heath, D., 1999; "Coherent Measures of Risk." *Mathematical Finance*, 9(3), 203–228.

Arzac, E. R., 1997; "PERCs, DECs, and Other Mandatory Convertibles." *Journal of Applied Corporate Finance*, 10(1), 54–63.

Asquith, P., 1995; "Convertible Bonds Are Not Called Late." *Journal of Finance*, 50(4), 1275–1289.

Bakshi, G., Cao, C., and Chen, Z., 1997; "Empirical Performance of Alternative Option Pricing Models." *Journal of Finance*, 52(5), 2003–2049.

Bates, D. S., 2000; "Post-'87 Crash Fears the S&P 500 Futures Options Market." *Journal of Econometrics*, 94, 181–238.

Baubonis, C., Gastineau, G., and Purcell, D., 1993; "The Banker's Guide to Equity-Linked Certificates of Deposit." *Journal of Derivatives*, 1(2), 87–95.

Baxter, M. and Rennie, A., 1996; *Financial Calculus: An Introduction to Derivative Pricing.* Cambridge University Press, Cambridge, England.

Benzoni, L., 2001; "Pricing Options under Stochastic Volatility: An Empirical Investigation." Unpublished, University of Minnesota.

Bernstein, P. L., 1992; *Capital Ideas: The Improbable Origins of Modern Wall Street.* Free Press, New York.

Bernstein, P. L., 1996; *Against the Gods: The Remarkable Story of Risk.* John Wiley & Sons, New York.

Black, F., 1976; "The Pricing of Commodity Contracts." *Journal of Financial Economics*, 3(1/2), 167–179.

Black, F., 1989; "How We Came Up with the Option Pricing Formula." *Journal of Portfolio Management*, 15(2), 4–8.

Black, F. and Cox, J., 1976; "Valuing Corporate Securities: Some Effects of Bond Indenture Provisions." *Journal of Finance*, 31, 351–367.

Black, F., Derman, E., and Toy, W., 1990; "A One-Factor Model of Interest Rates and Its Application to Treasury Bond Options." *Financial Analysts Journal*, 46(1), 33–39.

Black, F. and Scholes, M., 1973; "The Pricing of Options and Corporate Liabilities." *Journal of Political Economy*, 81, 637–659.

Bliss, R. R., 1997; "Movements in the Term Structure of Interest Rates." *Federal Reserve Bank of Atlanta Economic Review*, 82(4), 16–33.

Bodie, Z., 1995; "On the Risk of Stocks in the Long Run." *Financial Analysts Journal*, 51(3), 18–22.

Bodie, Z. and Crane, D., 1999; "The Design and Production of New Retirement Savings Products." *Journal of Portfolio Management*, 25(2), 77–82.

Bodnar, G. M., Hayt, G. S., and Marston, R. C., 1998; "1998 Wharton Survey of Financial Risk Management by U.S. Non-Financial Firms." *Financial Management*, 27(4), 70–91.

Bollerslev, T., Engle, R. F., and Nelson, D. B., 1994; "ARCH Models." In R. F. Engle and D. L. McFadden (eds.), *Handbook of Econometrics*, vol. 4 of *Handbooks in Economics*, chap. 49, pp. 2959–3038. Elsevier Science, B.V., Amsterdam.

Boyle, P. P., 1977; "Options: A Monte Carlo Approach." *Journal of Financial Economics*, 4(3), 323–338.

Boyle, P. P., Broadie, M., and Glasserman, P., 1997; "Monte Carlo Methods for Security Pricing." *Journal of Economic Dynamics and Control*, 21(8–9), 1267–1322.

Boyle, P. P. and Emanuel, D., 1980; "Discretely Adjusted Option Hedges." *Journal of Financial Economics*, 8(3), 259–282.

Boyle, P. P., Evnine, J., and Gibbs, S., 1989; "Numerical Evaluation of Multivariate Contingent Claims." *Review of Financial Studies*, 2(2), 241–250.

Brealey, R. and Myers, S., 2000; *Principles of Corporate Finance*. Irwin McGraw-Hill, Burr Ridge, IL, 6th ed.

Brennan, M. and Schwartz, E., 1985; "Evaluating Natural Resource Investments." *Journal of Business*, 58, 135–157.

Brennan, M. J., 1991; "The Price of Convenience and the Evaluation of Commodity Contingent Claims." In D. Lund and B. Øksendal (eds.), *Stochastic Models and Option Values: Applications to Resources, Environment and Investment Problems*, Contributions to Economic Analysis, pp. 33–71. North-Holland, Amsterdam.

Brennan, M. J., 2000; "Real Options: Development and New Contributions." In Brennan and Trigeorgis (2000), chap. 1, pp. 1–10.

Brennan, M. J. and Schwartz, E. S., 1977; "Convertible Bonds: Valuation and Optimal Strategies for Call and Conversion." *Journal of Finance*, 32(5), 1699–1715.

Brennan, M. J. and Schwartz, E. S., 1990; "Arbitrage in Stock Index Futures." *Journal of Business*, 63(1), S7–31.

Brennan, M. J. and Trigeorgis, L. (eds.), 2000; *Project Flexibility, Agency, and Competition: New Developments in the Theory and Application of Real Options*. Oxford University Press, London.

Briys, E. and Bellala, M., 1998; *Options, Futures and Exotic Derivatives: Theory, Application and Practice*. Wiley Frontiers in Finance. John Wiley & Sons, Chichester, England.

Broadie, M. and Detemple, J., 1996; "American Option Valuation: New Bounds, Approximations, and a Comparison of Existing Methods." *Review of Financial Studies*, 9(4), 1211–1250.

Broadie, M. and Glasserman, P., 1997; "Pricing American Style Securities by Simulation." *Journal of Economic Dynamics and Control*, 21, 1323–1352.

Broadie, M., Glasserman, P., and Kou, S. G., 1997; "A Continuity Correction for Discrete Barrier Options." *Mathematical Finance*, 7(4), 325–349.

Brown, G. W., 2001; "Managing Foreign Exchange Risk with Derivatives." *Journal of Financial Economics*, 60(2–3), 401–448.

Burghardt, G. and Hoskins, W., 1995; "The Convexity Bias in Eurodollar Futures." *Risk*, 8(3), 63–70.

Campbell, J. Y., Lo, A. W., and MacKinlay, A. C., 1997; *The Econometrics of Financial Markets*. Princeton University Press, Princeton, NJ.

Carty, L. V., 1997; "Moody's Rating Migration and Credit Quality Correlation, 1920–1996." Tech. rep., Moody's Investors Service.

Chance, D. M., Kumar, R., and Todd, R. B., 2000; "The 'Repricing' of Executive Stock Options." *Journal of Financial Economics*, 57(1), 129–154.

Chicago Board of Trade, 1998; *Commodity Trading Manual*. Chicago Board of Trade.

Cochrane, J. J., 2001; *Asset Pricing*. Princeton University Press, Princeton, NJ.

Constantinides, G. M., 1978; "Market Risk Adjustment in Project Valuation." *Journal of Finance*, 33(2), 603–616.

Constantinides, G. M., 1984; "Warrant Exercise and Bond Conversion in Competitive Markets." *Journal of Financial Economics*, 13(3), 371–397.

Cooper, L., 2000; "Caution Reigns." *Risk*, 13(6), 12–14. South Africa Special Report.

Core, J. E and Guay, W. R., 2001; "Stock Option Plans for Non-Executive Employees." *Journal of Financial Economics*, 61(2), 253–287.

Cornell, B. and French, K. R., 1983; "Taxes and the Pricing of Stock Index Futures." *Journal of Finance*, 38(3), 675–694.

Cornell, B. and Shapiro, A. C., 1989; "The Mispricing of U.S. Treasury Bonds: A Case Study." *Review of Financial Studies*, 2(3), 297–310.

Coval, J. D. and Shumway, T., 2001; "Expected Option Returns." *Journal of Finance*, 56(3), 983–1009.

Cox, D. and Miller, H. D., 1965; *The Theory of Stochastic Processes*. Chapman and Hall, London.

Cox, J. C., Ingersoll, J. E., Jr., and Ross, S. A., 1981; "The Relation between Forward Prices and Futures Prices." *Journal of Financial Economics*, 9(4), 321–346.

Cox, J. C., Ingersoll, J. E., Jr., and Ross, S. A., 1985a; "An Intertemporal General Equilibrium Model of Asset Prices." *Econometrica*, 53(2), 363–384.

Cox, J. C., Ingersoll, J. E., Jr., and Ross, S. A., 1985b; "A Theory of the Term Structure of Interest Rates." *Econometrica*, 53(2), 385–408.

Cox, J. C. and Ross, S. A., 1976; "The Valuation of Options for Alternative Stochastic Processes." *Journal of Financial Economics*, 3(1/2), 145–166.

Cox, J. C., Ross, S. A., and Rubinstein, M., 1979; "Option Pricing: A Simplified Approach." *Journal of Financial Economics*, 7(3), 229–263.

Cox, J. C. and Rubinstein, M., 1985; *Options Markets*. Prentice-Hall, Englewood Cliffs, NJ.

Crabbe, L. E. and Argilagos, J. D., 1994; "Anatomy of the Structured Note Market." *Journal of Applied Corporate Finance*, 7(3), 85–98.

Credit Suisse Financial Products, 1997; "CreditRisk+." Tech. rep., Credit Suisse First Boston, London.

Culp, C. L. and Miller, M. H., 1995; "Metallgesellschaft and the Economics of Synthetic Storage." *Journal of Applied Corporate Finance*, 7(4), 62–76.

D'Avolio, G., 2001; "The Market for Borrowing Stock." Graduate School of Business Administration, Harvard University.

DeGroot, M. H., 1975; *Probability and Statistics*. Addison-Wesley, Reading, MA.

Derman, E., 1996; "Valuing Models and Modeling Value." *Journal of Portfolio Management*, 22(3), 106–114.

Derman, E. and Kani, I., 1993; "The Ins and Outs of Barrier Options." Goldman Sachs Quantitative Strategies Research Notes.

Derman, E. and Kani, I., 1994; "Riding on a Smile." *Risk*, 7, 32–39.

Dixit, A., 1989; "Entry and Exit Decisions under Uncertainty." *Journal of Political Economy*, 97, 620–638.

Dixit, A. K. and Pindyck, R. S., 1994; *Investment under Uncertainty*. Princeton University Press, Princeton, NJ.

Duffie, D., 1996; *Dynamic Asset Pricing Theory.* Princeton University Press, Princeton, NJ, 2nd ed.

Eberhart, A. C., 2001; "The Valuation of Employee Stock Options as Warrants and the Concurrent Valuation of Common Stocks." Working Paper, McDonough School of Business, Georgetown University.

Edwards, F. R. and Canter, M. S., 1995; "The Collapse of Metallgesellschaft: Unhedgeable Risks, Poor Hedging Strategy, or Just Bad Luck?" *Journal of Applied Corporate Finance*, 8(1), 86–105.

Edwards, F. R. and Ma, C. W., 1992; *Futures and Options.* McGraw-Hill, New York.

Emanual, D. C., 1983; "Warrant Valuation and Exercise Strategy." *Journal of Financial Economics*, 12(2), 211–235.

Eraker, B., 2001; "Do Stock Prices and Volatility Jump? Reconciling Evidence from Spot and Option Prices." Unpublished, Duke University.

Fleming, I., 1997; *Goldfinger.* Fine Communications, New York.

Forster, D. M., 1996; "The State of the Law after *Procter & Gamble v. Banker's Trust.*" *Derivatives Quarterly*, 3(2), 8–17.

French, K. R., 1983; "A Comparison of Futures and Forward Prices." *Journal of Financial Economics*, 12(3), 311–342.

Froot, K., Scharfstein, D., and Stein, J., 1994; "A Framework for Risk Management." *Journal of Applied Corporate Finance*, 7(3), 22–32.

Froot, K. A., 2001; "The Market for Catastrophe Risk: A Clinical Examination." *Journal of Financial Economics*, 60(2–3), 529–571.

Froot, K. A. and O'Connell, P. G. J., 1999; "The Pricing of U.S. Catastrophe Reinsurance." In K. A. Froot (ed.), *The Financing of Catastrophe Risk*, pp. 195–231. University of Chicago Press, Chicago.

Galai, D. and Masulis, R. W., 1976; "The Option Pricing Model and the Risk Factor of Stock." *Journal of Financial Economics*, 3(1/2), 53–81.

Garman, M. B. and Kohlhagen, S. W., 1983; "Foreign Currency Option Values." *Journal of International Money and Finance*, 2(3), 231–237.

Gastineau, G. L., Smith, D. J., and Todd, R., 2001; *Risk Management, Derivatives, and Financial Analysis under SFAS No. 133.* The Research Foundation of AIMR and Blackwell Series in Finance.

Géczy, C., Minton, B. A., and Schrand, C., 1997; "Why Firms Use Currency Derivatives." *Journal of Finance*, 52(4), 1323–1354.

Geman, H., Karoui, N. E., and Rochet, J. C., 1995; "Changes of Numeraire, Changes of Probability Measure and Option Pricing." *Journal of Applied Probability*, 32, 443–458.

Geske, R., 1979; "The Valuation of Compound Options." *Journal of Financial Economics*, 7(1), 63–81.

Goldman, B. M., Sosin, H. B., and Gatto, M. A., 1979a; "Path Dependent Options: Buy at the Low, Sell at the High." *Journal of Finance*, 34(5), 1111–1127.

Goldman, B. M., Sosin, H. B., and Shepp, L. A., 1979b; "On Contingent Claims That Insure Ex-post Optimal Stock Market Timing." *Journal of Finance*, 34(2), 401–413.

Graham, J. R. and Rogers, D. A., 2000; "Do Firms Hedge in Response to Tax Incentives?" Working Paper, Duke University.

Graham, J. R. and Smith, C. W., Jr., 1999; "Tax Incentives to Hedge." *Journal of Finance*, 54(6), 2241–2262.

Green, J., 1999; *Excel 2000 VBA.* Wrox Press, Birmingham, England.

Grenadier, S. R., 1996; "The Strategic Exercise of Options: Development Cascades and Overbuilding in Real Estate Markets." *Journal of Finance*, 51(5), 1653–1679.

Grenadier, S. R., 1999; "Information Revelation through Option Exercise." *Review of Financial Studies*, 12(1), 95–129.

Grinblatt, M. and Longstaff, F. A., 2000; "Financial Innovation and the Role of Derivative Securities: An Empirical Analysis of the Treasury STRIPS Program." *Journal of Finance*, 55(3), 1415–1436.

Grossman, S. J. and Stiglitz, J. E., 1980; "On the Impossibility of Informationally Efficient Markets." *American Economic Review*, 70(3), 393–408.

Gupta, A. and Subrahmanyam, M. G., 2000; "An Empirical Examination of the Convexity Bias in the Pricing of Interest Rate Swaps." *Journal of Financial Economics*, 55(2), 239–279.

Harris, M. and Raviv, A., 1985; "A Sequential Signalling Model of Convertible Debt Call Policy." *Journal of Finance*, 40(5), 1263–1281.

Harrison, J. M. and Kreps, D. M., 1979; "Martingales and Arbitrage in Multi-period Securities Markets." *Journal of Economic Theory*, 20, 381–408.

Haug, E. G., 1998; *The Complete Guide to Option Pricing Formulas*. McGraw-Hill, New York.

Haushalter, G. D., 2000; "Financing Policy, Basis Risk, and Corporate Hedging: Evidence from Oil and Gas Producers." *Journal of Finance*, 55(1), 107–152.

Heath, D., Jarrow, R., and Morton, A., 1992; "Bond Pricing and the Term Structure of Interest Rates: A New Methodology for Contingent Claims Valuation." *Econometrica*, 60(1), 77–105.

Henriques, D. B., 1997; "The Wealthy Find New Ways to Escape Tax on Profits." *The New York Times*, Dec. 1, C1.

Heston, S. L., 1993; "A Closed-Form Solution for Options with Stochastic Volatility with Applications to Bonds and Currency Options." *Review of Financial Studies*, 6(2), 327–343.

Ho, T. S. Y. and Lee, S. B., 1986; "Term Structure Movements and Pricing Interest Rate Contingent Claims." *Journal of Finance*, 41(4), 1011–1029.

Horwitz, D. L., 1996; "*P&G v. Banker's Trust*: What's All the Fuss?" *Derivatives Quarterly*, 3(2), 18–23.

Houweling, P. and Vorst, T., 2001; "An Empirical Comparison of Default Swap Pricing Models." Working Paper, Erasmus University.

Hsu, H., 1997; "Surprised Parties." *Risk*, 10(4), 27–29.

Huang, C. and Litzenberger, R., 1988; *Foundations for Financial Economics*. Elsevier Science Publishing Co., New York.

Huddart, S., 1998; "Patterns of Stock Option Exercise in the United States." In J. Carpenter and D. Yermack (eds.), *Executive Compensation and Shareholder Value*, chap. 8, pp. 115–142. Kluwer Academic Publishers, Norwell, MA.

Hull, J., 2000; *Options, Futures, and Other Derivatives*. Prentice-Hall, Upper Saddle River, NJ, 4th ed.

Ingersoll, J. E., Jr., 1977; "A Contingent-Claims Valuation of Convertible Securities." *Journal of Financial Economics*, 4(3), 289–322.

Ingersoll, J. E., Jr., 2000; "Digital Contracts: Simple Tools for Pricing Complex Derivatives." *Journal of Business*, 73(1), 67–88.

J. P. Morgan, 1997; "CreditMetrics—Technical Document." Tech. rep., J. P. Morgan & Co., New York.

J. P. Morgan/Reuters, 1996; "RiskMetrics—Technical Document." Tech. rep., J. P. Morgan & Co., New York. 4th ed.

James, J. and Webber, N., 2001; *Interest Rate Modeling*. John Wiley & Sons, Chichester, England.

Jarrow, R. A., 1996; *Modeling Fixed Income Securities and Interest Rate Options*. McGraw-Hill, New York.

Jarrow, R. A. and Oldfield, G. S., 1981; "Forward Contracts and Futures Contracts." *Journal of Financial Economics*, 9(4), 373–382.

Johnson, S. A. and Tian, Y. S., 2000a; "Indexed Executive Stock Options." *Journal of Financial Economics*, 57(1), 35–64.

Johnson, S. A. and Tian, Y. S., 2000b; "The Value and Incentive Effects of Nontraditional Executive Stock Option Plans." *Journal of Financial Economics*, 57(1), 3–34.

Jorion, P., 1995; *Big Bets Gone Bad: Derivatives and Bankruptcy in Orange County*. Academic Press, San Diego, CA.

Jorion, P., 2001; *Value at Risk*. McGraw-Hill, New York, 2nd ed.

Judd, K. L., 1998; *Numerical Methods in Economics*. MIT Press, Cambridge, MA.

Karlin, S. and Taylor, H. M., 1981; *A Second Course in Stochastic Processes*. Academic Press, New York.

Kealhofer, S. and Kurbat, M., 2002; "Predictive Merton Models." *Risk*, 15(2), 67–71.

Kemma, A. G. Z. and Vorst, A. C. F., 1990; "A Pricing Method for Options Based on Average Asset Values." *Journal of Banking and Finance*, 14(1), 113–129.

Kulatilaka, N. and Marcus, A. J., 1994; "Valuing Employee Stock Options." *Financial Analysts Journal*, 50, 46–56.

Lewis, M., 1989; *Liar's Poker*. Penguin, New York.

Litterman, R. and Scheinkman, J., 1991; "Common Factors Affecting Bond Returns." *Journal of Fixed Income*, 1(1), 54–61.

Litzenberger, R. H., 1992; "Swaps: Plain and Fanciful." *Journal of Finance*, 47(3), 831–850.

Longstaff, F. A. and Schwartz, E. S., 2001; "Valuing American Options by Simulation: A Least Squares Approach." *Review of Financial Studies*, 14(1), 113–147.

Lowenstein, R., 2000; *When Genius Failed: The Rise and Fall of Long-Term Capital Management*. Random House, New York.

Macaulay, F. R., 1938; *The Movement of Interest Rates, Bond Yields and Stock Prices in the United States Since 1856*. National Bureau of Economic Research.

Margrabe, W., 1978; "The Value of an Option to Exchange One Asset for Another." *Journal of Finance*, 33(1), 177–186.

McConnell, J. J. and Schwartz, E. S., 1992; "The Origin of LYONs: A Case Study in Financial Innovation." *Journal of Applied Corporate Finance*, 4(4), 40–47.

McDonald, R. L., 2000; "Real Options and Rules of Thumb in Capital Budgeting." In M. J. Brennan and L. Trigeorgis (eds.), *Project Flexibility, Agency, and Competition: New Developments in the Theory and Application of Real Options,* chap. 2, pp. 13–33. Oxford University Press, London.

McDonald, R. L., 2001; "The Tax (Dis)Advantage of a Firm Issuing Options on Its Own Stock." Working Paper, Finance Department, Kellogg School of Management, Northwestern University.

McDonald, R. L. and Siegel, E., 1986; "The Value of Waiting to Invest." *Quarterly Journal of Economics*, 101(4), 707–727.

McDonald, R. L. and Siegel, D. R., 1984; "Option Pricing When the Underlying Asset Earns a Below-Equilibrium Rate of Return: A Note." *Journal of Finance*, 39(1), 261–265.

McDonald, R. L. and Siegel, D. R., 1985; "Investment and the Valuation of Firms When There Is an Option to Shut Down." *International Economic Review*, 26(2), 331–349.

McMillan, L. G., 1992; *Options as a Strategic Investment*. New York Institute of Finance, New York, 3rd ed.

Mello, A. S. and Parsons, J. E., 1995; "Maturity Structure of a Hedge Matters: Lessons from the Metallgesellschaft Debacle." *Journal of Applied Corporate Finance*, 8(1), 106–120.

Merton, R. C., 1973a; "The Relationship Between Put and Call Option Prices: Comment." *Journal of Finance*, 28(1), 183–184.

Merton, R. C., 1973b; "Theory of Rational Option Pricing." *Bell Journal of Economics and Management Science*, 4, 141–183.

Merton, R. C., 1974; "On the Pricing of Corporate Debt: The Risk Structure of Interest Rates." *Journal of Finance*, 29(2), 449–470.

Merton, R. C., 1976; "Option Pricing When Underlying Stock Returns are Discontinuous." *Journal of Financial Economics*, 3(1), 125–144.

Merton, R. C., 1977a; "An Analytic Derivation of the Cost of Loan Guarantees and Deposit Insurance: An Application of Modern Option Pricing Theory." *Journal of Banking and Finance*, 1(1), 3–11.

Merton, R. C., 1977b; "On the Pricing of Contingent Claims and the Modigliani-Miller Theorem." *Journal of Financial Economics*, 5(2), 241–249.

Merton, R. C., 1990; "On the Mathematics and Economics Assumptions of Continuous-Time Models." In R. C. Merton (ed.), *Continuous-Time Finance*, chap. 3, pp. 57–93. Basil Blackwell, Cambridge, MA.

Merton, R. C., 1999; "Finance Theory and Future Trends: The Shift to Integration." *Risk*, 11(7), 48–51.

Miller, M. H., 1986; "Financial Innovation: The Last Twenty Years and the Next." *Journal of Financial and Quantitative Analysis*, 21(4), 459–471.

Modest, D. M. and Sundaresan, M., 1983; "The Relationship between Spot and Futures Prices in Stock Index Futures Markets: Some Preliminary Evidence." *Journal of Futures Markets*, 3(1), 15–41.

Modigliani, F. and Miller, M., 1958; "The Cost of Capital, Corporation Finance, and the Theory of Investment." *American Economic Review*, 48(3), 261–297.

Mood, A. M., Graybill, F. A., and Boes, D. C., 1974; *Introduction to the Theory of Statistics*. McGraw-Hill, New York, 3rd ed.

Morgenson, G., 1998; "Trimming Stock Options' Sails: Accounting Proposal Would Lift the Cost of Repricing." *The New York Times*, Aug. 20, D1.

Myers, S. C., 1977; "Determinants of Corporate Borrowing." *Journal of Financial Economics*, 5(2), 147–75.

Naik, V. and Lee, M., 1990; "General Equilibrium Pricing of Options on the Market Portfolio with Discontinuous Returns." *Review of Financial Studies*, 3(4), 493–521.

Neftci, S. N., 2000; *An Introduction to the Mathematics of Financial Derivatives*. Academic Press, San Diego, CA, 2nd ed.

Paddock, J. L., Siegel, D. R., and Smith, J. L., 1988; "Option Valuation of Claims on Real Assets: The Case of Offshore Petroleum Leases." *Quarterly Journal of Economics*, 103(3), 479–508.

Pan, J., 2002; "The Jump-Risk Premia Implicit in Options: Evidence from an Integrated Time-Series Study." *Journal of Financial Economics*, 63(1), 3–50.

Petersen, M. A. and Thiagarajan, S. R., 2000; "Risk Measurement and Hedging: With and Without Derivatives." *Financial Management,* 29(4), Winter 2000, 5–29.

Petrie, K. N., 2000; "Why Some Firms Use Collar Offers in Mergers." Working Paper, Terry College of Business, University of Georgia.

Pindyck, R. S., 1993a; "Investments of Uncertain Cost." *Journal of Financial Economics*, 34(1), 53–76.

Pindyck, R. S., 1993b; "The Present Value Model of Rational Commodity Pricing." *The Economic Journal*, 103(418), 511–530.

Pindyck, R. S., 1994; "Inventories and the Short-Run Dynamics of Commodity Prices." *Rand Journal of Economics*, 25(1), 141–159.

Rebonato, R., 1996; *Interest Rate Option Models.* John Wiley & Sons, Chichester, England, 2nd ed.

Reiner, E., 1992; "Quanto Mechanics." *Risk,* 5(3), 59–63.

Reinganum, M. R., 1986; "Is Time Travel Impossible? A Financial Proof." *Journal of Portfolio Management,* 13(1), 10–12.

Rendleman, R. J., Jr., 2002; *Applied Derivatives: Options, Futures, and Swaps.* Blackwell, Malden, MA.

Rendleman, R. J., Jr. and Bartter, B. J., 1979; "Two-State Option Pricing." *Journal of Finance,* 34(5), 1093–1110.

Rendleman, R. J., Jr. and Bartter, B. J., 1980; "The Pricing of Options on Debt Securities." *Journal of Financial and Quantitative Analysis,* XV(1), 11–24.

Richard, S. F. and Sundaresan, M., 1981; "A Continuous Time Equilibrium Model of Forward Prices and Futures Prices in a Multigood Economy." *Journal of Financial Economics,* 9(4), 347–371.

Ronn, A. G. and Ronn, E. I., 1989; "The Box Spread Arbitrage Conditions: Theory, Tests, and Investment Strategies." *Review of Financial Studies,* 2(1), 91–108.

Rooney, M., 1998; "Credit Default Swaps." Tech. rep., Merrill Lynch.

Ross, S. A., Westerfield, R., and Jaffee, D., 1996; *Corporate Finance.* Irwin/McGraw-Hill, Burr Ridge, IL, 4th ed.

Routledge, B. R., Seppi, D. J., and Spatt, C. S., 2000; "Equilibrium Forward Curves for Commodities." *Journal of Finance,* 55(3), 1297–1338.

Rubinstein, M., 1991a; "Double Trouble." *Risk,* 5(1), 73.

Rubinstein, M., 1991b; "One for Another." *Risk,* 4(7), 30–32.

Rubinstein, M., 1991c; "Somewhere Over the Rainbow." *Risk,* 4(10), 63–66.

Rubinstein, M., 1994a; "Implied Binomial Trees." *Journal of Finance,* 49(3), 771–818.

Rubinstein, M., 1994b; "Return to Oz." *Risk,* 7(11), 67–71.

Rubinstein, M. and Reiner, E., 1991a; "Breaking Down the Barrier." *Risk,* 4(8), 28–35.

Rubinstein, M. and Reiner, E., 1991b; "Unscrambling the Binary Code." *Risk,* 4(9), 75–83.

Ryan, M. D. and Granovsky, R. J., 2000; "Nikkei 225 Put Warrants." In J. C. Francis, W. W. Toy, and J. G. Whittaker (eds.), *The Handbook of Equity Derivatives,* chap. 17, pp. 368–394. John Wiley & Sons, New York, revised ed.

Saly, P. J., Jagannathan, R., and Huddart, S. J., 1999; "Valuing the Reload Features of Executive Stock Options." *Accounting Horizons,* 13(3), 219–240.

Samuelson, P. A., 1965; "Proof That Properly Anticipated Prices Fluctuate Randomly." *Industrial Management Review,* 6(2), 41–49.

Scholes, M., 1976; "Taxes and the Pricing of Options." *Journal of Finance,* 31(2), 319–332.

Scholes, M. and Wolfson, M., 1991; *Taxes and Business Strategy: A Planning Approach.* Prentice-Hall, Englewood Cliffs, New Jersey.

Schroder, M., 1988; "Adapting the Binomial Model to Value Options on Assets with Fixed-Cash Payouts." *Financial Analysts Journal,* 44(6), 54–62.

Schroder, M., 1999; "Changes of Numeraire for Pricing Futures, Forwards, and Options." *Review of Financial Studies,* 12(5), 1143–1163.

Schwartz, E. S., 1997; "The Stochastic Behavior of Commodity Prices: Implications for Valuation and Hedging." *Journal of Finance,* 52(3), 923–973.

Schwartz, E. S. and Moon, M., 2000; "Evaluating Research and Development Investments." In M. J. Brennan and L. Trigeorgis (eds.), *Project Flexibility, Agency, and Competition: New Developments in the Theory and Application of Real Options,* chap. 6, pp. 85–106. Oxford University Press, London.

Sharpe, W. F., 1976; "Corporate Pension Funding Policy." *Journal of Financial Economics*, 3(3), 183–193.

Sharpe, W. F., 1978; *Investments*. Prentice-Hall, Englewood Cliffs, NJ.

Shimko, D., 1993; "Bounds of Probability." *Risk*, 6, 33–37.

Siegel, D. and Siegel, D., 1990; *Futures Markets*. Dryden Press, Chicago.

Siegel, J. J., 1998; *Stocks for the Long Run*. McGraw-Hill, Burr Ridge, IL, 2nd ed.

Smith, C. W. and Stulz, R. M., 1985; "The Determinants of Firms' Hedging Policies." *Journal of Financial and Quantitative Analysis*, 20(4), 391–405.

Smith, D., 2002; "Two Common Textbook Misstatements about Bond Prices and Yields." Unpublished, Boston University School of Management.

Smith, D. J., 1997; "Aggressive Corporate Finance: A Close Look at the Procter & Gamble–Bankers Trust Leveraged Swap." *Journal of Derivatives*, 5(4), 67–79.

Sobehart, J. and Keenan, S., 2002; "The Need for Hybrid Models." *Risk*, 15(2), 73–77.

Spatt, C. S. and Sterbenz, F. P., 1988; "Warrant Exercise, Dividends, and Reinvestment Policy." *Journal of Finance*, 43(2), 493–506.

Srivastava, S., 1998; "Value at Risk Analysis of a Leveraged Swap." Working Paper, Carnegie-Mellon University.

Stein, J. C., 1992; "Convertible Bonds as Backdoor Equity Financing." *Journal of Financial Economics*, 32(1), 3–21.

Steiner, R., 1997; *Mastering Repo Markets*. FT Market Editions. Pitman Publishing, London.

Stigum, M., 1990; *The Money Market*. McGraw-Hill, New York, 3rd ed.

Stigum, M. and Robinson, F. L., 1996; *Money Market & Bond Calculations*. Richard D. Irwin, Inc., Chicago, IL.

Stoll, H. R., 1969; "The Relationship between Put and Call Option Prices." *Journal of Finance*, 24(5), 801–824.

Stoll, H. R., 1973; "The Relationship between Put and Call Option Prices: Reply." *Journal of Finance*, 28(1), 185–187.

Stulz, R., 1982; "Options on the Minimum or the Maximum of Two Risky Assets." *Journal of Financial Economics*, 10(2), 161–185.

Stulz, R., 1996; "Rethinking Risk Management." *Journal of Applied Corporate Finance*, 9(3), 8–24.

Sundaresan, S., 2002; *Fixed Income Markets and Their Derivatives*. South-Western, Cincinnati, OH.

Tavakoli, J. M., 1998; *Credit Derivatives: A Guide to Instruments and Applications*. John Wiley & Sons, New York.

Thatcher, K. L., Flynn, T., Ehrlinger, J., and Reel, M., 1994; "Equity Put Warrants: Reducing the Costs and Risks of a Stock Repurchase Program." Tech. rep., Salomon Brothers, New York.

Titman, S., 1985; "Urban Land Prices under Uncertainty." *American Economic Review*, 75(3), 505–514.

Triantis, A. and Borison, A., 2001; "Real Options: State of the Practice." *Journal of Applied Corporate Finance*, 14(2), 8–24.

Trigeorgis, L., 1996; *Real Options: Managerial Flexibility and Strategy in Resource Allocation*. MIT Press, Cambridge, MA.

Tuckman, B., 1995; *Fixed Income Securities*. John Wiley & Sons, New York.

Tufano, P., 1996; "Who Manages Risk? An Empirical Analysis of Risk Management Practices in the Gold Mining Industry." *Journal of Finance*, 51(4), 1097–1138.

Tufano, P., 1998; "The Determinants of Stock Price Exposure: Financial Engineering and the Gold Mining Industry." *Journal of Finance*, 53(3), 1015–1052.

Turnbull, S. M., 1987; "Swaps: Zero Sum Game?" *Financial Management*, 16(1), 15–21.

Vasicek, O., 1977; "An Equilibrium Characterization of the Term Structure." *Journal of Financial Economics*, 5(2), 177–188.

Wilmott, P., 1998; *Derivatives: The Theory and Practice of Financial Engineering*. John Wiley & Sons, Chichester, England.

Zhang, P. G., 1998; *Exotic Options: A Guide to Second Generation Options*. World Scientific, Singapore, 2nd ed.

Index